THE FINANCIAL SYSTEM AND THE ECONOMY

PRINCIPLES OF MONEY AND BANKING

FIFTH EDITION

MAUREEN BURTON AND BRUCE BROWN

PHI Learning Private Limited

New Delhi-110001

2009

To James Seth Burton (Uncle Jimmie) who was more like a father than an uncle.
—Maureen Burton

To Nina and Byron, and the optimism they embody.
—Bruce Brown

This Indian Reprint—Rs. 550.00
(Original U.S. Edition—Rs. 6589.00)

THE FINANCIAL SYSTEM AND THE ECONOMY—Principles of Money and Banking, 5th ed.
by Maureen Burton and Bruce Brown

ISBN-978-81-203-3958-3

Reprinted in India by special arrangement with M.E. Sharpe, Inc., 80 Business Park Drive, Armonk, NY 10504, U.S.A.

For sale in India, Pakistan, Bangladesh, Nepal and Sri Lanka Only.

Published by Asoke K. Ghosh, PHI Learning Private Limited, M-97, Connaught Circus, New Delhi-110001 and Printed by Rajkamal Electric Press, Plot No. 2, Phase IV, HSIDC, Kundli-131028, Sonepat, Haryana.

Brief Contents

Detailed Contents

Chapter 4   Financial Markets, Instruments, and Market Makers   67

Part Two Financial Prices

Part Three Financial Institutions

Chapter 8   An Introduction to Financial Intermediaries and Risk   159

Chapter 9   Commercial Banking Structure, Regulation, and Performance   181

Part Four **Financial Markets**

Chapter 13   **The Debt Markets**   283

Chapter 14   The Stock Market   315

Chapter 15   Securities Firms, Mutual Funds, and Financial Conglomerates   347

Chapter 16   How Exchange Rates Are Determined   375

Part Five Monetary Theory

Chapter 22 Aggregate Demand and Aggregate Supply 537

Part Six Monetary Policy

Chapter 23 The Challenges of Monetary Policy 561

Chapter 24   The Process of Monetary Policy Formulation   585

Chapter 25   Policy Implementation   609

Preface

INTRODUCTION TO THE TEXT

In early 2009, the economy is embroiled in a financial crisis that is unprecedented since the Great Depression. What started in the housing market spread throughout the entire financial system and wreaked havoc in the broader economy. The stock market has experienced the deepest bear market since the Great Depression, even surpassing the bursting of the stock market bubble in the early 2000s. The unemployment rate hit a 25-year high. As a result, rapid and revolutionary changes are occurring within the financial system and will continue to occur for some time.

Even before the current crisis, financial markets had been undergoing significant changes. Changes in information and computer technologies fostered the growth of new financial instruments and products. Many of the new products were thought to be creative ways to manage risk in a globalized environment. Technological changes also allowed for the unbundling of risks among financial market participants. Increased competition and globalization spurred on the changes. Regulations put in place during the Great Depression were removed. Financial institutions entered nontraditional venues. Laws forbidding the mergers of banks, securities firms and insurance companies were overturned. Mega-mergers occurred that changed the scope, size, and activities of financial institutions and created mega-firms that were "too big to fail."

Many of these changes have contributed to or facilitated the current crisis that financial markets are caught in. Managers of financial institutions must now make decisions in a new environment where caution can no longer be thrown to the wind. In 2009, financial market participants, policy makers, and regulators face new challenges as they continue to adapt to the changing environment in order to mitigate the ongoing financial crisis. No doubt the regulatory structure of the financial system will see a total overhaul as a result.

Given the economic climate, the motivation in developing this text is threefold.

- First, to give students an understanding of how the financial system works, how it affects the economy, and the role of policy makers and regulators.

- Second, to capture the recent changes in the financial system, some of which have contributed to the ongoing financial crisis, and some of which result from the crisis.

- Third, and most importantly, to present an analytical framework that enables students to understand and anticipate changes in financial markets and institutions as the financial system continues to evolve.

INTENDED AUDIENCE

The text is intended for an introductory undergraduate course in money and banking or financial markets analysis taught in either an economics or finance department. It may also be suitable for use in a financial markets course in an MBA Program.

CONTENTS OF THE TEXT

The Financial System and the Economy, fifth edition covers the traditional material found in a money and banking text and incorporates many of the recent changes and controversies within the financial services industry.

In addition, there are several unique features to this edition:

With regard to the ongoing financial crisis, we cover the origins and causes of the crisis including the development of subprime and Alt-A mortgages, the erosion of lending standards, the securitization of mortgages, and the development of credit derivatives. We look at financial bubbles and how they affect markets and lead to financial crisis. We focus on what policy makers have done to mitigate the crisis. We have expanded our coverage of financial instability including Hyman Minsky's long-term theory of financial instability.

With regard to specific actions taken as a result of the crisis, we have in-depth coverage on the following topics:

- In Chapter 12 on regulation, we cover the **Emergence Economic Stability Act**, of September 2008. We look at not only the uses of the first half of the bailout funds with regard to injecting capital into the largest financial institutions but also the plan on how to use the second half of the funds. We look at the Treasury's proposal to overhaul the regulatory system.

- In Chapter 13 on the debt markets, we look at the **Mortgage Bailout Plan** which is part of the **Financial Stability Plan.**

- In Chapter 21 on the financial aspects of the household, firm, and rest of the world sectors, we cover the **American Recovery and Reinvestment Act of 2009**—the $787 billion fiscal stimulus package that includes both increases in government spending and tax cuts.

- In Chapter 25 on monetary policy implementation, we look at the new special lending facilities created by the Fed in response to the crisis. We explore in detail the Fed's new tool kit and how the new lending has caused a doubling of the Fed's assets. We believe that this is something totally under the radar screen for many Americans.

ORGANIZATION OF THE TEXT

The Financial System and the Economy, fifth edition is organized in six parts:

Part One consists of a four chapter introduction. The student is introduced to the economy, money and credit, financial intermediaries, the Federal Reserve System, and financial markets and products.

Part Two consists of three chapters on interest rate determination, the term structure of interest rates, and the efficient market hypothesis. An alternative model of equilibrium based on the flow of funds among sectors and market efficiency is also presented.

Part Three consists of five chapters on financial institutions, financial innovation, financial instability, and regulation. Hyman Minsky's financial instability hypothesis is also covered.

Part Four consists of six chapters on financial markets including the debt and stock markets, securities firms, and also forwards, futures, and options markets. The determination of exchange rates and the international financial system are also covered.

Part Five has four chapters on monetary theory including the money supply process, the demand and supply of money and credit, and the financial aspects of the household, firm, government and foreign sectors. As a capstone chapter, the aggregate demand and supply model is also developed.

Part Six has four chapters that analyze monetary policy in an increasingly globalized environment. The chapters focus on the goals of monetary policy, the formulation of monetary policy by the Fed Open Market Committee, and the subsequent execution of the Policy Directive by the Trading Desk of the New York Fed. The growing need for greater international policy coordination is also addressed.

The Financial System and the Economy, fifth edition is designed to be flexible. After completing Part One, the instructor can emphasize financial prices (Part Two), financial institutions (Part Three), financial markets (Part Four), monetary theory (Part Five), or monetary policy (Part Six) depending on the focus of the class. In parts that are not being emphasized, chapters may be skipped.

PEDAGOGICAL FEATURES OF THE TEXT

In addition to presenting the material in a clear and concise manner, we have incorporated the following pedagogical tools to enhance the student's understanding.

- **Learning objectives** at the beginning of each chapter tell the student where the chapter is heading and what questions will be answered by studying the chapter.
- **Recap** sections are dispersed throughout each chapter to summarize analytical material the student should know before moving forward, and also to check that the student has mastered the preceding material.
- Highlight features include:
- **A Closer Look** feature that delves more deeply into the topic being discussed and provides enhancement material.
- **Looking Out** boxes that add relevant international material that show the interrelationships of global financial systems.
- **Looking Back** feature that provides historical background of the foundations of current economic circumstances.
- **Looking Forward** boxes that make projections about possible future situations within the arena of the financial system and economies.
- **Cracking the Code** feature that show students how to interpret the financial pages of daily newspapers, including stock, bond, Treasury bill, mutual fund, and foreign exchange quotes, and futures and options prices.
- **Key Terms** that are bold-faced in the text where they are first defined, listed at the end of each chapter, and also appear in the margins with definitions.
- **Summary of Major Points** that are chapter summaries intended to reinforce the chapter content and to aid in study for exams and quizzes, as well as to provide another check for students to make sure they have not missed an important concept of the chapter.
- End-of-Chapter materials that include:
- **Review Questions** and **Analytical Questions** that appear at the end of each chapter. Questions marked with a check mark can be answered with a short answer or a single number. Instructors may choose to use these objective questions for homework in larger sections.
- Annotated **Suggested Readings** that direct the student to related material and include relevant information available on the Internet.

SUPPLEMENTS TO THE TEXT

The Financial System and the Economy, fifth edition offers a comprehensive and well-crafted supplements package for the instructor.

- The test bank was carefully prepared by the authors and questions have been thoroughly tested on students.
- Microsoft PowerPoint slides have also been prepared by the authors and can be used to enhance lectures. The slides contain all of the exhibits in the text and additional lecture slides that follow the material covered in the text.

ACKNOWLEDGMENTS

Many people have made important contributions to this text. Special thanks go to Lynn Taylor, our Executive Editor at ME Sharpe, who was always supportive, enthusiastic, and helpful. She is a first rate editor. We also owe a debt of gratitude to Stacey Victor who did a great job handling the production aspects of the text. Both are delightful to work with.

Other people also deserve special recognition. As always, Professor Emeritus George Galbreath gave invaluable comments and insights, answered every question with thought and detail, and provided overall support and encouragement. Dr. Bryan Taylor, President of Global Financial Data in Los Angeles California provided much of the data and answered innumerable questions. Professor James Sutton also gave invaluable criticisms and suggestions. We are also grateful to our families and friends for their comfort, support, and understanding of our obsessive compulsive desires to create this text.

We are also indebted to many current and former students who have assisted us in a myriad of ways and enriched our lives. Roberto Ayala, Adam DeAvilan, Benton Wolverton, Naomi Rose Beezy, Ryanne Spady, Junyan Wang, Michael Medrano, and Duane A. Dohrman II.

PART 1

Introduction

CHAPTER ONE

Introduction and Overview

Learning Objectives

After reading this chapter, you should know:

The subject matter of economics and finance

The general role of the financial system in a modern economy

The major functions of financial markets and financial intermediaries

What saving is and its uses

How the financial system channels funds from lenders to borrowers

The role of the Federal Reserve and its regulatory and monetary policy responsibilities

WHAT THIS BOOK IS ABOUT

Why have financial institutions and financial regulations changed so dramatically in the last 25 years? Why do banks and others pay so much attention to what the Federal Reserve is doing? What is meant by the *globalization* of financial markets? How have technological changes affected financial markets? What are the complex financial instruments known as *derivatives*? Why have there been so many mergers between financial institutions? Why does the international value of the dollar fluctuate so much? Why does the economy experience periodic bouts of high unemployment and/or high inflation? What are the causes of the severe economic downturn in 2008 and 2009? What can policy makers do to mitigate this crisis that started in the financial system and spread to the broader economy?

We could go on, but you get the idea. This list of questions represents only a sample of the issues that motivate the discussions of theory, institutions, and policy found throughout the text. As the questions indicate, these matters affect many aspects of our lives every day.

This chapter begins your study of money and the financial system. It introduces the subject matter and provides an overview of the key concepts and relationships that are vital to understanding the system. Most of the details are ignored, and most terms are not rigorously defined and examined; this is the introduction! However, don't underestimate the importance of a good beginning.

ECONOMIC AND FINANCIAL ANALYSIS OF AN EVER-CHANGING SYSTEM

Economics
The study of how society decides what gets produced and how, and who gets what.

Economics is the study of how a society decides what gets produced, how it gets produced, and who gets what. More specifically, given unlimited wants on the part of society, economics is concerned with the following processes:

1. How scarce resources (land, labor, capital, and natural resources) are allocated in the production process among competing uses.[1]
2. How income generated in the production and sale of goods and services is distributed among members of society.
3. How people allocate their income through spending, saving, borrowing, and lending decisions.

Microeconomics
The branch of economics that studies the behavior of individual decision-making units such as households and business firms.

For convenience, economics is traditionally divided into the study of the causes and consequences of individual decision-making units such as households and business firms in a particular market, and the study of the causes and the effects resulting from the sum of decisions made by all firms or households in many markets. The former type of analysis is called **microeconomics**; the latter, more aggregative, type is called **macroeconomics**.

Macroeconomics
The branch of economics that studies the aggregate, or total, behavior of all households and firms.

Finance is the study of the financial or monetary aspects of production, spending, borrowing, and lending decisions. Finance deals with the raising and using of money by individuals, firms, governments, and foreign investors. We are familiar with our decisions to spend, borrow, lend, or save. Our everyday language includes such terms as *interest rates*, *checking accounts*, *debit cards*, *banks*, and *credit cards*. Finance in this context deals with how individuals manage money.

Finance
The study of how the financial system coordinates and channels the flow of funds from lenders to borrowers—and vice versa— and how new funds are created by financial intermediaries during the borrowing process.

At a macro level, finance is concerned with how the financial system coordinates and channels the flow of funds from lenders to borrowers and vice versa, and how new funds may be created during the borrowing process. The channeling and coordination process and its effects on the cost and availability of funds link developments in the financial system to developments in the rest of the economy. This aspect of financial analysis is emphasized in this text.

As you will soon learn, the production and sale of goods and services within the economic system are intimately related to the deposits, stocks and bonds, and other financial instruments that are bought and sold in the financial system. Thus, what happens on Wall Street can have a profound effect on what happens on Main Street and vice versa.

Because the financial system is vital to a healthy economy, the government regulates and supervises its operation. Such regulatory policy is aimed at promoting an efficient financial system. By establishing and enforcing operating regulations for financial markets and institutions, regulators seek to promote competition and efficiency while preserving the safety and soundness of the system.

Complicating our analysis of the interaction between the financial system and the economy is the fact that the financial system is not stagnant. It continually evolves and changes, sometimes at a faster pace than at other times. For various reasons (discussed in later chapters), the past several decades have seen rapid change, including the ongoing globalization of financial markets. The system is different than it was 20 years ago, and it will be different 20 years from now. The major forces behind these changes are changes in government regulations, advances in computer technologies, and innovations in the ways people spend, save, and borrow funds.

In recent decades, firms and individuals have developed new ways to raise and use money. Today, many manifestations of these financial innovations are all around us. For example, 24-hour automated teller machines (ATMs) are common, debit cards and credit cards are widely accepted at grocery stores, gas stations, and department stores, and home equity lines of credit allow home owners to borrow against the equity in their homes by writing checks as the need arises. Investors have an increasing array of mutual funds and other domestic and global financial instruments to choose from. Stocks and bonds can be purchased over the Internet at a fraction of the brokerage fees charged by full-service brokerage firms. None of these innovations were widely available in the mid-1980s.

New ways for financial and nonfinancial firms to manage risks also have been developed. Banks have merged with brokerage firms, insurance companies, and other firms that offer a whole host of financial and nonfinancial services. All this merger activity in the financial services industry has created new types of financial institutions that transcend national borders. Although still in an early stage in the United States, the use of smart cards and stored-value cards (as well as other ways to make electronic payments) is expected to explode in the very near future. These developments, most of which have been made possible because of changes in technology, have had or will have an impact on spending, saving, borrowing, and lending decisions. Not surprisingly, then, we shall closely examine the causes and consequences of these changes in the financial system.

Because of these financial innovations and other factors, U.S. Congress and the regulatory authorities such as the Federal Reserve have had to reconsider the costs and benefits associated with certain regulations. From the early 1970s until the late 1980s, regulatory changes were mostly in the direction of **deregulation**, which is the removing or phasing out of some existing regulations. Some regulations were eliminated because it was felt that they had become increasingly ineffective as firms and households found ways to get around them. Other regulations were removed because they were believed to inhibit competition and weaken rather than strengthen the financial system. During the late 1980s and early 1990s, however, crises in various financial markets, sometimes requiring taxpayer bailouts, led to attempts at *re-regulation*. By the mid-1990s, the recovery of the financial services industry and a booming economy led to the passage of major legislation that removed regulations forbidding interstate branching by banks. This, coupled with continuing advances in computer technologies,

Deregulation
The removing or phasing out of existing regulations.

fostered dramatic changes in the financial system. In the early 2000s, major legislation took effect that further deregulated the activities of firms in the financial services industry. The new legislation allowed banking, investment, and insurance services to be offered by one giant financial supermarket that made possible one-stop shopping for all their customers' financial services needs. As the financial system continues to evolve, we can expect that new and different ways of regulating will be introduced, analyzed, and tested, including the growth of international standards for financial institutions that participate in the global financial system. In 2008, the economy was experiencing an unparalleled banking crisis that some analysts thought was partially caused by the earlier deregulation. This crisis will undoubtedly hasten the passage of new legislation to regulate the financial system. Nevertheless, the goals of ensuring the safety and soundness of the financial system while fostering efficiency and competition will remain the same.

FINANCE IN OUR DAILY LIVES

Money
Something acceptable and generally used as payment for goods and services.

An individual's financial objective is to make payments when due and to manage funds efficiently until they are needed. To make payments we need money—that is, something that is acceptable in payment, whether it's for a cup of coffee or rent on a beach house.[2] While reading this book, keep in mind that only money can generally be used for payments.

In our daily lives, we receive income periodically (weekly, monthly, etc.), but our expenditures are more or less continuous, depending on our lifestyles. Given this lack of synchronization between the receipt of income and expenditures, we need to manage our money over, say, a month so that funds will be available when we make purchases of goods and services—called *consumption spending.* Income that is not spent on consumption is called saving. Part of household saving may be spent directly on investment goods, such as new houses.[3] With the remainder of saving, individuals will acquire financial assets, which also have to be managed.

Saving
Income not spent on consumption.

How might the funds not used for consumption or investment in new houses be managed? We could take currency (paper money), put it in an empty coffee can, and bury it in the backyard. We also could put the funds into a savings or money market account to earn interest. Other alternatives include buying corporate bonds, shares of common stock, Treasury bills, or other financial assets. The choices we make depend on how we wish to balance the key financial characteristics of concern to savers: the expected return (gain) and the risk of loss associated with acquiring and holding a particular asset. Some assets, such as Treasury bills, are relatively riskless; if you own such bills, you can be pretty sure the government will pay the interest and principal you are due. Other assets, such as bonds issued by new corporations not yet earning significant profits, may offer a much higher return, but they also carry the risk that the firm may fail and declare bankruptcy, meaning you will get nothing! Moreover, if an unexpected need arises and you need to get back the funds you originally loaned, you want your funds to be invested in liquid assets that can be converted quickly to cash without substantial loss. Balancing such considerations is the essence of managing a portfolio—a collection of financial assets—be it by an individual or by a financial institution.

What has just been described should be familiar, but to facilitate clarity and effective communication, the terminology employed in this text must be distinguished from colloquial use. *Income* is the flow of revenue (receipts) we receive over time for our services. With this income, we can buy and consume goods. If we have funds left over after consumption, we are saving, and we have to decide how to allocate those funds among the various types of financial assets available or invest them in real assets such as new

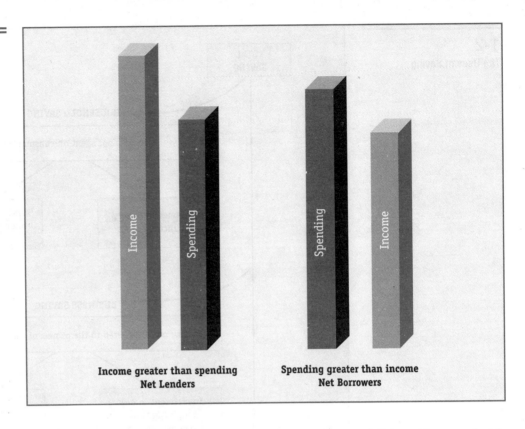

**Income greater than spending
Net Lenders**

**Spending greater than income
Net Borrowers**

Net Lenders
Spending units such as
households and firms whose
income exceeds their spending.

Net Borrowers
Spending units such as
households and firms whose
spending exceeds their income.

houses. If, however, we spend more than we earn, we have a deficit and have to decide how to finance it. When we spend less on consumption and investment goods than our current income, we are **net lenders.** If the opposite is true, we are **net borrowers.** Exhibit 1-1 portrays net lenders and net borrowers.

So far we have restricted our analysis to individuals and households, but business firms may also spend more or less than their income. Business firms do not spend on consumption, so all business income is saving except income distributed as dividends to the owners of the firms. With their saving, business firms make investment expenditures in capital and inventories or acquire financial assets. A firm's investment expenditures often exceed its available funds.[4] In this case, the firm incurs financial liabilities by issuing financial claims against itself. Note that every financial instrument is an asset to the owner (buyer) of the instrument and a liability to the issuer (seller). Exhibit 1-2 shows the uses of saving for households and business firms.

The fact that some people or business firms are in deficit positions while others are in surplus positions creates an opportunity or a need for a way to match them up. The financial system links up these net lenders and net borrowers. The government and foreign sectors may also spend more or less than their current available funds and hence be net borrowers or net lenders.

Recap   Economics studies how scarce resources are allocated among conflicting wants. Finance studies how the financial system coordinates and channels the flows of funds from net lenders to net borrowers. Net lenders spend less than their current income. Net borrowers spend more than their current income. Household saving may be used for investment in new housing or to acquire financial assets. Business saving may be used for investment in capital and inventories or to acquire financial assets. Financial instruments are financial assets to the holder of the instrument and financial liabilities to the issuer.

1-2
The Uses of Saving

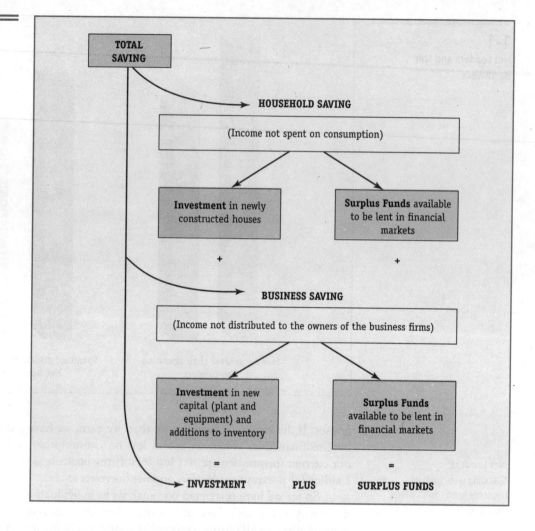

Financial Markets
Markets in which spending units trade financial claims.

Direct Finance
When net lenders lend their funds directly to net borrowers.

Financial Institutions
Firms that provide financial services to net lenders and net borrowers; the most important financial institutions are financial intermediaries.

Financial Intermediaries
Financial institutions that borrow from net lenders for the purpose of lending to net borrowers.

Indirect Finance
When net borrowers borrow from financial intermediaries that have acquired the funds to lend from net lenders.

INTRODUCING THE FINANCIAL SYSTEM

A well-organized, efficient, smoothly functioning financial system is an important component of a modern, highly specialized economy. The financial system provides a mechanism whereby a firm or household that is a net lender may conveniently make funds available to net borrowers who intend to spend more than their current income. The key word here is *conveniently*.

The financial system is composed of financial markets and financial institutions. Net lenders can lend their funds directly to net borrowers in **financial markets**. An example is the market for corporate bonds. General Motors can sell bonds to finance, say, the construction of a new plant in Mexico, and Emma from Kansas can purchase some of the bonds with the income she does not spend on goods and services. This is called **direct finance**. Purchasing stocks is another example of direct finance. **Financial institutions** are firms that provide financial services to net lenders and net borrowers. The most important financial institutions are **financial intermediaries**—various institutions such as banks, savings and loan associations, and credit unions—that serve as go-betweens to link up net lenders and net borrowers. Here the linkage between saver and borrower is indirect. For example, a household might deposit some surplus funds in a savings account at a bank, and the bank, in turn, might make a loan to a borrower. This is called **indirect finance**. Even though the ultimate lender is the spending unit

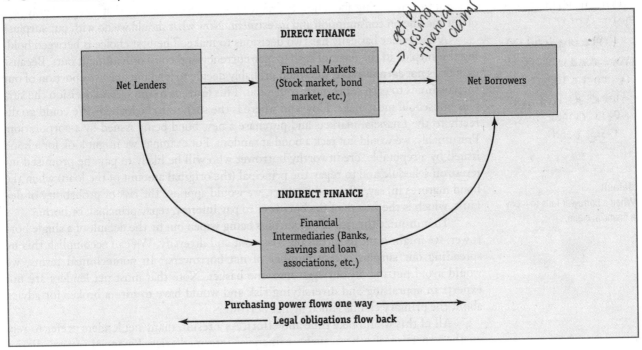

DIRECT FINANCE

Net Lenders

Financial Markets
(Stock market, bond
market, etc.)

get by issuing financial claims

Net Borrowers

INDIRECT FINANCE

Financial
Intermediaries (Banks,
savings and loan
associations, etc.)

Purchasing power flows one way ⟶
⟵ Legal obligations flow back

Financial Claims

Claims issued by net borrowers in order to borrow funds from net lenders who purchase the claims; assets to the purchaser, liabilities to the issuer.

with surplus funds, the borrower owes repayment of the loan to the financial intermediary, and the financial intermediary owes repayment of the deposit to the lender. Other financial institutions that are not financial intermediaries merely link up (for a fee) the net lenders to purchase the stocks or bonds issued by net borrowers.

Exhibit 1-3 pulls together the discussion on this point. Net lenders can lend funds either directly in the financial markets or indirectly through financial intermediaries. If they lend funds in the financial markets, they acquire direct, or primary, financial claims against the income of the borrower. Net borrowers borrow funds by issuing these **financial claims** in the market. To the holder/purchaser, the claims are assets owned; but to the issuer, the claims are liabilities owed. For example, the General Motors bonds mentioned previously are assets to Emma and liabilities to General Motors.

If net lenders lend funds through financial intermediaries, they acquire indirect, or secondary, financial claims on those intermediaries, which, in turn, acquire direct claims on net borrowers. Putting funds into a savings account is a classic example of acquiring a secondary claim on a financial institution. The institution will, in turn, make loans directly to a net borrower. Through lending activities, some financial intermediaries may also create new funds (money), which meet the needs of a growing economy. In either case, whether funds flow directly from net lenders or indirectly from intermediaries, credit is extended.

MORE ON FINANCIAL INTERMEDIARIES

One might ask, "Why do we need financial intermediaries? Why don't savers lend directly to borrowers?" To answer this, let us begin with the initial choices and decisions that we would face as a household. If we are working, we have a steady flow of income. If we spend only part of our income on consumption and investment goods, then we have a surplus and

Surplus owner's options:

1. Hold in form of cash, or lend out & gain interest?
   - Probably lend out.

2. How and where is it to be loaned?
   - look @ diff. ppl and choose less risky bond.

Default
When a borrower fails to repay a financial claim.

Transactions Costs
The costs associated with borrowing and lending or making other exchanges.

Liquidity
The ease with which a financial claim can be converted to cash without loss of value.

have funds available to lend in financial markets. If we spend more than our income, then we have a deficit and must borrow. Because deciding what to do with a surplus is more pleasant than worrying about how to finance a deficit, let us assume that we spend only part of our income on consumption and investment. Now what should we do with our surplus?

A net lender basically has two decisions to make. The first choice is between holding the surplus in the form of cash (paper currency and coin) or lending it out.[5] Because cash does not earn interest, we would probably decide to lend out at least a portion of our surplus funds to earn some interest income. This leads us to the second decision the surplus household must make: How and where is the surplus to be loaned? We could go directly to the financial markets and purchase a new bond being issued by a corporation. Presumably, we would not pick a bond at random. For example, we might look for a bond issued by a reputable, creditworthy borrower who will be likely to pay the promised interest on schedule and to repay the principal (the original amount of the loan) when the bond matures in, say, 10 years. In short, we would appraise the risk or probability of **default**, which is the failure of the borrower to pay interest, repay principal, or both.

To minimize the risk of our surplus being wiped out by the default of a single borrower, we might want to spread our risks out and diversify. We can accomplish this by spreading our surplus over a number of net borrowers.[6] In nontechnical terms, we would avoid putting all our eggs into one basket. Note that most net lenders are not experts in appraising and diversifying risk and would have to hire a broker for advice about the primary claims issued by net borrowers.

All of this would take time and effort. As a result, many net lenders prefer to rely on the expertise of others, such as financial intermediaries. Financial intermediaries acquire the funds of net lenders by offering claims on themselves. Thus, the net lender has actually made a loan to the financial intermediary and therefore has a financial claim on the intermediary in the amount of the surplus funds. To determine its profit, the financial intermediary subtracts what it pays to net lenders for the use of the funds from what it earns on the loans and other investments it makes with those funds.

Financial intermediaries pool the funds they acquire from many individual net lenders and use the funds to make loans to businesses and households, purchase bonds, and so forth. The intermediaries are actually lending out the surpluses they accept from individual net lenders while also appraising and diversifying the risk associated with lending directly to net borrowers. Because the intermediaries specialize in this kind of work, it is reasonable to presume that they know what they are doing and, on average, do a better job than individual net lenders could do. Financial intermediaries minimize the costs—called transactions costs—associated with borrowing and lending.

Another reason that net lenders often entrust their funds to financial intermediaries is that the secondary (indirect) claims offered by intermediaries are often more attractive to many lenders than primary (direct) claims available in financial markets. In many cases, for example, the secondary claims of intermediaries are insured by an agency of the federal government such as the FDIC.[7] Therefore, the risk of default associated with holding a secondary claim is often less than with a primary claim.

In addition, secondary claims are attractive because they are often more liquid than primary claims. **Liquidity** refers to the ease of exchanging a financial claim for cash without loss of value. Different types of claims possess varying degrees of liquidity. A claim that is easily exchanged for cash, such as a savings deposit, is highly liquid; exchanging a less-liquid claim involves more significant time, cost, and/or inconvenience. A rare oil painting is an example of a less-liquid asset.

Suppose you loaned funds directly to a small, obscure corporation, and the loan's term of maturity (the time from when you gave the firm the funds until it must pay back the principal) was two years. You have a financial claim in the form of a loan contract, and the corporation has your surplus funds. What would happen if after one year you suddenly wanted the funds back for some emergency expenditure? You might ask the corporation to pay you back at once, before the due date of the loan. If this option is closed because the corporation is unwilling or unable to pay off the loan immediately, you might try to sell the claim on the borrower to someone else who is willing to hold it until maturity. Although there are organized markets for the buying and selling of certain types of existing financial claims, such markets do not exist for all types of claims. The hassle associated with unloading the loan contract in a time of crisis is obvious. To avoid such inconvenience, many net lenders prefer to hold claims on financial intermediaries and let the "experts" worry about any problems.

DEPOSITORY INSTITUTIONS AND OTHER TYPES OF INTERMEDIARIES

Depository Institutions
Financial intermediaries that issue checkable deposits.

The most familiar type and the largest group of financial intermediaries are **depository institutions** consisting of commercial banks, savings and loan associations, credit unions, and mutual savings banks. Not surprisingly, their principal source of funds comes from the deposits of individuals, business firms, and governments, both domestic and foreign. Depository institutions are particularly popular with net lenders because the secondary claims purchased by net lenders from them—that is, the deposits—are often insured and therefore relatively safe. **Checkable deposits**, which as the name implies are subject to withdrawal by writing a check, are now offered by all depository institutions. Such deposits are money per se because they can be used in their present form as a means of payment. Other claims on depository institutions, such as savings deposits, are also quite liquid.

Checkable Deposits
Deposits that are subject to withdrawal by writing a check.

Other types of intermediaries offer specialized secondary claims. For example, insurance companies offer financial protection against early death (life companies) or property losses (casualty companies), while pension plans provide financial resources for retirement. All of these specialized intermediaries collect savings in the form of premium payments or contributions from plan participants. Each intermediary then uses the funds to purchase a variety of primary claims from net borrowers. Investment-type intermediaries (such as mutual funds and money market funds) pool the surplus funds of many small savers and invest them in financial markets, thereby offering the small savers greater opportunities to diversify than they would otherwise realize. Exhibit 1-4 highlights the various types of intermediaries.

Although our analysis covers intermediation in general, we pay particular attention to the role of depository institutions for several reasons. For one thing, depository institutions are by far the largest type of intermediary. They also are a central part of the process that determines the nation's money supply. Because one of our main objectives is to understand the nature and role of money in our economy, we will focus on the behavior of depository institutions and the process of intermediation in which they engage. By examining how money is provided, what it costs to obtain money when we need it, and what we can earn when we have enough of it to lend out, we will learn much about how money and the financial system affect our economy.

Recap   When net lenders lend directly to net borrowers, direct finance occurs. When net lenders put their funds in financial intermediaries, which then lend to net borrowers, indirect finance occurs. Financial intermediaries acquire the funds of net lenders by issuing claims on themselves. They use the funds to purchase the financial claims of net borrowers. The most important financial intermediaries are depository institutions that issue checkable deposits. Other financial intermediaries include life and casualty insurance companies, pension funds, mutual funds, money market mutual funds, and finance companies.

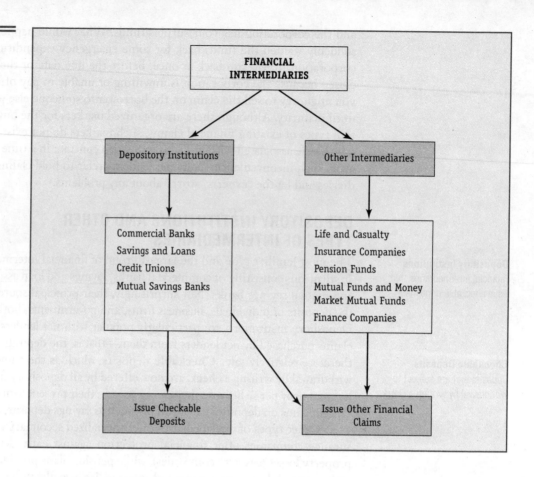

THE FEDERAL RESERVE SYSTEM

Federal Reserve (The Fed)
The central bank of the United
States that regulates the
banking system and determines
monetary policy.

The Federal Reserve (often referred to as "the Fed") greatly influences the way in which depository institutions serve as intermediaries and affect the money supply. Other financial markets and institutions are also greatly affected by the Federal Reserve. The Federal Reserve is a quasi-independent government agency that serves as our nation's central bank. Its influence begins with depository institutions and their role in the money supply process and spreads to other intermediaries and financial markets in general.

The Fed has a profound influence on the behavior of banks through 1) its regulatory policy and 2) its ability to affect interest rates and the total volume of funds available for borrowing and lending. In the past decade, depository institutions experienced a declining share of the funds available for borrowing and lending, while other financial and nonfinancial institutions have received an increasing share.[8] In addition, international financial flows (borrowing and lending that transcends national borders) have increased greatly. Because the Fed has more influence on domestic commercial banks and other depository institutions than on other financial institutions, there is concern that the Fed's ability to influence the economy through traditional avenues has actually declined. Nevertheless, the Fed continues to maintain a leading role in determining the overall health of the U.S. economy.

The Fed's influence on banks spreads through a number of channels to other financial intermediaries and to the transfer of funds from net lenders to net borrowers. By affecting interest rates and the volume of funds transferred from lenders to borrowers, the Fed can influence the aggregate, or total, demand for goods and services in the economy, and thus influences the robustness of the economy as a whole. This relationship is shown in Exhibit 1-5. The middle of this figure—the financial system and economic behavior of spending units—represents the essential anatomy or structure of the economy. The task before us is to learn how each part of the economy operates and how the collective activity of the parts is affected by the Fed's monetary policy—the Fed's efforts to promote the overall health and stability of the economy.

Monetary Policy
The Fed's efforts to promote the overall health and stability of the economy.

In terms of Exhibit 1-3, the Fed monitors the performance of the financial system and the economy with an eye toward augmenting or reducing the supply of funds flowing from lenders through financial markets and financial intermediaries to borrowers. Any action the Fed undertakes sets off a chain of reactions as depicted in Exhibit 1-5.

As we begin to think about the Fed's conduct of monetary policy and its effects on the economy, an analogy might be helpful. Think of the U.S. economy as a human patient. Just as a human body is made of many parts (arms, legs, torso), the U.S. economy is composed of many sectors (household, business, government, and foreign). Money and the acts of spending and saving and lending and borrowing are analogous to the flow of blood in the circulatory system of the body. We want to study how the flow of money and credit extension (borrowing and lending) affects the well-being of households, business firms, and the overall economy. By focusing on borrowing and lending money and on spending and saving, we will see how the major sectors of the economy interact to produce goods and services and to generate income.

The health of the U.S. economy varies over time. At times, the economy appears to be well and functioning normally; at other times, it appears listless and depressed; at still other times, it seems hyperactive—characterized by erratic, unstable behavior. By studying how all the key parts of the economy fit together, we should be able to learn something about the illnesses that can strike this patient. What causes a particular type of illness (say, inflation or unemployment)? How is the illness diagnosed? What medicines or cures can be prescribed? If more than one treatment is possible, which will work best? Are any undesirable side effects associated with particular prescriptions? Are the doctors who diagnose the problems and administer the treatment (the policy makers) ever guilty of malpractice?

All these questions depend in part on "what makes the patient tick" and how we define "good health." A human patient's health (or lack of it) is determined by the deviations, if any, from a well-established set of precise criteria involving body temperature, reflexes, blood chemistry, appetite, and so forth. For the economy, however, we have no well-established, precise criteria that allow us to judge its health. Rather, loosely defined

1-5
The Influence of the Fed's Monetary Policy

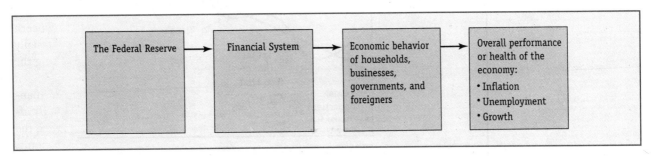

goals or objectives such as "full" employment or "low" inflation are used. If everyone agrees on these goals, including how to define and measure them, and the economy seems to be operating in the neighborhood of the goals, then we might say that the economy is in good health. If we are heading toward the goals, we would say that the economy's health is improving. If the economy seems to be deviating from the goals, we would say that its health is not good and that prescriptive measures may be necessary to improve matters.

THE ROLE OF POLICY: CHANGING VIEWS

Good health for the economy, as for humans, has both short- and long-run dimensions. Over the long run, we and policy makers would like to have the economy grow such that the quality of life and standard of living for an increasing population can improve. In the short run, we would like to minimize the fluctuations or deviations from the long-run growth path. In economics these short-run fluctuations of the economy are part of what is appropriately called the **business cycle**. Exhibit 1-6 illustrates the various stages of the business cycle and shows how they are related to the longer-run growth of the economy. The economy, like most of us, has its ups and downs. During a recovery or **expansion**, economic activity—as measured by the total quantity of goods and services being bought and sold—increases and unemployment falls. During a **recession** or contraction, economic activity decreases and unemployment rises. Just before the peak, all is bright and the economy/patient seems truly healthy. At the trough, all is bleak and the economy/patient appears quite ill. Over the longer run, we can calculate the average growth rate (trend), which smoothes out the expansions and contractions.

The key question is whether policy makers can, in fact, "manage" the economy successfully. Can they use monetary policy to minimize the short-run fluctuations of the economy over its long-run growth path? Can they use government spending and taxing decisions (**fiscal policy**) to speed up or slow down economic activity as needed? Can they, over time, change the growth rate of output? Because a look at the historical record does not provide an encouraging answer to this question, the appropriate role of policy in a complex modern economy is uncertain.

The medical profession requires considerable study and knowledge of causes and possible treatments before practitioners can diagnose and deal with an ailment. In eco-

Business Cycle
Short-run fluctuations in economic activity as measured by the output of goods and services.

Expansion
The phase of the business cycle in which economic activity increases and unemployment falls.

Recession
The phase of the business cycle in which economic activity decreases and unemployment rises.

Fiscal Policy
Government spending and taxing decisions to speed up or slow down the level of economic activity.

1-6
Long-Run Economic Growth and the Business Cycle

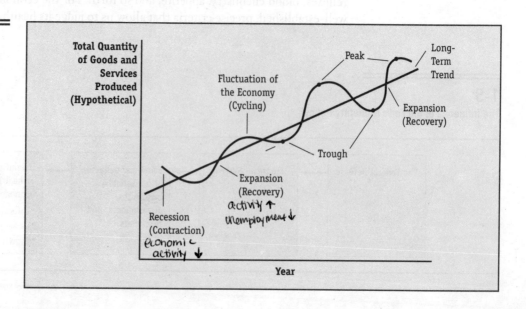

why are policy maker's goals hard to achieve?

- May not understand all causes of the problems.
- Reluctant to use known methods for fear of bad side effects.
3. The solution might not be known so they need to do more research.

nomics, despite the best efforts of eminent researchers, we still do not know how to cure some diseases; cures for all the economic ills we may encounter are simply not known.

Why are the goals that policy makers are trying to achieve so elusive? The answers are complex and fall into three possible areas.[9] First, the diagnosticians may not understand all the causes of the problems. What this really means is that we do not fully understand how the economy functions. Second, policy makers may be reluctant to use the currently known medicines to treat the patient because they have undesirable side effects, which may, in fact, be worse than the disease. Third, the cure for the problem may not yet be known, so more research will be needed to find a useful therapeutic approach. Thus far, we have assumed that the economy's illness can be cured only by doctors and their medicines. But could the patient get better without outside intervention?

Before the Great Depression of the 1930s, many economists tended to see the economy as inherently stable, having strong self-correcting tendencies. The prevailing belief was that the economy would never drift away from full-employment equilibrium for long; any disturbance or shock that pushed the economy away from full employment would automatically set in motion forces tending to move it back to full-employment equilibrium.[10] There was no need for corrective government action, then, because any movement away from equilibrium would be temporary and self-correcting. This view of the economy provided an economic rationale for the government to pursue a **laissez-faire,** hands-off policy.

Laissez-Faire
The view that government should pursue a hands-off policy with regard to the economy.

- the economy will self-correct when things get bad.

- Keynsian belief says that it will <u>not</u> fix itself, and it can continue to be bad for a while. (GD era beliefs)

The Great Depression altered this view of the economy's internal dynamics. Between 1929 and 1933, the unemployment rate increased from about 3 percent to about 25 percent. The downturn was experienced worldwide and persisted until the start of World War II. Few could argue, in the face of such evidence, that the problem was correcting itself. The economist John Maynard Keynes and others suggested that once the economy's full-employment equilibrium was disturbed, its self-correcting powers were likely to be overwhelmed by other forces. The net result would be that the economy could operate below full employment for some time.

This new perspective gave the government an economic rationale for attempting to stabilize overall economic activity. A consensus formed that a highly developed market economy, if left to itself, would be unstable. As a result, "activist" stabilization policy has been practiced by both Democratic and Republican administrations since the mid-1930s. Until the early 1980s, there had been relatively little debate about whether the government should intervene. Rather, the debate was about when, how, and to what degree the government should use its policies to help reestablish a full-employment, low-inflation equilibrium.

However, the economy's performance in the 1970s and the early 1980s gave rise to doubts about the government's ability to stabilize the economy. As Exhibit 1-7 shows, the growth trend of the economy was below that achieved in the 1960s, and the fluctuations around the trend were quite large. The unemployment and inflation rates were both higher in the 1970s and early 1980s than they had been in the 1960s. These developments raised many questions. Does the government know how to proceed to restore the patient's health? If it acts without adequate knowledge, can policy make things worse rather than better? Many people reverted to the pre-Depression view that "less government intervention in the economy is better." But reducing the role of government may be difficult. Attempts to do so in the 1980s resulted in larger government deficits, not less government.

Although the economy experienced healthy growth from about 1983 until the late 1980s, many believed that this growth was produced by large government deficits and increases in military spending. Chronic trade deficits, problem loans to less-developed countries, troubles within the savings and loan industry, and the collapse of the junk bond market were of concern to many.

1-7

Average Inflation,
Unemployment, and Growth
During Recent Decades

	Inflation	Unemployment	Growth (Output)
1960s	2.4%	4.75%	4.4%
1970s	7.0	6.25	3.2
1980s	5.5*	8.25	2.8
1990s	3.3	5.7**	3.7
2000–2008***	1.7	4.66	2.4

*Actually, if the early 1980s are not considered, inflation averaged just under 4 percent for the remainder of the decade.
**From mid-1997 through the rest of the decade, unemployment was below 5 percent.
***Annualized through second quarter 2006. Actually, after the second quarter of 2008, prices fell and there was moderate deflation (falling overall prices) for the remainder of the year. Unemployment also surged in the second half of 2008.

The recession of the early 1990s caused anxiety, not because of its depth or length, but because the recovery was so sluggish. Growth remained lethargic well into the first half of 1993. However, by early 1994, economic growth had accelerated and remained high throughout the remainder of the decade while inflation remained subdued. Toward the end of the 1990s, the long expansion resulted in an unemployment rate of 4 percent—the lowest rate in over 30 years. Surprisingly, there was little or no acceleration of inflation.

Stock and bond prices experienced extraordinary increases from the mid-1990s into early 2000, even though Alan Greenspan, then the Fed chair, voiced concern in December 1996 that an "irrational exuberance" was taking over in these markets. Despite a moderate correction of stock prices in October 1997, the stock market again closed at a record high in July 1998. To some, the Asian Crisis of 1997 meant good news for the U.S. economy, which was believed to be less likely to overheat. By late summer 1998, stock prices finally succumbed to the international financial problems. Stock prices plummeted about 20 percent, and questions surfaced about whether the U.S. economy could withstand a global downturn. The Fed responded by lowering interest rates three times in the fall of 1998. The fiscal year ended on September 30, 1998, with a widely publicized federal government budget surplus of $70 billion—the first surplus since 1969. By the end of calendar year 1998, lower interest rates had the desired effect, and the stock market rebounded strongly to new highs.

The economy continued to expand into the new millennium with the stock market reaching record highs in March 2000. However, there were clouds on the horizon that suggested the record-long expansion could not last forever. From March 2000 on, the technology-dominated NASDAQ index of stock prices plummeted, losing over 50 percent of its value by December 31, 2000, and the DOW, the best-known index of stock prices, ended the year 2000 down and continued to collapse in one of the worst bear markets in history. Worries that the economy was heading steeply down caused the Fed to take action to lower interest rates in early January 2001.

Many factors continued to threaten the record expansion, including falling profits, the prolonged effects of the bursting of the stock market bubble, escalating energy prices, announcements of significant layoffs, and drops in consumer confidence. The attack on the World Trade Center and the Pentagon in September 2001 resulted in further economic turmoil, and the U.S. government announced that a recession had actually begun in March 2001. All in all, the Fed took action to lower interest rates thirteen times from January 2001 through June 2003. During this time, rates went down to 45-year lows. Although the recession officially ended in November 2001, the economy languished in a jobless recovery throughout 2003. A large tax cut and a weak economy caused tax revenues to decline, while wars in Afghanistan and Iraq caused expenditures to balloon. The short-lived government surplus became a record government deficit.

By early 2004, the expansion had picked up pace, and the Fed's aggressive monetary policy continued to foster robust employment growth. In mid-2004, the Fed became concerned about inflation and began taking action to raise interest rates. By June 2006, the interest rate the Fed controls had been increased seventeen times to 5.25 percent. The Fed then held rates steady until September 2007. At that time, it became clear that the housing collapse and high oil prices were contributing to the severest financial crisis since the Great Depression and the Fed began what would be a long series of interest rate cuts. This aggressive action by the Fed was fostered by record collapses or the need for government bailouts of many large financial firms such as Countrywide, Bear Stearns, Indy Mac Bank, Lehman Brothers, Merrill Lynch, Fannie Mae, Freddie Mac, the American International Group (AIG), and Washington Mutual. In late September 2008, Congress, at the urging of the Treasury, the Fed and President Bush, passed the largest government bailout plan in history for the financial system. Under the plan, the government would inject up to $700 billion into financial markets to mitigate the crisis. The series of interest rate cuts by the Fed continued until December 2008. At that time, the target for the interest rate the Fed controls was at 0 to .25 percent—an historic low. Despite falling oil prices in late 2008, the economy had shed 2.6 million jobs in 2008, the unemployment rate soared, and many feared the economy was plunging into the worst downturn since the Great Depression. The major domestic automakers, on the doorstep of bankruptcy, requested and received a bailout from the government. The crisis continued to deepen in early 2009 and newly sworn-in President Obama promised an even bigger bailout to get the economy going again. The new administration also promised regulatory reforms to prevent such a catastrophic crisis in the future.

One thing is clear: monetary policy makers and those affected by changes in the financial environment—each of us—will make better decisions if we understand the concepts of money and credit extension and their effects on the financial system and the economy.

Summary of Major Points

1. Economics is concerned with how, given people's unlimited wants, scarce resources are allocated among competing uses, how income is distributed, and how people allocate their incomes through spending, saving, borrowing, and lending decisions.
2. Finance focuses on the financial side of these decisions—that is, the raising and using of funds by households, firms, and governments.
3. The financial system coordinates and channels the flow of funds from lenders to borrowers and creates new liquidity for an expanding economy.

The characteristics of this process have changed over time as innovations and changes in regulations have occurred.
4. Spending units that spend less than their current income on consumption and investment are called *net lenders*. Spending units that spend more than their current income are called *net borrowers*.
5. In allocating funds among the various types of financial assets available, net lenders are concerned about the expected return, the risk of loss, and the liquidity associated with acquiring and holding a particular asset.

6. Direct finance involves lending directly to net borrowers. Indirect finance involves lending to a financial intermediary, a type of financial institution that borrows in order to re-lend. Financial intermediaries issue claims on themselves. The lenders receive financial claims on the financial intermediaries, and the borrowers receive funds from the financial intermediaries.

7. Financial intermediaries exist because they help to minimize the transactions costs associated with borrowing and lending. The financial services provided include appraising and diversifying risk, offering a menu of financial claims that are relatively safe and liquid, and pooling funds from individual net lenders.

8. The most important types of financial intermediaries are the depository institutions: commercial banks, savings and loan associations, mutual savings banks, and credit unions. These institutions are central to the process of determining the nation's money supply. Other types of financial intermediaries are life and casualty insurance companies, pension funds, mutual funds and money market mutual funds, and finance companies.

9. The Federal Reserve is a quasi-independent government agency that serves as our nation's central bank. Its regulatory policy is aimed at promoting a smooth-running, efficient, competitive financial system. The Fed's monetary policy, which influences interest rates and the volume of funds available for borrowing and lending (credit extension), is directed at enhancing the overall health and stability of the economy. Although the Fed works primarily through depository institutions, its influence spreads from depository institutions to the financial system.

10. Views on the appropriate role of policy in the economy have varied over time. Throughout the middle and late 1980s, the economy experienced healthy growth that was accompanied by large trade and government deficits. After a recession in the early 1990s, economic growth resumed, and the economy achieved both low inflation and low unemployment with a record-long expansion into the new millennium. A recession had actually begun in March 2001, and although it officially ended eight months later, the recovery remained sluggish through 2003 despite aggressive expansionary monetary policy by the Fed. The recovery picked up steam in 2004, and the Fed took action to increase interest rates until mid-2006, when the possibility of a downturn again seemed on the horizon. Rates were held steady until September 2007. At that time, it became clear that the housing collapse had caused a severe crisis in the financial sector and the Fed responded by cutting interest rates to historic lows. This aggressive action by the Fed did not stop record collapses or government bailouts of many large financial firms and the largest financial bailout of the financial system in history. In early 2009, President Obama promised an even bigger bailout package to get the economy going again. Many feared the economy was plunging into a catastrophic downturn.

Key Terms

Business Cycle, p. **14**	Finance, p. **4**	Macroeconomics, p. **4**
Checkable Deposits, p. **11**	Financial Claims, p. **9**	Microeconomics, p. **4**
Default, p. **10**	Financial Institutions, p. **8**	Monetary Policy, p. **13**
Depository Institutions, p. **11**	Financial Intermediaries, p. **8**	Money, p. **6**
Deregulation, p. **5**	Financial Markets, p. **8**	Net Borrowers, p. **7**
Direct Finance, p. **8**	Fiscal Policy, p. **14**	Net Lenders, p. **7**
Economics, p. **4**	Indirect Finance, p. **8**	Recession, p. **14**
Expansion, p. **14**	Laissez-Faire, p. **15**	Saving, p. **6**
Federal Reserve, p. **12**	Liquidity, p. **10**	Transactions Costs, p. **10**

Review Questions

1. Provide a short discussion or definition of the following terms: *economics, finance, the financial system, net lenders, net borrowers, direct and indirect finance, financial markets, financial intermediaries, liquidity, business cycle, depository institutions,* and *monetary policy.*

2. Some people have money; some people need money. Explain how the financial system links these people together.

3. Discuss the statement: "Since I have high credit card limits, I have lots of money." Are credit cards money? Why or why not? (*Hint:* See Endnote 2.)

4. When are the surplus funds I have available to lend in financial markets equal to my saving?

5. Why do financial intermediaries exist? What services do they provide to the public? Are all financial institutions financial intermediaries?

6. What are transactions costs? Does financial intermediation increase or decrease transactions costs?

7. What is a depository institution? What is a checkable deposit? How does a depository institution differ from other intermediaries? Give three examples of depository institutions.

8. Why does the Fed monitor the economy? What actions can the Fed take to affect the overall health of the economy?

9. Why have views changed concerning the appropriate role of stabilization policies in managing the economy? Briefly discuss the historical evolution of these views.

10. What are the pros and cons of lending to my next door neighbor rather than putting my surplus funds in a bank?

11. Define *laissez-faire* and *fiscal policy.* Who determines fiscal policy? Who determines monetary policy?

Analytical Questions

Questions marked with a check mark (✓) are objective in nature. They can be completed with a short answer or number.

12. Rank the following assets in terms of their liquidity, from least to most liquid: cash, savings deposits, gold, a house, a rare oil painting, a checkable deposit. Explain your rank order.

✓13. Is each of the following an example of direct or indirect financing?
    a. John purchases stock from the biotech firm that employs him.
    b. Mary purchases a newly issued government security.
    c. John places $3,000 in a savings account at the local savings and loan.
    d. John receives a loan from Mary.
    e. John receives a loan from Friendly Savings Bank.

✓14. Bill's income is $4,000. He spends $3,000 on consumption and $300 on an investment in a newly constructed house. He acquires $700 in financial assets. What is his saving? What is the amount of surplus funds he has available to lend?

✓15. A firm spends $100,000 on investment in plant and equipment. It has available funds of $30,000 and borrows the additional funds from a bank. Is the firm a net borrower or a net lender? What is the amount of the surplus or deficit?

✓16. Diane Weil earns wages of $45,000 and interest and dividend income of $5,000. She spends $8,000 as a down payment on a newly constructed mountain cabin and lends $4,000 in financial markets. Assuming that Diane spends the remainder of her income on consumption, what is her saving? Is she a net lender or net borrower? What is her consumption?

✓17. Tech Corp had gross sales of $9 million and total expenses of $8.5 million. Assume that Tech wants to undertake a capital investment of $1 million. What is the minimum amount of bonds it would have to issue to do so? Assume that Tech pays out $300,000 in dividends. Now what is the minimum amount it would have to borrow?

✓18. What are the phases of a business cycle? Draw a graph of a typical business cycle and label the various phases.

✓19. The *misery index* is defined as the sum of the unemployment and the inflation rates. Use Exhibit 1-7 to calculate the misery index for each decade since 1960.

Suggested Readings

If the material covered in the text is to come alive and make sense to you, we suggest you try to read *The Wall Street Journal* and *Business Week* regularly. In fact, hardly a day goes by without a report on an issue that is in some way relevant to our subject. You might also consult *The New York Times, The Washington Post,* or *The Los Angeles Times;* all have good financial sections. Or you can browse the financial sections of *USA Today* (**http://www.usatoday.com**) or CNN (**http://www.money.cnn.com**) on the World Wide Web.

The *Federal Reserve Bulletin* presents policy issues of concern to the Board of Governors. Since 2006, *Federal Reserve Bulletin* articles have been published on the World Wide Web at **http://www.federalreserve.gov/pubs/bulletin/default.htm** as they become available.

A plethora of financial statistics can also be found in the Federal Reserve Bank Economic Database Web site (**http://www.research.stlouisfed.org/fred2/**).

A wealth of information about the current state of the economy and attempts at stabilization by the government can be found in *The Economic Report of the President.* It is published annually during the month of February by the U.S.

Government Printing Office and is available at the reference desk of most libraries. It is also available on the Internet at **http://www.access.gpo.gov/eop/**.

The Statistical Abstract of the United States contains summary data on income, expenditures, wealth, prices, and the financial system (among other things). It is published annually during December by the Census Bureau of the U.S. Department of Commerce. *The Statistical Abstract* is also available at the following Census Bureau Web page: **http://www.census.gov/compendia/statab/**.

The Survey of Current Business, published monthly by the Bureau of Economic Analysis, Department of Commerce, contains current business and income statistics. It is available on the World Wide Web at **http://bea.gov/scb/index.htm**. For a brief history of the Federal Reserve, go to **http://www.minneapolisfed.org/info/sys/history/**.

For more on monetary policy, see **http://www.minneapolisfed.org/info/policy/**.

For more information about business cycle expansions and contractions, see **http://www.frbsf.org/education/activities/drecon/2002/0205.html**.

Endnotes

1. When economists use the term *capital* in this context, they mean machinery and equipment that are used to produce other goods and services. For example, a sewing machine that produces shirts is capital.
2. Credit cards are not money. When a credit card is used, the user is taking out a loan by authorizing the institution that issued the credit card to make a payment with money on his or her behalf. Ultimately, the individual must pay credit card balances with money.
3. As used here, *investment in houses* refers to expenditures for new residential construction, where a service is rendered over a period of time.
4. Firms also make investment expenditures to replace worn-out capital.
5. There is another option. If we owe back debts, we could employ surplus funds to pay off those debts.
6. If we have only a small amount of surplus funds available, it may be extremely difficult to diversify to a significant extent. As we shall see in later chapters, small investors can use mutual funds to accomplish this objective.
7. The Federal Deposit Insurance Corporation (FDIC) enables the public to feel confident that funds deposited in a bank or savings and loan, up to a limit (currently $100,000), are safe. If the institution fails, the FDIC will step in and pay off the depositors. When financial institutions were failing daily during the early years of the Great Depression in the 1930s, the government became convinced of the pressing need for such an agency. See **http://www.fdic.gov/**.
8. Examples of very large nonfinancial institutions that have entered the lending business include General Electric (GE), Sears, and General Motors (GM), all of which now issue credit cards.

9. The complex answers are tackled in Part Six of the text.

10. *Equilibrium* is a concept used by economists to help analyze the economy. It refers to a state of the economy from which there is no tendency to deviate—a state of rest. Of course, in reality, the economy is constantly being bombarded with disturbances and is hardly ever "at rest." The concept of equilibrium, then, is an analytical device that helps us sort out the influences of many different factors, which, in the real world, are often all changing at the same time.

CHAPTER TWO

Money is like muck—not good unless you spread it.

—Francis Bacon

Money and Its Role in the Economy

Learning Objectives

After reading this chapter, you should know:

What the functions of money are

How the Fed defines the monetary aggregates M1 and M2 and the credit aggregate domestic nonfinancial debt (DNFD)

The evolution of the payments system

How the demand and supply of money influence the interest rate

How, in general, changes in money and credit influence the level of economic activity

CONCEPTUALIZATION: A KEY BUILDING BLOCK

As the week ends in the dormitory dining hall, Mary, the dining hall supervisor, calls Randy, the dishwasher, over and gives him his pay envelope. It should contain $50. Finding the envelope somewhat thicker than normal, Randy opens it and discovers five $10 tickets to the university's spring play next Saturday night. Tired and somewhat irritated, especially since he has already seen the performance, he tells Mary he wants money, not these tickets. Mary tries to persuade Randy to accept the tickets instead but fails and eventually produces a university check made out to Randy for $50.

A simple story. Yet it touches on most of the key issues addressed in this chapter: Why did Randy want money instead of the tickets? Why does he accept the check? Why aren't the tickets money? Why aren't they as good as money? As we shall see, the term *money* is used rather sloppily in everyday language.

The purpose of this chapter is twofold: first, to nail down the definition of money, and, second, to introduce money's importance, not only for Randy, but for the economy as a whole.

DEFINING MONEY

A good definition enables us to separate the thing being defined from all other things. Economists define *money* in terms of its specific functions within the financial system—by what it does. By specifying precisely what it does, we can distinguish money from everything else we observe in the financial system, even those things that at first glance appear quite similar. Of particular interest is what makes money unique: What does it do that other things do not?

The primary function of money, and the function that distinguishes it from all else in the financial system, is that it serves as a generally acceptable means of payment, or medium of exchange. As Chapter 1 stated, money is what we generally use to make payments and, thus, what is generally accepted as payment. The importance of money's function as a means of payment is so obvious that it is often overlooked.

Imagine a world without money where all goods were exchanged or traded by barter—by trading goods for goods. If you worked in a computer factory, you might be paid in keyboards, which would not only be difficult to exchange for other goods and services but also rather cumbersome to carry around. To buy groceries, for example, you would have to persuade the grocer to accept your keyboards for payment. There would be no reason for the grocer to do so, unless she had a use for additional keyboards or knew someone else who did. Finding such a double coincidence of wants, the situation when the grocer has what you want (groceries) and you have what she wants (keyboards), would often be extremely difficult. Thus, exchange under a barter system is costly in terms of search time—the time spent looking for someone who has groceries and wants computer keyboards. In general, the time and effort associated with barter make it a cumbersome and inefficient way to conduct transactions. It raises transactions costs, which are all costs involved with making exchanges. In turn, higher transactions costs hold down the volume of exchange in the economy.

This is why barter economies tended to be mostly agricultural. With the volume of trade relatively low and exchanges costly to carry out, one could never be sure of finding a double coincidence of wants. As a result, almost everyone produced the food and other items they needed to survive so that very few exchanges would be necessary. If some individuals decided to specialize and trade, they had an incentive to produce the goods that were easiest to trade rather than the goods that they were best at producing. For efficiency to occur, people should specialize in what they can most efficiently produce, which is ex-

Money
Anything that functions as a means of payment (medium of exchange), unit of account, and store of value.

Means of Payment (Medium of Exchange)
Something generally acceptable for making payments.

Barter
Trade of goods for goods.

Double Coincidence of Wants
A bartering situation in which each person involved in a potential exchange has what the other person wants.

Money, Exchange, and Economic Development

Most of us take for granted the existence of money; we have never experienced a barter system. How and why economies evolved from a primitive barter system to an advanced monetary system is a long story. The short, somewhat simplified version is that the high costs of barter exchange provided an economic incentive for people to devise a better system. Important in the early evolution of the system were the merchants who established trading posts or general stores. They purchased goods from farmers, often paying for the goods with a receipt that the farmer could later use at the store to purchase other items that the merchant had acquired from other farmers.

The receipts were an early form of money, as were the gold and silver nuggets that also came to be exchanged for goods and services at the trading posts and elsewhere. Eventually, as governments developed and the benefits of standardizing the money within an economy became apparent, governments came to produce and certify coins and paper notes (currency) as money.

By eliminating the need for a double coincidence of wants, the existence of money dramatically reduces the costs of conducting trade, thereby encouraging a larger volume of exchange. With more opportunities for exchange, it is no longer necessary for all of an economy's participants to individually produce the same goods to survive and prosper; because exchanges are faster and easier, labor time is not wasted in the trading process. People can now more easily specialize in the production of goods to which they are relatively best suited, trade these goods for money, and use the money to purchase goods produced by others. The development of the financial system and the resulting division of labor (and other resources) into the production of an increasing variety of goods are key ingredients in the process of economic development. The accompanying schematic diagram ties these several thoughts together.

```
┌─────────────────────────────────┐
│  Transactions costs             │
│  associated with barter         │
└─────────────────────────────────┘
             │
          encourage
             ↓
┌─────────────────────────────────┐
│  Development of money           │
└─────────────────────────────────┘
             │
          facilitates
             ↓
┌─────────────────────────────────┐
│  Exchange (trading)             │
└─────────────────────────────────┘
             │
          facilitates
             ↓
┌─────────────────────────────────┐
│  Specialization and division    │
│  of labor                       │
└─────────────────────────────────┘
             │
          facilitates
             ↓
┌─────────────────────────────────┐
│  Economic development           │
└─────────────────────────────────┘
```

actly what "money" in an economy encourages. Because money encourages specialization and trade, money is important in facilitating economic growth and development.

Fortunately, finding a double coincidence of wants is not necessary in today's economy because we do have something that serves as a generally acceptable means of payment—money. As a result, people can exchange goods and services for money and

handwritten note in margin: Only good system of barter is in an agricultural situation.

vice versa. To illustrate, Randy, the dishwasher, planned to exchange a week's labor for $50 and the $50 for groceries. If Randy had accepted the tickets—a type of barter transaction—he could not have eaten until he found a grocer who wanted tickets to the play. If he failed to do so by curtain time on Saturday, Randy would find that the tickets had become worthless and he would go hungry for the next week. A monetary exchange eliminates the need for a double coincidence of wants and thus facilitates trade by reducing the transactions costs involved.

Store of Value
Something that retains its value over time.

Something that becomes generally acceptable as a means of payment in exchange for goods and services will necessarily also function as a **store of value**. To be acceptable, something must store value or, more specifically, purchasing power, because people receive money and spend it at different points in time. In other words, there is a difference between the time people receive money and the time they spend it. If you are paid for your labor services today and do not need to purchase anything until tomorrow, you would presumably be unwilling to accept anything in payment that is likely to decline in value before you spend it. (Could Randy have sold the tickets to the play for $50 on Sunday, the day after the performance?) Conversely, people will accept something as a means of payment for goods and services when they believe they can easily exchange it for something else of like value in the near future.

We now know that money functions as a means of payment and store of value and what these functions mean. For monetary exchange to proceed in an orderly fashion, however, there must be some method of specifying the amount of money required to pay for a given quantity of a particular good. In other words, there is a need for an accounting unit, commonly referred to as a *unit of account*. Because all domestic prices and financial records, including debts, in the United States are expressed in dollars, the dollar serves as our monetary **unit of account**—it is the standard measure of value. To appreciate why it is convenient to have a standardized unit of account, imagine the poor grocer and the grocer's customers who, in the absence of money and a unit of account, would have to remember that one computer keyboard equals one gallon of milk, one crate of oranges equals 3 pounds of cheese, and so forth. A unit of account facilitates actual transactions throughout the economy by making it possible to compare the relative values of different goods and services and to keep records about prices and debts. Thus, $4 equals one gallon of milk or three pounds of cheese.

Unit of Account
A standardized accounting unit such as the dollar that provides a consistent measure of value.

In sum, money is whatever circulates in a modern economy as a generally acceptable means of payment. By necessity, money will also function as a store of value, and its unit of measurement will naturally become the unit of account and measure of value. The functions of money are portrayed in Exhibit 2-1.

Recap   Money can be defined by its functions. Money is anything that functions as a means of payment (medium of exchange), a unit of account, and a store of value. Money is acceptable in payment for goods and services.

THE MONETARY AGGREGATES AND DOMESTIC NONFINANCIAL DEBT

Given our definition, measuring the quantity, or stock, of money in an economy should be straightforward: add together those things that function as a means of payment. In reality, measurement is not quite so simple. There are at least two difficulties. First, what functions as a means of payment in an economy will change over time, so what is considered money will need to be revised as the economy's financial system evolves.

2-1
The Functions of Money

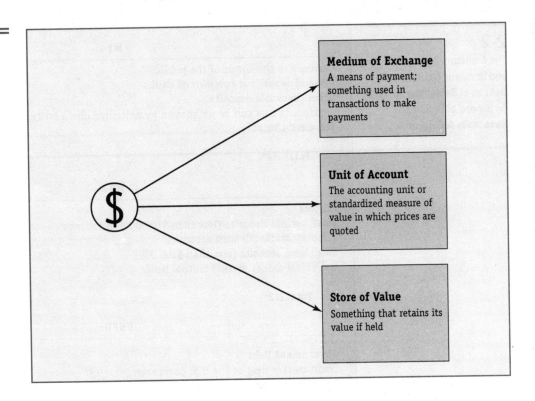

Medium of Exchange
A means of payment; something used in transactions to make payments

Unit of Account
The accounting unit or standardized measure of value in which prices are quoted

Store of Value
Something that retains its value if held

Money Market Deposit Accounts (MMDAs)
Financial claims with limited check-writing privileges, offered by banks since 1982; they earn higher interest than fully checkable deposits and require a higher minimum balance.

Monetary Aggregates
The measures of money—including M1 and M2—monitored and tracked by the Fed.

M1
Currency in the hands of the public plus checkable deposits.

M2
Everything in M1 plus other highly liquid assets.

Checkable Deposits
Deposits that are subject to withdrawal by writing a check.

Demand Deposits
Non-interest-earning checking accounts issued by banks.

For example, gold and silver coins were once money. Now they have been replaced by paper currency, coins made out of nonprecious metals, and checkable deposits. Second, some things may be difficult to classify; that is, some financial claims are on the borderline between being and not being a means of payment. For example, **money market deposit accounts (MMDAs)** that are issued by some depository institutions have limited check-writing privileges—up to three checks per month. MMDAs earn higher interest than most checking accounts and generally require a higher minimum balance. Because of the limited check-writing privileges, MMDAs have some characteristics of checking accounts even though they are primarily used as savings accounts by most individuals.

Monetary aggregates are collections of monetary assets. Today, the Fed keeps track of and monitors two monetary aggregates (M1 and M2). Changes in the monetary aggregates can provide useful information about how well the economy is doing. Exhibit 2-2 shows the composition of **M1** and **M2**. The aggregates comprise several different types of financial assets. Some items clearly serve as a means of payment (currency and checkable deposits), some are clearly not means of payment ("small" time deposits), and some are in between (money market deposit accounts).

The measure that *currently* corresponds most closely to the definition of money is **M1**. It consists of currency held by the public and checkable deposits.[1] Currency in the United States is issued by the U.S. Treasury and circulated by the Fed. **Checkable deposits** are deposits that can be withdrawn by writing a check to a third party. They consist of 1) **demand deposits**, which are non-interest-earning checking accounts issued by banks, and 2) other checkable deposits, which are interest-earning checking accounts issued by some depository institutions.

M1 contains the "monetary" assets that we use in transactions, and it is generally what we have in mind throughout the text when we refer to the *money supply*. All components of M1 are means of payment (transactions money).

Money and Its Role in the Economy   **27**

2-2

The Monetary Aggregates and Domestic Nonfinancial Debt as of September 30, 2008 (in Billions of Dollars, Seasonally Adjusted)

M1 =	
Currency in the hands of the public	$780.1
Demand deposits at commercial banks	351.9
Other checkable deposits	
(deposits that can be withdrawn by unlimited check writing)	316.1
Travelers' checks	5.8
Total M1*	**$1,453.8**

M2 =	
M1 plus	$1,453.8
Small savings deposits (less than $100,000) including	
money market deposit accounts	$4,033.5
Small time deposits (less than $100,000)	1,256.0
Individual money market mutual funds	1,026.2
Total M2	**$7,769.4**

DNFD =	
Government Debt	
Credit market debt of the U.S. government	$5,822.7
Credit market debt of state and local governments	2,231.3
Non-Government Debt	
Corporate bonds	3,703.8
Mortgages	14,559.0
Consumer credit (including bank loans)	2,590.5
Other bank loans	1,649.1
Commercial paper	401.8
Other debt instruments	2,021.3
Total DNFD	**$32,979.5**

*Components may not sum to total because of rounding.
Source: www.federalreserve.gov

Near Monies
Highly liquid financial assets that can easily be converted to transactions money (M1) without loss of value.

Domestic Nonfinancial Debt (DNFD)
An aggregate that is a measure of total credit market debt owed by the domestic nonfinancial government and private sectors.

M2 consists of everything in M1 plus some other highly liquid assets which can be converted to the items in M1 very easily without loss of value for the principal. The other highly liquid assets included in M2 are small savings and time deposits, MMDAs, and individual money market mutual funds (defined in Chapter 4). Even though these other assets are not used to make transactions, because they are all highly liquid, they are often referred to as **near monies**.

Because information about credit market activity can also provide useful information about the economy, the Fed keeps track of a broad measure of outstanding credit. This aggregate is **domestic nonfinancial debt (DNFD)**, which includes outstanding loans and debts accumulated in the present and past years. Take another look at Exhibit 2-2 for the components of DNFD. Items included in DNFD are such things as outstanding government debts, corporate bonds, mortgages, consumer credit, other banks loans, and commercial paper, which is defined in Chapter 4. Unlike the items included in M1 and M2, the components of DNFD are not money or near monies.

2-3

The Relative Size of the
Monetary Aggregates and
DNFD as of September 30,
2008 (Seasonally Adjusted)

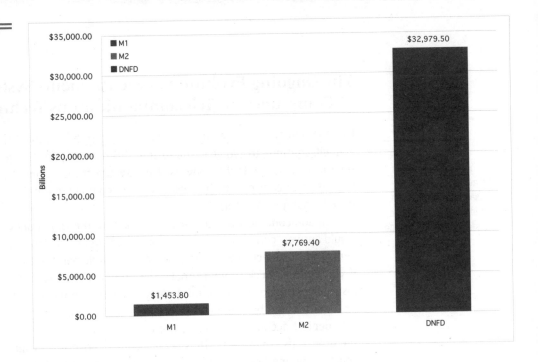

Specifically, DNFD refers to total credit market debt owed by the domestic nonfinancial sector, including the U.S. government, state and local governments, private nonfinancial firms, and households. Don't let the length of this definition confuse you. *Domestic* merely means U.S. entities, excluding foreign entities. *Nonfinancial debt* excludes the debt of financial institutions—those institutions that borrow solely to re-lend. The debt of financial institutions is excluded to avoid double counting.

For example, suppose Friendly Savings and Loan borrows surplus funds from small passbook savers and lends those funds to Jorge and Maria to buy their first home. If the debt of the financial institution were counted, both Jorge and Maria's mortgage debt and Friendly's debt to the passbook savers would be included in the aggregate. This would be double counting, because the ultimate transaction went from the passbook savers to Jorge and Maria with the savings and loan in between. Furthermore, Friendly's financial debt to the passbook savers is offset by the financial claim (mortgage) Friendly holds against Jorge and Maria.

Think of DNFD as a measure of the unpaid claims that lenders have against borrowers, excluding the debt of financial intermediaries. DNFD is probably the best measure of outstanding nonfinancial credit that we have. When credit flows increase, DNFD (the aggregate amount of debt outstanding) goes up. Likewise, when credit flows decrease, DNFD declines. Exhibit 2-3 shows the relative size of the monetary aggregates and DNFD. Exhibit 2-4 (p. 32) shows how the various aggregates have grown over time.

THE ECONOMY AND THE AGGREGATES

In the early and mid-1980s, M1 was the primary measure of money that the Fed watched. Targets were set for the growth rate of M1 that were thought to be consistent with the Fed's goal for the economy. The Fed monitored the targets to provide a barometer of economic activity. If M1 growth was above the target rate, the Fed would take actions that resulted in a slowdown in its growth, and vice versa. In either case, the goal

A Closer Look

The Ongoing Evolution of the Payments System: The Role of Computer and Telecommunications Technologies

Payments Mechanism
The means by which transactions are consummated; that is, how money is transferred in an exchange.

Like the human race, the current financial system has evolved from a primitive state and will continue to evolve in the future. This tendency to change has been influenced significantly by the technology used to execute transactions. The payments mechanism is the means by which transactions are completed—that is, how money is transferred among transactors.

If someone now asked you what makes up the U.S. money supply, we hope you would answer "currency held by the public and checkable deposits, the primary components of M1." Checkable deposits are payable on demand to third parties. For example, if you write a check to your grocer, the first two parties are you and the depository institution; the grocer is the third party. The check in payment for goods purchased is an order for your bank to debit (subtract) a certain number of dollars from your checkable deposit account. The dollars are then credited (added) to the deposit account of the grocer, the third party. Thus, a checkable deposit is a means of payment, and the check is the method used to transfer ownership of the deposit between parties to a transaction. The point is that the check itself is not money; if it were, printing presses would work around the clock! The balances in checkable deposits are money.

Electronic Funds Transfer System
The transfer of funds to third parties in response to electronic instructions rather than a paper check.

Over the years, computer and telecommunications technologies have greatly altered the way in which payments are made. Technological innovations are making checks much less important, and perhaps soon obsolete as a means of transferring purchasing power. Today, we are making an increasingly larger percentage of payments through an electronic funds transfer system. In this system, payments are made to third parties in response to electronic instructions rather than instructions written on a paper check. Note that an electronic funds transfer system does not eliminate the need for deposit accounts; it is just a more efficient way of transferring funds from one deposit account to another. To pay your grocery bill, for instance, your account is debited by the amount of your bill, and the grocer's account is credited by the same amount at the time of the exchange. The whole system is computerized so that no written checks are necessary. All you need is an account number and a debit card that you present to the grocer. The grocer, in turn, enters the prices of your purchases into a computer terminal (called a point-of-sale terminal), and at the end of the month, you receive a statement giving your current balance and a record of all the charges and deposits to your account. This is just like a checking account statement, but without the checks.

Point-of-Sale Terminal
A computer terminal that uses a debit card to electronically transfer funds from a deposit account to the account of a third party.

Stored-Value Cards
Plastic cards that have a magnetic strip that is swiped through a card reader to make payments; usually single use.

Other forms of electronic funds transfer systems are stored-value cards and smart cards. Stored-value cards are plastic cards that have a certain amount of funds embedded on a magnetic strip. The owner of the stored-value card has paid to have the funds transferred to the card. Stored-value cards look like credit cards and are swiped through a card reader when the owner wants to access the funds. As the funds are spent, the balance on the card is transferred electronically from the card to the card reader. Gift cards from your favorite store are an example of stored value cards. Stored-value cards are popular on college campuses to pay for such things are photocopying in the library, meals in the dining hall, and parking fees. They are also used to prepay for toll roads and generally have a single use.

Smart cards are much more sophisticated than stored-value cards in that they have a microprocessor chip embedded in them that stores information and usually includes a "digital signature." The stored information leads to greater security for someone who accepts a smart card for a payment because the digital signature is verified. Each time the card is used, the amount of the payment is deducted electronically from the card and credited to the recipient of the payment by a point-of-sale terminal that is equipped to do so. At some point, the recipient transfers smart card payments from the point-of-sale terminal to its bank. If transferred immediately, the payment is completed in a matter of seconds. The microprocessor checks the authenticity of the transaction by examining the digital signature that is embedded in the chip. Although the validity is authenticated, the transaction is kept anonymous as if cash were used. Some smart cards are issued by and accepted by a single institution only. Other smart cards are accepted by multiple institutions and multiple retailers. Although they have not caught on to a large extent in the United States, smart cards offer the possibility of replacing cash and checks to make most payments because they may be more convenient and cheaper to use.

Currently, many employers, in cooperation with banks, pay salaries by automatically crediting their employees' bank accounts rather than by issuing the customary check. Such automatic credits, referred to as direct deposits, are also a form of an electronic funds transfer system.

One of the best known and most popular forms of electronic transfer of funds is the automated teller machine (ATM). Your depository institution most likely has ATMs, which permit you to make deposits and withdrawals, even late at night when the institution itself is closed. In all probability, your college has several ATMs on campus. ATMs are also visible in grocery and convenience stores, at car washes, and at shopping malls. Recently, portable ATMs in vans have been established that can be moved to sporting event locations, concerts, and so on. As you may have guessed, the vans housing the ATMs have multiple security features that prevent theft. As the ownership of personal computers and modems has spread, it has become possible to conduct a large portion of one's financial transactions from home.

In conclusion, electronic funds transfer systems are nothing more than the application of computer and telecommunications technology to the entire area of financial transactions and services. The aim is to reduce the physical handling and labor costs associated with an ever-expanding volume of paper checks, deposit slips, and the like, as well as to provide increased convenience and service to the public. Transferring funds and making payments electronically is generally much cheaper than writing checks or using other paper instructions to transfer funds. The application of computer and telecommunications technologies thus greatly reduces the costs of making payments and improves the efficiency of the payments system. As questions regarding the privacy of financial records, security of the systems, and legal responsibilities are being resolved, new payments practices and electronic funds transfer systems are spreading rapidly. One thing is certain: In the future, more payments will be made electronically because they are cheaper and, in most cases, more convenient. The result will be further evolution in how money is used and, perhaps, changes in what functions as money. From barter to gold and silver coins to checkable deposits to electronic money, the evolution of money and the payments mechanism goes hand in hand with the development of an economy and computer and telecommunications technologies.

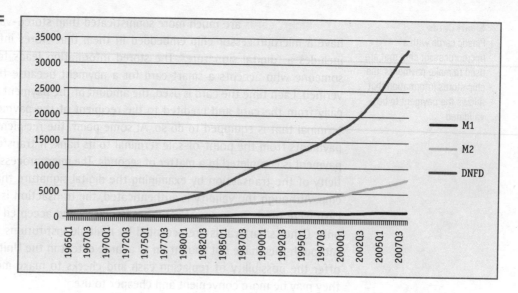

was to nudge the economy in the desired direction so that the objectives the Fed had set for the economy would be achieved.

During the late 1980s, M2 gained importance and prominence in the execution of monetary policy by the Fed. Throughout this period, the relationship between changes in M2 and economic activity seemed more stable than that between changes in M1 and economic activity. Consequently, the Fed watched the growth rate of M2 for signals about how well the economy was doing and deemphasized the role of M1. But in the early 1990s, the stable relationship between changes in M2 and changes in economic activity also seemed to break down. The growth rate of M2 moved in erratic and unpredictable ways. As a result, the Fed deemphasized the use of M2 as a policy indicator.

Beginning in the early 1990s, the Fed increasingly used changes in the growth rate of DNFD as an indicator of the direction of the economy. Changes in DNFD seemed, at least at that time, to have a stable relationship with changes in economic activity. If credit growth was increasing, then spending was likely to be going up. If credit extension was slowing, then the growth rate of economic activity was also likely to be slowing. By the late 1990s and continuing into the late 2000s, the Fed was using many other economic variables as barometers of economic conditions in addition to the monetary aggregates and DNFD. The monetary aggregates and DNFD were increasingly deemphasized in formulating policy and now are used primarily as informational variables along with many other indicators.

For our purposes, then, it is probably best to think of M1 as a measure of transactions money and M2 as a broader measure of money that, at times, has been closely related to economic activity. Likewise, DNFD, although not a monetary aggregate, is a broad credit aggregate that has also been closely related to economic activity and monitored by the Fed.

Recap   The Fed keeps track of two measures of money: M1 (transactions money) is currency in the hands of the public plus checkable deposits; M2 includes everything in M1 plus other highly liquid assets (near monies). In addition to M1 and M2, the Fed monitors DNFD, a broad measure of credit. DNFD includes public and private debt but excludes the debt of financial institutions to avoid double counting. Sometimes a given aggregate has been more highly correlated with the level of economic activity than at other times. Since the late 1990s, the monetary aggregates and DNFD have been deemphasized in monetary policy formulation.

Staying Ahead of the Counterfeiter

In the late 1990s, the United States issued redesigned currency (notes) for the first time since 1928. New $100, $50, $20, $10, and $5 bills featured larger presidential pictures (offset to the right), a colored security thread, color-shifting ink, and a watermark. By the late 1990s, technological innovations had made it easier for a counterfeiter to get reasonably good facsimiles of the old notes. The new notes were issued to make the currency more difficult to counterfeit. However, the new notes were not destined to have a long life of their own like their predecessors. In 2003, the United States issued another newly designed $20 bill; in 2004, a new $50 bill; in 2006, a new $10 bill; and in 2008, a new $5 bill. A redesigned $100 bill will follow. The newly designed notes have retained the features of the notes issued in the late 1990s but have additional safety measures, including faint shades of background colors. Different denominations have different background colors. For example, the new $20 bill has background colors of green, peach, and blue; the new $50 bill is red and blue; and the new $10 bill is orange, red, and yellow. Why are the notes being redesigned so soon after the late 1990s changes? You guessed it—to stay one step ahead of the counterfeiter. (The $2 and $1 bills will not be redesigned because they are not as desirable for counterfeiting.) But don't become too fond of the new currency. The government expects to issue newly designed notes every seven to 10 years. Of course, when new notes are issued, the old ones are still accepted in payment for goods and services and only slowly withdrawn from circulation as banks receive them and send them to the Federal Reserve to be replaced with the new notes. Thanks to the efforts of the government, counterfeited notes remain at low levels, estimated to be less than one percent of authentic U.S. currency worldwide.

The Demand for and Supply of Money

To understand money's role in the financial system, it is helpful to view money as an asset, much as someone might view an apartment house as an asset. The rental costs for apartments and the number of units constructed and rented are determined by two factors: the supply of apartments created by builders and the demand for apartments by renters. The analysis of money proceeds in a similar fashion. The interest rate is the cost to borrowers of obtaining money and the return (or yield) on money to lenders. Thus, just as rent is the cost to apartment dwellers and the return to the owner, the interest rate is the rental rate when money is borrowed or loaned, and it is known as the *cost of credit*.[2] By identifying and analyzing the factors affecting the demand for and supply of money, we gain considerable knowledge of both the "rental rate," or interest rate, associated with borrowing or lending money and the quantity of money that is demanded and supplied. As we shall see, changes in interest rates have a profound effect on economic activity.

Interest Rate
The cost to borrowers of obtaining money and the return (or yield) on money to lenders.

The Demand for Money

Quantity Demanded of Money
The specific amount of money that spending units wish to hold at a specific interest rate (price).

The **quantity demanded of money** is the specific amount of money that spending units wish to hold at a specific interest rate (price). If we hold other factors constant and allow only the interest rate to vary, we find there is an inverse relationship between the quantity demanded of money and the interest rate. Holding other factors constant is known as *invoking the ceteris paribus assumption.*[3] Thus, in this case, we conclude, ceteris paribus (a Latin term meaning "all things being equal"), that when the interest rate goes up, the quantity demanded of money goes down, and when the interest rate falls, the quantity demanded of money increases.

But why is this relationship between the quantity demanded of money and the interest rate inverse? The answer is quite simple if we consider that money (even in interest-earning checking accounts) generally earns less interest than nonmonetary assets (or near monies) such as savings accounts. Consequently, as the interest rate goes up, the opportunity cost of holding money goes up, and ceteris paribus, the quantity demanded of money goes down.[4] People conserve on their holdings of money balances and substitute holdings of other financial assets that pay a higher return. Thus, when the interest rate rises, "portfolio adjustments" decrease the holdings of money whose return has not increased or has increased less than that of nonmonetary assets.

Look at Exhibit 2-5, where we graph various interest rate–quantity demanded combinations to get a downward-sloping demand curve for money.

By the **demand for money**, we mean the entire set of interest rate–quantity demanded combinations—the entire downward-sloping demand curve. The demand for money by spending units is primarily determined by spending plans and by the need to pay for purchases. Spending plans and purchases, in turn, are influenced by income and generally go up when incomes go up. Thus, the demand for money to hold is positively or directly related to income. When our incomes go up, we hold more money for day-to-day transactions. (Melissa goes to the grocery store and takes her kids out for fast food more often after she gets a raise.) In addition to income and spending plans, other factors also affect the demand for money. These other factors include changes in inflation, changes in computer and telecommunications technologies that affect how we

Demand for Money
The entire set of interest rate–quantity demanded combinations as represented by a downward-sloping demand curve for money.

relationship

$I \uparrow \quad Q_{DM} \downarrow$

$I \downarrow \quad Q_{DM} \uparrow$

2-5
The Demand for Money

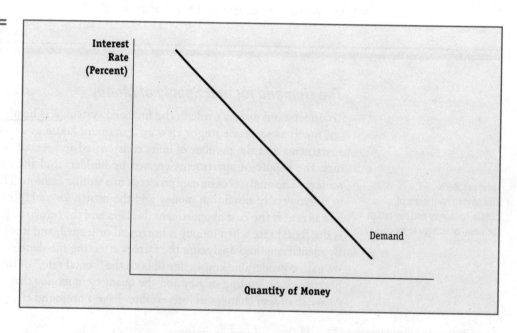

The quantity of money is measured on the horizontal axis, and the interest rate is measured on the vertical axis. Ceteris paribus, the quantity demanded of money is inversely related to the interest rate. As the interest rate falls, quantity demanded increases. As the interest rate rises, quantity demanded decreases.

2-6
Changes in the Quantity Demanded of Money Versus Changes in the Demand for Money

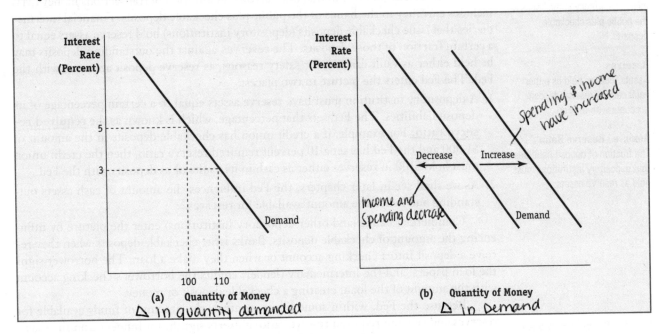

(a) **Quantity of Money** — Δ in quantity demanded

(b) **Quantity of Money** — Δ in Demand

Graph (a) illustrates a change in the quantity demanded of money due to a change in the interest rate. If the interest rate falls from 5 to 3 percent, quantity demanded increases from 100 to 110 and vice versa. Graph (b) illustrates a change in the demand for money. A shift of the money demand curve means that the demand for money has changed. A shift to the right means that the demand for money has increased, and a shift to the left means that the demand for money has decreased. If spending and income increase, the curve shifts rightward and quantity demanded increases for every interest rate. Likewise, if income and spending plans decrease, the curve shifts leftward as demand decreases.

make payments, and changes in the risk and liquidity of other financial instruments. We look at these other factors in Chapter 20.

In terms of Exhibit 2-5, when the demand for money changes, the entire demand curve shifts. For example, when the demand for money decreases, say, due to a decrease in incomes, the entire demand curve shifts to the left. Thus, we can see that changes in factors other than the interest rate affect the demand for money and cause the downward-sloping demand curve to shift. When the interest rate changes, we move along a single money demand curve, and there is a change in quantity demanded. Be certain you are clear about the difference between a *change in quantity demanded* and a *change in demand*. Exhibit 2-6 highlights the difference between changes in the quantity demanded of money and changes in the demand for money.

Recap   The demand for money is the amount that will be demanded at various interest rates. The quantity demanded of money is the amount that will be demanded at a specific interest rate. Among other factors, the demand for money is directly related to income. When income increases, demand increases, and vice versa. Ceteris paribus, the quantity demanded is inversely related to the interest rate. When the interest rate increases, the quantity demanded decreases, and vice versa. A change in demand is represented by a shift of the demand curve, while a change in quantity demanded is a movement along a demand curve due to a change in the interest rate.

The Supply of Money

Supply of Money
The stock of money (M1), which includes currency in the hands of the public plus checkable deposits.

The **supply of money** is a little more complicated than the demand for money and warrants a brief discussion. Recall that our narrowest definition of transactions money (M1) includes currency in the hands of the public plus checkable deposits. Financial intermediaries that issue checkable deposits (depository institutions) hold reserve assets equal to a certain fraction of those deposits. The **reserves** against the outstanding deposits may be held either as vault cash or, for safety reasons, as reserve deposit accounts with the Fed. The Fed enters the picture in two places:

Reserves
Assets that are held as either vault cash or reserve deposit accounts with the Fed.

1. A depository institution must have reserve assets equal to a certain percentage of its deposit liabilities. The Fed sets that percentage, which is known as the <u>required reserve ratio.</u> For example, if a credit union has checkable deposits in the amount of $1,000 and the Fed has set a 10 percent required reserve ratio, then the credit union must hold $100 in reserves either as cash in its vaults or as deposits with the Fed.

Required Reserve Ratio
The fraction of deposit liabilities that depository institutions must hold as reserve assets.

2. As we shall see in later chapters, the Fed influences the amount of cash assets outstanding and hence the amount available for reserves.[5]

Commercial banks (and other depository institutions) enter the picture by influencing the amount of checkable deposits. Banks issue checkable deposits when they receive a deposit into a checking account or when they make a loan. The borrower signs the loan papers, and the intermediary (lender) credits the borrower's checking account with the amount of the loan, creating a checkable deposit or money.

Quantity Supplied of Money
The specific amount of money that will be supplied at a specific interest rate.

Because the Fed, within some limits, controls the amount of funds available for reserves and sets the required reserve ratio, it exerts significant influence on the maximum amount of checkable deposits that depository institutions can create by making loans; hence, the Fed has significant influence on the money supply. Exhibit 2-7 depicts the relationship between the **quantity supplied of money** and the interest rate as a

---

2-7
The Supply of Money

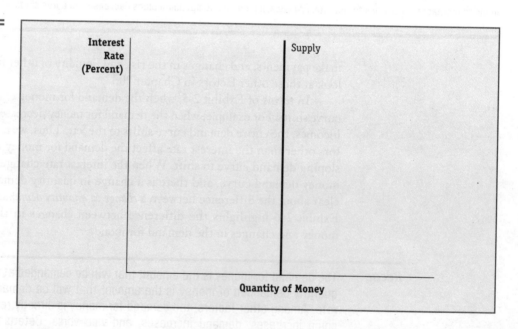

The quantity of money is measured on the horizontal axis, and the interest rate is measured on the vertical axis. The supply of money is depicted as a vertical line. The Fed influences the position of the vertical supply curve by determining the amount of cash assets available for reserves and by setting the required reserve ratio.

2-8
Changes in the Supply of Money

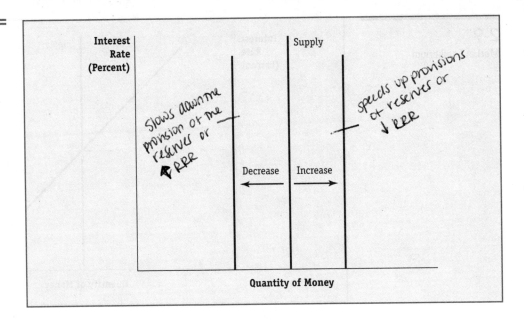

(handwritten notes on figure: "slows down the provision of the reserves or ↑RRR"; "speeds up provisions of reserves or ↓RRR"; axis labels: Interest Rate (Percent), Supply, Decrease, Increase, Quantity of Money)

An increase in the supply of money is depicted by a rightward shift of the vertical supply curve. If the Fed speeds up the provision of reserves or reduces the required reserve ratio, the supply of money increases. A decrease in the supply of money is depicted by a leftward shift of the vertical supply curve. If the Fed slows down the provision of reserves or increases the required reserve ratio, the supply of money decreases.

vertical line (supply curve).[6] The supply curve is vertical because of the Fed's ability to change the money supply, and, within limits, to control it.

As in the case of demand, the quantity supplied of money is the specific amount that will be supplied at a specific interest rate. By the supply of money, we mean the entire set of interest rate–quantity supplied combinations—the entire vertical supply curve. By changing the quantity of reserves available to the banking system or the required reserve ratio, the Fed can change the supply of money. Changes in the supply of money, initiated by the Fed, are reflected by shifts of the vertical supply curve, as depicted in Exhibit 2-8. If the Fed speeds up the provision of reserves or reduces the required reserve ratio, the money supply curve shifts to the right, and the supply of money increases. Likewise, if the Fed slows down the provision of reserves or increases the required reserve ratio, the money supply curve shifts to the left, and the supply of money decreases.

Recap   Depository institutions must hold reserve assets equal to a certain fraction of deposit liabilities—called the *required reserve ratio*—as set by the Fed. The Fed also influences the amount of cash assets outstanding and thus the amount available for reserves. These two factors give the Fed significant influence over the money supply.

Money, Interest Rates, and the Economy

Having previewed the factors that affect demand and supply, we are now in a position to see how the interaction between the supply of and demand for money determines its availability, or quantity, and its cost, or the interest rate. This is shown in Exhibit 2-9.[7] In this example, the market gravitates to i_e, or the equilibrium interest rate, where the quantity supplied of money equals the quantity demanded. If the interest rate is above i_e,

2-9
Market Equilibrium

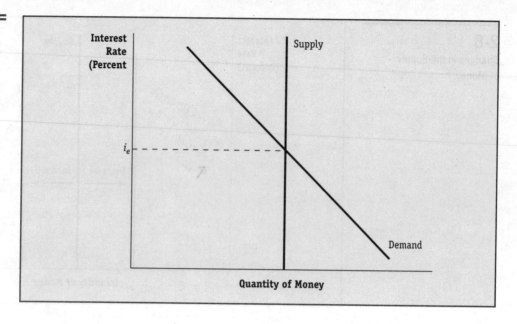

The market for money is in equilibrium when the quantity demanded is equal to the quantity supplied. This occurs at i_e where the demand and supply curves intersect.

there is an excess quantity supplied of money and, hence, downward pressure on the interest rate. If the rate is below equilibrium, there is an excess quantity demanded of money, and market forces will cause the interest rate to rise. Once the interest rate gravitates to i_e, the market will stay at the equilibrium rate until one of the curves shifts due to a change in either demand or supply.

Changes in the supply of or demand for money will affect the interest rate, just as changes in the supply of or demand for apartments will affect the rent of apartments. Ceteris paribus, if demand increases, the interest rate rises and vice versa. Exhibit 2-10 shows an increase in the demand for money due to increases in income or spending plans. This corresponds to a rightward shift of the demand curve. At the original interest rate, there is excess quantity demanded and upward pressure on the interest rate. The market gravitates to a new equilibrium at the higher interest rate, i'_e.

Likewise, if supply increases, ceteris paribus, the interest rate falls and vice versa. To illustrate, suppose that the Fed, through a stepped-up provision of reserves to depository institutions, succeeds in increasing the supply of money relative to the demand. As Exhibit 2-11 shows, this corresponds to a shift of the supply curve to the right. At the original equilibrium interest rate (i_e), there is excess quantity supplied and, thus, downward pressure on the interest rate. The market gravitates to a new equilibrium at a lower interest rate (i'_e), where quantity demanded is equal to quantity supplied.[8] Note that the analogy continues to hold: we would expect that an increase in the supply of apartments, with no change in demand, would result in a fall in rents and an increase in quantity demanded.

But what is the significance of the changes in interest rates caused by changes in the demand for or supply of money? Simply put, changes in the interest rate affect the aggregate (total) demand for goods and services. Because the Fed's influence comes from the supply side, we consider that case. If the supply of money increases due to the stepped-up provision of reserve assets by the Fed or a reduction in the required reserve ratio, the interest rate falls. The fall in interest rates reduces the cost of borrowing and would prob-

2-10

An Increase in the Demand for Money

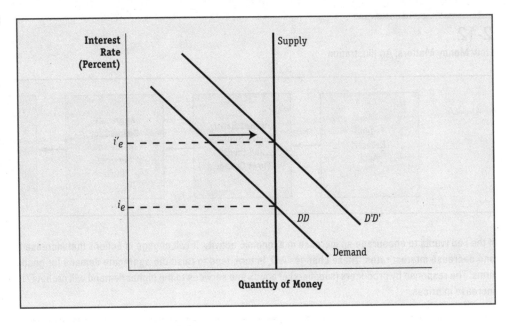

An increase in the demand for money leads to an increase in the interest rate from i_e to i'_e.

ably encourage some spending units in the economy to borrow more money and use it to purchase more goods and services. Credit would increase, and, more specifically, the increase in the supply of money would lead to an increase in the aggregate demand for goods and services. The increased demand for goods and services might lead to both an increase in the quantity of goods and services produced (supplied) and an increase in the general level of prices in the future, as the level of economic activity increases. The opposite would happen if the Fed took action to raise interest rates by reducing the supply

2-11

An Increase in the Supply of Money

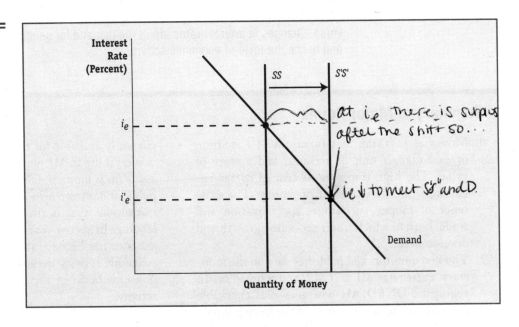

When the supply of money increases from SS to S'S', the equilibrium interest rate falls from i_e to i'_e.

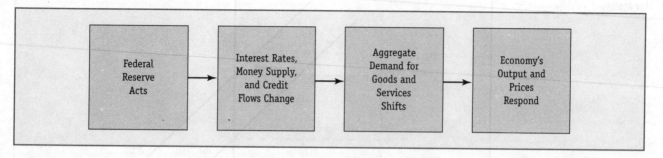

If the Fed wants to encourage an increase in economic activity, it will engage in actions that increase the money supply and credit flows and decrease interest rates. These changes will, in turn, tend to raise the aggregate demand for goods and services by households and firms. The response by producers (suppliers) of goods and services to the higher demand will probably include expansion of output and an increase in prices.

of money. Thus, by orchestrating changes in the interest rate via changes in the money supply, the Fed can speed up or slow down the level of economic activity. Exhibit 2-12 shows how the general relationships discussed in this section are important for the economy as a whole. Remember, this is just a first approximation that does not include many details; we do not expect you to understand all the specifics yet!

Recap   The interest rate is determined by the supply of and demand for money. Equilibrium occurs at the interest rate where the quantity demanded of money is equal to the quantity supplied. Changes in the supply of or demand for money (shifts of the supply or demand curves) affect the interest rate. Ceteris paribus, if demand increases, the interest rate rises and vice versa. Ceteris paribus, if supply increases, the interest rate falls and vice versa. Changes in interest rates affect the demand for goods and services in the economy and hence the level of economic activity.

Summary of Major Points

1. Money is anything that functions as a medium of exchange, a unit of account, and a store of value. The high transactions cost of barter encourages the development of money. The existence of money encourages specialization and trade, both of which foster economic growth and development.

2. The Fed monitors and publishes data on the monetary aggregates M1 and M2, and a broad credit aggregate, DNFD. M1 (currency plus checkable deposits) is the best measure of the money supply currently available for transactions purposes. M2 is everything in M1 plus some other highly liquid assets (near monies). DNFD includes all domestic public and private debt excluding debt of financial institutions that borrow for the purpose of relending. In recent years, the behavior of the aggregates has become a less reliable barometer of economic activity because of the less stable relationships between the aggregates and economic activity.

3. The payments mechanism is the means used to transfer money among transactors. Checks, for example, transfer ownership of checkable deposits. Innovations now being adopted suggest that an increasingly larger percentage of payments is being made with electronic funds transfer systems. Such innovations include debit cards, stored-value cards, smart cards, point-of-sale terminals, and ATMs. Smart value cards have microprocessor chips that allow anonymous, secure payments to be made.

4. The interest rate is the cost to borrowers of obtaining money and the return (or yield) on money to lenders. It is the cost of credit. Ceteris paribus, the quantity demanded of money and the interest rate are inversely related.

5. The demand for money is determined by the spending plans of spending units, which are usually positively or directly related to income. The supply of money is strongly influenced by the Fed through its control over cash assets available for reserves and the required reserve ratio.

6. The interaction between the supply of and the demand for money determines the equilibrium quantity of money and the equilibrium interest rate. In general, the initial effect of either an increase in the money supply or a decrease in money demand will be a fall in the interest rate, ceteris paribus. Conversely, the initial effect of either a decrease in the money supply or an increase in money demand will be a rise in the interest rate, ceteris paribus.

7. Changes in the money supply, credit, and the interest rate will generally alter the aggregate (total) demand for goods and services in the economy. Changes in aggregate demand will, in turn, affect the overall level of output and prices. More specifically, a rise in the money supply and/or credit flows and the accompanying fall in the interest rate will generally raise aggregate demand and lead to an expansion of output and some rise in prices. By orchestrating changes in interest rates via changes in the money supply, the Fed can speed up or slow down the level of economic activity.

Key Terms

Automated Teller Machine (ATM), p. **31**
Barter, p. **24**
Checkable Deposits, p. **27**
Demand Deposits, p. **27**
Demand for Money, p. **34**
Domestic Nonfinancial Debt (DNFD), p. **28**
Double Coincidence of Wants, p. **24**
Electronic Funds Transfer System, p. **30**

Interest Rate, p. **33**
Means of Payment (Medium of Exchange), p. **24**
Monetary Aggregates, p. **27**
Money, p. **24**
Money Market Deposit Accounts (MMDAs), p. **27**
M1, p. **27**
M2, p. **27**
Near Monies, p. **28**
Payments Mechanism, p. **30**
Point-of-Sale Terminal, p. **30**

Quantity Demanded of Money, p. **33**
Quantity Supplied of Money, p. **36**
Required Reserve Ratio, p. **36**
Reserves, p. **36**
Smart Cards, p. **31**
Store of Value, p. **26**
Stored-Value Cards, p. **30**
Supply of Money, p. **36**
Unit of Account, p. **26**

Review Questions

1. Discuss or define briefly the following terms and concepts: *means of payment, store of value, unit of account, barter, monetary aggregates, liquidity, nonfinancial debt, electronic funds transfer system,* and *risk*.

2. What are the functions of money? Which function do you think is most important?

3. Suppose we define *money* as that which serves as a store of value. Explain why this is a poor definition.

4. How does the Fed calculate M1, M2, and DNFD? Are these aggregates all money? Why or why not? Which contains the most liquid assets? Which is smallest? Which is largest? Which

monetary aggregate is most closely associated with transactions balances?

5. Why is the debt of financial institutions excluded from DNFD?

6. What is the payments mechanism? What changes are occurring in this mechanism? Why are they occurring? How do smart cards differ from stored-value cards?

7. Zoto is a remote island that has experienced rapid development. In contrast, Zaha is an island where growth has been sluggish and the level of economic activity remains low. How could the existence of money have affected these two outcomes?

8. Your friend took a class in money and banking two years ago and recalls that currency in the hands of the public is in M1. Explain to your friend why currency in the hands of the public is also included in M2.

9. Briefly define *the interest rate*, *reserves*, and *the required reserve ratio*.

10. Discuss the similarities between how the price of cell phones is determined in the market for cell phones and how the interest rate is determined in the market for money.

11. What is the difference between the demand for money and the quantity demanded of money?

12. What is the opportunity cost of holding money?

13. Chris and Harold Yoshida are a young couple with a growing income. What will happen to their demand for money over time?

14. In what form can a depository institution hold reserves? Who determines the amount of funds available for reserves? How does the Fed influence the amount of reserves a depository institution must hold?

Analytical Questions

Questions marked with a check mark (✓) are objective in nature. They can be completed with a short answer or number.

✓15. In which monetary aggregate(s) is each of the following assets included?
   a. Small savings and time deposits ($100,000)
   b. Money market deposit accounts
   c. Currency in the hands of the public
   d. Checkable deposits
   e. Individual money market mutual funds
   f. Institutional money market mutual funds
   g. Large time deposits
   h. Travelers' checks

16. Show on a graph how the interest rate and the quantity demanded of money are related. Do the same for the quantity supplied of money. When is the market for money in equilibrium?

✓17. Assume the market for money is originally in equilibrium. Explain what happens to demand, supply, quantity demanded, and/or quantity supplied, ceteris paribus, given each of the following events:
   a. The Fed lowers reserve requirements.
   b. Households increase their spending plans.
   c. Income falls due to a severe recession.
   d. The Fed steps up its provision of reserves to depository institutions.

✓18. Graph each case presented in question 17.

✓19. Ceteris paribus, what happens to the demand for money if incomes go down? Ceteris paribus, what happens to the supply of money if reserves go up? In each case, does the interest rate change? Graph each case.

✓20. Use a graph to show what happens to the interest rate if the demand for money is increasing while the supply of money is decreasing.

Suggested Readings

For an interesting discussion of many of the topics in this chapter, see the most recent Fed chair's "Monetary Policy Report to Congress" that is given in February and July of each year. The report and testimony of the chair is available on the Internet at **http://www.federalreserve.gov/**.

A beautiful book well worth the effort to locate is *Money: A History*, ed. Jonathan Williams (New York: St. Martin's Press, 1997).

For an extremely comprehensive look at money, see *A History of Money from Ancient Times to the Present Day*, 3rd. ed., Glyn Davies (Cardiff: University of Wales Press, reprinted 2005).

For an inclusive look at many of the topics discussed in this chapter, including the face of U.S. currency, counterfeiting, new currency designs, and the history of money, go to **http://www.minneapolisfed.org/econed/curric/money.cfm.**

An interesting discussion that deals with many topics about our nation's coins and currency is found in the testimony of Louise L. Roseman, director, Division of Reserve Bank Operations and Payment Systems, before a subcommittee of the U.S. House of Representatives, July 19, 2006. Roseman's testimony, the text of which is available on the Internet at **http://www.federalreserve.gov/boarddocs/testimony/2006/,** includes a discussion of the introduction of the new currency, a new dollar coin to be minted in 2007, and anticounterfeiting measures. Two useful Internet brochures can be accessed from the home page of the Atlanta Federal Reserve Bank at **http://www.frbatlanta .org/.** They are "Dollars and Cents: Fundamental Facts about U.S. Money" and "Paying for It: Checks, Cash, and Electronic Payments."

Another interesting site is **http://www.moneyfactory .com/.** For specific information on the newly redesigned currency, see **http://www.moneyfactory.com/newmoney/.**

For current statistical data on the monetary aggregates, see **http://www.federalreserve.gov/releases/H6/.**

For a more academic discussion of money, see Paul Dalziel, "On the Evolution of Money and Its Implications for Price Stability," *Journal of Economic Surveys* 14:4 (September 2000): 373–93.

For an interesting article on the development of barter, metal coins, and paper money, see Robert Ferris, "Money: A Pictorial History," *Business Credit* 98 (June 1996): 20–31.

Endnotes

1. M1 also includes travelers' checks, which account for a relatively small portion. For simplicity's sake, we ignore travelers' checks.
2. The market in which money is borrowed and loaned is called the *credit market*. In Chapter 6, we look in depth at interest rate determination from the perspective of the credit market, where the interest rate is determined by the supply of and demand for loanable funds.
3. In economics, we make the ceteris paribus assumption so that we can investigate the relationship between two variables without having changes in additional variables conceal that relationship.
4. The *opportunity cost* is the value of the next best alternative that is forgone.
5. Cash outside the Fed is either held by the public or deposited in a financial intermediary. If it is deposited, it serves as reserves for the financial intermediaries that issue checkable deposits, and it is considered a cash asset.
6. Some economists consider the money supply curve to be upward sloping instead of a vertical line. The reasoning is that when interest rates rise, depository institutions find innovative ways around reserve requirements in order to make more loans. The loans are more profitable because they are made at higher interest rates. In the process of making additional loans, more money is created.
7. As is commonly known, there are many interest rates in the economy, so speaking of "the interest rate" as if there were only one is an obvious simplification. Once the fundamentals have been developed, it will be much easier to extend our analysis to take into account the many different interest rates.
8. The ceteris paribus condition is very important here. For example, if the Fed takes actions that lead to increases in the money supply, then inflationary expectations may also increase. If inflationary expectations change, then the ceteris paribus condition is violated. In this case, increases in the money supply may lead to increases in interest rates because of the effect on inflationary expectations. Lenders will have to be compensated with higher interest to make up for the loss in the purchasing power of the money they have lent, a loss caused by inflation.

CHAPTER THREE

Speak softly and carry a big stick.

— Theodore Roosevelt

The Overseer: The Federal Reserve System

Learning Objectives

After reading this chapter, you should know:

How the Fed is organized

What the Federal Open Market Committee (FOMC) is

The most important functions of the Fed

The Fed's major policy tools

The controversy regarding Fed independence

UNRAVELING THE FED'S MYSTIQUE

"Stock Market Surges Following Fed Testimony," "Interest Rates Rise in Anticipation of Tighter Fed Policy," "Fed Approves Mega Bank Merger," "Fed Actions Prevent Crisis After Bank Failure": such headlines appear nearly every day in the nation's business and financial press. To help understand the prominent role of the Fed and its operations, we will examine its origin, role, organization, and policy tools. Many of the details regarding the formulation of policy and the precise linkages between policy actions and the economy will be examined in later chapters. For now, we want to focus on these questions: What is the Fed? Why does the Fed appear to have such great power and influence over the economy? Who does what within the Fed? Why do they do it?

ORGANIZATIONAL STRUCTURE OF THE SYSTEM

Federal Reserve System
The central bank of the United States that regulates the banking system and determines monetary policy.

Federal Reserve Act
The 1913 congressional statute that created the Federal Reserve System.

Lender of Last Resort
The responsibility of the Fed to provide an elastic currency by lending to commercial banks during emergencies.

Banking Reform Acts of 1933 and 1935
Statutes passed by Congress in response to the collapse of the banking system between 1930 and 1933.

Board of Governors
The seven governors of the Fed appointed by the president with Senate approval for 14-year terms.

The Federal Reserve System was created by Congress in 1913. Experience in the United States and abroad had finally convinced lawmakers that such an institution was needed to avoid the banking crises that had periodically plagued the economy. The main purpose of the Federal Reserve Act was simple. It created a central bank—a kind of bank for banks—that could lend funds to commercial banks during emergencies and thus provide these banks with the funds necessary to avoid insolvency and bankruptcy. An example of such an emergency is a major crop failure that makes it impossible for farmers to pay off their bank loans. The 1913 legislation referred to this role of the Fed as providing an "elastic currency"; today, it is often referred to as "the lender of last resort" function.

Over time, the responsibilities of the Federal Reserve have been expanded. In the midst of the Great Depression, it was clear that the limited scope and powers of the Federal Reserve System were not up to handling the nearly 8,000 bank failures that occurred during the 1930–1933 period. In the **Banking Reform Acts of 1933 and 1935**, Congress provided many of the additional policy tools and regulations that the Fed needed.

The most significant change during this period involved the underlying role of the Federal Reserve—that is, the Fed's purpose and objectives. The Fed moved into a new era because of the economic crisis of the Great Depression, the changing view of the role of government policy after this collapse (discussed in Chapter 1), and the new legislation that broadened its powers. The Federal Reserve System became a full-fledged central bank. Now more than a bank for banks, it was charged with contributing to the attainment of the nation's economic and financial goals. More specifically, it was to regulate and supervise the operation of the financial system in order to (1) foster a smooth-running, efficient, competitive financial system and (2) promote the overall health and stability of the economy through its ability to influence the availability and cost of money and credit. Let us first identify the major parts of the Federal Reserve System and then discuss its functions.

The core of the Federal Reserve System is the Board of Governors, located in Washington, D.C. The board consists of seven members appointed by the president with the advice and consent of the U.S. Senate. See "A Closer Look" on page 47 for brief biographical sketches of the board members as of January 2009. The full term of a board member is 14 years, and the terms are arranged so that one expires every two years. The long tenure and staggered terms were designed to insulate the board from day-to-day political pressures and encourage the members to exercise the same independent

The Board of Governors

- Chair Ben S. Bernanke (b. 1953). Took office on February 1, 2006, for a four-year term as chair; appointed to a full 14-year term on the board in February 2006; previously served on the board from 2002 to 2005.

  Background: Academics and government; served as chair of the President's Council of Economic Advisers from June 2005 to January 2006; professor of economics and public affairs, Princeton University, 1985 to 2002; assistant and associate professor of economics, Graduate School of Business at Stanford University, 1979 to 1985; visiting scholar at the Federal Reserve Banks of Philadelphia (1983–89), Boston (1989–90), and New York (1990–91, 1994–96); member of the Academic Advisory Panel of the New York Fed, 1990 to 2002; Ph.D. in economics from Massachusetts Institute of Technology, 1979.

- Donald L. Kohn (b. 1942). Took office in August 2002 to fill a full term ending January 31, 2016. Appointed to a four-year term as vice chair on June 23, 2006.

  Background: Public service at the Fed; staff adviser to the Board for Monetary Policy, 2001 to 2002; secretary of the Federal Open Market Committee, 1983 to 2002; director of the Division of Monetary Affairs, 1983 to 2001, and deputy staff director for Monetary and Financial Policy, 1983 to 1983; associate director, Federal Reserve Board's Division of Research and Statistics, 1981 to 1983; chief of capital markets, Federal Reserve Board's Division of Research and Statistics, 1978? to 1981; and economist, Federal Reserve Board's Division of Research and Statistics, 1975 to 1978;? financial economist, Federal Reserve Banks of Kansas City, 1970 to 1975;? Ph.D. in economics from the University of Michigan, 1971.?

- Kevin M. Warsh (b. 1970). Took office in February 2006 to fill an unexpired term ending January 2018.

  Background: Government and business; special assistant to the president for Economic Policy and executive secretary of the National Economic Council from 2002 until February 2006; member, executive director, and vice president of the mergers and acquisitions department of Morgan Stanley & Co. in New York; Juris Doctorate from Harvard Law School, 1995.

- Elizabeth A. Duke (b. 1952). Took office August 2008 to fill an unexpired term ending July 2012.

  Background: Business; senior executive vice president and chief operating officer of TowneBank, a Virginia-based community bank; executive vice president at Wachovia Bank and SouthTrust Bank; president and chief executive officer of Bank of Tidewater, Virginia Beach, Virginia; member of the Board of Directors of the American Bankers Association, 1999–2006; Chair of the Board of Directors of the American Bankers Association, 2004–2006; various civic positions; M.B.A. from Old Dominion University; graduate of the Stonier Graduate School of Banking and the Virginia Bankers School of Bank Management.

- Daniel K. Tarullo (b. 1952). Took office in January 2009 to fill an unexpired term ending January 31, 2022.

judgment that Supreme Court justices employ. In theory, a president would be able to appoint only two of the seven members on the board during a four-year term. In actuality, early resignations of board members have permitted recent presidents to name more than two new board members during a four-year term. We might also note that although board members cannot be reappointed if they serve a full term, they may be reappointed if the initial appointment was to fill an unexpired term due to an early resignation. Board members can be removed from office only under extraordinary circumstances. So far, it has never happened.

The president, with the advice and consent of the Senate, appoints one of the seven board members to be the chair for four years and another to be vice chair. The choice of the board chair is crucial, for experience shows that he becomes the chief spokesperson for the Fed and thus a strong force in U.S. economic policy making.[1]

Federal Reserve Banks

Reserve Bank
One of the 12 Federal Reserve Banks; each is located in a large city in its district.

The original Federal Reserve Act divided the nation into 12 districts. Each Federal Reserve Bank district is served by a Reserve Bank located in a large city in the district. Thus, as shown in Exhibit 3-1, we have the Federal Reserve Banks of Boston, New York, Philadelphia, Richmond, Cleveland, Atlanta, Chicago, Dallas, Kansas City, St. Louis, Minneapolis, and San Francisco. The three largest are the Reserve Banks of New York, Chicago, and San Francisco, which account for more than 50 percent of Fed assets. The 12 Reserve Banks have a total of 25 branches, located in major cities in the respective district. For example, the St. Louis Fed has branches in Memphis, Tennessee, Little Rock, Arkansas, and Louisville, Kentucky, while the Dallas Fed has branches in Houston, San Antonio, and El Paso, Texas. As we shall see in Chapter 9, all commercial banks that are federally chartered national banks must join the Federal Reserve System. State-chartered banks may join or not join as they choose. The member banks within a Reserve Bank district (say, the Boston district) elect six of the nine directors of that Reserve Bank, and the Board of Governors appoints the other three. These directors, in turn, appoint the president and other officials of that Reserve Bank.

The reason the original Federal Reserve Act created 12 Reserve Banks and provided for the election of directors by member commercial banks was to decentralize policy-making authority.[2] Considerable anti-Federalist sentiment existed in Congress at the time. Over time, the desire to decentralize authority has been stymied by the increased concentration of policy-making authority in Washington.

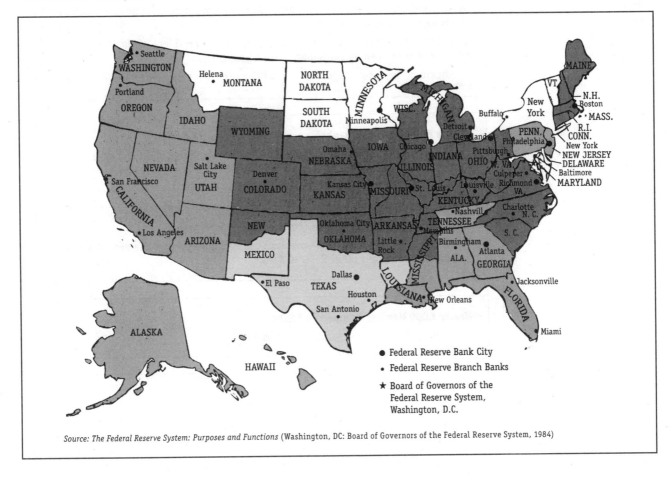

● Federal Reserve Bank City

• Federal Reserve Branch Banks

★ Board of Governors of the
   Federal Reserve System,
   Washington, D.C.

Source: The Federal Reserve System: Purposes and Functions (Washington, DC: Board of Governors of the Federal Reserve System, 1984)

Federal Open Market Committee (FOMC)

Federal Open Market Committee (FOMC)

The principal policy-making body within the Federal Reserve System.

The **Federal Open Market Committee (FOMC)** is the principal policy-making body within the Federal Reserve System. The FOMC formulates monetary policy and oversees its implementation. The committee has 12 members including all seven members of the board and five of the 12 Federal Reserve Bank presidents. The president of the New York Federal Reserve Bank always sits on the FOMC and is a permanent voting member. This is so because the New York Fed, as we shall see, implements monetary policy in accord with the FOMC's instructions. The remaining four seats are filled by the other Reserve Bank presidents who serve one-year terms on a rotating basis. Although only five Reserve Bank presidents have voting rights on the FOMC at any one time, all 12 presidents and their senior advisers attend FOMC meetings and participate in the discussions. By law, the FOMC determines its own internal organization. By tradition, it elects the chair of the Federal Reserve Board as chair of the FOMC, and the president of the New York Federal Reserve Bank as vice chair of the FOMC.

The FOMC gathers in closed meetings in Washington eight times a year (about every six weeks). At these meetings, the FOMC reviews current economic conditions,

Board of Governors

Seven members appointed by the president of the United States and confirmed by
the Senate for 14-year terms.

One of the seven governors is appointed chair by the president of the United
States and confirmed by the Senate for a 4-year term.

The Board of Governors appoints three of the nine directors to each Reserve Bank.

Twelve Federal Reserve Banks

Each with nine directors who appoint the Reserve Bank president and other
officers of the Reserve Banks.

Federal Open Market Committee (FOMC)

Seven members of the Board of Governors plus the president of the New York Fed
and presidents of four other Reserve Banks.

Nearly 3,000 Member Commercial Banks

Elect six of the nine directors to each Reserve Bank.

Policy Directive
A statement of the FOMC that
indicates its policy consensus
and sets forth operating
instructions regarding monetary
policy.

determines the appropriate stance of monetary policy, and evaluates the risks to its goals
of price stability and sustainable economic growth. Included in the minutes of an FOMC
meeting is the policy directive, which is usually a two- to four-paragraph statement.[3]
This statement represents a digest of the meeting, indicates the policy consensus of the
FOMC, and sets forth the operating instructions (or directive) to the Federal Reserve
Bank of New York regarding the conduct of monetary policy.

Since January 2005, minutes of an FOMC meeting are published three weeks after
the meeting, but interested parties do not have to wait for their release to find out what
the Fed intends to do. In early 1994, the Fed began announcing policy changes made at
FOMC meetings immediately following their conclusion. In addition to any policy
change, the Fed also makes a statement about what they believe the direction of the
economy to be with regard to inflation and economic growth. These changes have removed some of the secrecy that previously surrounded the specific contents of the
meetings.

In the next section, we look at what the Fed is charged with doing. Before moving
on, however, take a look at the outline of the Fed's organizational structure in Exhibit
3-2.[4]

Recap   The Federal Reserve System was created in 1913. It consists of 12 Reserve Banks. The Fed is
governed by the Board of Governors, whose seven members are appointed by the president to
14-year terms. The board chair is appointed to a four-year term. The FOMC is the major policy-
making body. It includes the seven Fed governors plus five Reserve Bank presidents. The presi-

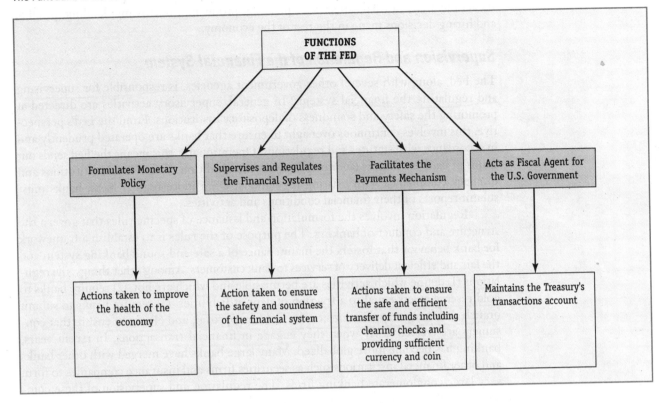

dent of the New York Reserve Bank is a permanent member of the FOMC, and the other four slots rotate yearly among the remaining 11 Reserve Bank presidents.

THE FED'S FUNCTIONS

Since its inception, the Fed's powers and responsibilities have gradually expanded. The current list of the Fed's responsibilities can be divided into four functional areas, depicted in Exhibit 3-3, and outlined in the following text.

Formulation and Implementation of Monetary Policy

A primary responsibility of the Federal Reserve is the formulation and implementation of the nation's monetary policy. The conduct of monetary policy has two objectives: first, to ensure that sufficient money and credit are available to allow the economy to expand along its long-term potential growth trend under conditions of relatively little or no inflation; second, in the shorter run, to minimize the fluctuations—recessions or inflationary booms—around the long-term trend.

In general, the Fed takes actions to affect the cost and availability of funds in the financial system.[5] More specifically, the Fed's actions have a direct effect on the ability of depository institutions to extend credit, on the nation's money supply, and on interest rates. Leaving many of the details for a later chapter, the key point here is that what the Fed does, or fails to do, has a pervasive effect on the environment in the financial system

Monetary Policy
The attempts by the Fed to stabilize the economy and to ensure sufficient money and credit for an expanding economy.

The Overseer: The Federal Reserve System **51**

and the overall health and performance of the economy. For example, by taking actions that increase the availability of funds, the Fed may bring about an expansion of the money supply and, in the short run, a decline in interest rates, or it can do the reverse. Its actions may, in turn, affect the spending, producing, borrowing, lending, pricing, and hiring decisions made in the rest of the economy.

Supervision and Regulation of the Financial System

The Fed, along with several other government agencies, is responsible for supervising and regulating the financial system.[6] In general, supervisory activities are directed at promoting the safety and soundness of depository institutions. From the Fed's perspective, this involves continuous oversight to ensure that banks are operated prudently and in accordance with statutes and regulations. Operationally, this means the Fed sends out teams of bank examiners (auditors) to assess the condition of individual institutions and to check compliance with existing regulations. On a more regular basis, banks must submit reports of their financial conditions and activities.

Regulation involves the formulation and issuance of specific rules that govern the structure and conduct of banking. The purpose of the rules is to establish a framework for bank behavior that fosters the maintenance of a safe and sound banking system and the fair and efficient delivery of services to bank customers. Among other things, the regulations (1) define which activities are permissible and which are not, (2) require banks to hold reserve assets equal to a fraction of deposit liabilities, (3) require banks to submit branch and merger applications to the Fed for approval, and (4) try to ensure that consumers are treated fairly when they engage in financial transactions. In recent years, banking has become more globalized. Many large banks have merged with other banks and other financial institutions such as securities firms and insurance companies to form very large conglomerate banking firms. The regulation and supervision of these complex firms is challenging for the Fed. In later chapters, we shall see how the rules and regulations have changed over time as the banking environment changes, and the implications of these changes.

With regard to consumers being treated fairly, the Fed is charged with ensuring that financial institutions comply with the Truth in Lending Act, the Fair Credit Billing Act, and the Equal Credit Opportunity Act. These statutes are designed to protect the customers of financial institutions from discrimination on the basis of race, sex, or age and from unfair or misleading lending practices. In addition, the Fed is responsible for ensuring compliance with the Community Reinvestment Act,[7] which seeks to increase the availability of credit to economically disadvantaged areas and to ensure nondiscriminatory lending practices. To carry out these responsibilities, the Fed monitors the advertising by institutions, investigates complaints from customers, reviews standard loan contracts used by institutions, and requires institutions to submit numerous reports summarizing their lending activities.

Another example of the Fed's supervisory and regulatory activities occurs when a bank encounters serious difficulties and is in danger of failing. The cause of the problem may be—and often is—related to fraudulent or misguided lending practices. Whatever the case, the Fed, along with the other relevant government agencies, tries to find an orderly solution that will preserve the public's confidence in the financial system. Often this has involved finding a merger partner for the weak or failing institution, lending funds to the institution to give it time to work out its problems, and in extreme cases, removing the bank's management.

3-4
The Check-Clearing System

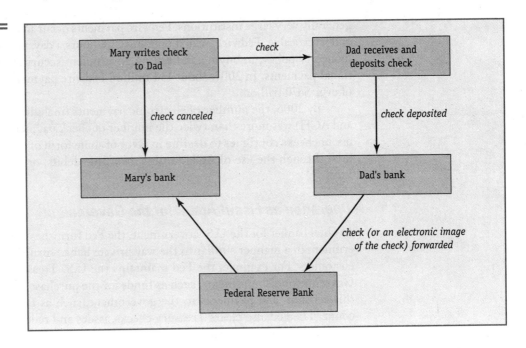

Facilitation of the Payments Mechanism

The **payments mechanism** is at the heart of the nation's financial system. Billions of dollars are transferred each day to pay for goods and services, settle debts, and acquire securities. Because any disruption of this mechanism could prove deleterious to the economy, the Fed is committed to the development and maintenance of safe and efficient means for transferring funds—that is, making payments.

Most obviously, the Fed facilitates the transfer of funds by providing currency and coin and clearing checks. As of late 2008, the value of currency (Federal Reserve notes) and coins in circulation was about $780 billion. As Exhibit 3-4 illustrates, the Fed plays a central role in the transfer of funds initiated by the writing of a check. The task is enormous. In 2007, the Fed cleared about 29 billion checks with a value over $41 trillion. Since October 2004, banks have been authorized to substitute an electronic image of a check for the actual paper check. Rather than physically transporting the original check, the electronic image can be sent almost instantaneously all over the country with the result being that the check-clearing process is expedited and the costs reduced.

The Fed also participates, along with private sector vendors, in the **automated clearinghouse (ACH)** function, which assists the government and private sectors in making automated debits and credits. Developed in the 1930s primarily as a way to disperse social security payments and salaries to government workers, the ACH continues to evolve into other government and private sector uses. The ACH is used by employers to make direct payments of payroll checks into checking accounts, and by consumers to authorize transfers for insurance premiums, mortgage payments, other bills, and certain online or telephone transfers. In 2006, private sector payments were about six times the value of government payments. In total, 14.6 billion ACH payments were made that year with a value of almost $31 trillion.

The Fed also operates **Fedwire**, an electronic system for transferring very large sums of funds (wholesaling funds) among about 9,500 Fedwire participants, which are generally very large institutions. Fedwire payments occur in real time, and they are final and irrevocable. Fedwire, which operates 21.5 hours a day, is also used in implementing monetary policy, in buying and selling government securities, and in making international payments. In 2007, about 134 million Fedwire payments were made with a value of over $670 trillion.

By 2006, the number of electronic payments (including debit cards, credit cards, and ACH) was more than twice the number of check payments. Moreover, the relative use of checks continues to decline in favor of some form of electronic transfer, whether it be through the use of ACH, online or offline debits, or through the use of a credit card.

Operation as Fiscal Agent for the Government

As chief banker for the U.S. government, the Fed furnishes banking services to the government in a manner similar to the way private banks furnish banking services to their customers. For example, the Fed maintains the U.S. Treasury's transactions account.[8] Government disbursements, such as funds for the purchase of a missile, are made out of this account, and payments to the government, such as taxes, are made into this account. The Fed also clears Treasury checks, issues and redeems government securities, and provides other financial services. It acts as the fiscal agent of the government in financial transactions with foreign governments and foreign central banks.

Finally, we would be remiss if we did not tell you about a proposal by the U.S. Treasury in March 2008 to overhaul the financial regulatory structure. Under the proposal, the power of the Fed would be greatly expanded to include the regulation of non-bank financial institutions. In addition to regulating the banking system, the Fed's new powers would include oversight of any financial institution or market whose financial practices could pose a threat to the financial system or the economy. Such institutions include insurance companies, hedge funds, pension plans, mutual funds, private equity firms, and virtually any other large financial institution whose failure might cause catastrophic effects. The purpose of this would be to prevent a nonbank financial institution from taking excessive risks if its failure would drag the entire economy down. Thus, if the proposal is adopted, the functions of the Fed will be expanded to include oversight of any financial institution whose failure would pose such a threat. We cover the details of the proposed overhaul in Chapter 12. It is expected that any changes to the current regulations and functions of the Fed will not be adopted for at least the next several years. However, the ongoing financial crisis involving the collapse, government bailout, or severe strains of such firms as Countrywide Bank, Indy Mac Bank, Bear Stearns, Lehman Brothers, Merrill Lynch, Fannie Mae, Freddie Mac, American International Group (AIG), and Washington Mutual will undoubtedly hasten the overhaul of the regulatory structure. Finally, the unprecedented government bailout of the financial system which Congress approved in late September 2008 and the proposed additional bailout by the Obama administration will bring much greater focus and attention to a plan to reform the regulatory structure.

The next section focuses on the tools the Fed has at its disposal to fulfill those responsibilities.

Recap	The major responsibilities of the Fed include setting monetary policy, regulating and supervising the financial system, facilitating the payments mechanism, and acting as fiscal agent for the U.S. government.

The Eurosystem: Europe's Central Bank

The European Union consists of 27 European countries that seek greater economic and monetary integration. Twelve of the 27 member countries have adopted a single currency called the *euro*. It replaced the national currencies such as the French franc, German mark, and Italian lira of the respective countries. The conversion began on January 1, 1999, and was completed on March 1, 2002.[1]

The Eurosystem is made up of the European Central Bank (ECB) and the national central banks of the 12 countries in the currency union. The ECB, created on June 1, 1998, has capital of 5 billion euro, which has been contributed on a pro rata basis by the national central banks. The Eurosystem formulates and implements monetary policy for the euro zone and is independent of control by any member country. In addition to directing monetary policy, the Eurosystem conducts foreign exchange operations and holds and manages the official foreign reserves of member countries. The ECB also operates a payment system called *TARGET*, which interlinks the national payment settlement systems of the countries in the European Union in order to promote smooth operation of the payments system.

The decision-making bodies of the Eurosystem consist of the Governing Council and the Executive Board. The Executive Board consists of the president, the vice president, and four other members, all appointed by the member countries. Minimum nonrenewable terms are eight years. The Governing Council consists of the Executive Board plus the governors of the national central banks of the member countries. A minimum renewable term for governors is for five years. The national central banks of the 12 countries in the currency union continue to perform many day-to-day monetary functions.

By law, the primary objective of the Eurosystem is to maintain price stability in the euro zone. The Eurosystem decides on a quantitative definition of price stability, such as 2 percent inflation or less, that is to be met over a medium time period—such as a few years. In addition, "two pillars" are used to achieve the goal. The first pillar is a quantitative reference value for the growth rate of a broad-based monetary aggregate, such as the M2 in the United States. The second pillar consists of a broad collection of indicators that policy makers consider to assess the outlook for price developments in the area as a whole. The former is similar to targeting a monetary aggregate to guide policy formulation. The latter is similar to using a more eclectic approach in policy formulation.

To achieve its goals, the Eurosystem uses tools similar to the Fed's, including open market operations, a lending facility like the discount window called a *standing facility*, and reserve requirements. The 12 national central banks hold the required reserves, carry out open market operations, and operate the standing facility. The Eurosystem must approve of the financial instruments that are allowed to be used in open market operations; must set reserve requirements and interest rates on standing facility loans; and must take actions that nudge interest rates and the monetary aggregates in one direction or the other as part of monetary policy. In many ways, the national central banks take on a role similar to the 12 Federal Reserve Banks, and the ECB takes on the role of the Board of Governors and the Federal Open Market Committee of the Federal Reserve System.

Endnotes

1. On May 1, 2004, the EU was expanded from 15 to 25 countries. The original countries were Austria, Belgium, Denmark, Finland, France, Germany, Great Britain, Greece, Ireland, Italy, Luxembourg, the Netherlands, Portugal, Spain, and Sweden. The countries that joined in 2004 included Cyprus, the Czech Republic, Estonia, Hungary, Latvia, Lithuania, Malta, Poland, Slovakia, and Slovenia. Of the original 15, Denmark, Great Britain, and Sweden decided not to participate in the euro. The 10 additional countries may participate in the euro at a later date but did not as of 2008. On January 1, 2007, the EU was further expanded from 25 to 27 countries when Bulgaria and Romania were admitted.

THE FED'S MAJOR POLICY TOOLS
Open Market Operations

Open Market Operations
The buying and selling of government securities by the Fed to change the reserves of depository institutions.

Open market operations represent the most important monetary policy tool at the Fed's disposal. These operations, which are executed by the Federal Reserve Bank of New York under the guidance and direction of the FOMC, involve the buying or selling of U.S. government securities by the Fed. When the Fed buys securities, reserves rise, and when the Fed sells securities, reserves fall. (Details of this concept are discussed in Chapter 19.) These operations are important because they have a direct effect on the reserves that are available to depository institutions. (Recall from Chapter 2 that depository institutions are required to hold reserve assets equal to a certain proportion of outstanding deposit liabilities.) Changes in reserves, in turn, affect interest rates and the ability of depository institutions to make loans and to extend credit. When banks or other depository institutions make loans, they create checkable deposits. Thus, changes in reserves also affect the money supply.

Since the mid 1990s, the Fed uses the fed funds rate in the implementation of monetary policy. The Fed sets a target for the fed funds rate that it believes will result in a structure of interest rates—and subsequently a level of spending and borrowing—consistent with the Fed's goals for the economy. The Fed then uses open market operations to affect the supply of reserves and the reserves market so that the actual fed funds rate is equal to or very close to the targeted fed funds rate. For example, if the actual fed funds rate, as determined by supply and demand, is higher than the targeted rate, the Fed will supply reserves, causing the rate to fall, and vice versa.

The Discount Rate and Discount Rate Policy

Because the Fed controls the amount of required reserve assets that depository institutions must hold, it also operates a lending facility called the *discount window* through which depository institutions in need of reserves can borrow from the Fed. It is through the discount window that the Fed fulfills its function as a "lender of last resort." In January 2003, a new policy was implemented that established primary, secondary, and seasonal credit programs for discount window borrowing. Each program has its own interest rate, but the bulk of the borrowing and lending is in the primary credit program at the primary credit rate.

Primary Credit Rate
The rate for short-term borrowing of reserves by the healthiest depository institutions from the Fed, also known as the discount rate.

Discount Rate
The rate that healthy depository institutions are charged for short-term borrowing of reserves from the Fed. Today, the primary credit rate is referred to as the discount rate.

Secondary Credit Rate
The rate for short-term borrowing of reserves from the Fed by depository institutions experiencing financial difficulties.

Under the primary credit program, loans are made to depository institutions that are healthy and sound. The loans in this program may be used to cover shortfalls of reserves or to expand credit. The **primary credit rate** was originally set by the Fed one percent above the targeted fed funds rate, which, as noted in the previous section, the Fed influences through open market operations. Because the primary credit rate is set above the fed funds rate, banks under normal conditions will not borrow at the discount window but rather in the fed funds market, where borrowing is cheaper. However, in the event of a liquidity shortage in the banking system, funds would be available at the discount window. It is the primary credit rate that today is often referred to as the discount rate. Going along with the colloquial use, when we use the term *discount rate* throughout the text, we mean the primary credit rate. The primary credit rate was maintained one percent above the fed funds rate until August 17, 2007. On that date, the Fed lowered the spread between the *primary credit rate* and the fed funds rate to 0.5 percent. In addition, banks were encouraged to borrow at the discount window by the Fed. These actions were taken due to deterioration in credit markets because of a financial crisis in the housing sector. (More on this crisis in Chapter 11).

Under the secondary credit program, loans are made to depository institutions that are having financial difficulties. The interest rate charged is called the **secondary credit rate,** and in mid-2008 it was set 0.5 percent higher than the primary credit rate. The loans can only be used to cover shortfalls of required reserves, not to expand credit. Since the secondary credit rate is higher than the primary credit rate, banks in this classification are charged a penalty rate for having financial troubles.

Seasonal credit is extended to small depository institutions that have recurring seasonal funding needs such as banks in agricultural or seasonal resort communities. The loans in this program allow the institutions to minimize their holdings of excess reserves throughout the year, despite seasonal needs. When the seasonal need arises, banks can borrow reserves in this program rather than holding quantities of excess reserves throughout the year or liquidating assets to meet seasonal needs. The seasonal credit rate is an average of various CD rates and the fed funds rate.

Prior to January 2003, the discount rate was set by the Board of Governors, and changes to it often lagged behind changes in other interest rates, particularly short-term rates. The discount rate now automatically responds to changes in the targeted fed funds rate, thus eliminating the lag.

Changes in the discount rate can have several possible effects on depository institution behavior and the economy. The most obvious of these effects is that the cost of borrowing funds (reserves) from the Fed changes. Increases in the discount rate raise the cost of borrowing, and decreases lower it. Occasionally, "exceptional circumstances" such as a crisis in the housing market, a natural disaster, a terrorist attack, the shutdown of a large manufacturer in a small community, or other developments over which an institution's management has no control may adversely affect an individual institution or the banking system as a whole. Borrowers may not be repaying existing loans, depositors may be withdrawing large amounts of funds, and fears over the safety and solvency of an institution may be growing.

In such circumstances, as they emphasized in August 2007, the Fed stands ready to be a lender of last resort through the primary and secondary credit programs. The Fed's willingness to be a lender of last resort is closely related to its regulatory and supervisory responsibilities and its overall desire to preserve the public's confidence in the safety and soundness of the financial system, in general, and depository institutions, in particular.

Reserve Requirements

Required Reserves
The amount of reserve assets that the Fed requires depository institutions to hold against outstanding checkable deposit liabilities.

Required Reserve Ratio
The fraction of deposit liabilities that must be held as reserve assets.

The major item on the liability side of depository institutions' balance sheets is deposits. The Fed requires depository institutions to hold required reserves equal to a proportion of checkable deposit liabilities. The Fed specifies the required reserve ratio, which is the fraction that must be held. Currently, the Fed is authorized to set the required reserve ratio anywhere between 8 and 14 percent. For example, if the required reserve ratio on checkable deposits is 10 percent, then for each $1.00 in checkable deposit liabilities outstanding, a depository must hold $.10 in reserve assets. During 2008, the required reserve ratio was 0 percent on the first $10.3 million of checkable deposits, 3 percent on checkable deposits of more than $10.3 million and less than $44.4 million, and 10 percent thereafter. For simplicity, we ignore the 0 and 3 percent requirements.[9] Beginning in October 2008, the Fed began paying interest on reserve balances of depository institutions in response to the ongoing financial crisis of 2008–2009.

There are no reserve requirements on time and savings deposits, although such requirements have often been imposed in the past. Rather than frequently changing the required reserve ratio, which can be disruptive to financial institutions, the Fed uses open market operations as its major instrument for implementing monetary policy.

Sweep Accounts
A financial innovation that allows depository institutions to shift customers' funds out of checkable accounts that are subject to reserve requirements and into highly liquid money market deposit accounts (MMDAs) that are not.

In recent years, the amount of required reserves held by banks and other depository institutions has fallen dramatically because of the introduction and growth of sweep accounts. A sweep account is a financial innovation that allows depository institutions to shift customers' funds out of checkable accounts that are subject to reserve requirements and into highly liquid money market deposit accounts (MMDAs) that are not. For example, funds that were "swept" out of checkable deposits and into MMDAs totaled $5.3 billion in January 1994, when they were first tracked by the Fed. By July 2006, the cumulative funds in retail sweep accounts was over $320 billion. Some analysts have expressed concern that the reduction in required reserves resulting from the growth of sweep accounts will make it more difficult for the Fed to implement monetary policy. The evidence does not seem to support this concern. Sweep accounts are discussed in greater depth in later chapters.

Given the major policy tools of the Fed, the Board of Governors determines the reserve requirements and the primary credit and secondary credit rates. They also supervise and regulate the banking system. The FOMC, made up of mostly the Board of Governors, directs open market operations and determines monetary policy.

Clearly, the board swings the most weight within the Federal Reserve System—and most observers agree that the chair swings the most weight on the board and is a powerful figure in U.S. policy circles. The board exercises general supervisory and budgetary control over the 12 Reserve Banks. The Reserve Banks deal directly with depository institutions and administer discount policy. In addition, they are an important part of the nation's check-clearing system and play a key educational role by providing financial institutions and the public with information on Fed policy and the workings of the financial system and the economy. Also note that to help deal with the crisis, the Fed temporarily expanded its tools from the traditional ones we cover here. We look in more detail at these new actions taken by the Fed in Chapter 25.

Recap	The Fed's main tools for implementing monetary policy are open market operations and setting the required reserve ratio and the discount rate. Open market operations are the most widely used tool.

Early Attempts at Establishing a Central Bank

The creation of the Fed in 1913 was not the first attempt to establish a central bank in the United States. Indeed, the first effort occurred back in 1791, when the Bank of the United States was given a 20-year charter with the government providing one-fifth of the start-up capital. The fledgling bank had elements of both a private and a central bank. Like other private banks, it made loans to businesses and individuals. Like a central bank, it issued banknotes backed by gold, attempted to control the issuance of state banknotes, acted as fiscal agent for the government, and was responsible for the aggregate quantity of money and credit supplied in the economy. However, the bank was not without its detractors, who alleged that it represented big city "moneyed" interests. Fear and distrust, the unpopularity of centralized power, and questions about the bank's constitutionality all contributed to pressures to dissolve the bank. Its charter was allowed to run out in 1811.

The war of 1812 brought renewed pressures for a central bank that could oversee the financing of the war. Congress chartered the Second Bank of the United States in 1816. This bank also acted as fiscal agent for the U.S. government and issued banknotes redeemable in gold. Friction persisted between those who wanted a strong central bank (Federalists) and those who supported a more decentralized system (anti-Federalists). After substantially reducing the bank's powers in the early 1830s, President Andrew Jackson vetoed the rechartering of the bank, and it went out of existence in 1836.

The National Banking Acts of 1863 and 1864 succeeded in establishing a uniform national currency, but the lack of a central bank meant that there was no easy way to regulate the amount of currency in circulation. Consequently, the country experienced periodic shortages that often led to financial crises. Such crises occurred in 1833, 1884, 1893, and 1903. Nevertheless, attempts at creating a central bank that could regulate the amount of currency in circulation were not successful until 1913, when the Fed was established.

The Federal Reserve System and the Question of Central Bank Autonomy

The Federal Reserve System is a quasi-government agency whose primary responsibility is to stabilize the economy. As explained earlier, Congress established the Federal Reserve as an independent agency to shield it from political pressures. The 14-year terms of the members of the board ensure that the members do not have to defend their actions to Congress, the president, or the public. In addition, the Fed does not depend on an appropriation from Congress for its funding. The Fed pays its own way from the interest income it earns on its holdings of government securities and its loans to depository institutions. Finally, the Fed is exempt from many provisions of the

Freedom of Information Act (1966) and "government in the sunshine" legislation, which call for government policy to be made in meetings open to the public. As a result, Fed policy makers usually meet in secret to formulate policy.

Nevertheless, the Fed is not completely outside the government. In the short run, its decisions regarding monetary policy are, in theory, not constrained by the whims of the president or Congress or by any partisan politics. However, in the long run, Congress can pass laws that the Fed must obey, or it could even abolish the Fed altogether.

Those who support Fed independence do so mainly on the grounds that anything less than independence will inject politics into monetary policy operations. This argument was put forth eloquently by Alan Greenspan, former chair of the Board of Governors:

> We have to be sensitive to the appropriate degree of accountability accorded a central bank in a democratic society. If accountability is achieved by putting the conduct of monetary policy under the close influence of politicians subject to short-term election-cycle pressures, the resulting policy would likely prove disappointing over time. That is the conclusion of financial analysts, of economists, and of others who have studied the experiences of central banks around the globe, and of the legislators who built the Federal Reserve. The lure of short-run gains from running the economy can loom large in the context of an election cycle, but the process of reaching for such gains can have costly consequences for the nation's economic performance and standards of living over the longer term. The temptation is to step on the monetary accelerator, or at least to avoid the monetary brake, until after the next election. Giving in to such temptations is likely to impart an inflationary bias to the economy and could lead to instability, recession, and economic stagnation. Interest rates would be higher, and productivity and living standards lower, than if monetary policy were freer to approach the nation's economic goals with a longer term perspective.[10]

Macroeconomic research tends to support Greenspan's views on central bank autonomy. As in the United States, almost all directors of foreign central banks are appointed by the government. Their terms, however, are often considerably shorter than the 14-year term of Fed governors. The shorter the term, the less independent the central bank is. In some countries, government officials actually sit on the governing board, central banks are mandated by law to give credit to the government, and politicians can easily replace central bank governors. In others, it may not be so easy.

By considering these factors, researchers have judged the independence of various central banks and found that inflation rates are lowest in countries with the most independent central banks.[11] Apparently, the more independent the central bank is, the less likely it is to expand (inflate) the economy in response to political pressure. Evidence also suggests that countries with the most independent central banks do not have higher long-run rates of unemployment. Thus, on both the inflation and the unemployment front, an independent central bank appears to enhance macroeconomic performance.

Despite the perceived advantages of an independent central bank, many people contend that the independence of the Fed is inconsistent with democracy. They argue that the president and Congress are held accountable for economic conditions. If unemployment is rising and inflation is rampant, the president and members of Congress will be driven from office at election time. Because the president and Congress are responsible for economic policy, they should have all the tools at their disposal. More generally, opponents of Fed independence argue that monetary policy, like other government policies, should be controlled by people directly responsible to the electorate.

In response to concerns about too much Fed autonomy and to facilitate the implementation of monetary policy, the Fed has become considerably more open in recent years. For example, even though it has no legislative requirement to do so, the FOMC releases edited minutes of its deliberations three weeks after meetings. As previously discussed, since 1994, the Fed announces policy changes immediately after the FOMC meetings rather than waiting for the publication of minutes and the policy directive, or for the policies to be implemented. Back in 1993, the Fed agreed to publish "edited" transcripts, not just minutes, of the FOMC meetings with a five-year delay.[12] And in February 2000, the FOMC amended the language in the announcement to more clearly communicate its judgment of the economic outlook in the foreseeable future. All of these actions confirm that the Fed is more open than in the past, while maintaining that the present system gives it the proper degree of accountability necessary to carry out monetary policy.

Recap	The Fed is a quasi-independent government agency set up to be somewhat autonomous and shielded from political pressures. If subject to political pressures, the Fed could pursue policies that would be politically advantageous in the short run but detrimental in the long run. Research shows that countries with the most autonomous central banks have the lowest inflation rates. The Fed has become more open in recent years.

In the next chapter, we look at the role of financial institutions and markets.

Summary of Major Points

1. The Federal Reserve System was established by an act of Congress in 1913. The original Federal Reserve Act was modified and strengthened in 1933 and 1935, following the economic and financial collapse during the Great Depression.

2. The Fed is charged with regulating and supervising the operation of the financial system to keep it running smoothly and efficiently, and with promoting the overall health and stability of the economy through its ability to influence the availability and cost of money and credit.

3. The Board of Governors, located in Washington, D.C., is the core of the Federal Reserve System. It is composed of seven members appointed by the president, with the approval of the Senate, for 14-year terms. The president appoints one of the governors as chair for a four-year term.

4. The country is divided into 12 districts. Each district is served by a Reserve Bank located in a large city within the district.

5. The Federal Open Market Committee (FOMC) is the chief policy-making body within the Fed. It is composed of 12 members: the seven members of the Board of Governors and five of the 12 presidents of the Reserve Banks. The president of the New York Federal Reserve Bank is a permanent voting member, and the other four slots rotate yearly among the remaining 11 Reserve Bank presidents.

6. The Fed's functions can be classified into four main areas: formulating and implementing monetary policy; supervising and regulating the financial system; facilitating the payments mechanism; and acting as fiscal agent for the government.

7. The FOMC directs open market operations, the major tool for implementing monetary policy. These operations involve the buying or selling of government securities—actions that affect the volume of reserves in the banking system as well as interest rates. When the Fed buys securities, bank reserves increase. This, in turn, encourages bankers to expand loans and, hence, the money supply.

8. The FOMC meets eight times each year in closed meetings in Washington. Policy changes are announced immediately after the meetings. The minutes of the FOMC meetings are released to the public three weeks later. They contain the policy directive, which is the set of instructions regarding the conduct of open market operations that is issued to the New York Fed. The New York Fed executes open market operations on behalf of the FOMC and the entire Federal Reserve System. The Fed currently targets the fed funds rate and uses open market operations to keep that rate close to or at the target. The Fed announces FOMC decisions immediately following the meeting, including a statement about its judgment about the economic outlook in the foreseeable future.

9. In January 2003, the Fed established primary, secondary, and seasonal credit rates for discount window borrowing of reserves from the Fed. The primary credit rate is for short-term borrowing by healthy financial institutions. The secondary credit rate is 0.5 percent higher than the primary credit rate and is the rate charged for borrowing reserves by troubled depository institutions. Through discount window borrowing, the Fed is prepared to serve as a lender of last resort.

10. The Fed requires depository institutions to hold reserve assets equal to a proportion of each dollar of deposit liabilities. The Fed's required reserve ratio specifies the proportion.

12. There is an ongoing debate concerning the autonomy of the Fed. The Fed and others argue that independence is essential to the pursuit of economic stability. Without Fed autonomy, politicians would be tempted to take action that benefit the economy in the short run but may hurt the economy in the long run. Opponents argue that such independence is inconsistent with our democratic form of government. In recent years, the Fed has become more open.

Key Terms

Automated Clearinghouse (ACH), p. 53
Banking Reform Acts of 1933 and 1935, p. 46
Board of Governors, p. 46
Discount Rate, p. 57
Federal Open Market Committee (FOMC), p. 49

Federal Reserve Act, p. 46
Federal Reserve System, p. 46
Fedwire, p. 53
Freedom of Information Act (1966), p. 60
Lender of Last Resort, p. 46
Monetary Policy, p. 51
Open Market Operations, p. 56

Payments Mechanism, p. 53
Policy Directive, p. 50
Primary Credit Rate, p. 57
Required Reserve Ratio, p. 58
Required Reserves, p. 58
Reserve Bank, p. 48
Secondary Credit Rate, p. 57
Sweep Accounts, p. 58

Review Questions

1. Discuss each of the four major functions of the Fed. Which do you believe requires Fed autonomy? Why?

2. List the major responsibilities of each of the following:

   a. the Board of Governors
   b. the 12 Reserve Banks
   c. the Federal Open Market Committee

3. Why was the Fed created? What effect should the existence of the Fed have on financial crises?

4. Why did Congress create 12 Federal Reserve Banks rather than one central bank?
5. What features of the Fed's structure serve to make it fairly autonomous? Is Congress able to wield any control over the Fed?
6. Why have the responsibilities of the Fed increased since its inception?
7. Discuss the major policy tools that the Fed can use to promote the overall health of the economy. What is the most widely used tool?
8. What are the primary and secondary credit rates? When do they change? How often does the Fed change the required reserve ratio? How often does the Fed engage in open market operations?
9. What are the arguments for increasing the *autonomy* of the Fed? What are the arguments for increasing the *accountability* of the Fed?
10. Suppose that the Fed were less independent. How could this affect monetary policy? Suppose that the Fed were more independent. How could this affect monetary policy?
11. Why is the president of the New York Fed a permanent member of the FOMC?
12. Is the Fed more accountable to Congress or to the president? Why? Who created the Fed? Who appoints the Fed chair?
13. How does each of the following affect the money supply?
    a. The Fed lowers the required reserve ratio.
    b. The Fed buys government securities.
14. What are sweep accounts? How do sweep accounts affect required reserves? Are balances in sweep accounts subject to reserve requirements?

Suggested Readings

For an excellent monetary history and a summary of the events leading up to the legislation establishing the Federal Reserve, see Milton Friedman and Anna Jacobson Schwartz, *A Monetary History of the United States, 1863–1960* (Princeton, NJ: Princeton University Press, 1963).

The concern about political pressure on the central bank was well founded given the early history of banks in the United States. For a relevant discussion, see Bray Hammond, *Banks and Politics in America from the Revolution to the Civil War* (Princeton, NJ: Princeton University Press, 1953).

U.S. Monetary Policy and Financial Markets by Ann-Marie Meulendyke (1998) is a readable discussion of Fed procedures and the conduct of monetary policy. It can be obtained free of charge from the Public Information Dept., Federal Reserve Bank of New York, 33 Liberty Street, New York, NY 10045.

"The Federal Open Market Committee and the Formation of Monetary Policy" features remarks made by Fed governor Susan Schmidt Bies at the Academic Speaker Series, University of Tennessee, Martin, Tennessee, February 3, 2005. See **http://www.federalreserve.gov/boarddocs/speeches/2005/20050207/default.htm.**

"The Role of Federal Reserve Banks in the Federal Reserve System" is a transcript of remarks made by William Poole, president of the Federal Reserve Bank of St. Louis, at the Annual Global Student Investment Forum, University of Dayton, Dayton, Ohio, March 30, 2006. See **http://www.stlouisfed.org/news/speeches/2006/03_30_06.htm.**

Poole's speech "Understanding the Fed," delivered at the Dyer County Chamber of Commerce Annual Membership Luncheon, Dyersburg, Tennessee, August 31, 2006, is also available online at **http://stlouisfed.org/news/speeches/2006/08_31_06.html.**

"Thoughts on Financial Stability and Central Banking" is a transcript of remarks made by Vice Chairman Roger W. Ferguson, Jr., at the Conference on Modern Financial Institutions, Financial Markets, and Systemic Risk, Federal Reserve Bank of Atlanta, Atlanta, Georgia, April 13, 2006. The text is available online at **http://www.federalreserve.gov/newsevents/speech/Kohn20060413a.htm.**

"The Federal Reserve in an Electronic World" is a transcript of remarks made by Governor Mark W. Olson at the 2005 Payments Conference, Federal Reserve Bank of Chicago, Chicago, Illinois, May 19, 2005. The text is available online at **http://www.federalreserve.gov/boarddocs/speeches/2005/200505193/default.htm.**

For an interesting history of the Fed, see James McAfee, "Historical Perspectives on Form and Function," *The Region*, Federal Reserve Bank of Minneapolis (September 2004). The article is also available online at **http://www.minneapolisfed.org/pubs/region/04–09/McAfee.cfm.**

Fedpoints is a reference series explaining the structure and functions of the Federal Reserve System and other relevant economic concepts. It is available online at **http://www.newyorkfed.org/aboutthefed/fedpoints.html.**

"The Independence of Central Banks" by Sun Bae Kim summarizes a study showing that countries with the most independent central banks have the lowest inflation rates. The study suggests that if the central bank has a reputation for controlling inflation, this can substitute for legal independence. The article can be found in the *Weekly Letter of the San Francisco Federal Reserve Bank* (December 13, 1991).

"An Independent Central Bank in a Democratic Country: The Federal Reserve Experience" by William McDonough offers a discussion of the historical development of central banking in the United States. McDonough writes about the need for the Fed to be somewhat independent of the day-to-day control of the government so that it will be less likely to succumb to short-term political pressures. The article can be found in the *Federal Reserve Bank of New York Quarterly Review* 19 (Spring 1994): 1–6.

For general information on the Fed, go to **http://www.federalreserve.gov** and **http://www.minneapolisfed.org/info/sys/.**

For a list of the 12 Federal Reserve Banks and Internet links to each, see **http://federalreserve.gov/otherfrb.htm.**

Minutes of the FOMC meetings are posted at **http://woodrow.mpls.frb.fed.us/info/policy/fomcmin.cfm** and **http://www.federalreserve.gov/fomc/#calendars.**

Information on open market operations can be found at **http://www.federalreserve.gov** or **http://www.newyorkfed.org.**

Endnotes

1. The Board has not yet had a female chair.
2. In addition, no two members of the Board of Governors may come from the same Reserve Bank district. This ensures that the board is not unduly influenced by any particular region of the country.
3. Excerpts from a policy directive are reprinted in Chapter 25.
4. In addition to the organizational structures mentioned in the body of the text, the Fed includes three advisory councils: the Consumer Advisory Council, the Federal Advisory Council, and the Thrift Institutions Advisory Council. Composed of representatives from each Federal Reserve District, they meet several times a year with the Board of Governors to provide advice on issues relating to the Fed's responsibilities in the banking, consumer finance, and depository institutions areas. Federal Reserve insiders say that, as the name suggests, the advisory councils have no real power and serve mainly as a medium for public relations and the exchange of information.
5. The tools the Fed has available to affect the cost and availability of funds are discussed in the next section.
6. Many of the agencies that regulate the financial system are discussed in Chapter 12. Here, it is sufficient for you to know that the Fed has the broadest set of responsibilities, some of which overlap with the activities of other regulatory agencies.
7. The Community Reinvestment Act is discussed in greater detail in Chapter 12.
8. The transactions account of the government held at the Fed is similar to a checking account. However, the balance in the government's transactions account is not included in any monetary aggregate and therefore is not "money."
9. The amount of checkable deposits against which the 3 and 0 percent applies is modified each year depending on the percentage change in checkable deposits. Because $44.4 million in deposits is a relatively small amount, we ignore the 3 and 0 percent requirements. The Fed may also set a required reserve ratio of up to 9 percent on nonpersonal time deposits. Currently, the Fed does not impose reserve requirements on time deposits.
10. Statement by Alan Greenspan before the Committee on Banking, Finance, and Urban Affairs, U.S. House of Representatives (October 13, 1993).
11. In addition to the Sun Bae Kim article in the Suggested Readings, see Alberto Alesina and Lawrence H. Summers, "Central Bank Independence and Macroeconomic Performance," *Journal of Money, Credit, and Banking* 25:2 (May 1993): 151–62. Note that some of the European central banks in these studies are now part of the Eurosystem. These studies pre-

date the formation of the European Central Bank. However, they were used as resources in determining the structure that the new central bank should take with regard to central bank independence.

12. The editing of the transcripts usually involves deleting a small amount of confidential material that pertains to foreign central banks or entities.

4

Financial Markets, Instruments, and Market Makers

The worst form of inequality is to try to make unequal things equal.

—Aristotle

Learning Objectives

After reading this chapter, you should know:

The various ways of classifying financial markets, including primary and secondary markets; money and capital markets, and spot and futures markets

The definitions and characteristics of the major financial market instruments

The functions of the key participants—the market makers

How the various sectors of financial markets are connected

GAME TALK

To understand the role of financial markets and instruments in the financial system, we need to understand the jargon employed by insiders, or market participants, when they describe and discuss the "action" in financial markets. Trade jargon is not unique to these insiders, but it is pervasive in many aspects of life, including football. As the following example shows, even in this favorite American pastime, the "players" need to understand the lingo.

The time is Saturday afternoon during fall, and the place is the gridiron. When the quarterback reads a blitz (or red-dog) and man-to-man coverage, it is critical for him to call an automatic at the line of scrimmage and hit the flanker on a fly pattern. Of course, if the blitz does not materialize, the quarterback may find that he has thrown the pass into the teeth of zone coverage where the free safety can easily pick off the ball.

Such is the jargon of football. Much of this lingo is fully understood only by insiders—players, coaches, and football aficionados. Outsiders have difficulty understanding the game because they don't know the jargon, just as outsiders often have difficulty understanding financial market discussions. In this chapter, we will learn about financial markets and instruments (chiefly in the United States) and the language their participants use so that we too can understand what they are talking about.

INTRODUCING FINANCIAL MARKETS

A market for financial claims (instruments) can be viewed as the process or mechanism that connects the buyers and sellers of claims regardless of where they happen to be physically located.[1] Financial markets can be classified in many different ways. One of the most popular classifications divides the financial markets into individual submarkets according to the type of financial instrument that is traded: stock market, corporate bond market, Treasury bill market, commercial paper market, and so forth. There is, however, at least one difficulty with this classification scheme; it suggests that the individual submarkets are separate, more or less unconnected, compartments. A central message of this chapter is that the markets for the individual financial claims are connected and in many respects alike.

Another classification system assigns the various financial markets to either the **money market** or the **capital market** based on the length of the term of the instruments traded there. The money market includes those markets where securities with original maturities of one year or less are traded. Examples of such securities include Treasury bills, commercial paper, and negotiable certificates of deposit (CDs). The capital market includes those markets where securities with original maturities of more than one year are traded. Examples here include corporate bonds, stocks, mortgages, and U.S. Treasury notes and bonds. Not surprisingly, some refer to the money market as the *short-term market* and the capital market as the *long-term market*.

Notice that, together, the money market and the capital market include all of the individual submarkets we identified in the first classification scheme. In this case, however, we are grouping instruments by their **term to maturity**, which is the length of time from when the instrument is initially issued until it matures.

A third way to classify financial markets is to categorize them as the primary market and the secondary market. The **primary market** is the market in which a security is initially sold for the first time. For example, if a firm needs to issue new bonds or stocks to finance investment in new equipment, the initial sale of these new securities occurs in

Money Market
The market for financial assets with an original maturity of less than one year.

Capital Market
The market for financial assets with an original maturity of greater than one year.

Term to Maturity
The length of time from when a financial security is initially issued until it matures.

Primary Market
The market in which a security is initially sold for the first time.

the primary market. Thus, the primary market is where the public (individuals or financial institutions) buys newly issued bonds or stocks from the firms issuing them. Once a firm has issued bonds or stocks, further trading—say, a sale of bonds a month later by an initial purchaser—occurs in the **secondary market**.

In practice, the selling of new securities in primary markets by the firms issuing them and the trading of older securities in secondary markets occur simultaneously. However, this does not negate the importance of secondary markets and, particularly, high-quality secondary markets. We assess the quality of a secondary market by the cost and inconvenience associated with trading existing securities. In high-quality secondary markets, securities are traded at relatively low cost and little inconvenience. Such characteristics facilitate the sale and purchase of existing securities and thereby contribute to an efficient allocation of financial resources and a smoothly functioning savings-investment process.

To illustrate the point, imagine a financial system like those in many less-developed countries, where formal secondary markets do not exist. Assume now that you want to sell a security you purchased several years ago when it was first issued, say, by LHT, Inc., an emerging high-tech firm. The absence of a secondary market means that you would first have to search for someone willing and able to purchase your LHT security and then negotiate a mutually acceptable price with that person. This process would obviously be quite time consuming and inconvenient, and the experience might discourage you from saving part of your income in this way in the future; that is, you would be less likely to buy LHT bonds in the future. If other people who own securities have similar experiences, LHT, Inc., and all firms like it will encounter some difficulty in financing future deficits, and the amount of borrowing and lending will be less than it otherwise would have been. Assuming that the deficits were to be used for planned additions to the firms' plant and equipment, the amount of investment will fall. Without this investment, there will be less future growth of output and employment in the industry and the economy.

The message in this example is that the lack of a smoothly functioning secondary market will inhibit the financing of planned deficits in the primary market and thus have an adverse effect on investment and economic growth over time. In general, the strength and viability of primary markets are direct functions of the quality of secondary markets. Although the secondary market does not generate additional funds for the economy as a whole, its importance stems from the positive effect that a well-developed secondary market has on the primary market.

Another way to classify financial markets is by whether the transactions they arrange occur instantly or in the future according to terms decided today; that is, by whether the markets are spot or futures and forward markets. In spot markets, financial instruments trade instantaneously, and the spot price is the price of a security or financial instrument for immediate delivery. We are all familiar with spot markets. For example, if I decide to buy a share of IBM stock, I check with my broker and find out today's price for the stock. Or I use my computer to check stock and bond prices online.

At other times, I may be interested in buying or selling financial instruments for delivery on some date in the future at a price determined today. In this case, I enter the **financial futures** or the **financial forward markets**, where transactions are consummated today for the purchase or sale of financial instruments on a date in the future. Financial futures agreements trade U.S. government securities of several maturities, several stock market indexes, and foreign currencies on future specific dates. All quantities and futures dates are standardized. Financial forward agreements are transactions that are consummated today for the purchase or sale of financial

Secondary Market
The market in which previously issued financial securities are sold.

The strength and viability of primary markets directly affects quality of the secondary markets.

Spot Markets
Markets in which the trading of financial securities takes place instantaneously.

Financial Futures Markets
Organized markets that trade financial futures agreements.

Financial Forward Markets
Markets that trade financial forward agreements usually arranged by banks or other brokers and dealers.

instruments on a date in the future where the quantities and delivery dates are not standardized. Banks and other dealers and brokers customize financial forward agreements for their customers. Financial futures and forward markets are also called derivative markets because the value of the financial instruments (the futures and forward agreements) "derive" their values from the underlying instruments such as the government security, the shares of stock, and so on that are traded on the future date. In recent years, other complex types of derivative instruments besides futures and forward agreements have been created and are becoming part of the burgeoning derivative markets.

Financial futures and forward markets fulfill two basic functions. First, futures and forward markets may be used to reduce the risk associated with future price changes by "locking in" a future or forward price today. In recent years, financial futures and forward markets have experienced enormous growth. As financial prices have become more volatile, net lenders and net borrowers have turned to financial futures and forward markets to deal with the greater risk of unanticipated price changes. Second, financial futures and forward markets can also be used to speculate. Speculation in financial securities is the buying or selling of securities in the hope of profiting from future price changes. The many intricacies and nuances of financial futures and forward (derivative) markets are covered in detail in Chapter 17.

Recap   Financial markets can be classified as money or capital markets, as primary or secondary markets, or as spot or futures and forward markets. Money markets trade financial instruments with an original maturity of one year or less. Capital markets trade financial instruments with an original maturity of more than one year. Primary markets trade newly issued financial instruments, and secondary markets trade previously issued financial instruments. In spot markets, the trading of financial instruments takes place instantaneously. In financial futures and forward markets, the terms of the trade including price are arranged today, but the transaction occurs at some date in the future.

MAJOR FINANCIAL MARKET INSTRUMENTS

Financial markets perform the important role of channeling funds from net lenders to net borrowers. Because the action in financial markets involves the trading of financial instruments, understanding the action requires us to be familiar with what is being traded. We first examine the securities traded in the money market and then look at those traded in the capital market.

Money Market Instruments

Although individuals can invest in many money market instruments, the money market is primarily a wholesale market where large institutions trade low risk, highly liquid short-term financial claims issued in denominations of $1 million or more.[2] The money market brings together borrowers such as financial and nonfinancial firms that have short-term borrowing needs with those lenders, including other financial and nonfinancial firms, that have short-term funds to lend. The money market has undergone significant changes in the past 40 years, with new financial instruments being introduced and the amount outstanding of other instruments increasing at a far more rapid pace than the level of economic activity. In Chapter 10, we discuss the reasons for this growth and evolution when we look at the driving forces behind financial innovation.

Money and Other Financial Claims

In Chapter 1, we saw that net lenders usually lend their surplus funds to net borrowers through the financial system (financial markets and financial intermediaries). Put another way, purchasing power is transferred from those who have it to those who need it. What is transferred, in fact, is current purchasing power, which is exchanged for another financial asset, or a future claim on money. In effect, net lenders "rent out" their surplus funds to net borrowers for a given period of time, much as a landlord rents out an apartment. In financial markets, the net lender acquires a financial asset, which is a claim on and liability of the borrower. The claim, an asset to the holder and a liability to the issuer, is really an IOU—a promise by the borrower to repay the original amount borrowed (the principal) plus "rent" (the interest) to the lender.

Financial claims, other than money, are issued by borrowers or financial intermediaries. The intermediaries issue claims on themselves and then, in turn, lend to borrowers. The financial system includes many different types of financial claims, reflecting the wide variety of borrowers and lenders and the tendency to tailor particular types of claims to the preferences and needs of the net lenders and net borrowers. Since the 1990s, the trend among net lenders has been to bypass depository institutions and to put a large share of their surplus funds into mutual funds, the most rapidly growing type of intermediary.[1]

Because all financial claims, whether they be bank deposits, stocks, or Treasury bills, are claims on money, they can in some sense be compared with one another as well as with money. Traditional standards of comparison include the risk and the liquidity of various claims.

Risk refers to the possibility or probability that the value of a claim will decline. One example of risk is the possibility that a borrower will default and fail to pay back all or part of the principal or the interest. This risk is similar to the risk that a renter will burn down the apartment building or fail to pay his rent and be difficult to evict. The higher the probability of receiving less money back than expected, the riskier the financial claim is relative to money.

The *liquidity* of a financial claim (or asset) is determined by how easy or difficult it is to convert the asset into money. The ease (or difficulty) is defined in terms of the cost and time associated with the conversion. If significant costs or considerable time is required to convert a particular type of asset to money, it is usually referred to as *illiquid*. As the costs and time required to exchange a particular asset approach zero, the liquidity increases, with money representing perfect liquidity.[2]

Endnotes

1. Mutual funds are investment pools in which a large number of shareholders purchase securities such as stocks and bonds.
2. During the middle of the nineteenth century, coal miners' wages in Staffordshire, England, were paid partly in beer! Commenting on this practice, Charles Fay, a historian, remarked: "This currency was very popular and highly liquid, but it was issued to excess and difficult to store" (*Life and Labour in the Nineteenth Century* (Cambridge: Cambridge University Press, 1920): 197.

The Principal Money Market
Instruments: Amount
Outstanding, End of Year
(in billions of dollars)

Type of Instrument	1960	1970	1980	1990	2000	2008[a]
Treasury bills	$37	$76	$200	$482.0	$647.0	$1,489[a]
Negotiable CDs	0	45	260	546.9	1,052.6[b]	2,384.9[ab]
Commercial paper[c]	5	35	99	558.0	1,602.0	1,555.3[ac]
Bankers' acceptances	1	4	32	52.0	9.0	0.0
Repurchase agreements and fed funds	1	22	102	324.0	1,197.0	2,118.1
Eurodollars	0.8	2.4	61.4	103.5	191.1	NA[d]

a. As of September 30, 2008.

b. Includes all large time deposits greater than $100,000.

c. Includes commercial paper issued by financial and nonfinancial firms.

d. Not available.

Sources: Federal Reserve Flow of Funds Accounts, Z.1 (December 11, 2008), at http://www.federalreserve.gov/releases/Z1/; the U.S. Treasury at http://www.fms.treas.gov/bulletin/b2006-3.pdf.

For now, we introduce and briefly describe each of the principal money market instruments. Exhibit 4-1 shows the dollar amount of the principal instruments outstanding at the end of 1960, 1970, 1980, 1990, 2000, and 2007. Exhibit 4-2 summarizes the typical maturities, major borrowers, and degree of secondary market activity for these instruments.

U.S. Treasury Bills

U.S. Treasury Bills (T-bills)
Short-term debt instruments of the U.S. government with typical maturities of three to 12 months.

U.S. Treasury bills (T-bills) are short-term debt instruments of the U.S. government with maturities of four weeks, 13 weeks, 26 weeks, and 52 weeks. Although the

The Money Market

Instrument	Typical Maturities	Principal Borrowers	Secondary Market
Treasury bills	3 to 12 months	U.S. government	Very active
Negotiable CDs	1 to 6 months	Depository institutions	Modest activity
Commercial paper	1 to 270 days	Financial and business firms	Moderately active
Bankers' acceptances	90 days	Financial and business firms	Limited
Repurchase agreements	1 day, and 2 days to 3 months typical; 6 months less typical	Banks, securities dealers, other owners of securities, nonfinancial firms, governments	None, but very active primary market for short maturities
Fed funds	Chiefly 1 business day	Depository institutions	Active brokers' market
Eurodollars	Overnight, 1 week, 1 to 6 months, and longer	Banks	None

minimum denomination is $1,000 and T-bills are sold in $1,000 increments, for institutional buyers the minimum amount is usually several million dollars. T-bills pay a set amount at maturity, have no explicit interest payments, and are sold in regularly scheduled auctions.[3] In reality, they pay interest by initially selling at a discount—that is, at a price lower than the amount paid at maturity. For instance, in April 2009, you might pay $9,770 to buy a one-year (52 week) Treasury bill that can be redeemed for $10,000 in April 2008; thus, the bill effectively pays $230 in interest ($10,000 − $9,770 = $230). The yield on such a bill is 2.35 percent or $230/$9,770 [(interest amount)/(purchase price)].

U.S. Treasury bills are the most liquid of all the money market instruments because they have an active secondary market and relatively short terms to maturity. They also are the safest of all money market instruments because there is no possibility that the government will fail to pay back the amount owed when the security matures. The federal government is always able to meet its financial commitments because of its ability to increase taxes or to issue currency in fulfillment of its scheduled payments.

Negotiable Certificates of Deposit (CDs)

A certificate of deposit (CD) is a short-term debt instrument sold by a depository institution that pays annual interest payments equal to a fixed percentage of the original purchase price. In addition, at maturity the original purchase price is also paid back. Prior to 1961, most CDs were not negotiable; that is, they could not be sold to someone else and could not be redeemed from the bank before maturity without paying a significant penalty. In 1961, with the goal of making CDs more liquid and more attractive to investors, Citibank introduced the first negotiable certificates of deposit (CDs). Such negotiable CDs could be resold in a secondary market, which Citibank created. Negotiable CDs have a maturity of one week to 12 months and have a minimum denomination of $100,000. In practice, the minimum denomination to trade in the secondary market is over $1,000,000. Most large commercial banks and many large savings and loans now issue negotiable CDs. In addition, smaller banks are able to borrow in the market by using brokers to sell their CDs.

Negotiable Certificates of Deposit (CDs)
Certificates of deposit with a minimum denomination of $100,000 that can be traded in a secondary market, most with an original maturity of one to 12 months.

Commercial Paper

Commercial paper, a short-term debt instrument issued by financial and nonfinancial corporations, has an original maturity of less than 270 days. Most commercial paper is issued with 30 to 60 day maturities and is supported by a backup line of bank credit. Prior to the 1960s, corporations usually borrowed short-term funds from banks to finance such things as inventories and day-to-day expenses. Since then, many corporations have come to depend on selling commercial paper to other financial intermediaries and other lenders for their immediate short-term borrowing needs. The growth of the commercial paper market since 1960 has been impressive and is partially due to the increase in commercial paper issued by nonfinancial firms. Initially, only large well-known corporations had access to the commercial paper market. In the late 1980s and early 1990s, medium and small firms found ways to enter this market by getting letters of credit from a bank that, for a fee, guaranteed payment in the event of default by the issuer. In addition, some financial intermediaries also get funds to invest and lend by issuing commercial paper.

Commercial Paper
Short-term debt instruments issued by corporations.

Bankers' Acceptances

Bankers' acceptances are money market instruments created in the course of financing international trade where the credit worthiness of one trader is unknown to the

Bankers' Acceptances
Money market instruments created in the course of international trade to guarantee bank drafts due on a future date.

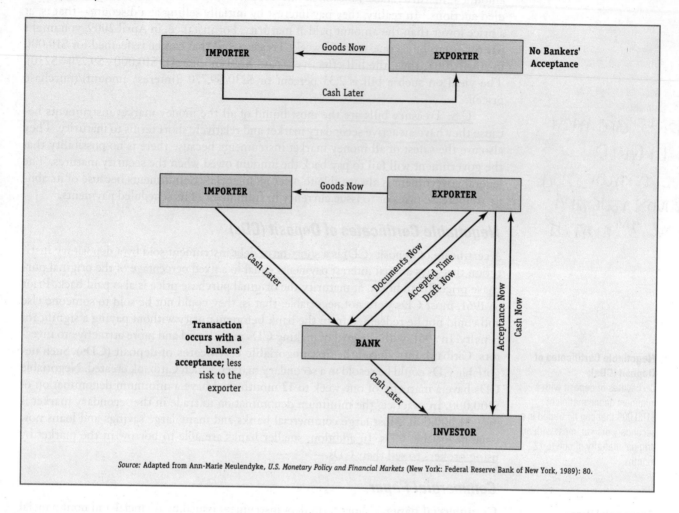

IMPORTER ← Goods Now ← EXPORTER   No Bankers' Acceptance

Cash Later

IMPORTER ← Goods Now ← EXPORTER

Cash Later

Documents Now

Accepted Time Draft Now

Acceptance Now

Cash Now

Transaction occurs with a bankers' acceptance; less risk to the exporter

BANK

Cash Later

INVESTOR

Source: Adapted from Ann-Marie Meulendyke, *U.S. Monetary Policy and Financial Markets* (New York: Federal Reserve Bank of New York, 1989): 80.

other. Typical maturities are from 30 to 180 days. Banks were first authorized to issue bankers' acceptances to finance the international and domestic trade of their customers by the Federal Reserve Act in 1913. Exhibit 4-3 depicts how bankers' acceptances work. A bankers' acceptance is a bank draft (a guarantee of payment similar to a check) issued by a firm and payable on some future date. For a fee, the bank on which the draft is drawn stamps it as "accepted," thereby guaranteeing that the draft will be paid. If the issuing firm fails to deposit the funds into its account to cover the draft by the future due date, the bank is obligated to pay the draft, making the draft more likely to be accepted when it is used to purchase goods abroad. The party that accepts the draft (often another bank) can then resell the draft in a secondary market at a discount before the due date, or it can hold the draft in its portfolio as an investment. Bankers' acceptances that trade in secondary markets are similar to Treasury bills in that they sell at a discount. The amount of bankers' acceptances outstanding increased by nearly 4,000 percent ($2 billion to $75 billion) between 1960 and 1984. Since 1984, however, the acceptance market has declined due to the growth of other financing alternatives and the increased trade in currencies other than the dollar. By March 2008, the amount of outstanding bankers' acceptances had fallen to $0.2 billion.

Repurchase Agreements

Repurchase Agreements
Short-term agreements in which the seller sells a government security to a buyer and simultaneously agrees to buy it back on a later date at a higher price.

Repurchase agreements are short-term agreements in which the seller sells a government security to a buyer and simultaneously agrees to buy the government security back on a later date at a higher price. In effect, the seller has borrowed funds for a short term, and the buyer ostensibly has made a secured loan for which the government security serves as collateral. If the seller (borrower) fails to pay back the loan, the buyer (lender) keeps the government security. For example, assume that a large corporation, such as IBM, finds it has excess funds in its checking account that it doesn't want sitting idly when they can earn interest. IBM uses these excess funds to buy a repurchase agreement from a bank. In the agreement, the bank sells government securities while agreeing to repurchase the government securities the next morning (or in a few days) at a higher price than the original selling price. The difference between the original selling price and the higher price for which the securities are bought back is, in reality, interest. The effect of this agreement is that IBM has made a secured loan to a bank and holds the government securities as collateral until the bank repurchases them when it pays off the loan. Repurchase agreements were created in 1969. Most repurchase agreements are overnight, although some are longer term. Almost all have a minimum denomination of $1 million. Outstanding repurchase agreements are now an important source of funds to banks.

Federal (Fed) Funds

Federal (Fed) Funds
Loans of reserves (deposits at the Fed) between depository institutions, typically overnight.

Federal (Fed) funds are typically overnight loans between depository institutions of their deposits at the Fed. This is effectively the market for excess reserves. A depository institution might borrow in the federal funds market if it finds that its reserve assets do not meet the amount required by law. It can borrow reserve deposits from another depository institution that has excess reserve deposits and chooses to lend them to earn interest. The reserve deposit balances are transferred between the borrowing and lending institutions using the Fed's wire transfer system. In recent years, many large depository institutions have used this market as a permanent source of funds to lend, not just when there is a temporary shortage of required reserve assets. As we saw in Chapter 2, the Fed has control over the cash assets available for reserves. The fed funds rate is the interest rate for borrowing and lending reserves in the fed funds market. If the Fed increases reserves, fewer depository institutions will need to borrow reserves and more will have excess reserves to lend. Ceteris paribus, the fed funds rate will fall and vice versa. In later chapters, we will see the importance of the fed funds rate in the implementation of monetary policy.

If Fed ↑ reserves then fewer deposit. institutions will need to borrow and more will have excess reserves to lend which will make fed funds rate ↓.

Eurodollars

Eurodollars
Dollar-denominated deposits held abroad.

Eurodollars are dollar-denominated deposits held in banks outside the United States. For example, if an American corporation makes a deposit denominated in U.S. dollars in a bank in England or some other foreign country, that is a Eurodollar deposit.[4] Eurodollar deposits are not subject to domestic regulations and are not covered by deposit insurance. Typical maturities are overnight to six months, and the average deposit is in the millions of dollars. The Eurodollar market started in the 1950s, when Soviet bloc governments put dollar-denominated deposits into London banks. The

Type of Instrument	1960	1970	1980	1990	2000	2008[a]
Corporate stock	$451	$906	$1,920	$3,530.0	$17,627	$19,648.4[a]
Mortgages	142	297	965	3,804.0	6,886	14,720.1[a]
Corporate and foreign bonds	75	167	319	1,704.0	4,991	11,261.5[a]
U.S. government securities[b]	240	372	863	3,052.0	5,773	8,534.9[ab]
U.S. government agency securities	10	51	170	1,445.9	4,345	8,072.9[a]
Municipal securities	71	144	337	983.0	1,481	2,669.0[a]

a. As of September 30, 2008.
b. Includes Treasury notes and bonds held by the public and intragovernmental holdings such as those held by the Fed and the Social Security Administration.
Source: Federal Reserve Flow of Funds Accounts, Z.1 (December 11, 2008), at **http://www.federalreserve.gov/releases/Z1/**; *Federal Reserve Bulletin*, various issues; *Banking and Monetary Statistics 1941–1970*, various issues.

funds were deposited in London because the governments were afraid that if the deposits were in the United States, they would be frozen in the event of a flare-up of Cold War tensions. Despite the easing of tensions, the Eurodollar market continues to thrive. Today, many corporations and investors hold Eurodollar deposits in a foreign country if they have trade-related dollar transactions in that country. Large corporations dominate the market. U.S. banks can also borrow Eurodollar deposits from their own foreign branches when they need funds to lend and invest. In recent years, borrowings of Eurodollars have become an important source of funds for domestically chartered banks.

CAPITAL MARKET INSTRUMENTS

The capital market is extremely important because it raises the funds needed by net borrowers to carry out their spending and investment plans. A smoothly functioning capital market influences how fast the economy grows. The principal capital market

Instrument	Typical Maturities	Principal Borrowers	Secondary Market
Corporate stock	—	Corporations	Very active for large corporations
Mortgages	15 to 30 years	Home owners and other investors	Moderately active
Corporate bonds	2 to 30 years	Corporations	Active
U.S. government securities			
Notes	2 to 10 years	U.S. government	Very active
Bonds	30 years	U.S. government	Very active
U.S. government agency securities	Up to 30 years	U.S. government agency	Active
Municipals	2 to 30 years	State and local governments	Active

instruments introduced in this section are listed in Exhibit 4-4, with the amounts outstanding at the end of 1960, 1970, 1980, 1990, 2000, and 2007. Exhibit 4-5 describes the typical maturities, principal borrowers, and degree of secondary market activity for these instruments.

Stocks

Stocks
Equity claims that represent ownership of the net assets and income of a corporation.

Preferred = Fixed pay
Common = Variable pay

Stocks are equity claims representing ownership of the net income and assets of a corporation. The income that stockholders receive for their ownership is called dividends. Preferred stock pays a fixed dividend, and in the event of bankruptcy of the corporation, the owners of preferred stock are entitled to be paid first after the corporation's other creditors. Common stock pays a variable dividend, depending on the profits that are left over after preferred stockholders have been paid and retained earnings set aside.[5] The largest secondary market for outstanding shares of stock is the New York Stock Exchange. However, a growing share of trading is occurring on the NASDAQ, an electronic trading platform, and on other online networks over the Internet. Several stock indexes measure the overall movement of common stock prices; the Dow Jones Industrial Average, perhaps the best known, is based on the prices of only 30 stocks. The Standard & Poor's 500 Stock Index is based on the prices of 500 stocks of the largest companies in the United States. The value of all outstanding stock was just over $20.1 trillion in early 2000, exceeding the value of any other type of security in the capital market. Note the dramatic increase in stock values between 1990 and early 2000—due to the very bullish stock market. In early 2000, the value of stocks began to fall in the deepest bear market in history, with the outstanding value of stocks falling to less than $11 trillion by the end of the third quarter of 2002. After three successive years of decline, the stock market began to recover, and by mid 2007, the value of outstanding equities reached just under $23 trillion. After this peak, the stock market fell to less than $19 trillion in mid 2008 as the ongoing financial crisis impacted most stocks and devastated the stocks of failing financial institutions. The amount of new stock issues in any given year is typically quite small relative to the total value of shares outstanding.

Mortgages

Mortgages
Loans made to purchase single- or multiple-family residential housing, land, or other real structures, with the structure or land serving as collateral for the loan.

Mortgages are loans to purchase single- or multiple-family residential housing, land, or other real structures, with the structure or land serving as collateral for the loan. In the event the borrower fails to make the scheduled payments, the lender can repossess the property. Mortgages are usually made for up to 30 years, and the repayment of the principal is generally spread out over the life of the loan. Some mortgages charge a fixed interest rate that remains the same over the life of the loan; others charge a variable interest rate that is adjusted periodically to reflect changing market conditions. Savings and loan associations, commercial banks, and mortgage brokers are the primary lenders in the residential mortgage market. In recent years, there has been a great deal of innovation in the mortgage market, including the introduction of interest-only loans, where the principal is not spread out over the life of the loan. Such loans reduce the monthly payment because no principal is paid. By making monthly payments more affordable, interest-only loans contributed to the housing boom of the early- and mid-2000s. Unfortunately, other innovations such as subprime mortgages directly led to the housing price collapse and mortgage crisis in the late 2000s. Subprime mortgages were made to borrowers at low initial interest rates that would later reset to higher rates, often making payments unaffordable for the borrower. These loans and falling housing prices led to the biggest housing bust and mortgage crisis in history. The crisis quickly spread to other domestic and global financial markets and is still plaguing the financial system in 2009. More on this ongoing crisis and the government response (or bailout) in later chapters.

Corporate Bonds

Corporate Bonds
Long-term debt instruments issued by corporations.

Corporate bonds are long-term bonds issued by corporations usually (although not always) with excellent credit ratings. Maturities range from two to 30 years. The owner receives an interest payment twice a year and the principal at maturity. Because the outstanding amount of bonds for any given corporation is small, corporate bonds are not nearly as liquid as other securities such as U.S. government bonds. However, an active secondary market has been created by dealers who are willing to buy and sell corporate bonds. The principal buyers of corporate bonds are life insurance companies, pension funds, households, commercial banks, and foreign investors. Bonds are rated by rating companies with regards to the probability of the issuing company being able to make payments when due. Bond issues with lower ratings are issued at higher interest rates to compensate for the increased risks.

U.S. Government Securities

U.S. Government Securities
Long-term debt instruments of the U.S. government with original maturities of two to 30 years.

U.S. government securities are long-term debt instruments with maturities of two to up to 30 years issued by the U.S. Treasury to finance the deficits of the federal government. Notes have an original maturity of two to 10 years; bonds have an original maturity between 10 and 30 years. At the present time, the Treasury sells newly issued fixed rate two-, three-, five-, and 10-year notes and 30-year bonds in regularly scheduled auctions. Government notes and bonds pay semiannual dividends and return the principal at maturity. An active secondary market exists, although it is not as active as the secondary market for T-bills. Despite this, because of the ease with which they are traded, government securities are still the most liquid security traded in the capital market. In 1997, the U.S. government began issuing inflation-indexed securities with returns that were adjusted in response to changes in inflation. Inflation-indexed securities currently are issued with five-, 10-, and 20-year maturities. The principal holders of government securities are the Federal Reserve, financial intermediaries, securities dealers, households, and foreign investors.

U.S. Government Agency Securities

U.S. Government Agency Securities
Long-term bonds issued by various government agencies, including those that support real estate lending and student loans.

U.S. government agency securities are long-term bonds issued by various privately owned government-sponsored agencies, including those that support commercial, residential, and agricultural real estate lending and student loans. Active secondary markets exist for most agency securities. Even though the agency securities do not have explicit government guarantees, most have an implicit government guarantee, and it is assumed the government will step in to support the market in the event of a default.

The two largest issuers of government agency securities are the Federal National Mortgage Association (Fannie Mae) and the Federal Home Loan Mortgage Corporation (Freddie Mac). Both are associated with the housing market. The proceeds from selling Fannie Mae and Freddie Mac securities are used to purchase mortgages. When the mortgages are purchased, new funds are provided to the mortgage market. Fannie Mae and Freddie Mac were caught up in the ongoing housing crisis that began in 2007. They had issued over $5 trillion in securities that would be paid from the payments on the mortgages they had purchased. When there were large defaults on the mortgages, Fannie Mae and Freddie Mac did not generate the revenue to make payments to the lenders who had purchased their securities. Given the implicit government guarantee, the U.S. government ended up taking over the two giants on September 7, 2008. Although the owners of the Fannie Mae and Freddie Mac securities did not lose, the shareholders of Fannie Mae and Freddie Mac were almost wiped out. As of late 2008, the fate of Fannie Mae and Freddie Mac is unknown.

The Government National Mortgage Association (Ginnie Mae), which is actually a U.S. government agency that is part of the Department of Housing and Urban Development (HUD), ensures the timely payment of principal and interest on mortgages. Thus, Ginnie Mae also facilitates greater lending in the mortgage market. Because Ginnie Mae is part of the government, Ginnie Mae securities are full faith and credit obligations of the U.S. government just as Treasury securities are, and thus there was no crisis in this market.

State and Local Government Bonds (Municipals)

State and Local Government Bonds (Municipals)
Long-term instruments issued by state and local governments to finance expenditures on schools, roads, and so on.

Revenue Bonds
Bonds used to finance specific projects with the proceeds of those projects being used to pay off the bondholders.

General Obligation Bonds
Bonds that are paid out of the general revenues and backed by the full faith and credit of the issuer.

State and local government bonds (municipals) are long-term instruments issued by state and local governments to finance expenditures on schools, roads, college dorms, and the like. An important attribute of municipals is that their interest payments are exempt from federal income taxes and from state taxes for investors living in the issuing state. Because of their tax status, state and local governments can issue debt at yields that are usually below those of taxable bonds of similar maturity. They carry some risk that the issuer will not be able to make scheduled interest or principal payments.[6] Payments are generally secured in one of two ways. **Revenue bonds** are used to finance specific projects, and the proceeds of those projects are used to pay off the bondholders. **General obligation bonds** are backed by the full faith and credit of the issuer; taxes can be raised to pay the interest and principal on general obligation bonds. Households in high tax brackets are the largest holders of state and local government bonds.

In the next section, we discuss market makers. They are among the most important participants in financial markets because they facilitate the flow of funds from net lenders to net borrowers, and vice versa.

Recap The major money market instruments are U.S. T-bills, negotiable CDs, commercial paper, bankers' acceptances, repurchase agreements, fed funds, and Eurodollars. The major capital market instruments are stocks, mortgages, corporate bonds, U.S. government securities, U.S. government agency securities, and municipals.

THE ROLE OF MARKET MAKERS

Market Makers
Dealers who link up buyers and sellers of financial securities and sometimes take positions in the securities.

The participants in financial markets are the buyers, sellers, and market makers. The market makers function as coordinators who link up buyers and sellers of financial instruments. The link involves arranging and executing trades. Market makers may make a market in only one type of security, say, Treasury bills, or in several different types of securities, including stocks and corporate and government bonds. Who are these market makers? Where are they located? Why do they exist? What does "making a market" entail? These are some of the questions to which we now turn.

Historically, since the Great Depression until 2008, the market makers had been investment banking firms. The main offices of these financial firms are in New York City, the financial capital of the United States. These offices are linked by telephone, telex, and the Internet to other major cities in the United States and the rest of the world where branch offices and regular customers are located. Like most enterprises, these firms are in business to earn profits. In this industry, profits are earned by providing financial services to the public. These services include giving advice to potential traders, conducting trades for the buyers and sellers of securities in the secondary market, and providing advice and marketing services to issuers of new securities in the primary market.

The packaging and marketing of newly issued stocks and bonds by a corporation in the primary market is *investment banking*. The term is potentially confusing, for it suggests that these market-making firms were banks; in fact, they were securities firms, not full-fledged banks, even though they provide some of the same services banks do. In recent years, in response to changing legislation that allowed them to do so, some large commercial banks have merged with securities firms that perform investment banking services. Furthermore, in response to the financial crisis of 2008, the five largest investment banks that dominated the industry, have either gone out of business (Lehman Brothers declared bankruptcy), been purchased by a commercial bank (J.P. Morgan purchased Bear Stearns; Bank of America purchased Merrill Lynch), or changed their charter to a bank holding company (Goldman Sachs and Morgan Stanley). Thus, the five leading investment bank titans no longer exist as independent entities and are now part of the commercial banking industry. The investment banking structure as we know it is in the process of evolutionary (or some may say revolutionary) change.

Despite this, we believe that these securities firms will still operate as separate parts of the larger financial conglomerate. They will employ brokers and dealers. A **broker** simply arranges trades between buyers and sellers for a fee. A **dealer,** in addition to arranging trades between buyers and sellers, stands ready to be a principal in a transaction. More specifically, a dealer stands ready to purchase and hold securities sold by investors in secondary markets. The dealer carries an inventory of securities and then sells them to other investors. When we refer to market makers in this text, we will be referring to dealers and the securities firms for which they work.

As a key player in financial markets, the market maker has an important role in our financial system. In particular, a market maker helps to maintain a smoothly functioning, orderly financial market. Market makers stand ready to buy and sell and adjust prices—literally making a market. Let us assume that there are 100,000 shares of a stock for sale at a particular price. If buyers take only 80,000 shares at that price, what happens to the remaining 20,000 shares? When such a short-term imbalance occurs, rather than making inconsistent changes in prices, the market maker takes a position (buys) and holds shares over a period of time to keep the price from falling erratically. Or the market maker may alter prices until all, or most, of the shares are sold. Thus, in the short run, market makers facilitate the ongoing shuffling and rearranging of portfolios by standing ready to increase or decrease their inventory position if there is not a buyer for every seller or a seller for every buyer. These actions enhance market efficiency and contribute to an evenly balanced financial system.

Market makers also receive, process, interpret, and disseminate information to potential buyers and sellers. Such information includes the outlook for monetary and fiscal policy; newly published data on inflation, unemployment, and output; fresh assessments of international economic conditions; information on the profits of individual firms; and analyses of trends and market shares in various industries. As holders of outstanding securities and potential issuers of new securities digest all of this information,

Broker
A person who arranges trades between buyers and sellers.

Dealer
A person who arranges trades between buyers and sellers and who stands ready to be a principal in a transaction; a market maker.

they may take actions that bring about a change in current interest rates and the prices of stocks and bonds.

To illustrate, assume that the political situation in the Middle East deteriorates, and experts believe a prolonged war, which would disrupt the flow of oil to the rest of the world, is likely. Analysts employed by the market makers would assess the probable impact on the price of oil, the effect on U.S. oil companies' profits, and so forth. Such information would be disseminated to and digested by financial investors and lead some of them to buy (demand) or sell (supply) particular securities.

In general, when something affects the supply of or demand for a good, the price of that good will be affected. In the financial markets, when something affects the supply of or demand for a security, its price will move to a new equilibrium and the market maker will facilitate the adjustment. As a quick perusal of the newspaper reveals, security prices change almost every day. Because of the activity of market makers, these changes usually occur in an orderly and efficient manner.

Why Market Makers Make Markets

The willingness of a market maker to make a market for any particular security will be a function of the expected profits and risks associated with buying, selling, and holding that type of security. The profits earned by a market maker flow mainly from the revenue generated by the price it charges for conducting a transaction, the number of transactions engaged in, and any capital gains or losses associated with the market maker's inventory of securities. Generally, a market maker charges a brokerage fee or commission for each transaction. The fee may be per item, such as five cents per share of stock; per trade, such as $7 per trade; or a specified percentage of the total value of the trade, such as .5 percent of the total proceeds from a sale of bonds. Market makers also collect a fee in some markets by buying a particular security at one price—the bid price—and selling the security at a slightly higher price—the "offer" or asked price. In this case, the revenue received by a market maker is a function of the spread between the bid and asked prices and the number of transactions in which the market maker and the public engage. Competition among market makers tends to minimize transactions costs to market participants.

To sum up, market makers play a key role in facilitating the buying and selling of securities by the public, as outlined in Exhibit 4-6. First, market makers assist in raising funds to finance deficits by marketing a borrower's new securities in the primary market. Second, they advise potential buyers and sellers of securities on the course of action likely to minimize costs and maximize returns. Third, they stand ready to buy or sell outstanding securities in the secondary market. To illustrate these various roles, Exhibit 4-7 summarizes the trading of a bond issued by All Purpose Enterprise Inc. (APEI), a typical firm that wants to expand its scale of operations by building a new plant and acquiring additional inventories. Note the coordinating and connecting role played by Merrill Lynch and Smith Barney.

Market Making and Liquidity

The quality and cost of services provided by market makers affect the transactions costs associated with buying or selling various securities. The costs and convenience associated with trading particular securities, in turn, affect the liquidity of these securities. Because transactions costs and liquidity affect portfolio decisions, the market-making function influences the allocation of financial resources in our economy. Some markets, such as the T-bill market, are characterized by high-quality secondary markets. The

Bid Price
The price at which a market maker is willing to buy securities.

Asked Price
The price at which a market maker is willing to sell securities.

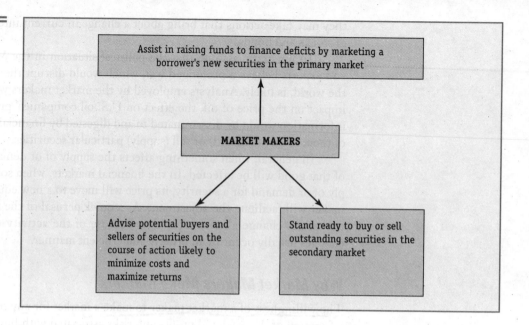

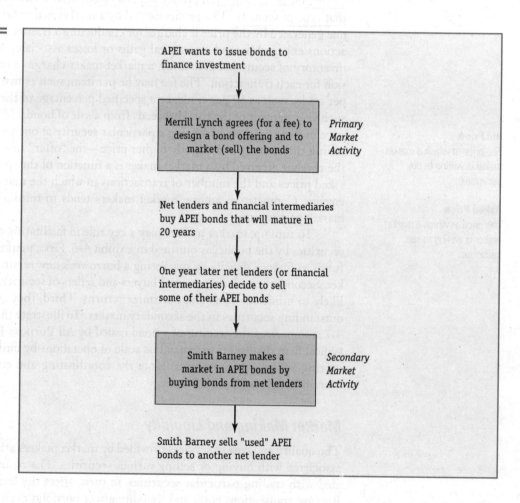

large volume of outstanding securities encourages many firms to make markets in Treasury securities, and the volume of trading and competition among market makers produces a spread between the dealer bid and asked prices of only 0.1 to 0.2 percent—well below the spread of 0.3125 to 0.5 percent associated with transactions in less actively traded, longer-term government securities.[7]

Substitutability, Market Making, and Market Integration

Market makers play another important but less obvious role in helping to integrate the various subsectors of financial markets. Market makers make markets in numerous financial instruments. In general, the trading floor of the typical market maker is a busy place. On the floor of the trading room, the specialist in T-bills sits near the specialist in corporate bonds, who, in turn, is only 20 feet from the specialist in mortgage-backed securities. Assuming that these people talk to one another, the activity in one market is known to those operating in other markets. With each specialist disseminating information to customers via telephone and continually monitoring computer display terminals, a noticeable change in the T-bill market (say, a half percentage point decline in interest rates on T-bills) will quickly become known to buyers and sellers in other markets. Such information will, in turn, influence trading decisions in these other markets and thus affect interest rates on other securities.

This spillover from one submarket to another is important in understanding the ties that bind the various compartments of financial markets together. The key concept underlying these linkages is the notion of substitutability. Whether they be bank managers or individuals allocating their own savings, portfolio managers monitor the expected returns on the array of financial assets available in financial markets. They compare the returns on assets in their portfolios to others available in the market. For example, if a higher, more attractive return becomes available on a Treasury bond as compared to a municipal bond already in the manager's portfolio, the manager may decide to sell the municipal security and buy the Treasury bond. This exchange of a lower-yielding security for a higher-yielding one is the essence of substitution. Assuming that many portfolio managers undertake similar actions, the net effect is to increase the supply in the municipal securities market and the demand in the Treasury bond market. Our market makers then act, in effect, as auctioneers, responding to such changes in supply and demand by changing the prices at which they are willing to buy or sell securities.

So far we have restricted our discussion to domestic financial markets. Yet for almost every domestic financial market, a corresponding foreign market exists. For example, there are markets for Japanese government securities, Hong Kong stocks, Canadian mortgage-backed securities, and Greek bonds. The same factors that affect the viability of domestic markets affect the substitutability between and among domestic and foreign instruments. Most financial markets are international in scope, as improvements in communication technologies have made the world a smaller place. Foreign instruments are good substitutes for domestic instruments in such a world, and vice versa. The activities of the market makers are critical to "greasing the wheels" that allow for this market integration.

Leaving the details aside, we have come full circle from the beginning of the chapter. We have seen that the numerous instruments traded in financial markets can be classified in many different ways; we have also seen that the separate markets for the individual instruments are linked by the activities of market makers and the willingness of traders to substitute among the alternative instruments available.

Before ending this discussion, note one other aspect about market makers. The traders obtain details on current interest rates, securities prices, and other information. Among many bits of data watched closely by all market makers is information relating to the operations of the Federal Reserve. In fact, if you asked these analysts and traders which type of information is most important, they would probably answer "information on Federal Reserve policy." Later in the text, we are sure you will be able to see why.

Summary of Major Points

1. The markets for particular types of financial claims are connected, not separate, entities. The connectedness of the markets results from the buying and selling (trading) of securities by the participants in the markets—that is, the substitution among available alternative instruments.

2. The money market is where securities with original maturities of one year or less are traded. The capital market is where securities with original maturities of more than one year are traded.

3. Primary markets are where new securities, issued to finance current deficits, are bought and sold. Secondary markets are where outstanding securities (issued earlier) are bought and sold. Secondary markets are important to the operation of an efficient financial system. Well-organized, smoothly functioning, high-quality secondary markets facilitate the trading of outstanding securities at relatively low cost and little inconvenience. This, in turn, facilitates the financing of planned deficits in primary markets.

4. The spot market is the market for the purchase or sale of securities for immediate delivery. In the futures and forward markets, contracts are entered into today to purchase or sell securities in the future at a price agreed upon today. Futures agreements are standardized with regards to quantities and delivery dates. Forward agreements are customized by banks and other brokers and dealers with regard to quantities and delivery dates to meet the needs of bank customers. Futures and forward markets are used to either reduce risk or speculate. Futures and forward markets are part of the grow-

ing derivatives markets where the financial instruments derive their values from some underlying instrument.

5. The principal money market instruments are U.S. Treasury bills (T-bills), negotiable certificates of deposit (CDs), commercial paper, bankers' acceptances, repurchase agreements, federal (fed) funds, and Eurodollars. The major capital market instruments are stocks, mortgages, corporate bonds, U.S. government securities, U.S. government agency securities, and state and local government bonds.

6. Market makers are the specialists who function as coordinators in financial markets and link up buyers and sellers of securities. They serve three important functions: (1) they disseminate information about market conditions to buyers and sellers; (2) they connect the various markets by buying and selling in the market themselves; and (3) they provide financial services that determine the quality of primary and secondary markets. In turn, the quality of the primary and secondary markets affects the ease or difficulty associated with financing deficits, lending surpluses, and, more generally, shifting into and out of various financial instruments.

7. Investment bankers assist corporations in the issuance of new stocks and bonds. Securities firms provide investment banking services. In recent years, securities firms and commercial banks have merged. In response to the financial crisis of 2008, the five largest investment banks have all either gone out of business or been assimilated into a commercial banking institution.

8. Dealers are market makers and their actions contribute to the smooth functioning of financial markets. They buy securities at bid prices and sell securities at asked prices. Their profit consists of the spread between the bid and asked prices and any price appreciation of the securities they hold.

9. Most domestic financial markets have a comparable foreign market, such as a foreign stock market. Market makers have assisted in integrating domestic and foreign financial markets.

Key Terms

Asked Price, p. **81**
Bankers' Acceptances, p. **73**
Bid Price, p. **81**
Broker, p. **80**
Capital Market, p. **68**
Commercial Paper, p. **73**
Corporate Bonds, p. **78**
Dealer, p. **80**
Derivative Markets, p. **70**
Eurodollars, p. **75**
Federal (Fed) Funds, p. **75**
Financial Forward Markets, p. **69**

Financial Futures Markets, p. **69**
General Obligation Bonds, p. **79**
Market Makers, p. **79**
Money Market, p. **68**
Mortgages, p. **77**
Negotiable Certificates of Deposit (CDs), p. **73**
Primary Market, p. **68**
Repurchase Agreements, p. **75**
Revenue Bonds, p. **79**
Secondary Market, p. **69**
Speculation, p. **70**

Spot Markets, p. **69**
State and Local Government Bonds (Municipals), p. **79**
Stocks, p. **77**
Term to Maturity, p. **68**
U.S. Government Agency Securities, p. **78**
U.S. Government Securities, p. **78**
U.S. Treasury Bills (T-bills), p. **72**

Review Questions

1. Distinguish between primary and secondary markets and between money and capital markets.

2. The secondary market for T-bills is active, and the secondary market for federal agency securities is limited. How does this affect the primary market for each security? Why are well-developed secondary markets important for the operation of an efficient financial system?

3. What is the difference between financial futures and financial forward markets? What are derivative markets? What are the ways derivatives can be used?

4. Discuss the major function of market makers in securities markets. What is the difference between a broker and a dealer?

5. If you call a local brokerage firm, you will find that the commission or brokerage fee charged for purchasing $10,000 of T-bills is less than the fee associated with purchasing $10,000 of, say, municipal bonds issued by the City of Cincinnati. Explain why.

6. Explain why it would be incorrect to view the various sectors of the financial markets as totally separate entities.

7. Define *commercial paper, negotiable certificates of deposit, repurchase agreements, bankers' acceptances, federal funds,* and *Eurodollars.* In what ways are they similar, and in what ways are they different?

8. What are mortgages?

9. Define and contrast *stocks* and *bonds.* What are the advantages of owning preferred stock? What are the advantages of owning common stock?

10. What is the difference between a government security and a government agency security? Which asset would you prefer to own if safety and liquidity were important to you?

11. Would you rather own the stocks or bonds of a particular corporation if you believed that the corporation was going to earn exceptional profits next year?

12. Why are municipals attractive to individuals and corporations with high incomes or profits?

13. Can the bid price ever be greater than the asked price?

Analytical Questions

Questions marked with a check mark (✓) are objective in nature. They can be completed with a short answer or number.

✓14. Rank the following financial instruments in terms of their safety and liquidity:
  a. U.S. T-bills
  b. Large negotiable CDs
  c. Mortgages
  d. Government bonds
  e. Government agency securities
  f. Commercial paper
  g. Eurodollars

✓15. In June 2010, John pays $9,800 for a one-year T-bill that can be redeemed for $10,000. What is the amount of interest earned? What is the yield?

Suggested Readings

Information on T-bills can be found at **http://www.trea surydirect.gov/indiv/products/prod_tbills_glance.htm.**

Fed funds transactions are discussed at **http://www.new yorkfed.org/.**

Two older books that may be of interest are *The Money Market*, rev. ed. (Homewood, IL: Dow Jones-Irwin, 1990), and *Handbook of Securities of the United States Government and Federal Agencies, and Related Money Market Instruments* (First Boston Corporation, July 1990).

Additional Fed publications explaining fed funds, repurchase agreements, and government securities can be accessed online at **http://www.newyorkfed.org/publications/result .cfm.**

For a discussion of the commercial paper market, see Mitchell Post, "The Evolution of the U.S. Commercial Paper Market Since 1980," *Federal Reserve Bulletin* (December 1992). For recent trends in the commercial paper market, see Pu Shen, "Why Has the Nonfinancial Commercial Paper Market Shrunk Recently?" *Economic Review*, Federal Reserve Bank of Kansas City 88:1 (First Quarter 2003): 55–76. Yields on financial and nonfinancial commercial paper can be seen at **http://www.economagic .com/fedbog.htm.**

Some articles dealing with the stock market boom of the late 1990s follow: Nathan S. Balke and Mark E. Wohar, "Why Are Stock Prices So High? Dividend Growth or Discount Factor?" *Federal Reserve Bank of Dallas Working Paper No. 00–01* (January 2000); Simon Kwan, "Three Questions About 'New Economy' Stocks," *FRBSF Economic Letter*, Federal Reserve Bank of San Francisco, No. 2000–15 (May 12, 2000); William R. Nelson, "Why Does the Change in Shares Predict Stock Returns?" *Finance and Economics Discussion Series*, Board of Governors of the Federal Reserve System, No. 1999–06 (1999).

Endnotes

1. The terms financial claims, instruments, or securities can be used interchangeably.
2. Many money market instruments such as U.S. government and agency securities are also sold in much smaller denominations for individual investors.
3. Individuals can bid on and purchase T-bills directly from the federal government at **www. treasurydirect.gov.**
4. Eurodollars must be distinguished from foreign deposits that are denominated in the currency of the host country. For example, a foreign deposit results when an American converts dollars to British pounds and deposits them in a bank in England with the deposit denominated in pounds.
5. Note that the board of directors of a corporation may choose not to pay common stockholders dividends even if the corporation has profits left over after preferred shareholders have been paid. In this case, the income that stockholders receive will be in the form of capital gains if the stock appreciates because of the retained earnings.

6. In mid-1995, investors in Orange County, California, found out firsthand about the risks of municipal bonds after the county declared bankruptcy in December 1994. The bankruptcy resulted from a $1.7 billion loss in the county's investment portfolio due to reckless risk taking in financial markets.
7. Spreads between dealer bid and asked prices for corporate bonds range up to 2 to 3 percent for securities with relatively low marketability.

PART 2

Financial Prices

CHAPTER FIVE

Change must be measured from a known baseline.

—Evan Shute

Interest Rates and Bond Prices

Learning Objectives

After reading this chapter, you should know:

What compounding and discounting are

Why interest rates and bond prices are inversely related

The major determinants of interest rates

The relationship between nominal and real interest rates

How interest rates fluctuate over the business cycle

THE PRESENT VERSUS THE FUTURE

State University currently charges students $5,000 a year for tuition. Following the appointment of an innovative financial officer, it offers enrolling freshmen a new way to pay four years' tuition—pay $18,000 today rather than $5,000 per year for four years. Would you participate in the plan? Following her third box office smash, a Hollywood sensation has just signed a multipicture contract. As compensation, the star has been offered either $6,000,000 today or $7,500,000 in five years. You are her financial adviser; what should she do and why? You win a million-dollar lottery and learn that the million dollars will be paid out in equal installments of $50,000 per year over the next 20 years. Would you be willing to trade this stream of future income for one payment today? How large would that payment have to be?

The purpose of the first half of this chapter is to provide the analytical framework needed to understand questions that involve comparing the present with the future, such as those just posed. The questions addressed are the keys to the second half of the chapter, where we will examine the determinants of interest rates and the relationships among interest rates, bond prices, economic activity, and inflation.

THE TIME VALUE OF MONEY

Money represents purchasing power; a person who has money can purchase goods or services now. If someone does not have money now and wants to make purchases, she can rent purchasing power by borrowing. Likewise, if someone else has money now and is willing to postpone purchases to the future, he can rent out purchasing power. Note carefully the role played by the interest rate here. Presumably, the willingness to postpone purchases into the future is a function of the reward—that is, the interest rate. In particular, the higher the interest rate, ceteris paribus, the greater the reward and, hence, the greater the willingness to postpone purchases into the future and lend in the present. Similar reasoning applies on the borrowing side. We can think of someone who wants to purchase goods and services but is short of the necessary funds as having two options: (1) borrow now and purchase now or (2) save now and purchase later. Because the willingness to borrow depends on the cost, among other things, we can conclude that the higher the interest rate, ceteris paribus, the less attractive option (1) appears and the more attractive option (2) becomes.

The central point to remember from this discussion is the role that the interest rate plays in linking the present and the future. Lending in the present enables spending in the future the sum of what is lent plus the interest earned. Borrowing in the present enables spending in the present but requires paying back in the future what is borrowed plus interest. Because the interest rate is the return on lending and the cost of borrowing, it plays a pivotal role in spending, saving, borrowing, and lending decisions made in the present and bearing on the future. The concept is called the time value of money. Simply put, the interest rate represents the time value of money because it specifies the terms on which a person can trade off present purchasing power for future purchasing power.

Time Value of Money
The terms on which one can trade off present purchasing power for future purchasing power; the interest rate.

COMPOUNDING AND DISCOUNTING
Compounding: Future Values

Compounding
A method used to determine the future value of a sum lent today

Compounding is a method used to answer a simple question: What is the future value of money lent (or borrowed) today? As illustrated in Exhibit 5-1, the question is forward looking; we stand in the present (today) and ask a question about the future. To see how it works, a few examples will be helpful.

5-1

Compounding: The Future Value of Money Lent Today

Payment Today $1,000	→	Future Value $1,060

Principal
The original amount of funds lent.

Suppose Joseph M. Student agrees to lend a friend $1,000 for one year. The friend gives Joe an IOU for $1,000 and agrees to repay the $1,000 plus interest in a year. The amount that is originally lent is called the principal—in this case, $1,000.

If the agreed interest rate is 6 percent, the friend will pay a total of $1,060 ($1,000 + $60). In this example, the amount of interest is $60 ($1,000 × .06 = $60).

This general relationship can be expressed as:

(A) Amount repaid = principal + interest.

The amount of interest can be expressed as

(B) Interest = principal × interest rate.

Substituting Equation (B) into Equation (A) yields

(C) Amount repaid = principal + (principal × interest rate).

Because each term on the right-hand side of Equation (C) has a common factor, it can be rearranged and rewritten as

(D) Amount repaid = principal × (1 + i),

where i is the interest rate. Using Equation (D) and our example, Joe's friend would repay

$$\$1,060 = \$1,000 \times 1.06.$$

We can rewrite Equation (D) as

(5-1) $$V_1 = V_0(1 + i)$$

where V_1 = the funds to be received by the lender (paid by the borrower) at the end of year 1 (a future value); and V_0 = the funds lent and borrowed now (a present value).

Imagine now that Joe's friend borrows for two years instead of one year and makes no payments to Joe until two years pass.[1] Here is where compounding comes into play. Compounding refers to the increase in the value of funds that results from earning interest on interest. More specifically, interest earned after the first year is added to the original principal; the second year's interest calculation is based on this total. The funds to be received at the end of two years, V_2, consist of the original amount of funds lent out, V_0, *plus* the interest earned the first year on the original amount, $i\,V_0$, *plus* the interest earned the second year on the amount of funds owed at the end of the first year [$i(V_0 + iV_0)$]. In our example:

Principal	+	Interest earned in first year	+	Interest earned in second year =
$1,000	+	.06($1,000)	+	.06[$1,000+.06($1,000)]=
$1,000	+	$60	+	$63.60=$1,123.60

In the second year, Joe earns interest not only on the principal (.06 × $1,000) but also on the interest earned in the first year [.06 × .06($1,000)]. In effect, the interest earned in the first year is reinvested. Expressed symbolically:

(5-2) $$V_2 = V_0 + iV_0 + i(V_0 + iV_0)$$

Using some simple algebra, this equation can be reduced to[2]

(5-3)
$$V_2 = V_0(1+i)^2$$

Equation (5-3) can be generalized for any sum of money lent (invested) for any maturity of n years:

(5-4)
$$V_n = V_0(1+i)^n$$

The future value of a sum of money invested for n years, V_n, is equal to the original sum, V_0, compounded by the interest rate $(1+i)^n$. In our last example, $V_0 = \$1,000$, $i = .06$, $n = 2$, and $V_2 = \$1,123.60$.

The formula in Equation (5-4) is actually quite easy to use. For example, most calculators have a y^x function, and $(1+i)^n$ is a y^x calculation. Using $(1+.11)$ for y and 10 for x, you should be able to verify that if Joe lends $1,000 for 10 years at an interest rate of 11 percent, he will receive \$2,839.42 at maturity: $\$2,839.42 = \$1,000(1.11)^{10}$.

Discounting: Present Values

Discounting
A method used to determine the present value of a sum to be received in the future.

Present Value
The value today of funds to be received or paid on a future date.

In effect, as shown in Exhibit 5-2, discounting is backward looking. It addresses this question: What is the present value of money to be received (or paid) in the future?

Consider the case of the movie star mentioned at the beginning of the chapter. She has been signed to a multipicture deal, and the studio has offered to pay her either $6,000,000 today or $7,500,000 in five years. Which option should she select?

To calculate the answer, we can simply rearrange Equation (5-4). In the previous example, we knew the present value, V_0, the interest rate, i, and the number of years, n, and we wanted to solve for the future value, V_n. Now we want to solve for the present value, V_0, of a sum to be received in the future ($7,500,000), so we can compare it to another present value (the $6,000,000). Accordingly,

(5-5)
$$V_0 = V_n/(1+i)^n$$

Assuming that we know the interest rate—say, it's 6 percent—the present value of $7,500,000 to be available in five years is

$$\$5,604,436.30 = \$7,500,000/(1 + .06)^5.$$

The present value of $6,000,000 received today for signing the multipicture contract is, obviously, $6,000,000. Given an interest rate of 6 percent, the present value of $7,500,000 to be received in five years is obviously less.[3] Accordingly, the movie star should take the $6,000,000 today. To see why more clearly, all you need to do is turn the discounting/present value problem into a compounding/future value problem; if the actress took the $6,000,000 today and invested it at 6 percent, she would have more than $7,500,000 in five years. To be exact, she would have $8,029,353.47 because $6,000,000 $(1 + .06)^5 = \$8,029,353.47$!

To be sure you are completely with us, close the book and ask yourself what the present value of $7,500,000 in five years, given an interest rate of 6 percent, really represents. It is the sum you would need to invest today, given a 6 percent interest rate, to have $7,500,000 in five years; that is, to have $7,500,000 in five years given an interest rate of

5-2
Discounting: The Present
Value of Money to Be
Received in the Future

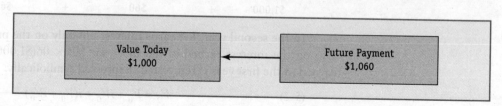

6 percent, you would have to invest $5,604,436.30 today. To nail everything down, assume the interest rate is 4 percent instead of 6 percent. Would you still advise the movie star to take the $6,000,000 today, or does the change in the interest rate point to a different option? Why or why not? The explanation and calculation are in endnote 4.[4]

Recap Compounding is finding the future value of a present sum. Discounting is finding the present value of a future sum. The future value, V_n, of a sum, V_0, invested today for n years is $V_0(1 + i)^n$. The present value, V_0, of a sum, V_n, to be received in n years is $V_n/(1 + i)^n$.

Interest Rates, Bond Prices, and Present Values

Although bonds issued by corporations and governments differ in a variety of ways, they generally share the following characteristics: they have an original maturity of more than 10 years, they have a face or par value (F) of $1,000 per bond, and the issuer (borrower) agrees to make equal periodic interest payments over the term to maturity of the instrument and to repay the face value at maturity. The periodic payments are called coupon payments (C) and are equal to the coupon rate on a bond multiplied by the face value of the bond. Note that the coupon rate, which usually appears on the bond itself, may not be the same thing as the current interest rate. The distinction between the coupon rate and the coupon payment and between the coupon rate and the interest rate is often a source of considerable confusion; bear with us and you can avoid the problem.

A bond represents a stream of future payments. Once the bond has been issued, the price the bond will trade at in secondary markets is the present value of the future stream of payments. To find its price, we need to compute the present value of each coupon payment and the present value of the final repayment of the face value on the maturity date. The appropriate formula is

Par Value
The face value printed on a bond; the amount the bond originally sold for.

Coupon Payments
The periodic payments made to bondholders, which are equal to the principal times the coupon rate.

$$\frac{C_i}{(1+i)^i} \cdots$$

used to compute the present value of a # of future payments

$$(5\text{-}6) \quad P = C_1/(1 + i)^1 + C_2/(1 + i)^2 + \cdots + C_n/(1 + i)^n + F/(1 + i)^n$$

where P = the price (present value) of the bond,
C = the coupon payment on the bond (C_1 in year 1, C_2 in year 2, etc.),
F = the face or par value of the bond,
i = the interest rate, and
n = the number of years to maturity (on a five-year bond, n = 5).

Notice that this formula is a descendant of Equation (5-5), with $P = V_0$ and $V_n = C$ or F. The only difference is that we use (5-6) to compute the present value of a number of future payments, such as occurs with a bond, and (5-5) to compute the present value of a single future payment. Suppose Jane is about to buy a bond that will mature in one year, has a face value of $1,000, and carries a coupon payment of $60, and the prevailing interest rate in the market is 6 percent. What is Jane willing to pay for this bond? Using Equation (5-6),

$$P = \$60/(1 + .06)^1 + \$1,000/(1 + .06)^1 =$$
$$\$56.60 + \$943.40 = \$1,000.$$

This tells Jane that the price of the bond or its present value is $1,000.[5] In other words, if the interest rate is 6 percent, the present value of receiving $1,060 in one year is $1,000, and this is what Jane (or anybody else) will pay for the bond. Because the coupon payment is $60, the coupon rate is 6 percent (6 percent = $60/$1,000). You might also note that when the price of a bond is equal to its par value ($1,000), the coupon rate is equal to the current interest rate.

Continuing with this example, Jane buys the bond for $1,000, and the next day the prevailing interest rate in the market rises to 8 percent. What effect does this have on the value (price) of Jane's bond? Remember that Jane's bond will pay her $1,060 in one year.[6] Imagine yourself with $1,000 to invest. How much would you pay for Jane's bond? Would you pay $1,000? We hope your answer is "no!" You could go out in the market and buy another bond yielding 8 percent for $1,000! Alternatively, you could buy Jane's bond. But you would do this if and only if it too was somehow made to yield 8 percent. How could this happen? The maturity of the bond (one year), the coupon payment ($60 per $1,000 of par value), and the par value ($1,000) are all fixed. They represent the contractual arrangements entered into by the bond issuer (borrower) at the time the bond was initially issued. What's left? The price of the bond! You and other investors would be willing to pay a price for the bond that, given the receipt of $1,060 at maturity, would represent a yield over the year of 8 percent. Using our Equation (5-5),

$$P = \$60/(1 + .08)^1 + \$1,000/(1 + .08)^1 =$$
$$\$55.55 + \$925.93 = \$981.48.$$

The amount $981.48 is the present value of $1,060 to be received in one year if the interest rate we use to discount the future sum is 8 percent.

Put somewhat more intuitively, if you bought Jane's bond for $981.48, you would receive $60 of interest at maturity plus a capital gain of $18.52; the gain is equal to the par value you get back at maturity ($1,000) minus the price you pay at the time of purchase ($981.48). Together, the interest and the capital gain ($60+$18.52 = $78.52) give us an 8 percent yield over the year ($78.52/$981.48 = .08). Thus, in this example, you buy the bond at a price below its par value. This is called a discount from par and raises the yield on the bond, called the yield to maturity, from 6 percent to 8 percent. In sum, as the market interest rate rises, the price of existing bonds falls. The lower yield to maturity on exist-ing bonds is unattractive to potential purchasers who can purchase newly issued bonds with higher yields to maturity. Therefore, the yield to maturity on previously issued bonds must somehow rise to remain competitive with the new higher level of prevailing interest rates. The yield on existing bonds rises when their prices fall. Hence, bond prices fall until the yield to maturity of the bond becomes equal to the current interest rate.

Suppose that instead of rising from 6 percent to 8 percent the day after Jane buys the bond, the interest rate in the market falls to 4 percent. You should now be able to do the arithmetic with the aid of Equation (5-6); the price (or present value) of Jane's bond will rise to $1,019.23. What does this represent? If any of us bought Jane's bond for $1,019.23, we would be paying a price above the par value. This is called a premium above par. At maturity, we would get $60 minus a capital loss of $19.23; the loss is equal to what we pay at the time of purchase minus the par value we receive at maturity ($1,019.23–$1,000 = $19.23). The $40.77 ($60–$19.23 = $40.77) represents a 4 percent yield over the year ($40.77/$1,019.23 = .04). Thus, as the market interest rate falls, the prices of existing bonds rise. The reason is that the higher yield to maturity on existing bonds is attractive to potential investors, and as they buy existing bonds, the bond prices rise, reducing their yield to maturity.

In general, then, there is an inverse relationship between the price of outstanding bonds trading in the secondary market and the prevailing level of market interest rates. As a result, we can say that if bond prices are rising, then interest rates are falling, and vice versa. One final point: for any given change in interest rates, the longer the term to maturity, the greater will be the change in the price of the bond. Thus, the prices of bonds that are going to mature in the very near future fluctuate much less than prices of longer term bonds. For example, if interest rates rise, the prices of bonds that are very close to maturity will not fall that much because the proceeds can shortly be reinvested at the new higher rates. This is not so for longer term bonds.

Discount from Par
When a bond sells below its face value because interest rates have increased since the bond was originally issued.

Yield to Maturity
The return on a bond held to maturity, which includes both the interest return and any capital gain or loss.

Premium above Par
When a bond sells above its face value because interest rates have decreased since the bond was originally issued.

Fluctuations in Interest Rates and Managing a Bond Portfolio

Why would the manager of a bond portfolio for a large pension fund be concerned about the likely direction of interest rates? Simply put, if rates rise sharply, for example, the value of the manager's portfolio, which contains previously purchased bonds, would fall significantly. This year's bonus for skillful management could go right out the window. Conversely, if rates fall, the prices of previously purchased bonds increase, and capital gains are in the offing. Such possibilities are what motivate managers and their advisers to pay so much attention to the factors that determine interest rates. More specifically, a portfolio manager who believes the Fed is about to engage in actions that will raise interest rates is likely to sell a considerable amount of bonds now to avoid the capital losses on bonds held that will accompany any rise in market yields. Conversely, the expectation of a fall in interest rates would encourage purchases of bonds now in anticipation of the capital gains that will accompany such a fall.[7]

Positioning the pension fund to take advantage of any change in interest rates requires our portfolio manager to understand the major factors determining movements in interest rates. Note that it is the expectation of interest rate changes that motivates the portfolio manager into action. After interest rates have changed, it is too late to take advantage of potential capital gains or to avoid potential losses. Of course, it is not too late to try to avoid making the same mistake again and again.

Recap   The price of a bond is the discounted value of the future stream of income over the life of the bond. When the interest rate increases, the prices of previously issued bonds decrease. When the interest rate decreases, the prices of previously issued bonds increase.

THE DETERMINANTS OF INTEREST RATES

In previous chapters, we emphasized the role of the financial system in coordinating and channeling the flow of funds from net lenders to net borrowers. The interest rate is of paramount importance because changes in the interest rate affect the amount of lending and borrowing, and vice versa. In the market for loanable funds, as in other markets, supply and demand represent the key to determining interest rates. This means, of course, that any change in interest rates will be the result of changes in supply and/or demand for loanable funds.

Demand for Loanable Funds
The demand for borrowed funds by household, business, government, or foreign net borrowers.

The **demand for loanable funds** originates from household, business, government, and foreign net borrowers who borrow because they are spending more than their current income. The downward-sloping demand curve indicates that net borrowers are willing to borrow more at lower interest rates, ceteris paribus.[8] Businesses borrow more at lower interest rates because more investment projects become profitable, ceteris paribus. Projects that would be unprofitable if the business had to pay 12 percent to borrow the funds become quite profitable if the funds can be had for only 2 percent. Consumers borrow more at lower interest rates, ceteris paribus, for such things as automobiles and other consumer durables.

Supply of Loanable Funds
The supply of borrowed funds originating (1) from household, business, government, and foreign net lenders or (2) from the Fed through its provision of reserves.

The total **supply of loanable funds** originates from two sources: (1) household, business, government, and foreign net lenders who are prepared to lend because they are spending less than their current income, and (2) the Fed, which, in its ongoing attempts to manage the economy's performance, supplies reserves to the financial system that lead to increases in the growth rate of money (and loans). We shall assume that the Fed's supply of funds is fixed at a particular amount for the time being. Adding the funds that net lenders are willing to supply to the Fed's supply of funds produces a supply curve for loanable funds that is upward sloping.

To illustrate how the behaviors of the Fed and net lenders interact, suppose that during the current period the Fed supplies reserves to the financial system leading to $300 billion of loanable funds being supplied to the market, and that this amount of funds will not increase or decrease as the interest rate changes. As for net lenders, suppose they are willing to lend $100 billion at a 4 percent interest rate, $200 billion at a 6 percent interest rate, and $300 billion at an 8 percent interest rate. Adding the fixed supply of loanable funds resulting from the Fed's supply of reserves to the interest-sensitive amount that will be supplied by net lenders, we get the total supply of funds of $400 billion at a 4 percent rate, $500 billion at a 6 percent rate, and $600 billion at an 8 percent rate. This is how the supply function shown in Exhibit 5-3 is calculated. Note that its upward slope reflects the changes in the quantity of funds supplied by net lenders at different interest rates, everything else remaining unchanged.

This indicates that net lenders are willing to supply more funds at higher interest rates because lending would be more profitable, ceteris paribus. As Exhibit 5-3 shows, the quantity of funds supplied equals the quantity of funds demanded at point E_1. The equilibrium interest rate in the market for loanable funds is 6 percent, and the equilibrium quantity of funds borrowed and lent is $500 billion.

From the point of view of our portfolio manager, it is not sufficient to know the equilibrium or current interest rate. What is really of concern is the potential for future changes in interest rates and the capital gains (increases in bond prices) or capital losses (decreases in bond prices) that will accompany such changes. Because any change in in-

5-3

The Supply of and Demand for Funds

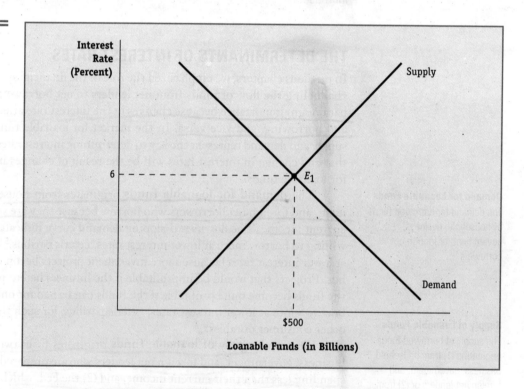

The interest rate is measured on the vertical axis, and the quantity of loanable funds is measured on the horizontal axis. At E_1, the quantity demanded is equal to the quantity supplied and the market is in equilibrium. The supply of and demand for loanable funds determine the interest rate.

terest rates will be the result of a change in either the supply of or demand for funds, let's take a close look at the major factors that can shift either of the curves.

Changes in the Demand for Loanable Funds

Gross domestic product (GDP) is the dollar value of final goods and services produced in the domestic economy in a year.[9] On the demand side, research has shown that movements in GDP represent a major determinant of shifts in the demand for funds. In particular, when GDP rises, ceteris paribus, firms and households both become more willing and able to borrow. Firms are more willing because the rise in GDP has improved the business outlook, encouraging them to expand planned inventories and engage in more investment spending such as purchases of plant and equipment. These new activities will have to be financed by borrowing. Households are more willing to borrow because the rise in GDP has increased their incomes and improved the employment outlook. These factors encourage them to increase their purchases of goods and services, particularly automobiles, other durable goods, and houses, which often require some financing. Firms and households are more able to borrow because the improved economic outlook and the rise in incomes will make it easier to make the payments on any new debt.

A positive relationship between changes in income and the demand for loanable funds means that both move in the same direction—when one rises, the other rises, and vice versa. Some students are puzzled by the positive relationship between GDP (income) and the demand for funds. They argue that these variables should be negatively related; for example, a drop in income, given expenditures, will increase a household's deficit, necessitating a rise in the demand for funds (borrowing). The problem with this reasoning is that expenditures are assumed to remain constant. In fact, the drop in income will lead to a reduction in expenditures. More generally, historical experience shows that the willingness and ability to borrow and spend will fall when income falls.

Another factor that affects the demand for loanable funds is an increase in the anticipated productivity of capital investments. Anticipated increases in productivity lead to a greater demand for capital investment and, hence, increase the demand for loanable funds.

The effect of an increase in the demand for funds resulting from a rise in income or an anticipated increase in the productivity of capital investment is shown in Exhibit 5-4. The demand for funds shifts from DD to $D'D'$. Previously, the quantity of funds supplied was equal to the quantity of funds demanded at point E_1; the equilibrium interest rate prevailing in the market was 6 percent, and the quantity of funds borrowed and lent was $500 billion. When the demand curve shifts to the right, ceteris paribus, a disequilibrium develops in the market. More specifically, at the prevailing 6 percent rate, the quantity of funds demanded exceeds the quantity supplied. Given this excess demand, the interest rate rises. The higher interest rate induces net lenders to increase the quantity of loanable funds they are willing to supply (a movement along the supply curve). Such changes in plans help to close the gap between quantity demanded and quantity supplied, and a new equilibrium is eventually established at point E_2, where the interest rate is 8 percent and the quantity of funds borrowed and lent is $600 billion. To sum up, we start with an equilibrium; demand increases, ceteris paribus, creating a disequilibrium; the interest rate goes up, and a new equilibrium is established.

Changes in the Supply of Funds

On the supply side, as you already know, one of the factors determining the supply of loanable funds is monetary policy. In particular, the Fed's ability to alter the growth rate of money in the economy means that it has a direct effect on the cost and availability of funds. To illustrate, a Fed-engineered increase in the supply of funds, as shown in

5-4
A Shift in the Demand for Funds

FACTORS That
Shift Supply
*Fed's monetary policy
• $S_M \uparrow \rightarrow I \downarrow$
$S_M \downarrow \rightarrow I \uparrow$

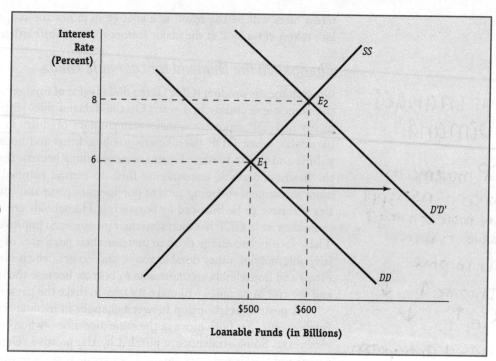

Exhibit 5-5, shifts the supply curve from SS to $S'S'$, ceteris paribus. This creates a disequilibrium: The quantity supplied of funds exceeds the quantity demanded of funds at the prevailing 6 percent interest rate. <u>The excess quantity supplied puts downward pressure on interest rates</u>. As interest rates fall, net borrowers and net lenders revise their borrowing and lending plans. For example, as the cost of borrowing falls, net borrowers will be induced to borrow a larger quantity (a movement along a demand curve). Such actions, which serve to narrow the gap between quantity supplied and quantity demanded, will continue until a new equilibrium is established at point E_2. The result is a fall in the interest rate from 6 percent to 4 percent and an increase in the quantity demanded from $500 billion to $550 billion. <u>In sum, the money supply growth rate and the interest rate are inversely related</u>, ceteris paribus. Holding other things constant, an increase in the money supply will lower the interest rate, and a decrease in the money supply will raise the interest rate via the effect of changes in the growth rate of the money supply on the supply of loanable funds.[10]

Another way to see this is to visualize financial intermediaries in the economy, particularly depository institutions, as having more funds to lend as a result of the Fed taking action to increase the money supply. The intermediaries will use these funds to acquire interest-earning assets such as securities and loans. If they demand more securities (bonds), this will raise the price of bonds and lower the interest rate on newly issued bonds and the yield to maturity on outstanding bonds, ceteris paribus. If the intermediaries want to extend loans, they will have to induce households and firms to borrow more than they are currently borrowing or planning to borrow. How can this be accomplished? If you said, "Lower the rates charged on loans," you are correct. Thus, the movement from E_1 to E_2 in Exhibit 5-5 is in response to a series of transactions, including the acquisition of securities, extension of loans, and accompanying changes in interest rates, that are at the heart of the operations of the financial system and its role in the economy.

The discussion of the determinants of interest rates, at least up to this point, can be summarized in a fashion that will prove quite convenient later on:

(5-7) $$i = f(\overset{+}{Y}, \overset{-}{M})$$

5-5

A Shift in the Supply of Funds

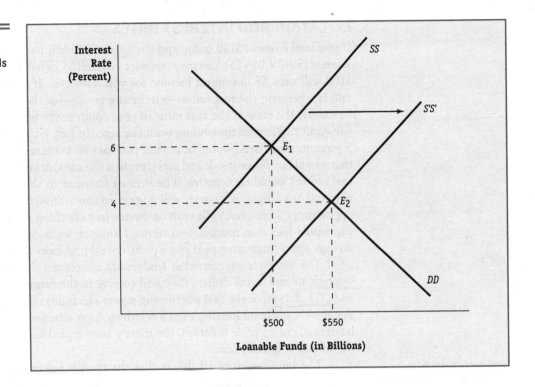

$$i = f\left(\overset{+}{Y}, \overset{-}{M}\right)$$

Equation (5-7), which is really a sentence written in shorthand, says the interest rate (i) is a positive function of income or GDP, Y, and a negative function of the money supply, M, ceteris paribus.[11] From the preceding discussion and accompanying graphical analysis, you should know that a rise in Y, holding other factors like M constant, will raise the demand for funds and, thus, the interest rate. Likewise, a rise in M, holding other factors like Y constant, will increase the supply of loanable funds and thus decrease the interest rate.

Of course, in the real world, other factors are not constant. Why is this important to keep in mind? Imagine that data released by the Fed indicate that both M and i are increasing. What could explain this seemingly paradoxical result? The answer is that the demand for funds must have increased by more than the increase in supply. This could result from an increase in income or, as you will learn in the next section, from an increase in expected inflation. We suggest graphing this case and others like it to make sure you understand the way in which Y, M, and i interact.

In Chapter 2, we saw that the interest rate could also be determined by the demand and supply of money. In reality, money is a stock variable that is measured at a point in time. Our model here deals with flows of loanable funds over time. Now would be a good time to read "A Closer Look" on p. 103, as it reconciles the two theories.

Recap The demand for loanable funds originates from net borrowers. The quantity demanded is inversely related to the interest rate, ceteris paribus. The supply of loanable funds originates from net lenders and from the Fed, which supplies reserves to the banking system. The quantity supplied is directly related to the interest rate, ceteris paribus. If incomes increase, the demand for loanable funds increases and the interest rate rises. Likewise, if the anticipated productivity of capital investment increases, the demand for loanable funds increases. If the money supply increases, the supply of loanable funds increases and the interest rate falls:

$$i = f(\overset{+}{Y}, \overset{-}{M})$$

INFLATION AND INTEREST RATES

If you lend a friend $100 today and she agrees to pay it back in one year with 5 percent interest ($100×.05=$5), you may consider yourself $5 richer and a shrewd financier. Your $100 will earn $5 of interest income for you. However, if during the year the inflation rate is 5 percent, the real value—purchasing power—of the funds lent plus interest will be exactly the same as the real value of your funds at the beginning of the year. As a result, your real reward for lending would be zero. In fact, if the inflation rate is higher than 5 percent, your friend would be paying you back an amount of money one year from now that would buy fewer goods and services than the amount you lent would buy today. Your real reward would be negative. The shrewd financier in this case would be your friend, not you! You might, of course, still engage in this transaction if it is your absolute best opportunity. If you hold idle cash or money in a checking account earning low interest, you would lose even more in real terms. However, we hope you would be able to find a savings opportunity that paid you a positive real (inflation-adjusted) return.

This example suggests that lenders are concerned about two things: (1) nominal interest, or how many dollars they will receive in the future in return for lending now; and (2) inflation, or the real purchasing power the funds will be worth upon repayment. For instance, a bond bearing even a relatively high interest rate may not be attractive to lenders if, due to price inflation, the money later repaid has less purchasing power than the money originally lent.

The implication of all this is that the market interest rate—called the nominal interest rate—is not an adequate measure of the real return on an interest-bearing financial asset unless there is assurance of price stability. Rather, the appropriate measure is the real interest rate, which is the return on the asset corrected for changes in the purchasing power of money. The real interest rate is the nominal interest rate minus the rate of inflation expected to prevail over the life of the asset. For example, if an investor expects inflation of 4 percent, an asset bearing 7 percent nominal interest will be expected to yield only approximately 3 percent in real terms. If inflation of 7 percent is expected, the investor would expect the asset bearing 7 percent nominal interest to yield nothing in real terms.

Money illusion occurs when investors react to nominal changes (caused by inflation) even though no changes in real interest rates have occurred. Financial investors who are not victims of money illusion will try to find an investment that pays the highest real return. Wise investors will concern themselves with the nominal market interest rate only insofar as it enters into their calculation of the real interest rate, which is the correct measure of the reward for lending and the cost of borrowing.

The above discussion can be summarized by some simple definitions written in the form of identities that are true by definition:

(5-8) $$i = r + p^e$$

Equation (5-8) says that the nominal interest rate has two parts: a real interest rate, r, and an inflation premium. The inflation premium is the amount of nominal interest that will compensate a lender for the expected loss of purchasing power accompanying any inflation. Accordingly, the inflation premium is equal to the expected inflation rate, p^e, and therefore, nominal interest rates rise or fall as expected inflation rises or falls, ceteris paribus. Rearranging Equation (5-8) produces

(5-9) $$r = i - p^e$$

One of the first economists to statistically analyze the relationship between inflation and nominal interest rates was Irving Fisher, a prominent economist of the early

Nominal Interest Rate
The market interest rate, or the real return plus the rate of inflation expected to prevail over the life of the asset.

Real Interest Rate
The interest rate corrected for changes in the purchasing power of money.

Money Illusion
When spending units react to nominal changes caused by changes in prices, even though real variables such as interest rates have not changed.

Inflation Premium
The amount of nominal interest added to the real interest rate to compensate the lender for the expected loss in purchasing power that will accompany any inflation.

Interest Rates: Which Theory Is Correct?
Reconciling Stocks and Flows

Liquidity preference is the name given to the theory based on the demand for and supply of money. It was developed by John Maynard Keynes in the 1930s. The supply of money is the stock of money, and the demand for money, or "preference for liquidity," is how much money spending units wish to hold. The supply of and demand for money are both measured at a point in time and refer to actual *stocks*. The stock of money is partially determined by the central bank through its control over the stock of reserves and reserve requirements. Also, remember from Chapter 2 that the demand for money is based on the spending plans of spending units. Demand is positively related to income, and quantity demanded is negatively or inversely related to the interest rate, ceteris paribus. The interest rate adjusts to equate the quantity supplied (stock) of money with the quantity demanded.

The loanable funds theory developed in this chapter is based on *flows* as opposed to stocks. Flows are measured through time, whereas stocks are measured at a point in time. Thus, if I offer you a job for $10,000, you will want to know whether this is per week, per month, or per year. Not so for stocks. If I give you a $10,000 savings account, there is no relevant time dimension. The loanable funds theory develops the argument that the interest rate is determined by the supply of and demand for loanable funds. The demand for loanable funds reflects borrowing plans by net borrowers, while the supply of loanable funds reflects lending plans by net lenders. Ceteris paribus, the quantity demanded of loanable funds is inversely related to the interest rate, while the quantity supplied of loanable funds is directly related to the interest rate. The interest rate adjusts to equate the quantity demanded of loanable funds with the quantity supplied.

To help you see that the theories complement each other, consider what happens when the Fed increases bank reserves. When reserves increase, banks create money by incurring deposit liabilities as they acquire loans as assets. In doing so, banks have simultaneously augmented the supply of loanable funds. According to liquidity preference, an increase in the supply of money, ceteris paribus, causes the interest rate to fall, while according to the loanable funds theory, an increase in the supply of loanable funds has the same effect. Likewise, if the Fed decreases the supply of reserves, you should be able to verify that both the stock of money and the supply of loanable funds decrease, leading to a higher interest rate. Again both theories predict that the interest rate changes in the same direction.

Next consider what happens when the demand for loanable funds increases, reflecting an increased desire by people to borrow more at every interest rate. Because banks acquire loan assets when they create checkable deposits, which are also money, an increase in the demand for loanable funds corresponds to an increase in the demand for money. According to both theories, an increase in the interest rate results. Likewise, a decrease in the demand for loanable funds translates to a decrease in the demand for money and a lower interest rate.

From an intuitive standpoint, we can reconcile the two theories by recognizing that when there is a change in a stock measured at different times, a flow has occurred; that is, a flow over time results in a change in a stock. For example, if I have a gallon of milk in the morning, go to the refrigerator for a glass of milk repeatedly throughout the day, and have half a gallon left at the end of the day, then I can safely say that I consumed half a gallon of milk during the day. Consumption of milk over the course of the day represents a *flow,* but the amount of milk in the refrigerator at a point in time is a *stock.* The change in the stock of milk as measured at two different points in time depicts the flow. If I save $100 per year, at the end of the year my stock of wealth will have increased by $100 (ignoring interest payments for the time being). Correspondingly, changes in the supply (flow) of loanable funds entail changes in the stock of money as measured at two different points in time. Likewise, changes in the demand (flow) of loanable funds entail changes in the demand for money. A theory stated in flows can always be reformulated in terms of stocks and vice versa.

twentieth century. The available evidence, such as that shown in Exhibit 5-6, does show that nominal interest rates are highly correlated with inflation and inflationary expectations.

Now suppose the commercial paper rate is 5 percent and the current and expected rate of inflation is 3 percent. This means that the expected real interest rate is 2 percent. What happens if borrowers and lenders revise their expectation of future inflation upward to 6 percent? If the commercial paper rate remains at 5 percent, they will expect the real interest rate to be minus 1 percent. This is the real cost of borrowing funds. The fall in the expected real cost of borrowing will produce a rise in the nominal demand for funds. The rise in demand should, in turn, put upward pressure on the nominal commercial paper rate.

What about lenders of funds in the commercial paper market? Initially, they would have expected a real return of 2 percent (.05 − .03 = .02). If the lenders also revise

5-6

Inflation and the Interest Rate, 1964–2008

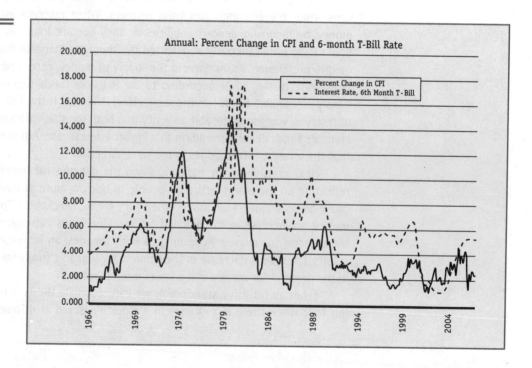

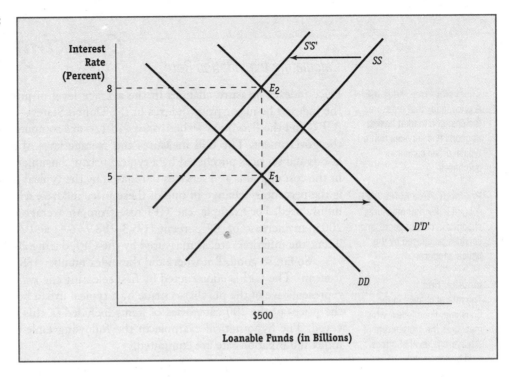

We begin, as in Exhibits 5-3, 5-4, and 5-5, with an initial equilibrium at point E_1 and a prevailing interest rate of 5 percent. If the expected inflation rate, p^e, is 3 percent, this nominal rate, i, implies a real rate, r, of 2 percent ($i=r+p^e$ or 5 percent=2 percent+3 percent). Assume now that p^e rises to 6 percent, ceteris paribus. At a 5 percent nominal rate, lenders will now expect a lower real rate (−1 percent instead of +2 percent). Accordingly, they will be willing to lend less, shifting SS to $S'S'$. As for the borrowers, the rise in p^e means that the expected real cost of borrowing at a 5 percent nominal rate has fallen (from +2 percent to −1 percent). In response, they will want to borrow more, shifting DD to $D'D'$. The eventual result of the fall in supply and rise in demand is an increase in the nominal rate equal to the change in inflationary expectations.

their expectations of inflation upward to 6 percent, it seems reasonable to presume that an expected real return of minus 1 percent would make them less willing to lend and would thus reduce the nominal supply of funds available in the commercial paper market. The reduction in supply would also put upward pressure on the nominal commercial paper rate.

The combined effect of the increase in demand and reduction in supply, as shown in Exhibit 5-7, is a rise in the interest rate from 5 to 8 percent. With expected inflation rising from 3 to 6 percent, the inflation premium and, therefore, the nominal interest rate rises by 3 percent, from 5 to 8 percent. In this example, the increase in the interest rate is equal to the increase in inflationary expectations. In an imperfect world—the real world—this may not always be the case, but we can be pretty certain that the direction of the change in interest rates will match the direction of the change in inflationary expectations.

In sum, expectations of inflation affect portfolio choices that help determine the demand and supply of loanable funds. Because interest rates respond to changes in demand and supply, and expectations of inflation affect demand and supply, we can conclude that expectations of inflation affect interest rates. Given this relationship, we can rewrite Equation (5-7) as follows:

$$(5\text{-}10) \qquad\qquad i = f(\overset{+}{Y},\, \overset{-}{M},\, \overset{+}{p^e})$$

Cracking the Code

Calculating the Inflation Rate

Consumer Price Index (CPI)
A price index that measures the cost of a market basket of goods and services that a typical urban consumer purchases.

Producer Price Index (PPI)
A price index that measures changes in cost of goods and services purchased by the typical producer.

Inflation rate
The rate of change in the Consumer Price Index, which measures the growth rate of the average level of prices paid by consumers.

Price indexes measure changes in the average level of prices of the items included in the index. The major price indexes in the United States—the **Consumer Price Index (CPI)** and the **Producer Price Index (PPI)**—are computed and published monthly by the government. The CPI measures the average level of prices of a market basket of goods and services purchased by a typical urban consumer. The PPI measures changes in the cost of goods and services purchased by the typical producer. The **inflation rate** is the percentage change in one of these price indexes, with the CPI being most commonly used. For example, the CPI rose from an average of 188.9 in 2004 to 195.3 in 2005, an increase of 3.4 percent (195.3–188.9=6.4) and 6.4/188.9=.034=3.4 percent). Thus, the inflation rate, as measured by the CPI, during 2005 was 3.4 percent.

So far, so good. But where did the index number 188.9 come from, and what does it mean? The CPI is constructed by first selecting the *market basket of goods and services* representative of the purchases made by a typical urban household. Then, each month, the prices of the 200 categories of items included in this same market basket are surveyed. The hypothetical example in the following table illustrates how the resulting index and inflation rate are computed.

Year	Total Cost of Market Basket	Consumer Price Index	Annual Inflation Rate
1982–84	$500.00	100.0	—
1990	653.5	130.7	—
1991	681.00	136.2	4.2%
1992	701.50	140.3	3.0
1993	722.50	144.5	3.0
1994	741.00	148.2	2.6
1995	762.00	152.4	2.8
1996	784.50	156.9	3.0
1997	802.5	160.5	2.3
1998	815.00	163.0	1.6
1999	833.00	166.6	2.2
2000	861.00	172.2	3.4
2001	885.50	177.1	2.8
2002	899.50	179.9	1.6
2003	920.00	184.0	2.3
2004	944.50	188.9	2.7
2005	976.50	195.3	3.4
2006	1,003.00	201.6	3.2
2007	1,036.50	207.3	2.8
2008	1,076.50	215.3	3.8

Source: U.S. Department of Labor, Bureau of Labor Statistics, **http://www.bls.gov/cpi/home.htm.**

The years 1982–1984 are the base period years for computing the index. Prices of the market basket in future years are compared to the prices of the same market basket in 1982–1984—that is, $500. The Consumer Price Index (CPI) in a given year is displayed in the following equation:

CPI = ([cost of the market basket in the given year]/[cost of the market basket in the base period]) × 100.

Accordingly, the CPI for 1982–1984 is 100, and for 2006, when the cost of the market basket rose to $1,076.50, the CPI is 215.3 because ($1,003.00/$500) 100 = 215.3. Literally, the CPI of 215.3 for 2008 means that prices were 115.3 percent higher in 2008 than in the 1982–1984 time period.

$$i = f\left(\overset{+}{Y}, \overset{-}{M}, \overset{+}{p^e}\right)$$

The nominal interest rate is positively related to the expected inflation rate. Now would be a good time to read the accompanying "Cracking the Code" on how to calculate the inflation rate.

Recap The nominal interest rate is the real interest rate plus the expected inflation rate. Money illusion occurs when investors react to nominal changes when no real changes have occurred. If expected inflation increases, the nominal interest rate will rise. Borrowers are then willing to pay an inflation premium, and lenders demand to be paid an inflation premium. Thus, nominal interest rates are correlated with expected inflation:

$$i = f\left(\overset{+}{Y}, \overset{-}{M}, \overset{+}{p^e}\right)$$

THE CYCLICAL MOVEMENT OF INTEREST RATES

Suppose that, like Rip Van Winkle, you slept for a long time, and when you woke up, you read this chapter and Chapter 1. You would find yourself well rested and—believe it or not—quite able to explain how interest rates move over the business cycle and why they move as they do.

Recall from Chapter 1 that the stages of the business cycle are the recession, trough, expansion, and peak. The recession phase is usually characterized by falling incomes, a drop in the inflation rate (especially in the later stages of the phase), and, not surprisingly, given the Fed's desire to stabilize the economy, a rising money supply growth rate. Using Equation (5-10), we hope you would predict that such developments generally produce a decline in interest rates during recessions. Conversely, during the expansion phase of the cycle, income is rising, inflation usually reaccelerates (especially in the later stages of the phase), and the Fed may be trying to slow money supply growth to prevent an inflationary boom from developing. Again referring to Equation (5-10), you should not be surprised to learn that interest rates usually rise as an economic recovery proceeds. Generally speaking, although not always, interest rates tend to fluctuate procyclically—that is, they move with the business cycle, rising during expansions and falling during recessions.[12]

This chapter contains an appendix on how the price of a special type of bond, a bond with no maturity called a *consol*, changes as interest rates change.

Summary of Major Points

1. The interest rate is the return on lending today (spending in the future) and the cost of borrowing today (repaying in the future). It links the present with the future. More directly, the interest rate represents the time value of money and specifies the terms under which one can trade present purchasing power for future purchasing power.

2. Compounding answers this question: What is the future value of money lent today? It is the increase in the future value of funds that results from earning interest on interest. Discounting answers this question: What is the present value of money to be received in the future? As long as the interest rate is positive, $1,000 received today is worth more than $1,000 to be received in the future. Discounting is the procedure used to compute the present value of funds to be received in the future. Here again the interest rate links the present with the future.

3. A bond represents a stream of future payments. The price of a bond will be equal to the present value of the discounted future stream of income. When the interest rate changes, the present value of the future payments will also change. When interest rates rise, the prices of outstanding bonds fall. Likewise, when interest rates fall, the prices of outstanding bonds rise.

4. Ceteris paribus, the quantity demanded of loan-able funds is inversely related to the interest rate. Ceteris paribus, the quantity supplied of loanable funds is directly related to the interest rate.

5. Changes in interest rates are the result of changes in the supply of funds and/or changes in the demand for funds. The supply of loanable funds results from the surpluses of net lenders and the provision of reserves by the Fed to the financial system. The demand for funds originates from the deficits run by net borrowers. The demand for loanable funds is positively related to income, Y, and positively related to anticipated increases in the productivity of capital investment. In general, anything that increases demand or reduces supply, ceteris paribus, will tend to raise interest rates. Anything that reduces demand or increases supply, ceteris paribus, will tend to lower interest rates. In summary,

$$i = f(\overset{+}{Y}, \overset{-}{M})$$

6. The nominal interest rate, i, is composed of a real interest rate, r, and an inflation premium, reflecting the expected inflation rate, p^e: $i = r + p^e$. In general, the willingness to lend and the willingness to bor-row depend on the real return to lending and the real cost of borrowing where $r = i - p^e$. In summary,

$$i = f(\overset{+}{Y}, \overset{-}{M}, \overset{+}{p^e})$$

7. Interest rates tend to fluctuate procyclically. As a recession proceeds, income and GDP fall, tending to reduce the demand for funds, and the Fed's efforts to stabilize the economy generally result in a rising growth rate of the money supply. Conversely, as an expansion takes hold, incomes and GDP rise, tending to increase the demand for funds. Often inflation reaccelerates, and to prevent an inflationary boom from developing, the Fed will slow money supply growth. Reflecting such developments, interest rates will tend to rise.

8. The Consumer Price Index measures the average level of prices of goods and services that the typical urban consumer purchases. The price index is 100 in the base year. The rate of change in the price index is the rate of inflation.

9. A *consol* is a perpetual bond with no maturity date. The price of a consol is equal to the coupon payment divided by the nominal interest rate. (See Appendix 5A.)

Key Terms

Compounding, p. 92
Consol, p. 110
Consumer Price Index (CPI), p. 106
Coupon Payments, p. 95
Demand for Loanable Funds, p. 97
Discount from Par, p. 96

Discounting, p. 94
Inflation Premium, p. 102
Inflation Rate, p. 106
Money Illusion, p. 102
Nominal Interest Rate, p. 102
Par Value, p. 95
Premium above Par, p. 96

Present Value, p. 94
Principal, p. 93
Producer Price Index (PPI), p. 106
Real Interest Rate, p. 102
Supply of Loanable Funds, p. 97
Time Value of Money, p. 92
Yield to Maturity, p. 96

Review Questions

1. Define the concepts of *compounding* and *discounting*. Use future values and present values to explain how these concepts are related.

2. Use the concept of present value to explain why a trip to Hawaii next year would be valued more to most people than the same trip in the year 2015.

3. Under what conditions will a bond sell at a premium above par? At a discount from par?

4. During the Great Depression of the 1930s, nominal interest rates were close to zero. Explain how real interest rates could be very high even though nominal interest rates were very low. (*Hint*: Prices fell during parts of the Great Depression.)

5. Assume that after you graduate, you get a job as the chief financial officer of a small company. Explain why being able to forecast the direction of interest

rate changes may be critical for your success in that position. Likewise, why are investment bankers concerned about future changes in the interest rate?

6. What factors affect the demand for loanable funds? The supply of loanable funds?

7. In general, discuss the movement of interest rates, the money supply, and prices over the business cycle.

8. A young couple is borrowing $100,000 to buy their first home. An older couple is living off the interest income from the $100,000 in financial assets they own. How does the interest rate affect each couple? If the interest rate increases, could that change the behavior of either couple? How and why?

Analytical Questions

Questions marked with a check mark (✓) are objective in nature. They can be completed with a short answer or number.

✓9. What is the present value of each of the following income streams?
   a. $100 to be received at the end of each of the next three years
   b. $100 to be received at the end of each of the next three years plus an additional payment of $1,000 at the end of the third year

✓10. What is the price of a bond that pays the income stream in question 9 (b)?

✓11. Assume that a bond with five years to maturity, a par value of $1,000, and a $60 annual coupon payment costs $1,100 today. What is the coupon rate? What is the current yield?

✓12. The nominal interest rate is 12 percent, and anticipated inflation is 8 percent. What is the real interest rate?

✓13. Graph the demand and supply for loanable funds. If there is an increase in income, ceteris paribus, show what happens to the interest rate, the demand for loanable funds, and the quantity supplied of loanable funds. If the Fed orchestrates a decrease in the money supply growth rate, ceteris paribus, show what happens to the interest rate, the supply of loanable funds, and the quantity demanded of loanable funds.

✓14. As an enrolling freshman, would you have been willing to pay $18,000 for four years' tuition rather than $5,000 per year for four years? (Assume you would be able to do so and that you have no fear of flunking out of college before you graduate.)

✓15. You win a million-dollar lottery to be paid out in 20 annual installments of $50,000 over the next 20 years. Assuming an interest rate of 6 percent, how large a payment would you accept today for this future stream of income?

✓16. Jake is given $10,000 in a CD that matures in 10 years. Assuming that interest payments are reinvested during the life of the CD, how much will the CD be worth at maturity if the interest rate is 5 percent? If the interest rate is 10 percent?

✓17. Henry and Sheree just had a baby. How much will they have to invest today for the baby to have $100,000 for college in 18 years if the interest rate is 5 percent? If the interest rate is 10 percent?

18. Use graphical analysis to show that if Y and M both increase, the interest rate may increase, decrease, or stay the same. In each case, what happens to the equilibrium quantity demanded and supplied?

19. Using Exhibit 5-6, determine in what years real interest rates were at their highest and lowest levels.

✓20. Assume that the price of a market basket of goods and services is $2,000 in the base period, $2,060 one year later, and $2,100 two years later. What is the price index in the base period? After the first year? After the second year? What is the rate of inflation in the first year? In the second year?

✓21. What is the price of a consol with a coupon payment of $200 per year if the interest rate is 10 percent? What is the interest rate on a consol if the coupon payment is $400 and the price of the consol is $8,000? (*See Appendix 5A.*)

✓22. I purchase a consol with a coupon payment of $100 when the interest rate is 10 percent. When I sell the consol, the interest rate has risen to 20 percent. What is the amount of my capital gain or loss? (*See Appendix 5A.*)

Suggested Readings

The article "The Cyclical Behavior of Interest Rates," *Journal of Finance* 52 (September 1997): 1519–42, offers an advanced discussion of interest rates.

A classic work dealing with interest rate determination is Irving Fisher, *The Theory of Interest* (New York: Macmillan, 1930). A more recent article, "The Fisher Hypothesis Revisited: New Evidence," finds that nominal interest rates are directly related to expected inflation rates and government borrowing. It can be found in *Applied Economics* 29 (August 1997): 1055–59.

For a basic discussion of the "Fisher Effect," see the Internet site **http://en.wikipedia.org/wiki/Fisher_hypothesis.**

For an interesting article on the relationship between interest rates and inflation, see Edward Renshaw, "Inflation and the Search for a Neutral Rate of Return on T-Bills," *Challenge* (November-December 1994): 58–61.

For an analysis of the relationship between interest rates and bond prices, see Dale Bremmer, "The Relationship Between Interest Rates and Bond Prices," *American Economist* 36 (Spring 1992): 85–86.

For information on estimating yields on Treasury securities, see **http://www.newyorkfed.org/aboutthefed/fedpoint/fed28.html.**

Information on interest rate calculations can be found online at **http://www.newyorkfed.org/education/interest_rates.html.**

Appendix 5A
The Inverse Relationship Between Bond Prices and Interest Rates: The Case of Consols

Consol

A perpetual bond with no maturity date; the issuer is never obliged to repay the principal but makes coupon payments each year, forever.

A type of bond called a consol has no maturity date. The issuer is not obligated to ever repay the principal but makes coupon payments each year forever. Thus, if I buy a consol today, I am entitled to receive the coupon payment forever but never to be repaid the principal. After some mathematical manipulation and simplification of Equation (5-6), found in endnote 13, such characteristics imply the following:[13]

$$i = C/P$$

The yield to maturity, or interest rate, i, on a consol is equal to the coupon payment, C, divided by the price of the bond, P. Suppose a new $1,000 face value consol is issued today and promises to pay $50 in interest each year. This is the coupon payment each year. Assuming the price of the new consol is $1,000, the $50 divided by the price shows that the consol yields 5 percent ($50/$1,000 = .05).

Now assume that a year later another $1,000 consol is issued by the same company. Suppose the prevailing level of interest rates in the economy has risen so that the new consol will have to pay $60 a year in interest to be competitive. Clearly, the new consol is a better investment than the one-year-old 5 percent consol.

Suppose that some unforeseen financial problems lead the owner of the old 5 percent consol to sell it. Who would be willing to purchase the old 5 percent consol, given that they could instead purchase a new 6 percent consol? The answer is nobody, at least not yet. The older consol will have to yield 6 percent to be sold, and it will sell if it can somehow be made to yield 6 percent.

The older consol cannot change the fact that it pays $50 a year in interest. However, the old consol can sell for a lower price. If the price drops to $833.33, then $50 a year interest would represent a yield of 6 percent ($50/$833.33 = .06). In fact, this is exactly what will happen. The owner of the old consol will offer the bond for sale at $1,000—the original price. Because no buyers appear, the market maker handling the transaction will lower the price. The price cutting will continue until buyers appear; this will occur when the price falls to $833.33, because at this point the yield on the old consol is competitive with the yield on new consols. Finally, what if the interest rate on new bonds falls to 4 percent? What will happen to the price of the old consol and why?[14]

Endnotes

1. If Joe received the interest earned on the loan after one year but left the principal, the total return over two years would be $120, or $60 each year. The average annual rate of return would be 6 percent [.06 = ($120/$1,000)÷2], which is simple interest. If, as in the example, no interest payment is made after one year—the funds being, in effect, re-lent or reinvested—the total return is $123.60, and the compound annual return is 6.18 percent [.0618 = ($123.60/$1,000)÷2]. The compound rate will always be higher than the simple rate due to the interest earned on interest.

2. For those who would like to work through all the steps, start with $V_2 = V_0 + iV_0 + i(V_0 + iV_0)$ $= V_0 + iV_0 + iV_0 + i^2V_0 = V_0 + 2iV_0 + i^2V_0 = V_0(1 + 2i + i^2) = V_0(1 + i)(1 + i) = V_0(1 + i)^2$.

3. We are also assuming that she expects the interest rate to be 6 percent for the next five years.

4. The present value of $7,500,000 to be received in five years, assuming an interest rate of 4 percent, is $6,164,453.30. This is obviously more than $6,000,000. Put another way, if the actress took the $6,000,000 today and lent it at 4 percent for five years, she would have only $7,299,917.41 at the end of the period rather than $7,500,000. The $6,164,453.30 is what she would need to lend today at 4 percent for five years to have $7,500,000 at the end of the period. In sum, the actress should take the $7,500,000 in five years rather than the $6,000,000 today.

5. Are you puzzled by the fact that the price of the bond in the marketplace equals the present value of the bond? If so, think of what happens in any market when a product is selling for less or more than buyers and sellers think it's really worth. If it is selling for less, quantity demanded will be greater than quantity supplied, and the price will rise in response. If it is selling for more, quantity demanded will be less than quantity supplied, and the price will fall in response. Equilibrium is reached when the prevailing price in the market is such that quantity demanded equals quantity supplied. So, too, in financial markets.

6. Technically, the time to maturity is now one year less a day, but to simplify, we ignore the one day.

7. In Chapter 16, we will see that the managers could also use financial futures markets to reduce the risk of losses from changes in interest rates.

8. The federal government's demand for loanable funds is less sensitive to changes in the level of interest rates than are the other sectors. The federal government does not necessarily borrow less at higher interest rates than at lower interest rates. Ceteris paribus, as interest rates rise, the government may actually borrow more because of higher interest payments on the outstanding national debt.

9. See any principles of economics text for a more detailed definition of GDP.

10. Later in the text, we shall see that continuous increases in the growth rate of the money supply can lead to inflation, changes in inflationary expectations, and possible increases in interest rates.

11. This equation is a reduced-form equation resulting from simultaneously solving a demand and supply equation for loanable funds.

12. The correlation between the business cycle and interest rates is far from perfect. For example, during the expansion that began in the early 1990s and ended in the early 2000s, interest rates did not behave in the same manner described.

13. From Equation (5-6), the price of a consol is equal to $P = C/(1 + i)^1 + C/(1 + i)^2 + C/(1 + i)^3 + C/(1 + i)^4 + \ldots = C[1/(1 + i) + 1/(1 + i)^2 + 1/(1 + i)^3 + 1/(1 + i)^4 + \ldots] = C(1/i) = C/i$. Therefore, $i = C/P$.

14. The old consol represents a future stream of income of $50 per year forever. At an interest rate of 4 percent, the price rises to $1,250 ($50/.04 = $1,250), and the lucky owner makes a capital gain of $250.

CHAPTER SIX

Time gives good advice.

—Maltese proverb

The Structure of Interest Rates

Learning Objectives

After reading this chapter, you should know:

What a yield curve is

What the expectations theory is

How expectations influence interest rates

What determines expectations

How term to maturity, credit risk, liquidity, and tax treatment affect interest rates

FROM ONE INTEREST RATE TO MANY

A familiar term we hope you have come to know and understand is the *interest rate*. Before you become too attached, however, the time has come to confess the obvious. Previous chapters have discussed in some detail what determines the interest rate as if there were just one interest rate. This simplification allowed us to abstract from many details and focus on the essential factors influencing interest rates in general. Of course, the real world is more complicated.

Numerous types of financial claims are traded in financial markets—Treasury bills, corporate bonds, municipal bonds, commercial paper, certificates of deposit, and Treasury notes and bonds, to name just a few. A glance at any newspaper reveals that the interest rates on the various types of financial claims differ. Lest you be overwhelmed by such differences, remember that our objective is to bring order to chaos. More specifically, we want (1) to explain the patterns and common threads that link the various interest rates together and (2) to identify the factors that explain the differences.

Simply put, interest rates generally move up and down together. All rates may not move by the same amount, and occasionally some rates may not even move in the same direction as the rest. As a result of such disparate movements, the spreads, or patterns of relationships, between rates can change. For example, the spread between Treasury bill rates and Treasury note rates may narrow while the spread between the rates on risky corporate bonds and the rates on those that are less risky may widen.

The purpose of this chapter is to study the factors that are primarily responsible for determining the relationships among interest rates. Financial analysts have isolated and identified four primary determinants of these relationships: (1) term to maturity, (2) credit risk, (3) liquidity, and (4) tax treatment.

Why is it important to know all of this, you ask? There are many possible responses, but this hypothetical example should suffice. Suppose you have $1 million available to purchase financial claims and you have narrowed your options to one-year Treasury notes yielding 3 percent, two-year Treasury notes yielding 4 percent, and two-year municipal notes yielding 2 percent. Which would you choose? More to the point, what would you need to know before you or any portfolio manager could make a rational decision? This chapter will provide answers to such questions.

THE ROLE OF TERM TO MATURITY IN INTEREST RATE DIFFERENTIALS

Treasury Notes
Securities issued by the U.S. government with an original maturity of 1 to 10 years.

Term Structure of Interest Rates
The relationship between yields and time to maturity.

Yield Curve
A graphical representation of the relationship between interest rates (yields) on particular securities and their terms to maturity.

The U.S. Treasury issues different types of securities—bills, notes, and bonds—as it manages the nation's debt or finances a government budget deficit, if any. The major characteristic distinguishing one type of Treasury security from another is the term to maturity. For example, Treasury **bills** have short terms to maturity of one year or less, while **Treasury notes and bonds** have long terms to maturity of one year or more.[1] We are interested in discovering what determines the relationship between interest rates on Treasury securities of different maturities. For example, what is the relationship between the interest rate on a Treasury security with a short term to maturity and the interest rate on a Treasury security with a long term to maturity? The pattern of relationships among interest rates and the time to maturity are usually referred to in financial markets as the **term structure of interest rates**.

The Yield Curve

A common analytical construct used as a framework for addressing this question is a yield curve. Formally, a **yield curve** is a graphical representation of the relationship between interest rates (yields) on particular financial instruments (securities) and their terms to maturity. Put another way, a yield curve visually represents the term structure of interest rates—that is, it shows how interest rates vary with the term to maturity.

When constructing yield curves for the purpose of examining the role of term to maturity in explaining interest rate differentials, analysts traditionally focus on Treasury securities. By concentrating on one particular type of security, we can control for factors other than term to maturity, such as riskiness and tax treatment, which could also affect the structure of yields.[2] In other words, focusing on Treasury securities permits us to isolate the effects of term to maturity. Although we use U.S. government securities, we could have used other types of assets to demonstrate yield curves. Other financial instruments (securities) that could be used include corporate bonds with the same default risk (and other non-maturity-related characteristics) or municipal bonds. Just be sure you understand that each individual asset is usually represented on a single yield curve, even though several yield curves may be drawn on one graph.

To construct yield curves, we begin with Exhibit 6-1. This table shows the interest rates on U.S. Treasury securities of different maturities prevailing on four different dates: January 16, 1981; January 29, 1993; June 1, 2003; and May 7, 2007. From this information, we can construct four different yield curves—one for each of the four dates. Term to maturity is always measured on the horizontal axis, while the return on an asset (yield to maturity) is measured on the vertical.

Using the data in Exhibit 6-1, the yield curves for the four dates are plotted in Exhibit 6-2. Notice that on January 16, 1981, the yield on three-month Treasury bills was 15.19 percent, while the yield on 10-year Treasury bonds was 12.53 percent. Thus, the slope of the yield curve at that time was negative, meaning that yields declined as the term to maturity increased. In contrast, on January 29, 1993, the yield curve had a positive slope, which means that yields rose with term to maturity. On this day, the yield on three-month Treasury bills was 2.92 percent, while the yield on 10-year Treasury bonds was 6.46 percent. Thus, the slope of the yield curve changed over time. Notice also that all 1993 yields were below all 1981 yields. This indicates that the level of the yield curve as well as the direction of the slope changed.

Next, look at the yield curve for June 1, 2003. On this date, the yield on three-month Treasury bills was less than 1 percent, while the yield on the 10-year security was 3.33 percent. Although upward sloping (slightly), the yield curve was much lower than in the previous years, reflecting the fact that in mid-2003, interest rates had fallen to 45-year lows. Finally, look at the yield curve for May 7, 2007. In this case, the two-, five-, and 10-year rates are all lower than the one-year rate of 4.92 percent. However, the total fluctuation over the entire maturity range is .37 percent (from 4.55 to 4.92 percent) and the yield curve is relatively flat. As you can see, there can be much variation in the shape and level among yield curves for the same financial instrument on different dates!

6-1

Interest Rates on Treasury Securities

Term to Maturity	January 16, 1981	January 29, 1993	June 1, 2003	May 7, 2007
3 months	15.19%	2.92%	0.92%	4.89%
1 year	13.91	3.41	1.01	4.92
2 year	13.15	4.24	1.23	4.68
5 year	12.69	6.08	2.27	4.55
10 year	12.53	6.46	3.33	4.64

Sources: Federal Reserve Bulletin and The Statistical Supplement to the Federal Reserve Bulletin, various issues (1981–2007).

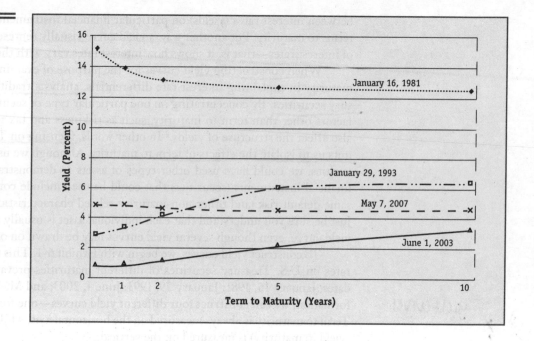

As mentioned earlier, the slope (shape) and position (level) of the yield curve are called the *term structure of interest rates*. We are interested in explaining what determines the term structure—that is, the shape of the yield curve and its level. Although much has been written to explain the term structure of interest rates, the conventional wisdom can be boiled down to expectations theory and some modifications of that theory. To simplify the explanation of the theory and the modifications, we shall assume that there are only two types of Treasury securities: T-bills with a short term to maturity (one year) and Treasury notes with a long term to maturity (two years). We shall develop our analysis in terms of the demand for and supply of these two securities.

In Chapter 5, we discussed interest rate determination in terms of the supply of and demand for loanable funds. By now you should be able to see that when we supply loanable funds, we demand financial securities, and when we demand loanable funds, we supply financial securities. Thus, developing our analysis of the expectations theory in terms of the demand for and supply of financial securities is consistent with our previous discussion.

- When we SUPPLY Loanable funds we DEMAND securities.
- When we SUPPLY securities we DEMAND loanable funds.

Recap
The yield curve is a graphical representation of the relationship between the interest rate (yield) and the term to maturity. Yield curves show how interest rates vary with term to maturity.

THE EXPECTATIONS THEORY

Expectations Theory
A theory holding that the long-term interest rate is the geometric average of the present short-term rate and the short-term rates expected to prevail over the term to maturity of the long-term security.

Simply put, the expectations theory postulates that (1) the yield curve is determined by borrowers' and lenders' expectations of future interest rates and (2) changes in the slope (shape) of the curve result from changes in these expectations. More specifically, the expectations theory postulates that the long rate is the geometric average of the current short rate and the future short rates expected to prevail over the term to maturity of the longer-term security.

To understand the expectations theory, let us begin by assuming that you have funds to lend for a two-year period. The current yield, i_1, on a one-year bill (a short-term security) is 5 percent per year, and the current yield, i_2, on a two-year note (a long-term security) is 5.99 percent per year. Now suppose that you and everyone else with funds available to lend expect that the yield on short-term (one-year) securities, i_1^e, will be 7 percent one year from now. Assuming that you have no preference as to holding one-year or two-year securities—that is, you do not have a preference for either short- or long-term securities—which would you acquire now? If you are a wise investor, we predict you will acquire the security with the higher expected rate of return. Think of yourself as having two options: Option A is to buy short-term (one-year) securities today and short-term securities again one year from now; Option B is to buy long-term (two-year) securities now. Which of the options gives the higher expected rate of return?

The answer is derived in two simple steps: (1) calculate the expected return from acquiring the one-year bill now and the one-year bill one year from now; (2) compare it with the 5.99 percent return you would earn by acquiring the two-year note now.

Geometric Average
An average that takes into account the effects of compounding; used to calculate the long-term rate from the short-term rate and the short-term rates expected to prevail over the term to maturity of the long-term security.

To calculate the expected return of the one-year bill now and the one-year bill one year from now, we find the geometric average of the two rates. We use the geometric average instead of the simple arithmetic average to take into account the effects of compounding as discussed in Chapter 5. In other words, the use of the geometric average assumes that the interest earned the first year will earn interest during the second year. More precisely, using the geometric average, the long rate, i_2, can be calculated as follows:

(6-1) $$(1 + i_2) = [(1 + i_1)(1 + i_1^e)]^{1/2}$$

Subtracting 1 from both sides of Equation 6-1 yields

(6-2) $$i_2 = [(1 + i_1)(1 + i_1^e)]^{1/2} - 1$$

Returning to our numerical example, if we perform these calculations, we find that the expected return associated with Option A is 5.99 percent. More specifically, plugging the present one-year rate and expected one-year rate into Equations (6-1) and (6-2) yields

$$(1 + i_2) = [(1 + .05)(1 + .07)]^{1/2} = [(1.05)(1.07)]^{1/2} = (1.1235)^{1/2} = 1.0599$$

and

$$i_2 = 1.0599 - 1 = .0599 = 5.99 \text{ percent}$$

This is the geometric average of the short rate now, i_1, and the short rate expected to prevail one year from now, i_1^e. The expected return from Option B—acquiring the two-year note—is also 5.99 percent. Because both options provide the same expected return, you and other lenders (buyers of securities) will be indifferent between the two options and perhaps will purchase both short-term and long-term securities. Because the long rate is, in fact, equal to the geometric average of the current short rate and the short rate expected to prevail one year in the future, we have an equilibrium configuration or term structure of interest rates. The associated yield curve is shown in Exhibit 6-3.

Our example does not prove the expectations theory postulated earlier; after all, we chose the numbers in the example. What happens when the numbers change?

To get the answer and in the process explain how the theory works, go back to our example and assume the one-year rate and two-year rate initially remain at 5 percent and 5.99 percent, respectively, but that expectations about future rates change such that the one-year rate expected to prevail one year from now rises from 7 to 9 percent. What would you and other potential purchasers of securities do, and how would those actions affect the term structure—that is, the slope and level of the yield curve in Exhibit 6-3?

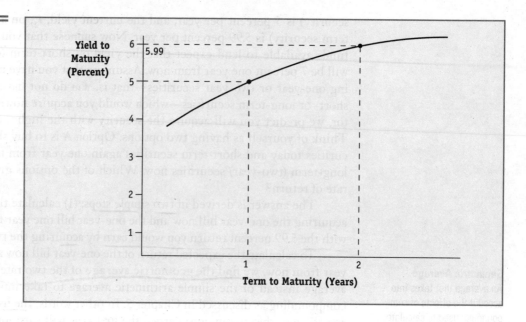

If the interest rate on a one-year security is 5 percent and the one-year rate expected to prevail one year from now is 7 percent, then the two-year rate is 5.99 percent. Because the future expected one-year rate is above the present one-year rate, the yield curve is upward sloping.

You and other financial investors would presumably first recalculate the expected return from Option A (buy short-term securities now and again one year from now) and compare it to the expected return from Option B (buy long-term securities now). We use Equation (6-2) to calculate the geometric average—the expected return—of Option A. The calculation reveals that the expected return is 6.98 percent: $.0698 = [(1.05)(1.09)]^{1/2} - 1$. Because this is higher than the 5.99 percent return associated with Option B, you and others will want short-term securities. In fact, those who own long-term securities will want to sell them and buy short-term securities. What will happen as the demand for long-term securities falls in the market? We hope you said the price of these long-term securities will fall and, thus, ceteris paribus, their yields will rise.

How far will this portfolio reshuffling go? Or, to put it somewhat differently, how high will long rates rise? Given our theory, and assuming the short rate remains at 5 percent and the expected short rate remains at 9 percent, the long rate will have to rise to 6.98 percent.[3]

Why 6.98 percent? This is the only rate that will equate the expected returns from Options A and B and thus leave financial investors indifferent between them. If investors are indifferent, there is no tendency to change, and an equilibrium configuration or term structure of interest rates is realized. More formally, a 6.98 percent interest rate on the two-year note, i_2, will make it equal to the geometric average of the prevailing 5 percent one-year rate, i_1, and the 9 percent one-year rate expected to prevail one year from now, i_1^e. The relationship between long-term interest rates and short-term interest rates depends directly on interest rate expectations; as i_1^e changes, i_2 will change relative to i_1.[4]

In our example, the adjustment in the long (two-year) rate from 5.99 to 6.98 percent as a result of the change in interest rate expectations was developed from the demand side of the market for securities, that is, from the point of view of the lender. But do not forget that the securities market also has a supply side. The expectations of the borrower are also important. Suppose you need funds for two years and can either issue a security for two years with an interest rate of 5.99 percent or issue a one-year security at 5 percent now and another one-year security one year from now at an expected 9 percent rate. Which option would you choose? Again, if you are a wise borrower, we assume you will choose the option that minimizes the cost of borrowing and thus maximizes utility or profits. Accordingly, you would issue a two-year security with an annual interest rate of 5.99 percent rather than sell two consecutive one-year securities having an expected average annual interest rate of 6.98 percent.

When borrowers believe that the average of current and expected future interest rates on short-term securities exceeds the rate on long-term securities, they will increase their current supply of long-term securities, thus tending to raise the long-term interest rate. In other words, because borrowers will want to issue two-year notes, the supply of the notes will increase (causing their price to fall), ceteris paribus, and thus higher interest rates will have to be paid on them. The market will be in equilibrium when the quantity of notes supplied equals the quantity of notes demanded.[5]

Taken together, the effects of interest rate expectations of investors and borrowers on the demand for and supply of securities, respectively, will determine the term structure of interest rates. More specifically, if, as in our example, expectations about future interest rates change such that future rates are expected to be higher, the original yield curve in Exhibit 6-3 will turn into the new yield curve in Exhibit 6-4. As the demand for long-term securities falls and the supply rises, the price of longs will fall, and the long rate will rise relative to the short rate, resulting in a steepening of the yield curve.

The last few paragraphs have been jam-packed with information. Let's try to summarize and nail down some implications of the key points. First, the hypothetical yield curve accompanying our initial example, shown in Exhibit 6-3, is positively sloped—that is, yields rise with term to maturity. The explanation for the slope of the yield curve

Positive slope = yields rise w/ term to maturity.

6-4
Hypothetical Yield Curve

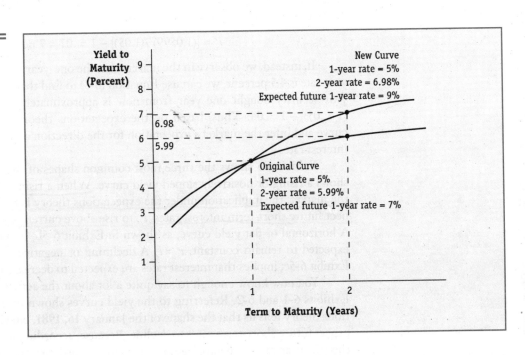

If the interest rate on a one-year security is 5 percent and the one-year rate expected to prevail one year from now increases to 9 percent, then the new two-year rate is 6.98 percent.

is directly related to the interest rate expected to prevail on short-term securities one year in the future—hence, the term *expectations theory*. More specifically, the positively sloped yield curve reflects expectations of a rise in the interest rate on short-term securities over the course of the year from the currently prevailing 5 percent to 7 percent.

Second, the new hypothetical yield curve accompanying our second example, where the expected future rate rose from 7 percent to 9 percent, is, as shown in Exhibit 6-4, even more positively sloped than the original curve. The explanation for the change in the slope is the change in future interest rate expectations. More specifically, the steeper slope reflects expectations of an even larger rise in the interest rate on short-term securities over the course of the year—that is, from the currently prevailing 5 percent to 9 percent rather than from 5 to 7 percent as in the previous example.

Third, the change in the slope of the yield curve, which accompanies a change in interest rate expectations, does not come about magically. Rather, it reflects changes in the supply of and demand for securities, which are induced by the change in interest rate expectations.

Fourth, assuming the expectations theory is basically correct, we can solve for the interest rate expected to prevail in the future by looking at the current structure of rates and doing some simple algebra. We start by squaring both sides of Equation (6-1):

(6-3A) $$(1+i_2)^2 = \{[(1+i_1)(1+i_1^e)]^{1/2}\}^2 = (1+i_1)(1+i_1^e)$$

We then divide through by $(1+i_1)$ to get

(6-3B) $$(1+i_2)^2/(1+i_1) = (1+i_1^e)$$

Subtracting 1 from both sides of the equation, we arrive at Equation (6-3):

(6-3) $$i_1^e = [(1+i_2)^2/(1+i_1)] - 1$$

Returning to our numerical example, if we know that the one-year rate is 5 percent and the two-year rate is 5.99 percent, as in our first example, we can plug the relevant numbers into Equation (6-3) and solve for i_1^e. Specifically,

$$i_1^e = [(1.0599)^2/(1.05)] - 1 = .07 = 7 \text{ percent.}$$

If, instead, we observe in the market that the one-year rate is 5 percent and the two-year rate is 4.5 percent, we can use Equation (6-3) to find that the expected rate on a one-year security bought one year from now is approximately 4 percent: $i_1^e = [(1 + .045)^2/(1 + .05)] - 1 = .04$. Thus, based on the expectations theory, you can look at the yield curve and infer the market's expectation for the direction and level of future short-term interest rates.

Exhibit 6-5 shows the three most common shapes of the yield curve. Exhibit 6-5a shows a rising or positively sloped yield curve. When a rising yield curve is observed in the market, the implication under the expectations theory is that market participants expect future short-term interest rates, i_s^e, to rise above current short rates, i_s; that is, $i_s^e > i_s$. A horizontal or flat yield curve, as shown in Exhibit 6-5b, implies that interest rates are expected to remain constant, $i_s^e = i_s$. A declining or negatively sloped yield curve, as in Exhibit 6-5c, implies that interest rates are expected to decrease in the future, $i_s^e < i_s$.

You now know enough to say quite a lot about the actual data and yield curves in Exhibits 6-1 and 6-2. Referring to the yield curves shown in Exhibit 6-2, the expectations theory tells us that the shape of the January 16, 1981, curve indicates that investors expect future short-term rates to decline. Because, according to the expectations theory, the two-year rate is the average of the current one-year rate and the one-year rate expected one year from now, the one-year rate expected to prevail one year from now must be less than the current one-year rate. Using the data in the table in Exhibit 6-1, the

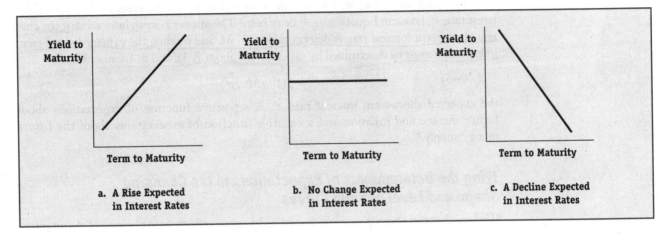

a. A Rise Expected
in Interest Rates

b. No Change Expected
in Interest Rates

c. A Decline Expected
in Interest Rates

expected one-year rate can be found by plugging the one- and two-year rates into Equation (6-3) and solving for the one-year expected rate. In this case, the one-year expected rate is 12.395 percent; since 12.395 percent = $.12395 = [(1 + .1315)^2/(1 + .1391)] - 1$.

According to the expectations theory, the shapes of the January 29, 1993, and June 1, 2003, curves indicate that, in both cases, investors expected future short-term rates to rise, but by different amounts. See if you can figure out the one-year rate that was expected to prevail one year from each of the three dates.[6] Finally, on May 7, 2007, the expectations theory suggests that investors expect little change in the level of interest rates.

Lastly, please note that the whole expectations theory is rather empty unless and until you can explain what determines future interest rate expectations and changes in those expectations. Otherwise, you have a theory explaining the term structure via expectations that are left unexplained.

Recap   According to the expectations theory, the long-term interest rate is the geometric average of the short-term rate and the short-term rates expected to prevail over the term to maturity. Given the one-year rate and the two-year rate, we can solve for the expected one-year rate one year from now.

DETERMINING INTEREST RATE EXPECTATIONS

Since expectations play such a pivotal role, then, the next question is what determines interest rate expectations. The answer is much easier than you might think. In the last chapter, we examined the determinants of the interest rate and developed a general expression—Equation (5-10)—that brought together the most important supply and demand influences on the interest rate.[7] This expression is now Equation (6-4):

(6-4) $$i = f(\overset{+}{Y}, \overset{-}{M}, \overset{+}{p^e})$$

where Y = national income or gross domestic product,
   M = the money supply, and
   p^e = inflationary expectations.

The signs over the variables indicate that a rise in income or inflationary expectations will tend to raise the interest rate and that an increase in the money supply will tend to reduce the interest rate.

Now, assuming that we want to know what determines the expected short-term interest rate, i_s^e, how can Equation (6-4) be of help? The answer is straightforward: if the current short-term interest rate is determined by Y, M, and p^e, then the expected short-term interest rate must be determined by expectations about Y, M, and p^e. In other words,

$$(6\text{-}5) \qquad\qquad i_s^e = f(\overset{+}{Y^e}, \overset{-}{M^e}, \overset{+}{p^e})$$

the expected short-term interest rate, i_s^e, is a positive function of expectations about future income and inflation and a negative function of expectations about the future money supply.[8]

Tying the Determinants of Expectations to the Changing Shape and Level of Yield Curves

We have learned that a positively sloped yield curve reflects expectations of rising interest rates. Using Equation (6-5), we can be even more specific; a positively sloped yield curve reflects expectations of some combination of future increases in income and inflation and possibly some reduction in the future growth rate of the money supply—developments that would all tend to raise future short-term interest rates. Conversely, a negatively sloped yield curve usually reflects expectations of some combination of future declines in income and inflation and possibly some accompanying increase in the future growth rate of the money supply—developments that would all tend to lower short-term interest rates in the future.

Next, ask yourself at what stage of the business cycle you would expect to observe a positively sloped yield curve. The answer is the stage when the future appears to hold some growth in income, a rise in prices, and perhaps slower growth of the money supply. This typically occurs at a business cycle trough and during the first half of a recovery. During the previous recession, real income fell, inflation decelerated, and the Fed responded with a more stimulative policy, resulting in a rise in the money supply growth rate. All of these developments contributed to a fall in the prevailing short-term interest rate and set in motion the forces of economic recovery. As the economy bottoms out and begins to recover, market participants expect future income and prices to rise as aggregate demand for goods and services increases, and they expect the Fed to be less stimulative so as to avoid an inflationary boom.[9] As a result, market participants expect future short-term interest rates to be higher than the prevailing level of short-term rates.

What about a negatively sloped yield curve? At what stage of the business cycle would market participants expect the future to bring a fall in income and inflation and Fed actions to increase the growth of the money supply? These developments usually occur around business cycle peaks including the late part of a recovery or expansion and the early part of a recession. Typically, income and prices have been rising quickly, and the Fed has moved to slow monetary growth—that is, "tighten" policy—to head off further surges in the inflation rate. As Equation (6-4) would lead one to predict, such developments have pushed up the prevailing level of short-term rates and set in motion forces that in the future are expected to lead to some slowdown in income, deceleration of inflation, and, after a time, a less restrictive monetary policy. Simply put then, future short-term rates are expected to be lower than the prevailing level of short-term rates; hence, we observe a negatively sloped yield curve.

Going back once again to Exhibit 6-2, we hope you are not surprised to learn that shapes of the yield curves somewhat coincide with what was going on in the economy at the time. For example, January 16, 1981, fell around a business cycle peak (the exact peak was July 1981).[10] January 29, 1993, fell during the lengthy beginning of a weak recovery. June 1, 2003, came after two and one-half years of economic weakness, a recession, and a jobless recovery. Finally, May 7, 2007 came at a time when the growth rate of the economy was faltering, and the Fed had stopped taking actions that raised short-term rates a year earlier. The change in the shape of the yield curve among the four dates reflects changes in interest rate expectations. The changes in interest rate expectations, in turn, reflect expected changes in the performance of the economy (income and prices) and expected changes in the stance of monetary policy (specifically, the money supply growth rate). Such changes are typically observed as the economy moves from one stage of the business cycle to another.

Recap	Because $i = f(\overset{+}{Y}, \overset{-}{M}, \overset{+}{p}{}^e)$, then $i_s^e = f(\overset{+}{Y}{}^e, \bar{M}^e, \overset{+}{p}{}^e)$. If Y^e, M^e, or p^e changes, then i_s^e changes. Changes in i_s^e cause the yield curve to shift.

Having identified and explained the major factors underlying the different shapes of the yield curves in Exhibit 6-2, we have one task left: to explain the different levels of the yield curves—that is, why all the rates prevailing in 1993, 2003, and 2007 were below the rates in 1981, why short-term rates were higher and long-term rates lower in 2003 than in 1993, and why short-term rates in 2007 were much higher (almost 4 percent) than in 2003 while, long-term rates were only about 1.5 percent higher than in 2003. We can address this issue in two parts:

1. In part, the difference in interest rates is due to the cyclical pattern of interest rates related to real economic activity and the supply of and demand for loanable funds. This part of the answer was discussed in Chapter 5. Expectations about the returns on financial securities and the returns to capital, the business outlook, and any other factors that influence the demand for and supply of funds will affect the level of the yield curve.

2. The second part of the answer is embedded in Equations (6-4) and (6-5). In 1993, inflationary pressures were lower than in the 1980s, and the economy was experiencing a mild recovery. In January 1981, the inflation rate was about 11 percent and was expected to fall to about 7 to 8 percent in coming years. Thus, in 1993 with the prevailing and expected inflation rates below those prevailing and expected in 1981, the inflation premiums embedded in both short- and long-term interest rates were considerably smaller than the inflation premiums embedded in short- and long-term rates in 1981. In 1993, Fed policy was keeping short-term rates abnormally low. Actual short-term rates were about equal to the inflation rate, yielding a real return of zero. The Fed adopted this strategy, which we will look at in more depth in a later chapter, to help the banking sector recover from massive losses experienced in the 1980s. But short-term interest rates could not remain so low forever, and the Fed increased them over the course of 1994. In 2003, the U.S. economy was struggling to pull itself out of a recession that had resulted from the bursting of the stock market bubble in early 2000, the terrorist attack on September 11, 2001, and the subsequent war against terror. Consequently, fears of deflation led to the lowest interest rates in 40 years, with the Fed reiterating that it did not see interest rates rising in the near future. However, by mid 2006, the Fed orchestrated 17 rate increases for short-term rates. Faced

with a global glut of capital, moderate growth rates, and subdued fear of inflation despite high oil prices in mid 2007, long-term rates had not increased nearly as much as short-term rates.

SOME NECESSARY MODIFICATIONS TO THE EXPECTATIONS THEORY

The expectations theory of the term structure provides a powerful and widely accepted explanation for the relationship between long- and short-term interest rates. However, many researchers, taking note of several historical and institutional features of financial markets, have argued that the expectations theory needs to be modified somewhat to make it a more complete explanation of the term structure. First, it has been observed that over the last 50 years, yield curves have almost always been positively sloped. Taken literally, this would imply that financial market participants have almost always expected short-term interest rates to rise. Given the ups and downs in the economy and the accompanying fluctuations in the supply of and demand for funds, this implication is difficult to accept. Second, an assumption underlying the expectations theory is that lenders and borrowers have no preference between long- and short-term securities; they would just as soon lend or borrow for short terms to maturity as for long terms to maturity. The implication that long- and short-term securities are close substitutes for one another has been questioned in light of observations suggesting that (1) many lenders have a preference for liquidity and thus prefer to hold short-term financial claims, which are usually more liquid than long-term financial claims; (2) many borrowers would prefer to issue long-term claims, thereby avoiding the need to issue and reissue short-term claims; and (3) short- and long-term borrowers have different purposes, such as borrowing for inventory versus borrowing for capital expenditures.

The question then is how does the expectations theory need to be modified in view of these observations? There is little doubt that many borrowers and lenders have preferred maturities, or what have come to be called preferred habitats, and that this creates a degree of segmentation between the short-term and long-term markets. Nevertheless, abundant evidence exists to support the proposition that the short- and long-term markets are not watertight compartments. More specifically, research suggests that investors, for example, are willing to switch preferred habitats from short-term financial claims to longer-term claims if a bonus or "sweetener" is associated with doing so. This sweetener or bonus is referred to as a liquidity premium; in essence, it is the extra return required to induce lenders to lend long-term rather than short-term. In other words, it is the amount of interest that is required to induce lenders to abandon their preferred habitats. The size of the premium is presumed to rise with the term to maturity; the longer the term, the larger the premium must be to induce lenders to give up their preference for liquidity.[11]

How the existence of liquidity premiums modifies the expectations theory of the term structure and yield curves can be illustrated with the help of Exhibit 6-6. Suppose the current short rate and expected short rate are both 5 percent. The expectations approach suggests that the yield curve would be flat (curve *A*). However, the preceding discussion suggests that the issuers of long-term bonds have to offer an interest premium to get investors to buy bonds having long-term maturities. The size of the premiums is presumed to rise with the term to maturity. Curve *B* in Exhibit 6-6 shows the size of the liquidity premium at each maturity. Curve *C* represents the yield curve actually observed. The components of the total yield (curve *C*) are the interest rate expectations (curve *A*) and the liquidity premiums (curve *B*).

Preferred Habitats

An expectations theory modification hypothesizing that many borrowers and lenders have preferred maturities, which creates a degree of market segmentation between the short-term and long-term markets.

Liquidity Premium

The extra return required to induce lenders to lend long-term rather than short-term.

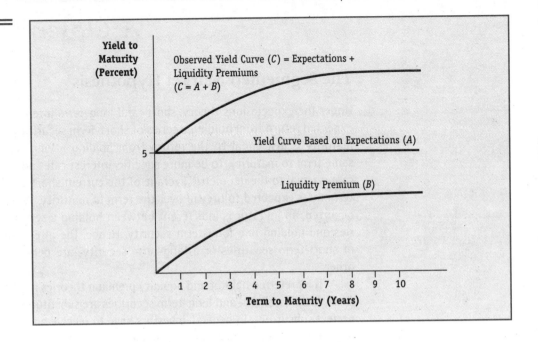

By way of contrast, note that the expectations approach would explain the shape of the yield curve depicted by curve C as indicating that market participants expect rates to rise over time.

So far this discussion has looked at the demand side of the market for securities. But let us not lose sight of the behavior of the suppliers of debt securities (borrowers) implied by this approach. Under normal circumstances, the demand for funds (supply of securities) is usually more fickle than the supply of funds. Changes in the demand for funds, which are driven by expectations, probably account for the largest part of the changes in interest rates. The existence of liquidity premiums means that borrowers are willing to pay them. But why would borrowers be willing to pay more to borrow for longer terms than they expect to pay by borrowing and reborrowing for short terms? Simply put, there is some chance that short rates will be higher in the future than the 5 percent expected rate assumed in our example. If higher-than-expected rates materialize, then borrowing and refinancing in the future would prove to be more expensive than borrowing for a longer term now. Also, the firm could suffer some difficulty in the future, which might reduce its credit rating and make it difficult to acquire funds later. By borrowing long-term, the adverse effects of such problems can be reduced.

In sum, the fact that yield curves have almost always been positively sloped over the past 50 years suggests that liquidity premiums do, in fact, exist. Theoretical considerations on both the supply and the demand side of the securities markets and a variety of empirical studies seem to support such a judgment. Consider again the relatively flat yield curve in May 2007, displayed in Exhibit 6-2. Given the modifications we have just made, it seems reasonable to revise our earlier conclusions based only on the expectations theory. When a liquidity premium is taken into account, it seems reasonable that the relatively flat yield curve of May 2007 may reflect constant or even slightly declining expected future interest rates. Some analysts believe the yield curve could be signaling a recession in the near future and Fed policy that leans towards interest rate decreases.

A Closer Look

The Segmented Market Hypothesis

Under the expectations theory, short- and long-term interest rates adjust until the expected return from holding a series of short-term securities over a certain term to maturity is just equal to the return from holding a long-term security with that same term to maturity. To be more specific, interest rates adjust until the long-term rate is equal to the geometric average of the current short-term rate and the short-term rates expected to prevail over the term to maturity. When full adjustment has occurred, an investor is indifferent between holding a series of short-term securities and holding one long-term security. Hence, the alternatives—holding a series of short-term securities or a long-term security—are perfect substitutes for each other.

The preferred habitat and liquidity premium theories modify this analysis. Under these theories, short- and long-term securities are substitutes for each other, but not perfect substitutes. In general, investors have to receive additional compensation for holding long-term securities that entail less liquidity.

The *segmented market hypothesis* takes the analysis a step further by hypothesizing that short- and long-term securities are not substitutes at all, either perfect or imperfect. Rather, under the segmented market hypothesis, markets for short- and long-term securities are completely separate. Accordingly, interest rates are determined by supply and demand factors in each separate market.

The segmented market hypothesis received renewed interest in 2000 because of the federal government surplus and the behavior of long-term interest rates. After 30 years of deficits, the federal government budget balance went into a surplus position in the late 1990s. (As noted in Chapter 1, the surplus disappeared a few years later after the terrorist attack on September 11, 2001.) During 2000, long-term rates declined much more so than short- and mid-term rates. Analysts hypothesized that this was due to the federal government's use of the government surplus to buy back long-term government securities. As the supply of long-term securities declined, their prices rose and long-term interest rates fell. The federal government was not buying back short- and mid-term securities; consequently, their rates were not affected by the same supply factors. As a result, the yield curve beyond a 10-year term became inverted during this time period.

Our discussion of the determinants of the relationship between short- and long-term interest rates (the term structure) can be easily summarized with the aid of Equation (6-6).

(6-6)
$$i_1 = f(\overset{+}{i_s}, \overset{+}{i_s^e}, \overset{+}{1})$$

The current long-term interest rate, i_1, is a function of the current short rate, i_s, the short rates expected in the future, i_s^e, and the liquidity premium, 1. The nature of the relationship between the long rate and each of the determinants is indicated by the sign over each variable. Thus, we would expect long rates to rise if current short rates rise, if expectations about future short rates are revised upward, or if liquidity premiums rise. "A Closer Look" discusses an alternative theory of how the shape and position of the yield curve is determined based on the segmented market hypothesis.

Recap

The expectations theory is modified by the fact that lenders may demand a liquidity premium to lend long-term and that borrowers may be willing to pay a liquidity premium to borrow long-term. Also borrowers and lenders may have preferred habitats (preferred maturities) that create a degree of segmentation between the short-term and long-term markets.

THE ROLE OF CREDIT RISK AND TAXES IN INTEREST RATE DIFFERENTIALS

The previous section dealt with interest rates on securities that were alike in every respect except one—term to maturity. Now we will extend our discussion and examine the relationship among interest rates on securities that have the same term to maturity but a different credit risk or taxability.

Credit Risk

Credit Risk
The probability of a debtor not paying the principal and/or the interest due on an outstanding debt.

The term credit risk refers to the probability of a debtor not paying the principal and/or the interest due on an outstanding debt. In effect, credit risk is a measure of the creditworthiness of the issuer of a security. Treasury securities are considered to have the least credit risk because they are backed by the federal government. The basic idea here is that in the unlikely event the federal government collapses, we can be reasonably sure the rest of the economy will have collapsed as well. The reverse is not true, because many individual firms can and do fail on a daily basis without the government collapsing. In contrast, corporate and municipal (state and local government) securities are viewed as being risky to some degree and are, therefore, analyzed and rated by firms that specialize in producing credit ratings. The three major credit-rating agencies, Standard & Poor's, Moody's, and Fitch Investors Service, evaluate a borrower's probability of default and assign the borrower to a particular risk class. With this information, a lender can determine to what degree a borrower will be able to meet debt obligations. Standard & Poor's, Moody's, and Fitch distinguish among several general classes of risk. Exhibit 6-7 reproduces the various credit ratings with a brief description of each. Bonds with below B ratings by the major credit rating services are not recommended for investment and are referred to as high-yield or junk bonds. They are highly speculative with regards to whether or not the interest and principal will be paid when due. Thus, because of high credit risk, junk bonds pay a very high yield.

Standard & Poor's, Moody's, and Fitch Investors Service
The three major credit-rating agencies that evaluate a borrower's probability of default and assign the borrower to a particular risk class. Visit their sites at **http://www.stockinfo .standardpoor.com, http:// www.moodys.com, and http://www.fitchratings.com.**

Junk Bonds
Highly speculative, high yield bonds with low credit ratings that are not recommended for investment because of high credit risk.

How are borrowers classified or rated? In the case of business firms, the credit-rating agencies examine the pattern of revenues and costs experienced by a firm, its degree of leverage (dependence on borrowed funds), its past history of debt redemption, and the volatility of the industry, among other things. A firm with a history of strong earnings, low leverage, and prompt debt redemption would get an Aaa rating from Moody and an AAA rating from Standard & Poor's or Fitch. A firm that has experienced net losses, has rising leverage, or has missed some loan payments would get a Baa or lower rating from Moody and a BBB or lower rating from Standard & Poor's and Fitch.

General Description	Standard & Poor's	Moody's	Fitch
Best quality	AAA	Aaa	AAA
High quality	AA	Aa	AA
Higher medium grade	A	A	A
Medium grade	BBB	Baa	BBB
Lower medium grade (speculative)	BB	Ba	BB
Not desirable investment (highly speculative)	B	B	B
Poor standing (high default risk)	CCC	Caa	CCC
Very high default risk	CC, C	Ca	C
(in default)	D	C	DDD, DD, D

The agencies also assign ratings to securities issued by state and local governments. Factors considered here include the tax base, the level of outstanding debt, the current and expected budget situation, and growth in spending.

To see how the credit ratings affect the spread between rates, let us make the reasonable assumption that most potential purchasers of securities would like to be compensated for risk taking. Based on real-world observations, we can say that investors are risk averse and, thus, must be rewarded or compensated with extra interest for accepting more risk. The extra return or interest is called a risk premium, and its size increases with the riskiness of the borrower. To illustrate, the prevailing rate on securities issued by borrowers rated Aaa is less than the rate on securities issued by borrowers rated Aa, the second highest rating. The spread between the two rates $(i_{Aa} - i_{Aaa})$ is the premium necessary to induce investors to accept the extra risk associated with Aa-rated securities relative to Aaa-rated securities. Similarly, the rates on Baa-rated securities are higher than the rates on A-rated securities, and so on down the credit ratings shown in Exhibit 6-7.[12]

When we plot the spread between the interest rates on securities of the same maturity, but possessing different credit risks, as in Exhibit 6-8, which depicts the spread between Baa-rated and Aaa-rated municipal bonds, we find that the spread varies over time as the perceived credit risks among the securities change. For example, if a default occurs in a major market, many investors may perceive lower-rated bonds as relatively more risky and respond by selling lower-rated issues and purchasing higher-rated issues. This movement to higher-rated securities is usually referred to as a "flight to quality." Put another way, if investors perceive that relative risks have changed, they will demand different risk premiums, and thus the rate spread among securities will change.

Taxability

The last major factor influencing the structure of interest rates is the taxability of securities. As you may know, interest income earned from securities issued by state and local governments is exempt from federal income tax, while interest earned from corporate securities is taxed at the same rates as other ordinary income.[13]

The marginal tax rate is the rate paid on the last dollar of income the taxpayer earns. Because the United States has a progressive tax rate structure, higher rates apply to additional income earned beyond given tax rate brackets. Income under the bracket

Risk Premium
The extra return or interest that a lender is compensated with for accepting more risk.

Marginal Tax Rate
The tax rate that is paid on the last dollar of income that the taxpayer earns.

6-8

The Spread between Baa Rated and Aaa Rated Municipal Bonds from 1980–2008

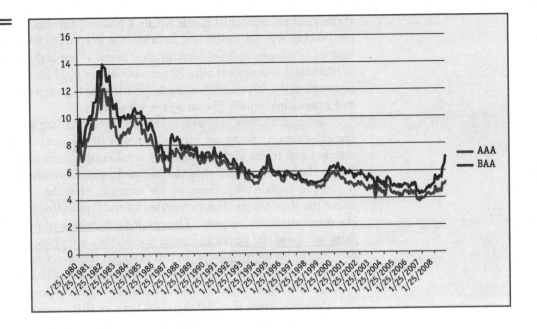

limits is taxed at lower rates. Interest income from bonds is additional income and is therefore taxed at the highest marginal rate that the taxpayer falls into. For bondholders who do not have much other income, interest income is taxed at a lower marginal rate than for bondholders whose other income puts them into a higher marginal tax bracket. This means, for example, that if you are in the 33 percent marginal federal income tax bracket, a 4 percent interest rate on a municipal bond is just as attractive as a 6 percent interest rate on, say, a taxable corporate bond; after taxes, both yield 4 percent.[14]

As we shall see, the tax-exempt status of municipal bonds makes them quite attractive to taxpayers in high marginal tax brackets. Financial intermediaries such as commercial banks and casualty insurance companies, which are subject to the 38 percent marginal corporate income tax rate, have traditionally been heavy purchasers of municipal securities.[15]

To see how the yields on municipals are related to the yields on other types of securities, the following simple equation is helpful.

$$\text{(6-7)} \qquad \text{after-tax yield} = i - it = i(1 - t)$$

where t = the marginal tax rate on interest income.

This says that the after-tax yield on a bond is equal to the interest rate earned, i, minus the portion that is taxed away, it; put another way, the after-tax yield is equal to the portion of the interest earned that is not taxed away: $i(1 - t)$.

Just as we care about our after-tax, take-home pay, rather than our before-tax gross pay, financial investors making portfolio decisions care about—and therefore compare—the after-tax returns on securities they might acquire. To see how this matters, suppose the rate on AAA-rated corporate bonds is 6 percent and the marginal tax rate of buyers is 33 percent, meaning that one-third of the interest income earned will be taxed away. If the only difference between the corporate bonds and AAA-rated municipal bonds is that the interest on corporate bonds is taxable while the interest on the municipal bonds is not ($t = 0$ percent), we would expect buyers to prefer the municipal securities to the corporate bonds as long as the rate on municipal bonds exceeds 4 percent.

If the yield on municipal bonds equals 4 percent, investors in the 33 percent marginal tax bracket will be indifferent because the corporate bond yields 4 percent [6 percent − (.33 × 6 percent) = 4 percent] after taxes. What if the marginal tax rate of buyers of municipal securities is only 20 percent? What yield on municipal bonds would leave investors in the 20 percent tax bracket indifferent between our 6 percent corporate bond and a municipal bond? The answer is 4.8 percent.[16]

In general, we would expect the buying and selling by investors—more formally, the substitution among securities—to result in the yield on municipals being approximately equal to the yield on similarly rated taxable securities, such as corporate bonds, minus the portion of the yield that is taxed away. Close the book for a moment and see if you can explain why. Suppose, for example, that the interest rate on municipals is above the after-tax yield on corporates for the typical investor; municipals are obviously the more attractive security. The resulting purchase of municipals and sale of corporates will raise the prices and lower the yields on municipals and lower the prices and raise the yields on corporates. In this example, the effect of the substitution toward municipals and away from corporates will be to equalize the interest rate on municipal securities with the after-tax return on similarly rated corporate securities.

We now know that the marginal tax rate that investors pay on interest income is the key to understanding the spread between the interest rates on tax-exempt municipal securities and the interest rates on taxable securities. We can also see that taxpayers, depending on their individual incomes, are in different marginal tax brackets, some high and some low. Thus, there is an average marginal tax rate somewhere between the high and the low marginal tax brackets. Because of substitution, the interest rate on municipal securities will gravitate to the rate that makes the "average" taxpayer (in the average marginal tax bracket) indifferent between municipals and similarly rated corporate securities.[17]

But why are those in high tax brackets, such as banks and rich individuals, especially attracted to municipals? Simply put, they are subject to a tax rate above the average marginal rate. To see precisely how this matters, assume that the average marginal tax rate is 20 percent, the rate on municipals is 4.8 percent, and the rate on corporates is 6 percent. The average investor—that is, the investor in the 20 percent marginal tax bracket—is indifferent between the two securities; both have an after-tax return of 4.8 percent. Not so the investor in a higher marginal tax bracket. Someone in the 33 percent marginal tax bracket, for example, would prefer the 4.8 percent return on the municipal security to the 4 percent after-tax return on the corporate security.

Recap   Other factors that affect the interest rates on different securities with the same maturity are credit risk and taxability of interest income. Taxpayers in marginal tax brackets above the average marginal tax bracket are particularly attracted to tax-exempt securities.

A final example shows how both credit risk and taxability play a part in determining yield to maturity. Under normal circumstances, yields on 20-year general obligation AAA-rated municipal bonds are less than 80 percent of yields on comparable Treasury securities. The yield spread mainly reflects the difference in the credit risk and the tax status accorded the earnings of the two assets. In December 1994, affluent Orange County, California, declared bankruptcy due to bond market losses in its investment pool. The bankruptcy created widespread uncertainty in the municipal bond market and the perception of greater risk. By year's end, the municipal bond market had gone into a tailspin, and according to *Business Week*, "municipal bonds [were] trading at yields unusually close to those on Treasury bonds, so after-tax yields for many long-term muni buyers [were] roughly one-third higher."[18] Although the tax status had not changed, the relative credit risk had, causing the spread between the two categories of securities to narrow. Buyers of municipal bonds demanded a larger risk premium, and as the after-tax yields reflect, they received it.

To sum up, the yields on municipal securities are typically, but not always, well below the yields on other securities with similar credit ratings and similar terms to maturity. The interest rate differentials observed are a reflection of the different tax treatment accorded the interest earned on each type of security and the different credit risk.

Summary of Major Points

1. The yield curve is a graphical representation of the relationship between interest rates (yields) on a particular security and its term to maturity. It is a visual depiction of the term structure of interest rates. A unique yield curve exists for each type of financial asset, such as government securities and corporate bonds, among others.

2. The most widely accepted explanation for the shape (slope) and position (level) of the yield curve is the expectations theory.

3. The expectations theory postulates that the long-term rate is the geometric average of the current short-term rate and the short-term rates expected to prevail over the term to maturity of the long-term security. The geometric average is the appropriate average to use in explaining the expectations theory because it takes into account the effects of compounding. The interest earned during the first year earns interest during the second year.

4. According to the expectations theory, the slope of the yield curve depends on the interest rates expected to prevail on short-term securities in the future. More specifically, a positively sloped yield curve reflects expectations of a rise in future short-term rates, relative to current short-term rates; a negatively sloped yield curve reflects expectations of a fall in future short-term rates, relative to current short-term rates.

5. Expectations about future short-term rates depend on expectations about future income, the money supply, and inflation. As expectations about these variables change, expected short-term rates will change, resulting in a change in the slope and level of the yield curve.

6. The fact that yield curves have almost always been upward sloping and that some borrowers and lenders appear to have preferred habitats has led to the view that the expectations theory is an incomplete explanation of the term structure of interest rates. Accordingly, the expectations theory has been modified to include and take into account term or liquidity premiums—the sweetener or bonus (extra return) needed to induce investors to acquire longer-term financial claims. In general, long-term rates will be determined by current short-term rates, expected short-term rates, and liquidity premiums.

7. *Credit risk* refers to the probability of a debtor defaulting—that is, not paying the principal or interest due on an outstanding debt. Standard & Poor's, Moody's, and Fitch—the three major credit-rating agencies—evaluate a borrower's probability of default and assign the borrower a risk classification.

8. Because investors are risk averse, they must be offered the bonus of extra interest to accept more risk. The extra return or interest is called a *risk premium*, and its size increases with the riskiness of the borrower.

9. Financial investors care about the after-tax return on their investments. Because the interest earned on municipal securities is exempt from the federal income tax, the yields on municipal securities are typically well below the yields on other (taxable) securities with similar credit ratings and similar terms to maturity.

Key Terms

Review Questions

1. Discuss the factors that determine the shape and level of a yield curve. How do term to maturity, credit risk, and tax treatment affect the interest rate on a particular asset?

2. Explain why a yield curve can be negatively sloped. Would interest rates be abnormally high or low? What would be the overall expectation of the direction of future short-term interest rates?

3. According to the expectations theory, how is the long-term interest rate determined? Why is the geometric average used instead of the simpler arithmetic average?

4. BBB-rated corporate bonds are riskier than AAA-rated bonds. Explain where the two yield curves will lie relative to each other. What could cause the spread to widen?

5. What determines expectations? Are expectations about future prices independent of expectations about future money supply growth rates? Why or why not?

6. Could the yield curve for municipals ever lie above the yield curve for government securities? (*Hint*: Consider all tax rates.) What effect would an increase in marginal tax rates have on the position of the yield curve for municipals?

7. Use the liquidity premium to give an explanation for why yield curves have most often been upward sloping over the past 50 years. Could a yield curve be upward sloping even if short-term rates were expected to remain constant? If interest rates are expected to fall dramatically, under what conditions would the yield curve still be upward sloping?

8. Define *preferred habitats*. Explain how this modification affects the expectations theory. What could cause market segmentation based on preferred habitats to break down? How is the market segmentation hypothesis different from the expectations theory?

9. Discuss the following statements: Over a typical cycle, the movement of the yield curve is like the wagging of a dog's tail. The entire tail wags, but short-term rates wag more often than long-term rates.

10. If yield curves became flatter (steeper), what does this say about expectations of future interest rates?

11. What would happen to the risk premium if the economy went into a strong expansion? A deep recession?

Analytical Questions

Questions marked with a check mark (✓) are objective in nature. They can be completed with a short answer or number.

✓12. If the current short-term rate is 5 percent and the expected short-term rate is 8 percent, what is the long-term interest rate? (Use the expectations theory.)

✓13. If the current short-term rate is 5 percent and the current long-term rate is 4 percent, what is the expected short-term interest rate? (Use the expectations theory.)

14. Rework questions 12 and 13 assuming that there is no compounding. (*Hint*: Use the simple arithmetic average instead of the geometric average.)

15. Assume that current interest rates on government securities are as follows: one-year rate, 5 percent; two-year rate, 6 percent; three-year rate, 6.5 percent; four-year rate, 7 percent. Graph the yield curve.

16. Given the yield curve in question 15, what is the expected direction of future one-year rates? Under what circumstances would one-year rates be expected to decline?

17. If a taxpayer's marginal tax rate is 33 percent, what is the after-tax yield on a corporate bond that pays 5 percent interest? If the average marginal tax rate of all taxpayers is 50 percent, will the taxpayer with the 33 percent marginal tax rate prefer a corporate or a municipal security? Assume equivalent safety and maturity.

18. Gather data from *The Wall Street Journal* on interest rates for today's government securities of various maturities. Graph the yield curve. (*Hint*: Check your answer by looking at the yield curve for Treasury securities that the *Journal* publishes daily in its Part C.)

19. What would happen to interest rates on municipal securities, given each of the following scenarios?
    a. The government increases marginal tax rates.
    b. The tax exemption on municipals is eliminated.
    c. Corporate profits fall severely.
    d. The federal government guarantees that the interest and principal on corporate bonds will be paid.
    e. A broader secondary market for government agency securities develops.

20. Draw the yield curve assuming that future short-term rates are expected to remain constant and the liquidity premium is positive. Now assume that net lenders increase their preference for short-term securities. Show what happens to the yield curve.

Suggested Readings

For information on current daily yields and yield curves on government securities, go to **http://www.ustreas.gov/offices/domestic-finance/debt-management/interest-rate/yield.html**.

Read about "The Living Yield Curve" on the Web at **http://www.smartmoney.com/onebond/index.cfm?story=yieldcurve&nav=dropTab**. This article analyzes normal, steep, inverted, and humped yield curves and allows you to compare yield curves on various dates.

For an interesting discussion of many issues touched on in this chapter, see the "Economic Outlook for the United States," remarks by Vice Chairman Roger W. Ferguson, Jr., at the Howard University Economics Forum, Washington, DC, March 3, 2006, at **www.federalreserve.gov/boarddocs/speeches/2006/20060303/default.htm**.

For a highly academic paper on yield curves, see "The Yield Curve and Predicting Recessions," by Jonathan H. Wright, *Finance and Economic Discussion Series: 2006–07*, Federal Reserve Board, February 2006, at **www.federalreserve.gov/pubs/feds/2006/200607/index.html**.

For a readable survey article on the yield curve by Tao Wu, see, "What Makes the Yield Curve Move" in the *Federal Reserve Bank of San Francisco Economic Letter*, No. 2003–15, June 6, 2003.

For a challenging and comprehensive book about the yield curve, see Moohrad Choudry, *Analysing and Interpreting the Yield Curve* (Singapore: John Wiley & Sons, 2004).

For an article that looks at the relationship between the slope of the yield curve and economic activity and inflation, see Arturo Estrella, Anthony P. Rodrigues, and Sebastian Schich, "How Stable Is the Predictive Power of the Yield Curve: Evidence from Germany and the United States," *Staff Reports*, No. 113, Federal Reserve Bank of New York (September 2000).

For an article that looks at measuring the yield curve, see Brian Sack, "Using Treasury STRIPS to Measure the Yield Curve," *Finance and Economics Discussion Series No. 2000–42*, Board of Governors of the Federal Reserve System (2000).

"Admiring Those Shapely Curves: The Gap Between Short-Term and Long-Term Interest Rates" is an article about how the shape of the yield curve can predict future economic growth. It can be found in *The Economist* (April 4, 1998): 83.

Many of the conclusions arrived at in this chapter are discussed in Burton Malkiel, *The Term Structure of Interest Rates* (Princeton, NJ: Princeton University Press, 1966).

Endnotes

1. Treasury bonds have an original maturity greater than 10 years. At the present time, the longest maturity of a newly issued fixed-rate Treasury security is 30 years. The Treasury now issues 5-, 10-, and 20-year inflation-indexed bonds with rates that vary with inflation.

2. Later in the chapter, we modify the analysis to account for differences in liquidity between short- and long-term financial securities.

3. For simplicity, we are assuming that the short-term rate does not change. In reality, because the demand for short-term securities increases, their price would rise. The portfolio reshuffling would result in a fall in the short rate in addition to a rise in the long rate.

4. Equation (6-2) is easily generalized for a long-term security, with, say, 10 years to maturity. In this case, the 10-year rate would be the geometric average of the current short-term one-year rate and the one-year rates expected to prevail over the next nine years. Thus, $i_{10} = [(1+i_1)(1+i_1^e)(1+i_2^e) \ldots (1+i_9^e)]^{1/10} - 1$, where i_n^e is the expected one-year rate n years from now.

5. For simplicity, we are ignoring the fact that the supply of short-term securities will also be reduced, causing their price to rise and their yield to fall.

6. Using the expectations theory to solve for the expected future short-term rate on January 29, 1993, we get 5.08 percent: $[(1 + .0424)^2/(1 + .0341)] - 1 = .0508$. Solving for the expected future short-term rate on June 1, 2003, we get 1.45 percent because $[(1 + .0123)^2/(1 + .0101)] - 1 = .0145$. Solving for the expected future short-term rate on May 7, 2007, we get 4.44 percent because $[(1 + .0468)2/(1 + .0492)] - 1 = .0444$.

7. Remember that this equation is a reduced-form equation derived from simultaneously solving a demand and supply equation for loanable funds.

8. An even deeper question is what determines Y^e, M^e, and p^e. A theory of how expectations are formed is covered in the next chapter.

9. In reality, the Fed may not put on the brakes until the economy is well into the recovery phase!

10. Note that negatively sloped yield curves have also been associated with abnormally high levels of interest rates when most market makers expect future interest rates to be lower. This was particularly true in 1981.

11. Of course, the lender who goes into the short-term market also faces the risk that interest rates could fall more than expected or rise less than expected. In this case, the lender would have been better off lending long. This is called the *reinvestment risk*. In general, it is believed that the liquidity premium outweighs the reinvestment risk.

12. For simplicity's sake, we have used Moody's ratings in this example. We could just as easily have used Standard & Poor's or Fitch's ratings.

13. In many states, interest on bonds issued by the investor's home state is also exempt from state income taxes. For example, California residents do not pay state income taxes on interest earned on bonds issued by California, but they do pay state income taxes on interest earned on bonds issued by Arizona. Although subject to federal income taxes, interest earned on federal government securities is exempt from state and local income taxes.

14. For simplicity's sake, we are assuming equivalent safety and maturity.

15. Commercial banks often feel subtle pressure to purchase the securities issued by municipalities in the immediate geographical area. With the bank's deposits coming from the local citizens, such purchases are viewed as an investment in the community the bank serves, an investment that demonstrates the goodwill and intentions of the bank.

16. 4.8 percent = 6 percent − (.20 × 6 percent).

17. Note that in actuality the yields on municipal securities are somewhat higher than one would expect after taking account of the average tax rate of all buyers. For the most part, the quality of the secondary market in municipal issues is not as good as the secondary market for Treasuries and many corporate issues. As a result, municipal securities possess somewhat less liquidity than other types of securities, and therefore the liquidity premium demanded by investors is larger on municipals than on other types of securities.
18. *Business Week* (December 26, 1994): 140.

7

Water seeks its own level.

Market Efficiency and the Flow of Funds Among Sectors

Learning Objectives

After reading this chapter, you should know:

How prices of different financial instruments are related

How expectations are formed

The difference between rational expectations and adaptive expectations

What the efficient markets hypothesis is and how it relates all financial prices

What the flow of funds among sectors is and how the flow of funds is affected when financial prices change

"STOCK PRICES RISE OVER 28 PERCENT WHILE BOND PRICES RISE OVER 9 PERCENT"

This was a typical newspaper headline reporting changes in financial prices during 2003. It is not always the case, however, that stock and bond prices move in these directions and by these magnitudes. For instance, in 2002, the headline would have read: "Stock Prices Fall over 20 Percent While Bond Prices Rise over 15 Percent." Other years are different—as different as day and night. The purpose of this chapter is simply to answer the question: Can these price movements among financial instruments be explained?

In the last chapter, we saw the important role that expectations play in determining bond prices. Expectations of GDP, money, and inflation affect expected interest rates, which then feed into actual interest rates and bond prices. In this chapter, we shall also see that expectations affect prices of all financial instruments. Because of their important role, economists have spent a great deal of time and energy in developing various theories of how expectations are formed by market participants.

We divide this chapter into three parts:

- First, we identify the relationship between bond prices and the prices of other financial instruments such as stocks or mortgages. You shall see that prices of all financial instruments adjust so that expected rates of return on all financial instruments are equalized after adjustments for varying degrees of risk and liquidity have been made.[1] Again, expectations play a central role.

- Second, recognizing the important role of expectations, we develop the theories of adaptive and rational expectations.

- Third, we take the analysis of how market participants form expectations one step further by developing the efficient markets hypothesis, which is based on the theory of rational expectations as applied to financial markets. We conclude that after full adjustment has occurred, prices of financial instruments are equal to their expected values, which equal the optimal forecasts of those variables given all available information.

Hopefully, the analysis will go a long way toward answering the question, "Can these price movements among financial instruments be explained?" found in the first paragraph of this chapter. We begin our discussion by relating expected rates of return to the prices of long-term financial instruments.

HOW EXPECTED RATES OF RETURN AFFECT THE PRICES OF STOCKS AND BONDS

Stocks and bonds are two major, long-term financial instruments. Stocks represent ownership of part of the issuing firm, whereas bonds represent debt of the issuer, whether it is a firm, government entity, or other net borrower. To streamline the analysis, we focus on how stock and bond prices are related while recognizing that the analysis could easily be extended to other long-term financial instruments such as mortgages.

A *portfolio* usually consists of many financial instruments, including both stocks and bonds. Market participants hold combinations of various financial assets rather than one asset to take advantage of gains from diversification. **Diversification** is the allocation of surplus funds to a variety of financial instruments instead of holding just one asset. As a famous saying in the world of finance goes, "Don't put all your eggs in one basket." Returns to holding two different assets may be positively or negatively correlated. Returns are positively (directly) correlated if they tend to move up or down

Diversification
The allocation of surplus funds to more than one financial instrument in order to reduce risk.

A Closer Look

The Benefits of Diversification

Assume there are two stocks with returns that are perfectly inversely (negatively) correlated. When the price of one increases by a certain percent, the price of the other decreases by the same percent. For example, SwimmingPools, Inc., pays a 16 percent return each year when temperatures are above average and zero percent in other years. SkiResorts, Inc., pays a 16 percent return each year when temperatures are below average and zero percent in other years. Assuming that half the time the temperatures are above average and half the time they are below average (a reasonable assumption given the nature of averages!), the expected return to holding either stock is 8 percent. If an investor chooses to hold one or the other, but not both, the expected return will be 8 percent, but the risk involves the fact that the return will fluctuate between either 0 or 16 percent. As the following table illustrates, smart investors will split their surplus funds equally between SwimmingPools and SkiResorts and earn an 8 percent return all of the time, thus eliminating all risk!

The expected return to owning a share of shock is the sum of each possible outcome multiplied by the probability of that outcome.

Stock	(a) Possible Outcomes	(b) Probability	(a) × (b)
SwimmingPools, Inc.			
(above average temps)	16%	.50	8%
(below average temps)	0%	.50	0
Expected return to owners	-	-	8
Return fluctuates between 0% and 16%			
SkiResorts, Inc.			
(above average temps)	0%	.50	0%
(below average temps)	16%	.50	8
Expected return to owners	-	-	8
Return fluctuates between 0% and 16%			

If an investor's surplus funds are split between SwimmingPools and SkiResorts, when temperatures are above average, half of the portfolio (the half invested in SwimmingPools) will earn 16 percent and half (the half invested in SkiResorts) will earn zero percent. As noted above, the expected return is the sum of the possible outcomes multiplied by their probabilities. In this case, the overall portfolio will earn 8 percent $(.16 \times .5 + 0 \times .5 = .08)$. The reverse is true for below-average temperatures, with SkiResorts earning 16 percent and SwimmingPools earning zero percent. Again, the portfolio split between the two firms earns 8 percent. Thus, the risk or the fluctuation of returns between zero and 16 percent has virtually been eliminated by diversification, or owning both companies. The portfolio earns 8 percent when temperatures are above average and 8 percent when temperatures are below average. Risk has been

eliminated because the returns to the two assets were perfectly inversely correlated. In the real world, few assets exhibit this property. It is also true that returns are
usually not perfectly positively (directly) correlated, meaning that the prices of two
stocks usually do not always change by the exact same percent. If stock prices are
perfectly correlated, risk is not reduced by diversification. In the case in which returns are correlated (either directly or inversely), but not perfectly so, risk can be
reduced (although not eliminated as in the case of perfect inverse correlation)
through diversification.

Thus, we can conclude the following:

- If returns to two assets held are perfectly negatively correlated, risk can be
  eliminated through diversification.
- If returns to two assets held are perfectly positively correlated, risk can *not* be
  reduced through diversification.
- If returns to two assets held are positively or negatively correlated, risk can be reduced
  for any given expected return but not eliminated through diversification.

together. For instance, if, as the economy improves, two stocks also tend to improve,
and vice versa, they are positively correlated. Note that the price of one stock may
be increasing 6 percent while the other is increasing 2 percent but that they are still
positively correlated even though the magnitude of the increase is different. To be positively correlated, the only thing that matters is that the change to each be in the same
direction.

Returns are negatively (inversely) correlated if the return on one asset increases
while the return on the other tends to decrease. To be negatively correlated, the only
thing that matters is that the change to each be in the opposite direction. Some financial
instruments do better in recessions, while most perform better in expansions. Returns
on financial instruments that improve over the business cycle are negatively correlated
with those that lose value. As long as returns among financial instruments are not perfectly correlated (that is, they do not change by the same magnitude and direction all
the time), then the risk or fluctuation of a combination or basket of assets with a given
expected return will be less than the risk for any one asset with the same expected return. Thus, one can earn a higher return for any level of risk or be exposed to less risk
for any given return by diversifying. Now would be a good time to read "A Closer Look"
on p. 139 to learn more about the benefits of diversification.

Assuming that an individual opts for a portfolio of various financial instruments
with different risks and returns, how would you go about managing such a portfolio?
More specifically, how would you decide whether to purchase and hold stocks or bonds
or some combination of both, and so on? We hope that you would compare the expected
rates of return on the different types of financial assets, selecting those with the highest
expected return consistent with the risk you are willing to take, while realizing that
by diversifying you can improve the expected performance or reduce the risk of your
portfolio.

Stocks

The size of a shareholder's ownership position depends on the number of stock shares owned. For example, if 1,000 shares are outstanding, a stockholder who owns 100 shares in effect owns 10 percent of the firm. The value of each share—and, therefore, the value of the stockholder's holdings in the corporation—depends on the prevailing price of the firm's stock. If, for example, the stock's price is $50 per share, the total value of the stockholder's 100 shares is $5,000, and the total value of the firm is $50,000 ($50×1,000 shares). If the stock price rises to $60 per share, then the value of the stockholder's 100 shares increases to $6,000 and the value of the firm increases to $60,000. Likewise, given an unforeseen fall in the stock's price to $40 per share, the values of the stockholder's shares and the firm decrease to $4,000 and $40,000, respectively. The key question, then, is, What determines the price per share?

Outstanding shares of stocks of publicly held companies are traded (bought and sold) on organized exchanges such as the New York Stock Exchange or by networks of brokers and dealers around the country. (More on this in Chapter 14.) Stock prices fluctuate daily, some going up, some going down, as financial investors buy and sell shares of various corporations. In part, those fluctuations occur because a share of stock represents a claim on the earnings of a firm. Tangible evidence of this sharing of earnings comes in the form of dividends, which are a distribution of profits to stockholders. If earnings prospects are improving, the share price and dividend paid per share may also be rising.[2] Financial investors will be attracted by the improved outlook (profitability) for the firm.

In general, as current and expected future earnings rise, stock prices also rise, and as current and prospective earnings decline, stock prices also decline. A growing economy means that sales, production, and incomes are expanding, while a declining economy means the opposite. Because expected earnings also rise when the economy is expected to grow and tend to fall when the economy is expected to contract, there is often a positive correlation between the growth of real national income and stock prices.[3]

What is the expected return on stocks? Generally speaking, the expected return on a share of stock, say, over a year, is the expected dividend plus the expected change in the price of the stock, all divided by the share price at the time of purchase. For example, if you pay $50 a share, the expected dividend is $1 per share, and you expect the price to rise $3 over the year, the expected return is 8 percent [($1+$3)/$50=.08=8 percent].[4] An 8 percent expected return would also result if the expected dividend is $4 and the expected capital gain is $0 because [($4+$0)/$50=.08=8 percent]. Now would be a good time to look at Exhibit 7-1, which examines this relationship.

Bonds

With regard to bonds, the expected return to a newly issued bond is the current interest rate. Recall from Chapter 5 that bonds represent long-term debt and pay a fixed annual coupon payment.[5] The coupon payment is the product of the face value of the bond multiplied by the coupon rate. Bondholders are entitled to be paid the coupon payment before dividends are paid to stockholders. The coupon rate is the interest rate at the time the bond is originally issued and usually appears on the bond itself. The coupon rate is not the same thing as the current interest rate if interest rates have changed since the bond was issued.

For example, if the face value of a bond is $1,000 and the coupon rate is 6 percent, then the coupon payment is $60, since $60 divided by $1,000 is equal to 6 percent

Expected Dividend	Expected Price Change [Capital Gain (+) or Loss (−)]	Expected Return
$3	−$2	($3+(−$2))/$50=2 percent
$3	$0	($3+$0)/$50=6 percent
$3	$2	($3+$2)/$50=10 percent
$3	$4	($3+$4)/$50=14 percent
$4	−$2	($4+(−$2))/$50=4 percent
$4	$0	($4+$0)/$50=8 percent
$4	$2	($4+$2)/$50=12 percent
$4	$4	($4+$4)/$50=16 percent

As the body of the text explains, the expected return of owning a share of stock for, say, one year is the expected dividend plus the expected capital gain or loss, divided by the share price at the time of purchase. Thus, when either factor changes, the expected return will change.

Assume that the stock originally costs $50 per share. The preceding table shows the rate of return for owning the stock given various expected dividends and expected price changes (the capital gains or losses).

If actual dividends or actual capital gains and losses turn out to be different from those expected, the actual return will be different from the expected. Needless to say, all investors hope that actual dividends and capital gains turn out to be higher than expected rather than the reverse.

($60 / $1,000 = .06). This coupon payment does not change even if interest rates change after the bond has been issued. However, the bond's price will change whenever interest rates change or if the issuer's ability to make the agreed-upon interest or principal payments comes into question.

As portrayed in Exhibit 7-2, the expected return on previously issued bonds is the coupon rate plus the expected percentage change in the bond's price over the course of the year.

Let's assume that you purchase a $1,000 newly issued 30-year bond described above with a 6 percent coupon rate. One year after the bond is issued, interest rates fall to 4 percent. The price of the bond with 29 years to maturity would increase to $1,339.67, because the present value of the 29 coupon payments of $60 plus the present value of the repayment of the $1,000 principle at maturity would equal $1,339.67.[6] In other words, as you saw in Chapter 5, prices of previously issued bonds adjust so that they pay the new prevailing interest rate. The expected return on the bond is equal to the coupon rate (6 percent) plus the expected percentage capital gain from the change in interest rates. In our example, the new interest rate is 4 percent, and the expected percentage capital gain is 34 percent [($1,339.67 − $1,000) / $1,000 = .34 = 34 percent]. Thus, the expected return to owning the bond over the year is the coupon rate (6 percent) plus the expected percentage capital gain (34 percent), or 40 percent.

To see how bond prices fit into the picture, assume that the current interest rate on bonds is 6 percent and that the expected return on stocks is 8 percent, with the typical stock costing $50 and the expected dividend equal to $4. We also assume for simplicity that (1) the expected capital gain is zero, (2) stocks and bonds have the same degree of liquidity,[7] (3) stocks are riskier than bonds, and (4) the portfolio managers must be

7-2
The Expected Return on Bonds

> **Expected Percentage Return on Bonds**
>
> = Coupon rate + Expected percentage change in the bond price
> = (coupon payment/bond price at the beginning of the year) + (expected bond price at the end of the year − bond price at the beginning of the year)/bond price at the beginning of the year)

compensated 2 percent for the additional risks of owning stocks. Under these conditions, when bonds pay a 6 percent return and stocks pay an 8 percent return, the typical portfolio manager is indifferent between stocks and bonds. He or she will presumably hold some of each because the risk-adjusted returns are equalized. Equation (7-1) depicts this situation:

(7-1)   Risk-adjusted return on stocks = risk-adjusted return on bonds
Nominal return on stocks − compensation for higher risk of owing stocks
= risk-adjusted return on bonds (8 percent − 2 percent) = 6 percent

Now suppose that the Fed decides to pursue a more expansionary monetary policy. The initial result of this is a decline in the interest rate on bonds to 4 percent and a reduction in the risk-adjusted return on bonds from 6 percent to 4 percent.[8] The fall in the interest rate will tend to raise stock prices through two channels.

First, the expected return on bonds is now below the risk-adjusted expected return on stocks. Given the substitutability of stocks for bonds in investors' portfolios and the higher expected return on stocks, the demand for stocks will rise, tending to raise stock prices. Within the confines of our simple example, we can even say how high stock prices will rise: stock prices will rise until the expected return on stocks is again 2 percent higher than the expected return on bonds (4 percent). This will occur when the price of our typical share of stock rises to $66.67, because the $4 expected dividend divided by $66.67 equals 6 percent ($4/$66.67 = .06).

Second, the fall in the interest rate will be expected to raise the demand for goods and services and increase the sales and earnings of firms. With earnings expected to rise, dividends will also be expected to rise. This reinforces the first effect. For example, if the dividend is expected to rise to $5 per share, then financial investors will be willing to bid up the price per share even further to $83.33 because $5 divided by $83.33 is equal to 6 percent ($5 / $83.33 = .06 = 6 percent).[9] Again, after stock prices have adjusted to the change in interest rates, the risk-adjusted return on stocks will be equal to the risk-adjusted return on bonds.[10]

Assuming that you and other portfolio managers would like to have owned the stock before all of this occurred, you can see now why actual and expected changes in the interest rate get so much attention in the stock market.

In the real world, many types of long-term financial instruments offer varying degrees of risk and liquidity. Because of the substitutability of various financial instruments, prices of financial instruments will adjust so that returns to owning different instruments are equalized after adjustments have been made for differences in risk and liquidity. In other words, in financial markets, risk- and liquidity-adjusted rates of return are equalized.

Recap   Prices of long-term financial instruments change as current and future expected earnings change. If interest rates fall, prices of previously issued bonds rise, and vice versa. If current and expected future earnings rise, ceteris paribus, stock prices also rise, and vice versa. In managing a portfolio, market participants compare expected rates of return and select those financial assets with the highest expected return consistent with varying degrees of risk and liquidity. As long as returns among various financial instruments are not perfectly correlated, diversification reduces risk for any given expected return. Stock and bond prices adjust until the portfolio manager is indifferent between stocks and bonds. If interest rates change, ceteris paribus, stock prices also change. When full adjustment has occurred, differences in returns on various financial instruments reflect differences in only risk and liquidity.

To reiterate, it is the expected return on bonds and the expected return on stocks that determine stock and bond prices. It should not surprise you that this is true of all financial instruments. Because expectations play such a central role, we turn now to a general theory of how price expectations are formed, which will then be applied to financial instruments.

The Formation of Price Expectations

The substantial research on the formation of price expectations suggests that the following factors are important in shaping the public's expectations of future prices as suggested in Equation (7-2):

(7-2)   Price expectations = f(current and past prices, expected change in national income, and expected changes in production costs)

This equation suggests that the formation of price expectations is both backward and forward looking. The idea that price expectations depend on the public's experience with prices, as reflected in current and past prices, is the backward-looking component. Expectations formed by looking back are typically called **adaptive expectations**. This experience is measured as a weighted average of past values because the recent past (say, the last one to two years) is likely to be more influential in forming expectations about the future than the more distant past. Thus, recent years are weighted more heavily than earlier years. For example, if the rate of inflation were 3 percent per year for 10 years and rose to 4 percent in the most recent two years, then the public will probably expect inflation in the coming year to be closer to 4 percent than to 3 percent.

It is unreasonable to believe that the public will take only the past into consideration when anticipating future prices. Thus, expected changes in costs of production and in national income also contribute to the formation of price expectations. For example, will the price of oil rise or fall? If the public expects a large rise in the price of oil, government expenditures, or bank reserves in the coming year, expectations of inflation may be raised to, say, 5 percent. Expectations formed by looking both backward and forward, using all available information, are typically called **rational expectations**. Exhibit 7-3 highlights the relationship between adaptive and rational expectations.

The **theory of rational expectations** states that, on average, expectations of financial prices will be equal to the optimal forecast. The **optimal forecast** is the best guess possible, arrived at by using all available information both from the past and about the future. Even if a forecast is rational, there is no guarantee that the forecast will be accurate. All that is necessary is that, *on average*, the forecast be equal to the optimal forecast. There is an aspect of randomness in financial markets that, more often than not, makes the forecast either a little short or a little wide of the mark. Thus, the forecast

Adaptive Expectations
Expectations formed by looking back at past values of a variable.

Rational Expectations
Expectations formed by looking both backward and forward.

Theory of Rational Expectations
The theory that expectations will, on average, be equal to the optimal forecast.

Optimal Forecast
The best guess possible arrived at by using all of the available information.

Adaptive Expectations	Rational Expectations
Expectations formed as a weighted average of past values	Expectations formed by looking at all available information
Usually more weight is given to more recent values of the variable	Looks at the past as well as all additional available information, such as information about expected changes in national income and costs
Backward looking	Backward and forward looking

error (the difference between the actual value and the forecast) will *on average* be zero. In any given time period, it is impossible to predict what the forecast error will be.

There is another reason besides randomness that the optimal forecast may deviate from what turns out to be the actual value of the forecasted variable: there may be one or more additional key factors that are relevant but not available at the time the optimal forecast is made. If the information is not available, then the forecast may be inaccurate. However, it is still rational because the decision maker makes use of all available information. This is different from the situation where market participants fail to use all available information because they are unaware of it or because it is too costly to do so. In this latter case, expectations formed in this manner are neither accurate nor rational.

The reasoning behind the rational expectations theory is that it is costly for market participants *not* to use all available information in forming price expectations. For example, if a producer ignores readily available information that interest rates are going up based on a change in Fed policy, then it may produce too much output, ignoring the effects that the interest rate hikes have on demand. Thus, the producer earns less profit than it otherwise would have. Or if a producer ignores the effect of higher oil prices on demand and costs, it may again produce more than the profit-maximizing output. In such cases, the errors are costly to management, employees, and stockholders and give a strong incentive to consider readily available information in the future.

An implication of rational expectations is that as new information becomes available, market participants should adjust expectations accordingly. The weight of current research on the formation of price expectations suggests that the public does not adjust its expectations instantaneously when new information becomes available. There are lags between the time that information becomes available and when it is fully incorporated into expectations. However, the evidence also suggests that as market participants (the public) have come to better understand the process of inflation, the lag in adjusting expectations has shortened considerably. Indeed, in recent years, the Fed has become more open about its policy stance; this is partly because the Fed believes that its policy will be more effective if market participants better understand what the Fed is doing and what it perceives about the future direction of the economy.

Another implication of rational expectations is that if there is a change in the way a variable moves, the way in which expectations of the variable are formed will also change. An example will help to clarify. In the early 1980s, changes in the monetary aggregate M2 were highly correlated with changes in national income. Therefore, changes in M2 played a major role in forming expectations about changes in national income. Since the late 1980s, changes in national income have not been highly correlated with changes in M2. Therefore, changes in M2 will not be given a large weight in forming expectations about changes in national income.

Adaptive expectations are formed by looking at current and past prices. Rational expectations are formed by looking at past prices and at all currently available information about the economy that may affect prices. The theory of rational expectations is that expectations of financial prices will be equal to optional forecasts, which are the best guesses possible, arrived at by using all available information. Because of randomness in financial markets, the actual value of a financial variable is usually different from the optimal forecast. However, the forecast error (the difference between the actual value of the variable and the optimal forecast) will on average be zero.

The Efficient Markets Hypothesis: Rational Expectations Applied to Financial Markets

Efficient Markets Hypothesis
This hypothesis states that when financial markets are in equilibrium, the prices of financial instruments reflect all readily available information.

The **efficient markets hypothesis** builds on the theory of rational expectations. Namely, when financial markets are in equilibrium, the prices of financial instruments reflect all readily available information. Financial markets are in equilibrium when the quantity demanded of any security is equal to the quantity supplied of that security. Returns reflect only differences in risk and liquidity. As in all markets, prices—in this case, prices of financial instruments—adjust to bring financial markets to equilibrium. In an efficient market, the optimal forecast of a security's price (made by using all available information) will be equal to the equilibrium price.

Let's assume that there is a financial instrument, say a share of stock, with an equilibrium return of 10 percent after adjusting for risk and liquidity. The stock clearly offers some combination of more risk and/or less liquidity than another financial asset whose equilibrium return is less than 10 percent. The dollar return in a given time period is equal to the price of the stock at the end of the time period minus the price at the beginning of the time period plus any dividend payment made during the time period. To express this return as a percentage, we need to divide the total return by the price at the beginning of the period, as in Equation (7-3), to get

$$(7\text{-}3) \qquad\qquad R = (P_{t+1} - P_t + D)/P_t$$

where
R = percentage return over the time period,
P_{t+1} = price of the stock at the end of the time period,
P_t = price of the stock at the beginning of the time period, and
D = dividend payments made during the time period.

If at the beginning of the time period we know the price and dividend payment of the stock, then the only unknown variable is the price of the instrument at the end of the time period (P_{t+1}). The efficient markets hypothesis assumes that expectations of future prices of financial instruments are rational. This is equivalent to assuming that the expected or forecasted price of the stock at the end of the time period will be equal to the optimal forecast of that variable arrived at by using all available information. Thus, if expectations are rational, the expected return on the stock will be equal to the optimal forecast arrived at by plugging in the optimal forecast for P_{t+1} into Equation (7-3).

Returning to our example, let's assume that company A announces new profit numbers that raise the expected price of the instrument at the end of the time period. The question is, How will today's price respond to the new higher expected price in the future? Assuming that the risk and liquidity of the financial asset have not changed and that the equilibrium return (based on that risk and liquidity) of A is 10 percent, the present price will adjust so that, given the new expected price, the return will still be 10 percent. Thus, the conclusion is that the current price will rise to a level where the optimal forecast of an instrument's return is equal to the instrument's equilibrium return.

To clarify, let's assume that the original price and expected price of A was $100 and that the dividend was $10. Using Equation (7-3), the original return would be 10 percent, which we assumed, given the risk and liquidity of A, was also the equilibrium return. Let's assume that based on the new higher profit numbers, the expected price increases to $115.[11] What will happen to the current price? Based upon our analysis, the current price should rise to a point where the expected return on A remains at its equilibrium return of 10 percent. In this case, we solve for the new current price based on an expected future price of $115 and a dividend of $10. Plugging the numbers into Equation (7-3), we get ($115 − P_t + $10)/$P_t$ = .10 or 10 percent. Solving for P_t, we get $113.63. Thus, the current price will immediately rise to $113.63, given the new higher expected price of $115. When the current price is $113.63, the expected return will be equal to 10 percent. At a price lower than $113.63, the expected return would be higher. For example, at the original price of $100, the expected return would be 25 percent ($115 − $100 + $10)/$100 = 25 percent). Funds would flow in this market by investors seeking the higher than equilibrium return of 15 percent based on risk and liquidity. As funds flowed in, the price of A would rise. Funds would keep flowing into the market, pushing the price up until the market returned to equilibrium. This occurs at a price of $113.63 because ($115 − $113.63 + $10)/$113.063 = 10 percent.

Two points are worth emphasizing. First, the equilibrium return is based on the risks and liquidity of this financial instrument relative to other financial instruments. Note that we are assuming that the risk and liquidity of A have not changed so that the equilibrium return to A relative to the risk and liquidity of other financial instruments is 10 percent. Second, *current* prices adjust whenever new information becomes available that changes current expectations about *future* prices.

The rationale behind the efficient markets hypothesis is straightforward. Namely, if current prices do not fully reflect any changes in expectations, then some market participants will earn less than what they otherwise would have. There will be unexploited opportunities to gain by purchasing those financial instruments that pay a return above equilibrium. The drive for profits ensures that all opportunities for profit will be exhausted and that prices of all financial instruments will adjust to the equilibrium return, which is the optimal forecast. Now would be a good time to read the "A Closer Look" on p. 148 about the implications of the efficient markets hypothesis.

The efficient markets hypothesis holds that the prices of all financial instruments are based on the optimal forecast obtained by using all available information. A **stronger version of the efficient markets hypothesis** holds that the prices of all financial instruments reflect the true fundamental value of the instruments. Thus, not only do prices reflect all available information, but this information is accurate, complete, understood by all, and reflects the market fundamentals. **Market fundamentals** are factors that have a direct effect on future income streams of the instruments. These factors include the value of the assets and the expected income streams of those assets on which the financial instruments represent claims. Thus, if markets are efficient, prices are correct in that they represent underlying fundamentals. In the less-stringent version of the hypothesis, the prices of all financial instruments do not necessarily represent the fundamental value of the instrument.

There have been extraordinary run-ups and collapses of stock or bond prices, known as bubbles, that do not seem to be related to market fundamentals. Such run-ups in stock prices occurred in Japan in the late 1980s and more recently in the United States in the late 1990s. Some economists point out that bubbles in financial markets can still be explained by rational expectations. It may be rational to buy a share of

Stronger Version of the Efficient Markets Hypothesis
The theory that the prices of all financial instruments not only reflect the optimal forecast of the financial instrument but also the true fundamental value of the instrument.

Market Fundamentals
Factors that have a direct effect on future income streams of the instruments, including the value of the assets and the expected income streams of those assets on which the financial instruments represent claims.

A Closer Look

Implications of the Efficient Markets Hypothesis

The efficient markets hypothesis is attractive from an intuitive sense. However, for most investors who want to believe they can consistently get above average returns, it is unattractive. The implications are that a hot tip will not pan out unless it is based on information not readily available; however, buying and selling stocks based on "insider" information (information available only to someone within the corporation) is illegal.

One implication of the efficient markets hypothesis is that prices of financial instruments reflect all readily available information. Thus, if information about an issuer is already expected, when an announcement of the information is made, the announcement will have little or no effect on the instrument's price. For example, if it is believed that the bankruptcy of a firm is eminent, prices of the stocks and bonds of the failing company will fall even before the actual bankruptcy is declared. Thus, prices of financial instruments change dramatically only when "unexpected information" becomes available.

Another implication of the efficient markets hypothesis is that it is impossible to beat the market (earn an above average return). This is so because current prices of financial instruments reflect the optimal forecast using all available information when markets are in equilibrium. If I read a favorable earnings report in the Sunday newspaper, by the time I buy the instrument on Monday morning, its price will already have adjusted so that I will not earn an above average return.

Whatever the available information, markets are always moving toward an equilibrium of sorts, which can mean moving toward or away from previous equilibriums as factors affecting supply and demand for securities or funds change. A market is really not efficient unless the available information is understood by significant participants. A learning curve exists in understanding, adapting to, and using information that is not equally shared, understood, or held with great and unvarying confidence, and this information is subject to imminent change; hence, volatility in the market is to be expected and may even be greater (1) the more information becomes available and (2) the faster it is disseminated.

The quality of information varies, and when traders are not sure of what they know or don't know, the market can be volatile even without any changes in the available information as confidence levels rise and fall. Add to this the rational or irrational emotions embodied in herd instinct, market momentum, market rotation, guru hypnosis, mythical mottos such as "buy on the rumor, sell on the fact," consensus forecasts, and so on. In areas of the market such as high tech stocks in the late 1990s and early 2000s, it is unlikely that participants interpreted the available information the same way.

With increased individual control over pension plans and the rise of managed mutual funds, individuals are now participants in the stock and bond markets more so than in the past. Many make little use of information except for minimal asset allocation based on the reputation of a popular guru or fund manager. Fund managers consequently engage in highly competitive behavior to report good earnings results.

Powerful mood swings of pessimism and optimism can by contagion sweep the markets and become part of the changing information that affects them.

For each person beating the average, someone is always being beaten by it. Whether someone can *consistently* beat the average is the question. John Maynard Keynes, the well-known economist, said that the true genius is the person who can accurately forecast what the average investor will believe about the direction of the economy or the future profitability of a corporation. In reality, forecasting what the average investor will believe is more important than forecasting what will actually happen.

One final note: When interest rates change, default risk also changes. For example, if the Fed takes action to increase interest rates, the economy slows and the risk of a default increases as the economy slows. Thus, the future income stream from the financial asset becomes less certain. This, in turn, affects both the risk premium that the lender will require and the price of the financial instrument.

stock at a high price if it is thought that there will be other investors in the future who would be willing to pay inflated prices (prices that exceed those based on market fundamentals) for the stock. This phenomenon is sometimes called "the greater fool" theory. Following this train of thought, subsequent collapses in stock prices occurred in Japan in the 1990s and in the United States in the early 2000s.

Other economists suspect that financial market prices may overreact before reaching equilibrium when there is a change in either supply or demand. That is, prices may rise or fall (overshoot or undershoot) more than market fundamentals would justify before settling down to the price based on fundamentals. In these cases, it may be possible for investors to earn above average returns or to experience above average losses.

Recap	The efficient markets hypothesis states that when financial markets are in equilibrium, the prices of all financial instruments reflect all readily available information. Prices of financial instruments are based on optimal forecasts. The rationale behind the hypothesis is that if prices do not reflect all available information, there will be unexploited profit opportunities. A stronger version of the efficient markets hypothesis holds that prices of financial instruments represent underlying or fundamental values of the assets and the expected income streams of those assets on which the financial instruments represent claims. Bubbles in financial markets where prices seem to exceed fundamental values can be rational if investors believe that other investors will buy the financial instrument at still higher prices. Some believe that financial prices overreact (overshoot or undershoot) in response to newly available information.

So far we have seen that according to the efficient markets hypothesis, financial prices adjust so that unexploited opportunities for profit are eliminated, and financial markets are in equilibrium when the prices of financial instruments are based on optimal forecasts using all available information. In equilibrium, differences in rates of return on financial instruments are based on differences in risk and liquidity. In the next section, we will take a broader look at the flow of funds among sectors such as the household, business, government, rest-of-the-world and financial sectors of the economy. We shall see that there are considerable links between the responses of spending units to changes in prices of financial instruments and the flow of funds among sectors.

Flow of Funds
A social accounting system that divides the economy into a number of sectors including the household, business, government, foreign, and financial sector.

Sources and Uses of Funds Statement
A statement showing the sources and uses of funds for any sector.

Sources of Funds
For any sector, income and borrowing.

Uses of Funds
For any sector, current spending and changes in financial instruments held.

Surplus Sector
A sector where the combined surpluses of the lenders are greater than the combined deficits of the net borrowers.

Deficit Sector
A sector where the combined deficits of net borrowers are greater than the combined surpluses of the net lenders.

The flow of funds is a social accounting system that divides the economy into a number of sectors and constructs a sources and uses of funds statement for each sector. The purpose of this section is to discuss the financial flows of funds among sectors and their relationship to the economy. We then construct a hypothetical sources and uses of funds table for the U.S. economy.

The four main sectors are the household, business, government, and rest-of-the-world sectors.[12] For any sector, the sources of funds are current income and borrowing. The uses of funds are current spending and changes in financial instruments held. Any sector is composed of spending units with surpluses (net lenders) and spending units with deficits (net borrowers). For any sector, the combined surpluses of the net lenders may be greater than the combined deficits of the net borrowers. In this case, the sector would be a surplus sector. If the combined deficits of the net borrowers are greater than the combined surpluses of the net lenders, then the sector is a deficit sector.

For *all* sectors combined, however, borrowing (the issuance of financial claims) must be equal to lending (the acquisition of financial assets). This is so because each financial claim, in turn, implies the existence of a complementary financial asset. However, in each individual sector, it is highly unlikely that the combined surpluses just equal the combined deficits. Thus, the economy is usually composed of surplus and deficit sectors where the combined surpluses of the surplus sectors is equal to the combined deficits of the deficit sectors for the economy as a whole. Exhibit 7-4 fleshes out these relationships.

Although the flow-of-funds accounts divide the economy into nine sectors, in Exhibit 7-5 we simplify to the household, business, government, and rest-of-the-world sectors. By adding a fifth sector, the financial sector, along with the others, we can see how intermediation facilitates the flows of funds from the surplus to the deficit sectors and vice versa. Note that for every use of funds, whether for acquiring financial assets or spending on goods and services, there must be a source, and every source is put to some

---

7-4
Surplus and Deficit Sectors

A Surplus Sector

The combined surpluses of all spending units in the sector > the combined deficits of all spending units in the sector

A Deficit Sector

The combined surpluses of all spending units in the sector < the combined deficits of all spending units in the sector

For All Sectors

The combined surpluses of the surplus sectors must equal the combined deficits of the deficit sectors

For example, if the household and business sectors are deficit sectors and the government and the rest-of-the-world sectors are surplus sectors, then the combined deficits of the household and business sectors must equal the combined surpluses of the government and rest-of-the-world sectors.

Likewise, if the business and government sectors are deficit sectors, and the household and rest-of-the-world sectors are surplus sectors, then the combined deficits must equal the combined surpluses.

7-5

A Hypothetical Sources and
Uses of Funds Statement for
the U.S. Economy (in Billions
of Dollars)

Sources of Funds	Uses of Funds
Households	
Disposable income: $8,200	Consumption spending on non-durables, durables, and
Net borrowing: $275	services: $8,100
	Investment spending on real assets: $375
Deficit = $275	
Business Firms	
Net revenues: $1,060	Net spending on real assets (plant and equipment): $1,225
Net borrowing: $220	Net spending on real assets (inventories): $55
Deficit = $220	
Government	
Tax receipts: $3,300	Government spending on goods and services: $1,190
	Government spending on transfer payments: $1,620
	Interest payments on the national debt: $260
	Surplus: $230
Rest-of-the-World	
Foreign purchases of U.S.	U.S. purchases of foreign goods and services: $1,470
goods and services: $1,170	
Net foreign purchase of U.S.	Net U.S. purchases of foreign financial assets: $240
financial assets: $805	
	Surplus = $265
Financial Intermediaries	
Net acquiring of financial	Net incurring of financial
assets: $1,080	liabilities: $1,080

The financial sector, composed of financial intermediaries, is included to show the extent of financial intermediation in the economy. Financial intermediaries acquire funds to lend by issuing claims on themselves. They use the funds to purchase financial instruments issued by borrowers. As you may have guessed, the extent of financial intermediation in an economy has a direct relationship on the extent of economic development.

use (if not spending on goods and services, then in acquiring financial instruments). Consequently, total sources and uses of funds are not only equal in each sector but also in the aggregate for all sectors taken together. Furthermore, the uses of funds by any one sector are the sources of funds for other sectors and vice versa.

For example, the sources for households are income and debt; for business firms, net revenues and borrowings; and for the government, taxes or borrowing. Likewise, each sector has two major uses for funds. Households use funds for spending on consumption and investment or for acquiring financial assets; firms use funds for investment or for acquiring financial assets; the government uses funds for government expenditures or for acquiring financial assets; and the rest-of-the-world sector uses funds to purchase U.S. goods or services or to invest in U.S. securities. The numbers we use in Exhibit 7-5 are hypothetical. As can be seen, the surpluses of the rest-of-the-world and household sectors exactly offset the deficits of the business and government sectors.

Looking Back

The Historical Pattern of Surplus and Deficit Sectors

Historically, the household sector was consistently a surplus sector. However, a relatively large surplus fell consistently in the early 1990s and became a deficit in 1997. After a small surplus in 1998, the household sector has continuously run a deficit through 2007.

The nonfinancial business sector has consistently been a deficit sector with the exception of a few years in the early and mid–1990s. The business sector ran a deficit over $850 billion in 2007, and it appears that it will also run a significant deficit in 2008. It is expected that in future years it will invariably remain a deficit sector.

The government sector was a deficit sector in almost all of the years from 1960 through 1997. During the first quarter of 1998, the combined federal, state, and local government budgets were in surplus for the first time since 1969. However, the surplus years for the government sector were short-lived. By 2001, the government was again a deficit sector. Partially due to the financial crisis, large deficits loom on the horizon.

Since 1982, the rest-of-the-world sector has also been a surplus sector. In the 1990s, the surplus of the rest-of-the-world sector increased from $100 billion in 1992 to $263.6 billion in 1997 to $442 billion in 2000 and to $854.5 billion in 2007.

The format in Exhibit 7-5 allows us to analyze flows of funds among sectors, how those flows are intermediated, and how the Fed can monitor and influence them. During expansions, both income and interest rates normally rise along with the relative intentions to deficit spend. In recessions, the reverse happens. Nevertheless, no sector of the economy can run larger deficits unless other sectors accept larger surpluses.

Recap   If the combined surpluses of net lenders are greater than the combined deficits of the net borrowers, then the sector is a surplus sector. If the combined deficits of the net borrowers are greater than the combined surpluses of the net lenders, then the sector is a deficit sector. For all sectors combined, the surpluses must be equal to the deficits.

PULLING IT ALL TOGETHER

In this chapter, we have looked at the efficient markets hypothesis based on the theory of rational expectations. We have seen that prices of financial instruments adjust so that risk- and liquidity-adjusted returns for all financial instruments are equalized. We then looked at the flow of funds among sectors where the combined surpluses of the surplus sectors are just equal to the combined deficits of the deficit sectors.

Let's return to the example discussed earlier of expansionary monetary policy, where the Fed takes action that leads to a fall in interest rates. When this occurs, there is a reshuffling of prices of financial instruments and some spending units decide to spend more in response to the decline in interest rates. Some spending units that were net lenders are enticed to become net borrowers. In the aggregate, the surpluses and deficits within any sector change so that a sector that was a surplus sector may become a deficit sector, or vice versa. Thus, actions by the Fed not only influence financial prices but also the flow of funds among sectors. The important point is that there are significant linkages between the response of spending units to changes in interest rates and the flow of funds among sectors.

This completes our look at the efficient markets hypothesis and financial prices. We return to stocks and bonds in Chapters 13 and 14. In the next section of the text, we look at financial institutions and their evolution.

Summary of Major Points

1. If returns to various financial assets are not perfectly correlated, holding a portfolio of diversified assets reduces risk for any given expected return or increases expected return for any given level of risk. Thus, investors generally opt for a portfolio of various financial instruments with different risks and returns.

2. Prices of long-term financial instruments such as stocks and bonds change as current and future expected earnings change. If interest rates fall or rise, prices of previously issued bonds rise or fall, respectively. If current and expected future earnings rise, stock prices also rise, and vice versa. Thus, it is the expected return on bonds and the expected return on stocks that determine stock and bond prices.

3. Market participants compare expected rates of return for various financial instruments and select a combination of those with the highest expected return consistent with varying degrees of risk and liquidity. In equilibrium, differences in returns on various financial instruments reflect differences in risk and liquidity only.

4. Adaptive expectations are formed by looking at current and past prices. Rational expectations are formed by looking at past prices and all currently available information about the economy that may affect prices. The theory of rational expectations is that expectations will be equal to optimal forecasts or the best guesses possible based on all available information.

5. The efficient markets hypothesis says that when financial markets are in equilibrium, the prices of all financial instruments reflect all readily available information. The rationale behind the hypothesis is that if prices do not reflect all available information, there will be unexploited profit opportunities.

6. Market fundamentals are factors that have a direct effect on future income streams of financial instruments. A stronger version of the efficient markets hypothesis holds that prices of all financial instruments reflect the true fundamental value of the instrument.

7. The efficient markets hypothesis does not imply that all participants in the market must know the optimal forecast; it is necessary for only a few savvy investors to know the optimal forecast. These savvy investors will then drive the price to the optimal forecast by exploiting opportunities for profit. The efficient markets hypothesis implies that it is impossible to maintain an above average return for a long period of time. Bubbles, investments based on insider information, and market overreaction to new information are exceptions to the efficient markets hypothesis.

8. The flow of funds is a social accounting system that divides the economy into sectors and constructs a sources and uses of funds statement for each sector. For the economy as a whole, the combined surpluses of the surplus sectors must equal the combined deficits of the deficit sectors. When interest rates change, spending changes and some net lenders become net borrowers and vice versa. Thus, when deficits and surpluses for individual spending units change, the flow of funds among sectors is affected.

Key Terms

Review Questions

1. Explain why stock and bond prices adjust until investors are indifferent between stocks and bonds, given varying degrees of risk and liquidity.

2. What is diversification? What is the expected return to a portfolio that is composed of a variety of financial assets?

3. If the returns to two different financial instruments are perfectly positively correlated, can holding a combination of the two reduce risk for any given return? Explain. If the returns to two different financial instruments are perfectly negatively correlated, can holding a combination of the two reduce risk for any given return? Explain.

4. When full adjustment has occurred, what do differences in returns on various financial instruments reflect?

5. If current and expected earnings rise, what happens to stock prices?

6. Interest rates are going up. What happens to the prices of previously issued bonds?

7. How do adaptive expectations differ from rational expectations?

8. Why is the actual value of a financial variable different from the optimal forecast of that variable? Assuming that expectations are rational, what, on average, will be the difference between the actual value and the optimal forecast?

9. What is the efficient markets hypothesis? How does it differ from the stronger version of the hypothesis?

10. What is the fundamental value of a financial instrument?

11. What is the rationale behind the efficient markets hypothesis?

12. Explain why the expected return on newly issued and previously issued bonds is the prevailing interest rate plus any expected capital gain or loss.

13. Must all market participants know the optimal forecast of a financial instrument for the price of the financial instrument to be driven to the optimal forecast?

14. What is a "bubble" in a financial market? Can financial prices ever overshoot or undershoot optimal values?

15. News comes out that leads investors to believe that there is more risk involved with owning financial instrument A. What will happen to its equilibrium return?

16. If the household, business, and government sectors are all deficit sectors, what does this imply about the rest-of-the-world sector?

17. Assume that in 2009, the U.S. government wants to significantly increase the government deficit. What does this imply about the other sectors?

Analytical Questions

Questions marked with a check mark (✓) are objective in nature. They can be completed with a short answer or number.

✓18. If the current price of a share of stock that pays a $1 dividend is $20, and if the expected capital gain

is $2, what is the expected return? What is the return if there is an expected capital loss of $2?

✓19. Assume the equilibrium return on a financial instrument is 10 percent, and the instrument pays no dividends or interest. If the current price is

$100 and the expected future price one year from now just increased from $110 to $120, what will happen to the current price? What if the expected future price decreases from $110 to $100?

✓20. Assume that the equilibrium return on a financial instrument is 10 percent. If the current price is $100 and the instrument does not pay interest or dividend, what is the price expected one year from now when the market is in equilibrium? If the equilibrium return on the instrument increases to 15 percent because the instrument is perceived as more risky, what happens to the current price, assuming the expected price one year from now does not change?

✓21. Assume that HappyDays, Inc., pays an 8 percent return during expansions and a zero percent return during recessions with certainty. SadDays, Inc., pays a zero percent return in expansions and an 8 percent return in recessions with certainty. Show how the fluctuation in return is eliminated if an investor splits his or her surplus funds equally between HappyDays and SadDays.

Suggested Readings

For a look at the historical development of the efficient markets hypothesis, see **http://www.investorhome.com/emh.htm.**

For a discussion of the development of the rational expectations theory, see **http://www.minneapolisfed.org/pubs/ar/ar1977.cfm?js=0.**

Current flow of funds data can be found on the Fed's Web site at **http://www.federalreserve.gov.** They make for interesting analysis because of the sometimes dramatic changes in the flows of funds among sectors.

An analysis of flow of funds data can be found at the Financial Markets Center, **http://www.fmcenter.org.**

For an interesting article about the efficient markets hypothesis, see Justin Fox, "Efficient Markets? Hah!" *Fortune* 139:4 (March 1, 1999).

Robert A. Haugen wrote two interesting books that offer a contrary view: *The Inefficient Stock Market: What Pays Off and Why*, 2nd ed. (Upper Saddle River, NJ Pearson Education, 2002), and *The New Finance: Overreaction, Complexity, and Uniqueness*, 3rd ed. (Upper Saddle River, NJ: Prentice Hall, 2003).

Endnotes

1. Additional factors that can affect the prices of financial instruments are term to maturity, the taxability of earnings, and other supply and demand conditions affecting particular markets. For our purposes here, *term to maturity* is encompassed under risk with, ceteris paribus, longer-term instruments entailing more risk. Also by expected rates of return, we mean *after-tax returns*.

2. If a company pays out only a small portion of its earnings as dividends, then it has retained earnings, which it invests back into the company. Ceteris paribus, this usually leads to higher profits later. If the expected returns from retained earnings exceed the risk-adjusted returns that shareholders could expect to receive on alternative investments made with the dividends, a firm's stock price will rise, and the owner will earn a larger capital gain when the stock is sold. In the 1990s, the trend among many companies was against paying dividends so that profits could be plowed back into the corporation, thus "growing" the corporation. Due to changes in tax laws in the early 2000s that favored dividends over capital gains, the trend has been reversed.

3. Real national income is national income adjusted for changes in price or inflation. For our purposes, real national income is equivalent to real GDP.

4. The specifics of this relationship are fleshed out in Equation (7-3) on page 146.

5. Coupon payments are usually made semiannually. We are assuming annual coupon payments here to simplify. The assumption does not substantively change the results.

6. Hopefully, you recall from Chapter 5 that after bonds are issued, the price of the bond is equal to the present value of the dividend payments and the repayment of principal at maturity.

Thus, $1,339.67 is the present value of the 29 future dividend payments of $60, and the repayment of the $1,000 principle in 29 years. We are assuming that dividends are paid only once a year. If interest rates have fallen, the price of the bond increases. If this bond were a consol, the price of the bond would equal $1,500.

7. If both stocks and bonds have highly developed secondary markets, the assumption that they have the same degree of liquidity is not that unrealistic.

8. As previously noted, the decline in interest rates to 4 percent causes the prices of previously issued bonds to rise so that their risk-adjusted return equals 4 percent instead of 6 percent. Thus, the return on previously issued bonds will equal the return on newly issued bonds.

9. A more formal approach to this relationship between stock prices and interest rates uses the present value (discounting) analysis developed in Chapter 5. Within this framework, the share price is viewed as the discounted present value of a firm's expected earnings (or dividends). Accordingly, a fall in the interest rate and/or a rise in the stream of expected earnings increases the expected value of the firm—that is, the share price—in the market.

10. If the interest rate rises to 8 percent, then, in equilibrium, the risk-adjusted return on stocks will rise to 10 percent, assuming that the typical investor must be compensated 2 percent for the additional risk of owning stocks. The price of a typical share will initially fall to $40 because $4 / $40 = .10 = 10 percent. Assuming the higher interest rate reduces demand and hence earnings, the dividend may be expected to fall to $3. If this is the case, the stock price falls further to $30 because $3 / $30 = .10 = 10 percent.

11. For simplicity's sake, we are assuming that despite the higher profit expectations, the dividend remains the same.

12. Historically, the rest-of-the-world sector has been called the foreign sector. We use the more up-to-date terminology currently used by the Fed.

8

Presume not that I am the thing I was.

—William Shakespeare

An Introduction to Financial Intermediaries and Risk

Learning Objectives

After reading this chapter, you should know:

The characteristics common to all types of
financial intermediaries (FIs)

The services provided by FIs

The types of risks FIs must manage

The principal assets and liabilities of the
major FIs

ARE ALL FINANCIAL INTERMEDIARIES MORE OR LESS ALIKE?

It is the last day of the month. Sandi and Dave have both been paid by their employers, and it's now time to pay the family's bills and save something for their upcoming vacation. Sitting at the kitchen table, they write checks on their account at HLT National Bank to Prudential Insurance Company for the premium due on Sandi's life insurance policy, APEI Credit Union for the car loan payment, and the local savings and loan (S&L) association for the mortgage payment. When these and other bills are paid, a check for the surplus funds to be saved is sent to their money market mutual fund account at Vanguard.

In this hypothetical series of transactions, Sandi and Dave dealt with five different financial intermediaries (FIs): a commercial bank, an insurance company, a credit union, an S&L, and a money market mutual fund. Why five instead of one? Can't one provide all of the relevant services? Put another way, how are these intermediaries similar to one another, and how do they differ? This chapter will examine the characteristics and roles of those institutions that provide the public with a wide range of financial services and play a central role in coordinating and channeling the flow of funds in the economy.

As we begin, we should emphasize that financial innovation, which is the creation of new financial instruments, markets, and institutions, has been the key to growth and survival in the financial services industry in the last 45 years.[1] Institutional details in the financial services industry are currently evolving at a rapid pace due to changes in technology and the globalization of finance. In a few years or sooner, Sandi and Dave may be paying their monthly bills as they sit in front of a computer terminal, and many of their payments may be made automatically from their checking account. After all, many households already do just that. In subsequent chapters, we analyze the forces that have previously produced major changes in the financial system and are likely to remain influential in the future.

Financial Innovation
The creation of new financial instruments, markets, and institutions in the financial services industry.

COMMON CHARACTERISTICS

Financial intermediaries (FIs) link up net borrowers and net lenders and, in the process, provide the public with a wide range of financial services. Recall from Chapter 1 that a *net lender* is a spending unit such as a firm or household for which spending on consumption and investment is less than income. Likewise, a *net borrower* is a spending unit for which spending is greater than income. The linking function involves the acquisition of financial claims on net borrowers by the FIs and the acquisition of claims on the FIs by net lenders. The net borrowers sell financial claims against themselves, which the intermediaries purchase. The financial claims may be signed loan papers, equities, or securities. In this context, when we say FIs make loans to net borrowers, the FIs are purchasing financial claims, which are the signed loan papers, from the net borrowers. The intermediaries get the funds to lend by selling their own financial claims that the net lenders purchase. The financial claims against the FIs include checking, time, and savings deposits, among others. Even though funds flow ultimately from net lenders to net borrowers, the intermediaries do more than act as a go-between. The net lenders acquire claims against the FIs, which sell their own liabilities; thus, the FIs are in debt to the net lenders.[2]

FIs, along with the investment banking and securities firms we met in the last chapter, make up the *financial services industry*. In the process of acquiring and providing funds, FIs provide the public with a wide range of financial services. FIs are by and large profit seeking.[3] In this context, this means that FIs provide financial services because

FIs as Firms

FIs are firms. We generally think of, say, manufacturing firms as acquiring inputs, including land, labor, and capital, and using these inputs to produce outputs. In the case of FIs, their inputs are their liabilities, or sources of funds. These funds are used to extend loans and acquire securities. Such financial claims are their assets and represent the outputs of the FIs. Banks, for example, incur deposit liabilities as a source of funds and use the funds to increase their asset holdings of loans and securities. Insurance companies receive premium payments from policyholders (inputs) and use the funds received to acquire assets—mainly loans and securities (outputs).

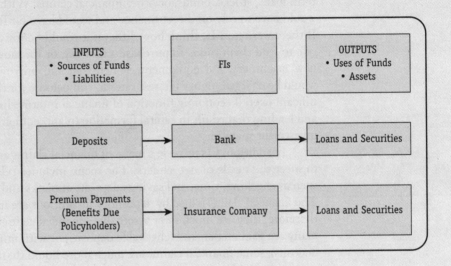

doing so is profitable. The quantity, quality, and type of financial services offered will expand or contract as the perceived profitability of this activity changes.

To illustrate, banks "hire" funds from depositors. The interest a bank pays on its deposits is a cost of doing business, akin to the wages a manufacturing firm pays its workers. The bank then lends out the funds it acquires to consumers, businesses, and governments. The interest earned on the loans represents revenue to the bank, akin to the revenue generated by a manufacturing firm's sales. Leaving some details aside, the difference between the interest earned and the interest paid is a primary determinant of the bank's profitability. If funds can be hired more cheaply by providing a new type of deposit service, FIs have an incentive to act accordingly. Similarly, if a particular type of lending turns out to be less profitable than expected, FIs have an incentive to lend less in this area or to attempt in some way to increase the expected revenue associated with such lending. As we shall see, the link between expected profitability and the specific services provided by FIs is a crucial part of the explanation of why FIs change over time.

The public demands financial services provided by FIs to reduce the risks and costs associated with borrowing, lending, and other financial transactions, and to fulfill the demand for various financial assets and services, including protection against the financial losses associated with various exigencies.

FIs use their expertise to appraise the risk of default associated with lending to particular borrowers. They usually do a better job of assessing these risks than individuals could do on their own. FIs pool the surpluses of many net lenders and lend to thousands of net borrowers. Diversification is spreading out the individual surpluses of net lenders among numerous borrowers. As long as the returns to different assets fluctuate differently diversification reduces the risk of losses for net lenders. Risk is diffused among thousands of borrowers, all of whom are not likely to default at the same time. The net lenders are no longer putting all of their eggs in one or a few baskets.

On the flip side, by buying the financial liabilities of net borrowers, the FIs provide borrowing opportunities for net borrowers. The liabilities may be long- or short-term loans, stocks, bonds, or other financial claims. Without the FIs, the net borrowers would have to rely on direct finance and would have far fewer or no borrowing sources. If there were no FIs, think how difficult it would be for most individuals to find someone to lend them funds to purchase a new car, or for most firms to borrow to purchase new machinery and equipment. When they did borrow, undoubtedly net borrowers would be charged higher interest rates to compensate for the greater risks. Thus, the significant overall economic function of financial intermediation is to facilitate borrowing and lending that result in capital formation (plant, equipment, and the like) and in other investment spending.

In addition, FIs provide a menu of financial claims and depository services tailored to meet the needs of net lenders. The menu includes relatively safe and liquid claims, such as checking, time, and savings deposits at banks and other depository institutions. The financial claims issued by depository institutions are insured up to $250,000 in 2009; therefore, they are much safer assets than financial claims that are not insured. Because many are paid on demand (checkable deposits) or with minimal hassle (time and savings deposits), some financial claims are much more liquid than other claims. If I make a loan to an individual borrower and an unexpected need arises whereby I need the funds back before the due date, the borrower may be unable or unwilling to pay me back early. Liquidity would not be a problem if I had my funds in insured checkable, savings, or time deposits.

FIs such as casualty and life insurance benefits offer the public a menu of contingent claims that provide some protection from the often catastrophic financial effects of theft, accidents, natural disasters, and death in exchange for regular premium payments. Again, the premium payments are collected from thousands of policyholders, and the guarantees spread out or diffused over the same policyholders.

With FIs playing such a vital role in the economy, it should not be surprising that they share another common feature. They are regulated by various levels and agencies of government. Government regulators establish and enforce operating regulations aimed at promoting a smooth-running, efficient financial system and protecting the public from fraud and other abusive practices. The regulators seek to promote competition in the market for financial services while preserving the public's confidence in the safety and soundness of the system.

Regulations represent an attempt to constrain or restrict an activity that might otherwise occur. In the financial system, regulations take on many forms. Entry into the industry is tightly controlled. For example, someone cannot just open a bank. A charter from the federal government or relevant state government is needed. There are

Diversification
The allocation of surplus funds to more than one financial instrument in order to reduce risk.

Contingent Claims
Claims such as casualty and life insurance benefits that offer the public protection from the often-catastrophic financial effects of theft, accidents, natural disasters, and death.

also restrictions on the particular types of assets and liabilities that specific FIs can acquire. S&Ls, for example, cannot acquire common stock. In the past, regulations limited the interest rates that FIs could pay on certain types of deposits and charge on certain types of loans. In addition, regulations have historically restricted the geographical areas in which some FIs could operate, although such restrictions have, for the most part, been eliminated.

Financial system regulations, examined in detail in Chapter 12, have had at least three major effects:

1. For quite a while, they tended to reinforce and encourage specialization by FIs in particular financial services. For example, life insurance companies stuck pretty much to providing life insurance, and S&Ls stuck to purchasing mortgages. More directly, the regulations tended to limit competition among different types of FIs.

2. Such specialization helps to explain the different types and mix of assets and liabilities that individual FIs hold.

3. Over time, FIs increasingly saw the benefits of diversifying. In other words, they saw that providing the public with a wider range of financial services could be profitable. Attempts to move in such a direction often involved innovations that got around some existing regulations, particularly restrictions that limited the range of services that FIs could provide and the competition among FIs in general. As you shall see in Chapters 9 and 12, legislation in late 1999 allowed commercial banks, securities firms, and insurance companies to affiliate under common ownership. Thus, one firm can offer its customers a complete range of financial services.

As we shall see, Sandi and Dave, whom we met at the beginning of the chapter, may be dealing with far fewer than five FIs if they do business with a one-stop financial conglomerate that offers an array of financial services.

Recap   FIs possess many common traits. In general, they are regulated, profit-seeking firms that provide the public with a wide range of financial services. These services help to reduce the risks associated with channeling funds from net lenders to net borrowers. The services provided include the appraisal and diversification of risk, the pooling of funds, and the provision of a menu of claims, including contingent claims, tailored to the needs of customers.

TYPES OF RISKS FACED BY ALL FIs

FIs are faced with different types of risk in varying degrees, depending on the composition of their assets and liabilities. We first review the types of risks common to all intermediaries and net lenders and net borrowers in general.

Credit or Default Risk

Default Risk
The risk that a borrower will be unwilling or unable to live up to the terms of the liability it has sold.

Credit or default risk is the risk that the borrower will be unwilling or unable to live up to the terms of the liability it has sold. Perhaps the borrower is a firm that uses the funds for expansion, but the business it thought would boom turns out to be a bust because of some unanticipated complication or a general slowdown in the economy. For whatever reason, when making a loan or buying a financial security issued by a borrower, the FI, whether it be a bank, mutual fund, or insurance company, is exposed to the risk that the borrower will default.

A primary function of the management of an FI is to evaluate the credit risk associated with purchasing the financial claims of net borrowers such as firms, individuals, and domestic and foreign governments. To do this, FIs employ experts in risk assessment who generally do a better job of assessing default risks than individuals could do on their own. Managers of FIs must be aware that they are making decisions under conditions of asymmetric information. **Asymmetric information** means that a potential borrower or issuer of securities knows more about the risks of an investment project than the FI's managers (the individuals who have to make the funding decision). Thus, the borrower and the lender do not have equal, or symmetric, information. After all, don't many of those who apply for a loan or issue securities obviously try to put their best foot forward and conceal any blemishes? In addition, those with the most to hide and those willing to take the biggest risks are often the most likely to be less than forthright and/or to pursue borrowing most diligently. If the net lenders fund these less-desirable borrowers, the result is an **adverse selection problem,** which increases the risk of default.

Asymmetric Information
When a potential borrower knows more about the risks and returns of an investment project than the bank loan officer does.

Adverse Selection Problem
When the least-desirable borrowers pursue a loan most diligently.

Moral Hazard Problem
When the borrower has an incentive to use the proceeds of a loan for a riskier venture after the loan is funded.

Moreover, after the loan is made or a security is purchase by an FI, it may be difficult to guarantee that the funds are used only for the stated purpose and not for a more risky venture. This so-called **moral hazard problem** results from the fact that once borrowers get the funds, they may have an incentive to engage in a more risky venture, because higher-risk ventures pay a higher return. After all, the borrowers are not risking their own funds. If the borrowers win, they keep the bigger profits; but if they lose, the lender bears the loss.

In reality, managing credit risk does not mean denying loans to all borrowers who may default or failing to make any investments that could go sour. Maintaining and enhancing profitability in the financial services industry, as in other industries, entails taking some risks. The future is uncertain. Unforeseen events can turn an otherwise profitable endeavor into a losing and perhaps bankrupt situation. Thus, a "good" credit risk can become a "bad" investment. A fact of economic life is that despite good intentions, decent planning, and a successful track record, some borrowers will default. Conversely, some who have experienced financial difficulties in the past will "turn the corner" and become quite profitable.

The task of financial managers is to lend and invest prudently. In general, this means gathering all relevant information on potential borrowers and using this information to avoid exposing the FI to excessive risk. The information should include income statements, credit checks, net worth, how funds are to be used, and so on. Recognize that the words *prudent* and *excessive* are somewhat nebulous. An FI's management team must establish guidelines that quantify the terms. Losses will occur. The trick is to cover the losses with profits on other loans and investments.

Interest Rate Risk

Interest Rate Risk
The risk that the interest rate will unexpectedly change so that the costs of an FI's liabilities exceed the earnings on its assets.

Another type of risk that must be managed is the **interest rate risk.** This is the risk that the interest rate will unexpectedly change so that the costs of an FI's liabilities exceed the earnings on its assets. This risk emanates from the relationship between the interest rate earned on assets and the cost of, or interest rate paid on, liabilities. An FI's profitability is directly related to the spread between these rates. FIs obviously strive for a large positive spread in which the return on assets significantly exceeds the cost of liabilities.

For example, FIs often borrow short term through savings deposits or commercial paper and make long-term loans or purchase long-term fixed rate financial assets, such as bonds or mortgages. When FIs borrow short and lend long, they are exposed to an interest rate risk. If the interest rate goes up, the cost of the short-term liabilities rises much more quickly than the returns on the long-term assets. Profits are reduced or can even turn into a losses.[4] This risk was a chronic problem for some intermediaries, particularly the S&L industry during the 1970s and 1980s, when the financial system was deregulated and interest rates fluctuated over a fairly wide range. FIs have responded to this changing environment in a variety of ways, including using adjustable rate loans. Rates on adjustable loans change as market interest rates change. FIs have also made extensive use of financial futures, options, and swaps options to hedge interest rate risk. These instruments will be analyzed in detail in Chapter 16.

Liquidity Risk

Liquidity risk is the risk that an FI will be required to make a payment when the assets that the intermediary has available to make the payment are long term and cannot be converted to liquid funds quickly without a capital loss. Such a situation could occur when depositors unexpectedly withdraw funds or when an insurance company incurs unexpectedly high claim losses as a result of an earthquake, fire, flood, or hurricane. All intermediaries may experience a sudden unexpected need for funds, but depository institutions are particularly vulnerable to a deposit run that can cause a financial crisis: their reserves are only a fraction of their liabilities and those liabilities are often payable on demand. The Fed stands ready to provide liquidity for depository institutions by acting as a lender of last resort. FIs can reduce their liquidity risk by holding highly liquid assets that can be converted quickly into the funds needed to meet unexpected withdrawals or contingencies. They can also make other arrangements such as backup lines of credit to meet unexpected needs.

Exchange Rate Risk

Economies have become increasingly international and global. As a consequence, many large FIs and other corporations maintain stocks of foreign currencies that are used in international transactions. In addition, some FIs may hold financial assets that are denominated in foreign currencies, such as foreign stocks or bonds. Exchange rates between various currencies fluctuate day-by-day and minute-by-minute based on the forces of supply and demand. We study the details of this in Chapter 22. An FI, like any holder of foreign exchange or foreign financial assets, is subject to an **exchange rate risk**, where changes in exchange rates cause the dollar value of foreign currency or foreign financial assets to fall. For example, assume that an FI holds 10,000,000 yen or a financial asset valued at 10,000,000 yen. If the exchange rate is $1 = 100$ yen, then 10,000,000 yen are worth $100,000 because (10,000,000 yen)/(100 yen) = $100,000/$1$. If the dollar exchange rate increases to $1 equals 200 yen, then the 10,000,000 yen are worth only $50,000 because (10,000,000 yen)/(200 yen) equals $50,000/$1$. A loss is incurred that is proportional to the amount of foreign currency or foreign financial assets that are held and to the change in the exchange rate. As you shall see in Chapter 16, foreign exchange forward contracts, futures, options, and swaps can be used to mitigate this risk. Exhibit 8-1 summarizes the types of risks faced by all intermediaries.

Recap   All FIs face several risks in varying degrees. Default risk is the risk that the borrower will not pay the financial claim. Asymmetric information is when a potential borrower knows more about the risks of an investment project than the lender. Adverse selection is when the least desirable borrowers pursue borrowing most diligently. Moral hazard is when a borrower has an incentive (the potential for higher profits) to use the borrowed funds for

> Default Risk—The risk that the borrower will not pay the principal and interest on a financial claim when due.
>
> Interest Rate Risk—The risk that changes in interest rates will reduce or eliminate a positive spread between assets and liabilities, thereby leading to potential losses.
>
> Liquidity Risk—The risk that an intermediary will need to make a payment and not have liquid funds available to do so because its long-term assets cannot be liquidated quickly without loss of value.
>
> Exchange Rate Risk—The risk that FIs that are holding stockpiles of foreign currencies or financial assets denominated in foreign currencies experience losses because of adverse changes in exchanges rate between the currencies.

a more risky venture. Interest rate risk is the risk that will occur when changes in the interest rate will turn a profitable spread into a loss. Liquidity risk is the risk that funds will not be available when needed. Exchange rate risk occurs when changes in exchange rates will cause the FI to experience losses in the dollar value of foreign currency or foreign financial assets.

A GUIDE TO FIs

The assets of FIs are financial claims such as loans and securities. The liabilities are financial liabilities such as deposits and borrowed funds. Various intermediaries hold different kinds of assets and liabilities. For any FI, net worth is the excess value of assets over liabilities. If the value of liabilities exceeds the value of assets, call the bankruptcy lawyer!

The nature of the liabilities sold by a particular type of FI bears a close relationship to the nature of the assets it acquires. More specifically, the maturity, stability, riskiness, and liquidity of an FI's liabilities affect the types of assets the FI chooses to purchase. In other words, the structure of an FI's assets and liabilities affects the exposure to the specific risks discussed in the preceding section and how it must manage each.

Deposit-Type FIs

Thrifts
Depository institutions known as S&Ls, savings banks, and credit unions.

Depository institutions include commercial banks, S&Ls, savings banks, and credit unions. The S&Ls, savings banks, and credit unions are called thrifts. As the term *depository institution* implies, a large portion of the liabilities of these FIs are deposits. The depository institutions have issued the deposits in order to obtain funds (inputs) that can be used to make loans and other investments (outputs). Deposit-type FIs are also important in the nation's money supply process because many of their deposit liabilities are checkable deposits.[5] Let's take a closer look at the institutions within this category.

Commercial Banks

Commercial Banks
Depository institutions that issue checkable, time, and savings deposit liabilities and, among other things, make loans to commercial businesses.

The word *bank* is derived from the Italian word *banca*, which refers to the "table, counter, or place of business of a money changer." Although modern banks bear little physical resemblance to ancient money changers, their functions remain quite similar. In modern parlance, **commercial banks** are typically defined as institutions that issue checkable deposit liabilities and extend loans to commercial businesses. These two characteristics help to differentiate banks from other FIs; but, of course, banks do many other things, too. For example, banks also issue time and savings deposits and offer many other types of loans, including mortgages and consumer loans. In addition, they provide electronic funds transfers, debit cards, international trade-related payments, credit cards, leasing, trust services, financial guarantees, and advisory and accounting services. Chapter 9 tells more about bank services.

A bank's success depends on many factors, but especially important is its ability to attract funds by offering deposit liabilities. Deposits fall into three categories: transactions deposits, savings deposits, and time deposits. **Transactions deposits** (checkable deposits) can be exchanged for currency and are used in transactions to make payments to others by transferring the deposit claim; the transfer is made by writing a check or making an electronic transfer. **Savings deposits** cannot be withdrawn by writing a check but are highly liquid. By custom, banks usually allow withdrawals on demand, although a waiting period could be required. **Time deposits** have a scheduled maturity, and if funds are withdrawn before that date, there is a penalty, usually the forfeiture of some interest that has already been earned. As you first saw in Chapter 2, another kind of account, a money market deposit account, has the characteristics of both transactions and savings deposits.[6] Deposits are by far the main source of bank funds; consequently, banks continually strive to increase deposits. In addition, in recent decades, banks have developed other nondeposit sources of funds such as borrowing in the fed funds, repurchase agreements, and Eurodollar markets. A bank's success depends on local and regional factors, such as the population and economic vitality of the bank's service area and its ability to attract deposits away from competing FIs or from banks in other geographical regions. National factors and monetary policy are also important in determining a bank's success.

A bank must decide how best to use its funds to meet its objectives. One obvious objective is to maximize profits. Stockholders will see to it that the bank's management does not lose sight of this goal. Banking can be a risky business, however, and the management and stockholders will also want to minimize the risks faced in the pursuit of profits. In particular, the bank will try to diversify its portfolio in a way that will ensure a considerable margin of liquidity and safety. Banks seek safety because they are highly leveraged institutions; that is, their assets are overwhelmingly supported by borrowed funds, which are either deposit or nondeposit liabilities. Banks hold a mix of loans (including business loans, consumer credit, and mortgages), government securities, municipal securities, corporate and foreign bonds, and other assets. In late 2008, banks' holdings of real estate loans (mortgages) were 75 percent greater than their holdings of business loans. This represents a dramatic change over the past 30 years, because business loans were traditionally the lending venue for banks, while mortgages were held primarily by S&Ls. It also made many banks vulnerable to the collapse in the subprime mortgage markets in 2007–2008. With the passage of legislation in 1999, banks may also underwrite and deal in municipal revenue bonds.

In addition to these interest-earning assets, banks also hold reserve (cash) assets to help meet their liquidity and safety objectives. Another reason that banks hold reserve assets is that the Fed forces them to do so. As we first saw in Chapter 3, the Fed sets reserve ratios that require banks to possess reserve assets equal to a certain percentage of checkable deposit liabilities.

Banks' concerns about liquidity are generated in part by the nature of their sources of funds. For example, checkable deposits, which are obviously payable on demand, can and often do fluctuate widely. Nondeposit liabilities have the potential to fluctuate even more. For example, if a bank's solvency is questioned or if another depository institution

Transactions Deposits
Deposits that can be exchanged for currency and are used to make payments through writing a check or making an electronic transfer.

Savings Deposits
Highly liquid deposits that can usually be withdrawn on demand but not by writing a check.

Time Deposits
Deposits that have a scheduled maturity and a penalty for early withdrawal.

offers more attractive rates, a bank can quickly lose some nondeposit funds such as fed funds, repurchase agreements, and Eurodollar borrowings that are usually placed for a relatively short time period.[7] When deposits and nondeposit liabilities fall, even the most solvent bank must have a cushion of liquidity to enable it to meet these withdrawals. Such liquidity needs can be satisfied by holding some highly liquid assets, such as Treasury bills and non-interest-bearing cash reserves. Banks may also hold liquid assets so they will be able to accommodate unexpected loan demand from valued customers. If profits were all that mattered, a bank would never hold a Treasury bill yielding, say, 5 percent if another equally safe asset such as a guaranteed student loan yielding, say, 6 percent were available. However, the liquidity of Treasury bills in effect provides an implicit return to banks in addition to the explicit yield.

Guided by its liquidity, safety, and earnings objectives, a bank must make portfolio decisions regarding the optimal mix of loans, securities, and reserves that it will hold. Simply put, this means the bank must decide on the best way to use its funds.

The *capital base* (or net worth) is the value of the bank's assets less the value of its liabilities. In general, the smaller the capital base, the more vulnerable the bank is to adverse developments. Assume that some of a bank's larger loans go sour. The borrowers default and fail to pay the principal and interest due. These defaults will reduce the cushion provided by the bank's capital base and push the bank toward insolvency and bankruptcy. For example, suppose the bank's capital base amounts to 8.4 percent of assets. Thus, for every $1,000,000 in assets, the bank holds only $84,000 in capital. If loans are 65 percent of assets, then loans amount to $650,000 ($.65 \times \$1,000,000$). The bank's capital will be gone if 12.9 percent of its $650,000 loans go sour because $84,000 is 12.9 percent of $650,000 ($\$84,000 = .129 \times \$650,000$). This is an equivalent way of saying that the bank has lost all of its capital. Thus, regulators are concerned that banks maintain adequate capital.

Savings Associations

Savings associations include S&Ls and savings banks. **Savings and loan associations (S&Ls)**, originally known as *building and loan associations*, were founded in the United States in the early 1830s. Their express purpose was to pool the savings of local residents to finance the construction and purchase of homes. **Savings banks** predate the S&Ls by about 20 years and are located mostly on the East Coast of the United States. Sixty percent are in New York and Massachusetts. Like S&Ls, savings banks were founded to encourage thrift and to help finance the construction and purchase of homes.[8]

Although the assets of S&Ls are much larger than those of savings banks, we discuss S&Ls and savings banks together as savings associations because their assets and liabilities have a similar composition and because the institutions share other commonalities. The major sources of funds for savings associations are time, savings, and checkable deposits. In the aggregate, these deposits accounted for about 65 percent of total liabilities on September 30, 2008. As in commercial banks, most deposits are insured for up to $250,000. Savings associations were first allowed to issue negotiable orders of withdrawal (NOW) accounts (interest-earning checkable deposits) nationwide in 1980. Checkable deposits make up a growing source of funds for savings associations. They use the funds mainly to acquire mortgage loans, which comprised about 58 percent of total assets held on September 30, 2008. Treasury, agency, and government-sponsored enterprises securities made up about 16 percent of assets.

Although they still specialized in mortgage lending, savings associations diversified somewhat during the 1980s into various forms of lending that had previously been prohibited by regulations. Other regulatory changes allowed the institutions to offer time deposits with rates that went up and down with rates on money market instruments, such as Treasury bills.

Prior to the 1980s, savings associations were not only prohibited from offering checkable deposits but also not allowed to pay rates on time and savings deposits that exceeded a ceiling rate set by regulators. In this earlier environment, small savings deposits were the major source of funds for savings associations. Small savers found passbook savings accounts attractive relative to the alternatives then available to them. The accounts were liquid, safe, insured stores of value with fixed interest rates. In the new environment, savings associations have more flexibility and now offer the public more diverse types of liabilities. As a result, there is more competition among banks, S&Ls, and savings banks to attract checkable and flexible rate time deposits.

During the 1980s, the S&L industry experienced multiple strains that came to be known as the *savings and loan crisis*. More than 500 institutions became insolvent and were seized by regulators during the late 1980s at the taxpayers' expense. The bailout also benefited taxpayers by maintaining the solvency of the financial system. The **Financial Institutions Reform, Recovery, and Enforcement Act (FIRREA) of 1989** attempted to resolve the crisis by creating a new federal regulatory structure, limiting the assets that S&Ls can acquire, and requiring S&Ls to maintain adequate capital. The final cost to the taxpayers for the bailout was approximately $124 billion, which was much less than initial estimates. (More on the S&L crisis in Chapter 11.) Although heavily committed to the mortgage market, savings banks were somewhat more judicious in their lending and consequently avoided some of the strains experienced by the S&Ls. Many savings and loans are again experiencing severe strains in the financial crisis of 2008. The collapse of Washington Mutual and buyout by J.P Morgan that was orchestrated by the Fed in September 2008 represented the largest failure of a depository institution in history.

The changes in the structure of the assets and liabilities of savings associations over time suggest that FIs' areas of specialization are increasingly overlapping. Furthermore, recent legislation now allows banks and savings associations to merge. Reflecting this trend, the word *bank* is often used generically by the press and the public to refer to commercial banks, S&Ls, and savings banks.

Credit Unions

Credit unions cater almost exclusively to small savers and borrowers. They are cooperative, nonprofit, tax-exempt associations operated solely for the benefit of members. By law, members must share a "common bond" such as through an employer, a church, or a labor union. In 2003, the "common bond" rules were relaxed so that credit unions can get a "community charter" that allows a more widespread and diverse membership. Although there are about 11,500 credit unions, most are small in size; 60 percent have total assets of $10 million or less. As in other depository institutions, deposits may be insured for up to $100,000.

Credit unions get most of their funds from members' savings accounts. In addition, as with S&Ls, regulatory changes first permitted credit unions to offer checkable deposits in 1980. Interest-earning checking accounts at credit unions are called *share drafts*, and they are now a significant liability for credit unions. As of September 30, 2008, about 30 percent of the assets held by credit unions were in the form of consumer loans to members, while about 42 percent were mortgages. Credit unions, which are tax-exempt, generally do not hold municipal securities.

Financial Institutions Reform, Recovery, and Enforcement Act (FIRREA) of 1989
An act that attempted to resolve the S&L crisis by creating a new regulatory structure, limiting the assets S&Ls can acquire, and requiring S&Ls to maintain adequate capital.

Credit Unions
Depository institutions that are cooperative, nonprofit, tax-exempt associations operated for the benefit of members who share a common bond.

The total funds acquired and loaned by credit unions have grown rapidly over the years. In 1970, for example, their assets totaled only $18 billion. The comparable late 2008 figure was $801.5 billion. Credit union assets increased almost fortyfold while prices increased a little more than fivefold! Being nonprofit institutions, credit unions have often offered depositors slightly higher rates and loan applicants slightly lower rates than have competing FIs. This advantage, along with the convenient locations of some credit unions (close proximity to businesses or the company cafeteria, for example), and the more recent relaxation of the "common bond" rules helps to explain their growth.

Recap	The major sources of funds for commercial banks are checkable, savings, and time deposits, plus nondeposit liabilities. The major uses of funds by banks include loans, government securities, and reserves. Because of legislation passed in 1999, banks have also been authorized to underwrite and deal in municipal revenue bonds. For S&Ls, the major sources of funds are time, savings, and checkable deposits, while the major use of funds is to make mortgage loans. Credit unions are tax-exempt and small in size but numerous. Their main sources of funds are share drafts and small savings accounts. They primarily make small personal and mortgage loans to their members.

Contractual-Type FIs

Contractual-type FIs have liabilities that are defined by contract. These contracts call for regular payments to be made to the FIs in exchange for future payments under specified conditions. As mentioned earlier, these claims are often referred to as *contingent claims*. The major contractual types of FIs are life insurance companies, property and casualty insurance companies, public pension funds, and private pension funds.

Life Insurance Companies
Intermediaries that offer protection against the financial costs associated with events such as death and disability in exchange for premiums.

Life insurance companies offer the public protection against the financial costs, losses, and reductions in income associated with death, disability, old age, and various other health problems. Based on the principle of risk sharing, the public makes payments, generally called *premiums*, in exchange for this protection. The companies lend out the funds collected to other households, businesses, and governments who are net borrowers by purchasing their securities (loans, stocks, and bonds). The insurance companies use the interest and dividend income received from the securities purchased, along with the premiums, to pay benefits to policyholders as they come due. The influx of premium payments is relatively steady and predictable; statisticians (actuaries) can predict fairly well the proportion of policyholders likely to become disabled, die, or become ill in a given year, so life insurance companies have a reasonably predictable stream of benefit payments to policyholders distributed over time. This allows these institutions to use a fairly large portion of their funds to acquire longer-term assets. Longer-term instruments generally provide higher yields than shorter-term assets but are not as liquid. Given the nature of the companies' liabilities, holding a large portion of liquid assets is not as essential for them as it is for banks. For example, on September 30, 2008, about 39 percent of life insurance companies' assets were corporate and foreign bonds, about 25 percent were equities, and at least 14 percent were other long-term securities. Thus, over 78 percent of their assets were long term. The liabilities are the policy benefits (reserves) that are due and will be paid to policyholders in the future.

Pension Funds
Tax-exempt intermediaries set up to provide participants with income at retirement in exchange for premiums.

Pension funds are tax-exempt institutions set up to provide participants with retirement income that will supplement other sources of income, such as social security benefits. Some pension plans are run by private corporations, and others are associated with federal, state, or local governments. In most cases, both employers and employees make contributions (pay premiums) to the pension fund. Like life insurance companies, pension funds have little need for a large amount of liquid assets. The number of people likely to retire each year is quite predictable. As a result, private pension funds and those associated with governments place a large percent of their funds—acquired through the contributions of employees and employers—into long-term assets. As of September 30, 2008, corporate equities, Treasury and agency securities, mutual funds, and corporate and foreign bonds (all long-term assets) made up over 75 percent of the assets of pension funds. Pension funds are the largest single class of investors in equities! The liabilities of pension funds are the policy benefits that will be paid out to policyholders in the future.

Property and Casualty Companies
Intermediaries that provide protection against the effects of unexpected occurrences on property.

Property and casualty companies provide protection against the untoward effects of unexpected occurrences on property, particularly automobiles and homes, in exchange for premiums. Two factors are relevant in trying to understand the composition of assets held by these FIs: (1) unlike pension funds, which are nontaxable, and life insurance companies, which are taxed at a very low rate, property and casualty companies are taxed at the full 38 percent corporate rate; and (2) compared to life insurance companies and pension funds, the stream of benefit payments made by these companies is less predictable. Accidents and natural disasters do not follow the more regular patterns of retirement and death. The Northridge, California, earthquake in 1994, Hurricane Opal in 1995, the attacks on the World Trade Center and the Pentagon on September 11, 2001, and Hurricane Katrina in 2005 account for some of the largest losses for property and casualty companies in history. Property and casualty companies need liquid assets to meet large and small exigencies. Tax considerations led these companies to hold over 28 percent of their assets in the form of tax-exempt municipal securities as of September 30, 2008. The need for liquidity helps to explain why over 7 percent of assets were held in the form of checkable deposits, currency, and repurchase agreements. The liabilities of property and casualty companies are the claims that will be paid out in the future.

Investment-Type FIs

The major types of intermediaries in the investment category are mutual funds, also known as *investment companies*, and money market mutual funds. Generally speaking, **mutual funds** acquire and pool funds from the public, invest the funds primarily in capital market instruments, and return the income received minus a management fee to the investors. Some funds invest in particular types of securities, such as corporate stocks and bonds, while others have broader asset portfolios that include stocks, bonds, mortgages, and so on. In the 1990s, mutual funds experienced tremendous growth. Small depositors poured money into mutual funds seeking higher returns than the low rates depository institutions were offering at the time. Mutual funds began expanding to offer other financial services previously provided by banks. Concern has been expressed regarding the adequacy of the regulation of mutual funds, given their tremendous growth in the 1990s (more on this in Chapter 19) and revelations of unethical and illegal trading by some mutual funds in the early 2000s. As of September 30, 2008, assets of mutual funds totaled $6,588.3 billion. The liabilities of mutual funds are the outstanding shares in the mutual fund.

Mutual Funds
Investment-type intermediaries that pool the funds of net lenders, purchase the long-term financial claims of net borrowers, and return the income received minus a fee to the net lenders.

Money market mutual funds, mentioned briefly in Chapter 2, are mutual funds that limit the type of financial claims they purchase. They acquire funds from

Money Market Mutual Funds
Mutual funds that invest in money market instruments.

individual investors and pool them to purchase money market instruments such as Treasury bills, bank CDs, and commercial paper. They do not invest in capital market instruments. The interest earned, minus a management fee, is then paid to investors. As of September 30, 2008, the assets of money market mutual funds were $3,376.5 billion. The liabilities of the money market mutual funds are the outstanding shares of the fund. Money market mutual funds came under severe stress in the financial crisis of 2007–2008. Nervous depositors were withdrawing funds from what were uninsured accounts. On September 19, 2008, the Treasury announced the creation of a plan that would insure money market mutual fund accounts for the next year, up to any account value. Money market mutual funds would pay a fee to participate in the insurance program.

Finance Company-Type FIs

Finance Companies
Intermediaries that lend funds to households to finance consumer purchases and to firms to finance inventories.

Finance companies such as Household Finance Corporation, Beneficial Finance, Commercial Credit Corporation, and the General Motors Acceptance Corporation lend funds to households to finance the purchase of consumer durables such as automobiles, appliances, and furniture or homes, and to businesses to finance inventories and the purchase or leasing of equipment. In the past, finance companies often loaned to borrowers considered risky by other types of FIs, particularly depository institutions. Today, finance companies lend to all types of borrowers. Their major sources of funds come from issuing long-term bonds (this source is by far the largest), selling commercial paper, and making bank loans. As of September 30, 2008, finance companies had assets of $1,910.0 billion, which were distributed somewhat equally among consumer credit, mortgages, and business loans.

Recap   Contractual-type intermediaries offer contingency claims in return for regular payments. They include life insurance companies, property and casualty companies, and pension funds. Investment-type intermediaries (mutual funds and money market mutual funds) pool funds from the public, invest the funds, and return the income received, less a management fee, to the investors. Finance company-type intermediaries purchase mortgages, and lend to households to purchase consumer durables and to businesses to finance inventories.

PULLING THINGS TOGETHER

FIs can be classified into four groups:
1. Deposit types (banks, S&Ls, savings banks, and credit unions)
2. Contractual types (insurance companies and pension plans)
3. Investment types (mutual funds and money market mutual funds)
4. Finance company types

Exhibit 8-2 summarizes the major types of assets and liabilities of the various FIs. Exhibit 8-3 shows the value of the assets held by each FI.

As Exhibit 8-3 shows, contractual-type FIs are now by far the largest group of FIs in terms of total assets, while pension plans are the single largest type of contractual FI. Banks are the largest FIs, with pension plans second. Each group can be distinguished from other groups by the financial services they specialize in and the composition of their assets and liabilities. Such factors also help to distinguish one member of a group

Type of Financial Intermediary	Primary Liabilities Sources of Funds	Primary Assets Uses of Funds
Depository Institutions		
Commercial Banks	Checkable, Savings, and Time Deposits	Loans, Mortgages, and Government Securities
Savings and Loan Associations	Checkable, Savings, and Time Deposits	Mortgages
Mutual Savings Banks	Checkable, Savings, and Time Deposits	Mortgages
Credit Unions	Checkable, Savings, and Time Deposits	Consumer Loans and Mortgages
Contractual Types		
Life Insurance Companies	Premiums	Corporate Bonds
Pension Funds	Employee and Employer Contributions	Stocks, Corporate Bonds, and Mortgages
Property and Casualty Insurance Companies	Premiums	Municipal and Corporate Bonds, and Government Securities
Investment Types		
Mutual Funds	Shares	Stocks and Bonds
Money Market Mutual Funds	Shares	Money Market Instruments
Finance Company Types		
Finance Companies	Bonds and Commercial Paper	Consumer and Business Loans, and Mortgages

from other members of the same group. More specifically, the composition of each FI's assets and liabilities depends mainly on (1) the range of financial services offered to the public; (2) any specialization in particular services offered to the public, perhaps as a result of custom; (3) the tax status of the institution; (4) the nature of the institution's liabilities; and (5) legal constraints or regulations governing the types of assets and liabilities that can be acquired.

Examples of these factors at work include the following:

1. S&Ls, reflecting custom and regulations, specialize in mortgage lending because they have a perceived competitive advantage and some tax advantages in that area.

2. Tax-exempt FIs, such as credit unions and pension funds, generally do not hold tax-exempt municipal securities, while institutions subject to the full corporate income tax, such as banks and property and casualty insurance companies, do hold such assets.

3. FIs such as life insurance companies that have a relatively steady and predictable inflow of funds and a fairly predictable stream of liabilities (payment outflows) hold more long-term and less-liquid assets than do FIs such as banks, which have a greater

	1970	1980	1990	2000	2008[a]
Depository Institutions					
Commercial banks	$505	$1,481.7	$3,337.5	$6,468.7	$12,272.5[a]
Savings associations	252	792.4	1,323.0	1,217.7	1,518.5[a]
Credit unions	18	67.6	217.2	441.1	801.5[a]
Contractual Types					
Life insurance companies	201	464.2	1,351.4	3,135.7	4,798.0[a]
Property and casualty companies	50	182.1	533.5	862.0	1,337.3[a]
Pension funds	170	786.8	2,767.7	7,511.9	9,110.7[a]
Investment Types					
Mutual funds	47	69.7	661.3	4,576.5	6,588.3[a]
Money market mutual fund	—	76.4	493.3	1,812.1	3,376.5[a]
Finance Company Types	64	196.9	547.0	851.2	1,910.0[a]

a. As of September 30, 2008.

Sources: Figures for 1970 are from the *Annual Statistical Digest,* Federal Reserve Board, 1991, various pages. Figures for 1980, 1990, 2000, and 2006 are from the *Flow of Fund Accounts, Z1*, Board of Governors of the Federal Reserve System, various years.

need for liquidity because a considerable portion of their liabilities (deposits) are payable on demand.

4. Banks do not hold corporate equities because regulations prohibit it.

In addition, the nature of an FI's assets and liabilities determines the degree to which it must manage specific risks. For example, an FI with a high percentage of long-term fixed rate assets must manage interest rate risks to a greater degree than an FI whose assets and liabilities do not have such a maturity configuration. Likewise, an FI with uncertain payment contingencies must manage the liquidity risk to a greater degree than an FI whose payments are more certain and stable.

Together, regulations and customs, or long-established practices existing from the time particular types of FIs began operating, can account for some of the differences among FIs. Nevertheless, while such distinguishing characteristics should not be ignored, it is equally important to keep sight of the "common threads" that bind all types of FIs together. Moreover, as this chapter has suggested, FIs are currently undergoing fundamental changes.

At the risk of oversimplification, we can say that banks are increasingly entering the markets for financial services traditionally provided by other FIs, which are increasingly trying to enter the markets traditionally served by banks. This process of homogenization and the trend toward "financial supermarkets" mean that, as noted earlier, Sandi and Dave, whom we met at the beginning of the chapter (and the rest of us), no longer have to deal with five different types of FIs. One FI may provide the services previously supplied by many.

The trend toward financial supermarkets or conglomerates eroded the effectiveness of various regulations and thereby led to fundamental changes in regulations and traditional competitive positions. The tendency toward consolidation of financial services was given new impetus by the **Gramm-Leach-Bliley Act (GLBA)**, which became

Gramm-Leach-Bliley Act (GLBA)

Legislation that removed decades-old barriers between banking and other financial services by creating financial holding companies that linked commercial banks with securities firms, insurance firms, and merchant banks; it was passed by Congress in November 1999 and became effective March 2000.

effective in March 2000. It removed decades-old barriers between banking and other financial services by creating *financial holding companies* that linked commercial banks with securities firms, insurance firms, and merchant banks. (More on the GLBA in Chapters 9 and 12.)

Even though banks and other intermediaries have experienced tremendous growth, they are losing ground to other nonfinancial institutions and direct financing venues, which have grown even faster. As previously mentioned, many corporate borrowers—both large and small—now borrow by issuing commercial paper rather than obtaining bank loans, and many nonfinancial corporations—Sears, AT&T, and General Motors, to name a few—now issue credit cards. In addition, more and more consumers bypass S&Ls to obtain mortgage loans directly from mortgage brokers.

Despite these ongoing developments, banks (and other depository institutions) probably are still the most important type of FIs because they have been central to the Fed's conduct of monetary policy and the determination of the money supply. We look at the Fed in the next chapter.

Summary of Major Points

1. In general, FIs are profit-seeking firms that link up net borrowers and net lenders and in the process provide the public a wide range of financial services. The linking or channeling function involves the acquisition of financial claims on borrowers by the FIs and the acquisition of claims on the FIs by lenders. FIs pool the surpluses of many net lenders and channel the funds to thousands of net borrowers. Risk is diversified because the net lenders are not putting all of their funds into one basket.

2. The quantity, quality, and type of financial services offered by FIs will vary with the perceived profitability of engaging in various activities.

3. FIs provide services to the public to reduce the risks and costs associated with borrowing and lending and other financial transactions. The claims on FIs are often more liquid and safer than claims on individual net borrowers would be. Some FIs also afford the public protection against the financial costs associated with various contingencies and fulfill the demand for various financial claims.

4. Most FIs are regulated. Historically, regulations tended to encourage specialization by certain types of FIs—in particular, financial services—and thus limited competition among different types of FIs. More recently, FIs have come to appreciate the benefits of diversifying and providing the public a wider range of financial services. This trend has led to various attempts to innovate around existing regulations, and competition has increased as a result. Recent legislation has allowed banks, insurance companies, and securities firms to affiliate under common ownership.

5. All FIs are exposed to various risks in varying degrees. Credit or default risk is the risk that a borrower will not live up to the terms of the liability it has sold. Asymmetric information is when a potential borrower knows more about the risks of an investment project than the lender. Adverse selection is when the least desirable borrowers pursue borrowing most diligently. Moral hazard is when the borrower has an incentive (the potential for higher profits) to use the borrowed funds for a more risky venture.

6. Interest rate risk is the risk that changes in the interest rate will turn a profitable spread into a loss. Liquidity risk is the risk that the FI will not have funds available to make required payments and will be unable to convert long-term assets to liquid funds quickly without a capital loss. Exchange rate risk is the risk that changes in exchange

rates will cause the FI to experience losses in the dollar value of foreign currency or foreign financial assets that the FI holds.

7. The differences among FIs manifest themselves in the financial services in which institutions specialize and in the composition of their assets and liabilities. The composition depends mainly on the range of financial services offered; any specialization in particular services, perhaps as a result of custom; the tax status of the institution; the nature of the FI's liabilities; and legal constraints or regulations.

8. The major types of FIs are deposit types, including banks, S&Ls, savings banks, and credit unions; contractual types, including insurance companies and pension plans; investment types, including mutual funds and money market mutual funds; and finance company types. The contractual-type group is the largest group, and commercial banks are the single largest FI.

9. The major sources of funds for commercial banks are checkable, savings, and time deposits, plus non-deposit liabilities such as fed funds, repurchase agreements, and Eurodollar borrowings. The major uses of funds for banks are loans, government securities, and reserves. The major sources of funds for S&Ls are time, savings, and checkable deposits. Their major use of funds is to make mortgage loans. Credit unions are tax-exempt, small in size, and numerous. Their main sources of funds are share drafts and small savings accounts. They primarily make small personal and mortgage loans to their members and invest in government securities. Savings banks, located mostly on the East Coast, lend heavily in the mortgage market.

10. Contractual-type intermediaries offer contingency claims in return for regular payments. They include life insurance companies, property and casualty companies, and pension funds. Life insurance companies and pension funds are able to invest in long-term assets because their payment outflows are relatively stable. Property and casualty companies must hold more liquid assets because they face more uncertainty with regard to their payment outflows. Investment-type intermediaries (mutual funds and money market mutual funds) pool funds from the public, invest the funds, and return the income received, less a management fee, to the investors. Mutual funds invest primarily in capital market instruments, including stocks and bonds. Money market mutual funds invest only in money market instruments. Finance company-type intermediaries lend to households to purchase consumer durables and homes, and to businesses to finance inventories.

Key Terms

Adverse Selection Problem, p. **164**

Asymmetric Information, p. **164**

Commercial Banks, p. **166**

Contingent Claims, p. **162**

Credit Unions, p. **169**

Default Risk, p. **163**

Diversification, p. **162**

Exchange Rate Risk, p. **165**

Finance Companies, p. **172**

Financial Innovation, p. **160**

Financial Institutions Reform, Recovery, and Enforcement Act (FIRREA) of 1989, p. **169**

Gramm-Leach-Bliley Act (GLBA), p. **174**

Interest Rate Risk, p. **164**

Life Insurance Companies, p. **170**

Liquidity Risk, p. **165**

Money Market Mutual Funds, p. **171**

Moral Hazard Problem, p. **164**

Mutual Funds, p. **171**

Pension Funds, p. **170**

Property and Casualty Companies, p. **171**

Savings and Loan Associations (S&Ls), p. **168**

Savings Associations, p. **168**

Savings Banks, p. **168**

Savings Deposits, p. **167**

Thrifts, p. **166**

Time Deposits, p. **167**

Transactions Deposits, p. **167**

Review Questions

1. List two services that FIs provide to the public. Why do intermediaries provide these services? What is a contingent financial claim? Give two examples.
2. "With financial intermediation, net lenders can earn a higher return on their surplus funds, and net borrowers can acquire funds at a lower cost." Explain how this seemingly contradictory statement can be true. (*Hint:* Consider a risk-free return.)
3. How are FIs like other firms? How are FIs similar to each other? How are they different?
4. If an FI has mainly long-term liabilities with few payment uncertainties, in what type of assets is it most likely to invest? Why?
5. What is a depository institution? What are the main types of depository institutions? What distinguishes them from other intermediaries?
6. Define default risk, asymmetric information, adverse selection, moral hazard, interest rate risk, liquidity risk, and exchange rate risk.
7. Identify the major contractual-type FIs. What are their main sources of funds (liabilities) and their main uses of funds (assets)?
8. What are the main sources of funds (liabilities) and uses of funds (assets) for finance company-type FIs?
9. Why does A-1 Student Auto Insurance Company need to hold more liquid assets than Senior Life Insurance Company? How do depository institutions manage liquidity risk?
10. John, a recent college graduate, is buying his first house. From which FIs could he obtain a mortgage loan?
11. How do money market mutual funds differ from mutual funds? How are money market mutual funds similar to depository institutions? As an investor, Sam holds both mutual funds and money market mutual funds. Holding which asset entails greater interest rate risk for him? Why?
12. Would a property and casualty company hold municipal securities in its portfolio of assets? What about a credit union and a life insurance company? Why or why not?
13. How can diversification reduce credit or default risk? In the event of widespread economic collapse, will diversification always reduce this risk?
14. What are the major determinants of an FI's liability structure? Give examples of each.
15. What was the purpose of the Financial Institutions Reform, Recovery, and Enforcement Act (FIRREA) of 1989? Why was the act needed?
16. Which FIs have deposit insurance?
17. What is a mutual savings bank? (*Hint:* See Endnote 8.)

Analytical Questions

Questions marked with a check mark are (✓) objective in nature. They can be completed with a short answer or number.

18. Explain whether each of the following situations involves asymmetric information, adverse selection, or moral hazard:
    a. I am financing a new car. In applying for a loan, I withhold information about my student loan, and the loan does not show up on my credit report.
    b. Just before quitting my job, I take out all the credit cards I can. I plan to run them up to the limit and declare bankruptcy.
    c. I take out a loan to manufacture a product. My costs end up being higher than expected, and there seems to be little market for my product. I am unable to repay the loan.

✓19. If a bank has assets of $100 million and liabilities of $95 million, what is its net worth? If 60 percent of its assets were loans, what percentage of the loans could go sour before the bank would lose all of its capital?

✓20. What type of risk does each of the following situations portray?
    a. After the attack on the World Trade Center, several major insurance companies did not

have sufficient cash assets available to meet casualty claims.

b. ABC Bank, located along the U.S.–Mexican border, was holding a large quantity of Mexican pesos when the value of the peso collapsed.

c. Friendly S&L specializes in fixed rate mortgages. There is a sharp increase in short-term interest rates.

d. A family needs funds immediately to meet a medical emergency. All of its assets are tied up in real estate.

e. I am planning a trip to Europe next summer and have exactly $5,000. At the present exchange rates, I will have a great time. Is there any doubt?

f. Chad takes a loan for an expensive racing truck and then loses his job.

Suggested Readings

Banking statistics for the latest quarter can be viewed at **http://www.fdic.gov/bank/statistical/index.html**.

For an interesting discussion titled "Modern Risk Management and Banking Supervision," see the remarks by Chairman Ben S. Bernanke at the Stonier Graduate School of Banking, Washington, DC, June 12, 2006, available online at **http://www.federalreserve.gov/newsevents/speech/bernanke/20060612a.htm**.

For a look at the effect of low interest rates on FIs, see "How Low Interest Rates Impact Financial Institutions," by John V. Duca, *Southwest Economy*, Federal Reserve Bank of Dallas, 6 (November/December 2003): 8–12. This article is available online at **http://dallasfed.org/research/swe/2003/swe0306b.html**.

For a rather academic look at how some banking institutions compete, see William R. Emmons and Frank A. Schmid, "When For-Profits and Not-for-Profits Compete: Theory and Empirical Evidence from Retail Banking," Federal Reserve Bank of St. Louis, Working Papers, 2004–004A, February 2004. This article is available online at **http://research.stlouisfed.org/wp/2004/2004-004.pdf**.

For a look at some issues relating to pension funds, see Simon Kwan, "Underfunding of Private Pension Plans." *Economic Letter*, Number 2003–16, Federal Reserve Bank of San Francisco, June 13, 2003. It is available online at **http://www.frbsf.org/publications/economics/letter/2003/e12003–38.html**.

For a look at how some nonfinancial firms also engage in financial intermediation, see Mitchell Merlin, "Trade Credit: Why Do Production Firms Act as Financial Intermediaries?" *Business Review*, Federal Reserve Bank of Philadelphia (3rd Quarter, 2003): 21–28. This article is available online at **http://www.phil.frb.org/files/br/brq303mb.pdf**.

The Journal of Financial Intermediation has numerous articles that deal with material in this chapter. It is available online at **http://www.olin.wustl.edu/jfi/**.

Endnotes

1. We take an in-depth look at financial innovation in Chapter 10.
2. For the time being, we are ignoring the money creation process by depository institutions, which may also generate funds that are lent to net borrowers. This process will be covered in depth in Chapter 19.
3. The exceptions, such as credit unions, will be discussed later in the chapter.
4. An FI can be exposed to losses if it has fixed rate liabilities, such as fixed rate CDs, and variable rate assets, such as variable rate loans. In this case, if interest rates fall, the return on assets falls, while the cost of liabilities does not.
5. To clarify, banks attract deposits (inputs) in order to make loans and other investments (outputs). Because banks hold reserve assets equal to only a fraction of their deposit liabilities when banks make loans, they create checkable deposits that are part of the money supply process.

6. To refresh your memory, money market deposit accounts are individual accounts authorized by Congress in 1982 that offer limited check writing (say, up to three checks per month) and generally pay higher interest than other checkable deposits.

7. Small depositors do not have to worry about the solvency of their bank as long as it is a member of the Federal Deposit Insurance Corporation (FDIC). Between 1980 and 2008, the deposits of all FDIC member banks were insured up to $100,000. In 2005, the limit on retirement accounts was increased to $250,000. In 2008, due to the ongoing financial crisis in the financial system, deposit insurance limits were temporarily increased to $250,000 on all accounts through the end of 2009.

8. The original savings banks were "mutuals," which meant that the depositors were really the owners of the institutions. They were actually benevolent philanthropic institutions set up to encourage the poor and the working class to save to relieve poverty and pauperism. The poor deposited whatever pennies they could, and the funds were managed by wealthy entrepreneurs. Today, roughly two-thirds of the savings banks retain this form of ownership, while one-third have sold stock and converted their ownership to stock savings banks.

THE BIGGEST INTERMEDIARY IN TOWN

CHAPTER NINE

9

A holding company is the people you give your money
to while you're being searched.

—Will Rogers

Commercial Banking Structure, Regulation, and Performance

Learning Objectives

After reading this chapter, you should know:

Who regulates whom in the banking system
and why

What a bank holding company is and why
virtually all large banks are now organized
as holding companies

What a financial holding company is

The reasons for the wave of bank mergers
following the regulatory changes of the 1990s

The nature of the evolutionary changes of the
banking system in recent years

THE BIGGEST INTERMEDIARY IN TOWN

The chief executive officer (CEO) convenes the regular Monday morning meeting of the managers of the bank's key divisions. As the division heads report, the managers learn that several large corporate customers are requesting short-term loans and that deposit growth has slowed in recent weeks. In response to this and other information, the CEO instructs the manager of the bank's liabilities to borrow more funds in the certificate of deposit (CD) market, and she directs the senior loan officer to pursue the corporate loan business aggressively by offering attractive terms on the requested loans. Since the slowdown in deposit growth appears to be related to increased competition from other financial intermediaries (FIs) in the area, particularly one large savings and loan (S&L), the managers endorse a major marketing plan designed to inform the public about several new services now available to depositors. The CEO also brings the committee members up-to-date on bank mergers among some key competitors. In addition, she discusses several possible mergers upper management is considering. Although mergers are supposed to exploit economies of scale and make the bank more profitable, committee members silently worry that they may translate to a loss of jobs. Finally, "the chief" directs the members of the committee to be "on their toes." Bank regulators have arrived to conduct their periodic examination of the bank's books and operations.

This story depicts the start of a fairly normal week at a bank. We hope it conveys the flavor of the dynamic world of banking and helps to introduce the issues to be examined in this chapter. What risks must banks manage? What competition do banks face in the markets for loans and deposits? What new services are banks offering? Why have there been so many bank mergers in recent years? What is a financial holding company? Who are the regulators, and what are the auditors looking for?

As discussed in Chapter 8, banks are one of the largest types of FIs and play an important role in transferring funds from lenders in our economy to borrowers. Banks borrow or hire funds from lenders and pay interest on the borrowed funds. They lend funds to borrowers and earn interest on the loaned funds. Ignoring some of the details for the moment, the excess of the interest earned on the loaned funds over the interest paid on the borrowed funds is the profit earned from financial intermediation.

As they "intermediate," commercial banks make a number of decisions. These decisions include (1) the interest rates they will pay to "borrow" or "hire" funds from depositors, (2) the types of deposits they will offer the public, (3) the interest rates they will charge to lend funds to borrowers, (4) the types of loans they will make, and (5) the types of securities they will acquire. Each of these decisions affects the borrowers' demand for funds (borrowing) from banks and/or the lenders' supply of funds (lending) to banks. Ultimately, we need to know much about the macroeconomic and microeconomic aspects of banking. On the macro side, how does bank behavior affect interest rates, the money stock, the volume of credit extended by banks, and economic activity? On the micro side, how do banks make the pricing and quantity decisions just mentioned, how do regulations affect such behavior, and how has bank behavior changed over time? We begin by examining the banking regulations that have led to our current commercial banking system. We then look at how the system's structure has been changing in recent years. Finally, we discuss bank efforts to increase profits and look at how banks have performed in this area over the last decade, particularly given the ongoing financial crisis of 2008 and 2009. Other issues are covered in succeeding chapters.

Again, we emphasize that banks, like many other firms and industries in our society, are continually changing and attempting to innovate. As a result, many institutional details will change somewhat as time passes. Nevertheless, we can look at how the banking system has evolved, provide a picture of the current system, and offer a glimpse at where the industry may be going.

THE BANKING REGULATORY STRUCTURE

As we saw in Chapters 1 and 3, the primary reason the banking system is regulated is to preserve its safety and soundness and ensure the fair and efficient delivery of banking services to the public. From the regulator's perspective, continuous oversight is needed to ensure that banks are operated prudently and in accordance with standing statutes and regulations. Broadly speaking, regulation involves the formulation and issuance of specific rules to govern the structure and conduct of banks.

For the most part, the regulatory structure prevailing at the beginning of the 1970s was inherited from and is the product of the 1930s. This structure was put in place as a result of events that precipitated the Great Depression. In October 1929, prices on the New York Stock Exchange collapsed. The Dow Jones Industrial Index, a measure of stock market values, stood at 200 in January 1928, rose to 381 in September 1929, and then collapsed. Eventually, the Dow reached a low of 41 in July 1932. From 1929 through 1933, more than 8,000 banks failed, industrial production fell more than 50 percent, and the nation's unemployment rate rose from 3 percent to 25 percent. At the time, people believed that these events were intimately connected and that the Great Depression was caused and/or severely aggravated by serious defects in the structure and regulation of the financial system. More specifically, the failure of many financial institutions was alleged to be the result of (1) "excessive and destructive competition" among banks, which had led to the payment of unduly high interest rates on deposits, and (2) the granting of overly risky loans, particularly those extended to stock market speculators. Further, it was believed that banks sought out such loans and the high yields they carried because of the high rates being paid on deposits. When the stock market crashed, the value of the speculators' portfolios collapsed, leading them to default on their bank loans. The banks, in turn, became insolvent (bankrupt) or were left so weakened that depositors rushed to withdraw their funds.

Given this diagnosis, the legislative and regulatory remedies established at the time are readily understandable.[1] Among the most widespread and ultimately pernicious "cures" was the establishment of maximum ceilings on the interest rates banks could pay on deposits. The ceilings, which were imposed under the **Glass-Steagall Act of 1933**, were popularly known as **Regulation Q**. Interest payments on demand deposits, which were the only type of checkable deposit in existence at the time, were prohibited, and interest payments on time and savings deposits were not to exceed the rate ceilings set by the relevant regulatory authority. The rationale for the ceilings was seductive and attractive: By holding down the rates on deposits (sources of bank funds), the rates on loans (uses of funds) could be held down. Banks would no longer need to seek out and grant high-risk, high-yield loans.

To further limit bank failures, the Glass-Steagall Act put deposit insurance into place with the creation of the **Federal Deposit Insurance Corporation (FDIC)**. As noted in Chapter 8, the deposits of most banks and other depository institutions were fully insured up to $100,000 between 1980 and 2008. In 2006, deposit insurance on retirement accounts was increased to $250,000. Due to the financial crisis in 2008 and to instill confidence into the system, deposit insurance was temporarily increased to $250,000 per account from September 2008 through the end of 2009. Beginning in 2010, deposit insurance limits will be adjusted for inflation every five years. The presence of deposit insurance eliminated **bank runs** or bank panics, in which depositors, fearing that their bank would fail, "ran" to get their funds out.

Glass-Steagall Act of 1933
Banking legislation that established Regulation Q interest rate ceilings, separated commercial and investment banking, and created the FDIC. It was enacted in response to the financial crisis that led to the Great Depression.

Regulation Q
Interest rate ceilings on deposits at commercial banks that were established during the Great Depression and phased out after 1980.

Federal Deposit Insurance Corporation (FDIC)
The federal agency that insures the deposits of banks and savings associations.

Bank Runs
When many depositors simultaneously attempt to withdraw their funds from a bank.

In addition, the Glass-Steagall Act separated commercial banking from investment banking. Investment banking is the underwriting and marketing of primary corporate securities. Banks were no longer allowed to own or underwrite corporate securities. Thus, the assets commercial banks could hold were effectively limited to cash assets, government securities, and loans. The commercial bank's role was to accept deposits paying up to the Regulation Q interest rate ceilings and to make predominantly commercial loans.

We have already seen that the Fed is the most important regulator of its commercial bank members. The Fed also sets reserve requirements and provides discount loan facilities for all depository institutions. Under the regulatory structure that prevailed from the 1930s until the early 1980s, the Fed shared regulatory responsibilities with two federal bodies—the **Comptroller of the Currency** and the FDIC—and with state banking departments. Prior to the 1980s, the scope of regulation included restrictions on entry, branching, types of assets and liabilities permitted, financial services that could be offered, and interest rates that could be paid on certain types of deposits and charged on certain types of loans. Today, banks have found ways around many of these regulations; many others have been relaxed if not totally eliminated. Recently, other regulations dealing mainly with bank capital requirements and risk management have become increasingly important. In Chapter 12, we look at major legislation in recent years that has drastically altered the structure of the banking system.

To aid in understanding this complex regulatory structure, it is useful to begin with the birth of a bank. Unfortunately (or should we say fortunately), none of us can just decide to open a bank tomorrow. Commercial banks in the United States are **chartered**; that is, they are given permission to engage in the business of commercial banking by either the federal government or one of the 50 state governments. When applying for a charter, the applicant must demonstrate a knowledge of the business of banking and have a substantial supply of capital funds.[2] If a bank's charter is granted by the federal government, the bank is called a **national bank.** The office of the Comptroller of the Currency is the federal government agency charged with chartering national banks. For example, Wells Fargo Bank of San Francisco is a federally chartered bank. A bank can also be chartered by a state banking authority. This system, in which commercial banks are chartered and regulated by the federal government or a state government, is usually referred to as the **dual banking system.** Think of it as a dual chartering system.

Banks that are federally chartered must belong to the Federal Reserve System and must subscribe to federal deposit insurance with the FDIC. The latter provides insurance for individual deposit accounts currently up to $250,000 per account and charges banks an insurance premium that varies with the reserves that the insurance fund has available. The premium is slightly more for high-risk banks. Thus, national banks are subject to the regulatory and supervisory authority of the Comptroller, the Fed, and the FDIC.

A state-chartered bank will be regulated by its state banking authority. If it chooses to join the Federal Reserve System, the state bank will also have to subscribe to federal deposit insurance, since all Fed members must have FDIC insurance. Thus, in this case, the state-chartered bank will be subject to regulation by the Fed and the FDIC. Finally, state banks may also subscribe to FDIC insurance without joining the Fed.[3]

One of the interesting and probably unique features of the system is that those being regulated can choose the regulator. In effect, they can "vote with their feet." By this we mean that banks can apply for either a state or a federal charter or attempt to shift from one to the other.

The decisions banks have made on chartering, branching, and membership in the Fed are captured in Exhibit 9-1. Presumably, these decisions are based on expected prof-

Comptroller of the Currency
The federal agency that charters national banks.

Chartered
Given permission to engage in the business of commercial banking. Banks must obtain a charter before opening.

National Bank
A bank that has received a charter from the Comptroller of the Currency.

Dual Banking System
The system whereby a bank may have either a national or a state charter.

The Origins of the Dual Banking System

How did we end up with a dual banking system? Actually, it was not the intent of Congress. The National Currency Act of 1863 and the National Banking Act of 1864 established the Comptroller of the Currency, which chartered national banks for the first time. The banknotes issued by the national banks circulated at full value and were backed by government bonds.

Prior to this time, all banks were chartered by the states. The state banks issued their own banknotes, which, under normal circumstances, were redeemable at face value in the bank's geographic trade area. Outside the bank's geographic area, the notes were often redeemable at less than face value. The acts also imposed a 10 percent tax on banknotes issued by state banks. The purpose of the restrictive tax was to make state banknotes so undesirable that state banks would be driven out of business. If they were unable to issue notes, then they could not make loans. A financial innovation—the acceptance of demand deposits—saved the state banks from extinction by allowing them to stay in business without issuing their own banknotes. The innovation foiled the plans of Congress to drive state banks out of business.

Incidentally, if you have any old state banknotes or national banknotes lying around your house, you may want to check out how much they're worth. At a mid-1990s show in St. Louis, Missouri, a $10 banknote from Platteville National Bank sold for $9,500.[a]

Endnote

a. "The Currency Dealer," *Greensheet Newsletter* (Torrance, CA: December 1995).

---

itability. The data in Exhibit 9-1 indicate that as of September 30, 2008, about 77 percent of all banks had state charters, while about 22 percent had national charters. The 1,556 national banks had 1,260,417 full-time equivalent employees, while the 5,590 state banks had only 692,008. Although state-chartered banks are more numerous, those that are nationally chartered tend to be larger. Most state-chartered banks do not belong to the Federal Reserve System, although larger state banks do tend to be Fed members.

Historically, most banks, especially smaller ones, found it more profitable to be state-chartered non-Fed members. State banking authorities were often viewed as being more friendly in regulating and supervising institutions and more lenient in allowing nonbanking activities than their federal counterparts. In addition, the reserve requirements, which specify that a bank must hold reserve assets equal to a portion of its deposit liabilities, were often lower for state-chartered/regulated banks than for national banks regulated by the Fed. Lower reserve requirements meant higher potential profits. Because a smaller amount of reserve assets were held, a larger proportion of deposit inflows could be used for loans and other interest-earning investments. (The required reserve ratio is now set by the Fed for all depository institutions and is the same for all depository institutions.) Larger banks, which usually were Fed members, often provided nonmembers with many of the services the Fed would normally have provided. Fed

	Number of Banks	Deposits (in Billions of Dollars)	Assets (in Billions of Dollars)
Total domestic banks	7,146	$7,778.51	12,050
National charter	1,556	5,134.85	8,334.90
State character	5,590	2,643.66	3,715.52

Source: Federal Deposit Insurance Corporation.

members also have to buy stock in the Fed equal to 3 percent of their assets. The stock pays dividends that are lower than what banks could earn by making loans.

Nearly all banks have elected to be part of the FDIC. Apparently, banks feel it is important to offer depositors the safety and peace of mind federal deposit insurance engenders. For those who think this point is trivial, recall that in the midst of the Great Depression—between 1929 and 1933 to be exact—more than 8,000 banks failed in the United States. As those banks failed, depositors in other banks rushed to withdraw their funds out of fear that the problems would spread. Such a bank run on even a healthy, solvent bank can cause severe difficulties, because the bank's asset portfolio may be illiquid, with not enough cash or liquid assets on hand to pay off the many depositors making withdrawals. Limiting cash withdrawals (to, say, $25 a week) or closing the bank temporarily, as often occurred, reinforced the public's perception that this bank and perhaps all banks were in serious difficulty. As the epidemic spread, such illiquid banks were often forced out of business, and the entire financial system was threatened.

In what must be judged one of the most successful pieces of legislation in history, Congress created the FDIC in 1933. This, by and large, halted the runs on solvent but illiquid banks and thus restored some stability to the banking and financial systems.[4] Deposit insurance was first made a "full faith and credit obligation" of the federal government in 1989. Prior to that year, the FDIC was on somewhat the same footing as private insurance companies in that the federal government was not required by law to pay off depositors if the FDIC ran out of funds in the face of widespread bank failures.

Clearly, having a dual banking system with a variety of regulatory authorities leads to a considerable overlap of responsibilities, with some institutions subject to regulation and supervision by as many as three regulatory authorities. In an attempt to minimize the overlap, primary regulatory responsibility for each category of banks has been assigned to one regulator, who then shares the resulting information. Regulatory responsibility has been distributed in the following manner: (1) the FDIC for state-chartered, insured banks that have not joined the Fed; (2) the Comptroller of the Currency for national banks, which also must be FDIC insured and Fed members; (3) the Fed for state-chartered, insured members of the Fed, and all bank and financial holding companies (more on them later); and (4) the states for state-chartered banks that do not subscribe to FDIC insurance or belong to the Fed. Exhibit 9-2 gives additional details for each category. The **Federal Financial Institutions Examinations Council (FFIEC)**, which was created by Congress in 1979, prescribes uniform principles, standards, and report forms for the federal examination of financial institutions by the Fed, the FDIC, and the Office of the Comptroller of the Currency. The FFIEC also makes recommendations to promote uniformity in the supervision of financial institutions.[5]

Some people believe that the current set of regulations, supervisory authorities, and statutes of the dual chartering system provides an incentive for local banks with state charters to adapt and structure their services so as to fulfill the needs of the local

Solvent
When a bank or other firm has assets worth more than liabilities (opposite of "bankrupt" or "insolvent").

Federal Financial Institutions Examinations Council (FFIEC)
A federal agency that prescribes uniform principles, standards, and report forms for the federal examination of financial institutions by the Fed, the FDIC, and the Office of the Comptroller of the Currency and that makes recommendations to promote uniformity in the supervision of financial institutions.

• **FDIC:**	Regulates state-chartered, insured non-Fed members and insured branches of foreign banks
• **Comptroller of the Currency:**	Regulates national banks that are not bank holding companies and federally chartered branches of foreign banks
• **Fed:**	Regulates state-chartered, insured members of the Fed, all bank holding companies, all financial holding companies, and branches of foreign banking organizations operating in the United States and their parent banks
• **States:**	Regulate state-chartered, non-FDIC-insured banks that are not Fed members

Sources: Federal Deposit Insurance Corporation.

community, while guidelines for federally chartered banks may relate to national and international concerns. They also argue that the dual system fosters competition and innovation among banks. Opponents of the dual system argue that the overlapping of regulatory agencies breeds considerable confusion and leads to lax enforcement; they maintain that this system gives banks considerable freedom to escape proper supervision and regulation. By the early 2000s, many of these discussions became irrelevant and obsolete because of ongoing changes in regulations, technological advances in the ways funds are transferred, and other financial innovations.

As Exhibit 9-3 shows, bank failures in the mid- and late 1980s were at the highest level since the inception of the FDIC in 1933. Between 1955 and 1981, bank failures averaged 5.3 per year. Between 1987 and 1990, they averaged a whooping 189 per year! Although still high in the early 1990s, in the period up to 2007, bank failures had fallen dramatically, with no banks failing from July 2004 until January 2007. In 2007, three banks failed—each merged with a healthy one. In 2008 the developing financial crisis was noticeably impacting commercial banks and there were 25 bank failures. Most dramatically, on Thursday evening, September 25th the FDIC took over Washington Mutual, separated it from its holding company, and sold nearly all of it to J.P. Morgan Chase for $1.9 billion. Washington Mutual had $307 billion in assets, making this by far the largest failure of a depository institution ever. Less than a week later, it appeared another huge depository institution, Wachovia, was about to be purchased by Citigroup. Wells Fargo made a superior offer on October 3, 2008. Less than three months earlier in July, Indy Mac Bank of Pasadena, California, with over $32 billion in assets, had been declared bankrupt and the FDIC was named as Conservator. A number of depositors with accounts in excess of the $100,000 insurance limit suffered losses. This seemed to fuel the ongoing crisis and financial instability. No such depositor losses were realized as a result of the resolution of problems at Washington Mutual and Wachovia.

When large bank failures escalated in 2008, many industry observers were extremely nervous. To what extent was this increase in bank failures the result of the ongoing financial crisis versus lax regulation? Some in Congress have viewed bank failures as a result of ineffective regulation. One could, however, argue the opposite—that bank failures reflect regulators doing their job and closing insolvent banks before they become even bigger problelms.[6] In Chapter 12, we look at ways regulators have implemented new and existing regulations to ensure adequate banking supervision. We also

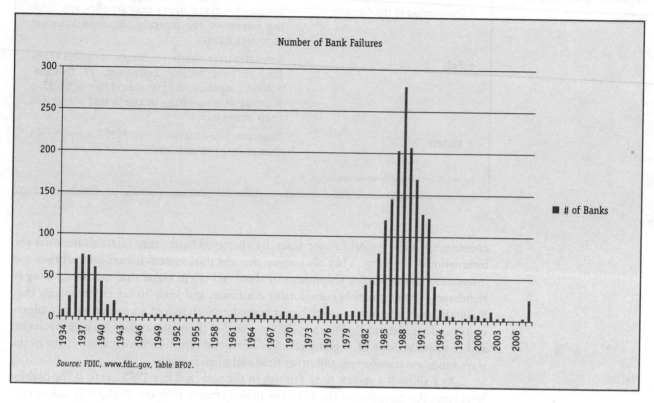

Number of Bank Failures

Source: FDIC, www.fdic.gov, Table BF02.

look at suggestions for overhauling the federal regulatory structure of banking and other financial services, in response to the ongoing changes that are occurring within the industry.

Recap

Federally chartered banks are called *national banks* and must belong to the Fed and subscribe to FDIC deposit insurance. State-chartered banks can, if they choose, belong to the Fed and/or subscribe to FDIC insurance. Nearly all banks subscribe to FDIC insurance. This dual banking system has allowed banks to choose their regulators. Seventy-seven percent of banks have state charters, while 23 percent have national charters. National banks tend to be much larger and have many more employees than state banks. Although the rate of bank failures was quite low from the 1990s until 2007, in 2008 several large depository institutions failed, including Countrywide Financial, Indy Mac Bank, Washington Mutual, and Wachovia Bank.

THE STRUCTURE OF THE COMMERCIAL BANKING SYSTEM

In establishing the statutes and regulations that have contributed to the evolution of the structure of the commercial banking system, Congress and the regulatory agencies were guided by several considerations. It was assumed that a large number of small banks would encourage competition and efficiency, which would result in conduct or behavior by firms that was beneficial to the public and society at large. At the same time, the more competitive the market, the greater the risk of failure of an individual firm from the pressure of intense competition. Although the public would be provided with the largest quantity of financial services at the lowest prices, more banks could fail in a highly competitive environment.

In contrast, a structure characterized by a few large firms would result in limited competition, inefficiencies, and fewer benefits for the public in the form of lower prices and improved quality and quantity of financial services.[7] At the same time, fewer banks would fail in a noncompetitive market. (Because of a lack of competition, banks could charge higher prices for their services and earn higher profits.) Nevertheless, with only a few large banks, the failure of just one bank could have major ramifications throughout the economy. With many small banks, the failure of one would not be catastrophic. Presumably, regulators attempt to balance all these considerations by encouraging bank behavior that is beneficial to society while at the same time ensuring the safety and soundness of the financial system.

Against this background, it should not be surprising that regulators were interested in monitoring and influencing, if not controlling, the structure of the market for banking services. In particular, regulators used their powers to control entry into the market, mergers among existing firms, and branching in an effort to maintain many small firms and a so-called competitive environment, while at the same time protecting small banks from excessive competition. But, as we shall see, the regulators' attempts to maintain a competitive environment often resulted in a noncompetitive environment. Even though there were many banks, each bank was shielded from competition.

A local environment can become more competitive in several ways. One way, of course, occurs when a new institution secures a charter and sets up in competition with the local banks. Competition can also increase if existing banks located elsewhere in the state are allowed to open new branch offices in the area. Although not always the case, the vast majority of states allow statewide branching.

Historically, however, branching generally had to stop at the state line. The **McFadden Act,** passed by Congress in 1927, prohibited federally chartered national banks from branching across state lines. It also required national banks to abide by the branching laws of the state in which they were located. State banks that are Fed members can operate only in the state that grants them a charter. Generally, other state-chartered banks could not open branches across state lines, although some states permitted entry by state-chartered banks that were not Fed members. Although it is now history, the McFadden Act is substantially responsible for the structure of the commercial banking system we have today.

Initially, state and federal restrictions on intrastate (multiple branches within one state) and interstate branching (branches within different states) were motivated by a desire to prevent undue concentration and reduced competition in banking. For example, it was believed that with unrestricted statewide branching, a few large city banks would open branches across a state and drive the small community banks out of business. The result would be a worrisome concentration of economic and perhaps political power in a few large institutions and a reduction in the quality and quantity of financial services available in smaller communities.

Concerns about size and concentration, along with the fear that more competition in local banking markets might lead to more bank failures, resulted in restrictions on entry and branching. This, in turn, led to a large number of small banks being located in relatively small communities. Despite the alleged competitiveness, many of these institutions have faced little or no competition because larger, and perhaps more efficient, banks were prohibited from entering the local market. Thus, entry and branching restrictions ultimately served to limit competition, not increase it. In part, this is why Congress, in 1994, decided to allow interstate branching. The McFadden Act was effectively

McFadden Act
The 1927 act by Congress that outlawed interstate branching and made national banks conform to the intrastate branching laws of the states in which they were located.

Size Distribution of
FDIC-Insured Banks as
of September 30, 2008

Asset Size	Number of Institutions	Percent of Total	Cumulative Percent	Total Assets	Percent of Total	Cumulative Percent
<$100 million	2,882	40%	40%	$156,361	1.3%	1.3%
$100 mil.–$1 bil.	3,755	53%	93%	1,088,258	9%	10.3%
$1 bil and up	509	7%	100%	10,805,794	89.7%	100.0%
Total	7,146			12,050,413		

Sources: Federal Deposit Insurance Corporation (http://www.fdic.gov) & Federal Reserve Statistical Release (http://www.federalreserve.gov)

Interstate Banking and Branching Efficiency Act (IBBEA)
Signed into law in September 1994, an act by Congress that effectively allows unimpeded nationwide branching.

abrogated in September 1994, when President Bill Clinton signed the **Interstate Banking and Branching Efficiency Act (IBBEA)**. The IBBEA has effectively allowed unimpeded nationwide branching since mid-1997.

Another reason for the enactment of the IBBEA was that Congress and the president were merely following the lead of the states. In 1985, the Supreme Court gave states the freedom to form regional banking pacts. Two years later, 45 of the 50 states allowed some form of interstate banking. More importantly, as we shall see in the next section, banks had, for all practical purposes, found ways to engage in interstate branching even before the law allowing branching was passed.

As Exhibit 9-4 shows, on June 30, 2007, there were 7,146 FDIC-insured banks in the United States. Of these, 40 percent had assets of less than $100 million each. Although $100 million might sound like a lot, it is small for a bank. At the same time, over 93 percent of FDIC-insured banks had assets less than $1 billion, while about 7 percent had assets greater than $1 billion.

A look at total banking assets for the industry reveals even more. The smallest 40 percent of all banks owned about 1.3 percent of total banking assets. The smallest 93 percent of banks had about 10.3 percent of total assets. About 7 percent of all banks had assets of more than $1 billion, but they owned about 89.7 percent of total banking assets! By any measure, it is clear that the industry is composed of a large number of very small banks and a small number of very large banks. As you might guess, most of the industry giants have extensive branching networks and are located in states that had liberal branching laws long before the IBBEA. But the numbers alone conceal additional relevant attributes of the banking structure—namely, that the numbers are changing dramatically as mergers occur and that virtually all of the large banks are organized as bank holding companies or as financial holding companies. To these subjects we now turn.

Recap
The McFadden Act of 1927 outlawed interstate branching by national banks. The act required national banks to abide by the branching laws of the state in which they were located. In 1994, the Interstate Banking and Branching Efficiency Act (IBBEA) effectively allowed unimpeded nationwide branching as of June 1, 1997. Today, there are a large number of very small banks and a small number of very large banks.

BANK HOLDING COMPANIES AND FINANCIAL HOLDING COMPANIES

Bank Holding Company
A corporation that owns several firms, at least one of which is a bank.

A **bank holding company** is a corporation that owns several firms, at least one of which is a bank. The remaining firms are engaged in activities that are closely related to banking.

If the holding company owns one bank, it is called a one-bank holding company. If it owns more than one, it is called, not surprisingly, a multi-bank holding company.

Many banks organize themselves into holding companies because they expect this organizational form to be more profitable than a simple bank would be. More specifically, this corporate form allows banks to diversify into other product areas, thus providing the public with a wider array of financial services, while reducing the risk associated with limiting operations to traditional banking services. In addition, prior to 1997, organizing as a bank holding company allowed banks to circumvent restrictions on branching and thus seek out sources and uses of funds in other geographical markets.

Thus, organizing as a bank holding company allowed banks to effectively circumvent prohibitions on intrastate and interstate branching, which have now been virtually eliminated, and to participate in activities that otherwise would be barred. Such activities include data processing, leasing, investment counseling, and servicing out-of-state loans. For a summary list of activities that bank holding companies can currently engage in, see Exhibit 9-5.

Almost all large banks are owned by holding companies. In January 2009, the largest holding company is J.P. Morgan Chase, which has over $2,251 billion in assets, over 200,000 employees, and a presence in more than 60 countries. Although the list is rapidly changing due to the ongoing financial crisis, the 25 largest bank holding companies as of

9-5

Allowable Activities for Bank Holding Companies (Federal Reserve Regulation Y—Through January, 2009, Revisions)

- Making, acquiring, brokering, or servicing loans, issuing and accepting letters of credit
- Real estate and personal property appraising
- Commercial real estate equity financing
- Check-guaranty services
- Collection agency services
- Credit bureau services

  Derivatives activities to transfer title to commodities underlying derivatives contracts instantaneously, on a pass-through basis
- Asset management, servicing, and collection activities
- Acquiring debt in default
- Real estate settlement services
- Leasing personal or real property
- Operating nonbank depository institutions
- Performing trust company functions
- Financial and investment advisory activities
- Providing feasibility studies
- Agency transactional services
- Investment transactions as principal including underwriting and dealing in government obligations, money market instruments, foreign exchange, forward contracts, options, futures, options on futures, swaps, and similar contracts
- Management consulting and counseling activities
- Courier services
- Printing and selling checks, deposit slips, etc.
- Insurance agency and underwriting
- Community development activities
- Issuing money orders, savings bonds, and travelers' checks
- Data processing

  Process, store, and transmit nonfinancial data in connection with their financial data processing, storage, and transmission activities

Source: Federal Reserve System, http://www.federalreserve.gov/regulations/default.htm.

Commercial Banks by Total Assets as of June 30, 2007

Rank	Bank Name	Location	Total Assts (Mil $)	Branches	
				Domestic	Foreign
1	BANK OF AMERICA, NATIONAL ASSOCIATION	CHARLOTTE, NC	1,252,402	5,835	123
2	JPMORGAN CHASE BANK, NATIONAL ASSOCIATION	COLUMBUS, OH	1,252,369	2,870	46
3	CITIBANK NATIONAL ASSOCIATION	LAS VEGAS, NV	1,132,840	1,006	365
4	WACHOVIA BK NATIONAL ASSOCIATION	CHARLOTTE, NC	524,113	3,167	12
5	WELLS FARGO BK NATIONAL ASSOCIATION	SIOUX FALLS, SD	428,724	4,076	3
6	U.S. BK NATIONAL ASSOCIATION	CINCINNATI, OH	221,026	2,836	1
7	SUNTRUST BANK	ATLANTA, GA	177,067	1,933	0
8	HSBC BK USA NATIONAL ASSOCIATION	WILMINGTON, DE	168,652	414	5
9	FIA CARD SVC NATIONAL ASSOCIATION	WILMINGTON, DE	143,218	0	1
10	NATIONAL CITY BANK	CLEVELAND, OH	138,415	1,430	1
11	REGIONS BANK	BIRMINGHAM, AL	132,667	2,203	0
12	BRANCH BANK & TRUST	WINSTON-SALEM, NC	121,998	1,431	0
13	BANK OF NY	NEW YORK, NY	108,157	8	9
14	STATE STREET BANK & TRUST	BOSTON, MA	101,555	2	10
15	PNC BK NATIONAL ASSOCIATION	PITTSBURGH, PA	93,805	953	0
16	KEYBANK NATIONAL ASSOCIATION	CLEVELAND, OH	89,930	1,159	1
17	LASALLE BK NATIONAL ASSOCIATION	CHICAGO, IL	77,062	138	1
18	CITIBANK SD NATIONAL ASSOCIATION	SIOUX FALLS, SD	76,686	0	0
19	CHASE BK USA NATIONAL ASSOCIATION	NEWARK, DE	74,073	2	0
20	COMERICA BANK	DETROIT, MI	58,668	382	1
21	BANK OF THE WEST	SAN FRANCISCO, CA	58,368	685	0
22	MANUFACTURERS & TRADERS TRUST	BUFFALO, NY	57,006	695	1
23	FIFTH THIRD BANK	CINCINNATI, OH	54,939	412	1
24	NORTH FORK BANK	MATTITUCK, NY	53,639	350	0
25	UNION BK OF CA NATIONAL ASSOCIATION	SAN FRANCISCO, CA	52,568	344	6

June 30, 2007 appear next to a list of the 25 largest banks in Exhibit 9-6a and b. Observe how the two lists overlap and see the additional assets that the bank holding companies add to the largest banks. Note that as of January 2009, J.P. Morgan Chase is the largest bank holding company and not Citigroup, which according to Exhibit 9-6b, was the largest bank hold company in June 2007.

Perhaps even more dramatic is the ongoing trend for bank holding companies to convert to **financial holding companies.** Under the Gramm-Leach-Bliley Act (GLBA) of 1999, bank holding companies, securities firms, insurance companies, and other financial institutions can affiliate under common ownership to form financial holding companies. A financial holding company can offer a complete range of financial services, many of which were previously prohibited. These activities include:

- Securities underwriting and dealing
- Insurance agency and underwriting activities
- Merchant banking activities
- Any other activity that the Fed determines to be financial in nature or incidental to financial activities

Financial Holding Companies
Holding companies that can engage in an even broader array of financial-related activities than bank holding companies, including securities underwriting and dealing, insurance agency and underwriting activities, and merchant banking activities; financial holding companies may engage in any other financial and nonfinancial activities as determined by the Fed.

Rank	Bank Name	Location	Total Assts (Mil $)
1	CITIGROUP INC.	NEW YORK, NY	2,220,866,000
2	BANK OF AMERICA CORPORATION	CHARLOTTE, NC	1,535,684,280
3	JPMORGAN CHASE & CO.	NEW YORK, NY	1,458,042,000
4	WACHOVIA CORPORATION	CHARLOTTE, NC	719,922,000
5	TAUNUS CORPORATION	NEW YORK, NY	579,062,000
6	WELLS FARGO & COMPANY	SAN FRANCISCO, CA	539,865,000
7	HSBC NORTH AMERICA HOLDINGS INC.	PROSPECT HEIGHTS, I	483,630,057
8	U.S. BANCORP	MINNEAPOLIS, MN	222,530,000
9	SUNTRUST BANKS, INC.	ATLANTA, GA	180,314,372
10	ABN AMRO NORTH AMERICA HOLDING COMPANY	CHICAGO, IL	160,341,966
11	CITIZENS FINANCIAL GROUP, INC.	PROVIDENCE, RI	159,392,731
12	CAPITAL ONE FINANCIAL CORPORATION	MCLEAN, VA	145,937,957
13	NATIONAL CITY CORPORATION	CLEVELAND, OH	140,648,168
14	REGIONS FINANCIAL CORPORATION	BIRMINGHAM, AL	137,624,205
15	BB&T CORPORATION	WINSTON-SALEM, NC	127,577,050
16	BANK OF NEW YORK COMPANY, INC.	NEW YORK, NY	126,457,000
17	PNC FINANCIAL SERVICES GROUP, INC.	PITTSBURGH, PA	125,736,711
18	STATE STREET CORPORATION	BOSTON, MA	112,345,777
19	FIFTH THIRD BANCORP	CINCINNATI, OH	101,389,721
20	KEYCORP	CLEVELAND, OH	93,490,903
21	BANCWEST CORPORATION	HONOLULU, HI	70,661,335
22	HARRIS FINANCIAL CORP.	WILMINGTON, DE	64,475,903
23	NORTHERN TRUST CORPORATION	CHICAGO, IL	59,609,734
24	COMERICA INCORPORATED	DETROIT, MI	58,945,727
25	MARSHALL & ILSLEY CORPORATION	MILWAUKEE, WI	58,327,527

- Any nonfinancial activity that the Fed determines is complementary to the financial activity and does not pose a substantial risk to the safety or soundness of depository institutions or to the financial system

Merchant Banking

Direct equity investment (the purchasing of stock) in a start-up or growing company by a bank.

Merchant banking is the making of direct equity investments (purchasing stock) in start-up or growing nonfinancial businesses. Under GLBA, financial holding companies will be able to own up to 100 percent of commercial, nonfinancial businesses as long as ownership is for investment purposes only, the financial holding company is not involved in the day-to-day management of the company, and the investment is for 10 years or less. Prior to the recent law, bank holding companies could own only 5 percent of a commercial company directly and up to 49 percent through certain subsidiaries.

To become a financial holding company, bank holding companies that meet certain criteria must file a declaration with the Federal Reserve.[8] The declaration must certify that, among other things, all of the bank holding company's depository institution subsidiaries are well capitalized and well managed. As of March 11, 2000, the effective date of the GLBA, 117 institutions were certified as financial holding companies. As of April 2008, over 647 financial holding companies were in existence.

To summarize, banks, under the holding company corporate umbrella, have been expanding the geographical areas they serve and the array of financial services they offer the public. Bank holding companies may also apply to become financial holding companies if they meet certain criteria. Under the financial holding company status, bank holding companies, insurance companies, and securities firms can affiliate under common ownership. In addition, financial holding companies can engage in an even broader array of financial and nonfinancial services than bank holding companies can. The expansion by banks into areas traditionally served by other, more specialized, FIs has been matched (as discussed in the last chapter) by other FIs and other nonfinancial institutions expanding into areas traditionally served mainly by banks, such as the checkable deposits offered by S&Ls and the credit cards offered by General Motors.

ONGOING CHANGES IN THE STRUCTURE OF THE BANKING INDUSTRY

The breakdown of barriers to intra- and interstate branching and to certain activities has resulted in increased competition in the financial services industry and considerable erosion in the domain and effectiveness of many long-standing financial regulations. The changes in the structure of U.S. banking and banking laws have been revolutionary and have resulted in a drastic decline in the number of banks in the past few years. Between 1980 and 2007, over 1,465 banks failed, about 9,800 mergers occurred, and about 4,700 new banks were started. The result was a net decline in the number of banks from over 14,400 to 7,146 in late 2008. After slowing in the immediately preceding years, the movement toward integration and consolidation among financial institutions in the financial services industry has increased due to the financial crisis of 2008 and the resulting mergers and takeovers of some extremely large banking institutions such as Washington Mutual and Wachovia.

A related trend is a significant increase in the share of total bank assets controlled by the largest banks. For example, in 1980, the 100 largest banking organizations (banks and bank holding companies) accounted for about one-half of total banking assets. By mid-2007, the largest 20 banks accounted for over half of all banking assets, the top ten banks held about 44 percent of assets, and the three largest banks controlled 25 percent of assets. The increased concentration of banking assets in the largest banks has resulted from the removal of branching restrictions, particularly across state lines, and from bank mergers. Despite the decline in the number of banks, the number of branches has actually increased since 1980.

In the 1990s, the pace and dollar volume of mergers increased significantly. Some of the largest mergers that took place during the early and mid-1990s include the Chase-Chemical Bank merger, the Wells Fargo-First Interstate merger, the NationsBank-Barnett merger, and the First Union-Core States merger. Although these mergers were the largest in history up to that time, they are much smaller than the more recent mergers of Citicorp and Travelers, Wells Fargo and Norwest, Banc One and First Chicago, and NationsBank and BankAmerica. These mergers have set a new standard for sheer size in U.S. banking organizations, and have been occurring not only between banks but also, like the Citicorp-Travelers merger, between banks and other companies in the financial services industry.[9] After the early 2004 combination of JP Morgan Chase and Bank One, the pace of mergers slowed somewhat; however, this slowdown seems unlikely to be a new trend. Exhibit 9-7 shows that while the number of banks has declined since the 1990s, the total number of bank branches has continued to grow. These divergent trends reflect the importance of bank mergers The accompanying feature titled "A Closer Look" examines some of the mega-mergers of the past decade.

In the latter half of 2008, merger and takeover activity was again on the rise, primarily as a result of the weakness of some large depository institutions such as Washington Mutual and Wachovia Banks. As the financial crisis developed it became increasingly

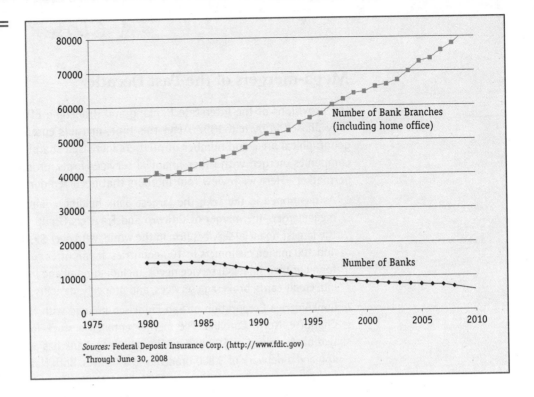

Sources: Federal Deposit Insurance Corp. (http://www.fdic.gov)
*Through June 30, 2008

evident that the structure of traditional investment banks would also not survive. Of the five largest traditional investment banks, none now exist in their original form. Bear Stearns was purchased by JPMorgan Chase, and Merrill Lynch by the Bank of America. In addition, Lehman Brothers filed for bankruptcy with part of it purchased by Barclays. Finally, Goldman Sachs and Morgan Stanley transformed themselves into bank holding companies.

Two things are certain: (1) the structure of the banking system is changing rapidly and looks far different than it looked 20 years ago; and (2) profit-seeking banks will continue to adapt to changing regulations and ever-transforming financial environments in ways that will produce further structural changes.

Finally, as we have seen, banks—under the financial holding company status—can enter the securities, insurance, and merchant banking industries and engage in other financial and nonfinancial activities as determined by the Fed. Banks were officially barred from these activities between 1933 and 2000, although many had found de facto ways into some of these areas through nonbank subsidiaries. We expect the trend for extensive financial integration and concentration to continue in the financial services industry.

THE EVOLUTION OF INTERNATIONAL BANKING

The environment for banks has also changed dramatically in the international arena. A striking increase in international borrowing and lending by domestic banks began in the 1970s with the expansion of world trade that occurred shortly after the first OPEC oil crisis.[10] Not only did the amount of international lending increase, but also the number of participating banks. Petrodollars, as they came to be known, flowed into the OPEC nations in payment for oil. In turn, the OPEC nations deposited a large part of

A Closer Look

Mega-mergers of the Past Decade

The provisions of the Interstate Banking and Branching Efficiency Act of 1994 were fully phased in by mid-1997. After this time, mergers entered a new era, as the size, geographical area, and number of mergers increased sharply. Moreover, bank holding companies merged with other financial services firms, producing mega-financial supermarkets. Here we review four mergers that occurred during the fall of 1998:

1. As mentioned in the text, the largest bank holding company resulted from another megamerger—the merger of Citicorp and Travelers Group. The new firm, Citigroup, is the largest financial services firm in the world, with over $2,200 billion in assets in 2007 and 100 million customers in 100 countries. It can offer customers one-stop shopping for all of their financial service needs, including retail and investment (securities) banking, credit cards, brokerage services, and property, casualty, and life insurance.

2. BankAmerica Corporation of San Francisco merged with NationsBank Corporation of Charlotte, North Carolina. The merger entailed a stock-for-stock swap between the two banks valued at $60 billion. The new megabank has assets in excess of $570 billion and a network of 3,800 branches in 27 states. Both NationsBank and BankAmerica had purchased securities firms in 1997. In 1991, San Francisco–based BankAmerica had purchased Security Pacific in what, at that time, was the largest ever bank merger. In 1997, NationsBank purchased Florida-based Barnett Bank and Missouri-based Boatman's Bancshares. The combined bank—called BankAmerica—is the second largest bank holding company in the country.

3. Ohio-based Banc One Corporation and First Chicago NBD Corporation swapped $30 billion of stock in order to merge. The result was the largest retail and commercial bank network in the Midwest. The new bank—called Bank One Corporation—has over 2,000 branches and assets in excess of $275 billion.

4. Minneapolis-based Norwest Corporation merged with San Francisco–based Wells Fargo to become the nation's sixth largest bank with assets over $191 billion and operations in 21 states throughout the West and Midwest. The new bank, known as Wells Fargo, is the nation's leader in offering banking services over the Internet.

   Although mergers continued at a rapid pace, the wave of mega-mergers subsided in late 1998 only to be revitalized in 2003 and 2004 with two of the largest mergers in history, which we review below.

1. On October 27, 2003, Bank of America, the third largest bank in the United States, announced that it was buying FleetBoston Financial Corporation, the nation's seventh largest bank, for about $47 billion. The new bank, with about $950 billion in assets, would be the second largest U.S. bank behind Citigroup. The merger gave Bank of America a foothold in New England, something that they had been lacking. The new bank had an estimated 180,000 employees and 5,700 branches.

2. On January 14, 2004, JP Morgan Chase, the nation's third largest bank, and Bank One Corporation, the nation's sixth largest bank, announced plans to merge in a $58 billion deal. The new bank has over $1.1 trillion in assets, over 145,000 employees, and 2,300 branches, making it the second largest bank behind Citigroup, leapfrogging over the new bank created by the Bank of America-FleetBoston merger in October 2003. JP

Morgan gained access to retail banking, while Bank One gained access to investment banking.

These mergers resulted from the desire to slash costs (and often employees), boost stock prices, and offer customers more diversified services. The trend is from traditional local banks with limited services to multiregional and national banks offering customers in a wider geographical area a larger menu of services, including bank accounts, loans, and investment and insurance services.

In 2008, the ongoing financial crisis that started in the subprime mortgage market and spread to the financial system as a whole ushered in another round of mega-mergers. This wave involved some of the oldest, most venerable names and included both commercial banks and investment banks.

1. On January 11th Bank of America announced plans to purchase Countrywide Financial for $4.1 billion in stock, and by July the transaction was completed.

2. On March 16th JPMorgan Chase announced plans to acquire Bear Stearns & Co. Inc. in a deal arranged by the Federal Reserve. This merger was completed June 2, 2008, with Bear Stearns' stock eventually purchased for $10 a share, up from the originally announced price of $2.

3. On September 14th Bank of America announces the purchase of the huge and famous investment bank, Merrill Lynch.

4. On September 15th the investment bank, Lehman Brothers, files for bankruptcy, with a large portion of the former investment bank purchased by the third largest U.K. bank, Barclays.

5. On September 25th after being put into receivership with the FDIC, the commercial banking operations of Washington Mutual were sold to JPMorgan Chase for $1.9 billion.

6. On October 3rd Wells Fargo announced its intention to purchase the Charlotte North Carolina based financial giant, Wachovia.

This most recent wave of mergers appears quite different than the earlier ones, with the combinations being arranged by government authorities to maintain financial stability. However from the perspective of the acquiring firms the incentive to merge is ultimately based on the promise of lower costs, wider customer base, and greater revenue and increased profit.

Write Off
Officially recognize a loan to a borrower who is not repaying, and not likely to repay in the future, as worthless.

Restructure (a Loan)
Change a loan to allow a borrower who would otherwise likely default to repay (e.g., allow the borrower to pay amounts currently due at some future date instead).

these funds in U.S. and European banks in exchange for deposit claims. Many U.S. banks began to loan funds denominated in dollars to less-developed countries. In the early 1980s, a crisis arose when the less-developed countries were unable to service their loans. As a result, many large banks had to **write off** or **restructure** these loans and incurred losses that took many years to be absorbed. Consequently, the 1990s and 2000s have seen less emphasis on growth, more caution, and greater stress given to asset quality and rate of return by banks.

In addition, a large number of foreign banks had made significant inroads into U.S. markets by the 1980s. Many of these foreign banks got caught up in the same types of problem loans as domestic banks in the 1980s, however, and their growth slowed considerably. Nevertheless, foreign banks still have a major presence in the United States. On June 30, 2007, 262 foreign banks from 50 different countries operated branches or offices in the United States. Branches of foreign banks controlled more than 19.8 percent ($1,845 billion) of banking assets in the United States. In addition, foreign banks had over 25 percent ownership interest in 68 U.S. commercial banks with about $738 billion in assets. Another 41 foreign banks operated agencies in the United States. An **agency of a foreign bank** is a more restrictive form of operation than a foreign branch in that the agency can raise funds only in the wholesale and money markets, whereas the branch of a foreign bank can accept retail deposits as well as borrow in the wholesale and money markets. An additional 149 foreign banks had representative offices in the United States.

Agency of a Foreign Bank
A U.S. banking office of a foreign bank that can only borrow funds in the wholesale and money markets and is not allowed to accept retail deposits.

Another indicator of an increase in international banking is the rapid growth in foreign office deposits of U.S. banks. In the second quarter of 2007 (April 1 to June 30), deposits in foreign offices increased by a record $143.3 billion (11.9 percent) and nondeposit liabilities increased by $128.3 billion (4.6 percent). In contrast, deposits in domestic offices declined by $3.2 billion (.05 percent).

In the 2000s, the banking system became truly international in scope. Advances in electronics and telecommunications allowed domestic and foreign bankers to participate in worldwide transactions without leaving home. Now, funds can be transmitted easily to virtually anywhere in the world. Deregulation has also made it possible for U.S. banks to open offices and enter foreign markets more easily than before, and vice versa.

In this new environment, bankers have discovered that there is tremendous competition for international transactions involving the electronic transfer of funds—and, consequently, profit margins are declining. Scores of banks from around the world can bid on loans with the result that the interest rate, and hence the return, are driven to rock-bottom levels. What appeared to be new lending opportunities have been somewhat disappointing because of the reduced profit margins. As a result, banks once again are looking to more traditional markets for expansion.

The time has come to round out our examination of commercial banking by focusing on the management of individual banks, with particular emphasis on the risks that banks face. In this way, we will gain a greater appreciation for what banks do and why.

Recap   Under the holding company corporate umbrella, banks have succeeded in expanding the geographical areas they serve and the array of financial services they offer the public. Barriers to interstate branching were removed in 1997 by the IBBEA. GLBA allowed banks, securities firms, and insurance companies to affiliate under common ownership and to provide their customers with an extensive array of financial services. Since the 1980s, the number of banks has declined because of bank failures and mergers. In the 1990s and early 2000s, many mega-mergers have occurred, and banking is becoming increasingly concentrated. Banking has become truly international in scope as well.

BANK MANAGEMENT: MANAGING RISK AND PROFITS

After the ribbon is cut and the new bank or branch opens, the bank's managers swing into action. In essence, it is the bank's balance sheet—assets, liabilities, and capital—that is "managed." The decisions involve what kinds of loans are to be made, what the prime rate should be, what interest rate to offer on one-year time deposits, and so forth. These decisions reflect an interaction between the bank's liquidity, safety, and earnings objectives and the economic and financial environment within which the bank operates.

To get a clearer picture of this interaction, it is useful to visualize bank management as having to face and deal with several types of risks and uncertainties, including credit or default risk, interest rate risk, liquidity risk, and exchange rate risk. A primary function of a bank loan officer is to evaluate or assess the default risk associated with lending to particular borrowers, such as firms, individuals, and domestic and foreign governments. To do this, the loan officer gathers all the relevant information about potential borrowers, including balance sheets, income statements, credit checks, and how the funds are to be used. As we shall see in Chapter 10, banks now can use credit derivatives to insure that returns to assets do not fall below a certain rate.

Bank managers must also manage interest rate risk. As noted in Chapter 8, a positive spread today can turn into a negative spread later when the cost of liabilities exceeds the return on assets. An example will illustrate the point. Suppose LHT National Bank is about to make a two-year loan to a local restaurant. The loan officer is satisfied that the credit risk is not excessive, and an interest rate of 7 percent is agreed upon. In effect, the bank, in view of the economic and financial outlook and its existing balance sheet, plans to finance the loan by issuing ("hiring") one-year time deposits paying 4 percent. The 3 percent spread will yield a handsome gross profit over the first year. What about the second year? As a great economic philosopher once said, "It all depends." At the end of the first year, the time deposit matures, and LHT has to "rehire" the funds needed to continue financing the outstanding loan to the restaurant. If the funds can be rehired at 4 percent, the spread will not change. However, suppose that the overall level of interest rates has risen dramatically, perhaps due to restrictive policy actions being pursued by the Fed, and the bank must now pay 10 percent on one-year time deposits. The 3 percent positive spread (7 percent minus 4 percent) in the first year of the loan is exactly offset by a 3 percent negative spread (7 percent minus 10 percent) in the second year. When various administrative and processing costs are considered, the loan turns out to be quite unprofitable.

Banks can use financial futures, options, and swaps to manage interest rate risk. These three instruments are discussed in later chapters, particularly Chapters 10 and 16. **Adjustable (variable) rate loans** can also be used to hedge interest rate risk. The basic idea is quite simple. The loan contract specifies that the rate charged on a loan—be it a consumer loan, business loan, or mortgage loan—will be adjusted up or down, say, once a year, as the cost of funds rises or falls. The aim, of course, is to preserve a profitable spread and to shift the interest rate risk onto the borrower.

Going back to our example, suppose the loan contract with the restaurant calls for an adjustable rate of three percentage points above the bank's cost of funds, instead of the fixed rate originally assumed. Such an arrangement produces the same 7 percent rate in the first year (4 percent plus 3 percent), but a 13 percent rate (10 percent plus 3 percent) in the second year. In effect, the bank has succeeded in shifting the interest rate risk to the borrower.[11] It is worthwhile emphasizing here that adjustable rate loans have become an important risk management tool. In the early 1990s, interest rates on liabilities fell faster than rates on assets, resulting in record bank profits. Imagine a positive spread becoming bigger over time.[12]

Like other intermediaries, banks need to manage liquidity risk. As noted in Chapter 8, a fairly large proportion of bank liabilities are payable on demand. Checkable deposits and savings deposits are two prominent examples. Banks must be prepared to meet unexpected withdrawals by depositors and to accommodate unexpected loan demands by valued customers. The resulting need for liquidity can be satisfied by holding some highly liquid assets, such as Treasury bills or excess reserves, or by expanding particular types of liabilities as needs develop. One way to expand liabilities is to attract large negotiable CDs, possibly by offering higher rates than those offered by the

Adjustable (Variable) Rate Loans

Loans where the interest rate is adjusted up or down periodically as the cost of funds to the lender changes.

competition. Other ways are to borrow more reserves from the Fed's discount facility or in the federal funds markets, or to increase borrowing in the repurchase agreements or overnight Eurodollar markets.

Finally, because banking has become more international in scope, some banks maintain stocks of foreign exchange that are used in international transactions and to service customers who need to buy or sell foreign currencies. If the exchange rate between two currencies changes, the value of the stocks of foreign exchange will also change. Thus, a bank, like any holder of foreign exchange, is subject to an exchange rate risk. As we shall see in Chapters 10 and 16, banks and other holders of foreign exchange now use exchange rate forward, futures, option, and swap agreements to hedge this risk.

BANK PERFORMANCE

Banks are facing increasing competition from other FIs and other nonfinancial corporations in a global environment. They have confronted a volatile economic and regulatory environment. In the face of such challenges, bank profitability, which was low in the 1980s, improved significantly in the 1990s. The strong profits were attributed to the strong economy that reflected favorably on bank assets, low interest rates, and growing sources of noninterest income.[13] Most analysts ascribed the better performance by banks to their more diversified portfolios and to their environment. The problem loans to less-developed countries such as Mexico, Brazil, and Argentina, which caused major loan losses for many large banks in the 1980s, were resolved. Banks have shored up capital due to new regulations. All of these factors led to record profit levels and high bank stock valuations.

Bank stocks performed below average in the late 1980s but did very well in the early 1990s and extremely well in the late 1990s. In the early 2000s, bank stocks declined as a result of the overall collapse of stock prices and the faltering economy. In the years following the 2001 recession, banks did quite well. By 2007 bank stock prices had surpassed their 1998 peak as the banking system became more profitable in the recovering economy. Up until 2007, the FDIC was reporting that the number of problem banks was declining and FDIC reserves for losses far exceeded that prescribed by law.[14] This changed dramatically in 2008 as bank profits plummeted. Although the financial crisis was centered in investment banking and insurance, commercial banks were adversely impacted as well with increased bank failures. As the crisis continued to unfold in early 2009, many of the nation's largest banks needed to be bailed out by the government.

Another major challenge facing banks as we enter the second decade of the new millennium is competition from other intermediaries and other nonfinancial companies that have taken an increasing share of intermediation. These nonbanks, as they have come to be called, face less regulation and, often, lower costs. Costs may be lower because nonbanks are less regulated than banks are with regard to what they can do and where they can locate. In addition, nonbanks do not face reserve requirements; nor do they have to maintain full-service branches. Banks' share of total intermediation is declining. Banks must increasingly adapt to a changing industry to maintain profits as well as to maintain market share. It is no wonder that banks are merging with other financial services firms including savings and loans, securities firms, and insurance companies, and expanding into areas previously prohibited to banks. One thing that is also clear is that the profitability and structure of the banking sector will be significantly altered as regulators, Congress, broad financial markets, and the economy at large work through the ongoing financial crisis of 2008.

In the next chapter, we look at financial innovation within the financial services industry.

Nonbanks
Other intermediaries and nonfinancial companies that have taken an increasing share of intermediation.

Bank management must deal with default risk, interest rate risk, liquidity risk, and exchange rate risk. Banks made record profits in the 1990s; then, after performing poorly in the early 2000s, resumed their upward trend until reaching a peak in 2007. Despite record profits over this period, banks' share of intermediation continued to decline. In 2008, bank profits and stock prices fell sharply, due to the ongoing financial crisis.

Summary of Major Points

1. Banking is a heavily regulated industry. Regulatory policy aims at promoting competition and efficiency, while preserving the safety and soundness of institutions. The Glass-Steagall Act of 1933 was enacted in response to the financial collapse of the Great Depression. The law established interest rate ceilings that could be paid to depositors, separated investment and commercial banking, and created the FDIC.

2. Banks in the United States are chartered by either the federal government or one of the 50 state governments. Federally chartered banks are called national banks and must belong to the Fed and subscribe to FDIC deposit insurance. State-chartered banks can, if they choose, belong to the Fed and/or subscribe to FDIC insurance. In fact, nearly all banks subscribe to FDIC insurance. Although only about 26 percent have federal charters and belong to the Fed, these banks tend to be the largest and have the most assets and banking offices.

3. The McFadden Act outlawed interstate branching by national banks. With regard to intrastate branching, the act required national banks to abide by the branching laws of the state in which they were located.

4. Restrictions were imposed on entry and branching as a result of fears that (1) more competition in local banking markets might lead to more failures and (2) letting big city banks enter markets served by small community banks might result in an unwanted concentration of power, to the detriment of smaller communities far from financial centers. These restrictions have resulted in a banking structure in which a large number of small banks control a small portion of total banking assets and a small number of large banks control the bulk of total banking assets. Many bank mergers occurred in recent years—some of them between banks and other financial services firms. Banking is becoming more heavily concentrated. As of June 1, 1997, the Interstate Banking and Branching Efficiency Act (IBBEA) of 1994 effectively allowed unimpeded nationwide branching. With the passage of the Gramm-Leach-Bliley Act of 1999, banks, securities firms, and insurance companies have been able to affiliate under common ownership and to offer the public a vast array of financial services under one umbrella since early 2000.

5. Under the holding company corporate umbrella, banks have been expanding the geographical areas they serve and the array of financial services they offer the public. The expansion by banks into areas traditionally served by other, more specialized, FIs has been matched by other FIs and nonfinancial institutions expanding into areas traditionally served mainly by banks. The result has been more competition in the financial services industry and considerable erosion in the domain and effectiveness of many long-standing regulations. Under GLBA, bank holding companies can be certified as financial holding companies. In addition to banking, financial holding companies can engage in securities underwriting and dealings, insurance activities, merchant banking activities, and other financial and nonfinancial activities determined by the Fed.

6. Banking has become internationalized as U.S. banks have increased their participation in international lending and domestic banks have faced competition from foreign banks. Branches of foreign banks now own over $1,845 billion or over 19 percent of U.S. banking assets. Electronic and telecommunication advances have helped to increase the competitiveness of international lending, thereby reducing the profit margin.

7. Bank managers supervise a bank's balance sheet. In the process, they have to face and deal with default risk, interest rate risk, liquidity risk, and exchange rate risk.

8. Regulators periodically audit (examine) banks. Conducting more of a management appraisal than a financial audit, the examiners pay particular attention to the quality of a bank's assets and, thus, how the bank is managing risk.

9. In the early 1990s, the cost of liabilities fell faster than the earnings on bank assets, resulting in record profits. The record profits continued into the late 1990s due to the strong economy, low interest rates, and increases in noninterest income. Bank stocks stumbled in the early 2000s but resumed an upward trend through 2007, surpassing previous highs. By 2008 the financial crisis was reducing bank profits and stock prices. A record number of vary large banks ran into difficulties, and were taken over by another institution.

Key Terms

Adjustable (Variable) Rate Loans, p. **199**
Agency of a Foreign Bank, p. **198**
Bank Holding Company, p. **190**
Bank Runs, p. **183**
Chartered, p. **184**
Comptroller of the Currency, p. **184**
Dual Banking System, p. **184**

Federal Deposit Insurance Corporation (FDIC), p. **183**
Federal Financial Institutions Examinations Council (FFIEC), p. **186**
Financial Holding Companies, p. **192**
Glass-Steagall Act of 1933, p. **183**
Interstate Banking and Branching Efficiency Act (IBBEA), p. **190**

McFadden Act, p. **189**
Merchant Banking, p. **193**
National Bank, p. **184**
Nonbanks, p. **200**
Regulation Q, p. **183**
Restructure (a Loan), p. **197**
Solvent, p. **186**
Write Off, p. **197**

Review Questions

1. We have stressed that the goals of efficiency and competition may conflict with the goals of safety and soundness. Give an example of when this could occur.

2. What is meant by a dual banking system?

3. What is a bank holding company? Why have most large banks become bank holding companies? What is a financial holding company? What must a bank holding company do to become a financial holding company?

4. What are the two major provisions of the McFadden Act? What was the motivation behind its passage?

5. What is the IBBEA? What was the motivation behind its passage?

6. How did multibank holding companies "get around" the McFadden Act before the passage of the IBBEA? Defend the following statement: The IBBEA did nothing more than endorse what was happening in the marketplace.

7. Critique the following statement: Since there are over 7,100 commercial banks in the United States, banking is obviously a highly competitive industry.

8. What is interest rate risk? Explain several ways that banks can reduce interest rate risk.

9. What is liquidity risk? Discuss ways in which banks deal with this risk. Does the development of nondeposit liabilities increase or decrease liquidity risk?

10. Identify two factors that have contributed to the growth of international banking. What factors contribute to reduced profit margins in this area?

11. Discuss the factors that have contributed to the revolutionary changes in the structure of U.S. banking in recent years. Which factors are most important? Could regulators have prevented many of the changes?

12. Will the revolutionary changes in banking increase or decrease the competitiveness of the industry? Why?

13. Discuss the following statement: The breakdown of barriers to interstate and intrastate banking means that competition in banking is decreasing.

14. What is the difference between a bank holding company and a financial holding company?

15. What is merchant banking?

Analytical Questions

Questions marked with a check mark (✓) are objective in nature. They can be completed with a short answer or number.

✓16. On September 30, 2008, what percentage of bank assets did the smallest 40 percent of banks control? What percentage of bank assets did the largest 7 percent of banks control?

✓17. Use Exhibit 9-1 to calculate the following:

    a. What percentage of state banks are members of the Fed?

    b. What percentage of banks are members of the Fed? What percentage of total deposits do they hold?

    c. What percentage of total assets do national banks own? What percentage of total deposits is in national banks?

    d. What percentage of total assets do state banks own?

Suggested Readings

For a great book on banking consolidation, see Gary A. Dymski, *The Bank Merger Wave: The Economic Causes and Social Consequences of Financial Consolidation* (Armonk, NY: M.E. Sharpe, 1999). Adam M. Zaretsky wrote a recent article on the same subject titled "Bank Consolidation: Regulators Always Have the Power to Pull the Plug," *The Regional Economist*, Federal Reserve Bank of St. Louis, January 2004.

For an interesting discussion of U.S. banking regulation and structure, or to ask your own question regarding the material in this chapter, see "Ask Dr. Econ," Federal Reserve Bank of San Francisco, available at: **http://www.frbsf.org/education/activities/drecon/askecon.cfm.**

For an in-depth look at technological advances in finance with special emphasis on the role of banks, see Jamie B. Stewart, Jr., "Changing Technology and the Payment System," *Current Issues in Economics and Finance*, Federal Reserve Bank of New York, 6, no. 11 (October 2000).

For a current look at bank profitability and other issues, see Til Schuerman, "Why Were Banks Better Off in the 2001 Recession?" *Current Issues in Economics and Finance*, Federal Reserve Bank of New York, 10, no. 1 (January 2004), and Alan Greenspan, *"The State of the Banking Industry"* Testimony Before the Committee on Banking, Housing, and Urban Affairs, U.S. Senate, April 20, 2004, **http://www.federalreserve.gov/boarddocs/testimony/2004/20040420/default.htm.**

Another interesting article is Robert R. Bliss and Mark J. Flannery, "Market Discipline in the Governance of U.S. Bank Holding Companies: Monitoring vs. Influencing," Working Paper No. WP-00-3, Federal Reserve Bank of Chicago (March 2000).

For a fascinating article about the sometimes harrowing experiences of a bank examiner, see David Fettig, ed., "Follow the Money," *The Region* 12, no. 2 (June 1998): 16–21, published by the Federal Reserve Bank of Minneapolis.

For a discussion of the trends likely to influence banking, see Dev Strischek, "Commercial Lending and Lenders in the 21st Century," *Journal of Lending and Credit Risk Management* 80, no. 12 (August 1998): 16–22.

For a glimpse into the future, see Robert T. Parry, "Financial Services in the New Century," *Federal Reserve Bank of San Francisco Economic Letter*, No. 98–15 (May 8, 1998).

For an interesting discussion of bank mergers, see Y. Amihud and G. Miller, eds., *Bank Mergers and Acquisitions* (Amsterdam: Kluwer Academic Press, 1998).

The Regulation and Supervision of Banks, Maximilian J.B. Hall, ed. (Northampton, MA: Edward Elgar, 2001), is a four-volume collection of 124 articles that span from 1973 to 1998.

For a look at "The Emerging Role of Banks in E-Commerce" see John Wenninger's article by the same name in *Current Issues in Economics and Finance*, Federal Reserve Bank of New York, 6, no. 3 (March 2000).

Two books that examine banking systems abroad may also be of interest. See *Islamic Banking*, by Mervyn K. Lewis and Latifa M. Algaoud (Northampton, MA: Edward Elgar, 2001), and *Banking and Financial Stability in Central Europe*, by Karl Petrick and David M.A. Green (Northampton, MA: Edward Elgar, 2001).

Endnotes

1. Subsequent research has seriously questioned this analysis. For example, it appears that the banks that were paying the very highest rates on deposits prior to the Great Depression were not the most likely to fail.

2. In addition, the applicant must be free of a criminal record.

3. In 1989, the FDIC was also given the responsibility of insuring the deposits of savings associations (S&Ls and savings banks) that wished to join. At that time, the FDIC was divided into two parts. The Bank Insurance Fund (BIF) insured commercial bank deposits of member banks, while the Savings Association Insurance Fund (SAIF) insured deposits of member savings associations. In 2006, BIF and SAIF were merged into one deposit insurance fund.

4. In 1985 some state- (as opposed to federally) insured S&Ls in Maryland and Ohio experienced "runs." Individual financial intermediaries, such as Indy Mac Bank, Washington Mutual, and Wachovia experienced runs in mid-2008, but these seemed firm-specific and concentrated among depositors with insured deposits in excess of $100,000 in one institution. Federal deposit insurance has proven effective in preventing any generalized run against the whole commercial banking system.

5. The FFIEC also prescribes uniform principles, standards, and report forms for the federal examination of savings and loans and credit unions.

6. In addition to what appeared to be lax regulation, many banks had problems during years of prosperity because leveraging was high and bad loans had been made to developing countries.

7. Note that this argument is in sharp contrast to one of the reasons given for the wave of bank mergers in recent years. Presumably, because of technological advances that began in the 1990s, large banks now can be more efficient than small ones. A recent study suggests, however, that most economies of scale are exhausted by the time banks reach the size of $10 billion to $25 billion in assets, which is certainly small by today's standards.

8. Banks that are not bank holding companies may apply simultaneously to become bank holding companies and financial holding companies.

9. This merger actually occurred prior to the passage of the Gramm-Leach-Bliley Act. Because it involved the merger of a bank and an insurance company, it would not have been legal without the ultimate passage of the GLBA.

10. OPEC stands for the Organization of Petroleum Exporting Countries, a cartel dominated by the Middle Eastern oil-producing nations.

11. Note that even though the interest rate risk for the bank has been reduced, default risk increases because the borrower is less certain of future payment obligations.

12. In a falling interest rate environment, a bank heavily into adjustable loans would be worse off than one that contracted at fixed rates on its assets.

13. In the early 1990s, profits rose mostly as a result of falling interest rates on liabilities, which lowered the cost of borrowing. The return on bank assets was also falling during the 1990s, but the cost of liabilities was falling faster, which resulted in increased profits.

14. The poor performance in the 1980s reflected troubled loans, which included loans to less-developed countries, and energy and commercial real estate loans. Concerns about the safety of the financial services industry, given the general climate surrounding the savings and loan crisis, were also quite prevalent.

10

CHAPTER TEN

Necessity is the mother of invention.

—Plato

Financial Innovation

Learning Objectives

After reading this chapter, you should know:

What financial innovation is and why it has
occurred at a rapid pace since the mid-1960s

How regulations, increased competition,
inflation, and volatile interest rates have
initiated financial innovations

The role of computer and information
technologies in fostering financial innovations

The major types of financial innovations in
recent years

THE ROAD FROM THERE TO HERE

Carol, a student at State University majoring in economics, is about to register for fall semester classes. She is interested in working overseas for a large financial institution, so she is attracted to a political science course (Pol Sci 505) that examines different political systems and how they influence the conduct of policy. The problem is that it is a graduate course, and undergraduates are not allowed to register for such courses. Undaunted, Carol meets with the instructor and convinces him that she is fully capable of handling the material. He tells her to register for Pol Sci 296, a listing usually reserved for special independent study courses, and to attend Pol Sci 505. In this way, Carol gets to take the course she desires and, in the process, evades the college regulation.

In recent semesters, State University has been experimenting by offering several classes over the Internet. This year, it is starting a virtual university where students can earn a degree without ever going to campus. This program will relieve the university's need for more classroom space and enable it to serve students who live in remote geographical areas far from campus. All in all, the university, driven to cut costs while serving more students, is finding creative ways to do so. Such adaptive or innovative behavior permeates many colleges today.

Innovation is also widespread in the economy at large. The driving force behind such behavior is reasonably straightforward: Participants in the economy (individuals and institutions) are simply trying to come as close as possible to achieving their objectives. The objective could be a well-rounded education likely to lead to a well-paying job for a student, maximum return at minimum risk for an investor, and maximum profitability for a financial firm. This process, referred to as *maximization*, is nothing more than the attempt of economic units to do the best they can given their objectives and the circumstances they face. If the circumstances pose a barrier to achieving an objective, there is an obvious incentive to find a way to surmount, or otherwise avoid, the obstacle. Likewise, if opportunities present themselves to increase profits, economic units have an incentive to pursue those opportunities. As the quotation at the beginning of the chapter suggests, such incentives give birth to the innovations we subsequently observe.

In our discussion of the financial system, we have repeatedly emphasized that change is an enduring characteristic. The current system is different from what it was 10 years ago, and it will be different 10 years from now. Financial innovation is the creation of new financial instruments, markets, and institutions in the financial services industry to increase profits. The major forces producing these changes include innovation in the ways people spend, save, and borrow funds in a globalized economy and innovation in the operations and scope of activities engaged in by financial intermediaries (FIs). In recent decades, computer and information technologies have played a major role in financial innovation. These advances have allowed for innovations in the way financial instruments are bought and sold, the creation of a variety of new financial instruments, and the globalization of financial markets that fulfill previously unmet services.

The purpose of this chapter is to develop a more complete understanding of the causes and consequences of the wave of financial innovation that has altered the U.S. financial system since the early 1960s. In Chapter 11, we look at the stresses and strains that the financial system faces and that are inherent in this dynamic environment.

MAJOR CAUSES OF FINANCIAL INNOVATION

Examples of innovative activity include the application of newly developed or existing technology in a new field or product area and the discovery and adoption of new methods of operating that legally evade rules and regulations. In both cases, the innovation increases profits. As we shall see, the adoption of new computer and information technologies and the avoidance of regulations have played key roles in the process of financial innovation since the 1960s. Two other factors have also been important in generating recent financial innovations: (1) FIs have faced increasing competition from other financial and nonfinancial institutions, causing them to innovate as part of a struggle to survive in a globalized environment, and (2) as prices, interest rates, and exchange rates have become more volatile, innovations have been developed to deal with this instability. All told, these factors have caused the period since the mid-1960s to be an era of rapid financial innovation, with one innovation leading to another and resulting in a restructuring of the entire financial services sector.

THE ANALYTIC FOUNDATIONS OF FINANCIAL INNOVATION

The incentive for FIs to engage in innovative activity flows from changes in the costs and benefits of innovating. On the cost side, one factor appears to have been particularly important. Since the 1970s, computer and telecommunications technologies have been increasingly available and powerful as well as less costly to adopt. As noted earlier, when discussing electronic funds transfer systems, these advances have reduced the transactions costs associated with managing, moving, and monitoring funds. They have also allowed for the globalization of financial markets where funds can be transferred fairly instantaneously and cheaply around the world.

The trading of financial claims is particularly receptive to computer advances because these claims are quite fungible (pronounced "FUHN-juh-bull"). Fungibility refers to the ease with which one item can be transformed into another. How does this characteristic fit in here? Think back to Carol and her professor at the beginning of the chapter. They innovated by essentially relabeling a course. This type of change is much easier and less costly than, say, turning an automobile plant into a computer factory. The situation is similar in the financial world where funds can be moved or transported and, in effect, relabeled relatively easily, making innovation less costly than it might be in other industries. Thus, applications of computer technologies to financial transactions have altered the nature and costs of financial transactions, have led to the creation of new financial instruments and institutions, and represent a major source of past and ongoing innovations in the financial services industry.

Turning to the benefits side, the interaction between the prevailing economic environment and the structure of financial regulations initially played the major role in financial innovation. Recall from Chapter 9 that Regulation Q put ceilings on interest rates that banks and savings and loans (S&Ls) could pay depositors. If innovating around these controls could avoid large losses and maintain profitability, then substantial ingenuity would be expended to find ways around the restrictions.

An example will help to clarify. Assume that you are a net lender with a savings deposit earning 5 percent, the ceiling rate, at HLT National Bank. Suppose that the rate on T-bills in the Treasury securities market is 8 percent. We would expect people to shift funds out of savings deposits and into T-bills. Such a removal of funds from banks and other intermediaries is called disintermediation.[1] The intermediaries are bypassed in the borrowing-lending process. As long as market interest rates are above Regulation Q ceilings, intermediaries subject to Regulation Q cannot effectively compete against open market instruments such as T-bills, commercial paper, and corporate bonds. Disintermediation follows as depositors take their funds out of intermediaries and invest them in open market instruments such as T-bills and commercial paper. The result is that banks are weakened as deposits flow out, and reduced profits or large losses loom on the horizon.

Prior to the late 1960s, interest rates rarely exceeded the Regulation Q interest rate ceilings. During the 1970s, interest rates were above the ceiling rates for significant periods of time, causing disintermediation to occur at an alarming rate. Savers with large balances had always been able to disintermediate and usually did so when market interest rates went above the Regulation Q limit. However, small savers with few alternatives were stuck earning the ceiling rate at depository institutions. Persistently high interest rates in the 1970s led to the development of money market mutual funds, which gave small savers an alternative to deposits in banks or other depository institutions subject to Regulation Q limits.

As discussed in Chapter 8, money market mutual funds pool funds from small investors, say, $5,000 from five individuals, and acquire money market instruments, such as T-bills and commercial paper, that small savers on their own cannot afford because of the high minimum denominations. The money market mutual fund passes the higher interest earned, minus a management fee, on to the small investors. For example, suppose you have $5,000 in a bank savings deposit yielding the Regulation Q ceiling rate of 5 percent, and the rate on commercial paper is 10 percent. You would like to transfer your funds from the depository institution, but the minimum denomination on commercial paper is $25,000, so you don't have enough to acquire the market instrument. The creation of money market mutual funds allows you to transfer your $5,000 to a fund that pools money from several small depositors and buys higher-denomination instruments while keeping a management fee. The money market mutual fund is an example of a financial innovation that created a new financial intermediary.

Now put yourself in the position of the bank's president. Profitable lending opportunities exist, but you are losing deposits through disintermediation and the transfer of funds to money market mutual funds.[2] You have an incentive to find a way to reverse the outflow of funds. The breakthrough occurs when your bank and other FIs develop new liabilities (discussed in the next section). Many of the new liabilities were created by taking existing bank liabilities from deposits subject to interest rate ceilings and relabeling them as liabilities not subject to the regulations. The newly created liabilities could pay the market interest rate, giving no incentive for depositors to disintermediate. However, the interaction between the prevailing economic environment and the structure of financial regulation—Regulation Q, in this case—produced rising benefits of innovation if Regulation Q limits could be avoided. Eventually, Regulation Q ceiling limits were removed, but before that happened, additional factors came into play, spurring further innovation by banks and other FIs.

Since the mid-1970s, banks and other FIs have been challenged by a sharp rise in competition from other domestic and global financial and nonfinancial institutions. In any industry with increased competition, profit margins generally decline, and cost-saving technological advances become more important. In a more competitive environment, the benefits of developing a new set of financial products and services are greatly increased. As you saw in Chapters 8 and 9, all FIs are becoming less specialized and more alike as they offer new products and services. For example, banks, under the auspices of bank and financial holding companies, now offer investment and financial advice, leasing, data processing, and tax planning. Look back at Exhibit 9–5 for a list of some activities now permitted for these companies. In recent years, the formation of financial holding companies has allowed banks to expand into insurance, securities, merchant banking, and other ancillary financial and nonfinancial activities that go far beyond the scope of those allowable under the bank holding company umbrella.[3] Thus, the greater the competition, the greater the drive to innovate to meet and beat the competition.

Finally, the greater volatility of price indexes, stock values, interest rates, exchange rates, and the like increases the risks—and, consequently, the costs—associated with intermediation. The increased risks make financial innovation to deal with this volatility more beneficial. New assets have been and are being developed to mitigate the risks associated with the greater price volatility. Financial forward, futures, and options markets are innovations that attempt to hedge interest rate and exchange rate risks. These instruments, called *derivatives*, are discussed shortly and are also the subject of Chapter 17. FIs now use them and other instruments to unbundle risk into its various parts. This allows those most willing and able to bear some of the risks of intermediation to do so, thus making financial markets more efficient. In addition, they allow financial and nonfinancial institutions to exploit every opportunity for profit from minute price differentials.

To summarize, the pace of innovation in the United States has been rapid over the past 45 years as the costs and benefits changed, as depicted in Exhibit 10-1. On the cost side, the malleability of financial claims and the application of emerging computer and telecommunications technology reduced the transactions costs associated with managing, moving, and monitoring funds. On the benefits side, three factors came into play:

1. The rise in interest rates increased the benefits in terms of higher profits associated with avoiding various regulations. For example, with market rates well in excess of

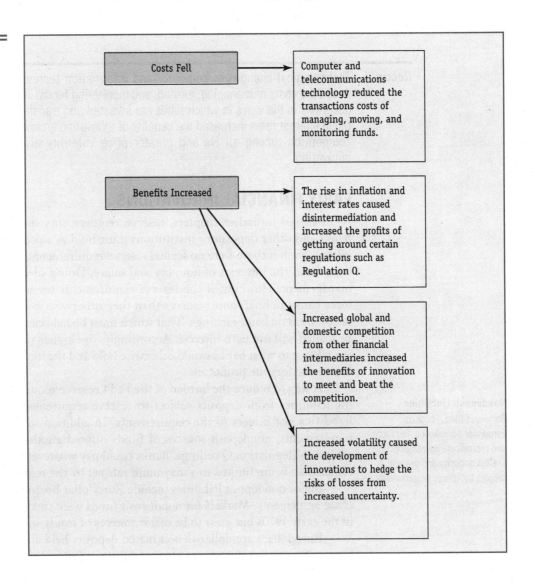

10-1

The Reasons for Financial Innovation over the Past 40 Years

Costs Fell → Computer and telecommunications technology reduced the transactions costs of managing, moving, and monitoring funds.

Benefits Increased →

The rise in inflation and interest rates caused disintermediation and increased the profits of getting around certain regulations such as Regulation Q.

Increased global and domestic competition from other financial intermediaries increased the benefits of innovation to meet and beat the competition.

Increased volatility caused the development of innovations to hedge the risks of losses from increased uncertainty.

Regulation Q ceiling rates on deposits, net lenders were induced to reduce their holdings of such deposits. The resulting disintermediation and its adverse effect on the profits of banks and other depository institutions prompted these FIs to find ways to create "new" liabilities not subject to the regulation.

2. Additionally, increased domestic and global competition from other FIs increased the benefits of financial innovation to "meet and beat" this competition.

3. Price and interest rate volatility increased the risks of financial intermediation and hence increased the benefits of developing new instruments such as futures and options to deal with these risks.

The regulatory structure played a pivotal role in generating financial innovation, but as we have seen, advances in computer and telecommunication technologies that reduce the costs of transferring funds were also significant. In the near future, advances in computer and information technologies are expected to be the predominant factor in the development of innovations.

A final note: Perhaps you have noticed that the benefits and costs of financial innovations are often interdependent. For example, changes in computer and information technologies have not only created cost-saving innovations but have also led to increased price volatility and increased competition in the provision of financial services that increase the benefits of innovating.

Recap   Technological changes in computer and information technologies have dramatically reduced the costs of managing, moving, and monitoring funds. These have led to numerous innovations in the ways in which funds are invested and transferred. In the 1960s and 1970s, rising interest rates increased the benefits of innovating around some regulations. Increased competition among all FIs and greater price volatility also increased the benefits of innovating.

EARLY FINANCIAL INNOVATIONS

As discussed in earlier chapters, reserve requirements specify the reserve assets that banks and other depository institutions must hold as a proportion of their deposit liabilities. Even if there were no formal reserve requirements, banks would still hold some reserves in the interests of liquidity and safety. Doing so would simply reflect prudent management. However, if the reserve requirements set by the regulatory authorities force banks to hold more reserves than they otherwise would, this excess constitutes a tax or drain on bank earnings. That which must be held cannot be loaned! What cannot be loaned will not earn interest. Accordingly, the higher that the reserve requirements are relative to what banks would otherwise hold and the higher the interest rates are, the higher the forgone profits are.

Nondeposit Liabilities
Borrowed funds, such as Eurodollar borrowings, fed funds, and repurchase agreements, that are not deposits and are not subject to reserve requirements.

A way to reduce the burden of the Fed's reserve requirements was to relabel existing liabilities from deposits subject to reserve requirements to so-called **nondeposit liabilities** not subject to the requirements. In addition to being exempt from reserve requirements, nondeposit sources of funds offered another advantage: they were not subject to Regulation Q ceilings. Banks could pay whatever rate prevailed in the market rather than being limited to a maximum rate set by the regulators.

Major nondeposit liabilities include Eurodollar borrowings, fed funds, and repurchase agreements. Markets for nondeposit funds were small and relatively unimportant in the early 1970s but grew to be major sources of funds, especially for large banks.

Eurodollars are dollar-denominated deposits held abroad. U.S. banks sometimes borrow Eurodollar deposits to obtain additional funds. Eurodollar borrowings by U.S.

Regulation D
A regulation that prescribed reserve requirements on some deposits.

banks provide an excellent example of a nondeposit source of funds that often represented a relabeling of liabilities to avoid Regulation Q (interest rate ceilings) and **Regulation D** (reserve requirements). The result has been a significant leak or hole in the regulatory dike and important shifts in the composition of bank liabilities (sources of funds) that spawned the growth of the Eurodollar and Eurocurrency markets.[4] "A Closer Look" on page 212 looks at the development of the Eurodollar market.

As we first discussed in Chapter 4, fed funds are essentially reserves that banks trade among themselves for periods of one to several days. The interest rate determined in the market for fed funds is called the *fed funds rate*. Like other market interest rates, it is determined by the forces of supply and demand. The demanders are banks and other depository institutions that need reserves (funds) to meet their reserve requirements, to meet unexpected withdrawal demands, or to finance loans. The suppliers are banks and other depository institutions that have surplus funds and no other immediate use for them.

In the 1960s, the fed funds market for overnight borrowing and lending of reserves began to experience tremendous growth.[5] It also changed considerably. Rather than borrowing just to meet temporary shortfalls in reserves, larger commercial banks came to look to the fed funds market as a permanent source of funds. They borrowed large amounts each and every day and funded assets, including long-term assets, on a continual basis with this source of funds. Small banks with fewer lending opportunities tended to be net lenders in this market.

Recall from Chapter 4 that an overnight repurchase agreement is an agreement in which a bank takes a government security from its asset portfolio and sells it with the simultaneous agreement to buy it back tomorrow at a price set today. The purchase price tomorrow is higher than the selling price today, with the difference being the interest that the lender receives from the bank. In reality, a repurchase agreement is a secured loan with the government security serving as collateral. Like fed funds, repurchase agreements became a significant new source of funds that large banks could access to get new funds to lend. These agreements were often "rolled over" on a daily basis, providing a "permanent" source of funds. As of September 30, 2008, the net amount of outstanding borrowings of fed funds and repurchase agreements by commercial banks was just over $678.4 billion.

Retail Sweep Accounts
A financial innovation that relabels deposit liabilities to nondeposit liabilities by "sweeping" balances out of transactions accounts that are subject to reserve requirements and into other accounts that are not.

A more recent innovation, a **retail sweep account** also involves the relabeling of deposit liabilities to nondeposit liabilities. First appearing in 1994, these accounts "sweep" balances out of transactions accounts that are subject to reserve requirements and into other deposits (usually money market deposit accounts) that are not.[6] Required reserves fall by the amount of funds in sweep accounts multiplied by the required reserve ratio. Balances in sweep accounts grew from $5.3 billion in January 1994 to $737 billion in March 2007. In the aggregate, required reserves dropped from about $60 billion in 1994 to about $41 billion in March 2007. As required reserves fall, ceteris paribus, banks have more funds to lend.

Another innovation that did not involve relabeling deposit liabilities but was no less important was the creation of negotiable certificates of deposit (CDs). The creation of a secondary market for large certificates of deposit in 1961 made them "negotiable" CDs. Thus, a corporation with excess funds, perhaps not having to make payroll until next week, could invest the funds in a negotiable CD with the knowledge that if the funds were needed before the CD matured, the CD could be sold in the secondary market. Although they were subject to the same reserve requirements that other CDs were, CDs with maturities of 30 to 89 days were exempted from Regulation Q ceilings in 1970. Reserve requirements on all negotiable CDs were eliminated by the end of 1973. Negotiable CDs are a particularly important source of funds for banks because a bank

The Development of the Eurodollar Market

In the 1970s, as we have seen, market interest rates frequently were above Regulation Q ceilings, causing disintermediation. Eventually, in 1980, Regulation Q was abolished on all but demand deposits. Corporations were still barred by regulation from holding negotiable orders of withdrawal (NOW) accounts and other interest-earning checkable deposits and, therefore, were left with their funds in short-term, no-interest demand deposits. Can you guess what happened? Corporate treasurers developed cash management techniques that would minimize their holdings of demand deposits. They moved liquid funds to money market instruments, such as commercial paper and T-bills. The banks responded with an all-out effort to maintain their liabilities and alleviate the disintermediation. They focused on getting corporations to convert what would otherwise be lost demand deposits into nondeposit liabilities. Even though the banks had to pay interest on the new liabilities, this was preferable to losing the liabilities altogether; if the liabilities were lost, the banks' ability to make loans would decrease. One of the ways banks converted demand deposits to nondeposit liabilities was through the use of Eurodollar deposits.

The following diagram shows how a demand deposit gets converted into a Eurodollar borrowing.

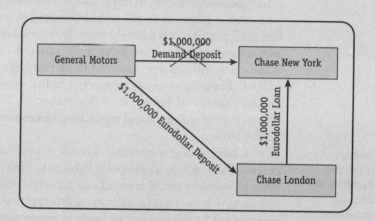

After its inception in the 1950s, the Eurodollar market was used to get around both Regulations Q and D. If market interest rates rose above the maximum rate that a bank—say, Chase—was allowed to offer on time deposits, disintermediation became a threat. Rather than sit idly by and watch its available funds dwindle and its ability to lend be constrained, the portfolio managers at Chase tried to persuade General Motors' financial officer to exchange the deposit at Chase New York for a deposit at the Chase branch in London. The deposit, which would be denominated in dollars and be free of reserve requirements and interest rate ceilings, would be known as a Eurodollar deposit.[a] The opportunity to evade some U.S. banking regulations by channeling funds through European banks encouraged the significant growth of the Eurodollar market.

As soon as General Motors deposited the funds in Chase's London branch, Chase's home office in New York would borrow the funds from its London branch. This is called a *Eurodollar borrowing*, a borrowing of dollar-denominated funds from Europe. As a nondeposit source of funds (liability), it is not subject to reserve requirements. Once Regulation Q was abolished on all but demand deposits, the Eurodollar market became one of the de facto vehicles that banks used to pay interest on corporate demand deposits. Corporate demand deposits were simply converted into overnight Eurodollar deposits.

Returning to our example, as a net result of this series of transactions, Chase Bank in New York, in effect, relabeled its demand deposit liability (owed to General Motors) as a Eurodollar borrowing (owed to General Motors) from its London branch. In the process, Chase New York reduced the volume of required reserves it had to hold. Assuming the reserve requirement on demand deposits was 10 percent, Chase New York could now lend more, even though its total liabilities had not changed. In addition, General Motors would earn and Chase would pay interest on the deposit.

In this example, General Motors converts a $1,000,000 demand deposit at Chase New York to a Eurodollar deposit at Chase London. Chase New York was holding $100,000 in required reserve assets against the $1,000,000 demand deposit. Chase New York borrows the Eurodollar deposit from Chase London. The Eurodollar deposit then becomes a $1,000,000 nondeposit liability, free of reserve requirements. General Motors earns interest on the deposit, and Chase New York has $100,000 in additional funds to lend.

One last point: Don't get the idea that the funds originally in Chase New York were withdrawn by General Motors, packed in a suitcase, flown to London, deposited, borrowed by Chase New York, and flown back to New York. We have traced out the relevant transactions in slow motion. In fact, the funds would never have left New York, and all the transactions could have occurred electronically, within minutes, using modern telecommunications technology.

Endnote

a. Prior to the development of the Eurodollar market, a deposit made in a foreign bank was usually denominated in the currency of the host country. For example, an American would take dollars, convert them to British pounds sterling, and deposit them in a bank in London. When the funds were withdrawn, the pound sterling had to be exchanged for dollars.

---

can advertise and attract additional deposits of negotiable CDs to extend its lending. This advantage was particularly significant when restrictions on branching realistically restricted the growth of checkable deposits to a certain geographical area. A bank could attract CD deposits by advertising high rates.[7]

The financial regulations and structures that had been designed during the Great Depression were increasingly ill suited to the changing economic and technological environment of the 1970s. As innovations weakened the effectiveness of various regulations, regulators recognized the difficulty, if not the impossibility, of controlling financial flows and the market for financial services. Accordingly, they decided to deregulate by dismantling the regulations.[8] The result was landmark legislation enacted by Congress in 1980 and 1982.[9] These laws phased out Regulation Q, expanded the asset and

Deregulate
The dismantling of existing regulations.

liability powers of banks and thrifts, allowed thrift institutions to offer checkable deposits, and established reserve requirements that applied to and were the same for all depository institutions.

Two other laws in the mid- and late 1990s further deregulated financial markets by eliminating most restrictions on interstate banking and allowing banks to merge with securities and insurance firms, thus effectively repealing the Glass-Steagall Act.[10] We look in much greater detail at all of these laws in Chapter 12, which deal with regulating the financial services industry.

Innovation within the financial system has proceeded due to unprecedented competition among banks and other financial institutions in a globalized financial environment. Advances in computer and information technologies have made the increased competition possible and have transformed the financial system into a global system. With the new technologies, funds can be transferred instantaneously around the globe at a very low cost. Thus, globalization of finance due to technological advances would have proceeded even without the concomitant growth in world trade.

Recap A major form of innovation that got around Regulations Q and D was the relabeling of deposit liabilities as nondeposit liabilities. Examples include Eurodollar borrowings, fed funds, repurchase agreements, and retail sweep accounts. The creation of negotiable CDs was another innovation that allowed banks to attract additional funds. Because market participants had found ways around many regulations, Congress passed two major deregulation statutes in the early 1980s that phased out Regulation Q ceilings, expanded the asset and liability powers of banks and thrifts, allowed all thrifts to offer checkable deposits, and established the same reserve requirements for all depository institutions. Two other laws in the 1990s removed most restrictions on interstate banking and allowed banks to merge with securities firms and insurance companies.

INNOVATIONS IN THE PAYMENTS SYSTEM

Innovations in the financial services industry have dramatically changed the nature of intermediation by creating new products, markets, and institutions. In recent years, these innovations have been made possible by advances in computer and information technologies. As Jamie B. Stewart, Jr., writes:

> I cannot recall a time of more fundamental and pervasive change in the financial services industry. Much of this change—and the pace at which it is taking place—is driven by extraordinary advances in computing and telecommunications technology. These advances in technology are not just evolutionary, they are revolutionary, and they are transforming virtually every aspect of commerce and banking.[11]

The payments mechanism is the means by which transactions are completed—that is, how money is transferred among transactors. The role of technology is perhaps nowhere more apparent or more important than in the innovations surrounding the payments system. The current payments mechanism has evolved from a primitive state and will continue to evolve in the future. This tendency to change, which we have already seen in those things functioning as a means of payment, is significantly influenced by the technology used to execute transactions.

Some of the more obvious innovations in the payments mechanism due to technological advances include such things as ATM machines, cash cards, debit cards, point-of-sale terminals, and home banking over the Internet. Other less-visible technology-related innovations include direct pay deposit and direct bill pay plans. Electronic payments account for about 90 percent of the dollar value of all transactions! In this system, payments are made to third parties in response to electronic instructions rather than instructions written on a paper check or by using currency.

Note that an electronic funds transfer system does not eliminate the need for deposit accounts; it is just a more efficient way of transferring funds from one deposit account to another. To pay your grocery bill, for instance, your account is debited by the amount of your bill, and the grocer's account is credited by the same amount at the time of the exchange. The whole system is computerized so that no written checks are necessary. All you need is an account number and a debit card that you present to the grocer. The grocer, in turn, enters the prices of your purchases into a computer terminal (called a *point-of-sale terminal*), and at the end of the month, you receive a statement giving your current balance and a record of all the charges and deposits to your account. This is just like a checking account statement, but you do not have to write all of those checks.

Technological innovations will eventually make checks much less important, or maybe even obsolete, as a means of transferring purchasing power. This is because paper checks are a much more costly way of making payments than electronic methods. However, as we saw in Chapter 3, starting in October 28, 2004, banks were authorized to substitute an electronic image of a check for the actual paper check to expedite the check-clearing process. Rather than physically transporting the original check, the electronic image can be sent almost instantaneously all over the country quickly and cheaply.

Currently, many employers, in cooperation with banks, pay salaries by automatically crediting them to their employees' bank accounts rather than by issuing the customary weekly, biweekly, or monthly check. Such automatic credits are also a form of an electronic funds transfer system. More than 60 percent of workers (and 95 percent of federal government employees) now receive their pay in this manner. The vast majority of Social Security recipients receive their payments through direct deposit. Also, you can file your tax return electronically and receive a tax refund that is directly deposited into your checking account.

Your depository institution most likely has automatic teller machines (ATMs), which permit you to make deposits and withdrawals even late at night, when the institution itself is closed. In all probability, your college campus and your favorite grocery stores have a few ATMs. ATMs, too, are a form of an electronic funds transfer system. As the ownership of personal computers and modems spreads, it will be possible to conduct a large portion of one's financial transactions from home. See the "Looking Forward" box for more information on the evolving concept of the "electronic purse."

Basically, electronic funds transfer systems are nothing more than the application of computer and information technologies to the entire area of financial transactions and services. Their aim is to reduce the physical handling and labor costs associated with an ever-expanding volume of paper checks, deposit slips, and the like, as well as to provide increased convenience and service to the public. As questions regarding the privacy of financial records, security of the systems, and legal responsibilities are resolved, new payments practices and electronic funds transfer systems will spread. The result will be further evolution in how money is used and, perhaps, changes in what functions as money. The evolution of money and the payments mechanism go hand in hand with the development of an economy.

Looking Forward

The Electronic Purse: An Innovation in the Making

Many banks have begun developing a new payments mechanism called the *electronic purse* or *stored-value card*. Prepaid cards for a single use have been available for many years. For example, some toll roads accept only a smart card in payment, college dorm cafeterias offer a prepaid smart card, libraries offer prepaid photocopy cards, and in many areas, phone companies sell prepaid calling cards.

The electronic purse will allow a single card the size of a credit card to be used in multiple locations to make many kinds of purchases. When making purchases, the card is passed through the merchant's point-of-sale terminal. Funds are deducted directly from the buyer's card and added to the point-of-sale terminal. Vendors can transfer the balances on their terminals to their bank accounts via a telephone transfer as frequently as they want. When the value on the card is spent, consumers can add additional funds to the card via a telephone transfer, an ATM machine, or a computer transfer. A personal identification number much like an ATM number can be used to validate that the card is being used by its owner.

The multiple-use smart card will have one or more computer chips embedded in it capable of storing and transferring information. The main benefit of the card to the consumer is convenience. Buying a cup of coffee, a newspaper, or a candy bar from a vending machine will no longer require fumbling for change. For merchants, the electronic card saves time and money in handling cash. Unlike checks, the card offers guaranteed payment and will most likely have lower transactions costs than those of credit cards or debit cards. For the issuer, there may be many benefits. For example, smart cards offer a potential source of fee income, and the issuer will earn interest on the unspent balances on the cards.

There are still many questions as to how smart cards will work. For instance, will transactions made on the cards be traceable? Such record keeping could help the police trace fraudulent use. Or should the use of the smart card be untraceable, like cash? Still other issues are whether the balances on smart cards will be covered by deposit insurance, whether nonbanks can issue the cards, and whether the cards will affect reserve management and the money supply. In the next few years, many of these questions will be resolved.

DERIVATIVES
Forward, Futures, and Option Agreements

Derivatives
Instruments such as forward, futures, options, swap, and other agreements that are routinely used to separate the total risk of a financial asset into subparts and that derive their value from the underlying assets.

Forward, futures, and option agreements are financial innovations used by financial institutions and others to reduce interest rate and exchange rate risks. They were developed in the 1970s and have grown exponentially since then. Since we devote all of Chapter 17 to these instruments, we provide here only a cursory description of each instrument and how it is used to reduce risks. Because these contracts derive their value from underlying assets, they are called **derivatives**. The underlying assets used in forward, futures, and option agreements include stocks, bonds, Treasury securities, stock market indexes, and foreign exchange.

Forward agreements are customized arrangements between two parties to trade a financial asset on a date in the future at a price determined today. The transactions costs of arranging forward agreements can be high because the amount of the financial instruments and delivery dates are customized. **Futures agreements** are standardized contracts where financial instruments are traded at a price determined today on a date in the future. They are bought and sold on organized exchanges. Because the contracts are standardized with regard to quantities and delivery dates, futures agreements cost much less than forward agreements. **Option agreements** give the buyer the right, but not the obligation, to buy or sell a standardized basket of financial securities at a price determined today on a standardized date in the future. The buyer of a **put option** has the right to sell the standardized basket. The buyer of the **call option** has the right to buy the standardized basket on the future date. In both cases, the buyer of the option will exercise the option (buy or sell) only if price changes in the underlying financial securities make it advantageous to do so. The seller of the option receives a premium because he/she will have to make a payment to the buyer if the price changes in such a way to make it advantageous for the buyer to exercise the option. The seller accepts the risk of a possible financial loss in exchange for the premium payment. As you shall see in Chapter 17, forward, futures, and option agreements are routinely used to hedge interest rate and exchange rate risk. The derivative contracts can be sold separately to the investors most willing and able to bear those risks. Two examples may help to clarify.

Consider the case where a domestic firm issues foreign bonds. Because the bonds will be repaid in a foreign currency and it is uncertain what the exchange rate between the dollar and the foreign currency will be on the due date, an exchange rate risk occurs. The firm can use a foreign exchange forward agreement to hedge this risk. With the foreign exchange forward agreement, the firm locks in today the number of dollars that will be exchanged for the foreign currency at the later date. It is now certain how many dollars it will receive for a given amount of foreign exchange.

In another example, a credit union has made two-year car loans funded by one-year deposits. Because it is unsure of what it will have to pay for the one-year deposits a year from now, it faces the risk that the interest rate will rise during the second year and the cost of the funds will exceed the rate on the car loans. For instance, say the credit union lends funds for two years at 8 percent funded by a one-year, 4 percent CD that has to be renewed at the end of one year. If the interest rate in one year turns out to be 9 percent, then the credit union will lose. It is only earning 8 percent on deposits it is paying 9 percent to borrow. The credit union can use futures or option contracts to hedge this interest rate risk.

Forward, options, and futures agreements can also be used to speculate about future prices. For example, when speculators believe stock prices are going down, they can sell a futures contract today that will guarantee them a certain price on the future date. If the speculators are correct and prices do go down, they will make a profit. Or, if I hold a large portfolio of stocks and I'm worried about prices falling, I can use a stock index futures contract or an option contract to hedge this risk and to reduce or eliminate my losses if stock prices do fall. More on this in Chapter 17.

Swap Agreements

Swap agreements are another type of derivative. An **interest rate swap** is a financial innovation that can be used to reduce the risk of future interest rate changes over a long period of time, sometimes up to 15 years. Swaps involve two parties that trade interest

Forward agreements
Customized arrangements between two parties to trade a financial asset on a date in the future at a price determined today.

Futures agreements
Standardized contracts where financial instruments are traded at a price determined today on a date in the future.

Option agreements
Standardized agreements that give the buyer the right, but not the obligation, to buy or sell a standardized basket of financial securities at a price determined today on a standardized date in the future.

Put option
An option where the buyer has the right, but not the obligation, to sell a standardized basket of financial securities at a price determined today on a standardized date in the future.

Call option
An option where the buyer has the right, but not the obligation, to buy a standardized basket of financial securities at a price determined today on a standardized date in the future.

Interest Rate Swaps
A financial innovation used to reduce the risk of future interest rate changes over a long period of time. Swaps involve two parties trading interest payment streams to guarantee that their respective payment inflows will more closely match their outflows.

payment streams to guarantee that their respective payment inflows will more closely match their outflows. Originating in 1982, this totally new instrument is used mainly by entities such as commercial banks, savings and loans, other intermediaries, government agencies, and securities dealers to reduce interest rate risk. The use of swaps is growing fast, particularly at large banks. Interest rate swaps make markets more efficient and reduce risks, but they are often complex. Because of their intricacy, we limit our discussion to a simple case.

Consider an example involving two commercial banks: Bank Two and Bank Three. Bank Two has long-term fixed-rate loans, such as mortgages, that it funds with floating or variable-rate money market accounts. The interest payments on money market accounts fluctuate with market interest rates, but the interest payments earned on the loans do not. The other bank—Bank Three—has made floating or variable-rate loans. The interest payments on these loans go up and down with an index of market interest rates, such as rates on government bonds. The bank funds these loans with long-term fixed-rate deposits. The interest payments on these deposits do not change.

Both banks make a profit on the spread, or the difference between what the banks earn on their loans and what they pay depositors for the use of their deposits. But there is a problem: As the loans and deposits are now configured, both banks have some interest rate risk. In other words, both banks are in a position in which a change in interest rates can cause them to experience a loss. If interest rates go up, Bank Two (with fixed-rate loans and variable-rate deposits) may end up paying more for the use of its deposits than it is earning on its loans. If interest rates go down, Bank Three (with variable-rate loans and fixed-rate deposits) may end up paying more for the use of its deposits than it is earning on its loans.

All is not lost, however. These two intermediaries can get together through an interest rate swap arranged by another bank. Bank Two and Bank Three can trade the interest payments on their deposits (liabilities), but not the principal payments. After the swap, Bank Two will be funding fixed-rate assets with fixed-rate liability interest payments, and Bank Three will be funding variable-rate assets with variable-rate instruments. Both can hedge risk by engaging in the swap. The interest payments that Bank Two receives are fixed because it has fixed-rate loans. After the swap, the interest payments it makes to fund the loans will also be fixed. A rise in interest rates will no longer put Bank Two in a losing position. Bank Three's earnings on its loans will continue to move up and down with market interest rates, but the interest payments it makes to fund the loans will also be flexible. A fall in interest rates will no longer put Bank Three in a losing position. Exhibit 10-2 illustrates this example of an interest rate swap.

We have described a simple interest rate swap, but as noted previously, these instruments can be—and usually are—complex.

A currency swap is an innovation whereby one party agrees to trade periodic payments in a given currency, over a specified period of time, with another party who agrees to do the same in a different currency. Currency swaps can be used to hedge against foreign exchange rate risk over a multiyear period. Thus, through the use of currency swaps, foreign exchange risk can be reduced for a significant period of time in the future.

Like many financial innovations, currency swaps originally developed as a means to circumvent regulation. In the past, many countries employed capital controls that delayed or forbade the conversion of earnings by a foreign company in a local currency into the domestic currency of the foreign company. The plan was to encourage greater foreign investment by domestically based foreign subsidiaries. By delaying the conversion of foreign-denominated earnings into the parent-company's domestic currency, countries hoped that foreign subsidiaries would engage in increased investment. An

Currency Swaps
A financial innovation used to hedge exchange rate risk over a long period of time, whereby one party agrees to trade periodic payments in a given currency with another party who agrees to do the same in a different currency.

This Year	
Bank Two	*Bank Three*
Two-year loans earn 9% fixed	Two-year loans earn 8% variable
Deposits cost 5% variable	Deposits cost 6% fixed

Next Year Rates Go Up—No Swap	
Bank Two	*Bank Three*
Loans earn 9% fixed ☹	Loans earn 12% variable
Deposits cost 9% variable	Deposits cost 6% fixed ☺

Next Year Rates Go Down—No Swap	
Bank Two	*Bank Three*
Loans earn 9% fixed ☺	Loans earn 5% variable
Deposits cost 2% variable	Deposits cost 6% fixed ☹

Next Year Rates Go Up—They Swap	
Bank Two	*Bank Three*
Loans earn 9% fixed ☺	Loans earn 12% variable ☺
Deposits cost 6% fixed	Deposits cost 9% variable

Next Year Rates Go Down—They Swap	
Bank Two	*Bank Three*
Loans earn 9% fixed ☺	Loans earn 5% variable ☺
Deposits cost 6% fixed	Deposits cost 2% variable

The swap allows both banks to be happy all the time!

example will make this clearer. Imagine a U.S. soft drink company has bottling and sales operations in China. If China delays the conversion of yuans into dollars, the bottling company will forgo interest earnings it could earn if it could convert yuans to dollars now. Thus, it makes sense for the soft drink company to borrow additional yuans, ask another Chinese company with U.S. subsidiaries to borrow dollars, and then the two companies can "swap" the proceeds from their respective loans. Each company gets immediate access to the currency that it wants and both innovate around the capital-control regulations. Like other regulations, currency controls have been greatly reduced or eliminated, but the innovation they spawned has not disappeared.

Credit Derivatives

A new type of derivative, the credit derivative contract, was first developed in the late 1990s and is used by banks and other lenders to unbundle credit risk—that is, to get someone else to bear the loss in the event of a default. Credit derivatives transfer the risk to another party that the return in a credit transaction (such as a loan) falls below a certain rate. The party that accepts the risk receives a fee for doing so, and if the return falls below the specified rate will have to make a payment to the other party. Credit derivatives derive their value from the underlying debt instruments such as loans. For the purchaser (beneficiary), credit derivatives are like insurance that hedges the default risk of the loans they hold. For the seller (guarantor), a risk is taken on in return for a fee. Banks enter into both sides of these agreements—either as guarantor (selling the insurance) or beneficiary (buying the protection)—as a way of diversifying their credit risk more broadly than across their own portfolio of loans.

As of September 30, 2008, the notional value of credit derivatives held by U.S. banks as guarantors was just $7.9 trillion, and the value held as beneficiaries was $8.3

Credit derivatives
Contracts that transfer the default risk of a loan or other debt instrument from the holder of the loan (beneficiary) to a guarantor who receives a fee for accepting the risk.

trillion. The twenty-five largest U.S. banks account for virtually 100 percent of these credit derivatives.[12] Although credit derivatives are only 7 percent of the derivatives market, they are the fastest growing segment of the market. The market is also global. In addition to banks, the main market participants are hedge funds, insurance companies, and pension funds. Until the current financial crisis, credit derivatives have been largely unregulated. Since collapses in this market have exacerbated the crisis of 2008–2009, this will undoubtedly change in the future.

The examples of derivatives (including forwards, futures, options, swaps, and credit derivatives) that we have just described are quite simple. Many derivatives in use today are far more complex and require the use of computers to evaluate their risk. Advances in the mathematical modeling of risk have made it possible to develop increasingly complex financial products and trading strategies. Indeed, "financial engineers" have used financial and mathematical models to create innovative and exciting "hybrid" financial instruments that meet the needs of and give new opportunities to financial market participants. If used properly, these new products and strategies increase the efficiency of the financial system.

That risk-averse, profit-seeking financial market participants are resourceful and ingenious in dealing with risk is not surprising. When risks increase (as they do when markets become more volatile), market participants develop new ways to "handle" or manage the risk. Thus, we have witnessed the phenomenal growth of swaps and other derivatives. Financial and nonfinancial corporations must now be aware of and take every opportunity to reduce risks. If they fail to do so, they may find that they are not playing on a level field. Even the most skeptical of players may become convinced that they should be using the flashy new derivative instruments rather than be vulnerable to risk. If prices settle down (become less volatile), the growth of these markets may slow, but it is doubtful they will ever disappear. Once such markets are so highly developed, they will continue to be a means to capitalize on even small opportunities to reduce risk.

Recap	Derivatives such as forward, futures, option, and swap agreements have allowed the risks associated with intermediation to be unbundled. (Forwards, futures, and options are covered in depth in Chapter 17.) Interest rate swaps entail two parties trading interest payment streams to guarantee that the inflows of payments will more closely match the outflows. Currency swaps involve trading a set of payments in one currency for a set of payments in a different currency. They are used to reduce a firm's exposure to foreign exchange risk. Currency swaps can be done for multiple-year periods. Credit derivatives transfer the risk to another party that the return in a credit transaction falls below a certain rate. The party that accepts the risk does so for a fee.

Securitization

Another financial innovation resulting from the current financial environment is the spread of securitization to many loan markets. Securitization is the process whereby relatively illiquid financial assets are packaged together and sold off to individual investors. In essence, securitization turns these relatively illiquid instruments into quite liquid investments called asset-backed securities. A market maker agrees to create a secondary market by buying and selling the securities. Securitization originated in the mortgage market in the late 1970s, when mortgage loans began to be packaged together and sold off to investors as securities, often with government insurance guaranteeing that the principal and interest would be repaid. Securitization became popular because

Securitization
The process whereby relatively illiquid financial assets are packaged together and sold off to individual investors.

Asset-Backed Securities
Securities that result from the process of securitization.

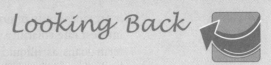

Securitization of Small Business Loans

In late 1993, small business loans were packaged into securities (securitization), and a secondary market for them was created. Indeed, a secondary market makes the securitization process much more successful because it increases the liquidity of the new securities. As is the case with all innovations, and true to our quotation at the beginning of this chapter, "necessity" did indeed give birth to this innovation.

In the early 1990s, small businesses were particularly hard hit by a credit crunch due to new capital adequacy requirements imposed on depository institutions by the Financial Institutions Reform and Recovery Act (FIRREA) of 1989. Under the new laws, banks and savings and loans (S&Ls) were required to hold more capital in an attempt to shore up the financial system. (The financial system was suffering severe strains due to the failure of the S&Ls at the time. We take an in-depth look at the provisions of the FIRREA in Chapter 12.) The situation was particularly critical because small businesses did not have the same access to the commercial paper market as did medium-size and large firms. For a long time, securitization of the small business loan market had not seemed feasible, because small business loans are particularly diverse and are often funded on a subjective basis. In other words, small business loans are by nature heterogeneous—a characteristic that did not make them good candidates for securitization.

Generally speaking, securitization develops most easily in markets in which financial assets are fairly homogeneous. For example, to be securitized and sold in a secondary market, mortgages are made to specific criteria regarding the income of the borrower and the loan-to-property value ratio. Under these circumstances, pools of mortgages are a fairly homogeneous lot. Vehicle loans, likewise, are made to certain income criteria, with the vehicles serving as collateral. In the case of small business loans that are packaged and sold as securities, the backing includes accounts receivable, inventories, and equipment.

In early 1993, Fremont Financial Corporation of Santa Monica, California, sold $200 million of variable-rate certificates backed by a pool of loans to small- and medium-sized businesses. Merrill Lynch underwrote the offering, which quickly sold out, with the securities being bought by insurance companies, pension funds, and other large investors. An active secondary market exists for business loans with payments guaranteed by the Small Business Association of the U.S. government. The novelty of the Fremont offering is that there was no federal government guarantee.

In general, as more small business loans become securitized, the risks involved in lending to small businesses will be spread among many investors, fast-growing companies will be funded, and income will be generated for the innovators. As former Fed chair Alan Greenspan put it, a secondary market for business loans "would be a major contribution to the financial vitality of this country."[a]

Endnotes

a. Kenneth H. Bacon and Eugene Carlson, "Market Is Seen in Small-Business Loans," *The Wall Street Journal* (October 18, 1993).

it provides a way of protecting against interest rate risk in an environment of increased interest rate volatility. No longer was the only option for an intermediary to hold long-term loans as illiquid assets. Rather, the loans could be packaged together as asset-backed securities and sold off in secondary markets. Even the creator of the security could invest in it, thus changing what were illiquid assets into highly liquid assets.

Since the mid-1980s, securitization has spread from the mortgage market to other markets, including credit card balances, vehicle loans and leases, accounts receivable, computer leases, home equity loans, student loans, railroad car leases, equipment leases, small business loans, and boat loans. Banks, finance companies, retailers, thrifts, and others issue asset-backed securities that provide them with new funds to lend. See the "Looking Back" feature for a discussion of the first securitization of small business loans.

Securitization has many advantages. Investing in asset-backed securities rather than individual securities offers reduced credit risk for investors because of the pooling of assets. The securities are also available in small denominations for investors who are unwilling or unable to invest larger sums. Securitization is an efficient way for borrowers and lenders to be brought together, and given its phenomenal growth since 1990, it now appears that securitization, which is a form of direct finance, will replace much of the lending that historically has gone through traditional intermediaries (indirect finance). The outstanding value of asset-backed securities increased from about $350 billion in 1991 to over $6.5 trillion at the end of 2006. We look at securitizations again in Chapter 15, when we discuss the role of government-sponsored enterprises in the mortgage-backed and other asset-backed securities markets.

The market for mortgage-backed securities ran into severe problems in the 2007–2009 time period when the bursting of the housing price bubble led to massive defaults and foreclosures for homeowners and bankruptcies and record losses for financial institutions. The federal government eventually took over Fannie Mae and Freddie Mac, the two largest government sponsored enterprises. In the next chapter, on the stresses and strains of the financial system, we look at the securitization of subprime mortgages and how that contributed to the ongoing financial crisis of 2007–2009.

The investor in mortgage-backed securities faces the risk that the mortgages will be prepaid before they mature because the property is sold or refinanced; prepayment will result in the return falling short of expectations.[13] To reduce this risk, an innovation known as **collateralized mortgage obligations** was developed. Collateralized mortgages redirect the cash flows (principal and interest) of mortgage-related products to various classes of bondholders, thus creating financial instruments with varying prepayment risks and varying returns. Those who are most risk averse can choose an instrument whose principal will soon be repaid. Those who are willing to bear more risk can choose an instrument whose principal will not be repaid until later. In exchange for more prepayment risk, the investor receives a higher return. Needless to say, such provisions make attractive choices available to a wider range of investors.

For a description of our financial future from one economist's perspective, see "Looking Forward."

Collateralized Mortgage Obligations
Securitizations that redirect the cash flows (principal and interest) of mortgage-related products to various classes of bondholders, thus creating financial instruments with varying prepayment risks and varying returns.

Recap   Securitization is the process whereby relatively illiquid financial assets such as loans are packaged together and sold off to individual investors. Securitization has spread from the mortgage market to many other markets, including vehicle loans, credit card loans, student loans, and others. Collateralized mortgage obligations allow the prepayment risks of mortgage-backed securities to be distributed among various classes of bondholders and turns relatively illiquid assets into liquid assets.

The Financial System of the Future

In this chapter, we have examined some of the ongoing changes in the financial system. We can still only guess what the future will bring. However, we believe that the following speculations are very interesting:

> Although financial functions will be the same, they will be looked at differently in the twenty-first century. Thus, we will not refer to "loans," "borrowings," or "securities," but to "claims on wealth" or "financial claims." We will avoid the term *banks* because banks, certainly as we know them, will not exist.... A key to the system will be "wealth accounts" in which companies and individuals will hold their assets and liabilities. These accounts will contain today's relatively illiquid assets such as buildings and vehicles as well as what we know today as stocks, bonds, other securities, and new types of financial claims. These accounts would also contain all forms of liabilities.... There will be no special need for retail financial branches because everyone will have direct access to his or her financial suppliers through interactive TV and personal digital assistants. True interstate banking will have arrived at last! Or more accurately, true "global banking" will have arrived, as every household will be a "branch."[a]

Endnotes

a. Charles S. Sanford, Jr., "Financial Markets in 2020," *Economic Review of the Federal Reserve Bank of Kansas City* (First Quarter 1994): 19–28.

OTHER CHARACTERISTICS OF THE FINANCIAL SYSTEM RESULTING FROM INNOVATION

Geographical barriers to deposit taking, loan granting, and the provision of other financial services have eroded. Lenders advertise and solicit credit card accounts and make mortgage loans nationwide. Loans can be obtained over the Internet. This is very different from 30 years ago, when lenders restricted mortgage lending to their immediate geographical area. Interstate branching is permitted nationwide, and some of the largest banks, operating through their holding or financial holding companies affiliates, provide many financial services nationwide and worldwide. Citigroup, the megacorporation created from the merger of Citicorp and Travelers, provides a vast array of financial services to more than 100 million customers nationwide and in more than 100 countries. The move to nationwide banking is being accompanied by an increasing level of international banking activity that complements the increased flows of funds among countries. The increased capital flows have also spawned new financial products. Small investors can now make liquid investments in global markets, including emerging economies, through what many would consider to be exotic mutual funds.

Finally, deregulation in the 1980s "let the genie out of the bottle," so to speak, and taught us that once introduced, a financial innovation will not go away, even if the factors that caused its inception disappear. We would be remiss, however, if we did not emphasize the role that credit derivatives and securitizations have played in exacerbating the ongoing financial crisis of 2008 and 2009. These innovations have allowed for financial instruments to grow much faster than the underlying economy and for losses to be magnified from what they would be otherwise when a bubble in a financial market bursts.

Recap   Geographical barriers for many financial services have been reduced. FIs have become increasingly less specialized and more automated and have expanded the range of financial services they offer.

This completes our look at the causes and consequences of financial innovations in the past 45 years. In the next chapter, we look at the stresses and the strains intrinsic to the financial system. We shall see that financial innovations can either contribute to or alleviate financial instability.

Summary of Major Points

1. Financial innovation is the creation of new financial instruments, markets, and institutions to increase profitability. Because financial claims are fungible and because other incentives have been present, since the early 1960s, a high level of financial innovation has occurred. This has happened because of changes in the benefits and costs of innovating. Many of the innovations, particularly those in more recent years, have been due to advances in information and computer technologies.

2. In the 1970s, much innovation centered on evading regulations. Restrictions included setting reserve requirements (Regulation D) and interest rate ceilings (Regulation Q), limiting entry, and separating commercial and investment banking.

3. In addition to information and computer technology advances, the incentives to innovate have included rising interest rates that led to disintermediation, volatile interest rates that increased interest rate risk, and increased competition.

4. The relabeling of deposit liabilities as nondeposit liabilities, which avoided both reserve requirements and interest rate ceilings, represented a major form of financial innovation. Included in this group of innovations are Eurodollar borrowings, fed funds, and repurchase agreements. In addition, the creation of a secondary market for CDs, making them "negotiable," was also an important innovation. Retail sweep accounts represent a more recent in-

novation beginning in 1994 that reduces required reserves by sweeping deposit liabilities into nondeposit accounts overnight.

5. Beginning in 1980, the banking system was deregulated. Regulation Q interest rate ceilings were phased out, and the asset and liability options for banks and thrifts were expanded. All depository institutions were allowed to offer interest-bearing checkable deposits, and reserve requirements were made the same for all intermediaries. Two other laws in the 1990s eliminated barriers to interstate branching and allowed banks, securities firms, and insurance companies to merge.

6. The financial sector is becoming more competitive. Derivatives such as financial forwards, futures, options, and swaps are increasingly being used to hedge risk and to unbundle risks. Collateralized mortgage obligations reduce the prepayment risk of mortgage-backed securities by redirecting the cash flows of mortgage-related products to various classes of bondholders. Interest rate and currency swaps allow participants to hedge interest rate and exchange rate risks. Credit derivatives allow for the unbundling of credit risk.

7. Securitization is the process whereby relatively illiquid financial assets are packaged together and sold off to individual investors. The new securities are backed by the payment flows of the original assets. Secondary markets make the asset-backed

securities highly liquid. Securitization is spreading from the mortgage market to many other markets including auto loans, credit card loans, small business loans, and student loans.

8. Geographical barriers for financial services are disappearing, and FIs are becoming less specialized and more concentrated. Profit margins from lending have been reduced. Financial transactions are becoming increasingly automated, and banks are expanding into other areas such as data processing and leasing. Mergers among large financial services firms are creating megafirms that offer one-stop shopping for all financial needs.

Key Terms

Asset-Backed Securities, p. **220**
Call Option, p. **217**
Collateralized Mortgage Obligations, p. **222**
Credit Derivatives, p. **219**
Currency Swap, p. **218**
Deregulate, p. **213**

Derivatives, p. **216**
Disintermediation, p. **207**
Financial Innovation, p. **207**
Forward Agreements, p. **217**
Fungibility, p. **207**
Futures Agreements, p. **217**
Interest Rate Swap, p. **217**

Nondeposit Liabilities, p. **210**
Option Agreements, p. **217**
Put Option, p. **217**
Regulation D, p. **211**
Retail Sweep Account, p. **211**
Securitization, p. **220**

Review Questions

1. Briefly discuss the incentives that have led to a rapid pace of financial innovation in the last 45 years.
2. What is *disintermediation?* When is it likely to occur? What factors can reduce it? If I take my funds out of my credit union and put them in a money market mutual fund, have I disintermediated? Why or why not?
3. Discuss the roles that technology and regulation play in aiding financial innovation. Will innovation always occur to exploit loopholes in regulations?
4. What are nondeposit liabilities? Give some examples. What are negotiable CDs? How do nondeposit liabilities differ from negotiable CDs? What are retail sweep accounts? What are *credit derivatives?*
5. What is Regulation Q? Regulation D? Discuss ways banks have found to get around both regulations.
6. What is securitization? How does it reduce interest rate risk? Name some types of liabilities that are now securitized.
7. Discuss some characteristics of the financial system in 2009 that make it different from earlier periods.

8. How have increased competition and price volatility affected financial innovation? What are some specific types of innovation that deal with these factors?
9. How do collateralized mortgage securities differ from mortgage-backed securities? Which has less risk?
10. Defend the following statement: Once an innovation appears, it will remain even after the impetus for its development disappears. Give an example.
11. Discuss how banks can reduce their reserve requirements.
12. Are financial claims more fungible today than in the past? Why?
13. Why didn't banks innovate to get around regulations in the 1940s and 1950s?
14. Explain why asset-backed securities are an example of direct finance. If a bank issues asset-backed securities, how does it get new funds to lend?
15. What are derivatives? Define forward, futures, and option agreements. What are the underlying instruments in these agreements?
16. What is the difference between a put and call option. Does the seller of an option hedge risk?

Analytical Questions

Questions marked with a check mark (✓) are objective in nature. They can be completed with a short answer or number.

17. Explain the process by which a group of credit card balances could be securitized.

✓18. Assume a reserve requirement of 10 percent. If Chemical Bank is successful in getting Microsoft to convert a $2 million demand deposit to a Eurodollar deposit, how much can Chemical Bank lend out because of this transaction?

Suggested Readings

Chairman Ben Bernanke of the Federal Reserve spoke (via satellite) at the Reserve Bank of Atlanta's 2007 Financial Markets Conference, May 17, 2007, on "Regulation and Financial Innovation." This address, which focuses on credit derivatives, is available online at **http://www.federalreserve.gov/boarddocs/speeches/2007/20070515/.**

The article titled "The Good, the Bad, and the Ugly" in the August 2, 2007, edition of *The Economist* magazine discusses the level of financial innovation in Great Britain.

Asani Sarkar explains the uses and importance of derivatives and currency swaps in the developing economy of India in "Indian Derivatives Markets." To find out how financial innovations such as derivatives and currency swaps are making an international economic impact, read Sarkar's article at **http://www.newyorkfed.org/research/economists/sarkar/derivatives_in_india.pdf.**

Curious about how swaps bolster corporate financing? For a complex look at the credit default swap market, see *New York Fed Staff Report No. 290*, July 2007, "Has the Credit Default Swap Market Lowered the Cost of Corporate Debt?" by Adam B. Ashcraft and João A. C. Santos. It can be found on the Web at **http://www.newyorkfed.org/research/staff_reports/sr290.pdf.**

The American Institute for Economic Research reports on the effects of financial innovation on the safety of your bank account. An increase in electronic transactions invariably leads to new forms of fraud; to find out how to protect your money, check out "How Safe is Your Bank Account?" at **www.aier.org/research/publications/research-reports/doc_download/1283-research-reports-2006-issue-07.**

The Chicago Federal Reserve offers a user-friendly way to look at the age of electronic banking, including information on ATMs, smart cards, and online banking. Take a look at **http://www.chicagofed.org/publications/electronicmoney/electronicmoney.pdf.**

For useful information and sources about financial innovation, see the *FRBSF Economic Letter*, "Financial Innovations and the Real Economy: Conference Summary," March 2, 2007. Here you will find discussions of how financial innovations relate to economic volatility, household debt, and more. It is available online at **www.frbsf.org/publications/economics/letter/2007/el2007–05.pdf.**

Gary Stern of the Minneapolis Fed discusses how increases in competition and globalization have spawned financial innovations in "Top of the Ninth Financial: Financial Innovation and the Fed," *The Region*, Federal Reserve Bank of Minneapolis, June 2007. The article is available online at **http://www.minneapolisfed.org/pubs/region/07–06/top9.cfm.**

Information on the repeal of the Glass-Steagall Act of 1933 can be found at **http://www.captive.com/newsstand/articles/article_1.html.**

For an explanation of why securitizations have grown so much, see O. Emre Ergungor, "Securitization," *Economic Commentary*, Federal Reserve Bank of Cleveland (August 15, 2003), at **http://www.clevelandfed.org/Research/Commentary/2003/0815.pdf.**

For a discussion of *Financial Innovation and Effective Risk Management*, see the remarks by Fed Governor Susan Schmidt Bies to the Financial Services Institute 2004, Washington, DC (May 6, 2004), at **http://www.federalreserve.gov/Boarddocs/Speeches/2004/20040506/default.htm.**

Some recent innovative trends in banking are summarized in "Recent Developments in Business Lending by Commercial Banks," by William F. Bassett and Egon Zakrajsek, *Federal Reserve Bulletin* (December 2003): 477–492. The article is also available online at **http://www.federalreserve.gov/pubs/bulletin/2003/12031ead.pdf.**

For a look at financial innovation in the 1980s and 1990s, see Philip Molyneux and Nidal Shamroukh, *Financial Innovation* (New York: John Wiley, 1999).

The topics of securitization and monetary policy are covered in Arturo Estrella, "Securitization and the Efficacy of Monetary Policy," Federal Reserve Bank of New York Conference on Financial Innovation and Monetary Transmission, May 2002, available online at **http://www.newyork fed.org/research/economists/estrella/securitization.pdf**.

For a look at "The Emergence of Electronic Communications Networks in the U.S. Equity Markets," see James McAndrews and Chris Stefanadis's article by the same name in *Current Issues in Economics and Finance*, Federal Reserve Bank of New York, 6, no. 12 (October 2000), also available online at **http://www.newyorkfed.org/research/current_issues/ci6–12.pdf**.

For a review of a study that forecasts what banks will look like in 2010, see "CFSI: A Glimpse of the Future," *The Banker* 148, no. 866 (April 1998): 12. Another interesting article is Eric R. Hake, "Financial Innovation as Facilitator of Merger Activity," *Journal of Economic Issues* 32, no. 1 (March 1998): 145–70.

Endnotes

1. Actually, the removal of funds from depository institutions is only half of disintermediation; the other half is the disposal of primary securities by the intermediaries to obtain the funds to pay the depositors. Disintermediation upsets the process by which resources are allocated to capital formation.
2. Be sure you are clear that *disintermediation* means the removal of funds from FIs into open market instruments such as government securities, stocks, or bonds. When funds are removed from depository institutions and put into money market mutual funds, disintermediation has not occurred because money market mutual funds are intermediaries.
3. Despite their efforts, banks' share of total intermediation has been declining, and as in any business that is losing market share, attempts to stop the "bleeding" become more profitable.
4. Actually, the Russians were the pioneers of the Eurodollar. For political reasons, they preferred dollar-denominated deposits with London banks rather than U.S. banks.
5. The fed funds market was started in the 1920s by some New York banks that borrowed and loaned reserves overnight among themselves. The market died out in the 1930s when most banks had excess reserves. It started up again in the 1950s but was so small as to be insignificant. In the 1960s, the market began to grow, and by the early 1970s, many large banks were looking to the fed funds market as a permanent source of funds—not just as a way to meet temporary shortfalls in required reserves.
6. Wholesale sweep programs have been in existence since the 1970s. With wholesale sweep programs, the depository institution sweeps funds in a business's demand deposit into a money market instrument such as a repurchase agreement, Eurodollar deposit, or money market mutual fund. For wholesale sweep accounts, the deposits are swept into an account that may or may not be a liability of the depository institution. For retail sweep accounts, the swept funds stay on the books of the depository institution.
7. In the 1980s particularly, financially distressed banks often offered higher rates on CDs to attract deposits.
8. In addition to the analytical factors, we should also mention that the general "political wind" had shifted in the late 1970s toward less regulation. This also contributed to the impetus for financial deregulation in the 1980s.
9. The two laws were the Depository Institutions Deregulation and Monetary Control Act of 1980 and the Garn-St. Germain Act of 1982.
10. The laws are the Interstate Banking and Branching Efficiency Act of 1994 and the Gramm-Leach-Bliley Act of 1999.
11. Jamie B. Stewart, Jr., "Changing Technology and the Payment System," *Current Issues in Economics and Finance*, Federal Reserve Bank of New York, 6, no. 11 (October 2000).
12. "OCC's Quarterly Report on Bank Derivatives Activities, First Quarter 2007," Comptroller of the Currency, Washington, DC 20219.
13. If the mortgage is going to be securitized in the near future, interest rate risk is not as important to the lender because the lender will not be holding the mortgage for an extended period of time over which the interest rate could change significantly. See **http://www.chicagofed.org/consumer_information/electronic_money.cfm**.

11

The advantage of a bad memory is that one enjoys several times the same good thing for the first time.
                                                                    —Friedrich Nietzsche

If you get into anybody far enough, you've got yourself a partner.

                        —Failed-then-jailed Texas Wheeler Dealer Billie Sol Estes

Financial Instability and Strains on the Financial System

Learning Objectives

After reading this chapter, you should know:

The ways in which financial intermediaries (FIs) deal with risk and why risk cannot be eliminated

What a debt deflation is and why it is so onerous

Why financial intermediation recurrently leads to financial instability and financial crisis

What the moral hazard problem is and how it may exacerbate financial crises

The causes of the great financial crisis of 2008

Other potential causes of future financial crises in a globalized financial system

MEMORY IS THE THING YOU FORGET WITH[1]

In the 1920s, Charles Ponzi, a Boston financier (or slick con man), convinced people that he was able to make huge sums of money by arbitraging Spanish postage stamps—that is, by buying the stamps in a low-cost market (Spain) and selling them in a high-cost market (Boston). The large difference between the selling price and the buying price would result in a capital gain.

Unfortunately for investors, instead of making capital gains, Ponzi was using the money enticed from new investors to pay off the high profits early investors had anticipated. Inevitably, people lost faith in his capability to pay off their investments, and Ponzi's empire collapsed as he became unable to attract new investors. Later, Ponzi engaged in a land scheme—selling swampland in Florida—that also eventually collapsed.

In the late 1990s, prices of Internet stocks increased exorbitantly in what came to be known as the "dotcom" bubble or fiasco, depending on how one looked at it. Small Internet companies launched initial public offerings (IPOs), selling newly issued shares of stock to the public for the first time. Investors fought to grab up stocks such as pets.com and etoys.com. Rumor had it that a company could just add "dotcom" to its name to see its stock soar. Companies without a product or any assets were snatched up in what was clearly a stock market frenzy. Technology became the latest hype, and the technology-laden NASDAQ composite stock index (a measure of the performance of technology stocks) increased about 525 percent in the five-year period from 1995 to 2000. The dotcom and other technology stocks were clearly in a stock market bubble. The bubble burst in early 2000, and the NASDAQ index gave back about 90 percent of the previous five-year gain over the next two and a half years. Internet companies failed, employees lost their jobs, and the paper wealth of investors in the dotcoms was destroyed. All of these factors contributed to the recession of the early 2000s. By late 2008, the NASDAQ was still about a third of its previous high in March 2000. The stock market bubble was not isolated to technology stocks, however. Broader stock markets were also caught up in an irrational bubble, but not as much as the NASDAQ. The bursting bubble encompassed global as well as domestic stock markets. Fortunately, however, it did not spread to other financial markets or institutions.

Although the early years of the new century were not good for stocks, they were good for the housing market. With interest rates driven to 45-year lows in response to the collapse of stock prices and the terrorist attack on the United States on September 11, 2001, housing prices soared into an unsustainable housing price bubble. The soaring prices caused many homeowners to take out large mortgages that they could not afford or could afford only if housing prices continued to soar. Lending standards were reduced so that even borrowers with low down payments and questionable credit scores could obtain mortgage loans. Many of the mortgages were made with adjustable "teaser" rates that would readjust sharply upward in a few years. Borrowers were confident that housing prices would continue to soar and that they could refinance at lower rates before the higher rates kicked in. They did not want to miss the opportunity to make a bundle in the housing market or to get a "piece of the American dream." Housing prices reached unsustainable levels relative to household incomes. Again, the housing boom was global in nature, with most developed countries seeing soaring prices in the early 2000s. The bubble peaked in 2006 and began to burst in 2007. Many homeowners saw severe decreases in their home prices, with the result being that they owed more on their mortgages than what their houses were worth; they were unable to afford the higher payments caused by the adjustable rates and could not refinance because they owed more than the total value of their property. A considerable amount of homeowners were left with few options other than to default on their home loans; mortgage lenders and other financial intermediaries suffered severe losses and went bankrupt, triggering a financial crisis in the mortgage market. Unfortunately the crisis in the mortgage market was not contained but spread to broader financial markets and the financial system at large. By September 2008, the financial system was caught in an unprecedented crisis. Policy makers feared a global collapse of the financial system which would have devastating effects on the economy. What began as excessive risk taking in the housing and mortgage markets spread to all domestic and global financial markets and threatened the entire global economy. Like all financial crises, the root cause was excessive risk taking. However, the crisis was compounded by the huge amount of leveraging and the explosion of complex derivative and securitized assets in a global economy. Although Band-Aid solutions were tried from August 2007 on, policy makers came to the conclusion that a comprehensive government bailout was needed. Congress passed and the president signed a $700 billion bailout plan on October 3, 2008. The Obama administration promised an even bigger bailout in early 2009. How long it will take for the economy to recover from this crisis remains to be seen.

How different were the financial institutions and individuals who participated in the housing bubble of the early 2000s from those who fell victim to the Ponzi scheme in the 1920s or the dotcom bubble of the late 1990s?[2] Perhaps they were really not all that different in their desire for a big payoff, their willingness to take a risk to achieve it, and their refusal to realistically evaluate that risk. Perhaps such behavior is part of human nature and hence endemic to financial institutions controlled by individuals.

In this chapter, we look at some of the reasons that strains and instabilities have recurrently plagued our financial system. We look at the role of moral hazard in causing financial crises. Finally, we will examine some famous and some not-so-famous stresses that have led to financial crises.

FINANCIAL INTERMEDIATION, RISK, AND FINANCIAL CRISES

You have seen that FIs have developed numerous ways to manage risk. For example, diversification reduces the risks of insolvency from widespread defaults in one sector or region of the economy. By not putting all of their eggs in one basket, FIs are less likely to run into problems. Another factor that reduces credit risk is the use of experts to evaluate and assess the creditworthiness of potential borrowers and potential investments. In recent years, credit derivatives that we discussed in Chapter 10 have also been used to mitigate credit risk.

Interest rate risk can be reduced through the use of adjustable rate (also called variable rate) loans or the judicious use of forwards, futures, options, and swap agreements, and securitizations. Coping techniques have become more refined as interest rates have become more erratic.

Forwards, futures, options, and swap agreements are also used to hedge exchange rate risk. In recent decades, foreign exchange rates have become more volatile, and finance has become more globalized. Both factors have caused this risk to increase significantly. Thus, we have seen the growing use of these agreements to hedge exchange rate risks. Forwards, futures, and options are the subject of Chapter 17.

In addition to borrowing funds from the Fed, depository institutions can rely on their ability to borrow nondeposit liabilities to meet liquidity needs. If liquidity is needed, funds can be purchased in the repurchase agreements, fed funds, or Eurodollar markets. This ability to borrow reduces the liquidity risk. Depository institutions can also issue new negotiable certificates of deposit. In a liquidity squeeze, all FIs can sell any available liquid assets in secondary markets.

Even though strategies to reduce risks are significantly developed and appear comprehensive, risk is impossible to eliminate because the future is highly uncertain. Risk is simply an inherent part of life. If an FI makes loans or purchases financial assets that involve only little or no apparent risk, it is passing up opportunities for profit. A relationship between a borrower and an FI that is established today may continue far into the future. The future circumstances the borrower and the FI find themselves in, however, may be far different from what they anticipated. What seems a sure bet today may turn out to be anything but that. Besides, if the entire economy collapses, even the most conservative FI is bound to see the value of its assets fall.

Risk is particularly acute and intensified in financial claims because payments from one party to another usually depend on a payment from a third party. For example, to make her house payment to the mortgage broker, Sally depends on receiving her paycheck from her employer. To pay the investor, the mortgage broker depends on getting the house payment from Sally, and so it goes. Financial claims are layered and depend on multiple parties fulfilling contracts or making payments that depend on still others fulfilling contracts. A default by one party sets off a chain reaction that can trigger multiple defaults. The more heavily spending units depend on payments from others, the greater the risk that a random default will lead to multiple defaults. Multiple defaults can lead to the freezing up of financial markets where lenders and borrowers no longer trust each other and lending dries up. What began in financial markets now spreads to "Main Street," as small businesses can no longer get loans to stay in business and consumers can no longer get loans to buy cars, etc. Workers are laid off, retirement accounts and wealth falls, and the situation further deteriorates.

Because of its very nature, the financial system will be chronically plagued by various strains, some of which will lead to multiple defaults and a financial crisis. We define a **financial crisis** as a critical upset in a financial market(s) that is characterized by sharp declines in asset prices and the default of many financial and nonfinancial firms.

Financial crises have occurred in the distant past (the Ponzi scheme) as well as the recent past (the dotcom and mortgage market crises). They will occur in the future. Like the business cycle, periods of severe strain are recurrent but not periodic. That is, they recur through time but not on a particular time schedule. Sometimes, long periods of time pass with no major strains; at other times, periods of stress occur very close together. Financial stresses vary in their severity. Sometimes, strains are isolated in one market, and other times they spread throughout the entire domestic and global financial system. The financial crisis of late 2008 is like the latter in that it burgeoned to threaten the entire system. When a crisis threatens the entire financial system, it is imperative for policy makers to seek a resolution to the crisis because of the deleterious effect of such a crisis on the economy. This is the reason for the unprecedented $700 billion Congressional bailout of the financial system in late 2008. Exhibit 11-1 depicts the anatomy of a financial crisis.

Many interrelationships exist. For example, a general slump in the economy can create a financial crisis. One party defaults because of a downturn in the economy and sets off a chain reaction of defaults. The financial crisis worsens the existing downturn and can result in a deep recession or depression. At other times, the causation may flow in the opposite direction. In this case, a financial crisis, such as a dramatic fall in stock prices or a random large bankruptcy that causes a chain reaction of defaults, leads to a general slump in business activity or a recession.

Many different factors may increase the probability of a financial crisis. First, for example, a sharp and unexpected rise in interest rates increases the likelihood of multiple defaults. Increases in interest rates raise the monthly payments of borrowers with variable rate loans. Payments may be going up at the same time the value of the assets such as houses that the borrowed funds were used to purchase are falling. For business firms that rely on short-term borrowings to fund inventories, costs will increase and,

Financial Crisis
A critical upset in a financial market(s) characterized by sharp declines in asset prices and the default of many financial and nonfinancial firms.

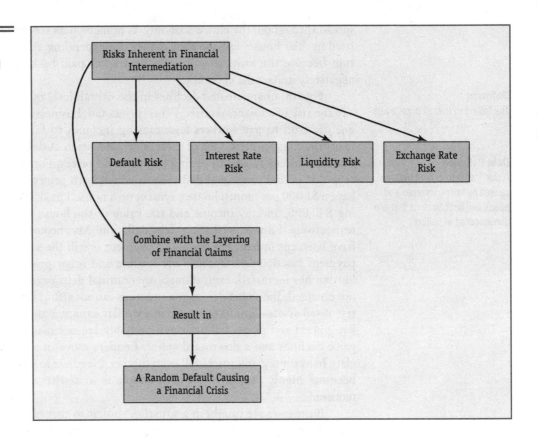

hence, profits will fall. Eventually, declining profits could lead to losses, reduced borrowing, and insolvency. For financial institutions such as banks that may rely on short-term borrowings or deposits to fund longer-term assets such as loans or mortgages, costs go up because of the higher interest rates that must be paid. At the same time, the value of the longer-term assets goes down. (Remember the inverse relationship between interest rates and the value of long-term fixed rate assets.) Moreover, when interest rates are rising, the most cautious borrowers will drop out of the market, postponing the investment or the large purchase until the future appears more certain. At such times, the adverse selection problem increases; that is, the pool of potential borrowers becomes more heavily weighted toward the less desirable borrowers—those who are more willing to take risks and have less secure financial positions.

Second, a fall in stock prices can set off a chain of events that increases the likelihood of a financial crisis. A fall in stock prices makes it more difficult for firms or individuals to borrow. Lower stock values reduce the net worth of firms, households, and stockholders. The value of possible collateral falls, the profit outlook dims, and potential borrowers appear less creditworthy. Households spend less because the falling stock prices have made them less wealthy. FIs may be hesitant to lend, given the new circumstances and the less certain future. Third, a fall in housing prices can set off a financial crisis in mortgage markets. If housing prices fall enough, homeowners will owe more than what their property is worth. Homeowners who find themselves in this position may walk away from their mortgage loans, leaving the lender holding the bag. The lender may try to sell the property, putting more downward pressure on housing prices, leading to more defaults on mortgage loans. The crisis in the mortgage market can spread throughout the entire economy, as homeowners see the wealth they had accumulated in their houses fall and thus reduce their spending. Also, if many lenders go bankrupt because the loans they have made are not paid back, job and income losses also negatively impact the economy.

Deflation
The falling of overall price levels.

Debt Deflation
A real increase in debt burdens caused by falling incomes and prices and debt burdens that are denominated in dollars.

Fourth, unanticipated declines in the overall level of prices (**deflation**) can intensify the risk of a financial crisis. When prices fall, businesses make less profit and consequently tend to pay workers less, causing incomes to fall as well. Deflation imposes many onerous burdens. One of these is debt deflation. A **debt deflation** is a real increase in debt burdens caused by falling incomes and prices. For example, assume we are in a "typical" period of general deflation in which both prices and incomes are falling. If I have a $1,000 per month house payment on a house I paid $100,000 for when I was making $40,000, and my income and the value of the house falls to $20,000 and $50,000 respectively, I am experiencing debt deflation. My income and the value of my house have been cut in half, but my house payment is still the same. In real terms, my house payment has doubled. Because my income and other prices have fallen, my real debt burden has increased, even though my nominal debt payment ($1,000 per month) has not changed. Individuals in such a situation cannot afford their house payments, so they try to sell assets—just as everyone in a similar situation also tries to sell. With the market glutted and prices falling, there probably are not many buyers, leading to further price declines and a downward spiral. Lenders move in and foreclose, individuals declare bankruptcy, and prices fall even further. Needless to say, the mood in the economy becomes highly pessimistic. This example is somewhat exaggerated, but you get the picture.

Businesses are caught in a situation similar to that of individuals. Businesses can't repay debt on inventories as the value of inventories drops below the amount of debt contracted to purchase them, the value of finished goods drops below the amount of debt contracted to purchase raw materials, and so on. As businesses contract, employment and incomes decline, and the economy continues in a downward spiral.

If the frequency of foreclosures and bankruptcies accelerates, which it usually does in a deflation, a debt deflation is under way, and losses for bad debts mount at FIs, potentially leading to their collapse. Fortunately, periods of deflation were not "typical" during the middle and late twentieth century. Not since the Great Depression has the United States experienced widespread debt deflation in which thousands of banks failed in response to a scenario similar to the one just described. The Depression prompted the government to put into place safety nets such as the Federal Deposit Insurance Corporation (FDIC) and the Federal Savings and Loan Insurance Corporation (FSLIC).[3] Eventually, in a deflation, when prices fall to low levels, the seeds of recovery are planted as buyers scrape together enough funds to start buying again at the depressed prices. In reality, this occurs when both input and output prices have adjusted to profitable terms of trade.

In the early years of the 2000s, the Fed feared the return of deflation. Because, the costs of deflation are potentially so high, the Fed acted aggressively to ward off even the slim possibility of it. As the Fed implied, the costs of inflation and deflation are not symmetrical in that the effects of deflation are potentially more destructive to the economy than the effects of a comparable amount of inflation.[4] Thus, the Fed drove interest rates to 45-year lows and held them there until the fear of deflation abated. The low interest rates fueled another crisis in the mortgage market that resulted from the bursting of the housing price bubble. As noted earlier, unfortunately, the mortgage crisis was not contained to the mortgage market but spread to other financial markets in what may be the greatest financial crisis and bailout in history. In early 2009, many analysts again were fearful of an oncoming deflation and this added to the urgency for policy makers to act.

Finally, in recent years, many financial crises have been global in nature, with a crisis in one country quickly spreading to others in the region and beyond. The growth in world trade, the removal of barriers to capital flows, and the increase in capital flows among nations has increased the likelihood of a financial crisis in one country spreading to other interdependent economies. Technology has exacerbated the problem in that hybrid financial claims are much more fungible due to advances in computer and information technologies. The risks of financial intermediation are magnified in a world of sophisticated global electronic funds transfers. Funds can move in and out of markets instantaneously, causing widespread losses and gains in various markets. The Mexican peso crisis of 1994, the Asian crisis of 1997–98, the 1998 crisis in Russia, and the 2001 crisis in Argentina are examples of financial crises in which the sudden and massive withdrawal of funds from the affected regions exacerbated the underlying causes of the crises.[5] Likewise, the extent to which global financial markets were intertwined with the subprime mortgage meltdown of 2007–2008 caught many analysts by surprise. Such fungibility of funds further contributes to financial instability. Now would be a good time to read the accompanying "A Closer Look" on the great financial crisis of 2008 and a theory of financial instability.

Consequently, because of the inherent risks of financial intermediation, a goal of regulators is to ensure the safety and soundness of the financial system. They do this in several ways, including creating a safety net for depositors (and possibly other investors). At the same time, regulators from various countries and international financial organizations are working together to establish guidelines and criteria for countries that wish to participate in the international financial system. They hope to increase international financial stability and to reduce the incidence of international financial crises. A secondary effect of these efforts, both domestically and globally, however, may be to encourage behavior that actually makes the system more prone to financial crises. We now turn to the problem of moral hazard, which can result in excessive risk taking.

Recap   A financial crisis is a critical upset in a financial market and is characterized by sharp declines in asset prices and widespread defaults. Financial crises occur from time to time because of the inherent risks in financial intermediation and because financial claims are layered. A debt deflation is a real increase in debt burdens caused by falling prices and incomes, leading to a downward spiral of foreclosures and bankruptcies. Financial crises can be triggered by sharp increases in interest rates, falls in stock prices, falls in home prices, or unanticipated decreases in the overall price level. A financial crisis in one economy can spill over to other economies. This effect is increased as economies become more interdependent due to the growth and fungibility of financial flows among countries.

THE PROBLEM OF MORAL HAZARD IN FINANCIAL INTERMEDIATION

The most severe financial crisis this country has ever experienced occurred during the Great Depression. During this period, which predated deposit insurance, more than one-third of the banks in the United States failed. To halt a series of bank runs in early 1933, President Franklin D. Roosevelt proclaimed a "bank holiday," shutting down all of the banks in the nation for one month. During this month, Congress passed the Glass-Steagall Act, which, among other reforms, established deposit insurance and created the Federal Deposit Insurance Corporation (FDIC). For the first time, small depositors did not have to worry about losing their deposits if their bank went belly-up. Soon, deposit insurance became available for small depositors in almost all depository institutions.

The Great Financial Meltdown of 2008

In the early 2000s, the housing market experienced an unprecedented boom as reflected in housing prices that increased nationwide and even worldwide. In many areas, housing prices roughly doubled in a five-year period. Part of the boom was caused by record low interest rates in the years following the dot.com bust and the terrorist attack on the World Trade Center on September 11, 2001. Part was caused by Congress that designed policies to increase homeownership among low income families.[a] In addition, innovation within the mortgage market also played a part. Two major innovations included the Alt-A (stated income) mortgages and subprime mortgages.

Alt-A mortgages were designed for borrowers with good credit who could not document or verify their income. Alt-A loans were made at higher interest rates than loans where income was fully documented and verified. Many observers felt that these types of loans were over-used and abused by borrowers who were overstating their incomes and less able to afford the payments on their loans than they claimed. Why, after all, would anyone pay the higher interest rate if they could document their income? The problem is accentuated if the interest rate is adjustable and, at a later date, interest rates and payments rise.

Subprime loans were an even worse innovation. Buyers with low credit scores and little or no down payments were given loans, often at low introductory (teaser) rates that would later escalate. When the introductory rate period ended (usually after a year or two), the loans would rise to very high rates to compensate the lender for the greater risks of the loans. This is a classic example of a Ponzi scheme. Borrowers could come out ahead only if property values continued to rise and they could borrow more to pay off current loan balances. Some loans even involved negative amortization, where the borrower ended up owing more at the end of the year than the original loan balance.

By 2006, the party abruptly ended as borrowers started defaulting at alarming rates, lenders were bankrupt, housing prices collapsed, mortgage lending evaporated, and many politicians were seeking some form of bailout for distressed borrowers. The crisis caused major problems not only for homeowners but for investors and financial institutions as well. Financial institutions that were holding large amounts of the worthless loans were experiencing strains as the value of their assets deteriorated. Many of the subprime loans had been pooled together to create new mortgage-backed securities that were sold to investors and other financial institutions. The new securities were backed by the payments on the subprime mortgages, many of which would not be made.

By late 2007, the crisis had already caused a slowdown in the U.S. economy and was beginning to spread beyond the mortgage markets. By early 2008, it was estimated that about 10 percent of all homeowners had negative equity in their homes, meaning they owed more than what the homes were worth. Such a situation encourages borrowers who run into problems to abandon their homes to foreclosures rather than trying to find ways to hold on to them. As lenders foreclose, more properties are

Subprime Mortgage

A mortgage loan made to a borrower with bad credit and little or no down payment.

Alt-A (Stated Income) Mortgage

A mortgage loan made to a borrower with good credit where the lender does not verify the income stated by the borrower.

vacant and deteriorating at a time when buyers are hesitant to jump into the market and funds for new mortgages are scarce. By the summer of 2008, a series of unprecedented collapses of financial institutions began that culminated in a massive government bailout of a financial system that was imploding. What started with innovation in the mortgage market ended with financial markets on the brink of collapse and the greatest government bailout in history. Below is a timeline that outlines some of the events that led up to the crisis and mammoth government bailout.

The Time Line Leading to the Financial Crisis of 2008

- In 2003–2006, many lenders offered subprime and Alt-A mortgages with low "teaser" rates. Borrowers would not be able to afford the payments when the rates reset higher in a few years. Many borrowers either did not know this or were relying on property values to continue to increase so that they could refinance at lower rates or, at worst, they could resell the homes for a profit.

- A massive housing price bubble peaked in July 2006. Nationwide, prices had more than doubled between January 2000 and mid 2006. Other areas of the country experienced even much greater increases.

- In early 2007, many subprime lenders went bankrupt, as borrowers could not afford to make the higher payments and were unable to refinance because they owed more than what their homes were worth. This had ripple effects on Wall Street and around the world because many of the "toxic" loans have been securitized into complex financial instruments and sold globally.

- In March 2007, Fed Chair Bernanke believed the crisis could be contained in the subprime market.

- In April 2007, New Century Financial, the nation's second largest subprime lender declared bankruptcy.

- In June 2007, housing prices experienced their first nationwide year-over-year decline since 1991. Neighborhoods across the country were becoming dotted with abandoned, foreclosed, and deteriorating homes.

- In August 2007, Ameriquest Financial, once the largest maker of subprime loans, went out of business.

- In September 2007, the Fed, for the first time in four years, began cutting interest rates, in what would be dramatic decreases over the next seven months.

- In October 2007, the Dow Jones Industrial Average, an index of stock prices, closed at an all time high. Treasury Secretary Henry Paulson warned that the housing crisis posed a significant risk to the economy.

- From late 2007 through September 2008, the Fed created several special lending facilities that extended the size and scope of Fed lending. Lending was extended to primary dealers in addition to depository institutions. (These lending facilities are discussed in Chapter 25.)

- In January 2008, a struggling Countrywide Financial was bought by Bank of America. Home sales fell to their lowest level in 25 years and prices continued to plummet.

- In February 2008, Congress passed and the President signed a stimulus plan to get the economy out of the doldrums by giving tax rebates to most households.

- On May 30, 2008, the Treasury arranged the sale of Bear Stearns, one of the five dominant investment banks, to J.P. Morgan for $10 a share, sweetening the deal with an unprecedented $29 billion loan from the Fed.

- On July 11, 2008, the FDIC seized IndyMac Bank in what was the second largest bank failure to date. Depositors with uninsured deposits (those over $100,000 in regular accounts or $250,000 in retirement accounts) lost uninsured deposits. Shareholders and other debtors were virtually wiped out. Initial cost estimates to the FDIC are $4 to $8 billion.

- On September 7, 2008, the federal government announced that it would take over Fannie Mae and Freddie Mac, the large government sponsored enterprises associated with the housing market. Together, Fannie and Freddie controlled over half the mortgages in the country and had over $5 trillion of government agency securities outstanding.

- On September 14, 2008, Bank of America announced the purchase of Merrill Lynch, another of the "big 5" investment banks, to prevent its collapse.

- On September 15, 2008, Lehman Brothers, the oldest (158 years) "big 5" investment bank files for bankruptcy.

- On September 18, 2008, the Fed sets up a rescue plan for American International Group Inc. (AIG), the world's largest insurance companies. The Fed injects $85 billion into the company in exchange for approximately 80 percent ownership. The Fed has virtually nationalized the insurance company to prevent its bankruptcy.

- Also on September 18, 2008, the Fed along with other central banks injects $180 billion into the financial system to shore up liquidity. The Dow Jones Industrial Average drops to 33 percent below the October 2007 all-time high.

- As of September 19, 2008, the Securities and Exchange Commission (SEC) outlawed the short selling of the stock of many of the largest financial firms at least through October 2, 2008 in an attempt to stabilize prices. The SEC believed that short selling exacerbated the price drops of financial stocks.

- On September 21, 2008, the Fed approved the conversion of Goldman Sachs and Morgan Stanley (the last two seminal investment banks) to bankholding companies. The conversion to the bankholding company status gave the firms greater access to borrowing from the Fed. The era of the large independent investment banking firm (separate from the commercial banking institution) that began in the Great Depression was effectively over.

- On September 24, 2008, money market mutual funds started to experience "runs" as panicked depositors withdrew funds. Interbank lending dried up and the Fed announced the creation of another emergency lending facility to provide liquidity to the markets. Financial markets were freezing up. The need for large scale action by the government became more imperative to prevent a total financial meltdown that would have disastrous effects for the global economy.

- On September 25, 2008, after a run on deposits, regulators seized Washington Mutual, which was the sixth largest banking organization and the largest savings and loan in the country. Washington Mutual was put into receivership with the FDIC. Most of the assets and liabilities were then sold to J.P. Morgan for $1.9 billion. Shareholders and unsecured bondholders are expected to lose virtually everything. This is the largest bank failure in history.

- On September 24 and 26, 2008, the Fed engages in massive concerted actions with other central banks to inject massive funds into a teetering global financial system. In total since the crisis began, $290 billion of swap agreements with other central banks have been authorized.

- On September 25, 2008, Washington Mutual was sold to JPMorgan Chase in a transaction worked out by the Office of Thrift Supervision (OTS) and the FDIC.

- On September 28, 2008, Congress worked through the weekend to reach an agreement on an estimated $700 billion bailout package for the financial system before the Asian markets opened on early Monday morning. The Band-Aid solutions to date had not worked and global financial markets were in danger of freezing up totally. Such a situation would be catastrophic for the economy.

- On Monday, September 29, 2008, the House of Representatives rejected the package and financial markets went into a tailspin. The Dow Jones Industrial Average falls 777 points, the largest one-day point drop in history. Politicians fight to get compromise legislation worked out to reassure the public and to prevent the freezing up of financial markets.

- On October 3, 2008, Congress passed and the President signed the Emergency Economic Stabilization Act of 2008. Because of the $700 billion bailout, the government deficit in 2009 could exceed $1 trillion. The Treasury was authorized to purchase up to $700 billion of "toxic" mortgage-backed and other securities in order to provide funds to intermediaries so that they could resume lending and prevent deterioration of the economy. Initially, a large part of the bailout funds were used to inject capital into the nation's largest banks rather than to buy "toxic" securities.

- In January 2009, the Obama Administration was working on a new, bigger bailout plan as the economy continued to deteriorate.

- After the bailout, turbulence is expected to continue in financial markets for at least the next several months and many more financial institutions are expected to fail. Policy makers and the population at large hope that the freefall of the financial system can be stopped and that the spillovers to the real economy in the form of a deep and long-lasting recession can be averted.

Endnotes

a. See Russell Roberts, "How Government Stoked the Mania," *Wall Street Journal*, October 3, 2008. A11.

Ever since the first deposit insurance statutes were enacted, there has been concern about the moral hazard problem that deposit insurance by its very nature causes.[6] In Chapter 8, we discussed moral hazard in terms of one borrower; that is, after getting the loan, a borrower may use the funds for a different, higher-risk project. In this chapter, the moral hazard problem refers to the reduction in market discipline experienced by FIs that stems from deposit insurance, a lender of last resort, and other practices of regulators.

Moral Hazard
The reduction in market discipline experienced by FIs that goes hand-in-hand with deposit insurance.

Increases in moral hazard go hand-in-hand with deposit insurance. For example, deposit insurance encourages banks (and other FIs) to make riskier loans; depositors do not keep close tabs on how banks are managing their funds—at least not as close as they would if their deposits were not insured. Insured banks take more risks because greater risks offer the possibility of higher returns, and after all, banks are highly leveraged—they are risking depositors' funds, as well as their own, and they get to keep all the winnings. Furthermore, loan officers do not have to lie awake at night worrying about losses when the funds (deposits) are insured. Well-managed banks are penalized because they have to help pay the losses incurred by poorly managed banks.

Even in light of all these concerns, until the 1980s, deposit insurance was widely viewed as an incredible achievement.[7] Despite the reduction in market discipline that resulted from it, the 1933 statute that established the FDIC was probably one of the

A Theory of Financial Instability

Financial Instability Hypothesis
Hyman Minsky's theory that (1) the mixture of hedge, speculative, and Ponzi spending units in the economy determines the economy's predisposition to a financial crisis, and (2) after sustained periods of prosperity, spending units tend to take on more debt, which may in time lead to another crisis.

Hedge Spending Unit
A spending unit such as a household or firm where the anticipated revenues (inflows) significantly exceed the anticipated payment obligations (outflows).

Speculative Spending Unit
A spending unit in which the funds coming in may potentially fall short of the payment outflows if there is an increase in interest rates.

Ponzi Spending Unit
A spending unit that must continuously increase its outstanding debt to meet its current obligations or payments.

The financial instability hypothesis, developed by the late economist Hyman Minsky, refers to the natural tendency for the financial system to undergo periodic waves of crises and bankruptcies. The financial crisis can lead to a general economic decline because lending falls and businesses that rely on borrowing to maintain their general scope of operation deteriorate. During an extended period of prosperity, the seeds of crisis spontaneously germinate as lenders become too overconfident that loans will be repaid. This overconfidence causes them to make bad loans, which eventually result in defaults, a subsequent reduction in credit extension, and the possibility of system-wide collapse.

To understand Minsky's theory, we first consider the financial condition of spending units (firms and households) within the economy. Minsky argues that at any moment in time, the economy is composed of a mix of three types of spending units—hedge, speculative, and Ponzi units.

A hedge spending unit is one where the anticipated revenues or incomes (inflows) significantly exceed the anticipated payment obligations (outflows). For example, a firm is a hedge spending unit if its normal or expected sales easily cover its costs, including loan payments to the bank, payroll, rent, and other expenses and, as far as we know, this situation is expected to prevail in the foreseeable future. A family is a hedge unit if its income is high enough to meet all of its debt payments, including mortgage, credit cards, car payments, etc. The likelihood of default or bankruptcy for a hedge unit is unlikely but possible if there is a sudden, unexpected drop in inflows.

A speculative spending unit is one where the funds coming in may potentially fall short of the payment outflows if there is an increase in interest rates. For example, a firm that must refinance a loan or reissue bonds in the near future may find that its payment outflows could exceed inflows if interest rates have increased. Or a household with a variable rate mortgage and car payment may feel strapped if there is a sudden spike in interest rates resulting in payment increases. Speculative units have more uncertainty than hedge units, even though over a long period, it is anticipated that payment inflows will exceed payment outflows. For speculative units, outflows could go up with no increase in inflows. The hedge unit cannot be hurt if the interest rate goes up, but the speculative unit can be.

Finally, a Ponzi spending unit (named after the Charles Ponzi we met in the introduction to Chapter 11) must continuously increase its outstanding debt to meet its current obligations or payments. It is willing to do so, because it anticipates a bonanza at some date in the future which will more than make up for the increased level of debt. If at any time the spending unit is unable to increasingly borrow additional funds, it cannot meet current outlays. The financial managers of Ponzi spending units most likely have trouble sleeping at night, although we are not certain whether the subprime borrowers and lenders in the housing market in the early 2000s did!

According to Minsky, it is the mixture of hedge, speculative, and Ponzi spending units at large that determines the overall financial health of the economy. If the economy is dominated by hedge spending units, then the underlying health of the economy is strong and the risk of widespread defaults and financial crisis is small. These spending units are not heavily dependent on the payments of others to meet their current payments.

On the other hand, if the economy is dominated by speculative spending units, the system is financially fragile and more highly dependent on borrowed funds. A random bankruptcy or an increase in interest rates can lead to more widespread defaults, which lead to more bankruptcies that can spread like wildfire throughout the economy.

Finally, if the economy is dominated by Ponzi units, bankruptcy is imminent unless these spending units can increasingly borrow additional funds. Under most circumstances, this seems highly unlikely. The degree of leveraging is extremely high. If for any reason spending units are unable to borrow additional funds, they default, leading to further defaults and widespread collapse. The greater this dependence is, the greater the potential for crisis. Spending units choose to become dependent enough on borrowed funds to become Ponzi units when a market (the stock market or the housing market, for instance) is in an irrational and exuberant bubble. Buyers are convinced that prices will continue to go up, no matter how unreasonable that may seem after the bubble bursts.

As suggested earlier, the enigma in the situation is that extended prosperity leads to an eventual collapse. As success continues, a growing number of spending units take on riskier—more leveraged—financial positions. Indeed, if expectations have been consistently substantiated in the past through the business expansion, there is no reason to suspect that they won't be validated in the future. The riskier or more highly leveraged position is actually rational behavior.

If households have not experienced a period of unemployment in several decades, then confidence grows, and they may increase their debt payments relative to their incomes, suspecting that their income flows will always continue. Why not buy the more expensive house your family can enjoy today and that will appreciate in the future? Likewise, firms are encouraged to increase their debt payments relative to inflows in the hopes of increasing profits. Why not expand operations using borrowed funds where you'll get to enjoy all the profits from that expansion? The longer the inflows meet or exceed the anticipated outflows, the greater this tendency becomes.

As a result of good times, spending units increase their debt payments to income ratios (debt-to-income ratios, for short). The economy as a whole moves into a more precarious and fragile position. Leveraging is the degree to which spending units rely on borrowed funds. With the degree of leveraging high, a random bankruptcy or a credit crunch—something that might go unnoticed in a hedge environment—can wreak havoc as the default of one unit leads to the default of another. A downturn is triggered and a domino effect pulls in the entire economy. The domino effect is not triggered if spending units are not highly leveraged.

Minsky believed that the boom-crises cycle repeats itself every 40 to 50 years. During a major downturn such as the one experienced during the Great Depression, widespread bankruptcies occur and there is massive deflation (falling prices) in real and financial assets. Lenders become unwilling to lend and borrowers become unwilling to borrow. Because credit extension is tightened, when the economy does begin to

Debt-to-Income Ratios
The debt payments of spending units relative to their incomes or inflows.

Leveraging
The degree to which a spending unit relies on borrowed funds.

recover, there is less debt than before the downturn and lenders are cautious about expanding debt or extending credit.

For several decades, spending units remember the downturn. Borrowers and lenders are unwilling to increase the amount of borrowing above very safe levels. Households and firms are not highly leveraged as spending units are cautious about taking outflows high relative to inflows. The economy is financially stable. But as all spending units increase their leveraging, the economy drifts to a less stable position. Lenders who refuse to go along with the increased lending will find that their market share is reduced and the downturn seems very far off, indeed.

At first, when a crisis occurs, the government may try one of several ways to prevent the downturn. The most prominent way is for the Fed to act in its role of lender of last resort or to simply supply liquidity through increasing reserves to the banking system. If the Fed intervenes swiftly and strongly, the downturn can be prevented. The original default can be limited to one area or sector of the economy.

Although Fed (or the U.S. government) intervention may prevent the downturn, the economy still remains in a fragile position. Spending units do not reduce their leveraging. The economy emerges with the same or higher level of debt, poised for another crisis when the government may again have to intervene. According to Minsky, financial crises may occur at increasingly close intervals as long as debt-to-income ratios remain high.

The knowledge that the Fed will perform a lender of last resort function or other bailout in a time of crisis may aggravate the propensity of bankers to engage in what becomes collectively risky lending. Bankers who do not participate (lend) liberally on the upswing will lose customers to their competitors. But the cumulative effect of all banks becoming more liberal in their lending is disastrous.

To summarize, it is in an extended recovery that the seeds of the downturn are planted. Spending units forget the lessons of the past as the past becomes more distant. They increase their outflows relative to their inflows. Debt-to-income ratios rise throughout the economy. The economy moves to a more vulnerable position, and some random event that would hardly be noticed in a different environment sets off a chain of bankruptcies and defaults that spread throughout the economy. Attempts by the Fed (or government) to prevent the downturn may aggravate the situation. When the downturn is prevented, the economy comes out of the financial crisis but remains in a highly leveraged and financially fragile position. A long-term cycle of boom and bust is an inherent part of a capitalist economy. How well do you think Minsky's theory explains the boom bust cycles the economy has been going through since the late 1990s? Can his theory explain the Great Financial Meltdown of 2008? It is the author's belief that it goes a long way in capturing the long-term endemic nature of financial crisis.

most successful pieces of legislation of the twentieth century. Much of the FDIC's success is often attributed simply to knowledge of its existence. That is, there have been no significant general runs on FDIC-insured banks because depositors know their funds are safe: a run would be a waste of time. For 50 years, the FDIC's losses were negligible, its reserves grew, and annually about two-thirds of all the insurance premiums paid in were refunded to the banks. As a result of the FDIC's success, Congress raised the insurance limit several times from the original $2,500 in 1934 to $100,000 per account at the present. We should note that the limit was raised to $100,000 in 1980 and that for a comparable amount of "real" or inflation-adjusted deposit insurance in 2008, the limit would be more than $200,000. In 2006, the deposit insurance limit for retirement accounts was increased to $250,000. Despite the moral hazard problem, beginning in 2010 and every five years thereafter, limits for both regular and retirement accounts will be adjusted to account for inflation. Finally, in response to the financial crisis of September 2008, the deposit insurance limit was raised to $250,000 until the end of 2009.

By the early 2000s, many banks, brokerage houses, insurance companies, and other financial services firms had consolidated into megafirms, the likes of which have never been seen before. A failure of a megafirm such as Citigroup, which was created from the merger of Citicorp and Travelers, would have catastrophic effects on the economy. In mid-2007, Citigroup had about $2.2 trillion in assets! Failure of such a firm would quickly exhaust the resources of any safety net such as deposit insurance. (In September 2008, the FDIC has assets of around $45 billion and insures deposits worth over $4 trillion.) A moral hazard problem exists if market participants believe that the effects of such a failure would be so catastrophic that a taxpayer bailout would be inevitable. Given the correlation between risk and return, the incentive is to take on riskier ventures whenever moral hazard is increased. Note that a higher average expected return induces investors to accept more risk. But—investors beware—this does not imply that a higher return will be realized for any given investment.

Moral hazard also became a concern among those who are designing an international framework for financial stability. As financial flows across national borders increase, excessive risk taking may occur if financial participants think that international financial organizations such as the International Monetary Fund (IMF) will bail out a country in crisis by acting as a lender of last resort or encouraging policies that prevent currency devaluation. In any case, if investors' losses are reduced or eliminated, a moral hazard problem will form, encouraging excessive risk taking. The previously mentioned currency crises in Mexico, Asia, Russia, and Argentina resulted in massive international financial support in an attempt to bail out the troubled economies. Indeed, investors did lose, but they would have lost more without the bailouts organized by the IMF.

Having considered the reasons that recurring financial crises plague the economy and looked at some of the factors that increase the probability of a financial crisis, we now turn our attention to other areas of concern. Please see "A Closer Look," about the collapse of the savings and loan industry in the 1980s.

Recap   Moral hazard results from the reduction in market discipline caused by the presence of deposit insurance. Moral hazard leads to excessive risk taking that can result in financial debacles. The existence of large megafirms could result in a moral hazard problem if market participants believe the firms' failure would cause enough havoc in the economy to prompt the government to step in and bail out the firms. The moral hazard problem may also exist in international markets if participants believe an international organization will bail out a country in crisis.

OTHER AREAS OF CONCERN

As the nation is so painfully finding out in late 2008, financial institutions and markets in the early 2000s face the potential for new and greater stresses and strains. Some of these new situations result from the changing composition of balance sheets, some

The Savings and Loan Debacle

Throughout most of the 1980s, the savings and loan (S&L) industry in the United States experienced severe strain. More than 1,500 institutions failed; many others downsized, and the industry as a whole shrank considerably. Taxpayers spent billions of dollars to bail out the industry because the financial crisis threatened the health and stability of the entire economy. Today the industry is far different from what it was at the start of the 1980s. The public at large has been disillusioned, questioning the safety and soundness of S&Ls and the financial system as a whole. The honesty and integrity of S&L owners, regulators, and even some members of Congress have been called into question.

As in most crises, the seeds of the S&L debacle were planted long before the first sprouts of trouble appeared. In many ways, the roots of the crisis can be found in the way S&Ls do business. Unless interest rates remain fairly stable for long periods of time, as they did from the early 1950s until the 1970s, it is risky to fund long-term loans or purchase long-term assets with short-term deposits. If interest rates rise, the cost of the funds borrowed over the short-term can increase above the amount long-term assets are earning. As you saw in Chapter 8, S&Ls were established for the express purpose of borrowing short from passbook savers and lending long in order to finance mortgage loans. That is, they were designed to engage in behavior that would be dangerous in an environment of volatile or rising interest rates.

From the early 1950s on, the U.S. economy experienced a slow upward drift in interest rates. Regulation Q, which put a ceiling on the interest rate that could be paid on deposits, applied to S&Ls as well as commercial banks. In fact, the ceiling for S&Ls was maintained at 0.5 percent above the ceiling for commercial banks. The purpose of this differential was to encourage savers to deposit funds into S&Ls, which then could be used to make mortgage loans, thus encouraging home ownership. With Regulation Q in place, the cost of the funds borrowed mostly from passbook savers was maintained at or below the ceiling limits. Small savers, at least for a time, had few alternatives to passbook savings accounts in depository institutions. Consequently, disintermediation (the removal of funds from FIs) was relatively minor when interest rates on other financial assets such as Treasury bills or commercial paper went above the Regulation Q limits. The other financial assets were generally unavailable to small savers who did not have the minimum amounts required to purchase them. For example, $10,000 is the minimum amount needed to purchase a Treasury bill. By the 1970s, however, small savers did have money market mutual funds as an alternative to passbook accounts in depository institutions.[a] Still, the situation fermented for some time before the crisis occurred. By the late 1970s and early 1980s, events had begun to unfold that would result in a total collapse of the industry and, as you shall see, a large taxpayer bailout.

To understand the burgeoning crisis, recall that nominal interest rates are approximately equal to real rates plus the expected inflation rate. In the late 1970s, high nominal rates reflected expectations about inflation and not high real rates. That is, the high nominal rates were the result of large inflation premiums. In fact, in the 1970s, real rates were often abnormally low and sometimes even negative despite the high nominal rates.

In late 1979, the Fed orchestrated a huge spike in already high nominal rates as part of a policy aimed at reducing inflation. Interest rates climbed far above the Regulation Q ceilings, which capped nominal rates while ignoring real rates. The spike in nominal rates caused severe disintermediation and/or the transfer of funds from S&Ls to money market mutual funds. Congress responded in 1982 by authorizing the S&Ls to offer money market deposit accounts that competed with money market mutual funds. Money market deposit accounts actually had an advantage over money market

Federal Savings and Loan Insurance Corporation (FSLIC)
The insurance company that insured the deposits in S&Ls until 1989, when it was dissolved because of insolvency.

mutual funds because they were insured by the Federal Savings and Loan Insurance Corporation (FSLIC).[b] This legislative change slowed the disintermediation and the transfer of funds from the S&Ls to money market mutual funds, but it was probably too little too late. Also, it left the S&Ls with another problem. S&Ls had mostly long-term fixed-rate assets, primarily low-rate mortgages that were then funded by high-interest variable-rate accounts. Thus, the S&Ls were hit with a double whammy: their profits fell as their costs of funds increased faster than their earnings on assets, and the value of their assets also fell. Recall that when interest rates rise, the value of long-term bonds falls. Long-term fixed-rate mortgages are similar to long-term bonds in that when interest rates rise, the value of long-term fixed-rate mortgages goes down.

In 1981, economists estimated that the S&L industry had a substantial negative net worth that was far greater than the assets of the Federal Savings and Loan Insurance Corporation (FSLIC) that insured the deposits of the sickly S&Ls. Rather than confronting the problem head on in the early 1980s, which would have required injecting taxpayer funds into the system at that time, Congress responded with actions that would eventually make the situation much worse. Under the Garn–St. Germain

Garn-St. Germain Act
A law that expanded the lending powers of the S&Ls in the early 1980s.

Act, it expanded the lending powers of the S&Ls into product lines that paid a high return but were unfamiliar to S&L managers and entailed a lot of risk. Capital requirements—the cushion against losses—were also lowered so that the S&Ls could aggressively enter the new lending arenas. Rather than having to hold capital equivalent to 5 percent of assets, S&Ls were required to hold capital equal to only 3 percent of assets.

With expanded lending powers and lower capital requirements, the industry went for broke and made new high-earning investments in such ventures as junk bonds and commercial real estate. Guess what happened? The S&Ls ended up losing a lot more and literally went broke. In late 1986, Congress granted the FSLIC $10.8 billion funded by borrowing against future deposit insurance premiums to be paid by the thrifts themselves. In 1988, the Federal Home Loan Bank, the equivalent of the Fed

Federal Home Loan Bank
The regulatory body of the savings and loan industry until 1989.

for S&Ls at the time, liquidated more than 200 insolvent thrifts by selling the institutions to individuals and firms. In the liquidation process, the buyers were compensated for the negative net worth of the institutions with an array of future guarantees and obligations, including tax breaks. None of these compensations required congressional authorization or appropriation and were later viewed with suspicion.

Finally, in 1989, Congress responded with the Financial Institutions Reform, Recovery, and Enforcement Act (FIRREA), which attempted to resolve the problem of widespread failures within the industry and insufficient insurance funds to settle the crisis. Over the course of the next decade, the total cost to the taxpayers was approximately $124 billion, which was much less than initial estimates. At the time of the bailout, the costs had already been incurred. The bailout shifted the costs from the owners and depositors of the failed thrifts to the public (taxpayers) at large. We should also point out that the bailout was to the benefit of taxpayers as well. We look at the specifics of the FIRREA and other recent regulatory measures in Chapter 12.

What can we conclude about the causes of the crisis? It is difficult to apportion blame, and doing so would not be productive anyway. Undoubtedly, the inherent problem of lending long and borrowing short when interest rates were rising was a major factor. Another factor was the extension of lending powers to the thrifts in the early 1980s. These new powers that allowed for more risk taking also seem to have attracted some dishonest individuals to the industry. Finally, regulators were slow to move in and shut down troubled thrifts, which caused eventual losses to be greater than they otherwise would have been. Congress was also slow to act. A lot of hard lessons were learned as taxpayer funds were diverted from potentially building better schools, roads, and infrastructure, among other more positive projects.

Endnotes

a. As you saw in Chapter 10, a person transferring funds from a depository institution to a money market mutual fund is not disintermediating but transferring funds from one type of intermediary to another.

b. The FSLIC was dissolved in 1989 as part of the S&L bailout. Since that time, S&Ls have been able to obtain deposit insurance from the FDIC.

---

result from activities that never show up on financial statements, and others result from the overall growth of the financial system relative to the economy.

National wealth consists of real assets such as houses, roads, infrastructure, and factories, plus net financial claims owed to Americans by foreigners. Domestic financial assets are not a part of national wealth because what is a financial asset to one party is a financial liability to another. Thus, domestic financial assets and liabilities cancel each other out.

In recent years, new financial products, new markets, and new institutions have proliferated. Financial flows and instruments had grown faster than national wealth and national income. In relative terms, the financial system is much larger than the real sector compared to their sizes a few decades ago. Derivatives allow new financial instruments to be created that base their claims on other financial assets, which base their claims on real assets. It is hoped that this potpourri of newly created instruments makes the financial system more efficient. However, the proliferation of financial instruments and the fungibility of financial claims in a global financial system augment the potential for new stresses and strains to the financial system. A crisis in one market quickly spreads to another through a contagion effect, and the unwinding of positions can take longer than in the past when the financial system was not so complex.

Financial intermediaries now engage in new kinds of behavior, called *off-balance-sheet activities*, as they seek to obtain additional revenues and profits from areas outside traditional borrowing and lending. **Off-balance-sheet activities** include standby lines of credit, overdraft protection, unused credit card balances, and other commitments for

Off-Balance-Sheet Activities
Activities such as standby lines of credit, overdraft protection, unused credit card balances, and other commitments for which a bank is liable but that do not show up on the balance sheet.

which the FI is liable but that do not show up on the balance sheet. **Standby lines of credit** guarantee that the bank will lend funds to a borrower in the future as agreed upon today. One example of a standby line of credit is a letter given to an issuer of commercial paper that guarantees to pay off creditors on the due date if the issuer cannot. If a bank gives a standby line of credit for a fee to an issuer of commercial paper and the issuer defaults, the bank experiences a loss just as if it had made a bad loan. The only difference is that this exposure never shows up on the balance sheet, whereas the loan-loss exposure does. Unused loan commitments of banks and savings associations totaled about $6.2 trillion as of June 30, 2004. The increase since 1990 has been due almost exclusively to an increase in unused credit card balances, which tripled as a percentage of total assets. In the next chapter, we shall see that banks must now consider off-balance-sheet activities in calculating capital requirements.

As we saw in the last chapter, a derivative is a financial contract whose value derived from the value of some other underlying asset, such as foreign exchange, bonds, equities, commodities, or an index. A derivative's value fluctuates with the value of the underlying asset. Examples of derivatives include financial futures, options, and combinations thereof. Derivatives are used by banks and others, including virtually every large corporation in the United States, to hedge, speculate, or arbitrage price differences. The use of derivatives allows for the unbundling of specific risks of financial assets into parts so that those more willing and able to do so bear the unbundled risks. Thus, the use of derivatives in this manner makes the financial system more efficient. As of June 30, 2008, five large banks represented 97 percent of the derivatives held by all banks. The value of the derivative contracts was about $182 trillion. Although this amount is extraordinarily high, many of these positions are offsetting positions used to reduce risk or to arbitrage to make a riskless profit. In these cases, there would be little or no risk. Thus, the net credit exposure to the banking system is only about $406 billion.

In recent years, derivatives have become even more complex. Powerful computers are often needed to assess the risks involved if one factor, say, an interest rate or exchange rate, changes by a small amount, perhaps only one-hundredth of 1 percent. Indeed, it is difficult, if not impossible, to understand all risks involved with extremely complex derivatives and all possible scenarios. For example, apparently many investors failed to understand that risks they were taking by investing derivative instruments based on subprime mortgage loans in 2008 and in the last chapter, we saw that credit derivatives played a significant part in the ongoing financial crisis. Nevertheless, derivatives will undoubtedly become even more complex in the future. Another problem is that even if they understand the risks, how can regulators be sure that institutions have proper oversight of their employees or operations to prevent the misuse of derivatives? Lax oversight could lead to large losses that catch management, regulators, and investors by surprise.

For these reasons, some analysts worry that derivatives may be too risky for banks. They believe that bank participation in these markets should be limited or that the market should somehow be regulated. Others go so far as to suggest that Congress ban the use of derivatives by banks altogether. This may be impossible because large banks could merely take this activity offshore, beyond the venue of the regulators. The concern is that some participants do not know enough about how derivatives work and the risks involved. If rates move by a small amount in an unanticipated direction, large losses can occur if derivatives are used for speculation. As you shall see in Chapter 17, you cannot lose if derivatives are used only to hedge. When losses have occurred, it was often because of insufficient oversight, both internally by management and externally by regulators.

Do market participants, including banks, have enough knowledge about them to be heavily involved? Can firms sufficiently oversee derivative activity? Will regulators be able to properly control these markets? Risks from derivatives currently do not show up on balance sheets. Will regulators be able to ensure that such risks are disclosed? What role did these instruments play in the financial collapse of 2008? These are questions to be answered in the near future.

Recap   The growth of the financial sector relative to the real sector, as well as the increased fungibility of financial claims, may exacerbate financial crises in the future. Off-balance-sheet activities such as standby lines of credit and unused credit card balances increase potential losses for financial institutions but do not show up on financial statements. Derivatives are financial contracts whose values are derived from the values of underlying assets, such as foreign exchange, bonds, equities, and commodities. Large banks and other financial and nonfinancial institutions are heavily involved in derivatives, and without proper oversight and regulation, large losses could occur.

In this chapter, we have come full circle from past stresses on the financial system and their resolution to the potential strains of the future. In Chapter 12, we look at the regulatory structure in place at the present time and possible areas of reform.

Summary of Major Points

1. FIs have developed numerous ways to reduce risks and deal with them. FIs use diversification and expert credit analysis to manage credit risk. They use adjustable rate loans, forwards, futures, options, swaps, and securitizations to manage interest rate risk. Liquidity risk is managed by the ability to borrow funds, and exchange rate risk is managed with forwards, futures, options, and swaps. Despite these measures and because of the uncertainty of the future and the interdependence of financial claims, financial crises will occur from time to time.

2. A financial crisis is a severe upset in a financial market that is characterized by sharp declines in asset prices and the failure of many financial and nonfinancial firms. Financial crises can be brought on by sharp increases in interest rates, decreases in stock or housing prices, or deflation. The financial system has been caught in an ongoing financial crisis in 2008 that began in the subprime mortgage market and spread to domestic and global financial markets. In September 2008, Congress passed the Emergency Stabilization Act of 2008, $700 billion taxpayer bailout, in an attempt to mitigate this crisis.

3. Deflation can be worse than inflation because it increases the real value of debts that are denominated in dollars. A debt deflation occurs when prices and incomes fall, increasing the real value of debts and resulting in foreclosures and bankruptcies. The last time the U.S. economy experienced depression was in the Great Depression, although the Fed was concerned that the economy could slip into a deflation in the early 2000s.

4. *Moral hazard* refers to the reduction in market discipline that comes with the presence of a safety net to prevent losses. The presence of deposit insurance or the belief that regulators will take mitigating actions in the event of a financial crisis creates moral hazard. With moral hazard, banks and other intermediaries have an incentive to invest in riskier loans and investment. This gradual increase in riskier activities resulted in many bank failures in the 1980s. Megamergers in the financial services industry may also lead to a moral hazard problem if market participants believe that the resulting firms are "too big to fail." The moral hazard problem also exists in international financial markets if participants believe that an international organization such as the IMF will bail out a country in

crisis, thus reducing losses from what they otherwise would be.

5. The financial sector has grown faster than the real sector, exposing the system to potential crisis because of its enormous size and the fungibility of financial claims. Off-balance-sheet activities such as standby lines of credit expose a financial institution to risks but do not show up on balance sheets. Derivatives are financial contracts whose values are derived from the values of other underlying assets, such as foreign exchange, bonds, equities, and commodities. Some large banks are heavily involved in derivatives, and concern has been expressed as to whether enough is known about the risks involved with this exposure.

Key Terms

Alt-A (Stated Income) Mortgage, p. **236**

Debt Deflation, p. **234**

Debt-to-Income Ratios, p. **241**

Deflation, p. **234**

Federal Home Loan Bank, p. **245**

Federal Savings and Loan Insurance Corporation (FSLIC) p. **245**

Financial Crisis, p. **232**

Financial Instability Hypothesis, p. **240**

Garn-St. Germain Act, p. **245**

Hedge Spending Unit, p. **240**

Leveraging, p. **241**

Moral Hazard, p. **239**

Off-Balance-Sheet Activities, p. **246**

Ponzi Spending Units, p. **240**

Speculative Spending Units, p. **240**

Standby Lines of Credit, p. **249**

Subprime Mortgage, p. **236**

Review Questions

1. Discuss ways in which each of the following risks can be reduced: default risk, interest rate risk, liquidity risk, and exchange rate risk.

2. Why does financial intermediation inherently involve risk? Are FIs better at evaluating risks than you are? Why or why not?

3. What is a financial crisis? Why does an economic downturn often lead to a financial crisis? Explain why the reverse is also true.

4. Can sharp increases in interest rates increase the risk of a financial crisis? Explain.

5. What is a debt deflation and why is it so onerous for the economy?

6. Is a financial crisis more likely to be triggered by inflation or deflation? Explain.

7. What does "too big to fail" mean? What are the costs of such a policy? Under what circumstances would your funds be safer in a large bank that made risky loans rather than in a small conservative local bank?

8. What is moral hazard? Why does deposit insurance inherently involve moral hazard? What factors contribute to moral hazard on the international level?

9. Discuss the factors that contributed to the S&L debacle during the 1980s.

10. Define *derivatives*. Why can they be risky?

11. S&Ls had limited experience making commercial loans, while commercial banks were extremely experienced in dealing with them. Explain how this difference could have exacerbated the adverse selection problem for the S&Ls in the 1980s.

12. Can derivatives cause massive losses if they are used only to hedge?

13. Discuss the reasons for the crisis in mortgage markets in the first decade of the 2000s.

14. What are some ways policy makers responded to the financial crisis of 2008–2009?

15. Define hedge, speculative, and Ponzi spending units. What is the financial instability hypothesis?

Analytical Questions

The questions marked with a check mark (✓) are objective in nature. They can be completed with a short answer or number.

✓16. If all prices and my income fall by 25 percent, by what percent does the real value of my debt increase?

✓17. List three factors that can cause a financial crisis.

Suggested Readings

For an interesting article about the causes of the most recent financial crisis, see "How Government Stoked the Mania," by Russell Roberts, *The Wall Street Journal*, Friday, October 3, 2008, p. A21. Another article dealing with the same topic is "Pressured to Take More Risk, Fannie Reached Tipping Point," by Charles Duhigg, *The New York Times*, October 5, 2008, p. A1. **http://www.fdic .gov**, the FDIC's home page, has numerous articles about deposit insurance, including deposit insurance reform initiatives.

http://www.ffiec.gov, the home page of the Federal Financial Institutions Examination Council, has other relevant information about deposit insurance and risk.

The Wall Street Journal discusses the effect of the subprime mortgage market on asset-backed securities. The article is available online at **http://online.wsj.com/article/SB1186 96582444395589.html?mod=googlenews_wsj.**

For a look at some of the challenges in managing financial risk, see Riccardo Rebonato, *Plight of the Fortune Tellers: Why We Need to Manage Financial Risk Differently*, Princeton University Press, 2008.

An article that underscores many of the points in this chapter is "The Natural Instability of Financial Markets," by Jan Kregel, Working Paper No. 523, The Levy Economics Institute of Bard College (December 2007). It is available online through **http://www.levy.org**.

An interesting article on financial fragility is "In Time of Tumult, Obscure Economist Gains Currency: Mr. Minsky Long Argued Markets Were Crisis Prone; His 'Moment' Has Arrived," by Justin Lahart, *The Wall Street Journal* (August 18, 2007): A1.

An interesting book that examines financial corruption and the ability of most Americans to invest their way to financial security is Roger Lowenstein, *Origins of the Crash* (East Rutherford, NJ: Penguin Books, 2004). For a look at the causes, consequences, and cures for instability in financial markets, see Colin Mayer, ed., *Financial Instability* (New York: Oxford University Press, 2001).

For a look at "The Federal Reserve Responds to Crises: September 11th Was Not the First," see Christopher J. Neely, Federal Reserve Bank of St. Louis, Working Papers 2003–034 (October 2003). It is available on the Internet at **http://research.stlouisfed.org/publications/review/04/ 03/Neely.pdf.**

Economic problems in Japan are discussed in "Sorting Out Japan's Financial Crisis," by Anil K. Kashyap, Federal Reserve Bank of Chicago, *Economic Perspectives*, 26, no. 4 (Fourth Quarter 2002): 42–55.

For an article that looks at a model of domestic financial crises, see Martin H. Wolfson, "Neoliberalism and International Financial Instability," *Review of Radical Political Economics* 32, no. 3 (September 1, 2000).

The global consequences of Asia's economic woes are discussed in "How the Asian Crisis Affected the World Economy: A General Perspective," by Xinshen Diao, Wenli Li, and Erine Yeldal, *Economic Quarterly*, Federal Reserve Bank of Richmond, 86, no. 2 (Spring 2000): 35–59. For a different perspective, see Joseph E. Medley, "The East Asian Economic Crisis: Surging U.S. Imperialism?" *Review of Radical Political Economics* 32, no. 3 (September 1, 2000).

For a look at alternatives for a new financial architecture, see Kenneth Rogoff, "International Institutions for Reducing Global Financial Instability," *Journal of Economic Perspectives* 13, no. 4 (Fall 1999): 21–42.

"The Cost of the Savings and Loan Crisis: Truth and Consequences" is discussed in an article by the same name by Timothy Curry and Lynn Shibut, *FDIC Banking Review* 13, no. 2 (December 2000).

The lender of last resort function is examined from a global perspective in "The Free Market Is a Lie," *New Statesman* (October 9, 1998): 4.

In "Two Crises: Inflationary Inertia and Credibility," Sebastian Edwards looks at the role of government and the financial crisis in Mexico. The article can be found in *The Economic Journal* 108, no. 448 (May 1998): 680–702.

Three recommended books on the S&L crisis are J.R. Barth, *The Great Savings and Loan Debacle* (Washington, DC: American Enterprise Institute, 1990); *The S&L Debate: Public Policy Lessons for Bank and Thrift Regulation* (New York: Oxford University Press, 1991); and Robert Emmet Long, ed., *Banking Scandals, The S&Ls and BCCI* (New York: H.W. Wilson, 1993).

For interesting reading on financial instability, try Hyman Minsky, *Stabilizing the Unstable Economy* (New Haven, CT: Yale University Press, 1986).

Martin Wolfson, *Financial Crises: Understanding the Postwar U.S. Experience*, 2d ed. (Armonk, NY: M.E. Sharpe, 1994), gives a comprehensive history of financial crises through the mid-1980s.

Endnotes

1. The quote is from Alexander Chase.
2. There are some differences. The Ponzi scheme was pure fraud. Despite some illegal activities, the crisis in the subprime lending and dotcom markets were not necessarily brought on by purely criminal activities.
3. Although not caused by debt deflation, the FSLIC failed during the 1980s savings and loan crisis, and taxpayers injected funds to save depositors from losses.
4. Former Fed chair Greenspan develops this argument in his remarks "Risk and Uncertainty in Monetary Policy," presented at the Meetings of the American Economic Association, San Diego, California, January 3, 2004. The remarks are available online at **http://www.federal reserve.gov/boarddocs/speeches/2004/20040103/default.htm.**
5. See the Suggested Readings, where you can find sources that look in detail at some of these financial crises.
6. The moral hazard problem pertains to any depository institution that offers deposit insurance, including S&Ls. We focus here on commercial banks.
7. The inception of deposit insurance in the early 1930s resulted in federal examination of state banks that are not members of the Fed. This, in turn, caused a sharp decrease in some of the activities that contributed to the bank failures of the 1930s.

12

The difficulty lies not so much in developing new ideas as in escaping from old ones.

—John Maynard Keynes

The people's right to change what does not work is one of the greatest principles of our system of government.

—Richard Nixon

Regulation of the Banking System and the Financial Services Industry

Learning Objectives

After reading this chapter, you should know:

Why regulation is needed in the financial services industry

Who regulates whom in the banking system

Some of the major pieces of legislation important to the banking industry today

Regulatory challenges facing Congress and the regulators

THE ROLE OF REGULATION

The ability of certain industries within a market economy to regulate themselves has been the subject of controversy for a long time. Some analysts believe that virtually no regulation is needed and that the market can handle practically every situation far better than a government regulatory agency. For example, they believe that airlines can regulate themselves better than a government regulatory agency can.[1] If an airline is unsafe, so the argument goes, it will experience more accidents than other airlines. As passengers become aware of this accident record, they will avoid flying on the unsafe airline, and it will be driven out of business. Likewise, the market can better regulate the financial services industry than any regulatory agency such as the Fed or the Office of Thrift Supervision can. According to this argument, a bank that takes too many risks will be driven out of business when cautious depositors become aware of the risks and withdraw their deposits or when the bank sustains losses and is unable to pay back depositors.

At the other extreme are those who believe that the economy needs a lot of regulation because the quest for profits is so strong that, without regulation, consumer welfare will likely be jeopardized. For example, an airline may skimp on costly maintenance to keep its planes in the sky because planes on the ground do not generate profit. Or a financial intermediary (FI) might take a large risk because the potential payoff is so big. After all, the bulk of the funds that the intermediary is risking belongs to the depositors.[2] Although the unsafe airline may eventually be driven out of business in a market economy, that doesn't bring back the loved ones who were killed in a plane crash because the airline failed to take reasonable safety precautions. Likewise, depositors may feel some satisfaction when the depository institution that lost their life savings is driven out of business, but the institution's demise does not reduce their pecuniary losses.

In Chapter 9, we discussed the Glass-Steagall Act, which was implemented in response to the financial collapse of the Great Depression. Glass-Steagall made the banking sector a highly regulated industry. Although the crisis in the Great Depression might suggest the need for some regulation, by the late 1970s sentiment in the United States had shifted to the belief that the economy had become a victim of over-regulation. This change led to a deregulation movement that continues in varying degrees today. Industries such as the airlines, trucking, and financial services have been **deregulated**.

After deregulation, some industries experienced severe stresses and bankruptcies, particularly in the 1980s. The financial services sector in particular went through the collapse of the savings and loan (S&L) industry, the largest wave of bank failures, and the most serious strains since the Great Depression. Some observers blamed deregulation at least to some extent for these problems. Others argued, however, that the failures were the result of previous regulations that had protected inefficient operations and that the problems would be resolved in time. Indeed, as we have seen, by the late 1990s, the banking system had recovered and made record profits. Although the industry did not fare as well in the downturn of the early 2000s, the recovery that followed pushed bank stock prices well above previous highs. Although the general trend was upward from 2001 to 2006, by October 2007, bank stock prices had fallen somewhat, primarily because of difficulties in residential mortgage markets. Most analysts were not prepared for the financial panic and crisis that would occur over the next year that would result in a series of the largest bank failures in history and a total collapse in financial stocks, and culminate in the unparalleled $700 billion bailout of the financial system.

Deregulate
The dismantling of existing regulations.

The banking system, composed of depository institutions, is a major part of the financial services industry. In this chapter, we focus primarily on the regulatory structure of the banking system today and look at the major pieces of legislation that have created it. We begin with deregulation acts in 1980 and 1982 that removed many of the regulations imposed in the Great Depression. We look at the regulatory structure that was implemented in response to the financial crises of the 1980s and to new regulations that were designed in response to technological changes and the globalization of financial markets. We also look at recent sweeping (and proposed) legislation that promises to overhaul the banking system and the financial services industry. Finally, because of the growing integration of banking and financial services firms, we summarize the major regulators of the financial services industry in general.

THE HOW AND WHY OF FINANCIAL SERVICES REGULATION

"Free to compete" means "free to fail." Because the failure of a significant number of FIs will undermine the public's confidence in the system, there is a potential conflict between the two objectives of regulation: competition and efficiency, on the one hand, and safety and soundness, on the other hand. The regulatory authorities attempt to balance these objectives, or at least so they tell us, by issuing regulations that govern banks and other financial intermediaries.

As you have seen, most, if not all, bank activities were regulated by various government regulators from the Great Depression in the 1930s until the 1980s. Given the despair and disruption accompanying the Great Depression, the financial regulators wrote regulations that limited "price" competition, restricted entry, controlled the various types of products and services that banks and other FIs could offer the public, and specified prudent capital positions for intermediaries. Specific regulations included Regulation Q interest rate ceilings, chartering and branching restrictions, assets and liabilities restrictions, and net worth requirements.

During the 1980s, banks and most other intermediaries were substantially deregulated. A series of financial crises followed that culminated in widespread insolvencies within the S&L industry and many bank failures.[3] The crises triggered attempts at reregulation and the thought that regulations needed to be overhauled.

Throughout this text, we have repeatedly emphasized the role of regulation in ensuring the safety and soundness of the financial system. Regulations were deemed necessary because of the nature of the financial system and the trade-off between high returns for net lenders versus safety and soundness. As you have seen, FIs can earn higher returns by assuming more risks. Indeed, some intermediaries offer higher returns for the acceptance of more risks. Historically, depository institutions—within limits—have offered a guaranteed, albeit lower, return.

When deciding how much risk to take on, an FI should evaluate the risks of an activity. Generally speaking, when the expected benefits outweigh the expected costs, the activity will, on average, be profitable to undertake. However, in the process of assessing the expected costs associated with various levels of risk, the intermediary considers only the costs to the stockholders, creditors, and depositors that would result from an investment or portfolio of investments going sour.[4] Because they are so highly leveraged, some FIs may fail to adequately consider how much risk they should take and may ignore the costs to the community at large that could result from the failure of the institution. The collapse of an FI not only affects those directly involved but could conceivably impede the smooth functioning of a local community or the entire economy.

The failure could lead to a bank run and a simultaneous financial collapse. Thus, we arrive at the crux of the problem: If left to decide the level of risk on their own, banks or other intermediaries will generally accept too much risk because they fail to consider the additional costs of failure that the community at large must bear. If banks and other intermediaries were left unregulated, the drive for profits might jeopardize the goals of safety and soundness for the system as a whole.

Prior to the 1980s, regulations encouraged specialization that resulted in the segmentation of the financial services industry. For many decades, the industry remained highly segmented. The limitations on portfolios were predicated on the alleged benefits of compartmentalizing FIs into various specialties. Insurance companies were to specialize in insurance and banks in banking and "never the twain shall meet." Thus, in the belief that competition needed to be limited among the compartments, the regulators effectively divided the financial markets.

Slowly, over time, however, barriers between intermediaries began to break down as financial institutions made inroads into each other's areas of specialty. The segmentation gave way as banks increasingly engaged in traditionally nonbanking activities, and nonbanks increasingly engaged in traditional banking activities. Finally, in 1999, landmark legislation underwrote the changes in the marketplace by allowing the full financial integration of banking, securities, and insurance firms as opposed to their segmentation into separate entities. Some analysts believe that this piece of legislation contributed to the financial crisis of 2008.

Historically, the regulatory structure was as segmented as the financial services industry. As the industry segmentation broke down, however, the regulatory segmentation failed to break down along with it.[5] Who said government bureaucrats were flexible anyway? Today, however, although the historical segmentation of regulatory responsibilities persists, we expect that the brute forces of events, (the financial crisis of 2008), will hasten the pace of change.

Regulation can focus on either financial markets (products) or financial institutions. For example, stocks, bonds, and futures are financial products that are regulated, and banks, S&Ls, and insurance companies are financial institutions that are regulated. In addition, sometimes a particular financial product or institution may be regulated by more than one agency, and a single agency may regulate more than one financial product or institution. Given this background, now would be a good time to look at the accompanying "A Closer Look" feature, which surveys the many agencies currently regulating the financial services industry. Many of these nonbanking system regulators are covered in more depth in subsequent chapters.

A final point needs to be reiterated. The regulatory structure of the financial services industry is in a process of ongoing change for several reasons, including the continuing evolution of the industry, resulting in new products and markets; the ongoing financial crisis of 2008 noted above; technological changes in the delivery of financial services; and the globalization of financial markets. All of these changes leave many concerns about the adequacy of current regulations. In early 2008, the U.S. Treasury announced a proposal to overhaul the U.S. financial regulatory structure. Now would be a good time to read the accompanying "Looking Forward" feature titled "A Proposal to Overhaul the Financial Regulatory Structure." Although we are not certain which of these proposals will be adopted, it seems clear that there will be major regulatory reform in the next few years.

Regulators in the Financial Services Industry

- **Banks:** We have already discussed the dual banking system in which federal and state-chartered banks exist side by side. Federal banks are regulated by the Office of the Comptroller of the Currency (OCC), the FDIC, and the Fed. State banks are regulated by the state banking commissioner and possibly the Fed and/or the FDIC, depending on whether they choose to be members of the Fed and/or subscribe to deposit insurance. With regard to reserve requirements, all banks are regulated by the Fed.

- **Bank holding companies and financial holding companies** are regulated by the Federal Reserve. However, unless the Fed suspects a problem, it relies on the reports of a subsidiary's functional regulator such as the Securities and Exchange Commission (SEC) or the state insurance commission.

- **Savings and loan associations:** S&Ls are regulated by the Office of Thrift Supervision (OTS) of the Treasury and, with regard to reserve requirements, the Fed. Those that subscribe to deposit insurance are also regulated by the FDIC.

- **Credit unions:** Federally chartered credit unions are regulated by the National Credit Union Administration, while those with state charters are regulated by state banking commissioners. The National Credit Union Share Insurance Fund insures deposits in credit unions up to $100,000. Because they are nonprofit, tax-exempt institutions, credit unions have generally engaged in less risk taking than their for-profit competitors, and consequently they have experienced much milder strains. They have larger reserves and fewer losses. Unlike other depository institutions, credit unions do not pay an insurance premium but put up capital equal to 1 percent of their insured deposits with the insurance fund. If this reserve is ever depleted because of losses, credit unions are required to replenish it out of capital.

- **Finance companies:** Finance companies must obtain permission to open an office for business from the state in which they want to operate. Once that permission is obtained, there are virtually no restrictions on branching. The Federal Trade Commission (FTC) regulates finance companies with regard to consumer protection. However, there are no restrictions on the assets they hold or how they raise their funds other than those generally applying to the issuance of securities.

- **Financial futures:** Financial futures are regulated by the Commodity Futures Trading Commission and the National Futures Association. The latter was set up by the industry for self-regulation.

- **Financial options:** Financial options are regulated by the SEC, which was established in 1933. Options on futures are regulated by the Commodity Futures Trading Commission. The Options Clearing Corporation has been set up by the industry for self-regulation.

- **Mutual funds:** The SEC was given regulatory control over mutual funds by the Investment Company Act of 1940. Regulations include requirements to publicly disclose financial information and restrictions on how business can be solicited. Mutual funds experienced tremendous growth in the 1980s and early 1990s. As a result, some observers believe that additional regulation may be needed for two reasons: (1) Sales offices for mutual funds are now allowed to be located inside commercial banks, even though the funds are not sold directly by the bank. Apparently, a significant portion of customers erroneously believe that mutual funds purchased in a bank are insured by the bank. (2) Mutual funds have grown to be a significant portion of total intermediation, while the regulatory structure has not grown at the same pace.

- Insurance companies: Insurance companies are regulated by the insurance commissioner of the state in which they do business.

- Pension funds: Pension funds are regulated by the Department of Labor. The Pension Benefit Guaranty Corporation provides insurance in the event that a pension plan is unable to pay the benefits defined in the pension agreement. The pension rights of more than 40 million Americans are protected by this insurance. In other words, if a plan cannot pay pension benefits because it invested the premiums poorly or because it was not funded properly to begin with, the Pension Benefit Guaranty Corporation will pay the benefits according to the contract and make up any payment deficiencies up to a limit.

- Stocks and bonds: Securities markets including brokers and dealers are overseen by the SEC. The SEC requires that companies fully disclose their financial condition before issuing bonds and while the bonds are outstanding. Likewise, issuers of new securities must register with the SEC and disclose all important financial information. If the equities are to be publicly traded, ongoing disclosure is required, and insider trading, which is trading of securities by those who have access to information about the companies involved before it is made public, is forbidden. Margin requirements specify the maximum percent of borrowed funds that can be used in a stock purchase. The Fed sets margin requirements for the purchase of stocks and bonds.

- Securities firms: Securities firms are regulated by the SEC, the New York Stock Exchange (NYSE), and other exchanges. In addition, securities firms are self-regulated by the National Association of Securities Dealers. The Securities Investor Protection Corporation insures retail customers of securities brokerage firms for up to $500,000 of their portfolios in the event the brokerage firm becomes insolvent.

- U.S. government securities: U.S. government and U.S. government agency securities are regulated by the Fed and the SEC.

- Government Sponsored Enterprises associated with the housing market (Fannie Mae and Freddie Mac) and the Federal Home Loan Banks: The Federal Housing Finance Agency (FHFA) was created in July 2008 in response to the ongoing financial crisis to oversee the agencies that dominate the secondary mortgage markets. Fannie Mae and Freddie Mac were put into conservatorship by the FHFA in September 2008.

Because the regulatory structure will continue to change as the financial services industry evolves, innovative regulations for new and existing markets and products may be just around the corner.

Recap   Regulation must balance the goals of competition and efficiency versus safety and soundness. FIs should balance the expected benefits and expected costs of assuming various levels of risk. Initially, regulation encouraged market segmentation and, hence, regulation was segmented. Although segmented markets are breaking down, regulations have been slower to change. Either financial products or financial institutions can be regulated. The regulatory structure is in the process of ongoing change because of the evolution of the financial services industry.

A Proposal to Overhaul the Financial Regulatory Structure

The subprime lending crisis of 2008 that spread to the entire global financial system highlighted lapses in the financial regulatory system. Even before this crisis, policy makers recognized the need to overhaul an outdated regulatory system. The globalization of finance and the plethora of financial innovations had made the financial system very different from what it was a few decades earlier. In March 2007, the U.S. Treasury "convened a blue-ribbon panel to discuss U.S. capital markets competitiveness." Out of this panel came the recognition that the competitiveness of the financial services industry was negatively impacted by an outdated regulatory structure. Therefore, in June 2007, the Treasury began work on a series of recommendations to modernize the regulatory system.

On March 31, 2008, Treasury Secretary Henry Paulson released the "Treasury's Blueprint for Financial Regulatory Reform."[a] The blueprint proposes a new regulatory framework that would be composed of three regulators, each with a different function. The goal of regulating by function was to make the regulatory structure more resilient to innovations within the financial system that could render current regulations inadequate or obsolete.

The first regulator would focus on financial stability across the entire financial system. This would protect against systemic risk, which is the risk that a collapse in one market will spread to the rest of the economy and result in a downturn. Not surprisingly, the Treasury recommends that the Fed perform this role. In doing so, the Fed's regulatory powers would be broadened from financial holding and bank holding companies to investment banks, insurance companies, hedge funds, private equity firms, and virtually any other financial institution or market whose financial practices could pose a threat to the financial stability of the economy. The Fed would have the power to oversee the capital adequacy, liquidity, and lending practices of any such financial institution or market.

The second regulator would concentrate on ensuring the safety and soundness of institutions such as banks and savings associations that had federally guaranteed deposit insurance. Presently, banks are regulated by the Office of the Controller of the Currency (OCC), and savings associations are regulated by the Office of Thrift Supervision (OTS). Under this proposal, banks and savings associations would both be chartered and regulated by the OCC and the OTS would be phased out.

The third regulator would protect consumers and investors from unfair lending practices and would monitor all financial institutions with regard to consumer protection. It would assume many of the roles of the Securities and Exchange Commission (SEC), which currently regulates stocks and bonds, and the Commodity Futures Trading Commission (CFTC), which currently regulates futures contracts. It would also take over many of the roles of banking and insurance regulators regarding disclosure. This would result in greater consistency in the disclosure to consumers of the risks involved with various financial products.

Finally, the report proposes maintaining the present state-level regulation of mortgage brokers and originators. However, it also recommends creating a Mortgage Origination Commission (MOC) to evaluate and oversee each state's regulation of the mortgage market. The MOC would then disclose states that were not adequately regulating mortgage brokers, and hence, whose mortgages may not be desirable for securitization. Concerning the mortgage crisis that began in 2006, it is now clear that many homebuyers who financed their purchase with a subprime loan did not understand the extent to which payments would increase over the next few years, and the buyers of the securitized loans were also not aware of how risky these loans were.

It is expected that the reforms to the financial regulatory system will be completed until sometime in 2009, and then adopted over the next several years after that. However, the ongoing financial crisis of 2008 may speed up the reform process and cause policy makers to take it far more seriously.

Endnotes

a. http://www.treasury.gov/press/releases/hp897.htm.

We now turn our attention to the most recent pieces of regulatory legislation: those governing the banking system from the 1980s to the early years of the new millennium.

DEPOSITORY INSTITUTIONS DEREGULATION AND MONETARY CONTROL ACT OF 1980 AND THE GARN–ST. GERMAIN ACT OF 1982: DEREGULATION IN THE EARLY 1980S

The burdens associated with complying with the regulations and the benefits associated with innovating around them produced numerous forms of adaptive behavior by banks and other FIs. For example, banks developed new types of liabilities to sidestep Regulation Q (interest rate ceilings that could be paid to depositors) and reserve requirements. These new types of liabilities included borrowings in the fed funds, negotiable CDs, repurchase agreements, and Eurodollar markets. Because these new types of liabilities were borrowings, not deposits, they were not subject to interest rate caps or reserve requirements. Banks also used the holding company corporate form to evade certain entry and branching restrictions and to engage in nonbanking activities. The financial regulations and structures that had been designed and erected during the Great Depression were increasingly ill suited to the changing economic and technological environment of the 1970s. As innovations weakened the effectiveness of various regulations, regulators recognized the difficulty, if not the impossibility, of controlling financial flows and the market for financial services. Accordingly, Congress decided to deregulate by dismantling the regulations. Landmark legislation enacted in 1980 and 1982 was the result.[6]

Depository Institutions Deregulation and Monetary Control Act of 1980 (DIDMCA)
The statute that removed many of the regulations enacted during the Great Depression; it phased out Regulation Q, established uniform and universal reserve requirements, increased the assets and liabilities that depository institutions could hold, authorized NOW accounts, and suspended usury ceilings.

The first legislation was the **Depository Institutions Deregulation and Monetary Control Act of 1980 (DIDMCA)**. Its numerous provisions reflect the compromises necessary to enact such an all-encompassing piece of legislation. As its title suggests, however, the major provisions of interest to us can be divided into two groups:

1. Deregulation

   a. The remaining Regulation Q ceilings were phased out over a six-year period that ended in 1986.

b. Asset and liability powers of banks and thrifts were expanded.
  (1) Assets: S&Ls and savings banks were allowed to extend loans to businesses and offer more services to customers.
  (2) Liabilities: All depository intermediaries were permitted to offer NOW accounts (interest-bearing checkable deposits) to households.
  (3) State **usury ceilings** (maximum interest rates FIs are allowed to charge borrowers on certain types of loans) were suspended.

2. Monetary control
  a. All depository institutions were subject to reserve requirements (so-called **universal reserve requirements**).
  b. Reserve requirements were to be the same on particular types of deposits across institutions (so-called **uniform reserve requirements**); this provision was phased in over an eight-year period that ended in 1987.

> **Usury Ceilings**
> Maximum interest rates that FIs may charge on certain loans.

> **Universal Reserve Requirements**
> Reserve requirements to which all depository institutions are subject.

> **Uniform Reserve Requirements**
> Reserve requirements that apply to particular types of deposits and are the same across all depository institutions.

In general, the deregulation provisions put some explicit price competition back into banking and permitted more competition among depository institutions. As a result, banks and thrifts would be more alike in terms of the products and services offered to the public. Congress hoped that the net result of more competition would be greater efficiency, an accompanying reduction in costs, and an improvement in the quantity and quality of financial services.

By mandating universal and uniform reserve requirements, the act strengthened the effectiveness of the regulatory process and expanded the powers of the Fed. Henceforth, when the Fed changed the amount of funds available for reserves, its control over the money supply and supply of loanable funds would be more direct. All in all, the DIDMCA was a landmark piece of legislation that brought many long overdue changes to the financial structure—changes that had been recommended by numerous federal studies over the previous 20 years.

Two years later, the Garn–St. Germain Depository Institutions Act of 1982 was enacted. Like its 1980 predecessor, the 1982 act had many provisions. Chief among them were those that speeded up the pace of deregulation by allowing depository institutions to offer two types of deposit accounts designed to compete directly with money market mutual funds: (1) money market deposit accounts, which have no rate ceiling and permit six third-party payments transactions per month, and (2) Super NOW accounts, which also have no rate ceiling but are fully checkable.

Since this legislation was enacted, competition among FIs and between FIs and the open market has increased dramatically. For example, depository institutions now offer rates on all deposit liabilities that are closely correlated with market rates. Such dramatic changes in the competitive environment within which banks and other FIs operate have noticeable effects on the portfolio behavior and operations of depository institutions.

Recap   Because market participants had found ways around many regulations, Congress passed two major statutes that deregulated financial markets. The DIDMCA in 1980 phased out Regulation Q ceilings and expanded the asset and liability powers of banks and thrifts. It also established uniform and universal reserve requirements for all depository institutions. The Garn–St. Germain Act of 1982, among other things, authorized money market deposit accounts and Super NOW accounts.

Basel Accord—The Introduction of International Capital Standards

Bank capital is the difference between bank assets and liabilities. It acts as a "cushion," protecting an FI from bankruptcy in the event of a decline in the value of its assets. Until

Looking Out

Basel Committee Announces 25 Core Principles for Effective Bank Supervision

The Asian meltdown of 1997–98 demonstrated how crisis prone the international financial system can be as financial markets become more globalized. Long before this crisis, the Basel Committee on Banking Supervision had related concerns and was meeting on a regular basis at the Bank for International Settlements in Basel, Switzerland. The committee consists of central bank governors from the G-10 countries. Its goal is to improve banking supervision at the international level and enhance international financial stability.

In September 1997, the Basel Committee announced 25 core principles that the committee believes must be in place for a supervisory system to be effective. In addition to the G-10 nations, 15 other emerging economies participated in the discussions. Supervisory authorities throughout the world were asked to endorse the principles by October 1998. Endorsement includes a review of current supervisory arrangements and the changes that would have to be implemented for a country to be in compliance with the principles.

The core principles address "the preconditions for effective banking supervision, licensing and structure, prudential regulations and requirements, methods of ongoing banking supervision, information requirements, formal powers of supervisors and cross-border banking."[a] They are intended to serve as a reference for regulators to apply when supervising banks in their countries. In addition, the principles are designed to be verifiable by domestic and international regulators and the market. It is hoped that if countries strengthen areas where they fall short of the core principles, domestic and international financial stability will be improved.

Endnotes

a. Press Release, Bank for International Settlements (September 23, 1997).

1980, banks were pretty much free to establish their own capital requirements as the Fed and other regulators pursued different avenues of control such as reserve requirements, asset restrictions, chartering, and Regulation Q. Since the deregulation of these traditional avenues of regulation in the early 1980s, regulators have attempted not only to impose stricter capital requirements but also to use them as a primary vehicle of regulation.

The trend toward stricter standards received further impetus in November 1988, when the United States and 11 other countries entered into the Basel Accord, which established uniform international capital standards for banks. The accord specified the amount of capital that banks must hold relative to assets. This standard was stricter than that imposed on U.S. banks at the time and involved risk-based capital standards for the first time. Thus, the amount of capital a bank was required to hold was based not only on total assets and liabilities but also on the measurable riskiness of those assets. Despite the regulators' efforts, many banks were holding less capital relative to assets than the

Basel Accord
A 1988 agreement among 12 countries that established international capital standards for banks.

Bank Capital Standards Under the Basel Accord (Basel I)

The Basel Accord established requirements for core capital and for total capital. Core capital is by definition the historical value of outstanding stock plus retained earnings. Total capital is core capital plus supplemental capital (loan-loss reserves plus subordinated debt). Subordinated debt is long-term debt that is paid off after depositors and other creditors have been paid in the event that the institution goes under. The amount of capital that must be held is based on the larger of two measures: one measure is based on risk-adjusted assets and the other on total assets.

The method based on risk-adjusted assets assigns different weights to different types of assets according to their risks. For instance, ordinary loans are counted at 100 percent of their value; mortgages are counted at 50 percent. Only half of the value of mortgages is counted because the property is held as collateral and repossessed in the event of default. Deposits between banks (interbank deposits) count at 20 percent, and T-bills and cash count at zero percent. In addition, off-balance-sheet activities that result in an obligation or potential obligation for the bank are also counted in risk-adjusted capital at their full value. For example, if a bank gives a standby letter of credit for $1,000, that letter of credit is counted at its full value ($1,000) in calculating risk-adjusted assets, even though it is not an asset. The reason for this is obvious. If the standby letter of credit is exercised, the bank stands to lose $1,000 just as if it had made a bad loan. For safety, a bank with off-balance-sheet activities that expose the bank to greater risk must maintain more capital. The risks of some activities such as futures, options, and swaps may be difficult to evaluate, however.

Once risk-adjusted assets have been determined, they are subject to two capital constraints: (1) core capital must be equal to at least 4 percent of risk-adjusted assets and (2) total capital must be equal to at least 8 percent of risk-adjusted assets. At the present time, risk-adjusted assets take into account only credit risk. They do not consider interest rate, liquidity, or exchange rate risks. Additional requirements that consider these risks may be implemented in the future.

In addition to the constraints based on risk-adjusted assets, banks are also subject to a leverage requirement stated in terms of total assets. In this case, all assets are weighted at 100 percent, and there is no accounting for off-balance-sheet activities. (The weight assigned to off-balance-sheet activities is zero.) According to the Basel Accord requirements, a bank must have core capital equal to at least 3 percent of total assets.

The use of international capital requirements has many desirable effects. All banks from the countries that abide by the standards are put on a more or less equal footing. The following table provides an example of how the standards are implemented under what has come to be known as Basel I.

Core Capital	$775,000
Stock issued	500,000
Retained earnings	275,000
Total Capital	1,535,000
Core capital	775,000
Loan-loss reserves	260,000
Subordinated debt	500,000

Risk-Adjusted Assets

Loans	$14,000,000 @ 100%	$14,000,000
Mortgages	3,500,000 @ 50%	1,750,000
Interbank deposits	2,000,000 @ 20%	400,000
Government securities	3,000,000 @ 0%	0
Reserves	1,800,000 @ 0%	0
Standby letters and other lines of credit	3,000,000 @ 100%	3,000,000
Total Risk-Adjusted Assets	$19,150,000	

Total Assets

Loans	$14,000,000 @ 100%	$14,000,000
Mortgages	3,500,000 @ 100%	3,500,000
Interbank deposits	2,000,000 @ 100%	2,000,000
Government securities	3,000,000 @ 100%	3,000,000
Reserves	1,800,000 @ 100%	1,800,000
Standby letters and other lines of credit	3,000,000 @ 0%	0
Total Assets	$24,300,000	

Core capital must equal at least 4% of risk-adjusted assets: 4% × $19,150,000 = $766,000

Total capital must equal at least 8% of risk-adjusted assets: 8% × $19,150,000 = $1,532,000

Core capital must equal at least 3% of total assets: 3% × $24,300,000 = $729,000

As noted in the body of the text, very large complex banking institutions will be subject to additional capital requirements under Basel II.

new regulations required. Thus, as a result of the accord, many U.S. banks had to alter their behavior—to shore up bank capital relative to assets—in the early 1990s to meet the stricter standards. "A Closer Look" explains these standards and gives an example of how they are implemented.

The original Basel Accord, now known as Basel I, is believed to have achieved its primary goal of promoting financial stability by imposing risk-based international standards for banks. However, as some banking institutions have become more complex and as risk-management strategies have become more sophisticated, the need for additional standards for the largest and most complex banking institutions has been recognized. These institutions use instruments and procedures whose risk is not adequately measured under Basel I.

Changes to the accord, known as Basel II (or officially, The International Convergence of Capital Measurement and Capital Standards: A Revised Framework), were issued by the Bank for International Settlements (BIS) in June 2004. As of mid-2007, details of U.S. implementation were still being negotiated by the "notice of proposed rulemaking" committee comprised of representatives from the primary U.S. regulatory authorities: the Federal Reserve, the Office of the Comptroller of the Currency, the Office of Thrift Supervision, and the Federal Deposit Insurance Corporation. In July 2007, these U.S. regulators agreed on a schedule for implementation and monitoring through 2008.

The basic objective of the Basel II framework is to more precisely measure the actual risks that banks face and determine required capital levels accordingly. A key aspect of the new framework is increased flexibility. It provides institutions with the opportunity to adopt approaches most appropriate to their situation.

Basel II consists of three primary components or "pillars." The first sets minimum capital requirements that firms are required to meet in order to cover credit, market, and operational risk. The second creates a new supervisory review whereby financial institutions have their own internal processes—processes that allow them to assess capital needs and to appoint supervisors to evaluate their overall risk profile in order to ensure adequate capital is held. The third aims to improve market discipline by requiring firms to publish details regarding their risks, capital, and risk management.

FINANCIAL INSTITUTIONS REFORM, RECOVERY, AND ENFORCEMENT ACT OF 1989—REREGULATION IN RESPONSE TO FINANCIAL CRISIS (BAILING OUT THE THRIFTS)

The Financial Institutions Reform, Recovery, and Enforcement Act (FIRREA) was signed into law in August 1989. The FIRREA was passed in response to the S&L crisis of the 1980s and was an attempt at reregulation following the deregulation and subsequent crises of the 1980s (see Chapter 11). The provisions of the FIRREA include the following:

1. An initial $50 billion was injected into the newly created Savings Association Insurance Fund (SAIF). The SAIF was established to provide insurance for the deposits of S&Ls, thereby replacing the Federal Savings and Loan Insurance Corporation (FSLIC). Additionally, the SAIF provided funding for the government takeover of failed S&Ls. The original $50 billion was raised by selling bonds known as bailout bonds, and the money was used to compensate institutions that took over a failed S&L by making up the difference between the value of the assets and liabilities of the defunct institution. Administration of the SAIF was made the responsibility of the Federal Deposit Insurance Corporation (FDIC). The FSLIC was dissolved. It had virtually gone bankrupt because of the crisis of the 1980s and was unable to cover the losses of insured deposits.

2. Two new government agencies were created. The Office of Thrift Supervision (OTS) was established to oversee the S&L industry, replacing the Federal Home Loan Bank Board. The Resolution Trust Corporation (RTC) was set up as a temporary agency to dispose of the properties of the thrifts that failed between January 1, 1989, and July 1, 1995. The FDIC was put in charge of the RTC, and the board of the FDIC was expanded from three to five members with the addition of the director of the OTS and an additional appointment by the president of the United States.

3. For the first time, deposit insurance was made a full faith and credit obligation of the federal government rather than the FDIC. Until 1989, neither Congress nor the taxpayers were legally required to bail out an insolvent deposit insurance company, whether it be the FDIC or the FSLIC. In reality, the government was de facto required to bail out a failed deposit insurer, as it did with the FSLIC, but only because

Office of Thrift Supervision (OTS)
An agency created by the FIRREA to replace the Federal Home Loan Bank Board as the overseer of the S&L industry.

Federal Home Loan Bank Board
The regulatory body of the S&L industry until 1989.

Resolution Trust Corporation (RTC)
An agency created by the FIRREA to dispose of the properties of the failed S&Ls.

failing to do so might cause a system-wide collapse. Contrary to what most Americans thought, there was no legal responsibility for the bailout. The new deposit insurance funds, the SAIF and the Bank Insurance Fund (BIF), both under the FDIC, were required to maintain reserves of at least 1.25 percent of insured deposits. Premiums paid are a percentage of total domestic deposits, including deposits of more than $100,000.

4. New regulations restricted the investments of S&Ls by limiting commercial mortgage lending and by phasing out junk bond investments by 1994. Investments in junk bonds had first been authorized in 1982 by the Garn–St. Germain Act. In addition, S&Ls were required to hold at least 70 percent of their assets as mortgages or mortgage-backed securities. Commercial real estate loans were restricted to 400 percent of total capital.

5. Capital requirements were imposed on the S&Ls. The requirements were similar to those placed on banks under the Basel I Accord. Risk-based capital standards were phased in, just as they had been for banks in participating countries (see "A Closer Look" on pages 263–264). Core capital for S&Ls was to be 3 percent, and total capital was to be at least 8 percent of risk-adjusted assets. These new requirements more than doubled the amount of capital that had to be held under the previous standards. To demonstrate the extent to which the industry has recovered, as of June 30, 2007, the total capital-to-asset ratio of S&Ls was 10.56 percent, which is higher than it was in the 1940–1970 period, when the ratio fluctuated around 7 percent.

FEDERAL DEPOSIT INSURANCE CORPORATION IMPROVEMENT ACT OF 1991—TIGHTENING UP DEPOSIT INSURANCE

Although it might seem that deposit insurance would solve the problem of excessive risk taking by protecting small depositors in the event of a depository institution's insolvency, deposit insurance actually increases the problem of excessive risk taking: it reduces market discipline because depositors no longer have to be concerned about the level of risk their bank engages in. This is the moral hazard problem introduced in Chapter 8. It occurs because the presence of deposit insurance causes financial intermediaries to take more risks than they otherwise would; they know that if they lose, their depositors will still get their funds back.[7] This encourages more risk because the greater the risk, the greater the possibility of higher returns. It's like going to Las Vegas to gamble with your neighbor's funds with the understanding that if you win, you get to keep the winnings and if you lose, your neighbor still gets paid back, but not by you.

Federal Deposit Insurance Corporation Improvement Act (FDICIA)

Legislation passed by Congress in 1991 to enact regulatory changes that ensure the safety and soundness of the banking and thrift industries. Regulators had long wished to merge the two separate deposit insurance funds, and the Federal Deposit Insurance Reform Act of 2005 accomplished this when signed into law by the president in early 2006.

In response to growing concerns about this problem, Congress passed the Federal Deposit Insurance Corporation Improvement Act (FDICIA) in 1991. The FDICIA attempted to secure the safety and soundness of the banking and thrift industries (S&Ls, savings banks, and credit unions) through several reforms. First, insurance premiums were scaled to the risk exposure of the banks or thrifts. However, in years when the insurance fund had adequate reserves, no institutions were charged premiums for deposit insurance despite their risk exposure. Second, FDICIA limited insurance coverage of regular and retirement accounts to a maximum of $100,000 per depository institution.[8] Third, the FDIC established a system that rated banks and savings institutions by their capital adequacy. Undercapitalized institutions were then categorized as undercapitalized, significantly undercapitalized, and critically undercapitalized, and institutions in each category subjected to appropriate treatment. The greater the degree of undercapitalization, the more severe the restrictions on the bank's operations. Fourth, the ability of foreign banks to use certain categories of deposits in the United States was limited, so they could only keep insured deposit accounts through insured U.S. subsidiary banks.

The fifth change required the FDIC to use the least costly method to resolve any insolvency. Previously, an insolvency could be resolved by either the **payoff method** or the **purchase and assumption method.** Under the payoff method, depositors of a failed institution are paid off, the assets are liquidated, and the institution is closed. Depositors with balances of more than $100,000 lose the balances over $100,000. Under the purchase and assumption method, an insolvency is resolved by finding a buyer for the failed institution. In this case, all deposit liabilities (even those above the $100,000 limit) are assumed by the purchasing institution, and depositors do not lose anything. The payoff method is usually cheaper for the FDIC. Being required to use the least costly method to resolve insolvencies makes the purchase and assumption method a more attractive alternative for disposing of insolvent banks that are "too-big-to-fail." Under the "too-big-to-fail" practice, which was adopted by FDIC regulators in 1984, the failure of a large bank would be resolved using the purchase and assumption method rather than the payoff method, thereby freeing the FDIC from insuring deposits of more than $100,000. Despite this provision, though, if the bank failure would result in a systemic risk (a risk to the entire financial system), the least costly method would not have to be used. An exception requires the approval of the U.S. Treasury in consultation with the president and the approval of two-thirds of the members of the Board of Governors of the Fed and the FDIC. Needless to say, an exception is unlikely to be granted unless the failure would cause serious adverse effects to the overall economy and the financial system. In the case of the failure of IndyMac Bank in July 2008, there were 10,000 depositors with balances over $100,000. In this case, the FDIC guaranteed 50 percent of the value of the deposits over $100,000. After the liquidation of IndyMac assets, it is not known if depositers with uninsured deposits will get any additional funds back.

FEDERAL DEPOSIT INSURANCE REFORM ACT OF 2005—MERGING DEPOSIT INSURANCE FUNDS

Regulators had long wished to merge the two separate deposit insurance funds, and the Federal Deposit Insurance Reform Act of 2005 accomplished this when signed into law by President George W. Bush in early 2006. Effective March 31, 2006, the Bank Insurance Fund and Savings Association Insurance Funds were merged into the new **Deposit Insurance Fund (DIF).** Additional changes include the following:

1. Increasing the coverage limit for retirement accounts to $250,000 while keeping the limit at $100,000 for ordinary accounts. In addition, both coverage limits were indexed to inflation beginning in 2010.

2. Setting a range from 1.15 percent to 1.50 percent, between which the FDIC Board of Directors may set the Designated Reserve Ratio (DRR), and allowing the FDIC to manage the pace at which the DRR varies within this range.

3. Eliminating the restrictions on premium rates based on the DRR and granting the FDIC Board the discretion to price deposit insurance according to risk for all insured institutions regardless of the level of the reserve ratio. This effectively eliminates cross-subsidization of more risky members of the insurance pool by healthier institutions.

4. Granting a one-time initial assessment credit (of approximately $4.7 billion total) to recognize institutions' past contributions to the fund.

The Reform Act and ancillary amendments also require completion or research that may affect future regulatory changes. The FDIC is required to study further potential

Payoff Method
The method of resolving a bank insolvency by paying off the depositors and closing the institution.

Purchase and Assumption Method
The method of resolving a bank insolvency by finding a buyer for the institution.

"Too Big to Fail"
The position adopted by FDIC regulators in 1984 whereby the failure of a large bank would be resolved using the purchase and assumption method rather than the payoff method.

Federal Deposit Insurance Reform Act of 2005
The Reform Act that merged the BIF and SAIF into the deposit insurance fund (DIF), increased the deposit insurance coverage for retirement accounts to $250,000, and adjusted coverage.

Deposit Insurance Fund (DIF)
Result of the combination of the Bank Insurance Fund and Savings Association Insurance Fund, effective March 31, 2006.

changes to the deposit insurance system, the appropriate deposit base in designating the reserve ratio, and its contingent loss reserving methodology and how it accounts for losses. In addition, the Comptroller General is required to study the federal bank regulators' administration of the prompt corrective action program and recent changes to the FDIC deposit insurance system, as well as the organizational structure of the FDIC. Given the ongoing financial crisis of 2008, many believe that the FDIC will need an injection of funds from Congress to resolve the number of insolvencies that are occurring.

Finally, please note as a result of the Basel Accord, the FIRREA, the FDICIA, and the Reform Act of 2005, banks and other depository institutions are now subject to both risk-based capital standards and risk-based insurance premiums. We turn now to the Community Reinvestment Act, which was actually passed in 1977 but had little impact until more recently.

Recap   The Basel Accord of 1988 established international capital standards for financial institutions. Basel II, signed by representatives of 13 countries, revised capital standards for more complex banking institutions. The FIRREA of 1989 bailed out the S&L industry, imposed new risk-based capital standards on S&Ls, and restricted the assets that S&Ls could hold. The FDICIA of 1991 imposed risk-based insurance premiums and eliminated the "too-big-to-fail" practice by requiring the FDIC to resolve insolvencies in the least costly way. The Reform Act of 2005 merged deposit insurance funds into the Bank Insurance Fund and indexed coverage limits for accounts.

COMMUNITY REINVESTMENT ACT—OUTLAWING DISCRIMINATORY LENDING PRACTICES

Community Reinvestment Act
Legislation passed by Congress in 1977 to increase the availability of credit to economically disadvantaged areas and to correct alleged discriminatory lending practices.

The original purpose of the **Community Reinvestment Act (CRA)** was to increase the availability of credit to economically disadvantaged areas and to correct alleged discriminatory lending practices. Minority borrowers and neighborhoods had long been the victims of **redlining**. Redlining refers to the practice of drawing a red line (or any colored line) around a certain area on a map and restricting the number or dollar amount of loans made in that area regardless of the creditworthiness of the borrower with respect to income or collateral.

The Community Reinvestment Act did not get much attention because it provided no means of enforcement for regulators to use. However, activist groups believed that many banks were not making significant efforts to comply with the law, and in recent years, many mainstream community groups have joined their calls for more stringent enforcement of the act.

Redlining
The practice of restricting the number or dollar amounts of loans in an area regardless of the creditworthiness of the borrower.

During the late 1980s and the 1990s, a means of enforcing the act became available with the wave of bank mergers and acquisitions that began in the late 1980s and accelerated in the late 1990s. In deciding whether to approve a bank merger or acquisition, the Fed now assesses how well the bank is meeting the CRA's lending criteria, and compliance statements are judged critically.[9]

In 1995, CRA regulations were revised to make them more objective and performance oriented, as well as to reduce compliance and reporting costs for many banks. Under the new rules, banks are divided into three classifications: large retail, small retail, and wholesale or limited-purpose institutions. Large and small retail banks are evaluated principally on their performance in assessment areas, whereas wholesale and limited-purpose institutions are evaluated based on their nationwide performance, as long as they have adequately addressed the needs of the assessment area. For large retail banks, current regulations establish performance goals for lending, investment, and service. Banks are rated "outstanding," "satisfactory," "needs to improve," or "substantial noncompliance." Most banks have received satisfactory or better ratings. Now all federal agencies responsible for supervising depository institutions conduct CRA examinations, and each institution's record is taken into account when considering an institution's application for deposit facilities. Bank performance in this area is often difficult to judge, however, because banks are required to practice nondiscriminatory lending while focusing on safety and soundness.

To the extent that the Community Reinvestment Act has forced financial institutions to recognize and respond to the changing demographics before they would otherwise have done so, the law has provided an important service to the industry and community. Many bankers found that as they developed new markets, products, and services to meet the needs of the community, these new activities would be quite profitable. However, some analysts also suggested that the CRA contributed to the financial crisis of 2008 by increasing the number of mortgages and other loans made to low income households that would later not be able to afford the loans.

INTERSTATE BANKING AND BRANCHING EFFICIENCY ACT OF 1994—THE DAWN OF NATIONWIDE BRANCHING?

Interstate Banking and Branching Efficiency Act (IBBEA)
A 1994 act that eliminated most restrictions on interstate bank mergers by June 1, 1997.

The **Interstate Banking and Branching Efficiency Act (IBBEA)** of 1994 eliminated most restrictions on interstate bank mergers and made interstate branching possible for the first time since the passage of the McFadden Act in 1927.[10] The law permits all bank holding companies to acquire banks anywhere in the nation as long as certain conditions are met. In addition, under the same conditions, banks in one state may merge with banks in another state, thus effectively branching. The conditions include meeting requirements for the safety and soundness of the institutions involved (they must be well capitalized and well managed) and making commitments to community reinvestment under the Community Reinvestment Act. Under no circumstances will banks be permitted to use a branch to generate deposits without considering community reinvestment needs. Prior to the law, some states had limited or put additional conditions on the acquisition of banks by out-of-state bank holding companies.

In addition, as of June 1, 1997, bank holding companies were permitted to convert their multiple banks in various states into branches of a single interstate bank. This reduced the costs of maintaining a separate board of directors for each bank and the costs of other duplicative overhead expenses. Whether significant savings will be realized remains to be seen.

We turn now to the final major piece of banking legislation in the twentieth century. With the passage of the Gramm-Leach-Bliley Act in 1999, the financial services industry of the twenty-first century is far different from that of the twentieth century.

THE GRAMM-LEACH-BLILEY ACT (GLBA) OF 1999—THE FINAL DEMISE OF GLASS-STEAGALL

Until 1999, the most significant piece of banking legislation in the twentieth century had been the Glass-Steagall Act of 1933, which separated investment and commercial banking, created the FDIC, and limited the range of assets and liabilities that a commercial bank could hold and issue. After 67 years, this act was effectively repealed with the passage of the Gramm-Leach-Bliley Act (GLBA) in November 1999. The new landmark legislation became effective March 11, 2000, and it significantly impacts the financial services industry. Rather than segmentation among financial service providers, the act allows for considerable financial integration in the financial services industry.

Major Provisions of the Gramm-Leach-Bliley Act

Financial Holding Companies (FHCs)
Bank holding companies that have applied for and been certified by the Fed to engage in a wide range of financial and nonfinancial activities, including securities, insurance, and merchant banking activities and other financial or nonfinancial complementary activities.

GLBA allows bank holding companies that meet certain criteria to be certified as **financial holding companies (FHCs)**. FHCs may engage in a broad array of financial and nonfinancial activities. To become an FHC, a bank holding company must file a declaration with the Fed that certifies that all of its depository institutions are well capitalized and well managed and have a "satisfactory" or better rating under the Community Reinvestment Act. An FHC may engage in the following activities:

1. Financially related activities including securities underwriting and dealing, insurance agency and underwriting activities, and merchant banking activities.

2. Other financial activities that the Fed determines to be financial in nature or incidental to financial activities.

3. Nonfinancial activities that the Fed determines are complementary to a financial activity and do not pose a substantial risk to the safety or soundness of depository institutions or the financial system.

The act also authorizes expanded powers for banks and their subsidiaries. Under the new law, banks are authorized to

1. underwrite and market municipal revenue bonds, and

2. own or control a "financial subsidiary" that engages in activities that national banks are not permitted to directly engage in if prior approval of the Office of the Controller of the Currency is received.

Under the GLBA, the Fed is given the ultimate responsibility for supervising FHCs. This is similar to its ultimate regulatory responsibility for bank holding companies. However, under the law, the Fed is to rely on reports of examination prepared by the subsidiary's primary functional regulator as much as possible. For example, the primary banking regulator may be the FDIC, the Fed, or the Office of the Controller of the Currency; for securities activities, the primary regulator is the Securities and Exchange Commission; and for insurance activities, the state insurance commissioner is the primary regulator. There are some exceptions, such as when the Fed believes that the activities of a subsidiary may pose a threat to an affiliated depository institution or if the subsidiary is in violation of any federal law that the Fed has jurisdiction to enforce.

As of March 2000, when the law became partially effective, 117 bank holding companies had been certified as FHCs. Full phase-in of the law became effective November 12, 2004, when financial subsidiaries of FHCs were allowed to engage in merchant banking activities. By April 2008, the number had increased to about 647.

Two important additional provisions of the GLBA protect consumers. The first requires that ATM operators post a notice of any fees that may be imposed and inform the consumer through an onscreen or paper message of the amount of the fee before the consumer is irrevocably committed to completing the transaction. The second includes a number of new requirements relating to the disclosure of financial information about consumers. Namely, financial institutions cannot sell information for marketing purpose and are required to disclose, prior to the opening of an account and at least annually thereafter, the institution's policies regarding the disclosure of nonpublic personal information to third parties.

A Time Line of Banking Legislation

During the twentieth century, the United States enacted a number of pieces of major banking legislation that shaped the industry and its evolution.

- **1913:** The Federal Reserve Act created the Federal Reserve System.
- **1927:** The McFadden Act prohibited interstate banking.
- **1933:** The Glass-Steagall Act established the FDIC as a temporary agency, separated commercial and investment banking, established Regulation Q interest rate ceilings, and set the interest rate ceiling on demand deposits at zero percent.
- **1935:** The Banking Act established the FDIC as a permanent agency.
- **1980:** The Depository Institutions Deregulation and Monetary Control Act (DIDMCA) authorized NOW accounts nationwide, thereby ending the monopoly of commercial banks on checkable deposits; phased out Regulation Q; established uniform and universal reserve requirements; granted new powers to thrifts; eliminated usury laws; and increased deposit insurance from $40,000 to $100,000 per account.
- **1982:** The Garn–St. Germain Act expanded the asset and liability powers of banks and thrifts; expanded the power of the FDIC to help troubled banks; and created money market deposit accounts and super NOW accounts.
- **1989:** The Financial Institutions Recovery, Reform, and Enforcement Act (FIRREA) authorized a taxpayer bailout of the S&L industry; brought deposit insurance for thrifts under the FDIC; created the Resolution Trust Corporation, a temporary agency to dispose of the assets of failed institutions; and imposed new restrictions on S&Ls.
- **1991:** The Federal Deposit Insurance Corporation Improvement Act (FDICIA) abolished the "too-big-to-fail" policy; limited brokered deposits; established new capital requirements for banks; established risk-based insurance premiums; gave the FDIC new powers to borrow from the U.S. Treasury; restricted activities of foreign banks; and insured state banks.
- **1994:** The Interstate Banking and Branching Efficiency Act (IBBEA) as of June 1, 1997, allowed virtually unimpeded interstate branching by adequately capitalized and managed banks that meet CRA requirements.
- **1999:** The Gramm-Leach-Bliley Act (GLBA) allowed banks, insurance companies, securities firms, and other financial institutions to affiliate under common ownership and to offer a complete range of financial services that had been previously prohibited; created financial holding companies (FHCs) that could engage in financially related activities, other financial activities, and complementary nonfinancial activities; expanded allowable activities for banks and their subsidiaries; and repealed key provisions of the 1933 Glass-Steagall Act that separated commercial and investment banking.
- **2005:** The Federal Deposit Insurance Reform Act of 2005 merged the Bank Insurance Fund and Savings Association Insurance Fund into a new Deposit Insurance Fund (DIF). It also increased the coverage limit for retirement accounts to $250,000 and indexed this limit for both retirement and ordinary accounts beginning in 2010.
- **2008:** The Emergency Economic Stabilization Act of 2008 authorized up to $700 billion to the U.S. Treasury to buy "toxic" assets. Among other things, the funds were used to shore up the capital of large banks that were in trouble, rather than buy toxic assets. The Act also established an insurance program for "troubled" assets.

THE EMERGENCY ECONOMIC STABILIZATION ACT OF 2008

The Emergency Economic Stabilization Act of 2008 (EESA) was passed and signed into law on October 3, 2008 in response to the financial collapse of 2008. The Act initially authorized the U.S. Treasury to purchase up to $700 billion of questionable "toxic" mortgage-backed securities under the "Troubled Assets Relief Program" (TARP). $250 billion was available immediately and an additional $100 billion would be available upon submission of a progress report about how the original funds were used. Congress had to authorize the use of the remaining $350 billion. As of early 2009, Congress was expected to authorize the additional $350 billion to be spent under the direction of the new Obama administration.

On October 14, 2008, the TARP program was revised by the Treasury and the initial $250 billion would be used to purchase preferred stock in American banks under the Capital Purchase Program (CPP). The Treasury decided that it would be better to directly inject capital into the banks rather than purchasing the toxic assets. By the end of October 2008, nine of the largest American banks applied for and received $125 billion. The thought was that by shoring up the capital of banks, banks would begin lending again and the financial system would recover. In November 2008, the Treasury authorized the use of $40 billion of TARP funds to purchase preferred stock in the insolvent American International Group (AIG) which had been taken over by the government. Also in November 2008, three large insurance companies announced plans to purchase depository institutions to give them access to TARP funds. Finally, in November, the Treasury secretary officially announced that the TARP funds would not be used at this time to purchase "toxic" assets but rather that the funds would be used in other ways such as the CPP to support the financial system. In December 2008, the Treasury authorized the use of TARP funds to bailout General Motors and Chrysler. Through December 2008, TARP money continued to be used to buy preferred stock in large and small banks. By early January 2009, about $305 billion in the bailout funds had been spent with approximately $200 billion used to buy preferred stock in banks, $40 billion used to bailout AIG, an additional $45 billion invested in Citigroup and Bank of America (who had both participated in the CPP program), and $20 billion invested with the automakers and their financing subsidiaries. Some analysts criticized that the bailout funds were not used for their original purpose and merely supported large institutions that had created the problems. They also argued that the banks were not increasing their lending as the Treasury had expected, given the injection of capital.

EESA also temporarily increased the deposit insurance limit to $250,000 on all depository institutions' accounts to prevent disintermediation.

In addition to the EESA, the Obama administration was proposing an additional $800 billion-plus stimulus plan for the weakened economy in early 2009.

However, the funds were used in a variety of ways to shore up the financial system including to inject capital into banks through the Capital Purchase Program (CPP).

Recap   The Community Reinvestment Act of 1977 was designed to eliminate discriminatory lending practices. The IBBEA of 1994 allowed unimpeded nationwide branching as of June 1, 1997. The GLBA of 1999 allowed for the certification of financial holding companies that could engage in banking, securities, and insurance activities. The GLBA effectively repealed the provisions of the Glass-Steagall Act, which separated commercial and investment banking. The EESA authorized $700 billion to bail out the financial system in response to the financial crisis of 2008 that was threatening the collapse of the entire financial system.

The Ongoing Bailout of the Banking System: Nationalization or Not?

As we have seen, the Emergency Economic Stability Act (EESA) authorized $700 billion in funds to bailout the financial system. The EESA created the Capital Purchase Program (CPP) whereby up to $250 billion was to be used to purchase preferred stock in American banks. By the end of October 2008, nine of the largest American banks applied for and received $125 billion and about 90 other banks applied for and had received an additional $75 billion. The thought was that by shoring up the capital of banks, banks would begin lending again and the financial system would recover.

By January 2009, about $305 billion in the bailout funds had been spent including the $200 billion used to buy preferred stock in the banks mentioned above, the $40 billion used to bailout the insurance giant AIG, an additional $45 billion invested in Citigroup and Bank of America (who had both participated in the CPP program and needed additional funding), and the $20 billion invested to bailout the auto makers and their financing subsidiaries.

Now regulators were debating about how to use the remainder of the $700 billion of funds that were authorized under the EESA. Below are some of suggestions:

- Should the government continue to inject capital into the banking system on an as needed basis? So far, such injections have been criticized because banks have not increased their lending and the fragile financial system remains in a semi-frozen state.

- Should the government nationalize the banks? Nationalization means different things to different people. Some analysts would say that some banks have already been nationalized, given the large equity stakes the government has due to the previous capital injections. In addition, in late February 2009, the government became the largest shareholder in Citigroup by increasing their common stock holdings to 36 percent. (Citigroup had been the nation's first and largest financial holding company before running into hard times.) Many analysts consider this amount of control by one stakeholder to be virtual nationalization. In addition, the government has already "virtually" nationalized AIG by their huge equity position and many consider that Fannie Mae and Freddie Mac have been nationalized because of their conservatorship by the government. On the other hand, it may not be as important as it seems. The government, through the Fed, or other regulator, has supervisory and regulatory power over the banks and thus can wield a great deal of control over their behavior, even without actual ownership.

- Should the government create a super "Bad" bank that would be owned by the government and that would purchase toxic assets currently choking the global financial system? This idea is similar to what was done in 1989 when the Resolution Trust Corporation (RTC) was created to deal with the bad mortgages and to dispose of the repossessed properties from the savings and loan crisis. So far, policy makers have not done this. However, if other attempts fail, it may opt for a similar plan.

Such are the ideas that have been floating around with regards to how to mitigate the ongoing banking crisis.

To give us some idea of how the remaining EESA funds will be used, the Treasury Department announced a new Financial Stability Plan in late February 2009. Note that this plan will undoubtedly be revised (or dumped) going forward in response to unfolding events. As of March 2009, the core of the Financial Stability Plan is the Capital Assistance Program (CAP) which is designed to make sure that banks have sufficient capital to meet current demands and additional demands in the event that the economy further deteriorates. The thought is that with the greater capital level, lending would actually increase as confidence would be restored. Banks would have sufficient capital to meet even deteriorating conditions in the economy that could lead to greater than expected further losses and additional bank failures without the plan.

Under the plan, qualifying financial institutions including all domestically owned banks, bank holding companies, financial holding companies, and savings and loans with assets greater than $100 billion would be required to undergo a one-time evaluation by federal regulators to determine if they have sufficient capital. Currently, there are nineteen such large institutions. Smaller banks and other depository institutions that are not required to participate in the CAP would be able to participate if they chose to. The institutions would be evaluated by their primary regulator, which may be the Fed, the FDIC, the Office of the Comptroller of the Currency, or the Office of Thrift Supervision, depending on the institution's charter. Each institution's capital must be found to be adequate to meet the challenging economic environment that is expected over the course of the next few years. The amount of capital each bank must have will be based on a "consensus" and a "worse than expected" scenario or forecast.

Thus, the plan is proactive rather than reactive. Rather than capital being injected as needed, the plan would try to see that banks have sufficient capital to meet current needs but also to withstand greater than expected losses if the current dire situation deteriorates even further. If an institution is found to need more capital, it will first be able to solicit private sources during the time its application for CAP funds is being reviewed. If it cannot raise the additional capital privately, it would get the needed capital from the CAP in exchange for newly-issued preferred stock in an amount between 1 and 2 percent of the institution's total risk-weighted assets. The terms of the preferred stock are:

- it will pay a 9 percent dividend annually and
- it will be convertible into common stock at a price that is 10 percent less than the common stock price on February 9, 2009.

If an institution needed "exceptional assistance," it could apply to issue preferred stock bought by the government in excess of the 1 to 2 percent limit. The conversion of the preferred stock to common stock would occur seven years after the security was issued if it had not been redeemed or converted to common stock at an earlier date. To be converted to common stock at an earlier date, the issuer must get the approval of the regulators.

Banks that had already participated in the CPP to shore up their capital would be able to also participate in the CAP. Banks could also trade their issuances of preferred stock under the CPP program for the preferred stock under the CAP program. This would give them greater flexibility with regards to converting the preferred stock to common stock. The conversion of securities from the CPP program to the CAP program would not be counted as part of the 1 to 2 percent of risk-weighted assets of the CAP program alone. Remember dividends to preferred stockholders are paid before common stockholders receive any dividends.

The deadline for an institution to apply to participate in the CAP is May 25, 2009 and the issuance of the new securities must be completed within six months of the application date.

Additional programs under the Financial Stability Plan include a Consumer Business Lending Initiative to aid secondary credit markets, a Public Private Investment Fund to raise private capital to buy legacy assets, and a Homeowner Affordability and Stability Plan to restrict or refinance mortgages to help families stay in their homes. We look at the proposal to help the mortgage problem in "A Closer Look: The Mortgage Bailout Plan" in Chapter 13 on page 303.

Is the CAP a form of nationalization of the banks or not? The debate continues and it will be interesting to see how the government extricates itself from these equity positions.

However, in a Treasury White Paper released in late February 2009, the Treasury states that "The economy functions better when banking organizations are well managed in the private sector. U.S. government ownership is not an objective CAP. However, to the extent that significant government stake in a financial institution is an outcome of the program, our goal will be to keep the period of government ownership as temporary as possible and encourage the return of private capital to replace government investment. In addition, any capital investments made by Treasury under this plan will be placed in a separate trust set up to manage the government's investment in US financial institutions. The objective will be to create value for the taxpayer as a shareholder over time."[a]

Updated details of all programs to restore confidence in the financial system can be found online at www.FinancialStability.gov. The "A Closer Look: The Fed's New Tool Kit" in chapter 25 on page 624 discusses the enormous special lending facilities created by the Federal Reserve in addition to the EESA to mitigate the ongoing crisis.

Endnotes

a. "Treasury White Paper: The Capital Assistance Program and It Role in the Financial Stability Plan," available online at the www.financialstability.gov.

OTHER POSSIBLE AREAS OF REFORMS

By the turn of the century, many regulatory changes had already occurred, including the following: (1) scaling insurance premiums to the risk exposure of banks, (2) limiting foreign deposit coverage, (3) intervening early when a bank begins experiencing problems so that measures will be taken before bank capital is fully depleted, (4) ending the practice of "too big to fail," (5) increasing capital requirements, (6) expanding interstate banking, (7) allowing banks, securities firms, and insurance companies to affiliate under common ownership, (8) authorizing FHCs to engage in many previously prohibited financial and nonfinancial services, and (9) merging the deposit insurance funds of banks and savings and loans into one Deposit Insurance Fund. Despite these regulatory changes, many analysts perceive that the banking crisis of 2008 intensified the need for further reform of the regulatory structure.

Look again at "A Closer Look" on page 257. Current regulatory responsibility for the banking system (including banks and S&Ls) is distributed among four supervisory agencies: the FDIC, the Office of the Comptroller of the Currency, the OTS, and the Fed. Look at how many other regulators there are in the financial services industry. Many analysts think that the present system causes duplication of regulatory functions and bureaucratic delays. They believe that multiple, decentralized supervisory agencies result in costly systems that potentially decrease the effectiveness and efficiency of bank supervision. In response to these concerns, the Treasury, the Fed, the FDIC, and state banking departments are working together to make bank regulations more consistent and to make bank examinations more efficient and less burdensome. At the present time, the impetus for additional major reforms in financial sector regulation has increased due to the ongoing crisis in the financial system in 2008. Congress is expected to make substantial regulatory changes in response to this crisis.

Although many regulatory changes have been made in recent decades, more will undoubtedly be needed and implemented in the future as financial markets continue to evolve and adapt to new technologies. Furthermore, some recent regulatory changes have reversed and nullified past restrictions. For example, the Grahmm-Leach-Bliley Act of 1999 effectively nullified a primary component of the 1933 Glass-Steagall Act, one of the most significant pieces of legislation to come out of the Great Depression. In 2008, the ongoing financial crisis is also facilitating the disappearance of the large investment banking firm. Note that Lehman Brothers has declared bankruptcy; Merrill Lynch has been bought by Bank of America; Bear Stearns has been bought by J.P. Morgan Chase, and Goldman Sachs and Morgan Stanley have converted their charters to bank holding companies. Although the goal, financial stability, may remain the same, regulations perceived as advancing this goal may change over time. Finally, profit-seeking financial firms will seek to exploit any regulatory anomaly. They may obey the letter of the law, but chances are they will circumvent the regulatory intent. Thus, firms may influence the nature of future regulatory changes deemed to be both prudent and effective. Creation of effective regulations requires anticipation of the likely responses of those being regulated.

This concludes our discussion of financial institutions. We next turn our attention toward financial markets.

Summary of Major Points

1. Because the failure of a depository institution has system-wide repercussions, Congress has enacted legislation to regulate the financial services industry with the goal of averting such a failure. A segmented financial services industry resulted in a segmented regulatory structure.

2. Regulation is by institution group or financial market (product). All depository institutions are regulated by the Fed with regard to reserve requirements. The FDIC also regulates banks and thrifts that opt for federal deposit insurance. Many other regulatory agencies regulate specific institutions. In addition, agencies such as the SEC regulate stocks and bonds. Other agencies regulate other financial products such as futures and options. Some product groups establish self-regulatory bodies. At the present time, no agency is in charge of regulating the money market. The regulatory structure is in an ongoing evolutionary process.

3. Beginning in 1980, the banking system was deregulated. The Depository Institutions Deregulation and Monetary Control Act (DIDMCA) of 1980 phased out Regulation Q interest rate ceilings and expanded the asset and liability options for banks and thrifts. All depository institutions were allowed to offer interest-bearing checkable deposits, and S&Ls and savings banks were allowed to make business loans. DIDMCA also expanded the powers of the Fed by authorizing uniform and universal reserve requirements.

4. The Garn–St. Germain Depository Institutions Act of 1982 allowed all depository institutions to offer money market deposit accounts with no interest rate ceilings, permitted limited check writing, and guaranteed insurance for accounts of up to $100,000. The act also authorized Super NOW accounts, which are checking accounts that pay a market interest rate.

5. The Basel Accord, an agreement among 12 countries, sets uniform international capital requirements for financial institutions as a primary vehicle of regulation. Requirements for core capital and total capital are based on risk-adjusted assets and total assets. Core capital is the historical value of outstanding stock plus retained earnings. Risk-adjusted assets are calculated by assigning different weights to different types of assets, depending on risk. Basel II is revising the original capital requirements to more effectively regulate complex banking institutions.

6. The Financial Institutions Reform, Recovery, and Enforcement Act (FIRREA) of 1989 attempted to resolve the S&L deposit insurance crisis. It created the Office of Thrift Supervision and assimilated the defunct FSLIC into the FDIC. New regulations restricted the investments that S&Ls could make, and capital standards similar to those imposed on banks by the Basel Accord were adopted. Deposit insurance was made a full faith and credit obligation of the U.S. government, and bonds, which would eventually be paid off by taxpayers, were sold to obtain the funds necessary to bail out the defunct S&Ls.

7. The Federal Deposit Insurance Corporation Improvement Act (FDICIA) of 1991 required higher deposit insurance premiums for banks and thrifts that undertake high levels of risk. The "too-big-to-fail" practice that had been in effect since 1984 was ended. Under the "too-big-to-fail" practice, the failure of large banks was resolved using the purchase and assumption method rather than the payoff method.

8. The Federal Deposit Insurance Reform Act of 2005 merged the two separate preexisting deposit insurance funds, one for banks and the other for S&Ls, into one Deposit Insurance Fund (DIF). It also indexed coverage limits to inflation, set a range for the size of the fund reserves, allowed the FDIC to choose the exact level of reserves and discretion to determine the speed of adjustment to desired reserve levels, and gave the FDIC more discretion in setting insurance premiums.

9. The Community Reinvestment Act of 1977 gained prominence in the late 1980s as the Fed used compliance with this act as a criterion for approving or disapproving bank mergers. The regulations were further revised in 1995, and now all banking regulatory agencies examine all depository institutions for CRA compliance. CRA requires banks to lend in economically disadvantaged areas and to end the practice of redlining.

10. The Interstate Banking and Branching Efficiency Act (IBBEA) of 1994 allowed interstate branching by mergers of well-capitalized and well-managed institutions as of June 1, 1997. Under this law, bank holding companies can also convert separate banks into branches.

11. With the passage of the Gramm-Leach-Bliley Act (GLBA) in 1999, the final vestiges of the Glass-Steagall Act separating investment and commercial banking were removed. The stage is set for full financial integration of the banking, securities, and insurance industries. The GLBA allows for bank holding companies to be certified as financial holding companies (FHCs) that can engage in financially related activities, including securities underwriting and dealing as well as insurance and merchant banking activities. The GLBA also allows FHCs to engage in other financial activities and complementary nonfinancial activities. Banks had previously found ways into the securities industry through bank holding company subsidiaries. They have been able to do this because the Fed has relaxed or weakened many of the provisions of Glass-Steagall.

12. The Deposit Insurance Reform Act of 2005 merged the Bank Insurance Fund (BIF) and the Savings Association Insurance Fund (SAIF) into the Deposit Insurance Fund (DIF). It also increased deposit insurance limits and indexed them to inflation.

13. The Emergency Economic Stabilizaton Act of 2008 (EESA) authorized the U.S. Treasury to purchase $700 billion in toxic mortgages and other assets that were causing the financial crisis and the drying up of credit extension. The $700 billion bailout was eventually used to shore up the capital of large financial institutions and for a variety of other uses.

14. Despite the enactment of higher capital standards and risk-based insurance premiums, many believe that the reforms do not go far enough in dealing with the moral hazard problem.

Key Terms

Review Questions

1. How is the failure of an FI different from the failure of a video rental store? What do these differences imply about the need for regulation?

2. Discuss the major provisions of the FIRREA and the Reform Act of 2005.

3. What is redlining? How is the Community Reinvestment Act supposed to affect it? What are the classifications for depository institutions and the ratings under the current regulations? Could my bank be violating the law if it fails to lend to businesses located in the deteriorating downtown area?

4. What is the Basel Accord? Why is it desirable to have uniform international capital standards for banks? What is the difference between Basel I and II?

5. What is the intent of the 25 core principles for effective bank supervision?

6. Some contend that the passage of the IBBEA is having little effect on the banking industry. What is the basis of their argument? On what date were banks allowed to branch across state lines by merging with a bank in a different state?

7. What are the provisions of the Deposit Insurance Reform Act of 2005?

8. Would a wealthy individual with bank accounts of more than $100,000 prefer the FDIC to use the purchase and assumption method or the payoff method to liquidate failed banks? Why?

9. What is core capital? How do risk-adjusted assets differ from total assets?

10. Who regulates money markets? Capital markets?

11. What are the major provisions of the Depository Institutions Deregulation and Monetary Control Act of 1980? The Garn–St. Germain Depository Institutions Act of 1982? Which act expanded the powers of the Fed? How?

12. Explain the difference between risk-based capital standards and risk-based deposit insurance premiums.

13. What are the regulatory responsibilities of the Securities and Exchange Commission? What is insider trading? Who sets margin requirements?

14. Identify three self-regulating agencies and explain which industries they regulate. Speculate as to why an industry would self-regulate.

15. Explain the function of each:

    (a) National Credit Union Share Insurance Fund; (b) Pension Benefit Guaranty Corporation; (c) Securities Investor Protection Corporation; (d) FDIC

16. Explain the difference between the purchase and assumption method and the payoff method of resolving a bank insolvency. What does "too big to fail" mean?

17. What are the major provisions of the GLBA? What is an FHC? How does a bank holding company become an FHC? What conditions must be met to become an FHC?

18. Was investment banking effectively separated from commercial banking prior to the passage of GLBA? Explain.

19. What were the provisions of and purpose for the Emergency Economic Stabilization Act?

Analytical Questions

Questions marked with a check mark are objective in nature. They can be completed with a short answer or number.

✓20. Assume that a bank has core capital of $1,000,000 and total capital of $2,000,000. Its total risk-adjusted assets are $25,000,000 and total assets are $30,000,000. According to the Basel Accord (Basel I), does the bank have adequate capital?

✓21. Assume that a bank has the following:

Stock issued	$15,000,000
Retained earnings	2,750,000
Loan-loss reserves	2,600,000
Subordinated debt	5,000,000

What is its core capital? What is its total capital?

Suggested Readings

For an interesting review of usury laws in history and the changing definition of usury, read Joseph Persky's article "From Usury to Interest," *The Journal of Economic Perspectives* 21, no. 1 (Winter 2007), pp. 227–36.

The Federal Deposit Insurance Corporation (FDIC), which regulates banks and savings associations that purchase deposit insurance from it, is an exception to regulatory segmentation. Visit its site at **http://www.fdic.gov/**.

To see how competition affects the behavior of bank regulators, take a look at "Competition Among Bank Regulators," found on the Web at **http://www.richmondfed.org/publications/economic_research/economic_quarterly/pdfs/fa112002/weinberg.pdf**. In this article, John A. Weinberg analyzes how federal and state regulators compete against one another in a "race to the bottom."

For information about the Office of Thrift Supervision, visit **http://www.ots.treas.gov/**.

Chairman Ben Bernanke's speech before New York University Law School examines the costs and benefits of regulation. Using Adam Smith's "Invisible Hand" theory, Bernanke delves into a short history of the banking system, regulations, and hedge funds. His speech, titled "Financial Regulation and the Invisible Hand," can be found online at **http://www.federalreserve.gov/boarddocs/speeches/2007/20070411/default.htm**.

To see further analysis of the FDICIA's effect on bank debt, see *Does the Market Discipline Banks? New Evidence from the Regulatory Capital Mix*, by Adam B. Ashcraft. This report can be found online at **http://www.newyorkfed.org/research/staff_reports/sr244.pdf**.

For a look at the debate concerning whether banks should be regulated, see Arthur J. Rolnick's report entitled "Deposit Insurance Reform: Market Discipline as a Regulator of Bank Risk," available online at **http://www.minneapolisfed.org/Research/studies/tbtf/market.cfm?js=0**.

John C. Dugan, Comptroller of the Currency, speaks before the Committee on Financial Services of the U.S. House of Representatives about the OCC's role in securing consumer protection. Here the Comptroller discusses the different functions of the OCC and the control it has over retail banking. To see the speech from June 2007, visit **http://www.occ.treas.gov/ftp/release/2007–57b.pdf**.

Executive Vice President William L. Rutledge discusses how Basel II should improve financial stability in his speech before the International Conference on Financial Stability and Implications of Basel II in May 2005. "Basel II: Risk Management and Financial Stability" is available online at **http://www.newyorkfed.org/newsevents/speeches/2005/rut050517.html**.

The Economist gives insight into the passing of Basel II and its international impact on bank capital in this article called "All Together Now," from the July 26, 2007edition. This article can be found online at **http://economist.com/research/articlesBySubject/displaystory.cfm?subjectid=348936&story_id=9554827**.

For an analysis of the effects of deregulation on small businesses, see Yuliya Demyanyk, Charlotte Ostergaard and Bent Sorensen's article "Banking Deregulation Helps Small Business Owners Stabilize Their Income" (April 2007), available at the St. Louis Federal Reserve Web site at **http://stlouisfed.org/publications/re/2007/b/pages/deregulation.html**.

For a discussion of recommendations for financial services regulation, see the testimony of Governor Mark W. Olson on the Financial Services Regulatory Relief Act of 2003, before the Subcommittee on Financial Institutions and Consumer Credit of the Committee on Financial Services, U.S. House of Representatives, March 27, 2003. The text of Olson's testimony is available online at **http://www.federalreserve.gov/boarddocs/testimony/2003/20030327/default.htm**.

For a discussion of Basel II, see L. Jacobo Rodriguez, "International Banking Regulation—Where's the Market Discipline in Basel II?" Cato Policy Analysis No. 455 (October 15, 2002), available online at **http://www.cato.org/pubs/pas/pa-455es.html.**

For an excellent book on the material in this chapter, see Ken Spong, *Banking Regulation: Its Purposes, Implementation, and Effects*, 5th ed. (Kansas City: Federal Reserve Bank of Kansas City, 2000). Hard copies are also free for the asking from the Federal Reserve Bank of Kansas City.

For a look at "The Future of Financial Intermediation and Regulation," see the article by Stephen Cecchetti in *Current Issues in Economics and Finance*, Federal Reserve Bank of New York, 5, no. 8 (May 1999).

Ann B. Matasar and Joseph N. Heiney analyze the effects of IBBEA in "Lemonade or Lemon? Riegel-Neal and the Consolidation of American Banking," *International Advances in Economic Research* 6, no. 2 (May 2000): 249–58.

For an analysis of the success of the Community Reinvestment Act, see Robert B. Avery, Raphael W. Bostic, and Glenn B. Canner, "CRA Special Lending Programs," *Federal Reserve Bulletin* (November 2000): 711–31; also see "Does the Community Reinvestment Act Influence Lending? An Analysis of Changes in Bank Low-Income Mortgage Activity," Working Paper No. WP-00–6, Federal Reserve Bank of Chicago (May 2000).

Information on the Community Reinvestment Act (CRA) is presented in "Bank Merger Policy and the New CRA Data," by Anthony W. Cyrnak, *Federal Reserve Bulletin* (September 1998): 703–14. A related article, "New Information on Lending to Small Businesses and Small Farms: The 1996 CRA Data," also appeared in the *Federal Reserve Bulletin* (January 1998): 1–21.

Endnotes

1. For the airline industry, the regulatory agency is the Federal Aviation Administration (FAA).
2. In a world with deposit insurance, the problem is even greater because the depositors will be paid off even if the venture fails.
3. Correlation does not imply causality, which means that deregulation did not necessarily cause the subsequent insolvencies.
4. Actually, as you have seen, in a world with deposit insurance, the intermediary may consider only the costs to the stockholders and creditors because large portions of the deposits are insured. In reality, bank managers may consider only the risk of losing their own jobs if investments go sour.
5. Perhaps the only exception to this is the creation of the SAIF under the auspices of the Federal Deposit Insurance Corporation (FDIC) in 1989. However, in 2006, SAIF and BIF were combined to form the DIF.
6. In addition to the analytical factors, as noted earlier, the general "political wind" had shifted in the late 1970s toward less regulation.
7. In Chapter 8, we discussed moral hazard from a micro standpoint. In that case, borrowers had an incentive to use borrowed funds for a more risky venture once loan funds had been received.
8. This limit is rather easy for many families to circumvent. For example, a family of four can open 14 different accounts, each with $100,000 deposit insurance coverage, thus effectively giving them $1.4 million in deposit insurance at every institution. In case you are wondering how four people can have 14 accounts, it is by grouping them together in different ways. Thus, each can have an individual account; then there can be six accounts with two people on each account (such as father and mother, and mother and oldest child), three accounts with three people each, and one account with all four. Note also since 2006, retirement accounts have been insured up to $250,000, and because of the ongoing financial crisis, the limit on all accounts has been increased to $250,000 through 2009.
9. We shall see that the Interstate Branching and Banking Efficiency Act of 1994 and the Gramm-Leach-Bliley Act of 1999 also emphasized compliance with the Community Reinvestment Act.
10. In Chapter 9, we saw that the McFadden Act outlawed interstate branching and made national banks conform to the intrastate branching laws of the states in which they were located.

PART 4

Financial Markets

13

Gentlemen Prefer Bonds.

—Andrew Mellon

The Debt Markets

Learning Objectives

After reading this chapter, you should know:

The characteristics of the bond and mortgage markets and how the markets function

How corporate bond, government bond, and mortgage markets have changed in recent years

The characteristics and advantages of municipal bonds

What government agency securities, mortgage-backed securities, and government-sponsored enterprises are

BONDS AND MORTGAGES: THE MAJOR DEBT MARKETS

Bonds (corporate and government) and mortgages are the major long-term financial instruments of the debt market. In Chapters 5 and 6, you saw that small changes in interest rates can cause large changes in the prices of these instruments. The longer the term to maturity, the greater the change in price for any change in the interest rate. In an era of volatile interest rates, price changes can be dramatic and bond and mortgage markets anything but dull. In recent years, there have been other noteworthy trends in both the bond and mortgage markets.

In this chapter, we first explore the government and corporate bond markets. What are the characteristics that all bonds have in common? How do the federal government, government agencies, and government-sponsored enterprises affect the bond market? What are the advantages and disadvantages of bonds to firms and to investors? What is the international bond market?

In the second half of the chapter, we look at the mortgage market, which is the largest debt market in the United States.[1] Residential mortgages, which will be our focus, make up the largest segment of the market. How has the mortgage market changed in recent years? What are the roles of the government and government-sponsored enterprises in the mortgage market? What are the risks of investing in mortgages? What are the economic consequences of the recent financial market instability related to the "subprime mortgage market meltdown."

THE BOND MARKET

Coupon Rate
The fixed interest rate stated on the face of a bond.

Par Value
The principal or face value of the bond, which is repaid in full at maturity.

Coupon Payments
The coupon rate on a bond multiplied by the face value of the bond; coupon payments are usually made every six months.

Standard & Poor's Investors Service
A credit-rating agency that analyzes and evaluates bonds and assigns them to a particular risk class based on the probability that the issuer will fail to pay back the principal and interest in full when due.

Moody's Investors Service
A credit-rating agency that analyzes and evaluates bonds and assigns them to a particular risk class based on the probability that the issuer will fail to pay back the principal and interest in full when due.

Bonds issued by net borrowers are bought by and sold to net lenders in the bond market. The issuer may be the U.S. government, an agency of the government, a state or local government, a domestic or foreign corporation, or a foreign government. Bonds are debt instruments with an original maturity of more than 10 years that are issued by private and public entities. They normally pay a fixed interest rate, the **coupon rate**, which is stated on the face of the bond. The principal, also called the **par value** or face value of the bond, is repaid in full at maturity. The **coupon payments** are equal to the coupon rate multiplied by the face value of the bond and are usually made every six months.

As first discussed in Chapter 6, two major credit-rating agencies, **Standard & Poor's** and **Moody's Investors Service**, analyze and evaluate bonds and assign them to one of nine risk classes based on the probability that the issuer will fail to pay back the principal and interest in full when due. The credit-rating agencies examine the pattern of revenues and costs experienced by a firm, its degree of leverage (dependence on borrowed funds), its past history of debt redemption, and the volatility of the industry, among other things. A firm with a history of strong earnings, low leverage, and prompt debt redemption would get the highest rating from Moody's and Standard & Poor's. A firm that has experienced net losses, has rising leverage, or has missed some loan payments would be rated much lower and so be required to pay a higher interest rate to investors.

Moody's and Standard & Poor's also assign ratings to municipal securities issued by state and local governments. Important factors in determining the rating include whether the bond issue is insured, the tax base, the level of outstanding debt, the current and expected budget situation, and the growth in spending. Bond ratings are beneficial to lenders because they help the lender determine the risk involved in purchasing a specific bond. Bonds rated below investment grade are not recommended for investment and are often referred to as *high-yield* or *junk bonds*, depending on one's perspective. Of course, their high yield results from their riskiness. "A Closer Look" on page 285 discusses some of the recent trends in the bond market.

A Closer Look

Recent Trends in the Bond Market

Bond markets in recent years can only be characterized as tumultuous at best, as the economy experienced unprecedented upheaval that began in the mortgage-backed securities markets. Overall, in late 2007 and 2008, bond prices rose as interest rates fell on worries of a sluggish economy that might depress interest rates and stock prices. The weakness in the economy accelerated in late 2008. The Fed made a series of historic interest rate cuts beginning in July 2007. The fed funds target rate was reduced from 5.25 percent in August 2007 to the range of 0 to .25 percent in December 2008. In January 2009, the Fed signaled that it did not intend to increase rates anytime soon.

As we saw in Chapter 5, interest rates and bond prices are inversely related. Therefore, it should be no surprise to money and banking students that bond markets and bond prices have been tremendously affected by the large interest rate declines in recent months. During late 2007 and 2008, bond prices rose and holders of previously issued bonds made large capital gains as interest rates fell. This was the opposite of what occurred from 2004 to 2006, when bond prices drifted lower as interest rates rose from their unusually low level in 2003 to the peak in mid-2007.

As of early 2009, several important factors were influencing bond markets. First was the ongoing difficulty in the residential mortgage markets. Increased risks on real estate-backed investments were causing a "flight to quality," increasing investor's demand for safe government bonds, not only in domestic markets, but also among global financial market participants. This pushed the prices of government securities up (and yields down) relative to other mortgage-related bonds and corporate bonds in general. Long-term Treasury yields fell into the 2 to 3 percent range. This drop in yields on Treasuries was much greater than the drop in yields for other securities. Thus, the risk premium for holding corporate bonds increased significantly and the spread between Treasury securities and corporate bonds widened as the crisis went forward in late 2008.

Second, the severely weakened economy saw real GDP contract 3.8 percent and the unemployment rate rise to over 7.2 percent in the last quarter of 2008. This would tend to push overall interest rates down on all securities as there was a reduced demand for borrowing in a faltering economy. However, counteracting these factors was the projected change in the size of the U.S. government's budget deficit. As the economy and tax revenues continued to decline into 2009, the government worked on a second stimulus package that was expected to amount to over $800 billion. The first stimulus package passed in September 2008 had been for $700 billion. It was expected that the decline in tax revenues and the increased bailout packages would cause the government deficit to explode. Without the second stimulus package, the deficit was expected to exceed $1.2 trillion for fiscal year 2009. Some analysts were predicting the deficit could go as high as $1.6 trillion. By itself, this represents a tremendous increase in the rate of issuance of new government securities, decreasing their price and increasing their returns. However, when all is considered, with the dire shape of the economy in early 2009, it was unlikely that rates would increase much over the next year.

Because of these factors and uncertainties, the issuance of new securities in U.S. capital markets declined dramatically over the first three quarters of 2008, falling about 25 percent from the first three quarters of 2007 to $4.2 trillion. As to be expected, the sharpest declines were in those sectors most adversely affected by the slowdown while at the same time, the issuance of Treasuries increased. Thus, private asset-backed securities, global credit default obligations, and corporate long-term issuances each fell about 88, 80, and 30 percent respectively. New corporate bond issues plummeted in the third quarter due in response to lower corporate profits, increased uncertainty, and widening spread with Treasuries. Defaults on corporate bonds increased and initial public offerings fell over 75 percent from the third quarter of 2007. Also, the issuance of Treasuries increased about 23 percent to $668.4 billion with the sharpest increase coming the third quarter of 2008. Not as likely to be expected, the issuance of federal agency mortgage-backed securities also soared to $1 trillion in the first three quarters of 2008. These are securities primarily issued by the government-sponsored enterprises, Fannie Mae and Freddie Mac that were taken into conservatorship by the government in September 2008. The soaring agency securities were issued by Fannie Mae and Freddie Mac to make up for the steep decline in private mortgage-backed and asset-backed securities, despite the conservatorship. The newly issued agency securities now have an explicit government guarantee. The market for private mortgage-backed and asset-backed securities actually went from bad to worse as the financial crisis of 2008 unfolded. The markets froze up and buying and selling stopped in late 2008. Finally, under the Emergency Economic Stabilization Act of 2008, the Treasury was authorized to purchase $700 billion of these mortgage-backed securities and other securities which now had become "toxic." However, as of early 2009, no "toxic" securities had been purchased and there were no plans to use the bailout funds to do so. Rather, after Congress passed the bill, the use of the bailout funds was changed. Instead of purchasing "toxic" securities, the funds were to be used to inject capital into banks and for other purposes. The issuance of long-term municipals remained virtually the same. Despite the weak economy, the low interest rate environment encouraged new issues of municipals, which were higher than what they would have been without the favorable rates. Employment in the securities industry also declined over 3 percent in the last half of 2008. To date, this is far less than the over 20 percent decline in employment in the late 2000 to 2003 period in response to the bursting of the stock market bubble.

Sources

Securities Industry and Financial Markets Association (SIFMA), *Research Quarterly*, November 2008 available online at http://www.sifma.org/research/pdf/RRVol3-10.pdf

Securities Industry and Financial Markets Association (SIFMA), *Research Report*, January 21, 2009 available online at www.sifma.org/research/pdf/RRVol 4-1.pdf

THE CORPORATE BOND MARKET

Bond Indenture
A document stating the terms under which a bond is issued.

Trustee
An expert (usually working for a bank or trust company) who interprets the provisions of a bond offering for investors and who sees that the terms and conditions of the offering are fulfilled.

As the name implies, corporations issue corporate bonds. Investment bankers design, market, and underwrite new corporate bond issues. The terms of the offering, along with many other provisions, are spelled out in the bond indenture when the bonds are issued. The indenture is made out to a trustee representing the investors who buy the bonds. The trustee usually works for a bond or trust company and is an expert in interpreting the provisions of the offering for the investor. The trustee also sees that the issuer fulfills the terms and conditions of the indenture.

Debenture Bonds
Bonds with no specific collateral backing but that have a general claim on the other unpledged assets of the issuer.

Subordinated Debenture Bonds
Bonds with no collateral backing that have a general claim after debenture bondholders have been paid.

Bonds may be backed by specific collateral such as real or personal property. The collateral can include plant, equipment, and financial assets that the issuing corporation owns. If the borrower cannot repay the lender, this collateral may be sold to raise money necessary to repay the debt. Debenture bonds are not backed by specific collateral but, in the event of a default, have a general claim on the issuer's otherwise unpledged assets. Finally, subordinated debenture bonds are not backed by collateral and have a general claim after debenture bondholders have been paid. Thus, in the event of a default, owners of subordinated debenture bonds are the last bondholders in line to receive any funds. As expected, other factors being equal, subordinated debenture bonds pay the highest return reflecting their greater default risk, followed by debenture bonds, and followed by bonds backed by collateral with the least default risk.

Some bonds also come with financial guarantees issued by insurance companies. The bond issuer pays a premium that guarantees the payment of interest and principal by the insurance company in the event the issuer defaults. In reality, the credit of the guarantor is substituted for the guarantee of the issuer. The bonds are issued at a lower interest rate than otherwise because of the guarantee. It is beneficial to the bond issuer to pay for the financial guarantee if the present value of the interest savings over the life of the bond is higher than the insurance premium. Interestingly, corporate bonds are less likely than municipal bonds to purchase such insurance. Although municipal bonds issued by government agencies typically have a lower default risk and would seemingly benefit less from such insurance than corporate bonds, the fact that interest income is normally exempt from state taxes for residents of the state selling the bonds implies that wealthy bond purchasers in small states may not be able to appropriately diversify their holdings. Bond insurers may diversify such risk across states while individual purchasers of bonds cannot. Purchasers of corporate bonds are better able to diversify and, therefore, less likely to benefit from bond insurance.

Call Provisions
Provisions spelled out in a bond indenture that allow the issuer to buy back the bonds at a specified price; bonds would tend to be called if interest rates had fallen since the bonds were initially issued.

Convertible Provisions
Provisions spelled out in a bond indenture that allow investors to convert the bonds to a specific number of shares of common stock.

Most corporate bonds are issued with call provisions. Call provisions allow the issuer to buy back the bonds before maturity at a specified price. Bonds tend to be called if interest rates have fallen since the bonds were initially issued. The issuer could issue new bonds at the lower rates to buy back the previously issued bonds. Other corporate bonds offer convertible provisions that allow investors to convert the bonds to a specific number of shares of common stock. Bonds that are callable offer higher coupon rates than comparable noncallable bonds, and bonds with convertible provisions offer lower comparable rates.

Zero-Coupon Bonds
Corporate bonds sold at a discount, with the difference between the amount paid for the bond and the amount received at maturity equal to the interest.

Some firms also issue zero-coupon bonds, which, as their name implies, do not have coupons and do not make coupon payments. Instead, the bonds are sold at a discount with the difference between the amount paid for the bond and the amount received at maturity being equal to the interest.[2] The advantage to the investor is that there is no risk that the interest earned over the life of the bond will have to be reinvested at a lower rate. A disadvantage to the investor is that the interest payments accrue over the life of

Cracking the Code

Corporate Bonds

The following table is a typical example of the way bond market information appears on *The Wall Street Journal Online*. The *WSJ* online edition provides reports of the most actively traded bonds on the New York Exchange. To view the most active investment-graded bonds, the most active high-yield bonds, and the most active convertible bonds for free, go to **www.wsj.com** and click on Markets Data Center, then select Bonds, Rates & Credit Markets. To understand the information provided, let us take a look at General Electric Capital Corp., one of the most active investment grade bonds as of November 2007. We will focus on the first bond in **bold** type.

New York Exchange

First, in column 1, you see the issuing company's name—General Electric Capital Corp (GE). Next to the name is the symbol GE.HDM and the coupon rate, or yield, 5.625 percent. It appears on the face of the bond and indicates the amount of interest that GE will pay the holder annually; in this case, the 5.625 percent indicates that $56.25 of interest will be paid annually (usually in semiannual installments) per $1,000 of face (or par) value of bonds held. The $56.25 is 5.625 percent of $1,000. Next is the maturity date, September 2017. At that time, GE will give the holder of the bond the last interest payment and $1,000 of principal per $1,000 of face (or par) value. As the name suggests, the face value appears on the face of the bond.

Next, we will look at the investment ratings provided by Moody's, S&P, and Fitch. General Electric has a triple A rating from Moody's, meaning that the company has a history of strong earnings, low leverage, and prompt debt redemption. (Note that the ratings from S&P and Fitch are not provided for GE.) The Weekly High, Low, Last, and Net Change in columns 6–9 refer to the price of the bond during the week from November 4, 2007 through November 9, 2007. The last column, "Yield %," presents the effective return on both coupon payments and principle if this bond were held until maturity in September 2017.

Note the price code in the bond market is different from the price code in the stock market. Bond prices are stated as percentages of 100, with 100 representing $1,000 face value. Hence, the closing price for the day

Issuer Name	Symbol	Coupon	Maturity	Rating.Moody's/ S&P/ Fitch	High	Low	Last	Change	Yield %
GENERAL ELECTRIC CAPITAL CORP	**GE.HDM**	**5.625%**	**Sep 2017**	**Aaa/—/—**	**104.084**	**98.241**	**102.084**	**0.596**	**5.349**
DEUTSCHE TELEKOM INTL FINANCE BV	HT.HA	5.750%	Mar 2016	A3/A–/A–	100.717	100.209	100.508	–0.934	5.672
LEHMAN BROTHERS HLDS	LEH.JAD	6.200%	Sep 2014	A1/—/AA–	102.765	95.620	95.620	–2.180	7.013
BEAR STEARNS & CO	BSC.GPS	6.400%	Oct 2017	A1/—/A+	98.131	94.335	95.163	–2.028	7.088
TIME WARNER	AOL.HL	6.500%	Nov 2036	Baa2/BBB+/BBB	95.736	94.915	95.266	–0.433	6.879
TIME WARNER	AOL.HK	5.875%	Nov 2016	Baa2/BBB+/BBB	100.331	97.683	100.331	2.137	5.827
INTL BUSINESS MACHINES CORP	IBM.KG	5.700%	Sep 2017	A1/A+/A+	102.610	102.066	102.610	0.300	5.354
CITIGROUP	C.HFD	5.875%	May 2037	Aa2/—/AA	90.875	89.359	90.875	1.058	6.579
KOHL'S CORP	KSS.GH	6.250%	Dec 2017	Baa1/BBB+/BBB+	100.125	99.519	99.999	–0.335	6.245
PROCTER & GAMBLE	PG.GY	4.950%	Aug 2014	Aa3/AA–/—	100.677	99.534	99.788	0.198	4.986

Source: *The Wall Street Journal Online* (November 12, 2007).

was 102.084, which means $1020.84. The weekly high was 104.084, which means $1040.84, and the weekly low was 98.241, which means $982.41. The closing price (102.084) was up .596 from the previous week's closing price. Thus, the previous week's closing price was 101.488, which means $1014.88. Therefore, the price of the bond has increased $5.96 during the past week.

Not so simple is the "Yield %" in the final column. In the past, financial publications reported the "current yield," which is simply the yearly coupon payment divided by the current price. For the General Electric bond we are considering, this would simply be 5.625/102.084 = 5.51 percent. This figure is not reported and is higher than the reported yield of 5.349 percent, because the bond is selling at a premium (since 102.084 > 100). Although the bond now costs $1020.84, in September 2017, only the $1,000 face value will be paid along with the final interest payment. Thus, the yield to maturity (Yield % reported) is smaller than the current yield (not reported). The opposite would be true for a bond selling at a discount. For example, consider the Lehman Brothers Holdings bond LEH.JAD. Its yield to maturity is reported as 7.013 percent, but its current yield would be 6.2/95.620 = 6.484 percent.

If a bond such as GE.HDM is selling at a premium, this implies interest rates have fallen since the bond was first issued. If a bond such as LEH.JAD is selling at a discount, this implies interest rates have risen since the bond was first issued. Only if a bond is selling at 100, or at par value, will the coupon yield be equal to the current yield.

the loan, and taxes must be paid on the amount of the interest earned each year, even though the interest is not paid until the bond matures. An advantage for the corporation is that interest payments are written off on an annual basis, even though they are not paid until the bond matures.

The secondary market in corporate bonds is a loosely connected array of brokers and dealers who buy, sell, and take positions in bonds in an over-the-counter market. In an over-the-counter market, brokers and dealers buy and sell bonds through computer links and over telephone lines. Although the bulk of bond trading takes place over the counter, some bonds are also bought and sold on organized exchanges such as the New York Stock Exchange.

Specific bonds trade with varying degrees of liquidity in the secondary market. Other factors being equal, the greater the expected liquidity, the lower the yield. Now would be a good time to read "Cracking the Code" on p. 288, which explains how to interpret corporate bond prices and yields as reported in the financial pages of popular newspapers or from online financial websites.

Recap Bonds are debt instruments that may be issued by domestic or foreign governments and corporations. The terms of a corporate bond issue are spelled out by the bond indenture and interpreted by the trustee. Some bonds are backed by real or financial assets that the corporation owns. Debenture bondholders are entitled to be paid before subordinated debenture bondholders but after bondholders with bonds that are backed by specific collateral. Bonds with call provisions allow the issuer to buy back the bonds before maturity. Bonds with convertible provisions allow investors to convert the bonds to a pre-specified number of shares of common stock. Zero-coupon bonds are sold at a discount. Secondary markets for bonds are primarily over-the-counter markets.

THE TREASURY NOTE AND BOND MARKETS

As you saw in Chapter 4, government securities consist of Treasury bills, notes, and bonds. Bills have an original maturity of one year or less, notes have an original maturity

Treasury Bonds

To understand how to read the accompanying table of developments that occurred in the government bond market on October 19, 2007 (taken from *The Wall Street Journal*), look at the highlighted line below. Under Rate (the first column) is 4.250. This is the coupon rate, and it indicates that the holder of this security receives $4.25 per year for each $100 (face or par value), usually paid in semiannual installments.

Maturity			Ask		
Rate	Mo/Yr	Bid	Asked	Chg	Yld
4.250	Nov 15 2012	100:15	100:16	+1	3.08

Source: *Wall Street Journal* (October 18, 2007).

The maturity date (second column) is Nov 15 2012. This simply indicates that the security will mature in November of the year 2012.

The next two columns give the Bid and Asked prices. The bid price is the price the market maker (dealer) is willing to pay to acquire this security. Prices are quoted in 32nds. Thus, 100:15 bid means 100 15/32, or $100.4688 per each $100. Hence, for a $1,000 bond, you need only to move the decimal point to find that the bid price is $1,004.688. The asked price is the price the dealer is asking when selling the security. In this case, the asked price is 100:16, which means 100 16/32, or $100.5 per $100. For a $1,000 bond, the asked price is $1,005.

The column Chg shows that the bid for this particular government security increased 1 on October 17, 2007, as compared with the close on the previous trading day. The change is also reported in 32nds, so the increase is really 1/32, or $0.03125 per $100, or $0.31 for a $1,000 dollar bond.

The last column gives the *yield to maturity* on an annual basis for this bond. It is 3.08 percent, which is the interest rate, or rate of return, on the bond. The yield to maturity takes into account the dollar return to the investor resulting from the coupon payment ($100 per year per $1,000 face value), the price appreciation or the depreciation between when the security is bought and when it matures, and the price paid.

In this case, there will be a depreciation at maturity; the security is selling at a premium: the market price of $1,005 exceeds the face value of $1,000.

Whenever the security sells at a premium, the yield to maturity is less than the coupon rate. Can you explain why the yield to maturity exceeds the coupon rate when the security sells at a discount (meaning the market price is less than the face value)?

---

of two to 10 years, and bonds have an original maturity of more than 10 years. U.S. government (or Treasury) notes and bonds are issued in the primary market by the Bureau of the Public Debt in minimum amounts of $1,000. Historically, Treasury notes and bonds were sold at a fixed coupon rate that did not change over the term of the security. Treasury bonds with maturities up to 30 years are currently sold in regularly scheduled competitive auctions. Issuance of new 30-year bonds was suspended in October 2001, but resumed in February 2006, so currently the 30-year bond is the newly issued fixed rate government security with the longest maturity. Treasury bonds and notes, like T-bills, are sold in other regularly scheduled auctions. The Treasury decides the maturity structure and the amount of the various offerings.

Treasury notes and bonds are a full faith and credit obligation of the U.S. government. Consequently, investors view these Treasury securities as being free from default risk. The federal government, with its power to tax or issue currency, will definitely pay back the principal and interest as scheduled. Because they are so highly liquid and free of default risk, interest rates on Treasury securities serve as a benchmark to judge the riskiness and liquidity of other securities.

However, Treasury notes and bonds are not free of interest rate risk. If the interest rate goes up after the issuance of securities but before their maturity, the value of the notes and bonds will go down. If they are sold before maturity, the investor will receive less than the face value of the security and experience a capital loss. This risk increases with the length of time to maturity, partially explaining why longer-term bonds typically pay a higher interest rate than shorter-term bills and notes.

The secondary market in Treasury notes and bonds is an over-the-counter market where a group of U.S. government securities dealers stands ready to buy and sell various issues of outstanding securities. Today, Treasury securities are sold in secondary markets somewhere in the world 24 hours a day. An extensive and very active secondary market makes Treasury notes and bonds highly liquid. The dealers' profits stem from the spread between the bid (buying) and asked (selling) prices. In the early 2000s, the Treasury bought back some higher interest long-term bonds with funds raised by issuing lower interest, shorter-term securities, to manage the maturity structure of the federal debt so as to reduce government financing costs. As the yield curve flattened in the mid-2000s, the benefit of substituting short-term debt for long-term diminished. However, in the financial meltdown of 2008, there has been a "flight to quality" which means that investors worldwide have sold riskier debt in favor of Treasury securities. Thus, prices of Treasury securities rose relative to other securities and yields, particularly short-term yields, fell dramatically.

A desirable feature of Treasury bonds is that the interest earned on them is exempt from state income taxes. Not all states have state income taxes, so this feature is particularly beneficial in states with high income tax rates. The "Cracking the Code" feature on p. 290 explains how to interpret the prices of Treasury bonds reported in major newspapers.

Separate Trading of Registered Interest and Principal Securities, or Treasury STRIPS, are fixed rate government securities first offered in 1984 and sold through depository institutions and government securities dealers. All newly issued Treasury fixed rate notes and bonds with maturities of 10 years or longer are eligible for the STRIPS program. STRIPS allow investors to register and trade ownership of the interest (coupon) payments and the principal amount of the security. The advantage of STRIPS is that the coupon and principal payments can be sold separately at a discount. STRIPS are sold in book entry form, meaning that the security is issued and accounted for electronically. The investor pays less today for the future payment than he or she will receive when the security matures. The interest the investor earns is the difference between what is paid today and what is received at maturity. Because the future payments are sold at a discount, the investor avoids the uncertainty that coupon payments may have to be reinvested at a lower interest rate because rates have fallen since the security was issued. The future payments of the STRIPS securities are direct obligations of the U.S. government.

U.S. Treasury Bonds have been popular with foreign investors because of their liquidity and perceived safety. The Looking Out feature on page 292 highlights the importance to foreign bond sales for both the United States. and other nations.

An inflation-indexed bond is a more recent hybrid, first offered for sale by the Treasury in January 1997. In September 2004, the term used by the Treasury for such securities was simplified to "inflation protected securities," resulting in the memorable acronym "TIPS." Inflation-indexed bonds, such as TIPS, are securities for which the principal amount is adjusted for inflation when an interest (coupon) payment is made, usually every six months. Although the interest rate does not change,

Treasury STRIPS
A type of government security that allows investors to register and trade ownership of the interest (coupon) payments and the principal separately.

Inflation-Indexed Bonds (e.g. Treasury Inflation Protected Securities, or TIPS)
Bonds whose principal amounts are adjusted for inflation at the time when coupon payments are made (usually every six months).

Looking Out

The International Bond Markets

As financial markets become more globalized, the international bond market plays an increasingly important role in the domestic bond market by augmenting the supply of funds available to the bond market and by increasing the array of bonds available to investors. The markets were experiencing the same stresses and strains as domestic bond markets due to the financial crisis in 2008. The international bond market consists of primary and secondary markets for Eurobonds and foreign bonds. We review each here.

Eurobonds

Eurobonds are bonds denominated in a currency other than that of the country where they are marketed. For example, dollar-denominated bonds sold outside the United States are called *Eurobonds*. Like the term *Eurodollar*, the term *Eurobond* has come to mean any bond denominated in the currency of the country from which it was issued, rather than that of the country where it is sold. The Eurobond market experienced tremendous growth in the 1980s, 1990s, and 2000s. No longer do domestic net borrowers have to look only to domestic net lenders or domestic financial intermediaries to obtain funds. Likewise, domestic net lenders have opportunities to supply funds denominated in dollars outside the United States. The Eurobond market has greatly expanded the borrowing sources for domestic borrowers. In addition, Eurobonds are less regulated than domestic bonds and offer some tax advantages.

Up to 1984, foreign purchasers of U.S. bonds were subject to a 30 percent withholding tax on all interest payments. Because of this, many Eurobonds were issued through subsidiaries of U.S. corporations in the Netherlands Antilles. This location was picked because of a treaty between the United States and the Netherlands Antilles that made non-U.S. investors exempt from the withholding tax. By effectively sidestepping the tax, the bonds could be offered at a lower rate. To issue Eurobonds, however, corporations had to have or establish a financial subsidiary in the Netherlands Antilles. This was too costly for many firms. In July 1984, the U.S. government repealed the withholding tax and authorized U.S. corporations to sell bonds directly to non-U.S. investors without the withholding tax. This greatly increased the volume of bonds sold directly to non-U.S. investors.

Foreign Bonds

Unlike Eurobonds, foreign bonds are denominated in the currency of the country in which they are underwritten and sold to investors, although the issuer of the bonds is from a foreign country. An example is a bond issued by a French corporation, denominated in dollars (as opposed to euros), and marketed in the United States by U.S. investment bankers. Foreign bonds denominated in dollars and marketed in the United States are called *Yankee bonds;* foreign bonds denominated in Japanese yen and sold in Japan are called *Samurai bonds;* and foreign bonds denominated in British pound sterling and sold in Great Britain are called *Bulldogs*. Domestic corporations with overseas operations often issue foreign bonds in the countries where the overseas operations are located in order to finance those operations.

the interest payments are based on the inflation-adjusted principal, and the inflation-adjusted principal is received at maturity. (In the event of deflation, the investor receives the original par value of the security.) Inflation-indexed bonds protect the investor from the ravages of inflation. Currently, five-year inflation-indexed securities are auctioned in April and October; 10-year inflation-indexed securities are auctioned in January, April, July, and October; and 20-year inflation-indexed securities are issued in January and July. There are limits to the amounts that households can purchase annually.

Recap

Treasury securities are sold in competitive auctions. They are considered to be free of default risk, and their interest rate serves as a benchmark to judge the risk and liquidity of other financial assets. The secondary market for government securities is a highly developed over-the-counter market. STRIPS are government securities that allow the investor to register and trade ownership of the coupon payments and the principal separately. The principal of inflation-indexed bonds such as Treasury Inflation Protected Securities (TIPS) is adjusted for inflation every six months. Although the interest rate doesn't change, the coupon payment is based on the inflation-adjusted amount, and the investor receives the inflation-adjusted principal at maturity.

MUNICIPAL BONDS

Municipal Bonds (munis)
Bonds issued by state, county, and local governments to finance public projects such as schools, utilities, roads, and transportation ventures; the interest on municipal securities is exempt from federal taxes and from state taxes for investors living in the issuing state.

Municipal bonds (munis) are bonds issued by state, county, and local governments to finance public projects such as schools, utilities, roads, and transportation ventures. The interest on municipal securities is exempt from federal taxes as well as from state taxes for investors living in the issuing state. This allows the issuer to borrow at a lower rate than if investors had to pay taxes on the interest earned.

Municipal bonds are particularly attractive to taxpayers in high-income tax brackets. The interest rate on munis will gravitate to the rate at which the marginal investor is indifferent between purchasing munis or purchasing other bonds of comparable maturity, liquidity, and risk on which the interest income is not tax exempt.[3] This rate is depicted in Equation (13-1), where t is the marginal tax rate of an investor just indifferent between buying a municipal bond versus an ordinary bond with taxable interest; i_b is the rate on comparable bonds; and i_m is the rate on munis.

(13-1)
$$i_b(1-t) = i_m$$

Taxpayers in a tax bracket higher than the marginal rate t can earn a higher return by investing in munis. The cost to the state, county, or local government issuer is t percent less than it would be if the interest income were not tax exempt. Thus, if the comparable corporate rate is 8 percent, the relevant marginal tax bracket is 25 percent, and the muni rate is 6 percent, taxpayers in a tax bracket above 25 percent can earn a higher after-tax return by investing in munis. In addition, in this case, municipalities can borrow at a 2 percent lower rate than if the interest income were not tax exempt. If the relevant marginal tax rate increased to 50 percent and the interest rate on taxable corporate bonds remained at 8 percent, then municipal bonds would need to pay only 4 percent.

General Obligation Bonds
Municipal bonds to be repaid out of general tax revenues.

As noted in Chapter 4, municipal bonds may be either *general obligation bonds* or *revenue bonds*. **General obligation bonds** are repaid out of general tax revenues. There has not been a default in the state-issued general obligation municipal bonds market in the last 100 years. This is not true for revenue munis issued by local and county governments. Repayment of *revenue bonds*, in contrast, is tied to the success of a specific

Revenue Bonds
Municipal bonds to be repaid out of the revenues from a specific project that the bonds support.

project that the bonds support. That is, the bondholder is paid back out of the cash flows of a particular project. There have been defaults on revenue bonds when specific projects did not generate the forecasted revenues.

As previously mentioned, muni bonds are more likely to be backed by a bond insurer than corporate bonds, with roughly half of such issues so insured. In early 2008 bond insurers such as Ambac, MBIA, Assured Guaranty, and FSA were receiving a great deal of scrutiny. Such insurers were previously believed to have effectively reduced default risk of municipal bonds. They insured bonds issued across many different states, and it seemed unlikely that many such issuers would default simultaneously. Thus, the insurers earned the highest "triple A" ratings, which then applied to the bonds they insured. Some insurers, specifically Ambac and MBIA, moved away from their specialty in government bonds and began to insure more risky bond-type securities backed by residential mortgages during the real estate boom years of 2002–2006. Falling real estate prices after 2006 increased the likelihood of default on such assets and threatened the insurers themselves. If the credit rating of a bond insurer were reduced, this would affect all the bonds they had previously insured, increasing the interest rate borrowers would be required to pay. As of early 2008, government agencies from New York and the United States were actively assisting bond insurers to retain their "triple A" credit ratings.

GOVERNMENT AGENCY SECURITIES

Government Agency Securities
Bonds issued by private enterprises that were publicly chartered by Congress to reduce the cost of borrowing to certain sectors of the economy, such as farming, housing, and student loans.

Government agency securities are issued by private enterprises that were publicly chartered by Congress to reduce the cost of borrowing to certain sectors of the economy. Government agency securities may be divided into two classes: government-sponsored enterprises and federally related institutions securities markets.

Areas where **government-sponsored enterprises (GSEs)** have been established include housing, farming, the savings and loan industry, and student loans. Among others, GSEs include the Federal Home Loan Banks, the Federal National Mortgage Association ("FannieMae"), the Federal Home Loan Mortgage Corporation ("Freddie Mac"), the Farm Credit System, and the Student Loan Marketing Association. All have historically been privately owned and issue long-term securities (bonds) to assist in some aspect of lending, such as funding mortgage loans, student loans, and farm credit. Many market participants assume that the government is a de facto guarantor of the payments and this did prove to be the case when Fannie Mae and Freddie Mac were put into conservatorship by the government in late 2008. We examine the GSEs that pertain to the mortgage market in more detail later in this chapter.

Government-Sponsored Enterprises (GSEs)
Private enterprises that have been chartered by Congress to reduce the cost of borrowing in such sectors as housing, farming, the savings and loan industry, and student loans.

Government-sponsored enterprises have experienced tremendous growth in the last two decades. Their outstanding credit market debt, which is composed mostly of long-term securities, increased from about $525 billion at the end of 1993 to over $3.15 trillion by the third quarter of 2008. Thus, the outstanding GSEs securities increased nearly 500 percent in the last 14 years.

In addition to government agency securities, the Federal Financing Bank, created in 1973, issues bonds to borrow for several federally related institutions. Among others, these institutions include the Commodity Credit Corporation, the General Services Administration, the Government National Mortgage Association, the Rural Telephone Bank, the Small Business Administration, and the Tennessee Valley Authority. The bonds issued by the Federal Financing Bank are backed by the full faith and credit of the U.S. government.

The yield spread between government agency securities and U.S. government securities reflects differences in liquidity and risk. The yield spread can be significant because secondary markets do not have the breadth and depth of Treasuries and, hence, agency securities are not as liquid as Treasuries.

Recap	Municipal securities are bonds issued by state, county, and local governments. The interest income on municipal securities is exempt from federal taxes and from state income taxes for investors living in the state where the municipals were issued. Municipal securities may be either general obligation bonds or revenue bonds. About half of such securities are insured by private companies, with their generally higher credit ratings applied to the issues, lowering the interest rates they must pay. Government agency securities are issued by government-sponsored enterprises and by the Federal Financing Bank.

THE ANATOMY OF MORTGAGES

Mortgage
A long-term debt instrument for which real estate is used as collateral and which results from loans made to individuals or businesses in order to purchase or refinance land, single- or multiple-family residential housing, commercial properties, or farms.

Collateral
The building (structure) or land that will be foreclosed on and repossessed if the borrower fails to make the scheduled payments; the lender then sells the property to recoup some or all of the losses.

Fixed Rate Mortgages
Mortgages where the interest rate remains the same over the life of the loan.

Variable Rate Mortgages
Mortgages where the interest rate is adjusted periodically to reflect changing market conditions.

A mortgage is a long-term debt instrument for which real estate is used as collateral to secure the loan in the event of a default by the borrower. If the borrower defaults, the property is usually sold to recoup some or all of the losses. Mortgages are assets to the holder (lender) and liabilities to the issuer (borrower) who signs the mortgage agreement. They are similar to bonds, with the caveat that the underlying real property or land serves as collateral.

Mortgages result from loans made to individuals or businesses to purchase land, single- or multiple-family residential housing, commercial properties, and farms. Mortgages may also be made to finance new commercial or residential construction. The building (structure) or land serves as collateral. Most mortgages are made to individuals to purchase residential property. Thus, households are the major borrowers in this market. In the third quarter of 2008, single- and multifamily residential mortgages totaled about $12 trillion, or 82 percent of all mortgages, which were about $14.7 trillion. Typically, borrowers pay a minimum down payment of 5 to 20 percent to purchase a property and take out a mortgage loan for the balance of the purchase price. During the housing bubble years from 2002 to 2006, down payments of less than 5 percent were not unheard of, but by the end of 2007, required down payments had moved back toward their previous levels.

Mortgages have either a fixed or a variable interest rate. With fixed rate mortgages, the interest rate does not vary over the life of the loan. Lenders are exposed to an interest rate risk—the risk that nominal interest rates will rise, causing the value of fixed rate mortgages to decline. In addition, if long-term fixed rate mortgages are funded with short-term deposits, the lending institution can experience a negative cash flow if the costs of liabilities rise above the earnings on assets. As mentioned in Chapter 4, with variable rate mortgages, the interest rate is adjusted as other market interest rates change. If rates move up, the interest rate on the mortgages increases, and vice versa. Thus, variable rate mortgages reduce the interest rate risk of holding long-term mortgages because, in the event that interest rates rise, loan payments and interest rates on the mortgages also rise. The interest rate on some variable loans adjusts every month, and others adjust less frequently, such as every 6 or 12 months. The rates adjust based on a mark-up or margin over some index that represents the cost of funds for the lender. The interest rates on newly issued variable mortgages is typically lower than the comparable newly issued fixed rate mortgage to reward the borrower for accepting the added risk that the rate can go up.

The Evolution of the Mortgage Market

Prior to the Great Depression, most mortgages were balloon mortgages on which only interest payments were made on a monthly basis and the entire principal was due at maturity. They required large down payments that averaged about 40 percent of the property value. At the end of the term (usually three to five years), the mortgage was usually renegotiated for a slightly lesser amount. Because of the economic havoc created by the Great Depression, many borrowers could not renegotiate the mortgages, and many lenders failed in the early 1930s. The widespread defaults caused the collapse of the mortgage market. The federal government stepped in and assisted homeowners by taking over the balloon payments and allowing borrowers to spread out the payment of both the principal and interest over a longer period of time. Thus, the first amortized mortgages were introduced. In addition, in 1934, the federal government established the Federal Housing Administration (FHA) to ensure the timely payment of principal and interest on long-term fixed rate mortgages that met the FHA's criteria. In 1944, Veterans Administration (VA) insured loans, similar to FHA loans, were established; they required no down payments for eligible veterans.

In the two decades after World War II, the mortgage market thrived and was dominated by savings and loan associations that held long-term mortgages funded with short-term deposits. By the late 1960s, an inflationary environment began to cause problems for savings and loans. The need to adjust asset maturities in the face of rising inflation and interest rates underscored the need for a secondary market. With a secondary market, the lender would not have to hold the mortgage until maturity but could sell it in the secondary market. Hence, the interest rate risk would be reduced. In 1968, the government established Ginnie Mae and rechartered Fannie Mae as a privately owned government-sponsored enterprise rather than as a government-owned enterprise. Advances in computer technologies and the emergence of mortgage-backed securities in 1970 fostered the growth of a secondary market.

By the 1980s, mortgage brokers and mortgage bankers were originating many mortgage loans that were then sold off in the secondary market to Fannie Mae, Freddie Mac, and other private issuers of mortgage-backed securities. Mortgage brokers and mortgage bankers originate mortgages but do not hold them as investments. Despite the collapse of the savings and loan industry in the 1980s, mortgage lending continued as other lenders, including commercial banks, stepped in to fill the void.

From 1982 until late 2008, the dollar value of outstanding mortgages increased from $1.6 trillion to over $14.7 trillion, an increase of more than 915 percent in nominal terms. During this same period, the consumer price index increased by about 103 percent, nominal GDP increased about 255 percent, and real GDP increased by about 106 percent. Thus, outstanding mortgages grew at a much faster rate than the overall level of prices and the levels of real and nominal economic activity.

Two other changes are noteworthy. First, in 1982, savings institutions held more than 35 percent of all outstanding mortgages. By late 2008, however, that number dropped dramatically to about 6 percent. Commercial banks that held approximately 18 percent of outstanding mortgages in 1982 first experienced an increase in their share of all mortgages held (to about 25 percent by mid-2004), then a decrease (to just over 15 percent by late 2008). Both institutions prefer to hold variable rate mortgages because of the reduced interest rate risk.

Second, the largest holders today of mortgages are GSEs and GSE-backed mortgage pools. In 1982, they held 23 percent of all mortgages. By late 2007, their share had increased to 41 percent of all mortgages. This does not include the mortgages that are federally insured by Ginnie Mae but held by private institutions. Except for ensuring the timely payment of principal and interest on VA and FHA loans, the federal government did not play an important role in the mortgage market before 1970. With the creation of Ginnie Mae and Freddie Mac and the growth of Fannie Mae, the federal government has had a major impact on the industry since the early 1970s. In addition, private issuers of mortgage-backed securities held around another 20 percent of mortgages in 2007. Such issuers were tiny in 1982. With Fannie Mae and Freddie Mac under conservatorship, there is a possibility that their operations will be curtailed in the future. If so, this may create an opportunity for private issuers of mortgage-backed securities, assuming these assets survive in the future.

By the middle of the first decade of the 2000s, mortgage market activity consisted of three distinct functions: originating, investing in, and servicing mortgages. Sometimes, one institution performs all three activities. At other times, an institution may perform only one or two of them. For example, a mortgage broker may originate loans only, while a bank may originate, invest in, and service the mortgages. A savings and loan may originate the loan and sell it in the secondary market, but continue to service the mortgage for a fee.

As discussed in Chapter 11, in the second half of 2007, a crisis that had been smoldering in the subprime mortgage market boiled over. Subprime mortgages are made to individuals with bad credit scores and little or no down payments. They are made at low introductory "teaser" interest rates that will "reset" much higher in two or three years. Supposedly, borrowers believed they would be able to refinance at lower rates or pull more money from a house that had appreciated in value to make ends meet. Lenders believed that if the borrowers defaulted, they could always repossess the house and sell it at a profit. As housing prices started to fall in 2006, many of the borrowers with subprime loans could not afford to make their payments, could not refinance, could not sell their homes, and owed more than their houses were worth. As a result, they defaulted on their mortgages, and lenders were left holding thousands of houses they could not sell at any price close to what they had lent. This turn of events sent the mortgage market into complete chaos, causing record losses and the collapse of many institutions. In early 2008, the crisis had spread to global bond markets and was far from resolved.

As a result of the crisis, we expect to see further changes in the structure of the mortgage market. We predict more government oversight and regulation, and the disappearance of subprime lending altogether. Lenders will be much more selective about the borrowers they lend to and more carefully evaluate their credit risk.

We should note that the separation of the three distinct functions mentioned above contributed to the problem by creating a moral hazard. A mortgage broker would originate the loan, then sell it to a lender, who then would securitize it off or sell it in the secondary market. The key players in this scenario—the mortgage originator, the lender, and the investor—were not as careful about the ability of the borrower to pay off the loan as they should have been, because they were not going to be holding the loan on their books for that long.

There are three main risks that go along with investing in mortgages

Default Risk

The risk that the borrower will not make the principal and interest payments as scheduled.

- The longer the term to maturity, the greater the default risk because the more distant future becomes more uncertain.
- The lower the down payment, the greater the default risk. The borrower has less to lose by defaulting.
- If interest rates rise, the default risk on variable rate loans increases because monthly payments rise and the borrower is less able to afford them.

Interest Rate Risk

The risk that interest rates rise and the value of long-term mortgages declines. If long-term mortgages are funded with short-term deposits, the spread between the earnings on assets and costs of liabilities narrows and may become negative.

- The longer the term to maturity, the greater the interest rate risk.
- Variable rate loans reduce the interest rate risk.

Prepayment Risk

The risk that mortgages will be prepaid early and that the funds will have to be reinvested at a lower return.

- Prepayment risk increases greatly when interest rates fall, particularly if they stay low for a significant period of time.
- Prepayment risk is much less for variable rate loans than for fixed rate loans.

Prepayment Risk
The risk that mortgages will be prepaid early and that the funds will have to be reinvested at a lower return.

An additional risk—the prepayment risk—is that mortgages will be prepaid early and that the funds will have to be reinvested at a lower return. This risk increases greatly when interest rates fall, particularly if rates stay low for a significant period of time as borrowers refinance their mortgages to take advantage of the lower rates. This risk has been lower for variable rate loans than for fixed rate loans because the interest rate on variable loans will fall along with other rates. Borrowers with variable rate loans may, however, refinance into fixed rate loans if the short-term rates upon which their variable rates are based increase more than longer-term interest rates. Exhibit 13-1 summarizes the risks of investing in mortgages.

Unlike a bond whose principal is repaid at maturity, the repayment of the principal on a mortgage is generally spread out over the life of the loan. Each month, a constant monthly payment is made that includes some part of the principal in addition to the interest payment. At the end of the loan, the mortgage has been fully repaid. This is known as amortization.[4] Mortgages have typically been made for up to 30 years, although 40-year mortgages are becoming more available and can help borrowers lower their monthly payments.

Amortization
The paying off of the principal of a loan over the life of the loan.

In recent years, shorter-term mortgages have also become more popular. Fixed term loans of shorter durations such as 15 or 20 years will result in higher monthly payments, but lower total interest expense over the life of a loan. Hybrid 30-year mortgages that offer fixed rates for an initial time period, such as one, three, five, seven, or 10 years, and variable rates thereafter, have also been developed. Lenders are willing to accept lower payments in the early years of such a loan since they face less interest rate risk than with a conventional fixed rate loan. If future interest rates increase with a variable rate, loan lenders may increase the rate they charge, but with a conventional fixed rate loan this would not be possible. Hybrid loans are most appropriate for individuals likely to move to a new home in the near future. In the home price bubble years from 2002 to 2006, such loans also allowed some buyers to purchase more expensive homes than may have been warranted by their income, since low initial "teaser" rates resulted in lower initial monthly payments. This would pose no threat if a buyer's income increased over time, home prices continued to increase, and/or low cost short-term financing remained available in the future. In an environment with stagnant incomes, falling home prices, and reduced availability of home financing as occurred in 2008, such loans could result in (1) homeowners being unable or unwilling to make mortgage payments, (2) increasing rates of foreclosure, and (3) home sales further depressing already low home prices.

Residential mortgages may also be insured by an agency of the federal government. The insurance guarantees the repayment of the principal and interest in the event that the borrower defaults. This eliminates the credit or default risk for the lender. The two federal agencies that guarantee mortgages are the **Federal Housing Administration (FHA)** and the **Veterans Administration (VA)**. For a .5 percent fee, the FHA insures mortgage loans made by privately owned financial institutions up to a certain amount that varies by state and county, depending on average housing costs.

In early 2009, the standard mortgage limit for FHA insured loans was $271,050, but for high cost areas limits were as high as $625,500 and based on a percentage of Freddie Mac loan limits. Higher limits of up to $544,185 exist for Alaska and Hawaii, and these limits may soon be applied to additional states such as California and New York. The FHA loan limit is generally adjusted in response to changes in housing prices. These limits differ from those that apply for "conforming loans" purchased by Freddy Mac or Fannie Mae, but without official government insurance. The conforming loan limit is $417,000 in 2009. FHA loans are designed to help low-income families purchase homes. Borrowers must meet certain conditions dealing with income and credit as defined by the FHA. With the government guarantee, the lender does not have to worry about the borrower defaulting. VA loans are similar to FHA loans but are designed to insure the principal and interest payments on loans made to veterans. The purpose is to help those who have served the country in the military to purchase homes. FHA and VA loans generally have small or no down payments.

Conventional mortgages have no federal insurance and are made by financial institutions and mortgage brokers. Conventional loans generally require a 5 to 20 percent down payment. Conventional mortgages may or may not require the borrower to purchase private insurance that would make the principal and interest payments in the event the borrower defaults. The borrower pays a higher interest rate to cover the cost of the insurance. Generally, when the down payment or equity in the property is less than 20 percent, lenders require borrowers to obtain private mortgage insurance. Private mortgage insurance is purchased from a privately owned insurance company.

Federal Housing Administration (FHA)
A federal agency that, for a .5 percent fee, insures mortgage loans made by privately owned financial institutions up to a certain amount if the borrowers meet certain conditions defined by the FHA.

Veterans Administration (VA)
A federal agency that, among other things, insures mortgage loans made by privately owned financial institutions up to a certain amount if the borrowers meet certain conditions, including being military veterans.

Conventional Mortgages
Mortgages made by financial institutions and mortgage brokers without the federal insurance that the principal and interest will be repaid.

Recap   Mortgages are long-term debt instruments used to purchase residential, commercial, and farm properties. The underlying property serves as collateral. Fixed rate mortgages carry the risk to the lender that nominal interest rates will rise and the value of the mortgages will fall. When the interest rate falls, borrowers will refinance at the lower rate, causing the lender to have to reinvest the funds at a lower rate. The interest rate on variable rate mortgages is adjusted as market rates change. The principal of a mortgage is generally amortized over the life of the loan. The principal and interest payments may be insured by the FHA or VA, which are agencies of the federal government. Conventional loans have no federal insurance and are made by financial institutions and mortgage brokers. Lenders may require borrowers with conventional loans to obtain private mortgage insurance.

THE SECONDARY MORTGAGE MARKET AND MORTGAGE-BACKED SECURITIES

Federal National Mortgage Association (Fannie Mae)
Formerly a privately owned government-sponsored enterprise that sold securities and used the proceeds to buy mortgages primarily of banks. It, along with Freddie Mac, was placed into conservatorship under the Federal Home Loan Mortgage Corporation, in September 2008.

Government National Mortgage Association (Ginnie Mae)
A government-owned enterprise that guarantees the timely payment of interest and principal on bundles of at least $1 million of standardized mortgages.

Mortgage-Backed Securities
Securities backed by a pool of mortgages; they have a low default risk and provide a steady stream of income.

Federal Home Loan Mortgage Corporation (Freddie Mac)
Formerly a privately owned government-sponsored enterprise that sold securities and used the proceeds to buy mortgages primarily of thrifts. It, along with Fannie Mae, was placed into conservatorship under its former regulator, Federal Home Loan Mortgage Corporation, in September 2008.

Secondary markets trade previously issued financial claims. Prior to 1970, only mortgages insured by the FHA or VA were sold in secondary markets, and these were sold directly to investors. The amount of market activity was very small. Congress had created the Federal National Mortgage Association (Fannie Mae) in 1938 but did not establish a secondary market for FHA and VA loans until 1972. Fannie Mae issued bonds and bought FHA- and VA-insured mortgages. Still, the market did not grow to any significant extent and was even declining because of a decrease in VA loans.

In 1968, Congress created the Government National Mortgage Association (GNMA, or Ginnie Mae). In 1970, Ginnie Mae began a program through which it guaranteed the timely payment of interest and principal on *bundles* of $1 million or more of standardized mortgages. Small denomination mortgages (mortgages up to the FHA and VA limits) were standardized with regard to the debt-to-income ratios of borrowers and the loan-to-value ratios of properties. The standardized mortgages were packaged together in a bundle to be resold in secondary markets. Thus, Ginnie Mae guaranteed (for a fee) that the mortgage bundles would be repaid. The guarantee was backed up by the full faith and credit of the U.S. government. Ginnie Mae fostered the creation of large secondary markets that increased the liquidity of previously illiquid mortgages. This made mortgages more attractive to investors, lowering mortgage interest rates and increasing the availability of home loans.

The secondary market in mortgages created by the Ginnie Mae guarantee operates as follows: Private financial institutions such as banks or savings and loans gather or pool several Ginnie Mae federally guaranteed mortgages into bundles of, say, $1 million. They then sell all or parts of the $1 million securities, called mortgage-backed securities, to third-party investors such as pension funds, mutual funds, or individual investors. The principal and interest on the mortgage-backed securities are paid from the payments that borrowers make on the original mortgages. If investors need their funds back before the securities mature, they can sell them in a secondary market for mortgage-backed securities. The secondary market for mortgage-backed securities operates similar to the secondary market in corporate bonds.

Despite the lack of default risk because of the government guarantee, Ginnie Mae securities are subject to an interest rate risk. Because they are long-term instruments, if the interest rate rises after the securities have been issued, the value of the securities will fall.

In 1970, Congress authorized Fannie Mae to purchase conventional (non-VA- or non-FHA-insured) mortgages. Congress also created the Federal Home Loan Mortgage Corporation (Freddie Mac) to lend further support to the VA, FHA, and conventional mortgage markets. Congress hoped to make housing more available by increasing the funds flowing into mortgages. The goal, which remains the same today, was to expand the opportunities for low- and moderate-income families to purchase homes. Although Fannie Mae purchased and held mortgages, it did not pool the mortgages to create a mortgage-backed security until 1981. ~~Freddie Mac issued its first mortgage-backed security in 1971.~~ It resulted from a pool of conventional mortgages. Fannie Mae primarily buys the mortgages of banks, while Freddie Mac primarily buys the mortgages of thrifts.

Fannie Mae and Freddie Mac were government-sponsored enterprises (GSEs). They were exempt from state and local corporate income taxes and had a $2.25 billion line of credit with the U.S. Treasury. Fannie Mae and Freddie Mac provided loanable funds to the housing sector. They purchased conventional loans, package or pool the mortgages together, and issued mortgage-backed securities (also called *government agency securities*) using the pool of mortgages as collateral. Some mortgages purchased by Fannie Mae and Freddie Mac were directly held by Fannie Mae and Freddie Mac as investments instead of being packaged and sold as mortgage-backed securities. ~~Both Fannie Mae and Freddie Mac were placed into conservatorship under the Federal Home Loan Mortgage Corporation in September 2008.~~ While these two entities are no longer investor-owned, and are instead officially now under the jurisdiction of the U.S. government, their actual activities with respect to mortgages have not changed much.

Both Fannie Mae and Freddie Mac ~~only purchase mortgages up to a certain limit, which in early 2009 was $417,000~~ as noted before. ~~Loans of this size or smaller are called conforming loans.~~ Since such loans are more liquid, ~~interest rates on them required by lenders are lower.~~ Loans larger than this limit are "nonconforming" or "jumbo" loans, which have higher interest rates. ~~The decline in home prices was particularly severe in high price markets, where most buyers would typically need a mortgage above $417,000,~~ such as in upscale neighborhoods in California or New York. The stimulus package passed by U.S. Congress in early 2008 included a temporary increase in this conforming loan limit to $729,000 with the objective of lowering interest rates on large mortgage loans, increasing demand for expensive homes, and limiting the decline in their prices, ultimately reducing the financial distress of individuals who had borrowed to purchase these expensive homes. The temporary increase ended on December 31, 2008.

Investors who purchase Fannie Mae and Freddie Mac mortgage-backed securities can sell them in secondary markets if funds are needed before the securities mature. The secondary markets for mortgage-backed securities are created by market makers who buy and sell previously issued mortgage-backed securities. Some mortgage-backed securities are traded on organized exchanges.

By September 30, 2008, the amount outstanding of federally related mortgage-backed securities totaled more than just under $5 trillion, up from $1.2 trillion in 1991 and $.18 trillion in 1982. Thus, these markets have experienced spectacular growth in the last two decades.

Collateralized Mortgage Obligations (CMOs)

As noted previously, ~~investors in mortgage-backed securities face the risk that the mortgages will be prepaid before they mature because the property is sold or refinanced and that the return will fall short of expectations.~~ To reduce this risk, ~~collateralized mortgage obligations have been developed by Freddie Mac.~~ **Collateralized mortgage obligations** redirect the cash flows (principal and interest) of mortgage-backed securities to various classes of bondholders, thus creating financial instruments with varying prepayment risks and varying returns. Those who are most risk averse can choose an instrument whose principal will soon be repaid. Those who are willing to bear more

A conforming loan is one equal or smaller in size than the conforming loan limit set by the Office of Federal Housing Enterprise Oversight (OFHEO). Since they can be more readily packaged and resold, interest rates on conforming loans (sometimes called "conventional" loans) are generally lower than for larger, jumbo, non-conforming loans.

Collateralized Mortgage Obligations
Securities developed by Freddie Mac that redirect the cash flows (principal and interest) of mortgage-backed securities to various classes of investors, thus creating financial instruments with varying prepayment risks and varying returns.

risk can choose an instrument whose principal will not be repaid until later and, hence, is subject to a greater prepayment risk. In exchange for more prepayment risk, the investor receives a higher return. Needless to say, such provisions make attractive choices available to a wider range of investors. However, CMOs have been caught up in the ongoing mortgage meltdown related to the financial crisis of 2008. It remains to be seen to what extent these markets will eventually recover.

Private Mortgage-Backed Securities

In 1984, some private groups started to issue their own mortgage-backed securities. The new securities did not rely on the backing of Ginnie Mae and were not issued by corporations such as Fannie Mae or Freddie Mac that had ties to the federal government. Such issuers of private mortgage-backed securities include, among others, commercial banks, mortgage bankers, and investment banking firms. Privately issued mortgage-backed securities may also be sold in secondary markets. Again, the secondary markets are created by market makers who trade the previously issued securities. Up until 2006, privately issued mortgage-backed securities expanded at a faster rate than GSE-backed securities. Thus the proportion of such "private label" mortgage-backed securities rose from 8.5 percent in 2003 to 18.7 percent in 2006.

This availability of funding through private mortgage-backed securities is related to the "subprime mortgage meltdown" discussed in Chapter 11. Lenders intending to quickly sell loans they originated became less interested in the creditworthiness of their borrowers. The proportion of nontraditional, nonprime loans among mortgages packaged in nonagency securitizations rose from 3 percent in 2002 to a peak of over 50 percent by 2006. This market froze up at the end of 2008 and it remains to be seen if and when it will recover.

Recap   Fannie Mae and Freddie Mac are GSEs that issue mortgage-backed (agency) securities and use the proceeds to purchase mortgages. Ginnie Mae guarantees the timely payment of principal and interest on mortgage-backed securities put together by private lenders. Ginnie Mae securities have an explicit government guarantee. Other private groups issue mortgage-backed securities without government involvement. Secondary markets trade previously issued mortgage-backed securities. Collateralized mortgage obligations redirect the cash flows (principal and interest) of mortgage-backed securities to various classes of bondholders, thus creating financial instruments with varying prepayment risks and varying returns. From 2003 to 2006, a relative increase in privately issued mortgage-backed securities fueled the increase in nonstandard loans and thus contributed to the mortgage market difficulties that surfaced in 2007–2008.

This completes our look at the bond and mortgage markets. This chapter contains two appendices on the pricing of bonds and mortgages. In the next chapter, we look at the stock market.

A Closer Look

The Mortgage Bailout Plan

In February 2009, President Obama announced a new Mortgage Bailout Plan to help struggling homeowners. The goal of the program is to help at-risk homeowners (homeowners in danger of losing their homes) to stay in their homes. The plan consists of two parts.

First, the government would commit to up to $200 billion to Fannie Mae and Freddie Mac to help lenders modify or refinance the loans of homeowners who have little or no equity. This part of the plan may help 4 to 5 million homeowners refinance to a lower interest rate and thus lower their payments. In early 2009, mortgage rates are close to historic lows because of the severe economic downturn. Under current standards, homeowners need 20 percent equity in their homes to refinance. Without the plan, homeowners with less than 20 percent equity in their homes would not be able to refinance. Many homeowners who had put down 20 percent, now have much less equity, given the collapse in property values. For example, say a homeowner bought a house for $300,000 with 20 percent down payment, an original loan amount of $240,000 and an interest rate of 6.25 percent. If the value of the home has fallen to $260,000, the homeowner would not be able to refinance to take advantage of the lower rates. With a market value of $260,000, he/she would only be able to borrow $208,000 despite owing almost $240,000. (Note very little of the principal is paid off in the first few years of a mortgage). The new plan allows such a homeowner to refinance at the current rates. At 6.25 percent, his/her original payment is $1477.73 for principal and interest. If they can refinance at 4.75 percent, his/her payment would fall to $1,251.96, a savings of $225.77 a month. Hopefully, homeowners who see their payments fall under this plan will increase their spending on other items and help to get the economy going again. The funding for this program comes from the Housing and Economic Recovery Act passed in August 2008.

Second, under the Homeowner Stability Initiative, the plan provides up to $75 billion to help homeowners in danger of losing their homes to foreclosure through a loan modification. It is expected that 3 to 4 million homeowners will be able to take advantage of this plan. The plan could consist of writing down principal for borrowers who are upside down (owe more than what their home is worth) or reducing interest payments so that at-risk homeowners will be able to keep their homes. Other options include extending the length of the loan to 40 years. All of the options result in lower house payments today and thus more homeowners could now afford to stay in their homes. If foreclosures are reduced, this helps support property values in the area, thus benefiting all homeowners in the area.

The Treasury developed uniform guidelines for both programs, and the guidelines (including a worksheet for homeowners at risk) are available online at www.financialstability.gov.

Summary of Major Points

1. Bonds are debt instruments issued by the U.S. government; an agency of the government; a state, county or local government; a domestic or foreign corporation; or a foreign government. The coupon payment is based on the par (face) value multiplied by the coupon rate. Bonds are rated by Moody's and Standard and Poor's with regard to creditworthiness.

2. The terms of a corporate bond issue are spelled out in the bond indenture. Some corporate bonds are backed by real or financial assets. Debenture bonds and subordinated debenture bonds are not. Most corporate bond issues have call provisions that allow the issuer to buy back the securities before maturity at a pre-specified price. Corporations also issue zero-coupon bonds that do not pay interest but are sold at a discount. Secondary markets trade previously issued corporate bonds.

3. Treasury securities are considered to be free from default risk. The secondary market for government securities is the largest secondary market in the world. Treasury bonds are subject to an interest rate risk. With its reintroduction in February 2006, the 30-year bond is once again the longest maturity of newly issued fixed rate securities issued by the U.S. Treasury.

4. STRIPS allow the coupon and principal payments of government securities to be sold separately at a discount. The principal amount of an indexed bond is adjusted for inflation when an interest (coupon) payment is made. The interest rate does not change, but the interest payments are based on the inflation-adjusted principal. The Treasury issues five-, 10-, and 20-year inflation-indexed securities.

5. Municipal bonds are issued by state and local governments. Interest income on municipal securities is exempt from federal taxes and from state taxes for investors living in the issuing state. General obligation bonds are repaid out of general tax revenues. Revenue bonds are repaid from the revenues of a specific project that the bonds support. Government agency securities are issued by private enterprises that are publicly chartered by Congress to reduce the cost of borrowing in specific areas.

6. Bond markets have grown significantly, fueled by increases in nonfinancial corporate bonds and increases in bonds issued by the Treasury and government-sponsored enterprises. Foreign entities have made substantial net purchases of domestic bonds, increasing the supply of funds flowing into this market.

7. Mortgages are long-term debt instruments used to purchase residential, commercial, and farm properties. The underlying property serves as collateral that the debt will be repaid. The principal of the loan is generally amortized over its life.

8. The timely payment of the principal and interest on a mortgage may also be insured for a fee by an agency of the federal government. The purpose of FHA-insured loans is to help low-income families purchase homes. The purpose of VA loans is to help veterans purchase homes. Conventional mortgages are made by financial institutions without government insurance.

9. Mortgages have a default risk, an interest rate risk, and a prepayment risk. The prepayment risk is the risk that the borrower will repay the loan early and that the funds will have to be reinvested at a lower rate.

10. With fixed rate mortgages, the interest rate remains the same over the life of the loan. With variable interest rate mortgages, the interest rate fluctuates over the life of the loan according to the general level of interest rates.

11. In recent decades, the government has become much more active in the mortgage market by guaranteeing the repayment of Ginnie Mae mortgages and sponsoring Fannie Mae and Freddie Mac. Fannie Mae and Freddie Mac were privately owned, government-sponsored enterprises that issued mortgage-backed (agency) securities and use the proceeds to purchase mortgage loans. Both were placed under the conservatorship of the Federal Home Loan Mortgage Corporation in September 2008, but their activities are largely unchanged. Private groups also issue mortgage-backed securities without an explicit or implicit

government guarantee. The rise of this market has coincided with an increase in the use of nonstandard, subprime mortgages. Secondary markets exist that trade previously issued mortgage-backed securities. Mortgage markets have experienced severe strains in the financial crisis of 2008–2009.

12. The price of a bond is the present value of the future cash flows associated with the bond. The discount factor used to determine the price of a bond includes a risk-free rate and a risk premium. Treasury bonds are considered to pay a risk-free rate of return. The risk premium encompasses both economy-wide and firm- or industry-specific risks. Economy-wide factors include the stance of monetary policy, expected inflation, and the level of economic activity. The major firm or industry factors include the capital structure of the firm, the economic outlook for the firm, and the credit rating of the bond issuance. (See Appendix 13A.)

13. The price of a mortgage is the discounted value of the future stream of monthly payments over the life of the instrument. When the interest rate increases, the prices of long-term mortgage securities decrease, and vice versa. Prices of mortgage-backed securities are determined by the prices of the mortgages that make up the pool that backs the security. (See Appendix 13B.)

14. The discount factor used to determine the price of a mortgage or mortgage-backed security includes a risk-free rate, a risk premium, and a premium for the higher servicing costs that mortgages entail. The risk premium includes the risk that the mortgage may be prepaid early when investment opportunities for the lender are less favorable. It also includes compensation for the lower liquidity of mortgages due to a less-developed secondary market. (See Appendix 13B.)

Key Terms

Amortization, p. 298
Bond Indenture, p. 287
Call Provisions, p. 287
Collateral, p. 295
Collateralized Mortgage
  Obligations, p. 301
Conforming Loans,
  p. 301
Conventional Mortgages,
  p. 299
Convertible Provisions,
  p. 287
Coupon Payments, p. 284
Coupon Rate, p. 284
Debenture Bonds, p. 287
Federal Home Loan
  Mortgage Corporation
  (Freddie Mac), p. 300
Federal Housing Administration
  (FHA), p. 299

Federal National Mortgage
  Association (Fannie Mae),
  p. 300
Fixed Rate Mortgages,
  p. 295
General Obligation Bonds,
  p. 293
Government Agency
  Securities, p. 294
Government National
  Mortgage Association
  (GNMA or Ginnie Mae),
  p. 300
Government-Sponsored
  Enterprises (GSEs), p. 294
Inflation-Indexed Bonds
  (Treasury Inflation Protected
  Securities, or TIPS), p. 291
Moody's Investors Service,
  p. 284

Mortgage, p. 295
Mortgage-Backed Securities,
  p. 300
Municipal Bonds (munis),
  p. 293
Par Value, p. 284
Prepayment Risk, p. 298
Revenue Bonds, p. 293
Standard & Poor's Investors
  Service, p. 284
Subordinated Debenture
  Bonds, p. 287
Treasury STRIPS, p. 291
Trustee, p. 287
Variable Rate Mortgages,
  p. 295
Veterans Administration (VA),
  p. 299
Zero-Coupon Bonds,
  p. 287

Review Questions

1. Define *par (face) value*, *coupon rate*, *coupon payment*, and *current yield*. What are *call provisions* and *convertible provisions*, and how do they affect the interest rates on newly issued securities?

2. What is a bond indenture? What is the role of the trustee?

3. What role do Moody's and Standard & Poor's Investors Services play in the bond market?

4. What is the difference between debenture bonds, subordinated debenture bonds, and bonds backed by specific collateral? What are zero-coupon bonds?

5. What are inflation-indexed bonds? How do they reduce the risk of holding long-term bonds? Does the interest rate on inflation-indexed bonds change after they have been issued?

6. Why are interest rates on Treasury securities used as benchmarks to judge the riskiness and liquidity of other securities?

7. What are the advantages of investing in STRIPS rather than Treasury securities that make regular coupon payments?

8. Are revenue bonds as safe as general obligation bonds?

9. What are the reasons for differences in interest rates between Treasury securities and government agency securities? Between Treasuries and municipals? When will a bond sell in the secondary market for its face value?

10. How is a mortgage similar to a bond? How is it different? What is the difference between a fixed interest rate and variable interest rate loan? What is amortization?

11. Explain the process by which a mortgage-backed security is created. What roles do Ginnie Mae, Fannie Mae, and Freddie Mac play?

12. If Sandi and Dave repay their mortgage early because they are refinancing or selling their home, what is the risk for the lender?

13. How can investing in a collateralized mortgage obligation entail less risk than investing in a mortgage-backed security? Can it ever entail more risk?

14. How would a fall in interest rates affect the value of previously issued mortgages?

15. What is the difference between the secondary market in mortgages and the secondary market in mortgage-backed securities?

16. Discuss what will happen to the discount factors used to determine prices of previously issued bonds sold in secondary markets, given the following scenarios (see Appendix 13A):

    a. A company's earnings report comes in much lower than expected.

    b. Your college is suffering from declining enrollments, particularly among students who want to live on campus. Revenue bonds have been issued to finance your college dorm.

    c. Fed policy turns expansionary.

    d. The performance of the economy is particularly strong.

17. What factors are important in determining the price of a previously issued bond? (See Appendix 13A.)

18. Discuss what would happen to the discount factor for mortgages under the following circumstances (see Appendix 13B):

    a. A recession is expected in the near future.

    b. The Fed has taken action to raise interest rates.

    c. International financial crises have caused an inflow of funds into the United States.

    d. The federal government is running a larger surplus than expected.

19. Technological advances have reduced the servicing costs on loans. What would happen to the discount factor applied to value mortgages and mortgage-backed securities and why? (See Appendix 13B.)

Analytical Questions

Questions marked with a check mark (✓) are objective in nature. They can be completed with a short answer or number.

✓20. Explain why the General Electric Capital Corporation bond in the "Cracking the Code" box on p. 290 is selling at a premium above par?

✓21. A Treasury bond pays a 4.250 percent coupon rate. What is the coupon payment per $1,000 face value? How is this related to its yield to maturity?

✓22. If the interest rate on a corporate bond is 10 percent, in equilibrium, what will be the rate on a muni with comparable risk, maturity, and liquidity if the marginal investor faces a marginal tax rate of 20 percent?

✓23. Assume that the risk-free rate is 5 percent and the risk premium for investing in mortgages is 2 percent. Also assume that it costs approximately 1 percent to service a mortgage loan. What will the discount factor for mortgages be? (See Appendix 13B.)

✓24. Will the following events increase, decrease, or leave the mortgage rate unchanged? (See Appendix 13B.)

a. The Fed lowers the interest rate because of a slowdown in economic activity.

b. Technological changes reduce the costs of servicing mortgage loans.

c. The default rate on mortgages increases because of falling property values.

Suggested Readings

Information regarding Treasury securities and auctions can be found on the Treasury's Web site at **http://www.treas.gov**.

The New York Fed describes the operation of the Treasury STRIPS program at **http://www.newyorkfed.org/about thefed/fedpoint/fed42.html**.

Basic information about inflation-indexed bonds can be found at **http://www.treasurydirect.gov/indiv/products/prod_tips_glance.htm**.

Information about FHA loans is available at **http://www.hud.gov/buying/index.cfm**; information about VA loans is available at **http://www.homeloans.va.gov/**.

Find information on the operations of the GNMA (Ginnie Mae) at **http://www.ginniemae.gov**.

Information about Fannie Mae and Freddie Mac can be found online at **http://www.fanniemae.com** and **http://www.freddiemac.com**.

Mortgage rates, the size of mortgage you can afford, and a payment calculator are available online at **http://www.mortgagequotes.com/**. Another site with similar information is **http://www.mtgprofessor.com/**.

For an insightful analysis of the "subprime mortgage meltdown" and its general impact on U.S. Debt markets, read the testimony of Sheila C. Bair, Chairman, Federal Deposit Insurance Corporation, before the Financial Services Committee, U.S. House of Representatives, on April 17, 2007 and again on September 5, 2007, available at **http://www.fdic.gov/news/news/speeches/**.

For a private-sector view of the mortgage difficulties and their impact on the economy, see "Meeting the Challenge: The Role of Real Estate Finance in Our Nation's Economy—A Report to the 110th Congress from the Mortgage Bankers Association," available at **http://www.mortgagebankers.org/files/Advocacy/2007PolicyAgenda-MeetingtheChallenge.pdf**.

To learn about Government-Sponsored Enterprises (GSEs) such as Fannie Mae and Freddy Mac, as well as residential mortgage-backed securities, visit the Web site of their former regulator, and current conservator, the Office of Federal Housing Enterprise Oversight (OFHEO), and read their working papers and annual report to Congress, available online at **http://www.ofheo.gov/**.

For a fresh and insightful discussion of the importance of the housing market for business cycles, see "Housing IS the Business Cycle," by Edward E. Leamer, NBER Working Paper No. 13428, 2007.

For a look at how the Federal Reserve Chairman views the economy in light of the mortgage market difficulties, see Ben Bernanke's January 10, 2008, speech, "Financial Markets, the Economic Outlook, and Monetary Policy," available online at **http://www.federalreserve.gov/newsevents/speech/bernanke20080110a.htm**.

To help understand inflation-indexed debt, see Brian Sack and Robert Elsasser, "Treasury Inflation-Indexed Debt: A Review of the U.S. Experience," *Economic Policy Review*, Federal Reserve Bank of New York (May 2004): 47–63.

For a complete look at all aspects of the bond market, see Frank J. Fabozzi, *Bond Markets: Analysis and Strategies*, 5th ed. (Upper Saddle River, NJ: Prentice Hall, 2004).

For a discussion of high-yield (junk) bonds, see Glenn Yago, *Beyond Junk Bonds: Expanding High-Yield Markets* (New York: Oxford University Press, 2003).

For an article that gives some perspective on the international bond market, see Jane D'Arista, "Assessing International Banking and Bond Markets," *Capital Flows Monitor* (December 19, 2000).

Mortgage-backed securities are the subject of "Remarks by Alan Greenspan," before a conference on mortgage markets and economic activity sponsored by America's Community Bankers, Washington, DC (November 2, 1999). Greenspan is a former Federal Reserve Chairman and the individual who some believe aided and abetted the housing price increase and related mortgage meltdown. His remarks are available on the Fed's Web site at **http://www.federalreserve.gov/board-docs/speeches/1999/19991102.htm.** It is instructive to compare his early comments with those after the housing bubble burst, for example in: "A Disappointed Greenspan Lashes out at Bush's Economic Policies," *The New York Times*, September 17, 2007, or in his memoir, *The Age of Turbulence: Adventures in a New World* (New York: Penguin, 2007).

A New York Fed publication on zero-coupon bonds (Fedpoint 42) is available online at **http://www.newyorkfed .org/aboutthefed/fedpoint/fed42.html.**

Appendix 13A
Factors That Affect Bond Prices

As you first saw in Chapter 5, the present value of the future income stream determines the price at which a bond currently trades, and this value is determined by the current interest rate, not the coupon rate. When interest rates change, prices of previously issued bonds change.

To find its present value and, thus, the price at which the bond trades in financial markets, we need to compute the present value of each coupon payment and the present value of the final repayment of the face value on the maturity date. The appropriate discount factor is the current interest rate on a security of equal risk, liquidity, and maturity.

The formula for the price of a previously issued bond is depicted in Equation (13A-1):

(13A-1) $$P = C_1/(1+i)^1 + C_2/(1+i)^2 + \ldots + (C_n + i)^n + F/(1+i)^n$$

where P = the price (present value) of the bond,
C = the coupon payment on the bond (C_1 in year 1, C_2 in year 2, etc.),
F = the face or par value of the bond,
i = the interest rate, and
n = the number of years to maturity (on a five-year bond, $n = 5$).

You can see that the price of a bond is equal to its par value only when the coupon rate is equal to the current interest rate.

The formula in Equation (13A-1) for determining bond prices is based on annual coupon payments. In reality, bonds usually make semiannual coupon payments.

When a bond pays semiannual coupon payments of $C/2$ (assuming that C is the annual coupon payment), and when this bond has n years to maturity, then $2 \times n$ payments (two payments per n year) will be made. The final payment at the end of n years will be equal to F. To find the present value (P) of the stream of income, we divide the interest rate (i) by 2, because two payments of $i/2$ over the course of the year will be equal to i. For example, if the coupon rate were 8 percent, then two semiannual payments of 4 percent would approximate an 8 percent annual return. The approximate discount factor for the final payment (F) is again $i/2$ because we are considering $2n$ periods.

Equation (13A-2) becomes

(13A-3) $$P = C/2/(1 + i/2)^1 + C/2/(1 + i/2)^{2n} + \ldots + (C/2 + i/2)^n + F/(1 + i/2)^{2n}$$

where P = the price (present value) of the bond,
   $C/2$ = the semiannual coupon payment on the bond,
   F = the face or par value of the bond,
   i = the interest rate, and
   $2n$ = the number of six-month periods to maturity (on a bond with five years to maturity, $n = 10$).

Note that we used the word *approximate* because semiannual coupon payments of 4 percent would be more than an 8 percent annual return if the effects of compounding are taken into account. That is, because the coupon payment made in the first half of the year would earn interest during the second six-month period, the annual return would actually be more than 8 percent.

In the case of bonds, the expected future cash flows (the coupon payment and the repayment of the face value at maturity) are known with certainty unless the corporation or government entity runs into financial difficulties and cannot meet its obligations. That is, unless the issuer defaults, the interest payments and the principal payments are known in advance, and there is no chance that they will be more or less. This is different from the case of stocks, whose cash flow payments in the form of dividends are uncertain.

Because of the federal government's power to print money and to tax, Treasuries are considered to be default risk free, and the long-term government bond rate has been regarded as the risk-free rate. In the case of Treasuries, the current Treasury bond rate is the discount factor that is used to find the prices of bonds with equivalent maturities. Thus, to find the price an investor would be willing to pay for a stream of income from a Treasury that has 10 years to maturity, the appropriate discount factor to use is the 10-year Treasury bond rate.

Many factors affect the risk-free rate. One of the most important is the stance of monetary policy. If the Fed increases the supply of reserves, short-term interest rates fall, and the supply of credit is expanded; long-term interest rates will usually fall as well, but by a smaller amount. Changes in inflationary expectations and the level of economic activity also affect long-term risk-free interest rates. If it is expected that inflation will increase in the coming years, then bond purchasers will require—and borrowers will be willing to pay—an inflation premium to compensate for the loss in purchasing power. Likewise, if income is increasing, this increases the demand for loanable funds and puts upward pressure on interest rates. In the real world, these factors are interrelated. For example, expansionary monetary policy may cause market participants to expect higher inflation. Rather than leading to lower interest rates, interest rates may rise despite the expansionary monetary policy. Likewise, a recession brought on by higher oil prices may lead to higher interest rates if the impact of the higher oil prices affects inflationary expectations more than the drop in income does. Other factors such as international capital flows and the amount of government borrowing also impact interest rates.

In the case of bonds that are not default risk free, investors require that a risk premium be added to the risk-free return. The sum of the risk-free return plus the risk premium will equal the appropriate discount factor to use in determining the price of a bond, as depicted in Equation (13A-2).

Factors That Affect the Risk-Free Rate	Factors That Affect the Risk Premium
• The stance of monetary policy • Changes in inflationary expectations • Changes in the level of economic activity • Changes in capital inflows • Changes in government borrowing	• The credit rating of the bond as determined by Moody's and Standard & Poor's • The economic outlook • The capital structure of the firm • Other firm-specific conditions • Losses in international markets

(13A-2)

$$d = R_F + R_P$$

where d is the discount factor, R_F is the risk-free rate, and R_P is the risk premium.

The question that remains is how the risk premium is determined. That is, what is the risk premium that investors require as compensation in order to purchase the bonds rather than Treasuries? A major factor that affects the ability of the bond issuer to make payments as prescribed is the level of economic activity. In a booming economy, sales, revenues, and cash flows all facilitate the timely payment of the corporation's obligations. Likewise, in a recession or depression, cash flows may fall short of what's needed to meet scheduled payments.

The capital structure of a firm is composed of debt and equity. Debt reflects borrowing, whereas equity reflects ownership in the form of stocks. The riskiness of a firm's capital structure is reflected by the firm's debt relative to its equity. Other things being equal, the higher the debt relative to equity, the greater the risk to bondholders and the higher the risk premium will be. The reason is that if a highly leveraged firm experiences a substantial decline in earnings, it may default on its debt obligations and be forced into bankruptcy. A firm with low debt relative to equity could weather a decline in earnings by cutting dividends to stockholders, which are residual claims, not contractual obligations. The highly leveraged firm does not have this option: it must pay its debt costs or fold. Therefore, firms that have considerable debt relative to equity will find the cost of debt financing relatively high.

Finally, there can be other firm- or industry-specific conditions that can affect the ability of a corporation to meet its debt obligations. To the extent that these factors exist, the risk premium is affected. Some of these factors are labor disputes, lawsuits such as those against the tobacco industry, losses in international markets, and oil shortages.

As you may have guessed, the credit rating of the issuing corporation will affect the risk premium because it should capture the firm, industry, and economic risk factors.

The factors that affect the risk-free return and the risk premium are summarized in Exhibit 13A-1.

Present-value tables and financial calculators can be used to simplify the process of finding bond prices.

Recap

The price of a bond is the discounted value of the future stream of income over the life of the bond. The discount factor used to determine the price of a bond includes a risk-free rate and a risk premium. Treasury bonds are considered to pay a risk-free rate of return. The risk premium encompasses both economy-wide and firm- or industry-specific risks.

Appendix 13B
Determinants of the Price of Mortgages in Secondary Markets

A large and active secondary market exists for mortgages and mortgage-backed securities. In this appendix, we discuss how the price of a previously issued mortgage is determined. Because mortgage-backed securities are, as is obvious, backed by mortgages, we will also be able to conclude how the prices of mortgage-backed securities are determined in secondary markets.

Like bonds, the price of a previously issued mortgage is simply the present value of the future stream of income from the ownership of the security. This consists of the monthly payment stream that includes both an interest and principal payment as depicted in Equation (13B-1).

(13B-1) $$P_M = MP/(1 + d_M)^n$$

where P_M = the price at which the security will trade in the secondary market,
  MP = the monthly payment (including both principal and interest),
  d_M = the monthly discount factor required by lenders in this market, and
  n = the number of months remaining on the loan.

Once the mortgage has been made, the original interest rate becomes irrelevant. Only the remaining monthly payments and the current discount factor are relevant in determining the mortgage's present value and, hence, the price at which the mortgage will trade.

Note that in Equation (13B-1), because we are considering monthly payments instead of annual payments, d_M represents the monthly discount factor. To find the monthly discount factor, d_M, we merely divide the annualized discount factor, d_M, by 12. For example, a mortgage with five years remaining to maturity would have 60 more monthly payments, payment one through 60 spread over five years. If the annualized discount factor is 9 percent, the monthly discount factor is .75 percent (9/12). The payment at the end of the first remaining year is the 12th payment and the present value of this payment is $MP/(1 + .0075)^{12}$. If annual payments (AP) were made instead of monthly payments, there would be five annual payments remaining, and the present value at the end of the first remaining year would be $AP/(1 + .09)^1$.

To find the price at which the mortgage will trade in financial markets, we need to compute the present value of each monthly payment remaining. The appropriate discount factor is the current interest rate on a security of equal risk, liquidity, servicing costs, and maturity. As noted before, servicing costs are the costs associated with collecting the monthly payments.

Because mortgages require the handling of monthly payments of principal and interest, mortgages have higher servicing costs than Treasury securities that make semiannual coupon payments. Lenders in the mortgage market must be compensated for these higher costs.

As summarized in Equation (13B-2), the annualized discount factor that is used to determine the present value includes three components: a risk-free return, a risk premium, and a premium for the higher servicing costs that mortgages entail:

(13B-2) $$d_M = r_F + r_P + r_{SC}$$

The risk-free return is composed of the return on a Treasury security of comparable maturity.[5] When the risk-free interest rate changes, the discount factor and, hence, the prices of previously issued mortgages also change.

The risk premium includes the return that the investor needs to be compensated for given the increased riskiness of owning mortgages. The risk premium includes compensation to the lender for the following possibilities:

- The borrower will default.
- The loan will be prepaid early when reinvestment possibilities for the lender are less favorable than when the mortgage was originally made.
- The lower liquidity of mortgages compared to Treasury securities will cause the lender to experience losses.

When the mortgage is federally insured, the risk premium will be lower than otherwise because the default risk is zero. In this case, the risk premium will include compensation for the prepayment risk and the lower liquidity of mortgages.

Treasury securities are considered to be default risk free, and the long-term government bond rate has been regarded as the risk-free interest rate. As noted earlier, the 10-year Treasury note rate has recently replaced the 30-year Treasury bond rate as the benchmark risk-free rate.

Many factors affect the risk-free rate. One of the most important factors is the stance of monetary policy. If the Fed increases the supply of reserves, short-term interest rates fall and the supply of credit expands. Ceteris paribus, long-term interest rates will fall, but usually not by as much as short-term rates. Changes in inflationary expectations and the level of economic activity also affect the long-term risk-free interest rate. If it is expected that inflation will increase in the coming years, lenders will require and borrowers will be willing to pay an inflation premium to compensate for the loss in purchasing power. Likewise, if income is increasing, this increases the demand for loanable funds and, ceteris paribus, puts upward pressure on interest rates.

In the real world, the factors that affect the risk-free interest rate are interrelated. For example, expansionary monetary policy may cause market participants to expect higher inflation. Rather than leading to lower interest rates, interest rates may rise despite the expansionary monetary policy. Likewise, a recession brought on by higher oil prices may lead to higher interest rates if the impact of the higher oil prices affects infla-

---

13B-1

Factors That Affect the Discount Factor for Mortgages

Factors That Affect the Risk-Free Rate
- The stance of monetary policy
- Changes in inflationary expectations
- Changes in the economic outlook and the level of economic activity
- Changes in government borrowing

Factors That Affect the Risk Premium
- Changes in the economic outlook and the level of economic activity (pertains to uninsured mortgages only)
- The prepayment risk that the mortgage will be prepaid early and that the reinvestment options for the lender will be less desirable than when the original mortgage was made (pertains to insured and uninsured mortgages)
- Changes in the relative liquidity of mortgages and mortgage-backed securities relative to Treasury securities

Factors That Affect Servicing Costs
- Any factors that affect the servicing costs of the loan such as changes in technology that reduce servicing costs

tionary expectations more than the drop in income. Other factors such as international capital flows and the amount of government borrowing also impact interest rates.

The risk premium with which investors need to be compensated in order to purchase the mortgages is affected by the borrower's ability to make the monthly payment. For insured mortgages, the risk premium is much lower than for uninsured mortgages. For uninsured mortgages, a major factor affecting the risk premium is the level of economic activity. In a booming economy, incomes and economic activity are increasing, thus reducing the number of defaults in the mortgage market. Likewise, in a booming economy, interest rates rise as does the prepayment risk. The reverse is true in downturns.

Changes in technology due to innovations reduce servicing costs. An example of such an innovation is the development of automatic payment deductions from a borrower's checking account. This saves the costs of sending out monthly statements and collecting and processing checks.

The factors that affect the discount factor are summarized in Exhibit 13B-1.

Note that as the economic outlook and the level of economic activity improve, the risk-free rate rises while the risk premium falls, and vice versa. Hopefully, you can explain why.

Recap
The price of a mortgage is the discounted value of the future stream of monthly payments over the remaining life of the loan. The price of a mortgage-backed security is based on the prices of the mortgages in the pool that backs the security. The discount factor includes a risk-free rate, a risk premium, and a premium for the higher servicing costs that mortgages entail. Treasury securities are considered to pay a risk-free rate of return. The risk premium encompasses economy-wide risks, the risk that the mortgage may be prepaid early when investment opportunities for the lender are less favorable, and a premium for the lower liquidity of mortgages. The premium for the higher servicing costs of mortgages is affected by changes in technology that reduce servicing costs.

Endnotes

1. Even though outstanding mortgages are the largest debt instrument, the value of equities (stocks) has in recent years exceeded the value of mortgages by a substantial amount. The reason is that as new mortgages are issued, old mortgages continue to mature, whereas equities have no maturity date. For example, on September 30, 2008, the outstanding value of domestic equities was just under $19.7 trillion, while the outstanding value of mortgages was about $14.7 trillion.
2. Zero-coupon bonds are similar to Treasury bills that are also sold at a discount.
3. As discussed in Chapter 6, the marginal tax rate is the tax rate on the last dollar of taxable income. Because the United States has a progressive income tax, the tax rate rises as income rises. Taxpayers, depending on their individual incomes, are in different marginal tax brackets, some high and some low. The average marginal tax rate is somewhere between the high and the low marginal tax brackets for all taxpayers. Because of substitution, the interest rate on municipal securities will gravitate to the rate that makes the average taxpayer (in the average marginal tax bracket) indifferent between municipals and similarly rated corporate securities.
4. The alternative to an amortized loan would be to make interest-only payments and to repay the principal in a balloon payment at the end of the loan. Although common prior to the Great Depression, this is unusual, but became more common again in the housing boom of 2004–2008 in the mortgage market.
5. The comparable maturity for a Treasury security and a mortgage are not the same as the terms to maturity. For example, because a 30-year mortgage payment includes both a principal and interest payment each month, the comparable term of the mortgage will actually be less than a 30-year Treasury that does not repay any of the principal until the end of 30 years.

Buy low, sell high!

The Stock Market

Learning Objectives

After reading this chapter, you should know:

The major characteristics of the stock market

How the organized exchanges and over-the-counter markets function

What the various stock indexes are and what each measures

How the value of a share of stock is determined

SPECULATIVE BUBBLES AND THEIR EFFECTS ON THE ECONOMY

In the past, a text on the financial system and the economy would not routinely include a chapter on the stock market, nor would it include a chapter on the bond and mortgage markets (Chapter 13). Such chapters would more likely be found in a text dealing specifically with capital market assets. Texts on the financial system traditionally focused on the banking system. So why include such chapters here?

At this time, there are compelling reasons to include chapters on the stock, bond, and mortgage markets—reasons that relate to the recent price volatility of these assets and the changing structure of capital markets. Many readers are likely aware of recent stock market ups and downs. The late 1990s saw a record stock market boom. Stock prices underwent dramatic increases despite some sharp sell-offs. Technological changes in the transfer of funds, increased globalization of financial markets, and other structural changes in the economy facilitated the flow of funds into equity investments around the world. In the early 2000s, the stock market collapsed when faltering economies, here at home and abroad, could not support the stratospheric prices of the late 1990s. Stock prices zoomed upward again in the period between 2003 and 2007 before dropping about 45 percent between October 2007 and January 2009.

At the same time, more households than ever were and are investing in the stock market, whether directly through brokers, employers, or online or indirectly through savings or retirement plans. In 2009, more than 100 million Americans owned shares of stock through individual investments or through mutual funds.

When stock price movements are more pronounced, as in the late 1990s, stock markets have greater potential for speculative bubbles that cannot be sustained. A **speculative bubble** is an irrational increase in prices accompanied by euphoric expectations. As you saw in Chapter 11, when market participants realize that the speculative bubble cannot be maintained, they tend to liquidate their positions, with the result that prices fall to lower levels than had the bubble not occurred in the first place. Such volatility in stock prices can cause financial instability as gains and losses are magnified. When the bubble bursts, as it did in the early 2000s, the resulting financial losses may spill over into the real sector, causing or contributing to unemployment and recession.

In Chapter 3, you saw that the Fed attempts to minimize fluctuations in output and prices around a long-term trend. In that chapter, we were concerned about output prices of goods and services. But, as the preceding discussion implies, the Fed must also be concerned about unstable stock and real estate prices. Volatile stock and real estate prices can affect employment, inflation, and the health and stability of the financial system. If a speculative bubble bursts and stock or real estate prices tumble, the real sector can be adversely affected for a considerable time. *The Economist* magazine aptly stated: "Just as champagne tastes wonderful until the bubbles go to your head, so financial bubbles tend to create nasty economic hangovers."[1]

The stock market rally of the late 1990s was interrupted briefly by a worldwide collapse of stock prices in October 1998. By early 1999, the market had fully recovered. In early 2000, the market reached a cyclical bull high and then turned down. An economic downturn began in early 2001 and was exacerbated by the attack on the World Trade Center and the Pentagon on September 11, 2001. The market experienced three down years (2000, 2001, and 2002) and the worst bear market in history. By the end of 2002, stock markets had bottomed, and stock prices began an upward trend in 2003, which continued until October 2007. Over this five-year period, the Dow Jones Industrial Average, the most famous measure of average stock prices, had nearly doubled. However, as noted earlier, in 2008 stocks were caught up in the same financial crisis as other financial markets. The precipitous drop in prices was due more to the financial crisis of

Speculative Bubble

An irrational increase in stock prices accompanied by euphoric expectations.

How Volatile Asset Prices Affect the Economy

In late 2008, it appeared the U.S. economy may be heading for (or in) a deep recession due to the ongoing financial crisis. The crisis began with falling real estate prices, which led to the collapse of the subprime mortgage and mortgage-backed securities markets and quickly spread to other domestic and global financial markets and assets. The United States had last experienced a recession in 2001, and the primary cause of this downturn seems to have been declining stock prices.

The 2001 recession ended a U.S. expansion of more than 10 years. Many analysts attribute part of the downturn to the cataclysmic collapse of the overvalued stock markets that began in 2000.[a] Stock prices, led by dot.com[b] and technology stocks, experienced record increases in the late 1990s. Some analysts believed that stocks were overvalued as early as 1995. Between 1995 and 2000, stock prices more than doubled. By 2000, it was becoming clear that stock valuations were in a speculative bubble. Markets collapsed, with the dot.com and technology sectors experiencing the largest and earliest price declines. The Federal Reserve Board responded by lowering interest rates 11 times in 2001. As noted earlier, the stock markets hit bottom by early 2003 but then recovered, with major stock indices nearly doubling from 2003 to 2007. This period of increasing stock prices seems to have been fueled by low interest rates and the interrelated general economic recovery. Low interest rates also fueled the housing market and resulted in increasing real estate prices. By late 2007, it appeared the real estate bubble was "bursting," just as some economists had been predicting. While falling stock prices may have caused the 2001 recession, falling home prices seemed primarily responsible for the downturn and eventual financial collapse in 2008.

Given these trends, it seems apparent that asset prices are undergoing more pronounced fluctuations than in the past. Some of the reasons for this could be technological modifications in how funds are transferred and other structural changes in capital markets.[c] For example, technological improvements in electronic funds transfer systems and increased globalization of capital markets allow funds to flow more freely and quickly around the world. Although this increased the efficiency of financial markets, the speed with which financial flows could occur increased price swings. Other innovations, such as securitization of mortgage loans, have also made financial assets more liquid than in the past. At the same time, more households than ever before are investing in the capital markets, whether directly through a broker, through their employer, or online, or indirectly through a savings or retirement plan. And in recent years, an unprecedented number of homeowners have refinanced their homes in order to extract funds from them to be used for consumption, home renovation, or other investments.

Volatile asset prices can affect the real sector via several channels. One channel is the link between changes in asset prices and wealth. When asset prices increase, nominal wealth increases. The increases in wealth, in turn, can lead to spending increases in the goods and services markets and a willingness to take on more debt. Exclusive shops on Rodeo Drive in Beverly Hills had exceptional years in the late 1990s after the historic run-up of stock prices. Apparently investors spent some of their profits on high-end luxury items or increased their level of debt to purchase luxury items. Similarly, the less affluent may notice large increases in the value of their retirement accounts, feel better off as a result, and therefore consume more now.

These increases in spending and debt in response to gains in wealth speed up the level of economic activity. If sustained, the increases in demand can also cause prices in the goods and services market to rise. Thus, inflation in asset markets may, after some time, spill over to cause inflation in the goods and services sector.

The flip side, of course, is that decreases in asset prices can trigger declines in spending and, eventually, price reductions in the goods and services markets. For example, if the value of an individual's stock portfolio falls from $100,000 to $50,000 when the market crashes, they experience a drop in wealth and subsequently may not take an expensive trip they had been planning. The reduced demand for vacation trips will slow economic activity and lead to prices being lower than they would otherwise have been. If asset prices are stable or change slowly, these spillovers do not affect spending, saving, borrowing, and lending decisions as dramatically as when asset prices are more unstable.

Volatile stock and real estate prices also affect the real sector through their effect on financial institutions and the financial system. The solvency of any institution that holds large amounts of stocks, bonds, and mortgages could be threatened if prices fall unexpectedly and significantly. Financial institutions, in particular, may see the value of their assets decline sharply, while their liabilities, which are denominated in dollars, do not fall in value. Entire industries may be affected. For example, the U.S. savings and loan industry experienced enormous losses in the 1980s because of declines in the value of mortgages and other capital market assets. The value of mortgages can fall when declining real estate values cause some borrowers to default, or when rising interest rates decrease the value of outstanding mortgages. The resulting savings and loan crisis caused unemployment and bankruptcies in the industry and required a taxpayer bailout.

In other episodes, globalized financial markets have facilitated capital flows that ultimately contributed to speculative bubbles. The Mexican financial crisis of 1994–1995 and the Asian financial crisis of the late 1990s are examples of situations in which stocks, supported by large capital inflows, became overvalued. When exchange rates could not be maintained, what began as currency crises quickly spread to other markets. Stock, bond, and real estate prices plummeted, causing widespread bankruptcies of financial and nonfinancial firms. The financial systems and real sectors of the affected economies collapsed. Unprecedented international intervention was needed as domestic and international investors withdrew funds from the crippled regions. It became clear that investors were able to reverse capital flows just as quickly as individual consumers were able to cancel their vacation plans when the value of their stock fell.

Endnotes

a. The downward pressure on the U.S. economy was also greatly exacerbated by the attacks on the World Trade Center and the Pentagon on September 11, 2001, and the resulting economic turmoil.

b. Dot.com stocks are those of Internet companies, many of which in the 1990s were small start-up companies that had never earned a profit.

c. In Chapter 6, we saw that prices of long-term fixed rate debt instruments, including bonds and mortgages, fluctuate a great deal in response to small changes in interest rates. Money market assets are short term and do not experience such price volatility when interest rates change. In this and the next chapter, we are referring primarily to capital market assets.

2008 rather than the bursting of a speculative bubble as in the earlier time period. The accompanying "A Closer Look" feature on p. 317 looks more closely at how volatile asset prices affect the economy.

THE ANATOMY OF STOCKS

Firms issue shares of stock when they need to raise long-term financial capital, usually for investment spending. If a corporation is publicly held, shares of stock are sold to the public. A share of stock represents equity in a corporation and entitles the owner to a share of the corporation's profits.[2] The stock may be **preferred stock** or **common stock.** Owners of preferred stock receive a fixed dividend to which they are entitled before owners of common stock can receive anything. The fixed dividend is similar to the interest payment that a bondholder receives. However, dividends must be paid to preferred stockholders only if the corporation earns a profit, whereas the corporation is liable for interest payments under all circumstances. In addition, interest payments to bondholders are tax write-offs for the corporation; dividend payments to preferred stockholders are not.

Common stockholders receive a variable dividend after preferred stockholders have been paid and retained earnings have been set aside. Retained earnings are profits not distributed to stockholders that are usually used to fund investment projects. In the 1990s, some "growth" companies such as Microsoft did not pay dividends. In this case, stockholders benefit from increases in the stock's price generated by putting the earnings back into the company or using the earnings to purchase back the company's own stock. In 2004, the popularity of not paying dividends was adversely affected by legislation that reduces taxation of most dividends received by households.[3] If a company buys back its own stock and does not resell it, the stock is retired. After shares of stock are retired, the remaining outstanding shares tend to appreciate in value. Common stockholders have voting rights within the firm, whereas preferred stockholders do not. Stockholders who own only a minuscule share of the outstanding stock of a firm do not usually exercise voting rights.

Investment bankers usually market new shares of stocks, or securities. One or more securities firms design and market the new securities offering. Sometimes, employees and individuals may purchase new shares of stocks directly from the company, thus bypassing investment banks. Stocks represent liquid claims because the shares can usually be sold relatively easily in secondary markets. Previously issued shares of stock are traded either on organized exchanges or over the counter. As you saw in Chapter 4, the marketing of newly issued shares represents primary market activity while the purchase or sale of previously issued securities represents secondary market activity. "Cracking the Code" deciphers the information about stock prices reported in major newspapers. As noted in Chapter 4, the investment banking industry is undergoing significant change with regards to organization and structure as a result of the financial crisis of 2008.

Households, state and local governments, foreigners, and a variety of financial institutions hold domestically issued stocks. The major financial institutions that own shares of stocks are mutual funds, private and public pension funds, and insurance companies.

Preferred Stock
Restricted equity claims with characteristics of both bonds and common stock. While dividends must be paid to preferred stockholders before common stockholders, preferred dividends are set at a specific level and do not increase if extraordinary profits are earned. Preferred stock holders generally do not have voting rights.

Common Stock
Equity claims representing ownership of the net income and assets of a corporation. Common stock holders are "residual claimants," since their dividends are paid out of profits remaining after payment of interest to lenders and dividends to preferred stock holders. Common stock holders may vote for the Board of Directors, and thus have the potential to exert control over decisions of managers.

The Stock Market **319**

Cracking the Code

The Stock Market

Here is a section from a typical stock page of a major newspaper. To begin cracking the code, look at the following entry for Gap Inc., the popular clothing store.

The name of the company is in the third column, followed by the company ticker symbol and then the regular annual dividend paid by Gap, in this case, $0.08. The price of the stock at the close of the preceding day's trading was $18.86 (from the column labeled Close). The dividend is usually divided by the closing price to get the current yield (or return). The dividend of $.08 divided by the closing price $18.86 gives a current yield of .4 percent ($.08/$18.86=.004%).

The column labeled PE indicates that the ratio of the price per share to the earnings per share of the company—that is, the price-to-earnings (P-E) ratio—is 19.92. The higher the earnings per share of the company

(given the price of the stock), the lower the ratio. Stocks with low PE ratios compared to other firms in the industry are sometimes thought to be undervalued, and stocks with high PE ratios are thought to be overvalued.

The Vol column tells us the number of shares traded (in hundreds) on a given day. Thus, 64162 means that 6,416,200 shares of Gap were traded on this particular day. The price of the stock at the close was, as mentioned, $18.86. In the last column, the closing price per share was down 0.16 ($0.16) from the close of the previous day.

To the left of the company's name are two columns headed High and Low. These are the high and low prices of the stock for the last 52 weeks. Gap had traded at a low price of 15.20 ($15.20) and at a high price of 21.39 ($21.39). Those of you who bought at 15.20 ($15.20) can smile.

52 Weeks

High	Low	Stock	Sym	Div	Yld.%	PE	Vol 100s	Close	Net Change
21.39	15.20	Gap Inc	GPS	0.08	0.4	19.92	64162	18.86	−.16

Source: The Wall Street Journal (October 16, 2007).

The value of corporate equities increased dramatically in the 1990s, reversed course in the early 2000s, resumed rising after 2003, and then fell dramatically from July 2007 until this writing in January 2009. Exhibit 14-1 traces the outstanding value of corporate equities since 1982.

After the banner years of the 1990s, stocks did not fare as well in the early 2000s, when the value of outstanding corporate equities fell for three consecutive years to just under $11 trillion by the end of the third quarter 2002. As noted earlier, in early 2003, the market again began rising and continued its upward trend until July 2007. On September 30, 2007, the outstanding value of domestic corporate equities was over $26 trillion. This was up from $11.9 trillion just five years earlier and from $2.6 trillion twenty years earlier.

In 2008 stock prices experienced large fluctuations and moved dramatically downward as the financial crises, the government bailout of the financial system, and the likelihood of a deep recession filled headlines. By the end of the third quarter of 2008, the value of outstanding corporate equities had fallen to $19.6 trillion.

Securities and Exchange Commission (SEC)

A government agency created by the Securities and Exchange Act of 1934 that regulates disclosure rules for companies that issue publicly traded shares of stock.

All companies that issue publicly traded shares of stock are regulated by the Securities and Exchange Commission (SEC), which was created by the Securities and Exchange Act of 1934. The SEC has broad disclosure requirements to protect investors by requiring companies to file numerous reports detailing their financial condition, information about key personnel, and any changes that would be important to stockholders. The SEC also has extensive authority to regulate secondary market activities.

14-1

The Value of Outstanding
Shares of Domestically
Issued Stock Since 1982
(Billions of Dollars at
Year's End)

Year	Corporate Equities
1982	$1,562.5
1983	1,856.0
1984	1,789.2
1985	2,270.4
1986	2,682.6
1987	2,710.3
1988	3,076.3
1989	3,819.7
1990	3,542.6
1991	4,863.4
1992	5,430.9
1993	6,306.2
1994	6,333.3
1995	8,495.7
1996	10,255.8
1997	13,201.3
1998	15,427.8
1999	19,522.8
2000	17,627.0
2001	15,310.6
2002	11,900.5
2003	15,618.5
2004	17,389.3
2005	18,512.0
2006	20,016.8
2007	22,445.0
2008*	16,023.8

*As of September 30, 2008.
Source: Flow of Funds of the United States, Z.1, Board of Governors of the Federal Reserve System, various issues.

STOCK OFFERINGS

Initial Public Offering (IPO)
When a corporation issues stocks publicly for the first time.

An initial public offering (IPO) is public offering of stock by a corporation for the first time. Many companies that have gone public in recent years are well known to college students. Some of them are Ben and Jerry's Ice Cream, California Pizza Kitchen, Martha Stewart Living, Omnimedia, Guess? and Krispy Kreme Doughnuts, as well as a rash of Internet start-up companies such as Google in 2004 and NetSuite in 2007. Stock prices often move dramatically on the first day of trading. For example, on the first day of trading, California Pizza Kitchen's stock jumped 35 percent, Krispy Kreme Doughnuts' stock jumped 75 percent, and Red Hat, Inc., an Internet company, saw its stock jump more than 80 percent. But these returns look puny compared to Google, whose stock rose from an initial $85 in August 2004 to $491.52 by mid-August 2007, a 478 percent return over a three-year period. On January 30, 2009, Google opened at $344.69 a share.

But the experience of the Internet offerings of the late 1990s teaches a sobering lesson. Most of their price jumps did not last through a general downturn in Internet stocks in mid-2000. For example, Red Hat debuted in mid-1999 at $15 a share, rose to $151.31 by late 1999, fell to $3.81 a share by August 10, 2001, and was trading at $14.70 a share on January 30, 2009.

Secondary Stock Offering
An offering of newly issued shares by a firm that already has outstanding publicly held shares.

A secondary stock offering is an offering of newly issued shares by a firm that already has outstanding publicly held shares. To bring new shares to the market, a

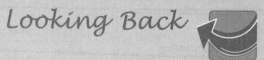

Looking Back

Famous Financial Quotations

"Stock prices could double, triple, or even quadruple tomorrow and still not be too high. Stocks are now, we believe, in the midst of a one-time-only rise to much higher ground—to the neighborhood of 36,000 for the Dow Jones Industrial Average."

—James K. Glassman and Kevin A. Hasset, "Dow 36000,"
The Atlantic Online (September 1999), http://www.theatlantic.com

"In a [stock] market like this, every story is a positive one. Any news is good news. It's pretty much taken for granted now that the market is going to go up."

—*The Wall Street Journal* (August 26, 1987), less than
two months before the largest percentage drop in stock prices in history

Although there have been many stock market crashes, the most famous occurred in 1929, heralding the Great Depression. Although it was not known at the time, output had actually turned down before the market crashed. The market crash came at the end of a decade of rising stock prices and what many now realize was a speculative bubble. The following are some quotations from around that time:

"There will be no interruption of our permanent prosperity."

—Myron E. Forbes, president, Pierce Arrow Motor Car Co. (January 12, 1928)

"I cannot help but raise a dissenting voice to statements that we are living in a fool's paradise, and that prosperity in this country must necessarily diminish and recede in the near future."

—E.H. Simmons, president, New York Stock Exchange (January 12, 1928)

"Stock prices have reached what looks like a permanently high plateau. I do not feel that there will soon, if ever, be a fifty- or sixty-point break below present levels, such as Mr. Babson has predicted. I expect to see the stock market a great deal higher than it is today within the next few months."

—Irving Fisher, one of the most prestigious economists
of the day (October 16, 1929)

"I believe that the breaks of the last few days have driven stock prices down to hard rock. I believe that we will have a ragged market for a few weeks and then the beginning of a mild bull movement that will gain momentum next year."

—Irving Fisher (October 22, 1929)

Shelf Registration
A procedure that permits a company to register a number of securities with the SEC and sell them over a two-year period rather than at the time of registration.

corporation must register the new issue with the SEC. Since 1982, the SEC has allowed corporations to register securities without immediately issuing them; this procedure is called shelf registration. Shelf registration permits a company to register a number of securities and sell them over a two-year period rather than at the time the shares are registered. This avoids the costs in time and money of several registration processes and allows the firm to respond quickly to advantageous market conditions.

Stocks represent equity in a corporation. Preferred stockholders receive a fixed dividend, and common stockholders receive a variable or no dividend. Firms issue stock to raise funds for long-term investment spending. An IPO is a public offering of newly issued stocks by a corporation that has not previously sold stocks to the public. A secondary stock offering is an offering of newly issued stocks by a firm that has publicly held stocks outstanding. Shelf registration permits a company to register new shares of stocks at the present time but to issue the new shares over a two-year period.

THE STOCK MARKETS

When most people think about the stock market, they think of New York City's Wall Street, an actual street in South Manhattan that is home to New York's financial district and is also the nation's financial center. For financial market participants, however, Wall Street has a much broader connotation that includes many different organized stock exchanges and a nationwide network of brokers and dealers who buy and sell stock over the counter. In recent years, the volume and values of stocks traded—whether on exchanges or over the counter—have increased dramatically. Large institutional investors such as pension funds, insurance companies, and mutual funds have come to dominate the market. The institutional investors tend to trade large blocks of stocks (more than 10,000 shares of a given stock or trades with a market value higher than $200,000). Institutional investors, who owned only 7.2 percent of all equities in 1950, now own over 60 percent of the market valuation of all stock. The expanded use of computers to execute trades has accommodated the increased volume of trading and facilitated an increase in program trading by institutional investors. Program trading allows institutional investors to preprogram computers to buy or sell a large number (basket) of stocks. The NYSE has recently changed the way it measures the amount of program trading. Using current mythology which results in lower values, approximately 30–35 percent of trades were the result of program trading in the early weeks of 2009.

Program Trading
The preprogramming of computers to buy or sell a large number (basket) of stocks, usually by institutional investors.

Despite the increase in institutional trading, a higher percentage of households have a stake in the stock market than ever before, usually through retirement funds, direct ownership, or ownership of mutual funds. In 1989, only 31.6 percent of households owned stock in some form, but by late 2007 that percentage had increased to more than 50 percent. While high, this percentage is still less than the comparable figure of 62 percent for home ownership. As of September 30, 2007, households owned stocks and mutual funds valued over $11.29 trillion. As Exhibit 14-2 shows, investing in the stock market has over time paid a higher total return than investing in the bond market or purchasing other financial assets. Other factors being equal, ownership of stocks entails a greater risk than ownership of bonds or other financial assets. Even though there is a higher expected return with stock ownership, there is no guarantee that any given investment will realize a higher return. Moreover, most financial assets issued by depository institutions offer the added advantage of deposit insurance. Stockholders own the excess, whether paid out in dividends or not, of what is left over after bondholders and other creditors have been paid fixed obligations. The residual may be huge, but then again it may fall short of expectations.

Margin Requirement
The percentage of invested funds that can be borrowed as opposed to being paid in readily available funds; currently, margin requirements are set by the Fed at 50 percent.

Investors do not have to put up funds equal to the full value of a stock purchase. Instead, they can purchase stocks on the margin ("buying on the margin") by borrowing. The **margin requirement** is the percentage of a stock purchase that can be borrowed as opposed to being paid in readily available funds. The current margin requirement, which is set by the Fed, has been 50 percent since 1974, and applies only to initial purchases. Buying on the margin allows an investor to amplify gains when the stock's price

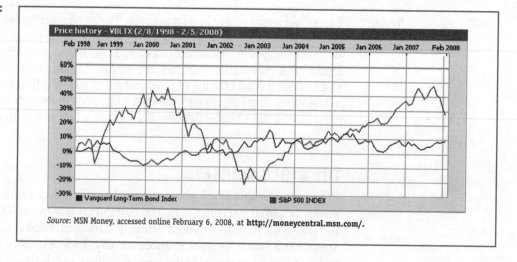

Source: MSN Money, accessed online February 6, 2008, at http://moneycentral.msn.com/.

goes up because the investor has control, in essence, over a larger number of shares. It is thought that margin buying fuels speculation in stocks and can be particularly dangerous in a stock market bubble.

The New York Stock Exchange and the National Association of Securities Dealers require member firms to impose a minimum 25 percent **maintenance margin requirement** (also know as "minimum maintenance" or "maintenance requirement") on their customers. The maintenance margin requirement is the minimum amount of equity the investor needs in his or her account relative to the market value of the stock. The maintenance requirement becomes relevant if the stock has been purchased using borrowed funds and if the stock's value falls so that the investor has less equity than the amount required by the maintenance margin. Many individual brokerage firms set higher margin requirements and vary those requirements, depending on the stocks and trading behavior of individual customers. For example, assume that an investor purchases a share of stock for $100 with $50 of his or her own funds and borrows the rest from a broker. If the stock falls to $80, the owner has $30 equity in the stock, considering that there is a $50 loan. If there is a 25 percent maintenance margin requirement imposed by a broker or the exchange, the owner must have at least $20 (.25×$80) equity in the stock. The owner has $30 equity, so all is well. If the stock falls to $60 per share, the owner's equity falls to $10 ($60 less the $50 loan). Because the owner is required to maintain a 25 percent margin, the owner is required to have $15 (.25×$60) in equity. The owner has only $10 equity, so a margin call for $5 will be made to the owner. If the owner fails to provide the additional funds, the stock will be sold to pay off the loan.

In a falling stock market, buying on the margin can present problems. As noted earlier, if the value of a stock falls to where the lender will put in a margin call that requires the investor to put up more funds, and if the investor fails to do so, the stock is sold at the low price so the lender can recoup part or all of its losses. The selling of the stock to recoup losses puts additional downward pressure on the flagging stock price.

In late 1999 and early 2000, margin credit grew much faster than the overall appreciation of the stock market. By early 2000, margin credit relative to the total value of stocks traded in the market reached a 29-year high. Raising margin requirements has also been proposed as a monetary policy tool to reduce speculative behavior that could fuel a stock market bubble, but the Fed did not choose to exercise this option in the bull market of the late 1990s. It is interesting to consider the similarity with the real estate bubble of 2003–2007, when lower required down payments and increased willingness by borrowers to assume debt and lenders to issue debt fueled price increases.

Maintenance Margin Requirement

The minimum amount of equity the investor needs in his account relative to the market value of his stock.

U.S. markets in the mid- to late 1990s also experienced unprecedented capital inflows to purchase U.S. equities. The magnitude of these inflows is dramatic and is part of the ongoing globalization of financial markets. Exhibit 14-3 shows the dollar value of net non-U.S. purchases of U.S. stocks since 1995.

Only life insurance companies and mutual funds purchased more U.S. equities than did non-U.S. purchasers. The inflows that many attributed to booming U.S. markets also contributed to those booming markets by increasing the demand for stocks. Without the inflow from abroad, demand for U.S. stocks would have been lower and equity prices not as high. Thus, it is difficult to say whether the inflows are the result of booming stock prices or if the inflows caused stock prices to boom. If foreigners sell U.S. equities or slow purchases, prices of U.S. equities will be lower than they otherwise would have been. Indeed, as Exhibit 14-3 shows, foreign purchases of U.S. equities

14-3
Net Non-U.S. Purchases of U.S. Stocks

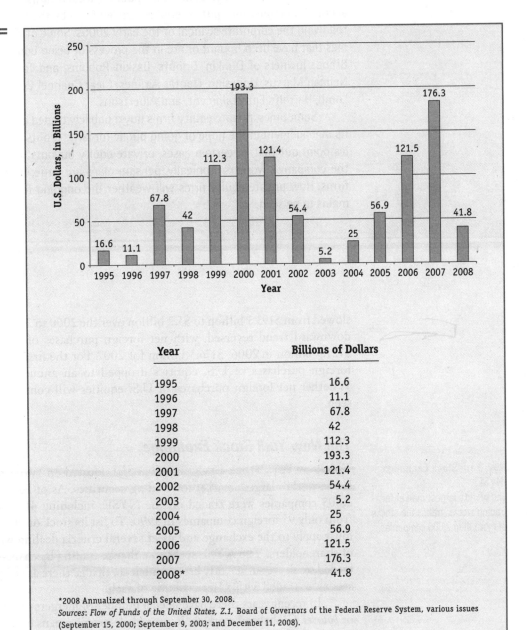

Year	Billions of Dollars
1995	16.6
1996	11.1
1997	67.8
1998	42
1999	112.3
2000	193.3
2001	121.4
2002	54.4
2003	5.2
2004	25
2005	56.9
2006	121.5
2007	176.3
2008*	41.8

*2008 Annualized through September 30, 2008.
Sources: Flow of Funds of the United States, Z.1, Board of Governors of the Federal Reserve System, various issues (September 15, 2000; September 9, 2003; and December 11, 2008).

A Closer Look

Private Equity Funds

Private equity funds have historically been a major source of funding for start-up companies and for firms that are in financial distress. Private equity funds are investment companies that buy publicly held companies and convert them to private ownership—usually through a limited partnership. Although the market for private equity started in the 1960s, it exploded by the middle of the first decade of the 2000s. This represents a significant change in the way corporations are owned. Private equity firms avoid the disclosure regulations that publicly traded firms face. They also avoid the accounting regulations put on publicly traded firms by the Sarbanes-Oxley legislation following the corporate scandal of the early 2000s. Some of the better known companies that have been bought or are in the process of being bought are Chrysler, Dunkin' Brands (owners of Dunkin' Donuts, Baskin-Robbins, and Togo's), Toys "R" Us, Hertz, Neiman Marcus, Univision, Qantas Airlines, Clear Channel Communications, Bausch & Lomb, Harrah's Entertainment, and Albertsons.

Sometimes, private equity firms buy a publicly traded company and then change its management in the hope of going public for large profits in a few years. Some critics point out that, in certain cases, private equity buyouts result in a loss of jobs for the company's workers. Ironically, pension plans are large investors in private equity firms. How private equity firms will weather the ongoing financial crisis of 2008 remains to be seen.

---

slowed from $193.3 billion to $5.2 billion over the 2000 to 2003 period. But in 2004, this downward trend reversed, with net foreign purchases of U.S. equities increasing to $121.5 billion in 2006, $176.3 billion for 2007. For the first three quarters of 2008, net foreign purchases of U.S. equities dropped to an annualized rate of $41.8 billion. Whether net foreign purchases of U.S. equities will continue to drop remains to be seen.

The New York Stock Exchange

New York Stock Exchange (NYSE)
The world's largest market for trading stocks; trades the stocks of more than 2,800 companies.

The New York Stock Exchange (NYSE), located on Wall Street in New York City, is the world's largest market for trading securities. As of February 2008, the stocks of 2,805 companies were traded on the NYSE, including 419 non-U.S. companies—up from only 95 foreign companies in 1990. To list its stock on the NYSE, the corporation must apply to the exchange and meet several criteria dealing with the size and number of shareholders. The NYSE seeks to enhance trading by ensuring that markets for any traded stock are sufficiently broad and deep, that is, there are a large number of different securities traded with a large volume of each.

In recent years there have been a number of mergers of different financial markets or *bourses*. Globalized markets, improved electronic means of trading, and the benefits of known and trusted "brand name" exchanges have all supported this general trend. The

NYSE has been a major player in these consolidations. The following is a list of recent changes that have transformed the NYSE, America's and the world's largest exchange:

- 12/15/05—NYSE Hybrid Market is launched, combining traditional auction and electronic trading.
- 12/30/05—The sale of permanent seats on the NYSE ends.
- 3/7/06—NYSE and ArcaEx (Archipelago Exchange), an online securities exchange used for trading both stocks and options, merge. ArcaEx became NYSE Arca.
- 7/17/06—NYSE Group acquires MatchPoint Trading, Inc., a financial services technology company specializing in call market trading and technologies.
- 9/18/06—NYSE Group buys an ownership stake in Marco Polo Network, an electronic platform for trading equities and derivatives listed on emerging market exchanges.
- 4/4/07—NYSE Group, Inc., and Euronext N.V. merge to form NYSE Euronext. Euronext had itself been previously formed by the merger of exchanges in Paris, Brussels, Amsterdam, and Lisbon, as well as the London International Financial Futures and Options Exchange (LIFFE). This move combines major marketplaces across Europe and the United States with long histories and established reputations.
- 12/11/07—NYSE opens an office in China, having been the first foreign exchange to receive such approval.
- 10/01/08—NYSE Euronext purchases the American Stock Exchange in order to capture a bigger share of the options and fund-trading businesses.

Although NYSE Euronext has become a huge publicly traded company, it still has a significant regulatory independent body.[4]

Each company whose stock is listed on the NYSE "Big Board" is assigned to a single post where a specialist in that stock manages the auction process. Orders for a specific stock are funneled to the appropriate post. If the post is surrounded by more brokers looking to buy the stock than to sell at the existing price, the stock's price will rise. If the reverse is true, the price will fall. In this way, the forces of supply and demand determine prices.

At the NYSE, orders may be electronically delivered to these trading posts, booths, or handheld computers in several different ways. More than 95 percent of buy or sell orders reach the specialist's workstation directly at the trading post via the Designated Order Turnaround System ("SuperDOT"), an electronic order-routing system. After the order has been executed, a report of execution is returned directly to the member

Designated Order Turnaround System (SuperDOT)
A computer system used for trades of fewer than 3,000 shares on the NYSE.

14-4
The Ten Largest Companies (Measured by Market Value) Traded on the Big Board, September 2007

Company Name	Symbol	Market Cap ($ billion)	NYSE Average Daily Volume
Mitsubishi UFJ Financial Group	MTU	$21,861.4	1,929,220
Banco de Chile	BCH	$3,572.9	17,457
Exxon Mobil Corp.	XOM	$502.9	26,807,800
General Electric Co.	GE	$425.5	40,500,900
Unibanco	UBB	$407.6	1,571,630
Total SA	TOT	$347.2	1,958,150
China Mobile	CHL	$337.4	2,595,390
Petrochina Co.	PTR	$325.1	785,178
AT&T, Inc.	T	$255.7	23,467,700
Royal Dutch Shell	RDS-B	$252.9	271,157

Source: http://www.nyse.com.

3M Company	International Business Machines Corp.
ALCOA, Inc.	Johnson & Johnson
American Express, Inc.	JPMorgan Chase & Co
AT&T, Inc.	Kraft Foods Inc.
Bank of America Corporation	McDonald's Corp.
Boeing Co.	Merck & Co., Inc.
Caterpillar , Inc.	Microsoft Corp.
Chevron Corp.	Pfizer, Inc.
Citigroup, Inc.	The Coca-Cola Company
E.I. DuPont de Nemours & Co.	The Home Depot, Inc.
ExxonMobil Corp.	The Proctor and Gamble Company
General Electric Co.	United Technologies Corp.
General Motors Corp.	Verizon Communications, Inc.
Hewlett-Packard Co.	Wal-Mart Stores, Inc.
Intel Corp.	Walt Disney Co.

Source: http://www.nyse.com. and www.ccn.money.com

firm office over the same electronic circuit that brought the order to the trading floor. Larger orders (more than 3,000 shares) are typically represented personally by floor brokers by one of three additional methods: i) Broker Booth Support System (BBSS), a sophisticated computer system used to receive orders on the Trading Floor, connected to specialist posts and broker handheld computers; ii) NYSE e-Broker, a wireless, handheld tool that enables floor brokers to submit and manage quotes and orders, track executions, and speed the flow of information between customers and the point of sale; and iii) NYSE Direct+, a high-speed electronic connection between NYSE member firms and the Exchange, enabling immediate electronic execution of customer orders.

When a new price is reached, this information is sent out over a ticker, a device which provides a constant stream of stock symbols and prices; each symbol consists of three or fewer letters representing the stock of a particular corporation. The ticker continuously posts stock prices electronically on displays in brokerage houses and on computer screens around the world.

On occasion, there have been large daily fluctuations in stock prices. During the week of October 12 to 16, 1987, the Dow Jones Industrial Average, an index of stock prices, fell 250 points. On Monday, October 19, 1987, it fell 508 points, or more than 20 percent. This was not only the largest point drop in history to that date but also by far the largest percentage drop. To give you some idea of its magnitude, the next largest percentage decline occurred on October 28, 1929, when the market fell 12.8 percent near the start of the Great Depression.[5] Although far from the largest percentage drop, the largest point drop to date in the Dow Jones Industrial average occurred on September 29, 2008 when the average fell 777 points in the ongoing financial crisis of 2008. Late 2008 was characterized by incredibly large swings in stock markets as the economy tried to work its way through the worst financial crisis since the Great Depression.

In response to the October 1987 crash, certain reforms were instituted to limit such severe declines. In particular, so-called **circuit breakers** were introduced to temporarily halt market trading if prices fall by a specified amount. During the halt, market makers have a chance to take positions and evaluate new information to provide support for the market. Bargains can be snatched up, stopping the free fall in prices. Originally, the new rules called for trading to be halted for half an hour if the market dropped 250 points from the previous day's close. If the market dropped 400 points, trading was to be halted for one hour.

Circuit Breakers

Reforms introduced in 1987 on the NYSE to temporarily halt market trading if prices change by a specified amount.

The circuit breakers that halt all market trading were first tripped on October 24, 1997, as stocks fell in response to the Asian crisis. Shortly thereafter, the point ranges were broadened to 350 and 550 points. At the time, many analysts called for switching to a percentage change system from the point change system because trading halts based on percentage changes would be more meaningful. The Dow had increased so dramatically throughout the 1990s that a 350- or 550-point change was not nearly as significant as when the Dow was at lower levels.

In response, the NYSE adopted a threshold percentage rule that took effect on April 15, 1998. The point threshold is adjusted quarterly, based on a percentage of the average closing level of the Dow Jones Industrial Average during the previous month, rounded to the nearest 50 points. The thresholds are as follows:

1. If the Dow declines 10 percent from the threshold before 2:00 P.M., the market will close for one hour; between 2:00 and 2:30 P.M., the market will close for 30 minutes; after 2:30 P.M., the 10 percent threshold is removed, and the market will continue trading.

2. If the Dow declines 20 percent from the threshold before 1 P.M., the market will close for two hours; between 1 and 2 P.M., for one hour; after 2 P.M., for the day.

3. If the Dow declines 30 percent at any time, the market will close for the day.

For the first quarter 2009, the 10 percent threshold was a 850-point decline, the 20 percent decline was 1,700 points, and the 30 percent threshold was a 2,600-point decline.

Circuit breakers also limit a form of program trading called **index-arbitrage trading**, which involves purchasing (or selling) a basket of stocks, usually through program trading, with the simultaneous selling (or purchasing) of a futures agreement in the same basket of securities. Index-arbitrage trading occurs when the price of the basket of stocks and the price of a futures agreement in those stocks diverge enough for someone to make a riskless profit (arbitrage) from buying in one market and selling in another. As you shall see in Chapter 16, spot prices and futures prices are highly correlated, and an arbitrageur can make a riskless profit if price differentials become out of alignment. NYSE Rule 80A provides for limitations on index-arbitrage trading in any component stock of the S&P 500 Stock Price Index on any day that the Dow Jones Industrial Average advances or declines at least 2 percent from its previous day's closing value.[6] Circuit breakers for index-arbitrage trading are triggered more frequently because of the smaller price change that is needed to trigger the circuit breaker than for those price changes that halt all market activity.

NASDAQ (National Association of Securities Dealers Automated Quotation System)

Formerly referred to as the "over-the-counter market," NASDAQ has evolved into a bona fide stock exchange. NASDAQ grew rapidly in the 1990s and 2000s and had become the main rival to the NYSE. Although the market capitalization of the stocks traded on the NYSE far exceeds that of stocks traded on the NASDAQ, the NASDAQ has been growing relatively faster in terms of the number of shares and dollar volume of trading.

Approximately 3,200 firms are listed on the NASDAQ exchange, of which 335 are from outside the United States. NASDAQ lists more companies and on average, trades more shares per day than the NYSE. NASDAQ listed companies have tended to be disproportionately small, young, technology companies in the past, but now a wide variety of firms are listed, including such high-tech giants as Apple Computer and Microsoft.

Historically, while trades on the NYSE took place at a physical location in New York, NASDAQ was used by securities dealers at various locations, only electronically connected. This lack of a central physical location slowed its general acceptance as

Index-Arbitrage Trading
The purchasing (or selling) of a basket of stocks, usually through program trading, with the simultaneous selling (or purchasing) of a futures agreement in the same basket of securities in order to make a riskless profit (arbitrage) from the price differential between the basket of stocks and the futures agreement.

National Association of Securities Dealers Automated Quotation System (NASDAQ)
An electronic stock market for trading securities. In 2002, it became an investor-owned corporation, completely independent of the National Association of Securities Dealers (NASD), which had founded it in 1971. It lists more companies and trades more shares on average than the NYSE

a financial market as real as those with trading floors in historic buildings. In 2000, NASDAQ opened the visually high-tech "MarketSite" in Times Square, New York City, but this location is primarily for public relations rather than actual trading.

NASDAQ was founded in 1971 by the National Association of Securities Dealers (NASD), who divested ownership in 2001. Now it is owned and operated by The NASDAQ Stock Market, a publicly traded corporation in its own right.

Until 1987, most NASDAQ trading occurred via the telephone, but during the October 1987 stock market crash, market makers often didn't answer their phones. As a result, an electronic method for dealers to enter their trades was established. The dealers or brokerage firms that make a market in a particular security or securities buy and sell the securities at publicly quoted prices. Unlike the NYSE, each stock has multiple market makers. The NASDAQ prides itself on its ability to objectively facilitate rapid trades with small transactions costs.

NASDAQ has been actively combining with other exchanges and has used its technological expertise to extend its international reach. In 1992, it joined with the London Stock Exchange to form the first intercontinental linkage of securities markets. More recently, in late 2007, it purchased old, established, but small regional exchanges in Philadelphia and Boston, and in early 2008, it was in the process of forming a strategic alliance with the large and dynamic Middle Eastern exchange Bourse Dubai Ltd. Although mergers have reduced the number of exchanges, competition between NASDAQ and the NYSE seems to be spurring each to lower fees, introduce new technology, and become more international.

Other Exchanges

American Stock Exchange (AMEX)
An historically important stock exchange located in New York City, recently merged with NASDAQ. It currently handles about 10 percent of all securities trades in the U.S. and is relatively important in small-cap stocks and exchange-traded funds (ETFs).

Over-the-Counter (OTC) Market
A network of securities dealers that trades stocks of companies not listed on an official exchange such as NASDAQ or the NYSE.

Historically, there were three nationally important stock exchanges, the NYSE, American Stock Exchange (AMEX), and Over-the-Counter (OTC) Market. The emergence of NASDAQ from the OTC market placed AMEX at a disadvantage. The NASDAQ merged with AMEX in 1998, but then sold AMEX to private investors in 2003.[7] In October 2008, NYSE Euronext purchased the AMEX, primarily for their expertise in futures trading and Exchange-Traded Funds (ETFs), and their presence in stock options trading.

Many regional stock exchanges in cities such as San Francisco, Boston, Philadelphia, and Chicago traded shares of companies listed on the national exchanges. Nearly all have been absorbed by the two remaining national stock markets, either directly or indirectly. For example, the San Francisco and Los Angeles stock exchanges merged in 1937 to form the Pacific Stock Exchange. This was purchased by Archipelago Exchange (ArcaEx), a vibrant and growing electronic exchange, in 2005. In 2006, ArcaEx was purchased by the NYSE in order to help it better compete with NASDAQ. In late 2007, NASDAQ first purchased the Boston Stock Exchange and, shortly thereafter, purchased the oldest U.S. stock market, Philadelphia. The only exchanges remaining other than the NYSE and NASDAQ tend to specialize in areas other than stocks. For example, the CME Group—formed from the 2007 merger of the Chicago Mercantile Exchange (CME) and the Chicago Board of Trade (CBOT)—specializes in futures contracts, while the New York Mercantile Exchange, Inc. (NYMEX) specializes in trading physical commodity futures, energy, and precious metals.

Many foreign countries also have stock exchanges with varying degrees of development and depth. Some European exchanges, such as the London Stock Exchange and Amsterdam Stock Exchange, predate those in the United States. The Nikkei Exchange in Tokyo, the London Stock Exchange, the DAX in Germany, and the Toronto Stock

Exchange in Canada are among the busiest exchanges around the world. In September 2000, the Amsterdam, Brussels, and Paris stock exchanges merged to form the Euronext Exchange, which as mentioned, subsequently merged with the NYSE in 2007. Even more cross-border mergers are expected, particularly in European countries that participate in the Euro. In recent years, many emerging economies have developed stock exchanges concomitant with the globalization of finance and the increase in capital flows. Stocks in smaller, less established firms not listed on either the NYSE or NASDAQ still trade in an over-the-counter manner, but with higher transactions costs and lower liquidity.

Consolidation has not been limited to the stock exchange. In July 2007, NASD and the member regulation, enforcement, and arbitration functions of the New York Stock Exchange were combined to form the Financial Industry Regulatory Authority (FINRA). FINRA is a nongovernmental regulator for all securities firms doing business in the United States. It oversees over 5,000 brokerage firms, about 172,000 branch offices, and more than 665,000 registered securities representatives and administers the largest dispute resolution forum for investors and registered firms. It also performs market regulation under contract for The NASDAQ Stock Market, the International Securities Exchange, and the Chicago Climate Exchange. FINRA has approximately 3,000 employees and operates from Washington, D.C., and New York, with 15 district offices around the country.

Financial Industry Regulatory Authority (FINRA)
A nongovernmental regulator for all securities firms doing business in the United States, overseeing more than 5,000 brokerage firms. It was created in July 2007 through the consolidation of NASD and the member regulation, enforcement, and arbitration functions of the New York Stock Exchange

Recap   U.S. and international stock markets have been evolving and adapting at breakneck speed. Adoption of new trading technologies and internationalization have coincided with two fundamental trends: 1) consolidation between and among domestic and global stock exchanges, and 2) the transformation of stock exchange ownership to corporate entities where the exchange is owned by the shareholders of the corporation. Regional exchanges have been absorbed by either the NYSE or NASDAQ, as have new technology-based exchanges such as ArcaEx and the historically important AMEX. At the present time, only the NYSE and NASDAQ remain as significant U.S. stock markets. Each has become internationally integrated and employs the latest trading technology. As stock markets have become investor-owned corporations, the nature of self-regulation has changed. The Financial Industry Regulatory Authority (FINRA) is currently the largest nongovernmental regulator of U.S. securities firms.

Stock Market Indexes

A stock market index measures the overall performance of the stocks included in the index. An index can be used to evaluate how well a specific stock or mutual fund is performing relative to the stocks represented in the index. Almost 100 indexes monitor stock prices. The Dow Jones Industrial Average (the Dow) measures movements in the stock prices of 30 of the largest companies in the country. The Dow, first introduced in 1896, is the oldest index in use today and is probably the most famous. The stocks in an index may include all the stocks traded on a particular stock exchange, selectively picked stocks, or stocks that fall into a particular class based on the value of outstanding shares.

The following list describes the major stock indexes reported in the popular media. As a quick glance shows, other indexes are far more broadly based than the Dow. Over the long run, however, the movement of the Dow has closely paralleled other more comprehensive indexes.

Dow Jones Industrial Average (the Dow)
An index that measures movements in the stock prices of 30 of the largest companies traded on the NYSE.

- The Dow Jones Industrial Average (the Dow or DJIA, for short) is an unweighted average of the sum of the daily closing prices of the stocks of 30 of the largest companies in the country, the "blue chips." The companies that make up the index are selected by Dow Jones & Company, which also publishes *The Wall Street Journal*. The companies are changed over time to reflect changes in corporate America. The 30 companies included in the index as of late 2007 are listed in Exhibit 14-5 (p. 328). Note that the index is larger than the sum of the daily closing prices of the 30 stocks. The number that the sum is divided by is adjusted to account for the effect of stock splits and stock dividends. Also, when one company is dropped and a new company added, the average is adjusted so that the new index is comparable to earlier values.

- The Dow Jones Transportation Average is calculated using the prices of 20 airline, trucking, and railroad stocks.

- The Dow Jones Utility Average is calculated using the prices of 15 gas, electric, and power company stocks.

- The Dow Jones 65 Composite Index is calculated from all stocks in the Dow Jones Industrial, Transportation, and Utility Averages.

- The Standard and Poor's 500 (the S&P 500 for short) is a weighted index of prices of 500 broad-based corporations. Stocks included in the index may be traded on the New York Stock Exchange (NYSE), the American Stock Exchange, or over the counter. They are selected by Standard and Poor's Corporation and changed over time as needed so that the index reflects general stock market conditions. As with other weighted

14-6

The Value of the DJIA, S&P 500, NYSE Composite, and NASDAQ (1985 through 2008) Billions of Dollars

	Dow Jones Industrial	S&P 500	NASDAQ Composite
1985	1,546.67	211.28	324.93
1986	1,895.95	242.17	348.83
1987	1,938.83	247.08	330.47
1988	2,168.57	277.72	381.38
1989	2,753.20	353.40	454.82
1990	2,633.66	330.22	373.84
1991	3,168.83	417.09	586.34
1992	3,301.11	435.71	676.95
1993	3,754.09	466.45	776.80
1994	3,834.44	459.27	751.96
1995	5,117.12	615.93	1,052.13
1996	6,448.27	740.74	1,291.03
1997	7,908.25	970.43	1,570.35
1998	9,181.43	1,229.23	2,192.69
1999	11,497.12	1,469.25	4,069.31
2000	10,786.90	1,320.28	2,470.53
2001	10,021.50	1,148.08	1,950.40
2002	8,341.63	879.82	1,335.52
2003	10,453.90	1,111.92	2,003.37
2004	10,783.01	1,211.92	2,175.44
2005	10,717.50	1,248.29	2,205.32
2006	12,463.10	1,418.03	2,415.29
2007	13,264.82	1,468.36	2,652.28
2008*	8,776.39	903.25	1,577.03

Source: Global Financial Data, Los Angeles, California.

indexes, the S&P 500 weights the stocks according to their relative values so that larger corporations contribute more to the index. Many analysts consider the S&P 500 to be a more meaningful index of overall stock market activity than the Dow.

- The New York Composite Index is a weighted average of the market value of all stocks traded on the NYSE. The index also reports four subgroup indexes representing industrial, transportation, utility, and finance stocks.

- The Wilshire Equity Index Value (the Wilshire 5000) is a weighted index of the value of all stocks listed on the NYSE, all stocks on the American Stock Exchange, and all over-the-counter stocks that are traded by NASDAQ members. As such, it includes virtually all companies in the United States and is the broadest measure of stock market activity. Today, the Wilshire 5000 includes over 6,800 stocks. When the index was originally created, it included 5,000 stocks (hence the name).

- The NASDAQ Composite Index, as its name suggests, is a weighted index that measures changes in prices of all stock traded by the NASDAQ system.

Exhibit 14-6 reports the value of the DJIA, the S&P 500, and the NASDAQ Composite from 1985 through 2008. Note the phenomenal increase in all of the indices. Exhibit 14-7 includes the daily averages of the stock market volume and the values

14-7

Daily Average of Stock Market Volume and Values Traded (1985 through 2008)

	Stock Market Volume (Daily Average, Millions of Shares)		Value Traded (Daily Average, Billions of Dollars)	
	NYSE	NASDAQ	NYSE	NASDAQ
1985	109.2	82.1	3.9	0.9
1986	141	113.6	5.4	1.5
1987	188.9	149.8	7.4	2
1988	161.5	122.8	5.4	1.4
1989	165.5	133.1	6.1	1.7
1990	156.8	131.9	5.2	1.8
1991	178.9	163.3	6	2.7
1992	202.3	190.8	6.9	3.5
1993	264.5	263	9	5.3
1994	291.4	295.1	9.7	5.8
1995	346.1	401.4	12.2	9.5
1996	412	543.7	16	13
1997	526.9	647.8	22.8	17.7
1998	673.6	801.7	29	22.9
1999	808.9	1,081.80	35.5	43.7
2000	1,041.60	1,757.00	43.9	80.9
2001	1,240.00	1,900.10	42.3	44.1
2002	1,441.00	1,752.80	40.9	28.8
2003	1,398.40	1,685.50	38.5	28
2004	1,456.70	1,801.30	46.1	34.6
2005	1,602.20	1,778.50	56.1	39.5
2006	1,826.70	2,001.90	68.3	46.5
2007	2,110.9	2,132.0	86.8	60.0
2008	2,609.4	2,259.3	82.4	59.4

Source: Securities Industry Association.

traded from 1985 through 2008. Again, note the phenomenal increase in both the volume and value of stocks traded. In the next section, we look at stock markets and mutual funds.

The Stock Market and Mutual Funds

Mutual funds are companies that pool the funds of many investors and then invest in several hundred or even thousands of stocks. In addition, some mutual funds invest in bonds or some combination of both stocks and bonds. The small investor who buys into the fund can own a small piece of the large basket of stocks and/or bonds. As we will see in Chapter 15, any individual can tap into the higher returns of the stock market while minimizing the risk of doing so by purchasing shares of a mutual fund.

For many investors, mutual funds may offer less risk and greater safety than individual stocks because of diversification. Because all securities do not perform equally well over the business cycle (returns are not perfectly correlated), diversification reduces risk. This greatly reduces the consequences of investing in a single company that fails (putting all of your eggs in one basket). If a mutual fund has invested in 1,000 companies, the risk that all of them will go under at once is much less than the risk that any one of them will be forced into bankruptcy. If only one or a few of the companies perform poorly, the overall returns to the mutual fund are hardly affected. Mutual fund companies offer highly trained professional management to research the best investments. This not only saves the individual investor time and effort but also is intended to improve the performance (yield) of the portfolio. No-load mutual funds are bought directly from the mutual fund company and do not involve a brokerage commission.

Indexed Mutual Funds
A mutual fund that holds the same basket of securities that are represented in an index such as the S&P 500 or the Wilshire 5000, so that the investor receives roughly the same return as the index to which the fund is tied.

Indexed mutual funds hold the same basket of securities that are represented in an index such as the S&P 500 or the Wilshire 5000. The investor receives roughly the same return as that of the index to which the fund is tied. For example, if an index appreciates 10 percent, a mutual fund holding the same stocks as in the index also appreciates 10 percent. Indexed mutual funds usually have relatively low costs because little trading occurs. Management fees are low because the mutual fund's holdings do not have to be actively managed. For investors who are satisfied with the return of the overall market, these funds may be a good bet because of their low costs. Often, actively managed funds earn lower returns than the indexed funds and involve significantly higher management fees and other costs.

Exchange-Traded Funds (ETFs)
A security created by a securities firm depositing into a fund that mirrors the holdings of stocks in an index.

In 1993, an alternative investment to indexed mutual funds called exchange-traded funds was developed. Exchange-traded funds (ETFs) are shares of a security (such as shares of stock) that mirror the holdings and, hence, the performance of an index. ETFs result from the deposit by a securities firm of a large basket of stocks into a fund that reflects the holdings of the index. The securities firm then receives a block of ETF shares against the basket of stock. The shares are then offered to individual investors. Because the shares mirror the holdings of stocks in an index, they offer approximately the same return (appreciation or depreciation) that the index does. In the last few years, a series of ETFs have been introduced that do not merely track an index, but track a function of the underlying index, for example following the index multiplied by two, or even negative one. Owning an ETF is like owning a share of stock rather than shares in a mutual fund. ETFs are traded on several exchanges and can be bought and sold through a broker anytime during the exchange hours for their trading price at that particular moment. When mutual funds are traded, they are bought or sold at end-of-day prices. Unlike mutual funds, ETFs can be bought with borrowed funds (margin buying) and sold short. Limit orders can also be placed. The dollar value of ETFs, which go by names such as Diamonds, iShares, Spiders, and Vipers, among others, has increased from their inception in 1993 to over $500 billion in 2007, or nearly half of the total index fund asset base. A disadvantage of ETFs is that a brokerage commission has to be paid to buy or sell them, which is avoided when no-load indexed mutual funds are bought directly. Both indexed mutual funds and ETFs may also have tax advantages for investors over other mutual fund investments.

| Recap | Stock market indexes measure movements in stock prices. The Dow is an index of 30 of the largest companies in the country. The S&P 500 is a weighted average of 500 broad-based companies and is considered to be a more meaningful index than the Dow. Mutual funds are investment companies that pool the funds of many investors and purchase securities. They allow for much greater diversification than investors could achieve on their own. Mutual funds now offer indexed mutual funds that hold the same basket of stocks as represented in a stock index. ETFs are securities that mirror the holdings of stock in a market index. |

THE VALUATION OF STOCKS

Should you buy a particular stock or not? It depends on whether you think it is your most profitable opportunity, given your tolerance for risk. At the present price at which it is trading, is the stock undervalued or overvalued? In this section, we will attempt to shed some light on these questions.

Given some of the material covered in Chapters 6 and 7, you will not be surprised to learn that the price of a share of stock in a firm should equal the present value of the expected future cash flows that the share will generate, where cash flows include both dividends and retained earnings. If we assume that the stock will be held indefinitely into the future (forever), then the current price of the stock will be equal to the present value of the expected cash flows, as portrayed in Equation 14-1.

(14-1)
$$P = C_1/(1+d) + C_2/(1+d)^2 + C_3/(1+d)^3 \cdots$$

where C_n is the expected cash flow in the nth year and d the discount factor (interest rate)[8] applied to find the present value or price (P).

If we expect the firm to earn a constant cash flow, ($C_1 = C_2 = C_3 = \ldots$), then Equation 14-1 simplifies to Equation 14-2.

(14-2)
$$P = C/d$$

Assuming that we can estimate the expected cash flow (C) and the discount factor (d), we can solve for the current value of a share of the stock. If the stock is trading at a lower price, the savvy investor will buy; if it is trading at a higher price, the investor will sell. If there is agreement about expected cash flows, the stock's price should converge to the value based on that expectation. In the real world, there are often very divergent opinions about future cash flows. That is the reason some people are buying and others are selling at any given moment.

A question that remains is how the discount factor is determined. For any stock, there is a required return needed by investors who purchase the stock. This is the equilibrium return that is based on a risk-free return plus a risk premium associated with owning the stock, as discussed in Chapter 7. The risk-free return is usually measured by the long-term government bond rate.

The risk premium is composed of two parts:

- A **market risk premium** based on historical data that shows how much on average the ownership of stocks pays over the risk-free return.
- A **firm-specific risk premium** that is measured by a coefficient called **beta**, which measures the overall sensitivity or variability of the stock's return relative to changes in the entire stock market.[9] Changes in the S&P 500 can serve as a proxy for changes in the whole market. Thus, if on average a 1 percent increase (or decrease) in the S&P 500 results in a 2 percent increase (or decrease) in a particular stock's price, then the beta for this stock is 2. This indicates that the stock in question is riskier than the average stock in the S&P 500 index because its value fluctuates more. On the other hand, if a 1 percent change in the S&P 500 generates a .5 percent change, the beta is .5, and the stock varies less than the S&P 500.

The capital asset pricing model uses the preceding analysis to develop a model of the return needed to own a share of stock based on the market and firm-specific risks. According to the capital asset pricing model, the return needed is equal to the risk-free return plus beta multiplied by the market risk premium, as depicted in Equation 14-3.

(14-3)
$$d = R_f + \beta(R_m)$$

where d is the discount factor, R_f is the risk-free return, β is beta for this particular stock, and R_m is the market risk premium with which investors must be compensated for owning stocks in general. The discount factor takes into account the risk-free return, the market risk premium, and the firm-specific variance of the return as measured by beta.

In the preceding example, if the risk-free return is 5.5 percent, the market risk factor based on historical data is 4 percent, and beta for this firm is 2, then d is equal to 13.5 percent [5.5+(2×4)=5.5+8=13.5]. The variable d, 13.5 percent, is the discount factor that we will plug into Equation 14-2 to find the present value of a share of the firm's stock. If the expected cash flow is $10 per year, the price of the stock will be $74.07, because $10/.135=$74.07.

Note that the risk-free return and the market risk premium are the same for all firms while beta is usually different and dependent on the variability of a firm's returns.

The assumption of a constant expected cash flow is rather limiting because—we hope—cash flows will grow over time. If we assume that expected cash flows grow at a constant percent, g, then we can modify Equation 14-2 to take into account this common growth rate. This is done in Equation 14-4:

(14-4)
$$P = C/(d - g)$$

where P is the stock price, C is the expected cash flow today, d is the discount factor, and g is the constant growth rate of future expected cash flows.

Thus, modifying the example, if cash flows are expected to grow 5 percent annually (g=.05), the new stock price will be $117.65 because [$10/(.135 − .05) = $117.65].

In Chapter 7, we considered the efficient markets theory, which laid much of the groundwork for this section. You saw that the prices of stocks and bonds adjust until the average investor is indifferent between stocks or bonds—in other words, until the risk-adjusted returns to owning stocks or bonds are equalized. In this section, we have expanded that analysis to consider a market risk of owning stocks versus bonds plus a firm-specific risk as measured by beta. The equilibrium return to owning stocks consists of a risk-free return, a risk premium for owning stock, and a firm-specific premium. Again, if the Fed takes action that causes interest rates to change, this changes

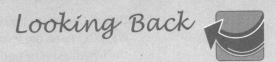
Looking Back

Could U.S. Stock Prices Be Justified?

As shown in Exhibit 14-6, by the end of the 1990s, U.S. stock prices as measured by indices had reached levels that would have been unimaginable at the start of the decade. Some analysts believe that the market had been in an irrational bubble that could not be sustained and look to the downturn in the early 2000s to support their claim. Others believe that the record increases were justified. They say that increases in information technologies have transformed the way firms do business, have increased worker productivity, and have promised increased cash flows that justified the high prices. Again, between 2002 and 2007, stock prices had almost doubled. After peaking in July 2007, the stock market fell over 35 percent by October 2008 in response to the global credit crisis. Were stock prices too high in 2007 and 1999, or too low in 2002 and 2008?

Although a definitive answer has not been found, several theories have been put forth that attempt to explain the relatively high stock valuations in 1999 and 2007. From the material in this chapter, we can see that the abnormally high stock prices could be justified under either or both of two conditions:

- first, if expected cash flows increased sufficiently to justify the high prices, and
- second, if the rate at which expected cash flows are discounted decreased enough to justify the high prices.

One theory holds that the high prices were justified if the growth rate of earnings increased from the 1.4 percent average over the past century to 2.4 percent in recent years and if the required rate of return fell from the 7.3 percent average over the last century to 6.6 percent.[a] This theory suggests that changes in stock market participation, consumer preferences, and earnings growth together could explain the higher prices. As noted elsewhere, a much larger percent of the population now participates in the market. Given increased life expectancies and uncertainty surrounding future social security payments, investors now have a longer time horizon for investments. Finally, given the growth of mutual funds, cash flows are less uncertain because of the greater extent of diversification that investing in mutual funds makes possible.

Another theory suggests that the high stock prices could be accounted for because of increases in productivity.[b] For example, productivity increased at an 8 percent annual rate in the 1960s, 2 percent in the 1970s, and 17 percent in the 1990s. Although many believe that the explosion of information technologies has increased worker productivity, these estimates seem unrealistic at best. They also raise another question. If volatile productivity growth can explain changes in stock prices, what are the factors that cause productivity growth to be so volatile?

A third theory is that a major technological innovation reduced the value of existing firms and caused a reduction in the stock market that continued until shares in new firms that make use of the technology make their way into the market.[c] The idea is that the information technology revolution began in the early 1970s with the invention of the microprocessor. However, older firms with existing technologies and capital were slow to adopt the changes and, hence, their values were reduced. The higher value of the new innovative firms was not reflected in stock markets because they did not offer tradable securities. Only after the new firms issued tradable stocks via IPOs would the value of new technologies be reflected in the market. To support the hypothesis, the authors show that most of the increased values in the stock market relative to gross domestic product since 1985 are the result of increases in the value of new firms. Firms that were already in existence by the early 1970s lost about half of their value in the early 1970s and have not fully recovered.

Finally, a fourth theory suggests that the run-up in stock prices was due to two factors:

- technological changes that were being assimilated into stock valuations, and
- structural changes such as financial liberalization that allowed for more widespread participation in stock markets.[d]

Both of these factors may help to explain the run-up in stock prices. In addition, there are learning curves for both the changes in technology and the increased participation that could help to explain market volatility.

In the bull market and new economy of the late 1990s, Internet stocks—referred to as dot-coms—experienced enormous gains. Some of these start-up companies had never made a profit, had never produced a product, and had virtually no real or financial assets. Then why were investors willing to pay such hefty prices? If you followed this chapter, you should be quick to answer: expected future cash flows. Of course, after spring 2000, when prices of many of the dot-coms collapsed, investors began to take a closer look and question whether or not the expected cash flows had been vastly overestimated. Perhaps some Internet stocks had been caught in a speculative bubble.

Other stocks that suffered significant losses at the time included media and telecommunications stocks. Indeed, the technology-laden NASDAQ index fell about 72 percent from February 2000 to February 2003 in the worst bear market in history.

Technology leaders such as Google and Apple, oil companies and other energy producers, along with financial firms led stock prices higher from 2003 to 2007. Time will tell if prices of these stocks were also pushed up beyond a sustainable, justifiable level.

Endnotes

a. John Heaton and Deborah Lucas, (1999), "Stock Prices and Fundamentals," *NBER Macroeconomics Annual*, 1999, 14(2), p. 213.
b. Robert E. Hall, (2000), "The Stock Market and Capital Accumulation," National Bureau of Economic Research (NBER), Working Paper 7180.
c. Bart Hobijn and Boyan Jovanovic, "The Information Technology Revolution and the Stock Market: Preliminary Evidence," Mimeo (New York University, 2000); and Boyan Jovanovic and Peter L. Rousseau, "Vintage Organization Capital," Mimeo (New York University, 2000).
d. Joseph Zeira, "Informational Overshooting, Booms, and Crashes," *Journal of Monetary Economics* 43, no. 1 (1999): 237–57.

the risk-free return of government bonds, and the financial prices of stocks and bonds adjust until the investor is again indifferent between stocks and bonds.

A point needs to be emphasized: future cash flows are, of course, unknown; therefore, it is the discounted value of expected cash flows that is used in stock valuation. You can see why cash flow and earnings reports get so much attention in the media. If earnings reports differ from what was forecasted, sharp price movements can occur immediately as investors take advantage of buying and selling opportunities. "Looking Back" on p. 337 discusses some of the current issues with regard to the performance of U.S. stock markets in recent years.

Recap   The value of a stock is the discounted present value of the expected future stream of cash flows that the stock will generate. Investors require a return that is the sum of a risk-free return plus a risk premium to account for the fact that stocks are riskier than government securities. In addition to a market risk premium, there is a firm-specific risk premium based on beta that measures the variability of a stock's return relative to the entire market. If cash flows grow by a constant percent, g, the price of a share of stock will be equal to $C/(d - g)$, where C is the original cash flow, d is the discount factor based on the market and firm-specific risks, and g is the constant growth rate of the cash flow.

We have completed our look at stocks. We hope you have a better understanding of these financial instruments. This chapter contains an appendix on how a firm that wishes to raise long-term financial capital chooses between issuing stocks or bonds. In the next chapter, we will examine securities firms, mutual funds, and financial conglomerates.

Summary of Major Points

1. In recent decades, prices of stocks have become more volatile. The Fed is concerned about this because of the potential for stock price bubbles and crashes to cause unemployment or inflation, or to affect the solvency of financial institutions and the financial system.

2. Stocks represent ownership in a corporation. Preferred stock pays a fixed dividend, and common stock may pay a variable or no dividend. Under normal circumstances, publicly held stocks are liquid financial assets that may be traded in organized markets such as the NYSE or NASDAQ. They may also be traded over the counter through computer networks and via telephone transactions.

3. Institutional investors in the stock market are primarily insurance companies, pension plans, and mutual funds. Program trading allows institutional investors to preprogram computers to buy or sell a market basket of stocks. Buying on the margin refers to buying stocks by using one's own funds and borrowed funds. At the present time, margin requirements for purchases are 50 percent. Exchanges set maintenance margins that must be maintained after the stock has been purchased. Shelf registration allows a corporation to register stocks that it can issue over the next two years.

4. The NYSE operates auction-type markets on which a specialist trades large blocks of shares at a specific post. Most smaller trades are made on the NYSE via the SuperDOT system, which is a computer system that sends buy or sell orders to the specialist's post.

5. After a wave of mergers and consolidation, two large international stock exchanges remain, the NYSE and NASDAQ. Both have responded to technological advances and increased globalization by merging with other exchanges, both small regional exchanges within the U.S. and large integrated exchanges in different countries. And both evolved from mutual ownership form to corporate form with publicly trade stock. The form of

regulation has changed as well, with the creation of Financial Industry Regulatory Authority (FINRA) from the consolidation of the regulation, enforcement, and arbitration functions of the New York Stock Exchange with the NASD. Some trading between larger institutional investors, or in stocks of small corporations not listed by the NYSE or NASDAQ, still takes place on an over-the-counter basis.

6. Stock market indexes measure movements in stock prices. The Dow is an index of 30 of the largest companies in the country. The S&P 500 is a weighted average of 500 broad-based companies and is considered to be a more meaningful index than the Dow. Mutual funds are investment companies that pool the funds of many investors and purchase securities, allowing greater diversification for small investors. Indexed mutual funds hold the same basket of stocks as represented in a stock index. ETFs are securities that mirror the holdings of stock in a market index and offer the same advantages of investing in individual stocks.

7. The value of a share of stock is the discounted present value of the expected future cash flows that the stock will generate. Investors require a return that is the sum of a risk-free return plus a risk premium to account for the fact that stocks are riskier than government securities. In addition to a market risk premium, there is a firm-specific risk premium based on beta that measures the variability of this stock's return relative to the entire market. If cash flows grow by a constant percent, the price of a share of stock will be equal to $C/(d - g)$, where C is the original cash flow, d is the discount factor based on the market and firm-specific risks, and g is the constant growth rate of the cash flows.

8. If firms want to spend more than their receipts, they must decide between internal or external financing. If the firm uses external financing, it can issue new stocks or bonds. If a firm chooses external debt financing, it must also decide whether the debt will be long term or short term. Issuing stock dilutes the ownership of the firm. Issuing debt has tax advantages because interest payments are a tax write-off, whereas dividend payments are not. Issuing debt increases the firm's leverage ratio, which makes the firm more vulnerable to a downturn in profits. (See Appendix 14A.)

Key Terms

American Stock Exchange (AMEX), p. 330

Beta, p. 336

Capital Asset Pricing Model, p. 336

Circuit Breakers, p. 328

Common Stock, p. 319

Designated Order Turnaround System (SuperDOT), p. 327

Dow Jones Industrial Average (the Dow), p. 331

Exchange-Traded Funds (ETFs), p. 334

External Financing, p. 343

Financial Industry Regulatory Authority (FINRA), p. 331

Firm-Specific Risk Premium, p. 336

Index-Arbitrage Trading, p. 329

Indexed Mutual Funds, p. 334

Initial Public Offering (IPO), p. 321

Internal Financing, p. 343

Leverage Ratio, p. 344

Maintenance Margin Requirement, p. 324

Margin Requirement, p. 323

Market Risk Premium, p. 336

National Association of Securities Dealers Automated Quotation System (NASDAQ), p. 329

New York Stock Exchange (NYSE), p. 326

Over-the-Counter (OTC) Market, p. 330

Preferred Stock, p. 319

Program Trading, p. 323

Secondary Stock Offering, p. 321

Securities and Exchange Commission (SEC), p. 320

Shelf Registration, p. 322

Speculative Bubble, p. 316

Review Questions

1. How could a stock market crash affect the economy?
2. Assuming that other factors remain constant, is common or preferred stock riskier to hold?
3. Assuming that other factors remain constant, which pays a higher return to the stockholder: common or preferred stock?
4. To which market index would you refer to see how well the stock market is performing? Why? Why do you think the movements of the Dow and the S&P 500 are highly correlated?
5. Why are mutual funds generally perceived to be less risky than holding a market basket of individual stocks?
6. What are institutional investors, and what impact do they have on stock markets? What is program trading?
7. Who currently owns the NYSE and NASDAQ? How has the ownership structure changed over time?
8. Are firms listed on the NYSE "big board" always larger than firms listed only by NASDAQ?
9. What are circuit breakers? How have the rules affecting them changed in recent years?
10. What is program trading? What is index-arbitrage trading?
11. How has the NYSE responded to the technological challenge posed by NASDAQ and the trend toward more global financial markets?
12. In a paragraph, explain how inflation in stock markets can spill over to inflation in output markets. Do the same for deflation.
13. What is buying on the margin? Does it increase or decrease the risk of large losses? What about gains?
14. Can newly issued Microsoft stock be offered in an IPO? Explain. What is the difference between buying stock in a secondary public offering or in the secondary market?
15. What are the differences between indexed mutual funds and ETFs?
16. How does a firm choose between debt and equity financing? What are the advantages and disadvantages of each? (See Appendix 14A.)

Analytical Questions

Questions marked with a check mark (✓) are objective in nature. They can be completed with a short answer or number.

✓17. If a share of stock pays a dividend of $3 and closes today at $36, what is the current yield?

✓18. What is the discount factor if beta is 1.2, the market risk premium is 5 percent, and the risk-free return is 4 percent?

✓19. If the expected cash flow is constant and equal to $10, what is the value of a share of stock with the discount factor in problem 18? If the cash flow is expected to grow 3 percent each year, what is the value?

✓20. If I bought $10,000 worth of stock by putting up 60 percent of the selling price and borrowing the rest, how much have I borrowed? If the stock falls to $3,000 and a margin call is put in for the difference between the value of the stock and the amount I have borrowed, how much will I have to put up?

✓21. New earnings figures suggest that cash flows will experience a $100 onetime increase because of a new product being brought online. If d is 15 percent and g is 3 percent, how much will the stock's value increase?

✓23. Jessie bought a share of stock for $100. She borrowed $50 from her broker. There is a 25 percent maintenance margin requirement established by the brokerage firm she does business with. The price of the stock falls to $80. Will her broker put in a margin call to her, asking her to put up more funds? If so, how much more? What if the price falls to $50? In each case, if so, how much more?

Suggested Readings

To access closing prices, number and dollar value of shares traded, as well as other information on NYSE-listed companies, search the exchange's database at **http://www.nyse .com.**

"A Guide to the NYSE Marketplace," published in June 2006, provides a great introduction to the New York Stock Exchange and stock trading in general. It is available online at **http://www.nyse.com/pdfs/nyse_bluebook.pdf.**

For a brief introduction to the NASDAQ, see the "NASDAQ Fact Sheet 2008," available online at **http://www .nasdaq.com/about/2008_Corporate_FS.pdf.**

To see how the founder of the Vanguard Group, Inc., John Bogel, feels about Exchange-Traded Funds (EFTs), see "What's Wrong with ETFs?" *Business Week*, April 30, 2007.

Partially in order to support the stock market, the Fed reduced its interest rate target by 1.25 percent within an eight-day period in early 2008. To see how these actions were viewed at the time, see "Desperate Measures" in *The Economist*, January 22, 2008.

For an interesting look at the stock market in the 1990s, see Maggie Mahar, *Bull! A History of the Boom, 1982–1999* (New York: HarperBusiness, 2004).

For a look at the consequences of the Fed's actions on the stock market, see "What Explains the Stock Market's Reaction to Federal Reserve Policy?" by Ben S. Bernanke and Kenneth N. Kuttner, Board of Governors of the Federal Reserve, Finance and Economics Discussion Series, 2004–16 (March 2004). It is available online at **http://www.fed eralreserve.gov/pubs/feds/2004/200416/200416pap .pdf.**

"Should the Fed React to the Stock Market?" is the question posed by Kevin J. Lansing in his article by the same name in *The Economic Letter,* Federal Reserve Bank of San Francisco, Number 2003-34 (November 14, 2003).

For a sobering look at the stock market, see J. Patrick Raines and Charles G. Leathers, *Economists and the Stock Market: Speculative Theories of Stock Market Fluctuations* (Northampton, MA: Edward Elgar, 2000).

For a discussion of the linkages between asset prices and monetary policy, see "Manias and How to Prevent Them: An Interview with Charles Kindleberger" and "Market Volatility and Monetary Policy," by John Balder, Jr., both in *Challenge* (November–December 1997): 21–31 and 32–52, respectively. Also see "Monetary Policy and Asset Prices," by Andrew J. Filardo, *Economic Review of the Federal Reserve Bank of Kansas City* 85, no. 3 (Third Quarter 2000): 11–38.

Technology has played a part in the formation of numerous stock market bubbles. For an in-depth look at technological innovation and stock market bubbles since the early 1900s, see Robert Shiller's *Irrational Exuberance* (Princeton, NJ: Princeton University Press, 2001).

For a historical look at a time when the New York Stock Exchange nearly collapsed, see Alec Benn, *The Unseen Wall Street, 1969–1975* (Westport, CT: Greenwood Publishing Group, 2000).

For a comprehensive view of the stock market and how it affects the economy, see John Charles Pool and Robert L. Frick, *Demystifying the Stock Market* (Winchester, VA: Durell Institute of Monetary Science at Shenandoah University, 1993).

One of the best resources for a layperson to learn about the stock market is William J. O'Neill, *How to Make Money in Stocks: A Winning System in Good Times or Bad*, 3rd ed. (New York: McGraw-Hill, 2002). Another good book is *One Up on Wall Street: How to Use What You Already Know to Make Money in the Market*, by Peter Lynch and John Rothchild, (New York: Simon and Schuster, 2000).

For a look at "Mutual Funds and the U.S. Equity Market," see the article by the same name by Eric M. Engen and Andreas Lehnert, *Federal Reserve Bulletin* (December 2000): 797–817.

For another point of view, see "The Long-Term Outlook for Stocks: Interview with Peter Diamond," *Challenge* 43, no. 2 (March–April 2000): 6–16.

Appendix 14A: The Choice Between Stocks and Bonds

In the process of investing and operating on a day-to-day basis, firms experience periods when expenditures exceed receipts. As a result, a firm must make several portfolio decisions regarding the financing of excess spending. First, should the spending be financed internally or externally? Internal financing is simply the spending of money balances on hand or the liquidation of financial or real assets owned by the firm to finance the excess. Internal financing is the largest source of funds for business firms.

As for external financing, there are two types: expanding equity or expanding debt. Thus, if a firm chooses external financing—perhaps because its financing needs exceed the internal funds available—it must then decide whether to issue new debt and/or equity.

External financing via equity involves issuing shares of common stock, thereby expanding the ownership in the firm. If the new shares are sold to existing shareholders, ownership is not diluted. Indeed, existing shareholders are sometimes given the first option to purchase the new shares. If the firm chooses external financing through borrowing, it must decide whether to issue long-term or short-term debt. For example, the firm must choose between loans or market instruments, such as commercial paper and corporate bonds. In general, each decision is guided primarily by the desire for profit maximization and the existing structure of financial liabilities. A firm will choose the option that minimizes the cost of funds.

For each firm, the prevailing financial environment, the stance of monetary policy, and so forth, will determine the overall cost of funds. The relative cost of alternative sources of financial capital and, therefore, the particular financing decision reached by a given firm, will be influenced by several considerations: (1) the particular type of expenditures being financed, (2) the current financial environment and expectations about the future environment, (3) the firm's financial structure, and (4) the tax laws. Traditionally, borrowing to finance inventories has taken the form of either short-term bank loans or the issuance of commercial paper. The usual maturity of the bank loans or commercial paper is one to six months, which is appropriate because inventories are typically not held for long periods of time. Fluctuations in inventory investment over the business cycle explain much of the variation in short-term debt accumulated by firms. The correlation is not perfect, however. For example, if many firms perceive prevailing long-term rates to be temporarily high relative to short-term rates, some firms will issue short-term debt to finance the initial phases of their investment spending on new capital. These firms expect that long-term interest rates will soon drop, at which point the firms will issue long-term debt to pay off the maturing short-term debt and finance subsequent phases of their investment spending. Thus, we see how current and expected financial environments play a role in firms' financing decisions.

From the mid-1970s until 1991, a substantial portion of externally financed investment spending, which by definition is the acquisition of capital (new plant and equipment), was financed by issuing long-term debt. Why long-term debt instead of equity? The answer is that U.S. tax laws tend to bias the financing decisions of business firms toward debt and away from equity. Interest paid on debt is a tax-deductible cost; therefore, it is subtracted from gross revenues before the corporate income tax is computed. Dividends paid to equity holders, however, are not tax deductible. Dividends must be paid from after-tax earnings. Thus, debt financing will initially be cheaper, on average, than equity financing. Equity financing may also entail higher transaction costs when it is initially issued. Additionally, equity financing dilutes the ownership of current shareholders.

Internal Financing
Spending money balances on hand or liquidating financial or real assets to finance spending that exceeds current receipts.

External Financing
The financing of spending that exceeds current receipts by expanding either debt or equity.

Debt financing also has a downside. Increasing debt is believed to expose a firm to more risk and therefore weaken its financial structure. The exposure to more risk can ultimately raise the overall cost of capital because the suppliers of funds require higher returns to compensate them for the additional risk.

The relationship among debt finance, risk, and the cost of capital is rooted in a common measure of the financial structure—the **leverage ratio,** or the ratio of debt to equity on a firm's balance sheet. Other things being equal, the higher the leverage ratio, the greater the risk to bondholders and stockholders. The reason is that if a highly leveraged firm experiences a substantial decline in earnings, it may default on its debt obligations and be forced into bankruptcy, possibly leaving its stockholders with nothing. A firm with a low leverage ratio could weather a decline in earnings by cutting dividends, which are residual claims, not contractual obligations. The leveraged firm does not have this option: it must pay its debt costs or fold. Hence, ceteris paribus, risk-averse investors will typically demand a higher yield on funds they lend to highly leveraged corporations. Firms that have considerable debt relative to equity will find the cost of debt financing (as well as equity financing) to be relatively high. As a result, they may decide to issue equity both to raise funds and to strengthen their balance sheets.

Another reason that firms issued new debt in the 1980s was to acquire the equities of other firms in whole or in part. Often referred to as mergers and acquisitions, this activity has sometimes been financed by the issuance of junk bonds that carry yields above those prevailing on higher-rated conventional corporate bonds. In this case, debt increases, but no new investment occurs. Whatever the benefits of this activity, the resulting expansion of debt relative to equities increases the leverage ratio of the corporate sector as a whole. This, in turn, generates concerns about increased risk—that is, the increased vulnerability of individual firms and the economy as a whole to adverse developments.

Starting in 1991 and lasting until early 1994, firms altered the trend of debt financing and issued new shares of stock instead. Because of lower interest rates on CDs, savers poured funds into mutual funds that soaked up the new stock issues. With stocks trading at high values, issuing relatively fewer shares could raise large amounts of funds. By mid-1994, the trend had reversed. Companies bought back record amounts of stock, and stock buybacks remained brisk a decade later. Companies were using earnings to purchase their own stock rather than to pay dividends. In the bull market of the late 1990s, this activity was also pushing stock prices even higher.

Leverage Ratio
The ratio of debt to equity on a firm's balance sheet.

Endnotes

1. "America Bubbles Over," *The Economist* (April 18–24, 1998): 67.
2. Corporations are legal entities that own the assets of the corporation. Stocks represent ownership of the legal entity rather than ownership of the assets directly.
3. Indeed, in January 2003, Microsoft announced that it would begin paying dividends for the first time.
4. NYSE Regulation, Inc., is a not-for-profit corporation with the official goals of strengthening market integrity and investor protection. NYSE Regulation is a subsidiary of NYSE Euronext and its board of directors, with a majority of directors unaffiliated with any other NYSE board. NYSE Regulation is thus relatively independent in its decision making.
5. Over time, movements in the Dow have been closely correlated with the overall movement of more broadly based stock market indexes.
6. The NYSE has proposed to the SEC that the relevant index should be changed to the NYSE Composite from the DJIA.

7. The NASDAQ purchased the online trading network Instinet in 2006. It then spun out Instinet, LLC as private agency broker, which was then acquired by Nomura Holdings, Inc., in 2007.

8. Terminology is not uniform in this area, with some writers using the term "discount factor" to mean $d=1/(1+r)$, in which case r would be called the "discount rate." We reserve the term "discount rate" to denote the rate set by the Fed, and use "discount factor" to denote $d =$ "rate of time preference," or the interest rate used to discount future payments.

9. The covariance between two variables is a measure of how the variables move together. The variance of a variable is a measure of how a variable moves relative to its mean. In reality, beta is the covariance between a specific stock's return and the market's return, all divided by the variance of the market's return.

10. Historically, dividends were subject to so-called double taxation. They were taxed as part of business income and taxed again as part of household income. Tax law changes in 2003 reduced taxes on dividend income that households receive.

15

People tell their friends about their winners and the IRS about their losers.

Securities Firms, Mutual Funds, and Financial Conglomerates

Learning Objectives

After reading this chapter, you should know:

What securities firms are and what financial services they provide

What the various types of mutual funds are

What hedge funds and real estate investment trusts (REITs) are

What the role of government-sponsored enterprises (GSEs) is

What financial conglomerates are and why they have grown so much in recent years

THE BOILER ROOM

Seth was a young, intelligent, upper-middle-class, frustrated college dropout who wanted to make a "quick, easy buck." In the fast-track economy of the 1990s, he saw many people had struck it rich in the stock market. From his apartment, Seth had been running a successful but illegal gambling operation that catered to college students who played cards between classes. His big chance came when a customer asked him to go to work for J.T. Marlin, a securities firm out on Long Island. He was told that like many other young stockbrokers in New York, he would be able to make $1 million within three years if he worked hard. Seth went for the bait.

He soon discovered that the securities he would be selling were bogus. The corporations issuing them had no assets or products, and the securities existed only on paper. Friends of Michael Brantley, the owner of J.T. Marlin, owned the fake corporations. The funds that were raised went to these friends, who then shared them with Brantley. In this way, the brokers working for J.T. Marlin could be paid commissions that exceeded the maximum allowed by securities regulations. Prices were pushed artificially high because of aggressive brokers who worked in a "boiler room" and created a false demand for the stock. Lies were told to potential investors about the prospects of the fake corporations, and unscrupulous brokers employed high-pressure sales techniques. Apparently, not all of the brokers knew the depths of the scam and chose to look the other way as they made millions.

After all the shares of the spurious corporations had been sold, the brokers no longer pushed the stock and its price fell through the floor. Investors were left with worthless securities. Many unsuspecting investors who hoped to make a killing in the market lost everything they had. Brantley, his friends, and the brokers who work for J.T. Marlin made a bundle.

Needless to say, the firm was violating many government regulations and committing many crimes. Regulators were hot on its trail. Eventually, J.T. Marlin was closed down and the owners hopefully brought to justice. For immunity and to save his father's career (his father was a judge), Seth Davis turned state's evidence.[1]

You may recognize that interesting plot if you saw the hit movie *The Boiler Room*. It is far from realistic in that the overwhelming majority of securities firms operate above board, and regulators are keeping closer watch over the industry, particularly since the mutual fund scandal of the early 2000s. The movie does, however, capture some aspects of how securities firms operate, particularly in a booming economy. Brokers can be aggressive and investors can be naive. Sometimes, buyers do minimal research into the quality of the securities they purchase. Finally, financial prices can change dramatically based on rumors or whims.

In this chapter, we consider securities firms—investment banks, securities brokers, and dealers. As noted, not many securities firms are like J.T. Marlin in that they do not deal with phony securities or pay illegal commissions. Instead, securities firms are important in the marketing of newly issued and previously issued financial claims. They "grease the wheels" in the raising of funds for net borrowers and the transferring of debt and equity securities among investors. Also, as mentioned in Chapters 4 and 11, the investment banking industry is in the process of ongoing change due to the collapse, mergers, or changing structure of the five seminal investment banks in the ongoing financial crisis of 2008.

We also look at mutual funds and government-sponsored enterprises (GSEs) in this chapter. Investment banks, brokers and dealers, mutual funds, and GSEs are the major financial institutions that make up the securities industry. Many of these firms are experiencing severe stress due to the financial crisis in 2008. As noted in Chapter 11,

Fannie Mae and Freddie Mac have been put into conservatorship by the federal government. These institutions have played central roles in the financial system and hence it is not surprising that many of them are under severe strain in late 2008.

The emergence of financial conglomerates is also discussed. Financial conglomerates meld together financial services once provided separately by several intermediaries and differing financial institutions. In this way, conglomerates offer a variety of financial services under one roof and operate on a nationwide and global basis. Note that the ongoing financial crisis of 2008 is hastening the emergence of financial conglomerates by encouraging mergers between healthy and distressed firms. For example, Bank of America purchased the investment bank Merrill Lynch and Countrywide Financial, and J.P. Morgan Chase Bank took over the investment bank Bear Stearns, with the injection of $29 billion from the federal government.

By structuring the text as we have, we hope to give you a more representative picture of the dynamic trends among major financial institutions and the key roles they play in the financial system. We also acknowledge the major changes going on within the securities industry and the incredible changes that will occur in the next few years because of the ongoing crisis.

SECURITIES FIRMS

Securities firms aid in the smooth functioning of the financial system. There are two main functions of securities firms: investment banking and buying and selling previously issued securities. Investment banking deals with the marketing of newly issued securities in the primary market. Brokers and dealers assist in the marketing of previously issued securities in the secondary market. Some securities firms provide both functions; others provide only one or the other.

During the 1990s, securities firms experienced tremendous growth as the average daily trading volume of U.S. securities increased 512 percent. In the bear market of the early 2000s, the industry shrank, only to rise again from 2003 to 2007. As noted above, these trends have reversed dramatically in 2008, as many security firms have bought, sold, and held many of the "toxic" securities that have caused the financial meltdown in 2008. At the same time, households have shifted their liquid financial assets away from bank deposits and into financial securities. The percentage of household financial assets in bank deposits fell from 55 percent in 1975, to 23 percent in 1990, and 16.3 percent in 2007. The corresponding value for direct mutual fund share ownership has increased from 3.5 percent in 1990 to nearly 12 percent in 2007.[2]

Investment Banks: The Primary Market

Investment Banks
Financial institutions that design, market, and underwrite new issuances of securities in the primary market.

We first discussed investment banks in Chapter 4. **Investment banks** are financial institutions that design, market, and underwrite new issuances of securities—stocks or bonds—in the primary market.[3] Merrill Lynch (part of Bank of America), Smith Barney (part of Citigroup), Morgan Stanley, and Goldman Sachs are some of the better-known investment banks. Their main offices tend to be in New York City, but they are electronically linked to branch offices in other major cities in the United States and around the world.

The design function of the investment bank is important because a corporation may need assistance in pricing the new financial instruments that it will issue in the open market. The corporation looks to the investment bank to provide advice about the design of the new offering. In return for their services, the investment bank is paid a fee. In addition to their primary market activity, many investment banks are also brokers and dealers in the secondary markets.

Google's Unusual Initial Public Offering

In August 2004, Google became a publicly traded company. The path for a typical company to "go public" is to have its initial offering of ownership shares (common stock) underwritten by a prestigious and well-connected investment bank or syndicate of banks. The lead investment bank determines an appropriate price and number of shares and thus the total monetary value of the offering. Investors rely on the reputation of the investment banks in deciding to invest or not. Investment banks charge a fee, typically between 4 and 7 percent, for underwriting the new issue and for standing ready to purchase stock in the new company if necessary. Investment banks might set a low initial price and then allocate these low-priced shares to preferred investors. If the price rapidly increases, these initial investors will personally benefit from the "pop." But Google was not a typical firm, and its founders, Larry Page and Sergey Brin, resolved to take the firm public in a way that would benefit it and its new owners more, and the investment banks less.

First, they choose to use an open Dutch auction method to determine the price. This involves potential investors submitting bids of the number of shares desired at different prices. For example, say a new company offered 100 shares of its stock for sale, and investors offered to purchase 30 shares at a price of $70 each, 60 shares at $60, 110 shares at $50, and 180 shares at a price of $40. Those investors willing to pay $70, $60 or $50 would be able to buy at the lowest price where quantity demanded was at least 100, that is, $50. At this price, a total of 200 shares would be demanded but only 100 were offered, so a method for allocating the 100 shares would be needed. For example, each investor could receive 100/200 or 50 percent of the shares they demanded. Thus, the three investors would purchase 15, 30 and 55 respectively.

Google's initial public offering took place on August 19, 2004, at a price of $85 per share, implying a total value of $23 billion. On the first day of trading, the share price jumped to $100, and by October of 2008, the price of one share of Google was worth more than $386 (down from its peak of $714 in December 2007).

Responsibilities for New Offerings

Initial Public Offering (IPO)
An offering of stocks or bonds to the public by a company that has not previously sold securities to the public.

There are two types of new offerings. When a company has not previously sold financial stocks or bonds to the public, the offering is an **initial public offering (IPO)**. The investment bank will try to establish an appropriate price by looking at stock prices of other firms in the industry with comparable characteristics. Because no previously issued securities are being publicly traded, it is usually much more difficult to determine the price at which securities in an IPO should be offered. In the case of bonds, investment banks look to the market prices of existing bonds with comparable maturity, risk, and liquidity. The issuer's existing degree of leverage (reliance or borrowed funds) is also a determinant of how much can be raised and at what price in the bond market.

Seasoned Issuance
The offering of new securities by a corporation that has outstanding previously issued securities.

When stocks or bonds have been previously issued, the offering is called a **seasoned issuance**. The price of the new issue should be the same as the market price of the outstanding shares. However, the investment bank must still anticipate how the new issue will affect the market price of the outstanding shares. Likewise, with a seasoned issuance of bonds, the investment bank must anticipate how the greater degree of leverage will affect the price at which the new bonds can be sold.

Timing. Timing is one of the most important factors affecting the selling price of new securities. For example, it may be a good time to sell newly issued shares if the corporation's outstanding stock were trading at relatively high prices, if favorable earnings reports have recently been issued, and if the economy is particularly strong. A relatively larger amount of funds can be raised by issuing fewer shares at a higher price than if the stock were trading at a lower price. Likewise, if long-term interest rates are relatively low and profit expectations are high, it may be a good time to issue bonds.

The role of the Securities and Exchange Commission. Once the amount, type, and pricing of securities have been established, the investment bank assists the corporation in filling out and filing the necessary documents with the **Securities and Exchange Commission (SEC)**. The SEC is a government regulatory agency that was created in 1934 to regulate the securities industry. Primary areas of regulation include setting "disclosure" requirements for new securities issues and monitoring illegal and fraudulent behavior in securities markets. As noted above, securities firms have played a central part in the financial crisis of 2008. An SEC ruling in 2004 that allowed for much greater leveraging (reliance on borrowed funds) among the largest investment banking firms has been cited as contributing to the crisis.

The SEC maintains active supervision of investment banks, particularly with regard to information that must be disclosed to potential investors. A corporation must go through the formal procedure of filing with the SEC if the securities issuance is higher than $1.5 million and if the term to maturity is more than 270 days. A **registration statement** must be filed with the SEC before the offering can be issued. This statement contains information about the offering, the company, and other disclosure information, including relevant information about management, what the funds will be used for, and the financial health of the corporation. Once the registration statement has been filed, the SEC has 20 days to respond. If the SEC does not object during the 20-day period, the securities can be sold to the public. The lack of an objection by the SEC in no way means that the new securities are of high quality or that the price is appropriate. It simply means that it appears that the proper information has been disclosed to potential investors. The **prospectus,** which is a subpart of the registration statement, must be given to investors before they purchase the securities. It contains all of the disclosures and pertinent information about the new offering that the SEC requires.

Credit rating. Investment banks also assist in obtaining a credit rating for the new bond issues from Standard & Poor's, Fitch's, or Moody's Investors Services. A trustee is selected to monitor whether or not the corporation fulfills the terms of the offering as outlined in the **bond indenture.** The terms of the offering along with many other provisions are spelled out in the bond indenture before the bonds are issued. Investment banks may also assist in arranging that the issuance of new stock is listed (traded) on an exchange and/or in the over-the-counter market.

Underwriting and marketing. Once the necessary steps to issue the new securities have been taken, the investment bank takes on the responsibility of underwriting and marketing the securities. In underwriting the security, the investment bank purchases the entire issuance at an agreed-upon price. It then assumes responsibility for marketing the newly issued securities. If the price at which the bank sells the securities is higher than the price it paid, the bank will earn a profit on the spread. If the securities sell for less than the agreed-upon price, the investment bank accepts the loss.

Securities and Exchange Commission (SEC)
The government agency that regulates the securities industry and monitors illegal and fraudulent behavior in securities markets.

Registration Statement
A statement that must be filed with the SEC before a new securities offering can be issued.

Prospectus
A subpart of the registration statement that must be given to investors before they purchase the securities.

Bond Indenture
A document that outlines the terms of a bond issuance.

Syndicate

A group of investment banks, each of which underwrites a proportion of new securities offerings.

Sometimes one investment bank may be reluctant to take full responsibility for a new issuance. In this case, the bank may form a **syndicate** by asking other investment banks to underwrite part of the new offering. The syndicate is merely a group of investment banks, each of which underwrites a portion of a new securities offering. In a syndicate, each participating investment bank earns the profit—or assumes the loss—on the portion of the new offering it underwrites.

Investment Banks and the Functioning of the Primary Market

As a key player in financial markets, investment banks facilitate the smooth and orderly functioning of primary markets. They stand ready to buy and sell and to adjust prices—literally making a market. If there are 100,000 shares of a stock for sale at a particular price, and if buyers take only 80,000 shares at that price, the investment bank that bought the securities may hold them for a time to keep the price from falling erratically. Or the investment bank may alter prices until all, or most, of the shares are sold. Thus, the investment bank enables the ongoing shuffling and rearranging of portfolios by standing ready to hold the securities if there is no immediate buyer. Although these actions can involve risk for the investment bank, they enhance market efficiency and contribute to an efficiently functioning financial system. The investment bank is rewarded with profits from fees for designing and assisting in the underwriting of the new securi-

15-1

U.S. Corporate Underwriting Activity, 1985–2008 (Billions of Dollars, Rounded)

Year	New Debt Issues	New Equity Issues	Total Underwritings
1985	$98	$33	$131
1986	217	57	274
1987	211	53	264
1988	201	37	238
1989	164	31	195
1990	169	24	193
1991	281	76	357
1992	386	102	488
1993	535	131	666
1994	390	77	467
1995	441	97	539
1996	584	152	736
1997	785	153	938
1998	1,107	153	1,260
1999	1,084	192	1,275
2000	1,076	205	1,281
2001	1,454	170	1,624
2002	1,400	154	1,554
2003	1,794	156	1,950
2004	2,086	203	2,290
2005	2,601	190	2,791
2006	3,148	191	3,339
2007	2774.3	247.5	3,021.8
2008	937.1	242.6	1,179.7

Source: Securities Industry and Financial Markets Association (SIFMA), **http://www.sifma.org/ research/statistics/other/keystats.pdf.**

ties and (as you saw earlier) from hopefully selling the securities at a higher price than what they paid for them.

Exhibit 15-1 shows U.S. corporate underwriting activity since 1985. Note that new debt issuances exceeded new equity issues in every year between 1985 and 2008, usually by increasingly larger amounts. Outstanding debt does not grow as fast as the new issuances would suggest because some debt issues mature each year, while equity issues do not mature. However, in some cases, stocks are bought back and retired by the corporations that issued them. Note also the relatively large issuances of equity in the late 1990s, when stock valuations were particularly high.

Private Placement

Private Placement
The sale of new securities to a limited number of large investors; because the number of investors is small, the underwriting process is avoided.

Investment banks also handle **private placement**. This is an alternative for a corporation issuing new securities that bypasses the process described previously and places the new securities offering privately. In a private placement, new securities are sold to a limited number of investors. Because the number of investors is small, they are of necessity very large investors such as commercial banks, insurance companies, pension plans, or mutual funds. Private placements occur more frequently with bonds than with stocks.

Private Equity

Private equity funds have historically been a major source of funding for start-up companies and for firms that are in financial distress. Private equity funds are investment companies that buy publicly held companies and convert them to private ownership—usually through a limited partnership. Although the market for private equity started in the 1960s, it expanded rapidly in the mid-2000s. This represents a significant change in the way corporations are owned. Private equity firms avoid the disclosure regulations that publicly traded firms face. They also avoid the accounting regulations put on publicly traded firms by the Sarbanes-Oxley legislation following the corporate scandal of the early 2000s. Some of the better known companies that have been bought or are in the process of being bought are Chrysler, Dunkin' Brands (owners of Dunkin' Donuts, Baskin-Robbins, and Togo's), Toys "R" Us, Hertz, Neiman Marcus, Univision, Qantas Airlines, Clear Channel Communications, Bausch and Harrah's Entertainment, and Albertsons.

Recap   Investment banks design, market, and underwrite the issuance of new securities (stocks and bonds) in the primary market. The securities may be an IPO or a seasoned offering. In addition to advising the issuer about market conditions and prospective prices, the investment bank assists in filing the necessary forms with the SEC so that the new securities can be sold publicly. A registration statement must be filed with the SEC. Part of the registration statement is the prospectus that contains information and disclosures about the issuance. The prospectus is distributed to investors. The SEC is concerned that appropriate information is disclosed to the public; approval by the SEC to sell the securities is in no way an endorsement of their quality or an acknowledgement that the price is proper. Private placement of securities to a limited number of investors is an alternative to going through the underwriting process. Private equity firms have recently increased in importance in funding start-ups and distressed companies.

BROKERS AND DEALERS: THE SECONDARY MARKET

Broker
An individual who arranges trades between buyers and sellers of securities for a fee.

Brokers and dealers make up brokerage firms, which are securities firms that also facilitate the smooth and orderly functions of secondary financial markets. **Brokers** arrange trades between buyers and sellers—that is, they arrange for a buyer to purchase securities from a seller. The broker charges a brokerage fee, or commission, for arranging the trade. **Dealers** are market makers who, in addition to arranging trades between buyers and sellers, stand ready to be a principal in a transaction and may maintain an inventory of securities. Dealers stand ready to purchase and hold previously issued securities sold by investors. Because the dealer carries an inventory of securities and then sells them to other investors, there is the risk that the price of the securities will fall and the brokerage firm will experience a capital loss.

Types of Orders

Three types of orders may be placed with brokerage firms: market orders, limit orders, and short sells. **Market orders** direct the broker or dealer to purchase or sell the securities at the present market price. **Limit orders** instruct the broker or dealer either to purchase the securities at the market price up to a certain maximum, if possible, or to sell the securities at the market price if it is above a certain minimum. Securities are bought at one price (the **bid price**) and sold at a higher price (the **asked price**).

A **short sell** instructs the broker or dealer to borrow shares of stocks and sell them today with the guarantee that the borrowed stocks will be replaced by a particular date in the future. The investor engages in a short sell if he or she believes that the stock's price is going to fall in the future and that the borrowed shares will be paid back with shares purchased in the future at the lower price. A high volume of short sells indicates that investors believe that the stock's price is going to fall. If the price does not fall, the buyer of the short sell must purchase the shares at a higher price and thus loses money. If many buyers of short sells are in this position, the market price is pushed even higher.

Margin Loans

Full-service brokerage firms not only arrange for the trading of securities but also give investment advice to potential investors. In addition, they may make loans, called **margin loans**, to investors to help them purchase securities. In this case, investors do not have to put up funds equal to the full value of the purchase. Instead, they can purchase stocks on the margin by borrowing. The **margin requirement** is the percentage of a stock purchase that can be borrowed as opposed to being paid in readily available funds. The current margin requirement, which is set by the Fed, has been 50 percent since 1974 and applies only to initial purchases. Many individual brokerage firms set margin requirements higher than 50 percent and vary them depending on the stocks being traded and the trading behavior of individual customers.

Brokerage Fees

Until 1975, all brokerage firms charged investors virtually the same brokerage fees for executing trades of financial securities. Brokerage firms distinguished themselves among investors by engaging in non-price competition. Some attempted to offer better and more attentive advice established through market research. Others had geographical advantages, name recognition, or other attributes that led to better customer relationships. All of this began to change when Congress passed the Securities Acts Amendment of 1975 that eliminated fixed commissions. Instead of engaging only in non-price competition, brokerage firms could compete by offering lower fees.

Discount brokerage firms provide only limited or no investment advice, but their fees are much lower than those of full-service brokerage firms. In recent years, because of increased competition among brokerage firms and the emergence of discount brokers

Dealer
An individual who arranges trade and stands ready to be a principal in a transaction.

Market Orders
Orders by an investor that direct the broker or dealer to purchase or sell securities at the present market price.

Limit Orders
Orders that instruct the broker or dealer to purchase securities at the market price up to a certain maximum or to sell the securities at the market price if it is above a certain minimum.

Bid Price
The price at which a dealer is willing to buy securities.

Asked Price
The price at which a dealer is willing to sell securities.

Short Sell
Investors' instructions to brokers or dealers to borrow shares of stocks and sell them today with the guarantee that the investors will replace the borrowed stocks by a date in the future.

Margin Loans
Loans to investors for which the proceeds are used to purchase securities.

Margin Requirement
The percentage of a stock purchase that can be borrowed.

Online Trading

What is online trading? In general, it means trading stocks, mutual funds, and money market shares via the Internet. Brokers and dealers, of course, use computers for most of their trading. However, online trading usually refers to an individual's use of computers for trading.

Online trading offers the public more control over trading and over their financial accounts. However, even more significantly, it offers lower fees for executing trades and hosting financial accounts. Online trading brokerage firms can do this because they use technology to automate these processes. This makes trading less costly and increases the volume that can be handled.

Before the Internet, only a few firms offered computerized trading, mainly through direct dial-up connections. The customer base was very small. However, with the explosive growth of the Internet, the number of online trading brokerage firms and customers has shot upward. The number of online accounts increased from zero in 1994 to about 10 million in 2000. Although the rate of growth in online trading accounts slowed in the early 2000s, some researchers estimated that as of 2008, the number of such accounts was nearing 50 million.

The increased popularity of online trading has brought about a new set of brokerage firms coming from three major sources. One source is discount brokerage firms seeking new ways to offer low-cost trading services. The second source is new companies created as online trading brokerage firms. The final source is existing full-service brokerage firms coming late into the online trading market; these firms have added online trading to their list of services to prevent the loss of customers to other online trading firms.

Even though many traditional full-service brokerage firms have added online trading to their list of services, they still have experienced a rapid decline in commission revenues. Consequently, these brokerage firms have concentrated on improving information services such as advising and consulting, while offering other advanced trading services such as making margin loans to their customers.

Other types of online traders include people who do not work for brokerage firms but still trade for a living—commonly called *daytraders*—and people who have other jobs to earn a living and trade only as frequently as they wish. The latter group includes people with savings who want to earn extra money in addition to their primary income, often to build funds for retirement. Both types of online traders use the services of online trading brokerage firms.

Daytraders, however, typically use specialized online trading firms because they need more sophisticated services. The brokerage firms used by daytraders provide more sophisticated software and more real-time, direct, and detailed access to information and stock exchanges. This is often referred to as *direct access trading*. An example of this is NASDAQ Level II quotes. Typically, the general public and other online traders see only one price at a time listed for a particular security (for example, IBM stock). NASDAQ Level II, however, shows several prices and volumes for recent trades of a particular stock. This level of information is of little use to most non-daytraders, although it is sometimes offered to those with big accounts who engage in heavy trading.

Online brokerage firms engaged in price wars in the mid- to late 1990s. However, pricing has stabilized, and firms now compete more on features such as ease of use and quality of information. This competition has brought about two new services to the online trading market: (1) trading in foreign stock markets and (2) using remote handheld devices, such as cellular phones and two-way pagers, to get online information and to execute online trades.

and online trading, brokerage fee revenues have fallen. In place of trading fees, brokerage firms are earning more from advising fees and from interest income on margin loans. The development of the Internet allows for the further evolution of securities marketing by allowing for online trading. "A Closer Look" on p. 355 explores the emergence of online trading.

In addition to regulation by the SEC, the securities industry is also self-regulated by the **Financial Industry Regulatory Authority (FINRA)**, which was created by the consolidation of regulatory functions of the National Association of Securities Dealers (NASD) and the New York Stock Exchange. Brokerage firms that are registered with the SEC must also purchase insurance for their customers from the **Securities Industry Protection Corporation (SIPC)**. SIPC is a nonprofit membership corporation that U.S. registered brokers and dealers are required by law to join. Congress established SIPC in 1970. Its purpose is to protect investors' securities from liquidation by the brokerage firm. Each investor is insured for $500,000. Note that this does not protect investors from losses because of falls in securities prices; however, it does protect the investor from losses resulting from the bankruptcy or insolvency of the brokerage firm.

The income of securities firms depends on the fees and commissions they generate in their day-to-day activities. As of December 31, 2008, the financial assets of security brokers and dealers were about $2,982.9 trillion, a sizable increase from $1,613 trillion just four years earlier in 2003, and $83.3 billion in 1982. These figures reveal the growth of trading within the industry, despite smaller commissions, as financial markets have created new types of financial instruments such as derivatives that first exploded and are now imploding in the financial crisis of 2008.

The Financial Industry Regulatory Authority (FINRA)
A nongovernmental regulator of the U.S. securities industry with authority over more than 5,000 brokerage firms. FINRA was created in July 2007 by consolidation of regulatory functions of the NASD and the New York Stock Exchange.

Securities Industry Protection Corporation (SIPC)
A nonprofit membership corporation established by Congress that provides insurance to protect investors' securities from liquidation by the brokerage firm.

Recap	Brokerage firms are important financial institutions because they facilitate the smooth functioning of securities markets. Brokers arrange the trading of financial securities among corporations and investors in exchange for a brokerage fee. Dealers not only arrange trades but also buy and sell financial securities for their own portfolios in order to make a market. Market orders direct the broker or dealer to purchase or sell the securities at the present market price. Limit orders instruct the broker or dealer either to purchase the securities at the market price up to a certain maximum if possible or to sell the securities at the market price if it is above a certain minimum. A short sell instructs the broker or dealer to borrow shares of stocks and sell them today with the guarantee that the borrowed stocks will be replaced by a date in the future. The investor engages in a short sell if he or she believes that the stock's price is going to fall in the future and that the borrowed shares will be paid back with shares bought at a lower price.

INVESTMENT COMPANIES

Investment Companies
Companies that own and manage a large group of different securities for investors who have purchased shares of the companies.

Unlike the securities firms just described, **investment companies** are financial intermediaries that raise funds from many small investors by selling shares in the company. The funds are then pooled together and used to purchase financial securities. Investment companies reduce risk for individual investors by purchasing hundreds or even thousands of different securities. This allows individual investors to diversify to a much greater extent than they would be able to by purchasing individual securities on their own. In addition, because large blocks of securities are bought and sold, the investment company can take advantage of volume discounts, and the transactions costs per share are lower than if smaller amounts of securities had been purchased or sold. Investors share in the gains and losses proportionate to the size of their investment.

Open-End and Closed-End Companies

Open-End
A mutual fund (type of investment company) that continually sells new shares to the public or buys outstanding shares from the public at a price equal to the net asset value.

Investment companies may be **open-end** or **closed-end**. An open-end fund continually sells new shares to the public or buys outstanding shares from the public at a price equal to the net asset value. The net asset value per share is found by subtracting the liabilities of the mutual fund from the market value of the securities that the fund owns and dividing the difference by the outstanding number of shares.

Closed-End
Investment companies that sell a limited number of shares like other corporations but usually do not buy back outstanding shares.

The vast majority of investment companies are open-end companies called **mutual funds**. Mutual funds that deal in money market instruments with an original maturity of one year or less are called **money market mutual funds**. They issue more shares as investors demand them. Because they buy and sell their own shares, mutual fund shares are not traded on organized exchanges. Mutual funds sell their own new shares to investors and stand ready to buy back outstanding shares.

Mutual Funds
Investment companies that pool funds from many small investors by selling shares.

Closed-end investment companies sell shares like other corporations, but usually do not buy back outstanding shares. Once the sale of a limited number of shares is completed, the fund is "closed" to new purchases, but the shares may be traded like shares of stock on organized exchanges. Because the price of a share of a closed-end fund is determined by supply and demand, it can differ from the net asset value.

Money Market Mutual Funds
Mutual funds that deal in money market instruments with an original maturity of one year or less.

Load and No-Load Companies

Some investment companies require that a **load**, or sales commission, be paid to a broker to buy into a fund. **No-load** funds are purchased directly from the mutual fund company without a broker or a sales commission.

Load
A sales commission paid to a broker to purchase mutual funds.

Both load and no-load companies deduct a percentage from the net asset value each year to administer the funds. The fees are usually in the range of 0.2 to 1.5 percent. Both types of funds may also deduct a fee called *12b-1* (named for the SEC regulation that authorizes the fee) for marketing and advertising expenses. By law, the load, administrative fees, and 12b-1 fees cannot exceed 8.5 percent of the investment for loaded funds. Finally, there can be a redemption fee, called a *back-end load*, to sell the investment company shares. An investor should know all of the fees before investing in a fund.

No-Load
Mutual funds that are purchased directly from the mutual fund company and are not subject to a load.

Growth of Investment Funds

Investment funds, particularly mutual funds, have experienced incredible growth since the late 1980s. One reason for this trend is legislation that gave individuals control over where their pension funds are invested, and many have chosen mutual funds. By 2007, over 45 percent of U.S. households owned mutual funds. Exhibit 15-2 shows the growth of mutual funds, money market mutual funds, and closed-end investment funds from

15-2
The Value of Outstanding Shares of Investment Companies, 1982–2008 (Billions of Dollars)

Year	Money Market Mutual Funds	Open-End Mutual Funds	Closed-End Investment Companies
1982	219.9	76.9	7.5
1983	179.5	112.1	7.4
1984	232.2	135.6	6.4
1985	242.4	245.9	8.3
1986	290.6	426.5	14.5
1987	313.8	480.2	21.3
1988	335.0	500.5	43.2
1989	424.7	589.6	2.5
1990	498.3	608.4	52.9
1991	535.0	769.5	71.2
1992	539.5	992.5	93.5
1993	589.6	1,375.4	116.1
1994	602.9	1,477.3	117.8
1995	745.3	1,852.8	134.4
1996	891.1	2,342.4	144.7
1997	1,048.7	2,989.4	149.4
1998	1,334.2	3,613.1	151.0
1999	1,578.8	4,538.5	152.1
2000	1,812.1	4,435.3	141.9
2001	2,240.7	4,135.5	139.5
2002	2,223.9	3,638.4	150.8
2003	2,016.4	4,654.2	205.6
2004	1,879.8	5,436.3	245.9
2005	2,006.9	6,048.9	270.7
2006	2,312.1	7,068.3	294.3
2007	3,053.2	7,798.3	318.9
2008	3,376.5	6,588.3	256.5

Sources: *Flow of Funds Account of the United States, Z.1,* Board of Governors of the Federal Reserve System, various issues.

1982 to 2007. Note that the rapid changes in the value of outstanding shares was due not only to additional funds flowing into or out of mutual funds but also to changes in market valuations. Also note that the dollar amounts invested in open-end mutual funds are much higher than those invested in closed-end investment companies.

Often, many types of mutual funds are offered by a single investment company. Investors can own several different funds within one investment company. They can choose the funds they prefer depending on their investment needs. Investors can also move their money in and out of various funds within one company at a relatively low cost. Some of the better-known and larger investment companies that you may have heard of are Fidelity, Vanguard, American Funds, Putnam, Janus, Franklin, and T. Rowe Price.

Exhibit 15-3 outlines various types of funds that investors can select, depending on their particular goals and risk tolerance.

Investment companies also create new funds that invest in several mutual funds. In reality, the investor purchases a **fund of funds.** For example, Vanguard's STAR fund

Fund of Funds
A mutual fund that invests in a portfolio of other mutual funds rather than individual stocks and/or bonds.

15-3
A Sample of the Types of
Mutual Funds

Stock Funds

Aggressive growth funds seek capital appreciation by investing in small companies with potential for growth; such funds are risky but often pay high returns.

Global equity funds invest in stocks from around the world, thereby achieving greater diversification than that achieved by investing in comparable stocks provided by one country; the downside is exposure to losses if exchange rates change adversely.

Growth and income funds invest in companies that are expected to grow and that pay dividends.

Income-equity funds invest in companies expected to pay high dividends.

Index funds invest in a market basket of stocks that replicates the basket included in a stock market index such as the S&P 500; index funds attempt to match the performance of the index.

Sector funds invest in stocks of particular industries such as biotechnology or health care; because diversification is less than that achieved in more broadly based funds, returns can be more volatile.

Socially conscious funds invest in companies they believe to be ethically responsible; depending on the specific values and goals, these funds may avoid stocks of companies involved with cigarettes, alcohol, gambling, weapons, or nuclear power; they may also avoid stocks of a country whose leadership they believe is repressive.

Bond Funds

Corporate bond funds invest only in corporate bonds.

Global bond funds invest in bonds from around the world; the exchange rate risk can be high.

Ginnie Mae funds invest in Ginnie Mae mortgage-backed securities.

High-yield bond funds invest most of their portfolio in junk bonds; these funds offer the potential for high returns but also entail high risk.

Long-term municipal bond funds invest in a broad base of municipal bonds; earnings are exempt from federal taxes.

State municipal bond funds invest in municipal bonds from one state; earnings are exempt from federal taxes and from state taxes for investors living in the issuing state.

U.S. government income funds invest in U.S. government bonds and government agency securities.

Stock and Bond Funds

Balanced funds invest in some combination of stocks and bonds to preserve principal, generate income, and achieve long-term growth.

Flexible portfolio funds can vary relative investments among stocks, bonds, and money market instruments depending on management.

Income mixed funds invest in stocks and bonds to earn high dividend and interest income.

Convertible securities funds invest in securities (such as preferred stock or bonds) that can be converted to common stock; such securities offer the potential to share in earnings if the company does very well by converting to common stock.

---

invests in nine different Vanguard funds. In general, 60 to 70 percent of investments are held in stock funds, 20 to 30 percent in bond funds, and 10 to 20 percent in money market mutual funds. The advantages to investors are that funds of funds achieve much greater diversification than if they invested in only one mutual fund, and they save the

Investment Companies

In *Barron's* weekly publication, *The Wall Street Journal*, or online, you can find quotations for open-end and closed-end mutual funds. The purpose of this "Cracking the Code" is to familiarize you with how to decipher those quotes.

FUND	NAV	Net Chg	YTD % Ret	3-Yr % Ret
American Century 1st				
EquIndex....................	5.31	−0.09	−9.1	16.2
EqGro........................	21.96	−0.31	−9.3	14.6
EqInc........................	7.31	−.011	−6.3	16.4
IncGro......................	26.82	−0.34	−7.2	13.9
LgCoVal....................	6.52	−0.15	−8.9	12.5
StrMod......................	6.49	−0.03	−5.3	25.4

Source: Barron's, March 3, 2008.

Open-End Mutual Funds

The following quotes are from the March 3, 2008, edition of *Barron's*, and show a group of six different mutual funds offered by American Century 1st. The funds differ by the amount of risk, and the name of each fund often describes the type of financial instruments in which it invests.

Look at the underlined row. In the first column, *Eq-Gro* is the name of the fund within the group of American Century 1st Funds. As the name (short for Equity and Growth) implies, this fund invests in growth stocks that are held in the hopes of high potential appreciation as opposed to current income from dividends. The second column gives the net asset value (21.96) as of the end of the previous week, February 29, 2008. The third column gives the net change in the net asset value from the previous Friday (−0.31), while the fourth column gives the year-to-date percent return to the fund (−9.3), which in this case is from January 1, 2008, to February 29, 2008. The fifth and final column gives the three-year percent return (+14.6). In this example, the net asset value is $21.96, down $0.31 from the previous Friday, the year-to-date percent return is negative 9.3 percent, and the three-year return from February 2005 to February 2008 is positive 14.6 percent in total.

Note that if you invest in the *EqGro* fund of the American Century 1st Funds, you are investing in one of six funds offered by American Century 1st Funds, not in a fund of funds. An investor can invest in one or more of the funds to tailor the amount of overall risk to his or her specific needs. Larger mutual fund companies offer far more than six different funds. For example, Fidelity Investments offers more than 175 different no-load mutual funds.

Closed-End Funds

Below is a portion of the closed-end funds section of the March 3, 2008, edition of *Barron's*. This portion looks at U.S. government bond funds. Look at the underlined row. In the first column is the fund's name, BR Enhcd Govt (EGF),

FUND NAME (SYMBOL)	Stock Exch	NAV	Mkt Price	Prem/ Disc	12 mos Yield
U.S. Government Bond Fund					
AllianceBernInc (ACG)	N	8.69	8.37	−3.7	8.1
BR Enhcd Govt (EGF)	N	18.01	17.37	−3.6	7.8
MFS Govt Mkes (MGF)	N	7.31	7.00	−4.2	5.9
WstAstInftMgt (IMF)	N	19.29	17.17	−11.0	4.3
WstAstClymrinfLnkOpp (WIW)	N	14.00	12.25	−12.5	6.1
WstAstClymrinfLnkSec (WIA)	N	13.90	12.28	−11.7	5.7

Source: Barron's, March 3, 2008.

for Blackrock Enhanced Government Fund, followed by the fund's ticker symbol (EGF). The second column gives a one-letter abbreviation of the exchange (N) on which the fund is traded. The N stands for the New York Stock Exchange. The third column gives the net asset value ($18.01). The fourth column gives the closing market price of the fund ($17.37) on Friday, February 29, 2008, the previous trading day. Because this is a closed-end fund, the market or closing price can be more or less than the net asset value. In this case, the net asset value ($18.01) is more than the market price of the fund

($17.37), and the fund is trading at a discount. The fifth column gives the percentage premium or discount (above or below the net asset value) at which the fund was trading the previous week (−3.6 percent). The current discount can be calculated: ($17.34 − $18.01)/$18.01 = −.036, or −3.6 percent. The final column gives the percentage 52-week market return (7.8 percent). For bond funds, the 52-week market return is based on the past 12-month income distributions as a percent of the current market price.

time and effort of investing in several different mutual funds on their own. A disadvantage is that costs can be high because both the individual funds and the fund of funds may charge fees. If investors pick different funds on their own, they can avoid the fund of funds fees.[4] By December 2008, there were over 8000 mutual funds that belonged to the Investment Company Institute (ICI), the national association of investment companies in the United States, with combined assets of $9.6 trillion. To put these numbers in perspective, note that stocks of only about 2,800 individual companies trade on the New York Stock Exchange.

| Recap | Investment companies are financial intermediaries that pool the funds of many investors to invest in several hundred or even thousands of stocks. For any given investment, investment companies offer greater safety and more diversification than investing in just one or a few company's stocks. Money market funds invest in financial instruments with an original maturity of one year or less. Some mutual funds invest in bonds or some combination of both stocks and bonds. An open-end fund continually sells new shares or buys shares from the public at the net asset value and is called a *mutual fund*. Closed-end investment companies sell a limited number of shares that may be traded on the open market and on organized exchanges. The value of open-end funds (mutual funds) greatly exceeds that of closed-end investment companies. The price of closed-end investment companies is determined by supply and demand and can differ from the net asset value. Mutual funds and closed-end investment companies can be either load or no-load funds and have experienced tremendous growth in recent years. |

HEDGE FUNDS

Hedge Fund
A nontraditional type of mutual fund formed as a partnership of up to either 99 or 499 wealthy investors with large minimum investments; attempts to earn maximum returns regardless of rising or falling financial prices.

Historically, a **hedge fund** was a nontraditional investment fund formed as a partnership of up to 99 "accredited" investors who invested in a variety of often risky securities. An accredited investor was one who had at least $1 million in investable assets. In April 1997, the SEC expanded the rules by allowing some hedge funds to raise money from 499 "qualified" investors. In this case, a *qualified investor* is an individual who has a minimum net worth of $5 million, or an institution such as a pension fund or mutual fund with at least $25 million in capital. Today, both types of hedge funds exist.[5]

For all hedge funds, a general partner usually organizes the fund and is responsible for making day-to-day trading decisions. Limited partners put up most of the funds but have limited or no say in the day-to-day decision making. Partners who buy into the hedge funds are wealthy individuals and institutions—minimum investments start around $250,000, and many hedge funds have much higher minimum requirements. Hedge funds may also limit withdrawals or require that funds be invested for a minimum time period, such as 10 years.

Because there are a limited number of wealthy investors, hedge funds are not regulated in the same way that traditional investment pools or mutual funds are. They are not required to file a registration statement and may engage in many trading strategies from which traditional mutual funds are barred. These strategies include borrowing funds to invest, purchasing many types of option and derivative instruments, short selling, and dealing in real estate and commodities.

Hedge funds attempt to earn high or maximum returns regardless of whether prices in broader financial markets are rising or falling. The funds trade securities and other creative financial instruments and try to outperform traditional investment funds by employing novel trading strategies.

In general, hedge funds use riskier investment strategies than traditional mutual funds, although some are less risky than others. As you have seen, the funds often rely on borrowed funds (leveraging) as well as the funds of the partners. This leverage increases the potential for profits but also magnifies the potential for losses. Short selling to take advantage of falling prices and the use of some risky financial instruments can also result in large losses if prices do not move in the anticipated direction. In general, hedge funds outperform other mutual funds when markets are falling.

Traditionally, hedge funds charge high fees and take a large percent of the profits. For example, some charge a 2 percent annual management fee and take 25 percent of the profits. The remainder of the profits is distributed to the partners based on their percentage of ownership in the fund.

Although the first hedge fund was established more than 50 years ago, the number and assets of hedge funds have grown tremendously since the mid-1990s. Domestic hedge funds now number more than 3,000. Under the 2001 U.S. Patriot Act, hedge funds are required to meet new anti-money-laundering restrictions to prevent money-laundering activities from funding terrorists. Offshore hedge funds are located outside the United States, and they are difficult for most U.S. investors to invest in because of certain tax consequences. The number of partners in offshore hedge funds is unrestricted.

At the present time, hedge funds are becoming more accessible for investors because of the development of *funds of hedge funds*. A fund of hedge funds invests in multiple hedge funds, each usually employing a different investment strategy. Because of pooling, they have lower required minimums for participation and offer less risk due to diversification into many hedge funds.

Some of the strategies employed by hedge funds include:

1. Selling borrowed securities (short selling) in the hope of profiting by buying the securities at a lower price on a future date
2. Exploiting unusual price differences between related securities in anticipation of making a profit when the prices come into more traditional alignment
3. Trading options and other derivatives
4. Borrowing to invest (leveraging) so that returns are increased

REAL ESTATE INVESTMENT TRUSTS

Real Estate Investment Trusts (REITs)
A special type of mutual fund that pools the funds of many small investors and uses them to buy or build income property or to make or purchase mortgage loans; pass-through institutions in which the rents from the income property and/or the interest income from the mortgages are passed through to shareholders.

A **real estate investment trust (REIT)** is a special type of mutual fund that pools the funds of many small investors and uses them to make investments. Whereas other mutual funds invest only in financial instruments, REITs may invest in real property as well. Their funds are used to buy or build income property or to make or purchase mortgage loans, unlike those of traditional mutual funds. Another difference is that to some extent, they also raise funds by taking out bank loans or issuing debt. REITs are pass-through enterprises in that rents from income property and/or interest income from the mortgages are passed through to shareholders. Shareholders are also entitled to any capital gains from the properties that the REITs own.

At least 75 percent of the assets of REITs must be either real property (generally commercial or industrial real estate) or mortgages. The majority of REITs invest in real property such as shopping malls, apartment complexes, hotels, golf courses, and other commercial buildings for income. REITs may either buy or provide the funding to build income property. The income from property provides a steady, dependable stream of income for investors. Some REITs either make or purchase mortgage loans on commercial property, and some do both.

REITs resulted from legislation passed by Congress in 1960. The intent of the legislation was to give small investors an opportunity to invest in commercial real estate. At that time, REITs could own income property but not manage it. REITs did not become very popular until 1986, when the restrictions on managing income property were removed. Now individual REITs have different characteristics and may be highly specialized, depending on the investment strategy and management style of the fund's manager. They are virtually diversified holdings of real estate investments that are professionally managed.

By law, REITs must return 95 percent of their earnings to shareholders each year. Therefore, if they want to expand, they must issue new equity or debt or take out bank loans. REITs are also attractive because most of their earnings (95 percent of which are passed through) are exempt from corporate federal and state income taxes, thereby avoiding double taxation and allowing for fairly predictable income streams.

Shares of REITs are traded on organized exchanges like shares of stock. Thus, they are liquid investments even though their equity is in real property and long-term mortgages. In recent years, the spreads between the bid and asked prices have narrowed significantly, signaling that the secondary markets are becoming more highly developed. Prices of REITs are determined by supply and demand. In this sense, they are like closed-end investment companies because the price can deviate from the underlying value of the assets owned.

Prices of REITs fell in the 1998–1999 period as investors flocked to high-tech stocks, and then again in 2007 and 2008, as a result of falling U.S. real estate prices. The total amount of U.S. REITs increased rapidly from $136 billion in 2003 to $403.7 billion in 2006, before falling back to $338.1 billion by December 31, 2007.

Recap   A hedge fund is a type of mutual fund that has fewer than either 99 or 499 wealthy investors. The SEC does not regulate these funds. Hedge funds attempt to earn high returns for their investors regardless of whether financial prices are going up or down. Hedge funds engage in risky investment strategies. A REIT is a type of mutual fund that pools the funds of many small investors and uses them to buy or build income property or to make or purchase mortgages. These funds are pass-through institutions in that the rents from the income property and/or the interest income from the mortgages are passed through to shareholders. Whereas other mutual funds invest only in financial instruments, REITs may invest in real property as well as financial instruments. Shares of REITs are traded on organized exchanges. By law, REITs must return 95 percent of their income to shareholders each year. REITs allow for the integration of commercial real estate markets and capital markets.

GOVERNMENT-SPONSORED ENTERPRISES

Government-Sponsored Enterprises (GSEs)
Publicly held corporations that are chartered by Congress.

Government-sponsored enterprises (GSEs), as the name suggests, are corporations that are sponsored or chartered by Congress. Despite the federal charter, most GSEs are privately owned and privately managed. Some GSEs have issued shares of stock that are publicly held like shares in other corporations, and the stocks of these GSEs are traded on organized exchanges.

GSEs issue short-term securities that sell at a discount and long-term bonds that pay semiannual coupon payments. The majority of the issuances are long term. The proceeds are used to assist in some aspect of lending that the federal government has deemed desirable. GSEs operate mainly in the areas of housing, farm credit, and student loans. The securities that GSEs issue, called *government agency securities*, are considered government securities for SEC purposes.

In most instances, the federal government has no legal obligation to guarantee the timely payment of interest and principal of GSE securities. However, many market

15-4

Financial Assets and Liabilities of Government-Sponsored Enterprises, 1982–2008 (Billions of Dollars)

Year	Total Financial Assets	GSE Securities Outstanding	Total Liabilities*
1982	254.8	205.4	249.1
1983	256.5	206.8	250.3
1984	297.7	237.2	291.0
1985	324.0	257.8	319.6
1986	346.4	273.0	342.8
1987	374.4	303.2	370.1
1988	421.7	348.1	416.1
1989	454.2	373.3	447.6
1990	477.6	393.7	469.1
1991	496.8	402.9	486.0
1992	552.3	443.1	538.7
1993	631.1	523.7	614.4
1994	781.8	700.6	761.7
1995	896.9	806.5	873.4
1996	988.6	896.9	964.1
1997	1,099.4	995.3	1,070.3
1998	1,403.8	1,273.6	1,368.1
1999	1,720.6	1,591.7	1,681.1
2000	1,969.4	1,825.8	1,922.5
2001	2,300.8	2,114.0	2,247.1
2002	2,543.3	2,339.9	2,475.6
2003	2,794.4	2,564.2	2,747.1
2004	2,882.9	2,613.0	2,818.0
2005	2,819.4	2,542.9	2,736.8
2006	2,872.9	2,590.5	2,782.0
2007	3,183.3	2,831.4	3,083.6
2008*	3,407.8	3,154.8	3,357.0

September 30, 2008

*Note: GSEs have other miscellaneous liabilities in addition to outstanding securities. The difference between total assets and total liabilities represents stockholder equity.

**Note: Student Loan Marketing Association (Sallie Mae) is included until 2004, when it was fully privatized.

Sources: Flow of Funds Accounts of the United States, Z.1, Board of Governors of the Federal Reserve System, Washington D.C., various issues.

participants assume that the government is the de facto guarantor of the payments. In the financial crisis of 2008 when Fannie Mae and Freddie Mac were put into conservatorship by the government, this was proved to be the case. Although shareholders in the company were expected to lose everything, the worth of the securities issued by them was never a question. The yield spread between government agency securities and U.S. government securities is due to differences in liquidity and risk. The yield spread can be significant because secondary markets do not have the breadth and depth of Treasuries. If market participants question the de facto government guarantee, the spread can also widen. Exhibit 15-4 shows the financial assets and liabilities of GSEs from 1982 to 2008. In recent years, GSEs have increased significantly in terms of their size and market share. This is particularly true with respect to lending in the housing sector.

The GSE Housing Market

Federal National Mortgage Association (Fannie Mae)
A former GSE that issues bonds now guaranteed by the U.S. government, and uses the proceeds to purchase mortgages or mortgage-backed securities of banks.

In late 2008 the two largest GSEs Federal National Mortgage Association (Fannie Mae), the Federal Home Loan Mortgage Corporation (Freddie Mac), were placed under the conservatorship of their regulator, the Federal Housing Finance Agency, FHFA (formerly the Office of Federal Housing Enterprise Oversight, OFHEO). Although Fannie Mae and Freddie Mac are in conservatorship, it appears their fundamental operations will not change much in the immediate future. These former GSEs had been exempt from state and local corporate income taxes and were supported by a line of credit with the U.S. Treasury.

Federal Home Loan Mortgage Corporation (Freddie Mac)
A former GSE that issues bonds now guaranteed by the U.S. government, uses the proceeds to purchase mortgages or mortgage-backed securities of thrifts.

Fannie Mae and Freddie Mac provide loanable funds to the housing sector by selling their own securities and using the proceeds to purchase mortgages or mortgage-backed securities in the secondary mortgage market. The securities that they issue are backed by the principal and interest payments on the mortgages or mortgage-backed securities that they have purchased. Before September 2008, Fannie Mae and Freddie Mac were privately owned and their stock traded on the New York Stock Exchange. When Fannie Mae and Freddie Mac were put into conservatorship, common and preferred stock holders lost even though those who had purchased the agency securities of Fannie Mae and Freddie Mac did not. The difference between Fannie Mae and Freddie Mac is that Fannie Mae primarily buys the mortgages of banks, while Freddie Mac primarily buys the mortgages of thrifts.

Congress created these GSEs in order to make housing more available by increasing the funds flowing into mortgages. The goal was to expand the opportunities for low- and moderate-income families to purchase houses. The U.S. Department of Housing and Urban Development (HUD) regulates these GSEs with regard to meeting this goal. In Chapter 11, we discussed recent issues involving the demise of Fannie Mae and Freddie Mac.

Government National Mortgage Association (Ginnie Mae)
A government-owned enterprise that, for a fee, gives an explicit government guarantee that Ginnie Mae bonds issued by private financial institutions will be repaid.

The Government National Mortgage Association (GNMA, or Ginnie Mae) is a U.S. government-owned corporation within the Department of Housing and Urban Development (HUD). As part of HUD, Ginnie Mae is more accurately characterized as a government-owned enterprise. For a fee, Ginnie Mae guarantees that the mortgages purchased with bond proceeds will be repaid and, hence, the bonds will be repaid. Unlike Fannie Mae and Freddie Mac, Ginnie Mae does not issue bonds. Other financial institutions such as banks, savings associations, or mortgage brokers issue the bonds that are guaranteed by Ginnie Mae, referred to as *Ginnie Mae bonds*. The minimum denomination for Ginnie Mae Bonds is $25,000. Unlike Fannie Mae and Freddie Mac, Ginnie Mae securities have always been fully backed by the U.S. government and, thus, have had no default risk.

The GSE Farm Loan Market

Federal Farm Credit Banks Funding Corporation (FFCBFC)

A GSE that issues bonds and discount notes to make loans to farmers to increase the funds flowing into agriculture.

The **Federal Farm Credit Banks Funding Corporation (FFCBFC)** issues bonds and discount notes and uses the proceeds to make loans to farmers in order to facilitate the funds flowing into agriculture. The bonds carry no explicit government guarantee that the principal and interest will be repaid. The FFCBFC ran into financial problems in the 1980s because many farmers defaulted on high-interest loans made in the late 1970s and early 1980s. Congress created the **Farm Credit Financial Assistance Corporation (FACO)** in 1987. FACO issues bonds and uses them to assist the FFCBFC. Unlike the bonds of the FFCBFC, FACO bonds do have an explicit government guarantee.

Farm Credit Financial Assistance Corporation (FACO)

A GSE that issues bonds to assist the FFCBFC, which was having financial problems at the time FACO was created.

Other GSEs

Financing Corporation (FICO)

A GSE created in response to the S&L crisis that issued bonds to help shore up the FSLIC.

In 1987, Congress created a new GSE, the **Financing Corporation (FICO)**, in response to the savings and loan crisis. The savings and loan crisis is covered in detail in Chapter 11. FICO was to issue up to $10.825 billion in 30-year bonds to help shore up the insurance company (the FSLIC) that at the time insured deposits in the failed thrifts. FICO was capitalized by nonvoting stock purchased by the 12 regional Federal Home Loan Banks. It is to be dissolved by 2026 or earlier. FICO was not successful in bailing out the failed thrifts, so additional legislation and the creation of another GSE was needed.

Resolution Trust Corporation (RTC)

A GSE created in 1989 in response to the savings and loan crisis that issued bonds and used the proceeds to dissolve or find buyers for the failed thrifts and their properties. The RTC went out of business on December 31, 1995, after completing its work.

In 1989, Congress created another GSE, the **Resolution Trust Corporation (RTC)**. The RTC was to dissolve or find buyers for the failed thrifts and liquidate the $450 billion of real estate properties owned by the thrifts being dissolved. Thirty-year bonds were issued to help finance the RTC, but the federal government did not explicitly guarantee the bonds. The RTC went out of business on December 31, 1995, after it had completed its work. By that time, it had resolved the insolvencies and closed more than 750 savings associations. In the financial crisis of 2008, some have suggested that Congress should create a similar institution to deal with the abundance of foreclosed properties. The Emergency Economic Stability Act of 2008 failed to do so.

The Student Loan Market

Student Loan Marketing Association (Sallie Mae)

A former GSE, fully privatized in 2004, that issues securities to purchase student loans, thus increasing the funds flowing into student loans and making them more liquid.

The **Student Loan Marketing Association (Sallie Mae)**, a publicly traded company, issues securities and uses the proceeds to purchase student loans. The securities are not backed by an explicit federal government guarantee. In fact, in 2004, Sallie Mae was fully privatized and is no longer officially a GSE. Despite this, the federal government guarantees repayment of many of the student loans. The purpose of Sallie Mae is to increase the funds flowing into student loans and to make student loans more liquid. The company, which is the nation's largest supplier of student loans, owns or manages student loans for more than 5 million borrowers.

Recap   GSEs are privately owned government-sponsored enterprises that issue financial securities. The funds that are raised are used to provide funds to areas that the government deems desirable, including housing, farm credit, and student loans. The major GSEs that pertain to the housing market were Fannie Mae and Freddie Mac. The FFCBFC issues securities and uses the proceeds to make loans to farmers. Congress created FACO in 1987 because of financial troubles of the FFCBFC. FICO and the RTC were created in response to the savings and loan crisis. Sallie Mae is a publicly traded company that issues securities and uses the proceeds to purchase student loans. Sallie Mae was privatized in 2004, while Fannie Mae and Freddie Mac were placed under conservatorship in 2008, so these three entities are no longer GSEs.

THE GROWTH OF FINANCIAL CONGLOMERATES

Financial Conglomerates
Firms that own and operate several different types of financial intermediaries and financial institutions on a global basis.

Financial conglomerates are firms that own and operate several different types of financial intermediaries and financial institutions. As a rule, they operate on a global basis. Financial conglomerates usually result from the mergers of several firms. For example, one financial conglomerate may own a commercial bank, a savings institution, a mutual fund, a pension fund, a securities firm, and an insurance company. The alleged advantages of forming financial conglomerates include taking advantage of economies of scale, economies of scope, and diversification.

The crisis of 2008, which drastically changed the financial landscape, appears to be hastening the formation of multifaceted conglomerates. The independent investment banking model seems fundamentally changed, with the five most notable independent investment banks either liquidated or merged with a commercial bank–based financial conglomerate.

Economies of Scale
Gains from bigness that may result from several firms being able to streamline management and eliminate the duplication of effort that would result from several separate firms.

Economies of scale, which are gains from bigness, may result when separate firms owned by a conglomerate and offering the same product are able to streamline management and eliminate duplication of effort. The conglomerate may have fewer boards of directors than if there were many separate firms. They may also share a common technology infrastructure.

Economies of Scope
Advantages to firms being able to offer customers several financial services under one roof.

Economies of scope refer to the advantages of a conglomerate's ability to offer several financial services under one roof. This one-stop shopping is supposedly an advantage to financial services customers and, hence, gives financial conglomerates the upper hand over several separate firms providing the same set of services. In addition, the subsidiaries can share information about customers and seek new customers from other subsidiaries.

Diversification
The branching out of financial conglomerates into several product lines to reduce the dependence of the conglomerates on any single product line.

Diversification refers to the branching out of the financial conglomerate into several product lines. Diversification reduces the dependence of the financial conglomerate on one service. This, in turn, reduces the risk of failure for the financial conglomerate. If one division is performing poorly, the conglomerate can still be earning a profit if other divisions pick up the slack. For example, if the credit card division is losing money, it can be subsidized by the insurance division for a while. If credit cards were the dominant product line of a financial services institution, losses in this area could affect the solvency of the institution. This is not so in the case of a financial conglomerate.

Financial conglomerates have been emerging in the financial world since the early 1970s. Some of the first attempts were started by nonfinancial giants, such as Sears, that bought financial subsidiaries. Not all of the early attempts met with success, particularly when a nonfinancial firm was purchasing financial institutions. For example, in 1981, Sears purchased Dean Witter Stock Brokerage and Coldwell Banker Real Estate, only to sell them in 1989 because of losses in these subsidiaries. Subsequently, Sears sold its remaining financial services, mainly its credit card division, to Citigroup. Sears merged with K-mart and formed Sears Holding Company in 2005. After an aborted attempt to transform itself into a financial firm such as Berkshire-Hathaway, it began to refocus on its retail operations.

Regulations dating back to the Glass-Steagall Act during the Great Depression attempted to prevent different types of financial firms from merging and providing a vast array of financial services. However, by the mid-1990s, many institutions were already finding loopholes in existing regulations in order to form financial conglomerates, and impetus was building to do so. In November 1999, Congress passed the Gramm-Leach-Bliley Act (GLBA), also known as the Financial Modernization Act. The passage of this law gave new impetus to the formation of financial conglomerates. The law effectively repealed Glass-Steagall and allowed for the formation of financial holding companies (FHCs). FHCs may

Citigroup

In 1998, Citicorp, the nation's second-largest bank holding company, announced that it would merge with Travelers Group, the parent company of Travelers Insurance and Salomon Smith Barney. Salomon Smith Barney (currently Smith Barney) was the nation's third-largest securities firm. Citigroup was on its way to becoming the quintessential financial conglomerate, operating globally and providing a vast array of financial services.

The 1998 merger occurred before the passage of GLBA and, in its present configuration, Citigroup would not be a legal entity if GLBA had not passed. Indeed, the Fed approved the merger in September 1998 with the understanding that Citigroup would divest itself of several banned services—such as insurance underwriting—within five years if Glass-Steagall were not repealed. But GLBA passed and the merger was consummated in October 1998. At that time, Citigroup had more than $700 billion in assets, more than 100 million customers, and a presence in more than 100 countries.

Citibank, which is owned by Citicorp, is the nation's second-largest bank. In addition to Citibank, Citigroup has nonbank subsidiaries that provide services such as investment banking; credit cards; global asset management; trust services; buying and selling stocks, mutual funds, and bonds for customers; consumer finance; commercial lending; mortgage banking; data processing; leasing; securities advising and management; and insurance services.

In 2000, Citigroup announced the purchase of Associates First Capital Corporation. The deal boosted Citigroup's consumer-oriented U.S. business lines and strengthened its international position. Three years later, Citigroup issued a credit card (together with Banamex) aimed at Mexicans living in the United States, bought a significant share of Shanghai Pudong Development Bank Co. Ltd., and through its subsidiary, ZAO Citibank, launched a new Russian credit card. In 2004, Citigroup acquired KorAm Bank, one of South Korea's largest commercial banks with 223 branches. It also purchased Washington Mutual Finance Corporation (from Washington Mutual, Inc.) and First American Bank of Texas. The next year, in 2005, Citigroup introduced a new debit card program in Egypt, mobile phone banking in Australia, financial services through post offices in Romania, and a dual-currency card in China. In 2006, it opened in Kuwait and Dubai; expanded equities operations in Russia, India, the Middle East, Brazil, and Canada; and acquired 20 percent stakes in Akbank in Turkey and Guangdong Development Bank in China.

In 2007, Citigroup's expansion and internationalization efforts were slowed by its massive U.S. mortgage market related losses. These forced CEO and chairman Charles Prince to resign. Vikram Pandit, formerly of the investment bank Morgan Stanley, is the current CEO.

The rationale behind the mergers and alliances was to take advantage of economies of scale and scope and diversification. Experts had forecasted that the Citicorp-Travelers merger would save at least $1 billion per year in expenses, but the actual results have been mixed. Citigroup stock suffered in the bear market of the early

2000s. Afterward, its stock price did better, rising to over $55 per share at the end of 2006. But more recently, problems associated with declining real estate prices and rising default rates punished Citigroup's 5.21 billion shares, so that by January 2009, they were trading around $10 a share.

own securities firms, banks, and insurance companies. They may also engage in ancillary financial and complementary nonfinancial enterprises. By March 2000, the effective date of GLBA, there were 111 FHCs; as of February 2008, there were 468.

Rather than maintaining the status quo of segmentation among financial service providers, the GLBA encourages considerable financial integration in the financial services industry and the formation of financial conglomerates. Many of these firms are transnational in that they offer a full range of financial services in many countries. "A Closer Look" on p. 368 discusses Citigroup, a financial conglomerate formed in 1998, before the passage of GLBA.

Since the 1990s, there have been three trends in financial markets: growth, consolidation, and globalization. These trends have been emphasized repeatedly throughout this text. We expect that these trends will continue in the future and that financial markets and institutions will be most influenced by these factors as they evolve. The financial crisis of 2008 seems to have encouraged the formation of financial conglomerates. For example, as a result of the crisis, Bank of America has purchased Countrywide and Merrill Lynch; and Wells Fargo has purchased Wachovia.

Recap   Financial conglomerates operate several different financial intermediaries and institutions that provide an array of financial services on a domestic and global basis. They result from consolidation in the financial services industry due to economies of scale, economies of scope, and diversification. Passage of the GLBA encouraged the formation of financial conglomerates. The financial crisis of 2008 may result in the increase of financial conglomerates.

This completes our look at financial institutions. You should now have a better understanding of their evolution and current state. In the next section of the text, we will direct our attention to the determination of exchange rates before considering financial forward, futures, and options markets.

Summary of Major Points

1. Investment banks design, market, and underwrite the issuance of new securities in the primary market. The newly issued securities may be an IPO or a seasoned offering. In addition to advising the issuer about market conditions and prospective prices for the new securities, the investment bank also assists in filing the necessary reports with the SEC so that the new securities can be sold publicly. The securities may be stocks or bonds. A registration statement must be filed with the SEC. Part of the registration statement is the prospectus that will be distributed to investors. The SEC is concerned that appropriate information about the issuance is disclosed to the public.

2. Mutual funds pool the funds of many investors to invest in several hundred or even thousands of stocks or bonds. Mutual funds may offer greater safety and more diversification than investing in one or a few stocks. Mutual funds have experienced tremendous growth in recent years. Money market mutual funds invest in securities with an original maturity of one year or less.

3. An open-end fund continually sells new shares or buys outstanding shares from the public at the net asset value. Closed-end investment companies sell a limited number of shares that may be traded openly. The price is determined by supply and demand and can differ from the net asset value. The net asset value per share is the difference between the market value of the shares of stock that the fund owns and the fund's liabilities, all divided by the outstanding number of shares. Mutual funds can be either load or no-load funds.

4. Government-sponsored enterprises (GSEs) are corporations that are sponsored or chartered by Congress. Most GSEs are privately owned and privately managed. Some GSEs have issued shares of stock that are publicly held like other corporations. The stocks of these GSEs are traded on organized exchanges. GSEs issue short-term securities that sell at a discount and long-term bonds. The majority of the issuances are long term. The proceeds are used to assist in some aspect of lending that the federal government has deemed desirable. The major areas in which GSEs have operated are housing and farm credit, and student loans. The securities that GSEs issue have been called *government agency securities.* In 2008 the two largest GSEs, Fannie Mae and Freddie Mac, were placed under a conservatorship by the Federal Housing Finance Agency, FHFA.

5. In most cases, the federal government had no legal obligation to guarantee the timely payment of in-

terest and principal of GSE securities. However, many market participants assumed that the government was the de facto guarantor of the payments. The yield spread between government agency securities and U.S. government securities reflected differences in liquidity and risk. In 2008, the federal government formally became the guarantor of debt issued by the two largest former GSEs, Fannie Mae and Freddie Mac.

6. Historically, a hedge fund is a type of mutual fund that has fewer than 99 very wealthy investors. In 1997, the number of investors was expanded to 499 for some hedge funds. The SEC does not regulate hedge funds. Hedge funds attempt to earn high returns for their investors regardless of whether financial prices are going up or down. Sometimes, hedge funds engage in risky investment strategies.

7. Real estate investment trusts (REITs) pool the funds of many small investors and use them to buy or build income property or to make or purchase mortgage loans. They are pass-through institutions in that the rents from the income property and/or the interest income from the mortgages are passed through to shareholders. At least 75 percent of the assets of REITs must be either real property (generally, commercial or industrial real estate) or mortgages. By law, REITs must return 95 percent of their earnings to shareholders each year. Shares of REITs are traded on organized exchanges like shares of stock.

8. Financial conglomerates are financial firms that provide an array of financial services that had been previously provided by several financial intermediaries and institutions. In theory, financial conglomerates offer economies of scale, economies of scope, and diversification. Changes in technology and regulations, as well as financial difficulties of stand-alone investment banks have given new impetus to the formation of financial conglomerates in recent years.

Key Terms

Review Questions

1. What are the functions of investment banks? Do they engage in primary or secondary market activity? What is a syndicate?

2. What is a prospectus? What are the differences among a prospectus, a registration statement, and a bond indenture?

3. What is the difference between a securities broker and a securities dealer? What roles do brokers and dealers play in the financial system?

4. How does a hedge fund differ from a traditional mutual fund? What are the two types of hedge funds and how are their requirements for participation different? What is the difference between a mutual fund and a money market mutual fund?

5. Are investment banks financial intermediaries? Explain why or why not.

6. The spread between the bid and asked price widens. What does this mean about the securities?

7. What is the difference between a load and a no-load mutual fund? Could a no-load fund ever result in higher total sales commissions and costs?

8. Miguel expects a stock's price to rise. Should he short sell the stock? Explain.

9. What is the difference between a market order and a limit order? What are the two types of limit orders?

10. What type of securities do GSEs sell? What is the purpose of GSEs? Who owns the GSEs? What happened to the federal government guarantee of securities issued by Fannie Mae and Freddie Mac in 2008?

11. What are some of the factors for the growth of mutual funds in recent years?

12. List some reasons that Henry should consider purchasing a fund of funds. Are there any reasons he should not?

13. How do REITs differ from other mutual funds? Are all REITs pretty much the same? What are their differences?

14. What is a financial conglomerate? Discuss the factors that contribute to the formation of financial conglomerates.

15. How does diversification reduce the risk that a financial conglomerate will fail? What is the difference between economies of scale and economies of scope?

Analytical Questions

Questions marked with a check mark (✓) are objective in nature. They can be completed with a short answer or number.

✓16. A mutual fund owns stocks with a market value of $1 billion and has liabilities of $1 million. What is the net asset value? If there are 2 million shares of stock outstanding, what is the net asset value per share?

✓17. What are some of the factors that determine the spread between the bid and asked price? If the bid-asked spread narrows, what does this mean?

✓18. What are the factors that determine the spread between agency securities and Treasuries? If agency and Treasury securities are perceived to have the same risk, why may there still be a positive spread between their prices?

✓19. Make a chart listing the similarities and differences among the following institutions: money market mutual funds, mutual funds, hedge funds, government-sponsored enterprises, and REITs.

✓20. Comment on the following: Frank calls his broker to complain that the stock the broker sold him has fallen in value and Frank has lost a lot of money. The broker says: "Look, I made money and the brokerage firm made money on the deal. Two out of three is not bad!"

Suggested Readings

Learn about the *Financial Industry Regulatory Authority (FINRA)* the largest nongovernmental regulator for all securities firms doing business in the United States (the successor to the NASD) by visiting their site at: **http://www.finra.org/AboutFINRA/CorporateInformation/index.htm.**

For information about investment banking and capital markets around the world, visit the site of Thomson Financial at **http://www.thomson.com/solutions/financial/.**

Learn more about GSEs at their Web sites: **http://www.freddiemac.com, http://www.fanniemae.com,** and **http://www.ginniemae.gov.** Other information on government-sponsored enterprises is available at the U.S. Department of Housing and Urban Development Web site at **http://www.hud.gov,** and the Office of Federal Housing Enterprise Oversight (OFHEO) Web site at **http://www.ofheo.gov/newsroom.aspx.** Recent changes to conforming loan limits are listed on the latter site at **http://www.ofheo.gov/media/hpi/AREA_LIST.pdf.**

For more on the former GSE, Sallie Mae, go to **http://www.salliemae.com.**

To learn more about mutual funds from the perspective of those who sell them, go to the Investment Company Institute site at **http://www.ici.org** and their 2007 Factbook at **http://www.icifactbook.org.**

For a discussion of exchange-traded funds (ETFs) and their benefits relative to mutual funds, see "Better Than Beta?" in *The Economist*, February 28, 2008.

For an academic view of hedge funds, read "Hedge Funds: Past, Present, and Future," by Rene Stulz in *The Journal of Economic Perspectives*, 21, no. 2 (Spring 2007).

The Federal Reserve Chair, Ben Bernanke, addresses the regulation of financial firms in a speech given May 15, 2007, accessible at **http://www.federalreserve.gov/newsevents/speech/bernanke20070515a.htm.**

To learn about Google's August 2004 Initial Public Offering, see the following articles in *Business Week:* "The How and Why of Google's Auction," May 3, 2004; "The A-B-Cs of Google's Auction," August 10, 2004; and "The Google IPO Marches On," August 13, 2004. Additional information is available in articles in *The Economist:* "A Cartel-Buster," May 6, 2004, and "Google's IPO Rollercoaster," August 20, 2004.

For a look at government-sponsored enterprises from an educated point of view, see the testimony of former Fed Chairman Alan Greenspan on government-sponsored enterprises before the Committee on Banking, Housing, and Urban Affairs, U.S. Senate, February 24, 2004. A transcript of the testimony is available online at **http://www.federalreserve.gov/boarddocs/testimony/2004/20040224/default.htm.**

For a recent overview of some issues relating to mutual funds, see John B. Carlson, Eduard A. Pelz, and Erkin Y. Sahinoz, "Mutual Funds, Fee Transparency, and Competition," *Economic Commentary*, Federal Reserve Bank of Cleveland (March 1, 2004), available online at **http:// www.clevelandfed.org/Research/Commentary/2004/03–01.pdf.**

For an engaging article on "Why We Do What We Do: The Views of Bankers, Insurers, and Securities Firms on Specialization and Diversification," see the panel discussion summary by the same name by Kevin J. Stiroh. The discussion session featured Tony Candito, Michael J. Castellano, and Richard Heckinger as presenters, and Darryll Hendricks as moderator. Stiroh's summary is available in *Economic Policy Review*, Federal Reserve Bank of New York, 6, no. 4 (October 2000): 81–87, and online at **http://www.newyorkfed.org/research/epr/00v06n4/0010stir .pdf.**

For a discussion of many of the topics in this chapter, see Dimitri B. Papadimitriou, ed., *Modernizing Financial Systems* (London and Basingstoke: Macmillan/St. Martin's Press, 2000).

For a historical look at the securities industry at a time of dramatic change, see Alec Benn, *The Unseen Wall Street, 1969–1975* (Westport, CT: Greenwood Publishing Group, 2000).

For a discussion of the size, number, behavior, regulation, and policy implications of hedge funds, see Barry Eichengreen and Donald Mathieson, "Hedge Funds: What Do We Really Know?" *Economic Issues*, International Monetary Fund, 19 (September 1999).

Endnotes

1. What the firm was doing would not have been illegal as long as there was no connection between the corporation issuing the stock and the securities firm. However, in reality, J.T. Marlin was undoubtedly committing many other acts of securities fraud.
2. Data are from the *2008 U.S. Statistical Abstract*, Table 1138; and *Flow of Funds Accounts of the United States, Z.1*, Board of Governors of the Federal Reserve System (March 6, 2008).
3. The Glass-Steagall Act of 1933 separated investment banking from commercial banking. As you have seen, this act was effectively repealed in 1999 with the passage of the Gramm-Leach-Bliley Act (GLBA). The passage of the GLBA is partially responsible for the emergence of financial conglomerates discussed later in this chapter.
4. With the Vanguard STAR Fund, Vanguard waives the fund of funds fee so that investors pay only the fees of the individual mutual funds.
5. As used here, *hedge fund* means any kind of private investment partnership. The most common meaning of *hedge* is to reduce risk. This can be misleading because hedge funds often engage in very risky activities.
6. The tax consequences include that net losses cannot be used to offset gains and that deferred interest payments are taxable in current years and investors are often not provided the information by the hedge fund that would allow them to make current tax payments and to avoid tax penalties. Offshore hedge funds are easily available to a small number of tax-exempt wealthy U.S. investors.

16

There are three main causes that dispose men to madness: love, ambition, and the study of foreign exchange.

—Walter Leaf, 1926

How Exchange Rates Are Determined

Learning Objectives

After reading this chapter, you should know:

What exchange rates are, and how they affect prices of imports and exports

How exchange rates are determined by supply and demand in the foreign exchange market

The factors that cause exchange rates to change

What the theories of purchasing power parity and interest rate parity are

THE MORE THINGS CHANGE, THE MORE THINGS STAY THE SAME

Throughout the early and mid-1980s, typical headlines in *The Wall Street Journal* told of the strong dollar, its detrimental effects on U.S. jobs, and the eventual efforts to bring down the "overvalued" dollar. By the mid-1990s, the dollar had fallen to record lows against many currencies and was at less than half its mid-1980s value against the Japanese yen. Headlines such as "Dollar Rises in Foreign Exchange Market as U.S. Interest Rates Surge" were replaced with "Dollar Sinks to New Low Against Yen." In the late 1990s, the dollar again strengthened against the yen and other major currencies. In the early 2000s, the dollar was still riding high, particularly against the newly created European Union currency, the euro. The dollar reversed course in early 2002, and except for a brief upturn in 2005, continued to decline in value versus the euro into early 2008. In January 2002, the dollar could purchase 1.17 euros, but by February 2008, it was worth only .68 euros, representing a decline of nearly 42 percent in value versus the euro over this period.

Just what does all of this mean to the average person? How do changes in the international value of the dollar affect job opportunities for recent college graduates and other workers? How are domestic interest rates linked with interest rates in the rest of the world? What happens to imports and exports when the value of the dollar changes? Perhaps most important, how are all of these questions and their answers related? Such questions about the dollar's value are often puzzling to the average person. Many diverse opinions exist about whether a strong dollar is good or bad for the economy, even though the implications of a strong dollar are not often fully understood.

Forty years ago, such questions and the interactions between the U.S. economy and the rest of the world were largely ignored by most bankers, stock market analysts, economists, accountants, corporate treasurers, policy makers—and textbook writers! The reasons were that trading of goods, services, financial securities, and currencies between the United States and other countries accounted for only a small portion of total transactions in the United States and that exchange rates between currencies were fixed by the central banks of the various countries and did not change on a day-to-day basis.

Today, the situation is much different for two simple reasons:

1. Cross-border trading of foreign currencies and financial instruments denominated in various currencies has increased much faster than the more visible explosion of international trade in goods and services.
2. The value of the dollar relative to other currencies changes daily.

Consequently, to ignore the globalization of financial markets in a study of the financial system would be a serious omission.

This chapter focuses directly on exchange rates and their determination. Although exchange rates are intricately linked with national aspects of financial markets, focusing directly on them in this chapter will help clarify the presentation. Throughout this chapter, keep in mind that exchange rates are prices, ultimately determined by forces of supply and demand.

DEFINING EXCHANGE RATES

The exchange rate is the number of units of foreign currency (money) that can be acquired with one unit of domestic money.[1] In other words, the exchange rate specifies the purchasing power of, say, the dollar in terms of how much it can buy of another currency. For example, if the yen/dollar exchange rate is 100 yen, this literally means that $1 will buy 100 yen.[2] If the exchange rate rises to 150 yen, meaning that $1 will now buy 150 yen, then the dollar is said to have appreciated relative to the yen. Because it will

Exchange Rate
The number of units of foreign currency that can be acquired with one unit of domestic money.

Foreign Currency (Money)
Supplies of foreign exchange.

Appreciated
Description of a currency that has increased in value relative to another currency.

Cracking the Code

How Movements in the Exchange Rate Affect the Dollar Price of Foreign Goods

Suppose a Japanese auto costs 2,000,000 yen in Japan. Ignoring transportation costs and the like, what will it cost in the United States? The answer is that the price depends on the exchange rate between the yen and the dollar. The middle row in the following table lists the beginning situation: If the auto costs 2,000,000 yen and $1 buys 100 yen, then as Equation (16-1) indicates, the dollar price will be $20,000 (2,000,000/100).

The top row in the table shows that when the dollar appreciates from 100 yen to 150 yen, the dollar price of the Japanese auto falls to $13,333 (2,000,000/150). In contrast, as illustrated in the third row, a depreciation of the dollar results in a rise in the dollar price of the Japanese auto.

Yen Price of Japanese Auto	Exchange Rate	Dollar Price of Japanese Auto
(1)	(2)	(1)/(2)
2,000,000 yen	$1 = 150 yen	$13,333
2,000,000 yen	$1 = 100 yen	$20,000
2,000,000 yen	$1 = 50 yen	$40,000

[handwritten notes:] $ ¥ 1:100 ratio → $ ¥ 1:50 ratio, Depreciation

now buy more yen, the dollar's purchasing power has risen. It has grown stronger. On the other hand, if the yen/dollar exchange rate falls from 100 yen to 50 yen, the dollar is said to have **depreciated** relative to the yen. Because it will now buy fewer yen, the dollar's purchasing power has fallen. It has grown weaker. Supplies of foreign currencies are called **foreign exchange.**

So what does all of this have to do with the price a U.S. importer will have to pay for Japanese autos? The following handy formula, linking prices and the exchange rate, provides the ingredients necessary to answer this question:

(16-1) U.S. dollar price of foreign goods
     = foreign price of foreign goods/exchange rate

It is easy to get things backward. To prevent this, it is useful to consider units. For example, the units in Equation 16-1 are: dollar/good=yen/good÷yen/dollar=yen/good×dollar/yen. Note that cancelling yen on the right-hand side leaves the units, dollar/good, the same on both sides.

The accompanying "Cracking the Code" feature uses this formula and the hypothetical figures already mentioned to illustrate the key point of this discussion—the U.S. dollar price of a foreign good is inversely related to the exchange rate. More specifically, as the dollar appreciates, ceteris paribus, the price of foreign goods in the United States falls, even if the foreign price in yen is constant. Conversely, as the dollar depreciates, ceteris paribus, the price of foreign goods in the United States rises.

[handwritten notes in left margin:]
• $ price of a foreign good is INVERSELY related to the exchange rate.
• $↑, P_{Fg}↓
• $↑, I↑, E↓
• $↓, I↓, E↑

Needless to say, the importer and its customers (whether they realize it or not) are affected by changes in the exchange rate. More generally, the exchange rate links the domestic and foreign markets for goods, services, and securities. As a result, changes in the exchange rate will have repercussions in all the domestic and foreign markets, including markets for both inputs and outputs. Thus, if the dollar appreciates, ceteris paribus, U.S. imports (which are now relatively cheaper than before) increase, and U.S. exports to foreign countries (which are now relatively more expensive) decrease. As the dollar becomes stronger, ceteris paribus, we lose domestic jobs in both the industries in direct competition with the imports and the industries that end up exporting less. Hopefully,

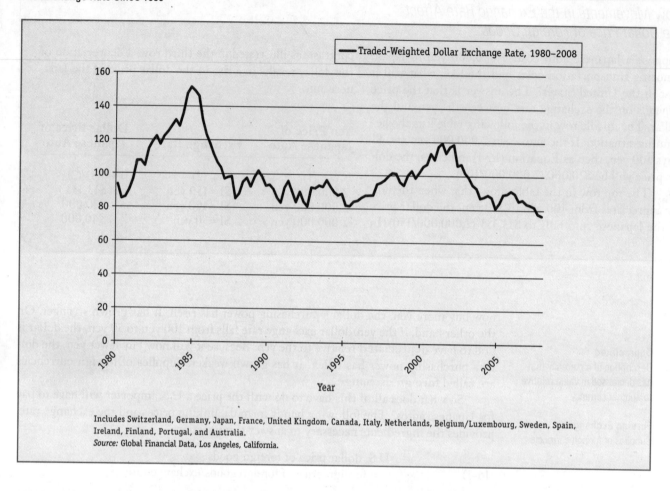

Traded-Weighted Dollar Exchange Rate, 1980–2008

Includes Switzerland, Germany, Japan, France, United Kingdom, Canada, Italy, Netherlands, Belgium/Luxembourg, Sweden, Spain, Ireland, Finland, Portugal, and Australia.
Source: Global Financial Data, Los Angeles, California.

we have given you some insight into how these fluctuations affect the U.S. economy. Exhibit 16-1 shows the wide fluctuations in the value of the exchange rate since 1980.

To understand these various linkages and repercussions, we must first examine what determines the exchange rate. Simply put, the exchange rate, like all prices, is determined by supply and demand. The United States and the rest of the world trade goods, services, and securities. This trading gives rise to a supply of and demand for the various currencies that are traded in the so-called foreign exchange market. More specifically, the supply of dollar-denominated funds comes from the demand by U.S. residents for foreign goods, services, and financial claims during a specific time period; the demand for dollar-denominated funds comes from the demand by foreign residents for U.S. goods, services, and financial claims over a period of time. For simplicity, in the remainder of this chapter, we will follow common usage and use the word *dollars* to represent dollar-denominated funds.[3]

Foreign Exchange Market
The market for buying and selling the different currencies of the world.

Recap   The *exchange rate* refers to the number of units of foreign currency that can be acquired with one unit of domestic money. The U.S. dollar price of foreign goods is equal to the foreign price of foreign goods divided by the exchange rate.

Cracking the Code

Finding the Yen/Euro Exchange Rate

If we assume $1 = 100 yen and $1 = .8 euros, then 100 yen = .8 euros. We can find how much 1 yen is worth by dividing both sides of the last equation by 100:

$$100/100 \text{ yen} = .8/100 \text{ euros}$$
$$1 \text{ yen} = 0.008 \text{ euros}$$

This is the euro/yen exchange rate.

Likewise, we can find out how much 1 euro is worth by dividing both sides of the equation by .8:

$$.8/.8 \text{ euros} = 100/.8 \text{ yen}$$
$$1 \text{ euro} = 125 \text{ yen}$$

DETERMINING EXCHANGE RATES

To understand how supply, demand, and exchange rates are related, it is best to begin with how the exchange rate between two currencies is determined. The general framework we develop is directly applicable to the more complex relationships among all national currencies. For example, suppose we know the yen/dollar rate is 100 yen and the euro/dollar rate is .8 euros. Then, as demonstrated in "Cracking the Code" (above), it must follow that the euro/yen rate is .008 euros. This "transitivity" allows us to confine our analysis to two monies. We begin by considering how the exchange rate between the U.S. dollar and the Japanese yen is determined, recognizing that our analysis could easily be extended to relationships among more than two currencies. Now would be a good time to look at Exhibit 16-2, which shows some of the basics of foreign exchange markets.

THE DEMAND FOR DOLLARS IN THE FOREIGN EXCHANGE MARKET

The demand for dollars in international financial markets originates from foreign purchases of U.S. goods, services, and securities. Drawing on Exhibit 16-2, we can write:

(16-2)

$$\text{Demand for dollars} = f(\overset{+}{\text{foreign demand for U.S. goods,}} \text{services, and securities})$$

The plus (+) sign over the expression simply means that the foreign demand for U.S. goods, services, and securities and the demand for dollars are positively related; when the former rises, the latter will also rise. When foreign demand for U.S. goods, services, and securities falls, the demand for dollars falls.

Now consider what happens to the quantity demanded of dollars/month when the exchange rate changes.[4] (Note that the quantity demanded is the amount of dollars that will be demanded at a specific exchange rate, and change in quantity demanded is depicted by movement along the demand curve for dollars). The answer is that, ceteris paribus, the quantity demanded is inversely related to the exchange rate, as depicted in Equation (16-3):

(16-3)

$$\text{Quantity demanded of dollars/month} = f(\overset{-}{\text{exchange rate}})$$

When the exchange rate goes up so the dollar becomes more expensive, ceteris paribus, the quantity demanded of dollars/month goes down, and vice versa. To see how and why the exchange rate and the quantity demanded of dollars/month are inversely

- Ex$_{rate}$ ↑ QD$_\$$ ↓

- Ex$_{rate}$ ↓ QD$_\$$ ↑

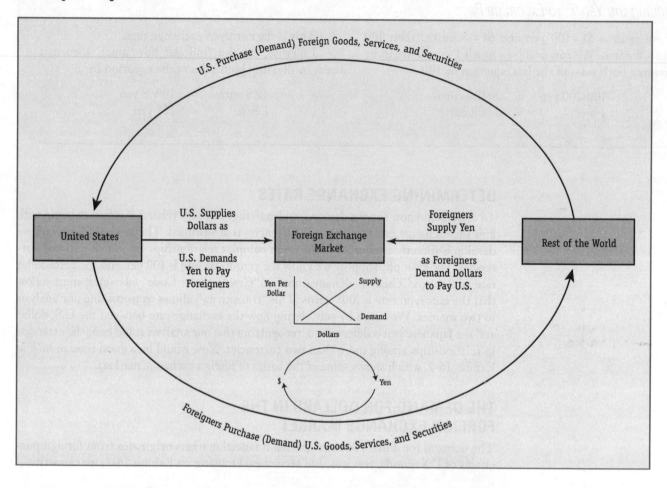

U.S. Purchase (Demand) Foreign Goods, Services, and Securities

United States

U.S. Supplies
Dollars as

U.S. Demands
Yen to Pay
Foreigners

Foreign Exchange
Market

Foreigners
Supply Yen

as Foreigners
Demand Dollars
to Pay U.S.

Rest of the World

Yen Per
Dollar

Supply

Demand

Dollars

\$ Yen

Foreigners Purchase (Demand) U.S. Goods, Services, and Securities

The foreign exchange market facilitates the trading of goods, services, and financial claims (securities) between countries. This global market is woven together by the market makers in foreign currencies—mostly, the foreign exchange departments of the largest commercial banks located in the world's major financial centers, such as New York, London, Frankfurt, and Tokyo. Without the ability to switch funds back and forth among the world's 100-odd currencies, Americans could not dine in London, sell hot dogs to Japanese tourists, buy imported digital video cameras, or export computers. Furthermore, they could not buy and sell foreign exchange to speculate on future price (exchange rates) movements.

related as shown in this expression, we need to examine how the exchange rate and changes therein affect foreign demand for U.S. goods, services, and securities.

Focusing only on goods to simplify matters, the answer will depend on how the exchange rate affects the prices of U.S. goods in foreign markets—that is, the yen price of U.S. goods in Japan. The following formula provides the key to the entire question:

(16-4)

$$\text{Yen (foreign) price of U.S. goods} = \text{dollar price of U.S. goods} \times \text{exchange rate}$$

For example, as in the "Cracking the Code" box on p. 381, if a bushel of U.S. wheat costs \$8 in the United States, and the yen/dollar exchange rate is 100 yen—

Cracking the Code

The Cost of a Bushel of U.S. Wheat in Japan

If a bushel of U.S. wheat costs $8 in the U.S. and the yen/dollar exchange rate is 100, then in Japan, assuming purchasing power parity holds, the bushel of wheat will cost 800 yen, calculated as follows:

Dollar price of U.S. goods × exchange rate = yen price of U.S. goods

$8 × 100 yen/dollar = 800 yen

If the dollar appreciates to 150 (implying depreciation of the yen), then a bushel of U.S. wheat will cost 1,200 yen:

$8 × 150 yen/dollar = 1,200 yen

[handwritten margin note:]
If $↑, P_wheat ↑,
QD_wheat ↓, QD_$ ↓

If $↓, P_wheat ↓,
QD_wheat ↑, QD_$ ↑

meaning that $1 buys 100 yen or, equivalently, from a foreign perspective, it takes 100 yen to buy $1—the bushel of wheat will cost 800 yen in Japan (8 × 100 yen = 800 yen).

If the dollar appreciates from 100 yen to 150 yen, this would raise the yen price of the bushel of wheat from 800 yen to 1,200 yen (8 × 150 yen). Following standard tenets of consumer demand theory, we can reasonably assume that foreigners, ceteris paribus, will respond to the price rise by reducing the quantity demanded of U.S. wheat /month (and U.S. goods, more generally), thereby reducing the quantity demanded of dollars/ month. Conversely, a depreciation of the dollar, from say, 100 yen to 50 yen, would lower the yen price of the bushel of wheat 800 yen to 400 yen (8 × 50 yen). Again, it is reasonable to assume that foreigners, ceteris paribus, will respond to the fall in the yen price by raising the quantity demanded of U.S. wheat/month (and U.S. goods, more generally), thereby raising the quantity demanded of dollars/month.[5]

To sum up to this point, the minus sign over the exchange rate in Equation (16-3) reflects the fact that, ceteris paribus, an appreciation of the dollar will raise the yen price of U.S. goods in Japan, thereby reducing the quantity demanded of U.S. goods and thus the quantity demanded of dollars/month. The reverse is also true.

Recap

[handwritten margin note:]
- D_$ = directly related to D_goods
- QD_$ = inversely related to E rate.

The demand for dollars is directly related to foreign demand for U.S. goods, services, and securities. The quantity demanded of dollars/month is inversely related to the exchange rate, ceteris paribus. The foreign price of U.S. goods is equal to the dollar price of U.S. goods times the exchange rate. If the dollar appreciates, the foreign price of U.S. goods increases, ceteris paribus.

THE SUPPLY OF DOLLARS IN THE FOREIGN EXCHANGE MARKET

So much for the demand side—what about supply? In international financial markets, the supply of dollars originates from domestic purchases of foreign goods, services, and financial securities, as depicted in Equation (16-5):

$$
(16\text{-}5) \quad \text{Supply of dollars/month} = f(\overset{+}{\text{U.S. demand for foreign goods, services, and securities}})
$$

As before, the plus sign over the expression means that U.S. demand for foreign goods, services, and securities and the supply of dollars in the foreign exchange market

$D_{FG} \uparrow, D_{\yen} \uparrow, S_\$ \uparrow$

$D_{FG} \downarrow, D_{\yen} \downarrow, S_\$ \downarrow$

are positively related. When the former rises, the latter rises. This occurs because when U.S. demand for foreign goods, services, and securities rises, the demand for yen to pay for those foreign goods, services, and securities also rises. But how do U.S. residents get more yen? The short simple answer is by supplying more dollars! (Remember, dollars are being supplied to purchase yen to purchase foreign goods.) You should be able to explain why a drop in the U.S. demand for foreign goods (in this case, Japanese goods) will lead to a decrease in the supply of dollars.

The next step is to consider how the quantity supplied of dollars/month is affected by changes in the exchange rate. (Note that quantity supplied is the amount of dollars that will be supplied/month at a specific exchange rate.) The answer is that, ceteris paribus, the quantity supplied is directly related to the exchange rate, as shown in Equation (16-6):

$$(16\text{-}6) \qquad \text{Quantity supplied of dollars/month} = f(\overset{+}{\text{exchange rate}})$$

To see why the exchange rate and the quantity supplied of dollars/month are positively related, ceteris paribus, consider how changes in the exchange rate affect U.S. demand for foreign goods, services, and securities. Focusing again only on goods for simplicity, we can draw on the "Cracking the Code" feature on p. 377 and the discussion of Equation (16-1). As you saw, the dollar price of foreign goods in the United States is equal to the yen price divided by the exchange rate. Thus, as shown in the feature, as the exchange rate rises, the dollar price of foreign goods falls. Accordingly, we would expect U.S. residents to increase the quantity demanded of foreign goods/month, which, in turn, will raise the quantity of dollars supplied/month to the foreign exchange market, ceteris paribus. Conversely, a fall in the exchange rate will raise the dollar price of foreign goods in the United States, thereby lowering the quantity demanded of foreign goods/month and, thus, the quantity supplied of dollars/month, ceteris paribus.[6]

We have established an inverse relationship between the quantity demanded of dollars/month and the exchange rate, ceteris paribus. In addition, given our assumptions, we have confirmed a direct relationship between the quantity supplied of dollars/month and the exchange rate, ceteris paribus. These relationships are graphed in Exhibit 16-3 on p. 384, which depicts the determination of the equilibrium exchange rate. The foreign exchange market "clears" at the exchange rate where the demand and supply curves intersect. At this exchange rate, the quantity demanded of dollars/month is equal to the quantity supplied of dollars/month, and we have market equilibrium (at point A). At any other exchange rate, there is either a surplus or a shortage of dollars. Market forces generated by the surplus or shortage will cause changes in the exchange rate, which will continue until equilibrium is reached.

Recap   The supply of dollars is directly related to U.S. demand for foreign goods, services, and securities. The quantity supplied of dollars/month is directly related to the exchange rate, ceteris paribus. The exchange rate adjusts until the quantity demanded of dollars/month is just equal to the quantity supplied/month in international markets.

We have made a good start, but our ultimate objective is to understand the causes and consequences of changes in the exchange rate resulting from changes in supply or demand. Accordingly, we need to examine the factors that can cause the supply and demand curves for dollars in the foreign exchange market to shift.

Cracking the Code

The Foreign Exchange Market

Suppose that you need pounds for an upcoming trip to England. You call your local bank, say, in Nashville, Tennessee, and place a buy order for 1,000 pounds. Most likely, your local bank does not have a foreign exchange department, so it will call its correspondent bank that specializes in international transactions and place an order for pounds with Citibank's foreign exchange department.[a]

Most foreign currency transactions in the United States are executed by the foreign exchange departments of the largest banks, which are linked via modern telecommunications with foreign exchange dealers around the world. Accustomed to handling transactions from around the globe daily, they stand ready to buy or sell dollars and foreign currencies at the prevailing exchange rate. Acting as auctioneers, they (and other dealers nationwide and worldwide) are prepared to adjust the exchange rate up as buy orders for dollars rise relative to sell orders, or adjust the exchange rate down as buy orders for dollars fall relative to sell orders. Of course, this is just another way of saying that the exchange rate will change as supply and/or demand changes.

So how much will your 1,000 pounds cost? If you could "crack the code" in the relevant table from an online source such as MSN Money, you could figure out the approximate cost. We have reproduced a portion of the foreign exchange table (GBPUS) that appeared on the MSN Money Web site **http://moneycentral.msn.com** on February 25, 2008. It shows the number of dollars required to buy one British pound. The table shows the rate at the end for the trading day, 1.96928, as well as the change.

GBPUS quote; February 25, 2008

1.96928	–.00155	–.08%
Previous Close	1.97083	
Open	1.97006	
Day's High	1.97083	
Day's Low	1.96271	

The first thing to note is this exchange rate is reported in U.S. dollars per British pound. Exchange rates are usually reported in foreign currency required to purchase one dollar—the convention we use throughout this book. To obtain this familiar form, we need to take the reciprocal of dollars per pound to get pounds per dollar: 1/1.96928 = .5078. This implies it takes slightly more than one half of a pound to purchase one dollar, or equivalently nearly two dollars to purchase one pound.

We can see that the amount of dollars required to purchase one pound decreased from 1.97083 to 1.96928 from the previous trading day's closing to the closing on February 25, a decrease of about .08 percent, (1.96928 – 1.97083)/1.97083 = –.000786 or approximately – .0008. This implies the dollar appreciated and pound depreciated. Similarly, we can calculate the amount of pounds one dollar can purchase and see it increased from .5074 to .5078, unsurprisingly a gain of approximately .08 percent.

Changes in the exchange rate have profound implications for any transactions between the two currencies. For example, suppose a hotel room in England costs 100 British pounds and this remains unchanged. If the pound/dollar exchange rate falls from .75 pounds/dollar in January, when an American family is planning their trip, to .5 pounds/dollar in July, when they arrive in England, the amount of dollars they must pay for the hotel room increased from $133.33 to $200. Likewise, at the close of business on February 25, 2008, the 1,000 pounds you need to purchase for your trip to London would cost 1000×1.96928=$1,969.28.

Endnotes

a. A correspondent bank is merely a large bank, usually located in an important financial center, which provides the smaller bank with various services.

CHANGES IN SUPPLY AND DEMAND AND HOW THEY AFFECT THE EXCHANGE RATE

Starting with supply, let's first consider how and why changes in the supply of dollars in the foreign exchange market affect the exchange rate. The initial question that needs to be addressed is what factors, in addition to the exchange rate, could cause U.S. residents to alter their demand for foreign goods, services, and securities, and thus their supply of

16-3
The Market for Dollars

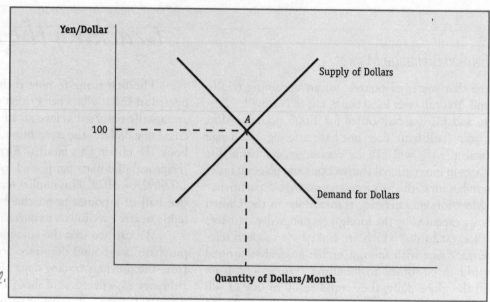

Yen/Dollar

100

Supply of Dollars

A

Demand for Dollars

Quantity of Dollars/Month

Factors that Δ
Supply $
~~~~~~~~~~
1. Δ in U.S. real income.
2. Δ in $ price of US.
   goods relative to
   $ price foreign goods.
3. Δ in foreign "r"
   relative to U.S. "r".

dollars in the foreign exchange market. In other words, what factors could cause the supply curve of dollars to shift? Previous research suggests that the following factors play a major role:

1. *Changes in U.S. real income.* Changes in U.S. real income and changes in the supply of dollars are positively related. The reason is that as real income grows in the United States, households and firms have more funds to spend and save. Accordingly, they will demand more U.S. goods, services, and securities and more foreign goods, services, and securities. Thus, as U.S. real income grows, ceteris paribus, the supply of dollars will increase because Americans now have more income to spend on imports. Likewise, as U.S. real income falls, ceteris paribus, the supply of dollars will decrease.

2. *Changes in the dollar price of U.S. goods relative to the dollar price of foreign goods.* Simply put, if the prices of U.S. goods rise relative to the dollar prices of foreign goods, ceteris paribus, U.S. residents will demand more foreign goods and, therefore, supply more dollars in the foreign exchange market because foreign goods are now relatively cheaper than U.S. goods. Holding the exchange rate constant, what could cause such changes in relative prices? If you said a higher inflation rate in the United States than in Japan, you are right! Likewise, using similar reasoning, if the inflation rate in the United States falls relative to that in Japan, U.S. residents will supply fewer dollars in the foreign exchange market, ceteris paribus.

3. *Changes in foreign interest rates relative to U.S. interest rates.* As foreign interest rates rise relative to U.S. rates, ceteris paribus, foreign securities become relatively more attractive. Accordingly, U.S. residents will buy more foreign securities and, thus, supply more dollars. Likewise, if foreign rates fall relative to U.S. rates, the supply of dollars decreases, ceteris paribus. To be more precise, U.S. residents will compare interest rates in the United States, i_{US}, with the expected return on foreign securities. As we shall see later in this chapter, the latter consists of the foreign interest rate, i_{FOR}, minus the expected appreciation (if any) in the value of the dollar.

For a graphical presentation of this analytical discussion of supply, see Exhibit 16-4. Study it carefully before moving on to the discussion of the demand for dollars.

Using the same logic and analytical framework we used for supply, we now ask what factors, in addition to the exchange rate, could cause foreigners to alter their demand for

16-4

Changes in the Exchange
Rate: The Role of Changes in
Supply

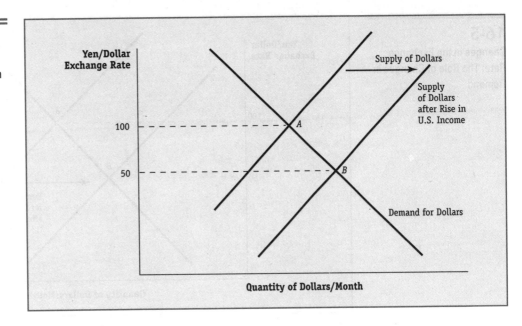

This exhibit begins with an initial equilibrium exchange rate of 100 yen. Assume that the equilibrium is now disturbed by a change in one of the factors that affect the supply of dollars, say, a rise in U.S. income, which increases the supply of dollars, as shown by the rightward shift of the supply curve. The new equilibrium at point *B* results in a depreciation of the dollar as the equilibrium exchange rate falls from 100 yen to 50 yen. Note that a rise in the prices of U.S. goods relative to the dollar prices of foreign goods, or a rise in foreign interest rates relative to U.S. interest rates, would have produced a similar increase in supply and depreciation of the exchange rate.

Factors that Δ
  Demand $

· Δ in foreign real income.

·· Δ in foreign price of foreign goods relative to foreign price of U.S. goods

·· Δ in U.S. "r" relative to foreign "r".

U.S. goods, services, and securities and thus their demand for dollars in the foreign exchange market. Remember that changes in the demand for dollars cause the demand curve for dollars to shift. We begin by identifying the major factors that can alter demand:

1. *Changes in foreign real income.* Ceteris paribus, changes in foreign real income and the demand for dollars are positively related. For example, if foreign real incomes rise, ceteris paribus, foreign firms and households will have more funds to spend and save. Accordingly, they will demand more of their own goods, services, and securities, as well as more imported goods, services, and securities. Thus, as foreign real incomes grow, ceteris paribus, the demand for dollars, reflecting the increased supply of yen to execute transactions, will grow. Following similar reasoning, if foreign incomes fall, the demand for dollars will also fall, ceteris paribus.

2. *Changes in the foreign (yen) price of foreign goods relative to the foreign price of U.S. goods.* Ceteris paribus, changes in, say, the yen price of Japanese goods relative to the yen price of U.S. goods and the demand for dollars are positively related. To see why, assume inflation accelerates in Japan, but there is no inflation in the United States. The Japanese inflation will raise the yen price of Japanese goods relative to the yen price of U.S. goods. As a result, foreigners will demand more U.S. goods and, thus, more dollars, ceteris paribus. If U.S. inflation rises relative to inflation in Japan, foreigners will demand fewer dollars, ceteris paribus.

3. *Changes in U.S. interest rates relative to foreign interest rates.* A positive relationship also exists between changes in U.S. interest rates relative to foreign rates and the demand for dollars. For example, suppose that, initially, the interest rate on both foreign

16-5

Changes in the Exchange
Rate: The Role of Changes in
Demand

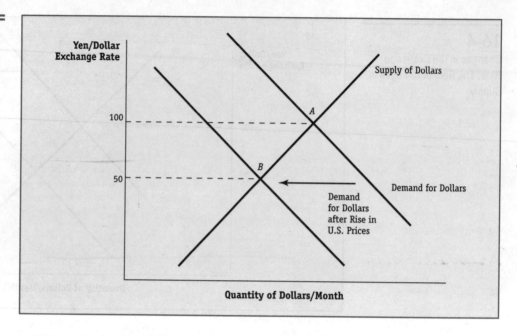

Assume that the initial equilibrium at point *A* is disturbed by a change in one of the factors that affects
the demand for dollars. In particular, suppose that the yen price of U.S. goods rises relative to the yen
price of foreign goods because of inflation in the United States. As a result, foreigners' demand for U.S.
goods declines, as shown by the leftward shift of the demand curve. The new equilibrium (point *B*) results in a depreciation of the dollar from 100 yen to 50 yen. Note that a fall in foreign incomes or a rise in
foreign interest rates relative to U.S. rates would have produced a similar leftward shift in the demand
curve and depreciation of the dollar.

government bonds and U.S. Treasury bonds is 6 percent. Portfolio managers in Japan, noticing the identical rates and recognizing the benefits of diversification, hold
some of both types of bonds in their portfolios. Now, interest rates in the United
States rise. As a result, the demand for U.S. securities rises, as does the demand for
dollars, ceteris paribus. Likewise, if interest rates in Japan fall, the demand for dollars
rises, ceteris paribus.[7] More on this later in the chapter.

These points are illustrated graphically in Exhibit 16–5. Study this exhibit carefully before moving on. Make sure that you note the similarities between the factors
that cause changes in the demand for dollars and the factors that cause changes in the
supply of dollars.

Recap   Increases in U.S. real income, in U.S. prices relative to foreign prices, and in foreign interest
rates relative to U.S. interest rates all increase the supply of dollars, and vice versa. Increases in foreign real income, in foreign prices relative to U.S. prices, and in U.S. interest
rates relative to foreign interest rates all increase the demand for dollars, and vice versa.

EXCHANGE RATES IN THE LONG RUN: THE THEORY
OF PURCHASING POWER PARITY

We have covered some important material. Now is a good time to stop and see how to
use this analysis. Suppose that the U.S. economy is expanding at a relatively slow pace,

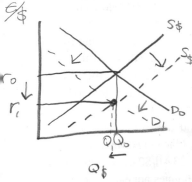

with real GDP growing at a 1 to 2 percent annual rate, compared to its potential growth trend of 2.5 to 3 percent. Against this background, the Federal Reserve decides that a rise in the aggregate demand for goods and services is in order. Accordingly, the Fed pursues a more stimulative monetary policy by taking action that causes interest rates to fall. The question we want to focus on in the present context is how the fall in U.S. interest rates will affect the exchange rate.

Believe it or not, the answer flows directly from the preceding discussion of changes in supply and demand. Ceteris paribus, the fall in U.S. interest rates relative to interest rates in Japan will lead to a depreciation of the dollar—that is, to a fall in the exchange rate. The reasoning is as follows: the fall in U.S. rates reduces the attractiveness of U.S. securities relative to foreign securities; as a result, foreigners will demand fewer U.S. securities and, thus, will demand fewer dollars in the foreign exchange market, while U.S. residents will demand more foreign securities and, thus, will supply more dollars in the foreign exchange market. In sum, the dollar depreciates as a result of the reduction in the demand for and rise in the supply of dollars induced by the Fed's actions. Try sketching out this scenario graphically as in Exhibits 16-4 and 16-5. If the Fed's policy works, output will expand, income will grow, and demand for imports will rise, all of which will potentially further weaken the dollar, especially if the policy fuels the expectation of inflation or actual inflation.

Taking our analysis one step further, consider the case in which the Fed policy and expanding economy causes an acceleration of the actual inflation rate in the United States. The theory of purchasing power parity asserts that in the long run, exchange rates adjust to different inflation rates among countries so that the *relative* purchasing power of various currencies is equalized. Thus, after full adjustment among all currencies, one currency, such as the dollar, will purchase the same market basket of goods and services in every country. In other words, an American student traveling in China can take the $1.25 they would normally spend on a can of Coke while in the United States, convert the $1.25 to the Chinese currency, and purchase an identical can of Coke in China.

Purchasing Power Parity
The theory that, in the long run, exchange rates adjust so that the relative purchasing power of various currencies is equalized.

To help clarify this theory, assume that inflation is 5 percent in the United States and 3 percent in the European Union. After the inflation and at the original exchange rate, relative prices in the United States are roughly 2 percent higher than those in the European Union.[8] As you saw earlier in the chapter, the European demand for the relatively more expensive U.S. exports will decline, and the U.S. demand for relatively cheaper U.S. imports will increase. Thus, the demand for dollars will decrease and the supply of dollars will increase. As a result, the dollar will depreciate in terms of the euro. The question is how much the dollar will depreciate. According to the purchasing power parity theory, the dollar should then appreciate by 2 percent, thus offsetting the higher U.S. inflation relative to the European Union (5 percent – 3 percent = 2 percent), leaving the relative purchasing power between the dollar and the euro unchanged.

The purchasing power parity theory is based on many, often unrealistic, assumptions. These assumptions include that all goods and services are identical and tradable, that there are no transportation costs and no barriers to trade such as tariffs, and that exchange rates are influenced only by relative inflation rates across the various countries. In reality, all goods such as Toyotas, Chevrolets, and BMWs are not identical, and therefore will not sell for the same prices. Furthermore, all goods are not tradable, and there are transportation costs and other barriers to trade. Try buying a fast-food imported hamburger or getting an imported haircut. Overall prices in one country may increase because of large price increases of nontradable goods such as housing, land, and nontradable services. In this case, a higher inflation in one country would not pass through to a depreciation of the currency.

In addition to the unrealistic assumptions, the purchasing power parity theory suffers from a lack of completeness because it neglects factors that can and do cause exchange rates to vary significantly over time. These factors include changes in productivity, economic growth, market structures, and technologies across countries, as well as shifts in factor supplies causing commodity price shocks. For example, countries with higher productivity growth or more competitive market structures, ceteris paribus, would experience relatively lower inflation and, hence, currency appreciation and vice versa. Finally, the purchasing power parity theory does not account for changes in tastes among countries. As preferences for another country's products increase, there is a tendency for that country's currency to appreciate. For example, if U.S. taste for French wine decreases (perhaps because of the development of the California wine industry), the supply of dollars would shift left (as Americans would need fewer euros to buy French wine), causing an appreciation of the dollar. Consequently, because of the unrealistic assumptions and the lack of completeness, a word of caution is needed: although there is a tendency for currencies of countries with higher relative inflation to

A Closer Look

The Big Mac Index and Purchasing Power Parity

Every year, *The Economist* newsmagazine publishes an interesting and fun Big Mac currency index based on the purchasing power parity theory. According to the theory, the dollar price of a Big Mac, the signature hamburger of the McDonald's chain, should be the same in all of the 120 countries around the world where the Big Mac is sold. The most recent table is from the July 5, 2007, issue of *The Economist*. To find the dollar price of a Big Mac, the price in the local currency is merely divided by the exchange rate. If the dollar price of a Big Mac is less than the $3.41 U.S. price, then the currency is thought to be undervalued relative to the U.S. dollar. Likewise, if the dollar price of a Big Mac is more, the currency is thought to be overvalued.

As the table shows, the dollar price of a Big Mac around the world varies from $1.45 in China to $7.61 in Iceland. Hence, according to the Big Mac index, the currency in China is thought to be undervalued by 57 percent [($1.45 − $3.41)/$3.41 = −.5748]. While the currencies of several Asian and other emerging economies appear to be undervalued, the currency of Iceland is, according to the Big Mac index, overvalued by 123 percent [($7.61 − $3.41)/$3.41 = +1.23]. The theory of purchasing power parity does not seem to be able to explain these disparities.

The Big Mac index is flawed by the unrealistic assumptions and the lack of completeness of the purchasing power parity theory. For example, not all Big Macs taste the same in all countries. Local customs and tastes dictate each region's recipe. In some countries, Big Macs are quite spicy. (In others, mayonnaise is served with McDonald's French fries.) Likewise, there can be differences in local sales taxes, trade barriers on beef, and differences in local labor and rent costs. Thus, more factors, in addition to purchasing power parity, need to be considered in explaining exchange rate differentials and movements.

Cash and Carry
The Hamburger Standard, July 2007

	Big Mac prices		Implied ppp† of the dollar	Actual dollar exchange rate July 2nd	Under(−) / over(+) valuation against the dollar, %
	in local currency	in dollars			
United States‡	$3.41	3.41			
Argentina	Peso 8.25	2.67	2.42	3.09	−22
Australia	A$3.45	2.95	1.01	1.17	−14
Brazil	Real 6.90	3.61	2.02	1.91	+6
Britain	£1.99	4.01	1.71§	2.01§	+18
Canada	C$3.88	3.68	1.14	1.05	+8
Chile	Peso 1.565	2.97	459	527	−13
China	Yuan 11.0	1.45	3.23	7.60	−58
Czech Republic	Koruna 52.9	2.51	15.5	21.1	−27
Denmark	Dkr 27.75	5.08	8.14	5.46	+49
Egypt	Pound 9.54	1.68	2.80	5.69	−51
Euro area**	€3.06	4.17	1.12††	1.36††	+22
Hong Kong	HK$ 12.0	1.54	3.52	7.82	−55
Hungary	Forint 600	3.33	176	180	−2
Indonesia	Rupiah 15,900	1.76	4.663	9.015	−48
Japan	¥280	2.29	82.1	122	−33
Malaysia	Ringgit 5.50	1.60	1.61	3.43	−53
Mexico	Peso 29.0	2.69	8.50	10.8	−21
New Zealand	NZ$4.60	3.59	1.35	1.28	+5
Peru	New Sol 9.50	3.00	2.79	3.17	−12
Philippines	Peso 85.0	1.85	24.9	45.9	−46
Poland	Zloty 6.90	2.51	2.02	2.75	−26
Russia	Rouble 52.0	2.03	15.2	25.6	−41
Singapore	S$3.95	2.59	1.16	1.52	−24
South Africa	Rand 15.5	2.22	4.55	6.97	−35
South Korea	Won 2,900	3.14	850	9.23	−8
Sweden	SKr33.0	4.86	9.68	6.79	+42
Switzerland	SFr6.30	5.20	1.85	1.21	+53
Taiwan	NT$75.0	2.29	22.0	32.8	−33
Thailand	Baht 62.0	1.80	18.2	34.5	−47
Turkey	Lire 4.75	3.66	1.39	1.30	+7
Venezuela	Bolivar 7,400	3.45	2.170	2.147	+1
Colombia	Peso 6,900	3.53	2.023	1.956	+3
Costa Rica	Colon 1,130	2.18	331	519	−36
Estonia	Kroon 30.0	2.61	8.80	11.5	−23
Iceland	Kronur 469	7.61	138	61.7	+123
Latvia	Lats 1.39	2.72	0.41	0.51	−20
Lithuania	Litas 6.60	2.61	1.94	2.53	−24
Norway	Kroner 40.0	6.88	11.7	5.81	+102
Pakistan	Rupee 140	2.32	41.1	60.4	−32
Paraguay	Guarani 10,500	2.04	3.079	5.145	−40
Saudi Arabia	Riyal 9.00	2.40	2.64	3.75	−30
Slovakia	Koruna 61.3	2.49	18.0	24.6	−27
Sri Lanka	Rupee 210	1.89	61.6	111	−45
UAE	Dirhams 10.0	2.72	2.93	3.67	−20
Ukraine	Hryvnia 9.25	1.84	2.71	5.03	−46
Uruguay	Peso 62.0	2.59	18.2	23.9	−24

†Purchasing-power parity; local price divided by price in United States   ‡Average of New York, Chicago, Atlanta and San Francisco   §Dollars per pound   **Weighted average of prices in euro area   ††Dollars per euro

Sources: McDonald's; The Economist

depreciate in the long run and vice versa, the trade-off is far from perfect, as the purchasing power theory suggests.

Now would be a good time to read the accompanying "A Closer Look" on the Big Mac Index, which attempts to test the purchasing power parity theory using McDonald's famous burger.

We have examined rather carefully the variety of domestic and foreign factors that, taken together, determine the exchange rate. We would be remiss if we failed to point out that changes in the factors that affect exchange rates are ongoing and, therefore, changes in exchange rates are ongoing. In other words, in reality, demands and supplies are changing all the time, so equilibrium is a constantly moving target. For example, changes in U.S. real incomes lead to changes in other countries' real incomes, which lead to changes in U.S. incomes, which lead to changes in . . . (and so on). The interrelationships and interactions are increasingly significant as the world's economies become more intertwined. In the next section, we look at how investors choose among financial instruments denominated in various currencies.

Recap   The theory of purchasing power parity asserts that exchange rates adjust to varying rates of inflation across countries so that relative purchasing power among various currencies is equalized. Although there is a tendency for countries with higher inflation to see their currencies depreciate, the correlation is far from perfect because of the limiting assumptions of the theory that do not hold in the real world.

CHOOSING AMONG DOMESTIC AND FOREIGN FINANCIAL INSTRUMENTS: THE THEORY OF INTEREST RATE PARITY

When comparing financial instruments denominated in the same currency, investors consider the return, the maturity, and the default risk. If instruments are denominated in different currencies, investors and borrowers must also consider the exchange rate risk, or the risk that the exchange rate between two currencies will change and alter the real return of the investment. For example, suppose that a U.S. investor converts dollars to Mexican pesos to make an investment denominated in pesos that earns a 10 percent nominal return. The investor expects the exchange rate to remain constant; but if the peso unexpectedly depreciates by 10 percent, the entire 10 percent return is wiped out when the pesos are converted back to dollars. Thus, exchange rate risk must be factored into any international investment.

In globalized financial markets, financial market players compare expected rates of return on instruments denominated in various currencies, including their own. To do so, they must convert all returns to an equivalent return in the domestic currency. The nominal rate of return in a domestic currency on an investment that is denominated in a foreign currency is the nominal foreign interest rate plus the expected change in the exchange rate, less an adjustment for risk that results from the uncertainty of the future exchange rate. Equation (16-7) depicts such a situation:

(16-7)
$$I_{US} = I_{FOR} + E$$

where I_{US} is the nominal U.S. return on an investment in a foreign instrument that earns the nominal foreign interest rate, I_{FOR}, and E is the expected percentage change in the exchange rate (depreciation of the dollar) plus an exchange rate risk factor that compensates for the uncertainty of the future exchange rate. For example, if the interest is 1 percent in Japan and 6 percent in the United States, then investors must expect the dollar to depreciate, and yen to appreciate by approximately 5 percent over the next year.

Suppose the exchange rate is 100 yen/dollar now, but expected to be 95 yen/dollar in one year. The dollar would be expected to depreciate 5 percent and the yen appreciate 5 percent, so E=.05=5 percent. A Japanese investor could choose to invest 100 yen at 1 percent in Japan and have 101 yen in one year, or exchange 100 yen for $1, invest this at 6 percent, and have 1.06 dollars in one year, which could be exchanged for approximately 101 yen (95×1.06) at the year's end. Similarly, an American could invest $100 in the United States and receive $106 in one year, or change the $100 into 10,000 yen to invest this in Japan. The American investor would then receive 10,100 yen in one year, which could be exchanged for $106 (approximately 10100/.95).

Lenders compare this nominal U.S. return, I_{US}, with the U.S. interest rate and choose the instrument that offers the highest return, while borrowers choose to borrow in the market that offers the lowest rate as expressed in their domestic currencies. Because of market adjustments, if the nominal U.S. return is greater than the nominal foreign return plus the exchange rate adjustment, lenders will supply more funds in the U.S. market, and borrowers will borrow more funds in foreign markets. The theory of interest rate parity asserts that the adjustments will continue until the U.S. and foreign nominal interest rates are equal, except for the expected exchange rate adjustment and an exchange rate risk factor. When interest rates have adjusted so that rates between countries differ only by the expected appreciation or depreciation of the currency, then interest rate parity has been reached and international financial markets are in equilibrium.

In reality, borrowers and lenders are making decisions based on the expected real return rather than nominal returns. The real interest rate (return) is the nominal return less expected inflation. At times, we may wish to express returns between nations in terms of real interest rates as opposed to nominal rates. To do so for the United States, we must subtract expected U.S. inflation from each nominal rate in Equation (16-7), as in Equation (16-8). In equilibrium, the real U.S. interest rate, R_{US}, will be:

Interest Rate Parity
The theory that in equilibrium, interest rates adjust so that after adjustments have been made for expected inflation and exchange rate risk, returns are equalized across countries.

(16-8)
$$R_{US} = I_{US} - P_{US} = I_{FOR} + E - P_{US}$$

where P_{US} is the expected U.S. inflation rate. Likewise, we can express the nominal foreign rate, I_{FOR}, in terms of the real foreign rate, R_{FOR}, plus the expected foreign inflation, P_{FOR}, to arrive at the equilibrium real U.S. interest rate in terms of the foreign real rate and domestic and foreign expected inflation. The results are summarized in Equation (16-9):

(16-9)
$$R_{US} = R_{FOR} + P_{FOR} + E - P_{US}$$

The degree of capital mobility is the ease with which funds can flow in and out of financial instruments denominated in different currencies. We can conclude that with greater capital mobility, the real U.S. and foreign interest rates will tend to be equalized after differences in expected inflation and expected changes in exchange rates, along with the uncertainty of these changes, have been taken into account. As you shall see in Chapter 17, foreign exchange futures, forward, and swap agreements can be used to hedge or reduce interest rate risk. In the next section of this chapter, we look at the often mysterious concept of the balance of payments that keeps track of the financial flows among nations.

Recap   Financial market participants compare expected rates of return on instruments denominated in different currencies. The expected nominal rate of return on a foreign investment is the foreign interest rate plus the change in the exchange rate less an adjustment for risk from the uncertainty of the future exchange rate. The expected real return includes an adjustment factor for expected inflation in both countries. In equilibrium, interest rates adjust so that after adjustments have been made for expected inflation and exchange rate risk, returns are equalized across countries.

Looking Back

The Causes and Consequences of Dollar Exchange Rate Movements Since 1980

The internationalization or globalization of the U.S. economy became apparent to all during the first half of the 1980s. During 1979 and 1980, the international value of the dollar reached a record low. As can be seen in Exhibit 16-1, by early 1985, the dollar had appreciated by more than 60 percent from its low.

What caused this appreciation? Most experts agree that it was a combination of several factors. First, in late 1979 and early 1980, the Fed embarked on a program of monetary restraint to lower the high inflation rate in the United States. This had the effect of raising interest rates in the United States—in particular, real interest rates—relative to real interest rates in the rest of the world. Second, in 1981, Congress enacted a large tax cut. The tax cut, along with the failure to cut spending, led to a larger government deficit, which also tended to raise real interest rates in the United States.

The rise in real U.S. interest rates induced by the monetary and fiscal policy actions, in turn, increased foreign demand for U.S. securities and, thus, the demand for dollars, while reducing U.S. demand for foreign securities and, thus, the supply of dollars in the foreign exchange market. As a result, the rise in U.S. real interest rates relative to real rates in the rest of the world helped produce a substantial appreciation of the dollar.

What were the consequences of the dollar's appreciation? Simply put, the rise in the international value of the dollar had a dramatic effect on the U.S. economy. As one would predict, based on the discussion in this chapter, the appreciation tended to raise the prices of U.S. goods in foreign markets, discouraging exports, and tended to lower the prices of foreign goods in the United States, encouraging imports. The result was a substantial increase in the current account deficit. By 1985, the United States was buying $150 billion more goods and services from abroad than it was selling abroad. Naturally, this deterioration in U.S. international competitiveness reduced employment and output in the United States relative to what they would have been. (Actually, employment and output initially decreased, but by 1985, both were on the rise. In 1985, the current account deficit was rising, the budget deficit was rising, GDP was rising, and employment was rising!) The lower import prices encouraged by the appreciation also tended to dampen the inflation rate in the United States.

Beginning in early 1985, U.S. policy makers in coordination with major U.S. trading partners agreed to a concerted effort to lower the value of the dollar. Central banks would supply dollars and demand their own currencies. The pressure to intervene came from the realization that the U.S. economy was severely uncompetitive. The "overvalued" dollar was causing a record trade deficit, and U.S. jobs were being lost in domestic exporting industries and industries that suffered from competition from imports. The value of the dollar did fall consistently in the late 1980s due both to central bank intervention and to falling U.S. interest rates that reduced the demand for U.S. securities. The trade deficit also fell, but not as fast or as far as economists had expected, given the depreciation of the dollar. By the early 1990s, the dollar was about 50 percent lower than in 1985, but the trade deficit, although reduced, still persisted. In the short run, the percentage decrease in the demand for foreign products was less than the percentage decrease in the exchange rate, although this condition was not expected to persist in the long run.

In the early 1990s, the desire to reduce the government budget deficit led to contractionary fiscal policy. At the same time, the Fed pursued a relatively easy monetary policy due to the weak economy and reduced fears of inflation. These policies produced lower interest rates and depreciation of the dollar. In mid-1993, despite these circumstances, the trade deficit began to widen. No doubt this was due to the mild recovery of the U.S. economy and the faltering of many foreign economies.

The demand for imports increased in the recovering domestic economy, while the demand for exports decreased in the stumbling foreign economies. With U.S. interest rates at low levels relative to those of the rest of the world, particularly a united Germany, some economists wondered how far and for how long the dollar would fall.

By mid-1995, the dollar was again on the rise. U.S. interest rates had risen above foreign rates due to the strength of the U.S. economy and tightening actions taken by the Fed. The relatively higher U.S. interest rates led to increasing capital inflows. Continued strengthening of the U.S. economy raised expectations that the Fed would continue taking actions that would lead to increases in interest rates. Uncertainty abroad and the exceptionally strong performance of the U.S. economy led to further strengthening of the dollar.

During late 1997 and early 1998, the financial crisis in Asian economies caused the ongoing appreciation to escalate. A "flight to quality" in international financial markets triggered by the crisis in Asia often meant a flight into dollars and dollar-denominated financial instruments. Finally, in late fall 1998, the overvalued dollar did plummet as the Fed on two occasions took action that lowered interest rates.

By mid-1999, the dollar was again on the rise as an overheating U.S. economy continued to demonstrate incredible resilience. By late 2000, the dollar was stronger than it had been since 1986. The trade deficit was also very high, buoyed by a booming U.S. economy. As the economy fell into recession in 2001, the Fed orchestrated numerous cuts in the interest rate, and the Bush administration had a significant tax cut passed by Congress. Ceteris paribus, the hope was that falling interest rates and a tax decrease would work together to offset the strong recessionary tendencies the economy was experiencing. The U.S. economy was experiencing expansionary monetary policy, which led to falling interest rates. The tax cut combined with increased government spending to fight a war in Iraq caused the budget surplus to reach a record deficit. Although these actions would normally cause a fall in the value of the dollar, it was not until 2002 when this began to occur.

The dollar fell against most major currencies from 2002 until the end of 2004, but in late 2004 and early 2005, it began to rise again. This may have been due to the apparent strength of the U.S. economy and the belief that this strength, at least in comparison to Europe, would continue. From 2005 to 2008, the dollar began to decline versus other currencies such as the euro. This seems related to the developing weakness of the U.S. economy related to declining real estate prices and the connected financial problems. Federal Reserve interest rate cuts, at a time when interest rates in other countries were either stable or increasing, put further downward pressure on the dollar into 2008. Where the dollar will end up, given the severity of the global financial crisis that is manifesting itself in late 2008, remains to be seen.

DEFINING THE BALANCE OF PAYMENTS AND ITS INFLUENCE ON THE EXCHANGE RATE, THE FINANCIAL SYSTEM, AND THE U.S. ECONOMY

Balance of Payments
The record of transactions between the United States and its trading partners in the rest of the world over a particular period of time.

Credit
In the balance of payments, any item that results in a payment by foreigners to Americans.

Merchandise Exports
Foreign purchases of U.S. goods.

Debit
In the balance of payments, any transaction that results in a payment to foreigners by Americans.

Merchandise Imports
U.S. purchases of foreign goods.

Current Account
Transactions that involve currently produced goods and services, including the balance of goods and services.

Net Transfer Payments
In the current account, the difference between transfer payments received from and transfer payments made to foreigners.

Trade Balance
The difference between merchandise exports and imports.

Trade Deficit
Status when merchandise imports are greater than exports.

Trade Surplus
Status when merchandise exports are greater than imports.

Balance of Goods and Services
Net exports of services plus the trade balance.

The supply and demand forces that determine the exchange rate are reflected in the **balance of payments.** Simply put, the balance of payments for the United States is the record of transactions between the United States and its trading partners in the rest of the world over a particular period of time, such as a year. It is a record of the international flow of funds for purchases and sales of goods, services, and securities.

The accounting procedure underlying the balance of payments is based on a standard double-entry bookkeeping scheme, such as that used by business firms or households to record receipts and payments. This means that receipts (sources of funds such as income or borrowing) will, by definition, equal payments (uses of funds). In the balance of payments, all transactions that result in payments by foreigners to Americans are recorded as receipts; they are **credit** or plus items. Examples of such transactions include foreign purchases of U.S. goods (called **merchandise exports**), foreign purchases of U.S. securities (in effect, exports of securities), and expenditures by foreign tourists in the United States (in effect, exports of services). All transactions resulting in payments by Americans to foreigners are recorded as payments; they are negative or **debit** items. Examples of such payments include U.S. purchases of foreign goods (called **merchandise imports**), U.S. purchases of foreign securities (in effect, imports of securities), and expenditures by U.S. residents traveling abroad.

Over the years, government statisticians and analysts have found it useful to divide the balance of payments into several parts by grouping various types of receipts and payments into particular accounts. These accounts are discussed below and shown in Exhibit 16-6, which provides a simplified and hypothetical balance of payments for the United States. Note that for now, we will ignore government transactions in foreign currencies—the so-called Official Reserve Account of the balance of payments. This complication will be taken up when we discuss international policy in Chapters 18 and 26. The balance of payments may seem imposing at first, but as we take a closer look at the various accounts, you will find that it is not so formidable.

The Current Account

The **current account** brings together transactions that involve currently produced goods and services. It is composed of exports and imports of goods and services and **net transfer payments** (also called *net unilateral transfers*). The difference between merchandise exports and imports, often referred to in news reports as the **trade balance,** is taken by many observers to be an important indicator of a country's ability to compete internationally in the production and sale of goods. When merchandise imports are greater than exports, as they have been in the United States for some years, a country has a **trade deficit,** suggesting some deterioration in international competitiveness. It could just as well suggest an improvement in the country's ability to attract foreign investment. The hypothetical figure in Exhibit 16-6 shows a U.S. trade deficit—indicated by (4) in the exhibit—of $200 billion. In contrast, if exports are greater than imports, as has been the case in Japan for some time, a country has a **trade surplus,** suggesting that it is competing successfully in the world economy or that its citizens are investing heavily abroad.

When net exports of services (5) involving tourism, transportation, insurance, and financial services are added to the trade balance (4), we get the **balance of goods and services** (6), which is often referred to as *net exports.* If net exports are negative, as they have been in the United States throughout the 1980s, 1990s, and 2000s, then we are buying more goods and services from foreigners than they are buying from the United

16-6

A Hypothetical and Simplified Balance of Payments for the U.S. Economy in the Year 2009 (in Billions of Dollars)

Account	Component	Receipts from Foreigners — Use of $ by foreigners	Payments to Foreigners — Source of $ by foreigners	Balance
Current	(2) Merchandise exports	+$400		(4) Balance of trade: (2)+(3) = −$200
	(3) Merchandise imports		−600	
	(5) Net exports of services	+$50		(6) Balance of goods and services: (4)+(5) = −$150 = net exports
	(7) Net unilateral transfers		−$30	(1) Balance on current account: (6)+(7)=−$180
Capital	(9) Capital inflows	+$280		(8) Balance on capital account: (9)+(10)=$180
	(10) Capital outflows		−$100	
		Total uses	Total sources	
Balance of Payments		+$730	−$730	(1)+(8)=0

States. Relatively speaking, the result is that GDP and, thus, production and employment in the United States are lower than they would have been if net exports had been less negative, ceteris paribus.[9]

Net transfer payments are the difference between transfers received from foreigners and transfers made to foreigners, including payments such as U.S. government aid to foreigners, aid from foreign governments to the United States, and private charitable relief. Adding net unilateral transfers (7) to the balance of goods and services, or net exports (6), yields the **balance on current account** (1), which in our example is in deficit by $180 billion.

The Capital Account

The **capital account** summarizes the financial flow of funds and securities between the United States and the rest of the world. The globalization of the U.S. financial system—a fancy term to describe the tremendous growth of international lending and borrowing—is reflected in a surge of U.S. investment in international stocks, bonds, and mutual funds in the recent decades, as well as the increased borrowing abroad by U.S. entities to fund the U.S. current account deficit.

Purchases of U.S. financial securities by foreigners and, more generally, borrowing from foreign sources by U.S. firms and residents, result in **capital inflows** into the United States; these are receipt (credit or plus) items in the capital account, as shown in Exhibit 16-6. Purchases of foreign financial securities by U.S. residents and borrowing by foreigners from U.S. banks and other sources result in **capital outflows** from the United States; these are payment (debit or negative) items in the capital account. In our

Balance on Current Account
The balance of goods and services plus net unilateral transfers.

Capital Account
The financial flow of funds and securities between the United States and the world.

Capital Inflows
Purchases of U.S. financial securities by foreigners and borrowing from foreign sources by U.S. firms and residents.

Capital Outflows
Purchases of foreign financial securities by U.S. residents and borrowing by foreigners from U.S. banks and other domestic sources.

hypothetical example in Exhibit 16-6, the balance on capital account (8), which is equal to the difference between capital inflows and capital outflows, is in surplus by $180 billion—and the United States is experiencing a **net capital inflow**.

Recap
The balance of payments for the United States is the record of transactions between the United States and its trading partners in the rest of the world over a particular time period. The balance of payments consists of the current account and the capital account. The current account brings together transactions involving currently produced goods and services. It includes the balance of goods and services and unilateral transfers. The capital account measures the flow of funds and securities between the United States and the rest of the world.

So much for the components of the balance of payments. What do they have to do with the exchange rate and U.S. markets? Believe it or not, the various tools of analysis necessary to answer this question have already been developed. All we need to do is to bring them together.

THE BALANCE OF PAYMENTS AND THE EXCHANGE RATE

Take a careful look at the bottom line in Exhibit 16-6. Not surprisingly, it says that the balance of payments balances; the hypothetical $180 billion deficit in the current account (1) is exactly offset by a $180 billion surplus in the capital account (8).[10] Another way of saying the same thing is that the sum of all the items in the Payments to Foreigners column is exactly equal to the sum of all items in the Receipts from Foreigners column.

To see why this equality is not just the result of bookkeeping gimmickry and why it relates directly to the determination of the exchange rate and the role it plays in our economy, note that all items in the Receipts column represent foreign demands for U.S. goods, services, and securities—the very items that determine the demand for dollars in the foreign exchange market. Similarly, all items in the Payments column represent U.S. demands for foreign goods, services, and securities—the very items that determine the supply of dollars in the foreign exchange market. Assuming that the exchange rate is flexible and free to move in response to any change in demand or supply, the exchange rate will move to that rate where the quantity of dollars demanded/month is equal to the quantity of dollars supplied/month. Put in terms of Exhibit 16-6, the equilibrium exchange rate will change until the sum of all items in the Receipts column, which reflects the quantity of dollars demanded/month, is equal to the sum of all items in the Payments column, which reflects the quantity of dollars supplied/month. While the uses of funds are always equal to the sources (for every source, there is a use), the intended uses and sources may differ significantly, and these differences in plans and intentions move the exchange rate.

While examining the factors determining exchange rates, you learned that a fall in U.S. interest rates relative to foreign rates would tend to decrease the foreign demand for U.S. securities and, thus, the demand for dollars. You also learned that a fall in U.S. rates relative to foreign rates would tend to increase the U.S. demand for foreign securities and, thus, the supply of dollars. In balance of payments terminology, the relatively lower U.S. interest rates would cause increased capital outflows and decreased capital inflows. The fall in the demand for dollars and the increase in the supply of dollars, in turn, would lead to a depreciation of the dollar.

If capital outflows rise and capital inflows fall, the capital account surplus in Exhibit 16-6 will fall. If nothing happens to the current account, the balance of payments will no longer balance. Obviously, something else must change. What happens is this: As the exchange rate depreciates, a number of adjustments in foreign demands and U.S. demands ensue. Among the most important is a decrease in the current account deficit, reflecting, in large part, a decrease in the trade deficit. To be more specific, the depreciation of the dollar will tend to decrease the yen (foreign) price of U.S. goods abroad, thus increasing U.S. exports. The depreciation will also tend to raise the dollar price of foreign goods in the United States, thus decreasing U.S. imports and the trade deficit. From a purely domestic perspective, the fall in U.S. interest rates pulls foreign funds from the U.S. financial system, leads to a depreciation of the dollar, and tends to increase foreign demand for U.S. output and, thus, increase U.S. employment relative to what it otherwise would have been.

So why shouldn't a country cut its interest rates relative to its trading partners, reduce the value of its currency, and stimulate exports in order to increase its rate of growth? Note, this process depends on reducing imports and increasing exports, i.e., the country producing more and consuming less. Another problem, especially important for small countries, is that the increased price of imports in domestic currency terms can fuel inflation. We will explore such issues in Chapter 26.

This chapter has focused on the theory of exchange rate determination, and the following one will examine the relevant international institutions and their development. Although increased globalization has blurred the distinction between international and national goods and financial markets, these two chapters give us an opportunity to focus directly on international aspects and clarify international issues.

Recap   The exchange rate adjusts until the quantity demanded of dollars/month is just equal to the quantity supplied/month in international financial markets. If the intended sources and uses of dollars differ, changes in the exchange rate will bring them into equality. In the following chapter, we will consider the international financial system and recent changes in it.

Summary of Major Points

1. The exchange rate is the number of units of foreign money (currency) that can be acquired with one unit of domestic money. If the exchange rate rises, the dollar is said to have appreciated relative to other currencies. If the exchange rate falls, the dollar has depreciated.

2. The dollar price of foreign goods is equal to the foreign price of foreign goods divided by the exchange rate. The foreign price of U.S. goods is equal to the dollar price of U.S. goods multiplied by the exchange rate. Accordingly, depreciation of the dollar will lower the price of U.S. goods in foreign markets and raise the price of foreign goods in the United States. An appreciation will raise the price of U.S. goods in foreign markets and lower the price of foreign goods in the United States.

3. The exchange rate is a price—the price of one national currency in terms of another—and is determined by supply and demand. The demand for dollars in the foreign exchange market reflects the demand by foreign residents for U.S. goods, services, and financial claims. The supply of dollars comes from the demand by U.S. residents for foreign goods, services, and financial claims.

4. The demand for dollars in the foreign exchange market shows an inverse relationship between exchange rate and the quantity demanded of dollars/month. This demand curve shifts rightward if foreign income increases, if the foreign inflation rate is higher than the U.S. rate, or if the foreign interest rate falls relative to the U.S. interest rate. The supply of dollars in the foreign exchange market

shows a positive relation between the exchange rate and the quantity supplied of dollars/month. This supply curve shifts rightward if U.S. income increases, if the U.S. inflation rate is higher than the foreign rate, or if the U.S. interest rate falls relative to the foreign interest rate.

5. A depreciation of the dollar can result from one or more of the following: a fall in U.S. interest rates relative to foreign interest rates, a rise in U.S. income, a fall in foreign income, and/or more inflation in the United States than abroad. An appreciation of the dollar can result from one or more of the following: a rise in U.S. interest rates relative to foreign interest rates, a fall in U.S. income, a rise in foreign income, and/or less inflation in the United States than abroad.

6. If the exchange rate is flexible and thus free to move in response to any change in the demand for or supply of dollars, the exchange rate will move to that rate where the quantity of dollars demanded/month is equal to the quantity of dollars supplied/month. According to the purchasing power parity theory, exchange rates adjust in the long run so that the relative purchasing power of various currencies is equalized. The purchasing power parity theory is based on the assumption that goods are identical and tradable, and that there are no transportation costs or barriers to trade. Also, the theory ignores changes in tastes, productivity, economic growth, market structures, and technologies across countries. Thus, there are many other factors that affect exchange rates. Although there is a tendency for

countries with relatively high inflation rates to experience currency depreciation, the correlation is not nearly as perfect as the purchasing power parity theory implies.

7. The nominal rate of return on a foreign investment is the foreign interest rate plus the expected change in the exchange rate less an adjustment for risk from the uncertainty of the future exchange rate. The expected real return includes an adjustment factor for expected inflation in both countries. In equilibrium, when interest rate parity is achieved, interest rates adjust so that after adjustments have been made for expected inflation and exchange rate risk, returns are equalized across countries.

8. The balance of payments is the record of transactions between the United States and its trading partners in the rest of the world over a particular period of time. It keeps track of the flow of funds for the purchases of goods, services, and securities. Ignoring official government transactions, it is composed of the current account and the capital account. If a change, such as a policy-induced rise in U.S. interest rates relative to foreign interest rates, results in capital inflows and a larger capital account surplus, it will also result in an appreciation of the dollar. In turn, the appreciation of the dollar will tend, among other adjustments, to reduce U.S. exports and to increase U.S. imports. These adjustments will tend to produce a larger current account deficit, which will rebalance the balance of payments.

Key Terms

Appreciated, p. 376

Balance of Goods and Services, p. 394

Balance of Payments, p. 394

Balance on Current Account, p. 395

Capital Account, p. 395

Capital Inflows, p. 395

Capital Outflows, p. 395

Credit, p. 394

Current Account, p. 394

Debit, p. 394

Depreciated, p. 377

Exchange Rate, p. 376

Foreign Currency (Money), p. 376

Foreign Exchange, p. 377

Foreign Exchange Market, p. 378

Interest Rate Parity, p. 391

Merchandise Exports, p. 394

Merchandise Imports, p. 394

Net Capital Inflow, p. 396

Net Transfer Payments, p. 394

Purchasing Power Parity, p. 387

Trade Balance, p. 394

Trade Deficit, p. 394

Trade Surplus, p. 394

Review Questions

1. Define *exchange rate, foreign currency*, and *foreign exchange market*.
2. Distinguish between a change in the quantity demanded of foreign exchange and a change in demand for foreign exchange. Do the same for the quantity supplied and the supply of foreign exchange.
3. Explain the relationship between the supply of dollars in the foreign exchange market and debit items in the balance of payments. Do the same for the demand for dollars in the foreign exchange market and credit items in the balance of payments.
4. Defend the following statement: The balance of payments always balances.
5. Explain how the trade balance, the balance of goods and services, and the balance of payments differ.
6. How is a surplus in the current account related to a deficit in the capital account? How is a deficit in the current account related to a surplus in the capital account?
7. If interest rates in the United States were lower than rates in the rest of the world, would the United States be more likely to be experiencing a net capital inflow or a net capital outflow? Ceteris paribus, would the current account be in surplus or deficit?
8. If the demand for U.S. exports falls because of a change in foreign tastes, what will happen to the exchange rate? What will happen to the trade balance and the balance of goods and services?
9. What would happen to the exchange rate if foreigners decided to sell U.S. securities, perhaps because of an increase in the perceived risk of investing in the United States?
10. What is the difference between the trade balance and the current account balance?
11. What are the assumptions of the purchasing power parity theory? What are the reasons that the theory may not offer a complete explanation of exchange rate differentials?
12. What is interest rate parity?

Analytical Questions

Questions marked with a check mark (✓) are objective in nature. They can be completed with a short answer or number.

✓13. If a hotel room in downtown Tokyo costs 20,000 yen per night and the yen/dollar exchange rate is 100, what is the dollar price of the hotel room? If the yen/dollar exchange rate increases to 150, what happens to the dollar price of the hotel room?

✓14. If a hotel room in downtown Los Angeles costs $100 per night and the yen/dollar exchange rate is 100, what is the yen price of the hotel room? If the yen/dollar exchange rate increases to 150, what happens to the yen price of the hotel room?

✓15. Assume that the dollar appreciates by 10 percent in terms of the Mexican peso. Explain what happens to the dollar price of tequila from Mexico after the appreciation. What happens if the dollar depreciates by 10 percent? Assume the peso price of tequila in Mexico is unchanged.

✓16. If a bottle of rare French wine sells for 40 euros in Paris and the exchange rate is 0.9 euros/dollar, how much will the bottle of wine sell for in New York City? Assume purchasing power parity holds.

✓17. Use graphs to show what happens to the demand for and supply of dollars in the foreign exchange market in the event of each of the following:
   a. Domestic income rises.
   b. Foreign income rises.
   c. Domestic inflation rises relative to foreign inflation.
   d. Domestic interest rates rise relative to foreign interest rates.

✓18. Use graphs to demonstrate that when both domestic and foreign incomes are rising, we cannot be sure of the direction of exchange rates.

✓19. If merchandise exports are $600 and merchandise imports are $500, what is the trade balance?

✓20. If there is a surplus of $100 in the capital account, no unilateral transfers, and a $50 deficit in the net exports of services, what is the trade balance?

21. If \$1 = 150 yen and 1 yen = 75 British pounds, what is the pound/dollar exchange rate? What is the dollar/pound exchange rate?

22. If the yen/dollar exchange rate is 125, how much will 25,000 yen cost in dollars? If the dollar appreciates to 150 yen/dollar, how much will the 25,000 yen cost in dollars?

23. If the yen/dollar exchange rate is 125, how many yen will \$15,000 be worth? If the dollar depreciates to 100 yen/dollar, how many yen will \$15,000 be worth?

24. Explain how, according to the purchasing power parity theory, exchange rates will adjust if inflation in the United States is 3 percent and inflation in Japan is 1 percent.

25. If nominal interest rates fall by 2 percent in the United States, ceteris paribus, explain what will happen to exchange rates to achieve interest rate parity

Suggested Readings

For detailed information on the balance of payments, go to http://www.newyorkfed.org/aboutthefed/fedpoint/fed40.html.

Although we ignored (for the time being) government transactions in foreign currencies, the *Federal Reserve Bulletin Statistical Supplement* includes data on international transactions on a quarterly basis. The January 2008 supplement is available online at http://www.federalreserve.gov/pubs/supplement/2008/01/default.htm.

Before he became the Federal Reserve Chairman, Ben Bernanke gave an interesting and relevant speech: "The Global Saving Glut and the U.S. Current Account Deficit," March 10, 2005. It is available online at http://www.federalreserve.gov/boarddocs/speeches/2005/200503102.

To understand the importance of the U.S. current account deficit, see "Financial Globalization and the U.S. Current Account Deficit" by Matthew Higgins and Thomas Klitgaard, in the Federal Reserve Bank of New York publication *Current Issues in Economics and Finance*, December 2007, available online at http://www.newyorkfed.org/research/current_issues/ci13–11.html.

For an interesting discussion about the relationship between the government and trade deficits, see the remarks by Governor Edward M. Gramlich, "Budget and Trade Deficits: Linked, Both Worrisome in the Long Run, but Not Twins" at the Los Angeles Chapter of the National Association for Business Economics Luncheon, Los Angeles, California, March 31, 2004. The remarks are available online at http://www.federalreserve.gov/boarddocs/speeches/2004/20040225/default.htm.

Beth J. Harpaz wrote an article about the effects of a weak dollar on a college student traveling in Italy in 2004. Titled "Strategies for Coping with the Weak Dollar," this Associated Press article, dated March 25, 2004, is available online

at http://www.euroquest.com/PressReleases/Museum Pass/MuseumPass%200n%20MSNBC.pdf.

Since 1986, *The Economist* has been making the study of real exchange rates a bit more spicy by tracing the dollar price of Big Macs around the world, as discussed in the body of the chapter. See the full text of the 2007 Big Mac Index article, "Sizzling—Food for Thought About Exchange Rate Controversies," *The Economist* (July 5, 2007).

An interesting variation of the Big Mac Index is the Starbucks Index: "Burgers or Beans—A New Theory Is Percolating Through the Foreign-Exchange Markets" can be found in the July 15, 2004 edition of *The Economist*. The article examines real exchange rates by considering the dollar price of a Starbucks tall latte in some of the 32 countries in which it is now sold. Information about *The Economist* can be found online by accessing http://www.economist.com.

We suggest the following free publications from the New York Fed: *Basics of Foreign Trade and Exchange and Balance of Payments* (Fedpoints 40), and *All About the Foreign Exchange Market in the United States*. For those of you who prefer comic books, request *The Story of Foreign Trade and Exchange*. All three are available by writing to the Federal Reserve Bank of New York, Public Information Department, 33 Liberty Street, New York, NY 10045. You can view the Fedpoints and other New York Fed publications online at http://www.newyorkfed.org.

Another Fed publication available online is *Strong Dollar Weak Dollar, Foreign Exchange Rates and the U.S. Economy*, Federal Reserve Bank of Chicago. It is available at http://www.chicagofed.org/publications/strongdollar/strongdollar.pdf.

For a look at the implications of the euro, see Robert A. Mundell, *The Euro as a Stabilizer in the International Economic System* (Norwell, MA: Kluwer Academic Press, 2000).

Endnotes

1. Remember our earlier warnings about market jargon? Well, the problem is acute in the international sphere. For example, note that the definition of foreign currency includes foreign coin, paper currency, and checkable deposits; in contrast, our definition of currency in the United States includes paper currency and coin only (Chapter 2).

2. Exchange rates can also be expressed from the other direction. For example, if $1 will buy 100 yen, then 100 yen will buy $1 and 1 yen will buy $.01 [1/(100 yen)=$.01].

3. In Chapter 2, we defined the dollar as a unit of account by which exchange values of goods and services could be measured. In this chapter, we are talking about the flow of funds—that is, the supply and demand of dollar-denominated funds—not dollars. So, when we use the term *dollars*, we really mean *dollar-denominated funds*.

4. In Chapters 2 and 5, we saw that the interest rate can be determined by either a stock model (the supply of and demand for money) or a flow model (the supply of and demand for loanable funds/month). Exchange rate determination is an analogous situation in that the exchange rate can be explained using a stock model (dealing with the supply of and demand for foreign exchange at a particular moment), or a flow model (dealing with flows of foreign exchange over a particular time period). In this chapter, we have opted for the flow model, noting that just as with all stock and flow models, each can generally be converted into the other without loss of substance. We hope you recall that over time, flows generate changes in stocks and that by measuring stocks at two points in time, a flow over time can be determined. For simplicity, we arbitrarily picked one month as our time period. The quantity demanded of dollars/month is the amount of dollars that will be demanded at a specific exchange rate.

5. Actually, we are also assuming that the demand for wheat, and U.S. products in general, is relatively elastic with regard to the exchange rate—that is, as the exchange rate changes, ceteris paribus, quantity demanded/month changes by a larger percentage than the exchange rate, causing total dollar expenditures to fall when the exchange rate increases and to rise when the exchange rate decreases. This is a reasonable assumption in the long run, although demand for U.S. products may be relatively inelastic in the short run.

6. We are also making the reasonable assumption that, ceteris paribus, the quantity demanded of foreign goods/month by U.S. residents changes by a larger percentage than the percentage change in the exchange rate. Thus, as the exchange rate appreciates, the quantity supplied of dollars/month also increases. And as the exchange rate depreciates, the quantity supplied of dollars/month also decreases. This assumption, which is reasonable in the long run, may not hold in the short run.

7. These examples of supply and demand shifters generally assume constant future expected exchange rates and future expected inflation. Without this simplification, results become more complicated. For example, an increase in the nominal U.S. interest rate could correspond with a decreased demand for U.S. dollars by foreigners if they expect higher U.S. inflation in the future and a depreciating U.S. dollar. This would be the opposite of what we would expect with future expected inflation and exchange rate constant.

8. To be more precise, the U.S. relative prices would increase by 1.05/1.03−1=.01942, or 1.942 percent over European prices. We follow standard convention in rounding this to 2 percent.

9. Don't let the terminology confuse you: *Less negative* refers to a smaller trade deficit of goods and services, meaning either more exports or fewer imports and, hence, ceteris paribus, more U.S. jobs and production in either the domestic exporting industries or those industries competing with imports. If the United States were running a trade surplus of goods and services, the greater the surplus, the greater would be the stimulus to U.S. GDP.

10. We are ignoring any official government transactions in foreign exchange markets until Chapter 18.

17

Never let the future disturb you. You will meet it, if you have to, with the same weapons of reason which today arm you against the present.

—Marcus Aurelius

Forward, Futures, and Options Agreements

Learning Objectives

After reading this chapter, you should know:

The difference between a forward contract and a futures contract

The scope and nature of organized financial futures and options markets

The relationship between spot and futures prices

The difference between put and call options

The reasons for the astounding growth of financial forward, futures, and options agreements in recent years

A SINGLE SOLUTION

It is 5:10 P.M. on Friday, the last day of a month in late 2009. The CEO's meeting with his staff has run later than usual, and a sense of uneasiness pervades the room. Doz-All, a newly emerging conglomerate, is involved in diversified financial and manufacturing areas. The mortgage banking division has committed to make $10 million in loans at 7 percent to be funded in 60 days; $25 million in bonds issued 10 years ago for start-up money is maturing in three months, and the company plans to pay off the existing bondholders by issuing new bonds. The newly formed international division is converting $20 million to Japanese yen to invest in Japanese securities over the next few months. The stock adviser points out that although the corporation has a diversified stock portfolio, there is a general fear that the market may be heading down.

All of these situations expose the corporation to risks—the risks that interest rates (and hence bond prices), stock prices, or foreign exchange rates will move in an unexpected direction, causing the corporation to experience a loss. The senior vice president appears tired. She cannot help but perceive that the risks associated with everyday business seem to have escalated in recent years.

In the past two decades, financial prices such as interest rates, stock prices, and exchange rates have become more volatile. This increased volatility has created greater risks.[1] The chief financial officer (CFO) is a young business school graduate whom senior management has come to rely on. He assures them that there are ways to deal with the increased risk, although doing so will cost money. In this case, however, his recommendations are the source of the tension felt in the room. To reduce Doz-All's risk exposure, the CFO is recommending that the corporation use the financial forward, futures, or options markets. In days long past, futures and options on agricultural products and commodities were considered to be highly risky, and forward agreements, which could be costly, had other drawbacks. Could the new financial forward, futures, and options markets that have emerged in the past 30 years actually be used to reduce or manage the risks inherent in everyday business?

In this chapter, we explore financial forward, futures, and options contracts. We shall see that risk-averse financial intermediaries and corporations increasingly use these markets in their everyday business for just this purpose—to reduce the risks associated with price fluctuations. The adage "necessity is the mother of invention" aptly applies, because financial forward, futures, and options markets have experienced incredible growth in the past three decades in response to increased price volatility.

FORWARD TRANSACTIONS

Financial Forward Contract
An agreement in which the terms, including price, are completed today for a transaction that will occur in the future.

A financial forward contract is an agreement between two parties to buy or sell an agreed-upon amount of a financial asset on a date in the future at a price determined today. Financial forward transactions can be used to hedge the risks associated with price changes of any financial instrument. Although virtually all financial prices have become more volatile in recent decades, forward agreements are primarily and most widely used to deal with the risks created by price fluctuations in foreign exchange markets. Thus, foreign exchange forward markets are the focus of this section.

The exchange rate is the price of one currency in terms of another. As you have seen in earlier chapters, *exchange rate risk* is the risk that changes in the exchange rate will cause someone to experience unexpected losses. The more unpredictable and unstable that exchange rates are, the greater the exchange rate risk is. Exchange rates have become much more volatile since the major industrialized countries adopted the flexible exchange rate system in 1973.[2] Also, as international trade has increased and as financial markets have become more globalized, the demand for foreign financial instruments has soared. This has led to the increased trading of foreign currencies with more volatile prices and a dramatic increase in exchange rate risk for market participants. These participants have found ways to hedge this greater exchange rate risk through the development of forward markets.

Hedge
An investment made to reduce risk.

In Chapter 16, we discussed how exchange rates are determined by supply and demand in the foreign exchange market. In that chapter, we were referring to *spot rates*—that is, the exchange rates of foreign currency for immediate delivery. In financial forward agreements, the terms (including prices and amounts) are completed today for a transaction that will occur on a specified date in the future. Financial intermediaries, acting as brokers or agents, can link up two parties in a forward transaction. As noted earlier, the most common type of financial forward agreement is the forward agreement in foreign currencies (foreign exchange). These agreements have been highly developed by large commercial banks to provide services to their customers who will need or receive foreign currencies on a future date. In this case, the bank is one of the two parties in the forward transaction. Commercial banks also sometimes hold large amounts of foreign currencies and hence can use forward markets to hedge their own exchange rate risk.

Large banks have many customers that operate on a global basis. These customers may know that they will receive and/or need foreign currencies on a future date. The foreign currencies are used by the bank's customers to purchase or to pay for goods, services, and financial instruments. For example, perhaps one U.S. company will be liquidating its holding of French stocks in six months to pay off a maturing domestic bond issue, while another U.S. company plans to increase its investment in Europe. The first company will be receiving euros; the latter company will need euros. Another customer may be an importer, an exporter, or a securities firm that sells domestic and foreign financial instruments globally. Large banks buy and sell not only foreign exchange at spot rates for present delivery but also foreign exchange for future delivery at a forward rate. The forward rate for a foreign currency will gravitate toward the *expected* future spot exchange rate for that currency. The forward rate is affected by the same factors that affect spot rates as discussed in Chapter 16. These factors, which affect the supply and demand for foreign exchange, include expected inflation and interest rate differentials between the two countries, the economic outlook in both countries, and domestic and foreign monetary and fiscal policies. The forward rate can be used as a market-based forecast of the future spot rate.

Forward Rate
The price today for a delivery on a future date.

A bank buys foreign exchange forward agreements from some customers and sells foreign exchange forward agreements to others. The bank engages in these forward agreements to earn profits and to provide a service to its customers who wish to hedge the exchange rate risk. The profit comes from buying the currency at one price, the bid price, and selling the currency at a slightly higher price, the asked price. Large banks have a long history of providing exchange facilities for foreign currencies as a service to their customers. These currency exchange facilities predate flexible exchange rates. Forward agreements arranged by large banks were a natural outgrowth of this trade-facilitation service under the post-1973 flexible exchange rate system.

A typical foreign exchange forward agreement works as follows: The forward agreement is a contract with a bank to purchase or sell on a future date a specific amount of foreign exchange at a forward rate (exchange rate) determined today. For example, assume that a customer of Citibank is to receive 1 million euros in six months and another customer will need 1 million euros in six months. Both customers know the present spot rate but are worried that unknown future changes in the exchange rate could reduce their profits. Citibank can enter into a forward agreement with each that will hedge this risk. The agreements will also earn a small profit for Citibank. Just as in spot markets, Citibank buys forward contracts at one rate and sells forward contracts at a slightly higher rate. The difference between the bid and asked prices represents the profit margin on the transaction. If the forward rate for Citibank to buy euros from a customer with a delivery date in six months is 1 euro = $1.559, then 1 million euros can be sold to the bank by a customer for $1,559,000 (1,000,000 × 1 euro = 1,000,000 × $1.559). Thus, 1 euro=$1.559, which is the bid price.[3] A customer that will be receiving 1 million euros in six months may enter into this transaction to reduce the risk that the euro will depreciate and that she will receiver fewer than $1,559,000 in exchange for the 1 million euro. For example, if the euro depreciated to 1 euro=$1.558, then, without the forward agreement, the customer would be able to sell the euro for only $1,558,000 instead of $1,559,000.

Assume that the forward rate (exchange rate) for Citibank to sell euros with a delivery date in six months is 1 euro = $1.560. This is the forward asked price. A customer who will need 1 million euros in six months may enter into a forward agreement in order to reduce exchange rate risk. The 1 million euros will cost the customer $1,560,000 (1,000,000 × 1 euro = 1,000,000 × $1.56) in six months. A customer needing 1 million euros in six months may enter into this transaction to reduce the risk that the euro will appreciate and that he will have to pay more than $1,560,000 for 1 million euros. For example, without the forward agreement, if the euro appreciated to 1 euro = $1.565, then 1 million euros would cost the customer $1,565,000 instead of $1,560,000.

The profit to Citibank in the forward markets is, as noted previously, just as in spot markets: Citibank buys at one forward rate (the bid price) and sells at a slightly higher forward rate (the asked price). The bank makes a profit on the difference between the bid and asked prices multiplied by the number of euros bought and sold. In this case, the profit on the forward transactions in 1 million euros is $1,000 ($1,560,000 − $1,559,000). Exhibit 17-1 highlights these relationships.

The one-, three-, and six-month forward rates for major foreign currencies such as the euro, the British pound, the Canadian dollar, the Japanese yen, and the Swiss franc are reported daily in *The Wall Street Journal*, along with the spot exchange rates. The accompanying "Cracking the Code" feature on p. 407 discusses how to read the spot and forward exchange rates reported by the *Journal*. Note that for both spot and forward rates, only one exchange rate is reported. This is the midrange rate between the bid and the asked prices.

If the bid and asked spot exchange rates six months from now are equal to the current forward rates, the customers both buying and selling forward agreements would be no better or no worse off financially. In addition, they may have slept more soundly at night because of the reduced exchange rate risk. In six months, the actual bid and asked spot exchange rates may be more or less than the forward rates today. In this case, one of the customers will be worse off and one will be better off than without the forward agreement, depending on how rates diverged from what was expected. However, both customers are willing to give up the opportunity to gain in exchange for reducing the risk of being worse off.

17-1

Citibank Engages in Forward Agreements

6-Month Forward Rates Today	
Bid (buy) Price	Asked (sell) Price
1 euro=$1.559	1 euro=$1.560
1,000,000 euros=$1,559,000	1,000,000 euros=$1,560,000

Profit to Citibank from buying and selling 1,000,000 euros at today's forward rates = $1,000 = ($1,560,000 − $1,559,000).

Cracking the Code

Foreign Exchange Spot and Forward Rate Quotations

The following foreign exchange quotations for Friday, March 8, 2008, were reported in *The Wall Street Journal* on Monday, March 10, 2008. Spot rates are reported for about 180 countries, but forward rates are reported for only the major foreign currencies including the British pound, the Canadian dollar, the Japanese yen, and the Swiss franc. For both spot and forward exchange rates, the rate that is reported is the midrange rate between the bid and the asked prices. The name of the country and its currency appear in column 1. Column 2 gives the midrange rates for the current day in terms of U.S. dollars per unit of foreign currency. Column 3 gives the midrange rates in terms of foreign currency per U.S. dollar.

For example, the Column for six-month forward rate for the British pound is highlighted. On Friday, March 8, 2008, the midrange of the six-month forward bid and asked rates was 1 British pound=$1.9857. Column 3 is merely the reciprocal of column 2. Thus, on March 8, 2008, the six-month forward rate was $1=.5036 British

pounds (1 British pound/$1.9587=$1.9587/$1.9587=$1). The final column gives the year-to-date percent change in the U.S. dollar. In this case, since the beginning of 2008, the change in the six-month forward dollar rate was negative. Thus, the six-month forward rate has depreciated 0.5 percent against the British pound. Note that the spot rate of the British pound (top row) depreciated 1.4 percent over the same period.

Country/ currency	Fri, March 8, 2008		US$ vs. YTD chg (%)
	in US$	per US$	
UK (Pound)	2.0146	.4965	−1.4
1-mo forward	2.0100	.4975	−1.2
3-mos forward	2.0005	.4999	−0.9
6-mos forward	*1.9587*	*.5036*	*−0.5*

Source: The Wall Street Journal (March 10, 2008): C11.

The problem is that today it is not known which one will lose and which one will gain without the forward agreement. Both customers can reduce the uncertainty of the future exchange rate by engaging in a forward agreement with Citibank today. Thus, for reducing the possibility of a loss, they are both giving up the opportunity to gain. However, as noted earlier, the forward rate will converge to the market's general expectation of the future spot rate. Thus, market participants will give up the opportunity to gain only if there were unexpected changes in the future spot rate.

An example may help to clarify. As depicted in Exhibit 17-2, assume the current bid and asked spot rates in six months are 1 euro=$1.549 and 1 euro=$1.550. This is different from the respective forward rates of 1 euro=$1.559 and 1 euro=$1.560 of six months previous. Without the forward agreement, Customer A, receiving the 1 million euros, would be able to exchange them for only $1,549,000, or $10,000 less than the $1,559,000 the euros could be exchanged for with the forward agreement. This customer would be better off with the forward agreement and worse off without it. Without the forward agreement, Customer B, needing or buying the 1 million euros, would pay only $1,550,000, or $10,000 less than the $1,560,000 the euro would cost if she entered into the forward agreement. This customer would be worse off with the forward agreement and better off without it. However, because the future rate is uncertain, with the forward agreement both have hedged the risk of being worse off.

Any market participant who holds supplies of foreign currencies is exposed to exchange rate risk. This includes financial and nonfinancial firms that operate in many countries with many different currencies. Because the forward agreements arranged between banks and their customers are often not perfectly offsetting matches, the bank can be exposed to an exchange rate risk. For example, if one customer is to receive

	Current Spot Rates	Forward Rates Six Months Previous
Bid	1 euro = $1.549	1 euro = $1.559
Asked	1 euro = $1.550	1 euro = $1.560

No forward agreement (exchanges at current spot rates):
Customer A receives 1,000,000 euros and exchanges them for $1,549,000.
Customer B needs 1,000,000 euros and pays $1,550,000 for them.

With forward agreement entered into six months earlier:
Customer A receives 1,000,000 euros and exchanges them for $1,559,000.
Customer B needs 1,000,000 euros and exchanges $1,560,000 for them.

Reconciling:
With no forward agreement, Customer A receives $10,000 less ($1,549,000 versus $1,559,000), and Customer B pays $10,000 less ($1,550,000 versus $1,560,000). Customer A is worse off and Customer B is better off.

With the forward agreement, Customer A receives $10,000 more ($1,559,000 versus $1,549,000), and Customer B pays $10,000 more ($1,560,000 versus $1,550,000). Customer A is better off and Customer B is worse off.

1 million euros in six months and another needs 900,000 euros in six months, the bank can still arrange the forward agreements with both, but it is then subject to an exchange rate risk on the difference between what the receiving customer will receive and what the customer who needs euros will need. In this case, the amount of exposure to the bank is for 100,000 euros (1 million euros received less 900,000 euros needed). If the euro depreciates from 1 euro=$1.55 to 1 euro=$1.54, then 100,000 euros would fall in value $1,000 from $155,000 to $154,000. Likewise, if the euro had appreciated from 1 euro=$1.55 to 1 euro=$1.56, then 100,000 euros would increase in value $1,000 from $155,000 to $156,000.

Forward agreements can also be used to speculate about future exchange rates. The speculator may be a customer of the bank or the bank itself. If the speculator thought that the future spot price in six months would be lower than the current six-month forward rate, he would enter into a forward agreement to sell foreign exchange at the higher forward rate. If the speculator was correct, he could enter the spot market in six months and purchase the foreign exchange at a lower price than he sold it for in the forward market. Likewise, if the speculator thought that the future spot price of the currency would be higher than the current forward rate, he would enter into a forward agreement to buy the currency in six months. If correct, the speculator buys the currency in the forward market at a lower price than what it can be resold for in the spot market. Indeed, it is the buying and selling by speculators that causes the forward rate to converge to the market's expectation of future spot prices.

Limitations of Forward Agreements

As you have seen, forward transactions can reduce the risks of future price changes, which reduce profit. But, as with most things in life, appearances may not reveal the whole picture. The forward market in foreign currencies works well because large banks have developed the market. For other financial instruments such as stocks and bonds, forward markets are not so highly developed. In this case, there are two general problems with arranging forward agreements:

1. Finding partners may be difficult; the transactions costs may be high and outweigh the possible gain. Finding partners who want the exact amount of the financial instrument on the exact date can be difficult at best.[4]

2. One party to the agreement may default, that is, not keep his or her part of the agreement. The party who is likely to default is the one that is worse off down the road by entering into the forward agreement earlier. Getting compliance may require legal action and may be costly if not impossible.[5]

Futures Contracts
Standardized agreements in agricultural and commodity markets to trade a fixed amount of the product or commodity on specific dates in the future at a price determined today.

Although volatile prices of financial instruments other than foreign exchange may lead to large losses that could be reduced with forward agreements, the forward markets are not highly developed. Consequently, the costs of finding a partner and then enforcing the forward contract may be prohibitively high. But all hope is not lost! To minimize the costs and risks involved with arranging forward transactions, standardized agreements called **futures contracts** have been developed for many types of financial instruments, including stocks, government securities, and foreign currencies.

Recap

Forward contracts are agreements to buy or sell something at a price determined today for delivery on a later date. Forward agreements between individual market participants are arranged by intermediaries. Forward markets are not highly developed for financial instruments other than foreign currencies.

FINANCIAL FUTURES

Because agricultural and commodity markets historically have experienced large price fluctuations, futures markets in these products evolved more than a century ago. In the case of agricultural products, demand is relatively stable, and price fluctuations are related to weather: bad weather greatly reduces supply and leads to higher prices, and vice versa. Prices of commodities such as oil, copper, and gold fluctuate because of large changes in supply or demand.

Financial Futures Markets
Organized markets that trade financial futures including the Chicago Board of Trade, the Chicago Mercantile Exchange, and the London International Financial Futures Exchange.

As noted earlier, prices of financial securities, stocks, and foreign currencies have become unstable during the past 30 years. Consequently, **financial futures markets**, which trade futures in financial instruments, appeared and are now used by most major financial institutions and other large corporations to manage the risk of losses because of price fluctuations of financial instruments.

Financial futures are contracts in which two parties agree to trade standardized quantities of financial instruments on standardized future dates, according to the terms (including the price) that are determined today. Financial futures can be used to reduce the risk associated with future price changes of financial instruments.

Financial Futures
Standardized futures contracts that trade financial instruments on a future date according to terms (including the price) determined today.

Futures contracts differ from forward agreements in that the amounts and delivery dates are standardized, whereas for forward agreements they are not. Forward agreements for specific amounts and dates are negotiated with commercial banks and other financial intermediaries. Futures contracts with standardized amounts and dates are traded on the floors of organized exchanges for a small fee.

Financial futures markets trade a wide variety of contracts in underlying financial instruments such as government securities (Treasury bills, notes, and bonds), stock market indexes, Eurodollars, and numerous foreign currencies.[6] The contracts are traded on major exchanges around the world. For example, financial futures are traded on the Chicago Board of Trade, the New York Board of Trade (formerly the New York Cotton Exchange and now part of the Intercontinental Exchange), the Chicago Mercantile Exchange, the Australian Securities Exchange, and the Singapore Exchange. In early 2004, EUREX US became the first foreign-owned futures and options market to begin trading on U.S. soil. The purpose of EUREX is to provide more direct access to investment opportunities in U.S. Treasury futures for European customers. In April 2007, EUREX merged with the New York Stock Exchange. Futures markets for various currencies and U.S. government securities are available virtually 24 hours a day, somewhere in the world. Often these markets use electronic communication networks to provide information and execute trades. Thus, as you saw in Chapter 14, the floor of the exchange may soon be replaced by a system of electronic trading where futures trading can be executed 24 hours a day in "cyberspace" from a personal computer. "A Closer Look" lists information about the most actively traded financial futures.

A futures contract trades a fixed amount of the instrument for delivery on specific dates in the future. For example, Treasury bond futures trade in contracts of $100,000 face value for delivery in March, June, September, and December over the course of the following year. There are four prices today for delivery of $100,000 of Treasury bonds on the four future dates. Likewise, Treasury bill futures, which trade in contract amounts of $1 million, are also available for delivery on the same dates at prices set today. Note that the futures contract can be bought or sold on any given day between now and the future delivery date. The predicament for the buyers and sellers is that the spot price on the delivery date may be different from the futures price agreed on today.

The seller of a September $1 million T-bill future has the right and obligation to deliver $1 million in T-bills in September for a price set today. The purchaser of the $1 million September T-bill future has the right and obligation to buy $1 million in T-bills in September at a price set today. Hence, both parties know the terms of a transaction that will occur in September, a point in time in the future, and the risk to either party of a price change between now and then is eliminated. The buyer rarely takes physical possession of the securities on the delivery date. Likewise, the seller rarely delivers. If the price changes, the buyer or the seller merely settles up financially for any changes in value.[7]

If the price of T-bills rises between now and September, the seller has given up an opportunity to make a profit because she agreed to sell at the lower futures price established today. If the spot price falls in September, the buyer has given up the right to purchase the securities at the lower price in the spot market because he agreed to the higher futures price today. Without the futures contract, however, either party could lose if the price changes in an adverse direction.

Let's consider a simple numerical example. Assume that the futures price is $96,000 for the delivery of $100,000 of Treasury bonds next December. The seller agrees to deliver, and the buyer agrees to pay this much. (Make sure you are clear that December is the *delivery date* of the securities, not their *maturity date*, which may be several years hence.) When December actually arrives, if the spot price is $97,000, the seller still must make good on the contract for $96,000, even though he could sell them for $97,000 in the spot market. The buyer still pays $96,000 for the Treasury bond contract, even though she would have had to pay $97,000 for the same contract in the spot market. In this example, the seller is worse off by $1,000, and the buyer is better off by $1,000. (Remember that the securities are not usually physically delivered, but a financial settlement is made between the buyer and the seller.)

However, if the spot price is $95,000 when December arrives, the seller gets to sell at $96,000 even though he would get only $95,000 in the spot market. The buyer has to pay $96,000 even though she could have paid $95,000 to buy in the spot market. The seller is better off by $1,000, and the buyer is worse off by $1,000. Again, a financial settlement is usually made between the buyer and the seller.

The point is that at the time of the agreement, neither party knows what the spot price will be on the future date. Both were willing to accept the known outcome as opposed to an uncertain future spot price even though after the fact one could have been

A Closer Look

Futures, Exchanges That Trade Financial Futures, and Minimum Amounts

Consider for a moment the many types of futures markets that exist: grains and oil seeds (including corn, oats, soybeans, wheat, barley, flaxseed, and canola); livestock and meat (including cattle, hogs, and pork bellies); food and fibers (including cocoa, coffee, sugar, cotton, and orange juice); metals and petroleum (including copper, gold, platinum, palladium, silver, crude oil, heating oil, gasoline, natural gas, brent crude, and gas oil); interest rates (including 10-year agency and 10-year, five-year, and two-year U.S. Treasury notes, 30-day federal funds, Eurodollars, one-month LIBOR, Euroyen, and Treasury bonds); currencies (including Australian dollars, British pounds, Canadian dollars, euros, Japanese yen, Mexican pesos, and Swiss francs); and indexes (including Dow Jones Industrial and mini Dow Jones, NASDAQ 100, S&P Composite, and S&P Mini).[a]

Grain and commodities futures have been around for some 100 years. Financial futures including interest rate, currencies, and stock index futures are a relatively recent innovation (during the last 30 years) that has experienced tremendous growth.

The accompanying table shows some of the major financial futures and the contract size, along with the futures exchange.

Endnotes

a. Our list includes both financial and other futures because we believe you may find them interesting. Because these are information items only, we are not defining all of the terms.

Type of Future	Contract Size	Exchange* at Which Trading Occurs
Interest Rate		
10-year Interest Rate Swaps	$100,000	CBOT
10-year U.S. Treasury notes	$100,000	CBOT
2-year U.S. Treasury notes	$200,000	CBOT
30-day federal funds	$5 million	CBOT
5-year Treasury	$100,000	CBOT
Eurodollar	$1 million	CME
LIBOR—one month	$3 million	CME
Euroyen	100 million yen	CME
U.S. Treasury bonds	$100,000	CBOT
Currencies		
Australian dollar	$100,000 Australian	CME
British pound	£62,500 British	CME
Canadian dollar	$100,000 Canadian	CME
Euro	125,000 euro	CME
Japanese yen	12.5 million yen	CME
Mexican peso	500,000 pesos	CME
Swiss franc	125,000 S. francs	CME
Index Futures		
Dow Jones Industrial	$10 x DJIA	CBOT
NASDAQ 100	$100 x Index	CME
Goldman S. Index	$250 x Nearby Index	CME
U.S. Dollar Index	1,000 x Index	NYBOT
Russell 2000 Index	500 x Index	CME

*Exchanges: CBOT (Chicago Board of Trade); CME (Chicago Mercantile Exchange); NYBOT (New York Board of Trade)
Source: http://www.barrons.com.

Cracking the Code

Futures Prices

Toward the back of the Money and Investing section of *The Wall Street Journal*, you will find a table entitled "Futures Prices." Part of the Interest Rate Futures section of this table for Wednesday, March 12, 2008, is reproduced here. We can crack the code to futures prices by looking at the highlighted row starting on the left with April under "30 Day Federal Funds (CBT)."

The 97.665 in column 2 means that on March 12, the agreed-upon opening price for April delivery of Treasury bills was 97.665 percent of the face value of the contract. The low price for that day (column 4) was 97.650.

The high for the day (column 3) was 97.695 percent, and the settle for the day (column 5) was 97.680. The .025 in column 6 indicates that there was a .025 change from the previous day. To verify this, we would have to check the preceding day's newspaper to see whether the settle price was 97.655 (97.680–.025=97.655). Note that 30-day federal funds sell at a discount, which is reflected in the price being less than 100 percent of the contract amount. For the fed funds contract, the contract amount (face value) is $5 million. The open interest is the number of contracts outstanding for the month of July—in this case, 84,280.

30 Day Federal Funds (CBT)—$5,000,000; 100 daily average

	High	Low	Settle	Chg	Open Int
March	97.280	97.310	97.275	97.290	.015	65,263
April	**97.665**	**97.695**	**97.650**	**97.680**	**.025**	**84,280**

Source: The Wall Street Journal (March 13, 2008): C10.

better off without the agreement. Because the contracts are standardized with respect to type (90-day T-bills, 10-year Treasury notes, and the like) and quantity ($1 million and $100,000 contract sizes), and because volume is large, brokerage fees for buying and selling futures are relatively small.

So far, we have been discussing futures in which the parties are hedging, or reducing, the risk of a price change in the future. Futures markets can also be used for speculation. Consider the case in which ABC Government Securities (a firm that specializes in trading government securities) believes that the spot price of T-bills is going to be much higher in September than today's futures price. If ABC holds this belief firmly, it can put its money behind the belief and buy a futures contract. If ABC is correct, it can resell the futures contract at the higher spot price on the delivery date.

Contrarily, if the firm believes the price will be lower, it can sell a futures contract to make its profit. If ABC's guess is right, it can go into the spot market in September and purchase the T-bills at the lower price for immediate delivery to the buyer of the future. The difference between the futures price and what ABC pays in the spot market is its profit—ABC is good at counting this.

Futures prices are reported daily in most major newspapers. Now would be a good time to read the "Cracking the Code" feature on futures prices.

Because financial futures are written only in standardized contract amounts for delivery on a few specific dates, a perfect offsetting transaction between the buyer and seller, as in forward markets, is rarely made. For example, suppose a bank has loans that will be repaid next August and suspects that interest rates are heading down. The bank may have to reinvest the funds at a lower rate. The bank can buy a September T-bill futures contract today to hedge this risk. If interest rates do move down, the funds will be reinvested in August at a lower rate, but the reduction in earnings from the level the bank is currently receiving will be at least (partially) offset by the profit made on the September futures contract. (Recall that T-bills are sold at a discount, and, as with other securities, if interest rates go down, the price of the newly issued T-bills goes up.) Even though the standardized contracts do not provide an exact match (either by amount or by date), they do provide an offsetting transaction that reduces risk. Because a perfect match need not be found, the high transactions costs of finding a unique trading partner, as in forward agreements, are greatly reduced.

The futures price is set by bidding and offering in an auction-like setting on the floor of the exchange. Each financial instrument that is traded usually has its own **pit** (trading area on the floor) where authorized brokers gather to buy and sell for their customers. Bid and asked prices (to buy or sell) are called out until the brokers become aware of the prices in the market. The most favorable transactions (from the point of view of both the buyers and sellers) are consummated. Once an agreement is struck in the pit, the transaction becomes depersonalized, and the agents of the buyer and seller never meet again for that transaction. Instead, a **clearinghouse**, operated by the exchange, takes on the responsibility of enforcing the contract. Both the buyer and the seller rely on the clearinghouse to execute the transaction. Specifically, the seller looks to the clearinghouse to deliver, and the buyer looks to the clearinghouse to pay the amount due on the delivery date. In this way, the default risk associated with a forward transaction is greatly reduced because the clearinghouse of the exchange assumes the obligation.

The futures contract is a standardized agreement to make a trade at a later date. In exchange for the small brokerage fee, the clearinghouse of the organized exchange guarantees that the terms will be met. To facilitate this guarantee, the exchange requires buyers and sellers of futures to put up a **performance bond**, called a **margin requirement,** set by the exchange. Brokers are required to collect margin requirements from their customers before they make any futures purchases or sales. Note that the performance bond or margin is required of both the seller and the buyer and that the brokerage fee plus the margin requirements are relatively small compared to the dollar value of the futures agreement. An example of how financial futures can be used by a firm, LHT, Inc., to hedge interest rate risk is given in the accompanying "A Closer Look" feature on p. 414.

In summary, financial futures markets have experienced spectacular growth in the past 30 years, because the financial world has become a much more volatile place and financial futures can be used to reduce risks associated with this volatility. Because interest rate swings are larger, the prices of government securities (or the value of any fixed-rate instrument) oscillate more rapidly and over a broader range. Stock prices now fluctuate over a wider range, and flexible exchange rates have increased the movement of currency prices, while foreign trade in goods, services, and securities has escalated sharply. Futures markets may be used to hedge all of these risks. We now turn to how the futures price is determined.

Pit
The trading area on the floor of an organized exchange (such as the Chicago Board of Trade) where authorized brokers gather to buy and sell for their customers.

Clearinghouse
The part of an organized exchange that takes on the responsibility of enforcing a contract after the agreement is struck.

Performance Bond
A bond required by an organized exchange from both the buyer and the seller of a futures agreement to ensure that both parties abide by the agreement.

Margin Requirement
The amount that brokers must collect from their customers before they make any futures purchases or sales.

Recap   Financial futures are standardized contracts in which two parties agree to trade financial instruments at a future date according to terms, including the price, that are determined today. Financial futures are different from forward agreements because the quantities and delivery dates are standardized and, thus, the brokerage fees are relatively small. Financial futures markets exist for government securities, stock market indexes, Eurodollars, and foreign currencies. Both the buyer and the seller have obligations and rights. Financial futures can be used to hedge the risk of future changes in prices or to speculate. Organized exchanges trade the standardized contracts.

LHT Inc. Enters the Futures Market

Let's consider an example in which financial futures are used to hedge. Assume that LHT Inc. issued bonds 10 years ago and that those bonds will mature in a year. When the bonds come due, LHT Inc. will not be in a position to pay off the debt. Instead, it will issue new bonds (borrow) to raise the funds to pay off the owners of the original bonds.[a] Let's further assume that LHT fears that interest rates could rise over the next year, causing the new bonds to be issued at a higher interest rate. If this scenario materializes, the firm will have to make higher interest payments on the new bonds, which will cut sharply into profits. But something as important as profits need not be left to the vicissitudes of unknown interest rates one year from now! LHT can protect itself against an undesirable increase in rates by selling a T-bill future today. The T-bill futures agreement will oblige LHT to deliver so many T-bills on a later date, say, in one year, at a price set today. If the interest rate does rise over the course of the year, as LHT expects, the spot price of the T-bills will fall. (Remember the inverse relationship between the price of securities and the interest rate that we discussed in Chapter 5.) LHT can buy the T-bills in the spot market at the lower price for delivery to the purchaser of the futures contract who pays the higher price agreed on earlier. If the interest rate does rise, the loss due to issuing new bonds at a higher interest rate is offset by the profit that LHT makes on the T-bill futures contract.

But what happens if LHT Inc. is wrong about the direction of the interest rate over the next year and the interest rate falls or, equivalently, the price of T-bills rises? LHT takes a loss on the T-bill future because it buys the T-bills in the spot market at the *higher* price to deliver to the buyer of the futures contract for the *lower* price previously agreed on. However, LHT is not really worse off. The loss in the futures market is offset by the savings on the new bonds the corporation issues at a lower rate because interest rates have fallen.

As you have seen, the securities usually are not actually delivered physically. Instead, the buyer or seller of the futures agreement merely pays any price difference between the spot price and the futures price. In this case, if the interest rate does go up, LHT receives a payment from the seller of the T-bill futures agreement that offsets the loss incurred by having to issue bonds at the higher interest rate. If the interest rate goes down, LHT makes a payment to the seller of the T-bill futures agreement but issues the new bonds at the lower interest rate.

LHT Inc. has successfully used the futures market to reduce the risk of losses if interest rates go up while sacrificing the possibility of gains if interest rates go down—a trade that the firm may be happy to make. Can you explain what happens if interest rates stay the same over the course of the next year? Think about it before checking the answer in endnote b.[b]

Endnotes

a. Borrowing to repay maturing debt is called *rolling over* and is actually quite common.
b. LHT Inc. buys T-bills in the spot market to deliver to the purchaser of the futures contract at the same price for which it sold the contract. Aside from a small brokerage fee to purchase the futures contract (that can be thought of as an insurance premium), LHT Inc. is no worse off.

DETERMINING THE FUTURES PRICE

Financial futures are traded each day on exchanges around the world. The exchange delivers or accepts for delivery the futures contract at the specified future time and place at a price agreed on today. The buyer or seller merely accepts the risk of a price change of the contract and agrees to pay off any financial losses or to receive any financial gains. There are several different futures prices, depending on the expiration date of the futures contract. In this section, we pose the question, How are those prices determined? We hope that buzzers and alarms are going off in your head and that your immediate response is "supply and demand." Of course, you are right! But, in this case, it may prove beneficial to look a little more closely at what determines the supply and demand for financial futures and, hence, their prices.

Perhaps the first and most important thing to point out is that the futures price and the spot price are highly correlated—that is, they move up and down together. This is not accidental but due to actions of individuals called **arbitrageurs** who seek a riskless profit.

Consider what happens if a futures contract for Treasury bonds to be delivered in three months is much higher than the present spot price. An arbitrageur could purchase the Treasury bonds in the spot market while selling a futures contract. She could hold the bonds purchased in the spot market for delivery at the later date to fulfill the futures contract. Granted, she would incur some **carrying costs** in holding the Treasury bonds (or the gold or whatever), but as long as the futures price is higher than the current spot price plus the carrying costs, she would make a riskless profit. (Carrying costs generally consist of the interest costs for the use of the funds to purchase the securities, less the interest earned on the securities while the arbitrageur is holding them, plus other transactions costs of the exchange.) On the other hand, if the futures price were below the spot price plus carrying costs, arbitrageurs (who owned some of the securities) would buy futures, driving the futures price up, and sell in the spot market, driving the spot price down. Can you explain how a riskless profit would be made?[8]

When and if such an opportunity for riskless profit opens up, arbitrageurs move in, purchase in the spot market (driving up the price), and sell in the futures market (driving down the price), and vice versa. As the delivery date of the futures contract comes closer, the length of time in which funds are borrowed to establish the position is reduced. Therefore, as the delivery date nears, the carrying costs are reduced, and the futures price approaches the spot price. Arbitrage continues until the futures price is bid up (down) to the spot price plus carrying costs—a phenomenon called **convergence.** Thus, on the last day before the expiration date, the futures price is practically equal to the spot price—the carrying costs are negligible since only one day is left. Hence, because futures prices are highly correlated with spot prices and because convergence occurs, futures prices are ultimately determined by the spot prices of the underlying contract instruments. Now would be a good time to read "A Closer Look," which discusses stock index futures and the October 1987 crash of the stock market.

Arbitrageurs
Traders who make riskless profits by buying in one market and reselling in another market.

Carrying Costs
Interest costs for funds used to purchase the security underlying a futures contract plus any transactions costs.

Convergence
The phenomenon in which the futures price is bid up or down to the spot price plus carrying costs; the futures price approaches the spot price as the expiration date draws nearer.

Recap   The futures price is determined by supply and demand. If the futures price is higher than the spot price plus the carrying costs, an arbitrageur will sell a futures agreement and, at the same time, purchase securities in the spot market. The increased supply of futures will push the price down until the difference between the spot price and the futures price is equal to the carrying costs. If the futures price is lower than the spot price plus carrying costs, arbitrageurs (who own some of the underlying instruments) will buy futures and

Stock Index Futures and the '87 Crash

A stock market index such as the Dow Jones Industrial Average is an index that measures price changes of a market basket of stocks included in the index. Stock index futures are contracts that give the purchaser (seller) the right and obligation to purchase (sell) a multiple of the value of the index on some specified date in the future at a price determined today. Stock index futures are available for several indexes of stock market activity, and the futures contract calls for the delivery of the cash value of a multiple of a particular stock index.

Perhaps the two most prominent stock index futures are the futures contracts for the S&P 500 and the NYSE Composite Indexes. In both cases, the contract size is $500 times the index on the delivery date. The financial futures contracts are available for the quarterly dates (during March, June, September, and December) over the next two years. For example, if Jamal purchases a December contract for the S&P 500, this gives him the right and obligation to receive on the delivery date $500 times the value of the S&P 500 stock index on that date. The price for the future delivery is negotiated today. Let's say Jamal negotiates a price today of $275,000, which he will pay on the delivery date. Consider the two cases for the delivery date on which the S&P Index is (1) 525 or (2) 575. If it is 525, the seller pays $262,500 (500×$525) but receives $275,000 from Jamal. If it is 575, Jamal pays $275,000 but receives $287,500 (500×$575). In the first case, the seller makes a profit. In the second case, Jamal makes a profit. If $500 times the value of the index is greater than the futures price, the buyer of the futures makes a profit. If it is less, the seller makes a profit.

As with all futures, the spot and futures prices move up and down together. In the case of stock index futures, arbitrage prevents the futures price from deviating a tremendous amount from the spot price. For instance, if the futures price is far higher than the spot price, an arbitrageur could make a riskless profit by buying a market basket of stocks that made up the index while selling a futures contract. As long as the futures price exceeds the spot price plus the cost of carrying the inventory of stocks, the arbitrageur could make a riskless profit. By doing so, however, she would be increasing the demand for stocks in the spot market (pushing up the index) and increasing the supply of futures contracts (pushing down their price). As in other futures markets, arbitrage would keep the spot and futures price in close alignment with one another.

But wouldn't it be difficult to recognize every opportunity for arbitrage and go into the spot market to purchase the market basket of stocks that make up the stock index? After all, in the case of the S&P 500, one would have to purchase (or sell) 500 different stocks. Not even the largest of most small investors can do this. As you saw in Chapter 14, however, the advent of sophisticated computer technology has allowed brokerage houses and institutional investors (such as mutual funds and pension plans) to program automatic purchases and sales of stock index market baskets into a computer. Sales or purchases can be triggered automatically when the stock index futures price gets out of alignment with the spot price. This *pro-*

gram trading allows every opportunity for arbitrage to be exploited immediately. As advantageous as this may seem to the brokerage house that uses it, program trading can be controversial.

During the week of October 12–16, 1987, the Dow Jones Industrial Average fell 250 points, and on Monday, October 19, 1987, it plummeted 508 points, or more than 20 percent—the largest percentage drop in history and the largest point drop to that time. Could program trading have been the culprit in this major downturn?

Consider what would happen if a stock index futures suddenly fell steeply. Program trading would trigger spot market sales of the stocks that made up the index, as well as purchases of index futures. A major fall in the futures price could bring about large sales (and plummeting prices) in the spot market for stock. *Stop orders* (or orders to automatically sell if the stock price falls to a certain level) would be triggered, which would cause further plummeting of spot prices and could reverse the trend of purchases in the futures market. Indeed, the October 1987 crash was triggered by program trading and stop orders.

To prevent a reoccurrence of the 1987 crash, many exchanges have put in circuit breaker restrictions that, among other things, limit computerized program trading if the index falls more than a certain amount on any day. They have been activated many times.

Other analysts are less concerned about program trading than about the cause of the fall in futures prices to begin with. If futures prices fall because of the expectation that spot prices will be falling, the arbitrage causing the present spot price to fall may simply be rational price adjustment in a declining market. By restricting computerized trading, we may be treating only the symptoms of a problem without treating the cause. Maybe the market, like a virus, should be allowed to run its course, or maybe a little preventive medication will stop a mild virus from turning into a severe infection. Opinions about the extent of intervention needed continue to differ.

---

sell in the spot market. The futures price will go up, and the spot price will come down until the difference equals the carrying costs. As the delivery date nears, the spot and the futures prices converge.

OPTIONS

In the previous sections, we pointed out that business firms (financial and nonfinancial) or individuals can use the futures market to reduce the risk of price changes inherent in everyday business. Thus, if they need to buy or sell a financial instrument in the future, they can use the futures market to offset any possible loss due to an unanticipated price change between now and the day when they will be making the purchase or sale. An unattractive feature of the futures market, however, is that it also eliminates a possible gain from a price change.

Disadvantage!

For example, consider the case in which Michael needs to borrow $1 million in a month. He knows what the interest rate is today, but is concerned that it will be higher in a month. He can sell a T-bill future for $1 million that gives him the right and obligation to sell the T-bills in 30 days at a price determined today. If the interest rate goes up, he borrows at a higher rate, but the price of the T-bill futures contract falls and he makes a profit. This profit offsets the higher borrowing costs (and accomplishes his goal of reducing the risk of losses if the interest rate goes up). If the interest rate goes down, Michael gains by borrowing at a lower rate. However, he loses money on the T-bill futures (because lower interest rates cause the T-bill futures price to rise and he is locked into selling at the lower price). Therefore, to reduce the risk of losses from the interest rate rising, he forgoes the chance of a gain if the interest rate falls.

Could there be another way to get risk protection from a loss without giving up the possibility of a gain? If you said, "Surely there must be because markets are so quick to respond to changing needs and conditions," you are correct (or, as we shall see, almost correct). We now turn our attention to options to demonstrate how our friend Michael can use them to reduce the risk of an interest rate increase over the next month without forgoing a gain if rates fall.

Options are similar to futures in that they are used to reduce the risk of future price changes or to speculate. Options give the buyer the right, but not the obligation, to buy or sell an instrument in the future for a price determined today. The agreed-upon price is called the **strike price**. This right continues until an expiration date specified in the contract. Options exist for many agricultural products, commodities, individual stocks (such as AT&T, IBM, and EDS), and many other financial instruments. Now would be a good time to read the accompanying "A Closer Look" on options.

In addition, options are available on the major types of futures contracts, including stock index futures, currency futures, and interest rate futures. These options, aptly called **options on futures,** give the buyer of the option the right, but not the obligation, to buy or sell a futures contract up to the expiration date of the option. As you have seen, at the delivery date of a futures contract, the futures price converges to the spot price of the underlying financial instrument. Hence, on the delivery date, the investor should be indifferent between hedging with a futures contract or hedging with the underlying debt instrument. Option contracts are often written on futures contracts rather than on the underlying debt instruments themselves because the futures contracts are often more liquid than the underlying financial instruments. This is because the secondary markets for most financial instruments are not as highly developed as the futures markets. Options are available for specific dates in the future, often for the two closest months and then for March, June, September, and December for the next nine months. As in the case of futures, the clearinghouse of the exchange enforces the contract and, for a fee, takes on the default risk.

Many of the similarities between futures and options stop here, however. There are two kinds of options, and we will briefly outline each of them, focusing mainly on financial options.

Put Options

Put options give the buyer of the option the right, but not the obligation, to sell a standardized contract of a financial instrument or a futures agreement at a strike price determined today. The seller has the obligation, but not the right, to buy the contract if the buyer exercises it before the expiration date.[10] Therefore, Michael, who has to borrow $1 million in the next month, can hedge the risk of a future interest rate increase by buying a put option on, say, a T-bill or Treasury bond contract. If the interest rate does go up, he exercises the option at a profit to offset the loss incurred by having to

---

Options
Standardized contracts that give the buyer the right, but not the obligation, to buy or sell an instrument in the future at a price determined today.

Strike Price
The agreed-upon price in an options contract.

Options on Futures
Options that give the buyer the right, but not the obligation, to buy or sell a futures contract up to the expiration date on the option.

Put Options
Options that give the buyer of the option the right, but not the obligation, to sell a standardized contract of a financial instrument at a strike price determined today.

More About Options

Options are available for hundreds of individual domestic and foreign stocks, for many stock indexes (both broad based and sector indexes), for exchange-traded funds (ETFs), and for foreign currencies. Most options must be exercised in less than one year. However, there are long-term options (both equity and index) whose specified time to exercise the option is more than one year. The New York Stock Exchange ARCA Options trading system, the Chicago Board Options Exchange, and the Philadelphia Stock Exchange are among the largest options exchanges in the United States. The International Securities Exchange, which was the first electronic options exchange, was launched in May 2000, and today it rivals the options trading and products of the other exchanges. The Chicago Board Options Exchange also makes an options market for Treasury securities that can be used to hedge interest rate risk.

Barron's has a wealth of information about options, prices, and the exchanges they trade on available for free online at **www.barrons.com**.

---

borrow at the higher rate. Like futures, financial options are written only in standardized contract amounts for delivery on a few specific dates, and a perfect offsetting transaction is rarely found. Nevertheless, risk is still reduced. Unlike futures, put options allow the risk of an interest rate increase to be hedged without losing the possibility of a gain if the interest rate goes down. If rates do fall, Michael simply does not exercise the option. He has used put options to reduce the risk of an interest rate increase when he has to borrow in the future. Put options could also be used to reduce the risk of a price decrease by anyone who has to sell a financial instrument in the future.

Call Options

Call Options
Options that give the buyer of the option the right, but not the obligation, to buy a standardized contract of a financial instrument at a strike price determined today.

Call options give the buyer the right, but not the obligation, to buy a financial instrument at a strike price determined today anytime before the expiration date. Note that the buyer has the right, but not the obligation, to buy. The buyer exercises the option (buys the instrument or futures contract at the strike price) only if it is in his or her interest to do so—that is, only if the price of the financial instrument is higher than the strike price. If the price of the financial instrument or futures contract falls, the buyer is not obliged to exercise the option and will let it expire. The option allows the buyer to limit the losses from a price increase without limiting his or her ability to take advantage of a price decrease.

Recap   Options give the buyer of the option the right, but not the obligation, to buy or sell an instrument in the future for a price determined today. Put options give the buyer the right, but not the obligation, to sell a standardized contract at a price determined today anytime before the expiration date on the option. A call option gives the buyer the right, but not the obligation, to buy a financial instrument at a price determined today anytime before the expiration date on the option.

The Option Premium

You might ask, however, why any individual or firm would hedge risk with futures that limit both losses and gains when they could use options that limit only losses. If you said, "Because futures must be cheaper," you may have a future as an economist! Futures cost very little—basically, only a small brokerage fee, which is low because the contracts are standardized and the volume in the market is very large. Both parties to the agreement have rights and obligations. With options, however, one party has rights with no obligations, and the other party has obligations with no rights. From the buyer's position, put or call options give the right but not the obligation to sell or buy the contract at the agreed-upon price if the buyer exercises the option. In addition to paying the exchange a brokerage fee, the party with the rights but no obligations (the buyer) pays an **option premium** to the party with the obligations but no rights (the seller). Make sure you are clear that the buyer of a put option has the *right*, but not the *obligation*, to sell, while the buyer of a call option has the *right*, but not the *obligation*, to buy.

The premium is the reward to the seller of either a put or a call option for accepting the risk of a loss with no possibility of a gain. In the case of interest rate options, for the hedger to be better off, the loss from the interest rate increase that the hedger avoids must be larger than the put option premium. In addition to the option premium, the option still entails a small brokerage fee for arranging the trade.

So far, we have been discussing situations in which options are used to hedge. As you might have guessed, put and call options can also be used to speculate. Needless to say, speculation in this manner can be extremely costly because option premiums are often quite substantial (costing several thousand dollars). If the option is not exercised, the buyer of the call or put option loses the option premium. Hedgers can think of the option premium as an insurance premium, limiting the amount of losses they will incur if a financial instrument must be purchased or sold at a later date. For speculators, the option premium is the amount that they are willing to bet when they believe that the price will change significantly from the strike price, thereby creating potential profit. As with hedgers, for the speculator to benefit from purchasing the option, the price must increase (in the case of call options) or decrease (in the case of put options) enough to more than cover the option premium. The downside to options, of course, is the option premium, which can be quite substantial, as compared to the usually small brokerage fee for buying or selling a futures contract. Economists are famous for saying: "There is no such thing as a free lunch!" If options are used to exploit gains while limiting losses, this is certainly true.

In summary, someone who needs to buy a financial security or instrument in the future can hedge the risk of an inopportune price increase by paying an option premium to purchase a call option, which gives the buyer the right to purchase the instrument at a price agreed on today up to the expiration date of the option. On the other hand, someone who needs to sell a financial security or instrument in the future can hedge the risk of a price decrease by paying a premium to purchase a put option, which gives the buyer the right to sell the contract at a price agreed on today up to the expiration date. The sellers of the call or put options are not hedging but merely accepting risk for a price—in this case, the option premium. The buyer of a call or put option is hedging

Option Premium
The premium paid by the buyer of an option to compensate the seller for accepting the risk of a loss with no possibility of a gain.

risk without giving up any potential for gains, as in the case of futures. Like futures, options can also be used to speculate about future price changes.

DETERMINING THE OPTION PREMIUM

As in all unregulated markets, the price to buy either a call or a put option (the option premium) is determined by the forces of supply and demand. Unlike futures markets, in which both parties to the transaction can be hedgers, in the case of options only one party to the transaction can be a hedger. For call and put options, the buyer can be a hedger. Both of these parties could also be speculators, but our point is that the seller of a call or put option can never be hedging. The seller is merely accepting risk for a premium—the option premium.

For any given options contract, the option premium will generally be higher when

1. The price of the contract instrument is more volatile.
2. The expiration date of the option is further into the future.
3. The strike price relative to the spot price for put options is higher, or the strike price relative to the spot price for call options is lower.

Eurodollars and T-bills are available in $1 million contracts for delivery on the same dates. Volatility in the price of the contract instrument affects the option premium. If the price of Eurodollars fluctuates more than the price of T-bills (all other factors being equal), the option premium for the Eurodollar option will be higher than the option premium for the T-bill option. Because of the greater volatility, the probability that the seller of the Eurodollar call or put option will lose is higher, and therefore the premium must be higher to compensate.

Second, time influences the option premium because the further into the future the expiration date is, the more time there is for the price to fluctuate and, hence, the more risk that the option will be exercised. Also, the further we look into the future, the more uncertain things become. Therefore, the more time there is before the expiration date, the higher the option premium will be.

Third, the strike price also affects the premium. If the strike price for a call option is very low relative to the spot price, it is much more likely that the spot price will go above the strike price and that the option will be exercised. Hence, the lower the strike price for a call option, the higher the option premium will be. For a put option, the higher the strike price, the more likely it is that the spot price will be lower than the strike price and that the buyer will exercise the option. Therefore, the higher the strike price for a put option, the higher the option premium will be.

Finally, note that the option still entails a small brokerage fee (for arranging the option) in addition to the option premium.

Recap The option premium is paid by the party who has rights but no obligations. The seller of the option receives the premium to compensate for accepting the risk of a loss with no possibility of gain. For any given options contract, the option premium will generally be higher when the price of the contract instrument is more volatile, the expiration date of the option is further in the future, or the strike price relative to the spot price for put options is higher or the strike price relative to the spot price for call options is lower.

One final note: We have looked at financial options and have seen that they can be used by business firms for managing risk due to price changes. Like forward and futures

A Closer Look

The Collapse of a California County and a British Bank

What do Barings Bank of London and Orange County, California, have in common? Not much to the casual observer, but events in late 1994 and early 1995 put the two close together in the history books forever. Within the span of a few months, both institutions were brought to their knees by massive losses sustained in the derivatives market.

We begin in affluent Orange County, located just south of Los Angeles. Robert Citron, a Democrat, had served as county treasurer for more than 24 years in this traditionally Republican county. As such, he managed the county's investment pool. Starting in the late 1980s, the pool began to grow rapidly from less than $1 billion to more than $8 billion as many other municipalities outside the county and other public entities opted to join the pool. They were attracted by its high return and the impressive earnings record that Citron had amassed. He was considered brilliant for consistently earning an above-average return, and others sought to share his good fortunes.

But all was not well, as wise investors should have suspected. After all, what is the probability of earning significantly above-average returns for several years in a row without taking more risks? Unfortunately, as Citron and the county found out all too late, the probability is not high. When all was said and done, Citron claimed to have had an "incomplete" understanding of the risks inherent in the financial instruments—or, as some would say, exotic derivatives—in which he was dealing. Having leveraged the $8 billion portfolio to $20 billion, he bet that interest rates would continue to fall in 1994. When the Fed began to raise rates in February, Citron failed to reverse his position. The pool owned securities whose value fell as rates rose. As rates continued upward, Citron faced reelection in June and denied to his constituency that the investment pool was in trouble. After his victory, he still tried to hold on, and by the time Wall Street refused to extend any more credit, the county was unable to come up with the funds needed to pay bondholders and was forced into bankruptcy. The portfolio was liquidated—that is, the securities whose value had fallen were sold—resulting in a $1.7 billion loss. Thus, the largest municipal bankruptcy in history had occurred in one of the country's wealthiest counties.[a]

Another unlikely candidate for bankruptcy was Barings, a prestigious British investment banking house that had been around for 233 years. Like Orange County, Barings was brought down by one individual. Nick Leeson was only 28 years old and, by most accounts, seemed to be on the fast track to success if not already there. He headed the futures trading department in Barings' Singapore branch. In 1994, his bonus topped $1 million—not bad for a kid who had grown up on the other side of the tracks. Who could guess that by late February 1995, he would be on the run and that Barings would be in bankruptcy? Here's how it happened.

Apparently, Leeson bought enough futures in a three-week period beginning in late January 1995 to have a $27 billion exposure. The transactions appeared normal because Barings had been taking large hedge positions for years in Nikkei Stock index futures—positions that were used to arbitrage even minute price differences between stocks traded in Singapore and Osaka, Japan. Around January 26, Leeson switched from a hedged position to a speculative position. No one knows for sure what his thinking was, but it is suspected that he thought the Kobe earthquake would stimulate the Japanese economy and push up the Nikkei. As events unfolded, however, his strategy proved wrong; he sold call options to raise cash for margin calls. In this situation, he was betting the Nikkei would settle into a narrow range. By February 20, his losses had accumulated to $700 million, and Barings put up more cash to cover his deficit. Barings believed that the margin call was for a corporate customer whose funds would be deposited in a few days. When Leeson couldn't produce the funds, he fled, leaving behind a note that said, "I'm sorry." By this time, the loss amounted to $900 million—more than all of Barings' capital. The Bank of England put Barings into bankruptcy. Less than a month had elapsed since the start of the fiasco. Leeson was eventually apprehended, extradited to Singapore, and sentenced to prison for three and a half years.

The Orange County and Barings examples are not unique.[b] As *Business Week* put it, "In the easy-money boom, too many securities executives lost the ability or will to scrutinize high-energy traders or guard against unethical salespeople. Too many bankers and CFOs [chief financial officers] neglected to ask whether they understood the complexity—or the downside—of the highly leveraged derivatives they were using to hedge financial risks."[c] In such a world, the value of derivative contracts can fluctuate wildly from even small changes in stock, bond, or currency prices. What should be done to protect investors and institutions? For now that remains an unanswered question. But one thing is certain: both Barings' executives and the board of supervisors of Orange County regret not keeping a closer eye on the situation.

Endnotes

a. If the county could have held on until mid-1995, when rates turned back down, the losses would have been much smaller.

b. In April 1994, Procter & Gamble sustained a $102 million after-tax loss in an interest rate swap. Also in April of that same year, Kidder Peabody found that one of its traders had parlayed a $210 million loss. After the loss, Kidder Peabody was sold to Paine Webber.

c. "The Lesson from Barings' Straits," *Business Week* (March 13, 1995): 30–32.

---

contracts, options can be used to reduce the risks of price changes in future time periods. All of the markets that we have been discussing—financial forward, futures, and options—are examples of derivatives. As you saw in Chapter 11, derivatives are financial contracts whose values are derived from the values of other underlying instruments, such as foreign exchange, bonds, equities, or an index. For example, the value of a financial futures contract in Treasury bonds derives its value from the underlying bonds. There are many kinds of derivatives, and those described in this chapter are relatively simple. Don't forget however, that derivatives can be used for speculating as well as hedging risk. In this case, they may increase risk, rather than reduce or manage it. "A Closer Look" gives an example of how derivatives brought down an otherwise healthy British investment bank and a wealthy southern California county.

This chapter contains one appendix that examines foreign exchange futures markets.

Summary of Major Points

1. In forward markets, the terms of a transaction (including the price) that will occur on a future date are arranged today. Forward transactions are used to reduce the risk that future price changes will eliminate profit. Forward agreements between individual parties are arranged by intermediaries. Forward agreements can have high transactions costs because they usually require the exact matching of two parties and because each party has a default risk in that the other party may not fulfill the agreement.

2. In financial markets, forward contracts in the most widely traded currencies have been established by large commercial banks. The bank is an actual participant in the agreement. In addition to buying and selling foreign currencies at spot prices, the banks also buy and sell the major currencies at forward rates. There does not have to be an exact matching of two parties. When there is not an exactly offsetting match, the bank has some exposure to exchange rate risk. Foreign currency forward agreements can be used to hedge exchange rate risk or to speculate about future currency values.

3. Financial futures are standardized contracts between two parties to buy or sell financial securities, such as government securities, stock indexes, Eurodollars, and numerous foreign currencies, on a future date at a price determined today. They are traded on major exchanges and are used to hedge interest rate risks, exchange rate risks, and the risk that stock prices will change. They can also be used to speculate about future price changes.

4. Because futures contracts are standardized, they have low transactions costs and high volume. They often do not provide an exact offsetting match with regard to the quality, the quantity, or the due date of the contract. The clearinghouse of the exchange enforces the contract and, for a fee, takes on the default risk. Both the buyer and the seller put up performance bonds. Arbitrageurs ensure that the futures price is equal to the spot price plus carrying costs. The futures price converges to the spot price on the delivery date.

5. Options are financial contracts that can also be used to hedge or speculate. They are available for many of the same financial instruments as futures. In addition, two kinds of options are offered for buying or selling futures contracts. A call option gives the buyer of the option the right, but not the obligation, to purchase the contract by the expiration date at a price determined today. A put option gives the buyer of the option the right, but not the obligation, to sell the contract by the expiration date at a price determined today. The buyer of a call or put option pays an option premium because she or he has rights but no obligations. The seller of the call or put option takes on the risk that the option will be exercised for a price, the option premium. Futures limit both gains and losses while options limit losses without limiting gains.

6. The option premium depends on the volatility of the financial instrument in the contract (such as T-bills), the difference between the strike price and the spot price, and the length of time until the expiration date on the option.

7. A foreign exchange futures market trades standardized contracts to buy or sell some amount of foreign exchange on a future date at a price determined today. These futures are widely used to hedge risks involving the delivery of one currency that must be converted to another currency at a later date. (See Appendix 17A.)

Key Terms

Arbitrageurs, p. 415

Call Options, p. 419

Carrying Costs, p. 415

Clearinghouse, p. 413

Convergence, p. 415

Financial Forward Contract, p. 404

Financial Futures, p. 409

Financial Futures Markets, p. 409

Foreign Exchange Futures Contract, p. 427

Forward Rate, p. 405

Futures Contracts, p. 409

Hedge, p. 405

Review Questions

1. Define *financial futures*, *forward agreements*, and *options*. What are the advantages and disadvantages of each?
2. How do spot markets differ from forward markets? How do spot markets differ from futures markets?
3. A government report forecasts both higher inflation and higher interest rates in the future. Yvette needs to borrow money in six months. What can she, as a future borrower, do now to protect herself from the risk of an increase in the interest rate? What if she is the lender?
4. Why do both the buyer and the seller of futures contracts have to put up performance bonds? When does the seller profit? When does the buyer profit? How is the clearinghouse protected from losses?
5. Explain why the futures price is very close to the spot price on the day before the delivery date of a futures contract.

6. How do arbitrageurs and speculators differ?
7. Explain how arbitrage causes the futures and spot prices to converge.
8. Explain the difference between call and put options. Does the buyer or the seller of an option pay the option premium? Why does the seller of an option take on the risk?
9. What are options on futures?
10. Explain how an investor could use a stock index future to hedge the risk of a fall in stock prices.
11. Assume that an intermediary uses futures only to hedge risk but never to speculate. Is it as vulnerable to losses as an intermediary that uses futures to speculate? Explain.
12. What factors determine the size of the option premium?

Analytical Questions

Questions marked with a check mark (✓) are objective in nature. They can be completed with a short answer or number.

13. Angela buys a Treasury bond futures agreement for $94,000. On the delivery date, the spot price is $95,000. Does she win or lose? By how much? If Angela bought the futures contract to hedge, can she lose? Explain. (Hint: What if she is willing to give up the opportunity for gain to reduce the risk of loss?)
14. IBM sells a Treasury bond futures agreement for $94,000. On the delivery date, the spot price is $95,000. IBM sold the futures agreement to speculate. Does IBM win or lose? Explain.
✓15. A firm buys a December $100,000 Treasury bond call option with a strike price of 110. If the spot price in December is $108,000, is the option exercised?
✓16. A firm buys a December $100,000 Treasury bond put option with a strike price of 110. If the

spot price in December is $108,000, is the option exercised?
✓17. An investment firm buys a December $100,000 Treasury bond put option with a strike price of 105. If the spot price in December is $108,000, is the option exercised?
✓18. An investment firm buys a December $100,000 Treasury bond call option with a strike price of 105. If the spot price in December is $108,000, is the option exercised?
✓19. If the settle price for a T-bill futures contract is 96.75, what is the percent discount?
✓20. A brokerage house purchases an S&P 500 futures agreement for $300,000. On the delivery date, the S&P 500 Index is 575. Does the brokerage house make a profit? What if the S&P 500 is 625?
21. If I buy a T-bill future for $950,000 and interest rates go up between now and the delivery

date, what will happen to the price of the T-bill future? Will I make money or lose money? Explain.

22. Assume that you will inherit a $1 million trust fund from your family when you turn 21 next year. Interest rates are high right now, and you fear they may be lower in a year. Explain in detail how you can use futures or options to alleviate your fears.

23. Ruben is exporting Colombian coffee to the United States. He will be paid $100,000 in six months, but he is concerned about how much of his domestic currency (Colombian pesos) he will receive for the $100,000. Explain in detail how he can reduce the risk that, in six months, the peso will depreciate in value against the dollar and he will receive fewer pesos than he anticipates. (See Appendix 17A.)

Suggested Readings

From the home page of the *Wall Street Journal* (**www.wsj.com**), a wealth of information about futures that can be accessed for free. *Barron's*, the weekly financial magazine, has an abundance of free information about both futures and options available at **www.barrons.com.**

The Chicago Board of Trade Web site, available at **http://www.cbot.com,** provides information about options trading.

Find information on the trading of futures and options at the Chicago Mercantile Exchange at **http://www.cme.com.**

Shalini Patel and Paula Tkac look at the futures market in their article "The Past, Present, and Future of Futures," *EconSouth*, Federal Reserve Bank of Atlanta, 9, no. 3 (Third Quarter, 2007).

A book that some consider the authority on futures and options is John Hull's *Options, Futures, and Other Derivatives*, 6th ed. (Upper Saddle River, NJ: Prentice Hall, 2006).

For a look at some of the material covered in this chapter, see Jeffery W. Gunther and Thomas Siems, "Debunking Derivatives Delirium," *Southwest Economy*, Federal Reserve Bank of Dallas, Issue 2 (March/April 2003). The article is available online at **http://www.dallasfed.org/research/swe/2003/swe0302b.pdf.**

"An Option for Anticipating Fed Action," by John B. Carlson, William R. Melick, and Erkin Y. Sahinoz, looks at how options on federal funds futures can be analyzed to gauge public expectations of future Fed actions. The article is available in *Economic Commentary*, Federal Reserve Bank of Cleveland (September 1, 2003), and online at **http://www.clevelandfed.org/Research/Commentary/2003/0901.pdf.**

For a comprehensive analysis of futures markets, see A.B. Malliaris, *Foundations of Futures Markets: Selected Essays of A.G. Malliaris* (Northampton, MA: Edward Elgar, 2000).

For a collection of 70 articles written on options over the past 25 years, see *Options Markets*, ed. George M. Constantinides and A.G. Malliaris (Northampton, MA: Edward Elgar, 2001).

For a discussion of the risks that derivatives pose for banks, see Chapter 7 of Franklin R. Edwards, *The New Finance: Regulation and Financial Stability* (Washington, DC: The AEI Press, 1996): 120–147.

Two comprehensive and somewhat technical articles are "Money Market Futures" and "Options on Money Market Futures," both found in *Instruments of the Money Market*, 7th ed., ed. Timothy Q. Cook and Robert K. LaRoche (Richmond, VA: Federal Reserve Bank of Richmond, 1993).

Appendix 17A
The Foreign Exchange Futures Market

In the body of this chapter, we discussed foreign exchange forward agreements that are offered by large banks to allow their customers to hedge exchange rate risk. In addition to these forward markets, large futures markets that trade foreign exchange futures contracts have also developed to hedge exchange rate risk. Both forward and futures agreements in foreign currencies facilitate cross-border trading in goods, services, and financial claims. Both achieve similar results. This appendix looks at foreign exchange futures contracts.

Foreign Exchange Futures Contract
A standardized contract to deliver a certain amount of a foreign currency on a date in the future at a price determined today.

A foreign exchange futures contract is a standardized contract to deliver a certain amount of a foreign currency on a date in the future at a price determined today. The agreed-upon price is the futures price. Like spot markets, foreign exchange futures markets have experienced remarkable growth due to the tremendous increase in trade and foreign investment, as well as the volatility of exchange rates. Foreign exchange futures markets have been organized since the mid-1970s and allow importers, exporters, and investors in foreign securities to hedge. Like other futures markets, they also provide the opportunity for speculation.

The foreign exchange markets, including both spot and futures markets, actually form the largest market in the world in terms of the volume of transactions. Spot markets do not have a single location, such as the New York Stock Exchange, but are located at large banks in the world's financial centers—London, New York, Tokyo, and Frankfurt. Large banks in financial centers in other countries are usually linked to the major banks in one of the financial centers, which, in turn, are linked by telephone, telex, or the Internet. Standardized futures contracts are traded on the Chicago Mercantile Exchange and require a relatively large minimum purchase. In reality, one worldwide foreign exchange market (either spot or futures) is open somewhere in the world 24 hours each day. Because supplies and demands change from day to day, exchange rates (both spot and futures prices) fluctuate day-to-day, hour-to-hour, and even minute-to-minute! The relationship between the spot and futures exchange rate is the same as the relationship between any spot and futures price in that they are highly correlated and converge as the delivery date nears.

Foreign exchange futures markets, like all futures markets, offer the opportunity to hedge risk or to speculate. Importers and exporters often enter into agreements to deliver goods in the future for a price determined today. Because the price is agreed on today without knowing the future spot exchange rate, there is a risk that the exchange rate between the two currencies will change between now and the delivery date. Thus, there is a possibility that the anticipated profit could be eliminated or, worse yet, that a loss could occur. This risk is referred to as *exchange rate risk*.

To hedge, an importer can enter the foreign exchange futures market. An example will help to clarify. Assume that Jean is exporting computers to a firm (Choca Firm) in Switzerland that plans to resell them at a profit. Choca Firm previously specialized in Swiss chocolates but now is trying to diversify by importing computers. Jean agrees to deliver 500 computers in September, three months from now, at a price of $1,000 per computer, or $500,000. Choca Firm will have to come up with $500,000 in September to pay for the computers.[10] Checking the exchange rate today, Choca finds that the Swiss franc/dollar rate is 1.1 Swiss francs. If the exchange rate stays the same (highly unlikely), Choca Firm would have to pay 550,000 Swiss francs (500,000×1.1) in September for the $500,000. This is great because Choca is confident that it can resell the computers for 600,000 Swiss francs, making a nice profit. But what if the Swiss franc depreciates (or, in other words, if the dollar appreciates) between now and September? If the Swiss franc/dollar rate changes to 1.2 Swiss francs (a depreciation of the Swiss franc and appreciation of the dollar), Choca Firm will have to pay 600,000 Swiss francs (500,000 × 1.2) for the $500,000 and will lose all of its profit. Worse yet, if the dollar appreciates to 1.3 Swiss francs, the importer will have to come up with 545,000 Swiss francs (500,000 × 1.3), incurring a sizable loss! Thanks to organized futures markets, Choca can hedge this risk by buying a standardized foreign exchange futures contract in dollars.

For example, today a futures contract for delivery of dollars in September is selling for 1.105 Swiss francs. If Choca Firm purchases this contract, it knows that it will pay 1.105 Swiss francs for the delivery of $1 in September, or 552,500 (500,000 × 1.105) Swiss francs for $500,000, regardless of what the spot exchange rate is in September. For Choca Firm or any importer interested in importing computers rather than speculating on future spot exchange rates, this offers a simple way to reduce exchange rate risk.

Another use of foreign exchange futures markets is to hedge risk when foreign securities are purchased. For example, foreign purchasers of U.S. government securities know they will be delivered so many dollars in, say, 90 days when the security matures. Can you explain how selling a futures contract hedges the exchange rate risk in this case?[11] No wonder the growth of these markets has paralleled the growth of trade in goods, services, and financial securities.

Endnotes

1. For example, small changes in interest rates can lead to large changes in the prices or value of long-term fixed-rate assets such as bonds or mortgages.
2. With the fixed exchange rate system of the Bretton Woods Accord, under normal circumstances, there was no exchange rate risk. When situations were not normal—when there was a currency crisis—there could be substantial exchange rate risk if a country was seriously considering changing the value of its currency.
3. The exchange rate can also be expressed as $1 = .64 euro (1 euro/1.559 = $1.559/1.559 = $1 = .64 euro).
4. Note that in the case of foreign exchange forward markets, large banks are actually the partners to forward transactions—namely, the bank buys currency from one customer and resells all or part of it to another in two separate forward contracts between each customer and the bank. The point is that the transactions are not between the two customers.
5. The risk of default is greatly reduced when one of the partners to the forward transaction is a large bank, as in the case of the foreign exchange forward markets.
6. As you saw in Chapter 4, Eurodollars are dollar-dominated deposits held abroad.
7. If the price of a futures contract changes, the buyer or seller settles up financially for any changes in value, usually by executing an opposing transaction. For example, if Suzanne purchases a futures contract, rather than taking delivery on the delivery date, she can sell a futures contract involving the same asset for the same delivery date. The sale effectively cancels out the purchase. Or if she had sold a futures contract, she can purchase a futures contract with the same delivery date, effectively canceling out the sale. Most futures contracts are settled in this manner: purchases in the futures market are reversed by sales in the futures market; sales in the futures market are reversed by purchases in the futures market. This fact does not alter the analysis, however.
8. Likewise, forward prices cannot diverge from spot prices by more than the carrying costs.
9. In this chapter, we are limiting our discussion to American options, which can be exercised anytime before their expiration date. European options can be exercised only on the expiration date of the option.
10. In this example, we are assuming that the importer must exchange domestic currency for the foreign currency—that is, Choca Firm must pay for its imports with the currency of the exporting country. The situation could work in reverse. In that case, the exporter would be paid in the currency of the importing country and have to exchange it for the exporting country's currency. Either way, the risk is the same; the only difference is in who bears the risk.

11. For example, assume that a Japanese firm purchases a U.S. government T-bill for $9,900. The T-bill sells at a discount, and the Japanese firm knows it will receive $10,000 in three months. The yen/dollar exchange rate on the date of the purchase is 110. Thus, the Japanese firm pays 1,089,000 yen (110 yen×$9,900) for the T-bill. If the exchange rate is the same in three months, the T-bill will return 1,100,000 yen for a profit of 11,000 yen. It is highly unlikely; however, that the exchange rate will be the same, and if the yen depreciates, the Japanese firm could see its profit reduced or even incur a loss. To hedge this risk, the firm can sell a futures contract today that agrees to deliver $10,000 three months from now at a yen price agreed on today. In this way, the firm will know exactly how many yen it will receive for the $10,000.

18

The dollar is our currency, but your problem.

—John Connolly, U.S. treasury secretary
to his European counterparts, 1971

The International
Financial System

Learning Objectives

After reading this chapter, you should know:

How and why the international financial
system is changing

The role of the international financial system
under the Bretton Woods Accord

How the present managed floating exchange
rate system works

The role the dollar plays in the international
financial system

The birth and growing importance of the euro

The roles of the International Monetary Fund,
the World Bank, and the Bank for International Settlements

A DRAMATIC METAMORPHOSIS

The international financial system consists of the numerous rules, customs, instruments, facilities, markets, and organizations that enable international payments to be made and funds to flow across borders. In recent years, the international financial system has experienced tremendous growth. New financial instruments have been created, and the volume of transactions has exploded. The dramatic metamorphosis of international financial markets is driven by technological changes, the growth in world trade, and the breakdown of barriers to financial (capital) flows.

From an economic standpoint, developments in the international financial system have made financial markets more efficient because funds (financial capital) can more easily flow around the world to wherever they will earn the highest return. Over time, as resources are allocated more efficiently, both developed and developing countries should experience increased economic growth. As a result, living standards around the world should rise more than they otherwise would have.

A more globalized environment can also entail costs. A disturbance in one financial market or in one country can have immediate effects on other countries and the entire international financial system. As Alan Greenspan once put it, "These global financial markets, engendered by the rapid proliferation of cross-border financial flows and products, have developed a capability of transmitting mistakes at a far faster pace throughout the financial system in ways that were unknown a generation ago."[1] An example is the turmoil in international capital markets during 2007 and 2008 caused by declining real estate prices in the United States. Since much of the financing for subprime mortgages ultimately came from foreign banks and financial firms, they were some of the biggest losers. Between April and December of 2007, Japanese financial institutions lost over $5.5 billion in the U.S. subprime mortgage market. Banks with the largest write-offs over this period include Swiss-based bank UBS, with losses totaling $11.45 billion for the last three months of 2007, and Bank of China, with losses expected to total $2.79 billion. By the summer of 2008, financial markets around the world were reeling as the crisis spread from the mortgage markets to global financial markets at large.

The international financial system includes the international money and capital markets and the foreign exchange market. The international money market trades short-term claims with an original maturity of one year or less; the international capital market trades capital market instruments, including stocks, bonds, mutual funds, and mortgages, with an original maturity of more than one year. In recent years, many new international financial products have been created to facilitate the increased financial flows. These include various types of mutual funds that allow individuals to invest in developed and emerging economies.

A crucial part of the international financial system is the foreign exchange market, where foreign currencies are bought and sold in the course of trading goods, services, and financial claims (securities) among countries. As you have seen in earlier chapters, this global market is woven together by the dealers in foreign currencies—mostly, the foreign exchange departments of the largest commercial banks located in the world's major financial centers such as New York, London, Frankfurt, and Tokyo. By April 2007, the average daily volume in foreign exchange markets was $3.2 trillion, an increase of over 70 percent from three years before.

In the post–World War II period, the international financial system has operated under two distinct exchange rate regimes. The specific exchange rate regime affects the trading of all international financial instruments. During the first regime from 1944 to 1973, major industrial countries maintained a system of fixed exchange rates, and currency values rarely changed. Under the second regime, which has been in effect since

1973, exchange rates fluctuate daily in response to changes in supply and demand (market forces). As we shall see, governments also intervene in this flexible exchange rate system.

In the preceding chapters on financial markets, we discussed many aspects of the international financial system, and in Chapter 16 we directly considered the market for foreign exchange. In this chapter, we examine the international exchange rate systems in effect since 1944. These exchange rate systems provide a framework in which the international financial system operates. We also discuss the unique role that the dollar still plays in the international financial system. Finally, we look at the international organizations that seek to provide a framework for financial stability as the cross-border trading of all types of financial instruments continues to grow.

THE INTERNATIONAL FINANCIAL SYSTEM FROM 1944 TO 1973

From the end of World War II until the early 1970s, the major economies of the world participated in a fixed exchange rate system, with the U.S. dollar functioning as the official reserve currency. Other countries defined their currencies in terms of the U.S. dollar and agreed to buy or sell dollars to maintain the agreed-upon exchange rates.[2] The dollar, in turn, was defined in terms of gold. During the postwar period, 1 ounce of gold was set equal to $35, and the United States agreed to convert any unwanted dollars of foreign central banks into gold. In cases of fundamental imbalances, an orderly procedure was established to make adjustments in exchange rates and thereby avoid the disruptive changes that had occurred between World War I and World War II

This fixed exchange rate system was established by the Bretton Woods Accord of 1944, which was worked out by representatives from the major industrialized countries who met at Bretton Woods, New Hampshire, to design a new international financial system. Under the Bretton Woods Accord, if the trade deficit of a country other than the United States increased, that country effectively increased the supply of its currency in international markets. The increased supply put downward pressure on the exchange rate. To maintain the agreed-upon exchange rate, the country's central bank had to purchase the excess supply of its currency using dollars.

An example will help clarify this concept. Assume that the exchange rate between the dollar and the British pound was set at $1 = 1/2 = .5$ pounds, but supply and demand were causing the market value of the two currencies to gravitate to $1 = 2/3 \cong .67$ pounds. Perhaps, ceteris paribus, Britain's trade deficit had increased significantly in recent months, causing Britain's balance of payments on current and capital accounts to move into a deficit position.[3] The smaller supply of dollars relative to pounds in international markets puts upward pressure on the exchange rate of the dollar, while the larger relative supply of pounds puts downward pressure on the value of the pound. In such a case, the Bank of England, the central bank of Great Britain, would intervene in the market by buying pounds with dollars until the market value of the two currencies converged at the agreed-upon exchange rate. By changing the supply of dollars and pounds outstanding, the Bank of England could manipulate the market value of the dollar in terms of the pound. In this manner, the values of the dollar and pound could be maintained at the agreed-upon exchange rate of $1 = .5$ pounds.

Such government transactions in foreign currencies were measured in the Official Reserve Account of the balance of payments. We ignored this account in Chapter 16. You can now see that by supplying dollars and demanding pounds, the Bank of England would run a surplus in the Official Reserve Account that would just equal the deficit in the current and capital accounts of the balance of payments. Hence, under fixed exchange

---

Fixed Exchange Rate System
An exchange rate system in which currency values do not fluctuate.

Official Reserve Currency
The currency used by other countries to define their own currency; the U.S. dollar was the official reserve currency under the Bretton Woods Accord.

Bretton Woods Accord
A 1944 agreement negotiated by the major industrialized countries that established fixed exchange rates with the U.S. dollar serving as the official reserve currency.

Official Reserve Account
The balance of payments account that records official government transactions in the foreign exchange market to bring the balance of payments into balance.

The Gold Standard

During the late nineteenth and early twentieth centuries, the United States, along with the other major world economies, was on a gold standard that lasted about 30 years. Under the gold standard, the amount of currency in circulation was backed by gold. Each country defined its currency in terms of gold and agreed to buy or sell unlimited quantities of gold at a preestablished price called the *par value*.

A gold standard is a type of fixed exchange rate system. For example, if one ounce of gold in the United States is equal to $20 and one ounce of gold in England is equal to 5 British pounds, then the pound/dollar exchange rate is .25; that is, $1 equals .25 British pounds. The dollar and the pound will always trade in this fixed ratio as long as both countries redeem their currencies in gold at the par value.

A gold standard comes under strain if countries experience different growth rates. For instance, suppose that a gold standard was in existence and that the United States was growing faster than its neighbors. In that case, the United States would find that imports were increasing faster than exports. In the foreign exchange market, the quantity supplied of dollars would be greater than the quantity demanded. Foreigners would present the dollars to the U.S. Treasury to be redeemed for gold, and the United States would lose its gold supply. As the United States lost gold, its money supply would fall with resulting depressing effects on output, jobs, and so on.

If policy makers wanted to keep the U.S. economy growing faster than economies in the rest of the world, they would be under pressure to devalue the U.S. currency. A devaluation is an increase in the number of dollars that must be presented to the Treasury to receive an ounce of gold. Fear of devaluation would cause more of the currency to be presented for redemption. Holders of dollars would convert the dollars to gold, and if devaluation did occur, they would convert the gold back to more dollars than they started with! This would exacerbate the gold loss and result in periodic financial crises as gold redemptions were suspended and the par values among currencies had to be redefined. In fact, scenarios like this actually occurred and led to the end of the gold standard.

rates, it was (and always is) official government transactions in foreign exchange markets that brought the balance of payments into balance at the fixed exchange rate.

Because the Bank of England was maintaining the fixed exchange rate by buying pounds with dollars, Great Britain could continue to maintain the fixed rate only so long as it had or could acquire sufficient dollars to support the value of its currency as needed. If Great Britain (or another foreign country) ran a persistent deficit in its current and capital accounts, its central bank would eventually run out of dollars and have to **devalue**, or decrease the value of, its currency in terms of the dollar in order to reflect the diminished value of the pound. Devaluation occurs when the monetary authorities reduce the value of a country's currency under a fixed exchange rate system. In terms of our analysis, the pound is devalued if the official rate is changed from $1

Devalue
Under a fixed exchange rate system, to decrease the value of a country's currency.

per .5 pounds to $1 per .67 pounds. At the original rate, each pound was worth $2, but at the latter rate, after the devaluation, each pound is worth about $1.5. The need to devalue could be accelerated if speculators sensed an impending necessity to devalue and consequently increased the supply of pounds from what it would be otherwise. The alternative to devaluing would be for Great Britain to run a severely contractionary policy designed to lower prices in pounds and make British goods more desirable. As exports increased and imports decreased, the value of the pound would be restored to the agreed-upon exchange rate.

As you have seen, in the decades immediately after World War II, the U.S. dollar served as the official reserve currency. Unlike Great Britain in our example, the United States was eventually in the unique position of being able to run persistent balance of payments deficits on the current and capital accounts. Initially, the United States was running sizable trade surpluses financed by capital outflows under the Marshall Plan. Foreign central banks sought to accumulate stockpiles of dollars to function as international reserves. During this period, a "dollar shortage" occurred as countries scrambled for dollars not only for reserves but also to rebuild their economies.

Once foreign central banks had acquired sufficient reserves, the ability of the United States to run chronic deficits in the balance of payments on current and capital accounts was also limited. In this case, the dollar, ceteris paribus, would become overvalued in terms of one or more foreign currencies. Under the Bretton Woods Accord, the United States would lose gold as the unwanted dollars were presented for conversion. The United States would then pressure foreign central banks to **revalue,** or increase the value of, their currency in terms of the dollar.

Revaluation occurs when the monetary authorities increase the value of a country's currency under a fixed exchange rate system. For example, the pound is revalued if the official rate is changed from $1 = .67 pounds to $1 = .5 pound. In the original case, each pound was worth $1.50, while in the latter case, each pound is worth $2. Ceteris paribus, the revaluation would, in time, reduce the U.S. balance of payments deficit on current and capital accounts and slow the flow of unwanted dollars abroad. In turn, the gold outflow would diminish.

A foreign central bank might be hesitant to revalue, however, because revaluation could adversely affect its country's economy. Among other things, revaluation could reduce net exports and have a negative impact on employment. Note that whether the United States was running a persistent surplus or a persistent deficit in its balance of payments on current and capital accounts, the foreign central bank had to change the value of its currency in terms of the U.S. dollar. The foreign central bank had to act because, under the Bretton Woods Accord, if the United States changed the value of the dollar, the change would affect the relationship between the dollar and all other currencies, even though the dollar might have been out of alignment with only one or a few of the foreign currencies. Consequently, foreign central banks would pressure the United States to correct the imbalance by reducing its deficit on the current and capital accounts. Note the irony of the situation and the potential for a stalemate in which each country is pressuring the other to take action.

A balance of payments deficit on current and capital accounts could also be caused by increases in the capital outflows of a country, ceteris paribus. If a country experienced a net capital outflow, this had the same effect as an increase in the trade deficit of the same magnitude. Ceteris paribus, an increased net capital outflow from the United States comes from an increase in direct foreign investment by U.S. individuals or firms. Likewise, if a country experienced an increased net capital inflow, this had the same effect on the balance of payments on current and capital accounts as an increase in the trade surplus.

Revalue
Under a fixed exchange rate system, to increase the value of a country's currency.

As you have seen in Chapter 16, ceteris paribus, such capital flows resulted from changes in domestic interest rates relative to foreign rates.

During the 1960s and 1970s, some countries, including the United States, expanded their economies and their domestic money supplies relatively faster than others, such as Japan and Germany. The United States experienced inflationary pressures in the mid- to late 1960s as a result of monetary and fiscal policies associated with the Great Society's War on Poverty and the Vietnam War buildup. Consequently, some central banks outside the United States accumulated more dollars than they wished to hold as reserve assets. Rather than revaluing their currencies, they asked the United States to convert these unwanted dollars to gold; up until 1971, foreign central banks could still receive gold from the Federal Reserve in exchange for their dollars.

As more and more central banks requested conversion, it became clear that the United States would not be able to continue to redeem the dollars in gold. Expecting a devaluation in the dollar, speculators rushed to change their dollars into currencies such as the West German mark. This caused the Bundesbank to stop providing marks for dollars. In late 1971, the United States suspended the international conversion of dollars into gold. At the same time, the dollar was devalued by setting the value of 1 ounce of gold equal to $42 rather than the $35 that had been in effect since the inception of the Bretton Woods Accord. Hence, the "official value" of the dollar was reduced from $1 = 1/35 ounce of gold to $1 = 1/42 ounce of gold, even though the United States was no longer redeeming dollars with gold, even for central banks. In 1973, most countries abandoned fixed exchange rates altogether, and the value of the dollar began to float. The Jamaica Agreement of 1974 officially adopted floating exchange rates, underscoring what had been done unofficially in 1973.

A final comment is in order. During the Bretton Woods period, the amount of cross-border trading of financial assets such as stocks, bonds, and mortgages was much lower than it is today. Under normal circumstances, exchange risk was minimal during this period, but many countries had capital controls that did not allow the purchase of foreign financial instruments. Also, technology was such that it did not foster cross-border financial flows.

Recap The international financial system consists of the arrangements, rules, customs, instruments, facilities, and organizations that enable international payments to be made and funds to flow across borders. The international financial system includes the international money and capital markets and the foreign exchange market. The Bretton Woods Accord of 1944 established fixed exchange rates among major world currencies. The U.S. dollar, which was backed by gold, served as the official reserve currency, and other countries defined their currencies in terms of the dollar. If a country other than the United States had a deficit in its balance of payments, it used supplies of dollars to purchase its own currency to maintain fixed exchange rates. If a country other than the United States had a surplus in its balance of payments, it demanded dollars to maintain the value of its currency. The system broke down in late 1971, when the United States suspended the international conversion of dollars to gold. A flexible exchange rate system was adopted in 1973. In the Bretton Woods period, cross-border investment in financial instruments was much less frequent than it is today.

THE MANAGED FLOAT EXCHANGE RATE SYSTEM SINCE 1973

The demise of the Bretton Woods Accord initiated a new era in which the exchange rates of major industrialized countries are no longer fixed. Rather, these countries participate in a **floating (flexible) exchange rate system,** in which exchange rates fluctuate by the minute and the hour as market forces change.

Like other major currencies, the exchange rate of the U.S. dollar is determined by demand and supply in international markets. The supply of dollars per month reflects the U.S. demand for foreign goods, services, and securities. Ceteris paribus, the quantity of dollars supplied is a positive function of the exchange rate. The demand for dollars reflects the foreign demand for U.S. goods, services, and securities. Ceteris paribus, the quantity demanded is a negative function of the exchange rate. The market gravitates to the equilibrium exchange rate where quantity demanded is equal to quantity supplied.

From an initial equilibrium, if U.S. incomes, U.S. inflation, or foreign interest rates rise, ceteris paribus, U.S. demand for foreign goods, services, and securities will increase, and so will the supply of dollars. The market will gravitate to a new equilibrium at a lower exchange rate that corresponds to a depreciation of the dollar.

Likewise, if foreign incomes, foreign inflation, or U.S. interest rates rise, ceteris paribus, foreign demand for U.S. goods, services, and securities will increase, and so will the demand for dollars. The market will gravitate to a new equilibrium at a higher exchange rate that corresponds to an appreciation of the dollar. Because we live in a very dynamic world, the factors that determine supply and demand are always changing. Hence, exchange rates change by the minute.

To summarize, factors such as domestic and foreign incomes, inflation rates, and interest rates affect exchange rates, and "flexible" exchange rates immediately adjust to changing market conditions and expectations. "A Closer Look" on p. 438 reviews the basics of exchange rate determination under flexible exchange rates as first presented in Chapter 16.

Our story does not end here, however. Market forces are not the only factor that affects exchange rates. In addition, central banks may intervene in the foreign exchange market by buying and selling currencies to influence exchange rates. Thus, the present international monetary system can be more correctly characterized as a **managed float exchange rate system** because exchange rates are allowed to fluctuate in accordance with supply and demand; however, central banks may intervene if a currency is thought to be over or undervalued. This system is distinctly different from the fixed exchange rate system under the Bretton Woods Accord.

Interestingly, central banks have intervened more often under the managed float than under the previous fixed exchange rate system, which required them to intervene to maintain the agreed-upon exchange rate. Sometimes central banks have intervened more frequently than at other times. Often, central banks of major countries have agreed to pursue similar exchange rate policies and have coordinated their interventions as part of the implementation of monetary policy. Central bank intervention is discussed more fully in Chapter 26.

One final point needs to be made. Under the managed float exchange rate system, many small countries peg the value of their currencies to the U.S. dollar or some other major currency or basket of currencies. By doing so, a small country reduces the risk that the value of its currency will fluctuate unpredictably. If the exchange rate of a small country fluctuates unpredictably, the value of real or financial assets denominated in that currency will also fluctuate unpredictably. By tying the value of its currency to the U.S. dollar or a basket of other major currencies, a small country can reduce this risk. A financial crisis can result, however, if the country cannot maintain the fixed exchange rate. Both the Mexican peso crisis of 1994 and the Asian crisis of 1997–1998 occurred when the affected countries were unable to maintain an exchange rate that they had fixed in terms of the dollar. In both cases, the eventual depreciation of the currencies triggered

The Foreign Exchange Market

In the accompanying graphs (a) and (b), the quantity of dollars is measured on the horizontal axis, and the exchange rate (euros per dollar) is measured on the vertical axis. The quantity supplied of dollars per month, reflecting U.S. demand for foreign goods, services, and securities, is, ceteris paribus, a positive function of the exchange rate, while the quantity demanded of dollars per month is a negative function of the exchange rate. In this case, quantity demanded is equal to quantity supplied at point A, producing an equilibrium exchange rate of .9 euros. Assume now that the initial equilibrium at point A in graph (a) is disturbed by one of the following developments: (1) the euro price of U.S. goods and services rises relative to the euro price of foreign goods and services because of inflation in the United States, (2) foreign interest rates rise relative to U.S. interest rates, or (3) foreign incomes fall relative to U.S. incomes. The result is a reduction in the demand for U.S. goods, services, and financial instruments by foreigners and thus a reduction in the demand for dollars—shown as a leftward shift of the demand function in graph (a).

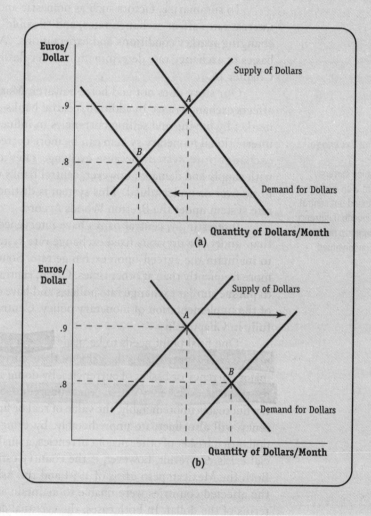

The new equilibrium at point *B* results in a depreciation of the dollar from .9 euros to .8 euros.

Next, assume that the economy is again at the initial equilibrium exchange rate of $1 = .9 euros as in graph (b). The equilibrium is disturbed by one of the following developments: (1) a rise in U.S. income, (2) a rise in U.S. prices relative to the dollar prices of foreign goods, or (3) a rise in foreign interest rates relative to U.S. interest rates. As a result, U.S. demand for foreign goods, services, and securities increases, as does the supply of dollars—shown as a rightward shift of the supply function in graph (b). The new equilibrium at point *B* results in a depreciation of the dollar as the equilibrium exchange rate falls from .9 euros to .8 euros.

In reality, a shock such as an increase in foreign interest rates relative to U.S. rates will shift the demand for dollars left (as foreigners want to invest less in dollar-denominated assets) and the supply of dollars right (as Americans will want to invest more in euro-denominated assets). Both shifts will cause the value of the dollar to fall. The relative magnitudes of the two shifts can be seen by the change in the volume of foreign exchange transactions. If the leftward shift in dollar demand is larger, exchange transactions will fall, but if the rightward shift in supply is larger, then the volume of foreign exchange transactions will increase.

widespread losses, the failure of many financial and nonfinancial firms, and financial crises. Exhibit 18-1 on p. 440 gives the exchange rate arrangements for most countries in the world.

Managing Exchange Rate Risk Under the Managed Float

Under flexible exchange rates, when market participants enter into contracts to receive or supply so much foreign currency on a future date, there is an exchange rate risk because the future spot exchange rate is unknown.[4] Market participants may be importers or exporters who will receive or who need a given amount of foreign exchange on a future date, or they may be investors who have purchased or who plan to purchase foreign financial securities that will mature in the future. If the exchange rate changes unexpectedly between now and the future date, the anticipated profits of an exporter, importer, or investor could be reduced. Worse yet, a loss could be incurred. Thus, under flexible exchange rate systems, market participants are exposed to substantial exchange rate risk.

In recent years, international financial markets have developed hybrid instruments including foreign exchange forward, futures, options, and swap agreements to hedge exchange rate risk. These instruments, which are all forms of derivatives, can be used to reduce the risk of unforeseen price changes. In this case, the prices are exchange rates. Thus, these markets can reduce exchange rate risk.

Forward, futures, options, and swap agreements effectively lock in today's exchange rate for a transaction that may or will occur in the future, thus reducing the risk that changes in the exchange rate will alter expected outcomes.

The development of foreign exchange forward, futures, options, and swap agreements coincides with the tremendous growth in trade and capital flows, coupled with the increased volatility of exchange rates under the managed float exchange rate system. Because these instruments can reduce exchange rate risks, they may facilitate trade in goods, services, and financial claims.

1. Exchange arrangements with no separate legal tender, another country's currency as legal tender (10 countries)

Ecuador, El Salvador, Kiribati, Marshall Islands, Micronesia, Montenegro, Palau, Panama, San Marino, Timor-Leste

2. Currency board arrangements (13 countries)

Bosnia and Herzegovina, Brunei Darussalam, Bulgaria, Djibouti, Estonia, Hong Kong SAR, Lithuania

ECCU (6 countries): Antigua and Barbuda, Dominica, Grenada, St. Kitts and Nevis, St. Lucia, St. Vincent and the Grenadines

3. Other conventional fixed-peg arrangements (70 countries)

Against a single currency (49 countries)

Angola, Argentina, Aruba, Bahamas, Bahrain, Barbados, Belarus, Belize, Bhutan, Bolivia, Cape Verde, Comoros, Egypt, Eritrea, Ethiopia, Guyana, Honduras, Jordan, Kuwait, Latvia, Lebanon, Lesotho, Macedonia, Maldives, Malta, Mauritania, Mongolia, Namibia, Nepal, Netherlands Antilles, Nigeria, Oman, Pakistan, Qatar, Rwanda, Saudi Arabia, Solomon Islands, Suriname, Swaziland, Syria, Trinidad and Tobago, Turkmenistan, Ukraine, United Arab Emirates, Uzbekistan, Venezuela, Vietnam, Yemen, Zimbabwe

CFA franc zone (14 countries)

WAEMU

Benin, Burkina Faso, Côte D'Ivoire, Guinea-Bissau, Mali, Niger, Senegal, Togo

CEMAC

Cameroon, Central African Rep., Chad, Congo, Rep. of Equatorial Guinea, Gabon

Against a composite (7 countries)

Fiji, Libya, Morocco, Samoa, Vanuatu, Iran, Seychelles

4. Pegged exchange rates within horizontal bands (5 countries)

Within a cooperative arrangement

Cyprus, Denmark, Slovak Republic

Other band arrangements

Hungary, Tonga

5. Crawling peg (6 countries)

Azerbaijan, Botswana, China, Iraq, Nicaragua, Sierra Leone

6. Crawling bands (1 country)

Costa Rica

7. Managed floating with no predetermined path for the exchange rate (48 counties)

Afghanistan, Algeria, Armenia, Bangladesh, Burundi, Cambodia, Colombia, Croatia, Czech Rep., Dominican Rep., Gambia, Ghana, Georgia, Guatemala, Guinea, Haiti, Indonesia, India, Jamaica, Kazakhstan, Kenya, Kyrgyz Rep., Laos, Liberia, Madagascar, Malawi, Malaysia, Mauritius, Moldova, Mozambique, Myanmar, Papua New Guinea, Paraguay, Peru, Romania, Russia, São Tomé and Príncipe, Serbia, Singapore, Sri Lanka, Sudan, Tajikistan, Tanzania, Thailand, Tunisia, Uganda, Uruguay, Zambia

8. Independently floating (35 countries)

Albania, Australia, Brazil, Canada, Chile, Congo, Iceland, Israel, Japan, Korea, Mexico, New Zealand, Norway, Philippines, Poland, Slovenia, Somalia, South Africa, Sweden, Switzerland, Turkey, United Kingdom, United States

Euro Area (13 countries, as of April 2007)

Austria, Belgium, Finland, France, Germany, Greece, Ireland, Italy, Luxembourg, Netherlands, Portugal, Slovenia, Spain

Source: IMF Annual Report—2007, Appendix, Table 11–9.

The Path to a Single European Currency

In 1979, the European Monetary System was established to increase exchange rate stability among countries in Western Europe. Under the system, individual currencies had limited flexibility, and central banks intervened by buying and selling currencies if exchange rates moved outside a narrow band. If fundamental imbalances existed, exchange rates were changed to correct the imbalances. In that same year, the European Currency Unit (ECU) was created. The ECU was an accounting unit made up of a weighted basket of currencies. The weights were determined by the gross domestic product and other real and financial variables of the participating countries. It was hoped that the ECU would eventually lead to the creation of a single currency.

In the Maastricht Treaty of 1991, 15 European countries agreed to a plan to adopt a single European currency by no later than 1999.[a] During the phase-in period, the countries maintained exchange rates within a narrow range of the ECU.[b] As of January 1, 1999, 11 countries participated in the currency union. Exchange rates of the 11 participating countries were fixed and no longer fluctuated even within a narrow range. In addition, the newly established European Central Bank, together with the national central banks, formed the Eurosystem that took over the formulation of monetary policy. Although the new currency did not yet circulate, all newly issued stocks and government bonds, bank accounts, corporate books, credit card payments, and mortgages could be figured in euros.[c]

The euro began circulating on January 1, 2002. Europeans exchanged their own national currencies for euros. After March 1, 2002, the national currencies were no longer accepted as money within participating "eurozone" nations.

To participate in the single currency, countries had to meet certain criteria, including having annual budget deficits not greater than 3 percent of their GDP and a government debt less than 60 percent of GDP or moving toward that goal. Of the 15 countries that signed the Maastricht Treaty, Great Britain, Denmark, and Sweden decided not to participate in the currency union. Greece became the twelfth country to participate in the currency union when it was able to join in 2001. In 2006, Slovenia and Cyprus were admitted, and then in 2008, Slovenia joined the eurozone. By 2008, 15 member states with over 320 million people were in the eurozone.

In giving up their national currencies, participating countries have surrendered the right to determine their own national interest rates, exchange rates, and monetary policies. In addition, they have given up some control over the size of their budget deficits. For example, countries may not be able to run fiscal deficits as large as they would like or to lower interest rates as much as they would like in the face of unemployment, and they definitely will not be able to devalue national currencies!

Despite these potential disadvantages, the participating countries supported the common currency to reduce transactions costs associated with making exchanges and to support greater economic integration. It was hoped that such a reduction would translate to higher economic growth rates. In describing the creation of the euro, a *Business Week* magazine contributor stated: "The potential benefits are limitless—and so are the risks."[d]

Endnotes

a. The following countries signed the Maastricht Treaty: Austria, Belgium, Denmark, Finland, France, Germany, Great Britain, Greece, Ireland, Italy, Luxembourg, the Netherlands, Portugal, Spain, and Sweden.
b. A currency crisis in 1992 caused the range to be widened from 2.5 percent to 15 percent.
c. Recall the discussion of the Eurosystem in Chapter 4.
d. "The Euro," *Business Week* (April 27, 1998): 90–94.

The Role of the Dollar Under the Managed Float

Under the Bretton Woods Accord, the dollar played a dominant role in the international financial system because it served as the official reserve currency. Under the managed float system, the dollar has continued to play an important role in the international financial system. Because of its relative stability, the dollar continues to serve as the major reserve currency.

In addition to serving as a reserve asset, the dollar is sometimes used as a medium of exchange and a unit of account in international markets. Exchanges between two currencies of small countries often take place through dollars rather than directly. For example, Peru might convert its currency to dollars and use the dollars to purchase the currency of South Africa rather than using its own currency to purchase the currency of South Africa directly. Prices of standardized contracts of raw materials and commodities are often quoted in dollars. For example, the price of oil from the Middle East is still typically quoted in dollars, and the dollar is also usually the medium of exchange through which oil is bought and sold around the world. The dollar is accepted for payments in many faraway places and has been widely used in countries experiencing political and economic unrest in the past, such as Russia, Ukraine, and Mexico.

The dollar also acts as a store of value. As you have seen, 50 to 60 percent of all U.S. currency and more than 70 percent of $100 bills are held abroad. The dollar is demanded as a store of value because of the political stability of the United States and the dollar's acceptance over time.

Although the dollar is no longer the official reserve asset, the demand for dollars to be used in international financial markets (either as reserves or for other uses) has continued to grow. Indeed, the demand for dollars has grown faster than domestic real incomes due to the increase in trade, capital flows, and real incomes around the world.

The importance of the dollar as a foreign exchange currency has fluctuated since the end of Bretton Woods, falling for two decades after 1973, increasing from 1993 to 2001, then again falling in recent years. While the British pound, Japanese yen, and Swiss franc all serve as reserve currencies, the biggest challenger to the dollar is the euro. Since its introduction in 1999, the euro's share in official foreign exchange reserves has increased from 17.9 to over 27 percent in March 2008. Over this same period, the pound's share has risen from 2.9 to 5 percent, the yen's share has fallen from 6.4 to 3 percent, and the dollar's share has fallen from 70.9 to about 63 percent.

Within this changing environment, several international organizations are developing unique roles in the international financial system. These organizations include the International Monetary Fund, the World Bank, and the Bank for International Settlements. They seek to foster stability in the international financial system so that the benefits of trade and cross-border trading of financial instruments can be realized.

Just as the financial system has evolved to deal with the growth in trade and capital flows, these organizations are redefining their roles in the increasingly globalized economy. It is to these organizations that we now turn.

Recap

Since 1973, major industrialized countries have participated in a managed float exchange rate system. The value of a currency is determined by supply and demand, but governments intervene by buying and selling (demanding and supplying) currencies to affect currency values. Small countries often tie the value of their currencies to the dollar or some other major currency. Foreign exchange forward, futures, options, and swap agreements have been developed to allow market participants to hedge exchange rate risks. Under the managed float, the dollar is still the major international reserve asset, although other currencies also serve as international reserves, and the euro has emerged as a serious competitor to the dollar. Both the euro and the dollar are demanded in international financial markets because of their perceived stability. They serve as a medium of exchange, a unit of account, and a store of value in some international markets.

MAJOR INTERNATIONAL FINANCIAL ORGANIZATIONS

As you have seen, the Bretton Woods Accord of 1944 established the fixed exchange rate system that remained in effect until the early 1970s. In addition, the meetings at Bretton Woods resulted in the creation of the International Monetary Fund (IMF) and the World Bank. Although the fixed rate exchange system has not survived, the IMF and World Bank did not meet a similar fate, as will be discussed in this chapter. Indeed, in recent years, both have gained in stature; another international organization, the Bank for International Settlements (BIS), is also discussed. The BIS predates the IMF and the World Bank and is the oldest major international financial institution in existence today.

International Monetary Fund (IMF)
An organization created in 1944 to oversee the monetary and exchange rate policies of its members, who pay quotas that are used to assist countries with temporary imbalances in their balance of payments.

World Bank
An investment bank created in 1944 that issues bonds to make long-term loans at low interest rates to poor countries for economic development projects.

The International Monetary Fund (IMF)

The purposes of the International Monetary Fund are:

to promote international monetary cooperation . . . ; to facilitate the expansion and balanced growth of international trade . . . ; to promote exchange stability . . . ; to assist in the establishment of a multilateral system of payments . . . ; to make its general resources temporarily available to its members experiencing balance of payments difficulties under adequate safeguards . . . ; and to shorten the duration and lessen the degree of disequilibrium in the international balances of payments of members.[6]

As such, the IMF is a voluntary institution owned and directed by the countries that choose to join. The IMF is much like an overseer of the monetary and exchange rate policies of its members. Member countries agree to exchange their currencies freely with other foreign currencies, to keep the IMF informed of changes in financial and monetary policies that may affect other members, and to adjust these policies based on the recommendations of the IMF for the greater common good.

When joining the IMF, each country is assessed a quota (membership fee) based on its economic importance and the amount of its international trade. A country's voting rights in the organization are proportionate to the amount of its quota. At the IMF's inception, the total quota (subscription) was $8.8 billion, of which the U.S. share was 31 percent. Thus, the United States controlled 31 percent of the votes. Quotas are revised every five years to ensure that the IMF has adequate funds at its disposal. As of February 2008, 185 countries (including all major countries of the world) were members of the IMF, and the total subscription was roughly $338 billion. The amount of the subscription has grown as more countries have joined the IMF and larger quotas have been assessed. Over the years, the U.S. share has fallen to 16.79 percent. Therefore, the United States today controls 16.79 percent of the votes. The IMF is headquartered in Washington, D.C., and has approximately 2,700 employees from more than 141 countries. Other offices are in Paris, Geneva, Switzerland, and at the United Nations in New York.

The IMF administers the pool of funds generated by the quotas to assist member countries that, because of deficits in their balance of payments, do not have enough foreign exchange to pay all of the claims that are being presented to them. Members can borrow from the pool of funds to resolve temporary imbalances. This influx of funds gives them time to change their economic policies so that balance of payment deficits are resolved in an orderly manner with minimal damages to themselves and to other countries. Members must request assistance and abide by IMF policy recommendations if receiving the funds. In addition to the pool of funds generated from the quotas, the IMF also has standby agreements to borrow supplemental funds, if needed, from the wealthiest members.

Special Drawing Rights (SDRs)

International reserve assets created by the IMF to supplement other international reserves.

In 1969, the IMF created **special drawing rights (SDRs),** which are international reserve assets that supplement other international reserves. SDRs were created in response to a shortage in international reserves. At that time, the Bretton Woods Accord was still in effect, and the dollar was the official reserve asset. The value of the SDR is a weighted average of the U.S. dollar, the euro, Japanese yen, and British pound sterling, so it fluctuates daily.

As of the end of January 2008, members held a total of 21.5 billion SDRs. Since each SDR was worth about 1.6 U.S. dollars, the outstanding dollar value of all SDR holdings was about $34 billion, representing about 1 percent of nongold international reserves of the member countries. SDRs are bookkeeping entries not backed by other reserve assets, and they provide the international financial system with additional liquidity. Central banks use SDRs, rather than other national currencies, to make payments to other member countries.

In the past, SDRs have been distributed to members of the IMF according to their quotas. Although only two distributions have been made since their inception, additional SDRs can be created and distributed if the IMF determines that there is a long-term global need for additional international reserves. The last distribution was in 1981. In September 1997, the IMF proposed an additional one-time allocation to spread the SDRs more equitably among members; such an allocation requires the approval of 85 percent of IMF voting power. Although 77.3 percent of IMF voting power did indeed approve it, the United States—which holds more than 17 percent of the power—opposed the distribution, so it has not taken place. Since the last allocation, 41 countries have joined the IMF and, hence, have never received an allocation.

The activities of the IMF can be divided into two distinct periods: the Bretton Woods era and the period since the managed float. During the Bretton Woods era, the IMF's activities centered on monitoring the fixed exchange rate system and assisting countries in maintaining it. The IMF would often make loans to countries to finance short-term deficits in their balance of payments so that the fixed exchange rates could be maintained. If long-term problems existed, the fixed exchange rates were adjusted to correct the imbalances. When making loans, the IMF often recommended that the recipient country change the domestic policies that had contributed to its balance of payments deficit. As already noted, loans were contingent on the borrower's acceptance of the IMF's recommendations.

When fixed exchange rates were abandoned in 1973, the IMF no longer had a fixed rate system to monitor, so its role changed. Now the IMF, in an advisory capacity, oversees economic policies that affect the balance of payments and exchange rates. In addition, the IMF provides information to members about countries that are experiencing balance of payments difficulties that could result in financial crises. Finally, the IMF continues to provide financial assistance to members that experience short-term balance of payments problems. As before, the financial assistance is contingent on the recipient's promise to reform its economic policies and adopt the IMF's recommendations. The IMF played a key role in resolving the international debt crisis that afflicted less-developed countries in the 1980s, the Mexican peso crisis of 1994–1995, and the Asian crisis of the late 1990s. Intervention by the IMF has also prevented many financial crises from occurring. For a discussion of the IMF's role in the Asian crisis of the late 1990s, see the accompanying "A Closer Look" feature on p. 446.

In the 2000s, the growing economic integration of the world's goods, services, and capital markets has created new opportunities and challenges for the IMF. It is taking a leading role in defining and fostering a stable international financial system.

The World Bank

Like the IMF, the World Bank was created in 1944 at Bretton Woods, is headquartered in Washington, D.C., and has 185 member countries as of 2008. The similarities stop there, however. The World Bank is an investment bank that issues bonds and uses the proceeds to make long-term, low-interest-rate loans to poor countries for economic development projects. The bonds have the highest credit rating because the World Bank's 185 member countries guarantee repayment.

The World Bank is really two organizations: the **International Bank for Reconstruction and Development (IBRD)** and the **International Development Association.** The latter makes interest-free loans with a maturity of 35 to 40 years to the world's poorest countries (in 2008 countries with a Gross National Income per capita below $1,065); about 50 percent of these loans go to African nations. The IBRD makes the bulk of its 12- to 15-year low-interest-rate loans to "middle income" countries with per capita incomes above $1,065 per year. However, as the World Bank points out, over 70 percent of the world's poor, those who live on less than $2 per day, live in these middle income countries. These countries may have private borrowing opportunities, but at much higher rates of interest. The interest rate charged is slightly above the rate the bank pays to borrow when it issues the bonds.

Many of the loans financed by the World Bank are used to build infrastructure: electric power plants, roads, and the like. The bank also finances projects to improve drinking water, waste disposal, health care, nutrition, family planning, education, and housing. In addition to loans, the bank provides technical assistance. Many countries that borrowed from the World Bank in the past have developed sufficiently and no longer need assistance. Thus, the bank can direct its aid to other poor countries.

The World Bank focuses on public projects rather than directly assisting private enterprises in developing countries. Another organization, the **International Finance Corporation,** seeks to mobilize funding for private enterprises. Although legally separate from the World Bank, the corporation is associated with it and is the organization through which the World Bank encourages small business development. The International Finance Corporation has also helped to establish stock markets in many developing countries, thus increasing the ability to attract international capital flows.

International Bank for Reconstruction and Development (IBRD)
A bank that makes 12- to 15-year loans to poor, but not the poorest, countries, charging an interest rate just above the rate at which the bank borrows.

International Development Association
An association that makes interest-free loans with a maturity of 35 to 40 years to the world's poorest countries.

International Finance Corporation
An organization that mobilizes funding for private enterprise projects in poor countries.

The Role of the IMF in the Asian Crisis

The IMF was created at the end of World War II to assist countries that were experiencing a financial crisis. The goal was to contain the crisis and prevent it from spreading to the global financial system.[a] The IMF assists countries that are experiencing a financial crisis by providing large-scale liquidity. In addition, the IMF can provide technical assistance to help policy makers find a resolution to the crisis.

The Asian crisis of 1997 arose out of a situation in which the currencies of Southeast Asia were pegged to the dollar and, thus, had appreciated along with the dollar. Given large current account deficits and relatively small supplies of international reserves, the currencies became overvalued. In addition, the countries were enjoying significant capital inflows and had large short-term loans denominated in U.S. dollars. If the currencies were devalued, more domestic currency would be required to pay back the dollar-denominated loans. The result would be many defaults and bankruptcies.

Throughout the crisis, the IMF played a significant role in helping the countries of Southeast Asia find a solution to their problems. Beginning in late 1997, the IMF recommended that the overvalued currencies be devalued. After the initial round of devaluations and the breaking of the dollar peg, the IMF called for the Asian nations to substantially increase their interest rates in an attempt to stop the continuing slide of currency values. In addition, the IMF made short-term loans to provide liquidity to the stricken economies. The goals of the rescue plans were to stabilize currency values, restore investor confidence, and reestablish the nations' access to international capital flows.

The IMF assistance did not come without strings attached. The IMF required the countries to pursue contractionary fiscal policies designed to cut consumption. The fall in consumption would lead to a decrease in imports and a reduction in the current account deficits. This policy recommendation was fairly typical for the IMF in such a situation.

In addition, the IMF required the governments to introduce structural changes into their financial systems, in particular, to improve the regulation and oversight of their banks. In the future, the countries were also to avoid becoming so dependent on short-term financing (especially from abroad) to prevent their financial systems from being so vulnerable to changes in market sentiment.

By mid-1998, some economies in Southeast Asia were on the road to recovery, although they were far from experiencing healthy growth. Without loans from the IMF, the crisis would have persisted. It is also highly likely that the countries would have defaulted on their short-term U.S. dollar loans.

Although the IMF had some success in alleviating the crisis, its policies have been criticized. Some critics complain that the rescue plans did not go far enough because they did not entail a restructuring of the short-term debt and left corporate sectors in a very fragile financial position. Without such a restructuring, the currencies continued to depreciate, and bankruptcies persisted longer than had a restructuring plan been part of the rescue package. At the other extreme, some critics argue that the crisis would have had a greater long-term, positive impact if it had been allowed to run its course without intervention from the IMF, although the short-term pain would have been greater. Still other critics argue that the crisis could have been prevented or at least mitigated if the IMF had warned the international financial community earlier about the problems of the troubled economies. [b]

Overall, the Asian crisis has caused the IMF to reconsider its role as an international financial organization, particularly as it relates to imposing structural reforms on its members and to fostering a stable international financial system.

The crisis also spawned the creation of the Financial Stability Forum to promote global financial stability.

Endnotes

a. A major rationale for intervening in financial crises was that an international financial crisis could lead to a military conflict. World leaders were painfully aware of the contribution of Germany's problems with hyperinflation in the 1920s to the rise of Hitler and subsequent world war.

b. Others believe that early warning systems may cause some crises to occur that otherwise would not.

The Bank for International Settlements (BIS)

Bank for International Settlements (BIS)
An international financial organization that promotes international cooperation among central banks and provides facilities for international financial operations.

The **Bank for International Settlements (BIS)** is an independent international financial organization, headquartered in Basel, Switzerland, that was created in 1930, which was 14 years before the Bretton Woods Accord. As such, it is the world's oldest international financial organization. The purpose of the BIS was "to promote the cooperation of central banks and to provide additional facilities for international financial operations."[7] The BIS was originally established to monitor and administer the reparations that the countries defeated in World War I were required to pay to the victorious nations. In addition, the BIS was to provide specialized services to central banks and, through them, to the international financial system.

Since 1960, the BIS has become an important international monetary organization with expanding functions. The BIS acts as a trustee for many international financial agreements and monitors compliance with the agreements. It is very active in identifying, negotiating, and monitoring international standards for banking regulation and supervision. The BIS seeks to establish international reporting standards for financial institutions and to assist countries in developing safe and sound financial practices. It encourages cooperation among member and nonmember central banks.

At the present time, 55 countries are members of the BIS, and the bank's directors come from the central banks of 13 countries (Belgium, Canada, China, France, Germany, Italy, Japan, Mexico, the Netherlands, Sweden, Switzerland, the United Kingdom, and the United States) and the European Central Bank. Central bankers from Belgium, France, Germany, Italy, the United Kingdom, and the United States are permanent members of the board of directors. A country does not have to be a member of the BIS to have an account with the bank, and central banks of 130 countries have deposit accounts with the BIS totaling around 6 percent of world foreign exchange reserves as of September 2007. The bank has 550 employees from 50 countries.

In addition to acting as a bank for central banks, the BIS is a meeting place where central bankers consult on a monthly basis. Since the early 1960s, a group of 11 nations (Belgium, Canada, France, Germany, Italy, Japan, the Netherlands, Sweden, Switzerland, the United Kingdom, and the United States), widely known as the *G-10*, has held regular monthly meetings at the bank to discuss international financial matters including financial stability. As financial markets have become more globalized, these informal meetings have taken on more importance and led to greater international cooperation. In Chapter 12, we discussed the details of the Basel Accord of 1988 that established international standards for banking regulation among the 12 nations that signed the agreement. The agreement was negotiated at the BIS.

At the present time, the BIS is expanding its relationships with central banks in emerging economies and, thus, is increasing its stature in the international financial system.

A FRAMEWORK FOR INTERNATIONAL FINANCIAL STABILITY

Financial Stability Forum (FSF)
An organization of representatives of central banks, Treasury departments, and international financial institutions created in 1999 to promote international financial stability through the exchange of information and to foster cooperation in international financial supervision and surveillance.

Leaders from Canada, Germany, France, Italy, Japan, the United Kingdom, and the United States (known as the *G-7 countries*), have met annually since 1975 to discuss common concerns, including the international financial system. Discussions before and after meetings are sometimes broadened to include leaders from other countries, including but not limited to the leaders of the G-10 countries mentioned earlier, who also meet annually. The financial crisis in Asia of the late 1990s revealed several deficiencies in the international financial system. As a result, the G-7 nations created the **Financial Stability Forum (FSF)** in early 1999 to promote international financial stability through the exchange of information and to foster cooperation in financial supervision and surveillance. The Financial Stability Forum consists of representatives of central banks, Treasury departments, and international financial institutions.

The FSF currently has 26 representatives from 12 countries, as well as 15 additional members from international organizations such as the World Bank and the IMF. Serviced by a small secretariat at the BIS in Basel, Switzerland, the FSF sponsors regularly scheduled meetings and occasionally special meetings centered on specific issues such as financial reporting and auditing.

In February 2008, the FSF's Working Group on Market and Institutional Resilience sent its recommendations to the G7 finance ministers and Central Bank governors concerning matters such as: international supervision and oversight, the originate to distribute model of asset-backed securities, the uses and role of credit ratings, market transparency, regulatory response to changes in risks, and regulatory authorities' ability to respond to crises.

The G-7 leaders agree that as a prerequisite for participating in a stable international financial system, a country must have sound economic policies that foster noninflationary growth. Emerging countries that want to take advantage of increased international capital flows need support and encouragement to develop stable financial systems and markets that are appropriately supervised both internally and externally. Developing countries must establish banking systems that encourage the appropriate amount of risk taking. The system may include deposit insurance and a lender of last resort, but it should still allow private lenders to bear the costs of their decisions as well as to reap the rewards. If lenders know that national or international regulators will bail them out in the case of failure, they are likely to engage in too much risk taking. The case in which lenders are encouraged to take too many risks because they know they will be bailed out is an example of the moral hazard problem confronting institutions.

At the same time, the financial system should be strong enough that private failures rarely spill over to the entire financial system.

In addition to establishing healthy national financial systems, countries must also standardize the reporting of qualitative and quantitative information about their financial markets, institutions, laws, and regulations. Reporting of fiscal conditions should include information about international reserves, external debt (both short and long term), and the health of the banking sector. At the same time, financial and non-financial institutions should adopt international accounting standards that allow for effective international comparisons. International standards should be developed for auditing, disclosure, bankruptcy, corporate governance, and the valuation of stocks, bonds, and other assets.

Finally, organizations such as the IMF and BIS should work with the Financial Stability Forum to see that the international financial system is more transparent and that surveillance is more open.

Recap	The IMF, the World Bank, and the BIS all have unique roles in the international financial system. The IMF promotes exchange rate stability, oversees the international financial system, and lends to member countries experiencing temporary balance of payments deficits. The World Bank promotes the economic development of the world's poorest countries by raising funds to make development loans. The BIS acts as a bank for central banks and seeks to establish and monitor international reporting and capital standards for financial institutions and to assist countries in developing safe and sound financial practices. The FSF, consisting of representatives of central banks, monetary authorities, and international financial institutions, meets regularly to exchange information and foster cooperation in financial surveillance and supervision in order to promote global financial stability.

Summary of Major Points

1. The international financial system consists of the arrangements, rules, customs, instruments, facilities, and organizations that enable international payments to be made and funds to flow across borders. The international financial system has experienced tremendous growth in recent years because of the increase in trade in goods, services, and financial instruments; technological advances; and the removal of barriers to capital flows. The system is composed of the international money and capital markets and the foreign exchange market.

2. The Bretton Woods Accord of 1944 established fixed exchange rates between the U.S. dollar and other major currencies. Under the accord, foreign countries defined their currencies in terms of the U.S. dollar and agreed to buy or sell dollars, the official reserve asset, to maintain the agreed-upon exchange rates. The dollar, in turn, was defined in terms of gold, and the United States agreed to convert any unwanted dollars of foreign central banks into gold.

3. Under fixed exchange rates, if a country other than the United States had a deficit in its balance of payments on current and capital accounts, it used supplies of dollars to purchase its own currency and maintain the exchange value. Likewise, if such a country had a surplus in its balance of payments on current and capital accounts, it demanded dollars to maintain or support the value of its currency. Persistent deficits and surpluses caused foreign countries to devalue or revalue their currencies, respectively.

4. The United States was in the unique position of being able to run persistent deficits in its balance of payments on current and capital accounts while foreign central banks were accumulating dollars to serve as international reserves. Once foreign central banks had acquired sufficient reserves, the ability of the United States to run deficits in its balance of payments on current and capital accounts was also limited. Eventually, the United States was unable to continue to convert dollars into gold, and

the Bretton Woods system of fixed exchange rates collapsed in 1973. It was replaced by a system of flexible exchange rates. During the Bretton Woods period, trade in goods, services, and financial instruments was much lower than it is today.

5. Under flexible exchange rates, the value of the dollar is determined by the demand for and supply of dollars, and the exchange rate will gravitate to the value at which quantity demanded is equal to quantity supplied. The demand for dollars is determined by foreign demand for U.S. goods, services, and financial instruments. The supply of dollars is determined by U.S. demand for foreign goods, services, and financial instruments. Ultimately, the demand for and supply of dollars are determined by domestic and foreign incomes, inflation rates, and interest rates.

6. Since 1973, the major industrialized countries have participated in a managed float exchange rate system. Under a managed float, market forces determine exchange rates, but governments may intervene by demanding or supplying currencies to affect exchange rates. Smaller countries often tie the value of their currencies to the dollar or some other major currency.

7. The dollar is very important in the international financial system because it serves as the major international reserve asset. Other currencies that serve as international reserves include the Japanese yen, the British pound, and especially the euro, which is emerging as a serious competitor to the dollar. In addition, dollars are demanded in international financial markets to serve as a medium of exchange, a unit of account, and a store of value. Even though the dollar is no longer the official reserve currency, the international demand for dollars has increased because of the growth of trade in goods, services, and capital flows.

8. Foreign exchange forward, futures, options, and swap markets are used by market participants to hedge exchange rate risk. They effectively allow those who will need or will receive foreign exchange in the future to lock in an exchange rate today.

9. The IMF is an international organization owned and operated by its 185 member countries. It promotes exchange rate stability, oversees the international financial system, and lends to member countries experiencing temporary balance of payments deficits. In addition to quotas from its members, the IMF has lines of credit from the major industrial countries to lend, if needed, to member countries with balance of payments difficulties. SDRs are an international reserve asset created by the IMF to supplement the supply of international reserves.

10. The World Bank promotes the economic development of the world's poorest countries by raising funds to make development loans. A total of 185 countries belong to the World Bank. Whereas the World Bank funds public projects, the International Finance Corporation seeks to encourage private enterprise and development. The corporation is separate from the World Bank but works closely with it.

11. The BIS acts as a bank for central banks and seeks to establish and monitor international reporting and capital standards for financial institutions and to assist countries in developing safe and sound financial practices. The Financial Stability Forum, created after the Asian financial crisis, consists of representatives from central banks, Treasury departments, and international financial institutions. It meets regularly to establish and maintain a framework for international financial stability.

Key Terms

Bank for International
   Settlements (BIS), p. 447
Bretton Woods Accord,
   p. 433
Devalue, p. 434
Financial Stability Forum
   (FSF), p. 448

Fixed Exchange Rate System,
   p. 433
Floating (Flexible) Exchange
   Rate System, p. 437
International Bank for
   Reconstruction and
   Development (IBRD), p. 445

International Development
   Association, p. 445
International Finance
   Corporation, p. 445
International Financial System,
   p. 432

Review Questions

1. What is the international financial system, and how has it changed in recent years? What opportunities does the new system offer? What are the challenges?

2. Identify and explain three differences between the international monetary system under the Bretton Woods Accord and the managed float exchange rate system that replaced it.

3. Why did the Bretton Woods Accord break down?

4. What was the role of the dollar under the Bretton Woods Accord?

5. Why has the demand for dollars in international financial markets continued to grow, even though the dollar is no longer the official reserve currency?

6. When a country ran a deficit in its balance of payments under the Bretton Woods Accord, how was that deficit resolved?

7. Leticia is a small country that is experiencing a deficit in its balance of payments. The value of Leticia's currency is tied to the U.S. dollar, which has been appreciating. What options could the IMF recommend to correct the imbalance in Leticia's balance of payments?

8. Under flexible exchange rates, what happens if a country experiences a deficit in its balance of payments? How long can a deficit in the balance of payments persist?

9. Why and how do central banks intervene in foreign exchange markets under the managed float exchange rate system?

10. How do the roles of the IMF and the BIS differ? How are they similar? What is the primary function of the World Bank?

11. What is the difference between the types of projects financed by the World Bank and those funded by the International Finance Corporation?

12. What factors have contributed to the increase in capital flows among countries?

13. What is the contagion effect? Why is it more pronounced today than it was 30 years ago?

14. What were the causes of the Asian crisis? What did the IMF do to mitigate the Asian crisis?

15. Explain how foreign exchange futures contracts can be used to reduce exchange rate risk. Is there exchange rate risk under both fixed and flexible exchange rate systems? Explain.

16. Use Exhibit 18-1 to define *pegged exchange rates*, *currency board*, and *exchange agreements with no separate legal tender*. How many countries have currency boards?

17. What is the Financial Stability Forum? Why was it created?

Analytical Questions

Questions marked with a check mark (✓) are objective in nature. They can be completed with a short answer or number.

✓19. Suppose the United States has capital inflows of $100 billion and capital outflows of $200 billion. What is the balance on the capital account?

✓20. Go online and find today's yen/dollar exchange rate. Has the dollar appreciated or depreciated since March 5, 2008, when $1 equaled 104.03 yen?

✓21. Graphically demonstrate what would happen to the exchange rate in each of the following situations:

a. The U.S. trade deficit increases, ceteris paribus.

b. The U.S. trade deficit decreases, ceteris paribus.

c. Capital outflows increase, ceteris paribus.

d. Capital inflows increase, ceteris paribus.

Suggested Readings

Visit the sites of the World Bank, the International Monetary Fund, and the Bank for International Settlements at **http://www.worldbank.org**, **http://www.imf.org**, and **http://www.bis.org/index.htm**.

More information about the Financial Stability Forum can be found at **http://www.fsforum.org/home/home .html**.

Stanley Fischer, who served as deputy director of the IMF during the Asian crisis, gives an insightful look at many of the issues discussed in this chapter in *IMF: Essays from a Time of Crisis—The International Financial System, Stabilization, and Development* (Cambridge, MA: MIT Press, 2004).

For a book that looks at the somewhat controversial history of the Bank for International Settlements, see James C. Baker, *The Bank for International Settlements: Evolution and Evaluation* (Westport, CT: Quorum Books, 2002).

For a comprehensive and detailed look at some issues pertaining to global policy making, see Claudio Borio and William R. White, "Whither Monetary and Financial Stability: The Implications of Evolving Policy Regimes," *Monetary Policy and Uncertainty: Adapting to a Changing Economy*, BIS Working Paper, No. 147, Federal Reserve Bank of Kansas City (February 2004): 131–211. The paper is also available online at **http://ssrn.com/abstract=901387**.

"Identifying the Role of Moral Hazard in International Financial Markets" is the subject of a paper by the same name by Steven B. Kamin, International Finance Discussion Papers, Board of Governors of the Federal Reserve, 2002–736 (September 2002). It is available online at **http:// www.federalreserve.gov/pubs/ifdp/2002/736/default .htm**.

An article that looks at the role of the U.S. dollar in the global financial system is Stephan Schulmeister's "Globalization Without Global Money: The Double Role of the Dollar as National Currency and World Currency," *Journal of Post Keynesian Economics 22*, no. 3 (Spring 2000): 365–396.

For a discussion of "The IMF and Global Financial Crises" see Joseph Joyce's article by the same name in *Challenge* 43, no. 4 (July–August 2000): 88–107. For another interesting article, also in *Challenge*, see Jane D'Arista's "Reforming International Financial Architecture," 43, no. 3 (May–June 2000): 44–82.

For a blending of theory and application to the changing international financial system, see Hans Visser, *A Guide to International Monetary Economics*, 2nd ed. (Northampton, MA: Edward Elgar, 2000).

For an in-depth look at the Asian crisis, see Uri Dadush, Dipak Dasgupta, and Marc Uzan, eds., *Private Capital Flows in the Age of Globalization: The Aftermath of the Asian Crisis* (Northampton, MA: Edward Elgar, 2000).

For a pessimistic view about the global financial system, see James L. Clayton, *The Global Debt Bomb* (Armonk, NY: M.E. Sharpe, 1999).

For a comprehensive article on the IMF, see Jane Sneddon Little and Giovanni P. Olivei, "Rethinking the International Monetary System: An Overview," *New England Economic Review*, Federal Reserve Bank of Boston (November 1999): 3–24.

Endnotes

1. Remarks by Alan Greenspan before the 34th Annual Conference on Bank Structure and Competition at the Federal Reserve Bank of Chicago, May 7, 1998.
2. In this chapter, when we refer to *dollar* or *dollars*, we also mean *dollar-denominated deposits*.
3. Recall from Chapter 16 that the *current account* measures transactions that involve currently produced goods and services (exports and imports) and net transfer payments. The *capital account* measures the financial flows of funds and securities among countries.
4. We hope you recall that the spot exchange rate is the exchange rate of foreign currency for immediate delivery.
5. *Annual Report of the Executive Board for the Financial Year Ended April 30, 2004* (Washington, DC: International Monetary Fund): 102.
6. See the home page of the IMF at **http://www.imf.org**.
7. From article 3 of the original statute creating the Bank for International Settlements.

PART 5

Monetary Theory

19

The Fed, Depository Institutions, and the Money Supply Process

How do you make a million? You start with $900,000.

—Stephen Lewis to Morton Shulman

Learning Objectives

After reading this chapter, you should know:

How the Fed can affect the supply of reserves in the banking system

How changes in the supply of reserves or reserve requirements affect the ability of depository institutions to expand loans and deposits

What the monetary base is

What the money multiplier is and its historical context

What affects the Fed's ability to control the money supply and credit

WHERE MONEY COMES FROM

Suppose that during one month, say, April, the Fed conducts a large open market operation; it sells government securities through its trading desk at the New York Fed. About a month later, in conjunction with its regular weekly release of pertinent financial data (usually on a Thursday afternoon), the Fed reports that the money stock fell during the month of May. The purpose of this chapter is to help you understand the relationship between these two events: the open market sale and the subsequent fall in the money stock.

Much of the groundwork for this chapter has already been laid. In Chapter 2 we examined the definition, measurement, and role of money in the economy; in Chapter 3, we introduced the Federal Reserve and the tools it uses in conducting the nation's monetary policy; and in Chapters 8 through 12, we examined various aspects of the behavior of financial intermediaries, with particular focus on depository institutions.

As you have seen, depository institutions include banks, savings and loan associations, credit unions, and mutual savings banks. They issue checkable deposits and hold reserve assets equal to a fraction of deposit liabilities. Taken together, depository institutions make up the banking system.

This chapter focuses on the ways in which the operations of the Fed affect the banking system and the ways that depository institutions, in turn, influence the supply of money and credit in the economy.

THE FED AND BANK RESERVES
Open Market Operations

Open Market Operations
The buying and selling of government securities by the Fed.

Open market operations refer to the buying and selling of government securities by the Fed. When the Fed engages in open market operations, a link is created between the Fed's actions and the nation's money supply. Open market operations affect the supply of reserves available to depository institutions. The volume of reserves has a direct effect on the banking system's ability to extend loans and thereby expand checkable deposits and the supply of money. In addition, open market operations have an impact on the liquidity of the financial system, and more broadly, they affect the supply of credit in the economy. Look at Exhibit 19-1 to make sure you are clear about these steps.

The New York Federal Reserve Bank buys or sells U.S. government securities on behalf of the Fed and under the guidance and direction of the Federal Open Market Committee (FOMC). Such day-to-day transactions are an extremely important monetary policy tool. In general, open market operations initially influence the financial system in two ways. First, they affect the amount of reserves in the banking system.[1]

19-1
The Money Supply Process

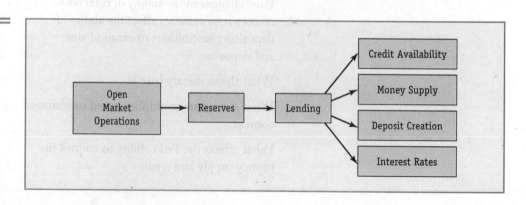

Second, they affect the level of interest rates, particularly short-term interest rates, such as the federal funds rate and Treasury bill rates. We use the word *affect* because, as you shall see, changes in other factors can have an impact on both reserves and interest rates. For now, we are going to focus on the effect of open market operations on reserves. There are two rules to remember:

1. When the Fed buys securities, reserves of depository institutions rise.
2. When the Fed sells securities, reserves of depository institutions fall.[2]

For example, suppose that the Fed wants to add $1,000 to the supply of reserves in the banking system. The trading desk at the New York Fed, which is run by the manager of the Fed's portfolio of securities, will buy $1,000 of, say, Treasury bills (or Treasury bonds) from a group of dealers (market makers) with whom it does business regularly. The Fed pays for these securities by issuing checks to the sellers, whom we shall treat as part of the public at large. The sellers, in turn, deposit their checks in, say, HLT National Bank. These checks are then cleared through the Fed's check-processing network (see Exhibit 3-4 to refresh your memory about this process). In this case, HLT sends the checks or, as we saw in Chapter 3, electronic images of the checks to the Federal Reserve Bank in its district. The Fed then credits HLT's deposit balance at the Fed, which is a component of HLT's reserves. (Remember that reserves can be held in two forms—vault cash and deposits at the Fed.)

After the open market purchase, the Fed has $1,000 more in securities, and the dealers, who are the public, have $1,000 less in securities. In return for selling the securities to the Fed, the public gets checks worth $1,000 from the Fed, which for now we assume are deposited in HLT National. The deposits are an asset to the public and a liability to the bank. After HLT sends the check or electronic image of the check to the Fed for collection, the bank's deposit balance at the Fed—a component of its reserves—is credited with $1,000. In this case, reserves, deposits, and the money supply have all risen simultaneously by $1,000.

To generalize, when the Fed buys Treasury bills from the public, it pays with checks drawn on itself. In effect, the Fed "creates" the funds out of thin air! Using the power granted by Congress, the Fed pays for the securities with a stroke of its pen. The public exchanges these checks for deposits at depository institutions, which send the checks to the Fed for collection. The Fed, in turn, credits the reserve accounts of the depository institutions. For the depository institutions, both reserve assets and deposit liabilities have increased. Thus, through its purchase of securities, the Fed has augmented the supply of bank reserves. The rise in reserves enables HLT and other depository institutions to expand their lending, thereby increasing the supply of money and credit in the economy.

T-accounts are simplified balance sheets used to focus on changes in assets and corresponding changes in liabilities.[3] Exhibit 19-2 shows T-accounts for the Fed, the public, and HLT National. It traces the transactions and changes that occur as a result of the Fed's open market purchase. The Fed has experienced an equal change in assets and liabilities. See if you can work through an open market sale of securities by the Fed and the fall in reserves that results.[4]

As discussed in Chapter 3, the Fed controls the amount of required reserve assets that depository institutions must hold. Because of this, it also operates a lending facility called the *discount window* through which depository institutions caught short of reserves can borrow.

Like open market operations, changes in discount loans affect the volume of reserves in the banking system. When the Fed makes a discount loan to a depository institution, reserve assets increase by the full amount of the loan. When a discount loan is

FED		PUBLIC		HLT NATIONAL BANK	
Assets	Liabilities	Assets	Liabilities	Assets	Liabilities
(1) +$1,000 securities purchased from the public	(3) +$1,000 deposit due HLT	(1) −$1,000 securities sold to the Fed (2) +$1,000 deposits in the form of checks received from Fed and deposited in HLT		(3) +$1,000 reserves in the form of deposits at the Fed	(2) +$1,000 deposits by the public

extended, the effect on reserves is the same as an open market purchase. Likewise, when a discount loan is paid off and borrowing from the Fed is reduced, the effect on reserves is the same as an open market sale. Although the Fed has complete control over the volume of open market operations, it cannot totally control the amount of borrowing from the discount window, which must be initiated by depository institutions. Changes in recent years have discouraged discount lending, except in cases where the solvency of an institution is threatened. The Fed can thus use the discount window to fulfill its function as a lender of last resort while at the same time deemphasizing the use of the discount window for day-to-day borrowing to meet reserve requirements.

Other Factors That Change Reserves

Before moving on, we need to elaborate on two points. First, factors other than open market operations and discount loans can affect reserves. Second, the Fed can and does respond to changes in reserves caused by these other factors with offsetting open market operations. That is, if another factor causes an unexpected increase in reserves, the Fed can use an open market sale to decrease reserves. Likewise, if an unexpected decrease in reserves occurs, the Fed can use an open market purchase to increase reserves.

To clarify, let us consider an example of how one of the many factors affects the volume of reserves in the banking system and what the Fed can do about the effects. The federal government keeps most of its transactions balances in "tax and loan accounts" at various commercial banks throughout the country. Shortly before the federal government wants to make a payment, funds are transferred from the commercial banks to the government's account at the Fed. (Remember from Chapter 3 that the Fed is the fiscal agent for the U.S. government.) A check is then written by the government on the account at the Fed. Initially, reserves of commercial banks fall and the government's transactions account at the Fed increase. When the government actually spends the funds, reserves at commercial banks will again rise, as checks drawn on the government's account at the Fed are deposited into commercial banks. The net result of this series of transactions is that deposits and reserves in the banking system are lower than they otherwise would be during the period when the government's deposits are removed from the commercial banks and before they are redeposited by the recipients of government checks.

Now suppose the Fed, given its current policy stance, does not want reserves and deposits to decrease. What can it do? The answer is that it can buy securities to offset the impact of the decline in reserves on the banking system. Likewise, if some other

Offsetting Open Market Operations
Open market purchases or sales to offset changes in the monetary base caused by other factors.

factor unexpectedly causes reserves to increase, the Fed can use an open market sale to offset the impact on the banking system.

In general, these offsetting open market purchases and sales are designed to counter movements in the reserves of depository institutions caused by other factors to maintain existing reserve conditions in the banking system. The Fed does not change its policy stance every day, but other factors that affect reserves are always changing; as a result, the Fed conducts large amounts of day-to-day offsetting open market purchases and sales. In sum, even though a variety of factors including discount loans can affect the volume of reserves in the banking system, the Fed's powerful tool—open market operations—enables it to offset the impact of these other factors and thus greatly influence the reserves of depository institutions. The first appendix to this chapter looks in some detail at the other factors that influence reserves.

The rules we laid out at the beginning of this section should now be much clearer. Understand that in examining the first link in Exhibit 19-1, we have traced the transactions in slow motion. In practice, most of the transactions are conducted electronically and occur quickly. Regardless of timing, however, the essential point is that through its open market operations, the Fed can inject or remove reserves from the banking system.

LOAN AND DEPOSIT EXPANSION BY THE BANKING SYSTEM

Now we want to examine the second linkage in Exhibit 19-1. More specifically, we want to see how changes in reserves affect the volume of deposits and loans in the banking system. To simplify, we employ a balance sheet (and T-account) for a bank in our hypothetical banking system.[5]

Prototype Balance Sheet for a Bank

Assets	Liabilities
Reserves	Checkable deposits
Loans	

On the assets side are reserves and loans. For simplicity, we ignore other assets. On the liabilities side, we shall assume that there are only checkable deposits, the major component of the nation's money supply. We are ignoring other deposit and nondeposit liabilities and net worth. Thus, we are focusing only on changes in assets and liabilities resulting from the various transactions we discuss.

Look at Exhibit 19-3, which begins where Exhibit 19-2 left off. HLT begins with the $1,000 of new **total reserves** and $1,000 of new deposit liabilities, which resulted from the open market purchase described in the previous section. Where do we go from here? HLT is not in business to hold idle funds as reserves; it uses funds deposited with it to acquire assets that earn interest income. If the Fed insists that HLT hold **required reserves** equal to 10 percent of its checkable deposit liabilities, the remaining 90 percent of reserves are **excess reserves**. In this example, required reserves are $100 (10% × $1,000) and excess reserves (total reserves minus required reserves) are $900 ($1,000 − $100).

Given their desire for profits, we assume that HLT and other depository institutions in our system will not wish to hold any excess reserves and will, therefore, use such funds to acquire assets. In our simple model, loans are the only assets that are acquired. Assuming that new loan customers are readily available, we are ready to consider the first stage of what will be a multistage process of loan and deposit expansion.

Total Reserves
Required reserves plus excess reserves.

Required Reserves
The amount of reserve assets that the Fed requires a depository institution to hold.

Excess Reserves
Reserves over and above those required by the Fed.

HLT National Bank			
Assets		**Liabilities**	
Total reserves	$1,000	Checkable deposits	$1,000
Loan	900	New checkable deposits	900
Total assets	$1,900	Total checkable deposits	$1,900

Beginning where Exhibit 19-2 left off, HLT has just seen both its total reserve assets and its checkable deposits increase by $1,000. Assuming the bank was loaned up to begin with, this represents an increase of $100 in required reserves and $900 in excess reserves. The bank can safely lend out its excess reserves. When a loan is made, the proceeds are disbursed by creating a checkable deposit. The bank's assets increase by the amount of the loan.

It just so happens that an old friend, J.P. Young, needs $900 to purchase a new audio system. Given the excess reserves it has on hand, HLT agrees to lend J.P. $900. He signs a loan contract, which HLT puts in its vault, and HLT credits $900 to J.P.'s deposit balance. The loan contract is an asset, and the deposit balance is a liability. Exhibit 19-3 also shows the T-account entries for HLT after this transaction.

Combining this stage with the initial situation, HLT's balance sheet shows a $900 rise in assets—the $900 loan is added to the original $1,000 in reserves. On the liability side, there is also a $900 increase—the new $900 deposit in J.P.'s account is added to the original $1,000 deposit. Because deposits increase when the $900 loan is made, $900 of money has been "created."

Remember, however, that J.P. did not borrow the money to keep in his account. J.P. writes a check for $900 to pay I.M. Loud, Inc., for the audio equipment. We will assume that I.M. Loud, Inc., does its banking at Second National Bank. Accordingly, I.M. Loud deposits the check received from J.P. in its deposit account at Second National. Second National credits I.M.'s account, and when the check is cleared, the Fed will debit (decrease) HLT's deposit account at the Fed by $900 and credit (add to) Second National's deposit account at the Fed by the same amount. HLT will, in turn, debit J.P.'s account for $900 for the check written to I.M. This series of transactions is shown in Exhibit 19-4.

So what is the net effect of those transactions on the supply of money and credit in the economy? When J.P. writes a check for $900 against his account at HLT, this reduces HLT's deposit liabilities and reserve assets by $900. (The $900 in reserve assets is credited to I.M. Loud's bank, Second National.) If we sum up the charges on HLT's

HLT National Bank				Second National Bank			
Assets		**Liabilities**		**Assets**		**Liabilities**	
Total reserves	$100	Checkable deposits	$1,000	Total reserves	$900	Checkable deposits	$900
Loan	900						
Total	$1,000		$1,000		$900		$900

Loaned Up
Situation when a bank has no excess reserves left to serve as a basis for lending.

balance sheet (bottom row), we see that the initial $1,000 deposit inflow is balanced by a $100 rise in reserves and a $900 rise in loans. HLT is now fully loaned up, which means that it has no excess reserves left to serve as a basis for lending. The entire $100 of reserves it holds is considered *required reserves*. HLT responded to the initial deposit inflow by expanding its loans and deposits by 90 percent of the inflow. Thus, HLT, and indeed any individual depository institution, can make additional loans and thereby "create" deposits equal to its excess reserves.

The process has not ended, however. Take a close look at Second National's balance sheet. It is clearly not loaned up. It has $810 of excess reserves. Just as HLT did, Second National will react to the deposit inflow ($900) by setting aside enough to meet the Fed's reserve requirement and lending out the rest. In this case, given our assumption of a 10 percent reserve requirement, it will keep $90 as required reserves and will have $810 of excess reserves. The excess reserves will serve as the basis of lending to, say, Jane Collins, who happens to need exactly $810 to pay her fees at State University. Jane gives a check to the university, which then deposits it in Third National Bank, as depicted in Exhibit 19-5. As was the case before, the clearing of the check results in the Fed's crediting Third National's account at the Fed by the same amount. Second National will, in turn, debit Jane's account by the same $810, leaving it fully loaned up with the original gain of $900 in deposits on the liability side of its balance sheet and a rise of $90 in required reserves and $810 in loans on the asset side of its balance sheet. (Again, $810 in total reserve assets has been credited to Third National, State University's bank, because Jane's check is written to State.) You should now be able to describe what will happen in the next stage.

We have shown that each individual bank was able to increase its earning assets by the amount of the excess reserves that resulted from a deposit inflow. Why, then, can't an individual bank (or other depository institution for that matter) expand deposits by more than its excess reserves (90 percent of the inflow)? In general, a bank cannot assume that new deposits created in conjunction with loans will be spent and redeposited in its coffers.

19-5
Transactions of Second National Bank and Third National Bank

Second National Bank

Assets		Liabilities	
Total reserves	$900	Checkable deposits	$ 900
Loans	810	Checkable deposits	810
Total	$1,710		$1,710

The proceeds of the loan from Second National are spent and deposited in the university's account at Third National. Second National loses $810 in reserve assets, and the $810 deposit of the loan proceeds is extinguished. The resulting balance sheets of Second National and Third National are as follows:

	Second National Bank				Third National Bank		
Assets		Liabilities		Assets		Liabilities	
Total reserves	$90	Checkable deposits	$900	Total reserves	$810	Checkable deposits	$810
Loans	810						
Total	$900		$900		$810		$810

Rather, it should expect to lose reserves equal to the loans extended and deposits created. If it loaned out, say, $1,000 (100 percent of the inflow) and subsequently lost $1,000 of reserves, it would find itself with the original $1,000 inflow of deposits on the liability side. If you think this is okay, you've forgotten one important factor—the Fed's reserve requirements. All depository institutions must have $100 of required reserves for each $1,000 of checkable deposits. To ensure that it meets the requirement, an individual institution will normally limit lending and deposit creation to its excess reserves.

As the loans of one depository institution increase, however, the use of the loan proceeds by the borrower leads to a deposit inflow at another institution. A deposit inflow increases total deposit liabilities and reserve assets. The depository institution will adjust to the inflow of reserves and deposits by expanding its loans and "creating" additional deposits. Subsequently, the individual institution will lose reserve assets and the additional deposit liabilities as the borrower uses the loan proceeds to pay for a purchase. However, one institution's loss is another's gain. Note that as this process occurs, the total volume of reserves in the banking system does not change. Instead, at each stage deposits rise and the composition of total reserves in the banking system changes: required reserves rise and excess reserves fall.

The size of these changes can be stated precisely. As deposits flow through the banking system, the change in deposits at each depository institution can be represented as the change in required reserves plus the change in excess reserves. The change in required reserves is equal to 10 percent of the deposit inflow, and the change in excess reserve assets is equal to 90 percent of the deposit inflow. Hence, the change in loans and deposits created by each depository institution is equal to 90 percent of the inflow to that institution. In our example, the $1,000 increase in deposits at HLT is followed by a $900 increase in deposits at Second National, which is followed by an $810 increase in deposits at Third National. Taken together, that is, adding up the changes in all the individual balance sheets, the increase in total deposits in the banking system at each stage as loans are extended is 90 percent of the new deposits created at the previous stage. This means that, ultimately, the new deposits created at subsequent stages approach zero, and the process ends.[6]

Perhaps the most important aspect of the process to keep in mind is that the total expansion of loans and deposits ($1,000 + $900 + $810 + . . .) is much greater than the initial injection of reserves into the banking system. In fact, the expansion of loans and deposits turns out to be a multiple of the initial injection of reserves. Some simple algebra presented in the next section will help confirm this point.

Recap   Open market purchases increase the supply of reserves, while open market sales decrease the supply of reserves. Changes in other factors can also affect reserves. Depository institutions lend out excess reserves and, in the process, create money. Any one institution can safely lend only its excess reserves. When the proceeds of a loan are spent, however, deposits and reserves flow into another depository institution, which responds by expanding loans and creating additional deposits. Deposits and the money supply expand by a multiple of the injection of reserves.

THE SIMPLE MULTIPLIER MODEL OF THE MONEY SUPPLY PROCESS

In our simple example, the process of creating money and credit from increases in reserves will end when all reserves in the banking system become required reserves—that is, when the banking system is fully loaded up. This situation is reached gradually as individual depository institutions create deposit liabilities and at the same time increase assets (loans in this case) in response to deposit inflows. When no excess reserves are left in the banking system, new loans cannot be made and new deposit creation ceases. The net result of the actions taken by individual depository institutions for the banking system and the economy as a whole can be illustrated with the aid of a simple model.

Required Reserve Ratio (r_D)
The fraction of deposits that depository institutions are required to hold as required reserves.

Required reserve assets, RR, are, by definition, equal to the **required reserve ratio**, r_D, multiplied by the amount of deposit liabilities, D:

$$(19\text{-}1) \qquad RR = r_D \times D$$

Excess reserves, ER, are, by definition, equal to total reserves, TR, minus required reserves, RR.

$$(19\text{-}2) \qquad ER = TR - RR$$

If total reserves equal required reserves, there are no excess reserves to serve as the basis of lending. In this case, when the banking system is fully loaned up (when ER equals zero),

$$(19\text{-}3) \qquad TR = RR = r_D \times D$$

Rearranging terms yields

$$D = TR / r_D$$
$$\text{or}$$
$$(19\text{-}4) \qquad D = 1 / r_D \times TR$$

Simple Money Multiplier
The reciprocal of the required reserve ratio, $1/r_D$.

Total deposits are equal to the quantity of reserves multiplied by the reciprocal of the required reserve ratio. We shall refer to $1/r_D$ as the **simple money multiplier**.

For any change in reserves, TR, the change in deposits, D, is equal to the change in the multiplier multiplied by the change in reserves. Assuming excess reserves equal zero, we can rewrite Equation (19-4) as

$$(19\text{-}5) \qquad \Delta D = 1/r_D \times \Delta TR$$

Because we assumed that r_D was fixed at 10 percent (.1) in our example, the simple money multiplier is 1/.1, which is equal to 10. Therefore, the increase in deposits resulting from the $1,000 increase in reserves will be $10,000, assuming depository institutions hold no excess reserves. Although in our example reserves increased by $1,000, make sure you understand that the simple money multiplier works in both directions. If reserves decrease by $1,000, assuming depository institutions hold no excess reserves, there would be a corresponding decrease in deposits of $10,000.

Fractional Reserve Banking System
A banking system in which individual banks hold reserve assets equal to a fraction of deposit liabilities.

The simple multiplier process is a reflection of what is called the **fractional reserve banking system**. A depository institution must hold reserve assets equal to some fraction of deposit liabilities. The fraction it must hold is determined by the reserve requirements set by the Fed. If the reserve requirement is 100 percent, any increase in deposits would result in an identical dollar-for-dollar increase in required reserves. In this case, the simple money multiplier would equal 1. If the reserve requirement is less than 1, however, a given dollar increase in deposits will result in the need to hold required reserves equal to only some fraction of the increase in deposits. The remaining fraction of reserve assets is excess reserves and can serve as the basis of lending, which becomes new deposits as described before. In this latter case, the total change in deposits is greater than the amount of required reserves, and therefore, the multiplier is greater than 1. In general, the change in deposits and credit, which accompanies a given change in reserves, will be inversely related to reserve requirements. That is, for a given change

19-6

The Required Reserve Ratio and the Simple Money Multiplier

r_D	Simple Money Multiplier $(1/r_D)$
.05	$1/.05 = 20$
.10	$1/.10 = 10$
.20	$1/.20 = 5$
.25	$1/.25 = 4$
.50	$1/.50 = 2$

in reserves, the smaller the required reserve ratio is, the larger the change in deposits and credit will be. Exhibit 19-6 shows various combinations of required reserve ratios and the resulting simple money multiplier.

The whole process can be viewed as an inverted pyramid (∇). The original injection by the Fed leads to increased reserve assets and deposit liabilities and provides individual depository institutions with excess reserves. They adjust to this abundance of reserves by expanding loans and deposits. The deposits, when spent by loan recipients, flow to other depository institutions (higher up on the pyramid), which, in turn, expand loans and deposits. The process continues because profit-maximizing institutions are, in general, not interested in holding non-interest-earning excess reserves. As a result, the original injection of reserves—the foundation of the inverted pyramid—can support a multiple expansion in loans and deposits, as in Exhibit 19-7. The whole process is not

19-7

An Inverted Pyramid Representing the Money Supply and the Monetary Base

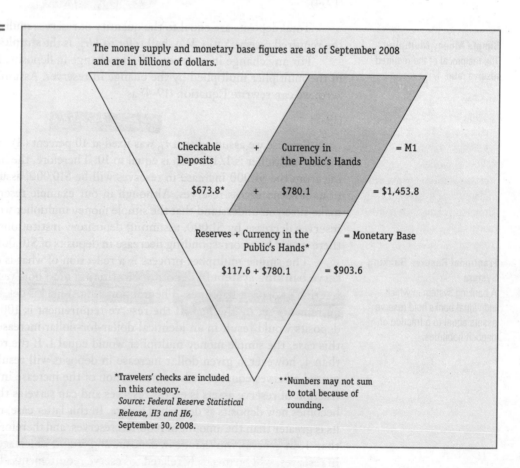

The money supply and monetary base figures are as of September 2008 and are in billions of dollars.

Checkable Deposits $+$ Currency in the Public's Hands $= M1$

$\$673.8*$ $+$ $\$780.1$ $= \$1,453.8$

Reserves $+$ Currency in the Public's Hands* $=$ Monetary Base

$\$117.6 + \$780.1$ $= \$903.6$

*Travelers' checks are included in this category.
Source: Federal Reserve Statistical Release, H3 and H6, September 30, 2008.

**Numbers may not sum to total because of rounding.

19-8

The Multiple Expansion of Deposits and Loans in the Banking System with an Initial Increase in Reserves of $1,000 and a Multiplier of 10

	Total Deposits	Required Reserves	Excess Reserves	Total Reserves	Loans	Total Assets RR+ER+Loans TR+Loans
Initial reserves provided	$1,000	$100	$900	$1,000	—	$1,000
Expansion						
Stage 1	$1,900	$190	$810	$1,000	$ 900	$1,900
Stage 2	2,710	271	729	1,000	1,710	2,710
Stage 3	3,440	344	656	1,000	2,439	3,439
Stage 4	4,100	410	590	1,000	3,095	4,100
Stage 5	4,690	469	531	1,000	3,690	4,690
Stage 6	5,220	522	478	1,000	4,221	5,200
Stage 7	5,700	570	430	1,000	4,680	5,700
Stage 8	6,130	613	387	1,000	5,130	6,130
Stage 9	6,510	651	349	1,000	5,517	6,510
Stage 10	6,860	686	314	1,000	5,859	6,860
.	.	.	.	.	.	.
.	.	.	.	.	.	.
.	.	.	.	.	.	.
Stage 20	8,900	890	110	1,000	7,902	8,900
Final	$10,000	$1,000	$0	$1,000	$9,000	$10,000

Source: Adopted from *Modern Money Mechanics* (Chicago: Federal Reserve Bank of Chicago, 1992).

Through a multistage, multiple expansion process, deposits grow to a total of 10 times the new reserves supplied to the banking system by the Fed through the open market purchase. The initial injection of reserves results in HLT National Bank and the banking system as a whole having an additional $1,000 of reserves, of which $100 represents required reserves and $900 represent excess reserves. In Stage 1, HLT makes a $900 loan and in the process expands deposits by a like amount. As a result, deposits in the banking system have now risen by $1,900—the initial $1,000 plus the $900. The deposits (proceeds of the loan) are spent and flow to another bank (Second National). The $900 inflow of deposits and reserves increases Second National's excess reserves by $810 and its required reserves by $90. For the banking system as a whole, the change in total reserves remains $1,000, but required reserves are now $190—the $100 held by HLT plus the $90 held by Second National—and excess reserves are $810 (remember that HLT lost its $900 of excess reserves when it made a loan). In Stage 2, Second National makes a loan for $810, raising the total expansion of loans in the system to $1,710 ($900 + $810) and the total expansion of deposits to $2,710 ($1,000 + $900 + $810). The process continues at each stage until excess reserves equal zero and required reserves equal the amount of initial reserves supplied.

---

unlike a family tree. A husband and wife have children, who in turn have children, and so forth.

Exhibit 19-8 shows in tabular form the expansion of loans, deposits, and reserves for our example in which the injection of reserves is $1,000, the required reserve ratio is .1, and the multiplier is 10. Note that at each stage, excess reserves decline and required reserves increase. At the final stage, excess reserves have fallen to zero, and required reserves are equal to the initial reserves supplied. At each stage, deposits expand by 90 percent of the deposit expansion at the previous stage. This process occurs because when the proceeds of a loan are spent and redeposited in another depository institution, required reserve assets equal to 10 percent of the new deposits must be held and 90 percent can serve as the basis of lending.[7] Again, the cumulative process continues until there are no excess reserves left to serve as the basis of lending—a point attained in our example when the total expansion of deposits has reached $10,000.

Recap $ER = TR - RR$. If depository institutions are loaned up ($ER = 0$), then $TR = RR = r_D \times D$. The simple money multiplier is $1/r_D$ because $\Delta D = 1/r_D \times \Delta TR$. Fractional reserve banking results in an expansion of deposits equal to a multiple of the increase in reserves. If depository institutions lose reserves, deposits fall by a multiple of the loss.

SOME COMPLICATING REALITIES IN THE MULTIPLIER MODEL

In the above model, we assumed that depository institutions never hold any excess reserves. When deposits flow in and reserve assets increase, depository institutions continue to lend by creating new deposit liabilities until excess reserves equal zero. In fact, depository institutions do hold excess reserves, and the amount fluctuates over time. The excess reserves are a leakage from the flow of increases in deposits and credit extension. The effect of this leakage is similar to the effect of an increase in reserve requirements. The amount of loans and deposits created at each stage will be reduced by the volume of excess reserves held. The net effect will be to lower the simple money multiplier.

Second, we have ignored currency. If the stereo dealer (I.M. Loud) in our example exchanges J.P.'s $900 check for a $675 deposit at Second National and $225 of currency from the vault at Second National, the net change in the reserves of Second National is less than J.P.'s check. Second National has an increase in its reserve account at the Fed of $900, a reduction in vault cash of $225, and a net change in reserves of $675.[8] In other words, the stereo dealer exchanges the $900 check for a deposit equal to three-fourths of the amount of the check and currency equal to one-fourth of the amount. This reduces the flow of reserves and deposits from Second National to subsequent depository institutions by 25 percent and, hence, reduces the overall expansion of the money supply.[9]

Modifying the Multiplier Model

As a result of these implications, the actual multiplier is not as simple as the one presented in Equation (19-4). We can develop a somewhat more realistic multiplier model by taking into account the factors already mentioned. Let us see what happens when we recognize that depository institutions hold excess reserves.

Now total reserves, TR, are equal to required reserves, RR, against checkable deposits, $r_D \times D$, plus excess reserves, ER.

$$TR = RR + ER$$

or

(19-6) $$TR = (r_D \times D) + ER = r_D D + ER$$

Next assume that depository institutions hold excess reserve assets equal to a constant proportion of checkable deposit liabilities, D. For example, say they hold a few cents of excess reserve assets per dollar of deposits. Given this assumption, we can define ER as equal to eD, where e is the ratio of excess reserves held to checkable deposits, ER/D. More directly, e is the ratio of excess reserves depository institutions choose to

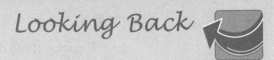

The Evolution of the Money Multiplier

Perhaps you had to study this chapter carefully to assimilate the material on the money multiplier. If so, you are not alone. Economists had grappled with ideas about how an increase in reserves led to a multiple increase in deposits and money for a long time before a clear, complete explanation emerged.

During the eighteenth century, writers such as John Law (1671–1729) and Alexander Hamilton (1755–1804) noticed that bank deposits were a multiple of the underlying cash base and inferred from this that banks create deposits. They did not see that the multiple resulted from the successive lending and redeposit of excess reserves. This idea was first put forth in 1826 by James Pennington (1777–1862), who recognized that a given increase in the reserve base causes deposits to multiply as the reserve increase shifts from bank to bank. It was left to Robert Torrens (1780–1864) to trace Pennington's notion of deposit expansion to its logical conclusion in 1837 (resulting in what we refer to as the *simple money multiplier* in this chapter). Thomas Joplin (1790–1847) clarified how expansion proceeds as one bank loses excess reserves to another, which then also expands. Alfred Marshall (1842–1924) provided the algebraic model for the simple multiplier that takes into account excess reserves—Equation (19-9) in this chapter. Finally, in 1921, Chester Phillips (1882–1976) "stated the theory with a power, precision, and completeness unmatched by his predecessors."[a]

Two steps remained to complete the analysis. First, the notion of a currency drain as deposits expand was developed by several economists between the 1930s and the 1950s. Finally, the work of James Meade, Milton Friedman, Anna Schwartz, and Phillip Cagan in the 1950s and early 1960s incorporated a currency drain into the money multiplier and fully explained the relationship between changes in the monetary base and changes in money. Thus, not until the early 1960s was the money multiplier fully expounded.

Now, don't you now think you mastered the material rather quickly?

Endnotes

a. The quotation is from Thomas M. Humphrey, "The Theory of Multiple Expansion of Deposits: What It Is and Whence It Came," *Economic Review of the Federal Reserve Bank of Richmond* (March–April 1987): 3–11. Much of the material presented in this feature is based on Humphrey's article.

---

maintain relative to the size of their deposit liabilities. Substituting this expression into Equation (19-6) yields

(19-7)
$$TR = r_D D + eD = (r_D + e)D$$

Solving this equation for D yields

(19-8)
$$D = 1/(r_D + e)\ TR$$

And in terms of changes in reserves and deposits, we have

$$(19-9) \qquad \Delta D = 1/(r_D + e)\Delta TR$$

Equation (19-9) defines the new relationship between deposits and reserves. Two things are important to note about this relationship. First, the multiplier in Equation (19-9), $1/(r_D + e)$, is smaller than the simple multiplier, $1/r_D$, in Equation (19-5). For example, if r_D is .10 and e is .02, the multiplier is 8.33 [$1/(.10 + .02) = 8.33$], rather than 10 ($1/.10 = 10$). Second, the multiplier is not under the complete control of the Fed. Depository institutions can control the excess reserve ratio, e, which suggests that control by the Fed is not a matter of simple arithmetic.

Having shown that depository institutions can affect the multiplier through e, let us examine how the public can affect the money supply through its currency-holding behavior. Recall that the total money supply (M) is equal to checkable deposits, D, plus currency in the hands of the public, C. Let us assume that the public also desires to maintain its currency holdings as a constant proportion of its checkable deposits. Currency held by the public, C, is equal to cD, where c is the desired ratio of currency to checkable deposits, C/D. Thus, we can write:

$$(19-10) \qquad M = D + C = D + cD = (1 + c)D$$

Taking account of the public's desire to maintain its currency holdings equal to cD, we can see that open market purchases of securities by the Fed may result in an increase of both reserves and currency in the hands of the public. As members of the public sell securities, their checkable deposits increase, and they exchange some of those deposits for currency to maintain the desired currency-to-deposits ratio, c.

We define the **monetary base**, MB, as the sum of reserves and currency in the hands of the public, $TR + C$. Although open market purchases initially show up as increases in reserves, which lead to new lending and deposit creation, the reserves become severely depleted as the newly created deposits are exchanged for currency to maintain the desired currency-to-deposits ratio.[10] Thus, when the Fed engages in open market operations, both reserves and currency in the hands of the public can change. In reality, open market operations change the monetary base. The multiplier is affected because some of the newly created deposits are exchanged for currency. Making the appropriate substitution for reserves from Equation (19-7) and substituting cD for C, as noted previously, we arrive at Equation (19-11):

$$\begin{aligned} MB &= TR + C \\ &= (r_D + e)D + cD \\ (19-11) \qquad &= (r_D + e + c)D \end{aligned}$$

Rearranging terms, we get

$$(19-12) \qquad D = [1/(r_D + e + c)]MB$$

Equation (19-12) shows the relationship between the monetary base and deposits. By combining Equations (19-10) and (19-12), we can derive the relationship between the monetary base and the money supply, M:

$$\begin{aligned} M &= D + C \\ &= [1/(r_D + e + c)]MB + C \\ &= [1/(r_D + e + c)]MB + cD \\ &= [1/(r_D + e + c)]MB + c[1/(r_D + e + c)]MB \\ &= [1/(r_D + e + c)]MB \times (1 + c) \\ (19-13) \qquad &= [(1 + c)/(r_D + e + c)]MB \end{aligned}$$

Monetary Base
Reserves plus currency in the hands of the public; denoted as MB.

In terms of changes in the monetary base and the money supply, and assuming r_D, e, and c remain constant, we have

(19-14) $$[(1+c)/(r_D + e + c)]\Delta MB = \Delta M$$

Equation (19-14) defines the change in the money supply in terms of the monetary base and the expanded multiplier, which we will now refer to as simply the **money multiplier**. Taking account of another complication (the currency drain) has reduced the multiplier; if c is equal to .3, the multiplier is $(1+.3)/(.1+.02+.3)=3.1$, rather than the 8.33 in Equation (19-9). Because we are using $M1$ as our measure of the money supply, our money multiplier is actually the $M1$ multiplier. In Appendix B of this chapter, we develop the $M2$ multiplier. Exhibit 19-9 presents the factors that cause the money multiplier to change.

To summarize, the money multiplier in this more complete model is the multiple of the change in the monetary base by which the money supply will change. Thus, in our example, when the Fed uses open market purchases to increase the monetary base by $1,000, the money supply will increase by $3,100. The new money multiplier takes account of excess reserves and the currency drain. In the simple money multiplier case, the simple multiplier is the multiple by which a change in reserves leads to a change in deposits and loans without considering other factors.

Money Multiplier
The multiple of the change in the monetary base by which the money supply will change.

19-9
Factors That Affect the Money Multiplier

An Increase in . . .	Caused by . . .	Results in . . .
c (the desired ratio of currency to checkable deposits)	The decision by the public to increase holdings of currency relative to deposits	A decrease in the money multiplier and a decrease in the money supply
e (the ratio of excess reserves held to checkable deposits)	The decision by depository institutions to hold more excess reserves	
r_D (the required reserve ratio)	The decision by the Fed to increase the required reserve ratio	

A Decrease in . . .	Caused by . . .	Results in . . .
c	The decision by the public to decrease holdings of currency relative to deposits	An increase in the money multiplier and an increase in the money supply
e	The decision by depository institutions to hold fewer excess reserves	
r_D	The decision by the Fed to decrease the required reserve ratio	

The Money Multiplier During the Great Depression

You might be interested to learn that between 1929 and 1933, bank holdings of excess reserves rose from $25 million to more than $2 billion; at the same time, the currency-to-deposits ratio increased from approximately 17 percent to 33 percent.[a] Why do you think these changes occurred? Borrowers were defaulting on loans as the Great Depression deepened, and depositors became wary of banks as thousands of them failed. Solvent banks found few attractive loan opportunities and tried to regain the public's confidence by staying liquid—that is, by holding excess reserve assets. People, however, had lost their faith in the banking system and responded by withdrawing funds, thus increasing their holdings of currency.

In this chapter, you have seen that the multiplier is equal to $(1+c)/(r_D+e+c)$ and that the multiplier times the monetary base is equal to the money supply. Without knowing any of the facts, the multiplier tells us that if r_D and total reserves remain roughly unchanged, checkable deposits, and, therefore, the money supply, will decline as e rises. Although it is not as clear from the formula, the multiplier will also decline if c rises as the public withdraws deposits and reserves from the banking system.

Because these processes were not really understood in the 1930s, the money supply fell by about one-third between 1929 and 1933 due to the rise in both e and c and the resulting fall in the money multiplier. The drop in the money supply was hardly the type of antidepression policy one would have hoped for.

It is possible that the Fed could have moderated or reversed the decline in the money supply by sufficiently lowering r_D or raising total reserves. The Fed could have provided banks with additional reserves through open market purchases or by lending reserves to banks and serving as a lender of last resort. Thus, the Fed could have offset the drop in the multiplier by increasing the monetary base. A sufficient volume of such actions would have forestalled the decline in the money supply. That the Fed did not respond in this fashion is one of the reasons the Fed is often blamed for aggravating the Great Depression. In fact, it actually raised reserve requirements, believing this would help to restore the public's confidence in the banking system.

Of course, today our understanding of what determines the money supply and its importance in the economy is much greater than it was in the depression era. Thus, it is likely that such a rise in e and c today would produce a much more aggressive Fed reaction.

Endnotes

a. Until 1980, banks were the only financial intermediaries that issued checkable deposits.

Recap   The monetary base is reserves, *TR*, plus currency in the hands of the public, *C*. The money supply will be equal to the monetary base, *MB*, times the money multiplier. The actual money multiplier is more complicated than the simple money multiplier because depository institutions may hold excess reserves, *ER*, equal to some fraction of deposits, and the public may withdraw cash as deposits expand to maintain a desired currency-to-deposits ratio, C/D. Taking both effects into account, the money multiplier is $(1+c)/(r_D+e+c)$. $\Delta M = \Delta MB[(1+c)/(r_D+e+c)]$.

The Fed's Control over the Money Supply

We could go on adding complications, but we hope you get the point. When the Fed engages in open market operations, reserves and the monetary base change. Compare Equations (19-5) and (19-14). In Equation (19-14), the multiplier is smaller and the Fed's control of the money supply is not so straightforward. The public, rather than the Fed, controls c, and depository institutions determine e.

Because c and e vary over time, the multiplier linking the monetary base and the money supply is not perfectly stable or predictable, especially in the short run. And what does that mean? It means that even if the Fed can control the monetary base, it may find controlling the money supply somewhat more difficult, especially in the short run. Over a longer period, fluctuations in the c and e ratios—and thus the multiplier—tend to offset one another. That is, a large increase is offset by a large decrease in some other period. Consequently, the Fed's ability to predict the money multiplier and control the money supply improves considerably over a longer time period.

The multiplier model presented in this chapter yields many insights into the money supply process, the interaction among depository institutions, and the effect of Fed actions. You should recognize, however, that it is really a "sausage grinder" model—the Fed increases the monetary base, you crank the handle, and loans, deposits, and currency held by the public come out at the other end. This model leaves out some of the points developed in earlier chapters. Nevertheless, when the Fed engages in open market operations, the effects ripple through the entire financial system, affecting loans, deposits, credit availability, currency held by the public, and the monetary aggregates.

Remember that depository institutions are firms, and like all other firms, they are interested in maximizing profits. Given this objective, firms will consider the costs and revenues associated with alternative courses of action, such as lending versus not lending or borrowing reserves versus not borrowing reserves. The multiplier model simplifies away such notions. In particular, the cost of deposits and the return on loans—in other words, interest rates—were ignored. We simply assume that depository institutions always have customers ready, willing, and able to borrow.

The model also fails to consider the creative ways in which banks and other depository institutions get around reserve requirements when the banking system is demanding more reserves than the Fed is willing to supply. The Eurodollar market is a prime example of a way that a bank can change a deposit liability with its corresponding reserve requirement into a nondeposit liability free of a reserve requirement. Credit extension can continue, even without the Fed feeding additional reserves into the system.

Given the preceding clarifications, some economists suggest that teaching this multiplier model should be done only from a historical perspective. They believe that in the complex financial system today, the model is merely a historical artifact with little relevance to the way depository institutions behave. We believe that if it is viewed with caution, the model gives some insight into the workings of the banking system.

In the next chapter, we look at the demand for money and credit. We also put demand and supply together to see how the public, the Fed, and the banking system jointly interact to determine a money market equilibrium. This chapter contains two appendices. The first is on other factors that affect the monetary base. The second develops the relationship between changes in the monetary base and changes in $M2$ (the $M2$ multiplier).

Summary of Major Points

1. The Fed's open market operations affect the amount of reserves in the banking system: when the Fed buys securities, reserves of depository institutions rise; when the Fed sells securities, reserves of depository institutions fall. Depository institutions must hold reserve assets, in the form of vault cash or deposits at the Fed, equal to a certain percentage of their deposit liabilities. The amounts that must be held are required reserves; any amounts held in addition to that are excess reserves.

2. For a depository institution, a deposit inflow increases total deposit liabilities and total reserve assets. Part of the reserves will be required and part will be excess. A depository institution can adjust to the inflow of reserves by expanding its loans and "creating" additional deposits equal to the amount of excess reserves that result from the deposit inflow.

3. As the proceeds of a loan are spent, the lending institution loses reserves. However, another depository institution gains reserves. The reserves lost by the lending institution flow to another as the funds are spent. The new depository institution gains deposit liabilities and reserve assets. This depository institution, too, can expand loans and create additional deposits in the amount of the excess reserves that flow to it.

4. Following an initial injection of reserves, the total volume of reserves in the banking system does not change. However, the composition of reserves changes; as deposits expand at each stage, required reserves rise and excess reserves fall.

5. The total expansion of loans and deposits is a multiple of the initial injection of reserves into the banking system. In the simplest model, which ignores excess reserves and currency, the multiplier is equal to $1/r_D$, that is, the reciprocal of the required reserve ratio. The simple multiplier is the multiple of the change in reserves by which deposits change. Thus, the lower the reserve requirements are, the larger the multiplier is. The higher reserve requirements are, the smaller the multiplier is.

6. The monetary base is reserves plus currency in the hands of the public. In a more elaborate model, excess reserves and currency drains are taken into account; the money multiplier is the multiple of the change in the monetary base by which the money supply will change. It is smaller than the simple multiplier and is influenced by the behavior of the Fed, depository institutions, and the public. This means that the money multiplier is not totally under the Fed's direct control and is not perfectly stable or predictable, especially in the short run.

7. Even if the Fed can control the monetary base, it may have difficulty controlling the money supply in the short run. Over a longer period (three to six months), the fluctuations in the multiplier tend to offset one another, and the Fed's ability to predict the multiplier and thus control the money supply improves considerably.

8. Other factors that affect bank reserves and the monetary base can be identified from the balance sheet of the Fed. The major assets of the Fed are gold, special drawing rights SDRs, other assets denominated in foreign currencies, discount loans, government securities, and float. The major liabilities of the Fed are Federal Reserve notes, bank deposits of reserves, and deposits of the U.S. Treasury. An increase in any of the assets of the Fed will increase the monetary base. An increase in any of the liabilities of the Fed will decrease the monetary base. The Fed exerts considerable influence on reserves and the monetary base through open market operations. (See Appendix 19A.)

9. The M2 multiplier tells us how much M2 will increase when the Fed increases the monetary base (MB). The M2 multiplier, which is calculated as M2/MB, is larger than the M1 multiplier because M2 contains small savings and time deposits, overnight repurchase agreements and Eurodollars, and individual money market mutual funds. (See Appendix 19B.)

Key Terms

Excess Reserves, p. 459
Federal Reserve Float, p. 477
Fractional Reserve Banking
   System, p. 463
Loaned Up, p. 461
Monetary Base, p. 468

Money Multiplier, p. 469
Offsetting Open Market Opera-
   tions, p. 458
Open Market Operations, p. 456
Repurchase Agreement, p. 475
Required Reserve Ratio (r_D), p. 463

Required Reserves, p. 459
Reverse Repurchase Agreement,
   p. 475
Simple Money Multiplier,
   p. 463
Total Reserves, p. 459

Review Questions

1. Briefly explain why the Fed does not have precise control over the money supply.
2. If the public chooses to hold no currency, does the Fed control the money supply? If depository institutions choose to always loan up, does the Fed have precise control? If both of these situations occur, does the Fed have control?
3. If a depository institution has excess reserves, how much can it safely lend?
4. What are offsetting open market operations? When would the Fed use an offsetting open market purchase? An offsetting open market sale?
5. Explain how open market purchases and sales influence interest rates. To increase the money supply, should the Fed use an open market purchase or sale?

6. Comment on John D. Rockefeller's statement, "I believe that the power to make money is a gift from God." Do depository institutions really create money? Explain.
7. If e increases given c and r_D, how can the Fed offset this change in e?
8. In what form can a depository institution hold its required and excess reserves? What are the possible uses of currency outside the Fed? (Hint: See Endnote 10.)
9. If discount loans increase, what happens to the monetary base?
10. What are the major assets and liabilities of the Fed? (See Appendix 19A.)

Analytical Questions

Questions marked with a check mark (✓) are objective in nature. They can be completed with a short answer or number.

✓11. Assume that the Fed sets the required reserve ratio equal to 10 percent. If the banking system has $20 million in required reserve assets, what is the amount of checkable deposits outstanding?
✓12. If $r_D = .25$, what is the simple money multiplier? If reserves increase by $100, how much do deposits increase?
✓13. If $c = .35$, $r_D = .10$, and $e = .10$, what is the money multiplier? If a depository institution's excess reserves increase by $400, how much can it safely lend? Ceteris paribus, how much money will the banking system create?
✓14. If $c = .25$, $r_D = .10$, $e = .05$, and the Fed sells $100 in securities to the public, what happens to re-

serves, the monetary base, and the money supply after the change has worked its way through the entire banking system? Use T-accounts to explain your answer.
✓15. Using the same ratios as in question 14 and again using T-accounts, explain what happens to reserves, the monetary base, and the money supply if the Fed buys $100 in securities from the public.
✓16. In each of the following fictitious examples, tell whether the money multiplier will increase, decrease, or stay the same:

   a. Depositors become concerned about the safety of depository institutions, and there is no deposit insurance.
   b. Depository institutions do not see any creditworthy borrowers.

c. The Fed lowers the required reserve ratio.

d. Larger amounts of currency are demanded by the public to use in the "underground economy."[11]

e. Depository institutions believe that overall default risk has decreased.

✓17. Assume that a depository institution has excess reserves of $100 and the required reserve ratio is 10 percent. What is the amount of checkable deposits at the depository institution resulting from new loans based on the excess reserves? Why is this amount different from the maximum amount of $1,000 in checkable deposits that can be generated by the banking system as a whole?

✓18. Suppose that you find $100 in the attic of an old house you have just purchased. You deposit the $100 in your checking account at Bank of America. Use a T-account to show what happens to the bank's assets and liabilities. What is the maximum amount that Bank of America can lend from this deposit given a required reserve ratio of 10 percent?

✓19. Suppose that you withdraw $1,000 in cash from your Bank of America checking account for a weekend trip to Las Vegas. Use a T-account to show the impact on the bank's assets and liabilities. Given a required reserve rate of 10 percent, what is the impact on bank lending?

✓20. By definition, narrow banking requires 100 percent reserve backing for checkable deposits. What is the money multiplier in this case?

✓21. If M2 is $4 trillion and the monetary base is $500 billion, what is the M2 multiplier? (See Appendix 19B.)

Suggested Readings

For a description of the money creation process using T-accounts and a discussion of the factors affecting reserves, see *Modern Money Mechanics*, rev. ed. (Federal Reserve Bank of Chicago, 1992).

For a discussion of a simulation model of the money creation process, see Norman E. Cameron, "Teaching Tools: Simulating Money Supply Creation in Class," *Economic Inquiry* 35 (July 1997): 686–693.

For a historic look at the role of money from the Fed's perspective, see "The Money Supply" online at **http://www .newyorkfed.org/aboutthefed/fedpoint/fed49.html**

Another valuable source for the material in this chapter is Tom Humphrey, "The Theory of Multiple Expansion of

Deposits: What It Is and Whence It Came," *Economic Review of the Federal Reserve Bank of Richmond* (March–April 1987): 3–11.

Links to historical estimates of the U.S. monetary base, calculated on both a seasonally adjusted basis and a non-seasonally adjusted basis, can be found at **http://research .stlouisfed.org/fred2/categories/45.html**.

Fedpoint 4 describes the repurchase and matched-sale transaction, initiated at the trading desk of the New York Fed, at **http://www.newyorkfed.org/aboutthefed/ fedpoint/fed04.html**.

Appendix 19A
Other Factors That Affect the Monetary Base

So far you have seen that the Fed, through open market operations, can change reserves and the monetary base. Although initially altering reserves, open market operations ultimately tend to change both reserves and the amount of currency held by the public. Although the Fed undoubtedly has enormous influence over reserve assets, other factors also affect them. This appendix identifies the various other factors that can affect reserves (and the monetary base) and shows how, despite these other factors, the Fed still exerts considerable influence over reserves, the monetary base, interest rates, and lending. The Fed monitors the net effect of movements in the other factors and uses open market operations to offset any net increase or decrease in the monetary base resulting from movements the Fed deems undesirable. Because the monetary base is the ultimate source of liquidity for the entire financial system, we frame our analysis in terms of it, rather than reserves, recognizing that reserves are merely the monetary base less currency in the hands of the public. Because the whole story flows from an examination and subsequently a rearrangement of the consolidated balance sheet for the entire Federal Reserve System—shown in Exhibit 19A-1—we shall begin by describing the major items shown there.

Major Assets of the Federal Reserve

The assets of the Federal Reserve are shown in the top portion of Exhibit 19-A1.

Gold and Special Drawing Rights (SDRs) Certificate Accounts and Other Assets Denominated in Foreign Currencies

The gold and special drawing rights (SDRs) certificate accounts and the other assets denominated in foreign currencies reflect the Fed's holdings of international reserves.[12] Changes in this account involve fairly complex transactions among the Fed, the Treasury, the International Monetary Fund (IMF), and foreign governments. Nevertheless, you simply need to recognize that acquisitions of gold, SDRs, or other assets denominated in foreign currencies will increase this asset account for the Fed and raise international reserves in the United States. Conversely, sales of gold, SDRs, or other assets denominated in foreign currencies will lower this asset account for the Fed and reduce international reserves.

Loans

As discussed in the body of this chapter, the various Federal Reserve Banks make discount loans to depository institutions via the discount window. Any changes in discount loans also change the volume of reserves and the monetary base.

Securities

Repurchase Agreement
An arrangement whereby the New York Fed agrees to buy securities from the securities dealers with whom it regularly does business and the dealers agree to repurchase the securities on a specific day in the near future.

Reverse Repurchase Agreement
An arrangement whereby the New York Fed agrees to sell securities to the securities dealers with whom it regularly does business and agrees to repurchase the securities on a specific day in the near future.

The Fed acquires or sells government securities through its open market operations. The Fed can buy or sell securities in either of two ways. First, it can buy or sell securities outright. An outright trade, other things being equal, represents a permanent addition or subtraction of reserves from the banking system. Second, the Fed can buy or sell through repurchase agreements or reverse repurchase agreements. As discussed in Chapter 4, a repurchase agreement is an arrangement whereby the buyer, in this case the New York Fed, agrees to buy securities from the securities dealers with whom it regularly does business, and the dealers agree to repurchase the securities on a specific day in the near future. Most repurchase agreements are for one day, but from time to time they run for more than one day. By using a repurchase agreement, the Fed can increase reserves temporarily, other things being equal, for a specific period of time.

Also, as discussed in Chapter 4, nonbank dealers are highly leveraged firms that generally borrow funds to finance their holdings or inventories of government securities. From the dealer's point of view, a repurchase agreement is a method by which the Fed finances the dealer's inventory of securities. Securities sold to the Fed under repurchase agreements will be available to the dealer to sell when the repurchase agreement matures. The New York Fed can also execute a reverse repurchase agreement, which is the opposite of a repurchase agreement. In this case, the Fed agrees to a temporary

19A-1

The Fed's Balance Sheet as of November 27, 2007 (in Millions of Dollars)

Assets

1 Gold certificate account	$11,037
2 Special drawing rights certificate account	2,200
3 Coin	1,165
4 Securities, repurchase agreements, and loans	825,747
Securities held outright	779,693
U.S. Treasury[a]	779,693
Bills[b]	267,019
Notes and bonds, nominal[b]	470,984
Notes and bonds, inflation-indexed[b]	36,911
Inflation compensation[c]	4,779
Federal agency[b]	0
Repurchase agreements[d]	46,000
Loans	54
5 Items in the process of collection	1,563
6 Bank premises	2,114
7 Other assets[e]	39,024
8 Total Assets	**882,848***

Liabilities

9 Federal Reserve notes net if Federal Reserve Bank Holdings	783,675
10 Reverse repurchase agreements[f]	34,272
11 Total deposits	19,576
Depository institutions	14,477
U.S. Treasury—General account	4,711
Foreign—Official accounts	97
Other	291
12 Deferred credit items	2,878
13 Other liabilities and accrued dividends[g]	5,904
14 Total liabilities	**846,305***

Capital Accounts

15 Capital paid in	18,278
16 Surplus	15,457
17 Other capital accounts	2,809
18 Total capital	**36,543***

*Note: Components may not sum to totals because of rounding.

[a] Includes securities lent to dealers, which are fully collateralized by other U.S. Treasury securities.

[b] Face value of the securities.

[c] Compensation that adjusts for the effect of inflation on the original face value of inflation-indexed securities.

[d] Cash value of agreements, which are collateralized by U.S. Treasury and federal agency securities.

[e] Includes assets denominated in foreign currencies, which are revalued daily at market exchange rates.

[f] Cash value of agreements, which are collateralized by U.S. Treasury securities.

[g] Includes exchange-translation account reflecting the daily revaluation at market exchange rates of foreign exchange commitments.

Source: Federal Reserve Statistical Release, H.4.1, *Factors Affecting Reserve Balances* (November 28, 2007). Available online at **http://www.federalreserve.gov/releases/h41/20071129/**.

sale of securities to dealers, which is matched by an agreement to repurchase the securities on a specific day in the near future. Again, most reverse repurchase agreements are for one day. Such transactions temporarily reduce reserves in the banking system. You will see in a few moments how repurchase agreements can come in handy.

Float (Items in the Process of Collections)

Federal Reserve float is an asset item arising from the accounting conventions underlying the Fed's check-clearing procedures. To review, suppose that you live in New York and send a check for $100 drawn on your account at a New York City bank or other depository institution to your mother, who lives in Chicago. She receives the check and deposits it in her bank account. Her bank credits her checkable deposit balance and sends the check or an electronic facsimile of the check to the Federal Reserve Bank of Chicago for collection. At this point, the check becomes a cash item in the process of collection for her bank. The Chicago Fed sends the check to the New York Fed, which returns the check to your bank. Then, your deposit account is debited. For the two commercial banks (yours and hers), the Fed completes the transfer of funds arising from the check by increasing the deposit account of the Chicago bank at the Chicago Fed and lowering the deposit account of the New York bank at the New York Fed. Remember that deposit accounts at the Fed are part of reserves and the monetary base. When all of these transactions are completed, the total amount of deposits, reserves in the banking system, and the monetary base will be, other things being equal, as it was before. The only difference will be in the location of the deposits and reserves (commercial bank deposits at Federal Reserve Banks). Chicago will have gained and New York will have lost deposits and reserves.

Because it takes time to transfer the check physically, the Fed typically credits the Chicago commercial bank's account at the Chicago Fed before it debits the account of the New York bank at the New York Fed. Thus, for a short time (usually a day), the deposit and reserves in question appear on the balance sheets of both banks. As a result, the Fed is, in effect, providing credit to the banking system through this procedure.[13] In late 2004, the Fed authorized commercial banks to submit electronic images of checks rather than the actual paper checks. As electronic technology is applied to the check-clearing process, the volume of float is likely to fall.[14]

Major Liabilities of the Federal Reserve

Now that we have sorted out the Fed's major asset accounts, let us briefly examine its major liability and capital accounts in Exhibit 19-A1.

Federal Reserve Notes

Federal Reserve notes are the paper money in circulation. These notes constitute about 90 percent of the currency in circulation in our economy. The other 10 percent of total currency in circulation consists mainly of coins minted by the Treasury. Federal Reserve notes may be either currency in the hands of the public or vault cash. If held as vault cash, they are part of reserves.

Bank Deposits

As you have already learned, banks may hold reserves in the form of vault cash or in the form of deposits at the Fed. Such deposits, which account for the majority of bank reserves, are assets for the institutions and liabilities for the Fed. These deposit balances are held at a bank's district Reserve Bank, and they rise or fall as the Fed credits or debits the bank's balance.

Deposits of the U.S. Treasury

Deposits of the U.S. Treasury are the Treasury's money account. The Treasury pays its bills by writing checks on its deposit balance at the Fed. When this happens, Treasury deposits decline. If tax receipts rise (as they do around major tax dates, such as April 15) or the Treasury issues and receives payment for securities to finance a deficit, the Treasury's deposits at the Fed rise. The level of Treasury deposits rises and falls with the ebb and flow of government receipts and expenditures.

The Monetary Base Equation

With all relevant items defined, we can develop a monetary base equation, which states the monetary base according to the factors that increase or decrease it. As mentioned earlier, we frame the analysis in terms of the monetary base because it is the foundation of liquidity for the economy. By subtracting currency held by the public from each side of the equation, we could express the equation in terms of reserves instead of the monetary base.

The first thing to notice about Exhibit 19A-1 is that the largest asset item is the securities account and the largest liability accounts are Federal Reserve notes and deposits (reserves) of depository institutions. The second thing to notice is that although the values of all items on the balance sheet change somewhat over time, the largest and therefore the most significant changes occur in the largest items.

To bring together all of the key items that affect the monetary base and thus derive the monetary base equation, we can rearrange the Fed's balance sheet. We know that total assets, TA, equal total liabilities and capital, TL:

(19A-1) $$TA = TL$$

On the liability side of the Fed's balance sheet, we have currency issued by the Fed, C^*, Treasury deposits, TD, depository institution deposits at the Fed, DF, and all other liabilities and capital, OL.

(19A-2) $$TL = C^* + TD + DF + OL$$

Note that in this case, C^* includes both currency in the hands of the public and vault cash. Because total reserves, TR, include vault cash, VC, plus deposits at the Fed, DF, while C is currency in the hands of the public, if we add DF to C^*, we get the monetary base, $TR + C$. Therefore, substituting $TR + C$ into Equation (19A-2) for $DF + C^*$, we get

(19A-3) $$TL = TR + C + TD + OL$$

Rearranging terms, we can express the monetary base—reserves, TR, plus currency in the hands of the public—in terms of the other items:

(19A-4) $$MB = TR + C = TL - TD - OL$$

Using Equation (19A-1), we can rewrite Equation (19A-4), substituting TA for TL:

(19A-5) $$MB = TR + C = TA - TD - OL$$

Total assets are equal to the gold and SDR account, reflecting international reserve holdings, IR; plus loans, L; plus government securities held, GS; plus float, F; plus other assets, OA:

(19A-6) $$TA = IR + L + GS + F + OA$$

The final step is to substitute Equation (19A-6) into Equation (19A-5), which gives us the monetary base equation:

(19A-7) $$MB = TR + C = IR + L + GS + F + OA - TD - OL$$

An increase in any of the items with a plus sign before it will raise the monetary base (and most likely reserves), and an increase in any of the items with a minus sign before it will lower the monetary base. Note that all items with a plus sign are from the asset side of the Fed's balance sheet and that the items with minus signs are from the liability side of the Fed's balance sheet.[15]

Appendix 19B
The M2 Multiplier

In the body of this chapter, we developed the money multiplier to calculate a change in the monetary base. In reality, because we were considering money to be currency, C, plus deposits, D, we were developing the multiplier for $M1$.[16] The $M1$ multiplier tells us how much $M1$ will increase when there is an increase in the monetary base; $M1$ will increase by the multiplier times the change in the monetary base.

In carrying out monetary policy, the Fed may be more interested in the behavior of $M2$ or another aggregate than in the behavior of $M1$. In this appendix, we develop the $M2$ multiplier, which tells us how much $M2$ will increase when the Fed increases the monetary base. In other words, $M2$ will increase by the $M2$ multiplier times the change in the monetary base. As we saw in Chapter 2, $M2$ is:

Currency in the hands of the public (C)
Checkable deposits (D)
Small savings and time deposits (D^*)
Overnight repurchase agreements
Overnight Eurodollars
Money market deposit accounts
Individual money market mutual funds $\left.\right\} = MI$

To simplify, we will consolidate the last four items together as money market instruments, MI. Equation (19B-1) illustrates this relationship.

$$(19B\text{-}1) \qquad M2 = C + D + D^* + MI$$

We also assume that spending units have desired D^*/D and MI/D ratios, just as they have a desired C/D ratio. The $M2$ multiplier is the ratio of $M2$ to the monetary base, MB. With the use of Equations (19-2), (19-11), and (19B-1), we can derive the $M2$ multiplier:

$$(19B\text{-}2) \qquad M2/MB = (C + D + D^* + MI)/(RR + ER + C)$$

To express this multiplier in notation that is similar to the $M1$ multiplier developed in the chapter, we multiply Equation (19B-2) by $(1/D)/(1/D)$, which is equal to 1. The result is derived in Equation (19B-3).

$$M2/MB = (C/D + D/D + D^*/D + MI/D)/(RR/D + ER/D + C/D)$$
$$(19B\text{-}3) \qquad = (c + 1 + D^*/D + MI/D)/(r_D + e + c)$$

Rearranging the terms yields Equation (19B-4):

$$(19B\text{-}4) \qquad M2/MB = (1 + c + D^*/D + MI/D)/(r_D + e + c)$$

Multiplying both sides of Equation (19B-4) by the monetary base and expressing the result in terms of changes yields:

$$(19\text{B-}5) \qquad \Delta M2 = (1 + c + D^*/D + MI/D)/(r_D + e + c)\Delta MB$$

Equation (19B-5) defines the relationship between changes in the monetary base and changes in $M2$. Thus, the $M2$ multiplier is equal to $(1 + c + D^*/D + MI/D)/(r_D + e + c)$. It is similar to the $M1$ multiplier except that the numerator is larger by the magnitude $D^*/D + MI/D$. Therefore, the $M2$ multiplier is larger than the $M1$ multiplier, which is also apparent because $M2$ is larger than $M1$. As can be seen from Equation (19B-5), the $M2$ multiplier is positively related to both the D^*/D and MI/D ratios. Like the $M1$ multiplier, the $M2$ multiplier is inversely related to the required reserve ratio, r_D; the currency-to-deposits ratio, c; and the excess reserve ratio, e.

Endnotes

1. Shortly, you shall see that open market operations usually also affect currency in the hands of the public.
2. We should point out that when the Fed buys or sells "anything else" such as gold or foreign exchange, reserves also change. The buying and selling of securities is the primary tool used to change reserves.
3. The basic balance sheet identity is total assets equal total liabilities plus net worth. Expressed in terms of changes, this identity implies that the change in assets must equal the change in liabilities plus the change in net worth. In the examples in this chapter, we assume that the entity's net worth does not change. Thus, in each case, a change in assets must be matched by a corresponding change in liabilities. By dealing only with changes, we can ignore other details and concentrate instead on the essential transactions.
4. If you do it correctly, the entries should be identical to those in Exhibit 19-2, except that they all should carry opposite signs (+changes to –, and – changes to +).
5. Note that we could have used the balance sheet of any depository institution; we chose to use a bank in our example because banks make up the largest class of depository institutions.
6. To illustrate $0.9 \times \$1,000 = \$900$; $0.9 \times \$900 = \$810$; $0.9 \times \$810 = \$729$; $0.9 \times \$729 = \$656.10$; $0.9 \times \$656.10 = \$590.49$; and so on.
7. In reality, the same expansion occurs whether the proceeds of a loan are spent and redeposited in another depository institution or in the same institution that made the loan.
8. Second National exchanges the $900 check for an increase of $900 in its reserve account at the Fed. However, the vault cash of Second National has gone down by $225. If Second National replenishes its vault cash by drawing on its account at the Fed, its reserve account has a net change of $675.
9. Other factors also complicate the simple multiplier. For example, until December 1990, depository institutions were required to hold reserves against some time and saving deposits. If State University decided to hold, say, one-fifth of the tuition payments it received from Jane and others in the form of large negotiable CDs rather than checkable deposits, then required reserves, checkable deposits, and $M1$ would initially fall. Reserve requirements were less on large negotiable CDs than on checkable deposits. The narrowly defined money aggregates fell as checkable deposits were exchanged for CDs, which are not included in $M1$. Total reserves in the system did not change, although required reserves decreased. In late 1990 and early 1991, reserve requirements on virtually all time and savings deposits were eliminated. However, to the extent that checkable deposits are exchanged for time and savings deposits, as checkable deposits grow, the multiplier can still be affected.
10. The monetary base can also be defined as reserve deposits at the Fed, DF, plus currency outside the Fed, C^*. This is so because currency outside the Fed is either in the vaults of depository institutions, where it is part of reserves, or in the hands of the public. Thus, reserves include deposits at the Fed plus vault cash, VC, and vault cash plus currency in the hands of the public is currency outside the Fed. The following equation summarizes this relationship and illustrates the difference between C and C^*: $TR + C = DF + VC + C = DF + C^*$, and $VC + C = C^*$.

11. The underground economy consists of activities including cash transactions to avoid taxes and illegal activities that are not reported in the National Income and Product Accounts and, hence, do not show up in gross domestic product (GDP) and other measures of economic activity.

12. As you saw in Chapter 18, SDRs are international reserve assets created by the International Monetary Fund.

13. All of this is analogous to the way individuals use float. Many of us write checks and send them off to pay bills, even though at that specific moment we do not have enough funds in our accounts to cover the checks. Knowing that it takes time for a check to clear, we plan to add funds to our accounts in time to cover the checks.

14. On the Fed's balance sheet, float is actually the difference between a cash item in the process of collection (an asset) and a deferred-availability cash item (a liability). The asset item always exceeds the liability item because the Fed credits the deposit (reserve) account of the bank, sending a check for collection to the Fed before it debits the deposit (reserve) account of the bank on which the check is drawn.

15. The plus items are sometimes called *factors supplying reserves* or *sources of reserves*, and the minus items are called *factors absorbing reserves* or *uses of reserves*. A table in the *Federal Reserve Bulletin* reports the data in this fashion.

16. For simplicity, we are following our convention of ignoring travelers' checks.

20

Money is like muck—not good unless it be spread.

—Francis Bacon

The Demand for Real Money Balances and Market Equilibrium

Learning Objectives

After reading this chapter, you should know:

Why the demand for money is really a demand for real money balances

What transactions and precautionary demand for real balances are

How the demand for real balances is related to the level of real income and the interest rate

Other determinants of the demand for real money balances

How changes in the demand and/or supply of real balances affect the market equilibrium and the interest rate

The theories of monetarism and Keynes's speculative demand for money

WHERE IS ALL THE MONEY?

On September 30, 2008, *M*1 was $1,453.8 billion. Of this, roughly $780.1 billion was currency and the remainder was checkable deposits. This money was used to support a gross domestic product (GDP) of approximately $14.4 trillion, resulting in a velocity of about 10.0. Given that there were about 126 million households in this country at that time, the average holding of *M*1 per household was $11,358, and the average holding of currency per household was $6,095.

If you are from an average household, you probably find these figures relatively high. The authors and the people we know, who are mostly professors, students, government bureaucrats, and other professionals, just don't seem to hold that much in money balances. Although our evidence is hardly scientific, we have been asking our students, colleagues, and friends for many years and get answers that leave us in a quandary. So, you may wonder, where is all this money?

Possibly a little investigation can shed some light on the situation. Corporations, as we all know, are forbidden by law to hold interest-earning checkable deposits. We can speculate that a large portion of outstanding demand deposits, which totaled $351.9 billion in September 2008, are held by corporations. We also know that other checkable deposits, which totaled $316.1 billion, must be held by households. Thus, the average household balance held in interest-earning checking accounts amounted to $2,749. This figure certainly seems more realistic.

This explanation of where the outstanding checkable deposits are seems "somewhat reasonable," but what about those large outstanding holdings of currency? Where are they located? Part of the explanation is that most businesses (particularly the corner grocer, dry cleaner, and the like) need some currency. Additionally, estimates are that more than 50 percent and perhaps as much as 60 percent of U.S. currency in circulation is held outside the United States. Indeed, four countries have withdrawn their own national currencies from circulation and use the dollar exclusively in transactions. These four countries that have "dollarized" are Ecuador, Guatemala, El Salvador, and Panama. Moreover, many speculate that large amounts of currency are needed to support the illegal activities of the underground economy such as drug trafficking, and some currency—particularly coin—is held by collectors. In addition, some otherwise legal activities are conducted with currency in order to evade taxes, which in itself is illegal. Nevertheless, why the amount of currency outstanding per household has been growing consistently since 1960 remains a mystery.

In this chapter, we discuss the determinants of how much money households and firms want to hold at a given moment in time. Additionally, we analyze equilibrium in the market for money balances. Although we may be unable to resolve the enigma of the missing currency conclusively, we do explain a lot about the demand for money and equilibrium in the money market.

THE DEMAND FOR REAL MONEY BALANCES

Wealth may be held either in real assets, such as houses, gems, and rare oil paintings, or in financial assets, such as stocks, bonds, mutual funds, and money. From this perspective, money is viewed as just one of many real or financial assets in which households may hold their wealth. When relative rates of return on the various assets change, households adjust their portfolios toward those real or financial assets that offer a relatively higher return.[1] Therefore, as the returns on some assets rise, ceteris paribus, households will hold relatively more in those assets (either real or financial) that yield a higher return and less in the assets whose relative yield has decreased. Money, however, is exceptional among financial assets because it alone functions as a means of payment (medium of exchange), as well as a store of value. Therefore, we single out money for special attention.[2]

The demand for money is actually a demand for **real money balances**, or the quantity of money expressed in real terms. Real money balances, or real balances for short, are adjusted for changes in purchasing power. We can define a real money balance as the nominal money supply, *M*, divided by the overall price level, *P*, as in

(20-1) $$\text{real money balances} = M/P$$

P is a price index that measures changes in the overall price level. Examples of price indexes include the consumer price index (CPI) and the producer price index (PPI).

To see why the demand for money is really a demand for real balances, consider the following example. What would happen if all prices, including input prices and output prices, quadrupled tomorrow? In nominal terms, everything would cost four times as much, but households and firms would be making four times as much money. Households and firms would demand to hold four times as much nominal money to make the same real transactions as before. The demand for nominal money balances would quadruple. Referring back to Equation (20-1), the numerator and the denominator both increase by a factor of 4, leaving the demand for real balances unchanged

(20-1A) $$(M\Delta/P\Delta = 4M/4P = M/P)$$

Note that we are ignoring the effect of price changes on financial assets and liabilities. When the overall price level rises, net borrowers pay back their debts with "cheap" dollars, and the net lenders receive back less in real terms than they loaned. Because for every financial liability there is a corresponding financial asset, the benefit to the borrower that owes the financial liability offsets the loss to the lender that owns the financial asset.

Because the demand for money is a demand for real money balances, nominal money demand is proportional to the overall level of prices. If the price level increases by 10 percent, the nominal demand for money increases by 10 percent, and the demand for real balances remains unchanged. Likewise, if the price level decreases by 10 percent, nominal demand decreases by 10 percent, and the demand for real balances remains unchanged.[3] Sometimes we use the expression "the demand for money" for short to mean the demand for real money balances or just real balances. But don't be confused; the demand for money is always a demand for real balances because of the proportionality between nominal money demand and the overall price level. Having established this relationship, we turn our attention to the factors that motivate households and firms to hold real money balances.

Households' Demand for Real Money Balances

There are basically two motives behind households' demand to hold real money balances. First, households need money to consummate transactions. Someone who purchases real assets, nondurable goods and services, or financial assets must supply in exchange a means of payment that is generally acceptable to the seller. Money is the means of payment. Because financial transactions occur frequently (probably several times a day) and income is typically received less frequently (say, weekly or monthly), households hold an inventory of real balances to get from one income-receiving period to the next. We call this first motive for holding real money balances the **transactions motive.**

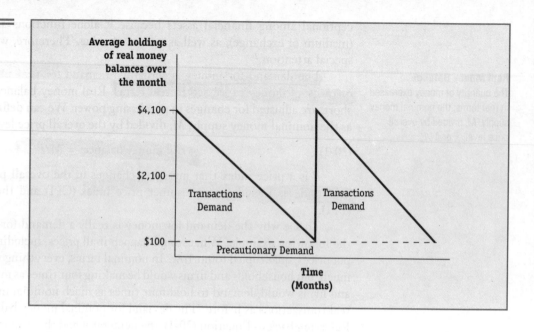

20-1

Real Money Holdings by a Typical Household

Exhibit 20-1 illustrates the transactions motive for holding real money balances by showing a typical relationship among income receipts, financial transactions, and holdings of real money balances. The peaks in the holdings of real balances each month represent paydays, and the gradual decline in the holdings of real balances between paydays reflects spending on goods and services and other transactions. Note that the exhibit shows that the typical household has some real money balances left over at the end of each month. This reflects the second motive for holding real money balances, the precautionary motive. Households try to hold some real money balances—the most liquid asset there is—as a precaution against unforeseen developments.

The transactions and precautionary motives for holding real money balances are analogous to reasons that households keep an inventory of food on hand. In general, it is costly and inconvenient to run to the store every time we want to eat. Accordingly, the typical household buys groceries once a week and then uses them several times a day throughout the week. As in Exhibit 20-1, the inventory of food runs down and is replenished at the next shopping trip. Because we don't like an empty refrigerator, especially when guests drop in unexpectedly, most of us try to keep some food on hand as a precaution.[4]

In addition to fulfilling the transactions and precautionary motives, we can think of real money balances as yielding a stream of services to households and, in the case of interest-earning checkable deposits, some interest income. These are the benefits of holding real money balances. The stream of services that real balances yield is defined by the time and distress saved by having money on hand for immediate use. The value or benefits of such services can be seen by examining what would happen if a household held all its financial assets in the form of bonds instead of holding real money balances. When the household wanted to purchase goods or make a payment, it would first have to sell bonds and acquire money. More specifically, the household would have to call a brokerage firm, pay a brokerage fee, and wait for the money to actually arrive.[5] The benefits of holding real money balances are thus both monetary (saving the brokerage fee and earning interest on checkable deposits) and nonmonetary (the time and inconvenience of waiting for money to arrive when it is needed but is not there).

Precautionary Motive
A motive for holding money based on the desire to protect against unforeseen developments.

Benefits of Holding Real Money Balances
The stream of services that real balances yield defined as the time and distress saved by having money on hand for immediate use.

The cost of holding real money balances is the additional forgone interest that holding nonmonetary financial assets, such as stocks or bonds, would have yielded. When money does pay interest, as in the case of interest-earning checkable balances, the interest rate yield on real money balances is generally less than what could be earned on other less-liquid financial assets. These other assets must pay a higher return, ceteris paribus, to compensate for the loss in liquidity and greater risk.[6]

But how much money should a household keep on hand given both the benefits and costs of holding real money balances? From an economist's point of view, the household should increase its holdings of real money balances as long as the benefits of doing so outweigh the costs. When we apply this rule to the transactions demand for real balances by households, two conclusions follow:

1. Ceteris paribus, the interest rate on nonmonetary assets and the quantity demanded of real money balances are inversely related; that is, as the interest rate increases, quantity demanded decreases, and vice versa. This relationship exists because if the interest rate on nonmonetary assets increases, the opportunity cost of holding real money balances also increases, and households will demand to hold less.

2. Ceteris paribus, the brokerage fee (the cost of transferring from nonmonetary to monetary assets) and the quantity demanded of real money balances is directly related. This relationship exists because if the brokerage fee increases, the household will make fewer calls to the broker and, hence, will hold a larger quantity of real money balances.

We leave the mechanics of demonstrating these particular results to the chapter appendix. Although the analysis is quite cumbersome, our abstract rules translate into behavior in the real world fairly easily. We now turn to the demand for real money balances by business firms.

Firms' Demand for Real Money Balances

Production, investment spending, and sales generate a variety of financial transactions. Over the past 30 years, universities have turned out large numbers of capable graduates trained in the intricacies of money and finance. In addition, the use of new technologies—computers, spreadsheet software, telecommunications—has become a routine necessity for firms. Cash management, in particular, and balance sheet management, more generally, have become highly sophisticated. As foreign activity by U.S. firms has increased, international financial transactions have expanded in size and importance. Nevertheless, the basic factors determining business holdings of real money balances can still be viewed in fairly straightforward terms.

Firms, like households, want (demand) real balances to consummate transactions, such as the regular, expected payments for factor services and tax payments. The payments to the factors include wages, salaries, rent, and the like. In addition, firms need money for transactions that cannot be perfectly anticipated. The timing of some transactions may be uncertain. A firm may not know when a certain delivery will be made or when it will have to pay for that delivery. Transactions balances are used to pay for normal day-to-day operations, even though the exact time of these payments may be difficult to predict.

Some transactions may be totally unexpected, as in the case of a bill for repairing equipment that broke down or expenses related to an unforeseen strike. Expenses, whether anticipated or not, must be paid. As a result, firms need some money and/or liquid assets such as Treasury bills (T-bills) as a precaution against these contingencies. Like households, firms have both transactions and precautionary motives for demanding real money balances.

Firms experience two flows of real money balances: expenditures that generate outflows of funds and receipts that generate inflows of funds. The basic problem is that these flows are not synchronized. Thus, when expenditures exceed receipts, a firm must have money either on hand or immediately accessible so that it can meet its financial obligations. Of course, if receipts exceed expenditures, the firm's financial manager must decide how much of the surplus to hold as real money balances and how much to use to acquire interest-bearing financial assets, such as T-bills and certificates of deposit (CDs).

The points just made are fairly obvious. But what determines the amount of real money balances that firms should hold? In essence, the basic framework is similar to that employed by households in deciding the size of real money balances to hold. That is, firms analyze the benefits and costs of holding real money balances.

For firms, the benefits of holding real money balances are the stream of services that money balances provide. Being able to make payments when they are due is a definite plus and a necessity if a firm is to retain its business reputation and integrity.[7] Indeed, a firm's long-run survival often depends on making payments in a timely fashion. The opportunity cost of holding real money balances is the forgone interest from retaining money in lieu of less-liquid, higher-earning assets. Real money balances held by firms (currency and demand deposits) do not, as of this writing, earn explicit interest. In any case, the relative interest rate differential between money and nonmonetary assets is the opportunity cost.

In deciding the optimum amount of money balances to hold, a cash manager will want to minimize money holdings subject to the constraint of having enough money on hand or accessible when needed. The cash manager will also attempt to maximize the return earned on the other financial assets held in place of money. In reality, firms, like households, will hold additional real money balances only if the benefits of doing so are greater than the costs, as depicted in Exhibit 20-2. We turn now to a discussion of interest rates, income, and real money balances.

20-2

How Households and Firms Decide What Amount of Real Balances to Hold

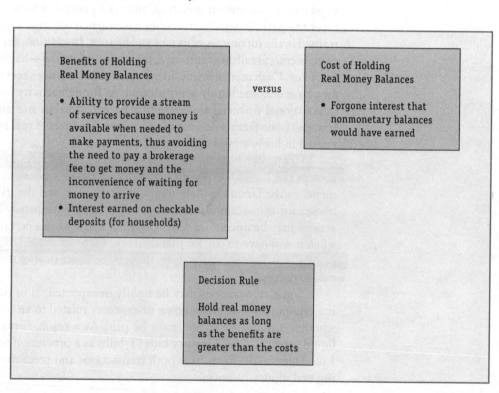

Benefits of Holding
Real Money Balances

- Ability to provide a stream of services because money is available when needed to make payments, thus avoiding the need to pay a brokerage fee to get money and the inconvenience of waiting for money to arrive
- Interest earned on checkable deposits (for households)

versus

Cost of Holding
Real Money Balances

- Forgone interest that nonmonetary balances would have earned

Decision Rule

Hold real money balances as long as the benefits are greater than the costs

Will Checks Go the Way of the Dinosaur?

Throughout this text, you have seen that it has become easier for consumers to make payments electronically, thus bypassing the use of checks or currency. For example, in Chapter 2, we described how point-of-sale terminals allow consumers to make purchases using debit cards and how consumers can pay some bills via phone transfers. In addition, a general-use prepaid card called an *electronic purse* is just around the corner and may replace currency in many uses. The electronic purse will most likely reduce the use of checks.

In addition to these innovations, many banks now issue check cards. A check card allows users to pay for a purchase by making a withdrawal from their checking account without writing a check. Check cards look like ATM cards but have a credit card symbol (such as VISA) in a corner. Instead of writing a check to make a purchase, a check card can be presented anywhere the VISA credit card is accepted. But it is not a credit card because there is no borrowing. A personal identification number (PIN) is needed for use.

A check card has many advantages. It is convenient because it is similar to paying with a credit card. It is flexible in that it may be used in places that accept credit cards but won't take checks. It saves the time of writing a check and usually doesn't require additional identification as checks do. It allows the owner to get cash from a huge network of ATM machines around the world. Some check cards also offer other carrots such as travel insurance when tickets are purchased with the card, warranty services on goods purchased with the card, and so on. A monthly statement of every transaction makes record keeping easy. The costs vary from bank to bank, but most banks offer deals that for the majority of people are cheaper than using debit machines or paper checks.

What are the disadvantages? Identifying the disadvantages seems rather difficult at this time, which suggests that checks may indeed be going the way of the dinosaur.

Recap The demand for money is a demand for real money balances (M/P). Real money balances are adjusted for changes in purchasing power. Households demand real money balances to fulfill the transactions and precautionary motives. The benefit of holding money balances is the stream of services that having money on hand provides. The cost is the forgone interest that holding nonmonetary financial assets would have yielded. Firms demand real balances to make transactions because inflows and outflows are not perfectly synchronized. Firms will minimize their holdings of money subject to the constraint of having money balances available when needed. Both households and firms will demand money balances as long as the benefits are greater than the costs.

THE INTEREST RATE, REAL INCOME, AND REAL MONEY BALANCES

The opportunity cost of holding currency or checkable deposits is the forgone interest that is given up when money balances are held. Currency and demand deposits earn no interest, and other checkable deposits earn less than various less-liquid financial assets. As the interest rate increases, ceteris paribus, the opportunity cost also increases.[8] Likewise, if rates fall, ceteris paribus, the opportunity cost falls.

At higher interest rates, spending units substitute into other less-liquid assets that yield a higher return.[9] In other words, at higher interest rates, households and firms will cut back on the quantity of real money balances they hold because there is a greater reward for doing so. Jose is not concerned about the idle $2,000 sitting in his checking account earning 2 percent if the rate on money market deposit accounts is 3 percent. If the rate on money market deposit accounts goes up to 10 percent, however, while the rate on checkable deposits increases to only 3 percent, he will likely try to hold a smaller average balance in his checking account.

In light of the preceding discussion, you can see the inverse relationship between the quantity demanded of real money balances and the interest rate on nonmonetary assets, ceteris paribus. This relationship is summarized in Equation (20-2). The negative sign over the interest rate specifies the inverse or negative relationship between the interest rate and the quantity demanded.

$$(20\text{-}2) \qquad \text{quantity demanded of real money balances} = f(\overset{-}{\text{interest rate}})$$

In this analysis, we are following the convention of defining the quantity demanded as the amount of real balances that will be demanded as a function of a specific interest rate. If the interest rate increases, ceteris paribus, the quantity demanded of real money balances decreases, and vice versa. If any other factor affecting demand changes, the demand for real balances changes.[10] The demand for real balances is the quantity demanded at every interest rate.

Now is a good time to look at Exhibit 20-3, which is a demand curve showing an inverse relationship between "the interest rate" and the quantity demanded of real money balances. Real money balances are measured on the horizontal axis, and the interest rate on nonmonetary financial assets is measured on the vertical axis. If the interest rate changes, ceteris paribus, we move along the demand curve as the quantity demanded of real money balances changes. Note that the demand curve is drawn holding other factors, including the price level, constant. For an alternative theory of why the quantity of real money balances demanded and the interest rate are inversely related, see "A Closer Look," which discusses Keynes's theory of liquidity preference.

20-3
A Demand Curve for Real Money Balances

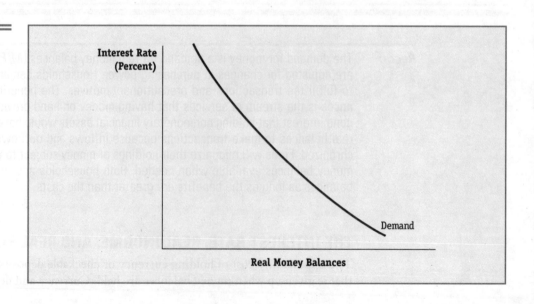

A Closer Look

Keynes's Speculative Demand for Money

So far, we have considered the quantity demanded of money to be inversely related to the interest rate, ceteris paribus, because money earns a lower rate of interest than nonmonetary financial assets. As the interest rate increases, the opportunity cost of holding money increases, and vice versa. Money is one of many financial assets that an individual may hold. As interest rates change, so do the relative rewards of holding various financial and real assets. Individuals adjust their portfolios to reflect these changes.

We would be remiss, however, if we did not introduce you to another theory that also results in an inverse relationship between the quantity demanded of money and the interest rate, ceteris paribus. This theory is known as *liquidity preference*. It involves the *speculative demand for money* and is attributable to John Maynard Keynes, perhaps the most influential economist of the twentieth century.

To simplify, Keynes assumed that individuals can hold their wealth in either bonds or money. Bonds earn the market rate of interest, and money earns no interest or less than the market rate of interest. Moreover, the price of bonds fluctuates when interest rates change. As you saw in Chapter 5, when interest rates rise, bond prices fall, and vice versa. Hence, when interest rates fall, individuals holding bonds experience capital gains, and when rates rise, individuals holding bonds experience capital losses. Consequently, from this analysis, Keynes concluded that if individuals expect interest rates to rise in the future, they are hesitant to buy bonds today because they will experience capital losses if their expectations are fulfilled and interest rates do rise. Hence, people prefer to hold money instead of bonds if they expect interest rates to rise. Likewise, individuals who expect interest rates to fall will prefer to buy bonds today so they will experience a capital gain if interest rates do indeed fall.

A caveat of this theory is that if interest rates are high, more and more individuals will come to believe that rates will be going down in the future and will therefore prefer to buy bonds today in the hope of a capital gain when interest rates do fall. Consequently, because individuals hold either bonds or money, when interest rates are high, the quantity demanded of money will be low. If interest rates are low, more and more individuals will believe rates will be rising in the future and will prefer to avoid holding bonds today out of fear of future capital losses. Hence, when interest rates are low, ceteris paribus, the quantity demanded of money will be high.

Keynes added one final twist. When interest rates are abnormally low, virtually everyone could come to believe that interest rates will be going up in the future. In this case, all individuals would prefer to hold money balances instead of bonds. This argument has a theoretically interesting implication for monetary policy. If the Fed increases the supply of reserves to the banking system, and the money supply, in turn, increases, individuals normally use part of the increase in money to buy bonds, thus increasing the demand for bonds. In the case of abnormally low rates, however, individuals fearing capital losses would choose to hold the increase in money instead of buying bonds. Without an increase in the demand for bonds to push up their prices,

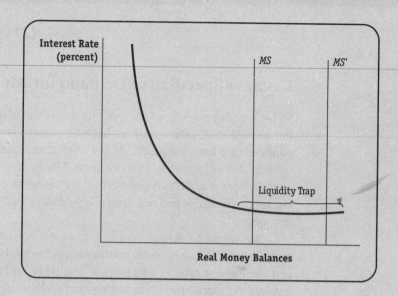

bond prices and, consequently, interest rates would not change. Thus, the Fed would be unable to increase the quantity of real output demanded by lowering interest rates and increasing interest-sensitive spending. When the Fed increases the money supply, individuals would merely hold the increase as "idle" money balances. The economy, which would be flooded with liquidity, would be in what is known as a *liquidity trap*.

Although economists can describe a liquidity trap, they do not know whether the economy has ever actually been in one. (Keynes couldn't find one.) Nevertheless, this possibility was one reason that Keynes preferred an active fiscal policy—changing government spending or taxes—to a policy that worked solely through changing interest rates. If an economy is in a recession and a liquidity trap, monetary policy will be unable to lower interest rates and stimulate interest-sensitive demand. To see why, take a look at the accompanying graph. Note that the interest rate, which measures the overall level of rates, is measured on the vertical axis. In a liquidity trap, the demand for real money balances curve becomes horizontal.

Later economists have questioned altogether the validity of Keynes's speculative demand for money. They point out that the theory implies that when interest rates are low, individuals prefer to hold money as opposed to bonds, waiting to buy until interest rates are up and bond prices are down. The problem is that the theory just does not seem realistic for the average person. How many "average people" do you know who hold money, say, in their checking accounts in lieu of bonds when interest rates are low because they fear a capital loss?[a] Apparently, many economists did not think they knew any. The point became somewhat moot because other economists showed that, ceteris paribus, there would still be an inverse relationship between the quantity demanded of money and the interest rate if money is viewed as one of many financial assets in which wealth can be held.

Endnote

a. Keynes was also writing during the Great Depression, when a liquidity trap seemed particularly unlikely. If the Fed was successful in increasing the money supply, is it plausible that people would just hold this money and not spend it in the middle of a depression?

So far, we have considered the demand for real money balances for a given income. Now we want to look at what will happen to demand if income changes. We begin with households. The amount of nominal money that a household demands at a point in time is directly related to its income. We can now extend that analysis to real money balances by recalling that real money balances are nominal money balances divided by a price index. Likewise, real income is nominal income divided by a price index. It is income adjusted for changes in prices. As real income increases, households on average are going to engage in more transactions and, hence, demand more real money balances. Households will also want to hold more real money balances to fulfill the precautionary motive. As real income decreases, the reverse is true. A high-income person is much more likely to carry around a few $100 bills in a purse or wallet for a "rainy day" than a less-well-off person. Thus, like the transactions motive, precautionary demand for real money balances is also directly related to real income.

Real Income
Nominal income divided by a price index.

The relationship between the household demand for real money balances and real income is not strictly proportional. That is, a doubling of real income does not result in a doubling of the demand for real balances. From an intuitive standpoint, households are able to conserve on real money balances as income increases so that an increase in real income results in a less than proportional increase in the demand for real balances.[11]

Turning to business firms, we would expect that as businesses expand production and sales, their transactions will increase, thus giving rise to increased demand for real money balances. Taking our analysis a step further, as real output expands and contracts, real income, in the aggregate, moves in the same direction. That is, if production and sales increase, real income also increases, and if production and sales decrease, real income decreases. Hence, like household demand, the demand for real balances by firms is directly related to real income.

This direct relationship between real aggregate income and the demand for real money balances by business firms appears to be borne out by the data. However, the data also strongly suggest that business money holdings have generally risen less than might have been expected as output and sales rose. Can you guess why? The most important reason is that during the 1970s and 1980s, interest rates generally trended up. Higher interest rates increased the opportunity costs of holding money balances and encouraged firms, like households, to economize on their cash positions. With the aid of their banks, firms developed better ways of managing inflows and outflows so that the flows were better synchronized and the timing of cash payments was more certain. As a result, a portion of the funds that otherwise would have been held as money balances was used to expand operations, acquire other financial assets, pay off existing debts, and so forth. When interest rates fell in the 1990s, the innovations that firms had developed in response to the high-interest environment of the 1970s and 1980s did not disappear. Instead, firms continued to use these techniques to exploit even minute price differentials.

The desired accumulation of real money balances for both households and business firms is summarized in Equation (20-3). The plus sign over real income signifies the direct or positive relationship between real income and demand.

$$\text{(20-3)} \qquad \text{demand for real money balances} = f(\overset{+}{\text{real income}})$$

Exhibit 20-4 shows various demand curves for real money balances. Real money balances are measured on the horizontal axis, and the interest rate is plotted on the vertical axis. Note that for every level of real income, there is a different demand curve, showing an inverse relationship between the quantity of real money balances demanded and the interest rate, ceteris paribus. If real income increases, the demand curve for real

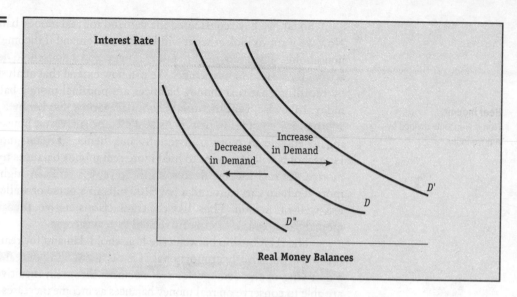

Each demand curve is drawn for a different level of real income. For simplicity, we are referring only to real income as a determinant of the position of the demand curve, recognizing that the level of production and sales is also a determinant. (Because production and sales are highly correlated with real income, this analysis is not significantly affected.) Because a direct relationship exists between the demand for real money balances and real income, if real income changes, the demand curve shifts. If the interest rate changes, ceteris paribus, there is a change in the quantity demanded of real money balances and a movement along a single curve.

money balances shifts to the right and there is an increase in demand. If real income decreases, the demand curve shifts to the left and there is a decrease in demand.

Recap   The demand for real money balances by households and firms is directly related to real income. That is, increases in real income increase demand while decreases in real income decrease demand. Likewise, ceteris paribus, quantity demanded is inversely related to the interest rate. The interest rate is the opportunity cost associated with holding real money balances. Increases in the interest rate, ceteris paribus, decrease quantity demanded, while decreases in the interest rate, ceteris paribus, increase quantity demanded.

ADDITIONAL FACTORS AFFECTING THE DEMAND FOR REAL MONEY BALANCES

Although real income is the major factor that determines the demand for real money balances, demand can also be affected by other factors, including the following:

1. Wealth
2. Payment technologies such as the introduction of ATM machines, debit cards, and credit cards
3. Expected inflation
4. The risk and liquidity of other financial assets

In turn, changes in these factors cause the demand curve for real money balances to shift.

As with real income, changes in wealth are directly related to changes in the demand for real money balances. As wealth increases, ceteris paribus, the demand for real balances also increases, and vice versa. At the same time, the widespread availability of ATM machines, allowing funds to be easily transferred between checking and savings balances, reduces the demand for real money balances. Jose will hold fewer real balances if he can transfer funds from his savings account to his checking account 24 hours a day at an ATM machine. Likewise, the widespread availability of credit cards may reduce the need to hold money balances by firms and households and thereby reduce both the precautionary and transactions motives for holding real money balances from what they otherwise would be.

Inflation reduces the value and purchasing power of money. Assuming that a household starts out with a given amount of nominal money balances, if inflation occurs, then the value of the real money balances will fall. The larger the initial money balances are, the greater is the risk of incurring losses if inflation should occur. Expectations of higher inflation, therefore, reduce the demand for real money balances, ceteris paribus. Increased uncertainty about future inflation rates will also reduce the demand for real money balances.

If the liquidity of other financial assets increases, they are better substitutes for real money balances and can be held instead of real money balances. Consequently, increases in the liquidity of other financial assets reduce the demand for real money balances. Therefore, when financial innovations increase the liquidity of other assets and create new highly liquid substitutes for money, the demand for real money balances decreases from what it otherwise would be.[12]

If the risk of holding other assets increases, the demand for real money balances increases, ceteris paribus. For example, if the stock and bond markets become more volatile, the demand for real money balances increases. Likewise, if the risk of holding money increases, the demand for other financial assets increases. Can you explain what happens if the risk of holding other financial assets decreases?

Exhibit 20-5 summarizes the factors that affect the demand for money. Having completed our discussion of the demand for real money balances, we are ready to put demand and supply together. After all, it takes both to make a market.

20-5

Factors That Affect the Demand for Real Money Balances

An Increase in . . .	Will Cause the Demand for Money to . . .
Income	Increase
Wealth	Increase
Payment technologies	Decrease
Expected inflation	Decrease
Risk of other financial assets	Increase
Liquidity of other financial assets	Decrease

A Decrease in . . .	Will Cause the Demand for Money to . . .
Income	Decrease
Wealth	Decrease
Payment technologies	Increase
Expected inflation	Increase
Risk of other financial assets	Decrease
Liquidity of other financial assets	Increase

Other factors that affect the demand for real balances include wealth, payment technologies, expected inflation, and/or the risk and liquidity of other financial assets. If wealth increases or the risk of other financial assets increases, the demand for real money balances increases. If payment technologies improve, if inflation is expected to increase, or if the liquidity of other financial assets increases, the demand for money decreases.

EQUILIBRIUM IN THE MARKET FOR REAL MONEY BALANCES

In Chapters 3 and 19, you saw that the Fed, through the use of open market operations, exerts a great deal of influence over the supply of nominal money balances and interest rates. This implies that the Fed also exerts a great deal of influence over the supply of real money balances because real money balances are nominal balances divided by a price index. We can depict the supply of real money balances curve as a vertical line on the demand-supply plane.

So far in this chapter, you have seen that, ceteris paribus, the quantity demanded of real money balances is inversely related to the interest rate. By putting the supply and demand curves together as in Exhibit 20-6, we can describe how the interest rate is determined. Real money balances are measured on the horizontal axis, and the interest rate is on the vertical axis. Equilibrium occurs where the two curves intersect (point *A*) at an interest rate of 6 percent. At this rate, the quantity of real money balances demanded is equal to the quantity of real money balances supplied. If the interest rate is above 6 percent, quantity demanded is less than quantity supplied, and there is a surplus of real balances. Because of this surplus, the price of real money balances (the interest rate) will fall. If the interest rate is below 6 percent, quantity demanded is greater than quantity supplied, and there is a shortage of real money balances. Because of this shortage, the interest rate will rise. Thus, the interest rate is that rate at which the quantity demanded is equal to the quantity supplied and the market for real money balances is in equilibrium.

A couple of life's few absolutes are that the future is uncertain and that change is an inherent part of life. Consequently, either demand or supply will be changing

20-6

Equilibrium in the Market
for Real Money Balances

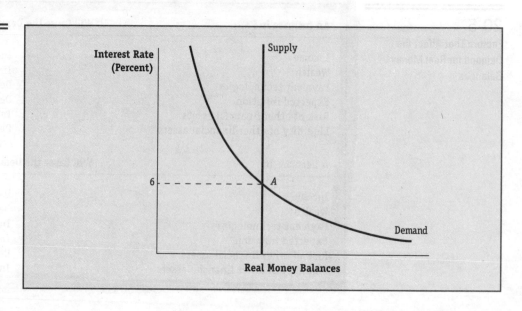

continuously in the dynamic world in which we live. Let's observe how interest rates will change in response to changes in the demand for or supply of real money balances. We begin with changes in supply.

Open market operations lead to changes in reserves that change the nominal money supply. If prices remain constant when the nominal money supply changes, the supply of real money balances will also change. Is it reasonable, however, to assume that the price level will remain the same when the nominal supply of money increases? Changes in the money supply are correlated with changes in the price level. However, changes in the rate of inflation today are most highly correlated with changes in the money supply one to two years ago. The immediate response to an increase in the growth rate of the nominal money supply is a less than proportional increase in the price level. For example, suppose that the nominal money supply increases at a faster rate than the price level. Then, because price changes usually lag, the supply of real balances also increases, as depicted in Exhibit 20-7. When the Fed increases the supply of reserves, ceteris paribus, the vertical supply curve of real money balances shifts to the right. When the Fed decreases the supply of reserves, ceteris paribus, the vertical supply curve shifts to the left. We should also note that as discussed in Chapter 19, other factors including changes in discount loans can and do change the supply of bank reserves, the monetary base, and the supply of real money balances.[13] A change in any of these factors, ceteris paribus, will shift the vertical supply curve of real money balances.

Assume that economic activity seems sluggish, that growth has been disappointing, and that the Fed has become convinced of the need to do something to speed up the economy. It decides to use open market purchases to increase bank reserves. The supply of real balances increases, and, in turn, the supply curve shifts to the right. Assuming that the demand for real money balances does not initially change, the interest rate falls and the market for real money balances moves to the intersection of the demand curve and the new supply curve (point *B*), as depicted in Exhibit 20-8.

20-7
A Change in the Supply of Real Balances

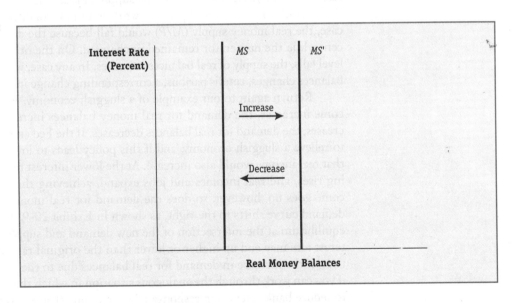

Assuming a given price level, when the money supply changes relative to that price level, the supply of real money balances also changes. If supply increases, the supply curve shifts to the right; if supply decreases, the curve shifts to the left. If the price level increases, however, the supply of real balances decreases, shifting the vertical supply curve to the left. If the price level decreases, the supply of real balances increases, shifting the vertical supply curve to the right.

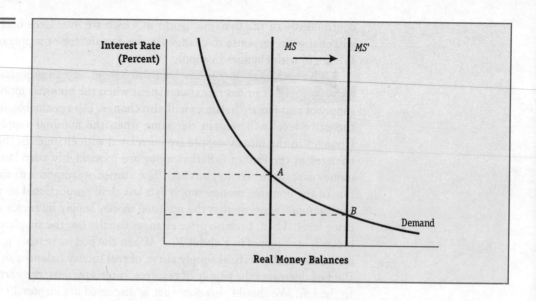

A change in reserves or the monetary base is not, however, the only factor that can change the supply of real money balances. Another factor is the price level. If there is a one-time change in the price level for a given nominal money supply, the supply of real money balances also changes. Note that this discussion applies to a one-time change in the price level, not to inflation, which is a sustained increase in the price level. As discussed previously, if there is a change in expected inflation, the demand for real money balances also changes.

Such a one-time change could be caused by a supply shock, such as a drought or a new labor contract. Prices rise, but the nominal money supply does not undergo a corresponding increase. In this case, the supply of real balances falls. For example, assume that overall prices increase 2 percent, while nominal money remains at $1 trillion. In this case, the real money supply (M/P) would fall because the denominator increased 2 percent while the numerator remained unchanged. On the other hand, if the overall price level falls, the supply of real balances increases. In any case, when the supply of real money balances changes, ceteris paribus, a corresponding change in the interest rate follows.

Return again to our example of a sluggish economy. We have seen that if real income increases, the demand for real money balances increases, and if real income decreases, the demand for real balances decreases. If the Fed engages in expansionary policy to relieve a sluggish economy, and if this policy leads to lower interest rates, it is hoped that real income would also increase. At the lower interest rate, interest-sensitive spending rises, and real incomes and jobs expand, achieving the desired results. As real income goes up, however, so does the demand for real money balances, and, hence, the demand curve shifts to the right, as shown in Exhibit 20-9. The market moves to a new equilibrium at the intersection of the new demand and supply curves (point C). The interest rate may end up higher or lower than the original rate, depending on the magnitude of the increase in demand for real balances due to the increase in real income. See if you can work through the analogous situation in which the Fed uses open market sales to reduce bank reserves in response to an economy that seems to be overheating. In this case, the interest rate initially rises, choking off interest-sensitive spending and resulting in a fall in real income. As real income falls, so does the demand for real money balances, and the demand curve shifts to the left. The interest rate may end up higher or lower than the original rate, depending on the magnitude of the decrease in the demand for real balances due to the decrease in income.

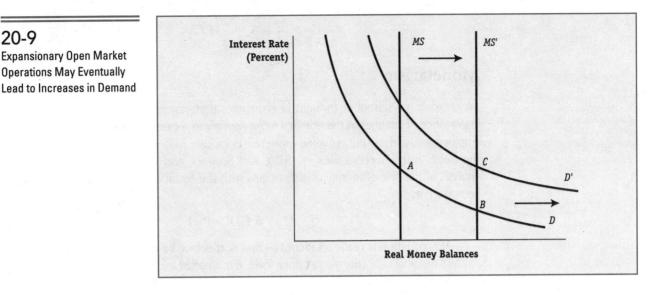

Look again at Exhibit 20-9, which depicts the situation in which real income, and hence the demand for real money balances, increase in response to lower interest rates. As you have seen, the demand for real balances can also increase for other reasons. For example, if wealth increases, if inflation is expected to subside, or if other financial assets become more risky and less liquid, the demand for real money balances increases. In this case, the demand for real balances curve shifts to the right. If the supply of real balances does not change, the interest rate rises. Such a situation is depicted in Exhibit 20-10. Likewise, if income decreases or other factors change (say, payment technologies improve), the demand curve shifts to the left and, ceteris paribus, the interest rate falls.

In any case, the market for real money balances always gravitates to the interest rate at which quantity demanded is equal to quantity supplied. When we observe interest rates constantly changing in our economy, they are responding to changes in supply and/ or demand. That is, they are moving up or down in response to increases or decreases (shifts) in supply and/or demand. "A Closer Look" examines the theory of monetarism,

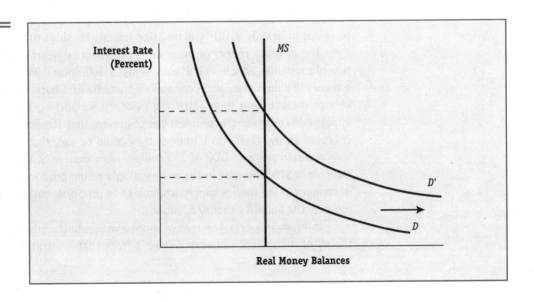

Monetarism

Monetarism is a school of thought in economics that, not surprisingly, emphasizes the importance of changes in the nominal money supply as a cause of fluctuations in prices, employment, and output. Leading monetarists include Milton Friedman (who received the Nobel Prize in economics in 1976), Karl Brunner, and Allan Meltzer. Monetarist analysis of the role of money usually begins with the *equation of exchange*, which can be written as

$$M \times V = \text{GDP} = P \times Y$$

This equation is really an identity—that is, it is true by definition. It says that the nation's nominal GDP (the overall price level, P, multiplied by the real level of output, Y) is equal to the money supply, M, multiplied by *velocity*, V, which is the number of times the money supply must "turn over" during a year to "mediate" all purchases of goods and services comprising GDP.[a] In effect, V is the average number of times the typical dollar component of the money supply is spent on final output through the economy in a year. An analogy may help. If there are nine players on a baseball team and the team scores 18 runs in one game, then each player, on average, scored twice—that is, each circled the bases twice. In this illustration, the total runs scored, 18, is akin to GDP, the nine players are analogous to the money supply, and the average velocity for each player is 2.

As the equation of exchange suggests, velocity is the crucial link between the money supply and economic activity. To illustrate, if the money stock is $1.3 trillion and velocity is 10, GDP will be $13 trillion ($1.3 trillion $\times$ 10 = $13 trillion); if velocity is 8, then GDP will be $10.4 trillion. Let's assume that the Federal Reserve can control M—that is, it can make the quantity of money equal to $1.3 trillion or whatever figure it believes is best for the economy's health. Furthermore, let's assume that the Fed would like to conduct monetary policy so that GDP comes as close as possible to a "full employment" figure, say, $13 trillion. Then the key to pulling this off will be the predictability of V. Will it be 8, 10, or some other figure? If the Fed has a GDP target of $13 trillion and believes velocity will be 10, it will aim for a money supply of $1.3 trillion. If, however, velocity turns out to be only 8, GDP will be $10.4 trillion—far short of the Fed's objective.

The *quantity theory of money* is the intellectual heart of monetarism. The equation of exchange, which, as it stands, is just a definitional identity, is transformed into a theory linking money and economic activity by first hypothesizing that V is reasonably predictable and then gathering evidence supporting this assertion. Why is this important? Let's take the simplest case. Suppose that V is stable (fixed). If policy makers could always count on V to be 9, they could be sure that a money supply of $1.44 trillion would produce GDP of $13 trillion. More generally, they would know that, for example, a $100 increase in the money supply would produce a $900 rise in GDP; that is, changes in the money supply would lead to proportional changes in GDP—this is, in essence, the quantity theory of money.

In many respects, the role of money within both monetarism and the quantity theory of money are not very different from that illustrated in Exhibit 3-6, Market

Equilibrium. Monetarists tend to prefer the simpler and more direct quantity theory approach because they believe that the detailed linkages between money and economic activity are either relatively unimportant or, given the complexities and interdependencies characterizing the economy, too hard to figure out. Thus, it is argued, focusing on M and V is appropriate and sufficient for analyzing the general role of money in the economy.

As we have noted previously, major structural changes in financial markets have not only skewed the relationship between narrowly defined monetary aggregates and the level of economic activity but also made it difficult for a central bank to use monetary targeting in the execution of monetary policy, as the theory of monetarism suggests. Because credit now emanates from so many sources other than depository institutions (mutual funds and finance companies, among them), the degree of credit restraint in operation at any particular time is difficult to measure by a standard money supply aggregate, such as $M1$ or $M2$, or a broader credit aggregate, such as domestic nonfinancial debt (DNFD).

Endnote

a. Consistent with general economic usage, we use the term GDP to refer to nominal GDP, which is equal to the total dollar value of all final goods and services produced by the economy during a year.

which is historically important in the development of monetary theory. Monetarism relates the nominal supply of money and changes therein to the level of economic activity.

Recap Open market operations or a one-time change in the overall price level for a given nominal money supply causes the supply of real balances to change. The market for real balances always gravitates to the interest rate at which quantity demanded is equal to quantity supplied.

A FINAL NOTE

In this chapter, we extended the discussion introduced in Chapter 2 by developing a theory of interest rate determination based on the supply of and demand for real money balances. Real money balances are measured at a point in time and refer to actual stocks. The interest rate adjusts to equate the quantity supplied (stock) of real money balances with the quantity demanded.

In Chapter 5, we developed the loanable funds theory in which the interest rate is determined by the supply of and demand for loanable funds. The supply of and demand for loanable funds are measured through time and refer to actual flows. The interest rate adjusts to equate the quantity demanded of loanable funds with the quantity supplied. As in Chapter 5, we can reconcile the two theories by recognizing that when there is a change in a stock measured at different times, a flow has occurred. Correspondingly, changes in the flow of loanable funds entail changes in the stock of real money balances as measured at two different points in time. Make sure you are clear about the difference between stocks and flows and that interest rates equate both the supply of and demand for loanable funds and real money balances.

In this and the previous chapter, we have analyzed the supply of and demand for real money balances. This chapter has one appendix about the transactions demand for money by households. In the next chapter, we look at financial aspects of the household, business, government, and rest-of-the-world sectors to help gain an understanding of how spending and financial decisions affect economic activity.

Summary of Major Points

1. The demand for money is really a demand for real money balances. Real money balances are the nominal supply of money divided by the price level. Changes in the overall price level lead to proportional changes in the demand for money and no change in the demand for real balances. Households demand real money balances to consummate transactions (transactions motive) and to fulfill the precautionary motive.

2. Holding real money balances involves both benefits and costs. The benefits are the interest payments that are earned on checkable deposits plus the stream of services that money balances provide. The costs are the forgone interest payments that holding nonmonetary financial assets would have yielded. Households and firms should adjust their holdings of real balances to the point where the marginal benefits of doing so are equal to the marginal costs.

3. Household demand for real balances is directly related to real income. Ceteris paribus, the quantity demanded of real balances is inversely related to the interest rate. A firm's demand for real money balances is directly related to its production and sales and its need to engage in transactions. Both are highly correlated with real income. The demand for real money balances is also affected by other factors, including changes in wealth, the advancement of payment technologies, expected inflation, the availability of near money substitutes, and the risk and liquidity of other financial assets.

4. The interest rate is determined by the demand for and supply of real money balances. If either demand or supply changes, the interest rate changes. The supply of real balances changes when the Fed uses open market operations to change the supply

of reserves to depository institutions. Changes in the overall price level for a given nominal money supply also cause the supply of real balances to change. If the Fed is successful in speeding up a sluggish economy by increasing the supply of real balances, the demand for real balances will also increase as real income increases.

5. Keynes's liquidity preference theory asserts that there is a speculative demand for money such that the quantity demanded of money is inversely related to the interest rate. The inverse relationship results because when interest rates are low, people will demand to hold money instead of bonds because they fear a capital loss when interest rates rise. Likewise when interest rates are high and bond prices low, people will hold bonds instead of money to take advantage of a capital gain when interest rates fall. When interest rates are abnormally low, the economy may be in a liquidity trap where the money demand curve becomes horizontal. In this case, increases in the supply of money do not cause the interest rate to fall, and monetary policy is less effective in affecting economic activity.

6. Monetarism is a theory that stresses the relationship between changes in nominal money and changes in GDP. Monetarists believe that the primary determinant of changes in GDP is the change in the supply of money because velocity is highly stable. More modern monetarists stress that although velocity may not be stable, it is sufficiently predictable.

7. The benefits of holding additional real money balances decline as additional calls are made to the broker each month. The cost of each call to the broker, however, is a constant amount per call. Calls

to the broker should be made as long as the benefits of doing so are greater than the costs. The optimum number of calls determines the average daily holding of real balances and, hence, the transactions demand for real money balances by households. (See Appendix 20A.)

Key Terms

Average Daily Holding
 of Funds, p. **505**
Benefits of Holding Real Money
 Balances, p. **486**

Cost of Holding Real Money
 Balances, p. **487**
Precautionary Motive, p. **486**
Real Income, p. **493**

Real Money Balances, p. **485**
Transactions Motive, p. **485**

Review Questions

1. What is a real money balance? If the nominal money supply increases 20 percent while prices increase 20 percent, what happens to the demand for real money balances? What happens to the supply of real money balances?

2. If real income increases 20 percent, what happens to the demand for real money balances? Is the change in demand proportional to the change in real income?

3. What is the difference between a one-time increase in prices and inflation? How does a one-time increase in prices affect the demand for real money balances? How does expected inflation affect the demand for real balances? How does a one-time increase in prices affect the real money supply?

4. Why do firms want to hold real money balances? Why do households? What factors determine the quantity of real balances that each wants to hold?

5. What happens to the demand for real balances if interest rates on time deposits rise relative to interest rates on checkable deposits?

6. Correct the following statement: "When the interest rate increases, the demand for real money balances decreases."

7. Changes in money were more highly correlated with changes in nominal GDP than with changes in either real GDP or inflation. Does this finding support or refute monetarism? Explain.

8. Using the liquidity preference theory, explain why the quantity demanded of money is inversely related to the interest rate. What is a liquidity trap?

9. When is the market for real money balances in equilibrium? If the Fed engages in open market sales, what happens to the supply of real balances?

10. Explain the transactions and precautionary motives for demanding real money balances.

11. What are the benefits of holding real money balances? What are the costs? What is the optimum amount of real money balances that households and firms will demand?

Analytical Questions

Questions marked with a check mark (✓) are objective in nature. They can be completed with a short answer or number.

✓12. Graph the supply and demand curves for real money balances. Explain what happens to the interest rate in each of the following situations:

 a. Credit cards become more widely used and accepted to make transactions.

 b. The economy is growing faster than the Fed thinks is desirable; therefore, the Fed sells bonds to the public.

 c. Many new near money substitutes are created.

 d. The overall price level falls while the nominal money supply remains constant.

 e. ATM machines become more accessible and more widely used.

f. The secondary markets for negotiable CDs and junk bonds collapse.

g. Inflation is expected to pick up in the coming year.

✓13. The graph in Exhibit 20-1 shows a typical household's real money holdings, assuming that real money balances are gradually depleted over the course of the month. Jacques gets paid on the first of each month but parties extensively over the next week and is broke for the remainder of the month. Graph Jacques's real money holdings over the course of a month.

✓14. Graphically show what happens to the interest rate if the Fed takes action that leads to a decrease in the supply of real money balances while the economy is in a liquidity trap.

15. What is the equation of exchange? If nominal GDP is $12 trillion and the money supply is $1.5 trillion, what is velocity? If the Fed increases the nominal money supply, what happens to nominal GDP? (*Hint:* First assume that velocity is constant and then relax this assumption.) Can we be sure of the direction of change in prices and real GDP?

✓16. Graphically show what happens to the real money supply if the price level rises while the nominal money supply remains constant. What happens to the real money supply if both the nominal money supply and the price level rise by the same percent?

✓17. If Sara earns $4,000 per month, the interest rate is 4 percent, and the cost of a call to the broker is $.75, what should be her transactions demand for real balances per month? (See Appendix 20A.)

✓18. Referring to question 17, if Sara's income increases to $6,000 per month, what happens to her demand for real money balances? (See Appendix 20A.)

Suggested Readings

For data on money and income, visit the Economic Statistics Briefing Room at **http://www.whitehouse.gov/fsbr/esbr.html**.

Bruce Champ provides an interesting discussion in "Private Money in Our Past, Present, and Future," *Economic Commentary*, Federal Reserve Bank of Cleveland (January 30, 2007). It is available online at **http://clevelandfed.org/Research/commentary/2007/010107.cfm**.

Monthly statistics on the U.S. money stock are available both seasonally adjusted (SA) and not seasonally adjusted (NSA). The data series, extending from 1959 to the last quarter of the current year, can be found at **http://research.stlouisfed.org/fred2/ categories/25**.

For a fun and interesting article about the stone money of Yap, see Michael F. Bryan, "Island Money," *Economic Commentary*, Federal Reserve Bank of Cleveland (February 1, 2004). The article is available online at **http://www.clevelandfed.org/Research/Commmentary/2004/0201.pdf**.

Electronic banking promises to revolutionize the demand for money in the next few years. For an interesting survey, see Christoslav E. Anguelov, Marianne A. Hilgert, and Jeanne M. Hogarth, "U.S. Consumers and Electronic Banking, 1995–2003," Board of Governors of the Federal Reserve System, *Federal Reserve Bulletin* (Winter 2004): 1–18. The article is available online at **http://www.federalreserve.gov/pubs/bulletin/2004/winter04_ca.pdf**.

For an article that concludes that inflation around 2 percent is optimal, see Milton Marquis, "Inflation: The 2% Solution," *Economic Letter*, Federal Reserve Bank of San Francisco (February 2, 2001).

For "Fun Facts About Money," including counterfeiting, a history of paper money, and printing currency, see **http://www.frbsf.org/federalreserve/money/funfacts.html**.

For a look at two views of the quantity theory that the author concludes are similar, see Thomas M. Humphrey, "Fisher and Wicksell on the Quantity Theory," *Federal Reserve Bank of Richmond Economic Quarterly* 83 (Fall 1997): 71–90.

William J. Frazer, Jr., *The Legacy of Keynes and Friedman* (Westport, CT: Praeger, 1994) looks at the monetary theories of each economist.

Thomas Mayer, *Monetarism and Macroeconomic Policy* (Brookfield, VT: Edward Elgar, 1990), provides easy-to-read coverage of the topic.

For a history of the uses and abuses of money and debt, see G. Leigh Skene, *Cycles of Inflation and Deflation* (Westport, CT: Praeger, 1992).

For some engaging reading on monetarism, see Milton Friedman's classic article entitled "The Quantity Theory of Money: A Restatement," in *Studies in the Quantity Theory of Money* (Chicago: University of Chicago Press, 1956).

For an early discussion about the determination of velocity, see Irving Fisher, *The Purchasing Power of Money: Its Determination and Relation to Credit, Interest, and Crises* (New York: Macmillan, 1911).

For interesting reading that concludes that by the end of 1995, more than half of the U.S. currency was held abroad, see Richard D. Porter, "The Location of U.S. Currency: How Much Is Abroad?" *Federal Reserve Bulletin* 82 (October 1996): 883–903.

Appendix 20A
The Transactions Demand for Money by Households

You have seen that a household should demand real balances for transactions as long as the benefits of doing so are greater than the costs. A problem arises in that both the benefits and the costs increase as more real balances are held. The purpose of this appendix is to shed light on how this abstract rule can be translated into behavior in the real world. We use a numerical example to illustrate this procedure. Again, we are assuming that the household can hold money balances or bonds and that it must call its broker, pay a fee, and wait to liquidate the bonds when it needs funds.

Let's consider a simple example in which the household earns a fixed income of $4,000 per month and can make from zero to two calls to its broker each month, as shown in Exhibit 20A-1. For simplicity, we will also assume that the price level is 1. If the household makes no calls, it puts $4,000 in its checking account and spends the funds evenly over the course of the month. On average, the household is holding half of its monthly income ($2,000) as nominal money balances. During the first 15 days of the month, the household is holding more than half of its income ($2,000), and during the last 15 days, it is holding less. Because the price level is 1, the household's average daily holding of funds ($2,000/1=$2,000) is its demand for real money balances during the month.

Average Daily Holding of Funds
A household's demand for real money balances during the month; the amount of each withdrawal divided by two.

If the household makes one call to the broker during the month, initially half of its income ($2,000) is used to buy bonds, and the other half is spent evenly over the first 15 days of the month. On the sixteenth day, the household calls the broker to sell the bonds and receives back the half of its income ($2,000) originally invested in those bonds. It then spends these funds ($2,000) over the last 15 days of the month. On average, the household holds one-quarter of its income ($1,000) as checkable funds. Because the price level is 1, this is its demand for real money balances ($1,000/1=$1,000).

If the household makes two calls per month, it initially puts two-thirds of its income in bonds ($2,667) and spends the other one-third ($1,333) during the first third of the month. One-third of the way through the month, the household calls the broker to sell $1,333 worth of bonds for funds to spend during the middle third of the month. The household calls the broker a second time two-thirds of the way through the month for the remainder of the funds ($1,333). Because the household is removing one-third of its income each time it calls the broker and spending that amount equally over one-third of the month (approximately 10 days), its average holding of real money balances is half of each withdrawal, which is one-sixth of its income ($666.67). Because the price level is 1, the demand for real money balances is $666.67/1=$666.67.

Following the same methodology, if three calls per month are made, the demand for real money balances is $500/1=$500. Having completed this rather mechanical exercise, let's now consider the benefits and the costs of making additional calls to the broker. We can make a few simplifying assumptions that will not change the conclusions:

The Number of Broker
Calls Per Month and
the Average Holdings
of Real Balances
(Transactions Demand
for Real Balances)

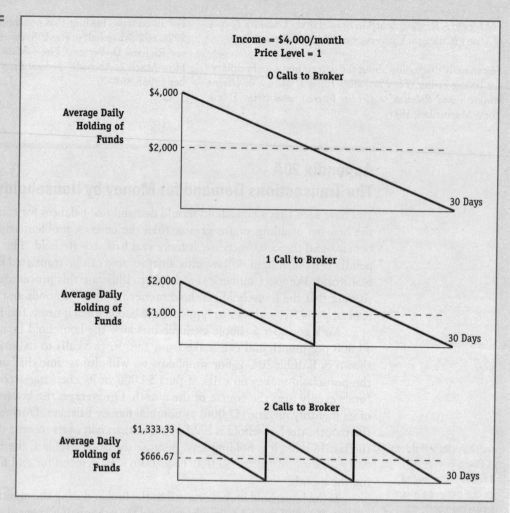

Income = $4,000/month
Price Level = 1

0 Calls to Broker

Average Daily
Holding of
Funds

$4,000

$2,000

30 Days

1 Call to Broker

Average Daily
Holding of
Funds

$2,000

$1,000

30 Days

2 Calls to Broker

Average Daily
Holding of
Funds

$1,333.33

$666.67

30 Days

1. We assume that the cost of a call to the broker (the brokerage fee, the time, and the inconvenience) is a constant amount per call regardless of how many calls are made.[14]
2. We assume that the benefit of an additional call to the broker is the additional interest that is earned on the larger amount of funds held in bonds during the month because of the call.

Armed with these two assumptions, we are now in a position to describe how many calls the household should make to the broker each month. Once we know this, we can determine the average daily balance and, hence, the real money balances that the household will demand each month for transactions. How so, you may ask? The number of calls determines how many time periods the month is divided into. If two calls are made, the month is divided into three time periods. If three calls are made, the month is divided into four time periods, and so on. The monthly income divided by the number of time periods gives the amount of funds at the start of each time period. Because the funds are spent evenly over the period, one-half of this amount is the average holdings of funds. If we divide the average holdings of funds by the price level, we get the quantity of real money balances that the household will demand for transactions.

In our example, if the household makes one call to the broker, the demand for real money balances decreases by $1,000, going from $2,000 to $1,000. The benefit of that first call is the interest earned on the $1,000 that is kept in bonds over the course of the month. If the household makes a second call, the demand for real money balances falls from $1,000 to $666.67, and the benefit of that second call is the interest that is earned on the additional $333.33 ($1000−$666.67) that is held in bonds over the course of the month. If the household makes a third call to the broker, the demand for real money balances falls from $666.67 to $500, and the benefit of the third call is the additional interest earned on $166.67 ($666.67−$500). We could keep going, but we hope you see the point. As additional calls to the broker are made, the benefit of each additional call, although positive, is decreasing. Total benefits are increasing but at a decreasing rate.

We now have all the pieces in place to make a decision. Recalling that we assumed that the cost of calls to the broker is a constant amount per call regardless of how many calls are made, we can say that calls should be made as long as the marginal benefits (the interest earned on the additional funds kept in bonds) are greater than the cost of the additional call. Because marginal benefits decrease as additional calls to the broker are made and costs per call are constant, the household will be exploiting all opportunities to be better off if it makes all calls when the marginal benefits are greater than the marginal costs. Exhibit 20A-2 shows the benefits and costs of additional calls. Assuming that the interest rate on bonds is 6 percent above the rate on money balances and the brokerage cost is $2.00 per call, one call should be made to the broker where the benefit is $5.00. If a second call is made, the benefit is $1.67 while the cost is $1.00. In this case, the quantity demanded of real money balances for transactions will be $1,000. In addition, the household will demand to hold a small amount of real money balances, say, $100, to fulfill the precautionary motive. In this case, then, the total quantity demanded of real money balances is $1,100 ($1,000+$100).

In this simple example, two factors can change the optimum number of calls to the broker per month: the cost per call and the interest rate. First, consider changes in the cost of brokerage calls.

Returning to Exhibit 20A-1, if the cost of brokerage calls falls to $1.00 per call, it is advantageous to make the second call, which has $1.67 in benefits. Again, the third call is not made. On the other hand, if the cost per call increases to $6.00, zero calls are made because the benefit of the first call is only $5.00. In this case, the household puts

20A-2

Benefits and Costs of Additional Calls to the Broker

Call	(A) Transactions Money if Call Is Not Made	(B) Demand for Money if Call Is Made	(A) − (B)	Benefit: Interest on Additional Bonds Held
0	$2,000	—	—	
1	2,000	$1,000	$1,000	$5.00 ($1,000×.005)
2	1,000	667	333	1.67 ($333×.005)
3	667	500	167	.86 ($167×.005)
4	500	400	100	.50 ($100×.005)

Benefits: The benefit of a call to the broker is the interest that is earned on the additional funds held in bonds because of the call. To illustrate, we will assume the interest rate is 6 percent per year or approximately 0.5 percent per month.

Costs: Assume the cost per call is constant at $2.00 per call. Eventually, the cost of an additional call will be higher than the benefits, and the call should not be made. In this example, only one call to the broker should be made because the second call costs $2.00 and the benefits are only $1.67.

20A-3
Benefits and Costs
of Call to the Broker
If the Interest Rate
Increases to 1 Percent
per Month

Call	(A) Transactions Demand for Money if Call Is Not Made	(B) Transactions Demand for Money if Call Is Made	(A) – (B)	Benefit: Interest Earned on Additional Bonds Held
0	$2,000	—	—	
1	2,000	$1,000	$1,000	$10.00 ($1,000×.01)
2	1,000	667	333	3.33 ($333×.01)
3	667	500	167	1.67 ($167×.01)
4	500	400	100	1.00 ($100×.01)

Costs: Assume that the cost per call is constant at $2.00 per call. In this case, the household should make two calls to the broker per month because the benefits of the second call ($3.33) outweigh the costs ($2.00). Hence, the quantity demanded of money for transactions is $667.

all of its income into its checking account and spends it evenly over the course of the month. Consequently, if the cost per call to the broker increases, households will make fewer calls. The average holdings of real money balances and, hence, demand will be greater. You should be able to analyze what will happen to the demand for real money balances if the cost per call to the broker decreases. Now would be a good time to look at Exhibit 20A-3, which illustrates what happens to the quantity demanded of real money balances if the interest rate per month increases from 0.5 percent to 1 percent. In this case, the benefits of each additional call double. If the cost per call is $2, the household makes two calls per month, and the quantity demanded of real money balances is $667. Therefore, as the interest rate increases, the quantity demanded of real money balances for transactions decreases from $1,000 to $667.

Endnotes

1. The yield or return on real estate includes the value of the stream of services that the assets provide plus any capital gain.
2. The value of money itself is measured in terms of the unit of account, which is an abstract measure of the exchange value. Another unique feature of money is that it has a fixed price in terms of the unit of account. For example, the value of a NOW account (money) is measured in dollars, which is the unit of account.
3. In this example, we are considering a one-time increase in the price level as opposed to inflation, which is a sustained increase in the price level. As you shall see, changes in inflation affect the demand for money.
4. As for the role of risk, note that we generally choose not to store food that tends to spoil quickly because when we need it, it might not be edible. The poorer and more susceptible our refrigeration system is to breakdowns, the greater this risk. Likewise, the greater the probability of inflation, the greater is the risk that money held for transactions and as a precaution will lose value. Therefore, the more prone the economy is to bouts of inflation, the fewer money balances we will hold. Instead, to hedge the risk of inflation, people might store value in the form of real assets.
5. The household could also hold savings or time deposits at banks or other financial intermediaries. In the case of savings accounts, the household members would have to make a trip to

the bank to remove the funds or transfer them over the phone or from a home computer. The household would incur record-keeping, time, and other transactions costs. In the case of time deposits, the same costs would be incurred, and the depositor might incur a penalty for removing the deposit before its maturity date.

6. Indeed, prior to the Depository Institutions Deregulation and Monetary Control Act of 1980 (DIDMCA), checkable balances paid no interest. Since that time, interest has been allowed on nonbusiness checking accounts, but it is less than the market rate of interest on other less-liquid assets.

7. Some firms may also be able to take a discount if they pay within a certain time period. The discount often amounts to 1 to 2 percent of the invoice. This translates into an annual return of 12 to 24 percent on the funds used to make the payment.

8. In this discussion, as in our analysis in Chapter 6, we are referring to "the interest rate" as representative of the overall level of interest rates, assuming that rates move up and down together depending on risk, liquidity, maturity, and tax treatment.

9. Even if interest rates on checkable deposits and on other market instruments increase by the same percentage amount, the opportunity cost of holding funds in checkable deposits increases. For example, assume that the T-bill rate is 5 percent and the rate on checkable deposits is 2 percent. If rates rise by 10 percent, the T-bill rate rises to 5.5 percent and the rate on checkable deposits to 2.2 percent. After the increase, the opportunity cost of holding checkable deposits, assuming that T-bills are the next best alternative, is 3.3 percent (5.5 percent less 2.2 percent). Before the increase, the opportunity cost was 3 percent (5 percent less 2 percent).

10. In this section, you will see that income is one of these "other factors" that will cause demand to change. In the next section, we look at additional factors.

11. Note that earlier we saw that if prices double, the demand for nominal money will also double, but the demand for real money balances will not change.

12. These innovations include home equity lines of credit on homes, which make even real assets more liquid.

13. Recall from Chapter 19 that the Fed can use offsetting open market operations to offset the impact of these factors.

14. For example, if the cost per call is $2 and three calls are made, total cost is $6. If four calls are made, total cost is $8.

21

The farmer's way of saving money: to be owed by someone he trusted.

—Hugh MacLennan

Financial Aspects of the Household, Business, Government, and Rest-of-the-World Sectors

Learning Objectives

After reading this chapter, you should know:

How economic and financial conditions influence household spending, saving, borrowing, and lending

What determines the volume of investment spending in the economy

How firms finance current production and investment

How the government's spending, taxing, and borrowing affect the financial system and the economy

How the spending, saving, borrowing, and lending of the rest-of-the-world sector affect the domestic financial system and the economy

TO SPEND OR NOT TO SPEND

Reflecting the weak economy, sales of new cars have been disappointing, and inventories of unsold cars are piling up on dealer lots. Given this situation, General Motors (GM), among others, decides to take some bold action. The prevailing interest rate on consumer loans for new automobiles is 4.5 percent. Beginning next Monday and lasting for the next 30 days, buyers of new GM cars will be able to finance their purchases by borrowing funds from GM's finance company subsidiary at a zero percent interest rate, and the price of all cars purchased will be reduced by $1,000. Jan and Dave, who had been planning to buy a new car next year, believe this deal is too good to pass up and decide to buy now. Because they must come up with $2,000 as a down payment on the $20,000 auto they want to buy (borrowing the other $18,000 from GM), Jan and Dave withdraw the necessary funds from their savings deposit at HLT National Bank.

After discussion, study, and months of agonizing, it is time to act. The board of directors of All Purpose Enterprise Inc. (APEI), one of the 10 largest companies in the nation, decides to undertake three separate actions: (1) sell a subsidiary whose profitability has consistently trailed other parts of the firm, (2) construct a new plant in India, and (3) extend an offer to purchase a medium-size firm specializing in telecommunications. With the economic outlook expected to improve in the months ahead and interest rates incredibly low, APEI, in effect, decides to restructure itself. It expects to increase its earnings in an improving economic climate by redeploying its assets. Because these actions will, on balance, require APEI to raise $2 billion of new funds, the company hires Smith Barney (part of Citigroup) of New York, a preeminent investment banker, to manage the tender offer for the telecommunications firm, the finding of a buyer for the subsidiary, and the issuance of the new bonds and stock necessary to finance the actions undertaken.

Between 1969 and 1997, the federal government budget was in a deficit position. The booming economy of the 1990s caused the federal budget to move into a surplus position in 1998, and large surpluses were projected to loom on the foreseeable horizon. The best way to use the surpluses became a topic of discussion and, in 2001, the Bush administration proposed a tax cut both to stimulate the economy and to reduce the projected surpluses. The discussion about the surplus disappeared after the September 11, 2001, attacks on the World Trade Center and the Pentagon. Increased military spending, new tax cuts, and a weak economy were expected to eliminate the projected surpluses at least in the near term. Sure enough, after having surpluses for four years, those surpluses quickly evaporated, and the budget went into a deficit position in 2001, which escalated to a record $500 billion in 2007, and was expected to exceed $1 trillion in 2009. Deficits also loomed over the foreseeable future.

In the early 2000s, the dollar was appreciating against both the yen and the euro. At the start of 2002, one dollar was worth about 130 yen and more than 1.1 euro. The dollar reversed course shortly thereafter. By early 2008, one dollar was worth only about 108 yen and .68 euro. Indeed, over the period from early 2002 to early 2008, the dollar fell about 38 percent against the currencies of its major trading partners.

Since 1982, the United States has run a continual deficit in the current account, dominated by a deficit in the balance of trade. The trade deficit with Japan and in the aggregate with the rest of the world has persisted regardless of whether the dollar was weak or strong. In recent years, a growing trade deficit with China received much media attention.

Although the preceding four scenarios seem unrelated, they are interdependent, and each affects the health of the economy and the functioning of the financial system.

In this chapter, we look at the financial aspects of the spending, saving, borrowing, and lending behavior of the household, firm, government, and the rest-of-the-world sectors. It is this behavior that ultimately determines aggregate demand.

HOUSEHOLD BEHAVIOR FROM A FINANCIAL PERSPECTIVE

The collection of real assets (houses, autos, and the like), financial assets (money, stocks, bonds, savings accounts, and so on) and liabilities (mortgages, consumer loans, and the like) is called a **portfolio.** One's portfolio can be displayed on a balance sheet, which measures the monetary value of a household's assets, liabilities, and **net worth** on a specific date. A portfolio is a stock concept because it measures the value of assets and liabilities held at a particular point in time. Aggregating over all households gives a balance sheet for the household sector, which reflects assets, liabilities, and net worth. Exhibit 21-1 shows the balance sheet entries of the household sector. Flows of spending, saving, borrowing, and lending that occur between given points in time cause balance sheet changes. The balance sheet transformations summarize the millions of spending, saving, borrowing, and lending decisions that households make in light of their objectives and constraints.

Consumption expenditures by households are by far the largest component of aggregate demand. In addition, when households spend money on investments such as houses, they also increase aggregate demand. Because household spending makes up more than 70 percent of aggregate demand, by its sheer size, household spending is extremely important in the macroeconomy. Our focus is on how and why the household spending flows change. Note that these changes are measured over an interval of time.

Research into consumer attitudes and behavior suggests that household portfolio decisions are guided by certain objectives such as happiness, good health, and a high standard of living. Leaving happiness and good health for the psychologists and physicians, economists traditionally focus on living standards, arguing that as households

Portfolio
The collection of real and financial assets and liabilities.

Net Worth
The difference between assets and liabilities at a point in time.

21-1
The Balance Sheet Entries of the Household Sector

Assets	Liabilities
Real estate	Real estate mortgages
Other real assets	Installment debt
Money	Other personal debt
Other financial assets	
	Net worth
Total assets	**Total liabilities plus net worth**

Like all balance sheets, the balance sheet for the entire household sector is arranged according to the fundamental identity that assets equal liabilities plus net worth. This means that the dollar value of the left column is identical to the dollar value of the right column. Other financial assets include time and savings deposits, stocks, bonds, mutual funds, money market mutual funds, and so forth. Not surprisingly, real estate holdings compose the largest portion of household assets, and mortgages on such real estate are the largest component of liabilities. Net worth measures the degree to which the value of assets exceeds the value of liabilities. Thus, net worth can be viewed as a measure of the financial health or wealth of households.

strive for a better quantity and quality of life, they will develop desired portfolios. Operationally, they will then spend, save, lend, borrow, or work to move their actual portfolios toward their desired portfolios. The point is that household behavior is purposeful, not haphazard. The result is a process characterized by consideration of alternatives, calculation of costs and benefits, and careful planning. Let's take a closer look at the process of financial decision making and what lies behind it.

Asset Accumulation: Spending and Saving

Real Assets
For households, durable goods and houses.

Households acquire **real assets** when they engage in consumption spending on durable goods or investment spending on newly constructed houses. If they have surplus funds left over to lend in financial markets, they acquire financial assets. In general, households desire real assets for the flow of services such assets provide. For example, a house (an investment good) provides shelter services over time. An auto provides transportation services, and a television provides entertainment services. Both the auto and the television are consumption goods. In addition, certain real assets such as houses and antiques may also be desired because of expected capital gains. The benefit or return associated with the acquisition of real assets is composed of the value of the flow of services together with any capital gain or loss. Such returns are analogous to and comparable with the returns on financial assets.

Financial Assets
Financial instruments such as stocks, bonds, and money, which serve as a store of value or purchasing power.

Financial assets, from the household perspective, serve as a store of value or purchasing power that can be used in the future, for example, to acquire real assets or pay for children's education. Financial assets, other than money, generally provide income to the holder in the form of interest and dividends and, sometimes, capital gains. This income supplements wages and salaries during the working years and supplements pensions during retirement. In fact, retirement constitutes a strong motive for households to be net lenders and thus accumulate financial assets during the working years. By doing so, households will be better able to maintain living standards in the retirement years.

Of course, retirement and future spending plans are not the only things that motivate the accumulation of financial assets. Equally important is the fact that we live in an uncertain world. Anyone can get laid off from a job, the refrigerator can break down, a medical emergency can occur, and so on. To cushion itself from the adverse effects of such happenings, a household will typically want to acquire some financial assets, especially liquid and safe assets such as savings deposits, Treasury bills, and money market mutual fund shares. These near monies can be converted into money quickly at little cost and involve little risk. The need for households to hold liquid assets for "a rainy day" has diminished somewhat in recent years as financial intermediaries have made so-called lines of credit (including home equity lines of credit) increasingly available to consumers. In essence, a line of credit is a promise by, say, a bank to lend you funds as you need them up to the amount for which you have been approved. Thus, if you have a $10,000 line of credit, all or part of these funds is available to you if and when the need arises. Changes in the size and composition of financial assets over time also reflect capital gains or losses on assets owned and household decisions to spend, save, borrow, or lend.

Money is also one of many financial assets households may possess. As you saw in the last two chapters, money is unique among financial assets in serving as a means of payment. Because of its unique position, we devoted all of Chapter 20 to the demand for real money balances. For now, we are merely reminding you that money is one of an array of financial assets a household may hold and that the demand for real money balances is directly related to income, while, ceteris paribus, the quantity demanded of real money balances is inversely related to the interest rate.

Liability Accumulation: Borrowing

Periodically throughout its lifetime, a household will consider spending (consuming) more than its current income or portfolio of financial assets can finance at that time. This is where borrowing and the accumulation of debt, or **financial liabilities**, come in. By examining the motives for borrowing and what limits the ability and willingness of households to borrow, we can highlight the important interdependencies inherent in household portfolio decisions.

A decision to borrow today is really two decisions: a decision to borrow today and a decision to repay what is borrowed plus interest in the future. The borrower is willing to trade off or borrow against future purchasing power for current purchasing power. Why would a household want to do this? Visualize a student couple whose current income is low but whose future income is expected to be higher. They desire to consume more now. Borrowing and spending now will raise consumption relative to current income and lower consumption in the future relative to income as the debts accumulated now are paid off. In the process, borrowing facilitates the smoothing out of household spending and consumption over time. Of course, households may also borrow to acquire knowledge and skills (education), which will lead to a higher future income. Likewise, they may borrow to acquire real or financial assets that are expected to rise in value over time.

Sounds great—but one question still needs to be answered. Because borrowing facilitates the acquisition of real and financial assets, and we generally prefer more rather than less, why not borrow continually and without limit? The answer, of course, is that households will not be able to borrow an unlimited volume of funds at the prevailing interest rate. The impediment to continuous borrowing, a **borrowing constraint**, comes from both the lenders—such as banks—and from the households themselves.

Borrowing Constraint
The impediment to continuous borrowing that may come from the lender's unwillingness to keep lending or the borrower's unwillingness to keep borrowing.

It is generally believed that as the ratio of debt or debt payments to income rises, the ability of a household to service or pay off additional debt is reduced. More specifically, the probability of default or delinquent payments on a loan rises. For this reason, financial intermediaries (FIs) are reluctant to grant new loans to heavily indebted borrowers. FIs require potential borrowers to fill out forms and undergo credit checks so that information on the household's balance sheet position and current and future income is available and can be used to gauge the riskiness of a potential loan. A household with little debt, a comfortable net worth position, and steadily growing income is obviously a more attractive borrower from a lender's perspective than a household with considerable debt, small net worth, and a highly volatile income stream.

The considerations that influence a lender's willingness to lend also influence a household's willingness to borrow. After all, households understand that if they become overextended and default on a loan, their future ability to borrow and spend will be severely impaired. Even if we disregard any legal repercussions, such a credit history will clearly make future potential lenders more reluctant to lend.

To summarize, households accumulate assets and liabilities in the process of attempting to maximize their well-being. The decisions they make and actions they take are the product of their objectives and the economic and financial environment in which they operate. Assuming that the objectives remain relatively constant, it is changes in the economic and financial environment that will lead to more or less spending and/or saving and, thus, more or less accumulation of real and financial assets and liabilities. The process is depicted in Exhibit 21-2.

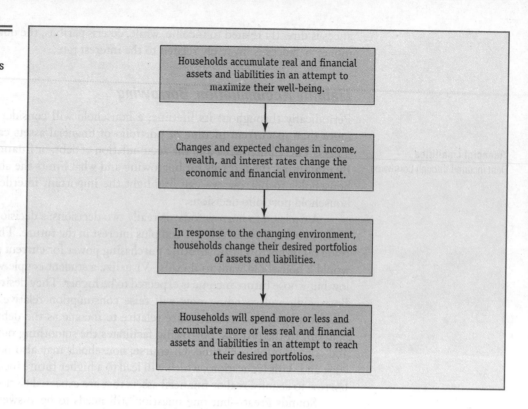

Households accumulate real and financial assets and liabilities in an attempt to maximize their well-being.

Changes and expected changes in income, wealth, and interest rates change the economic and financial environment.

In response to the changing environment, households change their desired portfolios of assets and liabilities.

Households will spend more or less and accumulate more or less real and financial assets and liabilities in an attempt to reach their desired portfolios.

HOW ECONOMIC AND FINANCIAL CONDITIONS INFLUENCE HOUSEHOLD ACCUMULATION OF ASSETS AND LIABILITIES

Household spending must be financed, whether via income, existing holdings of money, or borrowing. In addition, other financial or real assets can be a source of funds for spending, but they must be liquidated. Accordingly, fluctuations in household income and net worth (wealth) are usually directly associated with household willingness and ability to spend and borrow. It is important to note that although these variables tend to move together, the relationship between the aggregate variables is quite complex, with causation running in both directions. For example, while increases in household incomes surely encourage more consumption, it is also true that increases in aggregate consumption spending raise aggregate income.

Perhaps the most obvious financial determinant of spending and saving or borrowing and lending is the interest rate. Throughout this text, we have emphasized that the interest rate connects the present with the future. More specifically, it specifies the terms under which present purchasing power can be traded off for future purchasing power. To review, for the borrower who gets funds now and pays the principal plus interest in the future, the interest rate is the cost of borrowing and spending. For the lender who gives up funds now (forgoes some spending) and is paid the principal plus interest in the future, the interest rate is a reward for saving and lending. Thus, if interest rates rise as the result of the behavior of firms, government, or the rest-of-the-world sector, then both the cost of borrowing and the reward (return) for lending increase. Intuitively, we should expect households to respond by reducing their borrowing and spending on durables and housing and to increase their saving and, thus, their lending. In summary, changes (and expected changes) in income, wealth, and interest rates are the key forces driving household portfolio adjustments.

In late 2008 and early 2009, many households were experiencing painful adjustments in their portfolios as the crisis in the housing market caused the value of homes to plummet and some subprime mortgage loan rates were adjusting sharply higher. In addition, as the crisis spread to broader financial markets, households experienced losses in their savings and retirement accounts that led to massive reductions in household wealth.

Recap   Households accumulate assets and liabilities in an attempt to maximize their well-being. Assets may be real or financial. Households compare relative returns on real and financial assets. Money is one financial asset that is demanded for the stream of services that it yields. Households also incur financial liabilities. Changes and expected changes in income, wealth, and interest rates cause households to alter the composition of their assets and liabilities through portfolio changes.

FINANCIAL ASPECTS OF THE BEHAVIOR OF NONFINANCIAL BUSINESS FIRMS

Having devoted all of Part 3 to financial institutions, in this section we are restricting our analysis to nonfinancial firms. Business firms hold real assets such as plant and equipment and inventories. They also hold financial assets, including demand deposits and currency, as well as other highly liquid short-term financial assets such as money market mutual funds, negotiable certificates of deposit (CDs), foreign deposits, and trade credit. In addition, they hold time deposits, mutual funds, and other miscellaneous longer-term assets. Because business receipts and expenditures are not synchronized, firms use cash management techniques to move funds in and out of highly liquid short-term financial assets to minimize the costs of holding real money balances. We looked at the determinants of firms' demand for real money balances in Chapter 20. Taken together, these real and financial assets are what a firm owns.

Liabilities such as bonds outstanding; long-term mortgage loans owed; short-term debt, including business loans from banks and other financial intermediaries (FIs); and commercial paper outstanding represent what the firm owes. The funds acquired through such borrowing are used to finance current operations and the acquisition of new capital. The difference between the value of assets and liabilities is a business's net worth or

21-3

The Balance Sheet of the Business Sector

Assets	Liabilities
Real assets	**Equity**
Capital goods	Common stock
Inventories	
Financial assets	**Debt**
Currency, Checkable	Long-term
Deposits	
Money market mutual funds	Short-term
Certificates of deposit (CDs)	
Mutual funds	
Trade credit	
Other financial assets	Other financial liabilities
Total assets	**Total liabilities plus net worth**

owners' equity. As with households, changes in balance sheets at different points in time are caused by flows. Aggregating over all business firms gives a balance sheet for the business sector that reflects assets, liabilities, and net worth. See Exhibit 21-3 for the balance sheet entries of the business sector.

With this primer as background, it is natural to ask why firms wish to accumulate real assets. The simple answer is that real assets are used to produce goods and services and, therefore, earnings. Let's take a closer look at the key factors that underlie the accumulation of real assets.

The Accumulation of Real Assets by Firms: Capital and Inventories

A firm's most important real assets are its capital stock and inventories. We already know that capital is a key factor in the production process and that once existing factors are fully utilized, expanding production will require additional quantities of capital and/or other factors of production. If a firm is using only half of its existing capital, it would seem unlikely that investment spending would be high on the corporate priority list.

As depicted in Exhibit 21-4, business spending on new equipment, the construction of a new plant, and/or an increase in inventories is called **investment spending**. A firm's decision to invest, just like its decision to expand production, depends crucially on expected profits. If a firm finds that it can increase profits by expanding production, then output and sales rise. As production expands, capacity utilization increases, and at some point, the firm finds that it must undertake investment spending to expand further. If new equipment or a more modern plant can be expected to raise profits over time, a firm will invest.

Depreciation is the amount of investment that would be required to replace the capital stock worn out in the current production process. As a firm's existing capital stock depreciates, the firm must decide whether to replace it. If a firm's investment spending on capital is only as large as depreciation, the capital stock does not increase. **Net investment** increases the capital stock or inventories. Because the factors affecting replacement decisions are essentially the same as those affecting net investment, there is no real need for a separate analysis of investment spending that replenishes worn-out capital. Therefore, we shall focus on net investment, which is gross (total) investment minus depreciation.

From an economy-wide perspective, firms' decisions to invest play two key roles in the economy. First, investment spending is an important component of aggregate

Investment Spending
For businesses, spending on new equipment and capital or net additions to inventories.

Net Investment
Gross investment minus depreciation.

21-4
Business Investment

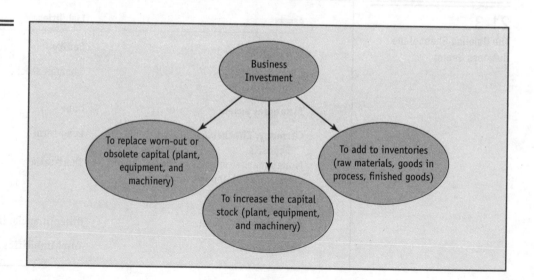

demand. Again, fluctuations in aggregate demand lead to changes in the overall price level and the level of real economic activity. Although investment spending is a much smaller component of aggregate demand than consumption, it is much more volatile than consumption spending. Hence, changes in investment spending are usually associated with fluctuations in business activity. Therefore, policy makers monitor investment spending closely, because decisions to invest or not to invest have important effects on real gross domestic product (GDP), unemployment, and prices. Second, increases in the capital stock raise the nation's productive capacity and enhance our standard of living and competitive position in the world economy.

Let's assume that a firm, which is currently using all of its existing capital, finds that it can increase profits by expanding production but must invest in new capital to do so. It begins by assessing the costs and revenues associated with various investment projects. Specifically, the firm will compare the rate of return on each project with the cost of financing that project. In making this comparison, both the rate of return and the cost of financing a project are typically expressed in annual percentage rates.

The cost side, specifically the cost of financial capital, can be kept fairly simple at this point. Suppose that the firm is considering a project that will cost $1 million. The firm can borrow the funds to finance the project, or it can use funds accumulated from past profits (retained earnings). If the firm borrows the $1 million, the cost of the funds will be the prevailing interest rate. If the firm uses funds from past profits, the cost of using the funds is measured by the return that the firm could earn if it loaned out the funds instead. Because the firm could lend out the funds at the prevailing interest rate, the interest rate is the cost of using the funds even though the firm is spending rather than lending them. This is an application of the notion of opportunity cost. The **opportunity cost** of holding or spending money is the return that one could have earned by using it in the next best alternative or opportunity. Whether the firm borrows or uses accumulated profits, the cost of funds is the prevailing interest rate. A final point should be noted: the interest rate that matters for investment decisions is the real interest rate, which is approximately the nominal interest rate minus the expected inflation rate. This is so because the real interest rate has been adjusted for expected inflation and represents the true opportunity cost of using funds. Another reason that the real interest rate is the relevant rate for investment decisions is that debts are denominated in dollars. If inflation is expected, a firm would be able to pay a higher nominal interest rate because the real value of its debt would be expected to fall. For example, if 5 percent inflation is expected, the firm would be willing to pay a 5 percent higher rate because the value of its outstanding debt would be falling by 5 percent in real terms. Also, if inflation does materialize, revenues coming into the firm would most likely increase.

As already discussed, whether a firm is willing to invest depends on a comparison of the cost of funds with the returns expected on the new capital goods. In general, the business outlook and the government's tax policy are important factors in the firm's assessment of the expected return on any particular investment project. The expected return is the present value of the future stream of returns likely to be associated with a particular project. The value of that stream is determined by the profits the project is expected to generate. Profits are a function of the productivity of the capital good, the price of the firm's output, the costs associated with operating and maintaining the capital good, and federal, state, and local taxes. If the business outlook is good, firms will expect demand for output to continue to grow, prices to rise, and, therefore, revenues to increase. On the other hand, if firms expect a long-lasting recession to begin shortly, the situation and outlook will not be conducive to investment: lower expected future sales will mean lower future profits; similarly, the future value of profits will also be lowered if the government is expected to raise corporate taxes.

Opportunity Cost
The return one could have earned by using funds in the next best alternative; for investment spending, the real interest rate.

In sum, the accumulation of capital by individual firms and, therefore, firms in the aggregate depends on the degree of capacity utilization, the business outlook, the government's tax policy, and the cost of financial capital (borrowing). Given firms' estimates of the returns on potential investment projects, the amount of investment spending on capital that will actually occur depends crucially on the prevailing financial environment, including the level of interest rates and the stance of monetary policy.

Like sales, planned inventories fluctuate over the business cycle. In particular, as the economy expands, inventory investment picks up in anticipation of higher sales. As the economy contracts, inventory investment may slow down in anticipation of slower sales. Firms must also finance their inventory stocks. Accordingly, firms take account of the cost of financing and holding inventories. The interest rate accounts for a large portion of that cost. In general, the higher the interest rate, the smaller is the upward adjustment in the stock of desired inventories in response to a surge in sales. The lower the interest rate, the larger is the upward adjustment in response to a surge. In sum and ignoring the details, we can conclude that current and expected sales are the primary determinant of the stock of planned inventories held by firms. Of course, the cost of financing inventories, the interest rate, also contributes to the decision.

Firms acquire real assets such as capital and additions to inventory. They also acquire financial assets (including money) and financial liabilities. Investment spending by the business sector is spending on capital or additions to inventories. The accumulation of capital depends on capacity utilization, the business outlook, the government's tax policy, and the cost of borrowing.

The Accumulation of Liabilities by Firms

Internal Financing
The spending of money balances on hand or the liquidation of financial or real assets to finance spending that exceeds current receipts.

In the process of investing and operating on a day-to-day basis, firms experience periods when expenditures exceed receipts. As a result, a firm must make several portfolio decisions, summarized in Exhibit 21-5, regarding the financing of excess spending. First, should the spending be financed internally or externally? **Internal financing** is simply the spending of money balances on hand or the liquidation of financial or real assets

21-5
Business Finance

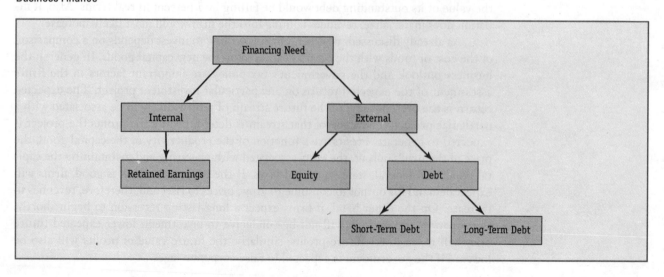

External Financing
Financing spending that exceeds
current receipts by expanding
either debt or equity.

owned by the firm to finance the excess. Internal financing is the largest source of funds for business firms. As for **external financing**, there are two types: expanding equity and expanding debt. Thus, if a firm chooses external financing, perhaps because its financing needs exceed the internal funds available, it must then decide whether to issue new debt and/or equity.

External financing via equity involves issuing shares of common or preferred stock, thereby expanding the ownership in the firm. If the firm chooses external financing through borrowing, it faces a third decision of whether to issue long-term or short-term debt. For example, the firm must choose between loans or market instruments such as commercial paper and corporate bonds. In general, each decision is guided primarily by the desire for profit maximization and the existing structure of financial liabilities. A firm will choose the option that minimizes the cost of funds.

For each firm, the overall cost of funds will be determined by the prevailing financial environment, the stance of monetary policy, and so forth. The relative cost of alternative sources of financial capital and, therefore, the particular financing decision reached will be influenced by several considerations: (1) the particular type of expenditures being financed, (2) the current financial environment and expectations about the future environment, (3) the firm's financial structure, and (4) the tax laws.

Traditionally, borrowing to finance inventories has taken the form of either short-term bank loans or the issuance of commercial paper. The usual maturity of the bank loans or commercial paper is one to six months, which is appropriate because inventories are typically not held for long periods of time. Fluctuations in inventory investment over the business cycle explain much of the variation in short-term debt accumulated by firms. The correlation is not perfect, however. For example, if many firms perceive prevailing long-term rates to be temporarily high relative to short-term rates, some firms will issue short-term debt to finance the initial phases of their investment spending on new capital. These firms expect that long-term interest rates will soon drop, at which point the firms will issue long-term debt to pay off the maturing short-term debt and finance subsequent phases of their investment spending. Thus, we see how current and expected financial environments play a role in firms' financing decisions.

Leverage Ratio
The ratio of debt to equity on a
firm's balance sheet.

The relationship among debt finance, risk, and the cost of capital is rooted in a common measure of the financial structure—the **leverage ratio**, or the ratio of debt to equity on a firm's balance sheet. Other things being equal, the higher the leverage ratio, the greater is the risk to bondholders and stockholders. The reason is that if a highly leveraged firm experiences a substantial decline in earnings, it could default on its debt obligations and be forced into bankruptcy, possibly leaving its stockholders with nothing. A firm with a low leverage ratio could weather a decline in earnings by cutting dividends, which are residual claims, not contractual obligations. The leveraged firm does not have this option: it must pay its debt costs or fold; hence, ceteris paribus, risk-averse investors will typically demand a higher yield on funds they lend to highly leveraged corporations. Firms that have considerable debt relative to equity will find the cost of debt financing (as well as equity financing) to be relatively high. As a result, they may decide to issue equity both to raise funds and to strengthen their balance sheets.

From the mid-1970s until 1991, a substantial portion of externally financed investment spending, which by definition is the acquisition of capital (new plant and equipment), was financed by issuing long-term debt. Why long-term debt instead of equity? The answer is that U.S. tax laws tend to bias the financing decisions of business firms toward debt and away from equity. Interest paid on debt is a tax-deductible cost and, thus, is subtracted from gross revenues before the corporate income tax is computed. Dividends paid to equity holders, however, are not tax deductible. Dividends must be paid out of after-tax earnings. Thus, debt financing will initially be cheaper, on average, than equity financing, which may also entail higher flotation costs. Equity financing also dilutes the ownership of current shareholders.

Debt financing also has a downside. Increasing debt is believed to expose a firm to more risk and, therefore, to weaken the firm's financial structure. The exposure to more risk can ultimately raise the overall cost of capital as the suppliers of funds require higher returns to compensate them for the additional risk.

Starting in 1991 and lasting until early 1994, firms altered the trend of debt financing and issued new shares of stock instead. Because of lower interest rates on CDs, savers poured money into mutual funds that soaked up the new stock issues. With stocks trading at high values, large amounts of funds could be raised by issuing relatively fewer shares. But by mid-1994, the trend had reversed itself. Companies bought back record amounts of stocks, peaking at more than $200 billion in 1998. Since then, stock buy-backs have continued and averaged between $40 and $50 billion per year between 2001 and 2004. Companies were using profits to purchase their own stock rather than pay dividends. In the bull market that lasted until early 2000, this activity was also pushing stock prices even higher. In addition, the capital gains of those who sold the stock back to the companies were subject to lower tax rates than dividends would have been. However, in 2004, taxes on dividends were significantly reduced, thus shifting household preferences toward dividends and away from capital gains.

Recap   Firms may use internal or external financing. Internal financing is the spending of money balances on hand. External financing involves expanding debt or equity financing. Firms choose the financing option that minimizes the cost of funds. The change in assets less the change in liabilities equals the change in net worth. Firms adjust their assets and liabilities in response to changes in expected profits, the business outlook, or interest rates.

FINANCIAL ASPECTS OF GOVERNMENT BEHAVIOR

Government spending on goods and services is a component of aggregate demand, just as consumption and investment expenditures are. Note that it is government spending on goods and services, not government outlays, that affect aggregate demand. Government outlays include government purchases of goods and services plus transfers, such as social security and unemployment benefits, and interest on the public debt. Transfers merely shift purchasing power from one group to another. Unlike changes in government purchases of goods and services, they do not represent changes in the demand for output.

If government spending increases, ceteris paribus, aggregate demand increases, and the public benefits from the increased spending, whether it be for higher education, national defense, better roads, or the space station. If the economy is at less than full employment, then the increase in government spending may also lead to increases in income and employment, as well as more consumption and investment spending. If the economy is at full employment and currently using all of its productive resources, then an increase in real government spending on goods and services will, of necessity, reduce real private spending or result in real borrowing from abroad.[1] The latter scenario may or may not lead to increased benefits for society as a whole.

If government spending decreases, ceteris paribus, aggregate demand decreases. Decreases in government spending usually also lead to decreases in income, increases in unemployment, and decreased benefits for society as a whole. If the economy is at full employment and currently using all of its productive resources, a decrease in real government spending on goods and services may result in increased real private spending or a reduction in real borrowing from abroad. The latter scenario may lead to increased benefits for society as a whole if the increased benefits of more real private spending or less borrowing from abroad outweigh the decreased benefits of less government spending.

Unfortunately, all increases in government spending must be financed either by tax increases or by the issuance of government securities, both of which can have a detrimental effect on the private sector. Ceteris paribus, increases in tax rates reduce disposable income. Because spending units have less income, consumption and investment spending decrease. Consumers and business firms are worse off, and aggregate demand is depressed from what it would be otherwise. If government securities are issued, you shall see that the economy can be adversely affected regardless of who purchases these securities. Interest rates may end up higher, and interest-sensitive spending on such things as investment in capital, inventories, and new houses may be negatively impacted. Likewise, the increased government spending may lead to higher inflation, which, if unanticipated, has detrimental effects on creditors and may debilitate the whole economy. Note that the real government expenditures on goods and services—rather than taxes—transfer goods from private to public use. Taxes in the aggregate merely influence whether the government allocates the goods with inflationary consequences.

Decreases in government spending can also be accompanied by decreases in taxes or a budget surplus that reduces the public debt. Both scenarios can have beneficial effects on the private sector. Ceteris paribus, decreases in tax rates increase disposable income. Because spending units have more income, consumption and investment spending increase. Consumers and business firms are better off, and aggregate demand is greater than it would be otherwise. If the government runs a surplus that reduces the public debt, interest rates may end up lower, and interest-sensitive spending on such things as investment in capital, inventories, and new houses may be favorably impacted. Likewise, the decreased government spending may lead to lower inflation, which can have beneficial effects on the aggregate economy.

Because the positive and negative impacts of increased or decreased government spending on the private sector are difficult to measure, judging whether the benefits outweigh the costs is a difficult task. In any case, before government spending is increased or decreased, the trick is to be sure that the benefits of that change are indeed greater than the costs.

The process of making decisions about government taxing and spending is complicated and frequently based on political rather than economic considerations. Taken together, individual policies aimed at many laudable objectives can add up to more government spending than either the president or Congress believes is economically sensible. Politicians are often reluctant to raise taxes or to cut spending on specific programs because both actions are likely to cost them votes. A moment's reflection on the implications of such behavior for the federal budget will help you understand why the government more often than not has run deficits since 1960, as shown in Exhibit 21-6. The **public debt** is the total of all past deficits less past surpluses and is sometimes referred to as the *national debt*.

Public Debt
The sum of all past government deficits less past surpluses.

To obtain a relative gauge of the growth of the government sector, analysts find it useful to view government outlays and receipts in relation to the general economy as a whole. We have used this approach in Exhibit 21-7, which shows federal outlays and receipts as a percentage of GDP since 1960.

Borrowing directly connects government actions to the financial system. Building on discussions in previous chapters, you can see that the government sector is similar to the household and business sectors because if outlays exceed receipts, the resulting deficit must

Fiscal Year	Receipts	Outlays	Surplus or Deficit (−)
1960	$ 92.5	$ 92.2	$ .3
1961	94.4	97.7	−3.3
1962	99.7	106.8	−7.1
1963	106.6	111.3	−4.8
1964	112.6	118.5	−5.9
1965	116.8	118.2	−1.4
1966	130.8	134.5	−3.7
1967	148.8	157.5	−8.6
1968	153.0	178.1	−25.2
1969	186.9	183.6	3.2
1970	192.8	195.6	−2.8
1971	187.1	210.2	−23.0
1972	207.3	230.7	−23.4
1973	230.8	245.7	−14.9
1974	263.2	269.4	−6.1
1975	279.1	332.3	−53.2
1976	298.1	371.8	−73.7
1977	355.6	409.2	−53.7
1978	399.6	458.7	−59.2
1979	463.3	503.5	−40.2
1980	517.1	590.9	−73.8
1981	599.3	678.2	−79.0
1982	617.8	745.8	−128.0
1983	600.6	808.4	−207.8
1984	666.5	851.8	−185.4
1985	734.1	946.4	−212.3
1986	769.1	990.3	−221.2
1987	854.1	1,003.9	−149.8
1988	909.0	1,064.1	−155.2
1989	990.7	1,143.2	−152.5
1990	1,031.3	1,252.7	−221.4
1991	1,054.3	1,323.8	−269.5
1992	1,198.5	1,479.4	−280.9
1993	1,275.1	1,525.8	−250.7
1994	1,374.4	1,561.4	−186.7
1995	1,463.2	1,637.1	−174.4
1996	1,587.6	1,698.1	−110.4
1997	1,723.4	1,752.2	−28.8
1998	1,721.8	1,652.5	69.2
1999	1,827.5	1,703.0	124.4
2000	2,025.0	1,788.0	236.9
2001	1,991.0	1,863.8	127.3
2002	1,853.2	2,010.1	−157.8
2003	1,782.3	2,157.6	−374.2
2004	1,880.3	2,293.0	−412.7
2005	2,153.9	2,472.2	−318.3
2006	2,407.3	2,655.4	−248.2
2007	2,568.2	2,730.2	−162.0
2008	2,523.6	2,978.5	−454.8
2009 estimate	2,357.0	3,543.0	−1,186
2010 estimate	2,533	3,236	−703
2011 estimate	2,825	3,323	−498

Source: The Budget of the United States Government, Fiscal Year 2009, Historical Tables (Washington, DC: U.S. Government Printing Office and the Congressional Budget Office); 22. Available online at http://www.whitehouse.gov/omb/budget and http://www.cbo.gov respectively.

Fiscal Year	Receipts	Outlays	Surplus or Deficit (−)
1960	17.9	17.8	0.1
1961	17.8	18.4	−0.6
1962	17.6	18.8	−1.3
1963	17.8	18.6	−0.8
1964	17.6	18.5	−0.9
1965	17.0	17.2	−0.2
1966	17.4	17.9	−0.5
1967	18.3	19.4	−1.1
1968	17.7	20.6	−2.9
1969	19.7	19.4	0.3
1970	19.0	19.3	−0.3
1971	17.3	19.5	−2.1
1972	17.6	19.6	−2.0
1973	17.7	18.8	−1.1
1974	18.3	18.7	−0.4
1975	17.9	21.3	−3.4
1976	17.2	21.4	−4.2
TQ	17.8	21.0	−3.2
1977	18.0	20.7	−2.7
1978	18.0	20.7	−2.7
1979	18.5	20.2	−1.6
1980	19.0	21.7	−2.7
1981	19.6	22.2	−2.6
1982	19.1	23.1	−4.0
1983	17.5	23.5	−6.0
1984	17.4	22.2	−4.8
1985	17.7	22.9	−5.1
1986	17.4	22.4	−5.0
1987	18.4	21.6	−3.2
1988	18.2	21.3	−3.1
1989	18.4	21.2	−2.8
1990	18.0	21.8	−3.9
1991	17.8	22.3	−4.5
1992	17.5	22.1	−4.7
1993	17.6	21.4	−3.9
1994	18.1	21.0	−2.9
1995	18.5	20.7	−2.2
1996	18.9	20.3	−1.4
1997	19.3	19.6	−0.3
1998	20.0	19.2	0.8
1999	20.0	18.7	1.4
2000	20.9	18.4	2.4
2001	19.8	18.5	1.3
2002	17.9	19.4	−1.5
2003	16.5	20.0	−3.5
2004	16.4	19.9	−3.6
2005	17.6	20.2	−2.6
2006	18.5	20.4	−1.9
2007	18.8	20.0	−1.2
2008	17.7	20.9	−3.2
2009 estimate	16.5	24.9	−8.3
2010 estimate	17.5	22.4	−3.3
2011 estimate	18.7	22.0	−1.6

*Percent for 2008–2009 are estimates.

Source: *The Budget of the United States Government, Fiscal Year 2009, Historical Tables* (Washington, DC: U.S. Government Printing Office and the Congressional Budget Office); 23–24. Available online at http://www.whitehouse.gov/omb/budget and http://www.cbo.gov respectively.

be financed by borrowing. Equation (21–1) ties government deficits to the government securities the U.S. Treasury must issue to finance the excess of outlays over receipts:

government outlays – government receipts
= new borrowing
= net new debt issued by the Treasury (bills, notes, and bonds)
(21-1)   = net government demand for loanable funds

In addition to borrowing to finance the current deficit, if some previously issued past debt is maturing and the government is not in a position to pay it off, that debt must be **rolled over**. That is, new borrowing called **refunding** must occur to refinance the part of the debt that is coming due. This type of new borrowing does not add to the public debt; only new borrowing to finance a current deficit increases the public debt.

If the federal government is running a surplus, it can use the surplus to pay off maturing debt, thereby eliminating the need to roll over or refund the debt. When the government runs a surplus, the value of the public debt is reduced by the amount of the surplus. In terms of Equation (21-1), net borrowing, net new debt, and the government demand for funds are all negative when the government runs a surplus. In the early 2000s, there was much discussion in the popular media about how the burgeoning government surplus should be spent. We hope you see that if the government spends the surplus, there is no surplus. The only other possibility is for the public debt to be reduced by the amount of the surplus.

Reflecting the paucity of surpluses after World War II and the relatively larger deficits, federal government debt outstanding totaled about $9 trillion on September 30, 2008. As noted in Chapter 13, part of the public debt is held by government agencies such as the Fed and the Social Security Administration. Of the estimated $10 trillion public debt, only $5.8 trillion was held by the public. The rest (about $4.7 trillion) was held by the Fed ($.5 trillion) and other government agencies ($4.2 trillion). Of the $4.3 trillion held by the public, foreigners held $2.9 trillion or over half the publicly held public debt.

The Treasury is the department responsible for managing the debt of the federal government. The Treasury must decide what maturities of securities should be issued—that is, how many bills, notes, and bonds—and when they should be issued.

The Treasury is by far the largest single borrower in financial markets, and, as we have seen, it dominates the market for securities because of the large outstanding volume of securities as well as the large initial offerings. To minimize the disruptions that its financing operations can cause in the market, the Treasury has **regularized** a large part of its financing activity. By this we mean that the Treasury announces its borrowing intentions well in advance and tends to borrow at regular intervals. For example, every Monday the Treasury sells new debt consisting of Treasury bills carrying 13- and 26-week maturities, and every Tuesday they sell new four-week bills. The Treasury uses these weekly sales of bills to refinance maturing bills—those issued three or six months previously. In effect, the government rolls over its old debt by paying with newly borrowed funds. In addition, the Treasury holds periodic auctions for two-, three-, five-, and 10-year notes. At the present time, the longest fixed-rate security the Treasury issues is the 30-year bond. Currently, five-, 10-, and 20-year inflation-indexed securities are auctioned several times a year.

Rolled Over
The result when the government borrows to pay off maturing debt.

Refunding
The refinancing of past government debt that is maturing.

Regularized
Describes the advanced announcements of Treasury intentions to borrow at standard intervals.

Recap Ceteris paribus, increases in government spending increase aggregate demand, and decreases in government spending decrease aggregate demand. Tax increases or increases in government borrowing are the costs of increased government spending. The public debt is the total of all past deficits less surpluses. If previously issued debt is maturing, it must be rolled over or refunded. Refunding does not add to the public debt. If the federal government is running a surplus, the public debt declines; if the federal government is running a deficit, the public debt increases.

Financial Effects of Government Borrowing

Simply put, government borrowing, and, thus, the budget deficit that generated it, can have a considerable impact on the availability and cost of funds to other borrowers. Likewise, a government surplus that reduces the public debt can free up loanable funds for other borrowers. In either case, the changes in the spending plans of other borrowers will, in turn, affect the overall pace of economic activity and inflation.

A rise in government borrowing represents an increase in the government's demand for funds. Recall that a rise in the demand for funds will, ceteris paribus, raise the interest rate. Again, as in Chapter 6, we assume that the interest rate refers to the overall level of interest rates. In this case, the interest rate on government securities initially rises because of the increase in government borrowing. In turn, interest rates on other securities such as corporate bonds, municipal bonds, and perhaps even mortgages are also pulled up. As the yield on government securities rises, financial investors seeking higher returns will be attracted to these securities. Some will rearrange their portfolios by selling, say, corporate bonds and buying government bonds. This selling of corporate bonds will tend to raise the rate on corporate bonds (lower the price), and the purchase of government bonds will tend to lower the rate on government bonds (raise the price). This process of substitution binds together all of the interest rates in financial markets and generally causes all interest rates to move up and down together. Thus, we can refer to the overall level of interest rates or the interest rate as moving up and down.

Why are we interested in this financial effect of government borrowing? We are interested because the rise in interest rates generated by the government's deficit financing will, ceteris paribus, tend to reduce the funds flowing to private borrowers such as firms and households, as well as municipal and state governments. This phenomenon is known as **crowding out**, which means that the rise in rates could induce some who had planned to borrow and spend to cancel, postpone, or reduce their spending and borrowing plans. More specifically, the rise in interest rates will tend to lower investment spending by some firms relative to what it otherwise would have been. This is because the firms find that the higher cost of financial capital now exceeds the expected return on some previously planned investment projects. Similarly, the rise in rates on mortgage and consumer loans will reduce spending by some households, particularly on consumer durables and housing, relative to what it otherwise would have been. The phrase "relative to what it otherwise would have been" is included to emphasize that consumption may increase even in the face of rising interest rates. However, the rise in interest rates will result in the increase in spending being smaller than it otherwise would have been.

A decrease in government borrowing represents a decrease in the government's demand for funds that will, ceteris paribus, tend to lower the interest rate. The interest rate on government securities falls because of the decrease in government borrowing. As the yield on government securities falls, financial investors seeking higher returns will be attracted to other securities. Some will rearrange their portfolios by selling, say, government securities and buying corporate bonds. This selling of government bonds will tend to raise the rate on government bonds (lower the price), and the purchase of corporate bonds will tend to lower the rate on corporate bonds (raise the price). As in the case of an increase in government borrowing, this process of substitution binds together all interest rates in financial markets and generally causes all interest rates to move up and down together.

Crowding Out
The reduction in private borrowing and spending due to higher interest rates that result from government deficit financing.

From the preceding analysis, ceteris paribus, when the government deficit increased, the interest rate increased, and when the government deficit fell, the interest rate decreased. A word of caution is in order: interest rates and deficits do not always move up and down together. In the real world where thousands of factors are changing at once, the relationship between interest rates and deficits can be obscured by a variety of factors. For example, on the demand side, decreases in the demand for funds by households and firms may offset the increase in the demand for funds by government. Indeed, this is exactly what we expect could happen in a recession. A cyclical drop in production and employment during a recession can lead, ceteris paribus, to an increase in the federal budget deficit. Tax receipts fall as household and business income falls, while government outlays rise mostly from increases in transfer payments such as unemployment compensation. The same cyclical drop in production that enlarges the deficit produces a reduction in household spending, particularly on housing and durable goods and in business investment spending. Because less spending typically means less borrowing, the increase in the government's demand for funds will offset a fall in demand by others, and interest rates can fall despite the rise in the budget deficit.

On the supply side, a fall in the total demand for funds, reflecting, say, a fall in the budget deficit, may not result in a decrease in interest rates if, at the same time, there is a decrease in the supply of funds. How could this occur? The supply of funds reflects the willingness of net lenders, both domestic and foreign, to supply funds and the Fed's provision of reserve assets to the economy.[2] Accordingly, if a fall in the government's deficit, and thus its borrowing, is accompanied by a decrease in the amount of funds supplied by the Fed, interest rates may not fall at all. Interest rates could even rise if the fall in the supply of funds generated by the decrease in reserves is relatively larger than the drop in demand.

Similarly, if foreign net lenders decide that U.S. financial claims are more attractive than foreign claims, there could be a rise in the foreign supply of funds. Large inflows of foreign funds into the United States during recent decades have played an important role in financing the U.S. government budget deficits. This inflow of funds from abroad have limited the rise in U.S. interest rates and the crowding out of consumption and investment spending that otherwise could have occurred.

Recap   Ceteris paribus, if the government deficit increases, the interest rate increases and may crowd out private spending. Ceteris paribus, if the government surplus increases, the interest rate decreases. However, other factors can often cause interest rates to move contrary to these predictions. During recessions, for example, even though the deficit is increasing, the interest rate may go down because of decreases in the demand for loanable funds by households or firms or increases in the supply of loanable funds orchestrated by the Fed. Likewise, both the interest rate and government surpluses may rise at the same time if the Fed is withdrawing funds from the U.S. economy. Inflows and outflows of foreign funds into the U.S. economy also affect the supply of loanable funds and the interest rate.

THE REST-OF-THE-WORLD SECTOR AND ITS EFFECT ON THE FINANCIAL SYSTEM

In Chapter 18, you saw that the exchange rate is the number of units of one currency that can be acquired with one unit of another. Like other prices, the exchange rate is determined by the forces of supply and demand. You saw that the demand for dollar-denominated funds is (1) directly related to changes in foreign income, (2) inversely related to changes in the foreign price of U.S. goods relative to the foreign price of foreign goods, and (3) inversely related to changes in foreign interest rates relative to U.S. interest rates. In turn, the supply of dollar-denominated funds is directly related to (1) changes in U.S. income, (2) changes in the dollar price of U.S. goods relative to the dollar price of foreign goods, and (3) changes in foreign interest rates relative to U.S. interest rates. Hence, changes in the exchange rate can come about from changes in either the foreign or the domestic economy.

Let's consider how changes in the exchange rate will feed back into the domestic economy regardless of their source. Think about the relationship between the exchange rate and the balance of trade in goods. Ceteris paribus, as the dollar appreciates, exports become more expensive for foreigners, while imports become cheaper for domestic residents. Being rational, foreigners reduce their purchases of the now more costly exports while spending units in the domestic economy substitute into the now cheaper foreign goods. The result is that as the dollar appreciates, exports decrease while imports increase. Given that net exports are by definition equal to exports minus imports, as the dollar appreciates, net exports fall, and as the dollar depreciates, net exports rise. Consequently, ceteris paribus, the relationship between net exports and the exchange rate is inverse.

Net exports are also a component of aggregate demand, along with consumption, investment, and government spending. Let's consider what happens to aggregate demand when the exchange rate changes. For example, if the dollar depreciates, then, ceteris paribus, net exports increase. Foreigners are purchasing more goods from the United States while domestic residents are purchasing fewer imports from abroad. In the United States, a depreciation in the dollar could mean more jobs and production and higher income than if the exchange rate remained unchanged. On the other hand, if the dollar appreciates, U.S. residents will, ceteris paribus, purchase relatively more goods from abroad; demand for domestic goods and services will be lower than it would be otherwise. This change could translate to fewer jobs, less production, and lower income in the United States. In other words, increases in the exchange rate, ceteris paribus, could lead to decreases in U.S. production, employment, and income, while decreases in the exchange rate could lead to increases in U.S. production, employment, and income. So changes in the exchange rate are, ceteris paribus, inversely related to U.S. production and employment. Exchange rate changes feed back to the domestic economy via their effect on net exports, which are directly related to changes in aggregate demand. Thus, in mid-2008, the depreciation of the dollar in terms of the currencies of our major trading partners has caused exports to increase at a far faster rate than our imports, causing our enormous trade deficit to fall slightly.

Now we can begin to see the linkages among economies clearly. In addition to domestic factors, such as monetary or fiscal policy or changes in the behavior of households and firms, any factor that affects net exports also affects aggregate demand and hence domestic GDP and the domestic price level. For instance, if foreign income (or the foreign price level relative to the U.S. price level or foreign interest rates relative to U.S. rates) changes, aggregate demand changes, causing domestic GDP and the price level to change. These changes then feed back to the foreign economy, which will, in turn, affect the domestic economy, and on it goes.

The rest-of-the-world sector clearly introduces additional complications that policy makers face in managing the domestic economy. Any policy action that affects the domestic economy will also affect the international economy, and the effects on the international economy will then feed back into the domestic economy. Likewise, developments in the international economy will affect the domestic economy. If a domestic economy is somewhat isolated from the rest of the world, this effect may be rather small; but as international trade and finance become more significant, as they have to the United States in the past 40 years, this effect also becomes more significant. Exhibit

21-8

Exports, Imports, and the Current Account Balance Since 1960 (in Billions of Dollars)

	(1) Exports	(2) Imports	(3) Net U.S. Exports of Goods and Services
1960	$27.0	$22.9	$0.4
1961	27.6	22.7	4.9
1962	29.1	25.0	4.1
1963	31.1	26.2	4.9
1964	35.0	28.1	6.9
1965	37.2	31.5	5.6
1966	40.9	37.1	3.9
1967	43.5	39.9	3.6
1968	47.9	46.6	1.4
1969	51.9	50.5	1.4
1970	59.7	55.8	4.0
1971	63.0	62.4	0.6
1972	70.9	74.2	−3.4
1973	95.3	91.2	4.1
1974	126.7	127.5	−0.8
1975	138.7	122.7	16.0
1976	149.5	151.1	−1.6
1977	159.4	182.4	−23.1
1978	186.9	212.3	−25.4
1979	230.2	252.7	−22.5
1980	280.8	293.8	−13.1
1981	305.2	317.8	−12.5
1982	283.2	303.2	−20.0
1983	277.0	328.7	−51.7
1984	302.4	405.1	−102.8
1985	302.0	417.3	−115.2
1986	320.6	453.3	−132.7
1987	363.9	509.1	−145.2
1988	444.1	554.5	−110.4
1989	503.3	591.5	−88.2
1990	552.4	630.3	−78.0
1991	596.8	624.3	−27.5
1992	635.3	668.6	−33.3
1993	655.8	720.9	−65.1
1994	720.9	814.5	−93.6
1995	812.2	903.6	−91.4
1996	868.6	964.8	−96.3
1997	955.4	1,056.9	−101.6
1998	955.9	1,115.9	−160.0
1999	991.3	1,251.8	−260.5
2000	1,096	1,475.8	−379.5
2001	1,035.1	1,401.7	−366.6
2002	1,006.8	1,433.1	−426.3
2003	1,048.9	1,543.8	−494.9
2004	1,164.5	1,797.8	−615.4
2005	1,309.4	2,023.9	−714.6
2006	1,467.6	2,229.6	−762.0
2007	1,641.4	2,350.0	−708.6
2008*	1,971.3*	2,677.9*	−706.5*

*Annualized through September, 2008.

Source: Federal Reserve Statistical Release, Z.1, Flow of Funds of the United States (March 6, 2008), current release and historical data. Available online at **http://www.federalreserve.gov/releases/z1/**.

21-8 shows exports, imports, and the trade balance since 1960. Striving (and sometimes failing) to manage such effects to preserve the health and stability of the economy must necessarily involve international considerations—more on this in a later policy chapter. For now, we turn to the effects of foreign demand for U.S. securities on domestic financial markets.

The Effects of International Events on the Interest Rate

Net Capital Inflow
Condition when the purchases of U.S. financial claims by foreigners exceed purchases of foreign financial claims by U.S. entities.

Net Capital Outflow
Condition when the purchases of foreign financial claims by U.S. entities exceed the purchases of U.S. financial claims by foreigners.

When purchases of U.S. financial claims by foreigners exceed purchases of foreign financial claims (securities) by U.S. residents, the United States experiences a **net capital inflow.** As a result, ceteris paribus, the supply of loanable funds is greater and the domestic interest rate is lower than they would be without the capital inflow. When net exports are positive (resulting in a surplus in the current account), there is a **net capital outflow,** making the supply of loanable funds lower and the domestic interest rate higher than they would be otherwise. Thus, net capital flows affect domestic interest rates through their impact on the supply of loanable funds.

In previous chapters, we considered the supply of loanable funds as consisting of the surplus funds generated by net lenders and increases in credit extension through financial intermediaries. Credit extension is often triggered by increases in reserve assets initiated by the Fed. We now are in a position to see that when foreigners purchase U.S. financial assets, they too are increasing the supply of loanable funds. Ceteris paribus, the inflow of funds from abroad leads to decreases in the interest rate. Likewise, decreases in foreign purchases of domestic financial assets lead to decreases in the supply of loanable funds and increases in the interest rate.

But, you may ask, why would foreigners want to increase or decrease their purchases of domestic financial assets? An obvious reason would be that U.S. interest rates had changed relative to the rest of the world, making U.S. securities more or less attractive relative to foreign securities. For example, if U.S. interest rates increase, ceteris paribus, funds will flow in from abroad to get the higher return. Note the paradox of the situation: the capital inflow causes interest rates to be lower than they would be otherwise, but this occurs because interest rates are relatively high to begin with. In addition, high U.S. interest rates relative to the rest of the world will increase the demand for dollar-denominated deposits and, hence, cause the dollar to appreciate relative to other currencies—and, as you have seen, changes in the exchange rate feed into net exports. It seems we have come full circle. Changes in the exchange rate affect net exports, which change aggregate demand. Changes in domestic interest rates affect capital flows, which also affect the exchange rate and, hence, net exports and aggregate demand. In the mid-2000s, U.S. financial instruments were in demand by foreigners for reasons other than interest rate differentials. For example, despite low U.S. interest rates, the government of the Republic of China purchased large amounts of U.S. government securities to maintain the exchange rate between the Chinese yuan and the U.S. dollar. This strategy makes products from China more attractive in the United States.

A related question is why domestic interest rates would be high or low relative to the rest of the world. Perhaps the supply of and demand for loanable funds will help to answer this question. If the interest rate equates the quantity demanded of loanable funds with the quantity supplied, then any factor that affects either demand or supply will also affect the interest. On the demand side, changes in the spending plans of households, firms, or the government will all affect the demand for loanable funds. On the supply side, changes in the surplus funds available from net lenders, credit extension by financial intermediaries, and capital flows from abroad will all change the supply of

The American Recovery and Reinvestment Act of 2009

With President Obama's signature, the American Recovery and Reinvestment Act (ARRA) of 2009 took effect on February 19, 2009. This law provides for a $787 billion stimulus package to bailout the economy which was mired in a deep downturn. As noted earlier, the downturn started with the mortgage crisis and subsequent financial crisis. It later spread to the broader economy as manifested by job loses, declining output, foreclosures, bankruptcies, and stock market losses. ARRA is the largest fiscal stimulus plan ever.

The new law enacts a series of spending initiatives and tax cuts. Tax cuts are about 37 percent of the total while spending increases are the remainder. Major categories, as reported by the Congressional Budget Office (CBO) are summarized as follows:[a]

Category	Billions[b] of Dollars
Food and farming	$26.4
Commerce	15.8
Defense	4.5
Energy and the environment	50.7
Government	6.7
Homeland security	2.7
Outdoors, Indian reservations and the arts	10.5
Labor and volunteering, health care and social services, education, social security	71.2
Oversight	.025
Military and veterans	4.2
Foreign relations	.6
Transportation and housing	61.1
Aid to states	53.6
Tax cuts	288.5
Individual aid	58.1
Individual health care aid	24.7
Health information technology	17.6
Aid to states for Medicaid	90.0
Total	$787.2[b]

The CBO estimates that because of the stimulus package, gross domestic product (GDP) will be increased between 1.4 percent and 3.8 percent *from what it otherwise is forecasted to be* by the fourth quarter of 2009, between 1.1 percent and 3.4 percent by the fourth quarter of 2010, between 0.4 percent and 1.2 percent by the fourth quarter of 2011, and by declining amounts in later years. If these increases materialize, the act will get the economy going again.

According to the CBO, ARRA is expected to increase the deficit by $787 billion between 2009 and 2019. The CBO estimated that while the stimulus would increase output, spending, and employment over the next few years, by 2019, GDP would actually be between .1 and .3 percent lower than without the package. The reason for the decrease in 2019 is because of higher interest rates and possible crowding out of

[a]Congressional Budget office at www.cbo.gov.
[b]Numbers do not sum to total because of rounding.

private expenditures due to the larger government debt. However, increases in GDP caused by the spending on infrastructure improvements, education, and research could offset any private sector losses due to crowding-out and cause GDP to be higher than what it would otherwise be without the stimulus package. In the near term, crowding-out is not an issue because of the large amount of slack and unused capacity in the economy. The possible .1 and .3 percent decreases in GDP in 2019 are small in comparison to the annualized 6.2 percent decrease in GDP the economy experienced in the last quarter of 2008. Many analysts also feared the downturn was far from the bottom and, thus, the current state of the economy merits the large stimulus package.

The Congressional Budget Office at www.cbo.gov offers a wealth of information about all of the stimulus packages to get the economy going. Another federal website that offers a wealth of information about the economy in the troubled times of 2009 and this piece of legislation in particular is www.recovery.gov.

---

loanable funds. In addition, variations in domestic inflationary expectations relative to foreign inflationary expectations will change the level of domestic rates relative to foreign rates.

To summarize, net exports affect the U.S. economy through their effect on aggregate demand. Output and prices are directly affected by changes in net exports. With regard to the financial side of the economy, ceteris paribus, net foreign demand for U.S. securities directly affects the supply of loanable funds and interest rates. If there is a net capital inflow, ceteris paribus, the exchange rate could be higher and net exports lower than they would be otherwise. Because of the large inflow of funds from abroad, we have focused on the net foreign demand for U.S. securities. Keep in mind that changes in the net domestic demand for foreign securities also affect the supply of loanable funds. Try working through the effects of an increase in foreign interest rates relative to U.S. rates. What happens to the domestic supply of loanable funds and the interest rate?

Recap   Net foreign demand for U.S. securities directly affects the supply of loanable funds and interest rates. If there is a net capital inflow, ceteris paribus, the exchange rate could be higher and net exports lower than they otherwise would be. Changes in the net domestic demand for foreign securities also affect the supply of loanable funds.

Summary of Major Points

1. Spending and saving decisions of households are based on their objectives and the economic and financial environment within which they operate. Assuming that the objectives remain relatively constant, it is changes in the economic and financial environment that lead to more or less spending and saving and, thus, more or less accumulation of assets and liabilities. Changes in income, wealth, and interest rates are the key forces driving household portfolio adjustments. Consumption spending by households is the largest component of aggregate demand.

2. Investment spending by individual firms—and, therefore, firms in the aggregate—depends on the degree of capacity utilization, the business outlook, the government's tax policy, and the cost of financial capital (borrowing). Given firms' estimates of the returns on potential investment projects, the amount of investment spending that will actually occur depends on the financial environment, including the level of interest rates and the stance of monetary policy. Like consumption spending, investment spending is a component of aggregate demand. Investment spending is more volatile than consumption spending.

3. Firms hold inventories of raw materials and finished goods to facilitate smooth and efficient production and to satisfy consumer demand. Accordingly, firms consider the interest rate, which is the cost of financing and holding inventories. In general, the higher the interest rate, the smaller will be the upward adjustment in the stock of desired inventories in response to a surge in sales, and vice versa.

4. Firms experience periods when expenditures exceed receipts. They must decide whether to finance the spending internally or externally. Assuming that a firm chooses external financing, it must then decide whether to issue new debt or equity. Debt financing offers tax advantages, but at the same time, financial leverage and its accompanying risks increase. Short-term borrowing is often used to finance inventories. Long-term borrowing is usually used to finance investment. If interest rates are expected to fall, short-term borrowing may sometimes be used for investment.

5. Politicians are sometimes reluctant to raise taxes or cut spending. Government outlays exceeded tax receipts between 1969 and 1997 and again from 2002 until the present. Increases or decreases in borrowing directly connect government actions to the financial system. If outlays exceed receipts, the resulting deficit must be financed by borrowing, carried out by the U.S. Treasury. Other maturing government debt must also be refunded.

6. Increases in the government deficit, ceteris paribus, push interest rates up by increasing the demand for loanable funds. Decreases in the government deficit or increases in the government surplus push interest rates down by decreasing the demand for loanable funds. Other factors operating on both the demand and the supply sides of the market for loanable funds may affect whether interest rates will indeed rise when the deficit rises. Expectations about the deficit affect the interest rate, particularly for long-term bonds, before the deficit changes. If the deficit causes interest rates to rise, private spending may be crowded out.

7. Net exports add to domestic demand. If net exports are positive, output and the price level could be higher than they would be otherwise. If net exports are negative, output and the price level could be lower than they would be otherwise. Net exports are inversely related to the exchange rate, ceteris paribus. If the exchange rate increases, ceteris paribus, net exports decrease, and vice versa. If the exchange rate increases, income from exports could decrease. Likewise, if the exchange rate decreases, income from exports could increase.

8. Foreign demand for U.S. financial assets has a significant effect on the domestic supply of loanable funds. To the extent that foreigners demand U.S. securities, the supply of loanable funds is increased and interest rates are lower than they would be otherwise.

Key Terms

Review Questions

1. Do assets equal liabilities for (a) an individual household? (b) the household sector as a whole? (c) the economy as a whole? Explain.
2. Both changes in income and changes in the interest rate affect spending. Which has a greater effect? Explain.
3. Explain the effect that each of the following variables has on household and/or business spending or saving:
   (a) Income; (b) Wealth; (c) The interest rate;
   (d) Capacity utilization; (e) Expectations;
   (f) Monetary policy; (g) Tax policy;
4. Define the following terms: *depreciation*, *net investment*, and *investment spending*.
5. Is money a financial asset?
6. What are some of the factors that determine whether a firm chooses internal or external financing? How is the leverage ratio related to the borrowing constraint?
7. Do most college students face a borrowing constraint? Explain.
8. My income is going up, but interest rates are also higher. Will I buy a new car?
9. Would a firm ever use short-term debt to finance long-term capital expenditures? (*Hint:* Consider all possibilities for expected long-term rates.)
10. How should the government decide whether to increase or decrease its purchases of goods and services? How does this procedure compare with the political process that is used?
11. How will a reduction in a government deficit affect aggregate demand? Do changes in transfer payments affect aggregate demand?
12. How can government expenditures be financed?
13. Assume a constant supply of loanable funds. When government deficit spending leads to increases in the demand for loanable funds, do interest rates always rise? Explain. (*Hint:* Consider the role of expectations.)
14. If the economy is at full employment and the government increases its purchases of goods and services, does this always lead to crowding out? Is crowding out good or bad for the economy?
15. Distinguish between public debt and a deficit.
16. When the U.S. Treasury issues government securities, who buys those securities?
17. Will increased government spending always lead to crowding out if the economy is not at full employment? (Consider the case in which the increased spending involves transfer payments rather than the purchase of goods and services.)
18. Discuss the following statement: If the Treasury increases its borrowing today, interest rates will always go up.
19. Briefly discuss the long-term effects of government borrowing and the public debt.
20. What is the relationship between net exports and aggregate demand, and between net exports and capital flows? If net exports increase, ceteris paribus, what happens to real GDP? If the domestic price level increases, ceteris paribus, what happens to net exports?
21. When the government balance is in surplus, does the government debt still have to be rolled over? Explain.
22. Why has the government regularized its borrowing?
23. What would happen to U.S. interest rates if, ceteris paribus, foreigners decided to sell some of the U.S. financial assets that they own?

Analytical Questions

Questions marked with a check mark (✓) are objective in nature. They can be completed with a short answer or number.

✓24. Assume that Rosemarie and Jack have the following assets at the end of the year:

House	$150,000
Stocks and bonds	10,000
Money	1,500
Furniture	3,500
Jewelry	2,000
Savings deposit	1,000
Car	10,000

What is the total of their real assets? What is the total of their financial assets? What are their total assets?

25. Assume that at the end of the year, Rosemarie and Jack have the following liabilities:

Mortgage loan	$120,000
Credit card debt	4,000
Car loan	6,000

What are their total liabilities? Assuming that the assets from question 24 and the preceding liabilities, what is their net worth?

Suggested Readings

A detailed analysis of the U.S. balance of payments can be found at **http://www.newyorkfed.org/aboutthefed/fed point/fed40.html.**

Check the data on consumer credit at **http://www.feder alreserve.gov/releases/g19/.**

Jose A. Lopez looks at borrowing by Spanish corporations in "Corporate Access to External Financing," *Economic Letter*, Federal Reserve Bank of San Francisco, 2007–31, October 19, 2007. The article is available online at **http:// www.frbsf.org/publications/economics/letter/2007/ e12007–31.html.**

In recent years, households have reduced their personal savings rate significantly. Alan Garner looks at this trend in "Should the Decline in the Personal Saving Rate Be a Cause for Concern?" *Economic Review*, Federal Reserve Bank of Kansas City, Second Quarter 2006. The article is available online at **www.kansascityfed.org/PUBLICAT/ ECONREV/er06q2.htm.**

To find information about specific companies, check Hoover's list at **www.hoovers.com.**

Current information on federal, and state, and local government finances can be found at **www.bea.doc.gov/news releases/glance.htm.**

The U.S. Treasury, which is responsible for managing the debt of the federal government, can be accessed at **www .treas.gov.** Upcoming auction schedules of Treasury securities can be found at **http://www.treasurydirect.gov/ instit/annceresult/press/press.htm.**

For a look at "The Impact of Exchange Rate Movements on U.S. Foreign Debt," see the article by the same name by Cedric Tille, *Current Issues in Economics and Finance*, Federal Reserve Bank of New York 9, no. 1 (January 2003). The article is available online at **http://www.ny.frb.org/ research/current_issues/ci9–1.html.**

Every three years, the U.S. government surveys consumer finances. The latest survey available (2007), as well as earlier surveys, are available online at **http://www.federalre serve.gov/pubs/oss/oss2/scfindex.html.**

For a look at the relationship between investing households and bankers, see John Hackett, "Luring Investors Back to the Market," *U.S. Banker* (June 2001): 28–34.

For insight into the relationship between households and firms, see Franklin Allen, "Financial Contagion," *Journal of Political Economy* 108, no. 1 (February 2000).

Endnotes

1. As in previous chapters, the term *real* before a variable means that the variable has been adjusted for changes in the price level. In this case, the real amount of government spending (adjusted for price changes) has increased.
2. Recall from Equation (6-2) that $i = f(\bar{M}, \overset{+}{Y}, \overset{+}{p^e})$, where i equals the interest rate, M equals the money supply, Y equals income, and p^e equals expected inflation. You can also think of the rise in government spending or cut in taxes, which necessitates more government borrowing, as raising Y and, thus, the demand for funds.
3. In the actual flow of funds, there is a rather large instrument discrepancy due to measurement errors.

CHAPTER TWENTY-TWO

One man's wage rise is another man's price increase.

—Harold Wilson

Aggregate Demand and Aggregate Supply

Learning Objectives

After reading this chapter, you should know:

The determinants of aggregate demand and aggregate supply

Why the aggregate demand curve is downward sloping and what causes it to shift

Why the short-run aggregate supply curve is upward sloping and the long-run aggregate supply curve is vertical

What causes the short-run and long-run aggregate supply curves to shift

How short-run and long-run aggregate supply are related

GDP UP 8 PERCENT: DOES THIS INDICATE AN ECONOMY IN GOOD HEALTH?

Over the four-year period from 1979 to 1982, nominal GDP increased, on average, by about 8 percent per year. Over the four-year period from 1997 to 2000, nominal GDP grew, on average, by about 6.7 percent per year. To the casual observer, these data might suggest that although the economy performed well in both periods, the performance was better in the first period. Nothing could be further from the truth!

The composition of the growth in nominal GDP was dramatically different across the two periods. From 1979 to 1982, prices rose about 8 percent per year, on average, while real GDP growth was essentially nil. In contrast, from 1997 to 2000, prices rose about 2.4 percent per year, while real GDP rose about 4.6 percent per year. With inflation lower and real growth higher, the economy obviously performed considerably better over the 1997 to 2000 period. Armed with these facts, it is natural to ask what accounted for this improvement. Was it good luck, deft policy adjustments by the Fed, or clever fiscal decisions by Congress and the president?

To answer this and related questions, we shall build on material developed in the previous chapter on the behavior of households, firms, the government, and the foreign sector. You shall see, for example, that an increase in demand, regardless of the source, will initially tend to lead firms to raise some combination of production, employment, and prices (depending on the shape of aggregate supply). We will also show how changes in aggregate demand and/or supply combine to produce changes in the overall price level and real GDP—the two factors that make up nominal GDP. Within the context of this overall discussion, we emphasize why the short-run effects of changes in aggregate demand or supply on output, employment, and prices differ markedly from the long-run effects. As you shall see, this point is crucial in explaining fluctuations in the economy's performance and the role of policy makers in aggravating or moderating such fluctuations.

AGGREGATE DEMAND

As its name implies, *aggregate demand* is the quantity of real goods and services that will be demanded at various price levels over a specific time period such as a year. We can arrive at aggregate demand by summing the total demands of each sector in the economy at a myriad of price levels. These demands, which have been discussed in some detail in Chapter 21, flow from the various spending, saving, borrowing, and lending decisions made by the household, firm, government, and rest-of-the-world sectors. Equation (22-1) illustrates the various components of aggregate demand:

(22-1)   aggregate demand = consumption + investment + government + net exports

Consumption demand originates with the household sector and includes intended purchases of durable goods, nondurable goods, and services. Consumer spending, which has a relatively stable growth rate (or stable with respect to income), is directly related to income and inversely related to the interest rate, ceteris paribus.

Gross investment demand emanates from the business and household sectors and includes intended expenditures for replacement and new capital, increases in inventories, and additions to the stock of houses. Like consumption, gross investment is directly related to income and inversely related to the interest rate, ceteris paribus. Unlike consumption, investment demand is relatively volatile, and swings in investment spending have been associated with turns in the business cycle.

Government demand includes intended purchases of goods and services such as roads, national defense, and education at the federal, state, and local levels. Transfers, such as social security payments and unemployment benefits, are excluded from aggregate demand because transfers merely shift purchasing power from one group to another without adding to or subtracting from the level of aggregate demand. Ceteris paribus, increases in government purchases increase aggregate demand, and decreases in such purchases reduce it. As you have seen, a complex decision-making process involving Congress and the president determines government purchases of goods and services. In recent years, government purchases, including those by state and local governments, have accounted for about 17 to 19 percent of real GDP.

Net exports represent the difference between exports and imports. Changes in net exports can be negative or positive. If the intended changes are positive, they add to aggregate demand; if negative, they reduce aggregate demand from what it otherwise would be. Ceteris paribus, net exports are inversely related to the exchange rate and to capital inflows.

The Aggregate Demand Curve

Having defined our terms, we now turn to how the quantity demanded of real GDP (aggregate demand) is related to changes in the overall price level. Look at Exhibit 22-1, which plots the relationship between the price level and aggregate demand using hypothetical figures. Real GDP is measured on the horizontal axis, and a price index, such as

22-1

The Aggregate Demand Curve

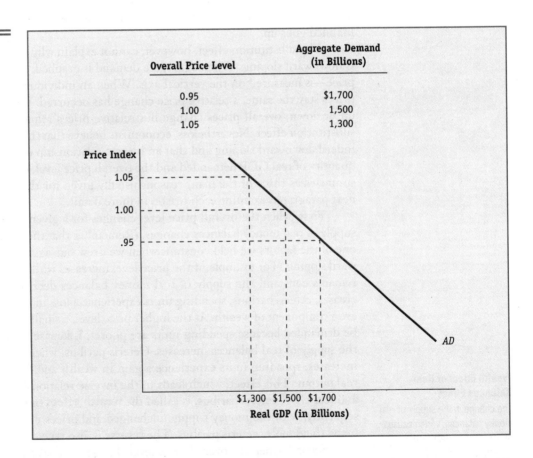

As the price level rises from 0.95 to 1.05, ceteris paribus, aggregate quantity demanded falls from $1,700 billion to $1,300 billion. The aggregate demand curve shows the relationship between total planned expenditures in the economy and the overall price level.

GDP Deflator
A price index that measures the overall changes in the prices of everything in GDP.

Aggregate Demand Curve
A curve showing the inverse relationship between the overall price level and the aggregate quantity of real output that will be demanded at various price levels, ceteris paribus.

the GDP deflator, is measured on the vertical axis. The **GDP deflator** measures overall changes in the prices of everything in GDP. Like other demand curves, the **aggregate demand curve** is downward sloping, indicating that, ceteris paribus, an inverse relationship exists between the aggregate quantity of real goods and services demanded and the overall price level. Thus, points on the aggregate demand curve show the quantities of real GDP that will be demanded at various price levels, assuming that all other factors except the price level are held constant. These other factors include the nominal money supply, expectations about future economic conditions, interest rates, taxes, and government purchases, among others.

Demand curves for individual products, such as hamburgers, baseballs, and dry cleaning, are downward sloping because of the *substitution effect*. As the price of hamburgers changes, ceteris paribus, hamburgers become either relatively cheaper or relatively more expensive than other goods and services. Ahmed and his friends substitute toward goods that are relatively cheaper and away from goods that are relatively more expensive. The result of such rational behavior is an inverse relationship between price and quantity demanded, ceteris paribus. For example, when the price of hamburgers goes up while the price of hot dogs remains unchanged, prudent shoppers substitute out of hamburgers and into hot dogs, which are now relatively cheaper.[1] The reverse happens when hamburger prices decline. Hamburgers are now relatively cheaper than hot dogs, and consumers find themselves enjoying more of the comparably cheaper burgers. Thus, when the price of hamburgers goes up, quantity demanded goes down, ceteris paribus, and when the price goes down, quantity demanded goes up.

The substitution effect, however, cannot explain why the aggregate demand curve is downward sloping. When aggregate demand is graphed, a price index—not a relative price—is measured on the vertical axis. When an individual price changes while other prices stay the same, a relative price change has occurred. When the price index moves up or down, overall prices change but relative prices remain unchanged. There is no substitution effect. Nevertheless, economists believe that the aggregate demand curve is indeed downward sloping and that an inverse relationship exists between the aggregate quantity of real GDP demanded and the overall price level, ceteris paribus. Exhibit 22-2 summarizes three of the main reasons usually given for this inverse relationship. The next paragraphs examine each reason in more detail.

First, when the overall price level changes for a given nominal money supply, the supply of real money balances changes. (Remember that the nominal money supply was one of the factors we held constant when we drew our aggregate demand curve downward sloping.) For example, if the price level increases while the nominal money supply remains constant, the supply of real money balances decreases. When the supply decreases, ceteris paribus, spending units experience a loss in wealth because real balances are a component of wealth. At the higher price level, a smaller quantity of real GDP will be demanded because spending units are poorer. Likewise, if the price level decreases, the supply of real balances increases. Ceteris paribus, when the supply of real balances increases, spending units experience a gain in wealth and demand a larger quantity of real output. This effect, which leads to the inverse relationship between the price level and real GDP, ceteris paribus, is called the **wealth effect** or **real balances effect**. Consequently, with the money supply unchanged and prices down, people can and do demand (buy) more, ceteris paribus. The reverse is also true.

Second, when the overall price level changes, ceteris paribus, domestic goods and services become relatively cheaper or relatively more expensive than foreign goods, which can lead to changes in net exports. For example, if the U.S. price level rises relative to

Wealth Effect or Real Balances Effect
The change in the supply of real money balances, which causes an increase or decrease in wealth, when the price level changes for a given supply of nominal money balances.

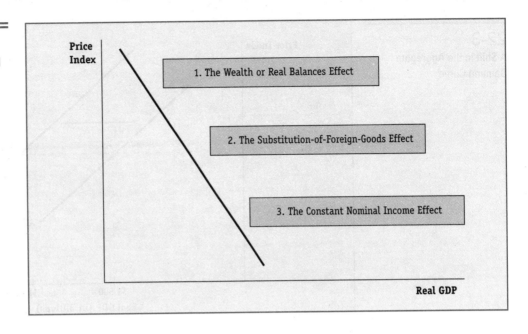

the foreign price level, U.S. goods are relatively more expensive than foreign goods. Purchasers substitute out of the relatively more expensive domestic goods and into the relatively cheaper foreign goods. Likewise, if the U.S. price level falls relative to the foreign price level, U.S. goods are relatively cheaper than foreign goods. Purchasers substitute out of the relatively more expensive foreign goods and into the relatively cheaper U.S. goods and services. As the price level rises, ceteris paribus, net exports fall, and as the price level falls, net exports rise. As the price level rises, the quantity demanded of real GDP falls because of the decline in net exports, and as the price level falls, quantity demanded increases. This effect, which, ceteris paribus, leads to the inverse relationship between the price level and the aggregate quantity of real GDP demanded, is called the **substitution-of-foreign-goods effect.**

Third, when we draw an aggregate demand curve, we consider what happens to the quantity demanded of real GDP as we vary the overall price level. Other factors, including nominal income, remain constant. By the equation of exchange, which we first discussed in Chapter 20, nominal income equals the overall price level multiplied by real GDP.[2] Hence, when the price level rises, the aggregate quantity demanded of real GDP must fall in accordance with the constant nominal income constraint. Simply put, less is demanded at higher prices because the funds run out sooner. We call this effect the **constant nominal income effect.**

Thus, the wealth effect, the substitution-of-foreign-goods effect, and the constant nominal income effect can explain why the aggregate demand curve is downward sloping. But what happens when aggregate demand changes? When aggregate demand changes, the entire set of relationships between the various price levels and the quantities demanded at those prices also changes. Simply put, if aggregate demand changes, the entire aggregate demand curve shifts. For example, if aggregate demand increases, the aggregate demand curve shifts to the right, and if aggregate demand falls, the aggregate demand curve shifts to the left. The mechanics of such shifts are shown in Exhibit 22-3. To complete our discussion of aggregate demand, we need to address briefly one last but crucial question: What causes aggregate demand to change?

Substitution-of-Foreign-Goods Effect
When changes in the domestic price level cause consumers to substitute into relatively cheaper foreign goods or out of relatively more expensive foreign goods.

Constant Nominal Income Effect
When changes in the price level necessarily cause the quantity demanded to change in the opposite direction to maintain constant nominal income.

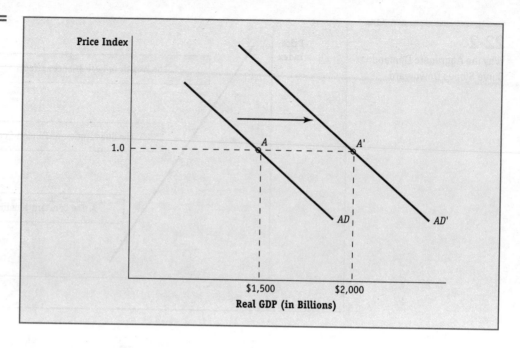

The first aggregate demand curve (*AD*) is identical to the one in Exhibit 22-1. If aggregate demand increases, the aggregate demand curve shifts to *AD'*. More specifically, the quantity demanded for goods and services at price level 1.0 rises from $1,500 billion to $2,000 billion, that is, from point *A* to point *A'*. The other points can be derived similarly.

What Causes Aggregate Demand to Change?

Changes in aggregate demand are the keys to understanding one side of the economy, so we turn now to identifying the primary causes of these changes.[3] As with any demand curve, the shape and position of the aggregate demand curve were initially determined by the factors we held constant, and it will change when and only when any of these factors changes.

From Equation (22-1), you can see that aggregate demand changes when any of its four components changes. If a component of aggregate demand increases while the others at least remain the same, aggregate demand is given a boost. If a component falls, aggregate demand also falls, and this decline may have undesirable ramifications for the economy as a whole.

A change in taxes, government spending, the money supply, interest rates, expected inflation, the economic outlook, and exchange rates can individually trigger changes in aggregate demand. We have already touched on the way that many of these catalysts activate fluctuations in the components of aggregate demand. For example, an increase in government spending, ceteris paribus, increases aggregate demand. Ceteris paribus, an increase in income tax rates decreases consumption expenditures, and an increase in corporate tax rates reduces the expected profitability of investment. Both would decrease aggregate demand. Changes in the money supply lead to changes in interest rates and liquidity within the entire financial system that affect consumption and investment spending. A change in expected inflation changes the demand for real money balances, ceteris paribus, and leads to changes in interest rates and stock prices. Moreover, a change in any of the factors usually affects the economic outlook, which then affects spending decisions. To round out our picture of what causes changes in aggregate demand at this time, we can safely link changes in any of the factors to changes in government spending and taxing decisions and to changes in the money supply and interest rates as initiated by the Fed. That is, monetary and fiscal policies can and do cause aggregate demand to fluctuate. The linkages between fluctuations in demand in the United States and the various stabilization policies of the federal government and the Fed will be taken up in greater detail in the policy chapters in Part 6. It is important to note, however, that sustained changes in aggregate demand usually have been the result of monetary and fiscal policy actions in the United States and, on occasion, of monetary and fiscal policy actions abroad. Finally, one of the reasons the federal government has reacted so strongly to mitigate the financial crisis of 2008–2009 is because of its effect on the economic outlook and aggregate demand, as households and businesses become more pessimistic about the future. Also, falling housing and stock prices effectively reduce the

22-4

A Schematic Overview of the Movements in Aggregate Demand

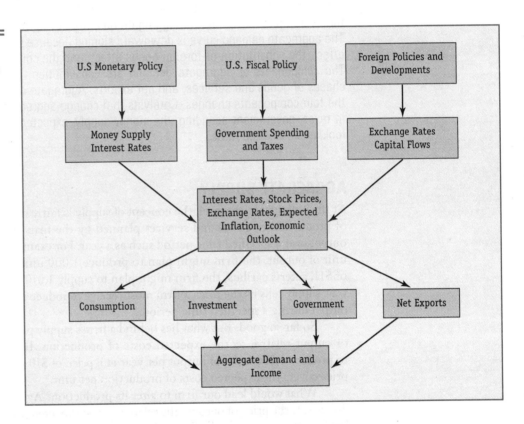

Policy actions in the United States and abroad are typically the source of major movements in aggregate demand. A policy action, such as a rise in the money supply engineered by the Fed, may lower interest rates in the United States. The resulting fall in the cost of financial capital will encourage consumption and investment spending, particularly the acquisition of real assets such as durable goods, houses, and plant and equipment. The increased spending will tend to increase production, sales, and profits, which will, in turn, tend to boost stock prices. On the international side, the fall in U.S. interest rates relative to foreign interest rates will tend to lower (or depreciate) the international value of the dollar. With import prices denominated in dollars rising and export prices denominated in foreign currencies falling, imports will tend to fall, and exports will tend to rise, boosting U.S. net exports. Thus, by affecting interest rates, exchange rates, stock prices, and, perhaps, expectations about future values of these magnitudes, policy alters aggregate demand in the United States.

wealth of households and in turn cause them to reduce their consumption expenditures and for aggregate demand to fall.

To summarize, the schematic diagram in Exhibit 22-4 brings together the essential parts of the story. Changes in U.S. monetary policy—and changes in fiscal policy—have a powerful impact on spending and, hence, on the components of aggregate demand through the effects on the financial system (interest rates and stock prices), international competitiveness (exchange rates), income, and expectations of future economic and financial developments.

Half of our demand and supply framework is now in place. To understand what happens to the price level and real output when aggregate demand shifts and how the price level and real GDP are ultimately determined, we need to develop the other half: a theory of aggregate supply.

Recap   *Aggregate demand* is the quantity of real goods and services that will be demanded at various price levels over a specific time period. There is an inverse relationship between the overall price level and the aggregate quantity of real output that will be demanded. The aggregate demand curve is downward sloping because of the wealth or real balances effect, the substitution-of-foreign-goods effect, and the constant nominal income effect. The components of aggregate demand are consumption, investment, government purchases of goods and services, and net exports. Aggregate demand changes when any of the four components changes. Catalysts that change aggregate demand include changes in taxes, government spending, the money supply, expected inflation, the economic outlook, and exchange rates.

AGGREGATE SUPPLY

At the individual firm level, the concept of supply is fairly straightforward. It is the level of production of goods and services planned by the firm at various prices per unit of output over a specified time period such as a year. For example, at a price level of $10 per unit of output, the firm might plan to produce 1,000 units of output. At a price level of $11, ceteris paribus, the firm might plan to supply 1,010 units of output. Put another way, supply tells us the price a firm must receive to induce it to produce various levels of output during a specified time period.

So far so good. But what lies behind a firm's supply plans? The answer is the price of output relative to the expected costs of production. If a firm is willing over time to produce 1,000 units of output per year at a price of $10 per unit, we can be sure this price covers the expected costs of production per unit.

What would lead our firm to alter its production? Again, the answer follows fairly directly. If the price of output falls relative to the expected price of inputs (which we will hold constant for now), the firm will ultimately reduce production because revenues are falling relative to costs.[4] Conversely, if the price of output rises relative to the fixed price of inputs, the firm will increase production because revenues per unit of output will be rising relative to costs per unit. Make sure that you understand that the price of the firm's output is changing while input prices remain constant.

The central analytical point of our discussion thus far is the key role played by relative prices. More specifically, the price of the output relative to the expected price of inputs drives a firm's production decisions; anything that alters this relative price will alter the quantity produced by the firm. In our example, a rise in output prices led to a rise in production, ceteris paribus, and a fall in output prices led to a decline in production. Thus, we see that there is a direct relationship between output price and quantity supplied.

From the Individual Firm to the Aggregate

Aggregate Supply Curve
The curve graphically depicting the relationship between the overall price level and the aggregate quantity of real GDP that will be supplied at various price levels.

These "microfoundations" of supply by individual firms provide the basics of aggregate supply. The **aggregate supply curve** for the economy as a whole depicts the level of output that all firms and others will produce at various price levels over a specified time period, such as a year. The price level at the aggregate level is not the price of a particular unit of output but the average of all output prices as captured by a price index. The quantity is not the amount of a particular good but the real output for the entire economy. As with aggregate demand, the price index is the GDP deflator, and our measure of real output is real GDP.

To see how firms in general and, therefore, aggregate supply react to a change in the price level, let's work through an example. Suppose aggregate demand for goods and services increases unexpectedly. What will happen? The answer—which can initially be confusing and a bit frustrating—is that some combination of prices, output, and employment will rise in the short run. Given the same factors of production, state of technology, and full employment, however, only prices will rise in the long run.

We should note that over time our "givens" (the factors of production and technology) do not remain constant. In Chapter 23, we take up the dynamic nature of their long-run response. In this chapter, we restrict our analysis to the more static situation in which the givens remain constant.

What accounts for the different short- and long-run responses of the economy? The brief answer is the behavior of firms as reflected in aggregate supply. A somewhat more detailed answer is the dynamics of firms' behavior and the resulting adjustments in aggregate supply over time. Soon we shall visualize what lies behind major fluctuations in the economy. By doing so, you will gain some insight into the difficulties that policy makers face in achieving the nation's goals.

Short-Run Aggregate Supply

Long-Run Equilibrium
When all prices have adjusted to shifts in aggregate supply or demand, and the flow of spending, saving, borrowing, and lending continues until something else changes.

Real Wage
The nominal wage divided by the overall price level.

Our analysis begins with the economy in **long-run equilibrium**. This term means that all prices (including wages) and quantities in the economy have fully adjusted to previous shifts in aggregate supply or demand; in addition, the configuration of interest rates, exchange rates, expectations, and relative prices is producing a flow of spending, saving, borrowing, and lending that will continue unless and until something changes. Included in the relative prices that have adjusted is the **real wage**, which is the nominal wage deflated by the price level. An important characteristic of this analytical convention (called *long-run equilibrium*) is that expected values are equal to actual values. Sales are coming in as expected, so there are no unexpected changes in inventories. Actual inflation is equal to expected inflation, so there are no unexpected changes in real interest rates or real wages. Resources, including labor, are fully employed. There is no tendency for the real wage to fall because there are no involuntarily unemployed workers willing to accept jobs for slightly lower nominal wages and, thus, ready to bid down the real wage.

Seldom, if ever, is the economy precisely in such a state, but that's less of a problem than you might think. The concept and characteristics of equilibrium will enable us to isolate and trace the effects of major shocks to the economy.

With the economy in long-run equilibrium, suppose that the Fed moves unexpectedly to raise aggregate demand by increasing the reserves of depository institutions through substantial open market purchases. The resulting rise in the money supply and initial fall in interest rates stimulate nominal spending and sales. The question for us is this: What happens to aggregate supply? Or, more specifically: How do firms respond to the increase in aggregate demand?

The rise in firms' sales produces an unexpected decline in inventories and puts unexpected upward pressure on output prices. Holding the prices of inputs fixed for now, firms in the aggregate, just like the individual firm already discussed, respond to the decline in inventories and rise in output prices relative to input prices by expanding output. Because more output requires more inputs, employment of labor and other factors of production will also expand. Since we started at a position of full employment, however, firms in the aggregate find it impossible to hire more workers without increasing the nominal wage. So, rather than remaining fixed as we initially assumed, the nominal wage begins to rise, albeit at a slower rate than output prices. Employment temporarily goes above sustainable full employment.[5] Workers temporarily perceive the increase in nominal wages—even though it is less than the increase in prices—to be an increase in real wages and agree to supply more labor.[6]

To sum up, the initial or short-run effect of a rise in demand will be an increase in the price level and an accompanying increase in output and employment. In other words, the quantity of goods and services supplied increases when the price level rises. The reason is that output prices are assumed to rise relative to input prices, providing the requisite incentive to raise production. Remember that a price index is measured on the vertical axis. When output prices rise, the overall price level rises. In this situation, however, we are assuming that, because input prices do not rise as quickly as output prices, relative prices are also changing.

What happens to the quantity of goods and services supplied in the short run if aggregate demand falls unexpectedly? The short answer is that there will be downward pressure on both the price level and the quantity of goods and services supplied. The reasoning parallels the preceding discussion: The unexpected fall in demand will produce an unexpected rise in firms' inventories and put downward pressure on output prices.[7] Firms respond to the rise in inventories and fall in output prices relative to input prices by reducing output. Reflecting the production cuts, employment of labor and other factors of production will fall. Thus, the initial or short-run effect of a fall in demand will be downward pressure on the price level and a reduction in output and employment. Here again, we see that the aggregate quantity of goods and services supplied will fall if the price level falls, reflecting a decline in output prices relative to input prices.

Short-Run Aggregate Supply Curve
A curve showing the direct relationship between the overall price level and the level of real output that will be supplied in response to changes in demand before full adjustment of relative prices has taken place.

The basic and essential features of short-run aggregate supply are nailed down graphically in Exhibit 22-5, which depicts the **short-run aggregate supply curve**, showing the direct relationship, ceteris paribus, between the overall price level and the aggregate quantity of real GDP supplied. The short-run aggregate supply curve is positively sloped; the aggregate demand curve shifts along a given positively sloped short-run aggregate supply curve. By tracing the short-run response of firms and, thus, the economy to shifts in aggregate demand, we, in effect, trace the short-run aggregate supply curve. Again, hypothetical figures are used. Study the exhibit carefully before moving on.

Recap
Aggregate supply is the amount of output that firms will supply at various prices for the economy as a whole. In the short run, there is a direct relationship between the overall price level and the level of output supplied. If aggregate demand increases, firms will supply more output in response to higher output prices. In the short run, input prices are fixed, and firms respond to higher output prices by offering more for sale. If aggregate demand falls, there will be downward pressure on the price level and the aggregate quantity of real goods supplied. Because output prices fall relative to input prices, firms will produce less.

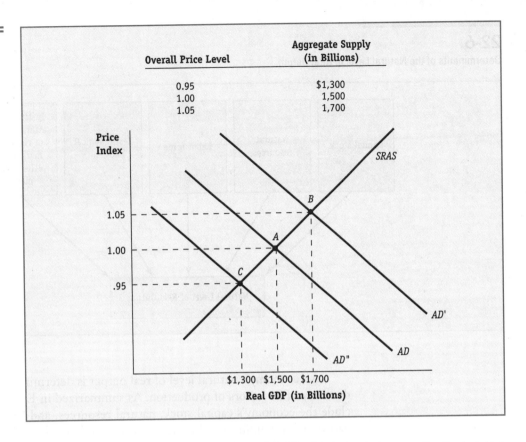

Overall Price Level	Aggregate Supply (in Billions)
0.95	$1,300
1.00	1,500
1.05	1,700

In the short run, shifts in aggregate demand generally lead to movements in the same direction in output, employment, and prices. Assume that the economy is in equilibrium at point *A* and aggregate demand increases (*AD* to *AD'*). With sales increasing, inventories falling, and output prices under upward pressure, firms respond by expanding output and employment. Input prices are assumed to be fixed or increasing relatively slower than output prices in the short run. Thus, output prices rise relative to input prices. The result for the economy as a whole is depicted by the movement from point *A* to point *B*. Output rises to $1,700 billion, and the price level increases to 1.05. Starting over again from point *A*, the result of a decline in aggregate demand (*AD* to *AD"*) is that the economy moves from point *A* to point *C*; output and the price level fall.

Long-Run Aggregate Supply

As discussed, it is entirely possible for the economy to move from one level of real output supplied (and demanded) to another in the short run. More generally, it is perfectly feasible for the economy to move from a position of long-run equilibrium (remember this is where we started our discussion of short-run aggregate supply) to a short-run equilibrium where the level of real output has changed.

The task before us is to explain (1) why at any particular time there is just one level of real output—called the **natural level of real output**—at which long-run equilibrium with a stable price level is possible; (2) why a short-run equilibrium, where the level of real output differs from the long-run natural level of real output, is a temporary, nonsustainable situation; and (3) how the economy moves back to long-run equilibrium. Put more simply, we want to understand what the natural level of output is and how and why the economy tends to move back toward this long-run norm whenever the level of output deviates from it.

Natural Level of Real Output
The level of real output that is consistent with long-run equilibrium, given the quantity and productivity of the economy's factors of production.

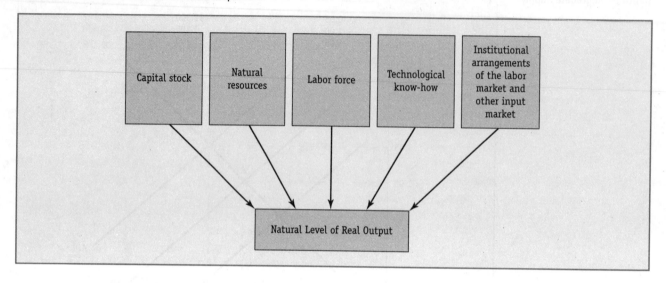

An economy's natural level of real output is determined by the quantity and productivity of its factors of production. As summarized in Exhibit 22-6, these factors include the economy's capital stock, natural resources, and labor force. In addition, the natural level is influenced by the technological know-how that production techniques embody and the institutional arrangements governing the operation of the labor market and other input markets. The natural level should not be thought of as an absolute limit on what the economy can produce. Rather, it is the level to which the economy would move, given its factors of production and current technology.[8] As discussed previously, the actual level of real output can increase in the short run if, for example, firms respond to a rise in demand by operating overtime using standby plant capacity and employing more people than usual. More people than usual may accept jobs because they mistake an increase in nominal wages for an increase in the real wage. That is, they fail to recognize for a time that output prices are actually going up faster than the nominal wage. Similarly, the actual level of real output can fall for a time, as occurs in a recession when workers are laid off and some portion of plant capacity is idled.

As we shall see, however, short-run equilibrium in which the actual level of output differs from the natural level of real output is not a long-run equilibrium and, thus, is not sustainable over time. When an economy is in long-run equilibrium, the prices of goods and services sold by firms will bear a consistent relationship to the prices of the inputs employed by firms. In particular, the prices of goods and services must be high enough to allow firms to cover their costs of production and earn a normal profit. Similarly, the prices of inputs—wages and salaries, in particular—must be high enough relative to the cost of living to make work worthwhile. The nominal cost of living can be measured by the prices of consumer goods, such as the consumer price index.

A helpful way to summarize the discussion to this point is to say that the economy is in long-run equilibrium when relative prices are correct—more specifically, when output prices are consistent and sustainable relative to input prices. As we pointed out at the beginning of the subsection on short-run aggregate real supply, the implication of saying that "relative prices are correct" is that all input and output prices in the economy have fully adjusted to previous shifts in aggregate supply or demand. The resulting configuration of interest rates, exchange rates, relative prices, and expectations is producing a flow of spending, saving, borrowing, lending, production, and employment that will continue unless and until something changes. A key characteristic of such a situation, which is crucial to everything that follows, is that actual values are equal to expected values. There are no surprises or unexpected developments. Actual sales are coming in as expected, and, thus, there are no unexpected changes in inventories or production.

Now suppose, for example, that output prices are expected to increase by 10 percent. With output prices expected to rise, input prices will rise proportionately in the long run to maintain the real incomes of the suppliers of the factors of production. With input prices rising in proportion to output prices, there will be no change in relative prices and, thus, no incentive for firms to produce more or for workers to work more. If output prices are expected to increase by 10 percent, the end result, depicted by the movement from point A to point B in Exhibit 22-7, will be a 10 percent increase in the price level from 1.00 to 1.10 with the economy continuing to operate at its natural level of real output. Actual prices will again be equal to expected prices, and, thus, there will be no unexpected changes in real wages or real interest rates; the economy will continue to operate at its natural level of real output, as shown in Exhibit 22-7.

In contrast, if actual values differ from expected values, adjustments in production, employment, spending, and so on, will occur. For example, if the actual price level turns out to be higher than expected, workers who bargained for and accepted a particular nominal wage rate based on an expected price level of 1.00 will, in time, come to realize that their real wages are lower than they anticipated. For example, if the price level turns out to be 1.05 rather than 1.00, workers will find that their real wages and real purchasing power are lower. Among other things, this will lead them to seek higher

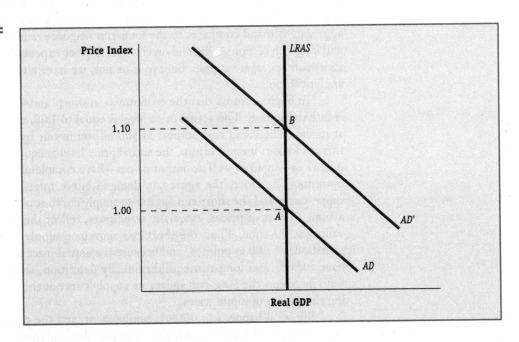

22-7
Long-Run Aggregate
Real Supply

Suppose that the economy is in long-run equilibrium at point A with the actual price level of 1.0 equal to the expected price level and the economy operating at its natural level of real output. Now assume that firms and suppliers of factors of production expect aggregate demand to increase, and this in fact occurs (with AD shifting to AD'). The economy responds to the anticipated rise in demand by moving up a given vertical long-run aggregate supply curve to point B.

nominal wages in an effort to restore their real wages and purchasing power. Any resulting wage increase will raise production costs, which, in turn, will affect employment, production, and output prices. By definition then, the situation when actual values differ from expected values cannot be a long-run equilibrium.

To sum up, we first discussed short-run aggregate supply in which input prices are initially assumed to be fixed or slower to change than output prices. In this situation, changes in output prices result in changes in relative prices and, thus, changes in production and employment. Second, we examined long-run aggregate supply in which input prices are not fixed and all input and output prices (and price expectations) have completely adjusted to various developments. The long-run aggregate supply curve is vertical at the natural level of real output, as shown in Exhibit 22-7. Along the long-run aggregate supply curve, there is no change in relative prices and the economy is operating at its natural level of real output, given the current technology and the quantity and productivity of the factors of production.[9] With these two building blocks in place, the final crucial question in our discussion of aggregate supply should be obvious: How is short-run aggregate supply related to long-run aggregate supply?

Long-Run Aggregate Supply Curve
The vertical curve through the natural rate of output to which the economy will return in the long run regardless of the price level.

Recap   In the long run, when input prices are flexible and full adjustment has occurred, the economy will gravitate to the natural level of real output. The natural level of real output is determined by the quantity and productivity of the economy's factors of production.

The Relationship Between the Short Run and the Long Run: Shifts in Short-Run Aggregate Supply

The task before us is, in effect, to integrate Exhibit 22-7 with Exhibit 22-5. More specifically, we need to show (1) how the short-run response of the economy to, say, a rise in aggregate demand compares to the long-run response, and (2) how the different short- and long-run responses depend on changes in price expectations and associated shifts in short-run aggregate supply. Believe it or not, we have already developed the requisite analytical tools.

To begin, assume that the economy is in short- and long-run equilibrium at point A in Exhibit 22-8. The actual price level is equal to 1.00, and the economy is operating at its natural level of real output: $1,500 billion in our hypothetical example. Because this is a long-run equilibrium, the actual price level is equal to the expected price level. All prices—input as well as output prices—have completely adjusted to previous developments. Therefore, the aggregate demand curve intersects the long-run aggregate supply curve and the short-run aggregate supply curve at point A. Note carefully that we assume that input prices, especially wage rates, reflect the price level expectations prevailing at the time. Thus, the short-run aggregate supply curve reflects price level expectations of 1.00 at point A, and because the actual price level is also equal to 1.00, we have a short- and long-run equilibrium. By definition, short-run aggregate supply always intersects the long-run aggregate supply curve at the expected price level governing the setting of input prices.

But what happens to output, employment, and the price level if there is an unexpected rise in the money supply and aggregate demand increases unexpectedly from AD to AD'? In the short run, the economy will move to point B. Intuitively, the rise in demand results in an unanticipated fall in inventories and a rise in the level of output prices relative to the level of input prices, which are assumed to be fixed in the short run or to rise more slowly than output prices. Firms respond to the rise in output prices and fall in inventories by expanding production and employment. They quickly find that

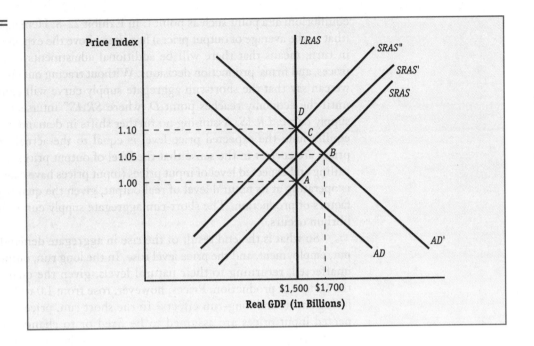

nominal wages, rather than remaining fixed as initially assumed, start to rise, albeit at a slower rate than prices. The result in our hypothetical example is a rise in the price level to 1.05 and a rise in real output to $1,700 billion.

At point *B*, the economy is in a short-run equilibrium. This is not a long-run equilibrium, however, so it is not sustainable. The reason is that the actual price level (1.05) is above the expected price level (1.00). Accordingly, input suppliers, such as workers, have suffered a decline in real income relative to what they expected, even though nominal wages may have risen. They will attempt to negotiate even higher wages and salaries, as will other input suppliers. The decline in their real income is the result of the unexpected price level increase, which exceeds the increase in nominal wages. With employment up and, thus, unemployment down, labor markets and the markets for other inputs, more generally, have tightened up so that the bargaining position of workers and other input suppliers has improved. We assume for now that firms and input suppliers base their revised expectations about future prices on the newly prevailing level of output prices—that is, 1.05. As a result of such adjustments, firms will experience a rise in current and expected input prices, leading to a shift in the short-run aggregate supply curve to *SRAS'*. (Note that *SRAS'* intersects the long-run aggregate supply curve, *LRAS*, at price level 1.05.) Again, the adjustment stops when the increase in wages catches up with the increase in the price level.

To understand why the short-run aggregate supply curve shifts as it does, it is useful to recall that the supply curve tells us what price level is required to induce firms to produce any particular level of output, given the level of expected input prices. Accordingly, if input prices are expected to rise, firms will require a higher output price to produce the same level of output. That is, the short-run aggregate supply curve will shift to the left.

In other words, firms revise their initial reaction to the original rise in demand. With input prices now expected to rise, the firms do not find it profitable to expand their output by as much as they did initially. The reduction in the aggregate quantity of real output supplied and the accompanying increase in the price level produce a new equilibrium at a point such as point *C* in Exhibit 22-8. Here again, the actual price level (that is, the average of output prices) has risen above the expected price level (1.05). This, in turn, means that there will be additional adjustments in price expectations, input prices, and firms' production decisions. Without tracing out all of the intermediate steps, we can say that the short-run aggregate supply curve will continue to shift to the left until the economy reaches point *D*, where *SRAS"* intersects the long-run aggregate supply curve, *LRAS*. Assuming no further shifts in demand, this is a point of long-run equilibrium: the expected price level is equal to the actual price level (1.10), relative prices are correct in the sense that the level of output prices is consistent with the prevailing and expected level of input prices (input prices have caught up), and the economy is operating at its natural level of real output, given the quantity and productivity of its factors of production. The short-run aggregate supply curve shifts left until this equilibrium occurs.

So what is the end result of the rise in aggregate demand? In the short run, output, employment, and the price level rose. In the long run, output and employment were unaffected, returning to their natural levels, given the quantity and productivity of the factors of production. Prices, however, rose from 1.0 to 1.1. What explains the differing short- and long-run effects? In the short run, price expectations and, thus, expected input prices are assumed to be fixed or to change more slowly than output prices. As a result, the economy moves up along the short-run aggregate supply curve (from point *A* to point *B* in Exhibit 22-8) as demand increases. Over time, as actual prices rise, expectations and thus firms' production decisions and workers' decisions to supply labor adjust, resulting in successive shifts in short-run aggregate real supply. Reflecting these adjustments and assuming no further shifts in demand, the economy moves back to the natural rate of unemployment (from point *B* to point *D* in Exhibit 22-8).

Demand-Pull Inflation
Sustained increases in the overall price level due to high levels of demand.

What we have just described and analyzed is a case of **demand-pull inflation.** Demand increases and "pulls" up prices. Note that from a policy maker's perspective, the short-run outcome (point *B*) is fairly attractive. Output rises, unemployment drops, and the increase in prices is not dramatic. In the long run (point *D*), the situation is much less pleasant. The result of boosting demand with, say, monetary or fiscal policy is that prices have risen while employment and output have returned to the natural levels prevailing initially (at point *A*). If policy makers are nearsighted, they will tend to focus on (and value) the short-run effects of boosting demand on the economy, ignoring or downplaying the longer-run inflationary effects. More on this point will follow in the next chapter, when we examine the effects of other economic scenarios and the Fed's response (monetary policy) from an aggregate demand and supply framework. Now would be a good time to read the accompanying "A Closer Look" on the Phillips Curve.

Recap   If the economy is in long-run equilibrium and aggregate demand increases, the economy will initially respond by moving to a short-run equilibrium at a higher price and output level above the natural rate of real output. Because this level of output is not sustainable, input prices will start to rise, shifting the short-run aggregate supply curve leftward. Over time, as input prices catch up with the higher output prices, the economy will move back to the natural rate of output at a higher price level.

In this chapter, we have completed a static analysis of aggregate demand and aggregate supply. This and earlier chapters have provided the framework for our discussion of monetary policy in Part 5.

The Phillips Curve

Our analysis so far suggests that there may be a trade-off between inflation and unemployment, which would imply that lower unemployment can be "bought" by the public's willingness to accept higher inflation. In 1957, A.W. Phillips noticed such a trade-off when analyzing British data for the 1861–1957 time period. Actually, Phillips's original work stressed the relationship between increases in the growth rate of wages and changes in the unemployment rate. When the unemployment rate was low, wages increased at a high rate. Likewise, when the unemployment rate was high, the rate of increase in wages was low or even negative.

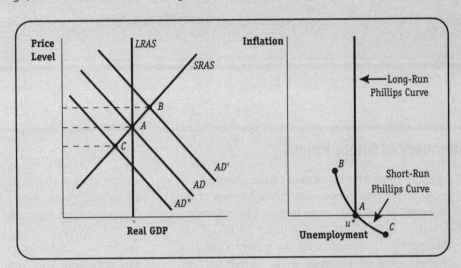

Later economists extended the analysis to suggest an inverse relationship between the rate of price changes (inflation) and changes in the unemployment rate. They could do so because of the strong correlation between changes in wages and changes in the overall price level. Thus, a low unemployment rate was associated with high inflation, and vice versa.

The concept was immediately embraced by economists and served as a springboard for much economic research over the next 20 years. But does the trade-off really exist? And, if so, can policy makers exploit it to achieve their goals?

Actually, we can use the analysis already developed to answer these questions. In the short run, a Phillips curve trade-off does exist. Starting from a point of long-run equilibrium, when there is an unanticipated increase in aggregate demand, the economy moves to a short-run equilibrium where the price level has risen, output has increased, and the unemployment rate has fallen. In the accompanying graphs, the economy moves from point A to B. The graph on the left is our familiar aggregate demand and aggregate supply model. In the graph on the right, the unemployment rate is measured on the horizontal axis, and the inflation rate is measured on the vertical axis; u^* is the unemployment rate that is expected when expected inflation is zero. This is the natural rate of unemployment. From the initial long-run equilibrium, if there is an unexpected

Phillips Curve
A curve suggesting a trade-off between unanticipated inflation and unemployment in the short run.

decrease in aggregate demand, the price level falls, output falls, and the unemployment rate increases; the economy moves from point A to C in each graph.

Thus, in the short run, there is a trade-off, but only if the increase or decrease in demand is unexpected. Once expectations about the actual price level have been adjusted, there is no longer a trade-off, as relative price adjustments bring the economy back to the natural level of output and the natural level of employment. Although a trade-off exists in the short run, in the long run the Phillips curve is vertical. The implication is again that myopic policy makers can buy "lower unemployment" in the short run by accepting more inflation, but not in the long run. As Robert Parry, former chief executive officer of the Federal Reserve Bank of San Francisco, put it, "A little inflation may get us more employment, but it would only be a temporary gain. The Fed simply doesn't have the power to push the economy beyond its capacity to produce goods and services for very long."[a]

Endnotes
a. "Fed Official Defends Rise in Rates," *Orange County Register* (October 9, 1994): 5.

Summary of Major Points

1. Aggregate demand is the sum of the quantities of goods and services demanded by each sector of the economy at various price levels. The aggregate demand curve shows the quantity of real GDP that people, businesses, and the government plan to purchase at various price levels. Ceteris paribus, quantity demanded is inversely related to the overall price level. The reasons for this inverse relationship include the wealth or real balances effect, the substitution-of-foreign-goods effect, and the constant nominal income effect.

2. The major causes of changes in aggregate demand (shifts of the aggregate demand curve) are changes in U.S. monetary and fiscal policies as reflected in changes in taxes and government expenditures or changes in interest rates and the money supply. Such policy changes have a powerful impact on spending plans through their effects on the financial system (stock and bond prices), our international competitiveness (exchange rates), and expectations of future economic and financial developments.

3. Firms' production decisions are guided by the price of their output relative to expected costs of production. A rise in output prices relative to input prices will lead firms to expand production, and a fall in output prices relative to input prices will lead firms to reduce production.

4. The short-run aggregate supply curve is positively sloped, ceteris paribus. It depicts the level of output firms will produce at various output price levels, assuming that input prices are constant or that changes in input prices lag changes in output prices. The assumption of constant or lagging input prices is what defines the short run and distinguishes the short run from the long run. Starting from a position of long-run equilibrium, an unexpected rise in demand will lead to a rise in output prices relative to input prices, an unexpected fall in inventories, and an accompanying increase in output and employment. In long-run equilibrium, expected values of sales, inventories, and prices are equal to actual values.

5. The long-run aggregate supply curve is vertical at the economy's natural level of real output. An economy's natural level of real output is determined by the quantity and productivity of its factors of production. What makes such a level of output "natural" is that it is sustainable in the sense that once output prices and input prices have fully adjusted to previous shifts in supply or demand, there is no tendency for the economy

to move away from this equilibrium level of output and employment.

6. If something causes actual values to differ from expected values, an economy's long-run equilibrium is disturbed, and adjustments in production, employment, spending, and so on, will occur. More specifically, after a disturbance (such as an increase in aggregate demand), some initial adjustments occur, producing a short-run equilibrium. As time passes, additional adjustments occur, particularly in price expectations, in input prices, and in the short-run aggregate supply curve, causing the economy to move toward a new long-run equilibrium.

7. In the short run, an unexpected rise in aggregate demand will, ceteris paribus, lead to a rise in output and employment and some rise in output prices. Subsequently, there will be an increased demand for inputs that results in higher input prices. The short-run aggregate supply curve shifts to the left, and firms post higher prices and produce less. In the long run, when output prices and input prices have fully adjusted to the initiating increase in demand, the economy will return to its natural level of real output. This is a case of demand-pull inflation. In the long run, a rise in demand pulls up prices but does not affect output and employment.

Key Terms

Aggregate Demand Curve, p. 540

Aggregate Supply Curve, p. 545

Constant Nominal Income Effect, p. 541

Demand-Pull Inflation, p. 552

GDP Deflator, p. 540

Long-Run Aggregate Supply Curve, p. 550

Long-Run Equilibrium, p. 545

Natural Level of Real Output, p. 547

Phillips Curve, p. 553

Real Wage, p. 545

Short-Run Aggregate Supply Curve, p. 546

Substitution-of-Foreign-Goods Effect, p. 541

Wealth Effect or Real Balances Effect p. 540

Review Questions

1. Explain the difference between aggregate demand and the aggregate quantity demanded of real output. Ceteris paribus, how is quantity demanded related to the overall price level?

2. Explain the wealth effect, the substitution-of-foreign-goods effect, and the constant nominal income effect.

3. What are the major sources of changes in aggregate demand? What are the short-run and the long-run effects?

4. What does investment spending consist of? How is investment spending related to the interest rate? Which is more volatile, consumption or investment? Which makes up a larger component of GDP?

5. Explain why only government purchases of goods and services, not transfers, are a component of aggregate demand.

6. What are net exports? How are they related to the exchange rate?

7. If prices and wages always change by exactly the same percentage and are expected always to do so, how is the short-run aggregate supply curve shaped? Make an argument that in this case, there is no such thing as a short-run aggregate supply curve. What is the real wage?

8. What is the GDP deflator?

9. Can the natural level of real output ever change? If so, when? How is the natural level of real output related to the long-run aggregate supply curve?

10. How do price expectations affect the position of the short-run aggregate supply curve?

11. What causes the short-run aggregate supply curve to shift left? Right?

Analytical Questions

Questions marked with a check mark (✓) are objective in nature. They can be completed with a short answer or number.

✓12. Graphically illustrate the difference between a change in aggregate demand and a change in the aggregate quantity demanded of real GDP. Illustrate an increase in aggregate demand and an increase in the quantity demanded of real GDP.

✓13. Use aggregate supply and aggregate demand curves to explain what will happen to prices, output, and employment, ceteris paribus, in each of the following situations:

  a. The government cuts spending.
  b. The Fed makes open market purchases.
  c. Corporate tax rates are increased.
  d. Interest rates abroad increase.

14. Why is the demand curve for wheat downward sloping? Why is the aggregate demand curve downward sloping? Explain why the reasons are different.

15. Draw a short-run aggregate supply curve. Why is the curve upward sloping? What causes the short-run aggregate supply curve to shift?

16. Use graphs to explain demand-pull inflation.

17. Assume that the economy is originally in long-run equilibrium and that there is a drop in demand. Use graphs to explain how and why the economy initially moves to a short-run equilibrium with unemployment. How does the economy return to long-run equilibrium?

18. Graph a Phillips curve. Explain why the long-run Phillips curve is vertical. Could there be more than one short-run Phillips curve? (*Hint: Consider a change in price expectations.*)

Suggested Readings

Current statistics on GDP growth, personal income, aggregate demand, and the government's finances are available online at **http://www.bea.gov/newsreleases/glance.htm.**

See price data and charts at the Economic Indicators page of the U.S. Government Printing Office Web site at **http://www.whitehouse.gov/fsbr/prices.html.**

Many principles of economics texts contain discussions of aggregate demand and aggregate supply. We recommend N. Gregory Mankiw, *Principles of Economics*, 4th ed. (Cincinnati, OH: South-Western College Publishing, 2007).

An article that touches on many of the topics in this chapter is "Evolving Inflation Dynamics and the New Keynes Phillips Curve," by Andreas Hornstein, *Economic Quarterly*, Federal Reserve Bank of Richmond, 93, no. 4 (Fall 2007): 317–339. The article is available on the web at **http://www.richmondfed.org/publications/economic_research/economic_quarterly/pdfs/fall2007/hornstein.pdf.**

"Fixing the New Keynesian Phillips Curve," by Richard Dennis, *Economic Letter*, Federal Reserve Bank of San Francisco, 2007–35, November 30, 2007, discusses an alternative view of inflation and monetary policy. **http://www.frbsf.org/publications/economics/letter/2006/el2006–18.html.**

Household debt burdens and their effects on consumer spending is the topic of "Property Debt Burdens," by Mark Doms and Meryl Motika, *Economic Letter*, Federal Reserve Bank of San Francisco, 2006–18, July 28, 2006. It is available on the Web at **http://www.frbsf.org/publications/economics/letter/2007/el2007–35.html.**

Two books that look at how the economy functioned in the 1990s are Joseph E. Stiglitz, *The Roaring Nineties* (New York, NY: W.W. Norton, 2004) and Alan S. Blinder and Janet L. Yellen, *The Fabulous Decade* (New York, NY: Century Foundation, 2004).

For an interesting article that looks at how the economy functions, see Alan S. Blinder, "A Core of Macroeconomic Beliefs?" *Challenge* (July–August 1998): 26–44.

Robert Lesson looks at "The Political Economy of the Inflation-Unemployment Trade-Off," *History of Political Economy* 29 (Spring 1997): 117–156.

For an interesting discussion of economic models versus recent economic performance, see Alan Greenspan, "Is There a New Economy?" *Vital Speeches of the Day* 64, no. 24 (October 1, 1998): 741–745.

E.P. Davis, *Debt, Financial Fragility, and Systemic Risk* (New York: Oxford University Press, 1993), looks at the financing behavior of households and businesses, which has generated high levels of debt since the 1970s, and its relationship to instability.

For a historical look at the inflation of the 1965–1979 era, see Thomas Mayer, *Monetary Policy and the Great Inflation in the United States* (Northampton, MA: Edward Elgar, 1999).

Endnotes

1. Note that the nominal price of hot dogs has not initially changed even though their relative price has changed.
2. In Chapter 20, we introduced the equation of exchange, which can be written as $M \times V = \text{GDP} = P \times Y$. This equation says that the nation's nominal GDP (the overall price level, P, multiplied by the real level of output, Y) is equal to the money supply, M, multiplied by velocity, V.
3. Shortly, you shall see that aggregate supply is the other side.
4. When we invoke the ceteris paribus assumption, we hold all other factors, including input prices, constant and allow only output prices to vary.
5. Sustainable full employment is the level that can be maintained without upward or downward pressure on wages and prices.
6. If a large percentage of workers works under a contractual collective bargaining agreement that holds nominal wages constant over the course of the agreement, an unexpected rise in the price level will result in increases in nominal wages that lag behind increases in the price level.
7. In the post–World War II period, prices have been much less flexible downward than upward. That is, prices are much more likely to rise in response to increases in demand than to fall in response to decreases in demand.
8. As the factors of production and technology change over time, the natural level of real output will also change.
9. Note that the vertical long-run aggregate supply curve will shift if the quantity and productivity of the factors of production change—more on this in Chapter 23.

23

Listen, there is no courage or any extra courage that I know of to find out the right thing to do. Now, it is not only necessary to do the right thing, but to do it in the right way and the only problem you have is what is the right thing to do and what is the right way to do it. That is the problem. But this economy of ours is not so simple that it obeys to the opinion of bias or the pronouncements of any particular individual.

—Dwight D. Eisenhower

The Challenges of Monetary Policy

Learning Objectives

After reading this chapter, you should know:

The goals of monetary policy, including economic growth, stable prices, full employment, and satisfactory external balance

How numerical goals are formulated and why they can differ in the short run and the long run

The monetary policy goals in terms of aggregate demand and aggregate supply

The monetary policy options available to respond to fluctuations in aggregate demand and aggregate supply

CAN THE BUSINESS CYCLE BE MITIGATED?

The Great Depression of the 1930s was by far the most severe downturn of the U.S. economy during the twentieth century. For more than a decade, output and employment remained considerably below the natural rate. Measured unemployment averaged more than 20 percent, and prices fell by more than 25 percent. During this painful period, macroeconomics underwent profound changes. Led by John Maynard Keynes, a school of thought was born that emphasized the need for government intervention to stabilize the level of economic activity. The problem, according to Keynes, was that only by accident would the level of aggregate demand be just sufficient to achieve full employment and stable prices. In the more likely situation, aggregate demand would be either too great or too little. Moreover, because relative price adjustments would occur only slowly, the economy could experience long bouts of either unemployment (too little demand) or inflation (too much demand).

The buildup for World War II in the early 1940s seemed to validate Keynesian theory. Almost overnight, the economy went to full employment, and measures were needed to "control" inflation. Based on such events, much of the academic community accepted Keynesian theory in the postwar period. During the 1960s, Keynesian policy prescriptions were put into practice by the government with some apparent success.[1] Although voices of dissent were always there, they became louder during and after the 1970s when the economy was plagued concurrently by high unemployment and high inflation, a condition that came to be known as **stagflation**. Economists struggled to understand the causes of and remedies for this dilemma, which Keynes believed could not happen.

Stagflation
A condition of concurrent high unemployment and high inflation.

Since the Great Depression, the U.S. economy has experienced 10 recessions. During these periods, output declined, unemployment increased, and the growth rate of prices generally fell. The economy also has experienced periodic bouts of rapid inflation. Some analysts believe that the government has been successful in reducing the length and magnitude of cyclical downturns and in lengthening cyclical expansions. A repetition of the Great Depression has been avoided, and the expansions of the 1980s and 1990s were of record length. Following a mild recession in early 2001–2002, the U.S. economy continued to expand until December 2007, when the economy entered another recession. This latest downturn was related to the financial crisis in the mortgage market stemming from the subprime loan debacle and the collapse of housing prices. By September 2008, what started in the mortgage markets spread to global financial markets and the financial system was on the brink of collapse as credit markets froze up. Policy makers worked frantically to prop up the failed system. In what was to date the largest bailout in history, policy makers enacted a $700 billion package to mitigate the crisis, and in early 2009 an even bigger stimulus was in the works. By the last quarter of 2008, the slowdown of the economy accelerated with the real GDP dropping at an annualized rate of almost 4 percent and unemployment rising to over 7 percent. Researchers generally agree that the vast majority of these economic contractions and expansions resulted from fluctuations in aggregate demand. For example, the latest slowdown is from the bursting of the housing bubble that caused consumers to slow their spending. Likewise, the collapse of stock prices in the early 2000s had the same effect on aggregate demand. However, shocks to aggregate supply (shifts of the aggregate supply curve) have occasionally been responsible for both recessions and inflations, as in the case of the supply shocks in the 1970s from increases in oil prices. Under such circumstances, analysis focusing only on aggregate demand may not be appropriate.

Since the early 1970s, international trade and finance have grown dramatically while barriers to capital flows have broken down. A flexible exchange rate system has replaced the fixed exchange rate system that was put into place in 1945. These factors have contributed to the increased volatility and relevance of exchange rates. The Fed has chosen on occasion to intervene in the foreign exchange market to smooth adjustments in the value of the dollar. Such intervention may interfere or conflict with the pursuit of other monetary policy goals. As you shall see, the Fed must be aware of the effects of its policies on the external balance of trade and capital flows, and in some cases may choose to ignore the effects of a declining dollar. For instance, in mid-2008, as the dollar reached record lows due to low U.S. interest rates, the Fed—at least up to late 2008—chose not to intervene.

At the same time, increased globalization means that the Fed must also respond to demand and supply shocks caused by events abroad. For example, on August 31, 1998, the Dow Jones Industrial Average fell 512 points, the largest point drop to that date. Most analysts attributed the drop to the financial and economic crisis in Russia, which followed on the heels of the Asian crisis. As you saw in Chapter 16, such a large drop in stock prices has the potential to destabilize the U.S. economy.

In this chapter, we look first at the macroeconomic goals and challenges of monetary policy. We then use an aggregate demand and supply framework to examine the specifics of how to achieve these goals if the economy experiences either a recession or excessive inflation. As the preceding discussion implies, what "should" be done in response to fluctuations in aggregate demand or aggregate supply is often unclear and controversial. This is particularly true in 2008, as policy makers scramble to respond to an unprecedented financial crisis.

THE GOALS OF MONETARY POLICY

Macroeconomic policy consists of (1) monetary policy, which involves the Fed's use of its policy instruments to affect the cost and availability of funds in the economy, and (2) fiscal policy, which involves alterations in government spending or taxes proposed and enacted by Congress and the president. As illustrated in Exhibit 22-4, the changes in fiscal and monetary policies that lead to changes in aggregate demand interact, in turn, with aggregate supply to produce changes in prices, real output, and employment.

In conducting monetary policy, the Fed works through the financial system. Recall that the Fed's primary tools for influencing the financial system include control of the monetary base, the required reserve ratio, and the primary and secondary credit rates. Monetary policy, in turn, influences the borrowing, lending, spending, and saving behavior of the household, business, government, and rest-of-the-world sectors. As depicted in Exhibit 23-1, the specific goals of monetary policy are to design and implement policies that will achieve sustainable economic growth, full employment, stable prices, and a satisfactory external balance. Some members of the Federal Open Market Committee (FOMC) and other analysts have stressed that maintaining stable prices is the primary goal of the Fed. Others have contended that employment levels in the economy must not be ignored. Now let's take a closer look at the rationales underlying these goals.

Economic Growth

The size of the "economic pie" divided up among a nation's citizens is determined by the quantity of goods and services produced. That is, the size is determined by real output or, specifically, real GDP. Simply put, if the size of a nation's economic pie and, thus, its potential standard of living are to rise over time, the productive capacity of the economy must expand. To use the terminology of Chapter 22, the natural level of real output (long-run aggregate supply) must increase.

Most economists agree that the growth of aggregate supply over time is determined primarily by the growth of capital, the labor force, and productivity. Thus,

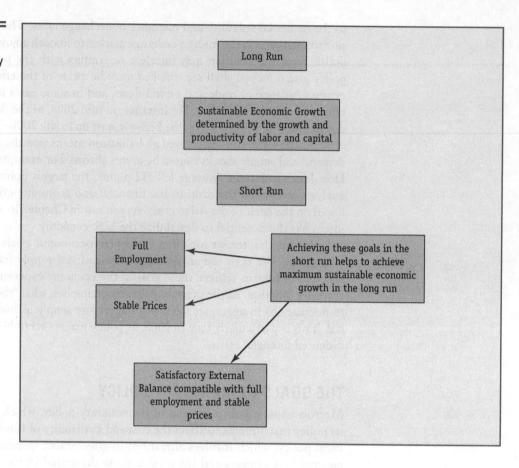

Long Run

Sustainable Economic Growth
determined by the growth and
productivity of labor and capital

Short Run

Full
Employment

Stable Prices

Achieving these goals in the
short run helps to achieve
maximum sustainable economic
growth in the long run

Satisfactory External
Balance compatible with full
employment and stable
prices

growth of the key inputs in the production process and technological improvements are the key to long-run growth of output. So far so good, but what determines the growth of capital, labor, and productivity?

The growth of the capital stock depends directly on the amount of investment spending undertaken by firms. By definition, the change in the capital stock is equal to net investment spending. The productivity of capital is thought to depend on the amount of resources devoted to research and development and on the resulting technological advances that lead to new and more productive plants and machines. Labor force growth flows from the growth of the population and from increases in the proportion of the population that participates in the labor force. The productivity of labor is thought to depend on the educational attainment and health of workers, the quantity and quality of the capital stock with which they work, and, perhaps, the competitive environment faced by firms and their employees.

In general, a thriving nation's productive capacity grows over time. Research shows that macroeconomic policy, through its effects on the determinants of economic growth, influences the pace of growth in a number of ways. While ignoring many of the detailed relationships and linkages, it is worth noting here that the government's tax policy affects both the willingness of firms to invest and engage in research and development and the willingness of households to work and save. Similarly, the level of interest rates resulting from the interaction of the monetary and fiscal policies pursued has a decisive influence on spending and saving decisions. Over time, such decisions affect an economy's growth potential; therefore, they affect aggregate supply.

Beyond these fairly obvious influences, we should also include the overall economic environment within which firms and households are making decisions. More

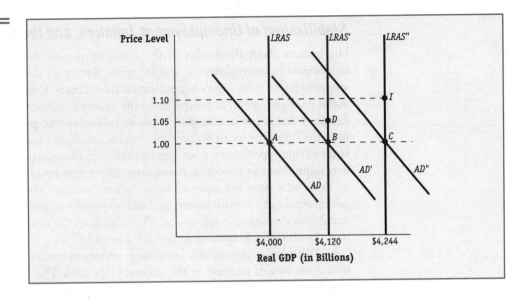

On the vertical axis is a price index, and on the horizontal axis is the level of real GDP. Assume that each year, the nation's natural level of real output, as measured by long-run aggregate supply (*LRAS*), grows by 3 percent. Thus, in year 1, *LRAS* is $4,000 billion; in year 2, *LRAS* is $4,000 billion × 1.03 = $4,120 billion; and in year 3, *LRAS* is $4,120 × 1.03 = $4,244. If aggregate demand also grows by 3 percent per year, then the economy will follow the path *A–B–C*, with 3 percent real GDP growth, a stable price level (1.00), and zero inflation. Alternatively, aggregate demand could grow faster than 3 percent, say, by 8 percent per year. Then, the economy would follow path *A–D–I*, with prices rising 5 percent per year. Thus, in general, the growth in aggregate demand relative to aggregate supply determines the price-output performance of the economy.

specifically, a stable environment is likely to be more conducive to farsighted planning and decision making that enhance an economy's long-run growth potential. Such an environment is characterized by consistently high rates of capacity utilization and employment and, thus, by real output that is growing at a steady, sustainable pace. Exhibit 23-2 depicts such a situation.

On the other hand, an unstable environment characterized by a series of inflationary booms and deflationary recessions is likely to inhibit long-run growth. In such a situation, aggregate demand almost always grows faster or slower than aggregate supply, thereby generating either inflationary pressures or an economic slowdown. Hence, the shorter-run stabilization objectives in the following discussion are not really separate and distinct from the long-run goals but support and complement the nation's pursuit of economic growth over the long run. Short-run fluctuations around the long-term trend influence the trend itself.

Recap   The goals of monetary policy are sustainable economic growth, full employment, stable prices, and a satisfactory external balance. Sustainable economic growth is determined by the growth and productivity of the labor force and capital stock. Policies that achieve full employment and a noninflationary environment help to achieve maximum sustainable growth.

Stabilization of Unemployment, Inflation, and the External Balance

Discussions about the health of the economy usually focus on recent and expected movements in unemployment and inflation. Rarely do the evening news and political speeches fail to note what's happening on these fronts. One reason society is concerned about unemployment, as measured by the unemployment rate, is fairly obvious: we understand that if the nation is to reach its full economic potential, all individuals must have the opportunity to become productive, employed members of society. In the absence of this opportunity, poor families and individuals experience financial distress and hardships. From an economic standpoint, output that could have been produced last year by those who were unemployed is lost forever and can never be made up. Against this background, it is readily understandable why our nation's leaders operate with a clear mandate regarding unemployment. The "Cracking the Code" feature on p. 570 explains how the official unemployment rate is measured.

What is less clear is why inflation generates so much concern. Simply stated, inflation is the rate of increase in the general price level. The consumer price index (CPI), which is discussed in the "Cracking the Code" feature on p. 106 in Chapter 5, is the most frequently cited measure of the price level in the United States. It measures the average level of prices of a typical market basket of goods and services that consumers purchase. However, the month-to-month percentage change in this index gives us a somewhat distorted measure of inflation because it fails to take into account the fact that the market basket on which the index is based will change as relative prices of the items in the index change. For example, if gas prices increase far more than other prices, consumers, where possible, will drive less and consume more of the other items whose prices have not increased as much. This substitution will not be taken into account; hence, the CPI tends to overstate inflation.

Because of this, the **personal consumption expenditure price index (PCEPI)** is actually the price index that the Fed monitors more closely in the formulation of monetary policy. The PCEPI measures the average increase in the prices of all domestic personal consumption. The base year is currently 2000. It is different from the CPI that uses a fixed basket of goods and services where the weights for the items in the basket are not changed for several years. The PCEPI uses an indexed method that compares the composition of expenditures on a given quarter's basket of goods and services to the last quarter. Thus, the weights of items in the PCEPI change, as consumers substitute out of things that have become relatively more expensive and into items that have become relatively cheaper. Thus, as prices change, some more than others, the PCEPI more accurately captures how consumers respond to those price changes. On average, since 2000, the PCEPI has risen about a third less than the CPI because of this substitution effect, which the CPI fails to capture. Like the core CPI, the core PCEPI leaves out the more volatile food and energy prices.

Measurement aside, why do policy makers worry about inflation? After all, if the prices of all goods and services double, but so do wages and salaries, isn't the nation as a whole unaffected? The short answer is no. To see why, it is useful to distinguish between expected inflation and unexpected inflation.

Suppose it's the year 2009 and households expect inflation to be about 3 percent in 2010. How will this expectation affect household behavior? First and foremost, the workers in the households will try to secure wage increases of at least 3 percent so that the purchasing power of their incomes will not decline. Ideally, of course, they would hope for a wage increase of more than 3 percent so that their real incomes would rise. Second, if they are net lenders, they will be looking for financial assets with nominal interest rates or nominal returns high enough to produce an adequate expected real

---

Personal Consumption Expenditures Price Index (PCEPI)

A price index measures the average change in the prices of all domestic personal consumption expenditures. The PCEPI changes the weights of items in the index as consumers substitute out of things that have become relatively more expensive and into items that have become relatively cheaper. Thus, it gives a better measure of inflation than the CPI, which does not.

return. For example, as discussed in Chapter 6, a nominal return of 7 percent, given expected inflation of 3 percent, is expected to produce a real return or real interest rate of about 4 percent. If inflation turns out to be close to 3 percent as expected, all is well. But what happens if prices actually rise by 5 percent?

First, the real wage of workers will fall because nominal wages will rise by a smaller percent than prices. The resulting change in output prices relative to input prices will, ceteris paribus, lead to an increase in firms' profits and encourage them to alter production and employment. As you saw in Chapter 22, the short-run aggregate supply curve slopes upward. That is, until expectations adjust to the unanticipated, higher price level, firms will offer more for sale than the natural level of real output. Second, the real return on financial assets acquired will be less than anticipated and perhaps even negative. In this case, borrowers who find that the actual real cost of borrowing is well below what they expected will benefit. Beyond these types redistribution, citizens living on fixed incomes, including many retirees, will find their purchasing power shrinking.

These simple examples illustrate a central reason why inflation, particularly unexpected inflation, is worrisome. Inflation redistributes income in arbitrary and unpredictable ways from workers to firms, from lenders to borrowers, and from those on fixed incomes to those with variable incomes that increase with inflation.

In addition, due to several features of the U.S. tax system, many firms and households will pay proportionately more taxes to the government in an inflationary environment. To illustrate, suppose that a household earns 4 percent interest on its surplus funds, the actual and expected inflation rate is zero, and the household is in the 25 percent tax rate bracket; then the household's after-tax real return is 3 percent, as Equation (23-1) shows:

	nominal interest rate	−	expected inflation rate	−	taxes	=	real after-tax return
(23-1)	.04	−	0	−	(.25 × .04)	=	.03, or 3%

Now suppose that, ceteris paribus, expected and actual inflation rises to 2 percent and the nominal interest rate rises from 4 to 6 percent to compensate lenders for the loss in purchasing power. The real after-tax return will again be the nominal rate minus the expected inflation rate and taxes. In this case, the real after-tax return equals 2.5 percent, as shown in Equation (23-2):

	nominal interest rate	−	expected inflation rate	−	taxes	=	real after-tax return
(23-2)	.06	−	.02	−	(.25 × .06)	=	.025, or 2.5%

Because nominal returns rather than real returns are taxed, inflation results in government taxes taking a larger portion of interest income than in a noninflationary environment. Inflation also reduces the real value of nominal money balances held. In this way, it acts as a tax on such holdings.

As for firms, standard accounting procedures base depreciation allowances on the historical cost of equipment and structures rather than on the replacement cost. In an inflationary environment, firms' depreciation allowances, which are deducted from revenues before taxable income is computed, are too small to replace the capital that wears out in the production process. More to the point, the too small allowances result in taxes being proportionately higher than in a noninflationary environment. Again, as in the prior examples, inflation redistributes income and can distort economic decision making.

Returning to the uncertainty theme already discussed with regard to economic growth, we note that researchers have also found that as the inflation rate rises, the variability of inflation tends to increase and the relationship among relative prices tends to become more volatile and difficult to predict. Consequently, pricing, production, saving, and investment decisions have to be made in a more uncertain environment. Firms and households are likely to be much more cautious about making long-term commitments to spend, save, produce, or invest; instead, they focus on near-term opportunities. This perspective does not enhance long-run stability and growth and can aggravate short-run instabilities and cyclical fluctuations.

Inflation can also have an adverse effect on the nation's international competitiveness and, thus, its role in the world economy and in world affairs. For example, if the prices of U.S. goods rise relative to prices of competing goods in the rest of the world, ceteris paribus, the demand for U.S. products will fall with attendant effects on domestic production and employment. Although the resulting depreciation of the dollar will help to offset and reverse the negative effects on the trade balance over time, there is no assurance that this will occur quickly. In the meantime, U.S. firms will lose a portion of their share of world markets.

As the U.S. economy becomes more globalized, monetary policy makers must be aware of the international effects of policy. For example, if the Fed embarks on a program of monetary restraint to slow the growth rate of the U.S. economy, real interest rates could rise relative to foreign rates. A substantial appreciation of the dollar and augmented capital inflows can result. The dollar's appreciation may have a dramatic effect on the economy through its effect on net exports. Net exports fall as the foreign prices of U.S. goods increase and the domestic prices of foreign goods decrease. As a result, employment and output in the United States would be less than they would have been otherwise.

If monetary policy makers establish policy goals for inflation and growth that are widely divergent from those of other countries, substantial fluctuations in exchange rates can result. In addition to the price effects on net exports and the interest rate effects on capital flows, fluctuations in exchange rates greatly increase the exchange rate risks of international trade and finance. Central bank intervention may then be needed to stabilize exchange rates, but such intervention can dampen or conflict with the pursuit of other policy goals.

Deflation
A drop in the overall price level as measured by a price index.

Last, policy makers must also be on the alert for deflation, or a falling overall price level—something the U.S. economy has not experienced since the Great Depression. Deflation is often worse than inflation because it can lead to debt deflation, defaults, and bankruptcies. When inflation levels are very low, the potential that the economy could slip into a deflation increases. In the late 1990s and early 2000s, inflation rates fell to their lowest levels in 40 years. Because prices of many commodities also fell dramatically, some economists were concerned about actual deflationary pressures. They believe that the Fed must be more concerned about deflation than inflation because the effects are not symmetrical. As experienced during the Great Depression and more recently in the 1990s in Japan, deflation can be more deleterious to an economy than inflation, particularly if it leads to a drop in asset prices and widespread bankruptcies. Because the effects of inflation and deflation on the economy may not be symmetrical, the Fed may be even more concerned about deflation than inflation.[2]

Finally, in late 2007 and early 2008, the Fed embarked on a policy to significantly lower interest rates. Foreign countries failed to follow suit, with the result that the dollar depreciated significantly against other key currencies. Because of the weak economy, the Fed did not pursue policies to strengthen the dollar; those policies would have involved raising interest rates in a deteriorating economy. Furthermore, the weakened dollar was fostering the sale of U.S. exports, mitigating the slowdown. Although the Treasury gave lip service to a strong dollar, it may have been pleased with the drop in the trade deficit.

To summarize, monetary policy can cause dramatic changes in exchange rates and the balances on the current and capital accounts—that is, the external balance—which then feed back to the domestic economy. Exchange rate volatility can necessitate central bank intervention. The bottom line is that in designing and implementing monetary policy, monetary policy makers must seek to achieve an acceptable external balance compatible with the domestic goals of full employment and stable prices. In Chapter 26, we take a more in-depth look at the international effects of monetary policy. You shall see that this increasingly globalized environment will necessitate increased coordination among countries as they establish policy goals. Monetary policy makers do not make policy decisions in a vacuum. They of are not oblivious to the domestic and international environment, nor do they aim at abstract, long-run theoretical goals. Rather, they have specific numerical objectives in mind for unemployment and inflation when they make policy adjustments that are consistent with the economic environment. It is to these objectives that we now turn.

Recap   Full employment is necessary for a nation to reach its economic potential. A stable price level is desirable because unexpected inflation redistributes income in arbitrary and unpredictable ways and causes distortions in the U.S. tax system. Monetary policy can cause changes in exchange rates and the external balance that feed back to the domestic economy. Monetary policy makers must secure an external balance that is consistent with the domestic goals of full employment and stable prices.

THE SOURCE OF NUMERICAL OBJECTIVES FOR UNEMPLOYMENT AND INFLATION

Employment Act of 1946
The first statute that directed policy makers to pursue policies to achieve full employment and noninflationary growth.

Humphrey-Hawkins Full Employment and Balanced Growth Act of 1978
A statute that required policy makers to pursue policies to achieve full employment and noninflationary growth.

Natural Rate of Unemployment
The rate of unemployment consistent with stable prices; believed to be about 4.0 to 4.5 percent.

General guidelines for policy makers are contained in the **Employment Act of 1946** and the **Humphrey-Hawkins Full Employment and Balanced Growth Act of 1978**. Both statutes direct policy makers to pursue policies consistent with achieving full employment and noninflationary growth. Briefly, this legislation, in effect, leaves it to policy makers, their staffs, and the economics profession at large to determine, for example, what unemployment rate is consistent with full employment and nonaccelerating inflation.

In the early years of the twenty-first century, most estimates of sustainable employment imply an unemployment rate of about 4.0 to 4.5 percent. Also called the **natural rate of unemployment**, this percentage is believed to be consistent with stable prices. The natural rate of unemployment is the unemployment rate that corresponds to the natural rate of real output discussed in Chapter 22. Economists believe that a measured unemployment rate much below this level will trigger inflation as labor shortages appear in some markets driving up wages and prices. The natural rate can change over time for various reasons, including the changing gender and age composition of the labor force and the changing safety net of benefits available to the unemployed.

In the late 1980s and early 1990s, the natural rate of unemployment was believed to be in the 5.5 to 6.0 percent range. Low unemployment in the mid-1990s with moderate inflation convinced many economists that the natural rate had fallen to the 5.0 to 5.5 range. In the late 1990s, unemployment continued to fall. By late 2000, actual unemployment had briefly fallen to 3.9 percent with no increase in actual inflation. Many economists believed that wage pressure would soon lead to price increases, but the inflation did not materialize. Since 2005, it was thought that the natural rate of unemployment was in the 4.0 to 4.5 percent range. As the economy slowed in late 2008 due to the ongoing financial crisis, actual unemployment increased to over 7 percent.

Cracking the Code

Measuring Unemployment

Statistics on the labor force, employment, and unemployment in the United States are gathered and published by the Bureau of Labor Statistics. Each month more than 65,000 households nationwide are surveyed. Based on their responses to a series of questions, individuals are classified as one of the following:

1. Unemployed (16 years or older, out of work, and actively looking for work)
2. Employed
3. Labor Force Participant (Employed plus Unemployed)
4. Not in the Labor Force (out of work and not actively looking for work; includes individuals who are under 16, retirees, disabled persons, and so-called discouraged workers who have lost their jobs and stopped looking for a job)

These data are then used to compute the unemployment rate, which is the percentage of the labor force unemployed:

unemployment rate = number of persons unemployed/labor force

To illustrate, in March 2008, 7.8 million people were unemployed, and the labor force totaled 153.8 million. Thus, the unemployment rate was 5.1 percent (7.8 million/153.8 million = 5.1 percent).

To appreciate the dynamics of the labor market and the relationship between the growth of the economy and unemployment, it is helpful to view the state of unemployment as a pool. Flowing into the pool are the new entrants to the labor force who have not yet found work and those who have recently lost or quit their jobs. Flowing out of the pool are those who have found jobs. If the inflow exceeds the outflow, the number in the pool rises. Conversely, if the outflow exceeds the inflow, the number in the pool falls. To understand the dynamics of unemployment, we must examine the causes and amounts of inflows relative to outflows. For example, from March 2007 to March 2008, the U.S. civilian labor force expanded by 900,000 people, reflecting the ongoing growth of the population. About 176,000 jobs were lost, which when combined with the growth in the labor force, meant that 1,076,000 additional people became unemployed over the course of the year, resulting in the unemployment rate jumping from 4.4 percent to 5.1 percent.

During the 2001–2002 recession, the labor force continued to grow, but job creation slowed dramatically as firms reacted to the fall in demand for their output and rising inventories by slashing production and laying off workers. The result was a large increase in the pool of unemployed people, and the unemployment rate rose sharply from 4.2 percent in 2001 to 6 percent by the end of 2002. Clearly, economic growth and unemployment are tightly connected. By late 2008, the unemployment rate had increased to 7.2 percent, showing the severity of the downturn.

Source: http://www.bls.gov/cps/.

On the inflation front, the problem is also complicated. Over time, policy makers desire price stability and often stress that this should be the primary objective of monetary policy. To some analysts, price stability means zero inflation, while others associate it with inflation rates in the 1 to 2 percent range. Many economists prefer 1 to 2 percent inflation because they believe that when actual inflation is zero, the economy could easily slip into a deflationary period. At the same time, goals, such as for inflation, are not selected in a vacuum. In setting the inflation goal over the near term, such as the next year or two, policy makers consider recent experience and attempt to balance their desire to reduce inflation further with their desire to minimize the accompanying and possibly adverse near-term effects on unemployment and output growth. Thus, recent historical experience, judgments about what is feasible, and the political environment all play a role. Times change and so do economic goals.

For example, in the 1950s and 1960s, inflation averaged 1 to 2 percent per year. In 1971, President Richard Nixon imposed a 90-day freeze on wages and prices because the inflation rate had "surged" to 3.5 percent. An inflation rate of 2 to 3 percent, considered moderate today, was worrisome then to policy makers. In contrast, during President Ronald Reagan's administration, the inflation rate fell dramatically from the double-digit levels prevailing at the beginning of the 1980s to below 3 percent by 1986. President Reagan claimed "victory" over inflation as the inflation rate settled down in the 3 to 4 percent range. In 1994, even though inflation still hovered in the 3 to 4 percent range, the Fed raised interest rates several times out of fear that rapid economic growth would cause inflation to rise again. In 2008, some economists believed that large federal bailouts of financial institutions would mean much higher inflation in the future. However, in late 2008 and early 2009, there were strong deflationary pressures from the housing market, oil markets, and the bankruptcies of retail firms in general. Given the deflationary pressures currently in the economy and the downward spiral the economy was caught in, these concerns were not given much merit at the time.

However, in the long run, after all adjustments have been completed, the goals of stable prices and full employment are believed to be perfectly compatible. Thus, there is no need for trade-offs between goals. But, we all live and policy makers act in the short run. History, as well as theory, tells us that policy makers' attempts to lower inflation can reduce output growth and increase unemployment for a time while attempts to raise output growth and employment can aggravate inflation. In this context, concerns about the short-run versus the long-run effects of policy actions and the price versus the output effects of policy actions in the short run do arise.

Finally, based on our historical experience, economists estimate that the potential long-run growth rate for real GDP is around 2.5 to 3.0 percent per year over time. Growth beyond 3.0 percent per year does not seem to be sustainable over a long period. Sustainable growth in the 2.5 to 3.0 percent range is compatible with the other numerical goals for full employment and stable prices. If the economy grows at this sustainable rate, the vertical long-run aggregate supply curve shifts to the right by 2.5 to 3.0 percent per year.

In sum, the prevailing economic and political environment and the nation's historical experience all play a role in setting the priorities that guide policy actions. Because the policy makers and the environment can change over time, so can the weight given to each priority. We turn now to the aggregate demand and supply framework to look at policy alternatives.

Recap General guidelines for numerical objectives are found in the Employment Act of 1946 and the Humphrey-Hawkins Full Employment and Balanced Growth Act of 1978. Full employment, as of 2008, was believed to be about 4.0 to 4.5 percent measured unemployment. The goal for inflation depends on recent experience and the political and historical environment. Price stability does not necessarily mean zero inflation but low inflation in the 1 to 2 percent range. Sustainable growth is thought to be in the 2.5 to 3.0 percent range.

CHANGES IN AGGREGATE DEMAND AND POLICY

From the perspective of an aggregate demand and aggregate supply framework, the obvious goals of monetary policy are to achieve successive long-run equilibriums with sustainable noninflationary growth. Such a situation occurs when the aggregate demand and long-run aggregate supply curves are both shifting to the right by the same relative magnitude. Look again at Exhibit 23-2, in which steady noninflationary growth is achieved because aggregate demand and long-run aggregate supply are both growing by 3 percent per year. Unfortunately, due to the extremely dynamic nature of the world, the economy may often fall short of achieving those goals. Consequently, policy makers

Looking Back

How History Has Affected U.S. and German Policy Goals

A nation's priorities depend in an important way on its history. In the United States, for example, the trauma of the Great Depression contributed to a political environment in which policy makers tended to emphasize economic growth and employment objectives for many decades after World War II. In contrast, after World War I, Germany experienced hyperinflation that contributed to economic and political dislocations, including Adolf Hitler's rise to power. After World War II, memories of this past ordeal led the former West Germany to emphasize the price stability objective. Such tendencies, in turn, govern policy making in the sense that they condition the direction in which policy makers are generally prepared to err. Accordingly, and not surprisingly, the tendency for policy makers to err on the expansionary side in the United States and the tendency for German policy makers to err on the restrictive side have resulted in the U.S. inflation rate generally being above the German inflation rate in the post–World War II period.

In addition to a nation's long-run historical experience, recent history also influences the priorities assigned to the various policy objectives. For example, the significant acceleration in inflation in the United States during the late 1970s clearly influenced priorities and actions. More specifically, the appointment of Paul Volcker as chair of the Board of Governors of the Fed in 1979 and the two recessions the nation endured in 1980 and 1982 can be linked to some degree to a consensus that inflation had to be brought down even at the cost of a temporary rise in unemployment and a retardation of economic growth. In 1994, recognizing the difficulty of curbing inflation if inflationary expectations take hold, the Fed took actions that increased interest rates five times despite little concrete evidence that inflation was or would be much above 3 percent in the foreseeable future.

Similarly, after the unification of Germany in 1990, the price stability goal remained preeminent, and the German inflation rate remained below 4 percent. By 1995, German inflation was below 2 percent.

Furthermore, when Germany joined the European Monetary Union and adopted the euro in 1999, it did so only on the condition that the primary goal of the European Central Bank be price stability.[a] Finally, to this day, changes in money play a foremost role in monetary policy to achieve the European Central Bank's primary goal of maintaining inflation equal to or below 2 percent. In the United States, monetary policy makers do not specify target ranges for the monetary aggregates and infrequently mention them in their meetings, choosing instead to focus on targeting the fed funds rate to achieve their policy objectives of maximum growth with price stability.

Endnotes

a. In mid-1990, residents of the former East Germany turned in their ostmarks, the currency of East Germany, for deutsche marks, the currency of West Germany. In 2002, residents of a United Germany exchanged deutsche marks for euros.

may need to react to changes or to initiate changes that guide or sometimes push the economy in the right direction.

In Chapter 22, we discussed demand-pull inflation, which occurs when an excessive level of aggregate demand pulls up the overall price level. Ceteris paribus, starting from a long-run equilibrium position, an unexpected shift to the right in the aggregate demand curve—an increase in demand—initially leads to increases in both output and the price level. The economy moves to a new short-run equilibrium along an upward-sloping short-run aggregate supply curve. The output level is not sustainable, however, and price level adjustments bring the economy back to long-run equilibrium at full employment and a higher price level.

Look at Exhibit 23-3, which illustrates the adjustment of the economy in response to an increase in aggregate demand. Initially, the economy is in long-run equilibrium at point *A*. The actual price level (1.00) is equal to the expected price level underlying the short-run aggregate supply curve, and the economy is operating at its natural level of real output ($1,500 billion). Subsequently, aggregate demand increases unexpectedly, shifting the aggregate demand curve from *AD* to *AD'*. In the short run, the economy will move to point *B*, with output rising to $1,700 billion and the price level increasing to 1.05.

Point *B* is not a long-run equilibrium, however, because the actual price level (1.05) is above the expected price level (1.00). As input suppliers respond to the unanticipated increase in prices, the expected price level increases to 1.05 and input prices increase. The short-run aggregate supply curve eventually shifts from *SRAS* to *SRAS"*. With input prices and, thus, production costs rising, firms will require a higher output price than was initially the case to induce them to produce a particular level of output. When the adjustment is completed, the economy will settle at a new long-run equilibrium at point *C*. (See if you can explain why this is the case.) In effect, the economy moves along the path *A–B–C* as shifts in short-run aggregate supply alter the initial short-run effects of a rise in aggregate demand. In the end, the increase in aggregate demand results in a rise in the price level (1.00 to 1.10) and no change in real GDP.

23-3
An Unexpected Increase in Aggregate Demand with No Fed Response

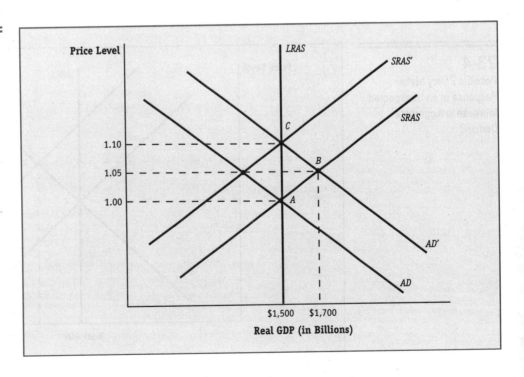

Normally, we would hope that the Fed would not unexpectedly increase the growth rate of the money supply when the economy was in a long-run equilibrium with stable prices and full employment. As we have pointed out, however, myopic policy makers may have an incentive to do so because such policies can lead to short-run, unsustainable gains in employment. In an election year, some politicians may find it desirable to push the unemployment rate below its natural level despite the concurrent and subsequent increases in the price level. If no other action were taken, price increases would eventually move the economy to a new long-run equilibrium with a higher price level, as in Exhibit 23-3.

Unexpected increases in aggregate demand can also come from other sources such as swells in household, business, or government spending and surges in net export demand. Regardless of the source, the Fed can use monetary policy and/or Congress can use fiscal policy to reduce the level of demand. For example, tighter monetary policy would reduce the growth rate of money and credit and at least temporarily raise short-term interest rates above what they would be otherwise. The appropriate fiscal policy would be to slow government spending or increase tax rates. In either case, the level of spending and, thus, aggregate demand would be reduced. The economy would then return to long-run equilibrium at a lower price level, perhaps more quickly than if the government did nothing. Exhibit 23-4 illustrates the path the economy would take to return to long-run equilibrium if the government intervenes.

In response to an unanticipated increase in aggregate demand, the economy moves from long-run equilibrium at point A to point B, ceteris paribus. Output is above the sustainable full employment level, and the price level has risen. If policy makers respond by using fiscal or monetary policy to reduce the level of demand, the economy will move back to long-run equilibrium at a price level (point A) that is lower than it would have been if the government had failed to act.

Note the irony of this situation when the increase in aggregate demand is due to an increase in the money supply. After generating the increase in aggregate demand, the Fed engages in contractionary policy to bring the economy back to long-run equi-

23-4
Possible Policy Maker
Response to an Unexpected
Increase in Aggregate
Demand

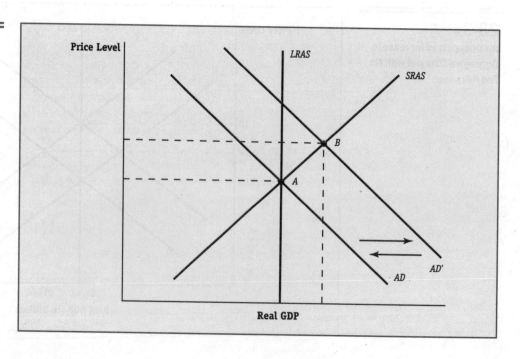

librium at the original point. We turn now to the equally sinister demand-induced recession.

Recap   Starting from full employment, an increase in aggregate demand initially leads to increases in both output and prices as the economy expands along the short-run aggregate supply curve. The higher level of output is not sustainable in the long run. Such unexpected increases in demand cause demand-pull inflation and can come from increases in spending in any sector. If policy makers do nothing, the economy returns to full employment at a higher price level. If policy makers engage in contractionary policies, the economy returns to full employment at the original price level.

DEMAND-INDUCED RECESSIONS

Whatever the source, the initial effect of an unexpected fall in aggregate demand is an unanticipated rise in inventories, ceteris paribus. In response, business firms cut production, employment, and prices. In the aggregate, output prices tend to fall relative to input prices, including wages, which do not fall immediately or fall slower than output prices in response to the reduction in demand. Exhibit 23-5 illustrates the case of a demand-induced recession.

Initially, the economy is in long-run equilibrium at point *A* at the intersection of the aggregate demand and long-run aggregate supply curves. The short-run aggregate supply curve is in the initial position of *SRAS*. The economy moves along the short-run aggregate supply curve (from point *A* to point *B* in Exhibit 23-5) into a recession.[3]

Once in a recession, the economy can take two possible paths from this short-run equilibrium back to a long-run equilibrium. First, with the actual price level (0.95) below the expected price level, firms and workers presumably will adjust their price expectations

23-5
Demand-Induced Recession

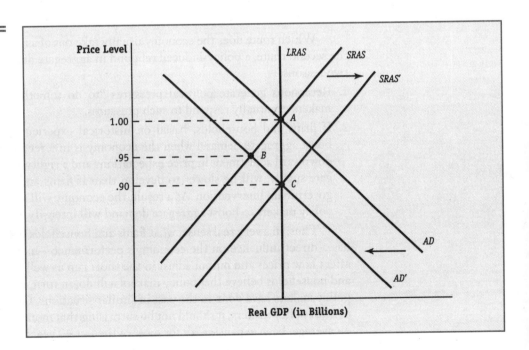

downward. This, along with the decline in the employment of labor and other factors of production, leads to decreases in nominal wages and other input prices. The short-run aggregate supply curve shifts to the right, reflecting the fall in production costs, and the economy returns to a long-run equilibrium at the natural rate of output (point *C*). Thus, following this path, the end result of a fall in aggregate demand (10 percent in Exhibit 23-5) is a proportional fall in the price level (1.0 to 0.9) with no effects on real output or employment.

An important question about this first possible path is how long it will take. The answer is that it depends on how quickly input and output prices adjust downward. This adjustment, in turn, depends on how individuals (firm managers as well as workers) formulate and thus modify their price expectations. Suffice it to say that the adjustment of prices and price expectations in the United States during recessions has usually been a sluggish process. Accordingly, policy makers have found it economically and politically difficult to wait for the economy to take the *B–C* path back to long-run equilibrium.

Such considerations suggest a second possible route out of the recession. Aggregate demand can be boosted, for example, through expansionary monetary and fiscal policies such that aggregate demand rebounds (from *AD'* back to *AD* in Exhibit 23-5). The economy returns to the natural level of real output and the initial price level (point *A*). Again, the appropriate monetary policy would be to increase the growth rate of the monetary and credit aggregates and to lower interest rates from what they would be otherwise. Likewise, the appropriate fiscal policy would be to increase the growth of government spending and/or reduce tax rates.

Recap   Starting from full employment, an unexpected drop in aggregate demand causes a demand-induced recession. Output and prices fall as the economy moves down a short-run aggregate supply curve. If policy makers do nothing, the short-run aggregate supply curve eventually shifts to the right as firms and workers adjust their price expectations downward. The economy returns to full employment at a lower price level. Policy makers can also choose to boost demand through fiscal or monetary policy. In this case, the economy returns to full employment at the original price level.

Which route does the economy usually take out of a recession? In modern history, the second route, a policy-induced rebound in aggregate demand, has predominated for two reasons:

1. Recessions generate political pressures "to do something," and, generally, policy makers eventually respond to such pressures.

2. If firms and households, based on historical experience, expect policy makers to boost aggregate demand when the economy is in a recession, then the first route, a downward adjustment in price expectations and a rightward shift of short-run aggregate supply, will be slower to develop than if firms and households did not expect government intervention. As a result, the economy will stagnate, and the pressure on policy makers to boost aggregate demand will intensify.

Thus, in a very real sense, what firms and households believe policy makers will do has a direct influence on the economy's performance—more specifically, these beliefs affect how prices and output adjust in the short run as well as the long run. What firms and households believe that policy makers will do, in turn, is heavily influenced by what policy makers have done in the past in similar situations. Given the short-run horizons of most policy makers, it should not be surprising that monetary and fiscal policies have, on average, been expansionary for most of the last 40 years.

A legacy of this interaction between policy makers and their constituents is that prices have risen more or less continuously since the end of World War II. However, the rate at which prices rise—that is, the inflation rate—has generally decelerated in recessions and accelerated in expansions. The expansion of the 1990s and the early 2000s is an exception; inflation rates fell for many years late into the expansion. For example, during 1998, more than six years into the expansion, the annualized rate of inflation fell to less than 1.5 percent.

So far, we have concentrated on developments that affect aggregate demand. To complete our examination, we need to analyze how developments that affect aggregate supply influence output, employment, and the overall price level in both the short and the long run.

Recap   If—based on historical experience—firms and households expect policy makers to boost aggregate demand in recessions, then a downward adjustment in price expectations and a rightward shift of the short-run aggregate supply curve will take a long time to materialize. In general, inflation accelerates in expansions and decelerates in recessions. An exception is the expansion of the 1990s, which was not accompanied by an acceleration of inflation.

CHANGES IN AGGREGATE SUPPLY AND POLICY

Supply Shock
Any event that shifts the short-run aggregate supply curve.

A **supply shock** is any event that shifts the aggregate supply curve. An example of an adverse supply shock is a significant rise in the price of oil, a key input widely used in production. Major crop failures and natural disasters such as earthquakes or serious floods are also examples of negative supply shocks. More generally, anything that destroys a significant portion of a nation's productive capacity or reduces the productivity of labor and capital is an adverse supply shock.

As in our analysis of the effects of shifts in aggregate demand, let's begin by assuming that the economy is in long-run equilibrium. Now suppose that an adverse supply shock occurs. For example, suppose, ceteris paribus, that the price of refined petroleum increases suddenly and substantially, as happened in 1974 when the price of refined petroleum increased by more than 70 percent, in 1980 when the price rose more than 50 percent, in 2004 when the price again rose more than 70 percent and again in 2008 when prices more than doubled from early 2007, reaching historic highs in both nominal and real terms.

Firms feel the effects of such a supply shock most immediately and directly. Simply put, input prices rise dramatically relative to what firms had expected. With costs of production higher, firms are unwilling to supply as high a level of output as before. More specifically, in the face of higher production costs, firms will, ceteris paribus, require a higher price level to produce the same level of output. Exhibit 23-6 shows the resulting leftward shift in the short-run aggregate supply curve.

With firms posting higher output prices, ceteris paribus, the quantity of real output demanded falls, and firms cut their production and employment. In the short run, the economy moves from point A to point B and experiences rising prices and falling output and employment. Policy makers are on the spot because the economy is experiencing both a recession and inflation. Real output has fallen below its natural level and prices have risen. In contrast to demand-pull inflation, the economy has now experienced so-called **cost-push inflation** triggered by increases in input prices.[4]

Cost-Push Inflation
Sustained increases in the overall price level, triggered by increases in input prices.

The problem from the policy makers' perspective is that monetary and fiscal tools work mainly on the aggregate demand side, while the more immediate problem

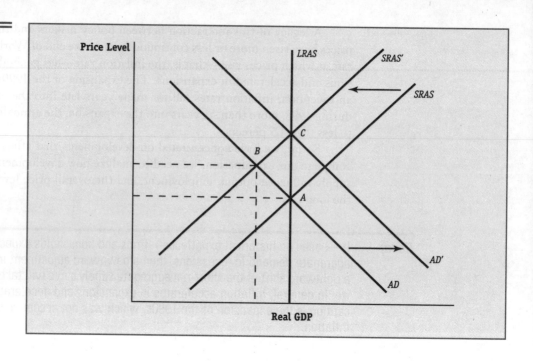

Accommodation
When policy makers increase
aggregate demand in response
to an adverse supply shock.

confronting them emanates from the supply side. What can be done? First, policy makers can boost aggregate demand via fiscal or monetary policy. If they do, the economy moves from point *B* to *C* in Exhibit 23-6. Assuming that this so-called **accommodation** is done quickly, the recession will be shorter in duration and less severe, but the inflation problem will be magnified as prices rise further. Second, policy makers can literally do nothing. With the economy at point *B* and aggregate demand unchanged, the idle plants and unemployment in the economy will eventually put downward pressure on wages and overall prices. As this occurs, the short-run aggregate supply curve will begin to shift to the right toward its initial position. Given enough time, the economy could return to a position close to its initial long-run equilibrium (point *A*). We say *close* because if the price of a major input is permanently higher, the natural rate of output may be reduced somewhat, but not permanently, as alternate inputs are developed or the output mix changes. However, because workers will be reluctant to accept lower wages in the face of higher heating and gasoline prices, the period of adjustment could be quite prolonged. It should not be surprising that policy makers have usually pursued an accommodating expansion in aggregate demand in response to an adverse supply shock.

Of course, supply shocks are not always adverse. In late 1985, the world petroleum market literally collapsed because of slow worldwide economic growth, weak demand, and the tendency for some OPEC members to cheat on their agreed-upon production quotas. With the price of crude petroleum falling from $24.09 in 1985 to $12.51 in 1986, countries such as the United States experienced a beneficial supply shock. The fall in production costs shifted the aggregate supply curve to the right, resulting in lower inflation and greater output growth than otherwise would have occurred. In real terms, prices were lower than they had been since the early 1970s. Prices stayed relatively low (except during the 1990–1991 Iraq war) until the start of the new millennium. However, fortunes tend to reverse courses. In 2003, oil prices started to increase dramatically. By July 2008, oil had topped $147 per barrel before dropping back to around $100 per barrel by September 2008. As noted earlier, such

Will the Fed Have More or Less Power to Affect the Economy in the Future?

In the 1990s, Japan and Mexico, among other nations, struggled to fight the ravages of deflation. The banking systems in both countries experienced near collapse because of falling asset prices. As prices fell, banks owed more to depositors than the value of their assets. Loans to buy property or stocks became worthless as the land and stock prices fell and borrowers defaulted. The monetary authorities seemed to have only limited ability to counter the breakdown of the economy as banks became unwilling to make new loans. In Japan, reluctant taxpayers were forced to inject funds into the insolvent system. In Mexico, the government, which had privatized the banking system in the early 1990s, was forced to adopt a costly loan purchase program to aid the ailing banks.

The United States did not experience a collapse in the 1990s, but if it had, the Fed, with its current powers, would have had less ability to affect the economy than in the past. The Fed and other central banks have seen a decline in their ability to control their domestic economies for the following reasons:

1. The banking system's share of intermediation is declining, and it is through the banking system that the Fed currently exerts its control.

2. Control over banks by the Fed is less stringent than in the past, as banks find new ways to attract deposits that are not subject to reserve requirements.

3. Global forces are more important than ever before.

As a *Wall Street Journal* article puts it:

> An even more pervasive myth is that central bankers have enormous powers to foster economic growth. Paul Volcker [chair of the Fed, 1979–1987] was wryly amused at magazine articles calling him the most powerful man on earth. He knew that global market forces were far more powerful than the Fed. But at least he had stronger controls in the early 1980s over the money supply than the Fed has today.[a]

But this may change in the future. Note that the Proposal to Overhaul the Financial Regulatory Structure discussed in Chapter 12 would expand the Fed's power over nonbank intermediaries and any financial institution whose acts could pose a threat to the financial stability of the United States. Perhaps this is in response to the Fed's decline in power and the need for a super agency that would have the power to address threats to the entire financial system. Furthermore, the Treasury and Fed's response to the financial crisis of 2008 has undoubtedly left the Fed with more power and we suspect that this will even increase in the years to come.

Endnote

a. George Melloan, "Don't Bank on the Fed to Ease Future Shocks," *The Wall Street Journal* (November 27, 1995): A17.

increases in the price of oil caused many observers to speculate that another cost-push inflation was on the horizon.

Recap   Adverse supply shocks shift the short-run aggregate supply curve to the left. Beneficial shocks shift it to the right. Adverse supply shocks cause rising prices and higher unemployment and are particularly difficult for policy makers to deal with. Given an adverse shock, an accommodating policy will increase employment but aggravate the inflation.

We have considered increases and decreases in aggregate demand and aggregate supply. Whatever the case may be, the goals and policy responses brought together in this chapter suggest ways to achieve full employment and stable prices. The formulation and implementation of policies to achieve these goals are the subjects of the next two chapters.

Summary of Major Points

1. The goal of monetary policy is to influence the overall performance of the economy. The size of the "economic pie" in the long run is influenced by the growth of the labor force and the capital stock and by increases in the productivity of these inputs. Government policies affect growth through the mix of monetary and fiscal policies and resulting tax and interest rate structures, which affect incentives to invest, work, and save. In addition, to the extent that government policies encourage a stable environment, growth is also affected.

2. In addition to economic growth, full employment, price stability, and a satisfactory external balance are also goals of monetary policy. Over the short run, economic growth depends on the growth of aggregate demand relative to aggregate supply, which determines the resulting fluctuations in output, employment, and prices. An unstable short-run environment is believed to have an adverse effect on long-run growth, and a stable short-run environment is believed to have a beneficial effect on long-run growth.

3. Full employment is a goal because if a nation is to reach its full economic potential, individuals must have an opportunity to become productive members of society. Price stability is a goal because inflation tends to redistribute income in arbitrary and unpredictable ways, especially if the change is unexpected. Inflation also contributes to uncer-

tainty and distortions in decision making. It can have an adverse effect on the nation's international competitiveness. When inflation rates are low, policy makers must also be on the lookout for deflation. Deflation is undesirable because it can cause a debt deflation, defaults, and bankruptcies. Monetary policy can cause dramatic changes in exchange rates and the balances in the current and capital accounts. Monetary policy must seek to achieve an acceptable external balance compatible with the goals of full employment and stable prices.

4. General guidelines for the macroeconomic goals are contained in the Employment Act of 1946 and the Humphrey-Hawkins Full Employment and Balanced Growth Act of 1978. Specific guidelines and setting priorities are the result of historical experience, judgments about what is feasible, and the political environment.

5. In the short run, an unexpected increase in aggregate demand produces demand-pull inflation and unsustainable increases in output. If policy makers do nothing, the economy returns to long-run equilibrium at a higher price level. If the government uses appropriate monetary or fiscal policy, the economy returns to long-run equilibrium at a price level lower than it otherwise would have been.

6. In the short run, an unexpected fall in aggregate demand will produce a recession. There are two possible paths to recovery. First, as time goes on,

price expectations will be revised downward, inflation will decrease, and the economy will recover as relative prices adjust. Alternatively, if policy makers and their constituents become impatient, demand can be boosted by expansionary monetary and fiscal policy. History shows that the second route has predominated.

7. Supply shocks cause a shift of the short-run aggregate supply curve. Adverse supply shocks pose a real dilemma for policy makers. Real output and employment fall while prices rise. An accommodating policy will moderate the recession but will aggravate the inflation. Cost-push inflation results when the overall price level increases due to increases in the cost of inputs.

Key Terms

Accommodation, p. **578**
Cost-Push Inflation, p. **577**
Deflation, p. **568**
Employment Act of 1946,
   p. **569**

Humphrey-Hawkins Full
   Employment and Balanced
   Growth Act of 1978, p. **569**
Natural Rate of Unemployment,
   p. **569**

Personal Consumption Expenditures Price Index (PCEPI),
   p. **566**
Stagflation, p. **562**
Supply Shock, p. **577**

Review Questions

1. What are the goals of monetary policy?
2. How are the goals of full employment and stable prices related to the long-run goal of economic growth? How can policy makers affect long-run growth?
3. Why do policy makers have to be aware of the external balance?
4. Explain why the short-run goal for inflation is not always zero percent.
5. What is deflation, and why do policy makers have to be concerned about it?
6. Does the natural level of unemployment ever change? If it does, explain why.
7. Explain why the numerical objectives of policy change.
8. What is a supply shock? What is the appropriate policy response to a negative supply shock? What determines whether policy makers should act or

do nothing in the face of adverse shocks to either aggregate demand or aggregate supply?
9. In the context of monetary policy, what is accommodation? If the Fed usually increases the money supply in response to decreases in aggregate demand, how will this affect the adjustment process?
10. Define both *cost-push* and *demand-pull inflation*.
11. How is the natural level of real output related to the natural rate of unemployment?
12. Can the economy experience a demand-pull inflation and a recession at the same time?
13. In the late 1990s, Congress and the president eliminated the federal deficit. What effect did this have on aggregate demand?
14. Can a person be employed but not be in the labor force? Can a person be unemployed but not be in the labor force?

Analytical Questions

Questions marked with a check mark (✓) are objective in nature. They can be completed with a short answer or number.

15. Use aggregate supply and aggregate demand curves to analyze a supply shock.

16. Use aggregate supply and aggregate demand curves to illustrate demand-pull and cost-push inflation.
✓17. The nominal interest rate is 6 percent, expected inflation is 3 percent, and the tax rate is 20 percent.

What is the real after-tax return? If the nominal interest rate and the expected inflation rate both decrease by 2 percent, what is the real after-tax return?

✓18. The nominal interest rate is 3 percent, but people expect prices to fall by 4 percent. What is the real interest rate? If the tax rate is 20 percent, what is the real after-tax return?

✓19. Draw the long-run aggregate supply curves for successive long-run equilibriums with a potential growth rate of real GDP at 2.5 to 3.0 percent per year. What is the sustainable growth rate of output over time?

20. Graphically demonstrate the appropriate Fed policy in response to a severe unexpected drop in aggregate demand.

21. Graphically demonstrate how changes in aggregate demand cause inflation or deflation (falling prices) in the short run. Explain why only the price level changes in the long run. What happens to the price level over successive long runs?

✓22. In each of the following cases, explain whether the individual is in the labor force, not in the labor force, employed, or unemployed:
   a. A 14-year-old truant who is looking for work
   b. A person who has started her own business
   c. A college student
   d. My retired mother who does volunteer work at a hospital
   e. A discouraged aerospace worker who has given up looking for a job
   f. A recent college graduate who is actively seeking a job

✓23. Use aggregate demand and aggregate supply curves to show what will happen to output and the price level if government spending is reduced at the same time the Fed takes action to increase the money supply.

Suggested Readings

Inflation and unemployment rates since the 1940s are available on the Internet at **http://research.stlouisfed.org/fred2/**.

Information on unemployment and inflation can also be found at **http://www.whitehouse.gov/news/fsbr.html**.

Data and tables on inflation can be seen at **http://www.clevelandfed.org/Research/Data/mcpipr.htm**.

In compliance with the Humphrey-Hawkins Act of 1978, the Fed must report its long-term goals to Congress in February and July of each year. See the latest Monetary Policy Testimony and Report to Congress by the chair of the Board of Governors of the Fed at **http://www.federalreserve.gov/boarddocs/hh/**.

Downloadable papers that describe the general purpose and goals of monetary policy can be found at **http://www.federalreserve.gov/pf/pf.htm**.

Robert Rich and Charles Steindel make "A Comparison of Measures of Core Inflation," *Economic Policy Review*, Federal Reserve Bank of New York, 13, no. 3 (December 2007).

Charles Steindel looks at "U.S. Policy and the Changing Global Landscape," *NABE News*, no. 186, April 2007.

Argia Sbordone looks at "Inflation Persistence: Alternative Interpretations and Policy Implications," *Journal of Monetary Economics* 54, no. 5 (July 2007).

For those interested in "How Theory Is Shaping Monetary Policy," see V.V. Chari and Patrick J. Kehoe's article by the same name in the Federal Reserve Bank of Minneapolis 2006 *Annual Report*. It is available online at **http://www.minneapolisfed.org/publications_papers/pub_display.cfm?id=3183**.

A highly recommended and comprehensive speech about monetary policy by former Fed chair Alan Greenspan highlights the risk management aspects of monetary policy during his tenure. The speech, titled "Risk and Uncertainty in Monetary Policy," was given before the American Economics Association, January 3, 2004, in San Diego, California. A transcript is available on the Internet at **http://www.federalreserve.gov/boarddocs/speeches/2004/20040103/default.htm**.

For a look at recent aspects of monetary policy, see Anthony M. Santomero, "Monetary Policy: Stability Through Change," *Business Review*, Federal Reserve Bank of Philadelphia (First Quarter 2004): 1–5. The article is available online at **http://www.phil.frb.org/files/br/brq104as.pdf**.

George A. Kahn and Scott Benolkin discuss "The Role of Money in Monetary Policy: Why Do the Fed and the ECB

See It So Differently?" *Economic Review*, Federal Reserve Bank of Kansas City, 92, no. 3 (Third Quarter 2007): 5–36. The article is available online at **www.KansasCityFed .org/PUBLICAT/ECONREV/PDF/3q07kahn.pdf.**

For a look at the systematic ways in which monetary policy affects the economy, see Michael Dotsey, "How the Fed Affects the Economy: A Look at Systematic Monetary Policy," *Business Review*, Federal Reserve Bank of Philadelphia (First Quarter 2004): 6–15. The article is available online at **http:// www.philadelphiafed.org/files/br/brq104md.pdf.**

The Federal Reserve Bank of San Francisco maintains a very thorough Internet site on U.S. monetary policy at **http://www.frbsf.org/publications/federalreserve/ monetary/.**

For an advanced look at monetary policy, see Carl E. Walsh, *Monetary Theory and Policy*, 2nd ed. (Cambridge, MA: MIT Press, 2003).

For an article that discusses the challenges of monetary policy given ongoing changes in financial markets, see

"Monetary Policy in a Changing World," by Thomas M. Hoenig, *Economic Review*, Federal Reserve Bank of Kansas City, 85, no. 3 (Third Quarter 2000): 5–10. It may be viewed and/or ordered on the World Wide Web at **http:// www.kc.frb.org/Publicat/econrev/er00q3.htm#hoenig.** For a discussion of the challenges of monetary policy given structural changes in the economy, see Robert T. Parry, "Monetary Policy in a New Environment: The U.S. Experience," *Economic Letter*, Federal Reserve Bank of San Francisco, 2000-31 (October 13, 2000).

For a discussion of Nobel laureate economist William Vickery's view that under normal conditions, inflation and unemployment are separable issues, see David Colander, "Macroeconomics: Was Vickery Ten Years Ahead?" *Challenge* (September–October 1998): 72–86.

Stephen G. Cecchitti, "Policy Rules and Targets: Framing the Central Banker's Problem," discusses many of the topics in this chapter. It can be found in *Economic Policy Review*, Federal Reserve Bank of New York, 4, no. 2 (June 1998): 1–14.

Endnotes

1. Keynes viewed fluctuations as originating with aggregate demand, and, as you have seen, under normal circumstances both fiscal and monetary policies affect demand. Although we consider both policies to be Keynesian, Keynes's preference was for fiscal policy.
2. A fascinating speech by Fed Chair Greenspan that highlights the asymmetrical differences between inflation and deflation is "Risk and Uncertainty in Monetary Policy," given before the American Economics Association, January 3, 2004, in San Diego, California. It is available on the Internet at **http://www.federalreserve.gov/boarddocs/speeches/2004/20040103/ default.htm**.
3. Technically speaking, *recession* is usually defined as a fall in real GDP lasting at least two consecutive calendar quarters. In actuality, the government maintains a Business Cycle Dating Committee to decide when the economy officially enters and leaves a recession.
4. We should note that a recession is not necessary to have cost-push inflation.

24

Comfort the afflicted and afflict the comfortable.

—Finley Peter Dunne

You must lose a fly to catch a trout.

—George Herbert

The Process of Monetary Policy Formulation

Learning Objectives

After reading this chapter, you should know:

The factors that guide the policy process

The various lags in the policy process

How and why the performance of the economy can differ from policy makers' objectives

What intermediate targets are and how they are related to the ultimate policy goals

How monetary policy is formulated by the Federal Open Market Committee (FOMC) and the major pitfalls of that process

SETTING THE STAGE

It's the regular mid-month meeting of the Federal Open Market Committee (FOMC). The chair orders the huge doors to the Fed's impressive conference room closed and calls the meeting to order. In his opening remarks, he suggests that the ensuing discussion focus on policy actions that will raise the inflation rate and increase the cyclical fluctuation of the economy over the next 12 to 18 months.

We hope that the last sentence has startled you! Something is wrong. Policy makers and professors consistently tell us that policy actions are directed at reducing the inflation rate and decreasing cyclical fluctuations. If this is so, however, why did the United States experience two recessions at the beginning of the 1980s, a recession at the beginning of the 1990s, a recession in the early 2000s, and a major slowdown beginning in 2008? Why do the unemployment and inflation rates periodically rise to unacceptable levels? Are maladies that strike the economy avoidable? Are they the result of bad luck or bad policy making? What role do economics and politics play?

In the last chapter, we discussed the major goals of monetary policy, which include sustainable economic growth, full employment, stable prices, and a satisfactory external balance. The Fed is charged with designing and implementing economic policies that will enhance the health and performance of the U.S. economy and achieve these goals. This chapter provides an overview of the monetary policy process with particular emphasis on what guides the plans of policy makers, how those plans get translated into actions, and how and why, despite good intentions, the performance of the economy can differ from policy makers' objectives. The discussion connects the world of theory to the real world in which policy is made. The approach is also general, leaving the specifics of policy to the next chapter.

THE POLICY PROCESS

The essential elements of the policy process and the problems surrounding the conduct of monetary policy can be illustrated with the aid of Exhibit 24-1. The policy goals, combined with the expected economic performance, guide policy actions, which then, in turn, alter spending, saving, borrowing, and lending decisions. Study this exhibit carefully because the rest of the chapter focuses in some detail on the elements and linkages it depicts.

At first glance, the challenges facing policy makers do not seem that imposing. Compare the expected performance of the economy to the goals. If the economy's performance is expected to be close to the goals, leave the policy unchanged; if the economy's performance is expected to fall well short of the goals, alter the policy accordingly. The reasoning is so simple and seemingly sensible that it leads one to wonder how policy and policy makers can ever go astray. Any policy maker, however, will tell you that making policy is both difficult and frustrating, laden with a never-ending series of problems and pitfalls. Obviously, we need to reflect a bit more deeply about the process depicted in Exhibit 24-1.

We begin with some specific questions about some basic generalities. How do policy makers figure out what the expected performance of the goal variables is likely to be? How do they decide what to do if they believe action is called for? Once they act, how do they know the actions taken are sufficient?

To begin, let's assume policy makers have already established goals and numerical objectives, as discussed in Chapter 23. The next step as depicted in Exhibit 24-1 is to determine the likely performance of the economy if policy remains unchanged. How do policy makers do this?

A Conceptual Overview of the Macroeconomic Policy Process

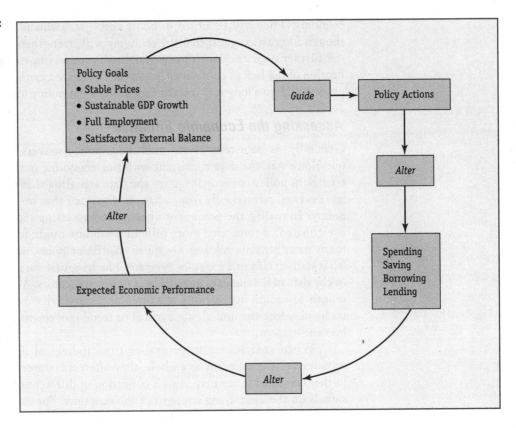

Policy Goals
• Stable Prices
• Sustainable GDP Growth
• Full Employment
• Satisfactory External Balance

Guide → Policy Actions

Alter

Spending
Saving
Borrowing
Lending

Alter

Expected Economic Performance

Alter

The basic approach is to use various statistical methods and models, judgment based on historical experience, and incoming data on the full range of factors comprising and determining aggregate demand and aggregate supply to develop a forecast for the variables of major concern such as real gross domestic product (GDP), inflation, the unemployment rate, and exchange rates. The data that are used include information about retail sales, industrial production, consumer confidence, business capital spending plans, wages, personal income, profits, and the external balance of payments. Long-term forecasts are currently made four times per year, in January, April, July, and October. The forecasts extend over a three-year period. If the incoming data and the forecasts suggest the economy's performance is deviating significantly from the goals and priorities, the policy makers will consider a change in policy to move the economy's likely performance closer to the goals.

Current Conditions versus Forecasts

Two aspects of the forecasts and incoming data used by policy makers deserve special note. First, forecasting is an imperfect science, so forecasting errors can be fairly large. The greater the volatility in economic variables, the larger the errors tend to be. Because of the possibility of significant errors, policy makers typically do not give heavy weight to forecasts in policy discussions.

Second, there is a strong tendency to focus on incoming data and to use them to guide policy. These figures, which define "current economic conditions," attract considerable media attention and generate much of the political pressure that periodically bears down on policy makers. For example, if the current data suggest that the economy is growing slowly, there will be considerable pressure on policy makers to stimulate the economy. They will be urged to boost aggregate demand and economic growth even though forecasts suggest that the economy will strengthen in six to nine months without further policy action. This nearsightedness and impatience, which are partly a reflection of the lack of confidence in the forecasts, are a critical part of the policy-making process and go a long way toward explaining what policy makers do or fail to do.

Assessing the Economic Situation

Generally, as data reports are published, policy makers ask themselves two simple questions: Are the data consistent with our economic outlook and desires, so that no change in policy is needed? Or are the data signaling that the economy's performance has deviated so markedly from what was expected that we should consider a change in policy? In reality, the process of filtering and assessing incoming data (much of which is estimated) is somewhat more difficult than one might imagine. The problem is that many monthly data releases are quite volatile or noisy, possessing a large element of what statisticians call *irregular variance*. The irregular variance or random fluctuations in the data make the data unreliable as policy indicators. As a result of potentially large month-to-month fluctuations, it is often necessary to have data for two to three months on hand before the underlying cyclical or trend movements in an individual data series become evident.

When analysts try to generalize from individual data series (or sectors of the economy) to the economy as a whole, they often encounter another problem. The noise in the individual series may cause a collection of different series to transmit conflicting signals on the underlying strength of the economy. For example, the data reported for February might show that retail sales are stronger than expected, suggesting that the rate of consumption spending is increasing. At the same time, new orders for capital goods and housing starts are weak, suggesting that the rate of business fixed investment and residential investment spending is slowing. Here again, if the economy is in fact deviating from its expected track, it will usually take several months of data releases covering the full spectrum of the economy's performance before the ambiguities in the monthly data are resolved. In sum, policy makers need time to recognize that a change in the economy's performance has occurred. This time between a significant and unexpected change in the economy's performance and policy makers' recognition of that change is called the **recognition lag** in the policy-making process.

Recognition Lag
The time it takes policy makers to recognize that a change in the economy's performance has occurred.

From Assessment to Action

As evidence begins to accumulate that the economy is deviating significantly from the desired path, a consensus develops among policy makers that policy needs to be altered. For example, if the economy is strengthening considerably and inflationary pressures are building, there is a need to reduce the growth of aggregate demand somewhat. At this point, the focus shifts from assessing the economy and considering whether anything needs to be done to deciding exactly what should be done. What policy tools should be used, how large or small should the policy adjustment be, and when should the policy change take place?[1]

Resolving these questions takes time, however. The net result is that policy actions can be paralyzed for a while, and policy makers may do too little too late. In any event, the policy-making process includes a **policy lag**—the time between the point when the need for action is recognized and the point when an adjustment policy is decided upon and set in motion.

Policy Lag
The time between the point when the need for action is recognized and the point when an adjustment policy is decided on and set in motion.

From Action to Effect

When policy makers act, does the economy respond immediately? In general, the answer is no. The policy action will set in motion a series of adjustments in the economy that will gradually alter the performance of the economy relative to what it would have been in the absence of any new policy actions. To illustrate, suppose that the economy has been growing quickly with inflation accelerating, and the Fed decides to pursue a more restrictive monetary policy. To cut the growth in aggregate demand, the Fed takes actions that reduce the supply of funds, and interest rates rise. Will firms cut their investment spending right away? Not necessarily. If a new plant is half completed, capacity utilization in its existing plants is high, and the demand for a firm's products is expected to remain fairly strong for the foreseeable future, then the firm (and other firms like it) will continue spending on investment projects. Gradually, however, as the rise in interest rates and reduction in the availability of funds slow the growth of aggregate demand, sales and capacity utilization will fall, and expectations about the future will be modified. At this point, investment spending plans will be reevaluated and possibly postponed or canceled, leading to a further deceleration in the growth of aggregate demand.

On the aggregate supply side, the slowing of the growth in aggregate demand will be associated with a downward revision in price expectations and an adjustment of wages and other input prices. Here again, historical experience suggests that this process will be gradual rather than instantaneous.

Impact Lag
The time between when an action is taken and when that action has a significant impact on economic variables.

The net result is an impact lag in monetary policy—that is, the time between when an action is taken and when that action has a significant impact on prices, employment, and output. How much time you ask? Available research suggests that significant effects generally begin to show up after six months to a year or more and continue accumulating for several years. However, some analysts suggest that one of the effects of the Fed's policy of increased openness in the last decade has been to shorten this lag, which is what the Fed hopes to do. Exhibit 24-2 brings together the various lags comprising the policy process. Now would be a good time to read the accompanying "A Closer Look" titled "Why the Fed Has Become More Open."

24-2

Lags in the Policy Process

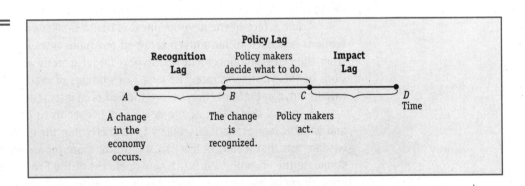

The economy begins to need corrective action at point A, but the need is not recognized until point B three months later. The time that elapses between point A and point B is called the *recognition lag*. Between point B and point C, policy makers think about what actions to take and reach a decision. The time that elapses between point B and point C is called the *policy lag*. Once action has been taken at point C, it takes time before the economy's performance is materially affected. The distance from point C to point D represents this *impact lag*.

A Closer Look

Why the Fed Has Become More Open

Throughout most of its history, the Fed has been a rather secretive organization surrounded by mystique. The Fed preferred to act covertly and to adjust policy gradually rather than abruptly, with the belief that such behavior minimized market disruptions and reduced the chance of a major policy error. Accordingly, the Fed did not announce policy changes immediately following FOMC meetings and the public did not find out about changes until the release of the minutes after the next FOMC meeting more than six weeks later. Thus, the Fed was using open market operations to change policy without the public's knowledge. Because open market operations are a complex blend of offsetting operations and those reflecting a change in the stance of policy, it was difficult to distinguish between the two.

All of this has changed in recent decades. As noted earlier, since 1994, the Fed has made public announcements immediately following all meetings whenever there were any changes in the fed funds rate target. In 2000, the Fed began making a statement after every FOMC meeting that included an assessment of the balance of risks to the economy. In 2002, a roll call vote was added so that the public could gauge the amount of dissent. In 2005, minutes of FOMC meetings were released with a lag of three weeks instead of six to seven weeks. Finally, in 2007, the Fed increased the number of times long-term economic projections were made from two to four times per year, and the economic projections were for three years rather than two. This openness constitutes a significant departure from the Fed's traditional behavior.

Why has the Fed abandoned its recalcitrant secretive behavior in favor of public disclosure? The reason seems to be the Fed's belief that if it better communicates current and future policy moves, there will be less uncertainty. A lower degree of uncertainty means more control over future expectations and, through this, more control over long-term rates. After all, these changes in long-term interest rates have the greatest impact on economic activity, and it is the long-term rate that the Fed is aiming to affect through changes in short-term rates.

A side effect of the new openness is that a smaller volume of open market operations is needed to hit a given targeted fed funds rate. The smaller volume results from the Fed's announcement of the new target directly and its effect on expectations of the short-term rate. The new expectations of market participants cause the rate to move in that direction before the Fed even intervenes.

A second side effect of the new openness seems to be a reduction in the long and variable lag for monetary policy to take effect in the economy. The conventional wisdom was that it took at least six months or more for an interest rate reduction to stimulate the economy. With the new openness of the Fed and the greater transparency, financial markets can more easily anticipate what the Fed will do and act accordingly and preemptively, thus reducing the lag.

Policy goals combined with expected economic performance guide policy actions. Policy makers tend to give more weight to incoming data about current economic conditions than to forecasts, which can be unreliable. The recognition lag is the time that it takes for policy makers to recognize that economic conditions have changed and that a policy change is necessary. The policy lag is the time between the recognition of the need for action and the implementation of the policy adjustment. The impact lag is the time that it takes for the policy action to have a significant impact on the economy.

PITFALLS IN POLICY MAKING

Despite good intentions, policy does not always produce an economic performance that closely coincides with the nation's economic objectives. There are no simple explanations for the periodic lack of correspondence between policy makers' plans and economic performance. As in all endeavors, honest mistakes can be made, analysis can be faulty, and unexpected events beyond the policy makers' control can occur. Against this background, let's briefly examine some of the most prominent problems affecting the successful conduct of policy.

Uncertainty and Lags

Our discussion of the impact lag for policy suggests that economic developments today are largely the result of policies pursued over the past several years. Logically, then, given such lags, policy makers can do little today to materially affect the current performance of the economy. What policy makers can do is affect the future performance of the economy. As we all know, however, the future cannot be known with certainty. Because economic forecasts, in particular, can be quite wide of the mark, policy makers cannot know for certain what, if anything, should be done today to improve the economy's future performance. To complicate matters further, the large month-to-month fluctuations in economic data that we discussed earlier prevent policy makers from knowing with certainty how the economy is currently performing.

The net result is that policy makers are generally quite cautious in adjusting policy. Unless there is a crisis, they prefer to move gradually rather than precipitously in the general direction suggested by the current data on the economy and the policy objectives. As understandable and reasonable as this approach sounds, some potentially serious pitfalls are lurking here.

To illustrate, imagine that you are in a shower (home, hotel, or dorm) adjusting the hot water faucet to attain the desired overall temperature of the water. The problem, especially in an older building without a modern plumbing system, is that there is often a lag between when you turn the hot water faucet and when the water becomes warmer. Moreover, the lag can vary, depending on how many other showers have been taken in the recent past, how many are currently being taken, and how much hot water is left in the tank. In other words, you lack the knowledge you need to fine-tune the hot water. When nothing happens after several gradual adjustments, you grow increasingly impatient and keep turning the knob. At some point, a rush of scalding water bursts out and burns you. You never intended to get burned, but it happened anyway.

Policy makers have the same problem. They don't really intend, for example, to raise the inflation rate (and get burned), but it happens. The economy is performing sluggishly and policy makers want to increase economic growth. They increase aggregate demand (turn up the heat), but nothing seems to happen. They—and the nation—become increasingly impatient and undertake further demand-increasing policy actions. Eventually, economic growth spurts ahead at an excessive pace, causing an unintended acceleration of inflation. Hopefully, increased knowledge will enable economic policy makers to take more precise actions, just as a modern plumbing system allows you to adjust the water temperature precisely.

In sum, the existence of lags in an uncertain world complicates policy makers' efforts to act appropriately in a timely fashion, regardless of whether contractionary or inflationary forces are building in the economy. More specifically, acting or failing to act today may aggravate inflation and cyclical fluctuations later. The economy may be destabilized rather than stabilized. In the case of recession, the push to do something now to improve the current situation as soon as possible interacts with the difficulties associated with lags and uncertainty and may lead to higher inflation later. In the case of inflationary pressures, the pressure not to do something now may, as they say, let the horse out of the barn. When there is pressure "to do something now" or "not to do something now," consistent formulation and implementation of policies conducive to economic growth and stability become even more problematic.

Data Revisions and Policy Regret

Some economic data series such as exchange rates, stock prices, and nominal interest rates are directly observable and not subject to revision. Other data, such as those on employment and unemployment, nominal and real GDP, and inflation rates, are based on sample estimates that may be subject to numerous revisions as more accurate information becomes available. We have already noted that such incoming data are subject to a great deal of white noise or random fluctuation. Policy decisions are based on incoming data that are available when the decisions are made. Data used in policy actions, such as those on output or overall prices levels, are often subject to numerous revisions. **Policy regret** occurs if revised data estimates suggest that some other course of action should have and would have been taken if the revised data had been available. For example, the Fed generally considers how far actual output is from potential output and how far actual inflation is from the inflation rate associated with stable prices. If actual output and inflation are subject to revisions, policy makers may experience policy regret. Indeed, each additional revision may imply a different optimal policy strategy. In addition, some economic concepts such as potential output and the inflation rate associated with stable prices may also be subject to revision but, as noted earlier in this chapter, we are considering these numerical goals as already having been established.

When revised data are used to evaluate past policy decisions, policy actions often appear to be overly accommodative or overly restrictive. In evaluating policy decisions, one must consider the data that were available when the decisions were made. If the data available at the time are used, policy decisions may seem more understandable. Because the Fed is aware of data revisions and the possibility of policy regret, the impetus would be to be more cautious in changing policy. Gradual change of policy reduces the effect of data uncertainty on policy recommendations. All policy actions are based on uncertain data and those that will be revised. However, some data are more uncertain than others. Some analysts suggest that the Fed could base policy actions on data that are less responsive to highly uncertain information or the Fed could respond to data that have been averaged over several time periods. Nevertheless, we hope that you can see how policy actions involve a great deal of skill and luck.

Globalization: A Financially and Economically Integrated World Economy

A new reality is having a profound influence on the conduct and effectiveness of domestic policies. Simply put, the economies of the world are becoming more interdependent.

Policy Regret
A situation in which policy actions based on available data would not have been taken if more accurate data revisions had been available.

What goes on in Tokyo, London, Hong Kong, Paris, and Frankfurt has an increasingly important effect on economic and financial conditions in the United States. Consequently, U.S. policy makers have somewhat less control over the performance of the U.S. economy than in previous eras, when the U.S. economy was more isolated from international trade and finance. As a result, the Fed has reached out to other central banks on an informal basis to coordinate monetary policy on numerous occasions. For example, in September 2001, the central banks of Canada, England, and the European Monetary Union engaged in a coordinated interest rate cut along with the Fed shortly after the attacks on the World Trade Center and the Pentagon. In December 2007, the Bank of Canada, the Bank of England, The European Central Bank, the Swiss National Bank, and the Fed announced coordinated measures to provide liquidity in short-term lending markets in response to the crisis in the mortgage markets. Again in September 2008, the same banks along with the Bank of Japan announced coordinated actions to provide liquidity to global financial markets. Later in the same month, the Fed announced further coordinated activities with the Reserve Bank of Australia, the National Bank of Denmark, the Bank of Norway, and the Bank of Sweden.

Such interdependencies have given rise to calls for increased cooperation and coordination among world policy makers. Although the difficulties some countries have in coordinating their domestic monetary and fiscal policies suggest that coordinating policies across countries will never be easy, the existence of globalization does highlight the new challenges and complexities facing policy makers. More on this in Chapter 26.

Policy makers are attempting to meet the challenges of globalization through informal discussions among the major industrialized countries and through international organizations such as the International Monetary Fund and the Bank for International Settlements. These dialogues suggest that to achieve a stable international financial system, countries around the world must have healthy financial systems with noninflationary policies. In addition, countries must standardize the reporting of information about financial markets, institutions, laws, regulations, international reserves, external debt (both short and long term), and the health of the banking sector. Finally, the surveillance of international organizations that oversee the international financial system must be more transparent and open. In such an environment, the full benefits of globalization could be reached while minimizing the costs. For now, we turn to the specifics of how monetary policy is formulated.

Recap   The existence of lags in an uncertain world complicates policy makers' efforts to act appropriately in a timely fashion. In a recession, the push to do something now to improve the current situation as soon as possible interacts with the difficulties associated with lags and uncertainty and may lead to higher inflation later. Data revisions may result in policy regret. In the face of inflation, the pressure not to do something now may cause further instability later. Increased globalization suggests the need for increased global coordination of monetary policy.

INTERMEDIATE TARGETS

Intermediate Target
The use of a target midway between the policy instruments and the ultimate policy goals.

Given these complexities, uncertainties, and time lags, the Fed has long used an **intermediate target** approach to the formulation and implementation of policy rather than focusing on the ultimate goals. The basic idea, illustrated in Exhibit 24-3, is that the Fed selects a variable—such as a monetary aggregate or an interest rate—that is in some sense midway between its policy instruments and the ultimate or final goals or targets of policy.[2] The intermediate target is then used to guide day-to-day open market operations.

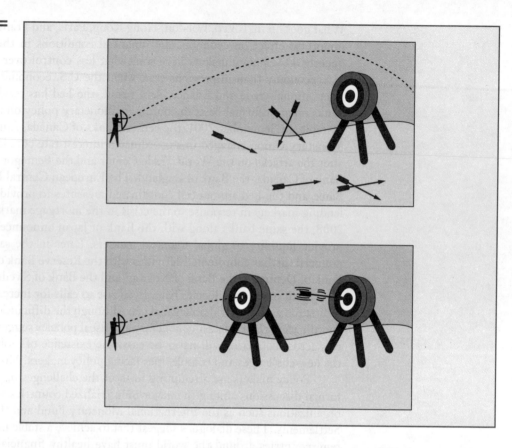

Why an intermediate target? Suppose you have a bow and arrow and want to hit the center of a target that you can barely see way off in the distance. The bow is your instrument, and the target you really want to hit is your final target. The distance and poor visibility make it difficult for you to hit the final target, so you select an intermediate target—a clearly visible target between you and the less-visible final target. You then align the intermediate target between you and the final target so that if you hit the center of the intermediate target, your arrow will continue on and strike the final target. In this way, you can hit the final target even though you can barely see it.

The rationale is that if the Fed hits the intermediate target, it will come reasonably close to achieving its economic objectives.

How does the Fed select a particular intermediate target and a particular range of values for that variable? For example, the Fed could pick domestic nonfinancial debt (DNFD), the broadest measure of credit, as an intermediate target and choose a growth rate range of 4 to 8 percent. Or it could use an interest rate as an intermediate target and select a target range such as 3.5 to 4.5 percent for nominal short-term rates. In any case, the basic criteria for selecting an intermediate target variable are related to the characteristics of economic data and policy actions we discussed earlier.

First, the variable should be reliably and, thus, predictably related to the goal variables. If a variable were not so related, hitting the intermediate target range would not necessarily help to achieve the goals, and selecting a target range for the intermediate variable consistent with the economic objectives would be virtually impossible. To illustrate, a sailor traveling between point A and point B will often find it useful to guide the ship by initially aiming for a buoy firmly anchored midway between the two points.

If the buoy were floating aimlessly instead of being anchored, it would not be a useful guide. Second, policy makers should be able to observe the intermediate target regularly. That is, the data about the target should be readily available. Third, the Fed should be able to hit the target range of the intermediate variable; that is, it should be able to control the intermediate variable with policy instruments with a reasonable degree of precision. Obviously, a variable that cannot be readily observed and controlled would be of little practical use to policy makers. Our intrepid sailor, for example, would find a navigation buoy of little use without a working compass and good visibility.

From the late 1970s until the early 1990s, the monetary aggregates and DNFD were monitored and used as intermediate targets to guide monetary policy because there was a stable relationship between changes in one or more of the aggregates and the level of economic activity. The Fed set growth target ranges for several aggregates to hedge its bets and to maintain as flexible a position as possible.

Despite setting target ranges for several aggregates, $M1$ was the most closely watched aggregate for use in policy formulation until the early 1980s. However, in the early 1980s, $M1$'s behavior became unstable and erratic, and the Fed de-emphasized its role as an intermediate target. In the mid-1980s, the Fed put more emphasis on changes in $M2$ because it seemed to have the strongest correlation with changes in economic activity. This relationship also became too unstable and unpredictable to be used in gauging policy. In the early 1990s, the strongest correlation seemed to be between changes in DNFD and changes in economic activity. However, the Fed's control over DNFD is far less precise than its control over the monetary aggregates because credit emanates from so many nonbanking sources. Hence, the ability to use DNFD in the implementation of monetary policy is severely limited.

The breakdown in the traditional relationships between monetary aggregates and economic activity caused an abandonment of the use of monetary aggregates as either targets or information variables in the early 1990s. In July 2000, the Fed even stopped providing projections about the growth rates of the monetary aggregates and DNFD.

Other models have fared no better in explaining the inflationary and growth processes. The result is that there is increasing reliance on a broad set of economic indicators to gauge monetary policy that is then implemented through changes in interest rates.

Consequently, since mid-1993, the Fed has emphasized interest rate targeting. Under such a regime, the Fed increases the interest rate target if it perceives a need to slow down the level of economic activity, and it decreases the target if it perceives a need to speed things up. The Fed carries out this procedure by announcing a target for the fed funds rate and using open market operations to hit the target. In this case, the fed funds rate is an operating target that is highly responsive to open market operations, the Fed's main policy tool. The Fed adjusts the fed funds rate with an eye toward raising or lowering other short- and long-term interest rates that are the intermediate target. Other short- and long-term interest rates adjust in response to changes in the fed funds rate. Note that the Fed has more direct control over the operating target than over the intermediate target. The accompanying "A Closer Look" feature on p. 596 discusses the use of operating targets since 1970.

Why has the relationship between some monetary aggregates and economic activity failed to survive over time? Many analysts attribute the breakdown to technological changes in the payments systems and the electronic transfer of funds and to financial innovations that resulted in the creation of new financial instruments and markets. Some believe that the definitions of the aggregates need to be revised and refined to take account of these changes. In addition, deregulation is also believed to have weakened the link between some monetary aggregates and economic activity by contributing to the decline in depository institutions' share of intermediation.

Operating Target
A target amenable to control by the policy tools and highly correlated with the intermediate target.

The Use of Operating Targets Since 1970

The ultimate goals of monetary policy are to affect the level of economic activity and the overall price level. As noted in the body of the text, monetary aggregates have historically been used as intermediate targets in the policy process because their behavior has often been related to both the ultimate policy goals and the policy tools that the Fed has available to influence those goals.

Until the 1980s, $M1$ had a stable and predictable relationship with nominal economic activity and, therefore, was the targeted aggregate. Even though control was imprecise in the short term, it was reasonably precise over a longer period, and changes in $M1$ were closely associated with changes in economic activity.

In the 1970s, the Fed sought to exploit the statistical regularity between changes in $M1$ and economic activity. It targeted the fed funds rate (the operating target) in an attempt to achieve the targeted growth rate range for $M1$ (the intermediate target). Under such a regime, if an increase in the demand for credit puts upward pressure on interest rates, including the fed funds rate, the Fed tends to be accommodating. That is, the Fed supplies reserves to the financial system to keep interest rates in their target range. Increases in the demand for credit were accommodated even though doing so led to an expansion of the money supply and caused the Fed to overshoot the $M1$ target range. When the Fed increased the interest rate target, the increase was usually not enough to choke off the demand for credit and keep the monetary aggregates in their target ranges. Consequently, because of the continual overshooting of the monetary aggregate target, this method was abandoned in late 1979.

In the early 1980s, the Fed focused on the level of nonborrowed reserves as the operating target. Nonborrowed reserves are total reserves less those reserves borrowed from the Fed at the discount window. The Fed was convinced that this method would give it more precision in hitting a monetary aggregate target and allow it to have greater direct control over inflation. If the demand for credit went up, the Fed would not increase the supply of nonborrowed reserves. As a result, the fed funds rate would go up. Note that, unlike today, the discount rate was set independently by the Board of Governors of the Fed, while the fed funds rate was determined by market forces. In turn, when the fed funds rate increased because of market forces, borrowing reserves at the discount window was relatively cheaper, assuming that discount rate changes were fairly infrequent. The result was that there was more borrowing at the discount window and less borrowing in the fed funds market than there would have been otherwise.[b]

In the mid-1980s, the relationship between $M1$ and economic activity started to break down, and the Fed began placing greater emphasis on other aggregates, particularly $M2$, as intermediate targets.[a] In the mid-1980s and early 1990s, the Fed used the level of reserves borrowed at the discount window as the operating target. Under this procedure, the Fed picked a level of borrowed reserves that it believed corresponded to the desired growth range of a monetary aggregate. If the demand for credit increased, pushing up the fed funds rate, then the demand for borrowed reserves at the discount window increased. This is so because the fed funds rate had increased relative to the discount rate. To maintain the target range for borrowed reserves, the Fed would be forced to increase the supply of nonborrowed reserves. Consequently, this regime was more accommodating to increases in credit than the regime that targeted nonborrowed reserves. Beginning in the mid-1980s, depository institutions became increasingly reluctant to borrow reserves from the Fed, thus weakening the link between borrowing from the Fed and the fed funds rate. Also, the fed funds rate was often higher than the discount rate because some banks, particularly large ones, were using the fed funds market as a permanent source of funds to lend, not just a back-up source when they were temporarily caught short of reserves.

In the early 1990s, the relationship between the aggregates and the level of economic activity broke down because past relationships no longer held. In the early 1990s, DNFD, the broadest measure of credit, seemed to be the monetary aggregate that was most closely related to economic activity. Because DNFD includes credit extension from sources outside the banking system, however, it is not that amenable to control by the Fed.

In the early 2000s, the Fed stopped announcing target ranges for the monetary aggregates and DNFD. As it stated in two monetary policy reports to U.S. Congress in 2000: "Given continued uncertainty about movements in the velocities of *M*2 and *M*3 (the ratios of nominal GDP to the aggregates), the Committee still has little confidence that money growth within any particular range selected for the year would be associated with the economic performance it expected or desired."[c]

Beginning in the June 2000 meeting and continuing at future meetings, the FOMC stopped establishing ranges for the growth of money and debt in future years. Owing to uncertainties about the behavior of debt and money, these ranges for many years have not provided useful benchmarks for the conduct of monetary policy.[d]

As a consequence of all these changes, today the Fed uses the fed funds rate as the operating target and explicitly announces its short-term objective for that target after each FOMC meeting.

Endnotes

a. In addition to M1 and M2, the Fed used to track another measure of money, M3. M3 is an even broader measure of money than M2 and consists of everything in M2 plus large time deposits, term repurchase agreements and term Eurodollars, and institutional money market mutual funds. The correlation between changes in M3 and economic activity also broke down in the 1990s. M3, a measure of money tracked by the Fed was discontinued by the Fed in March 2006.

b. Recall from Chapter 3 that, prior to January 2003, the discount rate was set by the Board of Governors and changed rather infrequently in response to requests from the Federal Reserve Banks. Changes in the discount rate usually lagged behind changes in other interest rates. At that time, the discount rate was often below other rates at which depository institutions could borrow reserves in the fed funds market. In January 2003, the primary credit rate (the discount rate at which the most creditworthy institutions can borrow) was set 1 percent above the targeted fed funds rate. In August 2007, the Fed approved a narrowing of the spread between the targeted fed funds rate and the primary credit rate to 0.5 percent. The purpose of the reduction in the spread was to mitigate the liquidity crisis caused by the subprime mortgage debacle, which spread to broader markets. The change was temporary but still in effect in late 2008. In either case, the discount rate is now above the fed funds rate and automatically changes whenever the fed funds target rate changes.

c. *Monetary Policy Report to the Congress* (February 17, 2000).

d. *Monetary Policy Report to the Congress* (July 20, 2000).

The Use of Interest Rates as Intermediate Targets

In the past, the use of interest rates as intermediate targets has been criticized for having either an inflationary or a recessionary bias. For example, let's assume that the Fed is targeting an interest rate at a given level and that aggregate demand increases. The increase in demand could emanate from the household, business, government, or foreign sector. In any case, the increase causes the demand for money and credit to increase also, as shown in Exhibit 24-4. The demand curve shifts from D to D', creating upward pressure on the interest rate because the quantity demanded is greater than the quantity supplied at the targeted rate, i_r. To maintain the interest rate target, the Fed will merely accommodate the increases in demand by supplying more reserves, causing money and credit to expand. Down the road, such accommodation can lead to inflation. If inflation does increase, this will put upward pressure on nominal interest rates. To fight this pressure, the Fed must ease even more, creating more pressure, and the cycle accelerates.

Likewise, if there is a comparable drop-off in aggregate demand, the Fed will reduce the supply of money to prevent the interest rate from falling. In this case, the drop in demand is exacerbated by the Fed's action, and the downturn is greater than it would be otherwise.

One final point needs to be emphasized. At any time, the Fed can control either an interest rate target or an aggregate target, but not both. For example, assume that the Fed has both a monetary aggregate target (M_T) and an interest rate target (i_T) and that the demand for credit suddenly increases, as depicted in Exhibit 24-5. In such a situation, if the Fed is more concerned about maintaining the interest rate target in the face of the increased credit demand, it must use open market operations to increase the supply of reserves. When it does so, credit and, hence, the monetary aggregates are allowed to expand, and the Fed overshoots the monetary aggregate target range as the money supply increases to M'. Serious overshooting of the monetary target can also defeat the interest rate target as inflation sets in. If the Fed is more concerned about hitting the monetary aggregate target range, then, in the face of increased demand for credit, it does not increase the supply of reserves. In this case, the Fed lets interest rates go up to i' and overshoots the target range. Thus, the Fed cannot have its way with both targets.

As noted earlier, since the early 1990s, the Fed has selected an interest rate target either because it believes that this target rate is most compatible with the ultimate goals for growth, employment, the price level, and the external balance or because the relationship between the monetary aggregates and economic activity is no longer stable and

24-4

Maintaining an Interest Rate Target

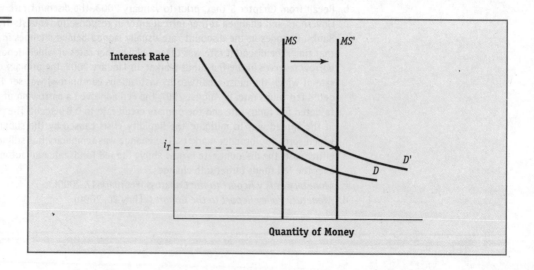

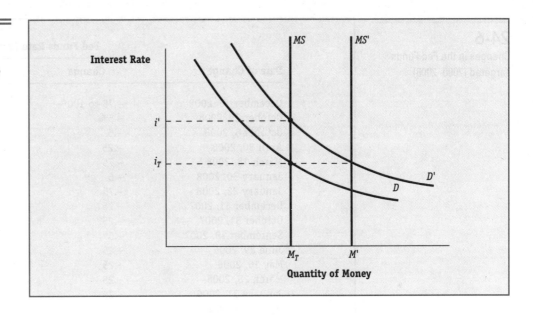

predictable. Exhibit 24-6 shows the fed funds targeted rate since 2000. At other times, a monetary aggregate or DNFD has been targeted because the Fed believes that doing so is the easiest way to achieve the ultimate policy goals.

Having examined the targets, we now turn to the specifics of how policy is framed.

Recap   The Fed uses intermediate targets to gauge policy. The intermediate target must be highly correlated with the ultimate target and must be amenable to control by the Fed. In recent years, the Fed has emphasized interest rates as intermediate targets and used the fed funds rate as an operating target. The Fed has chosen this path because of the instability in the relationship of the aggregates and the level of economic activity. The Fed cannot maintain both an interest rate target and an aggregate target at the same time in response to changes in demand.

FEDERAL OPEN MARKET COMMITTEE DECISIONS

Economic Projections
Goals for GDP, unemployment, and inflation over the next three years, set by the Fed four times each year.

Beginning in 1979, the FOMC published long-term economic projections (goals) twice a year for economic growth, unemployment, and inflation. The projections were made at the two-day meetings of the FOMC in January and June of each year and published in the semiannual *Monetary Policy Report to Congress*. In November 2007, the FOMC announced that it would begin establishing the long-term economic projections four times per year. Also, the projections would be established for the next three years rather than two. The reason for this change, as noted earlier, follows the trend since the mid-1990s of increased openness by the Fed in an effort to more clearly communicate its take on the economy and to help the public understand the basis for changes in monetary policy. The projection for economic growth would be based on projected changes in real GDP and the projection for changes in nominal GDP would be discontinued.

The FOMC currently uses the personal consumption expenditures price index (PCEPI) and the core PCEPI to develop projections for inflation. As noted in Chapter 23, the PCEPI gives a more accurate measure of inflation than the consumer price index (CPI) because the basket of consumer goods on which it is based changes each year to more accurately measure the items that consumers purchased that year. The core PCE

	Fed Funds Rate (Percent)	
Date of Change	**Change**	**New Level**
December 16, 2008	−.75 to 100%	0.25%
October 29, 2008	−.5%	1.00%
October 8, 2008	−.5	1.5
April 30, 2008	−.25	2.00
March 18, 2008	−.75	2.25
January 30, 2008	−.5	3
January 22, 2008	−.75	3.5
December 11, 2007	−.25	4.25
October 31, 2007	−.25	4.5
September 18, 2007	−.5	4.75
June 29, 2006	+.25	5.25
May 10, 2006	+.25	5
March 28, 2006	+.25	4.75
January 31, 2006	+.25	4.5
December 13, 2005	+.25	4.25
November 1, 2005	+.25	4
September 20, 2005	+.25	3.75
August 9, 2005	+.25	3.5
June 30, 2005	+.25	3.25
May 3, 2005	+.25	3
March 22, 2005	+.25	2.75
February 2, 2005	+.25	2.5
December 14, 2004	+.25	2.25
November 10, 2004	+.25	2
September 21, 2004	+.25	1.75
August 10, 2004	+.25	1.5
June 30, 2004	+.25	1.25
June 25, 2003	−.25	1
November 2002	−.5	1.25
December 11, 2001	−.25	1.75
November 6, 2001	−.5	2
October 2, 2001	−.5	2.5
September 17, 2001	−.5	3
August 21, 2001	−.25	3.5
June 27, 2001	−.25	3.75
May 15, 2001	−.5	4
April 18, 2001	−.5	4.5
March 20, 2001	−.5	5
January 31, 2001	−.5	5.5
January 3, 2001	−.5	6
May 16, 2000	+.5	6.5
March 21, 2000	+.25	6
February 2, 2000	+.25	5.75

For the six-year period 1995 through 2000, the fed funds rate target, which is established by the FOMC, fluctuated between 4.75 and 6.5 percent. Due to weakness in the economy in 2001 and prior to the terrorist attack on September 11 of that year, the target was reduced seven times. After the attack, the target was reduced four additional times in 2001 and once more in 2002. All in all, between May 15, 2000, and June 25, 2003, the fed funds targeted rate was reduced from 6.5 percent to 1 percent in the most expansionary monetary policy in history.

The targeted rate remained at 1 percent, a historic low, for more than one year—from June 23, 2003, to June 25, 2004—fueling a record boom in the housing market. In June 2004, "measured" increases of .25 percent began and continued until the rate reached 5.25 percent in June 2006. The rate remained at 5.25 percent for the next 15 months until September 2007, when it became clear that the crisis in the housing market (the bursting of the bubble in housing prices) could pull the economy into recession. The Fed continued to cut rates dramatically until a .75 to 1.00 percent cut in December 2008 resulted in a 0 to .25 percent rate, a full 5.0 to 5.25 percentage points lower than 15 months earlier. The effects of these dramatic cuts were expected to show up in mid to late 2009. However, the ongoing financial crisis convinced many that the economy was indeed in the worst recession in decades.

excludes the prices of energy and food, which are historically more volatile and less under the control of the Fed. The projections are for the current year and the following two years. In compliance with the 1978 Humphrey-Hawkins Act, the chair of the Fed reports these long-term forecasts to Congress in the *Monetary Policy Report to Congress* shortly after the meetings. Exhibit 24-7 below shows the projections presented to Congress in July 2008.

FOMC members believe that the forecasts are consistent with the long-term policy goals and are likely to emerge over the coming years. At the four other FOMC meetings over the course of the year (in addition to the meetings where the long-term projections are established), the long-term goals are reviewed and may be revised, but emphasis is on the short-term strategies.

24-7

Economic Projections of Federal Reserve Governors and Reserve Bank Presidents for 2008, 2009, and 2010

2008 Indicator	Range Percent	Central Tendency* Percent
Growth of Real GDP[b]	0.9 to 1.8	1.0 to 1.6
PCE prices (inflation)	3.4 to 4.6	3.8 to 4.2
Core PCE inflation	2.0 to 2.5	2.2 to 2.4
Unemployment	5.5 to 5.8	5.5 to 5.7
2009 Indicator	Range Percent	Central Tendency*
Growth of Real GDP[b]	1.9 to 3.0	2.0 to 2.8
PCE prices	1.7 to 3.0	2.0 to 2.3
Core PCE inflation	1.8 to 2.3	2.0 to 2.2
Unemployment	5.2 to 6.1	5.3 to 5.8
2010 Indicator	Range Percent	Central Tendency*
Growth of Real GDP[b]	2.0 to 3.5	2.5 to 3.0
PCE prices	1.6 to 2.1	1.8 to 2.0
Core PCE inflation	1.5 to 2.0	1.8 to 2.0
Unemployment	5.0 to 5.8	5.0 to 5.6

[a] The range for a variable in a given year includes all of the projections by the Fed governors and Reserve Bank presidents. The central tendency excludes the three highest and three lowest projections for each variable.
[b] Change from average for fourth quarter of previous year to average for fourth quarter of year indicated.
Source: *Monetary Policy Report to the Congress* (July 15, 2008). Available online at **http://www.federalreserve.gov/BoardDocs/HH/2008/July/fullreport.htm.**

Monetary Rules Versus Discretionary Risk Management

Monetary policy could be implemented following a prescribed rule such as targeting a given inflation rate, a given money supply growth rate, a certain interest rate, or some other criteria. Regardless of how the economy functions, the central bank would follow the prescribed rule, which would be set by some governmental authority. On the other hand, the central bank could be autonomous and maintain a great deal of discretion in the formulation of policy.

In recent years, the Fed has been chaired by a strong leader who has aspired to an "eclectic" approach to monetary policy with a great deal of discretion. This discretion has focused on risk management where the risks range from "well-defined to the truly unknown."[a] Hence, the full range of outcomes and their probabilities are not known. Accordingly, monetary policy involves a great deal of judgment in evaluating the different risks and their probabilities. Consequently, discretion is a mainstay in policy formulation.

Some analysts have always questioned, however, the amount of freedom a central bank should have in deciding monetary policy. The controversy can be summarized this way: should the Fed be tied to a simple policy rule, or should it have a great deal of discretion in deciding policy actions?

Perhaps the best-known advocate for rules is Nobel laureate Milton Friedman, who suggested that the money supply should grow at a steady, publicly stated rate. The growth rate in the money supply over the long run would compensate for the growth in output and, therefore, stabilize the price level. This would reduce the uncertainty about what the Fed was up to. Advocates of such a rule argue that the effectiveness of discretionary policy is limited by data measurement errors, unknown and variable lags, changing relationships among variables, and political pressures to ease policy. Thus, to stabilize the economy, the best the Fed can do is adopt a rule and stick with it, thus removing the uncertainty surrounding what the Fed does.

In recent decades, others have pointed out that there is a time inconsistency problem in monetary policy. For example, a time inconsistency problem exists if you eat dessert today but intend to diet tomorrow but when tomorrow comes, you decide not to diet. Another example is smoking, where pleasure is in the present. In both examples, the cost of the action (or inaction) includes health problems, shortened lifespan, and so on, which are in the future. In monetary policy, an example of a time inconsistency problem is the benevolent Fed's stimulation of the economy today in a recession while anticipating that it will slow the economy tomorrow to prevent an inflationary boom. When tomorrow comes, what seemed optimal before now appears less than optimal, and policy ends up having an inflationary bias. Furthermore, without a rule, market participants are always guessing what the Fed's next move will be, increasing uncertainty and instability, which is the opposite of what the Fed is supposed to do.

On the other hand, a strong case for discretion was perhaps best made by Chairman Alan Greenspan:

Uncertainty is not just an important feature of the monetary policy landscape: it is the defining characteristic of that landscape. As a consequence, the conduct of monetary policy in the United States at its core involves crucial elements of risk management, a process that requires an understanding of the many sources of risk and uncertainty that policymakers face and the quantifying of those risks when possible. It also entails devising, in light of those risks, a strategy for policy directed at maximizing the probabilities of achieving over time our goal of price stability and the maximum sustainable economic growth that we associate with it....

In implementing a risk-management approach to policy, we must confront the fact that only a limited number of risks can be quantified with any confidence....

As a result, risk management often involves significant judgment on the part of policymakers, as we evaluate the risks of different events and the probability that our actions will alter those risks. For such judgment, we policymakers, rather than relying solely on the specific linkages expressed in our formal models, have tended to draw from broader, though less mathematically precise, hypotheses of how the world works.

Some critics have argued that such an approach to policy is too undisciplined—judgmental, seemingly discretionary, and difficult to explain. The Federal Reserve should, some conclude, attempt to be more formal in its operations by tying its actions solely to the prescriptions of formal policy rules. That any approach along these lines would lead to an improvement in economic performance, however, is highly doubtful. Our problem is not the complexity of our models but the far greater complexity of a world economy whose underlying linkages appear to be in a continual state of flux. Rules by their nature are simple, and when significant and shifting uncertainties exist in the economic environment, they cannot substitute for risk-management paradigms, which are far better suited to policy-making. Were we to introduce an interest rate rule, how would we judge the meaning of a rule that posits a rate far above or below the current rate? Should policymakers adjust the current rate to that suggested by the rule? Should we conclude that this deviation is normal variance and disregard the signal? Or should we assume that the parameters of the rule are misspecified and adjust them to fit the current rate? Given errors in our underlying data, coupled with normal variance, we might not know the correct course of action for a considerable time. Partly for these reasons, the prescriptions of formal interest rate rules are best viewed only as helpful adjuncts to policy, as indeed many proponents of policy rules have suggested. In summary, then, monetary policy based on risk management appears to be the most useful regime by which to conduct policy. The increasingly intricate economic and financial linkages in our global economy, in my judgment, compel such a conclusion.[b]

Perhaps the best solution would be something in the middle such as limited discretion but with an absolute inflation cap. Under such a rule, the Fed would have unlimited discretion as long as inflation or monetary growth is kept below a certain level. If it goes above this level, the Fed would have to follow the monetary rule of maximum inflation. In reality, as noted in Chapter 3, the Fed is probably constrained by what is politically acceptable. Recall that what Congress has created, Congress can "uncreate," and if the Fed adopted a policy that was politically unacceptable, such as double-digit inflation, Congress could be quick to act. A popular suggestion and one followed by the Bank of England would be to announce an inflation target and implement policy so as to hit that target. With the Bank of England today operating via an explicit inflation target, policy makers' discretion is limited. Not so for the Fed.

Endnotes

a. "Risk and Uncertainty in Monetary Policy," remarks by Chairman Alan Greenspan at the Meeting of the American Economic Association, San Diego, California, January 3, 2004. Available online at http://www.federalreserve.gov/boarddocs/speeches/2004/20040103/default.htm.

b. "Monetary Policy Under Uncertainty," remarks by Chairman Alan Greenspan at a symposium sponsored by the Federal Reserve Bank of Kansas City, Jackson Hole, Wyoming, August 29, 2003. Available online at http://www.federalreserve.gov/boarddocs/speeches/2003/20030829/default.htm.

Once the long-term policy stance is set, the focus of the FOMC shifts to the immediate period. In most periods, the policy discussions center on the fed funds rate itself, as well as other interest rates. As noted previously, interest rates have gained center stage as intermediate targets since the mid-1990s.

At the same time, in the late 1990s and first decade of the 2000s, policy has been somewhat eclectic, and "the process of probing a variety of data to ascertain underlying economic and financial conditions has become even more essential to formulating sound monetary policy."[3] As a result, the Fed now looks at many indicators.

Despite the independence, strong leadership, and eclectic nature of the Fed, an old controversy of how much discretion the Fed should have continually resurfaces at various times, sometimes more strongly than others. Now would be a good time to read "A Closer Look" on rules versus discretion, which weighs in on the controversy.

Given its assessment of current economic conditions and the economic outlook, the FOMC comes up with short-term (usually quarterly) policy goals consistent with its longer-range goals. Against this background, the FOMC issues a policy directive to the Trading Desk of the New York Fed that guides the conduct of open market operations until the next FOMC meeting in approximately six weeks.[4] The policy directive states a specific fed funds rate that the New York Fed is to target. In the next chapter, we look at the specifics of how the directive is implemented.

Recap   The Fed sets long-term growth ranges for nominal and real GDP and prices. The long-term policy goals reflect recent and prospective inflationary and unemployment outlooks. Given the long-range goals, the short-term specifications are set that guide monetary policy between FOMC meetings. In recent years, the Fed has looked to interest rates to guide policy.

Summary of Major Points

1. In general, a comparison between the expected performance of the economy and the economic goals guides policy actions. More specifically, given the goals and corresponding numerical objectives, policy makers establish priorities among the goals, develop the expected performance of the economy, and implement particular policy actions. If the economy's performance is expected

to be close to the goals, policy is likely to remain unchanged. Conversely, if the economy's performance is expected to deviate markedly from the goals, policy will be altered.

2. Given the relatively large size of forecasting errors, policy makers tend to focus on incoming data and current conditions in considering policy adjustments.

3. The policy process involves three lags: the recognition lag, the policy lag, and the impact lag. The recognition lag is the length of time it takes for policy makers to recognize that an unexpected and significant change in the economy's performance has occurred. The policy lag is the time between the point when the need for action is recognized and when an adjustment policy is decided on and set in motion. The impact lag is the time between when an action is taken and when that action has a significant effect on prices, output, and employment.

4. The existence of lags in an uncertain world makes it difficult for policy makers to act appropriately in a timely fashion. Their actions today may increase price and cyclical fluctuations later, so they tend to be quite cautious in adjusting policy. Policy regret occurs when policy actions would not have been taken if data revisions had been available when the decisions were made. Policy regret can never be eliminated but can be reduced by basing policy actions on data that are less likely to be significantly revised or that are revised over several time periods.

5. The growing interdependence among the world's economies implies that U.S. policy makers have somewhat less control over the performance of the U.S. economy than previously, a factor that adds to the challenges and complexities facing policy makers.

6. Because of the complexities and lags involved with monetary policy, the Fed uses intermediate targets to try to achieve policy goals. The basic idea is that the Fed selects a variable, such as a monetary aggregate or an interest rate, midway between its policy instruments and the ultimate or final goals or targets of policy. The intermediate target is then used to guide day-to-day open market operations. The rationale is that if the Fed hits the intermediate target, it will come reasonably close to achieving its economic objectives.

7. In past decades, at times one aggregate has been more closely related to the level of economic activity than at other times. Since the early 1990s, the monetary aggregates have been deemphasized in favor of an interest rate target. The reason for this change is that the relationship between economic activity and the monetary aggregates had become unstable and difficult to predict since the early 1990s. The Fed has opted for an eclectic approach of looking at a variety of indicators to gauge policy. The Fed can control either an interest rate target or an aggregate target but not both simultaneously.

8. The FOMC develops long-term policy economic projections four times a year and chooses among short-term policy options to achieve their goals based on the projections. The major factors influencing the long-term policy decisions at any point in time include: (1) recent and prospective inflationary pressures, (2) the current and prospective pace of economic expansion, especially with reference to the economy's growth potential and degree of capacity utilization, and (3) recent and prospective movements in the unemployment rate.

9. The major factors influencing the selection of the short-term specifications are current economic and financial conditions such as recent data on inflation, real growth, the exchange rate, and prevailing expectations, including those about policy.

10. The FOMC issues a directive to the Trading Desk of the New York Fed that guides the conduct of monetary policy until the next FOMC meeting.

Key Terms

Economic Projections, p. **599**
Impact Lag, p. **589**
Intermediate Target, p. **593**

Operating Target, p. **595**
Policy Lag, p. **588**

Policy Regret, p. **592**
Recognition Lag, p. **588**

Review Questions

1. What are the ultimate targets of monetary policy?

2. What is an intermediate target? Why does the Fed use intermediate targets instead of focusing on the ultimate targets? What is an operating target?

3. What is the recognition lag? The policy lag? The impact lag?

4. How would the recognition, policy, and impact lags differ with regard to monetary and fiscal policy? What role does uncertainty play?

5. Are current incoming economic data or forecasts more important in guiding monetary policy? Why?

6. When is it most difficult to interpret incoming data? (*Hint:* Consider the case in which retail sales are weak but new orders for capital goods are strong, etc.)

7. What is *policy regret?* What are some of the strategies that the Fed could use to minimize policy regret?

8. Why can short-term goals sometimes differ from long-term goals? Why does the Fed now establish long-term economic projections four times a year rather than two times?

9. What is an irregular variance? How does it affect Fed behavior?

10. What are some common intermediate targets that the Fed has used to guide policy in recent years? Give two criteria for intermediate targets.

11. Why can't the Fed target both an interest rate and a monetary aggregate simultaneously?

12. Assume that the Fed is targeting the money supply and the demand for money falls. Explain why interest rates will fall.

13. Assume that the Fed is targeting an interest rate and the demand for money increases. Explain why the money supply will increase.

14. "The Fed should do everything it can to eliminate inflation." Do you agree? Explain.

15. Can using an interest rate as an intermediate target ever have an inflationary bias? Explain.

Analytical Questions

Questions marked with a check mark (✓) are objective in nature. They can be completed with a short answer or number.

16. Find the minutes of the most recent FOMC meeting, either at the library in the Federal Reserve Bulletin or on the Internet at **www.federalreserve.gov.** (Because the FOMC meets about every six weeks, minutes appear in 8 of the 12 monthly issues of the *Federal Reserve Bulletin*.) Summarize the policy directive.

✓17. Assume that the Fed is targeting an interest rate and aggregate demand drops. Show graphically why the Fed will have to reduce the supply of money to maintain the interest rate target.

✓18. Use a graph to explain why the Fed cannot target both an interest rate and a monetary aggregate at the same time, assuming that there is a drop in aggregate demand.

Suggested Readings

The minutes of each FOMC meeting, including the directive, are published in the *Federal Reserve Bulletin* each month immediately after the minutes are released. They make extremely interesting reading. This information is also available on the Web site of the Federal Reserve Board at **http://www.federalreserve.gov/.**

Two recent speeches by Fed governors that discuss the state of the U.S. economy and monetary policy in early 2008 are "The U.S. Economy and Monetary Policy," by Donald L. Kohn, available at **www.federalreserve.gov/newsevents/speech/kohn20080226a.htm,** and "Financial Market Turmoil and the Federal Reserve: The Plot Thickens," by Kevin Warsh, available at **www.federalreserve.gov/newsevents/speech/warsh20080414a.htm.** Another interesting read is the speech by Fed governor Frederic S. Mishkin to the Undergraduate Economics Association, Massachusetts Institute of Technology, Cambridge, Massachusetts, November 29, 2007, titled "The Federal Reserve's Enhanced Communication Strategy and the Science of Monetary Policy." It is available online at **http://www.federalreserve.gov/newsevents/speech/mishkin20071129a.htm.**

For a look at monetary policy, see "U.S. Monetary Policy: An Introduction, Parts 1, 2, 3, and 4," *Economics Letters*, Federal Reserve Bank of San Francisco, 2004–01, 02, 03, and 04 (January 16, 2004, January 23, 2004, January 30, 2004, and February 6, 2004, respectively).

An article that looks at the "rules versus discretion" debate is Douglas Clement, "The Veil of Discretion: Does the Fed Have Too Much Freedom," *The Region*, Federal Reserve Bank of Minneapolis, 18, no. 2 (June 2004): 10.

For a look at a risk management approach to policy, see "Monetary Policy Under Uncertainty," remarks by Chairman Alan Greenspan at a symposium sponsored by the Federal Reserve Bank of Kansas City, Jackson Hole, Wyoming (August 29, 2003). The remarks are available on the Internet at **http://www.kc.frb.org/Publicat/sympos/2003/pdf/Greenspan.0902.2003.pdf.**

For a look at issues involving policy regret, see Sharon Kozicki, "How Do Data Revisions Affect the Evaluation and Conduct of Monetary Policy?" *Economic Review*, Federal Reserve Bank of Kansas City, 89, no. 1 (First Quarter 2004): 5–35.

Stephen G. Cecchitti, "Policy Rules and Targets: Framing the Central Banker's Problem," discusses many of the topics in this chapter. It can be found in *Economic Policy Review*, Federal Reserve Bank of New York, 4, no. 2 (June 1998): 1–14.

Norman Frumkin's *Guide to Economic Indicators* (Armonk, NY: M.E. Sharpe, 2000) is a reliable reference tool for any reader.

For a look at the nature and consequences of uncertainty in monetary policy formation, see Jan Marc Berk's *The Preparation of Monetary Policy* (Norwell, MA: Kluwer Academic Press, 2000).

For a discussion that relates higher inflation in a country to a relatively larger financial sector, see Michael Frenkel, "Inflation and the Misallocation of Resources," *Economic Inquiry* 38, no. 4 (October 2000): 616–628.

For a fascinating, in-depth description of an FOMC meeting, see Laurence H. Meyer, "Come with Me to the FOMC," *The Region* (June 1998): 6–15, published by the Federal Reserve Bank of Minneapolis.

An easy-to-read and comprehensive book from which much of the material in this chapter is drawn is *U.S. Monetary Policy and Financial Markets* by Ann-Marie Meulendyke (1998). It can be obtained free for the asking from the Federal Reserve Bank of New York, 33 Liberty Street, New York, NY 10045.

Arturo Estrella and Frederic S. Mishkin ask, "Is There a Role for the Monetary Aggregates in the Conduct of Monetary Policy?" *Journal of Monetary Economics* 40, no. 2 (October 1997): 279–304.

For an interesting article that deals with topics in the chapter, see Alan S. Blinder, "Distinguished Lecture on Economics in Government: What Central Bankers Could Learn from Academics—and Vice Versa," *Journal of Economic Perspectives* 11 (Spring 1997): 3–19.

Endnotes

1. This aspect of the policy-making process, especially in the case of fiscal policy, can be agonizingly slow. It's one thing to decide to cut aggregate demand by reducing government spending and/or raising taxes. It's quite another to decide whose taxes to raise and exactly where spending should be cut. The latter inevitably involves political considerations.
2. Recall that the basic policy instruments that the Fed uses to manipulate the economy are open market operations, reserve requirements, and the discount rate, and that the major policy goals are full employment, stable prices, economic growth, and satisfactory external balance.
3. *Federal Reserve Bulletin* (September 1995): 853.
4. In the next chapter, you shall also see that the Fed, under the chair's leadership, can make an intermeeting adjustment.

25

Policy Implementation

The eyes see only what the mind is prepared to comprehend.
—Robertson Davies

Learning Objectives

After reading this chapter, you should know:

What the contents and format of the policy directive are

How open market operations affect the fed funds rate

How the Trading Desk reacts to new information

How required reserves are calculated

The difference between temporary and outright open market transactions

The Fed's new tools in response to the 2007–2008 financial crisis

A MORNING AT THE NEW YORK FED

System Open Market Account (SOMA)
The Fed's account of dollar-denominated Treasury securities, which are bought and sold by the Trading Desk to implement open market operations in accordance with policy directives.

Among other duties, each morning, William Dudley goes to work at the New York Fed with a specific job assignment—to implement the monetary policy of the United States. As manager of the Fed's System Open Market Account (SOMA), which contains the Fed's dollar-denominated assets acquired through open market operations, he interprets and executes the policy directives of the Federal Open Market Committee (FOMC).[1] Under his tutelage, the Fed operates a Trading Desk that buys and sells government securities from the SOMA to affect the fed funds rate and, eventually, the level of economic activity. Dudley arrives at the office and immediately meets with his staff; he is briefed on the opening level of interest rates that morning and any unusual events during the preceding night that may affect the supply of reserves to depository institutions. Late the previous afternoon, he consulted with his staff, securities dealers, and FOMC representatives. He must decide the direction, if any, that interest rates should be nudged to fulfill the FOMC policy directive. Around 9:30 A.M., he issues buy or sell orders to a room of securities dealers who work for the New York Fed.[2]

The traders use an electronic auction system called FedTrade to contact the primary securities dealers they work with and advise them that the Fed is either buying or selling. The primary dealers consist of large banks and securities dealers with whom the Fed deals directly. Exhibit 25-1 is a list of the primary dealers as of October 1, 2008. These dealers respond to the Fed's traders with offers to either sell or buy securities at various prices.

Primary Dealers
Large banks and securities dealers with whom the Fed directly engages in open market operations.

After a brief time, the Fed's traders gather in a room and announce their buy or sell offer prices. The manager tells the traders to discharge the most profitable transactions up to the amounts of the various Treasury securities that the Trading Desk is buying or selling. That is, if the Fed is buying, they execute the purchases up to the amount

---

25-1

Who Are the Primary Dealers? Primary Dealers as of October 1, 2008

Following is a list of the primary dealers that buy and sell securities directly with the Fed in the execution of monetary policy. In recent years, the number of primary dealers has fallen due to mergers among large financial institutions. Note that we expect further changes in this list, since Bank of America has purchased Merrill Lynch. In July 2008, Countrywide Securities Corporation was removed from the list as a result of its acquisition by Bank of America. Countrywide was a major player in the subprime lending debacle. On September 22, 2008, Lehman Bros. was removed from the list due to its bankruptcy. On October 1, 2008, Bear Stearns and Co. was removed from the list because of their acquisition by JPMorgan Securities, Inc.

BNP Paribas Securities Corp.	Dresdner Kleinwort Securities LLC
Banc of America Securities LLC	Goldman, Sachs & Co.
Barclays Capital Inc.	Greenwich Capital Markets, Inc.
Bear, Stearns & Co., Inc.	HSBC Securities (USA) Inc.
Canton Fitzgerald & Co..	JPMorgan Securities, Inc.
Citigroup Global Markets Inc.	Merrill Lynch Government Securities Inc.
Credit Suisse Securities (USA) LLC	Mizuho Securities USA Inc.
Daiwa Securities America Inc.	Morgan Stanley & Co. Incorporated
Deutsche Bank Securities Inc.	UBS Securities LLC

Source: Federal Reserve Bank of New York, **http://www.newyorkfed.org/markets/pridealers_listing.html.**

that the Fed wishes to buy at the lowest possible prices. If the Fed is selling on this day, they execute the transactions up to the amount that the Fed wishes to sell at the highest possible prices.

As the deals are consummated, reserves are either supplied or withdrawn from the banking system. In response to this change in reserves, it is hoped that interest rates move in the desired direction at approximately the desired magnitude. After lunch, Mr. Dudley decides whether additional purchases or sales in the open market are needed. Did interest rates overshoot or undershoot the desired target? In either case, an additional purchase or sale may be required, although usually it is not.

You may call this a simple story about an act with complex implications! Don't be fooled. Executing monetary policy is neither simple nor mundane. In a way, it is as much an art as a science, and the consequences are astronomical.

In the previous chapter, we looked at the difficulties in the policy process, focusing on how the FOMC makes decisions. In this chapter, we look at the intricacies of how those decisions are implemented by the Trading Desk of the New York Fed and how markets respond.

THE FOMC POLICY DIRECTIVE

Once the long-term policy stance has been set, the focus of the FOMC shifts to the immediate period. The policy discussions center on the fed funds rate itself, as well as other interest rates. As noted previously, interest rates gained center stage as intermediate targets from the early 1990s until the present. At the same time, policy has been somewhat eclectic, and "the process of probing a variety of data to ascertain underlying economic and financial conditions has become even more essential to formulating sound monetary policy."[3] As a result, the Fed now looks at many indicators.

Given its assessment of current economic conditions and the economic outlook, the FOMC comes up with short-term strategies consistent with its longer-range projections. Against this background, the FOMC issues a **policy directive** to the Trading Desk of the New York Fed that guides the conduct of open market operations until the next FOMC meeting approximately six weeks later. The directive, which is accompanied by a statement, is the link between the decisions formulating policy and the actions implementing policy. The policy directive and accompanying statement for the March 18, 2008, meeting of the FOMC is reproduced here.

Policy Directive
A statement issued by the FOMC to the Trading Desk of the New York Fed that directs monetary policy until the next FOMC meeting; in recent years, the policy directive has targeted a specific fed funds rate.

"The Federal Open Market Committee seeks monetary and financial conditions that will foster price stability and promote sustainable growth in output. To further its long-run objectives, the Committee in the immediate future seeks conditions in reserve markets consistent with reducing the federal funds rate to an average of around 2-1/4 percent."

The vote encompassed approval of the statement below:

The Federal Open Market Committee decided today to lower its target for the federal funds rate 75 basis points to 2.25 percent.

Recent information indicates that the outlook for economic activity has weakened further. Growth in consumer spending has slowed and labor markets have softened. Financial markets remain under considerable stress, and the tightening of credit conditions and the deepening of the housing contraction are likely to weigh on economic growth over the next few quarters.

Inflation has been elevated, and some indicators of inflation expectations have risen. The Committee expects inflation to moderate in coming quarters, reflecting a projected leveling-out of energy and other commodity prices and an easing of pressures on resource utilization. Still, uncertainty about the inflation outlook has increased. It will be necessary to continue to monitor inflation developments carefully.

Today's policy action, combined with those taken earlier, including measures to foster market liquidity, should help to promote moderate growth over time and to mitigate the risks to economic activity. However, downside risks to growth remain. The Committee will act in a timely manner as needed to promote sustainable economic growth and price stability.

Votes for this action: Messrs. Bernanke, Geithner, Kohn, Kroszner, and Mishkin, Ms. Pianalto, Messrs. Stern and Warsh.

Votes against this action: Messrs. Fisher and Plosser.[4]

The policy directive, along with the statement, is released to the public to communicate the FOMC's assessment of the risks to satisfactory economic performance in the foreseeable future. Note that each statement contains an evaluation of the risks with regard to sustainable economic growth and inflationary expectations (price stability). On March 18, 2008, the committee was very concerned about the weakened economic condition and less concerned about inflation. This is always not the case.

For example, on May 10, 2006, the committee was clearly more concerned about inflation and less about economic growth when it increased the fed funds rate. The policy directive and statement are below:

The Federal Open Market Committee seeks monetary and financial conditions that will foster price stability and promote sustainable growth in output. To further its long-run objectives, the Committee in the immediate future seeks conditions in reserve markets consistent with increasing the federal funds rate to an average of around 5 percent.

The vote encompassed approval of the paragraph below for inclusion in the statement to be released shortly after the meeting:

The Committee judges that some further policy firming may yet be needed to address inflation risks but emphasizes that the extent and timing of any such firming will depend importantly on the evolution of the economic outlook as implied by incoming information. In any event, the Committee will respond to changes in economic prospects as needed to support the attainment of its objectives.

Votes for this action: Messrs. Bernanke and Geithner, Ms. Bies, Messrs. Guynn, Kohn, Kroszner, Lacker, and Olson, Ms. Pianalto, Mr. Warsh, and Ms. Yellen.

Votes against this action: None.[5]

A third example from October 28, 2003, shows where the risks to economic growth and inflation are quite different from the other two cases. In this last example, the Fed maintained the targeted level of the fed funds rate. The policy directive and accompanying statement are below.

The Federal Open Market Committee seeks monetary and financial conditions that will foster price stability and promote sustainable growth in output. To further its long-run objectives, the Committee in the immediate future seeks conditions in reserve markets consistent with maintaining the federal funds rate at an average of around 1 percent.

The vote encompassed the substance of the following statements concerning risks that would be conveyed in the Committee's press release to be made available shortly after the meeting:

> The risks to the Committee's outlook for sustainable economic growth over the next several quarters are balanced; the risks to its outlook for inflation over the next several quarters are weighted toward the downside; and, taken together, the balance of risks to its objectives is weighted toward the downside in the foreseeable future.
>
> **Votes for this action:** Messrs. Greenspan, Bernanke, Ms. Bies, Messrs. Broaddus, Ferguson, Gramlich, Guynn, Kohn, Moskow, Olson, Parry, and Stewart. (Mr. Stewart voted as an alternate member.)
> **Votes against this action:** None.[6]

Thus, in October 2003, although the upside and downside risks to sustainable growth were roughly equal, in the FOMC's judgment, the probability of deflation, "an unwelcome fall in inflation" was greater than the probability of inflation.

Given the Fed's long history, the preceding releases of information to the public are a relatively recent phenomenon. In February 1995, the Fed formally adopted the practice begun in 1994 of announcing any changes in the targeted fed funds rate immediately following the FOMC meetings. By doing so, it eliminated questions and doubts about changes in policy. The announcements in 1994 occurred after a relatively long period of stable low interest rates. In these circumstances, a sudden shift to higher interest rates could have caught many market participants off guard and caused them to sustain real losses in the value of their portfolios. (Remember the inverse relationship between the interest rate and bond prices.) Thus, by announcing the increases, the Fed seems to have been attempting to give market participants a heads-up warning.

In December 1998, the FOMC also decided to announce any shift in its view of forthcoming developments in the economy. The shifts in perspective were communicated in a statement about the likelihood of future increases or decreases in the fed funds rate. The public was confused as to how to interpret the statement about future assessment of the balance of risks and its policy leanings. In an effort to achieve more openness, the Fed again modified its disclosure procedure in early 2000 to the format that is currently used. (Note that the language in the previous examples represents the new format adopted in early 2000.) In addition, an individual roll call of FOMC members' votes was added instead of just the outcome of the voting being reported. These moves have reduced the uncertainty and guesswork about Fed policy and its direction at the time of the FOMC meetings. So far, since the votes have been announced, the vast majority of times they have been unanimous or near unanimous; on those few occasions when they were not unanimous, there were at most two dissenters, but more often only one.

New monthly data on economic growth and inflation indicators—the unemployment rate, retail sales, industrial production, and the consumer and producer price indexes—are also released during the intermeeting period. The Fed, under the chair's leadership, can make an intermeeting adjustment. In the last decade, intermeeting changes occurred in October 1998, in response to a financial crisis in Russia; twice in early 2001, in response to a weak economy; once in September 2001, in response to the terrorist attacks on the World Trade Center and the Pentagon; twice in January 2008, in response to the further deepening of the housing crisis and once in October 2008 in response to the financial collapse. However, historically, an intermeeting change has

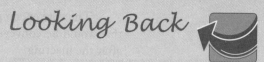
The Fed's Response to the Terrorist Attacks of September 11, 2001: America's Darkest Hour May Have Been the Fed's Finest

The terrorist attacks on the World Trade Center and the Pentagon on September 11, 2001, caused unfathomable despair and unparalleled loss of life and property. The attacks struck at the core of the U.S. financial system, destroying a part of the financial infrastructure, killing employees of major financial firms, and closing U.S. financial markets for one week. Communication networks were disrupted and backup systems in payment mechanisms were activated. Market participants had to conduct business from locations outside the nation's preeminent financial center. Uncertainties about payment flows disrupted the market for bank reserves. Depository institutions with excess reserves were not able to borrow through traditional venues. The result was a massive mushrooming of the effective demand for reserves. Float also increased considerably as air traffic came to a halt.

The Fed's first response to the attacks was to announce that it would supply all liquidity needed as a result of the disruption. The announcement was immediately followed by action. Increases in discount loans and open market operations supplied unprecedented liquidity to the financial system. Discount loans soared from around $200 million on September 11 to a record level of more than $45 billion on September 12. Reserve balances at Federal Reserve Banks jumped to more than $100 billion on September 12—an amount more than 10 times the normal level. Later in the week, open market operations were used to inject reserves as the record discount loans were repaid. Repurchase agreements (injecting reserves) peaked at $81 billion on September 14. The result of the Fed's swift action was a minimization of the fallout to the financial system from the attack and the avoidance of a financial crisis. By the end of September, reserve balances returned more or less to their pre-September 11 levels.

In addition, the Fed made an intermeeting change in the fed funds rate on the morning of September 17, shortly before the reopening of U.S. stock markets. It announced a corresponding decrease in the discount rate, as well. The Fed coordinated the decrease in interest rates with other central banks, including the European Central Bank and those in Canada, England, and Sweden. The Fed also arranged currency swap agreements with the European Central Bank, the Bank of England, and the Bank of Canada. The currency swaps, which totaled $68 billion, aided foreign banks in the respective countries whose U.S. operations were disrupted by the terrorist attack.

Prior to the attack, the fed funds and discount rates had been lowered a full three percentage points in a series of seven cuts since the beginning of 2001. This was the most aggressive easing in 20 years. After the attack, the Fed followed with three more cuts in addition to the one on September 17.

What were the results of such dramatic actions? The Fed's swift action caused payment mechanisms to return to normal within a few short weeks. As a result, the

U.S. financial system demonstrated profound resilience in response to the horrific events. By the first quarter of 2002, the economy had turned the corner, and moderate growth was returning much sooner than many analysts had expected. Many factors such as expansionary fiscal policy, continuing strength in consumer demand, automobile rebates, and declining inventories prompted the upturn. However, the Fed's lowering of interest rates also played a role in fostering the economic recovery. Looking back, few will say that the Fed was slow to respond to the crisis! Indeed, one of the saddest hours in U.S. history may be remembered as one of the Fed's finest.

been rare. Now would be a good time to read the accompanying "Looking Back" on the Fed's response to 9/11.

In the next section, we look at the specifics of how the directives are implemented.

Recap   At each FOMC meeting, a policy directive is sent to the New York Fed that directs the stance of monetary policy. In recent years, the Fed has targeted the fed funds rate. Nevertheless, the Fed has taken an eclectic approach and looked at a wide range of data to gauge economic and financial conditions. The New York Fed implements the policy directive by using open market operations. In addition to the policy directive, the FOMC issues a statement to the public stating the committee's expectation for the foreseeable future regarding the goals of price stability and sustainable economic growth.

THE RESERVES MARKET AND OPEN MARKET OPERATIONS

To implement the policy directive, the Trading Desk of the New York Fed tries to manage reserve levels of depository institutions so that the fed funds rate will be equal to the targeted rate. To do this, the Trading Desk develops estimates of the likely demand and supply of total reserves. The demand for reserves consists of (1) the demand for required reserves, plus (2) the demand for excess reserves. Depository institutions may demand excess reserves to avoid unintended shortages of required reserves. The supply of reserves has two major components: (1) borrowed reserves, which are reserves borrowed by depository institutions from the Fed's discount facility, and (2) nonborrowed reserves, which are reserves available in the open market. In equilibrium, the quantity demanded of reserves will equal the quantity supplied, making the market for reserves like any other market. Exhibit 25-2 reviews the basic reserve components and determinants.

But how does this equilibrium come about? Suppose that under current market conditions, including the current fed funds rate, the quantity demanded of reserves is greater than the quantity supplied. What will happen? Simply put, the excess quantity demanded would be reflected in the fed funds market, where reserves are bought and sold among depository institutions. Given the excess of quantity demanded over quantity supplied, market forces will cause the fed funds rate to rise. Likewise, if the quantity supplied

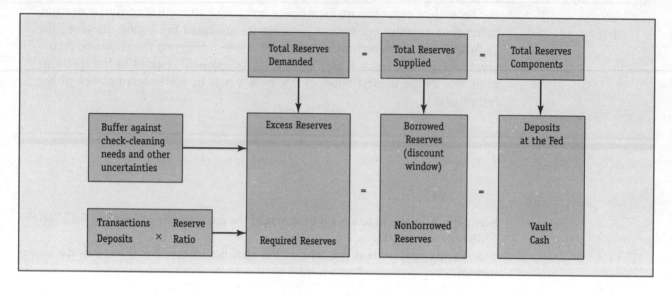

Total Reserves Demanded	=	Total Reserves Supplied	=	Total Reserves Components

Buffer against check-cleaning needs and other uncertainties → Excess Reserves

Borrowed Reserves (discount window)

Deposits at the Fed

=

Transactions Deposits × Reserve Ratio → Required Reserves

Nonborrowed Reserves

=

Vault Cash

of reserves at the current fed funds rate is greater than the quantity demanded, the fed funds rate will fall.

In recent years, the Fed has implemented policy by focusing its open market operations with an eye toward achieving the targeted fed funds rate. Suppose the directive calls for "maintaining the federal funds rate at an average of around 3 percent." Immediately after the FOMC meeting, the Trading Desk derives the reserve need, which is the difference, if any, between actual reserves and those projected to be needed to keep the fed funds rate at the desired level. The reserve need must be met with open market operations in order to fulfill the policy directive. If the Trading Desk supplies more than the reserve need, the fed funds rate will fall. If the Trading Desk supplies less than the reserve need, the fed funds rate will rise. Note that the reserve need may be negative because reserves may need to be withdrawn by open market sales to meet the directive.

Operationally, the manager of the Trading Desk begins the initial period following the FOMC meeting with the understanding that he needs to supply the reserve need on average over the weeks until the next FOMC meeting by conducting open market operations designed to carry out the policy directive. In practice, the manager must also consider other factors that affect reserves. The overwhelming majority of open market operations is designed to offset unexpected swings in the supply of reserves caused by a variety of "other factors." If not offset, these variations in reserves would induce an undesired change in the fed funds rate. The other factors that can affect reserves include changes on the Fed's balance sheet in such items as the float, Treasury deposits, gold, currency holdings, and international reserves.

As the weeks between FOMC meetings pass, various pieces of information accumulate. Each day, the Fed updates its estimates of the supply of reserves, given the previous day's change, if any, in the Fed's portfolio and new information on the other factors affecting reserves. Using updated information, the manager revises his or her

Reserve Need
The projected amount of reserves to be supplied or withdrawn by open market operations to reach or keep the fed funds rate prescribed by the policy directive.

estimate of the reserves that need to be supplied or absorbed to maintain the desired reserve conditions that coincide with the targeted fed funds rate. Thus, in response to the incoming data, the reserve need may be revised.

Finally, we should note that in recent years, required reserves have declined substantially and are continuing to decline. This is due to the widespread use of retail sweep accounts. A financial innovation that first appeared in 1994, **retail sweep accounts** "sweep" balances out of transactions accounts that are subject to reserve requirements and into other deposits (usually money market deposit accounts) that are not. **Wholesale sweep accounts** have been in existence since the 1970s. With wholesale sweep programs, the depository institutions sweeps funds out of a business's demand deposit into a money market instrument, such as a repurchase agreement, Eurodollar deposit, or money market mutual fund. For wholesale sweep accounts, the deposits are swept into an account that may or may not be a liability of the depository institution. For retail sweep accounts, the swept funds stay on the books of the depository institution. Required reserves fall by the amount of funds in sweep accounts multiplied by the required reserve ratio. Balances in retail sweep accounts grew from $5.3 billion in January 1994 to $641.9 billion in August 2004. Declines in required reserves are expected to taper off in future years, because all opportunities to reduce reserves will have been exploited. Indeed between mid-2007 and mid-2008, required reserves have hovered around $40 to $41 billion, down from almost $60 billion in 1994. Depositors are not affected because the funds are swept back into the transactions account when they are needed. Banks benefit because of the resulting reduction in required reserves that do not earn interest and because of the ability to make more loans and other investments with the funds that otherwise would be held as required reserves.

The significant decline in required reserves in recent years due to sweep accounts has raised concern that the fed funds rate may become more volatile and may affect the implementation of monetary policy. This increased volatility would result from depository institutions attempting to manage reserve accounts at the Fed with very low balances. Although there is some evidence that the fed funds rate has become more volatile with the growth of retail sweep accounts, the increased volatility does not seem to be significant enough to cause major disruptions in the fed funds market or general instability in financial markets. So far, the implementation of monetary policy has not been affected.

In October 2006, the **Financial Services Regulatory Relief Act** was signed into law, authorizing the payment of interest on reserve balances beginning in October 2011. However, because of the ongoing financial crisis, Congress moved the beginning date up to October 1, 2008. Thus, as of this date, depository institutions now earn interest on both required and excess reserves. The interest rate on required reserve balances is .1 percent below the fed funds rate. The law also gives the Fed the flexibility to eliminate required reserves altogether. Banks would still have to maintain some reserves at the Fed to clear payments among each other. At this time, it is believed that the Fed does not want to phase out reserve requirements.

However, the Fed has long advocated this policy of paying interest on reserves because it would make the banking system more efficient. With no interest paid on reserve balances, banks had an incentive to develop such mechanisms as sweep accounts to minimize their holding of reserves. With interest paid on reserves, this incentive is now gone. In reality, not being able to earn interest on required reserves represents a tax on banks and makes the banking system less efficient than it otherwise would be, because it uses resources to avoid the costly regulation. Congress had initially delayed this change until October 2011 because of the interest costs that the Fed will have to pay on reserve bal-

Retail Sweep Accounts
Retail accounts, created in 1994, with balances that have been swept out of deposit accounts subject to reserve requirements and into savings accounts that are not.

Wholesale Sweep Accounts
Wholesale accounts, created in the 1970s, with balances that have been swept out of deposit accounts subject to reserve accounts and into money market instruments such as money market mutual funds, Eurodollar deposits, and repurchase agreements.

Financial Services Regulatory Relief Act
An act signed into law in October 2006, authorizing the payment of interest on reserve balances beginning in October 2011, and, among other regulatory relief provisions, giving the Fed the authority to eliminate required reserves altogether. Banks would still maintain reserves at the Fed to clear payments among each other. It is believed that the Fed does not want to phase out reserve requirements at this time.

ances. Note that the Fed's earnings in the form of interest on the government securities that it holds and other fees that are now returned to the U.S. Treasury would be reduced.

To summarize, if the fed funds rate rises above the targeted rate, the Trading Desk increases the amount of reserves available to depository institutions in order to bring the fed funds rate back to the targeted level. Likewise, if the fed funds rate falls below the targeted rate, the Trading Desk decreases the amount of reserves. We are now in a position to look more closely at how required reserves are calculated.

| Recap | The Trading Desk calculates the reserve need to fulfill the policy directive. The reserve need is based on the discrepancy between actual reserves and projections of the amount that will be needed to fulfill the policy directive. The reserve need must be met with open market purchases or sales. As new data come in about interest rates, the Trading Desk may adjust the reserve need. New data about the economy may also lead to changes in the stance of monetary policy, which will also change the reserve need. The growth of retail sweep accounts since 1994 has reduced the amount of required reserves and led to concerns about (1) increased volatility of the fed funds rate, and (2) the Fed's ability to implement monetary policy using changes in the fed funds rate. So far, monetary policy does not seem to be affected. Beginning in 2011, Congress has authorized the Fed to pay interest on reserves. |

HOW THE DEMAND AND SUPPLY OF RESERVES ARE CALCULATED

Banks are required to hold reserve assets during a two-week maintenance period that corresponds to the two-week computation period. During the computation period, the actual amount of required reserve assets that must be held during the maintenance period is determined. During the two-week maintenance period, the actual average amount of reserves held must at least equal the amount of required reserves.

The average daily amount of required reserve assets that must be held is equal to the required reserve ratio times the average daily amount of deposits subject to reserve requirements. At the present time, only checkable deposits are subject to reserve requirements. Required reserves against checkable deposits will equal the checkable deposit balances multiplied by the reserve requirement ratio on such deposits. As of 2009, that ratio was zero percent on transaction deposits up to $10.3 million, 3 percent on transaction deposits between $10.3 and $44.4 million, and 10 percent on transaction deposits of more than $44.4 million. As first noted in Chapter 3, because $44.4 million is a relatively small amount of transactions deposits, we ignore the 0 and 3 percent requirements. By adding an allowance for excess reserves based on recent experience and any seasonal patterns, the staff of the New York Fed produces a path for the demand for total reserves including both required and excess reserves.

For example, if checkable deposits average $600 billion a day during the computation period, required reserve assets (deposits at the Fed plus vault cash) must average $60 billion a day during the maintenance period ($600 billion × 10 percent reserve requirement = $60 billion). If excess reserves have been averaging 1 percent of deposits, an additional $6 billion in excess reserves must be included in the path for total reserves that will be demanded ($600 billion × 1 percent excess reserves = $6 billion).

Between 1984 and July 30, 1998, a system called **contemporaneous reserve accounting** was used. Under such a system, the maintenance period, when the reserve assets must be held, more or less corresponds to the computation period. The two-week

Computation Period
The period during which the actual amount of required reserve assets that must be held during the maintenance period is determined.

Maintenance Period
The period during which the actual amount of reserves held must at least equal the amount of required reserves, as determined during the computation period.

Contemporaneous Reserve Accounting
A reserve accounting system under which the maintenance period—when the reserve assets must be held—more or less corresponds to the computation period when the amount of required reserves is determined.

25-3

Reserve Computations Under Contemporaneous and Lagged Reserve Accounting[a]

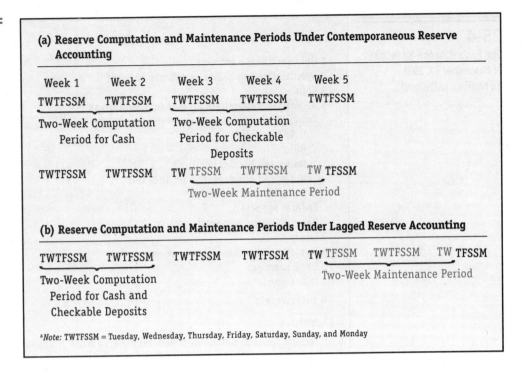

(a) Reserve Computation and Maintenance Periods Under Contemporaneous Reserve Accounting

Week 1	Week 2	Week 3	Week 4	Week 5
TWTFSSM	TWTFSSM	TWTFSSM	TWTFSSM	TWTFSSM

Two-Week Computation Period for Cash

Two-Week Computation Period for Checkable Deposits

TWTFSSM   TWTFSSM   TW TFSSM   TWTFSSM   TW TFSSM

Two-Week Maintenance Period

(b) Reserve Computation and Maintenance Periods Under Lagged Reserve Accounting

TWTFSSM   TWTFSSM   TWTFSSM   TWTFSSM   TW TFSSM   TWTFSSM   TW TFSSM

Two-Week Computation Period for Cash and Checkable Deposits

Two-Week Maintenance Period

[a]*Note:* TWTFSSM = Tuesday, Wednesday, Thursday, Friday, Saturday, Sunday, and Monday

Lagged Reserve Accounting
A reserve accounting system under which the maintenance period—when the reserve assets must be held—follows some time after the computation period—when the amount of required reserves is determined.

computation period starts two days before the two-week maintenance period. When one computation period ends, another immediately begins. The average daily balance of reserves held during the maintenance period must be equal to the average daily balance of reserves required during the computation period, with the exception that average vault cash in a two-week computation period counts as reserves in the maintenance period ending two weeks later. Prior to 1992, the lag in counting vault cash toward required reserves was two weeks longer. When one maintenance period ends, another immediately begins. Part (a) of Exhibit 25-3 illustrates how this reserve accounting method works in practice.

Beginning with the reserve maintenance period that started on July 30, 1998, the system was changed from contemporaneous reserve accounting to lagged reserve accounting. Under this system, the reserve maintenance period for depository institutions begins 30 days after the beginning of the two-week reserve computation period. When one computation period ends, another immediately begins, and a corresponding maintenance period begins 30 days later. Thus, depository institutions know the exact amount of required reserves that will be needed in the maintenance period before the maintenance period begins because the required reserves in any maintenance period are based on a two-week computation period that started 30 days earlier. The change makes it easier for depository institutions to calculate their required reserve balances for the current maintenance period.

With this system, the Trading Desk at the New York Fed can obtain more accurate information about required reserves, which is helpful in determining the overall demand for reserves by the banking system. Because the Fed currently implements monetary policy by targeting a fed funds rate, which is determined by the demand and supply of reserves, this change also makes the implementation of monetary policy easier.

25-4

The Fed's Balance Sheet as
of November 27, 2007
(in Millions of Dollars)

Assets

1 Gold certificate account	$11,037
2 Special drawing rights certificate account	2,200
3 Coin	1,165
4 Securities, repurchase agreements, and loans	825,747
Securities held outright	779,693
U.S. Treasury[a]	779,693
Bills[b]	267,019
Notes and bonds, nominal[b]	470,984
Notes and bonds, inflation-indexed[b]	36,911
Inflation compensation[c]	4,779
Federal agency[b]	0
Repurchase agreements[d]	46,000
Loans	54
5 Items in the process of collection	1,563
6 Bank premises	2,114
7 Other assets[e]	39,024
8 Total Assets	**882,848***

Liabilities

9 Federal Reserve notes net if Federal Reserve Bank Holdings	783,675
10 Reverse repurchase agreements[f]	34,272
11 Total deposits	19,576
Depository institutions	14,477
U.S. Treasury—General account	4,711
Foreign—Official accounts	97
Other	291
12 Deferred credit items	2,878
13 Other liabilities and accrued dividends[g]	5,904
14 Total liabilities	**846,305***

Capital Accounts

15 Capital paid in	18,278
16 Surplus	15,457
17 Other capital accounts	2,809
18 Total capital	**36,543***

*Note: Components may not sum to totals because of rounding.
[a]Includes securities lent to dealers, which are fully collateralized by other U.S. Treasury securities.
[b]Face value of the securities.
[c]Compensation that adjusts for the effect of inflation on the original face value of inflation-indexed securities.
[d]Cash value of agreements, which are collateralized by U.S. Treasury and federal agency securities.
[e]Includes assets denominated in foreign currencies, which are revalued daily at market exchange rates.
[f]Cash value of agreements, which are collateralized by U.S. Treasury securities.
[g]Includes exchange-translation account reflecting the daily revaluation at market exchange rates of foreign exchange commitments.
Source: Federal Reserve Statistical Release, H.4.1, *Factors Affecting Reserve Balances* (November 28, 2007). Available online at http://www.federalreserve.gov/releases/h41/Current/.

Part (b) of Exhibit 25-3 illustrates how this reserve accounting method works in practice.

The supply of total reserves can be determined by rearranging the Fed's balance sheet, which is displayed in Exhibit 25-4. The major items on the Fed's balance sheet can be summarized as follows:

Assets

Government securities held
Gold and special drawing rights (SDRs) accounts, which reflect international reserve
  holdings
Discount loans
Float
Other assets

Liabilities

Reserve balances of depository institutions with the Fed
Currency outside the Fed
Treasury deposits
Other liabilities

TRADING DESK MARKET TECHNIQUES

Each day, the Fed must decide whether to buy or sell securities outright or on a temporary basis. If bought or sold on a temporary basis, the transaction generally is reversed
the next day or within two weeks. The manager deals with the various factors that affect
reserves on a day-to-day basis, attempting to smooth out random fluctuations while
meeting the guidelines put forth by the FOMC in the policy directive.

Outright Transactions in the Market

Outright Transactions
Open market purchases that
supply reserves or open market
sales that withdraw reserves.

In general, the manager uses outright transactions when he/she wants to provide or absorb reserves over relatively long time spans. Thus, outright transactions are typically used
when projections show that a reserve need or reserve excess is likely to persist. Most outright transactions are technical operations designed to preserve existing reserve conditions against the background of the changing seasonal and secular (long-term) reserve
needs of the economy. An example of a seasonal reserve need occurs every year between
Thanksgiving and Christmas, when a rise in currency in circulation drains reserves from
the banking system. Meanwhile, the requirements of a growing economy create an ongoing reserve need for more currency. Although most outright transactions are conducted to
meet these seasonal and ongoing needs, in the past on rare occasions, the manager has used
outright transactions to underscore the thrust of policy or to signal a change in policy.

The Trading Desk makes far more outright purchases than outright sales because
of the growing demand for currency. Nevertheless, outright purchases in the open market, which supply reserves, typically account for no more than 10 percent of total Fed
transactions. Even though outright purchases usually account for less than 10 percent of
total Fed transactions at any time, the Fed's portfolio of securities consists mainly of
those bought outright because the temporary purchases wash out over time.

The Trading Desk manager can buy Treasury bills (T-bills) and federal agency
security issues in the secondary market. The Trading Desk stopped adding to its portfolio of agency securities in 1981. Consequently, the Fed's holdings of agency securities
declined to zero in December 2003, because agency securities were not replaced as they
matured. However, to support the mortgage market and the financial system in general
given the ongoing crisis, the Trading Desk began purchasing Fannie Mae and Freddie
Mac agency securities on January 5, 2009. Exhibit 25-5 shows the SOMA's current holdings of securities in early February 2009.

Security Type	Total Par Value
U.S. Treasury Bills (T-Bills)	$18,422,636.7
U.S. Treasury Notes and Bonds (notes/Bonds)	412,913,510.2
U.S. Treasury Inflation-Indexed Securities (TIPS)	39,377,689.8
Federal Agency Securities[1]	29,915,000.0
Total SOMA Holdings	**$500,628,836.7**

1. Fannie Mae, Freddie Mac, and Federal Home Loan Bank

Source: Federal Reserve Bank of New York. Available online at **http://www.newyorkfed.org/markets/soma/sysopen_accholdings .html.**

By law, the manager is not allowed to add to the Fed's portfolio by purchasing new securities directly from the Treasury. He may, however, roll over maturing securities in whole or in part into new issues.

Traditionally, the largest portion of outright transactions in the secondary market is in T-bills. The huge size of the secondary market in T-bills and its considerable depth, breadth, and liquidity enable it to absorb large transactions smoothly. The desk also manages the composition of the portfolio with the main goal of ensuring that the portfolio has a high degree of liquidity in case liquidity is needed. Thus, a key objective of the FOMC is to maintain the average maturity of securities held in the SOMA at a relatively short length.

Note that outright sales, even of T-bills, are relatively infrequent. As mentioned earlier, the growing demand for currency means that there will be more outright purchases than sales. Because sales are so rare, when they do occur, they tend to impart the kind of negative impact on market psychology the Trading Desk prefers to avoid when entering the market.

Temporary Transactions

The Trading Desk uses temporary transactions when it wants to supply or absorb reserves for relatively short periods, usually no longer than a few weeks. Typically, the need to conduct such transactions arises from swings in the various other factors affecting the supply of reserves, such as the float and Treasury balances. If the reserve need is for only a short period, the Trading Desk opts for temporary transactions because they are cheaper to execute than outright transactions. Two types of temporary transactions are used: repurchase agreements and reverse repurchase agreements.

When arranging repurchase agreements, the Trading Desk buys securities on a self-reversing, temporary basis. The seller, often a government securities dealer, agrees to buy the securities back from the Trading Desk on or before a specified date. Note that the term *repurchase agreement* has the opposite meaning to the Fed that it does to securities dealers. In Chapter 4, you saw that dealers use the term *repurchase agreements* to refer to the practice of borrowing money to finance their holdings of securities by selling the securities temporarily with an agreement to repurchase them at a later date.

To the Fed, the term refers to the temporary purchase of securities. Usually repurchase agreements are done overnight or for short periods of 2 to 14 days, although the Trading Desk can legally use repurchase agreements up to a maturity of 90 days. Because repurchase agreements provide reserves, they can be used to offset a temporary reserve drain arising from one or more of the other factors affecting reserves. If such drains were not fully offset, the supply of reserves would decline relative to the demand, reserve conditions would tighten, and the fed funds rate would rise. A repurchase agree-

Looking Forward

E-Money and Monetary Policy

There is some concern that the evolution of the payments system to an e-money system will reduce the ability of the Fed to execute monetary policy through traditional channels. Namely, the growth of e-money may supplant traditional payment mechanisms. E-money is privately created "money" that uses the Internet to execute payments. E-money bypasses both the use of currency and reserves. Depository institutions, other intermediaries, and nonfinancial firms may create e-money. E-money consists of credits similar to I.O.U.s that are used to make payments and are accepted in payment for goods and services. The firms that create e-money settle with each other rather than with the central bank. The concern is that if more payments are made in this way, the demand for currency and reserves will fall (and could theoretically fall to zero), thus reducing the ability of the Fed to control interest rates by changing the monetary base.

We are very far from the scenario in which the demand for reserves and currency becomes so insignificant that it interferes with the conduct of monetary policy. The demand for currency continues to increase, driven by both the growth of cash transactions in the United States and the international demand for dollars. However, this trend may slow in the future with the widespread adoption of smart cards to make payments.

The demand for reserve balances has rapidly decreased in recent years due to lower reserve requirements and the growth of retail sweep accounts. These developments do not seem to have reduced the Fed's ability to control interest rates.

Because a high proportion of e-money could displace traditional payment mechanisms in the future, the Fed's job in forecasting the demand for reserves and currency and thus implementing monetary policy may become more difficult. Consequently, e-money could have far-reaching implications for central banks.

System Repurchase Agreement
When the Trading Desk of the Fed buys securities on a self-reversing, temporary basis in order to supply reserves on a temporary basis.

Reverse Repurchase Agreements
The Fed's simultaneous sale and purchase of securities for delivery the next day or in a few days to withdraw reserves on a temporary basis.

ment used to supply reserves on a temporary basis is called a system repurchase agreement. The securities that are purchased go into the Fed's system account.

Reverse repurchase agreements are arranged by the Trading Desk when the manager wants to drain reserves temporarily from the banking system. Technically, when initiating reverse repurchase agreements, the manager sells securities and simultaneously purchases the same securities for delivery the next day or perhaps several days later. Like their repurchase agreement counterpart, reverse repurchase agreements are most often used to maintain existing reserve conditions by offsetting other factors that have changed reserves. More specifically, they are usually used to offset temporary reserve excesses arising from the other factors, which, if not offset, would lead to an undesired, albeit temporary, easing in reserve conditions.

Note that the bulk of open market operations involve temporary transactions as opposed to outright purchases and sales. In the case of temporary transactions, government, agency securities, and mortgage-backed securities are used. Although the Trading Desk may enter the market several times in a day, in recent years it has normally entered the market only once per day, as described earlier.

The Fed's New Tool Kit

Throughout this text, we have discussed the ongoing upheaval in financial markets spawned by the crisis in the subprime lending market. The financial crisis rapidly spread to other domestic and global markets, demonstrating the interconnectedness of global financial markets. In light of the pressures on short-term markets, where a severe shortage in the supply of credit was apparent, the Fed in late 2007 and early 2008 announced a series of measures to mitigate the crisis. For the United States, these new measures include the establishment of a Temporary Auction Facility, Primary Dealer Credit Facility, and a Term Securities Lending Facility. Note that these measures came before the widespread bailouts and multiple failures of financial firms. They also predate the $700 billion bailout by Congress (the Emergency Economic Stabilization Act [EESA] discussed in Chapter 12) to promote the safety and stability of the financial system in September 2008. In addition, while the bailout was being negotiated by Congress with the help of the Treasury and the Fed, the Fed created a new lending facility, the Asset-Backed Commercial Paper Money Market Mutual Fund Liquidity Facility that was designed to help money market mutual funds experiencing severe strains. In addition, in late 2008, the Fed created the Commercial Paper Lending Facility, the Money Market Investor Funding Facility, and the Term Asset-Backed Securities Loan Facility, all of which were designed to facilitate liquidity and new lending in troubled financial markets. These actions by the Fed are unprecedented attempts to prevent a widespread financial collapse. They also had the effect of greatly increasing the assets on the Fed's balance sheet, as they all represented loans by the Fed (assets for the Fed) or direct purchase by the Fed of financial instruments (other than Treasuries) to support the financial system. Between early 2008 and 2009, the assets of the Fed approximately doubled in size from just under $1 trillion to almost $2 trillion as a result of the special programs to address the financial crisis. What follows is a brief discussion of each of these new programs.

The Temporary Auction Facility (TAF)

Temporary Auction Facility (TAF)
A program begun in December 2007, whereby the Fed auctions funds to depository institutions for 28 or 84 days. Designed to provide liquidity to the financial system.

Through the Temporary Auction Facility (TAF), the Fed directly auctions funds to all depository institutions that are eligible to borrow at the discount window. The Fed announces the amounts and timings of the auctions, and bids are accepted through the local Reserve Banks. The original term of the loans was twenty-eight days. In August 2008, the Fed began auctioning both 28 and 84-day loans TAF funds. Prepayment of the loans is not allowed. Both competitive and noncompetitive bids are accepted in a single-price auction method. The interest rate on the loans is fixed at the stop-out rate as determined by the supply and demand bidding process. The bid amount of a single bidder is limited to 10 percent of the offering. The minimum bid for funds is $5 million, with additional increments of $100,000.

This facility is designed to ensure that liquidity is provided when other short-term markets such as the federal funds market are under stress. These injections of funds into the market by the Fed supplements open market operations and discount loans. Discount loans are usually overnight loans. Whereas open market operations are limited to the 17 or so primary dealers, all depository institutions eligible to borrow at the primary credit rate through the discount window can borrow through the TAF. In addition, a broader range of collateral is accepted when funds are borrowed through the TAF than at the discount window, and there is less of a stigma from borrowing at the TAF than at the discount window. When borrowing occurs at the TAF, reserves are injected into the system. How long the program will continue depends on credit market conditions, as it has no expiration date. In early February 2009, the Fed had outstanding loans amounting to over $400 billion through this facility.

The Primary Dealer Credit Facility (PDCF)

Primary Dealer Credit Facility (PDCF)
A program begun in March 2008, whereby primary dealers can borrow overnight from the Fed at the primary credit rate. Designed to increase liquidity and to provide support for the financial system.

In March 2008, the Fed began a program called the Primary Dealer Credit Facility (PDCF), where primary dealers can borrow directly from the Fed. The new credit facility operates similarly to the way that banks borrow from the Fed at the discount window. The PDCF hopes to improve the ability of primary dealers to provide funds for participants in the mortgage-backed security meltdown due to the housing crisis. The PDCF will provide overnight funding to primary dealers in exchange for a specified range of collateral that includes all Treasury and agency securities, all investment-grade corporate securities, municipal securities, mortgage-backed securities, and some asset-backed securities. Because these are direct loans by the Fed, the amount of reserves in the system will increase by the amount of the loans. The rate charged on the overnight loans is the same as the primary credit rate charged for borrowing at the discount window. The PDCF will remain in operation for a minimum period of six months and may be extended as needed to ensure the smooth functioning of financial markets in a time of crisis. As of January 2009, the PDCF is authorized to loan to primary dealers through October 30, 2009. This is the first time that Fed lending has been extended to nonbanks. The creation of this facility resulted from the bailout of the investment banking house, Bear Stearns, and the subsequent takeover by JPMorgan. By early 2009, the credit outstanding was just over $30 billion.

The Term Securities Lending Facility (TSLF)

Term Securities Lending Facility (TSLF)
A program where the Fed auctions government securities to primary dealers for a 28-day or longer period in exchange for less liquid and less credit-worthy securities such as mortgage-backed securities. Designed to increase liquidity without increasing reserves.

Also in March 2008, the Fed created a Term Securities Lending Facility (TSLF) that would lend up to $200 billion of Treasury securities to primary dealers for a term of 28 days, as opposed to an overnight loan under the PDCF. Auctions have been held weekly since March 27, 2008, and acceptable collateral includes federal agency debt and agency mortgage-backed securities, as well as non-agency mortgage-backed securities. Although 28-day loans are currently made, the maximum term is 90 days. The minimum bid is $10 million, with $10 million increments thereafter. Note that the TSLF does not lend funds directly to primary dealers. Rather, they auction off Treasuries in exchange for less-liquid securities. The lending rate is usually between 7 and 15 basis points, which represents the price primary dealers are willing to pay for the greater liquidity. The lending fee can be thought of as approximately equivalent to the spread between the Treasuries that are borrowed and the interest rate for the less desirable pledged collateral over the term of the loan. The purpose of this lending facility is to improve the liquidity of the primary dealers who choose to participate. Rather than holding illiquid mortgage-backed securities, primary dealers would now be holding liquid Treasuries. Because the same amounts of securities are outstanding from the Fed, there is no impact on reserves. In July 2008, the Fed authorized the auction of up to $50 billion of Treasury securities options to borrow from the TSLF. The Fed intended to use the options program before periods when it anticipates elevated stress in financial markets. The $50 billion in authorized options to borrow in TSLF is in addition to the $200 billion limit in the TSLF program. Like the PDCF, the TSLF is authorized to operate through October 30, 2009. In early February 2009, the Fed held about $120 billion of dealer securities through this program which they accepted in exchange for the more liquid Treasuries.

The Asset-Backed Commercial Paper Money Market Mutual Fund Liquidity Facility

Asset-Backed Commercial Paper Money Market Mutual Fund Liquidity Facility (AMLF)
A new lending facility where commercial banks or bank holding companies could borrow from the AMLF to purchase asset-backed commercial paper from money market mutual funds. Designed to reduce the strains on money market mutual funds due to disintermediation.

On September 19, 2008, the Fed announced the creation of a new lending facility, the Asset-Backed Commercial Paper Money Market Mutual Fund Liquidity Facility (AMLF). The purpose of this facility was to assist money market mutual funds that were experiencing severe disintermediation as depositors withdrew uninsured deposits. Depository institutions and bank holding companies could now borrow from this facility at the primary credit rate and use the proceeds of the loans to purchase high quality asset-backed commercial paper from money market mutual funds. On the same day, the Treasury announced a temporary program that would extend deposit insurance to money market mutual fund deposits that paid a premium for the coverage. Note that there was no limit on the amount of coverage per account, as there is at commercial banks. The Treasury thought there was a need for such a program to stop the run on money market mutual funds that would further cripple the global financial system. By early February 2009, the Fed had lent just over $16 billion to depository institutions and bank holding companies for this purpose.

The Commercial Paper Funding Facility (CPFF)

The Commercial Paper Funding Facility (CPFF)
A special lending facility designed to support the commercial paper market through effectively purchasing outstanding commercial paper and giving greater assurance that commercial paper will be able to be rolled over when it matures.

The Commercial Paper Funding Facility (CPFF) was created to support the commercial paper market at a time when it was experiencing severe strains. The volume of outstanding commercial paper had fallen, rates on longer term paper had increased significantly, and a large amount of commercial paper had to be rolled over on an overnight basis. Investors were hesitant to purchase commercial paper, and this was further crippling financial and nonfinancial firms that relied on the issuance of commercial paper for their financing needs. The CPFF was designed to increase the funds to this market and to insure both issuers and investors in commercial paper that funds would be available to pay investors when newly issued commercial paper was maturing. In early February 2009, the Fed had purchased about $260 billion of commercial paper under this facility.

The Money Market Investor Funding Facility (MMIFF)

The Money Market Investor Funding Facility (MMIFF) supported a private plan to provide liquidity to U.S. money markets by funding the purchase of short-term CDs and commercial paper from money market mutual funds and money market investors. If money market mutual funds had a liquidity squeeze from investors who wanted to redeem shares, the fund could sell short-term CDs and commercial paper to the MMIFF in order to raise the funds to meet the redemptions. The presence of such a Fed-created funding facility helps to restore confidence for money market investors and increase their willingness to invest in money market instruments. The MMIFF complements the CPFF and the AMLF to improve liquidity and funding in short-term credit markets.

The Term Asset-Backed Securities Loan Facility (TALF)

The Term Asset-Backed Securities Loan Facility (TALF) was designed to support the asset-backed securities markets which were collateralized by student loans, auto loans, credit card loans, and loans guaranteed by the Small Business Administration. Under the program, the New York Fed will lend an amount up to $200 billion to the issuers of asset-backed securities. The asset-backed securities will serve as collateral for the Fed. The issuers can then use the proceeds of the loans to issue new asset-backed securities. Due to the financial crisis, new issuances of asset-backed securities have declined. Such issuances provide new funds to lending for consumer credit and SBA loans, which are vital to the adequate function of credit markets.

Note that the TAF, PDCF, and TSLF make loans to depository institutions and other financial institutions as part of the lender of last resort function of the Fed. All provide liquidity to sound financial institutions. A second set of programs, including the AMLF, CPFF, MMIFF, and TALF support specific financial markets such as the commercial paper and the asset-backed securities markets. In addition, the Fed has also created assets on their balance sheets to assist in the bailout of Bear Stearns and American Insurance Group (AIG). Finally, the Fed has also started directly purchasing up to $500 billion of longer-term agency securities (primarily Fannie Mae, Freddie Mac, and Federal Home Loan Bank securities) to hold in its portfolio.

The complexity of policy procedures, coupled with the political milieu within which policy makers operate and muddle, puts a considerable premium on understanding the relationship among the economic goals the Fed is loosely charged with achieving, the intermediate target approach embraced by the Fed, the economic analysis provided by the FOMC, the policy directive, incoming data, reserve projections, and, finally, open market operations. Exhibit 25-6 above provides a field guide to the Fed's open market operations. By understanding the process, market participants can minimize the risk of misinterpreting Fed actions and statements and thus be better positioned to anticipate and deal with Fed policy.

Fed Activity	Translation	Implication
1. No Fed buying or selling.	The Fed is not expected to intervene.	A reserve add or intervene drain is not required or (a) it can be accommodated later when more information is available or (b) market conditions begin to more clearly reflect or indicate the need.
2. The Fed uses reverse repurchase agreements.	The Trading Desk sells Treasury securities to primary dealers. Buyers agree to sell them back at a specified time, usually the next day, which temporarily absorbs reserves.	A reserve drain is required, which may mean that either (a) the drain is consistent with prevailing Fed policy and necessary to prevent undesired fed funds rate declines or (b) the Fed has tightened.
3. The Fed engages in system repurchase agreements.	The Trading Desk provides funds (reserves) in exchange for Treasury securities with an agreement that dealers will repurchase them, usually the next day, which temporarily increases reserves.	Reserves must be added, which may mean that either (a) the increase is consistent with prevailing policy and necessary to prevent undesired fed funds rate increases or (b) the Fed has eased.
4. The Fed makes outright sales.	A permanent transaction has occurred with no resale agreements. The Fed sells Treasury securities in the open market, absorbing reserves. Bills only are sold.	Reserves are drained out of the banking system. Such a move is usually not associated with a change in policy but is conducted seasonally and occasionally when underscoring a policy move toward restraint.
5. The Fed makes outright purchases.	The opposite of an outright sale has occurred. The Fed buys securities in the open market with no repurchase agreements on the part of the sellers, injecting reserves permanently.	Reserves are permanently added. The action is usually not associated with policy implications but is conducted seasonally to provide for economic growth. Can occasionally signal policy moves toward easing.

Recap   To change reserves, the manager of the Trading Desk may use open market purchases or sales, repurchase agreements, or reverse repurchase agreements. System repurchase agreements provide reserves for a few days. They are used to offset a temporary reserve drain. A reverse repurchase agreement is used to temporarily withdraw reserves from the system for a few days. If the change is thought to be permanent, outright purchases or sales are more likely to be used.

Our next and final chapter examines the global implications and linkages of monetary policy. However, before moving on, now would be a good time to read "Looking Forward," which discusses the concept of e-money and its impact on monetary policy.

Summary of Major Points

1. The FOMC issues an operating directive to the Trading Desk of the New York Fed, which deals with how open market policy is to be implemented. In recent years, the policy directive has targeted a specific fed funds rate. Since 1994, the Fed has announced policy changes immediately following FOMC meetings.

2. The staff of the New York Fed estimates the amount of the reserve need to fulfill the policy directive. Given the directive, the manager of the open mar-

ket Trading Desk then decides whether reserves should be added or removed from the system. The Trading Desk also makes other purchases or sales to neutralize or offset changes in other factors affecting reserves. In recent years, required reserves have declined because of the introduction of retail sweep accounts. This trend may change because the Fed now pays interest on reserves.

3. During a maintenance period, banks hold reserve assets that correspond to the amount of required reserves. The amount of required reserve is based on the amount of checkable deposits in a computation period multiplied by the required reserve ratio. Prior to 1998, a system of contemporaneous reserve accounting was used. Since July 1998, the reserve maintenance period begins 30 days after the beginning of the two-week reserve computation period (lagged reserve accounting). In the maintenance period, the average daily amount of reserves must equal the average daily amount of required reserves during the computation period.

4. The manager of the Trading Desk may use outright purchases or sales in the open market to change reserves. The transactions are usually in the secondary market in T-bills. In recent years, there have been far more outright purchases than sales because of the growing need for currency.

5. Alternatively, system repurchase agreements or reverse repurchase agreements may be used to change reserves. System repurchase agreements and reverse repurchase agreements are not restricted to government securities but may employ government agency securities or mortgage-backed securities. A repurchase agreement provides reserves until it matures in a few days. Repurchase agreements are used to offset a temporary reserve drain. A reverse repurchase transaction is used to temporarily withdraw reserves from the system. If the change is thought to be of a seasonal or secular (longer-term) nature, the manager is more likely to use outright purchases than if the need for reserves is thought to be temporary.

6. The seller of the repurchase agreement (usually a government securities dealer) agrees to buy the securities back from the Trading Desk on or before a specified date. In a reverse repurchase transaction, the manager of the Trading Desk sells securities and simultaneously purchases them back for delivery on a later date.

7. In response to the financial crisis of 2008–2009, the Fed has created numerous special lending facilities to provide additional liquidity to the financial system.

Key Terms

Asset-Backed Commercial Paper Money Market Liquidity Facility (AMLF), p. **626**

Commercial Paper Funding Facility (CPFF), p. **626**

Computation Period, p. **618**

Contemporaneous Reserve Accounting, p. **618**

Financial Services Regulatory Relief Act, p. **617**

Lagged Reserve Accounting, p. **619**

Maintenance Period, p. **618**

Money Market Investor Funding Facility (MMIFF), p. **627**

Outright Transactions, p. **621**

Policy Directive, p. **611**

Primary Dealers, p. **610**

Primary Dealer Credit Facility (PDCF), p. **625**

Reserve Need, p. **616**

Retail Sweep Accounts, p. **617**

Reverse Repurchase Agreements, p. **623**

System Open Market Account (SOMA), p. **610**

System Repurchase Agreement, p. **623**

Temporary Auction Facility (TAF), p. **624**

Term Asset-Backed Securities Loan Facility (TALF), p. **627**

Term Securities Lending Facility (TSLF), p. **625**

Wholesale Sweep Accounts, p. **617**

Review Questions

1. What should the Trading Desk do if the fed funds rate falls below the targeted rate?

2. Explain what is meant by the *reserve need.*

3. For what purposes are system repurchase agreements and reverse repurchase agreements likely to be used?

4. For what purposes are outright purchases and sales likely to be used?

5. What is the computation period? What is the maintenance period?

6. When and why would the Fed accommodate a rise in reserve demand by supplying more reserves?

7. What characteristics of Treasury bills make them desirable for use in outright transactions by the Trading Desk?

8. The float increases unexpectedly. Will the Fed typically respond with outright purchases or temporary purchases?

9. Why have required reserves fallen in recent years? Will the trend continue?

10. Under lagged reserve accounting, how does the computation period correspond with the maintenance period? Under contemporaneous reserve accounting, how does the computation period correspond with the maintenance period? What are the advantages of a lagged reserve accounting period?

11. Why and how has the Fed become more open about monetary policy decisions in recent years?

12. What are the special lending facilities created by the Fed in response to the financial crisis of 2007–2009? What does each do? Why were they created?

Analytical Questions

Questions marked with a check mark (✓) are objective in nature. They can be completed with a short answer or number.

✓13. Assume that checkable deposits are $500 billion, desired excess reserves are 1 percent of deposits, the required reserve ratio is 10 percent, and the amount of reserves is $50 billion. What is the reserve need to maintain the existing reserve conditions?

14. Describe what the Fed should do to meet the reserve need in question 13.

✓15. The Fed anticipates a seasonal reserve need of $10 billion over the next month. Is it more likely to use outright purchases or temporary transactions to meet this need? If the Fed supplies $20 billion in reserves, what will happen to the fed funds rate?

16. Explain the following statement: Even though outright purchases account for less than 10 percent of Fed transactions, the Fed's portfolio of securities consists mainly of securities bought outright.

✓17. Assume that the demand for required plus excess reserves is $50 billion, the level of discount borrowing is $100 million, and the actual level of nonborrowed reserves is $49 billion. What is the reserve need if the existing degree of pressure on reserve positions is to be maintained? What will happen if the Fed supplies fewer reserves than the reserve need?

18. What are the implications of the following Fed activities?

   a. The Fed sells securities using reverse repurchase agreements.

   b. The Fed buys securities using system repurchase agreements.

   c. The Fed makes outright purchases for the system account.

Suggested Readings

Information on open market operations and their important role from a monetary policy perspective is available online at **http://www.newyorkfed.org/aboutthefed/fedpoint/fed32.html.**

Check out the Fed's temporary transactions, such as repurchase agreements and reverse repurchase agreements, at **http://www.newyorkfed.org/aboutthefed/fedpoint/fed04.html.** Another interesting discussion about Fed openness is a speech by Fed Governor Frederic S. Mishkin to the

Undergraduate Economics Association, Massachusetts Institute of Technology, Cambridge, Massachusetts, November 29, 2007. Titled "The Federal Reserve's Enhanced Communication Strategy and the Science of Monetary Policy," the speech is available online at **http://www.federalreserve.gov/newsevents/speech/mishkin20071129a.htm.**

Fed Governor Frederic S. Mishkin discussed "The Federal Reserve's Tools for Responding to Financial Disruptions" in a speech at the Tuck Global Capital Markets Conference, Tuck School of Business, Dartmouth College, Hanover, New Hampshire, on February 15, 2008. The speech is available online at **http://www.federalreserve.gov/newsevents/speech/mishkin20080215a.htm**.

"Understanding the Recent Changes to Federal Reserve Liquidity Provision" is the subject of an article on the Web site of the Federal Reserve Bank of New York, available at **http://www.newyorkfed.org/markets/Understand_Fed_lending.html**.

For a discussion of "Declining Required Reserves, Funds Rate Volatility, and Open Market Operations," see the paper by the same name by Selva Demiralp and Dennis Farley, *Finance and Economics Discussion Series*, Board of Governors of the Federal Reserve System, 2003–27 (July 2003). The paper is available online at **http://www.federalreserve.gov/pubs/feds/2003/200327/200327abs.html**.

Each year, the March and September issues of the *Federal Reserve Bulletin* contain the Fed's "Monetary Policy Report to the Congress," as mandated by the Humphrey-Hawkins Act of 1978. These reports make for interesting reading regarding monetary policy and the economic outlook. The Monetary Policy Report is available on the Internet at **http://www.federalreserve.gov/boarddocs/hh/**.

For an interesting discussion on monetary policy under different Fed chairs, see Cjristina D. Romer and David H. Romer, "Choosing the Federal Reserve Chair: Lessons from History," *Journal of Economic Perspectives* 18 (Winter 2004): 129–162.

For a discussion of Nobel laureate economist William Vickery's view that under normal conditions, inflation and unemployment are separable issues, see David Colander,

"Macroeconomics: Was Vickery Ten Years Ahead?" *Challenge* (September–October 1998): 72–86.

For a discussion of the challenges of monetary policy given structural changes in the economy in the 1990s, see Robert T. Parry, "Monetary Policy in a New Environment: The U.S. Experience," *Economic Letter*, Federal Reserve Bank of San Francisco, 2000–31 (October 13, 2000).

"Open Market Operations in the 1990s," by Cheryl L. Edwards, contains a thorough and comprehensive overview of this topic and can be found in the *Federal Review Bulletin* (November 1997): 859–874.

Chapters 6 and 7 of *U.S. Monetary Policy and Financial Markets* (1998), by Ann-Marie Meulendyke of the Federal Reserve Bank of New York, contain much valuable information on the execution of open market operations.

Canada, the United Kingdom, and New Zealand have conducted monetary policy without reserve requirements for several years. In the United States, required reserves have fallen significantly in recent years because of deposit sweeping. An article that looks at both issues is "Monetary Policy Without Reserve Requirements: Case Studies and Options for the United States," by Gordon H. Sellon, Jr. and Stuart E. Weiner, *Economic Review*, Federal Reserve Bank of Kansas City (Spring Quarter 1997): 5–30.

As mentioned in the chapter, the monthly *Federal Reserve Bulletin* contains the "Minutes of the FOMC Meetings" and the "Monetary Policy Report to Congress." In addition, the *Bulletin* contains many statements to Congress by the Fed chair and other Fed governors. This information may also be accessed on the Web site of the Federal Reserve Board at **http://www.federalreserve.gov**.

Endnotes

1. As executive vice president of the Markets Group at the New York Fed, in addition to managing the SOMA account, Mr. Dudley also oversees foreign exchange trading operations and account services to foreign central banks.
2. Since April 5, 1999, the Trading Desk has been entering the market during a 10-minute period around 9:30 A.M. Between 1997 and April 1999, the Trading Desk entered the market at 10:30 A.M. Prior to 1997, the Trading Desk entered the market at 11:30 A.M. The changes, which reflected the desire to enter the market at the most opportune time, were possible because of technological advances that led to the earlier receipt of critical data.
3. *Federal Reserve Bulletin* (September 1995): 853.
4. The policy directive and statement are available in the FOMC meeting minutes on the Internet at **http://www.federalreserve.gov/monetarypolicy/fomcminutes20080318.htm**.
5. The policy directive and statement are available in the FOMC meeting minutes on the Internet at **http://www.federalreserve.gov/fomc/minutes/20060510.htm**.
6. The policy directive and statement are available in the FOMC meeting minutes on the Internet at **http://www.federalreserve.gov/fomc/minutes/20031028.htm**.

26

If countries don't discipline themselves, the world market will do it.

—Morris Offit, Offitbank

Monetary Policy in a Globalized Financial System

Learning Objectives

After reading this chapter, you should know:

How international trade and capital flows affect monetary policy in a globalized financial system

The limitations of domestic monetary policy under fixed and flexible exchange rate systems

Why monetary policy will most likely require increased global coordination in the future, regardless of the exchange rate system

MONETARY POLICY AND THE GLOBALIZATION OF FINANCE

We have seen that one of the most important roles of the Fed is to formulate and implement the nation's monetary policy. The Fed attempts to ensure that sufficient money and credit are available to allow for a stable and healthy financial system. In this way, the economy can expand in accord with its long-run growth potential with little or no inflation and with minimal fluctuations in output and employment.

We have also seen that financial markets have experienced ongoing and dramatic changes. The financial system is experiencing a dramatic metamorphosis, driven by technological improvements in computers and telecommunications, the breakdown of barriers to capital flows, and an increasingly globalized environment. As a result, the international financial system has experienced inordinate growth, and economies have become much more interdependent in just a few short years. Never has the interdependencies of the world economies been more clear than in the ongoing financial crisis of 2008–2009. What began in U.S. mortgage markets spread around the globe as "toxic" mortgage-backed securities that were sold into global markets, threatening financial institutions around the world and causing a global recession that left policy makers scrambling to fix the broken economy.

In this final chapter, we look at the policy implications of the continuing growth of international trade and the globalization of the financial system. We consider the effects of monetary policy under both fixed and flexible exchange rate systems. You shall see that the globalization of finance may, of necessity, change the modus operandi of the Fed even though the goals of monetary policy remain the same. In this financial crisis, major central banks of the world have consulted with each other on a continuous basis and acted to provide liquidity to global markets to an unprecedented extent. In October 2008, major central banks also announced a coordinated interest rate cut in what may be the beginning of a new era of global monetary policy coordination.

MONETARY POLICY UNDER FIXED EXCHANGE RATES FROM 1944 TO 1973

Bretton Woods Accord
The 1944 accord that established a fixed exchange rate system among major industrialized countries, making the U.S. dollar the official reserve asset.

Fixed Exchange Rate System
System in effect when countries agree to buy or sell their currency to maintain fixed exchange rates with other currencies.

Official Reserve Asset
The asset (such as the dollar or gold) by which other countries define the value of their currency; used as international reserves.

As you saw in Chapter 18, from 1944 until 1973, the major economies of the world participated in the Bretton Woods Accord, a fixed exchange rate system with the U.S. dollar serving as the official reserve asset. Other countries defined their currencies in terms of the dollar and bought or sold dollars to maintain the fixed exchange rates. Supporters of the Bretton Woods Accord believed that the fixed exchange rate system offered several advantages.

One advantage was that under some conditions, inflation and unemployment could be self-correcting. If inflation or unemployment accelerated in one country relative to the rest of the world, market forces in international markets would come into play and cause the inflation and unemployment to be reduced.

Under a fixed exchange rate system, when a country experienced inflation higher than that of its trading partners, its balance of payments would go into a deficit position as net exports fell and capital outflows increased. Net exports would fall because the country's domestic prices were relatively higher than prices in the rest of the world, leading to a decrease in exports and an increase in imports. If the inflation were due to increases in the money supply, lower interest rates initially could also lead to a net capital outflow as foreign financial securities became more attractive than domestic securities. The net capital outflow would further increase the deficit in the balance of payments. Under the Bretton Woods Accord, the inflation-ridden country would be forced to buy back its currency to maintain fixed exchange rates. The act of buying back its currency tended to reduce the country's domestic money supply and inflationary pressures, increase domestic interest rates, and improve the trade imbalance. Thus, inflation would be self-correcting.

Likewise, if unemployment in a country increased, income would fall, causing imports to decrease and, assuming that exports remained constant, net exports to increase. The balance of payments would move into a surplus position, and the country would experience an increase in international reserves. If policy makers allowed the increase in international reserves to also increase the domestic money supply, the level of economic activity would speed up and employment would increase. Note that if the increase in international reserves did not lead to expansion of the domestic money supply, employment would not rise.

Another advantage of a fixed exchange rate system was that it minimized exchange rate risk. This is the risk that changes in the exchange rate might cause the value of foreign currencies or foreign financial instruments to fall. Under a fixed rate system, such as the Bretton Woods Accord, currency values did not change under normal circumstances. Therefore, exchange rate risk was very small and related only to the probability that the monetary authorities would redefine the currency in terms of the official reserve asset. Ceteris paribus, lower exchange rate risk is an advantage because it leads to increases in trade, capital flows, and economic efficiency. As you saw in Chapters 17 and 18, derivatives can be used to hedge exchange rate risk. Under a fixed exchange rate system, there is less need for derivatives because exchange rate risk is lower than under flexible exchange rates. Because derivatives involve some fees, the transactions costs of exchanging currencies are also reduced.

Despite these advantages, the Bretton Woods system also entailed some disadvantages. The ability of foreign countries to pursue their own monetary policies was limited because each country had to support its currency if market forces caused the currency's value to deviate from the agreed-upon exchange rate. For example, when a country wanted to pursue a more expansionary policy, its monetary authorities would increase the supply of reserves available to the banking system. Interest rates would fall and the monetary and credit aggregates would increase. This policy might result in a deficit in the balance of payments on current and capital accounts for two reasons. First, an increase in domestic income causes imports to increase. If the expansionary policy also causes domestic prices to increase, then exports decrease at the same time. Thus, net exports (exports minus imports) would decrease due to the rise in domestic income. Second, because of the falling interest rates, the country would also experience a capital outflow that would further contribute to the deficit in the balance of payments on current and capital accounts.

The central bank of the deficit country would then have to use its supplies of dollars to purchase its own currency to maintain the agreed-upon exchange rate. The act of buying back its currency would at least partially undo the stimulatory effects of the injection of reserves and would limit the monetary authorities' ability to pursue an expansionary policy. If the country ran out of dollars, it might have to devalue its currency. Devaluation entails discreet changes in the official exchange rate by the central bank but can destabilize financial markets and the domestic economy.

Likewise, if a country wished to pursue contractionary policies relative to those of the rest of the world, its balance of payments on current and capital accounts would move toward a surplus position. Net exports would increase as imports fell relative to exports. If prices also fell due to the contractionary policies, exports would increase. The higher interest rate would also lead to a capital inflow. Both factors would put upward pressure on the exchange rate. The ability of the monetary authorities to limit the growth of the money supply would be reduced by the necessity to supply the country's currency to maintain fixed exchange rates. The supplying of the currency would at least partially undo the contractionary effects. After a time, if the trade surplus and capital inflow persisted, the country would be under pressure to revalue its currency. In a **revaluation**, the monetary authorities increase the value of a currency relative to the official reserve asset. Again, financial markets and the economy would be destabilized. Although a country that is running a balance of payments deficit and losing international reserves must at some point devalue, the situation is different for a balance of payments surplus. If a country is running chronic surpluses, it does not have to revalue. Because a country can always print more money, the country could keep supplying its own currency, although this is a highly unlikely scenario.

As we noted earlier, under normal circumstances, exchange rate risk is lower with fixed exchange rates. When the situation is not normal, however, this advantage can turn into a major disadvantage. If a country is running a deficit in the balance of payments and devaluation seems likely, market participants will attempt to supply more of the currency to the central bank in exchange for dollars, the official reserve asset. By supplying more of the currency, however, market participants will further deplete the country's international reserves. Devaluation, which may have been only a possibility, would become a necessity. Thus, the expectation of devaluation may become a self-fulfilling prophecy.

For example, suppose that market participants expect the value of the peso to fall from $1 = 3.5 pesos to $1 = 7 pesos. Before the devaluation, an investor could exchange 350 pesos for $100 at the exchange rate of $1 = 3.5 pesos. If the investor is correct and the peso is devalued, the $100 will net 700 pesos after the devaluation. Note that the investor starts with 350 pesos and ends up with 700 pesos! As savvy investors exchange pesos for dollars, the country loses more of its international reserves, and the need to devalue becomes more imminent. In an attempt to stop the outflow of international reserves, policy makers may make the situation worse by denying that devaluation is a possibility. In this manner, the situation goes from bad to worse as devaluation is postponed until the problem becomes critical.

Another disadvantage of the Bretton Woods system was that it could be maintained only if all countries were willing and able to support their currencies and, if necessary, to periodically and orderly revalue or devalue them. As you have seen, foreign central banks had to adjust their currencies in terms of the dollar because the dollar was the official reserve asset. As long as foreign central banks were accumulating dollars to serve as international reserves, the United States could pursue expansionary domestic policies that resulted in balance of payment deficits on current and capital accounts. There was no need to worry about exchange rate pressures on its own or foreign currencies. Once foreign countries had acquired sufficient reserves, persistent U.S. deficits on current and capital accounts would result in the need for foreign countries to revalue their currencies. By the same token, persistent U.S. current and capital accounts surpluses would result in the need for foreign countries to devalue.

The need to periodically revalue or devalue was also related to the divergent domestic monetary and fiscal policies pursued by the Bretton Woods countries. Over time, if different countries pursued different policies, some countries would expand relatively faster than others, leading to exchange rate imbalances. For example, expansionary fiscal or monetary policy could cause one country to grow faster than another. Likewise, contractionary fiscal and monetary policy could cause a country to grow at a slower rate.

To the extent that countries experienced different growth rates, inflation rates, and interest rate structures, imbalances in the current and capital accounts would persist. If a country had more expansionary policies than the United States, it would experience chronic deficits in the current and capital accounts as well as the need to devalue. If a country had more contractionary policies, it would experience persistent surpluses and the need to revalue. If countries refused to make the necessary changes in their exchange rates, the system of fixed exchange rates established at Bretton Woods would break down.

As you saw in Chapter 18, the system did eventually break down when it became clear that the United States would not be able to continue to redeem dollars in gold. The breakdown occurred because U.S. policy makers were pursuing more expansionary policies than were some foreign economies, notably Germany and Japan. The result was an outflow of gold from the United States. With the suspension of the international conversion of dollars to gold in late 1971 and the official establishment of flexible exchange rates in 1974, the Bretton Woods fixed exchange rate system came to an end.

Recap The Bretton Woods Accord of 1944 established fixed exchange rates among major world currencies with the U.S. dollar serving as the official reserve asset. Supporters of the system believed that inflation and unemployment would, under some circumstances, be self-correcting and that exchange rate risk would be reduced. The need to maintain fixed exchange rates limited the ability of a country to pursue its own monetary policy. If a country wished to pursue more expansionary policies, lower domestic interest rates and higher income could lead to a deficit in the balance of payments. The need to buy back one's own currency would thwart the expansionary policies.

MONETARY POLICY UNDER FLEXIBLE EXCHANGE RATES SINCE 1974

Flexible Exchange Rate System
An exchange rate system in which the value of a currency is determined by supply and demand.

Under a flexible exchange rate system, market forces determine the value of a nation's currency. For the U.S. dollar, this means that the exchange rate is determined by the demand for and supply of dollars in international markets. The supply of dollars/month reflects U.S. demand for foreign goods, services, and securities. Ceteris paribus, quantity supplied is a positive function of the exchange rate. The demand for dollars reflects foreign demand for U.S. goods, services, and securities. Ceteris paribus, quantity demanded is a negative function of the exchange rate. The market, if left alone, will gravitate to the exchange rate where quantity demanded is equal to quantity supplied. As you saw in Chapters 16 and 18, factors such as domestic and foreign income, inflation rates, and interest rates affect exchange rates, and "flexible" exchange rates immediately adjust to changing market conditions and expectations.

Depreciation
A decrease in the value of a currency in terms of another currency under a flexible exchange rate system.

Appreciation
A rise in the value of a currency in terms of another currency under a flexible exchange rate system.

With the enactment of a flexible exchange rate system in late 1974, countries in some ways gained more control over their own monetary policies. No longer would a monetary objective or policy be compromised by a country's need to maintain the agreed-upon exchange rate as it was under the Bretton Woods Accord. No longer would a country have to support its domestic currency if market forces were causing the currency to depreciate or appreciate. As discussed in Chapter 16, depreciation occurs when the value of a currency falls in terms of another currency under a flexible exchange rate system. Appreciation occurs when the value of a currency rises in terms of another currency.

If monetary policy makers in a country are pursuing more expansionary policies than those of their neighbors, the balance of trade can move into a deficit position, with resulting deterioration in the balance of payments. Likewise, if a more contractionary policy is pursued, the balance of payments can move into a surplus position. Even though the country no longer has to defend its currency to maintain fixed exchange rates, it must consider other international ramifications of its monetary policy. Perhaps the most

Dollarization and Currency Boards

Full Dollarization
Abandonment of a country's own currency to adopt another country's currency as its official currency.

Full dollarization occurs when a country abandons its own currency in order to adopt another country's currency as its official currency. The adopted currency becomes the medium of exchange and unit of account. The U.S. dollar is the currency that has been most widely adopted and used by other countries. Although the U.S. dollar is the most widely dollarized currency, the term *dollarization* is generic and, in many cases, has little to do with the United States or the U.S. dollar. For example, Greenland has adopted the Danish krone; Vatican City, the Italian lira; Tuvalu, the Australian dollar; and so on.

Since 1999, El Salvador, Ecuador, and Guatemala have dollarized by adopting the U.S. dollar and abolishing their domestic currencies. Argentina has seriously considered full dollarization. (Panama dollarized in the early twentieth century.) Full dollarization with the U.S. dollar is discussed as a way to help developing countries, particularly those in South and Latin America, to overcome monetary and exchange rate volatility and to stabilize prices.

There are both benefits and costs to full dollarization. On the benefits side, there can be no balance of payment crises or speculative attacks on the domestic currency if the currency does not exist. The increased stability should lead to increased capital inflows, lower interest rates, and greater investment and growth. Lower interest rates also reduce the government's cost of financing the public debt. Another possibility is increased trade and financial integration with the United States and reduced inflationary expectations.

Seigniorage
The difference between the cost of producing and distributing currency and any revenues earned.

The costs of full dollarization include the loss of the identity associated with one's national currency. Many of the European countries that participate in the euro had a difficult time giving up their domestic currencies. Seigniorage is a more direct cost. Seigniorage is the difference between the cost of producing and distributing currency and any revenues earned through the distribution. For example, the Fed issues currency by purchasing government securities that earn interest. The interest goes to the Fed and eventually to the government. On the other hand, the currency issued by the Fed does not pay interest. The amount of interest earned on the government securities less the cost of producing the Federal Reserve notes is seigniorage. If a country fully dollarizes with U.S. dollars, that country forgoes earning seigniorage and the United States earns additional seigniorage that is related to the amount of U.S. dollars circulating in the foreign country. If electronic payments reduce the use of currency in the future, the amount of seigniorage will be reduced.

Another cost of full dollarization is that the country that dollarizes loses the ability to pursue an autonomous monetary policy. Small countries that wish to become more integrated with larger economies to increase trade and attract capital inflows have limited ability to pursue an independent monetary policy anyway.

Currency Board
An organized body within a country with the sole responsibility and power to define the value of the country's currency.

A close alternative to full dollarization is the creation of a currency board. A currency board is an organized body within a country with the sole responsibility and power to defend the value of a country's currency. The currency board pegs or fixes the currency value to the value of the currency of the dominant trading partner. The country commits to a fixed exchange rate, and the currency is fully convertible with the pegged currency. The government cannot print money unless it is backed by reserves of the currency to which it is pegged. Finally, the currency board has the power to force the government to eliminate a budget deficit that may be inflationary.

A currency board can achieve many of the benefits of full dollarization. Also, the value of the seigniorage from issuing one's own currency is not lost. The problem is that the currency board may not be perceived to be as permanent as full dollarization. Given the perception that the currency board could be abolished or modified, the full benefits of increased trade and investment and lower interest rates would not be realized. The currency could still be subject to speculative attacks if speculators sold the currency at the preset price, putting tremendous pressure on the currency board to devalue. In 1991, Argentina established a currency board that fixed the Argentina peso with the U.S. dollar and experienced a severe financial crisis in early 2002. Despite the presence of the currency board, there is less certainty with a currency board than with full dollarization. The increased uncertainty leads to higher interest rates, lower investment, and slower growth than would likely occur otherwise. Argentina, Bulgaria, Bosnia, and Hong Kong have had successful currency boards.

Finally, it should be noted that dollars already circulate and are widely used in many of the countries that could benefit from full dollarization. To the extent that the dollar displaces the national currency, seigniorage is already reduced.

---

important effects are capital flows and the potential depreciation or appreciation of its currency. Depreciation and appreciation, in turn, can feed back to the domestic economy and cause changes in the growth rate of income through net exports.

If international trade and capital flows are small relative to the aggregate level of economic activity, monetary authorities may have greater latitude in the execution of policy. International trade and capital flows have increased significantly since 1970, however, so policy makers must consider how their policies will affect foreign countries and what the feedback to the domestic economy will be. For example, in 2007, U.S. exports were about $1,600 billion, while imports were roughly $2,300 billion in an economy where gross domestic product (GDP) was about $13,800 billion. In 1960, exports were roughly $25.3 billion and imports $22.8 billion, while gross national product (GNP) was $526.6 billion. Thus, in 1960, exports and imports were 4.8 and 4.3 percent of GNP, respectively ($25.3/$526.6 and $22.8/$526.6). By 2007, exports had grown to 11.6 percent of GDP ($1,600/$13,800), and imports had increased even more to 16.7 percent of GDP ($2,300/$13,800). In some ways, U.S. monetary authorities have always recognized that their monetary policies can affect interest rate, inflation, and growth in other countries. In recent decades, U.S. policy makers have also become increasingly aware that foreign events can at times influence the U.S. economy and, hence, the formulation and effects of policy.

Coincidentally, with the growth in trade in the 1970s, governments began to remove barriers to international capital flows. The dismantling was virtually complete by the 1980s. In addition, major breakthroughs in telecommunications technologies and the electronic transfer of funds now allow funds to be transferred almost instantaneously anywhere in the world. These two factors have created a worldwide foreign exchange market where the buying and selling of different currencies take place and the "wheels are greased" for international trade and capital flows among nations. In 2007, the foreign exchange market traded more than \$3.2 trillion every day—the equivalent of nearly \$500 per day per person in the world—making it the largest market in the world. Because enormous sums of funds flow with lightning speed, the ability for funds to find their highest return is greatly increased. From an economic standpoint, economic efficiency is enhanced when funds flow to the location with the highest risk-adjusted return.

Capital flows jeopardize or weaken the intended effects of monetary policy. To illustrate, we will consider the case of contractionary monetary policy, in which the Fed raises interest rates to slow the level of economic activity. If U.S. interest rates move up relative to interest rates abroad, ceteris paribus, foreigners will demand more U.S. financial instruments—which will then pay a relatively higher return—and less of their own financial instruments—which will then pay a relatively lower return. The demand for dollars increases and puts upward pressure on the exchange rate. Capital flows in from abroad as the dollar appreciates. The augmented supply of funds from abroad causes U.S. interest rates, although higher than before the Fed acted, to be lower than they otherwise would be. Thus, slowing the level of economic activity is more difficult because of the offsetting effect of capital flows on the supply of loanable funds.

In addition, because of the reduced demand for foreign financial instruments, ceteris paribus, there is also a tendency for prices of foreign financial instruments to fall and foreign interest rates to rise. Changes in the supply of and demand for financial instruments cause capital flows that will bring real interest rates between countries into closer alignment. Given a change in U.S. interest rates, freer capital movements will bring about immediate changes in the exchange rate and eventual interest rate adjustments in foreign economies.

Continuing with our example of contractionary U.S. policy, if the increase in the domestic interest rate causes the dollar to appreciate, the dollar price of foreign goods falls while the foreign price of U.S. goods rises. The result is a decrease in exports and an increase in imports. Thus, net exports will also fall in response to an appreciation of the exchange rate. This latter effect reinforces the contractionary effects of a rise in domestic interest rates.

At the same time that these forces are working to decrease net exports, two other effects are working in the opposite direction—to increase net exports. First, the increase in domestic interest rates could cause a reduction in domestic demand as the demand for interest-sensitive expenditures falls. The reduction in aggregate demand decreases the demand for imports, thereby increasing net exports from what they otherwise would be. Second, if the slowing of the economy causes domestic prices to fall relative to foreign prices, then, ceteris paribus, both foreign and domestic customers have an incentive to switch to domestically produced goods and services. These two effects work to increase net exports and to mitigate the decline in net exports that results from the appreciation of the dollar.

Nevertheless, in most cases, the decrease in net exports caused by the appreciation of the dollar will be larger than the increase in net exports resulting from these two additional factors. Hence, the total effect of contractionary monetary policy is to decrease net exports. Although that may not always be the case, we usually assume that higher U.S. interest rates lead to an appreciation of the domestic currency, capital inflows, a decrease in net exports, and a larger trade deficit (or smaller trade surplus). Exhibit 26-1 provides a schematic diagram of the results of U.S. contractionary monetary policy under flexible exchange rates.

The impact of U.S. monetary policy also depends on the monetary and fiscal policies of other countries. If other central banks attempt to slow their economies when the U.S. monetary authorities are doing so, resulting effects on exchange rates depend on

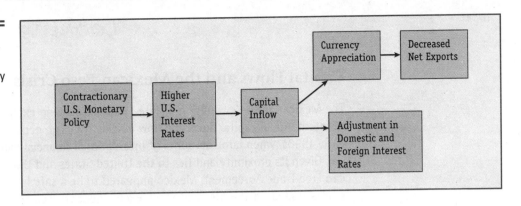

the relative magnitudes of the interest rate changes among the various countries. Thus, we can conclude that interest rates and exchange rates are determined jointly by the monetary and fiscal policies of the various interdependent countries and the resulting market forces.

In summary, the growth of trade and capital flows has occurred in a world that switched from fixed to flexible exchange rates. Because central banks are no longer necessarily committed to maintaining the value of their respective currencies, policy makers have more independence in formulating and executing monetary policy. A country's ability to run a monetary policy far different from that of its neighbors is limited by the increased interdependence of economies and the ease with which capital flows across borders. Capital flows and changes in the exchange rate offset the effects. The more important trade is to the domestic economy and the greater the ease with which capital flows between nations, the larger the effects. Thus, for the United States, external factors are likely to dampen the effects of any Fed actions that result in relative interest rate or income changes. In the near term, an increase in U.S. rates relative to foreign rates usually increases the exchange rate of the dollar and capital inflows, ceteris paribus. Similarly, a decrease in U.S. rates relative to foreign rates usually leads to decreases in the exchange rate of the dollar and capital outflows, ceteris paribus. Note that as a result of capital flows, these financial adjustments to U.S. monetary policy action will occur in advance of the slower response of output and prices.

Thus, the crux of the dilemma is that under fixed exchange rates, countries are limited in running their own monetary policies because of the need to maintain the value of their currency. Under flexible exchange rates, countries can also be limited. If a country tries to run a policy that is different from the rest of the world, capital and real flows will occur and will complicate the results and jeopardize that policy. What does all of this mean for the future? In a nutshell, it means that in all probability, nations will have to be more concerned about coordinating their monetary policies. The next section looks at the specifics.

Recap
Under flexible exchange rates, the value of a currency is determined by supply and demand. Flexible exchange rates free a country from the need to supply or demand dollars to maintain fixed exchange rates. In this way, flexible exchange rates allow policy makers more freedom in pursuing policies that diverge from those of other countries. At the same time, however, policy makers must also be concerned about the effects of their domestic policies on exchange rates and capital flows. Under flexible exchange rates, a country can pursue its own policy, but if it differs from policies in the rest of the world, changes in net exports and capital flows can mitigate the intended effects of the policy.

Capital Flows and the Mexican Peso Crisis

The Mexican peso devaluation of late 1994 is a striking example of the implications of international capital flows and how quickly they can occur. The story begins in the early 1990s, when large amounts of international financial capital poured into Mexico. Given its proximity and ties to the United States and the proposed North American Free Trade Agreement, Mexico appeared to be a safe haven. The market value of stocks traded on the Mexican stock exchange increased from $4 billion in 1985 to over $200 billion in 1993. In 1993, it was estimated that foreigners owned around 75 percent of the stocks traded on the exchange.[a] But the bubble could not last forever.

In the second half of 1994, Mexico began to experience capital outflows that resulted in a dramatic loss of international reserves, particularly the dollar. By December 20, 1994, Mexico found it necessary to devalue the peso by 15 percent from 3.50 to 4.00 pesos per dollar. Despite this move, the loss of international reserves continued, and three days later, when this exchange rate could not be maintained, the peso was allowed to float freely. The result was a 50 percent depreciation of the peso, massive capital outflows from Mexico, falling stock prices, skyrocketing interest rates, and an international financial crisis.

The capital outflow caused Mexico to lose most of its international reserves. Reserves fell from $17.1 billion on November 1, 1994, to $3.8 billion by January 30, 1995. There were fears that the government would default on the Tesobonos, which were dollar-indexed government bonds issued in pesos with maturities up to a year. Foreign investors, many of whom were in the United States, held half of the Tesobonos. President Bill Clinton authorized a $20 billion rescue package that would enable Mexico to redeem all maturing Tesobonos with U.S. dollars. (An additional rescue package later arranged by Clinton amounted to $30 billion.) As a result of the crisis, Mexico experienced a severe recession.

In addition to political instability in Mexico, many analysts believe that the crisis was caused by two international events. The first was the reversal of Japanese capital flows into Mexico in response to the domestic crisis in Japan. The second was the rise in U.S. interest rates orchestrated by the Fed starting in early 1994. Both caused capital flows out of Mexico and contributed to the subsequent crisis. Writing in *The Columbia Journal of World Business,* Michael Adler made three observations about the crisis:

1. Markets are extremely sensitive to uninsured risks and react quickly and massively when risks are perceived to rise.

2. Any rush to sell in one sector of the market produces liquidity shortages that cause selling pressures to cascade into other market sectors. [As a result of the Mexican peso crisis, other emerging markets and even other developed economies also experienced international capital outflows.]

3. Markets need some kind of insurance when governments, by suddenly changing the interest rate environment as the Federal Reserve did . . . can confront investors with the risk of ruin.[b]

As we noted in this chapter and in Chapter 18, the potential for crisis is augmented because capital flows are larger and more volatile than in the past.

Endnotes

a. Tom Petruno, "Global Money—Free Flows, Free Falls," *The Los Angeles Times* (March 19, 1995): A11.
b. Michael Adler, "Mexico's Devaluation: The Beginning, Not the End, of Its Problems," *The Columbia Journal of World Business* (Spring 1995): 112–120.

THE GLOBALIZATION OF MONETARY POLICY

A new reality is having a profound influence on the conduct and effectiveness of domestic policies. Simply put, the economies of the world are becoming more interdependent. What goes on in Tokyo, London, Hong Kong, Paris, and Buenos Aires has an increasingly important effect on the financial system and the economy in the United States. Consequently, U.S. policy makers have somewhat less control over the performance of the U.S. economy than in previous eras, when the American economy was more isolated from international trade and finance. As Alan Greenspan said about the effects of the ongoing crises in Russia and Asia on the U.S. economy: "It is just not credible that the United States can remain an oasis of prosperity unaffected by a world that is experiencing greatly increased stress."[1]

Such observations have given rise to calls for cooperation and coordination among world policy makers. Although the difficulties some countries have in coordinating their domestic monetary and fiscal policies suggest that coordinating policies across countries will never be easy, the existence of globalization does highlight the new challenges and complexities facing policy makers.

As you first saw in Chapter 18, policy makers are attempting to meet the challenges of globalization through informal discussions among the major industrialized countries and through international organizations such as the International Monetary Fund and the Bank for International Settlements. The dialogues suggest that to achieve a stable international financial system, countries around the world must have healthy financial systems with noninflationary policies. In addition, countries must standardize the reporting of information about financial markets, institutions, laws, regulations, international reserves, external debt (both short and long term), and the health of the banking sector. Finally, the surveillance of international organizations that oversee the international financial system must be more transparent and open. In such an environment, the full benefits of globalization could be reached while minimizing the costs.

When considering the future, one must consider a wide range of possibilities. In the broadest sense, major world economies will either remain on a version of the present system of flexible exchange rates or return to a version of fixed exchange rates. In either case, the ramifications for monetary policy will be considerable.

A fixed exchange rate system can be sustained only if the growth and inflation rates of the participating countries are similar and only if devaluations and revaluations occur in an orderly manner. To maintain the system for any period of time, both the monetary policies and the fiscal policies of the participating countries must be coordinated. As you have seen, divergent monetary and fiscal policies will lead to different growth rates of income, different inflation rates, and different interest rate structures. If economies grow at different rates, changes in net exports and interest rates will cause exchange rate pressures.

Looking Out

The Eurosystem

One of the best examples of increased cooperation and coordination in the formulation of monetary policy is the Eurosystem. As you saw in Chapter 16, the Eurosystem consists of the European Central Bank and the central banks of the 15 countries (as of 2008) that participate in the euro, Europe's single currency. As such, the Eurosystem implements and carries out monetary policies for the eurozone, with the primary goal of achieving price stability. To do this, the Eurosystem decides on a quantitative definition of price stability, such as 2 percent inflation or less.

In addition, "two pillars" are used to achieve the goal. The first pillar is a quantitative reference value for the growth rate of a broad-based monetary aggregate, such as *M*2 in the United States. The second pillar consists of a broad collection of indicators that policy makers use to assess the outlook for price developments in the area as a whole. The former is similar to targeting a monetary aggregate to guide policy formulation. The latter is similar to using a more eclectic approach in policy formulation.

To achieve its goals, the Eurosystem uses tools similar to the Fed's, including open market operations, a lending facility like the discount window called a *standing facility*, and reserve requirements. The 15 national central banks hold the required reserves, carry out open market operations, and operate the standing facility. The Eurosystem must approve of the financial instruments that are allowed to be used in open market operations. The system also sets reserve requirements and interest rates on standing facility loans. In addition, it takes actions that nudge interest rates and the monetary aggregates in one direction or the other as part of monetary policy.

The current chairman of the European Central Bank (ECB) is Jean-Claude Trichet. In early 2008, he had an opportunity to prove that the ECB's primary goal is price stability. In the wake of several large rate cuts by the U.S. Federal Reserve, the ECB has held its rates steady, and as theory would predict, the euro has increased dramatically versus the U.S. dollar. When asked why he was not lowering interest rates in the face of the financial sector difficulties, Mr. Trichet stated: "There is no contradiction between price stability and financial stability."[a]

Endnote

a. Dougherty, Carter. "In Europe, Central Banking Is Different." *The New York Times,* March 6, 2008.

If the participants' monetary and fiscal policies are similar, however, it is possible for them to reap large benefits from the increased trade and integration that fixed exchange rates could encourage. Increased trade would allow the countries to enjoy a higher standard of living, and capital flows would allow surplus funds to flow to their highest return. The downside is twofold: Countries that value their independence or have divergent goals with respect to unemployment and inflation would not do well under a fixed exchange rate system. In addition, countries may not have the political discipline to stick with fixed exchange rates if domestic problems become paramount.

Under flexible exchange rates, capital flows limit a country's ability to execute policies that deviate significantly from those of the rest of the world. Thus, incentive exists for nations to cooperate to find a workable policy acceptable to all. There is already a great deal of monetary policy coordination among developed countries. Some coordination is spearheaded by international organizations such as the International Monetary Fund, which was created at the Bretton Woods Conference, and the Bank for International Settlements in Basel, Switzerland. Informal groups of major trading partners meet regularly to discuss policy regimes and options and often communicate and work together to coordinate policies. One group, called the G-7 nations, includes the United States, the United Kingdom, France, Germany, Japan, Canada, and Italy. In a "managed" flexible exchange rate system, exchange rates are determined by the forces of supply and demand, with occasional central bank intervention. The central banks of the G-7 nations have frequently intervened by buying and selling in currency markets to affect exchange rates since 1971.[2]

On occasion, the U.S. Treasury and the Fed intervene in the foreign exchange market to restore orderly conditions or to influence exchange rates. Since the mid-1980s, they have pursued intervention, coordinated with the governments and central banks of the other G-7 countries, on several occasions. Given the large volume of foreign currency transactions, intervention by the central bank to directly affect exchange rates would have to be on a very large scale, even for a central bank. Therefore, intervention affects the market primarily by influencing market sentiment, although on occasion several central banks will try to directly affect exchange rates through coordinated intervention.

An example of coordinated intervention occurred in 1985, when leaders of France, Germany, Japan, Great Britain, and the United States met and decided to intervene in foreign exchange markets to reduce the value of the dollar. At that time, U.S. interest rates were high relative to those in the rest of the world, causing large capital inflows and a strong dollar. The strong dollar fueled trade deficits that were having a negative impact on U.S. employment. The plan was named the *Plaza Accord* after the hotel where the meeting took place. Since then, these nations and others have met on a more or less regular basis in an attempt to coordinate economic policy and to open international markets.

Two later examples of coordinated intervention occurred in mid-1998 and mid-2000. The first involved intervention by the United States and Japan to boost the value of the Japanese yen. On June 17, 1998, the Fed bought about $2 billion worth of yen in the first intervention on behalf of the yen in six years. At that time, the value of the yen had been declining for three years, and the exchange rate was near an eight-year low. On June 16, 1998, the yen/dollar exchange rate was $1 = 142 yen. After the intervention on June 17, 1998, the yen appreciated to $1 = 137 yen. There were two major reasons for the intervention. First, the sagging yen put additional pressures on the struggling economies of Southeast Asia, which needed to sell their goods to Japan. The weak yen made goods from Southeast Asia more expensive in Japan. Second, there was fear that the weak yen would pressure China to devalue its currency. A Chinese devaluation could set off another round of devaluations and defaults throughout Southeast Asia, intensifying the Asian crisis just as the stricken economies were beginning to recover. A unique aspect of this episode is that China had asked the United States and Japan to intervene. While the intervention appeared to impact exchange rates in the very short run, this was not true for the long run, and by late August of 1998, the yen was trading at $1 = 145 yen. Later that year, in the fall of 1998, the value of the yen in terms of the dollar did fall dramatically; however, the fall was not directly related to the intervention in June 1998.

The second example involved intervention by the G-7 major industrialized nations, including the United States, to boost the value of the euro. As noted in the body of the text, the G-7 nations include Canada, Germany, France, Italy, Japan, the United Kingdom, and the United States. The euro was launched on January 1, 1999, at a debut price of $1.17 against the dollar. By September 2000, the euro had fallen more than 28 percent to $.8439 against the dollar. Many analysts felt the euro was significantly undervalued but feared that a speculative attack on the new currency would drive its value down even further. On September 22, 2000, the G-7 nations initiated a concerted intervention by buying euros in currency markets. The initial result was an increase in the value of the euro to more than $0.88 against the dollar. However, the increase was short-lived. Within two weeks, the euro began a downward slide and by late October was trading at its all-time low. Several reasons were posited for the failure of the intervention. First, the European Central Bank followed the intervention with only a small increase in interest rates, and some felt that larger interest rate increases were necessary to support the currency. Second, with presidential elections in the United States in early November 2000, U.S. Treasury officials reiterated on several occasions that there was no change in the U.S. position on the strong dollar. Finally, others felt there were imbalances in the euro zone economies that would require structural changes in labor markets and tax laws before the euro would appreciate.

When central banks and governments decide to intervene in foreign exchange markets, they do so for three reasons:

1. To resolve a severe but temporary liquidity crisis and to stabilize international financial markets

2. To signal that regulators believe exchange rates are deviating significantly from fundamental underlying values (that is, the dollar is overvalued or undervalued because of speculation in the market)

3. To signal a change in exchange rate policy or to clarify an existing policy

When the Fed participates in an intervention, it does so by purchasing or selling dollars for other foreign currencies. Because the dollars go through the banking system, reserves are either augmented or decreased. They are augmented when the Fed buys foreign currencies with dollars. Reserves are decreased when the Fed buys dollars with foreign currencies that it has previously accumulated.

To limit the effects on reserves, the Fed can engage in *sterilization*. In this process, the full amount of the foreign exchange operation is offset by an open market operation so that the monetary base is unaffected by the foreign exchange operation. For example, suppose that the Fed in conjunction with Japan decides that the dollar is overvalued and the yen is undervalued. To prop up the value of the yen, the Fed sells dollars to purchase yen. If the transaction is unsterilized, the monetary base increases, and the domestic money supply and interest rates are affected. If the transaction is sterilized, the Fed uses open market sales to offset the increase in the monetary base. In general, in the United States, foreign exchange transactions are sterilized.

It is difficult to predict how the Fed will execute monetary policy in the future. Its current intermediate targets may no longer be relevant or effectively related to the level of economic activity in a globalized financial system. Within this system, the Fed must increasingly consider domestic exchange rates, capital flows, and foreign policies. Although the Fed's function will remain the same, it may have to work with new procedures and regulations, some of which will be international in scope.

Mutual interdependence is an unalterable fact in modern monetary policy. In the past, the Fed has responded to limit the damage of foreign financial shocks. In the future, it will also need to help ensure that U.S.-based shocks, such as the "mortgage

A New Kind of Monetary Policy Coordination

In the decades surrounding the euro's creation, the primary goal of monetary policy coordination was to limit exchange rate fluctuations. If a country's central bank pursued a relatively expansionary policy, increasing its money supply and reducing interest rates, then this country's currency would depreciate. For a group of integrated nations, such fluctuations were to be avoided for several reasons: i) The prospect of gains by successfully timing exchange rate changes could lead to destabilizing capital inflows and outflows. ii) Such fluctuations could lead to sudden changes in the direction of international trade and unnecessarily high adjustment costs in affected industries. A country which previously had a comparative advantage in one industry might suddenly find itself an importer of this product as a result of a sudden and unanticipated currency appreciation. iii) Most important for the countries that planned to adopt the euro, such fluctuations would complicate the transition to a single currency.

In more recent years, a new type of monetary policy coordination has become increasingly important—the maintenance of liquidity of internationally traded financial assets. Starting in late 2007 and continuing into 2008, representatives of the Fed have met with their counterparts from many central banks in order to maintain the liquidity of U.S. real estate–backed financial securities.[a] Foreign financial firms have been large investors in such securities, so any financial difficulties that might require them to rapidly liquidate their assets could significantly depress prices. With prices of such assets reduced to levels considered abnormally low, only investors in distress (or with a different assessment of the true long-term price of such securities) would consider selling. The prospect of falling asset prices, intertwined with reduced liquidity, could potentially cause a financial crisis that would seamlessly transcend national borders. Central banks are currently coordinating their efforts to maintain liquidity and forestall such a scenario. By the end of September 2008, the Fed had negotiated currency and asset swap agreements with the European Central Bank, the Bank of England, the Bank of Canada, the Bank of Japan, the Swiss National Bank, the Bank of Japan, the National Bank of Denmark, the Bank of Norway, the Reserve Bank of Australia, and the Bank of Sweden, totaling a whopping $620 billion. In late October 2008, the Fed announced additional swap agreements with the central banks of Singapore, Mexico, Brazil, and South Korea. Such agreements represent attempts to maintain liquidity in global financial markets and to enhance the smooth functioning of the global financial system. Many large central banks also announced a coordinated interest rate cut that same month.

Interestingly, as central banks have become more involved with maintaining liquidity for specific asset classes, they have become less involved with maintaining stable exchange rates. To be sure, recent increases in the value of the euro and the concomitant decreases in the dollar have brought requests from those adversely impacted to halt and even reverse the trend, but unlike such episodes in the past, there seems little attempt to harmonize the monetary policies pursued by the ECB and the Fed.

Finally, as we saw in Chapter 25, the Fed also coordinated interest rate decreases with the European Central Bank and those in Canada, England, and Sweden immediately following the terrorist attack on September 11, 2001. The Fed also arranged currency swap agreements with the European Central Bank, the Bank of England, and the Bank of Canada, totaling $68 billion to aid foreign banks in countries whose U.S. operations were disrupted by the attack.

Endnote

a. Federal Reserve Press Release, May 2, 2008.

meltdown," don't adversely impact foreign financial markets in a way that could ultimately boomerang back to the United States in an amplified or more virulent form. The Fed will have to design policies for a world with increasing trade and minimal barriers to international capital flows that can occur with great speed.

In conclusion, we can say that whether the world returns to fixed exchange rates or maintains the current flexible exchange rate regime, some policy coordination will be needed. Although flexible exchange rates increase the potential independence of monetary policy, the increasing openness of world trade and finance has heightened the interdependencies among nations. Flexible exchange rates allow a central bank to set its interest rates somewhat independently of other countries, but capital mobility means that a change in the interest rates relative to other countries is compensated for by changes in exchange rates and capital flows. Thus, a central bank's freedom to set interest rates is only as great as its acceptance of the foreign exchange rate movements and the capital flows connected with a change in interest rates. Amid all of the uncertainties, one factor seems highly probable: Monetary policy in the future will most likely involve more global coordination and cooperation whether it be under fixed or flexible exchange rates.

Recap   In the future, countries will be required to coordinate their monetary policies whether exchange rates are fixed or flexible, as countries become more interdependent due to the growth of trade and capital flows. In the past, cooperation between central banks was centered on exchange rate stability. Recently, such cooperation has been employed to maintain liquidity of specific classes of internationally traded securities such as those backed by U.S. real estate loans.

Summary of Major Points

1. The Bretton Woods Accord of 1944 established fixed exchange rates between the U.S. dollar and other major currencies. Supporters of the fixed exchange rate system believed that under some circumstances, inflation and unemployment would be self-correcting.

2. The need to maintain the value of the currency under fixed exchange rates limited the ability of a country to pursue its own monetary policy independent of other participants in the agreement.

3. Because countries had divergent monetary and fiscal policies, exchange rate imbalances persisted. Eventually, the United States was unable to maintain the conversion of dollars into gold, and the Bretton Woods system of fixed exchange rates collapsed in 1971. It was replaced by a system of flexible exchange rates.

4. Under flexible exchange rates, the value of the dollar is determined by the demand and supply of dollars. Flexible exchange rates freed countries from

the need to support their currencies to maintain fixed exchange rates. Each country in some ways gained greater latitude in adjusting its domestic monetary policy.

5. Even though countries do not have to support their currencies under flexible exchange rates, they must be aware of the effects that their monetary and fiscal policies have on the exchange rate, capital flows, and net exports. Monetary policy must be executed with an understanding of the international ramifications and the feedbacks to the domestic economy. This is particularly true if net exports are a relatively large component of aggregate demand and if capital flows are unrestricted.

6. Trade has increased because of the concerted efforts of developed nations since World War II.

These efforts result from the recognition of the gains from trade to all trading partners. Capital flows have also increased because of the removal of capital barriers and because of technological advances that have increased the speed of such flows.

7. Under flexible exchange rates, there is an incentive for countries to work together to coordinate monetary policy. Indeed, there is already considerable monetary policy coordination, particularly among such groups as the G-7 countries. Regardless of whether exchange rates are fixed or flexible, monetary policy in the future will most likely entail increased global coordination as economies become more interdependent because of the growth in trade and capital flows.

Key Terms

Appreciation, p. **637**
Bretton Woods Accord, p. **634**
Currency Board, p. **638**
Depreciation, p. **637**
Devaluation, p. **635**

Exchange Rate Risk, p. **635**
Fixed Exchange Rate System, p. **634**
Flexible Exchange Rate System, p. **637**

Full Dollarization, p. **638**
Official Reserve Asset, p. **634**
Revaluation, p. **635**
Seigniorage, p. **638**

Review Questions

1. Briefly explain the Bretton Woods exchange rate system. When was it created? When and why did the system collapse?

2. Under the Bretton Woods system, the U.S. dollar was the official reserve asset. How did this affect the U.S. balance of payments on current and capital accounts? Could the United States experience large balance of payments deficits on current and capital accounts indefinitely?

3. Assume that you work at the central bank of a small country that is considering an expansionary monetary policy to speed up the level of economic activity. Given fixed exchange rates, advise the president of your country what will happen to net exports if the country pursues a policy of monetary expansion. What action will the central bank have to take to support the agreed-upon exchange rate? How will that action affect the expansionary policy?

4. Argue that fixed exchange rates are preferable to flexible exchange rates. Then present the opposite argument.

5. For each of the following situations, assuming fixed exchange rates, tell what will happen to the balance of payments on current and capital accounts in the United States, ceteris paribus:
   a. Domestic income increases.
   b. Domestic interest rates fall.
   c. Foreign income increases.
   d. Foreign interest rates fall.
   e. Domestic inflation increases.
   f. Foreign inflation increases.

6. For each of the situations in question 5, tell what will happen to the exchange rate, assuming flexible exchange rates.

7. Explain whether you agree or disagree with the following statement: Flexible exchange rates allow nations to pursue their own monetary policies.

8. What are the advantages of fixed exchange rates? What are the disadvantages? Does it matter if the country is large or small?

9. Briefly explain how interest rates on instruments of comparable risk and maturity will tend to be equalized in a world without capital barriers.

10. Under a flexible exchange rate system, what effect does contractionary monetary policy have on the exchange rate?

11. Why is a country limited in executing its own monetary policy under a fixed exchange rate system? How is it limited under a flexible exchange rate system?

12. How can monetary policy coordination among countries increase the degree to which monetary policy can be used to pursue macroeconomic goals under fixed exchange rates? Under flexible exchange rates?

13. Could high U.S. interest rates affect investment spending in foreign countries? Explain.

14. What is the Eurosystem? Briefly discuss how the Eurosystem conducts monetary policy.

15. What is full dollarization? How does it differ from a currency board? What is seigniorage?

Analytical Questions

Questions marked with a check mark (✓) are objective in nature. They can be completed with a short answer or number.

✓16. Use graphs to demonstrate what will happen to the value of the dollar in terms of the Japanese yen in each of the following situations:

a. U.S. income increases.
b. Japanese income increases.
c. U.S. interest rates fall.
d. Japanese interest rates fall.
e. U.S. inflation increases.
f. Japanese inflation increases.

✓17. If the nominal U.S. interest rate is 10 percent and U.S. inflation is 6 percent, what is the real U.S. interest rate? What is the real U.S. rate in terms of foreign interest rates?

✓18. The Fed exchanges $1 million for 139 million yen. If the Fed sells $1 million worth of T-bills in the open market, what will happen to domestic interest rates and the money supply? If the Fed does not do the open market sale, what will happen to domestic interest rates and the money supply? In which case is the foreign exchange transaction sterilized?

Suggested Readings

Adam S. Posen and Arvind Subramanian call for more monetary policy in "A Global Approach Is Needed to Beat Inflation," in the Op-Ed section of the *Financial Times*, August 21, 2008. The article is available online at **http://iie.com/publications/opeds/oped.cfm?ResearchID=992.**

The "Monetary Policy Report to the Congress" always has a section on the external (rest-of-the-world) sector. The report is available online at **http://www.federalreserve.gov/boarddocs/hh/.**

Check out foreign exchange rate data at **http://www.federalreserve.gov/releases/h10/update//** or **http://research.stlouisfed.org/fred2/categories/15.**

The National Bureau of Economic Research Working Paper Series presents preliminary work by top researchers in economics. Two relevant recent papers are: #13815, "A Long Term Perspective on the Euro," by Michael Bordo and Harold James, 2008, which places the development of the euro in historical context; and #13736, "Global Forces and Monetary Policy Effectiveness," by Jean Boivin and Marc Giannoni, 2007, which finds that nations still appear to have the ability to employ monetary policy despite globalized capital markets.

In their IMF Working Paper no. 07/279, "Financial Globalization and Monetary Policy," Michael Devereux and Alan Sutherland find that price stability brings additional benefits in a more globalized world and should remain the primary focus of central bankers.

A recently published collection of academic papers, *International Monetary Policy After the Euro*, 2005, edited by the Nobel Prize–winning economist Robert Mundell, together with Paul Zak and Derek Schaeffer, presents a variety of positions regarding the impact of the euro on global monetary policy.

For a survey that looks at international monetary policy coordination since the end of Bretton Woods, see "International Coordination of Macroeconomic Policies: Still Alive in the New Millennium?" by Laurence H. Meyer, Brian M. Doyle, Joseph E. Gagnon, and Dale W. Henderson, *International Finance Discussion Papers Number 723* (April 2002). The paper is available online at **http://www .federalreserve.gov/pubs/ifdp/2002/723/ifdp723.pdf.**

For a paper that shows that business cycles were more coordinated in the post-Bretton Woods era, see "International Business Cycles Under Fixed and Flexible Exchange Rate Regimes," by Michael A. Kouparitsas, WP 2003–28, Federal Reserve Bank of Chicago (November 29, 2003). The paper is available online at **http://www.chicagofed.org/ publications/workingpapers/papers/wp2003–28.pdf.**

For students interested in a "famous" fixed exchange rate system, the gold standard, see *The Key to the Gold Vault,* published by the New York Fed in 1991 (revised 2003). It is free for the asking from the Public Information Depart-ment, Federal Reserve Bank of New York, 33 Liberty Street, New York, NY 10045 and available online at **www .newyorkfed.org/education/addpub/goldvaul.pdf.**

Two interesting *Fedpoints* published by the Federal Reserve Bank of New York are "Federal Reserve in the International Arena" (June 2003) and "Balance of Payments" (June 2004). Both are available online at **http://www.new yorkfed.org/aboutthefed/fedpoints.html.**

For a discussion of "Short-Run Independence of Monetary Policy Under Pegged Exchange Rates and Effects of Money on Exchange Rates and Interests," see the article by Lee E. Ohanian and Alan C. Stockman, *Journal of Money, Credit, and Banking* 29, no. 2 (November 1997): 783–806. Enrique G. Mendoza's "Comment on Short-Run Independence of Monetary Policy Under Pegged Exchange Rates" can be found in the same issue, 807–810.

For a broad view of critical international financial events since World War II and their effects on U.S. monetary policy, see Paul Volcker and Toyoo Gyohten, *Changing Fortunes* (New York: Times Books, 1992).

Endnotes

1. Speech by Alan Greenspan at the University of California, Berkeley (September 4, 1998).
2. Actually, the G-7 nations resulted from the 1986 expansion of a group of five (G-5) nations that had consulted since the flexible exchange rate system was put into place in the early 1970s. When Russia participates, it is referred to as the G-8. The original G-5 nations were the United States, the United Kingdom, France, Japan, and West Germany.

Glossary

A

Accommodation When policy makers increase aggregate demand in response to an adverse supply shock.

Adaptive Expectations Expectations formed by looking back at past values of a variable.

Adjustable (Variable) Rate Loans Loans where the interest rate is adjusted up or down periodically as the cost of funds to the lender changes.

Adverse Selection Problem When the least-desirable borrowers pursue a loan most diligently.

Agency of a Foreign Bank A U.S. banking office of a foreign bank that can only borrow funds in the wholesale and money markets and is not allowed to accept retail deposits.

Aggregate Demand Curve A curve showing the inverse relationship between the overall price level and the aggregate quantity of real output that will be demanded at various price levels, ceteris paribus.

Aggregate Supply Curve The curve graphically depicting the relationship between the overall price level and the aggregate quantity of real GDP that will be supplied at various price levels.

Alt-A (Stated Income) Mortgage A mortgage loan made to a borrower with good credit where the lender does not verify the income stated by the borrower.

American Stock Exchange (AMEX) An historically important stock exchange located in New York City, that merged with the NASDAQ in 1997 but was sold to private investors in 2003. It currently handles about 10 percent of all securities trades in the U.S. and is relatively important in small-cap stocks and exchange-traded funds (ETFs).

Amortization The paying off of the principal of a loan over the life of the loan.

Appreciated Description of a currency that has increased in value relative to another currency.

Appreciation A rise in the value of a currency in terms of another currency under a flexible exchange rate system.

Arbitrageurs Traders who make riskless profits by buying in one market and reselling in another market.

Asked Price The price at which a dealer (market maker) is willing to sell securities.

Asset-Backed Commercial Paper Money Market Mutual Fund Liquidity Facility (AMLF) A new lending facility where commercial banks or bank holding companies could borrow from the AMLF to purchase asset–backed commercial paper from money market mutual funds. Designed to reduce the strains on money market mutual funds due to disintermediation.

Asset-Backed Securities Securities that result from the process of securitization.

Asymmetric Information When a potential borrower knows more about the risks and returns of an investment project than the bank loan officer does.

Automated Clearinghouse (ACH) A function of the Fed that assists the government and private sectors in making automated direct payments of payroll checks into checking accounts, and allows to authorize transfers for insurance premiums, mortgage payments, other bills, and certain online or telephone transfers.

Automated Teller Machine (ATM) A machine that permits a depositor to make deposits and withdrawals to an account even when the financial institution is closed.

Average Daily Holding of Funds A household's demand for real money balances during the month; the amount of each withdrawal divided by two.

Average Marginal Tax Rate The average of the marginal tax rates of all taxpayers.

B

Balance of Goods and Services Net exports of services plus the trade balance.

Balance of Payments The record of transactions between the United States and its trading partners in the rest of the world over a particular period of time.

Balance on Current Account The balance of goods and services plus net unilateral transfers.

Bank for International Settlements (BIS) An international financial organization that promotes international cooperation among central banks and provides facilities for international financial operations.

Bank Holding Company A corporation that owns several firms, at least one of which is a bank.

Bank Runs When many depositors simultaneously attempt to withdraw their funds from a bank.

Bankers' Acceptances Money market instruments created in the course of international trade to guarantee bank drafts due on a future date.

Banking Reform Acts of 1933 and 1935 Statutes passed by Congress in response to the collapse of the banking system between 1930 and 1933.

Barter Trade of goods for goods.

Basel Accord A 1988 agreement among 12 countries that established international capital standards for banks.

Benefits of Holding Real Money Balances The stream of services that real balances yield defined as the time and distress saved by having money on hand for immediate use.

Beta A measure of the overall variability of a stock relative to changes in the entire stock market.

Bid Price The price at which a dealer (market maker) is willing to buy securities.

Board of Governors The seven governors of the Fed appointed by the president with Senate approval for 14-year terms.

Bond Indenture A document stating the terms under which a bond is issued.

Borrowing Constraint The impediment to continuous borrowing that may come from the lender's unwillingness to keep lending or the borrower's unwillingness to keep borrowing.

Bretton Woods Accord A 1944 agreement negotiated by the major industrialized countries that established fixed exchange rates with the U.S. dollar serving as the official reserve currency.

Broker An individual who arranges trades between buyers and sellers of securities for a fee.

Business Cycle Short-run fluctuations in economic activity as measured by the output of goods and services.

C

Call Options Options that give the buyer of the option the right, but not the obligation, to buy a standardized contract of a financial instrument at a strike price determined today.

Call Provisions Provisions spelled out in a bond indenture that allow the issuer to buy back the bonds at a specified price; bonds would tend to be called if interest rates had fallen since the bonds were initially issued.

Capital Account The financial flow of funds and securities between the United States and the world.

Capital Asset Pricing Model A model that asserts that the value of a share of stock includes a risk-free return, a market risk premium, and a firm-specific risk premium that is based on beta.

Capital Inflows Purchases of U.S. financial securities by foreigners and borrowing from foreign sources by U.S. firms and residents.

Capital Market The market for financial assets with an original maturity of greater than one year.

Capital Outflows Purchases of foreign financial securities by U.S. residents and borrowing by foreigners from U.S. banks and other domestic sources.

Carrying Costs Interest costs for funds used to purchase the security underlying a futures contract plus any transactions costs.

Chartered Given permission to engage in the business of commercial banking. Banks must obtain a charter before opening.

Checkable Deposits Deposits that are subject to withdrawal by writing a check.

Circuit Breakers Reforms introduced in 1987 on the NYSE to temporarily halt market trading if prices change by a specified amount.

Clearinghouse The part of an organized exchange that takes on the responsibility of enforcing a contract after the agreement is struck.

Closed-End Investment companies that sell a limited number of shares like other corporations but usually do not buy back outstanding shares.

Collateral The building (structure) or land that will be foreclosed on and repossessed if the borrower fails to make the scheduled payments; the lender then sells the property to recoup some or all of the losses.

Collateralized Mortgage Obligations Securities developed by Freddie Mac that redirect the cash flows (principal and interest) of mortgage-backed securities to various classes of investors, thus creating financial instruments with varying prepayment risks and varying returns.

Commercial Banks Depository institutions that issue checkable, time, and savings deposit liabilities and, among other things, make loans to commercial businesses.

Commercial Paper Short-term debt instruments issued by corporations.

Common Stock Equity claims representing ownership of the net income and assets of a corporation. Common stockholders are "residual claimants," since their dividends are paid out of profits remaining after payment of interest to lenders and dividends to preferred stockholders. Common stockholders may vote for the Board of Directors, and thus have the potential to exert control over decisions of managers.

Community Reinvestment Act Legislation passed by Congress in 1977 to increase the availability of credit to economically disadvantaged areas and to correct alleged discriminatory lending practices.

Compounding A method used to determine the future value of a sum lent today.

Comptroller of the Currency The federal agency that charters national banks.

Computation Period The period during which the actual amount of required reserve assets that must be held during the maintenance period is determined.

Conforming Loans One equal or smaller in size than the conforming loan limit set by the Office of Federal Housing Enterprise Oversight (OFHEO). Since they can be more readily packaged and resold, interest rates on conforming loans (sometimes called "conventional" loans) are generally lower than for larger, jumbo, nonconforming loans.

Consol A perpetual bond with no maturity date; the issuer is never obliged to repay the principal but makes coupon payments each year, forever.

Constant Nominal Income Effect When changes in the price level necessarily cause the quantity demanded to change in the opposite direction to maintain constant nominal income.

Consumer Price Index (CPI) A price index that measures the cost of a market basket of goods and services that a typical urban consumer purchases.

Contemporaneous Reserve Accounting A reserve accounting system under which the maintenance period—when the reserve assets must be held—more or less corresponds to the computation period when the amount of required reserves is determined.

Contingent Claims Claims such as casualty and life insurance benefits that offer the public protection from the often-catastrophic financial effects of theft, accidents, natural disasters, and death.

Conventional Mortgages Mortgages made by financial institutions and mortgage brokers without the federal insurance that the principal and interest will be repaid.

Convergence The phenomenon in which the futures price is bid up or down to the spot price plus carrying costs; the futures price approaches the spot price as the expiration date draws nearer.

Convertible Provisions Provisions spelled out in a bond indenture that allow investors to convert the bonds to a specific number of shares of common stock.

Corporate Bonds Long-term debt instruments issued by corporations.

Cost of Holding Real Money Balances The additional forgone interest that holding nonmonetary financial assets would have yielded.

Cost-Push Inflation Sustained increases in the overall price level, triggered by increases in input prices.

Coupon Payments The periodic payments made to bondholders, which are equal to the principal times the coupon rate.

Coupon Rate The fixed interest rate stated on the face of a bond.

Credit Derivatives Contracts that transfer the default risk of a loan or other debt instrument from the holder of the loan (beneficiary) to a guarantor who receives a fee for accepting the risk.

Credit In the balance of payments, any item that results in a payment by foreigners to Americans.

Credit Risk The probability of a debtor not paying the principal and/or the interest due on an outstanding debt.

Credit Unions Depository institutions that are cooperative, nonprofit, tax-exempt associations operated for the benefit of members who share a common bond.

Crowding Out The reduction in private borrowing and spending due to higher interest rates that result from government deficit financing.

Currency Board An organized body within a country with the sole responsibility and power to define the value of the country's currency.

Currency Swaps A financial innovation used to hedge exchange rate risk over a long period of time, whereby one party agrees to trade periodic payments in a given currency with another party who agrees to do the same in a different currency.

Current Account Transactions that involve currently produced goods and services, including the balance of goods and services.

D

Dealer An individual who arranges trade and stands ready to be a principal in a transaction.

Debenture Bonds Bonds with no specific collateral backing but that have a general claim on the other unpledged assets of the issuer.

Debit In the balance of payments, any transaction that results in a payment to foreigners by Americans.

Debt Deflation A real increase in debt burdens caused by falling incomes and prices and debt burdens that are denominated in dollars.

Debt-to-Income Ratios The debt payments of spending units relative to their incomes or inflows.

Default Risk The risk that a borrower will be unwilling or unable to live up to the terms of the liability it has sold.

Default When a borrower fails to repay a financial claim.

Deficit Sector A sector where the combined deficits of net borrowers are greater than the combined surpluses of the net lenders.

Deflation A drop in the overall price level as measured by a price index.

Demand Deposits Non-interest-earning checking accounts issued by banks.

Demand for Loanable Funds The demand for borrowed funds by household, business, government, or foreign net borrowers.

Demand for Money The entire set of interest rate–quantity demanded combinations as represented by a downward-sloping demand curve for money.

Demand-Pull Inflation Sustained increases in the overall price level due to high levels of demand.

Deposit Insurance Fund (DIF) Result of the combination of the Bank Insurance Fund and Savings Association Insurance Fund, effective March 31, 2006.

Depository Institutions Deregulation and Monetary Control Act of 1980 (DIDMCA) The

statute that removed many of the regulations enacted during the Great Depression; it phased out Regulation Q, established uniform and universal reserve requirements, increased the assets and liabilities that depository institutions could hold, authorized NOW accounts, and suspended usury ceilings.

Depository Institutions Financial intermediaries that issue checkable deposits.

Depreciated Description of a currency that has decreased in value relative to another currency.

Depreciation A decrease in the value of a currency in terms of another currency under a flexible exchange rate system.

Deregulate The dismantling of existing regulations.

Deregulation The removing or phasing out of existing regulations.

Derivative Markets Financial futures markets where the value of the financial instruments (the futures and forward agreements) "derive" their values from the underlying instruments such as the government securities, the shares of stock, etc., that are traded on the future date; financial futures and forward markets, among others, are examples of derivative markets.

Derivatives Instruments such as forward, futures, options, swap, and other agreements that are routinely used to separate the total risk of a financial asset into subparts and that derive their value from the underlying assets.

Designated Order Turnaround System (SuperDOT) A computer system used for trades of fewer than 3,000 shares on the NYSE.

Devaluation Under fixed exchange rates, a reduction in the

value of a currency by the monetary authorities relative to the official reserve asset.

Devalue Under a fixed exchange rate system, to decrease the value of a country's currency.

Direct Finance When net lenders lend their funds directly to net borrowers.

Discount from Par When a bond sells below its face value because interest rates have increased since the bond was originally issued.

Discount Rate The rate that healthy depository institutions are charged for short-term borrowing of reserves from the Fed. Today, the primary credit rate is referred to as the discount rate.

Discounting A method used to determine the present value of a sum to be received in the future.

Disintermediation The removal of funds from a financial intermediary.

Diversification The allocation of surplus funds to more than one financial instrument in order to reduce risk.

Domestic Nonfinancial Debt (DNFD) An aggregate that is a measure of total credit market debt owed by the domestic non-financial government and private sectors.

Double Coincidence of Wants A bartering situation in which each person involved in a potential exchange has what the other person wants.

Dow Jones Industrial Average (The Dow) An index that measures movements in the stock prices of 30 of the largest companies traded on the NYSE.

Dual Banking System The system whereby a bank may have either a national or a state charter.

E

Economic Projections Goals for GDP, unemployment, and inflation over the next three years, set by the Fed four times each year.

Economics The study of how society decides what gets produced and how, and who gets what.

Economies of Scale Gains from bigness that may result from several firms being able to streamline management and eliminate the duplication of effort that would result from several separate firms.

Economies of Scope Advantages to firms being able to offer customers several financial services under one roof.

Efficient Markets Hypothesis This hypothesis states that when financial markets are in equilibrium, the prices of financial instruments reflect all readily available information.

Electronic Funds Transfer System The transfer of funds to third parties in response to electronic instructions rather than a paper check.

Emergency Economic Stabilization Act of 2008 (EESA) A law enacted in September 2008 in response to the ongoing financial crisis that authorized the U.S. Treasury to purchase up to $700 billion of "toxic" securities in order to bailout the U.S. financial system.

Employment Act of 1946 The first statute that directed policy makers to pursue policies to achieve full employment and non-inflationary growth.

Eurodollars Dollar-denominated deposits held abroad.

Excess Reserves Reserves over and above those required by the Fed.

Exchange Rate The number of units of foreign currency that can be acquired with one unit of domestic money.

Exchange Rate Risk The risk that changes in the exchange rate can adversely affect the value of foreign exchange or foreign financial instruments.

Exchange-Traded Funds (ETFs) A security created by a securities firm depositing into a fund that mirrors the holdings of stocks in an index.

Expansion The phase of the business cycle in which economic activity increases and unemployment falls.

Expectations Theory A theory holding that the long-term interest rate is the geometric average of the present short-term rate and the short-term rates expected to prevail over the term to maturity of the long-term security.

External Financing The financing of spending that exceeds current receipts by expanding either debt or equity.

F

Farm Credit Financial Assistance Corporation (FACO) A GSE that issues bonds to assist the FFCBFC, which was having financial problems at the time FACO was created.

Federal (Fed) Funds Loans of reserves (deposits at the Fed) between depository institutions, typically overnight.

Federal Deposit Insurance Corporation (FDIC) The federal agency that insures the deposits of banks and savings associations.

Federal Deposit Insurance Corporation Improvement Act (FDICIA) Legislation passed by Congress in 1991 to enact regulatory changes that ensure the safety and soundness of the banking and thrift industries. Regulators had long wished to merge the two separate deposit insurance funds, and the Federal Deposit Insurance Reform Act of 2005 accomplished this when signed into law by the president in early 2006.

Federal Deposit Insurance Reform Act of 2005 The Reform Act that merged the BIF and SAIF into the deposit insurance fund (DIF), increased the deposit insurance coverage for retirement accounts to $250,000, and adjusted coverage.

Federal Farm Credit Banks Funding Corporation (FFCB-FC) A GSE that issues bonds and discount notes to make loans to farmers to increase the funds flowing into agriculture.

Federal Financial Institutions Examinations Council (FFIEC) A federal agency that prescribes uniform principles, standards, and report forms for the federal examination of financial institutions by the Fed, the FDIC, and the Office of the Comptroller of the Currency and that makes recommendations to promote uniformity in the supervision of financial institutions.

Federal Home Loan Bank Board The regulatory body of the savings and loan industry until 1989.

Federal Home Loan Bank The regulatory body of the savings and loan industry until 1989.

Federal Home Loan Mortgage Corporation (Freddie Mac) Formerly a privately owned government-sponsored enterprise that sold securities and used the proceeds to buy mortgages, primarily of thrifts. It, along with Fannie Mae, was placed into conservatorship under its former regulator, Federal Home Loan Mortgage Corporation in September 2008.

Federal Housing Administration (FHA) A federal agency that, for a .5 percent fee, insures mortgage loans made by privately owned financial institutions up to a certain amount if the borrowers meet certain conditions defined by the FHA.

Federal National Mortgage Association (Fannie Mae) Formerly a privately owned government-sponsored enterprise that sold securities and used the proceeds to buy mortgages, primarily of banks. It, along with Freddie Mac, was placed into conservatorship under the Federal Home Loan Mortgage Corporation in September 2008.

Federal Open Market Committee (FOMC) The principal policy-making body within the Federal Reserve System.

Federal Reserve (The Fed) The central bank of the United States that regulates the banking system and determines monetary policy.

Federal Reserve Act The 1913 congressional statute that created the Federal Reserve System.

Federal Reserve Float The excess in reserves that results from a check being credited to one bank (or other depository institution) before it is debited from another.

Federal Reserve System The central bank of the United States that regulates the banking system and determines monetary policy.

Federal Savings and Loan Insurance Corporation (FSLIC) The insurance company that insured the deposits in S&Ls until 1989, when it was dissolved because of insolvency.

Fedwire An electronic system for irrevocably and instantaneously transferring very large sums of funds (wholesaling funds) among about 9,500 Fedwire participants, which are generally very large institutions.

Finance Companies Intermediaries that lend funds to households to finance consumer purchases and to firms to finance inventories.

Finance The study of how the financial system coordinates and channels the flow of funds from lenders to borrowers—and vice versa—and how new funds are created by financial intermediaries during the borrowing process.

Financial Assets Financial instruments such as stocks, bonds, and money, which serve as a store of value or purchasing power.

Financial Claims Claims issued by net borrowers in order to borrow funds from net lenders who purchase the claims; assets to the purchaser, liabilities to the issuer.

Financial Conglomerates Firms that own and operate several different types of financial intermediaries and financial institutions on a global basis.

Financial Crisis A critical upset in a financial market(s) characterized by sharp declines in asset prices and the default of many financial and nonfinancial firms.

Financial Forward Contract An agreement in which the terms, including price, are completed today for a transaction that will occur in the future.

Financial Forward Markets Markets that trade financial forward agreements usually arranged by banks or other brokers and dealers.

Financial Futures Markets Organized markets that trade financial futures agreements including: Chicago Board of Trade, the Chicago Mercantile Exchange, and the London International Financial Futures Exchange.

Financial Futures Standardized futures contracts that trade financial instruments on a future date according to terms (including the price) determined today.

Financial Holding Companies Holding companies that can engage in an even broader array of financial-related activities than bank holding companies, including securities underwriting and dealing, insurance agency and underwriting activities, and merchant banking activities; financial holding companies may engage in any other financial and nonfinancial activities as determined by the Fed.

Financial Industry Regulatory Authority (FINRA) A nongovernmental regulator of the U.S. securities industry with authority over more than 5,000 brokerage firms. FINRA was created in July 2007 by consolidation of regulatory functions of the NASD and the New York Stock Exchange.

Financial Innovation The creation of new financial instruments, markets, and institutions in the financial services industry; new ways for people to spend, save, and borrow funds; changes in the operation and scope of activity by financial intermediaries.

Financial Instability Hypothesis Hyman Minsky's theory that (1) the mixture of hedge, speculative, and Ponzi spending units in the economy determines the economy's predisposition to a financial crisis, and (2) after sustained periods of prosperity, spending units tend to take on more debt, which may in time lead to another crisis.

Financial Institutions Firms that provide financial services to net lenders and net borrowers; the most important financial institutions are financial intermediaries.

Financial Institutions Reform, Recovery, and Enforcement Act (FIRREA) of 1989 An act that attempted to resolve the S&L crisis by creating a new regulatory structure, limiting the assets S&Ls can acquire, and requiring S&Ls to maintain adequate capital.

Financial Intermediaries Financial institutions that borrow from net lenders for the purpose of lending to net borrowers.

Financial Liabilities Debt incurred through borrowing.

Financial Markets Markets in which spending units trade financial claims.

Financial Services Regulatory Relief Act An act signed into law in October 2006, authorizing the payment of interest on reserve balances beginning in October 2011, and, among other regulatory relief provisions, giving the Fed the authority to eliminate required reserves altogether. Banks would still maintain reserves at the Fed to clear payments among each other. It is believed that the Fed does not want to phase out reserve requirements at this time.

Financial Stability Forum (FSF) An organization of representatives of central banks, Treasury departments, and international financial institutions created in 1999 to promote international financial stability through the exchange of information and to foster cooperation in international financial supervision and surveillance.

Financing Corporation (FICO) A GSE created in response to the S&L crisis that issued bonds to help shore up the FSLIC.

Firm-Specific Risk Premium A risk measured by beta that shows the overall sensitivity of the stock's return relative to changes in the entire market.

Fiscal Policy Government spending and taxing decisions to speed up or slow down the level of economic activity.

Fixed Exchange Rate System An exchange rate system in which currency values do not fluctuate.

Fixed Rate Mortgages Mortgages where the interest rate remains the same over the life of the loan.

Flexible Exchange Rate System An exchange rate system in which the value of a currency is determined by supply and demand.

Floating (Flexible) Exchange Rate System An exchange rate system in which currency values are determined by supply and demand and fluctuate in response to changes in supply and demand.

Flow of Funds A social accounting system that divides the economy into a number of sectors including the household, business, government, foreign, and financial sector.

Foreign Currency (Money) Supplies of foreign exchange.

Foreign Exchange Futures Contract A standardized contract to deliver a certain amount of a foreign currency on a date in the future at a price determined today.

Foreign Exchange Market The market for buying and selling the different currencies of the world.

Foreign Exchange Supplies of foreign currencies.

Forward Agreements Customized arrangements between two parties to trade a financial asset on a date in the future at a price determined today.

Forward Rate The price today for a delivery on a future date.

Fractional Reserve Banking System A banking system in which individual banks hold reserve assets equal to a fraction of deposit liabilities.

Freedom of Information Act (1966) A 1966 law that requires more openness in government and more public access to government documents.

Full Dollarization Abandonment of a country's own currency to adopt another country's currency as its official currency.

Fund of Funds A mutual fund that invests in a portfolio of other mutual funds rather than individual stocks and/or bonds.

Fungibility The ability of one type of financial instrument to be easily converted into another.

Futures Agreements Standardized contracts where financial instruments are traded at a price determined today on a date in the future.

Futures Contracts Standardized agreements in agricultural and commodity markets to trade a fixed amount of the product or commodity on specific dates in the future at a price determined today.

G

Garn-St. Germain Act A law that expanded the lending powers of the S&Ls in the early 1980s.

GDP Deflator A price index that measures the overall changes in the prices of everything in GDP.

General Obligation Bonds Municipal bonds to be repaid out of general tax revenues.

Geometric Average An average that takes into account the effects of compounding; used to calculate the long-term rate from the short-term rate and the short-term rates expected to prevail over the term to maturity of the long-term security.

Glass-Steagall Act of 1933 Banking legislation that established Regulation Q interest rate ceilings, separated commercial and investment banking, and created the FDIC. It was enacted in response to the financial crisis that led to the Great Depression.

Government Agency Securities Bonds issued by private enterprises that were publicly chartered by Congress to reduce the cost of borrowing to certain sectors of the economy, such as farming, housing, and student loans.

Government National Mortgage Association (Ginnie Mae) A government-owned enterprise that guarantees the timely payment of interest and principal on bundles of at least $1 million of standardized mortgages.

Government-Sponsored Enterprises (GSEs) Private enterprises that have been chartered by Congress to reduce the cost of borrowing in such sectors as housing, farming, the savings and loan industry, and student loans.

Gramm-Leach-Bliley Act (GLBA) Legislation that removed decades-old barriers between banking and other financial services by creating financial holding companies that linked commercial banks with securities firms, insurance firms, and merchant banks; it was passed by Congress in November 1999 and became effective March 2000.

H

Hedge An investment made to reduce risk.

Hedge Fund A nontraditional type of mutual fund formed as a partnership of up to either 99 or 499 wealthy investors with large minimum investments; attempts to earn maximum returns regardless of rising or falling financial prices.

Hedge Spending Unit A spending unit such as a household or firm where the anticipated revenues (inflows) significantly exceed the anticipated payment obligations (outflows).

Humphrey-Hawkins Full Employment and Balanced Growth Act of 1978 A statute that required policy makers to pursue policies to achieve full employment and noninflationary growth.

I

Impact Lag The time between when an action is taken and when that action has a significant impact on economic variables.

Index-Arbitrage Trading The purchasing (or selling) of a basket of stocks, usually through program trading, with the simultaneous selling (or purchasing) of a futures agreement in the same basket of securities in order to make a riskless profit (arbitrage) from the price differential between the basket of stocks and the futures agreement.

Indexed Mutual Funds A mutual fund that holds the same basket of securities that are represented in an index such as the S&P 500 or the Wilshire 5000, so that the investor receives roughly the same return as the index to which the fund is tied.

Indirect Finance When net borrowers borrow from financial intermediaries that have acquired the funds to lend from net lenders.

Inflation Premium The amount of nominal interest added to the real interest rate to compensate the lender for the expected loss in purchasing power that will accompany any inflation.

Inflation Rate The rate of change in the Consumer Price Index, which measures the growth rate of the average level of prices paid by consumers.

Inflation-Indexed Bonds (e.g. Treasury Inflation Protected Securities, or TIPS) Bonds whose principal amounts are adjusted for inflation at the time when coupon payments are made (usually every six months).

Initial Public Offering (IPO) An offering of stocks or bonds to the public by a company that has not previously sold securities to the public.

Interest Rate Parity The theory that in equilibrium, interest rates adjust so that after adjustments have been made for expected inflation and exchange rate risk, returns are equalized across countries.

Interest Rate Risk The risk that the interest rate will unexpectedly change so that the costs of an FI's liabilities exceed the earnings on its assets.

Interest Rate Swaps A financial innovation used to reduce the risk of future interest rate changes over a long period of time. Swaps involve two parties trading interest payment streams to guarantee that their respective payment inflows will more closely match their outflows.

Interest Rate The cost to borrowers of obtaining money and the return (or yield) on money to lenders.

Intermediate Target The use of a target midway between the policy instruments and the ultimate policy goals.

Internal Financing The spending of money balances on hand or the liquidation of financial or real assets to finance spending that exceeds current receipts.

International Bank for Reconstruction and Development (IBRD) A bank that makes 12- to 15-year loans to poor, but not the poorest, countries, charging an interest rate just above the rate at which the bank borrows.

International Development Association An association that makes interest-free loans with a maturity of 35 to 40 years to the world's poorest countries.

International Finance Corporation An organization that mobilizes funding for private enterprise projects in poor countries.

International Financial System The numerous rules, customs, instruments, facilities, markets, and organizations that enable international payments to be made and funds to flow across borders.

International Monetary Fund (IMF) An organization created in 1944 to oversee the monetary and exchange rate policies of its members, who pay quotas that are used to assist countries with temporary imbalances in their balance of payments.

Interstate Banking and Branching Efficiency Act (IBBEA) A 1994 act that eliminated most restrictions on interstate bank mergers by June 1, 1997.

Investment Banks Financial institutions that design, market, and underwrite new issuances of securities in the primary market.

Investment Companies Companies that own and manage a large group of different securities for investors who have purchased shares of the companies.

Investment Spending For businesses, spending on new equipment and capital or net additions to inventories.

J

Junk Bonds Highly speculative, high yield bonds with low credit ratings that are not recommended for investment because of high credit risk.

L

Lagged Reserve Accounting A reserve accounting system under which the maintenance period—when the reserve assets must be held—follows some time after the computation period—when the amount of required reserves is determined.

Laissez-Faire The view that government should pursue a hands-off policy with regard to the economy.

Lender of Last Resort The responsibility of the Fed to provide an elastic currency by lending to commercial banks during emergencies.

Leverage Ratio The ratio of debt to equity on a firm's balance sheet.

Leveraging The degree to which a spending unit relies on borrowed funds.

Life Insurance Companies Intermediaries that offer protection against the financial costs associated with events such as death and disability in exchange for premiums.

Limit Orders Orders that instruct the broker or dealer to purchase securities at the market price up to a certain maximum or to sell the securities at the market price if it is above a certain minimum.

Liquidity Premium The extra return required to induce lenders to lend long-term rather than short-term.

Liquidity Risk The risk that an FI will be required to make a payment when the intermediary has only long-term assets that cannot be converted to liquid funds quickly without a capital loss.

Liquidity The ease with which a financial claim can be converted to cash without loss of value.

Load A sales commission paid to a broker to purchase mutual funds.

Loaned Up Situation when a bank has no excess reserves left to serve as a basis for lending.

Long-Run Aggregate Supply Curve The vertical curve through the natural rate of output to which the economy will return in the long run regardless of the price level.

Long-Run Equilibrium When all prices have adjusted to shifts in aggregate supply or demand, and the flow of spending, saving, borrowing, and lending continues until something else changes.

M

M1 Currency in the hands of the public plus checkable deposits.

M2 Everything in M1 plus other highly liquid assets.

Macroeconomics The branch of economics that studies the aggregate, or total, behavior of all households and firms.

Maintenance Margin Requirement The minimum amount of equity the investor needs in his account relative to the market value of his stock.

Maintenance Period The period during which the actual amount of reserves held must at least equal the amount of required reserves, as determined during the computation period.

Managed Float Exchange Rate System A system in which currency values fluctuate with changes in supply and demand but central banks may intervene if currency values are thought to be overvalued or undervalued.

Margin Loans Loans to investors for which the proceeds are used to purchase securities.

Margin Requirement The percentage of invested funds that can be borrowed as opposed to being paid in readily available funds; currently, margin requirements are set by the Fed at 50 percent.

Marginal Tax Rate The tax rate that is paid on the last dollar of income that the taxpayer earns.

Market Fundamentals Factors that have a direct effect on future income streams of the instruments, including the value of the assets and the expected income streams of those assets on which the financial instruments represent claims.

Market Makers Dealers who link up buyers and sellers of financial securities and sometimes take positions in the securities.

Market Orders Orders by an investor that direct the broker or dealer to purchase or sell securities at the present market price.

Market Risk Premium The risk based on historical data that shows how much on average the ownership of stocks pays over a risk-free return.

McFadden Act The 1927 act by Congress that outlawed interstate branching and made national banks conform to the intrastate branching laws of the states in which they were located.

Means of Payment (Medium of Exchange) Something generally acceptable for making payments.

Merchandise Exports Foreign purchases of U.S. goods.

Merchandise Imports U.S. purchases of foreign goods.

Merchant Banking Direct equity investment (the purchasing of stock) in a start-up or growing company by a bank.

Microeconomics The branch of economics that studies the behavior of individual decision-making units such as households and business firms.

Monetary Aggregates The measures of money—including M1 and M2—monitored and tracked by the Fed.

Monetary Base Reserves plus currency in the hands of the public; denoted as *MB*.

Monetary Policy The attempts by the Fed to stabilize the economy and to ensure sufficient money and credit for an expanding economy.

Money Anything that functions as a means of payment (medium of exchange), unit of account, and store of value.

Money Illusion When spending units react to nominal changes caused by changes in prices, even though real variables such as interest rates have not changed.

Money Market Deposit Accounts (MMDAs) Financial claims with limited check-writing privileges, offered by banks since 1982; they earn higher interest than fully checkable deposits and require a higher minimum balance.

Money Market Mutual Funds Mutual funds that deal in money market instruments with an original maturity of one year or less.

Money Market The market for financial assets with an original maturity of less than one year.

Money Multiplier The multiple of the change in the monetary base by which the money supply will change.

Money Something acceptable and generally used as payment for goods and services.

Moody's Investors Service A credit-rating agency that analyzes and evaluates bonds and assigns them to a particular risk class based on the probability that the issuer will fail to pay back the principal and interest in full when due.

Moral Hazard Problem When the borrower has an incentive to use the proceeds of a loan for a riskier venture after the loan is funded.

Moral Hazard The reduction in market discipline experienced by FIs that goes hand-in-hand with deposit insurance.

Mortgage A long-term debt instrument for which real estate is used as collateral and which results from loans made to individuals or businesses in order to purchase or refinance land, single- or multiple-family residential housing, commercial properties, or farms.

Mortgage-Backed Securities Securities backed by a pool of mortgages; they have a low default risk and provide a steady stream of income.

Mortgages Loans made to purchase single- or multiple-family residential housing, land, or other real structures, with the structure or land serving as collateral for the loan.

Municipal Bonds (munis) Bonds issued by state, county, and local governments to finance public projects such as schools, utilities, roads, and transportation ventures; the interest on municipal securities is exempt from federal taxes and from state taxes for investors living in the issuing state.

Mutual Funds Investment-type intermediaries that pool the funds of net lenders, purchase the long-term financial claims of net borrowers, and return the income received minus a fee to the net lenders.

N

National Association of Securities Dealers Automated Quotation System (NASDAQ) An electronic stock market for trading securities. In 2002, it became an investor-owned corporation, completely independent of the National Association of Securities Dealers (NASD), which had founded it in 1971. It lists more companies and trades more shares on average than the NYSE.

National Bank A bank that has received a charter from the Comptroller of the Currency.

Natural Level of Real Output The level of real output that is consistent with long-run equilibrium, given the quantity and productivity of the economy's factors of production.

Natural Rate of Unemployment The rate of unemployment consistent with stable prices; believed to be about 4.0 to 4.5 percent.

Near Monies Highly liquid financial assets that can easily be converted to transactions money (M1) without loss of value.

Negotiable Certificates of Deposit (CDs) Certificates of deposit with a minimum denomination of $100,000 that can be traded in a secondary market, most with an original maturity of one to 12 months.

Net Asset Value The difference between the market value of the shares of stock that the mutual fund owns and the liabilities of the mutual fund all divided by the outstanding number of shares.

Net Borrowers Spending units such as households and firms whose spending exceeds their income.

Net Capital Inflow Condition when the purchases of U.S. financial claims by foreigners exceed purchases of foreign financial claims by U.S. entities (capital outflows) and when there is a surplus in the capital account.

Net Investment Gross investment minus depreciation.

Net Lenders Spending units such as households and firms whose income exceeds their spending.

Net Transfer Payments In the current account, the difference between transfer payments received from and transfer payments made to foreigners.

Net Worth The difference between assets and liabilities at a point in time.

New York Stock Exchange (NYSE) The world's largest market for trading stocks; trades the stocks of more than 2,800 companies.

No-Load Mutual funds that are purchased directly from the mutual fund company and are not subject to a load.

Nominal Interest Rate The market interest rate, or the real return plus the rate of inflation expected to prevail over the life of the asset.

Nonbanks Other intermediaries and nonfinancial companies that have taken an increasing share of intermediation.

Nondeposit Liabilities Borrowed funds, such as Eurodollar borrowings, fed funds, and repurchase agreements, that are not deposits and are not subject to reserve requirements.

O

Off-Balance-Sheet Activities Activities such as standby lines of credit, overdraft protection, unused credit card balances, and other commitments for which a bank is liable but that do not show up on the balance sheet.

Office of Thrift Supervision (OTS) An agency created by the FIRREA to replace the Federal Home Loan Bank Board as the overseer of the S&L industry.

Official Reserve Account The balance of payments account that records official government transactions in the foreign exchange market to bring the balance of payments into balance.

Official Reserve Asset The asset (such as the dollar or gold) by which other countries define the value of their currency; used as international reserves.

Official Reserve Currency The currency used by other countries to define their own currency; the U.S. dollar was the official reserve currency under the Bretton Woods Accord.

Offsetting Open Market Operations Open market purchases or sales to offset changes in the monetary base caused by other factors.

Open Market Operations The buying and selling of government securities by the Fed to change the reserves of depository institutions.

Open-End A mutual fund (type of investment company) that continually sells new shares to the public or buys outstanding shares from the public at a price equal to the net asset value.

Operating Target A target amenable to control by the policy tools and highly correlated with the intermediate target.

Opportunity Cost The return one could have earned by using funds in the next best alternative; for investment spending, the real interest rate.

Optimal Forecast The best guess possible arrived at by using all of the available information.

Option Agreements Standardized agreements that give the buyer the right, but not the obligation, to buy or sell a standardized basket of financial securities at a price determined today on a standardized date in the future.

Option Premium The premium paid by the buyer of an option to compensate the seller for accepting the risk of a loss with no possibility of a gain.

Options on Futures Options that give the buyer the right, but not the obligation, to buy or sell a futures contract up to the expiration date on the option.

Options Standardized contracts that give the buyer the right, but not the obligation, to buy or sell an instrument in the future at a price determined today.

Outright Transactions Open market purchases that supply reserves or open market sales that withdraw reserves.

Over-the-Counter (OTC) Market A network of securities dealers that trades stocks of companies not listed on an official exchange such as NASDAQ or the NYSE.

P

Par Value The principal or face value of the bond, which is repaid in full at maturity.

Payments Mechanism The means by which transactions are consummated; that is, how money is transferred in an exchange.

Payoff Method The method of resolving a bank insolvency by paying off the depositors and closing the institution.

Pension Funds Tax-exempt intermediaries set up to provide participants with income at retirement in exchange for premiums.

Performance Bond A bond required by an organized exchange from both the buyer and the seller of a futures agreement to ensure that both parties abide by the agreement.

Personal Consumption Expenditures Price Index (PCEPI) A price index measures the average change in the prices of all domestic personal consumption expenditures. The PCEPI changes the weights of items in the index as consumers substitute out of things that have become relatively more expensive and into items that have become relatively cheaper. Thus, it gives a better measure of inflation than the CPI, which does not.

Phillips Curve A curve suggesting a trade-off between unanticipated inflation and unemployment in the short run.

Pit The trading area on the floor of an organized exchange (such as the Chicago Board of Trade) where authorized brokers gather to buy and sell for their customers.

Point-of-Sale Terminal A computer terminal that uses a debit card to electronically transfer funds from a deposit account to the account of a third party.

Policy Directive A statement issued by the FOMC to the Trading Desk of the New York Fed that directs monetary policy until the next FOMC meeting; in recent years, the policy directive has targeted a specific fed funds rate.

Policy Directive A statement of the FOMC that indicates its policy consensus and sets forth operating instructions regarding monetary policy.

Policy Lag The time between the point when the need for action is recognized and the point when an adjustment policy is decided on and set in motion.

Policy Regret A situation in which policy actions based on available data would not have been taken if more accurate data revisions had been available.

Ponzi Spending Unit A spending unit that must continuously increase its outstanding debt to meet its current obligations or payments.

Portfolio The collection of real and financial assets and liabilities.

Precautionary Motive A motive for holding money based on the desire to protect against unforeseen developments.

Preferred Habitats An expectations theory modification hypothesizing that many borrowers and lenders have preferred maturities, which creates a degree of market segmentation between the short-term and long-term markets.

Preferred Stock Restricted equity claims with characteristics of both bonds and common stock. While dividends must be paid to preferred stockholders before common stockholders, preferred dividends are set at a specific level and do not increase if extraordinary profits are earned. Preferred stockholders generally do not have voting rights.

Premium above Par When a bond sells above its face value because interest rates have decreased since the bond was originally issued.

Prepayment Risk The risk that mortgages will be prepaid early and that the funds will have to be reinvested at a lower return.

Present Value The value today of funds to be received or paid on a future date.

Primary Credit Rate The rate for short-term borrowing of reserves by the healthiest depository institutions from the Fed, also known as the discount rate.

Primary Dealer Credit Facility (PDCF) A program begun in March 2008, whereby primary dealers can borrow overnight from the Fed at the primary credit rate. Designed to increase liquidity and to provide support for the financial system.

Primary Dealers Large banks and securities dealers with whom the Fed directly engages in open market operations.

Primary Market The market in which a security is initially sold for the first time.

Principal The original amount of funds lent.

Private Placement The sale of new securities to a limited number of large investors; because the number of investors is small, the underwriting process is avoided.

Producer Price Index (PPI) A price index that measures changes in cost of goods and services purchased by the typical producer.

Program Trading The preprogramming of computers to buy or sell a large number (basket) of stocks, usually by institutional investors.

Property and Casualty Companies Intermediaries that provide protection against the effects of unexpected occurrences on property.

Prospectus A subpart of the registration statement that must be given to investors before they purchase the securities.

Public Debt The sum of all past government deficits less past surpluses.

Purchase and Assumption Method The method of resolving a bank insolvency by finding a buyer for the institution.

Purchasing Power Parity The theory that, in the long run, exchange rates adjust so that the relative purchasing power of various currencies is equalized.

Put Options Options that give the buyer of the option the right, but not the obligation, to sell a standardized contract of a financial instrument at a strike price determined today.

Q

Quantity Demanded of Money The specific amount of money that spending units wish to hold at a specific interest rate (price).

Quantity Supplied of Money The specific amount of money that will be supplied at a specific interest rate.

R

Rational Expectations Expectations formed by looking both backward and forward.

Real Assets For households, durable goods and houses.

Real Balances Effect (Wealth Effect) The change in the supply of real money balances, which causes an increase or decrease in wealth, when the price level changes for a given supply of nominal money balances.

Real Estate Investment Trusts (REITs) A special type of mutual fund that pools the funds of many small investors and uses them to buy or build income property or to make or purchase mortgage loans; pass-through institutions in which the rents from the income property and/or the interest income from the mortgages are passed through to shareholders.

Real Income Nominal income divided by a price index.

Real Interest Rate The interest rate corrected for changes in the purchasing power of money.

Real Money Balances The quantity of money expressed in real terms; the nominal money supply, M, divided by overall price level, P, or M/P.

Real Wage The nominal wage divided by the overall price level.

Recession The phase of the business cycle in which economic activity decreases and unemployment rises.

Recognition Lag The time it takes policy makers to recognize that a change in the economy's performance has occurred.

Redlining The practice of restricting the number or dollar amounts of loans in an area regardless of the creditworthiness of the borrower.

Refunding The refinancing of past government debt that is maturing.

Registration Statement A statement that must be filed with the SEC before a new securities offering can be issued.

Regularized Describes the advanced announcements of Treasury intentions to borrow at standard intervals.

Regulation D A regulation that prescribed reserve requirements on some deposits.

Regulation Q Interest rate ceilings on deposits at commercial banks that were established during the Great Depression and phased out after 1980.

Repurchase Agreement An arrangement whereby the New York Fed agrees to buy securities from the securities dealers with whom it regularly does business and the dealers agree to repurchase the securities on a specific day in the near future.

Required Reserve Ratio (r_D) The fraction of deposits that depository institutions are required to hold as required reserves.

Required Reserves The amount of reserve assets that the Fed requires depository institutions to hold against outstanding checkable deposit liabilities.

Reserve Bank One of the 12 Federal Reserve Banks; each is located in a large city in its district.

Reserve Need The projected amount of reserves to be supplied or withdrawn by open market operations to reach or keep the fed funds rate prescribed by the policy directive.

Reserves Assets that are held as either vault cash or reserve deposit accounts with the Fed.

Resolution Trust Corporation (RTC) A GSE created in 1989 in response to the savings and loan crisis that issued bonds and used the proceeds to dissolve or find buyers for the failed thrifts and their properties. The RTC went out of business on December 31, 1995, after completing its work.

Restructure (a Loan) Change a loan to allow a borrower who would otherwise likely default to repay (e.g., allow the borrower to pay amounts currently due at some future date instead).

Retail Sweep Accounts Retail accounts, created in 1994, with balances that have been swept out of deposit accounts subject to reserve requirements and into savings accounts that are not.

Revaluation Under fixed exchange rates, an increase in the value of a currency by the monetary authorities relative to the official reserve asset.

Revalue Under a fixed exchange rate system, to increase the value of a country's currency.

Revenue Bonds Bonds used to finance specific projects with the proceeds of those projects being used to pay off the bondholders.

Reverse Repurchase Agreement An arrangement whereby the New York Fed agrees to sell securities to the securities dealers with whom it regularly does business and agrees to repurchase the securities on a specific day in the near future.

Risk Premium The extra return or interest that a lender is compensated with for accepting more risk.

Rolled Over The result when the government borrows to pay off maturing debt.

S

Saving Income not spent on consumption.

Savings and Loan Associations (S&Ls) Depository institutions established for the purpose of pooling the savings of local residents to finance the construction and purchase of homes; have offered checkable deposits since 1980.

Savings Associations Savings and Loan Associations and Savings Banks.

Savings Banks Depository institutions set up to help finance the construction and purchase of homes; located mainly on the East Coast.

Savings Deposits Highly liquid deposits that can usually be withdrawn on demand but not by writing a check.

Seasoned Issuance The offering of new securities by a corporation that has outstanding previously issued securities.

Secondary Credit Rate The rate for short-term borrowing of reserves from the Fed by depository institutions experiencing financial difficulties.

Secondary Market The market in which previously issued financial securities are sold.

Secondary Stock Offering An offering of newly issued shares by a firm that already has outstanding publicly held shares.

Securities and Exchange Commission (SEC) A government agency created by the Securities and Exchange Act of 1934 that regulates disclosure rules for companies that issue publicly traded shares of stock.

Securities Industry Protection Corporation (SIPC) A nonprofit membership corporation established by Congress that provides insurance to protect investors' securities from liquidation by the brokerage firm.

Securitization The process whereby relatively illiquid financial assets are packaged together and sold off to individual investors.

Seigniorage The difference between the cost of producing and distributing currency and any revenues earned.

Shelf Registration A procedure that permits a company to register a number of securities with the SEC and sell them over a two-year period rather than at the time of registration.

Short Sell Investors' instructions to brokers or dealers to borrow shares of stocks and sell them today with the guarantee that the investors will replace the borrowed stocks by a date in the future.

Short-Run Aggregate Supply Curve A curve showing the direct relationship between the overall price level and the level of real output that will be supplied in response to changes in demand before full adjustment of relative prices has taken place.

Simple Money Multiplier The reciprocal of the required reserve ratio, $1/r_D$.

Smart Cards Plastic cards with a microprocessor chip that are used to make payments; the chip stores information that allows the payment to be validated.

Solvent When a bank or other firm has assets worth more than liabilities (opposite of "bankrupt" or "insolvent").

Sources and Uses of Funds Statement A statement showing the sources and uses of funds for any sector.

Sources of Funds For any sector, income and borrowing.

Special Drawing Rights (SDRs) International reserve assets created by the IMF to supplement other international reserves.

Speculation The buying or selling of financial securities in the hopes of profiting from future price changes.

Speculative Bubble An irrational increase in stock prices accompanied by euphoric expectations.

Speculative Spending Unit A spending unit in which the funds coming in may potentially fall short of the payment outflows if there is an increase in interest rates.

Spot Markets Markets in which the trading of financial securities takes place instantaneously.

Stagflation A condition of concurrent high unemployment and high inflation.

Standard & Poor's Investors Service A credit-rating agency that analyzes and evaluates bonds and assigns them to a particular risk class based on the probability that the issuer will fail to pay back the principal and interest in full when due.

Standby Lines of Credit Lines of credit (commitments) for which a bank is liable but that do not show up on the balance sheet.

State and Local Government Bonds (Municipals) Long-term instruments issued by state and local governments to finance expenditures on schools, roads, and so on.

Stocks Equity claims that represent ownership of the net assets and income of a corporation.

Store of Value Something that retains its value over time.

Stored-Value Cards Plastic cards that have a magnetic strip that is swiped through a card reader to make payments; usually single use.

Strike Price The agreed-upon price in an options contract.

Stronger Version of the Efficient Markets Hypothesis The theory that the prices of all financial instruments not only reflect the optimal forecast of the financial instrument but also the true fundamental value of the instrument.

Student Loan Marketing Association (Sallie Mae) A former GSE, fully privatized in 2004, that issues securities to purchase student loans, thus increasing the funds flowing into student loans and making them more liquid.

Subordinated Debenture Bonds Bonds with no collateral backing that have a general claim after debenture bondholders have been paid.

Subprime Mortgage A mortgage loan made to a borrower with bad credit and little or no down payment.

Substitution-of-Foreign-Goods Effect When changes in the domestic price level cause consumers to substitute into relatively cheaper foreign goods or out of relatively more expensive foreign goods.

Supply of Loanable Funds The supply of borrowed funds originating (1) from household, business, government, and foreign net lenders or (2) from the Fed through its provision of reserves.

Supply of Money The stock of money (M1), which includes currency in the hands of the public plus checkable deposits.

Supply Shock Any event that shifts the short-run aggregate supply curve.

Surplus Sector A sector where the combined surpluses of the lenders are greater than the combined deficits of the net borrowers.

Sweep Accounts A financial innovation that allows depository institutions to shift customers' funds out of checkable accounts that are subject to reserve requirements and into highly liquid money market deposit accounts (MMDAs) that are not.

Syndicate A group of investment banks, each of which underwrites a proportion of new securities offerings.

System Open Market Account (SOMA) The Fed's account of dollar-denominated Treasury securities, which are bought and sold by the Trading Desk to implement open market operations in accordance with policy directives.

System Repurchase Agreement When the Trading Desk of the Fed buys securities on a self-reversing, temporary basis in order to supply reserves on a temporary basis.

T

Temporary Auction Facility (TAF) A program begun in December 2007, whereby the Fed auctions funds to depository institutions for 28 or 84 days. Designed to provide liquidity to the financial system.

Term Asset-Backed Securities Loan Facility (TALF) A special lending program to issuers of asset-backed securities that were collateralized by student loans, auto loans, credit card loans, and loans guaranteed by the Small Business Administration. The proceeds of the loans could then be used to issue new asset-backed securities.

Term Securities Lending Facility (TSLF) A program where the Fed auctions government securities to primary dealers for a 28-day or longer period in exchange for less liquid and less credit-worthy securities such as mortgage-backed securities. Designed to increase liquidity without increasing reserves.

Term Structure of Interest Rates The relationship between yields and time to maturity.

Term to Maturity The length of time from when a financial security is initially issued until it matures.

Theory of Rational Expectations The theory that expectations will, on average, be equal to the optimal forecast.

Thrifts Depository institutions known as S&Ls, savings banks, and credit unions.

Time Deposits Deposits that have a scheduled maturity and a penalty for early withdrawal.

Time Value of Money The terms on which one can trade off present purchasing power for future purchasing power; the interest rate.

Too Big to Fail The position adopted by FDIC regulators in 1984 whereby the failure of a large bank would be resolved using the purchase and assumption method rather than the payoff method.

Total Reserves Required reserves plus excess reserves.

Trade Balance The difference between merchandise exports and imports.

Trade Deficit Status when merchandise imports are greater than exports.

Trade Surplus Status when merchandise exports are greater than imports.

Transactions Costs The costs associated with borrowing and lending or making other exchanges.

Transactions Deposits Deposits that can be exchanged for currency and are used to make payments through writing a check or making an electronic transfer.

Transactions Motive A motive for holding money based on the need to make payments.

Treasury Notes Securities issued by the U.S. government with an original maturity of one to 10 years.

Treasury STRIPS A type of government security that allows investors to register and trade ownership of the interest (coupon) payments and the principal separately.

Troubled Assets Relief Program (TARP) The program under the EESA that initially authorized the U.S. Treasury to purchase up to $700 billion of "toxic" mortgage-backed securities from financial institutions. The TARP program was revised ten days after the EESA was signed. Under the revised TARP program, the Treasury would use the bailout funds to purchase newly-issued preferred stock in troubled institutions.

Trustee An expert (usually working for a bank or trust company) who interprets the provisions of a bond offering for investors and who sees that the terms and conditions of the offering are fulfilled.

U

U.S. Government Agency Securities Long-term bonds issued by various government agencies, including those that support real estate lending and student loans.

U.S. Government Securities Long-term debt instruments of the U.S. government with original maturities of two to 30 years.

U.S. Treasury Bills (T-bills) Short-term debt instruments of the U.S. government with typical maturities of three to 12 months.

Uniform Reserve Requirements Reserve requirements that apply to particular types of deposits and are the same across all depository institutions.

Unit of Account A standardized accounting unit such as the dollar that provides a consistent measure of value.

Universal Reserve Requirements Reserve requirements to which all depository institutions are subject.

Uses of Funds For any sector, current spending and changes in financial instruments held.

Usury Ceilings Maximum interest rates that FIs may charge on certain loans.

V

Variable Rate Mortgages Mortgages where the interest rate is adjusted periodically to reflect changing market conditions.

Veterans Administration (VA) A federal agency that, among other things, insures mortgage loans made by privately owned financial institutions up to a certain amount if the borrowers meet certain conditions, including being military veterans.

W

Wholesale Sweep Accounts Wholesale accounts, created in the 1970s, with balances that have been swept out of deposit accounts subject to reserve accounts and into money market instruments such as money market mutual funds, Eurodollar deposits, and repurchase agreements.

World Bank An investment bank created in 1944 that issues bonds to make long-term loans at low interest rates to poor countries for economic development projects.

Write Off Officially recognize a loan to a borrower who is not repaying, and not likely to repay in the future, as worthless.

Y

Yield Curve A graphical representation of the relationship between interest rates (yields) on particular securities and their terms to maturity.

Yield to Maturity The return on a bond held to maturity, which includes both the interest return and any capital gain or loss.

Z

Zero-Coupon Bonds Corporate bonds sold at a discount, with the difference between the amount paid for the bond and the amount received at maturity equal to the interest.

Index

Italic page references indicate tables, charts, and graphs.

About the Authors

MAUREEN BURTON
CALIFORNIA STATE POLYTECHNIC UNIVERSITY, POMONA

Maureen Burton received a B.A. from the University of Missouri at Columbia in 1971, an M.A. from California State University Fullerton in 1979, and a Ph.D. from the University of California at Riverside in 1986. All were in economics. She taught at Chaffey College from 1984 to 1987 and at Cal Poly Pomona since 1987 where she is a full professor. At Cal Poly Pomona, she has served as Coordinator of the Graduate Program and a Chair of the Economics Department. She is currently the Chair of the Faculty Rights Committee for the Cal Poly Chapter of the California Faculty Association. In addition to other publications, she co-authored an introductory text *Economics* (Harper Collins, 1987) with S. Craig Justice and *An Introduction to Financial Markets and Institutions*, (South-Western College Publishing, 2002) with Reynold Nesiba and Ray Lombra, with a second edition to be published in 2010 by M.E. Sharpe. Her main areas of interest include monetary policy and financial crisis.

BRUCE BROWN
CALIFORNIA STATE POLYTECHNIC UNIVERSITY, POMONA

Bruce Brown is currently Associate Professor of Economics at Cal Poly. He earned his A.B. degree in economics from the University of California, Berkeley and M.A. and Ph.D. degrees from the University of California, Los Angeles. Bruce has taught a wide variety of students ranging from those at UCLA and USC where he has held visiting positions, to Santa Monica College. From 1997 to 2000 Bruce was Associate Professor of Economics at Niigata University in Japan and experienced the tail end of the "lost decade" firsthand. His eclectic research interests have resulted in publications concerning immigration, inter-industry wage differentials, Japan's health care system, and economic methodology. Bruce's current research concerns credit rationing as a result of asymmetric information.